Organization Change

Organization Change

A Comprehensive Reader

W. Warner Burke, Dale G. Lake,
Jill Waymire Paine

JB JOSSEY-BASS

Published by Jossey-Bass

A Wiley Imprint

989 Market Street, San Francisco, CA 94103-1741—www.josseybass.com

Jossey-Bass books and products are available through most bookstores. To contact Jossey-Bass directly call our Customer Care Department within the U.S. at 800-956-7739, outside the U.S. at 317-572-3986, or fax 317-572-4002.

Jossey-Bass also publishes its books in a variety of electronic formats. Some content that appears in print may not be available in electronic books.

Library of Congress Cataloging-in-Publication Data

Organization change : a comprehensive reader / [edited by] W. Warner Burke, Dale G. Lake, Jill Waymire Paine. – 1st ed.
      p. cm.
  Includes bibliographical references and index.
  ISBN 978-0-470-26056-2 (alk. paper)
  1. Organization change. I. Burke, W. Warner (Wyatt Warner), 1935– II. Lake, Dale G. III. Paine, Jill Waymire, 1974–
  HD58.8.O7227 2008
  658.4'06–dc22   2008015954

Printed in the United States of America
FIRST EDITION
PB Printing 10 9 8 7 6 5 4 3

The Jossey-Bass Business and Management Series

CONTENTS

Please note: all chapters designated *website* in the
table of contents may be accessed online
at www.josseybass.com/go.burke.

FOREWORD

I t may sound silly to state that change in the 1950s and '60s was new. After all, today we claim that change has joined the inevitabilities of death and taxes. We now fully realize that from our planet's origin change has always been with us. But codifying what we know about change has not always been with us. It is true that thinkers for centuries have made declarations about change, for example, Heraclitus (540–480 B.C.) apparently stated, "Nothing endures but change," and many centuries later Jonathan Swift (1667–1745) borrowed the thought and wrote it as "There is nothing in this world constant, but inconstancy."

Beyond commenting on change what is more recent is an attempt to understand change from a scientific perspective. What do we know about change and what can we predict? Early attempts had no doubt occurred, but the decades of the fifties and sixties ushered in a spurt of activity resulting in studying and writing about change. The two World Wars of the 20th century caused enormous change especially the second one, and behavioral science scholars during those times began to make more concerted efforts to document and understand change and what was happening in the world.

The prime example of this spurt of activity was Kurt Lewin and his followers in the 1940s. Lewin's ideas and penchant for action research were stimulants for many of the behavioral scientists of those times. I was among them. Even though the 50s decade has been characterized as a rather dormant time (perhaps needed rest from the war to end all wars), the times intellectually were heady and exciting. I was privileged to be a part of those times and to have worked with Douglas McGregor at M.I.T. and with my other colleagues across the Charles River at Boston University, Ken Benne and Bob Chin. We were also involved with the National Training Laboratories (NTL) at the time, an organization founded in 1947 by Lee Bradford, Ken Benne, and Ron Lippitt who were Lewin's followers. NTL became an organization if not social movement devoted to change particularly at the individual level and later in the sixties expanded these early change ideas to the organizational level creating what became known as organization development (OD).

NTL brought together many of us in the behavioral sciences at the time. With much interchange, ideas and debates burgeoned about change. As a player in those exciting times, one of my efforts was to engage Ken Benne and Bob Chin in a concerted effort to consolidate and codify what we were learning about change. Not just change in a random sense, but *planned* change. What did we know about deliberately steering change in a particular direction, and what were the levers for and barriers to bringing about change that was planned and directional? The attempt to answer, or at least respond intelligently to this and other related questions, was our first edition of *The Planning of Change* published in 1961. As we continued to learn, three additional editions were published, the fourth and final one in 1985.

That was more than twenty years ago, and one thing we know for certain is that change continues, and now at an even more rapid rate. Knowledge about change especially planned change has expanded considerably. It is past time for us to catch up once again. Thus, this volume edited by Burke, Lake, and Paine. This time the book on planned change, and a large one at that demonstrating the tremendous growth in knowledge, is even more selective and focused. Yes, the focus is once again on *planned* change but in this case on planned *organization* change more in keeping with the expertise of Burke and his colleagues, and responding to the need to contain and bound the focus of the literature that is covered. This volume, then, is not a fifth edition in the Bennis, Benne and Chin tradition but one that places emphasis on the importance of understanding organizations in more depth, in general, and planned organization change, in particular.

The tradition that continues with this volume, however, is the scholar-practitioner model and the Lewinian mandate that theory and practice should go together—there is nothing more practical than a good theory. Articles for this volume have been selected with this perspective in mind, that is, theory informs practice and practice informs theory.

Change is both old and new. Change has been with us from the beginning yet we continue to gain new insights about the nature of change. And this volume is old and new, containing classics from past literature and perhaps classics from the more recent literature for the future.

So, it is with nostalgia that I pass the mantle of this kind of book to my colleagues, yet, at the same time, with joy that something I helped to initiate continues.

Warren G. Bennis

PREFACE

During the middle of the year 2003, two of us (Burke and Lake) held a conversation about our past, our writings, our education, and our experience in working with organizations to bring about change. Among other memory exchanges, we reminisced about the four editions of *The Planning of Change*, edited by Bennis, Benne, and Chin, and how helpful these works had been to us. The fourth and last edition was published in 1985. Since that time, both Ken Benne and Bob Chin had passed away. We further discussed the possibility of picking up the mantle and producing a fifth edition. "Let's talk to Warren Bennis about this," we said. That summer, Bennis and Burke were conducting a program together in Japan, so there was the opportunity for a conversation about this possibility: a Burke, Lake, and Bennis fifth edition. Warren was excited about the idea and was in full support. But he stated that first, he would not be able to work with us on a fifth edition and therefore his name should not be on the cover, and second, perhaps we should not think about a fifth edition but a new book instead. Although we could incorporate some of the articles from these previous editions, much in the field had been developed and published since 1985, and a different version might be in order. Moreover, Warren said he would like to propose that our work be published in the Jossey-Bass management series, where he serves as consulting editor. Lake and Burke were delighted with Warren's graciousness and support, and so we went to work.

As we began the work, two very important considerations occurred to us. First, as an old friend of ours once said, "It is best to write about things you know." Since we believed that we knew more about *organization* change than we did about change in general, it made sense for us not only to emphasize organization change but also to stick with the idea of *planning* as well; thus we are writing about *planned organization change.* Our second realization was that this undertaking required a huge amount of work. We therefore asked Jill Waymire Paine, a graduate assistant for Burke at the time, to join us. In spite of her work on finishing her doctoral dissertation, fortunately she agreed to take on the project with us.

This book, then, is not a fifth edition; but we have incorporated chapters from the previous editions of *The Planning of Change* by Bennis, Benne, and Chin, and therefore this work is dedicated to Warren and to the memories of Ken and Bob. That is, we want to recognize the wonderful contributions that they made with those four editions. Both Burke and Lake personally worked with Benne and Chin in the 1960s, and we continue to cherish our relationship with Warren.

Now a word about this book on planned organization change. As noted earlier, we have included readings from as far back as the 1950s, chapters that we believe are classics and need to be in the portfolio of any scholar or practitioner who works in the field of planned organization change.

Back in the 1960s, Burke was engaged with Richard Beckhard and others in delivering for the NTL Institute for Applied Behavioral Science a program of training and development for aspiring organization development practitioners. Frustrating was the participants' request to have their "toolkit" filled with tricks of the trade. Our response was something like, "But wouldn't you like to also have some understanding about where these tools came from, why and how they might or might not work, and what might be the underlying research and theory that undergirds them?" A typical participant reply was, "No, I don't have that kind of time; just fill up the kit and teach me how to use the tools that you put there." This book, in part, is about tools—team building, large group intervention, and others—but it is much more about what is behind and supports the hammer and nails. Team building today is based in large measure on writings from the 1950s and 1960s. A number of these more important writings are included in this volume. But we have gone beyond some of the classics and have included chapters from the eighties and nineties, and even up to 2008. These inclusions were highly selective, and we believe that even if they are not classics already they will be in the future. In any case, we have attempted to include some of the best from the past and bring the world of knowledge about planned organization change up to date.

A look at the book's contents will show that we begin as we should: with the external environment. Most organization change begins with the recognition that the factors in an organization's external environment are in flux, and as a consequence of this, change forces are now impinging on the organization as never before. Dealing with these new forces is therefore the impetus for changing the organization to meet these new challenges as effectively as possible.

Understanding what actions to take comes from knowledge about organizations in general and organization change in particular. Part Two is therefore devoted to theory about and models of planned change. Putting this knowledge into action starts with diagnosis, the focus of Part Three. What is our current state or situation? How ready are we for this change effort, and how well are we equipped to deal with these external forces?

As we launch the change and begin to make interventions into the system, it is likely that we will encounter resistance. Part Four is an extensive coverage of this very human phenomenon. The nature of resistance takes form according to which levels in the organization we are considering: the individual, group, or work unit, or the total system.

Part Five is then devoted to the variety of interventions that we may consider and choose from to implement the changes we have planned. Again, these interventions are categorized according to organizational level: individual, group, and larger system.

Without leadership and teamwork, change is unlikely. Part Six is devoted to key roles that are critical to effective implementation of change: the leader, the follower, groups (that is, traditional work units in the hierarchy and self-managed groups that are less constrained by hierarchy), and the role of teamwork itself.

Once we are under way with our change effort, it's highly important to evaluate our progress. Are we making any difference? Is the organization really changing? Part Seven is devoted to understanding how to answer these questions.

Finally, we end the book in Part Eight by offering conclusions and discussing some needs for the future.

January 2008   W.W.B.
                                                          D.G.L.
                                                          J.W.P.

PART ONE

ENVIRONMENT AS STIMULUS FOR CHANGE

Editors' Interlude

The main thesis of the famous historian Arnold Toynbee (*A Study of History*) was that the wellbeing of a civilization depends on its ability to respond creatively to challenges (we would say, changes), human and environmental. In much of this book we will be looking at the theory and practice of planned organization change. Before we become immersed in the theory, case studies, practices, and the like of planned change for organizations, it is useful to explore the phenomena that create the conditions for change to occur. New beginnings do foreshadow later outcomes. Changes started by charismatic individuals will create paths to change and resistance quite different from those of changes begun by natural, catastrophic events. Similarly, maintaining the motivation to change will vary considerably depending on the source of change.

Figure P.1 summarizes the proposition that any instance of status quo—a person's skill set, a manufacturing process, an inventory management process, or even an organization's core processes—is susceptible to forces in the environment, leaders with new visions, and organization change planning. One or more of these conditions or a combination of them creates potential for change. Whether *planned* change results is not a given.

Sometimes it is quite easy to point to an event or condition that stimulates the need for change. In the last few years, the world has witnessed tsunamis, earthquakes, typhoons, hurricanes and watched as various governments and private organizations responded to change, sometimes haphazardly,

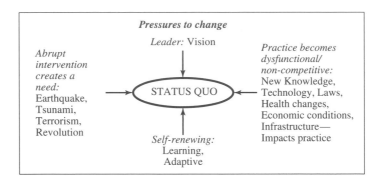

Figure P.1. Pressures to Change.

sometimes with planning as a way to mitigate future repetitions. For example, in Asia an intergovernmental commission was put together to measure ocean earthquakes for the purpose of predicting tsunamis. Some architectural and structural requirements were changed for ocean front buildings. However, the impact of earthquakes in Indonesia in November 2005 and May 2006 seemed to catch the government equally unprepared. Building structures and architecture have been radically altered in Japan and the United States in regions frequented by earthquakes. In Biloxi, Mississippi, as another example, well-intentioned persons tried to develop systematic attempts to reconfigure building permits to mitigate such future impacts as Katrina, but they ran afoul of the Federal Emergency Management Agency and essentially abandoned or tried to circumvent the new FEMA regulations. Nevertheless the stimulation to plan future changes was created by Katrina. Whether a natural disaster, a dramatic shift in geopolitical conditions, or a breakthrough in technology, the world has witnessed abrupt change in basic conditions that have *made visible the need for change*.

In still other instances, the need for change becomes visible slowly, not as easily identified as with a catastrophic event, the change becoming visible when long-standing practices become dysfunctional or technologically outdated. For example, most organizations in the late sixties and seventies could look around and see that word processors made more sense than IBM executive typewriters, even though massive skill training was required for the change. The change occurred. Other dysfunctional conditions usually become visible when organizations find they are no longer competitive or their products or services become less relevant. Government organizations, because their success or failure is at best only partially correlated to their funding, often continue well past their point of functional contribution. The classic example comes from the artillery division of the British army. In the First World War, the military determined that an artillery unit was to consist of loaders, an aimer, and discarders, in addition to three persons to hold the horses because of noise. Yes, you guessed it: the horse holders were still there at the start of the Second World War, even though the unit had been mechanized for a decade. Whether the need for change is abrupt, as with a tsunami or earthquake, or takes several years to reach a critical stage, as seems to be the case with global warming, at some point the conditions in the larger environment make the need for change visible enough to require a response from one or more entities. Responses obviously range from short-term fixes to the onset of planned change.

In other settings the stimulus to change often comes as a direct response to a *leader's vision* of how the organization should be changed. It should be noted, however, that a leader's vision is also typically a response to external environmental forces. In any case, John Young, in becoming CEO of Hewlett Packard, knew that HP was very good at inventing new ideas but not as skilled at turning them into marketable products. He challenged the entire organization to make "time-to-profitability" for new ideas the major focus of the company and was immensely successful at the time. Members of HP found they had to develop a new planned change process that did not stop at prototype, in order to introduce new ideas into the market quickly and successfully. Similarly, a large body of business biographies point to Jack Welch at GE, Herb Kelleher at Southwest Airlines, Howard Schultz at Starbucks, and Bill Gates at Microsoft as the sources of massive organizational change. These visionaries forced their organizations to develop new mind-sets and then to implement them. For example, Welch is well known for his introductions of new thrusts ("be number one or two in your markets," Workout, and adoption of Six Sigma) at GE; but how the planning processes at GE changed to accommodate these new thrusts is not as familiar. It is, however, an equally interesting story that recorded the early removal of more than two hundred highly trained strategic planners because their planning models could not respond to necessary change rapidly enough. Similarly, the organization had to develop a "real time, clock time" orientation toward change that went from identified opportunity to product more quickly than its competitors. It should be clarified, however, that an equally likely alternative to a leader's push for change is resistance (which is discussed in detail in Part Four).

In recent decades, some organizations have come to believe that change is the one constant they can count on in their businesses. They begin with the belief that today's practice should be a source for learning what is to come next. These organizations find ways to continuously reflect on and evaluate practice in order to improve or change it. Perhaps John Gardner (1964) was one of the first in modern times to identify the need for organizations to adopt a proactive stance toward change. In the early sixties he asserted, "It is a curious fact of history that no society has included in its charter a process for continuous renewal." More recently, Senge has referred to such organizations as *learning* organizations, while Fulmer called them *adaptive* organizations. Even more recently, Lawler and Worley (2006) have made the case for organizations to be *built for change* as opposed to *built to last*. Such organizations seem to have constructed into their core systems the ability to periodically *scan the environment*, determine what changes are needed in their own operations, and move forward with systematic, planned change. Shell Oil of Canada has been one of the leaders in continuously planning for their own change. They have had a system in place whereby each new venture by the company is followed by an independent, cross-discipline study team whose mission it is to determine what worked, what did not, and what was learned by the venture.

Such organizations (transformational, learning, self-renewing, built-to-change, or adaptive) argue for the importance of scanning the environment, planning change, implementing, and then revising on the basis of feedback, as necessities for survival. As of the time of this writing, only one organization has remained on the stock market's Standard and Poor's Index from its inception: General Electric. We believe this is no accident. It is there, first, because its assessment of the environment in the 1970s and 1980s led the company to get out of businesses in which it believed it could not be competitive, among them computers, personal electronics, and air conditioners, totaling $9 billion in sales. Second, it is there because it abandoned an outdated, slow-moving strategic planning process in order to change within a turbulent environment. Even though it may not be there for another decade, its lessons can be.

The four chapters that are included in this initial Part One are the classic by Emery and Trist (1965), Bennis's "Changing Organizations" (1966), and chapters from the more recent books by Foster and Kaplan (2001) and Pascale, Millemann, and Gioja (2000).

Emery and Trist were among the first to explain the nature of and how to scan the external environment for an organization. They described external environments in two broad categories: stable and dynamic. This "causal texture," they argued, provides necessary information to guide decision making for organizational executives.

The second chapter was written by Bennis in 1966 as a response to the dominant form of human organization at the time, namely, bureaucracy. Bennis argued that bureaucracies are suitable only in stable conditions and preclude organizations from being adaptive and responsive to an increasing rate of change in the external environment. Bennis's proposition was empirically supported one year later in the well-known study by Lawrence and Lorsch (1967) that is included in Part Three. The conclusion of Bennis's contribution consists of a series of predictions for organizations in the future that have proved to be largely accurate. More specifically, his forecast consists of a description of the current reality faced by organizations, with increased scale, turbulence and

interdependence in capital markets, enhanced education and increased job mobility among the general employee population, change in the psychological
contract and reduced commitment to work relationships, migration from manufacturing to more intellectual work, and a more decentralized, adaptive form
of organization.

The chapter by Foster and Kaplan, two McKinsey consultants, states that in
the twenty-first century external environments—particularly in the domain of
capital markets—external change now occurs more rapidly than organizations
can change in responding effectively. Moreover, they claim that nothing breeds
failure like success. In other words, the more efficient an organization becomes
operationally, the more it becomes locked into its ways of doing things. This
"cultural lock-in," as they call it, prevents change—especially needed
change—to respond to change in the organization's external environment.

The final chapter in Part One, about the external environment and internal
management of organizations, is the first chapter and therefore an overview of
the book *Surfing the Edge of Chaos: The Laws of Nature and the New Laws of
Business* by Pascale, Millemann, and Gioja. The book title tends to say it all,
and their initial chapter is a brief yet sweeping summary of change in the world
of science over the last two centuries. And where we are now is in the new
world science of *complexity*, which concerns the common properties of all living things. On the basis of the "nature of nature," as they call it, Pascale and
his colleagues describe a new management model. The model is based on four
fundamental or "bedrock" principles applicable to organizations, and particularly for these authors' business organizations. Drawing from the life sciences,
these principles, which are just as applicable to organizations as they are to
species, are that:

1. Equilibrium leads to death.
2. Innovation often occurs "on the edge of chaos".
3. Self-organization and emergence happen quite naturally.
4. Organizations can only be disturbed ("perturbed"), not directed.

And their primary point is that organizations either respond to change and
evolve or they die. The chapter, with its organizational examples, is an exposi-
tion of these ideas.

CHAPTER ONE

The Causal Texture of Organizational Environments

F. E. Emery
E. L. Trist (1965)

A main problem in the study of organizational change is that the environmental contexts in which organizations exist are themselves changing, at an increasing rate, and towards increasing complexity. This point, in itself, scarcely needs laboring. Nevertheless, the characteristics of organizational environments demand consideration for their own sake, if there is to be an advancement of understanding in the behavioral sciences of a great deal that is taking place under the impact of technological change, especially at the present time. This chapter is offered as a brief attempt to open up some of the problems; it stems from a belief that progress will be quicker if a certain extension can be made to current thinking about systems.

IDENTIFICATION OF THE PROBLEM

In a general way, it may be said that to think in terms of systems seems the most appropriate conceptual response so far available when the phenomena under study—at any level and in any domain—display the character of being organized, and when understanding the nature of the interdependencies constitutes the research task. In the behavioral sciences, the first steps in building a systems theory were taken in connection with the analysis of internal processes in organisms, or organizations, when the parts had to be related to the whole. Examples include the organismic biology of Jennings, Cannon, and Henderson; early Gestalt theory and its later derivatives such as balance theory; and the classical theories of social structure. Many of these problems could be represented in closed-system models. The next steps were taken when wholes had to be related to their environments. This led to open-system models.

A great deal of the thinking here has been influenced by cybernetics and information theory, though this has been used as much to extend the scope of closed-system as to improve the sophistication of open-system formulations. It was von Bertalanffy[1] who, in terms of the general transport equation that he introduced, first fully disclosed the importance of openness or closedness to the environment as a means of distinguishing living organisms from inanimate objects. In contradistinction to physical objects, any living entity survives by importing into itself certain types of material from its environment, transforming these in accordance with its own system characteristics, and exporting other types back into the environment. By this process the organism obtains the additional energy that renders it "negentropic"; it becomes capable of attaining stability in a time-independent steady state—a necessary condition of adaptability to environmental variance.

Such steady states are a very different affair from the equilibrium states described in classical physics, which have far too often been taken as models for representing biological and social transactions. Equilibrium states follow the second law of thermodynamics, so that no work can be done when equilibrium is reached, whereas the openness to the environment of a steady state maintains the capacity of the organism for work, without which adaptability, and hence survival, would be impossible.

Many corollaries follow as regards the properties of open systems, such as equifinality, growth through internal elaboration, self-regulation, constancy of direction with change of position, and so on—and by no means all of these have yet been worked out. But though von Bertalanffy's formulation enables exchange processes between the organism, or organization, and elements in its environment to be dealt with in a new perspective, it does not deal at all with those processes in the environment itself that are among the determining conditions of the exchanges. To analyze these, an additional concept is needed—*the causal texture of the environment*—if we may reintroduce, at a social level of analysis, a term suggested by Tolman and Brunswik[2] and drawn from S. C. Pepper.[3]

With this addition, we may now state a general proposition: that a comprehensive understanding of organizational behavior requires some knowledge of each member of the following set, where L indicates some potentially lawful connection and the subscript 1 refers to the organization and the subscript 2 to the environment:

$$L_{11}, L_{12}$$
$$L_{21}, L_{22}$$

L_{11} here refers to processes within the organization, the area of internal interdependencies; L_{12} and L_{21} to exchanges between the organization and its environment, the area of transactional interdependencies, from either direction; and L_{22} to processes through which parts of the environment become related to each other, that is, its causal texture, the area of interdependencies that belong within the environment itself.

In considering environmental interdependencies, the first point to which we wish to draw attention is that the laws connecting parts of the environment to each other are often incommensurate with those connecting parts of the organization to each other, or even with those that govern the exchanges. It is not possible, for example, always to reduce organization-environment relations to the form of "being included in"; boundaries are also "break" points. As Barker and Wright,[4] following Lewin,[5] have pointed out in their analysis of this problem as it affects psychological ecology, we may lawfully connect the actions of a javelin thrower in sighting and throwing a weapon; but we cannot describe in the same concepts the course of the javelin as this is affected by variables lawfully linked by meteorological and other systems.

THE DEVELOPMENT OF ENVIRONMENTAL CONNECTEDNESS (CASE ONE)

A case history, taken from the industrial field, may serve to illustrate what is meant by the environment becoming organized at the social level. It will show how a greater degree of system-connectedness, of crucial relevance to the organization, may develop in the environment, which is yet not directly a function either of the organization's own characteristics or of its immediate relations. Both of these, of course, once again become crucial when the response of the organization to what has been happening is considered.

The company concerned was the foremost in its particular market in the food canning industry in the UK and belonged to a large parent group. Its main product—a canned vegetable—had some 65 percent of this market, a situation that had been relatively stable since before the war. Believing it would continue to hold this position, the company persuaded the group board to invest several million pounds sterling in erecting a new, automated factory, which, however, based its economies on an inbuilt rigidity: it was set up exclusively for the long runs expected from the traditional market.

The character of the environment, however, began to change while the factory was being built. A number of small canning firms appeared, dealing not with this product or indeed with others in the company's range but with imported fruits. These firms arose because the last of the postwar controls had been removed from steel strip and tin, and cheaper cans could now be obtained in any numbers—while at the same time a larger market was developing in imported fruits. This trade being seasonal, the firms were anxious to find a way of using their machinery and retaining their labor in winter. They became able to do so through a curious side effect of the development of quick-frozen foods, when the company's staple was produced by others in this form. The quick-freezing process demanded great constancy at the growing end. It was not possible to control this beyond a certain point, so that quite large crops unsuitable for quick freezing but suitable for canning became available—originally from another country (the United States) where a large market for quick-frozen foods had been established. These surplus crops had been sold at a very low price for animal feed. They were now imported by the small canners at a better but still comparatively low price, and additional cheap supplies soon began to be procurable from underdeveloped countries.

Before the introduction of the quick-freezing form, the company's own canned product—whose raw material had been specially grown at additional cost—was the premier brand, superior to other varieties and charged at a higher price. But its position in the product spectrum now changed. With the increasing affluence of the society, more people were able to afford the quick-frozen form. Moreover, there was competition from a great many other vegetable products that could substitute for the staple, and people preferred this greater variety. The advantage of being the premier line among canned forms diminished, and demand increased for both the not-so-expensive varieties among them and the quick-frozen forms. At the same time, major changes were taking place in retailing; supermarkets were developing, and more and more large grocery chains were coming into existence. These establishments wanted to sell certain types of goods under their own house names and began to place bulk orders with the small canners for their own varieties of the company's staple that fell within this class. As the small canners provided an extremely cheap article (having no marketing expenses and a cheaper raw material), they could undercut the manufacturers' branded product, and within three years they captured over 50 percent of the market. Previously, retailers' varieties had accounted for less than 1 percent.

The new automatic factory could not be adapted to the new situation until alternative products with a big sales volume could be developed, and the scale of research and development, based on the type of market analysis required to identify these, was beyond the scope of the existing resources of the company either in people or in funds.

The changed texture of the environment was not recognized by an able but traditional management until it was too late. They failed entirely to appreciate that a number of outside events were becoming connected with each other in a way that was leading up to irreversible general change. Their first reaction was to make a Herculean effort to defend the traditional product; then the board split on whether or not to make entry into the cheaper unbranded market in a supplier role. Group HQ now felt they had no option but to step in. Many upheavals and changes in management took place until a "redefinition of mission" was agreed, and slowly and painfully the company reemerged with a very much altered product mix and something of a new identity.

Four Types of Causal Texture

It was this experience, and a number of others not dissimilar—by no means all of them industrial (and including studies of change problems in hospitals, in prisons, and in educational and political organizations)—that gradually led us to feel a need for redirecting conceptual attention to the causal texture of the environment, considered as a quasi-independent domain. We have now isolated four "ideal types" of causal texture, approximations to which may be thought of as existing simultaneously in the real world of most organizations—though, of course, their weighting will vary enormously from case to case.

The first three of these types have already, and indeed repeatedly, been described—in a large variety of terms and with the emphasis on an equally bewildering variety of special aspects—in the literature of a number of disciplines, ranging from biology to economics and including military theory as well as psychology and sociology. The fourth type, however, is new, at least to us, and is the one that for some time we have been endeavoring to identify. About the first three, therefore, we can be brief, but the fourth is scarcely understandable without reference to them. Together, the four types may be said to form a series in which the degree of causal texturing is increased, in a new and significant way, as each step is taken. We leave as an open question the need for further steps.

Step One

The simplest type of environmental texture is that in which goals and noxiants ("goods" and "bads") are relatively unchanging in themselves and randomly distributed. This may be called the *placid, randomized environment*. It corresponds to Simon's idea of a surface over which an organism can locomote: most of this is bare, but at isolated, widely scattered points there are little heaps of food.[6] It also corresponds to Ashby's limiting case of no connection between the environmental parts,[7] and to Schutzenberger's random field.[8] The economist's classical market also corresponds to this type.

A critical property of organizational response under random conditions has been stated by Schutzenberger, that there is no distinction between tactics and strategy; "the optimal strategy is just the simple tactic of attempting to do one's best on a purely local basis."[9] The best tactic, moreover, can be learned only by trial and error and only for a particular class of local environmental variances.[10] Although organizations under these conditions can exist adaptively as single and indeed quite small units, this becomes progressively more difficult under the other types.

Step Two

More complicated, but still a placid environment, is that which can be characterized in terms of clustering: goals and noxiants are not randomly distributed but hang together in certain ways. This may be called the *placid, clustered environment* and is the case with which Tolman and Brunswik were concerned; it corresponds to Ashby's "serial system" and to the economist's "imperfect competition." The clustering enables some parts to take on roles as signs of other parts or become means-objects with respect to approaching or avoiding. Survival, however, becomes precarious if an organization attempts to deal tactically with each environmental variance as it occurs.

The new feature of organizational response to this kind of environment is the emergence of strategy as distinct from tactics. Survival becomes critically linked with what an organization knows of its environment. To pursue a goal under its nose may lead it into parts of the field fraught with danger, while avoidance of an immediately difficult issue may lead it away from potentially rewarding areas. In the clustered environment the relevant objective is that of "optimal location," some positions being discernible as potentially richer than others.

To reach these requires concentration of resources, subordination to the main plan, and the development of a "distinctive competence," to use Selznick's[11] term, in reaching the strategic objective. Organizations under these conditions therefore tend to grow in size and also to become hierarchical, with a tendency towards centralized control and coordination.

Step Three

The next level of causal texturing we have called the *disturbed-reactive environment*. It may be compared with Ashby's ultrastable system or the economist's oligopolic market. It is a type two environment in which there is more than one organization of the same kind; indeed, the existence of a number of similar organizations now becomes the dominant characteristic of the environmental field. Each organization does not simply have to take account of the others when they meet at random but also has to consider that what it knows can also be known by the others. The part of the environment to which it wishes to move itself in the long run is also the part to which the others seek to move. Knowing this, each will wish to improve its own chances by hindering the others, and each will know that the others must not only wish to do likewise but also know that each knows this. The presence of similar others creates an imbrication, to use a term of Chein's,[12] of some of the causal strands in the environment.

If strategy is a matter of selecting the "strategic objective"—where one wishes to be at a future time—and tactics a matter of selecting an immediate action from one's available repertoire, then there appears in type three environments to be an intermediate level of organizational response: that of the *operation*, to use the term adopted by German and Soviet military theorists, who formally distinguish tactics, operations, and strategy. One has now not only to make sequential choices but to choose actions that will draw off the other organizations. The new element is that of deciding which of someone else's possible tactics one wishes to take place, while ensuring that others of them do not. An operation consists of a campaign involving a planned series of tactical initiatives, calculated reactions by others, and counteractions. The flexibility required encourages a certain decentralization and also puts a premium on quality and speed of decision at various peripheral points.[13]

It now becomes necessary to define the organizational objective in terms not so much of location as of capacity or power to move more or less at will, that is, to be able to make and meet competitive challenge. This gives particular relevance to strategies of absorption and parasitism. It can also give rise to situations in which stability can be obtained only by a certain coming-to-terms between competitors, whether enterprises, interest groups, or governments. One has to know when not to fight to the death.

Step Four

Yet more complex are the environments we have called *turbulent fields*. In these, dynamic processes, which create significant variances for the component organizations, arise from the field itself. Like type three and unlike the static types one and two, they are dynamic. Unlike type three, the dynamic properties arise not simply from the interaction of the component organizations but also from the field itself. The "ground" is in motion.

Three trends contribute to the emergence of these dynamic field forces:

1. The growth to meet type three conditions of organizations, and linked sets of organizations, so large that their actions are both persistent and strong enough to induce autochthonous processes in the environment. An analogous effect would be that of a company of soldiers marching in step over a bridge.

2. The deepening interdependence between the economic and the other facets of the society. This means that economic organizations are increasingly enmeshed in legislation and public regulation.

3. The increasing reliance on research and development to achieve the capacity to meet competitive challenge. This leads to a situation in which a change gradient is continuously present in the environmental field.

For organizations, these trends mean a gross increase in their area of *relevant uncertainly*. The consequences that flow from their actions lead off in ways that become increasingly unpredictable; they do not necessarily fall off with distance, but may at any point be amplified beyond all expectation. Similarly, lines of action that are strongly pursued may find themselves attenuated by emergent field forces.

THE SALIENCE OF TYPE FOUR CHARACTERISTICS (CASE TWO)

Some of these effects are apparent in what happened to the canning company of case one, whose situation represents a transition from an environment largely composed of type two and type three characteristics to one where those of type four began to gain in salience. The case now to be presented illustrates the combined operation of the three trends described above in an altogether larger environmental field involving a total industry and its relations with the wider society.

The organization concerned is the National Farmers Union of Great Britain, to which more than 200,000 of the 250,000 farmers of England and Wales belong. The presenting problem brought to use for investigation was that of communications. Headquarters felt, and was deemed to be, out of touch with county branches, and these with local branches. The farmer had looked to the NFU very largely to protect against market fluctuations by negotiating a comprehensive deal with the government at annual reviews concerned with the level of price support. These reviews had enabled home agriculture to maintain a steady state during two decades when the threat, or existence, of war in relation to the type of military technology then in being had made it imperative to maintain a high level of food without increasing prices to the consumer. This policy, however, was becoming obsolete as the conditions of thermonuclear stalemate established themselves. A level of support could no longer be counted on that would keep in existence small and inefficient farmers—often on marginal land and dependent on family labor—compared with efficient medium-size farms, to say nothing of large and highly mechanized undertakings.

Yet it was the former situation that had produced NFU cohesion. As this situation receded, not only were farmers becoming exposed to more competition from each other, as well as from Commonwealth and European farmers, but the effects were being felt of very great changes taking place on both the supply and marketing sides of the industry. On the supply side, a small number of giant firms now supplied almost all the requirements in fertilizer, machinery, seeds, veterinary products, and so on. As efficient farming depended on ever greater utilization of these resources, their controllers exerted correspondingly greater power over the farmers. Even more dramatic were the changes in the marketing of farm produce. Highly organized food processing and distributing industries had grown up dominated again by a few large firms, on contracts from which (fashioned to suit their interests rather than the farmer's) the farmer was becoming increasingly dependent. From both sides, deep inroads were being made on the farmer's autonomy.

It became clear that the source of the felt difficulty about communications lay in radical environmental changes that were confronting the organization with problems it was ill-adapted to meet. Communications about these changes were being interpreted or acted on as if they referred to the "traditional" situation. Only through a parallel analysis of the environment and the NFU was progress made towards developing understanding on the basis of which attempts to devise adaptive organizational policies and forms could be made. Not least among the problems was creating a bureaucratic elite that could cope with the highly technical long-range planning now required and yet remain loyal to the democratic values of the NFU. Equally difficult was developing mediating institutions, agencies that would effectively mediate the relations between agriculture and other economic sectors without triggering massive competitive processes.

These environmental changes and the organizational crisis they induced were fully apparent two or three years before the question of Britain's possible entry into the Common Market first appeared on the political agenda—which, of course, further complicated every issue.

A workable solution needed to preserve reasonable autonomy for the farmers as an occupational group, while meeting the interests of other sections of the community. Any such possibility depended on securing the consent of the large majority of farmers to placing under some degree of NFU control matters that hitherto had remained within their own power of decision. These included what they produced, how and to what standard, and how most of it should be marketed. Such thoughts were anathema, for however dependent farmers had grown on the NFU they also remained intensely individualistic. They were being asked, they now felt, to redefine identity, reverse basic values, and refashion organization—all at the same time. It is scarcely surprising that progress has been, and remains, both fitful and slow, and ridden with conflict.

VALUES AND RELEVANT UNCERTAINTY

What becomes precarious under type four conditions is how organizational stability can be achieved. In these environments, individual organizations, however large, cannot expect to adapt successfully simply through their own direct actions—as is evident in the case of the NFU. Nevertheless, there are some indications of a solution that may have the same general significance for these environments as have strategy and operations for types two and three. This is the emergence of *values that have overriding significance for all members of the field*. Social values are here regarded as coping mechanisms that make it possible to deal with persisting areas of relevant uncertainty. Unable to trace out the consequences of their actions as these are amplified and resonated through their extended social fields, people in all societies have sought rules, sometimes categorical (such as the Ten Commandments) to provide them with a guide and ready calculus. Values are not strategies or tactics; as Lewin[14] has pointed out, they have the conceptual character of "power fields" and act as injunctions.

So far as effective values emerge, the character of richly joined, turbulent fields changes in a most striking fashion. The relevance of large classes of events no longer has to be sought in an intricate mesh of diverging casual strands but is given directly in the ethical code. By this transformation a field is created that is no longer richly joined and turbulent but simplified and relatively static. Such a transformation will be regressive, or constructively adaptive, according to how far the emergent values adequately represent the new environmental requirements.

Ashby, as a biologist, has stated his view, on the one hand, that examples of environments that are both large and richly connected are not common, for our terrestrial environment is widely characterized by being highly subdivided[15]; and on the other that, so far as they are encountered, they may well be beyond the limits of human adaptation, the brain being an ultrastable system. By contrast the role here attributed to social values suggests that this sort of environment may in fact be not only one to which adaptation is possible, however difficult, but one that has been increasingly characteristic of the human condition since the beginning of settled communities. Also, let us not forget that values can be rational as well as irrational, and that the rationality of their rationale is likely to become more powerful as the scientific ethos takes greater hold in a society.

MATRIX ORGANIZATION AND INSTITUTIONAL SUCCESS

Nevertheless, turbulent fields demand some overall form of organization that is essentially different from the hierarchically structured forms to which we are accustomed. Whereas type three environments require one or another form of accommodation between like, but competitive, organizations whose fates are to a degree negatively correlated, turbulent environments require some relationship between dissimilar organizations whose fates are, basically, positively correlated. This means relationships that will maximize cooperation and that recognize no one organization can take over the role of "the other" and become paramount. We are inclined to speak of this type of relationship as an *organizational matrix*. Such a matrix acts in the first place by delimiting on value criteria the character of what may be included in the field specified—and therefore who. This selectivity then enables some definable shape to be worked out without recourse to much in the way of formal hierarchy among members. Professional associations provide one model of which there has been long experience.

We do not suggest that in other fields than the professional the requisite sanctioning can be provided only by state-controlled bodies. Indeed, the reverse is far more likely. Nor do we suggest that organizational matrices will function so as to eliminate the need for other measures to achieve stability. As with values, matrix organizations, even if successful, will only help to transform turbulent environments into the kinds of environment we have discussed as clustered and disturbed-reactive. Though, with these transformations, an organization could hope to achieve a degree of stability through its strategies, operation, and tactics, the transformations would not provide environments identical with the originals. The strategic objective in the transformed cases could no longer be stated simply in terms of optimal location (as in type two) or capabilities (as in type three). Rather, it must now be formulated in terms of *institutionalization*. According to Selznick, organizations become institutions through the embodiment of organizational values that relate them to the wider society. As Selznick has stated in his analysis of leadership in the modern American corporation, "the default of leadership shows itself in an acute form when *organizational* achievement or survival is confounded with *institutional* success"; "the executive becomes a statesman as he makes the transition from administrative management to institutional leadership."[16]

The processes of strategic planning now also become modified. Insofar as institutionalization becomes a prerequisite for stability, the determination of policy will necessitate not only a bias towards goals that are congruent with the organization's own character but also a selection of goal-paths that offer maximum convergence as regards the interests of other parties. This became a central issue for the NFU and is becoming one now for an organization such as the National Economic Development Council, which has the task of creating a matrix in which the British economy can function at something better than the stop-and-go level.

Such organizations arise from the need to meet problems emanating from type four environments. Unless this is recognized, they will only too easily be construed in type three terms, and attempts will be made to secure for them a degree of monolithic power that will be resisted overtly in democratic societies and covertly in others. In the one case, they may be prevented from ever under-taking their missions; in the other, one may wonder how long they can succeed in maintaining them.

An organizational matrix implies what McGregor[17] has called Theory Y. This in turn implies a new set of values. But values are psychosocial commodities that come into existence only rather slowly. Very little systematic work has yet been done on the establishment of new systems of values, or on the type of criteria that might be adduced to allow their effectiveness to be empirically tested. A pioneer attempt is that of Churchman and Ackoff.[18] Likert[19] has suggested that, in the large corporation or government establishment, it may well take some ten to fifteen years before the new type of group values with which he is concerned could permeate the total organization. For a new set to permeate a whole modern society, the time required must be much longer—at least a generation, according to the common saying—and this indeed must be a minimum. One may ask if this is fast enough, given the rate at which type four environments are becoming salient. A compelling task for social scientists is to direct more research onto these problems.

SUMMARY

- A main problem in the study of organizational change is that the environmental contexts in which organizations exist are themselves changing—at an increasing rate, under the impact of technological change. This means that they demand consideration for their own sake. Towards this end a redefinition is offered, at a social level of analysis, of the causal texture of the environment, a concept introduced in 1935 by Tolman and Brunswik.

- This requires an extension of systems theory. The first steps in systems theory were taken in connection with the analysis of internal processes in organisms, or organizations, which involved relating parts to the whole. Most of these problems could be dealt with through closed-system models. The next steps were taken when wholes had to be related to their environments. This led to open-system models, such as that introduced by Bertalanffy, involving a general transport equation. Though this enables exchange processes between the organism or organization and elements in its environment to be dealt with, it does not deal with those processes in the environment itself that are the determining conditions of the exchanges. To analyze these, an additional concept—the causal texture of the environment—is needed.

- The laws connecting parts of the environment to each other are often incommensurate with those connecting parts of the organization to each other, or even those that govern exchanges. Case history one illustrates this and shows the dangers and difficulties that arise when there is a rapid and gross increase in the area of relevant uncertainty, a characteristic feature of many contemporary environments.

• Organizational environments differ in their causal texture, both as regards degree of uncertainty and in many other important respects. A typology is suggested that identifies four "ideal types," approximations to which exist simultaneously in the real world of most organizations, though the weighting varies enormously:

1. In the simplest type, goals and noxiants are relatively unchanging in themselves and randomly distributed. This may be called the placid, randomized environment. A critical property from the organization's view-point is that there is no difference between tactics and strategy, and organizations can exist adaptively as single, and indeed quite small, units.

2. The next type is also static, but goals and noxiants are not randomly distributed; they hang together in certain ways. This may be called the placid, clustered environment. Now the need arises for strategy as distinct from tactics. Under these conditions, organizations grow in size, becoming multiple and tending towards centralized control and coordination.

3. The third type is dynamic rather than static. We call it the disturbed-reactive environment. It consists of a clustered environment in which there is more than one system of the same kind, that is, the objects of one organization are the same as or relevant to others like it. Such competitors seek to improve their own chances by hindering each other, each knowing the others are playing the same game. Between strategy and tactics there emerges an intermediate type of organizational response, what military theorists refer to as operations. Control becomes more decentralized to allow these to be conducted. On the other hand, stability may require a certain coming-to-terms between competitors.

4. The fourth type is dynamic in a second respect, the dynamic properties arising not simply from the interaction of identifiable component systems but from the field itself (the "ground"). We call these environments turbulent fields. The turbulence results from the complexity and multiple character of the causal interconnections. Individual organizations, however large, cannot adapt successfully simply through their direct interactions. An examination is made of the enhanced importance of values, regarded as a basic response to persisting areas of relevant uncertainty, as providing a control mechanism, when commonly held by all members in a field. This raises the question of organizational forms based on the characteristics of a matrix.

• Case history two is presented to illustrate problems of the transition from type three to type four. The perspective of the four environmental types is used to clarify the role of Theory X and Theory Y as representing a trend in value change. The establishment of a new set of values is a slow social process requiring something like a generation—unless new means can be developed.

Notes

1. L. von Bertalanffy, "The Theory of Open Systems in Physics and Biology," *Science* 111 (1950): 23–29.

2. E. C. Tolman and E. Brunswik, "The Organism and the Causal Texture of the Environment," *Psychol. Rev.* 42 (1935): 43–47.

3. S. C. Pepper, "The Conceptual Framework of Tolman's Purposive Behaviorism," *Psychol. Rev.* 41 (1934): 108–33.

4. R. G. Barker and H. F. Wright, "Psychological Ecology and the Problem of Psychosocial Development," *Child Development* 20 (1949): 131–43.

5. K. Lewin, *Principles of Topological Psychology* (New York: McGraw-Hill, 1936).

6. H. A. Simon, *Models of Man* (New York: Wiley, 1957), p. 137.

7. W. Ross Ashby, *Design for a Brain* (London: Chapman & Hall, 1960), chap. 15. sec. 4.

8. M. P. Schutzenberger, "A Tentative Classification of Goal-seeking Behaviours," *J. Ment. Sci.* 100 (1954): 100.

9. Ibid., p. 101.

10. Ashby, p. 197.

11. P. Selznick, *Leadership in Administration* (Evanston. Ill.: Row and Peterson, 1957).

12. I. Chein, "Personality and Typology," *J. Soc. Psychol.* 18 (1943): 89–101.

13. Lord Heyworth, *The Organization of Unilever* (London: Unilever, 1955).

14. Lewin.

15. Ashby, p. 205.

16. Selznick, pp. 27, 154. Since the present paper was presented, this line of thought has been further developed by Churchman and Emery in their discussion of the relation of the statistical aggregate of individuals to structured role sets: "Like other values, organizational values emerge to cope with relevant uncertainties and gain their authority from their reference to the requirements of larger systems within which people's interests are largely concordant" (C. W. Churchman and F. E. Emery, *Operational Research and the Social Sciences* [London: Tavistock Publications, 1965]).

17. D. McGregor, *The Human Side of Enterprise* (New York, Toronto, London: McGraw-Hill, 1960).

18. C. W. Churchman and R. L. Ackoff, *Methods of Inquiry* (St. Louis: Educational Publishers, 1950).

19. R. Likert, *New Patterns of Management* (New York, Toronto, London: McGraw-Hill, 1961).

CHAPTER TWO

Changing Organizations[1]

Warren G. Bennis (1966)

THE IDEA OF CHANGE

Not far from where the new Government Center is going up in downtown Boston, a foreign visitor once walked up to an American sailor and asked why the ships of his country were built to last for only a short time. According to the foreign tourist, "The sailor answered without hesitation that the act of navigation is making such rapid progress that the finest ship would become obsolete if it lasted beyond a few years. In these words, which fell accidentally from an uneducated man, I began to recognize the general and systematic idea upon which your great people direct all their concerns."

The foreign visitor was that shrewd observer of American morals and manners, Alexis de Tocqueville, and the year was 1835. He would not recognize Scollay Square today. But he caught the central theme of our country: its preoccupation, its *obsession* with change. One thing, however, *is* new since de Tocqueville's time: the prevalence of newness, the changing scale and scope of change itself, so that, as Oppenheimer said, "the world alters as we walk in it, so that the years of man's life measure not some small growth of what was learned in childhood, but a great upheaval."

Numbers have a magic all their own, and it is instructive to review some of the most relevant ones. In 1789, when George Washington was inaugurated, American society comprised fewer than four million persons, of whom 750,000 were black. Few persons lived in cities; New York, then the capital, had a population of 33,000. In all, 200,000 individuals lived in what were then defined as "urban areas"—places with more than 2,500 inhabitants. In the past ten years, Los Angeles has grown by 2,375,000, almost enough to people present-day Boston. In July 1964, the population of the U.S. was about 192 million. The U.S. Census Bureau estimates that the population in 1975 will be between 226 and 235 million and that in 1980 it will be between 246 and 260 million. World population was over three billion in 1964. If fertility remains at present levels until 1975 and then begins to decline, the population of the world will reach four billion in 1977, five billion by about 1990.

In 1960, when President Kennedy was elected, more than half of all Americans alive were over thirty-three years of age and had received their formative experiences during the Great Depression or earlier. By 1970, only ten years later, more than half of all Americans alive will be under twenty-five and will have been born after World War II. In one short decade the median age of the United States will have dropped by a full eight years—the sharpest such age drop recorded in history.

Observe the changes taking place in education. Thirty years ago, only one out of every eight Americans at work had been to high school. Today four out of five attend high school. Thirty years ago, 4 percent or less of the population attended college. Now the figure is around 35 percent, in cities about 50 percent.

Consider one more example of social change. We are all aware of the momentum of the Scientific Revolution, whose magnitude and accelerating rate—to say nothing of its consequences—are truly staggering. By 1980 science will cut an even wider path, for in that year the government alone will spend close to $35 billion on research and development: $10 billion on arms and arms control, $7 billion on basic research, and $18 billion on vast civilian welfare programs and new technology.

"Everything nailed down is coming loose," an historian said recently, and it does seem that no exaggeration, no hyperbole, no outrage can realistically appraise the extent and pace of modernization. Exaggerations come true in only a year or two. Nothing will remain in the next ten years—or there will be twice as much of it.

And it is to our credit that with the pseudo-horror stories and futuristic fantasies about *accelerations* of the rate of change (the rate of obsolescence, scientific, and technological unemployment) and the number of "vanishing" stories (the vanishing salesman, the vanishing host, the vanishing adolescent, the vanishing village) these phenomenal changes have failed to deter our compulsive desire to invent, to overthrow, to upset inherited patterns and comfort in the security of the future.

No more facts and numbers are needed to make the point. We can *feel* it on the job, in the school, in the neighborhood, in our professions, in our everyday lives. Lyndon Johnson said recently, "We want change. We want progress. We want it both at home and abroad—and we aim to get it!" I think he's got it.

CHANGING ORGANIZATIONS

How will these accelerating changes in our society influence human organizations?

Let me begin by describing the dominant form of human organization employed throughout the industrial world. It is a unique and extremely durable social arrangement called "bureaucracy," a social invention, perfected during the industrial revolution to organize and direct the activities of the business firm. It is today the prevailing and supreme type of organization wherever people direct concerted effort toward the achievement of some goal. This holds for university systems, for hospitals, for large voluntary organizations, for governmental organizations.

Corsica, according to Gibbon, is much easier to deplore than to describe. The same holds true for bureaucracy. Basically, bureaucracy is a social invention that relies exclusively on the power to influence through rules, reason, and the law. Max Weber, the German sociologist who developed the theory of bureaucracy around the turn of the century, once described bureaucracy as a social machine. "Bureaucracy," he wrote, "is like a modern judge who is a vending machine into which the pleadings are inserted together with the fee and which then disgorges the judgment together with its reasons mechanically derived from the code."

The bureaucratic "machine model" Weber outlined was developed as a reaction against the personal subjugation, nepotism, cruelty, and capricious and subjective judgments that passed for managerial practices in the early days of the industrial revolution. The true hope for man, it was thought, lay in his ability to rationalize, to calculate, to use his head as well as his hands and heart. Bureaucracy emerged out of the need for more predictability, order, and precision. It was an organization ideally suited to the values of Victorian Empire.

Most students of organizations would say that the anatomy of bureaucracy consists of the following "organs": a division of labor based on functional specialization, a well-defined hierarchy of authority, a system of procedures and rules for dealing with all contingencies relating to work activities, impersonality of interpersonal relations, and promotion and selection based on technical competence. It is the pyramidal arrangement we see on most organizational charts.

Allow me to leapfrog to the conclusion of my chapter now. It is my premise that the bureaucratic form of organization is out of joint with contemporary realities; new shapes, patterns, and models are emerging that promise drastic changes in the conduct of the corporation and of managerial practices in general. In the next twenty-five to fifty years we should witness, and participate in, the end of bureaucracy as we know it and the rise of new social systems better suited to twentieth-century demands of industrialization.

REASONS FOR ORGANIZATIONAL CHANGE

I see two main reasons for these changes in organizational life. One has been implied earlier in terms of changes taking place in society, most commonly referred to as the population and knowledge explosions. The other is more subtle and muted—perhaps less significant, but for me profoundly exciting. I have no easy name for it, nor is it easy to define. It has to do with humankind's historical quest for self-awareness, for using reason to achieve and stretch potentialities and possibilities. I think that this deliberate self-analysis has spread to large and more complex social systems, to organizations. I think there has been a dramatic upsurge of this spirit of inquiry over the past two decades. At new depths and over a wider range of affairs, organizations are opening their operations up to self-inquiry and analysis. This really involves two parallel shifts in values and outlooks, between the people who make history and those who make knowledge. One change is the scientist's realization of an affinity with "men of affairs," and the other is the latter's receptivity and newfound respect for "men of knowledge." I am calling this new development *organizational revitalization*. It is a complex social process that involves a deliberate and self-conscious examination of organizational behavior and a collaborative relationship between managers and scientists to improve performance.

To you who have profited as Alfred P. Sloan fellows here at MIT from Mr. Sloan's magnificent vision this new form of collaboration may be taken for granted. For myself, I have basked under the light of Prof. Douglas McGregor's foresight and have simply come to regard reciprocity between the academician and the manager as inevitable and natural. But I can assure you that this development is unprecedented, that never before in history, in any society, have humans in the organizational context so willingly searched, scrutinized, examined, inspected, or contemplated—for meaning, for purpose, for improvement.

I think this shift in outlook has taken a good deal of courage from both partners in this encounter. The manager has had to shake off old prejudices about "eggheads" and long-hair intellectuals. More important, the manager has had to make himself or herself and the organization vulnerable and receptive to external sources and to new, unexpected, even unwanted information—which all of you know is not an easy thing to do. The academician has had to shed some of his natural hesitancies. Scholarly conservatism is admirable, I think, except to hide behind, and for a long time caution has been a defense against reality. It might be useful to dwell on the role of academics and their growing involvement with social action, using the field of management education as a case in point. Until recently, the field of business was disregarded by large portions of the American public, and it was unknown to or snubbed by the academic establishment. Management education and research were at best regarded there with dark suspicion, as if contact with the world of reality—particularly monetary reality—was equivalent to a dreadful form of pollution. In fact, the academic has historically taken one of two stances toward the Establishment, *any* Establishment: that of rebellious critic or of withdrawn snob. The former (the rebel) can be "bought," but only in paperback books under such titles as *The Power Elite, The Lonely Crowd, The Organization Man, The Tyranny of Testing, Mass Leisure, The Exurbanites, The Life and Death of Great American Cities, The American Way of Death, Compulsory Mis-Education, The Status Seekers, Growing Up Absurd, The Paper Economy, Silent Spring, The Child Worshippers, The Affluent Society, The Depleted Society*. On the basis of these titles and reports of their brisk sales, I am thinking of writing one called *Masochism in Modern America*, practically a guaranteed success.

The withdrawn stance can be observed in some of our American universities, but less so these days. It is still the prevailing attitude in many European universities. There the university seems intent to preserve the monastic ethos of its medieval origins, offering a false but lulling security to its inmates and sapping the curriculum of virility and relevance. Max Beerbohm's whimsical and idyllic fantasy of Oxford, *Zuleika Dobson*, dramatizes this: "It is this mild, miasmal air, not less than the grey beauty and the gravity of the buildings that has helped Oxford to produce and foster, eternally, her peculiar race of artist-scholars, scholars-artists. . . . The buildings and their traditions keep astir in his mind whatsoever is gracious; the climate enfolding and enfeebling him, lulling him, keeps him careless of the sharp, harsh, exigent realities of the outer world. These realities may be seen by him . . . but they cannot fire him. Oxford is too damp for that."

"Adorable dreamer," said Matthew Arnold, in his valedictory to Oxford, "whose heart has been so romantic! Who has given thyself so prodigally, given thyself to sides and to heroes not mine, never to the Philistine! . . . what teacher could ever so save us from that bondage to which we are all prone . . . the bondage of what binds us all, the narrow, the mundane, the practical."

The intellectual and the manager have only recently come out of hiding and recognized the enormous possibilities of joint ventures. Remember that the idea of the professional school is new; this is true even in the case of the venerable threesome—law, medicine, and engineering—to say nothing of such recent upstarts as business and public administration. It is as new as the institutionalization of science, and even today this change is not greeted with unmixed joy. Colin Clark, the economist, writing in a recent *Encounter*, referred to the "dreadful suggestion that Oxford ought to have a business school."

It is probably true that we in the United States have had a more pragmatic attitude toward knowledge than anyone else. Many observers have been impressed with the disdain European intellectuals seem to show for practical matters. Even in Russia, where one would least expect it, there is little interest in the "merely useful." Harrison Salisbury, the *New York Times* Soviet expert, was struck during his recent travels by the almost total absence of liaison between research and practical application. He saw only one great agricultural experimental station on the American model. In that case, professors were working in the fields. They told Salisbury, "People call us Americans."

There may not be many American professors working in the fields, but they can be found, when not waiting in airports, almost everywhere else: in factories, in government, in less advanced countries, more recently in backward areas of our own country, in mental hospitals, in the State Department, in educational systems, and in practically all the institutional crevices Ph.D. recipients can worm their way into. They are advising, counseling, researching, recruiting, interpreting, developing, consulting, training, and working for the widest variety of clients imaginable. This is not to say that the deep ambivalence that some Americans hold toward the intellectual has disappeared, but it does indicate that academic man has become more committed to action, in greater numbers, with more diligence, and with higher aspirations than at any other time in history.

Indeed, Fritz Machlup, the economist, has coined a new economic category called the "knowledge industry," which he claims accounts for 29 percent of the gross national product. And Clark Kerr, the president of the University of California, said not too long ago, "What the railroads did for the second half of the last century and the automobile did for the first half of this century may be done for the second half of this century by the knowledge industry: that is, to serve as the focal point of national growth. And the university is at the center of the knowledge process."

CHANGES IN MANAGERIAL PHILOSOPHY

Now let us turn to the main theme and put the foregoing remarks about the reciprocity between action and knowledge into the perspective of changing organizations. Consider some of the relatively recent research and theory concerning the human side of enterprise that have made such a solid impact on management thinking, and particularly upon the moral imperatives that guide managerial action. I shall be deliberately sweeping in summarizing these changes as much to hide my surprise as to cover a lot of ground quickly. (I can be personal about this. I remember sitting in Professor McGregor's class some seven years ago, when he first presented his new theories, and I remember the sharp antagonism his Theory X and Theory Y analysis then provoked. Today, I believe most of you would take these ideas as generally self-evident.)

It seems to me that we have seen over the past decade a fundamental change in the basic philosophy that underlies managerial behavior, reflected most of all in the following three areas:

1. A new concept of *human*, based on increased knowledge of humans' complex and shifting needs, which replaces the oversimplified, innocent push-button idea of the human
2. A new concept of *power*, based on collaboration and reason, that replaces a model of power based on coercion and fear
3. A new concept of *organizational values*, based on humanistic-democratic ideals, that replaces the depersonalized mechanistic value system of bureaucracy

Please do not misunderstand. The last thing I want to do is overstate the case. I do not mean that these transformations of human, power, and organizational values are fully accepted or even understood, to say nothing of implemented, in day-to-day affairs. These changes may be light-years away from actual adoption. I do mean that they have gained wide intellectual acceptance in enlightened management quarters, that they have caused a tremendous amount of rethinking and search behavior on the part of many organizations, and that they have been used as a basis for policy formulation by many large-scale organizations.

I have tried to summarize all the changes affecting organizations, resulting both from the behavioral sciences and from trends in our society, in a chart of human problems confronting contemporary organizations (Table 2.1). These problems (or predicaments) emerge basically from twentieth-century changes, primarily the growth of science and education, the separation of power from property and the correlated emergence of the professional manager, and other kinds of changes that I will get to in a minute. The bureaucratic mechanism, so capable of coordinating men and power in a stable society of routine tasks, cannot cope with contemporary realities. The chart shows five major categories, which I visualize as the core tasks confronting the manager in coordinating the human side of enterprise.

Table 2.1. Human Problems Confronting Contemporary Organizations.

	Problem	Bureaucratic Solutions	New Twentieth-Century Conditions
Integration	The problem of how to integrate individual needs and management goals.	No solution because of no problem. Individual vastly oversimplified, regarded as passive instrument or disregarded.	Emergence of human sciences and understanding of man's complexity. Rising aspirations. Humanistic-democratic ethos.
Social influence	The problem of the distribution of power and sources of power and authority.	An explicit reliance on legal-rational power but an implicit usage of coercive power. In any case, a confused, shifting complex of competence, coercion, and legal code.	Separation of management from ownership. Rise of trade unions and general education. Negative and unintended effects of authoritarian rule.
Collaboration	The problem of managing and resolving conflicts.	The "rule of hierarchy" to resolve conflicts between ranks and the "rule of coordination" to resolve conflict between horizontal groups. "Loyalty."	Specialization and professionalization and increased need for interdependence. Leadership too complex for one-man rule or omniscience.
Adaptation	The problem of responding appropriately to changes induced by the environment of the firm.	Environment stable, simple, and predictable; tasks routine. Adapting to change occurs in haphazard and adventitious ways. Unanticipated consequences abound.	External environment of firm more "turbulent," less predictable. Unprecedented rate of technological change.
"Revitalization"	The problem of growth and decay.	?	Rapid changes in technologies, tasks, manpower, raw materials, norms, and values of society all make constant attention to the processes of the firm and revision imperative.

First, the problem of integration grows out of our "consensual society," where personal attachments play a great part, where the individual is appreciated, in which there is concern for individual well-being—not just in a veterinary-hygiene sense but as a moral, integrated personality.

Second, the problem of social influence is essentially the problem of power, and leadership studies and practices reveal not only an ethical component but an *effectiveness* component: people tend to work more efficiently and with more commitment when they have a part in determining their own fates and have a stake in problem solving.

Third, the problem of collaboration grows out of the same social processes of conflict, stereotyping, and centrifugal forces that inhere in and divide nations and communities. They also employ the same furtive, often fruitless, always crippling mechanisms of conflict resolution: avoidance or suppression, annihilation of the weaker party by the stronger, sterile compromise, and unstable collusions and coalitions. Particularly as organizations become more complex, they fragment and divide, building tribal patterns and symbolic codes that often work to exclude others (secrets and noxious jargon, for example) and on occasion to exploit differences for inward (and always fragile) harmony. Some large organizations, in fact, can be understood only through an analysis of their cabals, cliques, and satellites, their tactics resembling a sophisticated form of guerrilla warfare, and a venture into adjacent spheres of interest is taken under cover of darkness and fear of ambush.

(The university is a wondrous place for these highly advanced battle techniques, far overshadowing their business counterparts in subterfuge and sabotage. Quite often a university becomes a loose collection of competing departments, schools, and institutes, largely noncommunicating because of the multiplicity of specialist jargons and interests and held together, as Robert Hutchins once said, chiefly by a central heating system, or as Clark Kerr amended, by the questions of what to do about the parking problem.)[2]

Fourth, the real *coup de grâce* to bureaucracy has come as much from our turbulent environment as from its incorrect assumptions about human behavior. The pyramidal structure of bureaucracy, where power was concentrated at the top—perhaps by one person or a group who had the knowledge and resources to control the entire enterprise—seemed perfect to "run a railroad." And undoubtedly, for tasks like building railroads, for the routinized tasks of the nineteenth and early twentieth centuries, bureaucracy was and is an eminently suitable social arrangement.

Nowadays, due primarily to the growth of science, technology, and research and development activities, the organizational environment of the firm is rapidly changing. Today it is a turbulent environment, not a placid and predictable one, and there is a deepening interdependence among the economic and other facets of society. This means that economic organizations are increasingly enmeshed in legislation and public policy. Put more simply, it means that the government will be in just about everything, more of the time. It may also mean, and this is radical, that maximizing cooperation, rather than competition between firms—particularly if their fates are correlated—may become a strong possibility.

Fifth and finally, there is the problem of revitalization. Alfred North Whitehead sets it neatly before us: "The art of free society consists first in the maintenance of the symbolic code, and secondly in the fearlessness of revision. . . . Those societies which cannot combine reverence to their symbols with freedom of revision must ultimately decay." Organizations, as well as societies, must be concerned with those social conditions that engender buoyancy, resilience, and fearlessness of revision. Growth and decay emerge as the penultimate problem where the environment of contemporary society is turbulent and uncertain.

FORECAST OF ORGANIZATIONS OF THE FUTURE

A forecast falls somewhere between a prediction and a prophecy. It lacks the divine guidance of the latter and the empirical foundation of the former. On thin empirical ice, I want to set forth some of the conditions that will dictate organization life in the next twenty-five to fifty years.

The Environment

Those factors already mentioned will continue in force and increase. Rapid technological change and diversification will lead to interpenetration of the government—its legal and economic policies—with business. Partnerships between business and government will be typical. And because of the immensity and expense of the projects, there will be fewer identical units competing for the same buyers and sellers. The three main features of the environment will be interdependence rather than competition, turbulence rather than steadiness, and large-scale rather than small-scale enterprises.

Population Characteristics

The most distinctive characteristic of our society is, and will become even more so, its education. Peter Drucker calls us the "educated society," and for good reason: within fifteen years, two-thirds of our population living in metropolitan areas will have attended college. Adult education is growing even faster. It is now almost routine for the experienced physician, engineer, and executive to go back to school for advanced training every two or three years. Some fifty universities, in addition to a dozen large corporations, offer advanced management courses to successful people in the middle and upper ranks of business. Before World War II, only two such programs existed, both new and struggling to get students.

All of this education is not just "nice" but necessary. For as W. Willard Wirtz, the secretary of labor, recently pointed out, computers can do the work of most high school graduates—and they can do it cheaper and more effectively. Fifty years ago, education used to be regarded as "nonwork," and intellectuals on the payroll (and many staff workers) were considered "overhead." Today, the survival of the firm depends, more than ever before, on the proper exploitation of brain power.

One other characteristic of the population that will aid our understanding of organizations of the future is increasing job mobility. The lowered cost and growing ease of transportation, coupled with the real needs of a dynamic environment, will change drastically the idea of "owning" a job—or "having roots," for that matter. Participants will be shifted from job to job and even employer to employer with little concern for roots and homestead.

Work Values

The increased level of education and mobility will change the values we hold about work. People will be more intellectually committed to their jobs and will probably require more involvement, participation, and autonomy in their work.

Also, people will tend to be more "other-directed," taking cues, more from their immediate environment than from tradition. We will tend to rely more heavily on temporary social arrangements, on our immediate and constantly changing colleagues. We will tend to be more concerned and involved with relationships rather than with relatives.

Tasks and Goals

The tasks of the firm will be more technical, complicated, and unprogrammed. They will rely more on intellect than muscle. And they will be too complicated for one person to comprehend, to say nothing of control. Essentially, they will call for the collaboration of specialists in a project or team form of organization.

There will be a complication of goals. Business will increasingly concern itself with its adaptive or innovative-creative capacity. In addition, meta-goals—that is, supragoals that shape and provide the foundation for the goal structure—will have to be articulated and developed. For example, one metagoal might be a system for detecting new and changing goals; another could be a system for deciding priorities among goals.

Finally, there will be more conflict and contradiction among diverse standards of organizational effectiveness, just as in hospitals and universities today there is a conflict between teaching and research. The reason for this is the increased number of professionals involved, who tend to identify more with the goals of their profession than with those of their immediate employer. University professors can be used as a case in point. More and more of their income comes from outside sources, such as foundations that grant them money and industries for whom they consult. They tend not to be good "company men" because they divide their loyalty between their professional values and organizational goals.

Organization

The social structure of organizations of the future will have some unique characteristics. The key word will be "temporary"; there will be adaptive, rapidly changing *temporary systems*. These will be problem-oriented "task forces" composed of groups of relative strangers who represent a diverse set of professional skills. The groups will be arranged on an organic rather than a mechanical model; they will evolve in response to a problem rather than to programmed role expectations. The "executive" thus will become a coordinator or "linking pin" between various task forces, a person who can speak the diverse languages of research, with skills to relay information and to mediate between groups. People will be differentiated not vertically according to rank and status but flexibly and functionally according to skill and professional training.

Adaptive, problem-solving, temporary systems of diverse specialists, linked together by coordinating and task-evaluating specialists in an organic flux— this is the organizational form that will gradually replace bureaucracy as we know it. As no catchy phrase comes to mind, I call this an organic-adaptive structure.

Motivation

The organic-adaptive structure should increase motivation, and thereby effectiveness, since it will enhance satisfactions intrinsic to the task. There is a harmony between the educated individual's need for meaningful, satisfactory, and creative tasks and a flexible organizational structure.

There will, however, also be reduced commitment to work groups, for these groups, as I have mentioned, will be transient and changing. While skills in human interaction will become more important, due to the growing needs for collaboration in complex tasks, there will be a concomitant reduction in group cohesiveness. My prediction is that in the organic-adaptive system people will have to learn to develop quick and intense relationships on the job and learn to bear the loss of more enduring work relationships. Because of the added ambiguity of roles, more time will have to be spent on the continual search for the appropriate organizational mix.

In general, I do not agree with those who emphasize a new utopianism in which leisure, not work, will become the emotional-creative sphere of life. Jobs should become more rather than less involving; man is a problem-solving animal, and the tasks of the future guarantee a full agenda of problems. In addition, the adaptive process itself may become captivating to many.

At the same time, I think that the future I describe is not necessarily a "happy" one. Coping with rapid change, living in temporary work systems, developing meaningful relationships and then breaking them—all augur social strains, and psychological tensions. Teaching how to live with ambiguity, to identify with the adaptive process, to make a virtue out of contingency, and to be self-directing will be the task of education, the goal of maturity, and the achievement of the successful manager. To be a spouse in this era will be to undertake the profession of providing stability and continuity.

In these new organizations, participants will be called on to use their minds more than at any other time in history. Fantasy, imagination, and creativity will be legitimate in ways that today seem strange. Social structures will no longer be instruments of psychic repression but will increasingly promote play and freedom on behalf of curiosity and thought.

Bureaucracy was a monumental discovery for harnessing the muscle power of the industrial revolution. In today's world, it is a lifeless crutch that is no longer useful. For we now require structures of freedom to permit the expression of play and imagination and to exploit the new pleasure of work.

One final word: although I forecast the structure and value coordinates for organizations of the future and contend that they are inevitable, this should not bar any of us from giving the inevitable a little push here and there. And even though the French moralist may be right that there are no delightful marriages, just good ones, it is possible that if managers and scientists continue to get their heads together in organizational revitalization, they *might* develop delightful organizations—just possibly.

I started with a quote from de Tocqueville, and I think it would be fitting to end with one: "I am tempted to believe that what we call necessary institutions are often no more than institutions to which we have grown accustomed. In matters of social constitution, the field of possibilities is much more extensive than men living in their various societies are ready to imagine."

Notes

1. This chapter is taken from the first Douglas Murray McGregor Memorial Lecture of the Alfred P. Sloan School of Management, Massachusetts Institute of Technology. Published by MIT Press, Cambridge, Mass., February 1966. Used by permission.

2. For this observation, as well as for other major influences, I want to thank Prof. Kenneth D. Benne.

CHAPTER THREE

Survival and Performance in the Era of Discontinuity

Richard N. Foster
Sarah Kaplan (2001)

*This company will be going strong one hundred and even
five hundred years from now.*
—C. Jay Parkinson, president of Anaconda Mines, statement
made three years in advance of Anaconda's bankruptcy

In 1917, shortly before the end of World War I, Bertie Charles (or B. C., as he was known) Forbes formed his first list of the one hundred largest American companies. The firms were ranked by assets, since sales data were not accurately compiled in those days. In 1987, *Forbes* republished its original "Forbes 100" list and compared it to its 1987 list of top companies. Of the original group, sixty-one had ceased to exist.

Of the remaining thirty-nine, eighteen had managed to stay in the top one hundred. These eighteen companies—which included Kodak, DuPont, General Electric, Ford, General Motors, Procter & Gamble, and a dozen other corporations—had clearly earned the nation's respect. Skilled in the arts of survival, these enterprises had weathered the Great Depression, the Second World War, the Korean conflict, the roaring sixties, the oil and inflation shocks of the seventies, and unprecedented technological change in the chemical, pharmaceutical, computer, software, radio and television, and global telecommunications industries.

They survived. But they did not perform. As a group these great companies earned a long-term return for their investors during the 1917–1987 period 20 percent less than that of the overall market. Only two of them, General Electric and Eastman Kodak, performed better than the averages, and Kodak has since fallen on harder times (Figure 3.1).

One reaches the same conclusion from an examination of the S&P 500. Of the five hundred companies originally making up the S&P 500 in 1957, only

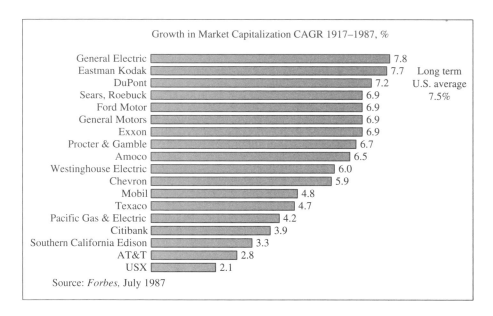

Figure 3.1. Long-Term Survivor Performance.

seventy-four remained on the list through 1997. And of these seventy-four, only twelve outperformed the S&P 500 index itself over the 1957–1998 period. Moreover, the list included companies from two industries, pharmaceuticals and food, that were strong performers during this period. If today's S&P 500 were made up of only those companies that were on the list when it was formed in 1957, the overall performance of the S&P 500 would have been about 20 percent less *per year* than it actually has been.

For the last several decades, we have celebrated the big corporate survivors, praising their "excellence" and their longevity, their ability to last. These, we have assumed, are the bedrock companies of the American economy. These are the companies that "patient" investors pour their money into—investments that would certainly reward richly at the end of a lifetime. But our findings—based on the thirty-eight years of data compiled in the McKinsey Corporate Performance Database—have shown that they do not perform as we might suspect. An investor following the logic of patiently investing money in these survivors will do substantially less well than an investor who merely invests in market index funds.

McKinsey's long-term studies of corporate birth, survival, and death in America clearly show that the corporate equivalent of El Dorado, the golden company that continually performs better than the markets, *has never existed.* It is a myth. Managing for survival, even among the best and most revered corporations, does not guarantee strong long-term performance for shareholders. In fact, just the opposite is true. In the long run, markets always win.

THE ASSUMPTION OF CONTINUITY

How could this be? How could a stock market index such as the Dow Jones Industrial average or the S&P 500 average—which, unlike companies, lack skilled managers, boards of experienced directors, carefully crafted organizational structures, the most advanced management methods, privileged assets, and special relationships with anyone of their choosing—perform better, over the long haul, than all but two of *Forbes's* strongest survivors, General Electric and Eastman Kodak? Are the capital markets, as represented by the stock market averages, "wiser" than managers who think about performance all the time?

The answer is that the capital markets, and the indices that reflect them, encourage the creation of corporations, permit their efficient operations (as long as they remain competitive), and then rapidly—and remorselessly—remove them when they lose their ability to perform. Corporations, which operate with management philosophies based on the assumption of continuity, are not able to change at the pace and scale of the markets. As a result, in the long term, they do not create value at the pace and scale of the markets.

It is among the relatively new entrants to the economy—for example, Intel, Amgen, and Cisco—where one finds superior performance, at least for a time. The structure and mechanisms of the capital markets enable these companies to produce results superior to even the best surviving corporations. Moreover, it is the corporations that have lost their ability to meet investor expectations (no matter how unreasonable these expectations might be) that consume the wealth of the economy. **The capital markets remove these weaker performers at a greater rate than even the best-performing companies do.** Joseph Alois Schumpeter, the great Austrian-American economist of the 1930s and 1940s, called this process of creation and removal "the gales of creative destruction." So great is the challenge of running the operations of a corporation today that few corporate leaders have the energy or time to manage the processes of creative destruction, especially at the pace and scale necessary to compete with the market. Yet that is precisely what is required to sustain market levels of long-term performance.

The essential difference between corporations and capital markets is in the way they enable, manage, and control the processes of creative destruction. Corporations are built on the assumption of continuity; their focus is on operations. Capital markets are built on the assumption of *discontinuity*; their focus is on creation and destruction. The market encourages rapid and extensive creation, and hence greater wealth building. It is less tolerant than the corporation is of long-term underperformance. Outstanding corporations do win the right to survive, but not the ability to earn above-average or even average shareholder returns over the long term. Why? Because their control processes—the very processes that help them to survive over the long haul—deaden them to the need for change.

THE REALITY OF DISCONTINUITY

This distinction between the way corporations and markets approach the processes of creative destruction is not an artifact of our times or an outgrowth of the dot com generation. It has been smoldering for decades, like a fire in a wall, ready to erupt at any moment. The market turmoil we see today is a logical extension of trends that began decades ago.

The origins of modern managerial philosophy can be traced to the eighteenth century, when Adam Smith argued for specialization of tasks and division of labor in order to cut waste. By the late nineteenth century, these ideas had culminated in an age of American trusts, European holding companies, and Japanese zaibatsus. These complex giants were designed to convert natural resources into food, energy, clothing, and shelter in the most asset-efficient way, to maximize output and to minimize waste.

By the 1920s, Smith's simple idea had enabled huge enterprises, exploiting the potential of mass production, to flourish. Peter Drucker wrote the seminal guidebook for these corporations in 1946, *The Concept of the Corporation*. The book laid out the precepts of the then-modern corporation, based on the specialization of labor, mass production, and the efficient use of physical assets.

This approach was in deep harmony with the times. Change came slowly in the twenties, when the first Standard and Poor's index of ninety important U.S. companies was formed. In the twenties and thirties the turnover rate in the S&P 90 averaged about 1.5 percent per year. A new member of the S&P 90 at that time could expect to remain on the list, on average, for more than sixty-five years. The corporations of these times were built on the assumption of continuity—perpetual continuity, the essence of which Drucker explored in his book. Change was a minor factor. Companies were in business to transform raw materials into final products, to avoid the high costs of interaction between independent companies in the marketplace. This required them to operate at great scale and to control their costs carefully. These vertically integrated configurations were protected from all but incremental change.

We argue that this period of corporate development, lasting for more than seventy years, has come to an end. In 1998, the turnover rate in the S&P 500 was close to 10 percent, implying an average lifetime on the list of ten years, not sixty-five! Drucker predicted the turning point with his 1969 book *The Age of Discontinuity,* but his persuasive arguments could not overcome the zeitgeist of the seventies. The seventies were, for many managers, the modern equivalent of the 1930s. Inflation raged, interest rates were at the highest levels since before World War II, and the stock market was languishing. Few entrants dared risk capital or career on the founding of a new company based on Drucker's insights. It was a fallow time for corporate start-ups. As the long-term demands of survival took over, Drucker's advice fell on deaf years.

The pace of change has been accelerating continuously since the 1920s. There have been three great waves. The timing and extent of these waves match the rise and fall of the generative and absorptive capabilities of the nation. The first wave came shortly after World War II, when the nation's military buildup gave way to the need to rebuild the consumer infrastructure. Many new companies entered the economy at this time and then rose to economic prominence during the 1940s and 1950s, among them Owens-Corning, Textron, and Seagram.

The second wave began in the 1960s. The rate of turnover in the S&P 90 began to accelerate as the federal defense and aerospace programs once again stimulated the economy, providing funds for the development of logic and memory chips, and later the microprocessor. They were heady days—"bubble days," in the eyes of some. The hot stocks were called "one-decision" stocks: buy them once and never sell them, and your future fortune was assured (Figure 3.2).

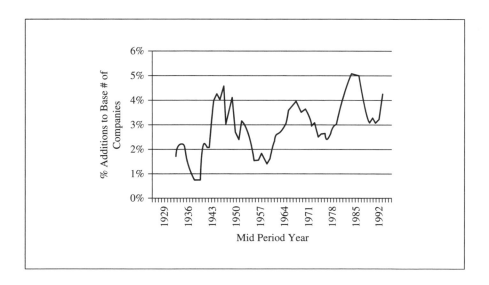

Figure 3.2. Change in the S&P 500 Seven-Year Moving Average.

The bubble burst in 1968. The New York Stock Exchange, which had risen to almost 1,000, did not return to that level again until the early 1980s. During this absorptive, or slack, period, when the country was beset with rising oil prices and inflation, and when bonds earned returns substantially greater than equities, few new companies joined—or left—the S&P 500. Interestingly enough, though, despite the worst economic conditions the nation had endured since the Depression, the minimum rate of corporate turnover did not drop to the low rate of turnover seen in the 1950s. The base rate of change in the economy had permanently risen.

Paul Volcker, chairman of the Federal Reserve Bank, finally led the charge that broke the back of inflation, and the number of new companies climbing onto the S&P 500 accelerated. In the 1980s, once again the S&P began substituting new high-growth and high-market-cap companies for the slower-growing and even shrinking-market-cap older companies. The change in the S&P index mix also reflected changes in the economic mix of business in the United States. When the markets collapsed in the late eighties and a short-lived recession hit the American economy in the early nineties, the rate of substitution in the S&P 500 fell off. But again, even at its lowest point the rate of turnover was higher than it was during the 1970s decline. The minimum level of change in the economy had been quietly building and was increasing again. This was even more evident as the technology-charged 1990s kicked into gear, accelerating the rate of the S&P index turnover to levels never seen before. By the end of the 1990s, we were well into what Peter Drucker calls the Age of Discontinuity. Extrapolating from past patterns, we calculate that by the end of the year 2020 the average lifetime of a corporation on the S&P will have been shortened to about ten years, as fewer and fewer companies fall into the category of "survivors" (Figure 3.3).

THE GALES OF DISCONTINUITY

The Age of Discontinuity did not arrive in the 1990s by happenstance. It arose from fundamental economic forces:

• The increasing efficiency of business, due to dramatic declines in capital costs. As industry shifted from goods to services, there was a concurrent decline in interaction and transaction costs. These costs declined because of the advent of information technology and the steady rise in labor productivity due to advances in technology and management methods.

• The increasing efficiency of capital markets, due to the increasing accuracy (and transparency) of corporate performance data.

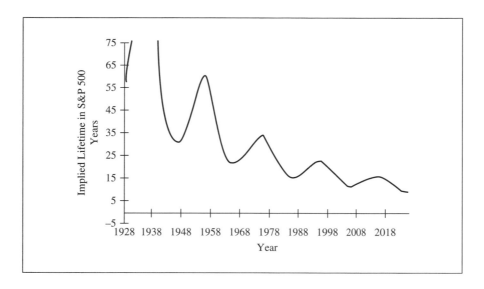

Figure 3.3. Average Lifetime of S&P 500 Companies.

• The rise in national liquidity, due to the improved profitability of U.S. corporations, and a favorable bias, unparalleled anywhere else in the world, toward U.S. equities.

• Strengthened fiscal management by the federal government, including an effective Federal Reserve, and reduced corporate taxes.

These forces have helped to create the likes of Microsoft, with a market capitalization greater than all but the top ten nations of the world (Microsoft's real assets make up about 1 percent of its market value). Computer maker Dell has virtually no assets at all. Internet start-up companies begin with almost no capital. For these companies, returns on capital are unimaginably large by previous standards. Productivity is soaring. The pipeline of new technology is robust. There are more than ten thousand Internet business proposals alone waiting for evaluation at venture capital firms, even after the NASDAQ collapse in March and April 2000. By all reports, the number (if not the quality) of these proposals is increasing all the time. Information technology is not nearing its limits. The effectiveness of software programming continues to grow; communications technology is just beginning. The global GDP will double in the next twenty years, creating approximately $20–$40 trillion in new sales. If, through the productivity improvements the Internet enables, the world can save 2 percent of the $25 trillion now produced, the market value of those savings will run into the trillions.

Incumbent companies have an unprecedented opportunity to take advantage of these times. But if history is a guide, no more than a third of today's major corporations will survive in an economically important way over the next twenty-five years. Those that do not survive will die a Hindu death of transformation as they are acquired or merged with part of a larger, stronger organization, rather than a Judeo-Christian death, but it will be death nonetheless. And the demise of these companies will come from a lack of competitive adaptiveness. To be blunt, most of these companies will die or be bought out and absorbed because they are too damn slow to keep pace with change in the market. By 2020, more than three quarters of the S&P 500 will consist of companies we don't know today—new companies drawn into the maelstrom of economic activity from the periphery, springing from insights unrecognized today.

The assumption of continuity, on which most of our leading corporations have been based for years, no longer holds. Discontinuity dominates.

The one hundred or so companies in the current S&P 500 that survive into the 2020s will be unlike the corporate survivors today. They will have to be masters of creative destruction, built for discontinuity, remade like the market. Schumpeter anticipated this transformation over a half century ago when he observed: "The problem that is usually being visualized is how capitalism *administers* existing structures, whereas the relevant problem is how it *creates* and *destroys* them."

THE NEED TO ABANDON THE ASSUMPTION OF CONTINUITY

How can corporations make themselves more like the market? The general prescription is to increase the rate of creative destruction to the level of the market itself, without losing control of present operations. As sensible as this recommendation is, it has proven difficult to implement.

Hundreds of managers from scores of U.S. and European countries have told us that although they are satisfied with their operating prowess, they are dissatisfied with their ability to implement change. "How do the excellent innovators do it?" they ask, presuming that excellent innovators exist. "What drives an innovation breakthrough?" Others question how one grows a company beyond its core business, and most fundamentally of all, "How do we find new ideas?"

The difficulties behind these questions arise from the inherent conflict between the need for corporations to control existing operations and the need to create the kind of environment that will permit new ideas to flourish—and old ones to die a timely death. This may require trading out traditional assets, challenging existing channels of distribution, or making dilutive acquisitions. But whatever the challenges, we believe that most corporations will find it impossible to match or outperform the market without abandoning the assumption of continuity. Author James Reston, in his book *The Last Apocalypse,* observed Europe's fear that the first millennium would have a fiery conclusion:

> When the millennium arrived the apocalypse did take place; a world did end, and a new world arose from the ruins. But the last apocalypse was a process rather than a cataclysm. It had the suddenness of forty years.

The current apocalypse—the transition from a state of continuity to a state of discontinuity—has the same kind of suddenness. Never again will American business be as it once was. The rules have changed forever. Some companies have made the crossing. Under Jack Welch, General Electric has negotiated the apocalypse and seen its performance benefit as a result. Johnson & Johnson is moving across the divide quickly, as we will see later. Enron has made strong progress by transforming itself from a natural gas pipeline company to a trading company. Corning has been successful in shedding its dependence on consumer durables and becoming a leader in high-tech optical fiber. In France, L'Oréal seems to be on the right track, having found a new way to organize itself and transfer beauty concepts from one economy to another. But these are the exceptions. Few have attempted the journey. Fewer still have made it to the other side successfully.

CULTURAL LOCK-IN

For half a century, Bayer aspirin drove the growth of Sterling Drug until Johnson & Johnson introduced Tylenol. Out of fear of cannibalizing its Bayer aspirin leadership, Sterling Drug refused to introduce its leading European non-aspirin pain reliever (Panadol) to the United States. Instead, it tried to expand its Bayer line overseas. This failure ultimately led to its acquisition by Kodak. Sterling Drug had become effectively immobilized, unable to change its half-century-old behavior out of fear. Its strong culture—its rules of thumb for decision making, its control processes, the information it used for decision making—blocked its progress and ultimately sealed its fate. It had locked itself into an ineffective approach to the marketplace despite clear signs that it needed to act in a new way.

"Cultural lock-in"—the inability to change the corporate culture even in the face of clear market threats—explains why corporations find it difficult to respond to the messages of the marketplace. Cultural lock-in results from the gradual stiffening of the invisible architecture of the corporation, and the ossification of its decision-making abilities, control systems, and mental models. It dampens a company's ability to innovate or to shed operations with a less-exciting future. Moreover, it signals the corporation's inexorable decline into inferior performance. Often, as in the case of Sterling Drug, cultural lock-in manifests itself in three general fears: the fear of cannibalization of an important product line, the fear of channel conflict with important customers, and the fear of earnings dilution that might result from a strategic acquisition. As reasonable as all these fears seem to be to established companies, they are not fears that are felt in the market. And so the market moves where the corporation dares not.

Cultural lock-in is the last in a series of "emotional" phases in a corporation's life, a series that mirrors remarkably that of human beings. In the early years of a corporation, just after its founding, the dominant emotion is passion—the sheer energy to make things happen. When passion rules, information and analysis are ignored in the name of vision: "We know the right answer; we do not need analysis."

As the corporation ages, the bureaucracy begins to settle in. Passions cool and are replaced by "rational decision making," often simply the codification of what has worked in the past. Data are gathered, analysis is performed, alternatives are postulated, and scenarios are developed. Attempts are made to avoid the game of information sculpting. Only when "rational" decision making is in vogue does all the relevant information flow to the right decision maker, at the right time, and in the right form to be easily analyzed and interpreted. Rational decision making is triumphant, at least for a while. This stage is often pictured as the normal state of the corporation, although in our experience, particularly as the pace of change increases, rarely does this ideal state accurately describe how the company actually operates.

Eventually, rational decision making reveals that the future potential for the business is limited. Often at this point, threatened by the prospects for a bleak future, the corporation falls back on defensive routines to protect the organization from its fate, just as defensive emotions emerge in our lives when we sense impending trauma. Management now sees the future filled more with trouble than with promise. Decisions are made to protect existing businesses. The fear of discarding the old for the new (product cannibalization), the fear of customer conflict, and the fear of earnings dilution through acquisition paralyze acts of creative destruction, and often effectively shield the corporation from the perception of future trouble—as well as the need to act—for a long time. Cultural lock-in is established, thwarting the emergence of a leader or team that might save the day.

Why does cultural lock-in occur? The heart of the problem is the formation of hidden sets of rules, or mental models, that, once formed, are extremely difficult to change. Mental models are the core concepts of the corporation, the beliefs and assumptions, the cause-and-effect relationships, the guidelines for interpreting language and signals, the stories repeated within the corporate walls. Charlie Munger, a longtime friend of and co-investor with Warren Buffett and vice chairman of Berkshire Hathaway, calls mental models the "theoretical frameworks that help investors better understand the world."

Mental models are invisible in the corporation. They are neither explicit nor examined, but they are pervasive. When well crafted, mental models allow management to anticipate the future and solve problems. But once constructed, mental models become self-reinforcing, self-sustaining, and self-limiting. And when mental models are out of sync with reality, they cause management to make forecasting errors and poor decisions. The assumption of continuity, in fact, is precisely the kind of disconnect with reality that leads corporations into flawed forecasting and poor decisions.

Mental models manifest themselves in corporate control systems. These systems are designed to ensure predictable goal achievement, whether it be cost control, the control of capital expenditures, or the control of the deployment of key personnel. Effective control means that an informed manager can be reasonably confident that unpleasant surprises will not occur.

Unfortunately, control systems can also create "defensive routines" in organizations, including the failure to challenge the status quo, the failure to encourage a diversity of opinions, failure to disagree with superiors (thereby displeasing them), communicating in ambiguous and inconsistent ways, and making these failures even when known "undiscussable." Change becomes impossible.

Corporate control systems also undermine the ability of the organization to innovate at the pace and scale of the market. Under the assumption of continuity, for example, the arguments for building a new business can be turned back, since its probable success cannot be proven in advance. Under these circumstances, it is more likely that ideas based on the incremental growth of current capabilities and mental models will be encouraged.

Corporate control systems limit creativity through their dependence on *convergent thinking*. Convergent thinking focuses on clear problems and provides well-known solutions quickly. It thrives on focus. Order, simplicity, routine, clear responsibilities, unambiguous measurement systems, and predictability are the bedrock of convergent thinking. Convergent thinking is tailor-made for the assumption of continuity. Convergent thinking can be effective at handling small, incremental changes and differences, but transformational changes completely flummox the system.

Discontinuity, on the other hand, thrives on a different kind of thinking, *divergent thinking*. Divergent thinking focuses on broadening—diverging—the context of decision making. It is initially more concerned with questions than getting to the answer in the fastest possible way. Divergent thinking places enormous value on getting the questions right, then relinquishes control to conventional convergent thinking processes.

Divergent thinking thrives as much on the broad search as on the focused search. It focuses as much on careful observation of the facts as on interpretation of the facts. It focuses as much on the skills of reflection (which require time away from the problem) as on the skills of swift decision making (which seek to avoid delay). We refer to these three skills—conversation, observation, and reflection—as the COR skills of divergent thinking. Unfortunately, conventional corporate control systems, built on the assumption of continuity, stifle the COR skills of divergent thinking, or kill it outright.

When mental models are out of sync with reality, corporations lose their early-warning system. Leaders with genuine vision are suppressed. As Ron Heifetz, director of the Program on Leadership at the Kennedy School of Government at Harvard, observed: "People who lead frequently bear scars from their efforts to bring about adaptive change. Often they are silenced. On occasion, they are killed."

Abbott Laboratories, for example, flush with the success of their strategy to build strong positions in the medical diagnostic and test equipment business, was anxious to avoid the shocks to the pharmaceutical industry posed by the emergence of Medicare and Medicaid in the early to mid-1970s. Yet it found itself with an incumbent CEO who squelched three potential successors seeking to change strategy.

Once cultural lock-in guides a company's decisions, in the absence of some great external shock the corporation's fate is sealed.

HOW THE MARKETS ENABLE CHANGE

Markets, on the other hand, lacking culture, leadership, and emotion, do not experience the bursts of desperation, depression, denial, and hope that corporations face. The market has no lingering memories or remorse. It has no mental models. The market does not fear cannibalization, customer channel conflict, or dilution. It simply waits for the forces at play to work out—for new companies to be created and for acquisitions to clear the field. The markets silently allow weaker companies to be put up for sale and leave it to the new owners to shape them up or shut them down. Actions are taken quickly on early signs of weakness. Only when governments are brought in, as with a bailout, does the market mimic a probable corporate response. Most of the time, the market simply removes the weak players, and in removing them improves overall returns.

Lacking production-oriented control systems, markets create more surprise and innovation than do corporations. They operate on the assumption of discontinuity and accommodate continuity. Corporations, on the other hand, assume continuity and attempt to accommodate discontinuity. The difference is profound.

REDESIGNING THE CORPORATION ON THE BASIS OF DISCONTINUITY

The right of any corporation to exist is not
perpetual but has to be continuously earned.
—Robert Simons

The market has pointed the way to a solution. In response to the tension that builds between the potential for improved performance and the actual performance of large businesses, in an era of increasing pace of change in the economy there are certain kinds of firms—particularly private equity firms, as we discuss in Chapter Seven—that have demonstrated the ability to change at the pace and scale of the market, and they have earned sustained superior returns for doing so. The two kinds of private equity firms—principal investing firms and venture capitalists—are quite different from each other, but each looks somewhat like the holding companies of the late nineteenth century. It is possible to imagine that they will form the seeds of the industrial giants of the twenty-first century.

These newly important firms have been able to outperform the markets for the last two to three decades, longer than any other company we know of. The difference between these partnerships and the conventional corporation is in their approach to organizational design. These financial partnerships have discovered how to operate at high levels of efficiency and scale while engaging in creative destruction at the pace of the market, exactly as Joseph Schumpeter envisioned. Created around the assumption of discontinuity, they have then determined how best to incorporate or fold in the requirements of continuity.

These firms never buy any company to hold forever. Rather, they focus on intermediate (four- to seven-year) value creation. Corporations, in contrast, concentrate on the very short term (less than eighteen months) for operations and the very long term (greater than eight years) for research.

Private equity firms make as much money by expanding the future potential of their properties as they do from increasing the properties' operating incomes. When a private equity firm invests in a company or buys all of the equity, it buys it with a take-out strategy in mind: management knows what it must do in the next four to seven years to build the property so that it has long-term value for the next buyer.

Finally, private equity companies think of their business as a revolving portfolio of companies in various stages of development. They realize they will sell some of their properties each year and buy others. They keep the pipeline full of new properties at the front end and supplied with buyers at the back end, cultivating both simultaneously (a skill at which they excel).

These firms differ from conventional corporations not only in their divergent thinking but also in the depth and speed of their research activities. Moreover, private equity firms allow each of the companies they buy to retain its own control systems. This allows the private equity firm to concentrate on creation and destruction to a far greater extent than do traditional corporations, and even to a greater extent than their own wholly or partially owned subsidiaries do.

THE ROAD AHEAD

Long-term corporate performance has not matched the performance of the overall markets because corporations do not adapt as fast as the markets do. This is due to the way they evolve, not because of the way they accomplish their day-to-day work. For historical reasons, as we have discussed above, corporations have been designed to operate—to produce goods and services—rather than to evolve. In order to evolve at the pace of the markets, they have to get better at creation and destruction, the two key elements of evolution that are missing.

Redesigning the corporation to evolve quickly rather than simply operate well requires more than simple adjustments; the fundamental concepts of operational excellence are inappropriate for a corporation seeking to evolve at the pace and scale of the markets. One cannot just add on creation and destruction; one has to design them in. And only if the corporation is redesigned to evolve at the pace and scale of the market will long-term performance improve. Markets perform better than corporations because markets allow new companies to enter more freely, and they force the elimination of those companies without competitive prospects more ruthlessly than corporations do. Moreover, markets do these things faster and on a larger scale than do corporations.

We believe that corporations must be redesigned from top to bottom on the assumption of discontinuity. Management must stimulate the rate of creative destruction through the generation or acquisition of new firms and the elimination of marginal performers, without losing control of operations. If operations are healthy, the rate of creative destruction within the corporation will determine the continued long-term competitiveness and performance of the company. Today's financial partnerships give us confidence that this realignment can work. They also suggest a way to do it.

To create new businesses at a faster rate, corporations also need to ponder the details of divergent thinking. Divergent thinking is a prelude to creativity. Many divergent thinkers possess apparently opposing traits: they may be passionate and objective, or proud and humble; they may be both extroverted and introverted; in negotiations they may be flexible and unyielding, attentive and wandering. They possess what Mihalyi Csikszentmihalyi, one of today's leading thinkers on creativity and the author of *Flow,* has called "a sunny pessimism." F. Scott Fitzgerald described it in this way: "The test of a first-rate intelligence is the ability to hold two opposed ideas in the mind at the same time, and still retain the ability to function. One should, for example, be able to see that things are hopeless and yet be determined to make them otherwise."

Managing for divergent thinking—that is, managing to ensure that the proper questions are addressed early enough to allow them to be handled in an astute way—requires establishing a "rich context" of information as a stimulus to posing the right questions. It requires control through the selection and motivation of employees rather than through control of people's actions; ample resources, including time, to achieve results; knowing what to measure and when to measure it; and genuine respect for others' capabilities and potential. It also requires the willingness to remove people from responsibility when it becomes clear they cannot perform up to standard. In the end, both divergent and convergent thinking must successfully coexist.

Next, to improve long-term performance the overall planning and control processes of the corporation need to be rethought. The conventional strategic planning process has failed most corporations. As practiced, it stifles the very dialogue it is meant to stimulate. New ways of conducting a dialogue and conversation among the leaders of the corporation and their inheritors are needed.

Finally, corporate control systems must be built that can manage to control operations and increase the rate of creative destruction. Control what you must, not what you can; control when you must, not when you can. If a control procedure is not essential, eliminate it. Measure less; shorten the time and number of intermediaries between measurement and action, and increase the speed with which you receive feedback.

The point is to let the market control wherever possible. Be suspicious of control mechanisms; they stifle more than they control. Let those who run a business determine the best mix of controls for their business (they know the system best) and shift the burden of integration to the corporate level, rather than designing uniform systems that have to be implemented throughout a corporation independent of the business. When such changes are implemented, the focus of the corporation will shift from minimizing risk, and thereby inadvertently stifling creativity, to facilitating creativity—and that is what is needed to strengthen long-term performance.

To implement these ideas, the role of leadership must be rethought. Ron Heifetz of Harvard says: "The adaptive demands of our societies require leadership that takes responsibility without waiting for revelation or request. One may lead perhaps with not more than a question in hand. A leader has to engage people in facing the challenge, adjusting their values, changing perspectives, and developing new habits of behavior."

If these steps are taken effectively, they will help prevent the emergence of cultural lock-in.

This book offers a clear storm warning to dot com companies: you have been born at a special time, one where all the elements of the ideal creative environment exist simultaneously. By focusing on ''getting the product out'' and ''building the website,'' you are following in the footsteps of millions of companies since the time of Adam Smith. You are blessed to exist at a time of rapid change, which gives you the opportunity to peer into the future and design your corporation accordingly. But after the early heady days of growth, your challenges will be the same as those of other companies of the past: to grow and avoid being trapped by cultural lock-in.

A NEW BEGINNING

The agenda outlined above is substantial. Not all companies will be willing to take it on. The first step is to recognize the description of the business world as an increasingly *discontinuous* place. In the following pages, we will lay out in more detail why we see the world as a place of discontinuity, and outline the specific problems—and solutions—corporations must address if they are to break the paradigm of underperformance over the long term and truly act as companies built on excellence. Building a company to last—managing to survive—is no longer enough in an age of discontinuity. The chapters that follow will help point the way.

CHAPTER FOUR

Management and the Scientific Renaissance

Richard Pascale
Mark Millemann
Linda Gioja (2000)

T here is a new scientific renaissance in the making. It will usher in new industries, alter how businesses compete, and change how companies are managed. This chapter explores the managerial implications of this new renaissance.

Scientific discovery shapes managerial thinking. Principles identified more than two hundred years ago, during an earlier scientific renaissance, have had wide influence on how managers think today. Derivative ideas from Newton's laws of motion and his early work on gas thermodynamics were literally lifted, equation by equation, and applied to the emerging field of economics.[1] When they were extended into the realm of enterprise, these applications shaped the practice of management and today's deep-seated beliefs about change.

We are entering another scientific renaissance. The magnets for the inquiry are called *complex adaptive systems*. Also known as "complexity science," this work grapples with the mysteries of life itself and is propelled forward by the confluence of three streams of inquiry: (1) breakthrough discoveries in the life sciences (for example, biology, medicine, and ecology); (2) insights of the social sciences (sociology, psychology, economics); and (3) new developments in the hard sciences (physics, mathematics, information technology). The resulting work has revealed exciting insights into life and has opened up new avenues for management.[2]

Efforts to understand life are as old as humanity itself. For uncounted millennia, they centered on the selective breeding of animals and plants to improve yields and reduce susceptibility to disease. By the time the first scientific renaissance ended in the 1880s, geneticist Gregor Mendel had unlocked the secrets of heredity.[3] Selective breeding, formerly an art, fell within the grasp of science.

A second milestone of great consequence was the discovery, in 1953, of the double helix of DNA by James Watson and Francis Crick.[4] By the end of the twentieth century, the vast new frontier they had opened was closing in on understanding, and possibly altering, the biochemistry of life.

For several decades after Watson and Crick's discoveries, efforts to decipher DNA sequences and other facets of living systems were thwarted by their enormous complexity. But powerful computers and arcane technology for observing microscopic organisms and genetic dynamics permitted considerable progress. A trickle of breakthroughs began. Among them was the capacity to identify particular genes that made a plant or animal resistant to disease or amplified desirable features. By the 1990s, Genentech, Amgen, Immunex, Monsanto, and a host of other firms were developing biotechnology to the point where patented pharmaceuticals and seeds had become commercial realities. These nascent capabilities are accompanied, in turn, by new challenges—business, ethical, and social.

LIVING SYSTEMS AND ORGANIZATIONAL CHANGE

Many subterranean streams have combined to form the current flow of interest in living systems. Most attention is galvanized by the extraordinary economic potential of biotechnology or the social consequences of vanishing rain forests and global warming. However, another tributary will prove as important as all the rest: understanding the mysteries of life will alter how we think about organizations, management, and social change.

Businesses, it turns out, can learn a great deal from nature. Besides providing an account of pathbreaking applications of living systems theory to management, this chapter reveals how cornerstone principles of the life sciences have been translated into practice and have considerably improved the odds of success in achieving discontinuous change.

THE NEW "LIFE" CYCLE

The industrial revolution was fueled by the earlier scientific renaissance. It was predicated on the machine model of take → make → break: taking raw materials, converting them into products, and eventually "breaking"—in two meanings of the word—both environmental and social balance through high-impact extraction and production techniques, and by fostering a spiral of obsolescence in which the products are used and discarded. Clear-cut forests, rusting machinery, and the heaping detritus of salvage yards are the fossil remains of this era.

The emerging life science model unfolds like a species in a new ecological niche: innovate → proliferate → aggregate. Nature favors adaptation and fleet-footedness. Most species compete when they must, but organisms strive when possible to reproduce more rapidly than their rivals and to dominate by sheer strength of numbers. Economists call this "increasing returns." Discovering a new niche and proliferating rapidly fosters ubiquity. One witnesses it in commerce when Microsoft Windows, or a brand franchise such as Amazon.com, or the QWERTY sequence of a keyboard, becomes the *lingua franca* for an industry or technology. Major families may join forces to create self-reinforcing arrangements. In nature, in the benevolent exchange between insects and plants, nectar is swapped for pollination services. In business, the merger of AOL with Time Warner is an effort to establish supremacy through aggregation in the e-business and communications industries.

OF COLONIES AND COMPANIES

Rapid rates of change, an explosion of new insights from the life sciences, and the insufficiency of the machine model have created a critical mass for a revolution in management thinking. The fallout of the scientific renaissance has fostered uncertainty and soul-searching.[5] Executives ask: How do we make practical sense of all this? How do we get the change and performance we need? Clues, it turns out, are to be found in the world of the termite.

Come with us to a remarkable structure: the twelve-foot-high mound of the African termite, home to millions of inhabitants.[6]

The mound is an architectural marvel. Naturalist Richard Conniff has described its perfect arches, spiral staircases, nurseries, storage facilities, and living quarters that vary with the status of individual termites. Tunnels radiate out from the mound more than 160 feet in any direction. These structures enable the termites to forage for grass, wood, and water within an 80,000-square-foot area without being exposed to predators.[7]

Within the mound, a ventilation system—operated by opening and closing vents—creates a motion similar to respiration. Oxygen is "inhaled" into the twelve-foot tower of mud, and carbon dioxide is "exhaled." The system also holds the internal temperature steady (plus or minus one degree Fahrenheit) even though the external climate ranges from freezing winters to 100-degree-plus summers. Humidity is constant at 90 percent.[8]

This organizational wonder—which evolved over 100 million years or so—is a tribute to an elaborate social structure. Every inhabitant obeys a series of genetically programmed *rules,* such as "Position yourself between the termite in front and the one behind, and pass on whatever comes your way." As a whole, members of the mound constitute a sophisticated society that makes it possible to meet the ever-changing needs of the colony.[9]

Entomologists have known about the workings of the termite for centuries. In the past two decades, though, a group of leading scientists has offered a different, intriguing perspective. They see the mound as a stunning example of a *complex adaptive system.*

A complex adaptive system is formally defined as a system of independent agents that can act in parallel, develop "models" as to how things work in their environment, and, most importantly refine those models through learning and adaptation.[10] The human immune system is a complex adaptive system. So are a rain forest, a termite colony, and a business.

Over the past several years, substantial literature has introduced the new science of *complexity.* This is a broad-based inquiry into the common properties of all living things—beehives and bond traders, ant colonies and enterprises, ecologies and economies, you and me. In aggregate, the coverage on this topic to date has achieved two significant things:

1. It has evoked wonder and excitement about the living world around us—how life surges and declines; how nature competes, cooperates, and thrives on change.

2. It has whetted some managerial appetites for a new approach that might help to unshackle the potential of people and organizations and has begun to challenge the machine model as a suitable management platform for the information age.

We aim to take a step beyond. This book describes a new management model based on the nature of nature, but it also does what no other book has done before. It distills, from the science of complexity, four bedrock principles that are inherently and powerfully applicable to the living system called a business. In brief, these principles are:

1. *Equilibrium* is a precursor to *death.* When a living system is in a state of equilibrium, it is less responsive to changes occurring around it. This places it at maximum risk.

2. In the face of threat, or when galvanized by a compelling opportunity, living things move toward the *edge of chaos.* This condition evokes higher levels of mutation and experimentation, and fresh new solutions are more likely to be found.

3. When this excitation takes place, the components of living systems *self-organize* and new forms and repertoires *emerge* from the turmoil.

4. Living systems cannot be *directed* along a linear path. Unforeseen consequences are inevitable. The challenge is to *disturb* them in a manner that approximates the desired outcome.

If properly employed, these principles allow enterprises to thrive and revitalize themselves. In contrast, the machine-age principles, although familiar and enduring, often quietly facilitate the stagnation and decline of traditional enterprises that are faced with discontinuous change.

The choice is that simple and that stark.

Complexity and *chaos* are frequently used interchangeably, even though they have almost nothing in common. The world is not chaotic; it is complex.

Humans tend to regard as chaotic that which they cannot control. This creates confusion over what is meant by the term *chaos*. From a scientific point of view, chaos is that unlikely occurrence in which patterns cannot be found or interrelationships understood.[11] A swarm of bees or the ants that overrun a picnic blanket may seem chaotic but they are actually only behaving as a complex adaptive system. E-commerce and the upending of traditional business platforms may feel "chaotic," but technically these innovations are complex.

LIVING SYSTEMS PIONEERS

Let us be clear. "Living systems" isn't a metaphor for how human institutions operate. It's the way it is.[12] Pioneering efforts by the companies described herein have demonstrated that ideas can produce a concrete bottom-line impact and profound transformational change. Indeed, some of the largest and most successful organizational transformations in recent years have been modeled on the principles of living systems. This chapter was largely inspired by business leaders who not only embraced those principles as their guidelines for change but also, through trial and error, found ways to translate them into concrete management practices.

Surfing the Edge of Chaos bridges theory and practice through six in-depth examples of living systems: British Petroleum, Hewlett-Packard, Monsanto, Royal Dutch/Shell, Sears, and the U.S. Army. We have observed leaders who explicitly or implicitly regarded their organizations as living systems and employed the four principles described above as a superior management platform in revitalizing their enterprises. We have seen executives consciously put these insights into practical use and create demonstrable successes that most probably could not have been achieved otherwise. Most business books have examples, but few take the long view and trace the ups and downs. We discuss both the successes and the failures.

There is no mystery—no secret formula, no magic potion—about the way the living systems model works. The examples identify insights about complex adaptive systems as they operate in the natural world and translate them to the world of business. Sensible lessons are gathered from observing the pitfalls and triumphs experienced by companies that have adopted the new model.

Our personal advisory relationships with the CEOs and other senior leaders in most of the six organizations provide intimate accounts of what transpired, not anecdotal or journalistic treatments. These accounts point toward practical design principles and processes and toward tools that can be used to unleash the potential of an organization. A fresh and unorthodox brand of leadership is necessary to initiate and shepherd an adaptive journey. Finally, we identify core disciplines that enable an organization to *sustain* its vitality once it has been reawakened.

Those are our promises for this undertaking.

We do not propose that the four principles stated earlier form a new silver bullet. The practices that stem from them are not foolproof; indeed, they are not always superior to traditional approaches. As we shall see shortly, a lot depends on the challenge faced and the magnitude of change sought.

"CONCRETE" EXAMPLES

In Mexico, Cemex, the world's third largest (and only global) cement company, dispatches its fleet of cement mixers on the basis of the same simple rules that govern how ants scavenge a colony's territory with ruthless efficiency. Cemex recognizes what homeowners know only too well: construction projects *never* proceed on schedule. Schedule a cement delivery in advance and you can bank on the site's being ready earlier (high-cost workers then hang around awaiting the delivery with nothing to do) or not being ready as planned (the cement then starts to harden in the truck).

Suppliers and customers alike have unhappily accepted this state of affairs for years. Logically speaking, how could it be otherwise when the construction site's state of readiness is dependent on so many unpredictable elements? But Cemex defies that logic. It promises to provide cement *where* you want it and *when* you want it, on two hours' notice. Cemex sells promises—not just cement—and uses them as compelling marketplace differentiators. And Cemex delivers.

How is it possible?

Cemex loads its fleets of cement trucks each morning and dispatches them with no preordained destination. The trick lies in how they make their rounds. Like ants scavenging a territory, they are guided to their destination by simple rules. Ants use chemical messages (called pheromones) to convey these instructions; Cemex uses an algorithm based on *greed* (deliver as much cement as rapidly as possible to as many customers as possible) and *repulsion* (avoid duplication of effort by staying as far away from other cement trucks as possible). It's scary to have a fleet loaded with—of all products—wet cement, which could harden before it is delivered. Yet the ant model works with remarkable efficiency. Cemex has obliterated competition in the eight nations where it operates (including the western and southwestern regions of the United States). Cemex's decision to emulate a living system delivers an incremental return of $388 million per year to the bottom line.[13]

A fluke? Hardly. In 1998, British Telecom introduced a similar system to dispatch its service fleet of eighty thousand vehicles. Savings in the first year: £250 million.[14] The U.S. Army employed the ant pheromone model to direct its drone ground surveillance coverage in Bosnia and Serbia (and to redirect drones when one was shot down). Coverage efficiency increased from 60 percent (using the old mainframe-based optimization model) to 87 percent (feeding the ant algorithm into a battle-hardened personal computer).[15]

Cemex has adopted one of the simplest applications of complexity science. Our corporate examples extend considerably beyond this realm. At Monsanto (now merged with Upjohn to form Pharmacia), CEO Robert Shapiro embraced the framework of living systems as the centerpiece of his efforts to reinvent a lackluster manufacturer of low-margin petrochemicals as a leading life-sciences enterprise.

As subtext to this story, Shapiro, a longtime McKinsey client, had to mind-wrestle with the partners of the formidable consulting firm. Instead of the top-down strategic reinvention that McKinsey was advocating, Shapiro persuaded the members of the consulting team to play the role of stewards and facilitators.

Over ten thousand Monsanto employees became involved in three hundred cross-business and cross-functional teams. Within that context, workers freed of top-side direction identified new business opportunities.

The campaign to implement these initiatives generated tensions that moved the company toward the edge of chaos. Self-organizing groups sparked dozens of breakthrough innovations and a staggering reduction in costs. Share price soared from $15 to $49. Along the way, Shapiro radically changed Monsanto's strategy and culture.[16]

Monsanto's transformation from an undifferentiated also-ran to a front-runner in genetically engineered crops affected the world community in unforeseen ways. Opposition to bioengineering mounted, changing the company's future.[17] Monsanto was confronted with another kind of disruptive change, one that was played out in the spotlight of media attention and shifting world opinion.

MANAGEMENT: PAST AND FUTURE TENSE

We have noted that contemporary business practices can trace their managerial heritage to the scientific work of Newton (irreducible and mathematical laws explaining the mechanics of nature) and Dalton (dividing complex molecules into individual atoms, and observing the interaction of molecules under pressure as the precursor to thermodynamics). As the *Wall Street Journal*'s Thomas Petzinger explains:[18]

> [From the 1680s onward] Isaac Newton was the new Moses, presenting a few simple equations—the laws of nature—which never failed in predicting the tides, the orbit or movement of any object that could be seen or felt. Output was exactly proportional to input. Everything was equal to the sum of its parts. Newton's mechanics seemed so perfect, so universal, that they became the organizing principles of all post-feudal society, including armies, churches, and economic institutions of every kind. . . . The very equations of economics, including many we use today, were built explicitly on the principles of mechanics and thermodynamics, right down to the terms and symbols. The economy was said to ''have momentum,'' was ''well oiled'' or ''gaining steam.''

As a model for everything, Newtonianism, it turned out, had limitations. It worked only within the narrow range of Newton's instruments.

The "laws of nature" fell to pieces in space, as Einstein's relativity physics showed, and at the subatomic level, as quantum physics showed. Scientists realized that however useful in solving smooth, mechanical problems, Newton's calculus was meaningless in understanding the vast preponderance of nature: the motion of currents, the growth of plants, the rise and fall of civilizations.

Einstein's insight into relativity—overturning, as it did, the orderly world of classical physics—exerted broad influence over many other disciplines. Early in the twentieth century, relativism was mirrored in art (Picasso and Pollack), poetry (T. S. Eliot), music (Stravinsky), literature (James Joyce), and interpretative religion. Object and observer became inseparable. Structure was connected to process, the medium to the message, doing to being. The rational and analytical were inseparable from the emotional and intuitive.[19]

Except in management. The reason is plain enough: if it ain't broke, don't fix it. For the greater part of the century, particularly from the 1950s onward, dazzling new technologies (electronics, engineered materials, computers, and bioengineering, to name a few) opened vast frontiers of commerce in which traditional management models flourished. Factor in fifty-five years without destructive global conflict and the result was the emergence of industrial economies with vast wealth, spending power, and consumer appetites. A good part of the twentieth century, excluding the Great Depression and the war years, may be regarded as an era of low-hanging fruit. In short, management didn't change because it didn't have to. True to Woody Allen's quip that 90 percent of life is just showing up, our large and lumbering corporations thrived because they showed up; their lack of agility was not a significant drawback, given their advantages of scale and the cornucopia of economic opportunity spread before them.

Then some unlikely startups, borne on the wings of new business models, proceeded to spoil the party. The newcomers—companies like Amazon.com, Southwest Airlines, Home Depot, and Nokia—ran rings around traditional companies mired in their comfortable equilibrium.

Gradually, a new consensus began to form within the ranks of management experts. It recognized that companies with talent and the instincts to innovate and collaborate can commercialize ideas and seize the high ground before slower, well-established rivals even spot the new hill. It held that by inspiring frontline workers to operate as independent agents, pursuing their own solutions with little central control, formidable business enterprises and social movements can emerge.

But beware: although this new agile species exploits some elements of complexity, a halfway understanding of what has transpired is likely to create more hazards than heroes. In other words, if you are hoping to skim this book to glean a few new tricks from the examples and resettle into the easy chair of the old mind-set, think twice. It would be akin to trading in a reliable workhorse like the World War II propeller-driven Spitfire for an F-18 but continuing to use inaccurate maps and a defective navigational system. You will just get to the wrong destination faster.

Corporations around the world now write checks for more than $50 billion a year in fees for "change consulting."[20] And that tab represents only a third of the overall change cost if severance costs, write-offs, and information technology purchases are included. Yet consultants, academic surveys, and reports from the "changed" companies themselves indicate that a full 70 percent of those efforts fail.[21] The reason? We call it *social engineering*, a contemporary variant of the machine model's cause-and-effect thinking. *Social* is coupled with *engineering* to denote how most managers today, in contrast to their nineteenth-century counterparts, recognize that people need to be brought on board. But they still go about it in a preordained fashion. Trouble arises because the "soft" stuff is really the *hard* stuff, and no one can really "engineer" it.

We will use *social engineering* repeatedly as a billboard phrase to highlight this managerial tradition. Its central premises are:

- *Leaders as head, organization as body.* Intelligence is centralized near those at the top of the organization, or those who advise them.
- *The premise of predictable change.* Implementation plans are scripted on the assumption of a reasonable degree of predictability and control during the time span of the change effort.
- *An assumption of cascading intention.* Once a course of action is determined, initiative flows from the top down. When a program is defined, it is *communicated* and *rolled out* through the ranks. Often, this includes a veneer of participation to engender buy-in.

That these familiar tenets of social engineering are not compatible with the way living systems work is probably self-evident. But as we noted earlier, the traditional approach does have its place. The tools associated with social engineering work well when the solution is known in advance and an established repertoire exists to implement it. These conditions apply in many situations, and it is not our intent to minimize them. However, even in such straightforward applications, if employee ownership of an initiative (for example, SAP) is a prerequisite for success, regarding each person as an intelligent "node" in a living system and involving him or her as such, improves implementation. We don't reject all the *tools* of social engineering in all cases but advocate the end of it as a *context*. Tools for control do not equal social engineering. What we are advocating is appropriate use of tools of the old paradigm, incorporated in a new management repertoire. Social engineering as a context is obsolete—period.

But that is not the focus or intent. Harder to handle are those nonroutine challenges where discontinuous change is sought. These challenges often demand a leap in capability, and solutions are unproven or unknown. In these instances, nimbleness and agility are essential, and tapping the full potential of the organization as a living system becomes imperative. This is not a "maybe" or a "sort of." It's a deal breaker. Facing such an adaptive challenge, we must throw out the old notion about how a business should be led, organized, and run. We must abandon familiar organizational principles and processes and adopt strange and unfamiliar ones. The lessons of living systems provide the best map for this new territory: a mental framework for seeing order in the disorder, powerful distinctions that accelerate change, mental hooks to rely on as we scale the cliffs of the worn-out business model to reach the business model of the future. Behaving like a gardener, not thinking like a mechanic, becomes the mantra of choice.

As a general rule, adults are much more likely to act their way into a new way of thinking than to think their way into a new way of acting. Many new—and some established—enterprises, such as those discussed herein, illustrate that rule. Despite many missteps along the way, they have evolved organizations and management approaches that smack more of a beehive than a bureaucracy. And as they have enacted this new reality, they have come to think differently.

BEYOND DILBERT

Is complexity science the dawning of a new age, or simply grist for Dilbert? Will old-line social engineers bolt a few showcase features of living science onto the traditional machinery, in much the same way as they compromised Total Quality Management and Self-Managed Teams? Overcoming these propensities is our quest. To be sure, the old order persists. But, to quote Petzinger:

> [The] new order is poised to overtake it—haltingly in some places, unevenly in others—but inexorably in every corner of the economy and society at large. How can we be so sure the Newtonian model is giving way to the natural one? Two reasons: for one, the marketplace leaves companies no choice. In an era when change arrives without warning and threatens to eradicate entire companies and industries overnight, organizations can survive only by engaging the eyes, ears, minds and emotions of all individuals and by encouraging them to act on their knowledge and beliefs. Second, and far more importantly, the new living systems model will thrive and persist because it bears more closely to what we are as humans.[22]

To repeat, living systems isn't a metaphor. It is the way it is.

This chapter is an effort to ensure that a dilution of these ideas doesn't happen. The lessons of complexity are simply too important to be lost or frittered away. We have seen how they can transmute the most leaden of organizations into the gold of a flexible, fast-reacting, innovative enterprise. We believe the story of those achievements must be told, in depth, and their significance must be made clear.

In other words, we have seen the future and have wrapped it between the covers of this book.

Notes

1. Alex Trisoglio, ''The Strategy and Complexity Seminar,'' unpublished, London School of Economics, July 1995, p. 3. This paper is a tour de force on the relationship of complexity to management. It is the best treatment on this subject encountered in the research.

2. See, for example, Mitchell Waldrop, *Complexity* (New York: Simon & Schuster, 1992). For a concise overview, see M. Gell-Mann, *The Quark and the Jaguar* (New York: Freeman, 1994); also, J. Cleveland, J. Neuroth, and P. Plastrik, *Welcome to the Edge of Chaos* (Lansing, MI: On Purpose Associates, 1996).

3. S. Kauffman, *At Home in the Universe* (Oxford, England: Oxford University Press, 1995), p. 37.

4. Ibid., pp. 38–65.

5. For an overview of this issue, see T. Petzinger, Jr., "A New Model for the Nature of Business," *Wall Street Journal*, February 26, 1999, pp. 81–82.

6. There is a considerable literature on these remarkable insects. See Edward O. Wilson, *The Insect Societies* (Cambridge, MA: Belknap Press of Harvard University Press, 1971); also Edward O. Wilson, *Sociobiology* (Cambridge, MA: Harvard University Press, 1975), pp. 33–37; Richard Conniff, "The Enemy Within," *Smithsonian*, October 1998, pp. 82–96.

7. Conniff, pp. 92–94.

8. Ibid., p. 96.

9. Ibid., p. 92.

10. See Gell-Mann, pp. 16–24; also Waldrop, pp. 294–299.

11. H. Sherman and R. Schultz, *Open Boundaries* (Reading, MA: Perseus, 1998), pp. 16, 67; Michael McMaster, *The Intelligence Advantage* (London: Knowledge Based Development, 1995), p. 19; Danah Zohar and Ian Marshall, *Who's Afraid of Schrüdinger's Cat?* (New York: Morrow, 1997), p. 103; Trisoglio, p. 20.

12. Richard Pascale, conversations with Stuart Kauffman, Santa Fe, NM, July 1998.

13. Peter Katel, "Bordering on Chaos," *Wired*, July 1997, pp. 98–107. Also see Thomas Petzinger, Jr., *The New Pioneers* (New York: Simon & Schuster, 1999), pp. 91–93; Anonymous, "How the Mexican Corporation Cemex Turned into an Industrial Giant," *Le Temps*, October 26, 1999, p. 31.

14. Pascale, notes from Bios Fellows meetings, Santa Fe, NM, July 1998.

15. Ibid.

16. Pascale, conversations at Monsanto with Robert Shapiro, Pierre Huchuli, and other senior executives, St. Louis, MO, Fontainebleau, France, and Frankfurt, Germany, September 4, 1997–October 18, 1999.

17. See, e.g., David Stipp, "The Voice of Reason in the Global Food Fights," *Fortune*, February 21, 2000, pp. 164–172; David Stipp, "Is Monsanto Worth a Hill of Beans?" *Fortune*, February 21, 2000, pp. 157–160; Michael Pollan, "Potato 3.0," *New York Times Magazine*, October 29, 1998, pp. 46–47.

18. T. Petzinger, *New Pioneers*, pp. 18–19.

19. Walter Isaacson, "Who Mattered—And Why," *Time*, December 31, 1999, p. 60.

20. Pascale, conversations with change practice consulting teams of Price Waterhouse Coopers and Andersen Consulting, Oxford, England, and Colorado Springs, CO, 1997–1999.

21. Pascale, conversations with David Schneider, partner, North American Change Practice, Price Waterhouse Coopers, Santa Fe, NM, March 1998; Pascale, Bios Fellows meetings, supra note 14; R. Eccles and N. Nohira, *Beyond the Hype* (Cambridge, MA: Harvard Business School Press, 1992), pp. 3–21; Darrel Rigby, ''What's Today's Special at the Consultant Cafe?'' *Fortune*, September 7, 1988, p. 162.

22. T. Petzinger, Jr.

PART TWO

THEORIES AND MODELS OF PLANNED ORGANIZATION CHANGE

Editors' Interlude

In Part One were chapters that helped us to learn about the characteristics of external environments, how these characteristics influence an organization, and, now in more recent times, why it is so difficult for organizations to keep pace with the change that is occurring in the larger world. This challenge, in turn, affects the context within which organizations must operate to ensure survival. Thus there is an increasing need to understand (1) change itself, (2) how to respond more rapidly to the changing dynamics of the external environment, and (3) how to lead and manage planned organization change more effectively.

Part Two, then, is an examination of the relationship between the organization and its environment and what must be done to ensure short-term survival and long-term survivability. In other words, we move from the external environment to the organization itself. The goal of this second section, a rather larger one with respect to the number of chapters included, is first to provide some fundamentals about organization—how to conceptualize and understand this kind of social system—and second to present some of the seminal work that help us to comprehend the nature of organization change.

Although there is no single theory that comprehensively explains an organization, much less organization change, the one that comes the closest is open-system theory. The theory is rooted in biology, especially cell biology and the original work of von Bertalanffy (1950). Metaphorically, then, an organization is viewed as an organism. For an organism to survive, whether a cell or an organization with myriad cells, there must be *input* to the cell from its external environment (for a cell it is oxygen, and for an organization it is capital); then *throughput* (for the cell, using oxygen for nourishment and for producing nutrients that sustain its life, and for the organization it is producing a product and/or service for an intended customer or user of this productivity to ensure survival); and finally, *output* (for the cell it is waste, those aspects of nutrients that are no longer useful for sustaining life—in fact, this elimination process helps to facilitate life—and for the organization it is the product and service themselves that constituents and customers choose to purchase or otherwise avail themselves of for some perceived value). This output then provides feedback to the system, which takes the form of input again. Yet this input is now in addition to the earlier input: the quality of the oxygen or the extent to which the organization's output is being used and/or purchased, and so on.

This cycle of input-throughput-output-feedback-input and so forth is simple yet profound in terms of what it helps to explain with respect to our understanding of organizations and organization change. The term *open* in this theory is the key to this understanding. A closed system, after all, exists only in the world of nonliving matter. As Katz and Kahn (1978), our primary translators of cell biology to organizations, so aptly noted, "open systems maintain themselves through constant commerce with their environment, that is, a continuous inflow and outflow of energy through permeable boundaries" (pp. 21, 22). In practical terms, the more an organization is insular the greater the risk of extinction.

When thinking about an organization, we usually consider the throughput aspects: the physical plant or building, the technology and its various parts (machine, communication tools, desks, and so on), jobs that people hold and the functions they perform, the structural and power hierarchy, the kinds of employees the organization attracts, and what is ultimately produced. All these parts, and additional ones not specified, compose a whole, and it is this whole that is critical to our understanding. Moreover, to the point: open-system theory significantly contributes to this kind of understanding, the parts and the whole. A closer look at this theory is warranted.

From von Bertalanffy's work (1950), Katz and Kahn (1978) described ten common characteristics that define open systems. Here we briefly consider these ten characteristics.

1. *Importation of energy.* All open systems take from their environments some form of energy—oxygen for the cell, money for the profit or nonprofit organization, stimulation for the human being, and even renewed supplies of

energy from other organizations or people for organizations themselves. As Katz and Kahn put it so succinctly, "no social structure is self-sufficient or self-contained" (p. 23).

2. *Throughput.* This is the process of transforming the energy from the external environment to something that is or will become useful for sustaining the system, for example, the human body converting sugar into heat, or the organization creating a new product or service.

3. *Output.* The system then exports some product into the environment— the human body exporting carbon dioxide, the organization providing for customers a product or service. As Katz and Kahn point out, some output may not be absorbed, for instance, by-products from a drug that may harm the human body, or secondary products (waste) that may harm the physical environment (mercury in the Hudson River).

4. *Systems as cycles of events.* Open systems follow the cycle of input-throughput-output, which continuously repeats itself. The business organization takes capital from the external environment, converts it into products and services that are marketed and sold, the revenues from these sales are then used to turn out further products and services, and so forth. Citing the early work of F. H. Allport (1962), Katz and Kahn point to the difference between a human body and an organization, regarding this cycle. The human body has physical boundaries, and its subparts are bounded within.

5. *Negative entropy.* "The entropic process is a universal law of nature in which all forms of organization move toward disorganization or death" (Katz & Kahn; p. 25). Unless deliberate effort is expended to prevent this process, that is, negative entropy, the organization will not survive. For survival to be ensured, the organization must import more energy from its external environment than it uses. Thus there is an extremely important need for any organization to monitor and take energy from its marketplace, whether for profit or not for profit.

6. *Information input, negative feedback, and the coding process.* This process of living systems is one of discerning from the environment what output from the organization is working (contributing to adequate if not high performance) and what output is not working. Based on feedback from the latter, corrections are made. Also, it should be noted that this discerning from the environment is selective. The organization cannot respond to everything in the environment, so *coding* occurs, that is, a process of simplifying the mass of random and perhaps confusing, if not contradictory, information.

7. *The steady state and dynamic homeostasis.* The organization's purpose of taking in energy to prevent entropy functions in such a way that it will maintain some constancy, consistency, or steady state. This process is one of

seeking homeostasis, to preserve the basic character of the system. Moreover, seeking a steady state is to prevent chaos, randomness, and a lack of direction. As Lewin (1947) explained, activity in the organization never results in a steady state over time. What may look like a steady state, or equilibrium as he labeled it, in reality is not. The relationship of the many parts of the system and the ratio of energy exchanges between the organization and its environment may look steady, but a closer look will reveal fluctuations, forces in the organization that drive or push the system toward its goals, and forces that prevent such movement. These ups and downs represent what Lewin called *quasi-stationary equilibrium.* Over time, operations in the organization may seem to be part of a steady state, but at any given moment the organization may be either "up" or "down" as it constantly seeks steadiness—equilibrium or homeostasis.

8. *Differentiation.* As they grow, open systems differentiate, that is, different functions are required to ensure long-term survival. At the outset of a business what is required is some operation—manufacturing a product or providing a unique service—and money. As the business grows, other functions are needed to sell the product or service, hire new employees (the human resource function), process information, and so on.

9. *Integration and coordination.* Naturally, as differentiation continues, coordinating all of these functions and integrating them for ultimate organizational effectiveness becomes necessary.

10. *Equifinality.* This final characteristic means that any given organization can reach its goals in more than one way. For any single goal there are typically numerous paths toward achievement of that goal.

The chapters in Part Two elaborate on the ideas and characteristics associated with open-system theory. For example, the initial chapter is Lewin's original piece (1947) on the notion of quasi-stationary equilibria referred to earlier. In the following chapter, "Mechanisms of Change," we continue with the thinking of Lewin about change with Schein's elaboration (1964) of Lewin's original three stages of change: unfreezing, changing, and refreezing. At the time, Lewin was somewhat sketchy with his three stages; he simply stated and briefly defined them. Schein's "mechanisms" for each of the stages help us to understand how these three actually need to work. And as we see from Chapter Fifteen, Burnes (2004) brings us up to date regarding the veracity of this earlier thinking of Lewin and elaborating by Schein.

Chapter Seven, the longest one in Part Two, is the classic by Chin and Benne (1967). We label it a classic contribution to the literature because of (1) the lasting nature of its content (the chapter was included in the second, third, and fourth editions of *The Planning of Change,* edited by Bennis, Benne, and Chin, the volumes that provided the basis for our work on this present volume); and

(2) the content itself. Chin and Benne provided us with ways of thinking about the overall process of planned changed. These ways, or strategies, of consciously and deliberately attempting to change an individual, a group, an organization, or even a community are in three categories: empirical rational, normative reeducative, and power coercive. The first strategy and the one most frequently used, they argued, rests on the assumption that people are rational and that the change strategy is seen as reasonable, that is, based on sound knowledge and precedence, and in their self-interest. If these criteria are met, people will adopt the proposed change. The *normative reeducative* strategy is based also on the belief that people are rational, but just as important, perhaps even more so, is the assumption that humans conform and are committed to sociocultural norms. Thus this strategy emphasizes education and involvement in that reeducative process—new and different ways of thinking about change and what may be needed. Moreover, this emphasis includes involvement in order to gain commitment to the change. In other words, change is not imposed. The final strategy is *power coercive* and therefore is based on the use of power, with several choices for the power holder: political, nonviolent resistance, or perhaps even violent tactics. It is likely that the greatest resistance to change is associated with this strategy. Besides adding to our understanding about different strategies of change, Chin and Benne have helped us to integrate our thinking with their broader and more comprehensive conceptual frameworks.

With the following chapter by McClelland (1965),* we consider change in a much more specific yet highly important way: motivation to change. McClelland's fundamental premise is that people can be convinced to become more motivated than they may currently be to achieve some goal. In other words, people can be *aroused to acquire* a particular motive that leads to change in behavior. McClelland's focus was on the need for achievement motive; he supports his premise with sound research and theory.

As we next return to planned organization change, we must consider the fact that organizations are complex, and not so easy to understand. It is therefore helpful to simplify them. One way is to consider organizations metaphorically. Earlier we referred to open-system theory and noted that this theory comes from cell biology. Consistent with this way of thinking, and since organizations are not closed systems, our metaphor of choice for the organization is the *organism.* Also consistent with open-system theory is the fact that an organism, starting with the basic cell, is dependent on and interacts with its external environment for survival.

In addition to helping us to simplify complexity, this metaphor of the organism can contribute to our understanding of organization change as well. That

---

*Chapter is included in the collection of readings on the *Organization Change: A Comprehensive Reader* website.

is, how the organization interacts with its external environment clarifies our thinking about the forces that impinge on and demand change for the organization (input), and then how the organization deals with these forces internally (throughput) and subsequently produces some product and/or services (output), which in turn interact with and have an impact on the external environment. This sequence is true of any living organism.

Thus, this metaphor is useful. And our Chapter Nine, from Morgan's book* *Images of Organizations* (1978), explains quite thoroughly the organization as an organism. Yet Morgan, who describes other metaphors for organizations, such as mechanical, political, and brain, cautions us about such thinking when he calls our attention to a metaphor as a useful way of "seeing" an organization and at the same time a way of "not seeing." A metaphor may oversimplify. With this chapter, then, Morgan explains the advantage of organism as metaphor and also addresses certain limitations, such as that an organism is a concrete fundamental of nature with tangible properties that can be seen and touched. An organization, however, is a social construction. With this limitation in mind and others that Morgan covers, we can nevertheless proceed with the organism as a way of considering any organization that is likely to be much more helpful than limiting.

In the years just after World War II, Great Britain brought about considerable technological change in a variety of industries. An example was coal mining. But this change regarding the way coal was extracted, the "long-wall method," caused problems and resistance on the part of miners. The new method removed coal faster and more efficiently but required more individual effort on the part of the miners rather than teamwork—their previous and preferred way of working. In other words, the *social* fabric of the workplace was profoundly changed. As Chapter Ten, by Trist, who was a primary consultant to the coal mining industry at the time, explains, human activities in the workplace are a combination of technology and social dynamics. Change efforts must consider both. Thus was born the concept of sociotechnical systems.

The next chapter by Greiner (1998)* may be considered more as a model than a theory; however, the writing is grounded in research and knowledge from the organization theory literature. The model is reflected in the title of Greiner's piece, "Evolution and Revolution as Organizations Grow"; in other words, organizations over time go through cycles or stages of change. Originally published in 1972, the article has stood the test of time and was republished as a *Harvard Business Review* classic in 1998 with updates, including a short retrospective entitled, "Revolution Is Still Inevitable." Greiner contends that there are five stages or phases in an organization's life cycle. Each stage at some point creates a crisis, revolutionary change or a jolt to the system occurs, and then a next phase ensues. In between these crises or perturbations, evolutionary change proceeds. The start-up phase is called creativity; the organization begins to grow. With growth (more people and complexity) a crisis of leadership eventually emerges and direction becomes a necessity, which later creates a crisis of autonomy. And so it goes with further crises of control, red tape, and then "who knows?" Greiner labels this last crisis with a question mark. Others have developed organizational life-cycle models, but Griener's remains perhaps the most popular. It seems to speak directly to executives' experiences, and with its grounding in the organization theory literature combines scholarship with practice.

The following chapter by Gersick (1991), like the earlier one by Chin and Benne, is sweeping and comprehensive. She compares models about change from six domains: adult, group, organization development, history of science, biological evolution, and physical science. She then concludes that the punctuated equilibrium paradigm helps to explain all of the domains, that is, an alternation between relatively long periods of time in which change occurs incrementally and adaptively, followed by brief periods of revolutionary upheaval occurrences. Gersick provides considerable theory and research support for her explanations. In addition to explications of equilibrium periods and revolutionary periods, she adds the component of deep structure, which refers to early implicit choices that a system makes about how it is to be organized and operated. These early choices constitute, deep within the structure and culture, almost immutable activities. This concept is not unlike what Foster and Kaplan refer to as "cultural lock-in"; see their Chapter Three in Part One.

Gersick cites the earlier chapter by Tushman and Romanelli (1985), which is our next entry. Chapter Thirteen provides support for Gersick's points of view; Tushman and Romanelli propose a punctuated equilibrium model of organization evolution to explain patterns of change they observed across quite a number of organizations and different industries. In other words, they provide evidence for their model and for what Gersick later explicated.

The periodical *Annual Review of Psychology* on occasion publishes articles on organizational change and development. One of the more recent ones (1999) is the summary of this field of organization change by Weick and Quinn,* our next entry in Part Two. They organize their review and summary in two primary ways: episodic change and continuous change. Of course, this language is essentially the same as revolutionary and evolutionary change. As might be expected, they cite the writings of Gersick and Tushman and Romanelli among many other references and point out that recent analyses of organization change concern the tempo of change—that is, the rate, rhythm, and patterns of work and change activities. Weick and Quinn also address the original three stages of Lewin's (unfreeze, change, and refreeze) and suggest that perhaps a more appropriate framework for today's rapid rate of change is freeze, rebalance, unfreeze. In other words, change happens all the time and quickly; thus it may be wise to "freeze" those changes that are useful, rebalance the system accordingly, and then move on to other changes (unfreeze).

The final chapter in Part Two is the recent one by Burnes (2004). It is our last entry in this section because he addresses the criticisms of Lewin's early work as being simplified and outdated, and refutes these criticisms with impressive evidence; and he helps to summarize much of the theoretical literature on organization change.

In summary, as we can see from the inclusions for Part Two there is a rich literature of theory about organization change. The primary concepts within this literature include open-system theory, organization as organism, motivation, punctuated equilibrium, deep structure, evolutionary/continuous and revolutionary/episodic or discontinuous change, and Lewin's three stages expanded by Schein as the mechanisms of change. Therefore, when significant change is needed, revolutionary methods need to be utilized. The change leader should "disturb" the system. Otherwise, continuous improvement will be the order of the day.

CHAPTER FIVE

Quasi-Stationary Social Equilibria and the Problem of Permanent Change

Kurt Lewin (1947)

1. THE OBJECTIVE OF CHANGE

The objective of social change might concern the nutritional standard of consumption, the economic standard of living, the type of group relation, the output of a factory, the productivity of an educational team. It is important that a social standard to be changed does not have the nature of a "thing" but of a "process." A certain standard of consumption, for instance, means that a certain action—such as making certain decisions, buying, preparing, and canning certain food in a family—occurs with a certain frequency within a given period. Similarly, a certain type of group relations means that within a given period certain friendly and hostile actions and reactions of a certain degree of severity occur between the members of two groups. Changing group relations or changing consumption means changing the level at which these multitude of events proceed. In other words, the "level" of consumption, of friendliness, or of productivity is to be characterized as the aspect of an ongoing social process.

Any planned social change will have to consider a multitude of factors characteristic for the particular case. The change may require a more or less unique combination of educational and organizational measures; it may depend upon quite different treatments or ideology, expectation and organization. Still, certain general formal principles always have to be considered.

2. THE CONDITIONS OF A STABLE QUASI-STATIONARY EQUILIBRIUM

The study of the conditions for change begins appropriately with an analysis of the conditions for "no change," that is, for the state of equilibrium.

From what has been just discussed, it is clear that by a state of "no social change" we do not refer to a stationary but to a quasi-stationary equilibrium—that is, to a state comparable to that of a river that flows with a given velocity in a given direction during a certain time interval. A social change is comparable to a change in the velocity or direction of that river.

A number of statements can be made in regard to the conditions of quasi-stationary equilibrium. (These conditions are treated more elaborately elsewhere.[1])

(A) The strength of forces that tend to lower the standard of social life should be equal and opposite to the strength of forces that tend to raise its level. The resultant of forces on the line of equilibrium should therefore be zero.

(B) Since we have to assume that the strength of social forces always shows variations, a quasi-stationary equilibrium presupposes that the forces against raising the standard increase with the amount of raising and that the forces against lowering increase (or remain constant) with the amount of lowering. This type of gradient, which is characteristic for a "positive central force field,"[2] has to hold, at least in the neighborhood of the present level. . . .

(C) It is possible to change the strength of the opposing forces without changing the level of social conduct. In this case the tension (degree of conflict) increases.

3. TWO BASIC METHODS OF CHANGING LEVELS OF CONDUCT

For any type of social management, it is of great practical importance that levels of quasi-stationary equilibria can be changed in either of two ways: by adding forces in the desired direction, or by diminishing opposing forces. If a change from the level L_1 to L_2 (the present to a new level) is brought about by increasing the forces toward L_2 (the new level), the secondary effects should be different from the case where the same change of level is brought about by diminishing the opposing forces.

In both cases, the equilibrium might change to the same new level. The secondary effect should, however, be quite different. In the first case, the process on the new level would be accompanied by a state of relatively high tension; in the second case, by a state of relatively low tension. Since increase of tension above a certain degree is likely to be paralleled by higher aggressiveness, higher emotionality, and lower constructiveness, it is clear that as a rule the second method will be preferable to the high-pressure method.

The group decision procedure that is used here attempts to avoid high-pressure methods and is sensitive to resistance to change. In the experiment by Bavelas on changing production in factory work, for instance, no attempt was made to set the new production goal by majority vote because a majority vote forces some group members to produce more than they consider appropriate. These individuals are likely to have some inner resistance. Instead, a procedure was followed by which a goal was chosen on which everyone could agree fully.

It is possible that the success of group decision and particularly the permanency of the effect is, in part, due to the attempt to bring about a favorable decision by removing counterforces within the individuals rather than by applying outside pressure.

The surprising increase from the second to the fourth week in the number of mothers giving cod liver oil and orange juice to the baby can probably be explained by such a decrease of counterforces. Mothers are likely to handle their first baby during the first weeks of life somewhat cautiously and become more ready for action as the child grows stronger.

4. SOCIAL HABITS AND GROUP STANDARDS

Viewing a social stationary process as the result of a quasi-stationary equilibrium, one may expect that any added force will change the level of the process. The idea of "social habit" seems to imply that, in spite of the application of a force, the level of the social process will not change because of some type of "inner resistance" to change. To overcome this inner resistance, an additional force seems to be required, a force sufficient to "break the habit," to "unfreeze" the custom.

Many social habits are anchored in the relation between the individuals and certain group standards. An individual P may differ in his personal level of conduct . . . from the level that represents group standards . . . by a certain amount. If the individual should try to diverge "too much" from group standards, he would find himself in increasing difficulties. He would be ridiculed, treated severely, and finally ousted from the group. Most individuals, therefore, stay pretty close to the standard of the groups they belong to or wish to belong to. In other words, the group level itself acquires value. It becomes a positive valence corresponding to a central force field with the . . . [forces] keeping the individual in line with the standards of the group.

5. INDIVIDUAL PROCEDURES AND GROUP PROCEDURES OF CHANGING SOCIAL CONDUCT

If the resistance to change depends partly on the value that the group standard has for the individual, the resistance to change should diminish if one diminishes the strength of the value of the group standard or changes the level perceived by the individual as having social value.

This second point is one of the reasons for the effectiveness of "group carried" changes[3] resulting from procedures that approach the individuals as part of face-to-face groups. Perhaps one might expect single individuals to be more pliable than groups of like-minded individuals. However, experience in leadership training, in changing of food habits, work production, criminality, alcoholism, and prejudices, all indicate that it is usually easier to change individuals formed into a group than to change any one of them separately.[4] As long as group standards are unchanged, the individual will resist changes more strongly the farther the person is to depart from group standards. If the group standard itself is changed, the resistance which is due to the relation between individual and group standard is eliminated.

6. CHANGING AS A THREE-STEP PROCEDURE: UNFREEZING, MOVING, AND FREEZING OF A LEVEL

A change toward a higher level of group performance is frequently short-lived; after a "shot in the arm" group life soon returns to the previous level. This indicates that it does not suffice to define the objective of a planned change in group performance as the reaching of a different level. Permanency of the new level, or permanency for a desired period, should be included in the objective. A successful change includes therefore three aspects: unfreezing (if necessary) the present level . . . moving to the new level . . . and freezing group life on the new level. Since any level is determined by a force field, permanency implies that the new force field is made relatively secure against change.

The "unfreezing" of the present level may involve quite different problems in different cases. Allport[5] has described the "catharsis" that seems to be necessary before prejudices can be removed. To break open the shell of complacency and self-righteousness, it is sometimes necessary to bring about deliberately an emotional stir-up. . . .

The experiments or group decision reported here cover but a few of the necessary variations. Although in some cases the procedure is relatively easily executed, in others it requires skill and presupposes certain general conditions.

Managers rushing into a factory to raise production by group decisions are likely to encounter failure. In social management as in medicine, there are no patent medicines, and each case demands careful diagnosis.

One reason why group decision facilitates change is illustrated by Willerman. . . .[6] [Willerman's study was concerned with] the degree of eagerness to have the members of a students' eating cooperative change from the consumption of white bread to whole wheat. When the change was simply requested, the degree of eagerness varied greatly with the degree of personal preference for whole wheat. In the case of group decision, the eagerness seems to be relatively independent of personal preference; the individual seems to act mainly as a "group member."

Notes

1. K. Lewin, "Problems of Group Dynamics and the Integration of the Social Sciences: I. Social Equilibria," *J. Hum. Relations*, vol. 1, no. 1, 1947.

2. Ibid.

3. N.R.F. Maier, *Psychology in Industry* (Boston: Houghton Mifflin, 1946).

4. Lewin, K. & Grabbe, P. (Eds.) (1945) Problems of Re-education, Journal of Social Issues, Vol. 1, No. 3.

5. G. W. Allport, "Catharsis and the Reduction of Prejudice," in Lewin and Grabbe (eds.), op. cit., 3–10.

6. K. Lewin, "Forces Behind Food Habits and Methods of Change," *Bull. Nat. Res. Coun.*, 1943, vol. 108, 35–65.

CHAPTER SIX

The Mechanisms of Change

Edgar H. Schein (1964)

The conceptual scheme shown in Figure 6.1 was developed to encompass the kinds of changes in beliefs, attitudes, and values that we regard as fairly "central" or "deep," changes that occur during socialization, therapy, and other processes involving the person's self or identity. The scheme also draws attention to a much-neglected problem, that of having to unlearn something before something new can be learned. Most of the kinds of changes we are concerned with involve attitudes or behaviors that are integrated around the self, where change implies the giving up of something to which the person has previously become committed and that he or she values.

Any change in behavior or attitudes of this sort tends to be emotionally resisted because even the possibility of change implies that previous behavior and attitudes were somehow wrong or inadequate, a conclusion that the change target would be motivated to reject. If change is to occur, therefore, it must be preceded by an alteration of the present stable equilibrium that supports the present behavior and attitudes. It is this step, difficult to pin down precisely, that we believe Lewin correctly saw as akin to "unfreezing"—making something solid into a fluid state. Any viable conceptual scheme of the influence process must begin with the process of unfreezing and thereby take account of the inherent threat that change represents. For any change to occur, the defenses that tend to be aroused in the change target must be made less operative, circumvented, or used directly as change levers.

Once the change target's present equilibrium has been upset, once he or she has become motivated to change, the person will seek information relevant to the dilemma. That is, he or she will seek cues as to the kind of changes to make in behavior or attitudes that will reestablish a comfortable equilibrium. Such information may come from personal or impersonal sources, from a single other person or an array of others, from a single communication, or from a

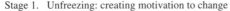

Stage 1. Unfreezing: creating motivation to change
                    Mechanisms: a) Lack of confirmation or disconfirmation
                                       b) Induction of guilt-anxiety
                                       c) Creation of psychological safety by reduction of
                                            threat or removal of barriers
Stage 2. Changing: developing new responses based on new information
                    Mechanism: a) Cognitive redefinition through
                                              (1) Identification: information from a single
                                                    source
                                              (2) Scanning: information from multiple sources
Stage 3. Refreezing: stabilizing and integrating the changes
                    Mechanisms: a) Integrating new responses into personality
                                       b) Integrating new responses into significant
                                            on-going relationships through reconfirmation

Figure 6.1. The Process of Influence and the Mechanisms Underlying Each Stage.

prolonged search. It is this process, the seeking out, processing, and utilization of information for the purpose of achieving new perceptions, attitudes, and behaviors, we have called "changing."

There remains the problem of whether the new behavior and attitudes fit well with the person's other behavior and attitudes, and whether they will be acceptable to significant others. The process of integrating new responses into the ongoing personality and into key emotional relationships leads ultimately to changes that may be considered to be stable. If the new responses do not fit or are unacceptable to important others, a new process of unfreezing is initiated and a new *cycle* of influence is thereby set up. *Stable* change thus implies a reintegration or a stage of "refreezing," to continue with Lewin's terminology. Just as unfreezing is necessary for change to begin, refreezing is necessary for change to endure.

Let us next examine some of the key mechanisms that can be identified in each stage of the influence process.

MECHANISMS OF UNFREEZING

Lack of Confirmation or Disconfirmation

The assumption that underlies a conceptual scheme such as the one proposed is that the change target's significant behavior, beliefs, attitudes, and values are organized around and supported by self-image. It is further assumed that the person presents himself or herself differently in different social situations. Therefore, it is the "operating self-image" that is relevant in any given situation.[1] This operating self-image does not exist in isolation but is usually integrated with the person's definition of the situation and image of the other people in the situation. For example, when a young man enters a classroom and adopts the appropriate self-image of "student," this image is integrated with his view of the larger situation as a school in which certain kinds of learning are supposed to take place, and with his image of others who are defined as teachers and fellow students.

Because of the interdependence of self-image, definition of the situation, and image of others in the situation, the process of unfreezing can begin by a failure of confirmation or actual disconfirmation in any one of the three aspects of the total situation.[2] The change target can be confronted with the information (1) that self-image is out of line with what others and the situation will grant or be able to sustain; (2) that the definition of the situation is out of line with "reality" as defined by others in the situation; (3) that image of the others is out of line with their image of themselves or of each other; and (4) one or more of the above in combination.

For example, a student entering the classroom may see herself as a passive listener only to discover suddenly that the teacher has called upon her; she may have defined the classroom as primarily a place to meet men and relax, but discover that the course is, in fact, "hard" and that the instructor defines the classroom as a place for active participation by students; she may have perceived the instructor as a *laissez faire* type of "good fellow," only to discover the instructor sees himself as a tough taskmaster determined to make his classroom into a real learning environment. Each of these types of information can be thought of as *disconfirmatory* of some assumption the student makes about self, the situation, and/or the others in the situation.

By contrast, *lack of confirmation* occurs when relevant information is lacking. Thus, if a student placed high value on himself as a ladies' man and defined classrooms as places to meet coeds, he would experience lack of confirmation if he discovered that there were no women among his fellow students. Another example might be the case of two students who initially reinforce in each other a self-image of indifference to learning and engage in horseplay during class meetings. If the teacher asks them to sit far apart, and if little opportunity to interact outside of class exists, one could say that these aspects of their self-image would subsequently be lacking in confirmation. In a situation where aspects of the self fail to be confirmed, one may predict that a *gradual* atrophy or unlearning of those aspects will occur.[3] In a situation where aspects of the self are actually disconfirmed, the person confronts a more immediate disequilibrium that requires some immediate change or new learning.

The Induction of Guilt Anxiety

The induction of guilt anxiety refers to the process wherein the person reacts to lack of confirmation or disconfirmation not by rejecting the information or its source but by feeling some sense of inadequacy or failure in self. The sense of inadequacy may (1) be felt in reference to a failure in living up to some ideal self-image, (2) result from a feeling of disappointing others whose reactions are valued, or (3) result from a failure to honor some obligation that has been assumed. Such feelings may be summarized by the concept of "guilt anxiety." Change will occur in the attempt to reduce, or more commonly to *avoid*, guilt anxiety.

Creation of Psychological Safety by Reduction of Threat or Removal of Barriers

Unfreezing can also occur through the reduction of threat or the removal of barriers to change. In these instances, one must assume that the change target already has some motive or desire to change but experiences a conflict that prevents the actual change from occurring. Either the change is inherently anxiety provoking because it brings with it the unknown or else it is perceived by the person to have consequences that he or she is unwilling or unable to bear. The change agent may in these instances (1) try to reassure the change target, or (2) try to help the change target bear the anxiety attendant upon change, or (3) attempt to show the target that the outcome is more palatable than may have been assumed.

MECHANISMS OF CHANGING

Cognitive Redefinition

The problem of learning a *new* response or changing an attitude can be thought of as a problem of seeking out *reliable* and *valid* information from a plethora of sources that may or may not be credible to the target. In making this assertion, we are limiting the learning or change situation to those situations governed by *social reality* as contrasted with *physical reality*[4]; that is, we are only considering situations in which validity is *consensually* judged in terms of the beliefs and attitudes of others.

How does the change target choose and make up his or her mind from the welter of sources available? In the typical, stable social situation, the person pays attention to those sources of information (other people) who confirm his or her present behavior and attitudes. If others fail to provide confirmation or actually disconfirm present attitudes, yet the person must continue to interact with them (for example, because the job demands it), we have a typical unfreezing situation with respect to those attitudes. The person knows something is wrong and that some kind of change is demanded, but the person does not automatically know what is wrong or how to correct the situation.

In order to determine what is wrong or how to change, the person must first reexamine certain assumptions or beliefs about self, others, and the definition of the situation. He or she must then decide if these assumptions are unwarranted or inconsistent with feelings and evaluations the others in the situation hold about themselves, the person, and the situation. *The first step in the change process, then, is to develop alternate assumptions and beliefs through a process of cognitive redefinition of the situation.*

This process involves (1) *new definitions* of terms in the semantic sense; (2) a *broadening of perceptions* or expanded consciousness, which changes the frame of reference from which objects are judged; and/or (3) new standards of *evaluation and judgment*. The new attitudes and behavior that are the eventual outcome of the influence process result from this intermediate step of cognitive redefinition.

From this perspective, the process of unfreezing can be viewed as *becoming open* to certain kinds of information that are actually or potentially available in the environment. The process of changing is the *actual assimilation* of new information resulting in cognitive redefinition and new personal constructs.[5] These in turn form the basis for new attitudes and new behavior.

In making cognitive redefinition pivotal to the change process, we have clearly allied ourselves with Gestalt theories of learning and have rejected reinforcement theories of learning. We would like to point out, however, that the reinforcement principle is very much relevant to the process of unfreezing and refreezing. The process of influence *begins* with the failure to obtain certain social reinforcements (lack of confirmation or disconfirmation); the process of influence *ends* with the reinforcement (confirmation) of new attitudes and behavior. The reinforcement principle cannot conveniently explain the actual mechanisms by which new assumptions, beliefs, or constructs develop and in turn lead to new attitudes and behaviors. We reject the notion of blind trial-and-error learning in the realm of social reality, favoring instead a position that makes the assimilation of information from the social environment the central process. The person does experiment in the process of change, but each experiment is based on some new definition of self, others, and the situation and has therefore already been preceded by some cognitive redefinition.[6]

The question arises whether this mechanism of change is always conscious or not. The answer is clearly negative. We have dramatic examples of cognitive redefinition in the realm of physical perceptions that occur entirely without awareness. There is no reason to doubt the existence of a similar process in the realm of social reality. The best examples come from psychophysical studies of judgments of weight or brightness. The entire frame of reference and pattern of judgments of the same stimuli can be altered simply by introducing an anchoring stimulus at either extreme of the scale.[7] The subject does not realize his judgments have changed, yet clearly cognitive redefinition has taken place. In the realm of social perception and rumor transmission, we have similar effects. Once certain key stimuli are introduced as anchors (for example, identifying a certain person in the story as black), the scale of judgment of other stimuli shifts, though the person may be completely unaware of the process.[8]

Let us turn now to the next problem, that of the *source of information* the person utilizes in redefining cognitions about self, others, and the situation. At one extreme, we have the acquisition of new information through a single source via some process of *identification*. The cues to which the person responds are those that come from a model to whom the person has chosen to relate emotionally. At the other extreme, we have the acquisition of new information through *scanning* a multiple array of sources, which may vary in salience and credibility but do not elicit the kind of emotional focusing implied by identification. The sources are usually other people, but they need not be physically present to exert an influence. Their information may have just as much potency in written or broadcasted form.

We have labeled these two extreme forms of information acquisition by the terms *identification* and *scanning*, recognizing that there are many forms, like imitation, which fall in between. Let us now examine each of these processes in greater detail.[9]

Cognitive Redefinition Through Identification

We can distinguish two basically different kinds of identification that have major consequences for the kind of influence or change produced in a change target. We have labeled these as *Type I* or *defensive* identification and *Type II* or *positive* identification. The conditions for, psychological processes of, and outcomes of these two types are shown in Table 6.1.[10]

Looking first at the *conditions* for identification, we note that *defensive identification* tends to occur in settings that the target has entered involuntarily and from which he or she cannot escape. The person usually experiences a sense of helplessness, relative impotence, fear, and threat. The relationship to the change agent is an imbalanced one in that the agent has most of the power. The agent usually occupies a formal position supported by institutionalized sanctions. The target's role is to change or learn and not to ask too many questions. The prototype of this relationship is the child *vis-à-vis* the powerful parent, or the concentration camp prisoner *vis-à-vis* a captor.

Positive identification, by contrast, tends to occur in situations where the target has entered voluntarily and from which the person feels free to leave. He

Table 6.1. Analysis of Two Types of Identification.

	Type 1 Defensive Identification	Type II Positive Identification
Conditions for the processes	Target is captive in the change situation	Target is free to leave situation
	Target role nonvoluntarily acquired	Target takes role voluntarily
	Agent in formal change agent position	Agent does not necessarily occupy formal role
	Target feels helpless, impotent, fearful, and threatened	Target experiences autonomy, sense of power, and choice
	Target must change	Target experiences trust and faith in agent
		Target can terminate change process
Psychological processes involved	Agent is primary source of unfreezing	Agent is usually not the source of unfreezing
	Target becomes position-oriented to acquire the agent's perceived power	Target becomes person-oriented because agent's power is seen to reside in personality, not position
	Target has limited and distorted view of agent and lacks empathy for agent	Agent will be chosen on the basis of trust, clarity, and potency
	Target tends to imitate limited portions of target's behavior	Target sees richness and complexity of agent as a person
		Target tends to assimilate what he or she learns from the model
Outcomes	New behavior in target is stilted, ritualized, restrictive, and narrowing	New behavior in target is enlarging, differentiated, spontaneous, and enabling of further growth
	New behavior is more likely to be acceptable to the influencing institution	New behavior is personally more meaningful but may be less acceptable to influencing institution

or she experiences a sense of autonomy and feels choices can be made. Instead of fear and threat *vis-à-vis* the change agent, the target experiences trust and faith. The power relationship is less tilted and is generally not supported by formal positions or institutional sanctions, though they may be present, as in the case of the psychotherapist. The prototype of this relationship is the mutual identification of husband and wife or close friends.

In terms of the *psychological processes* involved in the two types of identification, *defensive identification* generally implies a relationship in which the change agent operates as the primary source of unfreezing (provides the bulk of the discontinuing cues). The target responds to this situation by becoming preoccupied with the change agent's position or status, which is perceived to be the primary source of the change agent's power. This preoccupation with the position in turn implies a limited and often distorted view of the identification model. The change target tends to pay attention only to the power-relevant cues, tends to have little or no empathy for the person actually occupying the position, and tends to imitate blindly and often unconsciously only certain limited portions of the model's behavior. Or to put it another way, if existing attitudes and parts of the target's self are chronically and consistently disconfirmed in a coercive way, one solution for the target is to abandon them completely and to substitute those attitudes and values perceived to be a property of the powerful disconfirmer. . . .

Positive identification, by contrast, tends to be *person-* rather than *position-*oriented. The potential model is rarely the source of unfreezing and hence is less threatening. The model's power or salience is perceived to lie in some personal attributes rather than in some formal position. Because the change target feels free to leave the situation, he or she will use the criteria of trust and clarity to choose a model that in turn will lead to a fuller and richer view of the personality of the model. The person will tend to have empathy for the model and genuinely to assimilate the new information obtained from seeing the world through the model's eyes, rather than directly imitating behavior. Thus the target's new behavior and attitudes may not actually resemble the model's too closely. The whole process of identification will be more spontaneous, will be more differentiated, and will enable further growth rather than be compulsive and limiting.

Looking now at the *outcome,* we see that *defensive identification* leads to a more restricted, ritualized, and stilted set of responses and attitudes. On the other hand, *positive identification* leads to an enlarged, more differentiated, and fluid set of responses and attitudes. There is a greater likelihood of the latter process leading to psychological growth than is true of the former. However, the likelihood that the changes will be acceptable to the institution that has initiated the change process may be greater if defensive identification has taken place.

In both types of identification, the basic mechanism of change is the utilization of interpersonal cues coming from a change agent with whom the target identifies. These cues serve as the basis for redefining the cognitions the target holds about self, others, and the situation. But it is obvious that a great deal of change occurs through processes other than these two types of identification. Even in the most coercive institutions, defensive identification may account for only a small portion of the total change in the target. To gain a more balanced picture of change mechanisms, we must look at the other end of the information acquisition scale, the process we have called *scanning*.

Cognitive Redefinition Through Scanning

The process of *scanning* can best be differentiated from the process of *identification* by the degree to which the change target or learner focuses on multiple models, as contrasted with a single model in the social environment. Scanning thus involves a "cafeteria" approach to the utilization of interpersonal information, and the absence of strong emotional relationships between the change target and sources of relevant information. At the extreme, *scanning* implies attention to the *content* of the message regardless of the person, whereas *identification* implies attention to the *person* regardless of the content. In both cases, other people tend to be the primary source of information, but in scanning others become salient only in terms of their perceived relevance or expertness in solving the particular problem that is bothering the change target.

The contrast between *scanning* and *identification* can best be exemplified in a group engaged in group therapy or in human relations training. Let us assume that each member of the group is unfrozen with respect to some areas of self and is seeking information which will permit redefining the situation so as to reach a more comfortable equilibrium. An example of *defensive identification* would be the case of the group member who, because of great fear of the authority of the therapist or staff member in the group, attempts to change by mimicking and imitating what is perceived to be the staff member's behavior and attitudes. An example of *positive identification* would be the case of the group member who establishes a close emotional relationship with another group member or the staff member and attempts to view his or her own problems from the perspective of this other person. An example of *scanning* would be the case of the group member who looks to any source in the group for reactions which bear upon the particular problem perceived and attempts to integrate *all* the reactions obtained. To reiterate, when persons scan they relate themselves primarily to the information received, not to the particular source from which the information comes.

How does scanning compare with identification in the change outcome? In the case of scanning, the target may have a more difficult time locating reliable and useful information, but the solution eventually is likely to fit better into his or her personality because of the power to accept or reject information voluntarily. If the change goal is personal growth, the change agent should attempt to produce a setting conducive to scanning or positive identification, and avoid a setting conducive to defensive identification. If the change goal is the acceptance of a particular set of behaviors and attitudes, the change agent should attempt to produce a setting conducive to positive identification and provide the target with a good representative of the point of view to be learned. To achieve the latter change goal, defensive identification would be next best, and scanning would appear to be least likely to succeed.

Notes

1. The articles by Erving Goffman on "Face Work" and "Cooling," cited in *Interpersonal Dynamics* (eds. Bennis and Schein), are excellent analyses of the process of constructing, W.G., Schein, E.H., Berlew, D.E., & Steele, F. I. (Eds.) (1968), Rev. Ed., Interpersonal Dynamics, Homewood, Ill., Dorsey Press.

2. In the fairly common situation where information conflicts, where both confirming and disconfirming cues are available, the person probably tends to pay attention only to the confirming cues. As long as confirmation occurs, therefore, there are no real unfreezing forces present.

3. The best examples of lack of confirmation occurred in Communist-controlled POW camps, in which prisoners were systematically segregated from each other and their social structure undermined to such a degree that mutual mistrust led to virtually no meaningful communication. See E. H. Schein, "The Chinese Indoctrination Program for Prisoners of War," *Psychiatry,* Vol. 19 (1956), pp. 149–72. For a more extensive discussion of Communist indoctrination methods, see E. H. Schein with I. Schneier and C. H. Barker, *Coercive Persuasion* (New York: W. W. Norton, 1961), and R. J. Lifton, " 'Thought Reform' of Western Civilians in Chinese Communist Prisons," *Psychiatry,* Vol. 19 (1956), pp. 173–95.

4. L. Festinger, "Informal Social Communication," *Psychological Review,* Vol. 57 (1950), pp. 271–82.

5. We are using constructs here in the sense that G. A. Kelly, *The Psychology of Personal Constructs* (New York: W. W. Norton, 1955) defined them, as the beliefs, assumptions, and evaluations a person has about some object in the social world.

6. The best examples of this process were provided to us by the Chinese Communists. The prisoner changed his attitudes only after a prolonged process of unfreezing, the end result of which was a readiness to pay attention to the cues that cellmates were providing all along. Once he was paying attention to this category of information, the prisoner discovered that his meanings for words such as "crime" were different from theirs, and his standards of judgment based on his frame of reference were different from their standards because of their different frame of reference. Once he had redefined his own semantics and attempted to view the world from the

cellmates' frame of reference by applying their standards, he could accept himself as a guilty criminal and make a sincere confession.

7. H. Helson, "Adaptation-Level as a Basis for a Quantitative Theory of Frames of Reference," *Psychological Review,* Vol. 55 (1948), pp. 297–313.

8. G. W. Allport and L. Postman, *The Psychology of Rumor* (New York: Holt, Rinehart and Winston, 1947).

9. This analysis has been influenced by Kelman's excellent work on mechanisms of attitude change (H. C. Kelman, "Compliance, Identification, and Internalization: Three Processes of Attitude Change," *Conflict Resolution,* Vol. 2 [1958], pp. 51–60). We have not used his concepts of *compliance, identification,* and *internalization* because of our emphasis on deeper levels of change than those he deals with in his experiments. Kelman's concepts have greatly aided, however, in achieving some conceptual clarity in this area.

10. The analysis of identification follows closely Slater's analysis of personal and positional identification. Our analysis, however, deals more with adult processes whereas his focuses on childhood socialization. For an excellent analysis, see P. E. Slater, "Toward a Dualistic Theory of Identification," *Merrill Palmer Quarterly,* Behavior and Development, Vol. 7, No. 2. (1961), pp. 113–26.

CHAPTER SEVEN

General Strategies for Effecting Changes in Human Systems

Robert Chin
Kenneth D. Benne (1967)

D iscussing general strategies and procedures for effecting change requires that we set limits to the discussion for, under a liberal interpretation of the title, we would need to deal with much of the literature of contemporary social and behavioral science, basic and applied.

Therefore we shall limit our discussion to those changes that are planned changes—in which attempts to bring about change are conscious, deliberate, and intended, at least on the part of one or more agents related to the change attempt. We shall also attempt to categorize strategies and procedures that have a few important elements in common but that in fact differ widely in other respects. And we shall neglect many of these differences. In addition, we shall look beyond the description of procedures in common-sense terms and seek some genotypic characteristics of change strategies. We shall seek the roots of the main strategies discussed, including their variants, in ideas and idea systems prominent in contemporary and recent social and psychological thought.

One element in all approaches to planned change is the conscious utilization and application of knowledge as an instrument or tool for modifying patterns and institutions of practice. The knowledge or related technology to be applied may be knowledge of the nonhuman environment in which practice goes on or of some knowledge-based "thing technology" for controlling one or another feature of the practice environment. In educational practice, for example, technologies of communication and calculation, based upon new knowledge of electronics—audiovisual devices, television, computers, teaching machines— loom large among the knowledges and technologies that promise greater efficiency and economy in handling various practices in formal education. As attempts are made to introduce these new thing technologies into school situations, the change problem shifts to the human problems of dealing with the resistances, anxieties, threats to morale, conflicts, disrupted interpersonal communications, and so on that prospective changes in patterns of practice evoke in the people affected by the change. So the change agent, even though focally and initially concerned with modifications in the thing technology of education, finds himself or herself in need of more adequate knowledge of human behavior, individual and social, and in need of developed "people technologies," based on behavioral knowledge, for dealing effectively with the human aspects of deliberate change.

The knowledge that suggests improvements in educational practice may, on the other hand, be behavioral knowledge in the first instance—knowledge about participative learning, about attitude change, about family disruption in inner-city communities, about the cognitive and skill requirements of new careers, and so forth. Such knowledge may suggest changes in school grouping, in the relations between teachers and students, in the relations of teachers and principals to parents, and in counseling practices. Here change agents, initially focused on application of behavioral knowledge and the improvement of people technologies in school settings, must face the problems of using people technologies in planning, installing, and evaluating such changes in educational practice. The new people technologies must be experienced, understood, and accepted by teachers and administrators before they can be used effectively with students.

This line of reasoning suggests that, whether the focus of planned change is in the introduction of more effective thing technologies or people technologies into institutionalized practice, processes of introducing such changes must be based on behavioral knowledge of change and must utilize people technologies based on such knowledge.

TYPES OF STRATEGIES FOR CHANGING

Our further analysis is based on three types or groups of strategies. The first of these, and probably the most frequently employed by people of knowledge in America and Western Europe, are those we call empirical-rational strategies. One fundamental assumption underlying these strategies is that humans are rational. Another assumption is that people will follow their rational self-interest once this is revealed to them. A change is proposed by some person or group that knows of a situation that is desirable, effective, and in line with the self-interest of the person, group, organization, or community that will be affected by the change. Because the person (or group) is assumed to be rational and moved by self-interest, it is assumed that the person or group will adopt the proposed change if it can be rationally justified and if it can be shown by the proposer(s) that the person or group will gain by the change.

A second group of strategies we call normative-reeducative. These strategies build upon assumptions about human motivation different from those underlying the first. The rationality and intelligence of humans are not denied. Patterns of action and practice are supported by sociocultural norms and by commitments on the part of individuals to these norms. Sociocultural norms are supported by the attitude and value systems of individuals—normative outlooks that undergird their commitments. Change in a pattern of practice or action, according to this view, will occur only as the persons involved are brought to change their normative orientations to old patterns and develop commitments to new ones. And changes in normative orientations involve changes in attitudes, values, skills, and significant relationships, not just changes in knowledge, information, or intellectual rationales for action and practice.

The third group of strategies is based on the application of power in some form, political or otherwise. The influence process involved is basically that of compliance of those with less power to the plans, directions, and leadership of those with greater power. Often the power to be applied is legitimate power or authority. Thus the strategy may involve getting the authority of law or administrative policy behind the change to be effected. Some power strategies may appeal less to the use of authoritative power to effect change than to the massing of coercive power, legitimate or not, in support of the change sought.[1]

Empirical-Rational Strategies

A variety of specific strategies are included in what we are calling the empirical-rational approach to effecting change. As we have already pointed out, the rationale underlying most of these is an assumption that humans are guided by reason and that they will utilize some rational calculus of self-interest in determining needed changes in behavior.

It is difficult to point to any one person whose ideas express or articulate the orientation underlying commitment to empirical-rational strategies of changing. In Western Europe and America, this orientation might be better identified with the general social orientation of the Enlightenment and of classical liberalism than with the ideas of any one person. In this view, the chief foes to human rationality and to change or progress based on rationality were ignorance and superstition. Scientific investigation and research represented the chief ways of extending knowledge and reducing the limitations of ignorance. A corollary of this optimistic view of humans and their future was an advocacy of education as a way of disseminating scientific knowledge and of freeing men and women from the shackles of superstition. Although elitist notions played a part in the thinking of many classic liberals, the increasing trend during the nineteenth century was toward the universalization of educational opportunity. The common and universal school, open to all men and women, was the principal instrument by which knowledge would replace ignorance and superstition in the minds of people and become a principal agent in the spread of reason, knowledge, and knowledge-based action and practice (progress) in human society. In American experience, Jefferson may be taken as a principal, early advocate of research and of education as agencies of human progress. And Horace Mann may be taken as the prophet of progress through the institutionalization of universal educational opportunity through the common school.[2]

Basic Research and Dissemination of Knowledge Through General Education. The strategy of encouraging basic knowledge building and of depending on general education to diffuse the results of research into the minds and thinking of men and women is still by far the most appealing strategy of change to most academic people of knowledge and to large segments of the American population as well. Basic researchers are quite likely to appeal for time for further research when confronted by some unmet need. And many people find this appeal convincing. Both of these facts are well illustrated by difficulties with diseases for which no adequate control measures or cures are available—poliomyelitis, for example. Medical researchers asked for more time and funds for research, and people responded with funds for research, both through voluntary channels and through legislative appropriations. And the control measures were forthcoming. The educational problem then shifted to inducing people to comply with immunization procedures based on research findings.

This appeal to a combination of research and education of the public has worked in many areas of new knowledge-based thing technologies where almost universal readiness for accepting the new technology was already present in the population. Where such readiness is not available, as in the case of fluoridation technologies in the management of dental caries, a general strategy of basic research plus educational (informational) campaigns to spread knowledge of the findings does not work well. The cases of its inadequacy as a single strategy of change have multiplied, especially where "engineering" problems, which involve a divided and conflicting public or deep resistances due to the threat by the new technology to traditional attitudes and values, have thwarted its effectiveness. But these cases, though they demand attention to other strategies of changing, do not disprove the importance of basic research and of general educational opportunity as elements in a progressive and self-renewing society.

We have noted that the strategy under discussion has worked best in grounding and diffusing generally acceptable thing technologies in society. Some have argued that the main reason the strategy has not worked in the area of people technologies is a relative lack of basic research on people and their behavior, relationships, and institutions and a corresponding lack of emphasis upon social and psychological knowledges in school and college curricula. It would follow in this view that increased basic research on human affairs and relationships and increased efforts to diffuse the results of such research through public education are the ways of making the general strategy work better. Auguste Comte with his emphasis on positivistic sociology in the reorganization of society and Lester F. Ward in America may be taken as late-nineteenth-century representatives of this view. And the spirit of Comte and Ward is by no means dead in American academia or in influential segments of the American public.

Personnel Selection and Replacement. Difficulties in getting knowledge effectively into practice may be seen as lying primarily in the lack of fitness of persons occupying positions with job responsibilities for improving practice. The argument goes that we need the right person in the right position, if knowledge is to be optimally applied and if rationally based changes are to become the expectation in organizational and societal affairs. This fits with the liberal reformers' frequently voiced and enacted plea to drive the unfit from office and to replace them with those more fit as a condition of social progress.

That reformers' programs have so often failed has sobered but by no means destroyed the zeal of those who regard personnel selection, assessment, and replacement as a major key to program improvement in education or in other enterprises as well. This strategy was given a scientific boost by the development of scientific testing of potentialities and aptitudes. We will use Binet as a prototype of psychological testing and Moreno as a prototype in sociometric testing, while recognizing the extensive differentiation and elaboration that have occurred in psychometrics and sociometrics since their original work. We recognize too the elaborated modes of practice in personnel work that have been built around psychometric and sociometric tools and techniques. We do not discount their limited value as actual and potential tools for change, while making two observations on the way they have often been used. First, they have been used more often in the interest of system maintenance rather than of system change, since the job descriptions personnel workers seek to fill are defined in terms of system requirements as established. Second, by focusing on the role occupant as the principal barrier to improvement, personnel selection and replacement strategies have tended not to reveal the social and cultural system difficulties that may be in need of change if improvement is to take place.

Systems Analysts as Staff and Consultants. Personnel workers in government, industry, and education have typically worked in staff relations to line management, reflecting the bureaucratic, line-staff form of organization that has flourished in the large-scale organization of effort and enterprise in the twentieth century. And other expert workers—systems analysts—more attuned to system difficulties than to the adequacies or inadequacies of persons as role occupants within the system have found their way into the staff resources of line management in contemporary organizations.

There is no reason why the expert resources of personnel workers and systems analysts might not be used in nonbureaucratic organizations or in processes of moving bureaucratic organizations toward nonbureaucratic forms. But the fact remains that their use has been shaped, for the most part, in the image of the scientific management of bureaucratically organized enterprises. So we have placed the systems analysts in our chart under Frederick Taylor, the father of scientific management in America.

The line management of an enterprise seeks to organize human and technical effort toward the most efficient service of organizational goals. And these goals are defined in terms of the production of some mandated product, whether a tangible product or a less tangible good or service. In pursuing this quest for efficiency, line management employs experts in the analysis of sociotechnical systems and in the laying out of more efficient systems. The experts employed may work as external consultants or as an internal staff unit. Behavioral scientists have recently found their way, along with mathematicians and engineers, into systems analysis work.

It is interesting to note that the role of these experts is becoming embroiled in discussions of whether or not behavioral science research should be used to sensitize administrators to new organizational possibilities, to new goals, or primarily to implement efficient operation within perspectives and goals as currently defined. Jean Hills has raised the question of whether behavioral science when applied to organizational problems tends to perpetuate established ideology and system relations because of blinders imposed by their being "problem centered" and by their limited definition of what "a problem" is.[3]

We see an emerging strategy, in the use of behavioral scientists as systems analysts and engineers, toward viewing the problem of organizational change and changing as a wide-angled problem, one in which all the input and output features and components of a large-scale system are considered. It is foreseeable that with the use of high-speed and high-capacity computers, and with the growth of substantial theories and hypotheses about how parts of an educational system operate, we shall find more and more applications for systems analysis and operations research in programs of educational change. In fact, it is precisely the quasi-mathematical character of these modes of research that will make possible the rational analysis of qualitatively different aspects of educational work and will bring them into the range of rational planning—masses of students, massive problems of poverty and educational and cultural deprivation, and so on. We see no necessary incompatibility between an ideology that emphasizes the individuality of the student and the use of systems analysis and computers in strategizing the problems of the total system. The actual incompatibilities may lie in the limited uses to which existing organizers and administrators of educational efforts put these technical resources.

Applied Research and Linkage Systems for Diffusion of Research Results. The American development of applied research and of a planned system for linking applied researchers with professional practitioners and both of these with centers for basic research and with organized consumers of applied research has been strongly influenced by two distinctive American inventions: the land-grant university and the agricultural extension system. We therefore have put the name of Justin Morrill, author of the land-grant college act and of the act that established the cooperative agricultural extension system, on our chart. The land-grant colleges or universities were dedicated to doing applied research in the service of agriculture and the mechanic arts. These colleges and universities developed research programs in basic sciences as well, and experimental stations for the development and refinement of knowledge-based technologies for use in engineering and agriculture. As the extension services developed, county agents—practitioners—were attached to the state land-grant college or university that received financial support from both state and federal governments. The county agent and staff developed local organizations of adult farm men and women and of farm youths to provide a channel toward informing consumers concerning new and better agricultural practices and toward getting awareness of unmet consumer needs and unsolved problems back to centers of knowledge and research. Garth Jones has made one of the more comprehensive studies of the strategies of changing involved in large-scale demonstration.[4]

Not all applied research has occurred within a planned system for knowledge discovery, development, and utilization like the one briefly described above. The system has worked better in developing and diffusing thing technologies than in developing and diffusing people technologies, though the development of rural sociology and of agricultural economics shows that extension workers were by no means unaware of the behavioral dimensions of change problems. But the large-scale demonstration, through the land-grant university cooperative extension service, of the stupendous changes that can result from a planned approach to knowledge discovery, development, diffusion, and utilization is a part of the consciousness of all Americans concerned with planned change.[5]

Applied research and development is an honored part of the tradition of engineering approaches to problem identification and solution. The pioneering work of E. L. Thorndike in applied research in education should be noted on our chart. The processes and slow tempo of diffusion and utilization of research findings and inventions in public education is well illustrated in studies by Paul Mort and his students.[6] More recently, applied research, in its product development aspect, has been utilized in a massive way to contribute curriculum materials and designs for science instruction (as well as in other subjects). When we assess this situation to find reasons why such researches have not been more effective in producing changes in instruction, the answers seem to lie both in the plans of the studies that produced the materials and designs and in the potential users of the findings. Adequate linkage between consumers and researchers was frequently not established. Planned and evaluated demonstrations and experimentations connected with the use of materials were frequently slighted. And training of consumer teachers to use the new materials adaptively and creatively was frequently missing.

Such observations have led to a fresh spurt of interest in evaluation research addressed to educational programs. The fear persists that this too may lead to disappointment if it is not focused for two-way communication between researchers and teachers and if it does not involve collaboratively the ultimate consumers of the results of such research: the students. Evaluation researches conducted in the spirit of justifying a program developed by expert applied researchers will not help to guide teachers and students in their quest for improved practices of teaching and learning if the concerns of the latter have not been taken centrally into account in the evaluation process.[7]

Recently, attempts have been made to link applied research activities in education with basic researchers on the one hand and with persons in action and practice settings on the other through some system of interlocking roles similar to those suggested in the description of the land grant-extension systems in agriculture or in other fields where applied and development researchers have flourished.

The linking of research-development efforts with diffusion-innovation efforts has been gaining headway in the field of education with the emergence of federally supported research and development centers based in universities, of regional laboratories connected with state departments of education, colleges, and universities in a geographic area, and of various consortia and institutes confronting problems of educational change and changing. The strategy of change here usually includes a well-researched innovation that seems feasible to install in practice settings. Attention is directed to the question of whether or not the innovation will bring about a desired result, and with what it can accomplish, if given a trial in one or more practice settings.

The questions of *how* to get a fair trial and *how* to install an innovation in an already-going and crowded school system are ordinarily not built centrally into the strategy. The rationalistic assumption usually precludes research attention to these questions, for if the invention can be rationally shown to have achieved desirable results in some situations, it is assumed that people in other situations will adopt it once they know these results and the rationale behind them. The neglect of the above questions has led to a wastage of much applied research effort in the past.

Attention has been given recently to the roles, communication mechanisms, and processes necessary for innovation and diffusion of improved educational practices.[8] Clark and Guba have formulated very specific processes related to and necessary for change in educational practice following upon research. For them, the necessary processes are *development*, including invention and design; *diffusion*, including dissemination and demonstration; *adoption*, including trial, installation, and institutionalization. Clark's earnest conviction is summed up in this statement: "In a sense, the educational research community will be the educational community, and the route to educational progress will self-evidently be research and development."[9]

The approach of Havelock and Benne is concerned with the intersystem relationships between basic researchers, applied researchers, practitioners, and consumers in an evolved and evolving organization for knowledge utilization. They are concerned especially with the communication difficulties and role conflicts that occur at points of intersystem exchange. These conflicts are important because they illuminate the normative issues at stake between basic researchers and applied researchers, between applied researchers and practitioners (teachers and administrators), and between practitioners and consumers (students). The lines of strategy suggested by their analysis for solving role conflicts and communication difficulties call for transactional and collaborative exchanges across the lines of varied organized interests and orientations within the process of utilization. This brings their analysis into the range of normative-reeducative strategies, to be discussed later.

The concepts from the behavioral sciences upon which these strategies of diffusion rest come mainly from two traditions. The first is from studies of the diffusion of traits of culture from one cultural system to another, initiated by the American anthropologist Franz Boas. This type of study has been carried on by Rogers in his work on innovation and diffusion of innovations in contemporary culture and is reflected in a number of recent writers such as Katz and Carlson.[10] The second scientific tradition is in studies of influence in mass communication associated with Carl Hovland and his students.[11] Both traditions have assumed a *relatively passive recipient of input* in diffusion situations. And actions within the process of diffusion are interpreted from the standpoint of an observer of the process. Bauer has pointed out that scientific studies have exaggerated the effectiveness of mass persuasion since they have compared the total number in the audience to the communications with the much smaller proportion of the audience persuaded by the communications.[12] A clearer view of processes of diffusion must include the actions of the receiver as well as those of the transmitter in the transactional events that are the units of the diffusion process. And strategies for making diffusion processes more effective must be transactional and collaborative by design.

Utopian Thinking as a Strategy of Changing. It may seem strange to include the projection of utopias as a rational-empirical strategy of changing. Yet inventing and designing the shape of the future by extrapolating what we know of in the present is to envision a direction for planning and action in the present. If the image of a potential future is convincing and rationally persuasive to people in the present, the image may become part of the dynamics and motivation of present action. The liberal tradition is not devoid of its utopias. When we think of utopias quickened by an effort to extrapolate from the sciences of humankind to a future vision of society, the utopia of B. F. Skinner comes to mind.[13] The title of the Eight State Project, "Designing Education for the Future," for which this chapter was prepared, reveals a utopian intent and aspiration and illustrates an attempt to employ utopian thinking for practical purposes.[14]

Yet it may be somewhat disheartening to others, as it is to us, to note the absence of rousing and beckoning normative statements of what both can and ought to be in humanity's future in most current liberal-democratic utopias, whether these be based on psychological, sociological, political, or philosophical findings and assumptions. The absence of utopias in current society, in this sense, and in the sense that Mannheim studied them in his now-classical study,[15] tends to make the forecasting of future directions a problem of technical prediction, rather than equally a process of projecting value orientations and preferences into the shaping of a better future.

Perceptual and Conceptual Reorganization Through the Clarification of Language. In classical liberalism, one perceived foe of rational change and progress was superstition. And superstitions are carried from person to person and from generation to generation through the agency of unclear and mythical language. British utilitarianism was one important strand of classical liberalism, and one of utilitarianism's important figures, Jeremy Bentham, sought to purify language of its dangerous mystique through his study of fictions.

More recently, Alfred Korzybski and S. I. Hayakawa, in the general semantics movement, have sought a way of clarifying and rectifying the names of things and processes.[16] Although their main applied concern was with personal therapy, both (especially Hayakawa) were also concerned to bring about changes in social systems as well. People disciplined in general semantics, it was hoped, would see more correctly, communicate more adequately, and reason more effectively and thus lay a realistic common basis for action and changing. The strategies of changing associated with general semantics overlap with our next family of strategies, the normative-reeducative, because of their emphasis upon the importance of interpersonal relationships and social contexts within the communication process.

Normative-Reeducative Strategies of Changing

We have already suggested that this family of strategies rests on assumptions and hypotheses about humans and their motivation that contrast significantly at points with the assumptions and hypotheses of those committed to what we have called rational-empirical strategies. People are seen as inherently active, in quest of impulse and need satisfaction. The relation between humans and their environment is essentially transactional, as Dewey[17] made clear in his famous article on "The Reflex-Arc Concept." The human organism does not passively await given stimuli from the environment in order to respond. Humans take stimuli as furthering or thwarting the goals of their ongoing action. Intelligence arises in the process of shaping organism-environmental relations toward more adequate fitting and joining of organismic demands and environmental resources.

Intelligence is social, rather than narrowly individual. Humans are guided in their actions by socially funded and communicated meanings, norms, and institutions, in brief by a normative culture. At the personal level, people are guided by internalized meanings, habits, and values. Changes in patterns of action or practice are, therefore, changes not alone in the rational informational equipment of men and women, but at the personal level, in habits and values as well, and at the sociocultural level changes are alterations in normative structures and in institutionalized roles and relationships, as well as in cognitive and perceptual orientations.

For Dewey, the prototype of intelligence in action is the scientific method. And he saw a broadened and humanized scientific method as humankind's best hope for progress if people could learn to utilize such a method in facing all of the problematic situations of their lives. *Intelligence*, so conceived, rather than *reason* as defined in classical liberalism, was the key to Dewey's hope for the invention, development, and testing of adequate strategies of changing in human affairs.

Lewin's contribution to normative-reeducative strategies of changing stemmed from his vision of required interrelations between research, training, and action (and, for him, this meant collaborative relationships, often now lacking, between researchers, educators, and activists) in the solution of human problems, in the identification of needs for change, and in the working out of improved knowledge, technology, and patterns of action in meeting these needs. Humans must participate in their own reeducation if they are "to be reeducated at all." And reeducation is a normative change as well as a cognitive and perceptual change. These convictions led Lewin[18] to emphasize action research as a strategy of changing, and participation in groups as a medium of reeducation.

Freud's main contributions to normative-reeducative strategies of changing are two. First, he sought to demonstrate the unconscious and preconscious bases of human actions. Only as a person finds ways of becoming aware of these nonconscious wellsprings of attitudes and actions will he or she be able to bring them into conscious self-control. And Freud devoted much of his magnificent genius to developing ways of helping people to become conscious of the main springs of their actions and so capable of freedom. Second, in developing therapeutic methods he discovered and developed ways of utilizing the relationship between change agent (therapist) and client (patient) as a major tool in reeducating the client toward expanded self-awareness, self-understanding, and self-control. Emphasis upon the collaborative relationship in therapeutic change was a major contribution by Freud and his students and colleagues to normative-reeducative strategies of changing in human affairs.[19]

Normative-reeducative approaches to effecting change bring direct interventions by change agents, interventions based on a consciously worked out theory of change and of changing, into the life of a client system, be that system a person, a small group, an organization, or a community. The theory of changing is still crude, but it is probably as explicitly stated as possible, granted our present state of knowledge about planned change.[20]

Some of the common elements among variants within this family of change strategies are the following. First, all emphasize the client system and his or her (or its) involvement in working out programs of change and improvement for self (or itself). The way the client sees self and the problem must be brought into dialogic relationship with the way in which the client and the problem are seen by the change agent, whether the latter is functioning as researcher, consultant, trainer, therapist, or friend in relation to the client. Second, the problem confronting the client is not assumed *a priori* to be one that can be met by more adequate technical information, though this possibility is not ruled out. The problem may lie rather in the attitudes, values, norms, and the external and internal relationships of the client system and may require alteration or reeducation of these as a condition of its solution. Third, the change agent must learn to intervene mutually and collaboratively along with the client into efforts to define and solve the client's problem(s). The here and now experience of the two provide an important basis for diagnosing the problem and for locating needs for reeducation in the interest of solving it. Fourth, non-conscious elements that impede problem solution must be brought into consciousness and publicly examined and reconstructed. Fifth, the methods and concepts of the behavioral sciences are resources that change agent and client learn to use selectively, relevantly, and appropriately in learning to deal with the confronting problem and with problems of a similar kind in the future.

These approaches center in the notion that people technology is just as necessary as thing technology in working out desirable changes in human affairs. Put in this bold fashion, it is obvious that for the normative-reeducative change agent, clarification and reconstruction of values is of pivotal importance in changing. By getting the values of various parts of the client system along with his or her own openly into the arena of change and by working through value conflicts responsibly, the change agent seeks to avoid manipulation and indoctrination of the client, in the morally reprehensible meanings of these terms.

We may use the organization of the National Training Laboratories in 1947 as a milestone in the development of normative-reeducative approaches to changing in America. The first summer laboratory program grew out of earlier collaborations among Kurt Lewin, Ronald Lippitt, Leland Bradford, and Kenneth Benne. The idea behind the laboratory was that participants, staff, and students would learn about themselves and their back-home problems by collaboratively building a laboratory in which participants would become both experimenters and subjects in the study of their own developing interpersonal and group behavior within the laboratory setting. It seems evident that the five conditions of a normative-reeducative approach to changing were met in the conception of the training laboratory. Kurt Lewin died before the 1947 session of the training laboratory opened. Ronald Lippitt was a student of Lewin's and carried many of Lewin's orientations with him into the laboratory staff. Leland Bradford and Kenneth Benne were both students of John Dewey's philosophy of education. Bradford had invented several technologies for participative learning and self-study in his work in WPA adult education programs and as training officer in several agencies of the federal government. Benne came out of a background in educational philosophy and had collaborated with colleagues prior to 1943 in developing a methodology for policy and decision making and for the reconstruction of normative orientations, a methodology that sought to fuse democratic and scientific values and to translate these into principles for resolving conflicting and problematic situations at the personal and community levels of human organization.[21] Benne and his colleagues had been much influenced by the work of Mary Follett,[22] her studies of integrative solutions to conflicts in settings of public and business administration, and by the work of Karl Mannheim[23] on the ideology and methodology of planning changes in human affairs, as well as by the work of John Dewey and his colleagues.

The work of the National Training Laboratories has encompassed development and testing of various approaches to changing in institutional settings, in America and abroad, since its beginning. One parallel development in England that grew out of Freud's thinking should be noted. This work developed in efforts at Tavistock Clinic to apply therapeutic approaches to problems of change in industrial organizations and in communities. This work is reported in statements by Elliot Jaques[24] and in this volume by Eric Trist. Another parallel development is represented by the efforts of Roethlisberger and Dickson to use personal counseling in industry as a strategy of organizational change.[25] Roethlisberger and Dickson had been strongly influenced by the pioneer work of Elton Mayo in industrial sociology[26] as well as by the counseling theories and methodologies of Carl Rogers.

Various refinements of methodologies for changing have been developed and tested since the establishment of the National Training Laboratories in 1947, both under its auspices and under other auspices as well. For us, the modal developments are worthy of further discussion here. One set of approaches is oriented focally to the improvement of the problem-solving processes utilized by a client system. The other set focuses on helping members of client systems to become aware of their attitude and value orientations and relationship difficulties through a probing of feelings, manifest and latent, involved in the functioning and operation of the client system.[27] Both approaches use the development of ''temporary systems'' as a medium of re-education of persons and of role occupants in various ongoing social systems.[28]

Improving the Problem-Solving Capabilities of a System. This family of approaches to changing rests on several assumptions about change in human systems. Changes in a system, when they are reality-oriented, take the form of problem solving. A system to achieve optimum reality orientation in its adaptations to its changing internal and external environments must develop and institutionalize its own problem-solving structures and processes. These structures and processes must be tuned both to human problems of relationship and morale and to technical problems of meeting the system's task requirements, set by its goals of production, distribution, and so on.[29] System problems are typically not social *or* technical but actually sociotechnical.[30] The problem-solving structures and processes of a human system must be developed to deal with a range of sociotechnical difficulties, converting them into problems and organizing the relevant processes of data collection, planning, invention, and tryout of solutions, evaluation and feedback of results, replanning, and so forth, which are required for the solution of the problems.

The human parts of the system must learn to function collaboratively in these processes of problem identification and solution, and the system must develop institutionalized support and mechanisms for maintaining and improving these processes. Actually, the model of changing in these approaches is a cooperative, action-research model. This model was suggested by Lewin and developed most elaborately for use in educational settings by Stephen M. Corey.[31]

The range of interventions by outside change agents in implementing this approach to changing is rather wide. It has been most fully elaborated in relation to organizational development programs. Within such programs, intervention methods have been most comprehensively tested in industrial settings. Some of these more or less tested intervention methods are listed below. A design for any organizational development program, of course, normally uses a number of these in succession or combination:

1. Collection of data about organizational functioning and feedback of data into processes of data interpretation and of planning ways of correcting revealed dysfunctions by system managers and data collectors in collaboration.[32]

2. Training of managers and working organizational units in methods of problem solving through self-examination of present ways of dealing with difficulties and through development and tryout of better ways with consultation by outside and/or inside change agents. Usually, the working unit leaves its working place for parts of its training. These laboratory sessions are ordinarily interspersed with on-the-job consultations.

3. Developing acceptance of feedback (research and development) roles and functions within the organization, training persons to fill these roles, and relating such roles strategically to the ongoing management of the organization.

4. Training internal change agents to function within the organization in carrying on needed applied research, consultation, and training.[33]

Whatever specific strategies of intervention may be employed in developing the system's capabilities for problem solving, change efforts are designed to help the system in developing ways of scanning its operations to detect problems, of diagnosing these problems to determine relevant changeable factors in them, and of moving toward collaboratively determined solutions to the problems.

Releasing and Fostering Growth in the Persons Who Make Up the System to Be Changed. Those committed to this family of approaches to changing tend to see the person as the basic unit of social organization. Persons, it is believed, are capable of creative, life-affirming, self- and other-regarding and -respecting responses, choices, and actions, if conditions that thwart these kinds of responses are removed and other supporting conditions developed. Rogers has formulated these latter conditions in his analysis of the therapist-client relationship: trustworthiness, empathy, caring, and others.[34] Maslow has worked out a similar idea in his analysis of the hierarchy of needs in persons.[35] If lower needs are met, higher need-meeting actions will take place. McGregor[36] has formulated the ways in which existing organizations operate to fixate persons in lower levels of motivation and has sought to envision an organization designed to release and support the growth of persons in fulfilling their higher motivations as they function within the organization.

Various intervention methods have been designed to help people discover themselves as persons and commit themselves to continuing personal growth in the various relationships of their lives:

1. One early effort to install personal counseling widely and strategically in an organization has been reported by Roethlisberger and Dickson.[37]

2. Training groups designed to facilitate personal confrontation and growth of members in an open, trusting, and accepting atmosphere have been conducted for individuals from various back-home situations and for persons from the same back-home setting. The processes of these groups have sometimes been described as "therapy for normals."[38]

3. Groups and laboratories designed to stimulate and support personal growth have been designed to utilize the resources of nonverbal exchange and communication among members along with verbal dialogue in inducing personal confrontation, discovery, and commitment to continuing growth.

4. Many psychotherapists, building on the work of Freud and Adler, have come to use groups as well as two-person situations as media of personal re-education and growth. Such efforts are prominent in mental health approaches to changing and have been conducted in educational, religious, community, industrial, and hospital settings. Although these efforts focus primarily upon helping individuals to change themselves toward greater self-clarity and fuller self-actualization, they are frequently designed and conducted in the hope that personal changes will lead to changes in organizations, institutions, and communities as well.

We have presented the two variants of normative-reeducative approaches to changing as a way to emphasize their differences. Actually, there are many similarities between them as well, which justify placing both under the same general heading. We have already mentioned one of these similarities. Both frequently use temporary systems—a residential laboratory or workshop, "a temporary group with special resources built in, an ongoing system" that incorporates a change agent (trainer, consultant, counselor, or therapist) temporarily—as an aid to growth in the system and/or in its members.

More fundamentally, both approaches emphasize experience-based learning as an ingredient of all enduring changes in human systems. Yet both accept the principle that people must learn to learn from their experiences if self-directed change is to be maintained and continued. Frequently, people have learned to defend against the potential lessons of experience when these threaten existing equilibria, whether in the person or in the social system. How can these defenses be lowered to let the data of experience get into processes of perceiving the situation, of constructing new and better ways to define it, of inventing new and more appropriate ways of responding to the situation as redefined, of becoming more fully aware of the consequences of actions, of rearticulating value orientations that sanction more responsible ways of managing the consequences of actions, and so forth? Learning to learn from ongoing experience is a major objective in both approaches to changing. Neither denies the relevance or importance of the noncognitive determinants of behavior—feelings, attitudes, norms, and relationships—along with cognitive-perceptual determinants, in effecting behavioral change. The problem-solving approaches emphasize the cognitive determinants more than personal growth approaches do. But exponents of the former do not accept the rationalistic biases of the rational-empirical family of change strategies, already discussed. Since exponents of both problem-solving and personal growth approaches are committed to reeducation of persons as integral to effective change in human systems, both emphasize norms of openness of communication, trust between persons, lowering of status barriers between parts of the system, and mutuality between parts as necessary conditions of the reeducative process.

Great emphasis has been placed recently upon the releasing of creativity in persons, groups, and organizations as requisite to coping adaptively with accelerated changes in the conditions of modern living. We have already stressed the emphasis personal growth approaches put upon the release of creative responses in persons being reeducated. Problem-solving approaches also value creativity, though they focus more upon the group and organizational conditions that increase the probability of creative responses by persons functioning within those conditions than upon persons directly. The approaches do differ in their strategies for releasing creative responses within human systems. But both believe that creative adaptations to changing conditions may arise *within* human systems and do not have to be imported from *outside* them, as in innovation-diffusion approaches already discussed and the power-compliance models still to be dealt with.

One developing variant of normative-reeducative approaches to changing, not already noted, focuses upon effective conflict management. It is, of course, common knowledge that differences within a society that demand interaccommodation often manifest themselves as conflicts. In the process of managing such conflicts, changes in the norms, policies, and relationships of the society occur. Can conflict management be brought into the ambit of planned change as defined in this volume? Stemming from the work of the Sherifs in creating intergroup conflict and seeking to resolve it in a field-laboratory situation,[39] training in intergroup conflict and conflict resolution found its way into training laboratories through the efforts of Blake and others. Since that time, laboratories for conflict management have been developed under NTL and other auspices, and methodologies for conflict resolution and management, in keeping with the values of planned change, have been devised. Blake's and Walton's work represent some of the findings from these pioneering efforts.[40]

Thus, without denying their differences in assumption and strategy, we believe that the differing approaches discussed in this section can be seen together within the framework of normative-reeducative approaches to changing. Two efforts to conceptualize planned change in a way to reveal the similarities in assumptions about changing and in value orientations toward change underlying these variant approaches are those by Lippitt, Watson, and Westley and by Bennis, Benne, and Chin.[41]

Another aspect of changing in human organizations is represented by efforts to conceive human organization in forms that go beyond the bureaucratic form that captured the imagination and fixed the contours of thinking and practice of organizational theorists and practitioners from the latter part of the nineteenth through the early part of the twentieth century. The bureaucratic form of organization was conceptualized by Max Weber and carried into American thinking by such students of administration as Urwick.[42] On this view, effective organization of human effort followed the lines of effective division of labor and effective establishment of lines of reporting, control, and supervision from the mass base of the organization up through various levels of control to the top of the pyramidal organization from which legitimate authority and responsibility stemmed.

The work of industrial sociologists like Mayo threw doubt upon the adequacy of such a model of formal organization to deal with the realities of organizational life by revealing the informal organization that grows up within the formal structure to satisfy personal and interpersonal needs not encompassed by or integrated into the goals of the formal organization. Chester Barnard may be seen as a transitional figure who, in discussing the functions of the organizational executive, gave equal emphasis to his responsibilities for task effectiveness and organizational efficiency (optimally meeting the human needs of persons in the organization).[43] Much of the development of subsequent organizational theory and practice has centered on problems of integrating the actualities, criteria, and concepts of organizational effectiveness and of organizational efficiency.

A growing group of thinkers and researchers have sought to move beyond the bureaucratic model toward some new model of organization that might set directions and limits for change efforts in organizational life. Out of many thinkers, we choose four who have theorized out of an orientation consistent with what we have called a normative-reeducative approach to changing.

Rensis Likert has presented an intergroup model of organization. Each working unit strives to develop and function as a group. The group's efforts are linked to other units of the organization by the overlapping membership of supervisors or managers in vertically or horizontally adjacent groups. This view of organization throws problems of delegation, supervision, and internal communication into a new light and emphasizes the importance of linking persons as targets of change and reeducation in processes of organizational development.[44]

We have already stressed McGregor's efforts to conceive a form of organization more in keeping with new and more valid views of human nature and motivation (Theory Y) than the limited and false views of human nature and motivation (Theory X) upon which traditional bureaucratic organization has rested. In his work he sought to move thinking and practice relevant to organization and organizational change beyond the limits of traditional forms: "The essential task of management is to arrange organizational conditions and methods of operation so that people can achieve their own goals best by directing their own efforts toward organizational objectives."[45]

Bennis has consciously sought to move beyond bureaucracy in tracing the contours of the organization of the future.[46] And Shephard has described an organizational form consistent with support for continual changing and self-renewal, rather than with a primary mission of maintenance and control.[47]

Power-Coercive Approaches to Effecting Change

It is not the use of power, in the sense of influence by one person upon another or by one group upon another, that distinguishes this family of strategies from those already discussed. Power is an ingredient of all human action. The differences lie rather in the ingredients of power upon which the strategies of changing depend and the ways in which power is generated and applied in processes of effecting change. Thus, what we have called rational-empirical approaches depend on knowledge as a major ingredient of power. In this view, people of knowledge are legitimate sources of power and the desirable flow of influence or power is from people who know to people who don't know, through processes of education and of dissemination of valid information.

Normative-reeducative strategies of changing do not deny the importance of knowledge as a source of power, especially in the form of knowledge-based technology. Exponents of this approach to changing are committed to redressing the imbalance between the limited use of behavioral knowledge and people technologies and the widespread use of physical-biological knowledge and related thing technologies in effecting changes in human affairs. In addition, exponents of normative-reeducative approaches recognize the importance of noncognitive determinants of behavior as resistances or supports to changing— values, attitudes, and feelings at the personal level and norms and relationships at the social level. Influence must extend to these noncognitive determinants of behavior if voluntary commitments and reliance upon social intelligence are to be maintained and extended in our changing society. Influence of noncognitive determinants of behavior must be exercised in mutual processes of persuasion within collaborative relationships. These strategies are oriented against coercive and nonreciprocal influence, both on moral and on pragmatic grounds.

What ingredients of power do power-coercive strategies emphasize? In general, emphasis is upon political and economic sanctions in the exercise of power. But other coercive strategies emphasize the utilization of moral power, playing upon sentiments of guilt and shame. Political power carries with it legitimacy and the sanctions that accrue to those who break the law. Thus getting a law passed against racial imbalance in the schools brings legitimate coercive power behind efforts to desegregate the schools, threatening those who resist with sanctions under the law and reducing the resistance of others who are morally oriented against breaking the law. Economic power exerts coercive influence over the decisions of those to whom it is applied. Thus federal appropriations granting funds to local schools for increased emphasis upon science instruction tends to exercise coercive influence over the decisions of local school officials concerning the emphasis of the school curriculum. In general, power-coercive strategies of changing seek to mass political and economic power behind the change goals that the strategists of change have decided are desirable. Those who oppose these goals, if they adopt the same strategy, seek to mass political and economic power in opposition. The strategy thus tends to divide the society when there is anything like a division of opinion and of power in that society.

When a person or group is entrenched in power in a social system, in command of political legitimacy and of political and economic sanctions, that person or group can use power-coercive strategies in effecting changes they consider desirable without much awareness on the part of those out of power in the system that such strategies are being employed. A power-coercive way of making decisions is accepted as in the nature of things.

The use of such strategies by those in legitimate control of various social systems in our society is much more widespread than most of us might at first be willing or able to admit. This is true in educational systems as well as in other social systems.

When any part of a social system becomes aware that its interests are not being served by those in control of the system, the coercive power of those in control can be challenged. If the minority is committed to power-coercive strategies, or is aware of no alternatives to such strategies, how can they make headway against existing power relations within the system? They may organize discontent against the present controls of the system and achieve power outside the legitimate channels of authority in the system. Thus teachers' unions may develop power against coercive controls by the central administrative group and the school board in a school system. They may threaten concerted resistance to or disregard of administrative rulings and board policies, or they may threaten work stoppage or a strike. Those in control may get legislation against teachers' strikes. If the political power of organized teachers grows, they may get legislation requiring collective bargaining between organized teachers and the school board on some range of educational issues. The power struggle then shifts to the negotiation table, and compromise between competing interests may become the expected goal of the intergroup exchange. Whether the augmented power of new, relevant knowledge or the generation of common power through joint collaboration and deliberation is lost in the process will depend on the degree of commitment by all parties to the conflict to a continuation and maintenance of power-coercive strategies for effecting change.

What general varieties of power-coercive strategies to be exercised either by those in control as they seek to maintain their power or to be used by those now outside a position of control and seeking to enlarge their power can be identified?

Strategies of Nonviolence. Mohandas Gandhi may be seen as the most prominent recent theorist and practitioner of nonviolent strategies for effecting change, although the strategies did not originate with him in the history of mankind, either in idea or in practice. Gandhi spoke of Thoreau's *Essay on Civil Disobedience* as one important influence in his own approach to nonviolent coercive action. Martin Luther King was perhaps America's most distinguished exponent of nonviolent coercion in effecting social change. A minority (or majority) confronted with what they see as an unfair, unjust, or cruel system of coercive social control may dramatize their rejection of the system by publicly and nonviolently witnessing and demonstrating against it. Part of the ingredients of the power of the civilly disobedient is in the guilt that their demonstration of injustice, unfairness, or cruelty of the existing system of control arouses in those exercising control or in others previously committed to the present system of control. The opposition to the disobedient group may be demoralized and may waver in their exercise of control, if they profess the moral values to which the dissidents are appealing.

Weakening or dividing the opposition through moral coercion may be combined with economic sanctions—like Gandhi's refusal to buy salt and other British manufactured commodities in India or like the desegregationists' economic boycott of the products of racially discriminating factories and businesses.

The use of nonviolent strategies for opening up conflicts in values and demonstrating against injustices or inequities in existing patterns of social control has become familiar to educational leaders in the demonstrations and sit-ins of college students in various universities and in the demonstrations of desegregationists against *de facto* segregation of schools. And the widened use of such strategies may be confidently predicted. Whether such strategies will be used to extend collaborative ways of developing policies and normative-reeducative strategies of changing or whether they will be used to augment power struggles as the only practical way of settling conflicts will depend in some large part upon the strategy commitments of those now in positions of power in educational systems.

Use of Political Institutions to Achieve Change. Political power has traditionally played an important part in achieving changes in our institutional life. And political power will continue to play an important part in shaping and reshaping our institutions of education as well as other institutions. Changes enforced by political coercion need not be oppressive if the quality of our democratic processes can be maintained and improved.

Changes in policies with respect to education have come from various departments of government. By far most of these have come through legislation on the state level. Under legislation, school administrators have various degrees of discretionary powers, and policy and program changes are frequently put into effect by administrative rulings. Judicial decisions have played an important part in shaping educational policies, none more dramatically than the Supreme Court decision declaring laws and policies supporting school segregation illegal. And the federal courts have played a central part in seeking to implement and enforce this decision.

Some of the difficulty with the use of political institutions to effect changes arises from an overestimation by change agents of the capability of political action to effect changes in practice. When the law is passed, the administrative ruling announced, or the judicial decision handed down legitimizing some new policy or program or illegitimizing some traditional practice, change agents who have worked hard for the law, ruling, or decision frequently assume that the desired change has been made.

Actually, all that has been done is to bring the force of legitimacy behind some envisioned change. The processes of reeducation of persons who are to conduct themselves in new ways still have to be carried out. And the new conduct often requires new knowledge, new skills, new attitudes, and new value orientations. And, on the social level, new conduct may require changes in the norms, the roles, and the relationship structures of the institutions involved. This is not to discount the importance of political actions in legitimizing changed policies and practices in educational institutions and in other institutions as well. It is rather to emphasize that normative-reeducative strategies must be combined with political coercion, both before and after the political action, if the public is to be adequately informed and desirable and commonly acceptable changes in practice are to be achieved.

Changing Through the Recomposition and Manipulation of Power Elites. The idea or practice of a ruling class or of a power elite in social control was by no means original with Karl Marx. What was original with him was his way of relating these concepts to a process and strategy of fundamental social change. The composition of the ruling class was, of course, for Marx those who owned and controlled the means and processes of production of goods and services in a society. Since, for Marx, the ideology of the ruling class set limits to the thinking of most intellectuals and of those in charge of educational processes and of communicating, rationales for the existing state of affairs, including its concentration of political and economic power, are provided and disseminated by intellectuals and educators and communicators within the system.

Since Marx was morally committed to a classless society in which political coercion would disappear because there would be no vested private interests to rationalize and defend, he looked for a counterforce in society to challenge and eventually to overcome the power of the ruling class. And this he found in the economically dispossessed and alienated workers of hand and brain. As this new class gained consciousness of its historic mission and its power increased, the class struggle could be effectively joined. The outcome of this struggle was victory for those best able to organize and maximize the productive power of the instruments of production; for Marx this victory belonged to the now-dispossessed workers.

Many of Marx's values would have put him behind what we have called normative-reeducative strategies of changing. And he recognized that such strategies would have to be used after the accession of the workers to state power in order to usher in the classless society. He doubted if the ruling

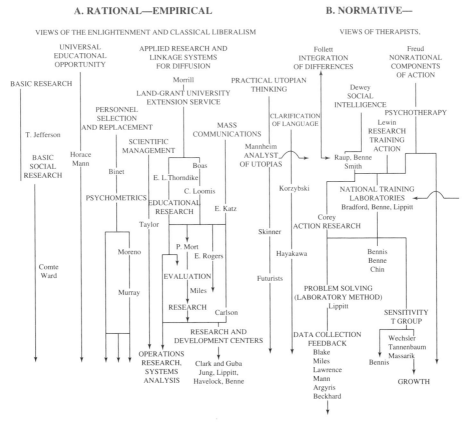

Figure 7.1. Strategies of Deliberate Change.

class could be reeducated, since reeducation would mean loss of their privileges and coercive power in society. He recognized that the power elite
could, within limits, accommodate new interests as these gained articulation and power. But these accommodations must fall short of a radical
transfer of power to a class more capable of wielding it. Meanwhile, he
remained committed to a power-coercive strategy of changing until the revolutionary transfer of power had been effected.

Marxian concepts have affected the thinking of contemporary men about
social change both inside and outside nations in which Marxism has become the
official orientation. His concepts have tended to bolster assumptions of the necessity of power-coercive strategies in achieving fundamental redistributions of
socioeconomic power or in recomposing or manipulating power elites in a society. Democratic, reeducative methods of changing have a place only after such
changes in power allocation have been achieved by power-coercive methods.
Non-Marxians as well as Marxians are often committed to this Marxian dictum.

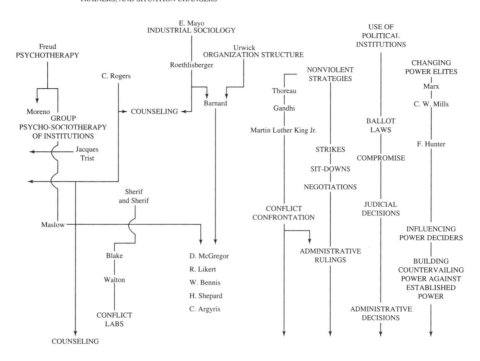

Figure 7.1. (continued)

In contemporary America, C. Wright Mills has identified a power elite, essentially composed of industrial, military, and governmental leaders, who direct and limit processes of social change and accommodation in our society. And President Eisenhower warned of the dangerous concentration of power in substantially the same groups in his farewell message to the American people. Educators committed to democratic values should not be blinded to the limitations to advancement of those values, which are set by the less-than-democratic ideology of our power elites. And normative-reeducative strategists of changing must include power elites among their targets of changing as they seek to diffuse their ways of progress within contemporary society. And they must take seriously Marx's questions about the reeducability of members of the power elites as they deal with problems and projects of social change.

The operation of a power elite in social units smaller than a nation was revealed in Floyd Hunter's study of decision making in an American city. Hunter's small group of deciders, with their satellite groups of intellectuals, front men, and implementers, is in a real sense a power elite. The most common reaction of educational leaders to Hunter's "discovery" has been to seek ways in which to persuade and manipulate the deciders toward support of educational ends that educational leaders consider desirable—whether bond issues, building programs, or anything else. This is non-Marxian in its acceptance of power relations in a city or community as fixed. It would be Marxian if it sought to build counterpower to offset and reduce the power of the presently deciding group where this power interfered with the achievement of desirable educational goals. This latter strategy, though not usually Marxian-inspired in the propaganda sense of that term, has been more characteristic of organized teacher effort in pressing for collective bargaining or of some student demonstrations and sit-ins. In the poverty program, the federal government in its insistence on participation of the poor in making policies for the program has at least played with a strategy of building countervailing power to offset the existing concentration of power in people not identified with the interests of the poor in reducing their poverty.

Those committed to the advancement of normative-reeducative strategies of changing must take account of present actual concentrations of power wherever they work. This does not mean that they must develop a commitment to power-coercive strategies to change the distribution of power, except when these may be necessary to effect the spread of their own democratically and scientifically oriented methods of changing within society (Figure 7.1).

Notes

1. Throughout our discussion of strategies and procedures, we will not differentiate these according to the size of the target of change. We assume that there are similarities in processes of changing, whether the change affects an individual, a small group, an organization, a community, or a culture. In addition, we are not attending to differences among the aspects of a system, let us say an educational system, which is being changed—curriculum, audiovisual methods, team teaching, pupil grouping, and so on. Furthermore, because many changes in communities or organizations start with an individual or some small membership group, our general focus will be upon those strategies that lead to and involve individual changes. We will sidestep the issue of defining change in this chapter. As further conceptual work progresses in the study of planned change, we shall eventually have to examine how different definitions of change relate to strategies and procedures for effecting change. But we are not dealing with these issues here.

2. We have indicated the main roots of ideas and idea systems underlying the principal strategies of changing and their subvariants in Figure 7.1 at the end of this essay. It may be useful in seeing both the distinctions and the relationships between

various strategies of changing in time perspective. We have emphasized developments of the past twenty-five years more than earlier developments. This makes for historical foreshortening. We hope this is a pardonable distortion, considering our present limited purpose.

3. Jean Hills, "Social Science, Ideology and the Purposes of Educational Administration," *Education Administration Quarterly* I (Autumn 1965), 23–40.

4. Garth Jones, "Planned Organizational Change, a Set of Working Documents," Center for Research in Public Organization, School of Public Administration (Los Angeles: University of Southern California, 1964).

5. For a review, see Ronald G. Havelock and Kenneth D. Benne, "An Exploratory Study of Knowledge Utilization."

6. Paul R. Mort and Donald R. Ross, *Principles of School Administration* (New York: McGraw-Hill, 1957). Paul R. Mort and Francis G. Cornell, *American Schools in Transition: How Our Schools Adapt Their Practices to Changing Needs* (New York: Bureau of Publications, Teachers College, Columbia University Press, 1941).

7. Robert Chin, "Research Approaches to the Problem of Civic Training," in F. Patterson (ed.), *The Adolescent Citizen* (New York: Free Press, 1960).

8. Matthew B. Miles, *Some Propositions in Research Utilization in Education* (March 1965), in press. Kenneth Wiles, unpublished paper for seminar on Strategies for Curriculum Change (Columbus, Ohio, Ohio State University). Charles Jung and Ronald Lippitt, "Utilization of Scientific Knowledge for Change in Education," in *Concepts for Social Change* (Washington, D.C.: National Educational Association, National Training Laboratories, 1967). Ronald G. Havelock and Kenneth D. Benne, "An Exploratory Study of Knowledge Utilization." David Clark and Egon Guba, "An Examination of Potential Change Roles in Education," seminar on Innovation in Planning School Curricula (Columbus, Ohio: Ohio State University, 1965).

9. David Clark, "Educational Research and Development: The Next Decade," in *Implications for Education of Prospective Changes in Society*, a publication of "Designing Education for the Future—an Eight State Project" (Denver, Colo., 1967).

10. Elihu Katz, "The Social Itinerary of Technical Change: Two Studies on the Diffusion of Innovation." Richard Carlson, "Some Needed Research on the Diffusion of Innovations," paper at the Washington Conference on Educational Change (Columbus, Ohio: Ohio State University). Everett Rogers, "What Are Innovators Like?" in *Change Processes in the Public Schools*, Center for the Advanced Study of Educational Administration (Eugene, Oregon: University of Oregon, 1965). Everett Rogers, *Diffusion of Innovations* (New York: Free Press, 1962).

11. Carl Hovland, Irving Janis, and Harold Kelley, *Communication and Persuasion* (New Haven: Yale University Press, 1953).

12. Raymond Bauer, "The Obstinate Audience: The Influence Process from the Point of View of Social Communication."

13. B. F. Skinner, *Walden Two* (New York: Crowell-Collier and Macmillan, 1948).

14. "Designing Education for the Future—an Eight State Project" (Denver, Colo., 1967).

15. Karl Mannheim, *Ideology and Utopia* (New York: Harcourt, Brace & World, 1946).

16. Alfred Korzybski, *Science and Sanity* (3rd ed.; International Non-Aristotelian Library, 1948). S. I. Hayakawa, *Language in Thought and Action* (New York: Harcourt, Brace & World, 1941).

17. John Dewey, *Philosophy, Psychology and Social Practice*, Joseph Ratner (ed.) (Capricorn Books, 1967).

18. Kurt Lewin, *Resolving Social Conflicts* (New York: Harper & Row, 1948). Kurt Lewin, *Field Theory in Social Science* (New York: Harper & Row, 1951).

19. For Freud, an interesting summary is contained in Otto Fenichel, *Problems of Psychoanalytic Technique* (Albany, N.Y.: NT Psychoanalytic Quarterly, 1941).

20. W. Bennis, K. Benne, and R. Chin, *The Planning of Change* (1st ed.; New York: Holt, Rinehart and Winston, 1961). R. Lippitt, J. Watson, and B. Westley, *The Dynamics of Planned Change* (New York: Harcourt, Brace & World, 1958). W. Bennis, *Changing Organizations* (New York: McGraw-Hill, 1966).

21. Raup, Benne, Smith, and Axtelle, *The Discipline of Practical Judgment in a Democratic Society*, Yearbook No. 28 of the National Society of College Teachers of Education (Chicago: University of Chicago Press, 1943).

22. Mary Follett, *Creative Experience and Dynamic Administration* (New York: David McKay Company, 1924).

23. Karl Mannheim, *Man and Society in an Age of Reconstruction* (New York: Harcourt, Brace & World, 1940).

24. Elliot Jaques, *The Changing Culture of a Factory* (New York: Holt, Rinehart and Winston, 1952).

25. William J. Dickson and F. J. Roethlisberger, *Personal Counseling in an Organization. A Sequel to the Hawthorne Researches* (Boston: Harvard Business School, 1966).

26. Elton Mayo, *The Social Problems of an Industrial Civilization* (Cambridge, Mass: Harvard University Press, 1945).

27. Leland Bradford, Jack R. Gibb, and Kenneth D. Benne, *T-Group Theory and Laboratory Method* (New York: John Wiley & Sons, 1964).

28. Matthew B. Miles, "On Temporary Systems," in M. B. Miles (ed.), *Innovation in Education* (New York: Bureau of Publications, Teachers College, Columbia University Press, 1964), pp. 437–492.

29. Robert R. Blake and Jane S. Mouton, *The Managerial Grid* (Houston: Gulf Publishing, 1961).

30. Jay W. Lorsch and Paul Lawrence, "The Diagnosis of Organizational Problems."

31. Stephen M. Corey, *Action Research to Improve School Practices* (New York: Bureau of Publications, Teachers College, Columbia University Press, 1953).

32. See contributions by Miles et al., "Data Feedback and Organizational Change in a School System," and Jay W. Lorsch and Paul Lawrence, "The Diagnosis of Organizational Problems."

33. C. Argyris, "Explorations in Consulting Client Relationships." See also Richard Beckhard, "The Confrontation Meeting."

34. Carl Rogers, "The Characteristics of a Helping Relationship."

35. Abraham Maslow, *Motivation and Personality* (New York: Harper & Row, 1954).

36. Douglas M. McGregor, "The Human Side of Enterprise," in W. Bennis, K. Benne, and R. Chin, *The Planning of Change* (1st ed.; New York: Holt, Rinehart and Winston, 1961), pp. 422–431.

37. Dickson and Roethlisberger, cited above.

38. James V. Clark, "A Healthy Organization." Irving Weschler, Fred Massarik, and Robert Tannenbaum, "The Self in Process: A Sensitivity Training Emphasis," in I. R. Weschler and E. Schein (eds.), *Issues in Training*, Selected Reading Series No. 5 (Washington, D.C., National Training Laboratories).

39. Muzafer and Carolyn Sherif, *Groups in Harmony and Tension* (New York: Harper & Row, 1953).

40. Robert Blake et al., "The Union Management Inter-Group Laboratory." Richard Walton, "Two Strategies of Social Change and Their Dilemmas."

41. R. Lippitt, J. Watson, and B. Westley, *Dynamics of Planned Change* (New York: Harcourt, Brace & World, 1958). W. Bennis, K. Benne, R. Chin, *The Planning of Change* (1st ed.; New York: Holt, Rinehart and Winston, 1961).

42. Lyndall Urwick, *The Pattern of Management* (Minneapolis; University of Minnesota Press, 1956).

43. Chester I. Barnard, *The Functions of the Executive* (Cambridge: Harvard University Press, 1938).

44. Rensis Likert, *New Patterns of Management* (New York: McGraw-Hill, 1961).

45. McGregor, pp. 422–431.

46. W. G. Bennis, "Changing Organizations."

47. H. A. Shephard, "Innovation-Resisting and Innovation-Producing Organizations."

CHAPTER TEN

Sociotechnical Systems

Origin of the Concept

Eric Trist (1981)

The sociotechnical concept arose in conjunction with the first of several field projects undertaken by the Tavistock Institute in the coal-mining industry in Britain. The time (1949) was that of the postwar reconstruction of industry in relation to which the Institute had two action research projects.[1] One project was concerned with group relations in depth at all levels (including the management/labor interface) in a single organization—an engineering company in the private sector. The other project focused on the diffusion of innovative work practices and organizational arrangements that did not require major capital expenditure but that gave promise of raising productivity. The former project represented the first comprehensive application in an industrial setting of the socioclinical ideas concerning groups being developed at the Tavistock. For this purpose a novel action research methodology was introduced. (The book describing the project became a classic [Jaques, 1951].) Nevertheless, the organization was approached exclusively as a social system. The second project was led, through the circumstances described below, to include the technical as well as the social system in the factors to be considered and to postulate that the relations between them should constitute *a new field of inquiry.*

Coal being then the chief source of power, much industrial reconstruction depended on there being a plentiful and cheap supply. But the newly nationalized industry was not doing well. Productivity failed to increase in step with increases in mechanization. Men were leaving the mines in large numbers for more attractive opportunities in the factories. Among those who remained, absenteeism averaged 20 percent. Labor disputes were frequent despite improved conditions of employment. Some time earlier, the National Coal Board had asked the Institute to make a comparative study of a high-producing, high-morale mine and a low-producing, low-morale, but otherwise equivalent mine. Despite nationalization, however, our research team was not welcome at the coal face under the auspices of the Board.

There were at the Institute at that time six postgraduate Fellows being trained for industrial fieldwork. Among these, three had a trade union background and one had been a miner. After a year, the Fellows were encouraged to revisit their former industries and make a report on any new perceptions they might have. One of these Fellows, Ken Bamforth, returned with news of an innovation in work practice and organization that had occurred in a new seam in the colliery where he used to work in the South Yorkshire coalfield. The seam, the Haighmoor, had become possible to mine "shortwall" because of improved roof control. I can recall now the excitement with which I listened to him. No time was lost in my going up to visit this colliery, where, since we were introduced by Ken, the local management and union readily agreed to our "researching" their innovation with a view to its diffusion to other mines. The area general manager (who had the oversight of some twenty mines) welcomed the idea. The technical conception of the new scheme was his, though the men, with union support, had proposed the manning arrangements.

The work organization of the new seam was, to us, a novel phenomenon consisting of relatively autonomous groups interchanging roles and shifts and regulating their affairs with a minimum of supervision. Cooperation between task groups was everywhere in evidence, personal commitment obvious, absenteeism low, accidents infrequent, productivity high. The contrast was large between the atmosphere and arrangements on these faces and those in the conventional areas of the pit, where the negative features characteristic of the industry were glaringly apparent. The men told us that in order to adapt with best advantage to the technical conditions in the new seam, they had evolved a form of work organization based on practices common in the unmechanized days when small groups, who took responsibility for the entire cycle, had worked autonomously. These practices had disappeared as the pits became progressively more mechanized in relation to the introduction of "longwall" working. This method had enlarged the scale of operations and led to aggregates of men of considerable size having their jobs broken down into one-man, one-task roles, while coordination and control were externalized in supervision, which became coercive. Now they had found a way, at a higher level of mechanization, of recovering the group cohesion and self-regulation they had lost and of advancing their power to participate in decisions concerning their work arrangements. For this reason, the book that overviewed the Tavistock mining studies was subtitled *The Loss, Rediscovery and Transformation of a Work Tradition* (Trist et al., 1963). The transformation represented a change of direction in organizational design. For several decades the prevailing direction had been to increase bureaucratization with each increase in scale and level of mechanization. The organizational model that fused Weber's description of bureaucracy with Frederick Taylor's concept of scientific management had become pervasive. The Haighmoor innovation showed that there was an alternative.

Those concerned with it had made an *organizational choice* (Trist et al., 1963). They could, with minor modifications, have extended the prevailing mode of working. They chose instead to elaborate a major design alternative. It was not true that the only way of designing work organizations must conform to Tayloristic and bureaucratic principles. There were other ways, which represented a discontinuity with the prevailing mode. The technological imperative could be disobeyed with positive economic as well as human results. What happened in the Haighmoor seam gave to Bamforth and myself a first glimpse of the "emergence of a new paradigm of work" (Emery, 1978) in which the best match would be sought between the requirements of the social and technical systems.

Some of the principles involved were as follows:

- The *work system,* which comprised a set of activities that made up a functioning whole, now became the basic unit rather than the single jobs into which it was decomposable.
- Correspondingly, the *work group* became central rather than the individual jobholder.
- *Internal regulation* of the system by the group was thus rendered possible rather than the external regulation of individuals by supervisors.
- A design principle based on the *redundancy of functions* rather than on the redundancy of parts (Emery, 1967) characterized the underlying organizational philosophy, which tended to develop multiple skills in the individual and immensely increase the response repertoire of the group.
- This principle valued the *discretionary* rather than the prescribed part of work roles (Jaques, 1956).
- It treated the individual as *complementary* to the machine rather than as an extension of it (Jordan, 1963).
- It was *variety-increasing* for both the individual and the organization rather than variety-decreasing in the bureaucratic mode.

Conceptually, the new paradigm entailed a shift in the way work organizations were envisaged. Under the old paradigm, engineers, following the technological imperative, would design whatever organization the technology seemed to require. This was a rule accepted by all concerned (Davis et al., 1955).

The "people cost" of proceeding in this way was not considered. Any people cost, it was presumed, could be compensated for first by improving the socio-economic conditions of employment and then by improving "human relations."

The movement under this latter title arose during the interwar period when the model of the technocratic bureaucracy was becoming entrenched. It failed to arrest the spread of work alienation after World War II (Baldamus, 1951, 1961; Walker and Guest, 1952). At the Glacier Metal Company, where Jaques (1951) carried out his research, it was observed that, despite the progressive personnel policies adopted and the far-reaching changes made in the character of management-labor relations, there was no reduction in the "split at the bottom of the executive chain." Nothing had happened to change the structure jobs. There was no change in the nature of the immediate work experience.

The idea of separate approaches to the social and the technical systems of an organization could no longer suffice for one such as myself who had experienced the profound consequences of a change in social/technical relations such as had occurred in the Haighmoor development. Work organizations exist to do work—which involves people using technological artifacts (whether hard or soft) to carry out sets of tasks related to specified overall purposes. Accordingly, a conceptual reframing was proposed in which work organizations were envisaged as sociotechnical systems rather than simply as social systems (Trist, 1950a). The social and technical systems were the substantive factors—the people and the equipment. Economic performance and job satisfaction were outcomes, the level of which depended on the goodness of fit between the substantive factors. The following research tasks emerged in the Tavistock program:

- The theoretical development of the core concept.
- Development of methods for the analytical study of the relations of technologies and organizational forms in different settings.
- A search for criteria to obtain the best match between the technological and social components.
- Action research to improve the match.
- Finding ways to measure and evaluate outcomes through comparative and longitudinal studies.
- Finding ways to diffuse sociotechnical improvements.

These tasks could not be carried out in a preplanned sequence. The research team had first to make an extensive reconnaissance of the field to locate relevant opportunities. It then had to become actively linked to them in ways that would sanction their study in a collaborative mode. The idiom of inquiry was action research (Trist, 1976b).

Sociotechnical studies needed to be carried out at three broad levels—from micro to macro—all of which are interrelated:

- *Primary work systems.* These are the systems that carry out the set of activities involved in an identifiable and bounded subsystem of a whole organization—such as a line department or a service unit (cf. Miller, 1959). They may consist of a single face-to-face group or a number of such groups, together with support and specialist personnel and representatives of management, plus the relevant equipment and other resources. They have a recognized purpose that unifies the people and the activities.

- *Whole organization systems.* At one limit, these would be plants or equivalent self-standing workplaces. At the other, they would be entire corporations or public agencies. They persist by maintaining a steady state with their environment.

- *Macrosocial systems.* These include systems in communities and industrial sectors, and institutions operating at the overall level of a society. They constitute what I have called ''domains'' (Trist, 1976a, 1979a). One may regard media as sociotechnical systems. McLuhan (1964) has shown that the technical character of different media has far-reaching effects on users. The same applies to architectural forms and the infrastructure of the built environment. Although these are not organizations, they are sociotechnical phenomena. They are media in Heider's (1942) as well as McLuhan's sense.

As the historical process of a society unfolds, individuals change their values and expectations concerning work roles. This changes the parameters of organizational design. Conversely, changes in technology bring about changes in values, cognitive structures, life-styles, habitats, and communications that profoundly alter a society and its chances of survival. Sociotechnical phenomena are contextual as well as organizational.

Not all social systems are sociotechnical. Emery (1959), following Nadel (1951), distinguished between ''operative'' and ''regulative'' institutions and proposed restricting the term ''sociotechnical'' to the former. Regulative organizations are concerned directly with the psychosocial ends of their members and with instilling, maintaining, or changing cultural values and norms; the power and the position of interest groups; or the social structure itself. Many such organizations employ technologies as adjuncts and have secondary instrumental systems that are sociotechnical. By contrast, organizations that are primarily sociotechnical are directly dependent on their material means and resources for their outputs. Their core interface consists of the relations between a nonhuman system and a human system.

There are mixed forms typified by the co-presence of psychosocial and sociotechnical ends, which may be congruent or conflicting. An example of the latter would be a prison with both an electronic surveillance system and a therapeutic community. Hospitals are inherently sociotechnical as well as psychosocial, which accounts for the complexity of some of their dilemmas.

From the beginning, the sociotechnical concept has developed in terms of systems since it is concerned with interdependencies. It has also developed in terms of open system theory since it is concerned with the environment in which an organization must actively maintain a steady state. Von Bertalanffy's (1950) paper on "Open Systems in Physics and Biology" became available at the time that the sociotechnical concept was being formulated. It influenced both theory-building and field projects, compelling attention alike to self-regulation and environmental relations. As regards the special role of technology, Emery put it as follows:

> The *technological component,* in converting inputs into outputs, *plays a major role in determining the self-regulating properties of an enterprise.* It functions as one of the major boundary conditions of the social system in mediating between the ends of an enterprise and the external environment. Because of this, the materials, machines and territory that go to making up the technological component are usually defined, in any modern society, as "belonging" to an enterprise, or are excluded from similar control by other enterprises. They represent, as it were, an "internal environment." This being the case, it is not possible to define the conditions under which such an open system achieves a steady state unless the mediating boundary conditions are in some way represented amongst the "system constants" [cf. von Bertalanffy, 1950]. The technological component has been found to play this mediating role and hence it follows that the open system concept, as applied to the enterprise, ought to be referred to the sociotechnical system, not simply to the social system [Emery, 1959].

SOURCE INFLUENCES

An interest in social and technical relations arose in my own thinking first at the macrosocial level, next at the whole organizational level, and thence at the level of primary work systems. This last, however, became the crucial level as regards the initiation of field projects that provided the concrete route through which the broader levels could again be reached.

Lewis Mumford (1934) in *Technics and Civilization* had introduced me to the idea of linking the two. Anthropology and cultural history suggested that, if the material and symbolic cultures of a society were not connected by any simple principle of linear causality (as some interpreters of Marx have implied), they were nevertheless intertwined in a complex web of mutual causality (Trist, 1950b). In the language of E. A. Singer (1959) they were coproducers of each other. The technological choices made by a society are critical expressions of its world view. As new technologies develop, new societal possibilities may or may not be taken up. The mode of their elaboration may be constructive or destructive. There are unanticipated consequences. In the period following World War II the information technologies of the second industrial revolution were already beginning to make themselves felt. It seemed not unlikely that there would be as big a cultural shift associated with them as with the energy technologies of the first industrial revolution.

As regards the whole organization level, the first industrial project in which I was involved made it impossible not to look at the relations between technical and social systems. This encounter was with the jute industry in Dundee, Scotland, where in the late 1930s I was a member of an interdisciplinary research team studying unemployment. The spinning section of the industry was being "rationalized," causing not only more unemployment but a deskilling of the remaining workers, along with an extension of managerial controls. As to alienation, workers in the interview sample would say that they might as well be unemployed, while the appearance of time-study personnel provoked a bitter reaction in the trade unions. In the changes taking place, the technical and social aspects were interactive. A new sociotechnical system emerged—that of a more controlling "technocratic bureaucracy" with very different properties from the earlier system in terms of which jute spinning had been, and jute weaving still was, organized.

Then came World War II. A new military sociotechnical system appeared in the form of the German Panzer Divisions, formidably competent in the way they linked men and machines to fit their purposes. The French army had failed to develop an equivalent system, despite de Gaulle's proposals. As the war proceeded, military technology gave increasing scope for, and prominence to, small group formations, recognizing their power to make flexible decisions and to remain cohesive under rapidly changing conditions. This led to a recasting of the role of junior officers and the kind of relations (more open and more democratic) best maintained between them and their men. In Britain the War Office Selection Boards to which I was attached were created to choose officers capable of behaving in this way (Murray, 1990). The Boards made extensive use of W. R. Bion's (1946) method of leaderless groups, which allowed leadership to emerge and rotate in a variety of group settings. All this opened up new areas of group dynamics—extended after the war when Bion (1950, 1961) introduced therapy groups at the Tavistock Clinic. A parallel influence was that of Lewin's (1939, 1951) experiments on group climates and group decision making, together with the beginnings of the National Training Laboratories at Bethel, Maine. These traditions became fused at the Tavistock. Bion focused on the unconscious factors obstructing the attainment of group purposes and on group creativeness; Lewin on the commitment to action consequent on participation and on the performance superiority of the democratic mode. Both emphasized the capacity of the small group for self-regulation, an aspect of systems theory that received increasing attention as cybernetics developed (Weiner, 1950).

GOING AGAINST THE GRAIN OF THE 1950s

To a number of us at this time, and certainly to me, it seemed that the small self-regulating group held the clue to a very great deal that might be improved in work organizations. Knowledge about this allowed considerable advances during and immediately after World War II. Experiences in industry in the reconstruction period had shown that sociotechnical relations were patterned on the breakdown of work into externally controlled one-person/one-job units and that top-down management hierarchies were being even more rigidly maintained than in the prewar period. The pattern of technocratic bureaucracy was increasing in strength.

Hence the interest of the Haighmoor development, which pointed to the existence of an alternative pattern going in the opposite direction to the prevailing mode. The Divisional Board, however, did not wish attention drawn to it. They feared the power change that would be consequent on allowing groups to become more autonomous at a time when they themselves were intent on intensifying managerial controls in order to accelerate the full mechanization of the mines. They refused to allow the research to continue and balked at Bamforth and myself referring to it in the paper that we published (Trist and Bamforth, 1951) on conventional longwall working. It would lead, they said, to expectations that could not be fulfilled; for, although autonomous groups might be successful on the Haighmoor shortwalls, they would not be feasible on the longwall layouts, which represented the prevailing method of mining. Later, this opinion was found to be false, though widely held. The Divisional Board's reaction suggested that any attempt to reverse the prevailing mode would be met with very serious resistance. To move in the opposite direction meant going against the grain of a macrosocial trend of institution building in terms of the model of the technocratic bureaucracy, which had yet to reach its peak or disclose its dysfunctionality.

Several major pioneer studies were carried out during the decade. They established a number of research findings of key importance; however, their effect on industrial practice was negligible. Neither what happened nor what failed to happen is widely known. These studies are reviewed here to provide a short account of what turned out to be the latency decade of the sociotechnical approach.

CONTINUATION OF THE MINING STUDIES

If the Haighmoor development had general meaning, it was reasonable to assume that similar developments would occur elsewhere. In fact, a parallel development in a more advanced form and on a larger scale emerged in another division of the National Coal Board (East Midlands), where one of the Area Managers, W. V. Sheppard (1949, 1951), was developing a method of continuous mining—a radical innovation designed on what appeared to be sociotechnical principles. There were two versions: the semimechanized (Wilson et al., 1951; Trist et al., 1963) and the fully mechanized (Trust, 1953a). The second was delayed because of teething troubles in an ingenious but somewhat underpowered cutter-loader invented by Sheppard. Faces were 100 and 120 yards in length, alternating advance with retreat and concentrated in one district so that only one main road needed to be maintained. Autonomous groups of twenty to twenty-five conducted all operations on one shift. There were three production shifts every twenty-four hours instead of one shift—the other two shifts had been concerned with coal face preparation and equipment shifting, which were now done in parallel with coal getting. All members were multiskilled and were paid the same day wage, which was then judged more appropriate for continuous mining than a bonus. Productivity and work satisfaction were unusually and consistently high. A beginning was made in spreading the new system to six pits. Emery (1952), who was over at the Tavistock on sabbatical from Australia, made a study of this process, paying special attention to required changes in the supervisor's role. After areawide appreciation conferences had been held for managers and undermanagers, an Area Training School was designed (Trist, 1953b) to which groups of eight (operators, foremen, and mechanics) from each pit scheduled to go over to the new system came for a week (during which they visited the original mine). They had sessions with everyone concerned from the area general manager to the face workers and the trade union secretary, who conducted the sessions in the new group organization. Members of these groups began to meet weekly to compare experiences. A kind of sociotechnical development center was created in the area workshops. This model was not picked up again for another twelve years, when something like it emerged both in the Norwegian Industrial Democracy Project (Thorsrud and Emery, 1964; Emery and Thorsrud, 1992) and the Shell Philosophy Project (Hill, 1971). It was a forerunner of "the deep slice" used by Emery (Emery, 1976) and by Emery and Emery (1974) in their method of Participative Design.

A study of overall area organization was made (Trist, 1953c). The incoming technology, in association with autonomous work groups, reduced by one the number of management levels underground. Group Centres between collieries and the area office were obviously redundant. Eventually, Divisional Boards between operating areas and the national headquarters in London also seemed unnecessary. These superfluous levels of management were based on narrow spans of control that implied detailed supervision of subordinates at all levels rather than the sociotechnical concept of boundary management, which was congruent with maximizing the degree of self-regulation through an entire organizational system. In the course of time, these levels were in fact eliminated. This showed how the sociotechnical concept could affect the organization as a whole and reduce the administrative overhead that has become so excessive in large technocratic and bureaucratic organizations.

Having reached the whole organization systems level, our research efforts (though on independent funds) were again stopped when a new divisional chairman took over. What had happened was seen in an entirely technological perspective—that of the new cutter-loader that had been introduced. Because machines of this type were judged not to be as good a bet for further mechanization as "shearing" machines, the whole project was regarded as not meriting continuation. Besides, granting more autonomy was not popular. The union regionally negotiated special pay for operators of new equipment. This broke up the unity of the face groups, which were further decimated when bonuses were introduced for various classes of workers. As time went on, the conventional system began to reinstate itself. Sociologically, this setback and the earlier one over the Haighmoor may be seen as examples of what Schon (1971) has called the "dynamic conservatism" of organizations.

A search of other coalfields produced only one, Durham, where the Divisional Board and the regional organization of the National Union of Mineworkers said they would like to proceed with social research into mining methods. Virtually all extant methods were available in the same low seam in a single area in the older part of the coalfield where customs were uniform and traditions common. Here, the research team found what the conventional wisdom had held to be impossible: the working of the conventional, semimechanized, three-shift longwall cycle by a set of autonomous work groups (locally known as "composite"). Groups of forty to fifty men interchanged the various jobs required, while alternating shifts in ways they felt best, and evolved an innovative pay system that seemed equitable to them. Output was 25 percent higher with lower costs (40 percent) than on a comparison face similar in every respect (conditions, equipment, personnel) except that of work organization. Accidents, sickness, and absenteeism were cut in half (Trist et al., 1963). Only one man left the composite faces in two years. Over the four-year period of the project, the conversion of an entire colliery with three seams from conventional to composite working was followed in detail. Much was learned about the conditions under which autonomous groups prosper and under which they fail. The potential of self-regulating groups in fully mechanized installations was studied and the research team began to collaborate in the design of sociotechnical systems for the most advanced technology then available. A meticulous study of a single face team was made by Herbst (1962). It explored the mathematical relations between a number of key variables.

A report was submitted to the National Coal Board (Trist and Murray, 1958). The results were not disputed. But the board's priorities were elsewhere—on the closing of uneconomical pits in the older coalfields and on carrying the union with it in implementing the national power-loading agreement, deemed critical for full mechanization. The board was not willing to encourage anything new that might disturb the delicately balanced situation as the industry contracted in face of the greater use of oil. On the union side, the Durham Miners' Association sent the report to their National Executive. No reply was received at the Tavistock Institute.

Hugh Murray[2] has since made an archival study of composite agreements in various British coalfields. There were quite a few of these in the mid-1950s, but they were regarded simply as wage settlements. There was no understanding that they might have implications for work organization.

In the late 1960s Murray carried out an action-research study of layouts using very advanced technology. He found that the coincidence of specialized work roles and high absentee rates was giving rise to wide-scale disruption of production processes. Men were posted to places in their specialty all over the mine through a "pit market." There was little cohesion in work teams. Efforts to introduce multiskilling, which would have afforded the basis for greater team cohesion, met with little success (Murray and Trist, 1969).

During the 1970s an experimental section based on autonomous groups was tried out in a mine in the American coal industry, with its room-and-pillar layouts and very different technology of roof bolting, continuous miners, and shuttle cars. Positive results were obtained comparable to those obtained earlier in Britain, not only as regards productivity but also safety, which was the reason for union collaboration. Although a second autonomous section was started, an attempt to diffuse this form of work organization to the mine as a whole encountered insuperable difficulties that were not foreseen by members of the Labor/Management Steering Committee or the research team (Trist et al., 1977; Susman and Trist, 1977). This project has been independently evaluated by Goodman (1979).

The difficulties centered on the resentment of those not included in the experiment toward the privileges of those who were. This resentment would not have become acute had not expansion of the mine led to some inexperienced new recruits winning places (and hence the top wage rate) on the second autonomous section when experienced men withdrew their bids at the last moment in order to stay with a foreman (who then deserted them). There was no infringement of seniority rules, but the issue split the union.

The project shows in great detail how unanticipated and uncontrollable events in the broader, as well as the immediate, context can influence outcome in the later stages of an action-research undertaking. For example, the union's national situation and leadership changed dramatically. The project also shows how the encapsulation of an innovation can prevent its diffusion and the dangers of applying classical experimental research design in the "moving ground" of a real-life field situation. Such a design was a condition of receiving initial support at the mine and from the sponsors of the national program of which it was a part.

STUDIES IN OTHER INDUSTRIES

Meanwhile, at the Tavistock, opportunities were sought in other industries. The first to arise was not only in another industry—textiles—but in another culture—India. In 1953 the late A. K. Rice (1953, 1958, 1963) paid his first visit to the Calico Mills in Ahmedabad during which time an automatic loom shed was converted from conventional to autonomous working, with results that surpassed expectations. Later, the change was diffused throughout the non-automatic weaving sheds in this very large organization, which employed nine thousand people. Rice did no more than mention through an interpreter the idea of a group of workers becoming responsible for a group of looms. The loomshed employees took up the idea themselves, coming back the next day with a scheme that they asked management's permission to implement. Terms regarding a progressive payment scheme were negotiated and the first trials of the new system began. As with the mines, major initiatives were taken by the workers themselves. The depth of their commitment became apparent when the Communist Party of India (orthodox) took offense at the "Ahmedabad Experiment," since it involved collaboration, and drafted a number of their members from various parts of the country into the city, already swollen with refugees from West Pakistan, to agitate against it. Though their families were threatened and attempts were made to set Hindu and Muslim workers against each other, the Calico's employees stood by an innovation that was largely their own creation.

Yet the group method, as it was called, did not spread to other mills as originally expected. I asked Shankalal Banker, the venerable leader of the Ahmedabad Textiles Union, about this when I was in Ahmedabad in 1973. He replied that the other owners did not want to share their power. Also, as Miller (1975) reports, the nonautomatic loomsheds gradually regressed to conventional ways of working. Training was not kept up. New middle managers, who knew little of what had originally taken place, took over. Senior management became preoccupied with marketing and diversification. The automatic loomsheds, however, retained the group method and their high level of per-formance and satisfaction with it.

The Tavistock workers sought to discover how far alternative organizational patterns existed in service industries. An instance was found in a large retail chain consisting of small stores run by four to six employees with shared tasks and all-round skills; the "manager" was a working charge-hand (Pollock, 1954). When, however, this organization enlarged its stores and extended its lines of sale, specialized jobs with several different statuses and rewards ap-peared, along with formal control mechanisms.

At roughly the same time, the opportunity arose to explore the possibility of an alternative organizational mode in a large teaching hospital. Advances in medical technology had turned the hospital into a "high pressure" center for intensive treatment, while reducing the length of patient stay and extending the range of diseases coped with. This had created severe problems in nurse training. The work system consisted of a set of tasks broken down into narrow jobs in a closely similar way to that in large-scale industry.

An attempt to introduce, in an experimental ward, the concept of a group of nurses becoming responsible for a group of patients met with both medi-cal and administrative resistance, though much was learned about the embodiment in social structure and professional culture of psychological de-fenses against anxiety (Menzies, 1960). Integrated ward teams have since been developed in Australia by Stoelwinder (1978; Stoelwinder and Clayton, 1978).

As the last years of the immediate postwar period came to a close in the early 1950s, the mood of the society changed from collaboration, which had fostered local innovation, to competition and an adversarial climate in management/labor relations, which discouraged local innovation. No further instances of an alternative pattern were identified. Nevertheless, the mining and textile studies had suggested that continuous production industries that were advancing in automation might develop requirements that could eventu-ally lead in a direction counter to the prevailing mode. Accordingly, analytic sociotechnical studies were instituted in chemical plants and power stations (Murray, 1960; Emery and Marek, 1962). These studies disclosed a basic change in the core shop-floor tasks: workers were now outside the technolo-gy—adjusting, interpreting, monitoring, etc. They had become managers of work systems. They needed conceptual and perceptual skills rather than ma-nipulative and physical skills. They usually worked interdependently with others because the essential task was to keep a complex system in a steady state. The opportunity to go over to an alternative pattern, however, did not seem to be under any "hot pursuit," though Bell (1956) had pointed to the possibility and Woodward (1958) noted the presence of fewer supervisors in continuous process than in mass production plants.

For a moment it looked as though a major action-research opportunity would be forthcoming in Britain. Richard Thomas and Baldwin (RTB), the largest complex in the British steel industry, were preparing to build the most modern steelworks in Europe. They wanted to break with many constraining precedents in management and with work practices that would inhibit taking full advantage of the most advanced equipment. The director of education and training invited the Tavistock to collaborate with him in evolving a new set of roles and decision rules, indeed a whole organizational structure, that would be a better match with the new technology. The method proposed was a series of participative workshops to be held in the RTB staff college, which would be attended by the different levels and functions of management, foremen, key operators, and shop stewards. But there were delays in site construction—the ground proved more marshy than expected—and huge additional expenditures were incurred, which worried the Treasury. The participative workshops were never held. In the end, an organizational structure and the various associated appointees were crash-programmed, and all the old roles and practices were reinstated with (as time showed) negative consequences of a severe kind (Miller and Rice, 1967).

There was a rising interest in sociotechnical relations among a number of social scientists concerned with industry in the British setting. In Scotland, Burns and Stalker (1961) observed a new management pattern, which they called "organismic" as contrasted with "mechanistic," in more technologically advanced industry. Woodward (1958) related changes in organizational structure to broad types of technology. Fensham and Hooper (1964) showed the increasing mismatch between conventional management and the requirements of a rationalized rayon industry. Such studies, however, were widely interpreted (not necessarily by their authors) as supporting a theory of technological determinism. There could be no organizational choice, as had been suggested by the Tavistock researchers.

In the United States[3] attention had been drawn to the counterproductive consequences of extreme job fractionalization (Walker and Guest, 1952). But concepts of job enlargement and rotation and, later, of job enrichment (Hertzberg et al., 1959), though concerned with sociotechnical relations, focused on the individual job rather than on the work system. In its orthodox form, job enrichment did not countenance participation but relied on experts brought in by management.

In continental Europe there were occasional signs of a concern with alternative organizational modes. Westerlund (1952) reported the introduction of small groups on the Stockholm telephone exchange. A similar transformation had been carried out in Glasgow by a telecommunications engineer (Smith, 1952). King (1964), from a training approach, had introduced groups with a good deal of scope for self-regulation in small textile firms in Norway. Van Beinum (1963) had completed his studies in the Dutch telecommunications industry. In the United States Davis (1957) introduced the concept of job design. This constituted a basic critique of industrial engineering and opened the way for systems change that could involve groups and encourage participation. A working relationship between him and the Tavistock group was established.

An opportunity for stocktaking occurred at an International Conference on Workers' Participation in Management in Vienna (Trist, 1958). Interest centered on co-determination in Germany and on the Yugoslav workers councils. The idea of involving workers directly in decisions about what should best be done at their own level seemed strange to those concerned with industrial democracy. Only marginal attention was paid to the idea that an alternative pattern of work organization to that prevailing might be on the horizon. In the end, however, it was not entirely ignored (Clegg, 1960).

Confusion regarding the forms and meaning of industrial democracy has persisted. Four different forms may be distinguished, all of which represent modes of participation and the sharing of power. They are:

1. *Interest group democracy,* i.e., collective bargaining, through which organized labor gains power to take an independent role vis-à-vis management.

2. *Representative democracy,* whereby those at the lower levels of an organization influence policies decided at higher levels (workers on boards, works councils).

3. *Owner democracy,* as in employee-owned firms and cooperative establishments where there is participation in the equity.

4. *Work-linked democracy,* whereby the participation is secured of those directly involved in decisions about how work shall be done at their own level.

These four forms may be found independently or together, in consonance or contradiction, and in different degrees in various contemporary industrial societies. The work-linked form has been the last to appear historically and is that with which the sociotechnical restructuring of work is associated (Trist, 1979b). It is the only approach that positively changes the immediate quality of the work experience. The other approaches, which have their own merits, do not affect the basic problem of worker alienation. Increasing congruency may be hypothesized among the four factors in the longer run. Organizational democracy would be a preferable term to industrial democracy.

CONCEPTUAL DEVELOPMENTS

A monograph by Emery (1959), who had returned to the Tavistock, put forward a first generalized model of the dimensions of social and technical systems, showing that, though they were multiple, they were not so numerous that analysis would become unmanageable. Eight dimensions were identified on the technical side, including level of mechanization/automation, unit operations, the temporo-spatial scale of the production process, and so forth.[4] On the social side, rigorous attention had to be paid to occupational roles and their structure, methods of payment, the supervisory relationship, the work culture, etc.—all of which belong to the "socio" rather than the "psycho" group (Jennings, 1947). The psycho group, concerned with interpersonal relations and Bion-type "basic assumptions" regarding group behavior, however important, did not represent the starting point. Appropriate structural settings had to be created before desirable social climates and positive interpersonal relations would have the conditions in which to develop.

The original formulation of social and technical relations had been made in terms of obtaining the best match, or "goodness of fit," between the two. In conjunction with the Norwegian Industrial Democracy project (Emery and Thorsrud, 1992), Emery reformulated the matching process (in terms of the more advanced systems theory that had become available) as the *joint optimization of the social and technical systems*. The technical and social systems are *independent* of each other in the sense that the former follows the laws of the physical sciences, while the latter follows the laws of the human sciences and is a purposeful system. Yet they are *correlative* in that one requires the other for the *transformation* of an input into an output. This transformation constitutes the functional task of a work system. Their relationship represents a *coupling* of dissimilars that can only be jointly optimized. Attempts to optimize for either the technical or social system alone will result in the suboptimization of the sociotechnical whole.

In the language of Sommerhoff (1950, 1969), a work system depends on the social and technical components becoming *directively correlated* to produce a given goal state. They are *co-producers* of the outcome (Ackoff and Emery, 1972). The distinctive characteristics of each must be respected else their *contradictions* will intrude and their *complementarities* will remain unrealized (Trist, 1981).

This logic was held to underlie job and organizational design. Failure to build it into the primary work system would prevent it from becoming a property of the organization as a whole. Emery (1967, 1976) further proposed that, at the most general level, there are two basic organizational design principles. Paradigm I, based on the redundancy of parts, is represented in all forms of bureaucracy (from the Pyramids onwards). Paradigm II, based on the redundancy of functions, is represented in self-managing groups leading to organizational democracy. This appears in emerging sociotechnical forms.

The conceptual advances were "directively correlated" with the involvement of the Tavistock research team in the action-research opportunities that occurred as the decade of the 1960s unfolded. A further round of developments took place in 1965 (Davis et al., 1965). *On Purposeful Systems* (Ackoff and Emery, 1972) has had far-reaching conceptual influence on subsequent work.

THE PATHFINDING ROLE OF THE NORWEGIAN INDUSTRIAL DEMOCRACY PROJECT

The hypothesis was made that no further advances could be expected until changes occurred in the "extended social field" of forces at the macrosocial level. Any happening of this kind would change the opportunities for, and meaning of, the efforts at the primary work system and whole organization levels. No one could foretell where and when this might occur, but such a happening could be expected from the increasing impact of the new information-based technologies.

The science-based industries were the "leading part" of the Western industrial system. They functioned as the principal change-generators and brought about many other changes, directly or indirectly (Emery and Trist, 1972/1973). Western societies were beginning what is often referred to as the second industrial revolution.

The anticipated happening occurred in 1962 in Norway, where little modernization of industry had taken place in comparison with other Scandinavian countries. Economic growth had slowed down; the largest paper and pulp company went bankrupt; Norwegian firms were being taken over by multinationals. In many other respects this very small country began to feel it had lost control of its own destiny. Its environment had become what Emery and I (1963) have called "turbulent."

A sudden demand for workers' control erupted in the left wing of the trade union movement. Neither the Confederation of Employers nor the Confederation of Trade Unions felt they understood what it was about. Having set up an Institute for Industrial Social Research at the Technical University in Norway, they asked it to conduct an inquiry into the matter. Given the political pressures, Einar Thorsrud, the director, who had close contacts with the Tavistock Institute, felt that the inquiry would be better undertaken in association with a group outside Norway, which had accumulated relevant experience. Accordingly, he invited the Tavistock to collaborate. Very soon Emery and I became, with Thorsrud, part of a planning committee composed of representatives of the two Confederations. The task was to work out a jointly evolved research design. Involvement of the key stakeholders in each step was a basic principle of the design.

The first inquiry undertaken was into the role of the workers' directors, whose existence was mandated by law both in state-owned enterprises and in those where the state had some capital (former German capital given to Norway by the Allies after World War II). Various members of the board were interviewed, including the workers' directors, the principal members of management and of the trade union organization. It was found that, whether the workers' directors were outstanding performers or not, their presence, though valued as enhancing democratic control, had no effect on the feelings of alienation on the shop floor or on performance (Thorsrud and Emery, 1964, 1969). Accordingly, it was proposed that a complementary approach be tried—that of securing the direct participation of workers in decisions about what was done at their own level. These findings were widely discussed throughout the two confederations and in the press. A consensus was reached that the mode of direct participation should be tried. The committee chose two sectors of industry that were not doing well and that were of strategic importance for the future of the economy (paper and pulp, and metal working). Criteria were established for selecting plants to conduct sociotechnical field experiments that would serve as demonstration projects. Joint committees within these sectors then chose likely plants that the research team visited to test their suitability and to secure local participation.

The research team made a study of the culture and history of Norwegian society. Industrialization had been late and more benign than in those European countries (or the United States) where industrialization had occurred earlier. Industrial relations were stable at the national level, where the two confederations accepted their complementarity. Norway had not passed through a period during which patterns of deference to authority had become entrenched. Traditions of egalitarianism were deep and had been more continuously maintained than in most Western societies. The hypothesis was made that this configuration would be favorable for the development of direct participation in the workplace. These favorable conditions were strengthened by the homogeneity of the society and by its small size. Members of key groups knew each other and overlapped. If they decided to move in a new direction, networks existed through which a wide support base could soon come into existence.

These contextual conditions permitted a series of four major sociotechnical field experiments involving work restructuring not only to be launched but, in three cases, to be sustained (Thorsrud and Emery, 1964, 1969). Yet the hypothesis that widespread diffusion into Norwegian industry would occur from high-profile field sites turned out to be wrong. They became encapsulated (Herbst, 1976). The diffusion took place in Sweden at the end of the decade—when the Norwegian results created great interest in the Employers and Trade Union Associations. Thorsrud was invited to visit. By 1973, between five hundred and one thousand work-improvement projects of various kinds, small and large, were going on in many different industries. A new generation of Swedes (better educated and more affluent) refused (by absenteeism and turnover) to do the dullest and most menial jobs. The importation of Southern Europeans created social problems. Something had to be done. Managers and unions took up the Norwegian approach and adapted it to their own purposes.

After that, shifts in the macrosocial field in Scandinavia recentered attention on the representation of workers on boards of management just when, in Germany, some interest appeared in direct worker participation. A number of laws have been passed in Norway and Sweden. In both countries a third of the members of the boards have to be workers' representatives.

THE SHELL PHILOSOPHY PROJECT

In Britain a large-scale sociotechnical project, begun by Shell (UK) with the Tavistock Institute in 1965, showed the need to develop a new management philosophy to establish values and principles that could be seen by all to guide work redesign, if commitment was to be secured not only from the various levels of management but also from the work force (Hill, 1971). This project began with a three-and-a-half day off-site meeting with the eleven most senior managers, the internal consultants, and four senior people from the Tavistock. It led to a whole series of two-and-a-half day, off-site residential conferences to discuss the original draft philosophy and to amend and ratify it. These conferences involved all levels of the organization, from the board to the shop floor and the outside trade union officials as well as the shop stewards.

After some four years, the advances brought about were arrested by an exceedingly complex situation within both the company and the industry. The ways in which the clock began to be turned back are described in Hill's (1971) book. The approach, however, was taken up by Shell in other countries—Australia, Holland, and, more recently, Canada. It appears to be characteristic of innovative processes that after a certain time particular implementive sites reach their limit. The burden of trailblazing is then taken up by others where favorable conditions emerge.

Meanwhile, what had happened regarding work restructuring and participation, especially in Sweden, created interest in the United States. Though one or two pioneer sociotechnical projects had been under way for some time in the United States, it was not until 1972 that wider public interest was awakened. Notions of work alienation were popularized by the media and associated with the threat of declining productivity in the face of Japanese and West German competition.

At an international conference held at Arden House in 1972, the term *quality of working life* (QWL) was introduced by Louis Davis. Although "industrial democracy" fitted most European countries, the term had dangerous connotations in the United States at that time. Along with "Work in America" (Special Task Force, 1973; O'Toole, 1974), which extended consideration to the mental health aspects of the workplace and the work/family interface, this conference set the tone for further developments. In Bateson's (1972) sense, it repunctuated the field. The two volumes of papers emanating from it (Davis and Cherns, 1975) became its standard reference work. Since then sociotechnical concepts and methods have become one input into a wider field concerned with changing social values and with studying the effects of values on organizations and their individual members. The age of resource scarcity coincided with increasing recognition that advanced industrial societies were producing conditions that were impoverishing the overall quality of life. The quality of life in the workplace is coming to be seen as a critical part of this overall quality. It is now less accepted that boredom and alienation are inherently a part of work life for the majority, or that they must perforce accept authoritarian control in narrow jobs. Examples can be pointed to in almost any industry of alternative forms of sociotechnical relations where these negative features do not have to be endured. For individuals and organizations alike, there is a choice.

In the 1950s the societal climate was negative toward sociotechnical innovation. Thirty years later, in the 1980s, the societal climate has become more positive (Walton, 1979). Nevertheless, in most Western countries the support base remains limited in the face of the persisting power of the technocratic and bureaucratic mode. Yet this mode is being experienced as increasingly dysfunctional in the more complex and uncertain conditions of the wider environment. Emergent values are moving in the direction of regarding personal growth and empowerment as human rights. All who wish them should have the opportunity to cultivate them. The workplace constitutes a key setting for this purpose. A Norwegian law of 1976 gives workers the right to demand jobs conforming to Emery's six psychological principles that shaped the original sociotechnical experiments of the Norwegian Industrial Democracy project:

1. Variety
2. Learning opportunity
3. Own decision power
4. Organizational support
5. Societal recognition
6. A desirable future

In 1981 a second international conference was held, this time in Toronto, Canada. The two hundred people attending the first conference in 1972 were almost entirely academics. In 1981, seventeen hundred to eighteen hundred people attended, most of whom were either managers or trade unionists. The real-world people were in the process of taking over. A large number of those present, including myself, expected a solid further development to take place during the 1980s. By and large, however, this has not happened. There has been much stagnation. Only in the last three or four years has the forward movement resumed. It cannot be said, even now, that it has become mainstream in any country. To make it so is the next task.

Notes

1. Through the Human Factors Panel of the then government's Productivity Committee or funds administered by the Medical Research Council.

2. Personal communication, 1977.

3. No attempt has been made to cover the work of the many colleagues who become involved in this field, from its opening up in the decade of the 1970s, in the United States, Canada, and many countries in Europe.

4. The others were the natural characteristics of the material, the degree of centrality of the various productive operations, the character of the maintenance and supply operations, and that of the immediate physical work setting.

References

Ackoff, R.L. and F.E. Emery. 1972. *On Purposeful Systems*. Chicago: Aldine-Atherton.

Baldamus, W. 1951. "Types of Work and Motivation." *British Journal of Sociology*, 2: 44–58.

—— 1961. *Efficiency and Effort: An Analysis of Industrial Administration*. London: Tavistock Publications.

Bateson, G. 1972. *Steps to an Ecology of Mind*. San Francisco: Chandler.

Bell, D. 1956. *Work and Its Discontents*. Boston: Beacon Press.

Bion, W.R. 1946. "The Leaderless Group Project." *Bulletin of the Menninger Clinic*, 10: 77–81.

—— 1950. "Experiences in Groups V." *Human Relations*, 3: 3–14.

—— 1961. *Experiences in Groups and Other Papers*. London: Tavistock Publications; New York: Basic Books.

Burns, T. and G.M. Stalker. 1961. *The Management of Innovation*. London: Tavistock Publications.

Clegg, H. 1960. *Industrial Democracy*. Oxford: Blackwell.

Davis, L.E. 1957. "Toward a Theory of Job Design." *Journal of Industrial Engineering*, 8: 19–23.

Davis, L.E., R.R. Canter and J. Hoffman. 1955. "Current Job Design Criteria." *Journal of Industrial Engineering*, 6: 5–11.

Davis, L.E. and A.B. Cherns. 1975. *The Quality of Work Life*, Vols. I and II. New York: Free Press.

Davis, L.E., F.E. Emery and P.G. Herbst. 1965. *Papers from the Socio-Technical Theory Project*. London: Tavistock Institute Document.

Emery, F.E. 1952. *The Deputy's Role in the Bolsover System of Continuous Mining*. London: Tavistock Institute Document 517.

———— 1959. *Characteristics of Socio-Technical Systems*. London: Tavistock Institute Document 527. Revised in *The New Paradigm of Work*. Canberra: Centre for Continuing Education, Australian National University, 1978. Also in *Design of Jobs*, edited by L.E. Davis and J.C. Taylor. Harmondsworth: Penguin Books, 1972. Vol. II, pp. 157–86.

———— 1967. "The Next Thirty Years: Concepts, Methods and Anticipations." *Human Relations*, 20: 199–237.

———— 1976. *Futures We Are In*. Leiden: Martinus Nijhoff. Chapter 4 reproduced in part, Vol. II, "The Second Design Principle: Participation and the Democratization of Work," pp. 214–33.

———— 1978. *The Emergence of a New Paradigm of Work*. Canberra: Centre for Continuing Education, Australian National University.

Emery, F.E. and M. Emery. 1974. *Participative Design: Work and Community Life*. Canberra: Centre for Continuing Education, Australian National University. Revised in Vol. II, "The Participative Design Workshop," pp. 599–613.

Emery, F.E. and J. Marek. 1962. "Some Socio-Technical Aspects of Automation." *Human Relations*, 15: 17–26.

Emery, F.E. and E. Thorsrud. 1992. Vol. II. "The Norskhydro Fertilizer Plant," pp. 492–507.

Emery, F.E. and E.L. Trist. 1963. "The Causal Texture of Organizational Environments." Paper presented to the International Psychology Congress, Washington D.C. Reprinted in *La Sociologie du Travail,* 1964, and in *Human Relations,* 18:21–32, 1965.

———— 1972/73. *Towards a Social Ecology: Contextual Appreciation of the Future in the Present*. London/New York: Plenum Press.

Fensham, F. and D. Hooper. 1964. *Changes in the British Rayon Industry*. London: Tavistock Publications.

Goodman, P.S. 1979. *Assessing Organizational Change: The Rushdon Quality of Work Experiment*. New York: Wiley.

Heider, F. 1942. "On Perception, Event Structure and Psychological Environment." *Psychological Issues*, I, 2.

Herbst, P.G. 1962. *Autonomous Group Functioning: An Exploration in Behaviour Theory and Measurement*. London: Tavistock Publications.

—— 1976. *Alternatives to Hierarchies*. Leiden: Martinus Nijhoff.

Hertzberg, F., B. Mausner and B. Snyderman. 1959. *The Motivation to Work*. New York: Wiley.

Hill, C.P. 1971. *Towards a New Philosophy of Management: The Company Development Programme of Shell U.K*. London: Gower Press. Excerpted, Vol. II. P. Hill and F. Emery, "Toward a New Philosophy of Management," pp. 259–82.

Jaques, E. 1951. *The Changing Culture of a Factory*. London: Tavistock Publications. Reissued 1987, New York: Garland.

—— 1956. *Measurement of Responsibility: A Study of Work, Payment and Individual Capacity*. New York: Dryden.

Jennings, H. 1947. "Leadership and Sociometric Choice." *Sociometry*, 10: 32–49.

Jordan, N. 1963. "Allocation of Functions Between Men and Machines in Automated Systems." *Journal of Applied Psychology*, 47: 161–65.

King, S.D.M. 1964. *Training Within the Organization: A Study of Company Policy and Procedures for the Systematic Training of Operators and Supervisors*. London: Tavistock Publications.

Lewin, K. 1939. "Patterns of Aggressive Behavior in Experimentally Created Social Climates." *Journal of Social Psychology*, 10: 271–99.

—— 1951. *Field Theory in Social Science: Selected Theoretical Papers*. New York: Harper and Row.

McLuhan, M. 1964. Understanding Media. New York: McGraw-Hill.

Melman, S. 1958. *Decision-Making and Productivity*. Oxford: Blackwell.

Menzies, I.E.P. 1960. "A Case Study in the Functioning of Social Systems as a Defence Against Anxiety." *Human Relations*, 13: 95–121. Vol. I, I. Menzies Lyth, "Social Systems as a Defense Against Anxiety: An Empirical Study of the Nursing Service of a General Hospital," pp. 439–62.

Miller, E.J. 1959. "Territory, Technology and Time: The Internal Differentiation of Complex Production Systems." *Human Relations*, 12: 243–72; also Tavistock Institute Document 526. Vol. II, pp. 385–404.

—— 1975. "Socio-Technical Systems in Weaving, 1953–1970: A Follow-Up Study." *Human Relations*, 28: 349–86. Revised, Vol. II, "The Ahmedabad Experiment Revisited: Work Organization in an Indian Weaving Shed, 1953–1970," pp. 130–56.

Miller, E.J. and A.K. Rice. 1967. *Systems of Organization*. London: Tavistock Publications.

Mumford, L. 1934. *Technics and Civilization*. Revised edition 1963. New York: Harcourt.

Murray, H. 1960. *Studies in Automated Technologies*. London: Tavistock Institute Document.

—— 1990. Vol. I, "The Transformation of Selection Procedures: The War Office Selection Boards," pp. 45–67.

Murray, H. and A.C. Trist. 1969. *Work Organization in the Doncaster Coal District.* London: Tavistock Institute Document.

Nadel, S.F. 1951. *The Foundations of Social Anthropology.* Glencoe, Ill.: Free Press.

O'Toole, J. (Editor). 1974. *"Work and the Quality of Life: Resource Papers for 'Work in America.'"* Cambridge, Mass.: MIT Press.

Pollock, A.B. 1954. *Retail Shop Organization.* London: Tavistock Institute Document.

Rice, A.K. 1953. "Productivity and Social Organization in an Indian Weaving Shed: An Examination of the Socio-Technical System of an Experimental Automatic Loomshed." *Human Relations,* 6: 297–329. Condensed, Vol. II, "Productivity and Social Organization: An Indian Automated Weaving Shed," pp. 106–29.

—— 1958. *Productivity and Social Organization: The Ahmedabad Experiment: Technical Innovation, Work Organization and Management.* London: Tavistock Publications. Reissued 1987, New York: Garland.

—— 1963. *The Enterprise and Its Environment: A System Theory of Management Organization.* London: Tavistock Publications.

Schon, D. 1971. *Beyond the Stable State.* London: Temple Smith.

Sheppard, W.V. 1949. "Continuous Longwall Mining." *Colliery Guardian,* 178.

—— 1951. "Continuous Longwall Mining: Experiments at Bolsover Colliery." *Colliery Guardian,* 182.

Singer, E.A. 1959. *Experience and Reflection,* edited by C.W. Churchman. Philadelphia: University of Pennsylvania Press.

Smith, F. 1952. *Switchboard Reorganization.* London: General Post Office (unpublished monograph).

Sommerhoff, G. 1950. *Analytical Biology.* Oxford: Oxford University Press.

—— 1969. "The Abstract Characteristics of Living Systems." In *Systems Thinking: Selected Readings,* edited by F.E. Emery. Harmondsworth: Penguin Books.

Special Task Force. 1973. *Report to the Secretary of Health, Education and Welfare on Work in America.* Cambridge, Mass.: MIT Press.

Stoelwinder, J.U. 1978. *Ward Team Management: Five Years Later,* Philadelphia: University of Pennsylvania, Management and Behavioral Science Center, Wharton School.

Stoelwinder, J.U. and P.S. Clayton. 1978. "Hospital Organization Development: Changing the Focus from 'Better Management' to 'Better Patient Care.'" *Journal of Applied Behavioral Science,* 14: 400–414.

Susman, G. and E. Trist. 1977. "An Experiment in Autonomous Working in an American Underground Coalmine." *Human Relations,* 30: 201–36. Revised and expanded, Vol. II, "Action Research in an American Underground Coal Mine," pp. 417–50.

Thorsrud, E. and F.E. Emery. 1964. *Industrielt Demokrati*. Oslo: Oslo University Press. Reissued in 1969 as F.E. Emery and E. Thorsrud, *Form and Content in Industrial Democracy: Some Experiences from Norway and Other European Countries*. London: Tavistock Publications.

—— 1969. *Mot en ny bedriftsorganisasjon. Oslo: Tanum*. Reissued in 1976 as F.E. Emery and E. Thorsrud, *Democracy at Work*. Leiden: Martinus Nijhoff.

Trist, E.L. 1950a. *"The Relations of Social and Technical Systems in Coal-Mining."* Paper presented to the British Psychological Society, Industrial Section.

—— 1950b. "Culture as a Psycho-Social Process." Paper presented to the Anthropological Section, British Association for the Advancement of Science. Vol. I, pp. 539–45.

—— 1953a. *Some Observations on the Machine Face as a Socio-Technical System*. London: Tavistock Institute Document 341.

—— 1953b. *An Area Training School in the National Coal Board*. London: Tavistock Institute Document.

—— 1953c. *Area Organization in the National Coal Board*. London: Tavistock Institute Document.

—— 1958. "Human Relations in Industry." Paper presented to the Seminar on Workers' Participation in Management, Congress for Cultural Freedom, Vienna.

—— 1976a. "A Concept of Organizational Ecology." *Bulletin of National Labour Institute* (New Delhi), 12: 483–96 and Australian Journal of Management, 2: 161–75.

—— 1976b. "Action Research and Adaptive Planning." In *Experimenting with Organizational Life: The Action Research Approach*, edited by A.W. Clark. London: Plenum.

—— 1979a. "Referent Organizations and the Development of Inter-Organizational Domains." Distinguished Lecture, Academy of Management 39th Annual Convention, Organization and Management Theory Division.

—— 1979b. "Adapting to a Changing World." In *Industrial Democracy Today*, edited by G. Sanderson. New York: McGraw-Hill-Ryerson.

—— 1981. "QWL and the '8os." Closing Address, International QWL Conference, Toronto. Vol. II, pp. 338–49.

Trist, E.L. and K.W. Bamforth. 1951. "Some Social and Psychological Consequences of the Longwall Method of Coal Getting." *Human Relations*, 4: 3–38.

Trist, E.L., G.W. Higgin, H. Murray and A.B. Pollock. 1963. *Organizational Choice: Capabilities of Groups at the Coal Face Under Changing Technologies: The Loss, Rediscovery and Transformation of a Work Tradition*. London: Tavistock Publications. Reissued 1987, New York: Garland. Chapters 13, 14 revised, Vol. II, "Alternative Work Organizations: An Exact Comparison," pp. 84–105. Chapters 19–22, Vol. I, "The Assumption of Ordinariness as a Denial Mechanism: Innovation and Conflict in a Coal Mine," pp. 476–93.

Trist, E.L. and H. Murray. 1958. *Work Organization at the Coal Face: A Comparative Study of Mining Systems*. London: Tavistock Publications.

Trist, E.L., G.I. Susman and G.R. Brown. 1977. "An Experiment in Autonomous Working in an American Underground Coal Mine." *Human Relations*, 30: 201–36.

van Beinum, H. 1963. *Een organisatie in beweging*. Leiden: Stanfert Kroese.

von Bertalanffy, L. 1950. "The Theory of Open Systems in Physics and Biology." *Science*, 3: 23–29.

Walker, C.R. and H. Guest. 1952. *The Man on the Assembly Line*. Cambridge, Mass.: Harvard University Press.

Walton, R.E. 1979. "Work Innovations in the United States." *Harvard Business Review*, 57: 88–98.

Weiner, N. 1950. *The Social Psychology of Organizing*. Reading, Mass.: Addison-Wesley.

Westerlund, G. 1952. *Group Leadership*. Stockholm: Nordisk Rotogravyr.

Wilson, A.T.M., E.L. Trist, F.E. Emery and K.W. Bamforth, 1951. *The Bolsover System of Continuous Mining*. London: Tavistock Institute Document.

Woodward, J. 1958. *Management and Technology*. London: Her Majesty's Stationery Office.

CHAPTER TWELVE

Revolutionary Change Theories

A Multilevel Exploration of the Punctuated Equilibrium Paradigm

Connie J. G. Gersick (1991)

Q uestions about change have commanded the attention of organization theorists for many years. How do individuals, groups, organizations, and industries evolve over time? How do they adapt or fail to adapt to changing environments? How can change be planned and managed? The need to understand change processes is particularly critical now, when dramatic alterations are under way in the economic, technological, social, and political features of our environment, and people in organizations are struggling to keep pace (Deal, 1985; Kimberly and Quinn, 1984).

Our research on these questions is inevitably directed by our basic assumptions about how change works. One paradigm that has heavily influenced our thinking about change processes is Darwin's model of evolution as a slow stream of small mutations, gradually shaped by environmental selection into novel forms. This concept of incremental, cumulative change has become pervasive; it is the way people have explained everything from geological erosion to skill acquisition. Within the field of evolutionary biology, however, Darwinian gradualism has been challenged. Natural historians Niles Eldredge and Stephen Gould (1972) postulate a very different view of evolution as *punctuated equilibrium*. They propose that lineages exist in essentially static form (equilibrium) over most of their histories, and new species arise abruptly, through sudden, revolutionary "punctuations" of rapid change (at which point—as in the Darwinian model—environmental selection determines the fate of new variations).

Similar new, empirically derived theories in a variety of different literatures echo the punctuated equilibrium argument. Examples in the social sciences include Kuhn's (1970) distinction between normal science and scientific evolution, Abernathy and Utterback's (1982) contrast between radical and evolutionary innovation in industry, Miller and Friesen's (1984) model of momentum and revolution in organizational adaptation, and Levinson's (1978) theory of adult development as an alternation between periods of stability and transition. In the physical sciences, Prigogine's Nobel Prize–winning work on order, chaos, and change in "self-organizing systems" provides a grand theoretical perspective.

This new way of thinking has far-reaching implications for organizational practice and theory about when and how change occurs and how it can be managed. More important, it offers some promising conceptual tools for understanding the issues facing organizations in an environment where incremental adaptation increasingly appears to be unequal to the economic, social, and ecological dislocations taking place (Halberstam, 1986; Kennedy, 1987; Loye and Eisler, 1987).

The aim of this article is to explicate the punctuated equilibrium paradigm in sufficiently broad terms to indicate its general applicability and its special potential to contribute to the study of organizations. I will also suggest issues for further research. My approach is to juxtapose similar theories from different research domains and to show how each suggests questions and insights for the others. Two premises underlie the article: (1) that there are important commonalities in the way many systems, including human systems, change; and (2) that we can benefit by comparing research findings from disparate areas because different facets of kindred processes may come into focus as the methodology and level of analysis vary.

The chapter is meant to provoke ideas, not to provide a comprehensive literature review. It is a selective exploration of one paradigm as reflected in six theories, each chosen to represent a different area and level of analysis: individual adult development (Levinson), group development (Gersick), organizational evolution (Tushman and Romanelli), history of science (Kuhn), evolutionary biology (Eldredge and Gould), and self-organizing systems (Prigogine and Stengers and the Brussels School).

KEY COMPONENTS OF THE PARADIGM: SHARED CONSTRUCTS

My argument that models from different fields have much to offer each other begins with the premise that they reflect common processes. Each theory examined here centers on the same paradigm, or basic gestalt, of evolution: relatively long periods of stability (equilibrium), punctuated by compact periods of qualitative, metamorphic change (revolution). In every model, the interrelationship of these two modes is explained through the construct of a highly durable underlying order or deep structure. This deep structure is what persists and limits change during equilibrium periods, and it is what disassembles, reconfigures, and enforces wholesale transformation during revolutionary punctuations. The tables in this section use the theorists' own words to document the degree to which these six models share the same paradigm and to show some of the specific features of each level of analysis.

The Punctuated Equilibrium Paradigm and How It Differs from Traditional Paradigms

Table 12.1 provides an overview of the six theories and suggests the range of fields in which the same paradigm has emerged. The statement of

Table 12.1. The Overall Punctuated Equilibrium Model as Described by Six Theorists.

Commonalities:

Systems evolve through the alternation of periods of equilibrium, in which persistent underlying structures permit only incremental change, and periods of revolution, in which these underlying structures are fundamentally altered.

Individuals: Levinson (1978, 49)

The life structure evolves through a relatively orderly sequence . . . [of] stable (structure-building) periods and transitional (structure-changing) periods.

Groups: Gersick (1988)

Teams progress in a pattern of "punctuated equilibrium," through alternating inertial change and revolution in the behaviors and themes through which they approach their work.

Organizations: Tushman and Romanelli (1985, 171)

Organizations evolve through convergent periods punctuated by strategic reorientations (or recreations) that demark and set bearings for the next convergent period.

Scientific fields: Kuhn (1970, 5–6)

Most scientists . . . spend almost all their time [doing normal science, which assumes] that the scientific community knows what the world is like. . . . [Scientific revolutions, which] lead the profession . . . to a new basis for the practice of science . . . are the tradition-shattering complements to the tradition-bound activity of normal science.

Biological species: Gould (1980, 184)

Lineages change little during most of their history, but events of rapid speciation occasionally punctuate this tranquility. Evolution is the differential survival and deployment of these punctuations.

Grand theory: Prigogine and Stengers (1984, 169–70)

The "historical" path along which the system evolves . . . is characterized by a succession of stable regions, where deterministic laws dominate, and of instable ones, near the bifurcation points, where the system can "choose" between or among more than one possible future.

commonalities at the top of the table offers a summary definition of the basic paradigm, derived from all the models. A look at the excerpts below it shows the striking similarities (and some differences) across models.

Table 12.2 shows how each theorist differentiates his or her model from traditional counterparts and indicates the extent to which this paradigm challenges premises inherent in traditional theories. Three main distinctions emerge. First, theorists contrast their work against concepts of change as a gradual blending of one form into another. This difference is not a simple question of the pace of change, as evenly spaced versus unevenly clumped. Gradualist paradigms imply that systems can "accept" virtually any change, any time, as long as it is small enough; big changes result from the insensible accumulation of small ones. In contrast, punctuated equilibrium suggests that, for most of systems' histories, there are limits beyond which "change is *actively prevented*, rather than always potential but merely suppressed because no adaptive advantage would accrue" (Gould, 1989, 124).

These models also dispute the ideas that (1) individual systems of the same type all develop along the same path and (2) systems develop in "forward" directions, as in the universal stage theories that dominate the current literatures on group and organizational development. Punctuated equilibria are not

Table 12.2. How Punctuated Equilibrium Models Differ from Traditional Counterparts.

Commonalities:
Systems do not evolve through a gradual blending from one state to the next. Systems' histories are unique. They do not necessarily evolve from lower to higher states, through universal hierarchies of stages, or toward preset ends.

Individuals: Levinson (1978, 40; 1986, 10)
Our findings led us [away] from the idea of a steady, continuous process of development to the idea of qualitatively different *periods* in development (1978, 40). Like Erikson and Freud, I define each period primarily in terms of its developmental tasks. . . . Unlike Piaget . . . I do not identify a particular structure as the . . . optimal one for a given period; the life structures generated in any period are infinitely varied. Phase 3 comes after phase 2 and to some extent builds upon it, but phase 3 is not necessarily more "advanced" (1986, 10).

Groups: Gersick (1989, 277)
Groups did not develop in uniform series of stages, nor through linear, additive building block sequences.

Project groups are all challenged to invent and generate a product, find ways to work together, deal with outside expectations, and pace themselves to meet deadlines. However, there appears to be no one best way to work.

(continued)

Table 12.2. (continued)

Organizations: Tushman and Romanelli (1984, 208)

Stage models [that] postulate a set of distinct and historically sequenced stages . . . dominate the literature on organizational evolution. [But] organizations do not evolve through a standard set of stages. . . . [They] may reach their respective strategic orientations through systematically different patterns of convergence and reorientation.

Scientific fields: Kuhn (1970, 170–171)

Perhaps science does not develop by the accumulation of individual discoveries and inventions. We may [also] have to relinquish the notion . . . that changes of paradigm carry scientists . . . closer and closer to the truth. . . . Nothing . . . makes it a process of evolution *toward* anything.

Biological species: Eldredge and Gould (1972, 84); Gould (1977, 36–37)

Evolution is not a stately unfolding [in which] new species arise from the slow and steady transformation of entire populations. . . . [It is] a story of homeostatic equilibria, disturbed only "rarely" . . . by rapid and episodic events of speciation.

Darwin explicitly rejected the . . . equation of what we now call evolution with any notion of progress. . . . Yet most laymen still equate evolution with progress . . . [a] fallacious equation [that] continues to have unfortunate consequences.

Grand theory: Prigogine and Stengers (1984, 207)

The way . . . biological and social evolution has traditionally been interpreted represents a particularly unfortunate use of . . . concepts . . . borrowed [unjustifiably] from physics. . . . The foremost example of this is the paradigm of optimization. Optimization models ignore both the possibility of radical transformations . . . that change the definition of a problem and thus the kind of solution sought—and the inertial constraints that may eventually force a system into a disastrous way of functioning.

---

smooth trajectories toward preset ends because both the specific composition of a system and the "rules" governing how its parts interact may change unpredictably during revolutionary punctuations. "The definition of the system is . . . able to be modified by its evolution" (Prigogine and Stengers, 1984, 189).

These models suggest that conflicting theories about organizational adaptability (such as resource dependency, Pfeffer and Salancik, 1978) and organizational rigidity (such as population ecology, Hannan and Freeman, 1977, 1984) are applicable at different times, depending on whether a system is in a period of transition or equilibrium. Finally, they suggest we use caution in applying theories based on universal "drivers" such as efficiency (e.g., see Williamson,

1983, 125), by proposing that systems' basic organizing principles are varied and changeable.

Deep Structure

Tables 12.3, 12.4, and 12.5 display excerpted summaries of the three main components of the punctuated equilibrium paradigm: *deep structure, equilibrium periods*, and *revolutionary periods*. The first of these, deep structure, is the most critical for understanding the models, and it is the hardest concept to define and communicate. (Kuhn, 1970, 174–210, and Levinson, 1986, discussed some of the difficulties.)

Each theorist explains this concept in language specific to his or her own research domain. I use the term *deep structure* (Chomsky, 1966) for its general appropriateness. The six sources together suggest a general explanation of its meaning. Systems with deep structure share two characteristics:

Table 12.3. Concepts of Deep Structure in Six Theories.

Commonalities:

Deep structure is a network of fundamental, interdependent "choices," of the basic configuration into which a system's units are organized, and the activities that maintain both this configuration and the system's resource exchange with the environment. Deep structure in human systems is largely implicit.

Individuals: Levinson (1986, 6)

Life structure: The underlying pattern or design of a person's life at a given time. . . . The life structure [answers the questions]: "What is my life like now? What are the most important parts of my life, and how are they interrelated? Where do I invest most of my time and energy?" The primary components of a life structure are the person's relationships with various others in the external world.

Groups: Gersick (1988, 17, 21)

Framework: A set of givens about the group's situation and how it will behave that form a stable platform from which the group operates. Frameworks may be partly explicit but are primarily implicit. They are integrated webs of performance strategies, interaction patterns, assumptions about and approaches toward a group's task, and outside context.

Organizations: Tushman and Romanelli (1985, 176)

Strategic orientation: Answers the question, What is it that is being converged upon? While [it] may or may not be explicit, it can be described by [five facets]: (1) core beliefs and values regarding the organization, its employees, and its environment; (2) products, markets, technology, and competitive timing; (3) the distribution of power; (4) the organization's structure; and (5) the nature, type, and pervasiveness of control systems.

(continued)

Table 12.3. (continued)

Scientific fields: Kuhn (1970)

Paradigm: Universally recognized scientific achievements that for a time provide model problems and solutions to a community of practitioners (viii). [Paradigms indicate] what a datum [is], what instruments might be used to retrieve it, and what concepts [are] relevant to its interpretation (122). [However, scientists] are little better than laymen at characterizing the established bases of their field. . . . Such abstractions show mainly through their ability to do successful research (47).

Biological species: Gould (1989); Wake, Roth, and Wake (1983, 218–219)*

Genetic programs: Stasis is . . . an active feature of organisms and populations . . . based largely on complex epistasis in genetic programs, and the resilient and limited geometries of developmental sequences (124).

[Living systems require very specific internal processes.]
The . . . conditions governing each internal process are provided by preceding processes within the system, [constituting a network of] circular interaction: [the activity of each element affects all]. Each . . . change of the system must remain within the . . . limits of the process of circular production and maintenance of the elements, or the system itself will decompose. No element can interact with the environment independently . . . and no independent change (evolution) of single elements can take place. . . . The same is true for the "activity" of the genes: they never "express" themselves in a direct, linear way. Thus organisms have evolved as systems resistant to change, even genetic change.

Grand theory: Haken (1981, 17)

Order parameters: Collective modes . . . which define the order of the overall system. . . . Order parameters . . . may be material, such as the amplitude of a physical wave, [or] immaterial, such as ideas or symbols. . . . Once . . . established, they prescribe the actions of the subsystems . . . at the microscopic level.

*The Wake et al. excerpt is from an article recommended by S. J. Gould (personal communication). It explains and expands on the excerpt from Gould.

(1) they have differentiated parts and (2) the units that compose them "work": they exchange resources with the environment in ways that maintain—and are controlled by—this differentiation (see Prigogine and Stengers, 1984, 154, 287). *Deep structure* is the set of fundamental "choices" a system has made of (1) the basic parts into which its units will be organized and (2) the basic activity patterns that will maintain its existence. Deep structures are highly stable for two general reasons. First, like a decision tree, the trail of choices made by a system rules many options out, at the same time as it rules mutually contingent options in. This characterization accords with organizational research on the tenacity of initial choices (Eisenhardt & Schoonhoven,

Table 12.4. Concepts of Equilibrium Periods in Six Theories.

Commonalities:

During equilibrium periods, systems maintain and carry out the choices of their deep structure. Systems make adjustments that preserve the deep structure against internal and external perturbations, and move incrementally along paths built into the deep structure. Pursuit of stable deep structure choices may result in behavior that is turbulent on the surface.

Individuals: Levinson

Structure-building periods: The primary task is to build a life structure: a man must make certain key choices, form a structure around them, and pursue his goals and values within this structure. To say that a period is stable in this sense is not . . . to say that it is tranquil. . . . The task of . . . building a structure is often stressful . . . and may involve many kinds of change. Each stable period . . . has distinctive tasks and character according to where it is in the life cycle (1978, 49). [Such periods] ordinarily last 5 to 7 years, 10 at most (1986, 7).

Groups: Gersick (1988)

Project groups' lives unfold in two main *phases*, separated by a transition period halfway between the group's beginning and its expected deadline. Within phases, groups approach their work using stable frameworks of assumptions, premises, and behavior patterns. As frameworks vary, specific activities and efficacy vary from group to group. During a phase, groups accumulate more or less work, learning, and experience within the boundaries of their framework, but (even when hampered by it), they do not change their fundamental approach to their task.

Organizations: Tushman and Romanelli (1985)

Convergent periods: Relatively long time spans of incremental change and adaptation which elaborate structure, systems, controls, and resources toward increased coalignment, [which] may or may not be associated with effective performance (173). [They are] characterized by duration, strategic orientation, [and] turbulence. . . . (179) During [these] periods . . . inertia increases and competitive vigilance decreases; structure frequently drives strategy (215).

Scientific fields: Kuhn (1970)

Normal science is directed to the articulation of those phenomena and theories that the paradigm already supplies (24). Three classes of problems—determination of significant fact, matching of facts with theory, and articulation of theory— exhaust . . . the literature of normal science, both empirical and theoretical. . . . Work under that paradigm can be conducted in no other way, and to desert the paradigm is to cease practicing the science it defines (34).

Biological species: Gould (1980)

Phyletic transformation [is] minor adjustment within populations [that is] sequential and adaptive (15). [It is a mode of evolution in which] an entire population changes

(continued)

Table 12.4. (continued)

from one state to another. [This] yields no increase in diversity, only a transformation of one thing into another. Since extinction (by extirpation, not by evolution into something else) is so common, a biota with [only this, and] no mechanism for increasing diversity would soon be wiped out (180).

Grand theory: Prigogine and Stengers (1984); Haken (1981)

In *stable regions*, deterministic laws dominate (169). All individual initiative is doomed to insignificance. . . . (206)

Under given external conditions, the individual parts of the system have . . . stable configurations . . . or oscillations. . . . [If] small perturbations [are] imposed upon the system . . . the individual parts of the system relax to their former state once the perturbation is removed, or they change their behavior only slightly when the perturbation persists (17).

Table 12.5. Concepts of Revolutionary Periods in Six Theories.

Commonalities:

Revolutions are relatively brief periods when a system's deep structure comes apart, leaving it in disarray until the period ends, with the "choices" around which a new deep structure forms. Revolutionary outcomes, based on interactions of systems' historical resources with current events, are not predictable; they may or may not leave a system better off. Revolutions vary in magnitude.

Individuals: Levinson (1986, 7)

Transitional periods ordinarily last about 5 years. [They] terminate the existing life structure and create the possibility for a new one. Primary tasks . . . are to reappraise the existing structure, explore possibilities for change in the self and the world, and move toward commitment to the crucial choices that form the basis for a new life structure in the ensuing period. The choices are . . . the major product of the transition.

Groups: Gersick (1989)

The *transition period* provides a compact, time-limited opportunity for radical progress by interrupting the inertial movement of phase 1. In successful transitions, groups stop the activity that has dominated the first half of their time, pull in new ideas (often involving outside contact), and reframe their accrued experience in ways that enable them to jump ahead. These transitions close with group agreement on some concrete goal that forms the basis for moving forward. The new or revised framework formed during transitions is the foundation for phase 2 work.

(continued)

Table 12.5. (continued)

Organizations: Tushman and Romanelli (1985)

Reorientations are relatively short periods of discontinuous change where strategies, power, structure, and systems are fundamentally transformed toward a new basis of alignment (173). *Recreations* are reorientations that also involve discontinuous change in core values which govern decision premises. . . . [They are] the most radical form of reorientation (179). During reorientations, organization inertia decreases, competitive vigilance increases; strategy drives structure (215).

Scientific fields: Kuhn (1970, 85)

Scientific revolution: a reconstruction of the field from new fundamentals . . . that changes some of [its] most elementary theoretical generalizations. . . . When the transition is complete, the profession will have changed its view of the field, its methods, and its goals . . . "handling the same bundle of data as before, but placing them in a new system of relations . . . by giving them a different framework" (Butterfield, 1949).

Biological species: Gould (1980, 182)

Speciation [is] the second mode [of evolution, which] replenishes the earth. New species branch off from a persisting parental stock.

Grand theory: Haken (1981, 17); Prigogine and Stengers (1984)

Bifurcation: At critical values of external parameters . . . [the system's] stability can get lost. . . . The total system tries to find a new global configuration. . . . The way the new state is reached seems universal. Because of internal fluctuations, the system tests different . . . "modes." Competition between different . . . modes sets in, and eventually one or a few kinds of modes win over. . . . The winners of this competition [can] entirely [prescribe] what the subsystems have to do.

Whenever we reach a bifurcation point, deterministic description breaks down. The type of fluctuation present in the system will lead to the choice of the branch it will follow [in a] stochastic process . . . (177).

1990; Gersick, 1988; Ginnett, 1987; Stinchcombe, 1965); early steps in decision trees are the most fateful. Second, as Wake et al. explained (see Table 12.3, Biological species), the activity patterns of a system's deep structure reinforce the system as a whole, through mutual feedback loops.

As Table 12.3 suggests, different kinds of systems face different "menus" of choices about how they will organize and run themselves. Identifying these sets of choices (which become the components of each system's deep structure) is an important part of theory building for specific punctuational models. For example, Tushman and Romanelli (1985) described five kinds of structural and performance choices that make up organizations' deep structures;

Levinson (1978), Gersick (1988), and Kuhn (1970) described categories of choices for individuals, groups, and scientific disciplines, respectively (see Table 12.3). This approach differs critically from that of universal stage theorists, who seek commonalities in the *outcomes* of choices and dismiss individual differences as "noise" (Gersick, 1988). Punctuational models identify common choice categories, but allow for infinite variety in individual systems' particular solutions. This is the difference between saying, for example, that all project groups progress through "forming, storming, norming, and performing" (Tuckman, 1965) and saying that all project groups are challenged to choose boundaries, norms, and work methods, but they vary in the sequence and manner in which they settle those choices.

Equilibrium Periods

If deep structure may be thought of as the design of the playing field and the rules of the game, then equilibrium periods might be compared loosely to a game in play. The stable integrity of the field and the rules and, thus, of the game itself does not mean that play is uninteresting, that every match is the same, or that scores and performances are static.

Within equilibrium periods, the system's basic organization and activity patterns stay the same; the equilibrium period consists of maintaining and carrying out these choices. As implied above, what "carrying out" means is different for different types of systems. In systems without intentionality, it can be a mechanical set of activities or a series of minor adjustments to the environment. Levinson, Gersick, Tushman and Romanelli, and Kuhn described the refinements and incremental steps human systems take during equilibrium periods, as they work to achieve goals built into their deep structures (see Table 12.4).

Systems in equilibrium also make incremental adjustments to compensate for internal or external perturbations without changing their deep structures (see Wake, Roth, and Wake, 1983). A classic example is provided by Citibank's "back office" efforts to process increasing floods of paperwork—before John Reed revolutionized the system—simply by hiring more people (Seeger, Lorsch, and Gibson, 1974).

It is important to note that human systems in equilibrium may look turbulent enough to mask the stability of the underlying deep structure. For example, a young adult's life structure may include the fundamental choice to test a variety of occupational options, resulting in a pattern of job changes that appears chaotic (Levinson, 1978). A project group may choose implicitly to subvert its task, or an organization may commit to a strategy it is not well equipped to accomplish, resulting in patterns of overt conflict, vacillation, or failure. However, the deep structure of chosen goals and activities remains in place.

One of the major questions generated by the punctuated equilibrium paradigm concerns the inertia that maintains a system's equilibrium. For organization theorists, a salient form of this question is: Why is it so hard for systems to make major changes? Tushman and Romanelli (1985) reviewed the impressive organizational literature on this observation. The theories included here discussed three barriers to radical change in human systems: cognition, motivation, and obligation.

Gersick, Tushman and Romanelli, Kuhn, Eldredge and Gould, and Prigogine and Stengers all discussed cognitive frameworks and the thoroughness with which they shape human awareness, interpretation of reality, and consideration of actions. As Kuhn stated, phenomena "that will not fit the box are often not seen at all" (1970, 24). Limits on the awareness of alternatives constrain change in behavior (Simon, 1976).

Several theorists also discussed motivational barriers to change. Levinson (1978) described the pain of loss, the uncertainty, and the fear of failure that accompany the anticipation of terminating a life structure and trying to define a new one. Gersick (1989) offered examples of groups' reluctance to take new steps in their projects, based on wishes to avoid losing opportunities, losing power struggles, or failing at more difficult tasks. Kuhn (1970, 78) described scientists' readiness to append "ad hoc modifications" to their theories, in an effort to erase contradictions that, if appreciated, could discredit their lives' work. The sunk costs incurred during a period of equilibrium, and fears of losing control over one's situation if the equilibrium ends, contribute heavily to the human motivation to avoid significant system change.

Lastly, Levinson (1978), Tushman and Romanelli (1985), and Kuhn (1970) discussed the inertial constraints of obligations among stakeholders inside and outside a system. Levinson's (1986) portrayal of the life structure as a set of relationships (see Table 12.3) points out how pervasively a system may be bound by others' expectations and needs. Kuhn (1970, 35) noted the inertial effects that scientific communities exert by carefully socializing students, granting legitimacy only to certain problems, and responding to research findings that fall outside the paradigm as failures that "reflect not on nature but on the scientist." As Tushman and Romanelli (1985, 177) suggested, even if a system overcomes its own cognitive and motivational barriers against realizing a need for change, the "networks of interdependent resource relationships and value commitments" generated by its structure often prevent its being *able* to change.

A final explanation for the stability of equilibrium periods is that systems benefit from this kind of persistence. For human systems, these benefits have to do with the ability to pursue goals and accomplish work. According to Kuhn (1970, 25), the practice of normal science—which prescribes what methods to use and promises that certain questions will ultimately reward pursuit— facilitates the solution of "problems that [scientists] could scarcely have imagined and would never have undertaken without commitment to the paradigm." This insight about normal science is paralleled for entrepreneurs, managers, task groups, and organizations when they respond to obstacles by inventing ways to persist with their goals, not by changing their basic direction.

Tushman and Romanelli (1985, 195), whose model defines equilibria as periods during which organizations become more internally consistent, proposed an additional reason for the adaptability of inertia. They suggested that ''selection processes favor . . . organizations whose strategic orientations are consistent with internal and external environmental demands.'' When the environment is reasonably stable, organizations that maintain equilibrium should become more and more thoroughly adapted to carry out their missions. By sticking to a course, a system can become skilled at what it does.

Revolutionary Periods

The third major component of the punctuated equilibrium paradigm is the revolutionary period. The difference between the incremental changes of equilibrium periods and revolutionary changes is like the difference between changing the game of basketball by moving the hoops higher and changing it by taking the hoops away. The first kind of change leaves the game's deep structure intact. The second dismantles it. The definitive assertion in this paradigm is that systems do not shift from one kind of game to another through incremental steps; such transformations occur through wholesale upheaval.

The discussions in the previous two sections should help explain why incremental changes in a system's parts would not alter the whole. As long as the deep structure is intact, it generates a strong inertia, first to prevent the system from generating alternatives outside its own boundaries, then to pull any deviations that do occur back into line. According to this logic, the deep structure must first be dismantled, leaving the system temporarily disorganized, in order for any fundamental changes to be accomplished. Next, a subset of the system's old pieces, along with some new pieces, can be put back together into a new configuration, which operates according to a new set of rules.

The example of removed basketball hoops suggests how changes to the core of a system's deep structure affect the whole system. The contrast with the gradualist paradigm is not, again, simply a matter of many incremental changes ''bunching up.'' According to punctuational paradigms, when basic premises change all the premises contingent on them are affected. This idea also contradicts the gradualist view of systems as never moving (or *having* to move) very far from their status quo during any one step. (Consider the fall of the Berlin Wall and the fate of initial predictions that Germany could take a very long time to reunite.) The same interdependence in deep structure that explains how it can unravel so rapidly once undermined also explains the relatively rapid close of a revolutionary period, once the basis for a new deep structure is found. As Gould (1983, 196) explained, with respect to biological organisms:

> If genetic programs were beanbags of independent genes, each responsible for building a single part of the body, then . . . any major change would have to occur slowly and sequentially as thousands of parts achieved their independent modifications. But genetic programs are hierarchies with master switches, and small genetic changes that happen to affect the switches might engender cascading effects throughout the body. Major evolutionary transitions may be instigated (although not finished all at once . . .) by small genetic changes that translate into fundamentally altered bodies.

This construction is supported by empirical findings about how systems undergo revolutionary change. Levinson, Gersick, Kuhn, and Prigogine and Stengers portrayed similar pictures of systems in transition periods, undergoing, first, a breakdown of the old equilibrium and a period of uncertainty about the future, before choosing a new basis around which to crystallize a new deep structure. In Levinson's (1978) and Gersick's (1989) terms, transition periods present two distinct tasks: terminating the old deep structure and initiating a new one.

Why should revolutions occur at all? The answers arise from the same features of deep-structured systems that generate inertia: the mutual interdependence of their parts and action patterns and the fact that deep structures determine how systems obtain resources from the environment. These features open up systems' deep structures to two basic sources of disruption: (1) *internal changes* that pull parts and actions out of alignment with each other or the environment and (2) *environmental changes* that threaten the system's ability to obtain resources.

The theorists covered here offer complementary reasons why human systems generate *internal* sources of strain and misalignment. Human systems tend to outgrow the deep structures that govern their perspectives and activities. As Levinson (1978) pointed out, a life structure appropriate for the developmental tasks of a person of twenty, just becoming independent of parents and entering adulthood, cannot meet the same person's needs when he or she is thirty and concerned with pursuing his or her own career and family. A project group's framework for starting a task is seldom appropriate to carry through the entire project (Gersick, 1988). An organization's growth strains its existing structures and practices (Tushman and Romanelli, 1985). Kuhn (1970) argued that the very pursuit of normal science makes paradigms obsolete, either by answering the interesting questions (and becoming routine engineering) or by finally running up against puzzles that the paradigm was never equipped to solve. In human systems, a deep structure formed at the beginning of a period is shaped by members' inexperience, their need to get started, and their untested expectations and goals. Eventually, human systems finish their deep structures' agenda, uncover their inadequacies, and generate new needs that the old structures cannot meet.

The *external environment* presents a less orderly source of change. Levinson (1978) noted that the social environment wants different things from a person of thirty and a person of forty, even if he or she is still in the same setting. Gersick and Hackman (1990) discussed the changes that may create mismatches between a group's framework and its environment. Tushman and Romanelli (1985, 205) provided a sophisticated picture of shifts that can make organizations' strategic orientation inappropriate for their environments, including (foreseeable) maturation in product life cycles and (unforeseeable) changes in the legal and social climate, or the invention of "substitute products and/or technologies."

Such internal or external shifts do not, by themselves, cause revolutionary change; they only create the need. This point is important to pursue because it has long been proposed that failure or goal blockage triggers change (e.g., March and Simon, 1958; Weiss and Ilgen, 1985)—a proposal that is challenged by the observation that groups and organizations may rely more heavily on old routines when faced with decline (Gladstein and Reilly, 1985; Greenhalgh, 1983; Staw, Sandelands, and Dutton, 1981). Punctuated equilibrium models suggest that failures may be extremely important in setting the stage for revolutionary change. But as long as events occur against the backdrop of the same deep structure, they are treated or interpreted in ways that preserve the system's inertia and, therefore, incremental solutions are sought. The handwriting on the wall cannot be read; events do not indicate to system members what they ought to be doing differently. It may be more useful to think of certain kinds of failures—those engendered by misalignments within a system's deep structure or between its deep structure and its environment—not as sufficient causes, but as major sources of energy for revolutionary change. Revolutions themselves seem to require decisive breaks in systems' inertia.

THE DYNAMICS OF REVOLUTIONS: OPPORTUNITIES FOR SYNERGY ACROSS MODELS

Having explained punctuated equilibrium in general, I would like to suggest the potential benefits that can be gained by comparing models from diverse domains. This section of the chapter attempts to take a step in that direction by examining one area, the dynamics of revolutionary change processes in organizational settings. The previous outline of revolutionary periods leads directly to what are perhaps the most interesting questions raised by the paradigm: (1) What triggers the onset of revolutionary periods? (2) How do systems function during revolutionary periods? (3) How do revolutionary periods conclude? This section is necessarily speculative; it touches several levels of analysis because organized human systems (and revolutions) are multilevel phenomena.

What Triggers Revolutionary Periods?

There may be many ways in which the inertia of an equilibrium period can be broken. The models included here indicate at least two: the attraction of newcomers to crisis situations and the system's arrival at key temporal milestones. Kuhn (1970) and Tushman and Romanelli (1985) discussed the first avenue of change. Kuhn stated that crises are necessary precursors to scientific revolutions. He described how the persistence of apparently unresolvable anomalies increasingly focuses scientists' attention on trouble spots. With the stage thus set, some individuals break through by inventing a new paradigm. These revolutionary thinkers are not a field's established experts, but "almost always . . . either very young or very new to the field whose paradigm they change. . . . These are the men who being little committed by prior practice to the traditional rules of normal science, are particularly likely to see that those rules no longer define a playable game and to conceive another set that can replace them" (1970, 90).

This analysis complements Tushman and Romanelli's identification of "performance pressures . . . whether anticipated or actual" (1985, 179) as the fundamental agents of organizational reorientation. Tushman, Newman, and Romanelli described as typical the scenario of an organization falling into serious trouble before responding by *replacing* its top management. They found that "externally recruited executives are more than three times more likely to initiate frame-breaking change than existing executive teams" (1986, 42).

Failures caused by inappropriate deep structures are destined to elude the (misdirected) efforts of current system members to correct them. Unless such failures kill the system, they command increasing attention and raise the likelihood that newcomers will either be attracted or recruited to help solve the problems. The newcomer has the opportunity to see the system in an entirely different context than incumbent members, and he or she may begin problem solving on a new path.

It is then the newcomer's explicit task to break the old deep structure and establish a new one. In scientific revolutions, Kuhn (1970) claimed, this is only possible when paradigm failures have caused enough crisis to generate receptivity to arguments that would otherwise be ignored; in fact, some scientists never relinquish the old paradigms and never understand the revolutionary new ones. When new executives are recruited to organizations in crisis, according to Tushman, Newman, and Romanelli (1986), it is up to them to break the grip of the old structure and reorient their organizations. One way new executives may facilitate this is by replacing their direct reports—literally removing sources of inertia.

A different trigger of change is presented in Levinson's and Gersick's models, in which system members use acute awareness of time to stop the inertia of equilibrium periods for *themselves*. Gersick found that project groups with life spans ranging from one hour to several months reliably initiated major transitions in their work precisely halfway between their start-ups and expected deadlines. Transitions were triggered by participants' (sometimes unconscious) use of the midpoint as a milestone, signifying "time to move." Although Levinson (1986, 5) proposed that transitions in adult development are stimulated by deficiencies in the current life structure, he also presented, as one of his most controversial yet robust findings, the discovery that each developmental transition "begins and ends at a well-defined modal age, with a range of about two years above and below this average." His report of the feelings men experience near age thirty, and again near age forty, closely parallel Gersick's findings about group members' sense of time at project midpoints, albeit on a different scale:

> At age 28 . . . a voice within the self says: "If I am to change my life . . . I must now make a start, for soon it will be too late" [1978,58].

> [Near age 40, a man's] need to reconsider the past arises in part from a heightened awareness of his mortality and a desire to use the remaining time more wisely [1978, 192].

These theorists propose that events "do not in themselves cause the start or end of a period" (Levinson, 1978, 55). Instead, the timing of the event determines its perceived significance and its potential to influence deep structure change. When people reach temporal milestones that are important to them, they change their views of their own situations, seeing a meaningful portion of their time as closed, and the next portion as imminent. Equilibrium periods are thus interrupted by strong, self-imposed signals.

This view is supported by research on the Einstellung effect: people's tendency to persist with the same approach to a problem or series of problems whether or not that approach is productive (Luchins, 1940). Ericsson and Simon reported (1984, 129) that such persistence is not inadvertent, but a deliberate choice to continue a strategy as long as the task appears to be the same. They found that "a number of experiments have reduced the Einstellung effect by marking the test problems as separate problems rather than a continuation of the sequence of problems presented before." Persistence as well as its converse are thus explained. When people feel that a temporal era has ended, they may consciously decide that the approaches they chose for that era are no longer valid. When individuals and groups are reminded, by temporal milestones, that their time is finite, they feel a sense of urgency to reevaluate past choices, pursue aspirations they have put off, and take new steps.

To date, people's attention to time has not been considered a factor in organizational reorientations. Organizations are not mortal like individuals, and they usually are not temporary in the same way as project groups. Nonetheless, there are reasons to consider the role of timing. Deadlines have been recognized as stimulators of organizational activity for many years (March and Simon, 1958). Certainly some organizations, such as start-ups backed by venture capital, are run much like time-limited projects. They have long-term goals (e.g., of five to ten years) by which they are expected to yield returns on investments; backers regularly evaluate such organizations' progress against time-linked targets.

Preliminary data from a field study by the author suggest that CEOs in start-up businesses do use temporal milestones in ways similar to project groups. Interviewed executives described being aware of problems for months without considering basic strategy changes—either as a conscious choice (as with Einstellung effects), or because their assumptions about their business kept them from realizing what was needed. For example, one executive said, "You'll do [strategic planning] as often as you need it," but immediately added that he sets a half-year time period within which he will not change directions. The excerpt that follows is from his description of his company's decision to shift its identity to a new product area, in order to improve its market valuation:

> Q: Did you decide that as soon as you talked to the financial analysts?
>
> No—it doesn't *happen* that way! (laughs) . . . After . . . collecting this data for the *first* half of the year, [we had] strategic review meetings [in the summer. That's when we said] well, let's—reset the direction for the business. . . . Just *shift* the direction of the company. . . . You'll do [strategic planning] I guess, as frequently as you need it, but—once you change the direction, you've got to give it six months or more before you can say, well, you know—"that didn't work, I've gotta try something else."

A second CEO's description of his company's response to a series of product failures illustrates that even serious, repeated problems can be persistently misdiagnosed for long periods of time. Until a temporal milestone gave this company the opportunity to redefine its product at a deep-structure level, the problems were seen as peripheral to the business:

> Six months ago, we had "tacky engineering problems," and we treated 'em [as such], not as a concept change. And we made a couple of bad errors. . . . We *patched* it. . . . [Our yearly] offsite session was almost all strategy . . . and in that session I think we came to grips with . . . these issues. . . . We all *understood* [that the product must include linkage systems]. Now we have strategic statements and technical statements and cost quotes . . . we can put it into effect. . . . We're in a different business today than we were six months ago.

Most likely, as Tushman and Romanelli (1985) suggested, the older the organization and the longer the executive team's tenure, the less often such milestones can break equilibrium and allow for changes of this magnitude. However, Levinson's research does show that individuals, at least, make far-reaching changes within time scales much grander than those of project groups or start-up organizations. The midlife transition, for example, is an often deeply wrenching shift, made near age forty, at the halfway point within the temporal context of an individual's whole expected life span.

Tushman and his associates (Tushman and Romanelli, 1985; Tushman et al., 1986) have stressed the importance of organizational leaders in managing reorientations. They reported that a small percentage of top executives do initiate reorientations without waiting for serious decline, without having to be replaced, and most important, with better results than executives hired in from outside. It is conceivable that, for some of those leaders, critical milestones in adult development, or in their long-range plans for their companies, coincide with important environmental shifts, thus priming them for revolutionary change in ways that elude others.

This section of the chapter has dealt with triggers of revolutionary periods: conditions that break a system's inertia and thereby allow revolutions to begin. According to Kuhn and Tushman and Romanelli, a system's members usually are unable to do this. When internal and/or external events make a system's deep structure obsolete, it usually takes a crisis, and the subsequent attraction of newcomers, to intervene and end equilibrium periods. In contrast, Levinson and Gersick suggested that when system members feel they have time limits, they set temporal boundaries determining when equilibrium periods will end, at which points they initiate their own transitions.

The contrast between these scenarios suggests the value of research to explore (1) whether temporal mechanisms are involved in the few cases where incumbents in organizations initiate their own reorientations and (2) whether there are ways, besides waiting for temporal milestones or replacing executives, to help organizational systems close equilibrium periods when revolutionary change is needed.

How Do Systems Function During Revolutionary Periods?

During equilibrium periods, organizational systems may make incremental changes because members want to try something new. This is not the case for change of revolutionary dimensions. System members do not begin revolutionary periods because they have a specific new idea to try, but because their equilibrium has been broken. Since they are no longer directed by their old deep structures, and do not yet have future directions, system members experience uncertainty, often accompanied by powerful feelings. This section of the chapter begins with the role of emotion in transition dynamics and moves to the related issues of environmental contact, cognition, and the dispersal of transitional changes throughout the system. Although transitions' outcomes are inherently unpredictable, the following points suggest some ways that future research might increase our chances to manage them well.

The Role of Emotion. Even in project groups of one hour's duration, the perception that a transition is imminent can pack a punch: "Once it passes the halfway point, that's when the panic sets in" (group member, quoted in Gersick, 1989, 287). Levinson (1978, 86) discovered that transitions in adults' lives are often profound crises. Feeling suspended and directionless, people fear "chaos, dissolution, [and] loss." Yet, he reported, transitions are also occasions for hope and anticipation of a better future. Tushman et al. (1986, 32) described organizational reorientations as inescapably risky and "painful to participants," yet potentially exhilarating, too. Evidence from the theories examined here suggests that emotion is more than an incidental by-product of transition dynamics; it often plays an important motivational role.

For example, the direct observation of project groups reveals a particular interplay of emotions and actions during successful transitions. In groups that move ahead at their transitions, the jolt of urgency registered at the midpoint usually includes enough fear of not finishing to help members complete agendas that have been productive, drop agendas that have not, and, at least temporarily, suspend power struggles. Although the choice of the midpoint (or some other milestone) may be calculated, part of its power to stop a group's equilibrium may well lie in the emotions people feel upon reaching it: research shows that strong negative emotion "interrupts . . . the normal program of behavior" (Isen, 1984, 180).

At the same time, such groups appear to feel enough optimism to initiate fresh search activities and to move forward on the basis of new ideas. Optimism is important because, as Kuhn (1970) and Tushman and Romanelli (1985) stressed, there is no way to prove, during a revolutionary period, that an idea will succeed. At inception, the central premises of a new paradigm or new strategic configuration are necessarily untested; their merit can only be demonstrated as the system rebuilds around them in the equilibrium period to come.

Kuhn further proposed that, among ideas competing to provide new scientific paradigms, the choice may ultimately rest on aesthetic appeal; an idea must feel right, at least to a small group, who will then risk investing the energy to pursue it. Tushman et al. (1986) discussed the importance of top executives' abilities to inspire confidence and enthusiasm for the new direction. Without an adequate combination of urgency and optimism, organizational systems at transition points may cling to old patterns, even while they clearly recognize the need to change, or they may simply quit. This hypothesis suggests the value of research on the effects of combined negative and positive emotions on performance, in situations calling for punctuational changes or turnarounds.

Environmental Contact. Urgency and optimism may also be important to another phenomenon that is often critical to transition dynamics: the influence of outsiders. Levinson (1978, 109) discussed important roles played by "transitional figures." These are people with whom adults in transition form special relationships, from whom they gain encouragement and learn new ways to live and work. Gersick (1988) found a similar occurrence of special interaction between project groups in transition and their external supervisors. Over half of the naturally occurring teams observed actively sought outside assistance during transition periods, partly to get help making choices and moving forward, and partly to check external requirements and increase the chances that their products would succeed in their environments. Previously this article reviewed the key role played by outsiders who are attracted or recruited to solve revolutionary crises in scientific disciplines and in organizations. Eisenhardt's (1989) research, showing the importance of a "trusted advisor" in helping organizations make major decisions fast and effectively, suggests transitional figures may also be critical in organizational reorientations where top executives remain in place.

The cognitive confusion and emotional distress of revolutionary periods may propel systems to seek outside help or to be especially receptive to outside influence at that time. The benefits provided by outsiders may include new cognitive perspectives, fresh awareness about the environment, and an energizing reassurance. Research on the role of outside advisors, and the effects of contrasting emotions in both help-seeking and help-providing behavior, may have important implications for the management of organizational transitions.

Cognition and the Dynamics of Insight. There is a moment that can be directly observed in project groups (Gersick, 1989), and occasionally documented in scientific disciplines (e.g., Gould, 1977), when a system in transition turns from confusion toward clarity. The system pivots on the insight around which a new deep structure will crystallize. It is clear that the articulation of a new vision is also central to organizational reorientation (Tushman and Romanelli, 1985). The six models examined here suggest several facets of this complex phenomenon.

Kuhn and Prigogine and his colleagues emphasize the unpredictability of a system in transition. Kuhn (1970) noted that perception is a subjective phenomenon: there is always more than one plausible way to interpret reality. Prigogine and Stengers (1984, 176) pointed to the objective unpredictability of the transition system itself, stating that it may follow "a number of equally possible paths," the choice of which will depend on a random fluctuation. In marked contrast to the relative predictability of equilibrium conditions, neither the mechanics of human cognition or the system itself absolutely "dictates" the outcome of a transition.

The situation, in line with the thinking of these theorists, is something like an Escher print: it incorporates several pictures simultaneously, none of which system members can distinguish as the transition begins. Prigogine's colleague Haken referred to this as *symmetry,* and he referred to the event that resolves it as *symmetry breaking:*

> Symmetry breaking is a wide-spread . . . behavior of complex systems, including the human brain. [For example] taking the black features [of an Escher graphic] as foreground, we recognize devils, whereas the white features as foreground let us see angels. . . . Pattern recognition can often be viewed as a sequence of symmetry-breaking events, in which at each branching point new information is needed to break the symmetry [and] make a unique decision possible [Haken, 1981, 19].

The construct of symmetry breaking helps researchers to understand the dawn of insight during transitions. Given a piece of information that provides a new way to look at it, a confusing puzzle can resolve into a coherent picture seemingly instantly. During the very swift transitions that can occur in project groups, this metaphor fits people's experience of things "falling into place." In more complex transitions, Kuhn and Gould offered intriguingly similar descriptions of the revolutionary turn toward a new structure beginning with a "keystone" (Kuhn, 1970, 56) or "key adaptation" (Gould, 1980, 191). In these cases, the new direction does not emerge all at once; instead, a catalytic change opens the door to it. Kuhn described critical insights that sometimes show the way to novel paths of investigation, leading to new paradigms. Gould described initial mutations that thrust a group of organisms into a new mode of life, thereby subjecting them to novel selective pressures, which then work toward full emergence of the new species.

Note that this model of insight formation illuminates some critical differences between the punctuated equilibrium paradigm and traditional universal-stage models of system evolution. First, systems' particular histories matter, because histories determine the unique array of information and conditions from which system members can select their new direction—the jumping-off place for the transition (Prigogine and Stengers, 1984). Second, systems' futures are unpredictable: the information used to "break the symmetry" of the transition period may come from a random environmental event or circumstance. These aspects of transitions both inject chance into the development process and explain how systems can adapt to entirely new features in their environments, rather than merely following their own teleology.

In the first section of the chapter, I described the relative speed with which transitions unfold and offered some general explanations for it. Why should people find insight quickly during transitions? The sheer urgency and discomfort of being without a functioning structure lend intensity to the search for new solutions. The dismantling of the old deep structure frees system members to search for symmetry-breaking information in new fields and to perceive material that they already knew in new ways. Further, as Tushman and his colleagues (1986) pointed out, an organization in transition is unstable on a number of fronts. If a new order does not take control relatively quickly, numerous vested interests may pull it toward its old structure; transition periods may end quickly by default.

A final contributor to the swift development of insight during transitions may have to do with the effects of time-awareness on perception. In their article on managerial problem solving and social cognition, Kiesler and Sproull (1982) noted that individuals automatically and continuously notice time and segment streams of stimuli into coherent units. The fineness of this segmentation and, thus, the level of abstraction and detail that is perceived changes automatically, in predictable ways. For example, experts segment events less finely and, thus, see "whole pictures"; conditions of uncertainty lead people to segment events much more finely, as they comb their surroundings for information.

Automatic changes in segmentation may be very important in the development of insight during transitions, especially transitions stimulated by temporal milestones. As system members perceive one era of their time to have closed and another era to have opened before them, their segmentation of the past and distant future should broaden. As those periods resolve into coherent blocks, system members' vision may shift suddenly from the trees to the forest. In project teams, this can be seen in members' characteristic transition summaries of what they have been doing and what is most important about where they need to go (Gersick, 1989). Simultaneously, the uncertainty of the transition may cause system members to segment the information that is *immediately* before them more finely. With that kind of search, according to Kiesler and Sproull, choices are made more rapidly.

The formation of insight is an important part of revolutionary periods in human systems. The dynamics of this process should be fertile soil for research on how to understand and foster the kind of divergent thinking that is critical for creative problem solving in general.

The Dispersal of Revolutionary Change Through the System. As Prigogine and Stengers noted (1984, 187), no one change can convert an entire system instantaneously. They portray reorganizations as beginning with a "nucleus," where the change must first become established firmly before it can take over the rest of the system. Furthermore, they reported that the more efficient a system's communication mechanisms are, the stronger and larger the nucleus must be if it is to result in a systemwide change, instead of being damped by its surroundings. Eldredge and Gould (1972) hypothesized similarly that speciation must begin rapidly and in populations that are small enough and isolated enough for the change to take hold, in order to avoid being diluted by the parent population.

It is intriguing to compare these ideas with the importance accorded top-executive teams in the work of Tushman and his colleagues. They proposed that, although convergent change during equilibrium periods can be managed through broad participation, top teams are the only instigators strong enough to mount successful reorientations (Tushman et al., 1986). It may be fruitful to explore whether executive teams who lead reorientations experience or seek isolation (either physical or social) from their own organizations, so that they can formulate changes and develop commitment to new directions.

How Do Revolutionary Periods Conclude?

It is essential to distinguish firmly between the *processes* of change in revolutionary periods and their *outcomes*—the new deep structures they bring about. One reason for this separation is that the substantive changes with which revolutionary periods conclude may differ widely in type, success, and scope. For example, Tushman and Romanelli (1985, 173, 179) found that *reorientations*, where "strategies, power, structure and systems" change, are less radical than *recreations,* where the "core values which govern decision premises" are also transformed. Levinson (1978) reported that transitions from one great era in life to the next (e.g., the age forty transition, between the eras of early and middle adulthood) are broader in magnitude than within-era transitions (e.g., at ages thirty and fifty). The group transitions that Gersick observed correspond to the milder kind of revolutions because they were contained within projects; more difficult revolutions must bridge wider gaps, as when one major project ends and another must be initiated.

Revolutionary periods may also vary in how much they benefit or harm a system. Levinson, Gersick, and Tushman and his colleagues all observed that a system may change significantly for the worse during a transition. This is consistent with the punctuated equilibrium paradigm's implication that systems do not inevitably evolve toward improvement.

Apart from the issues noted above, findings in two of the models examined here suggest that there are good reasons to keep revolutionary periods conceptually separate from revolutionary changes themselves. Levinson and Gersick have observed that a system may go through a clear, time-limited transition period, experiencing many of the unsettling processes described earlier, yet it can emerge at the end without having accomplished revisions in its deep structure. Both authors suggested that systems may undergo only mild change if their deep structures need little adjustment at the time the transition occurs. However, when system members back away from change "because of resignation, inertia, passivity, or despair" (Levinson, 1978, 52), the closing of the transitional opportunity often brings a sense of failure or stagnation. This emotional tone, and the absence of needed alterations, are likely to result in a period of persisting decline, lasting until the next transition or beyond (Gersick, 1989; Levinson, 1978).

These two models differ from that of Tushman and his colleagues, who define reorientations in terms of the changes themselves. According to Gersick's and Levinson's findings, systems that have undergone unsuccessful or abortive transitions are, indeed, different after revolutionary periods because they are weakened; however, such transitions would be invisible to researchers who are looking for new strategies or structures. The difference in Tushman and his colleague's definition of the construct may be a methodological artifact. Their use of historical archives to identify organizational reorientations, although offering the considerable advantage of access to larger samples, would seldom permit researchers a view of transition *processes* or of abortive transitions.

This issue has implications for practice and research and suggests the value of identifying organizational-level indicators that transition periods are under way. Only by separating the construct of a revolutionary period from accomplished changes is it possible to locate and study systems as they undergo transitions, when intervention may be most important, rather than waiting until the changes are complete.

DISCUSSION

The punctuated equilibrium paradigm offers a new lens through which theorists can make fresh discoveries about how managers, work groups, organizations, and industries both develop over time and react to changes in their environments. The construct of a deep structure that keeps systems basically stable during equilibrium periods offers a new way to understand systems' resistance to change. The idea that major change occurs through difficult, compact revolutions provokes interesting research questions and indicates the practical demands of adaptation to severe alterations in a system's environment or in its own growth. The emergence of the same paradigm in diverse fields has implications for theory and research methodology.

Methodological Implications

Methodological differences may account for some of the variety in different theorists' findings, and different methods may be needed to answer different questions. Levinson used intensive biographical interviews, which afforded him (1) the panoramic views of people's lives needed to place specific events within broad eras of continuity and change and (2) the intimate detail needed to create a rich portrait of the human experience of building structures and undergoing transitions. Turnover would present obstacles to using this technique at the organizational level. However, in those key organizations that kept their executive teams through reorientation periods, this type of interviewing would be invaluable for understanding the dynamics involved.

Gersick worked with more short-lived systems than individuals or organizations. The observation of project groups' entire life spans offered opportunities to study equilibrium and transition processes directly. The finding that transitions can be observed in brief laboratory simulations means that controlled hypothesis testing about these processes is possible (Gersick, 1989). It is difficult to establish naturalistic conditions in the laboratory, but good organizational simulations do exist (e.g., "Looking Glass," McCall and Lombardo, 1978). Laboratory studies could be especially useful for testing hypotheses on organizational stability and change and for trying intervention strategies.

The collection of documentary histories over very long time periods and for large, diverse samples by Kuhn and Tushman and his colleagues—similar to the study of fossil records by Eldredge and Gould—offers opportunities for insight about the structural conditions under which revolutionary change occurs and succeeds or fails. It affords a view of how revolutionary changes may spread to their surroundings or, in the case of defunct systems, of how they die out. Even though documentary data may be less available for individual and group histories, the work of these researchers suggests the rewards of using archives to study broad sets of structural variables among large samples.

Finally, the complementarity of these six models suggests the need and possibilities for multilevel research. Revolutionary change in large systems ultimately depends on comparably radical change among individuals and groups: conversely, individuals and groups attempting to make radical changes must be affected by the deep structures of the systems in which they are embedded.

Limitations of the Paradigm

There are at least two fundamental cautions to follow in applying the punctuated equilibrium paradigm. The first is to avoid assuming it is the only way systems change. Gould and Eldredge (1977, 19) themselves "never claimed either that gradualism could not occur in theory or did not occur in fact. Nature is far too varied and complex for such absolutes." Wake and his associates (1983) proposed that behavioral plasticity allows organisms to compensate for environmental changes without changing morphologically. In organizations, punctuational patterns may be most evident in systems that have confining deep structures; they may be least evident in highly flexible systems. Existing theory provides us with a ready-made map of how organizational structures vary on this dimension, from bureaucracies (Burns and Stalker, 1961) to clans (Ouchi and Price, 1978) and to "commitment strategy organizations" (Walton and Hackman, 1986). Weick's (1976) "loosely coupled systems," with their low internal interdependence, may be the least likely to fit the punctuated equilibrium paradigm.

The second caution is to avoid applying models from one research domain to another too freely or literally. Human systems, self-aware and goal-directed, have the capacity to "schedule" their own opportunities for revolutionary change (as with time-triggered transitions), to solicit outside perspectives, and to manage their histories in ways that are inconceivable for nonconscious systems. As much as theories from different domains have to offer each other, it would be a mistake to import constructs uncritically, rather than to use them to provoke questions about how they might apply in other settings.

Grand Theory

I have suggested specific research implications of each model examined here for the others. However, the most important implications of the punctuated equilibrium paradigm are suggested by the very diversity of the fields that have been affected by it. Scientists' assumptions about what change is and how it works must fundamentally influence how research is designed and how findings are interpreted. The punctuated equilibrium paradigm suggests three basic questions that can be asked of almost any model or set of findings: Do these data reflect a system in equilibrium or in transition? Do they depend on characteristics inherent in the system's parts, or in the deep structure that organizes them? How far can these conclusions be expected to hold, should the system undergo radical change?

Prigogine and Stengers (1984, 207; see Table 12.2), writing from the vantage point of physics, have argued that traditional deterministic paradigms have had "particularly unfortunate" effects on the social sciences. According to these authors, the search for optimizing, predictive trajectories that can be extrapolated to infinity is misguided because such approaches account neither for the extremes to which inertia may drive a system nor for the unpredictability of radical changes that rewrite the rules of the game. Finally, as Gould (1985) noted, efforts to unravel a system's workings by minutely dissecting its parts miss the point when the parts' behavior is determined by the deep structure that organizes them.

For organizational researchers and practitioners, there is the added challenge to the beliefs about how organizational systems can accomplish (or be helped to accomplish) change. On the one hand, the punctuated equilibrium paradigm proposes that fundamental change cannot be accomplished piecemeal, slowly, gradually, and comfortably. On the other hand, it holds promise that we may someday create new organizational forms that have not yet been impaired.

References

Abernathy, W., & Utterback, J. 1982. Patterns of industrial innovation. In M. Tushman & W. Moore (Eds.), *Readings in the management of innovation*, 97–108. Boston, MA: Pitman.

Burns, T., & Stalker, G. M. 1961. *The management of innovation*. London: Tavistock.

Chomsky, N. 1966. *Cartesian linguistics: A chapter in the history of rationalist thought*. New York: Harper & Row.

Deal, T. 1985. Cultural change: Opportunity, silent killer, or metamorphosis? In R. Kilmann, M. Saxton, & Roy Serpa (Eds.), *Gaining control of the corporate culture*, 292–331. San Francisco: Jossey-Bass.

Eisenhardt, K. M. 1989. Making fast strategic decisions in high velocity environments. *Academy of Management Journal*, 32, 543–576.

Eisenhardt, K. M., & Schoonhoven, C. B. 1990. Organizational growth: Linking founding team, strategy, environment and growth among U.S. semiconductor ventures (1978–1988). *Administrative Science Quarterly*, 35, 504–529.

Eldredge, N., & Gould, S. 1972. Punctuated equilibria: An alternative to phyletic gradualism. In T. J. Schopf (Ed.), *Models in paleobiology*, 82–115. San Francisco: Freeman, Cooper.

Ericsson, K. A., & Simon, H. A. 1984. *Protocol analysis: Verbal reports as data*. Cambridge, MA: MIT Press.

Gersick, C.J.G. 1988. Time and transition in work teams: Toward a new model of group development. *Academy of Management Journal*, 31, 9–41.

Gersick, C.J.G. 1989. Marking time: Predictable transitions in task groups. *Academy of Management Journal*, 32, 274–309.

Gersick, C.J.G., & Davis, M. D. 1990. Summary: Task forces. In J. R. Hackman (Ed.), *Groups that work (and those that don't): Creating conditions for effective teamwork*, 146–153. San Francisco: Jossey-Bass.

Gersick, C.J.G., & Hackman, J. R. 1990. Habitual routines in task-performing groups. *Organizational Behavior and Human Decision Processes*, 47, 65–97.

Ginnett, R. C. 1987. *First encounters of the close kind: The formation process of airline flight crews*. Unpublished doctoral dissertation. New Haven, CT: Yale University.

Gladstein, D. L., & Reilly, N. P. 1985. Group decision making under threat: The tycoon game. *Academy of Management Journal*, 28, 613–627.

Gould, S. J. 1977. Darwin's delay. In S. J. Gould, *Ever since Darwin*. New York: Norton.

Gould, S. J. 1980. *The panda's thumb*. New York: Norton.

Gould, S. J. 1983. *Hen's teeth and horse's toes*. New York: Norton.

Gould, S. J. 1985. *The flamingo's smile*. New York: Norton.

Gould, S. J. 1989. Punctuated equilibrium in fact and theory. *Journal of Social Biological Structure*, 12, 117–136.

Gould, S. J., & Eldredge, N. 1977. *Paleobiology*, 3, 115–151.

Greenhalgh, L. 1983. Organizational decline. *Research in the sociology of organizations*, vol. 2, 231–276. Greenwich, CT: JAI Press.

Greiner, L. E. 1972. Evolution and revolution as organizations grow. *Harvard Business Review*, 50(4), 3746.

Haken, H. 1981. Synergetics: Is self-organization governed by universal principles? In E. Jantsch (Ed.), *Toward a unifying paradigm of physical, biological, and sociocultural evolution*, 15–23. Boulder, CO: Westview Press.

Halberstam, D. 1986. *The reckoning*. New York: Morrow.

Hannan, M. T., & Freeman, J. 1977. The population ecology of organizations. *American Journal of Sociology*, 88, 929–964.

Hannan, M. T., & Freeman, J. 1984. Structural inertia and organizational change. *American Sociological Review*, 49, 149–164.

Isen, A. 1984. Toward understanding the role of affect in cognition. In R. Wyer & T. Srull (Eds.), *Handbook of social cognition*, vol. 3, 179–236. Hillsdale, NJ: Erlbaum.

Kennedy, P. 1987. *The rise and fall of the great powers*. New York: Random House.

Kiesler, S., & Sproull, L. 1982. Managerial response to changing environments: Perspectives on problem sensing from social cognition. *Administrative Science Quarterly*, 27, 548–570.

Kimberly, J., & Quinn, R. 1984. *New futures: The challenge of managing corporate transitions*. Homewood, IL: Dow Jones-Irwin.

Kuhn, T. S. 1970. *The structure of scientific revolutions* (2nd ed.). Chicago: University of Chicago Press.

Levinson, D. J. 1978. *The seasons of a man's life*. New York: Knopf.

Levinson, D. J. 1986. A conception of adult development. *American Psychologist*, 41, 3–13.

Loye, D., & Eisler, R. 1987. Chaos and transformation: Implications of nonequilibrium theory for social science and society. *Behavioral Science*, 32, 53–65.

Luchins, A. S. 1940. Mechanization in problem solving: The effect of Einstellung. *Psychological Monographs*, 54, 248.

March, J. 1981. Footnotes to organizational change. *Administrative Science Quarterly*, 26, 563–577.

March, J., & Simon, H. A. 1958. *Organizations*. New York: Wiley.

McCall, M. M., & Lombardo, M. M. 1978. *Looking Glass, Inc.: An organizational simulation*. Technical report 12. Greensboro, NC: Center for Creative Leadership.

Miller, D., & Friesen, P. 1984. *Organizations: A quantum view*. Englewood Cliffs, NJ: Prentice-Hall.

Mintzberg, H. 1981. Organization design: Fashion or fit? *Harvard Business Review*, 59(1), 103–116.

Ouchi, W. G., & Price, R. L. 1978. Hierarchics, clans, and Theory Z: A new perspective on organization development. *Organizational Dynamics*, 7(2), 24–44.

Pfeffer, J., & Salancik, G. 1978. *The external control of organizations*. New York: Harper and Row.

Prigogine, I., & Stengers, I. 1984. *Order out of chaos: Man's new dialogue with nature*. New York: Bantam Books.

Seeger, J. A., Lorsch, J. W., & Gibson, C. T. 1974. *First National City Bank operating group*. Cambridge, MA: President and Fellows of Harvard College.

Simon, H. A. 1976. *Administrative behavior* (3rd ed.). New York: Free Press.

Staw, B. M., Sandelands, L. E., & Dutton, J. E. 1981. Threat-rigidity effects in organizational behavior: A multilevel analysis. *Administrative Science Quarterly*, 26, 501–524.

Stinchcombe, A. 1965. Social structure and organizations. In J. March (Ed.), *Handbook of organizations*, 142–193. Chicago: Rand-McNally.

Tuckman, B. 1965. Developmental sequence in small groups. *Psychological Bulletin*, 63, 384–399.

Tushman, M., & Romanelli, E. 1985. Organizational evolution: A metamorphosis model of convergence and reorientation. In L. L. Cummings and B. M. Staw (Eds.), *Research in organizational behavior*, vol. 7, 171–222. Greenwich, CT: JAI Press.

Tushman, M. L., Newman, W. H., & Romanelli, E. 1986. Convergence and upheaval: Managing the unsteady pace of organizational evolution. *California Management Review*, 29(1), 29–44.

Wake, D. B., Roth, G., & Wake, M. H. 1983. On the problem of stasis in organismal evolution. *Journal of Theoretical Biology*, 101, 211–224.

Walton, R. E., & Hackman, J. R. 1986. Groups under contrasting management strategies. In P. S. Goodman (Ed.), *Designing effective work groups*, 168–201. San Francisco: Jossey-Bass.

Weick, K. 1976. Educational organizations as loosely coupled systems. *Administrative Science Quarterly*, 21: 1–19.

Weiss, H., & Ilgen, D. 1985. Routinized behavior in organizations. *Journal of Behavioral Economics*, 14, 57–67.

Williamson, O. 1983. Organizational innovation: The transaction-cost approach. In J. Ronen (Ed.), *Entrepreneurship*, 101–134. Lexington, MA: Heath.

CHAPTER THIRTEEN

Organizational Evolution

A Metamorphosis Model of Convergence and Reorientation

Michael L. Tushman
Elaine Romanelli (1985)

The saga of AT&T is but one example of the complexities and dynamics of organization evolution. This chapter builds on several literatures to increase our understanding of organizational evolution. The challenge to understand organizational evolution is not new. Weber (1952) and Merton (1968) postulated a near-irreversible momentum of increasing bureaucratization and goal-displacement, while Blau (1963) found evidence of bureaucratic flexibility and goal-succession. Shumpeter (1934) argued that organizations become ever more stable until replaced during "gales of creative destruction" (p. 87), while Chandler (1962) focused on heroic executives radically transforming their organizations as environmental conditions changed. Despite this long history of thought and debate, basic questions remain. We know relatively little about the nature and characteristics of organizational evolution, and even less about how patterns in organization evolution discriminate between those few organizations that prosper over time, and the majority that fail.

Partial redress of these weaknesses is evidenced in the intensifying interest in evolutionary or life-cycle aspects of organizational phenomena. First articulated by Starbuck (1965) and recently reemphasized by Aldrich and Pfeffer (1976), Kimberly and Miles (1980), and Child and Kieser (1981), the call for longitudinal, historical perspectives stems (1) from a pervasive dissatisfaction with static, cross-sectional views of organizations that illuminate covariant attributes to organizations, but tell little of the impact of history and precedent on current organization behavior; and (2) from simple curiosity for answers to such questions as, "How and why did this firm evolve? Why did certain firms succeed while others did not?"

Three fundamentally different organization evolution frameworks have been proposed. Ecological models emphasize change across populations of organizations as the result of net mortality driven by processes of environmental selection (Freeman, 1982; Hannan and Freeman, 1977). Adaptation models emphasize incremental change and moving equilibria as more effective organizations adapt to environmental threats and opportunities (Katz and Kahn, 1966; March and Simon, 1958; Quinn, 1981). Transformational models focus on metamorphic changes in organizations; organizations evolve through a series of fundamentally different periods or stages. Although much of this transformational literature postulates a predictable set of developmental stages (e.g., Greiner, 1972; Normann, 1977; Quinn and Cameron, 1983), others argue for nondeterministic patterns in the transformation of organizations (Filley and Aldag, 1980; Mintzberg and Waters, 1982). What remains lacking is a general theory of organization evolution that reconciles salient points of each of these three perspectives; a theory that examines both internal and external sources of organization inertia and change, and that recognizes the relative impacts of executive leadership on organization behavior over time.

This chapter develops a model of organization evolution that integrates these distinct evolutionary perspectives. We propose a *punctuated equilibrium* model of organization evolution. Organizations progress through *convergent* periods punctuated by *reorientations* that demark and set bearings for the next convergent period. Convergent periods refer to relatively long time spans of incremental change and adaptation that elaborate structures, systems, controls, and resources towards increased coalignment. These convergent periods may or may not be associated with effective performance. Reorientations are relatively short periods of discontinuous change where strategies, power, structure, and systems are fundamentally transformed towards a new basis of alignment. Where middle-level management interpolates structures and systems during convergent periods, *executive leadership* mediates between internal and institutional forces for inertia and competitive forces for fundamental change. It is executive leadership that initiates, shapes, and directs strategic reorientations.

The following sections elaborate these ideas and incorporate literature from multiple perspectives to clarify and support our model. Section One presents, with very little literature review, the basic ideas, terms, and logic of our organization evolution model. Sections Two through Four review literatures pertaining to convergence and inertia, forces for reorientation and metamorphic change, and the role of executive leadership in mediating these opposing forces for change and stability. Propositions are presented that formalize the basic ideas of our model. We conclude with a brief discussion of research, theoretical, and methodological implications of our punctuated equilibrium model of organization evolution.

I. CONVERGENCE AND REORIENTATION: A METAMORPHOSIS MODEL

Valuing of consistency that leads to competence;
the valuing of inconsistency that leads to learning; and both
that lead to increased effectiveness.
—Argyris and Schon, 1978

Our model of organization evolution is characterized by three defining constructs: (1) processes of *convergence* which operate, through incremental change mechanisms, to align and make consistent the complex of sociopolitical and technical-economic activities that support a firm's overall strategic orientation; (2) periods of *reorientation*, wherein patterns of consistency are fundamentally reordered toward a new basis of alignment; and (3) *executive leadership*, which serves as the key mechanism of intervention. This section presents an overview of the meaning of these constructs and the fundamental logic of our model.

Strategic Orientation, Consistency, and Convergence

The logical starting point for a model of organization evolution is the inception of a new firm. Through selective perceptions by founders of constraints and opportunities in the environment, basic decisions are made regarding what business the firm is in and how it will compete (Newman and Yavitz, 1983). Decisions regarding products, markets served, and normative postures regarding technology (i.e., technology leader vs. follower), human resources, and/or competitive timing (i.e., me-first vs. me-too) define a firm's strategic orientation. For example, where many firms produce similar products to similar market segments, some firms will be first-movers while others will consistently be followers (Miles, 1982; Miles and Snow, 1978).

A complex set of economic and political/social behaviors and activities are required to support a firm's strategic orientation (Zald, 1970). As economic entities, organizations must be *effective* and *efficient*. Organizations must be effective in producing a product or service that is desired by an external economy such that a flow of resources is maintained, and efficient with respect to internal resource utilization (Katz and Kahn, 1967). Organizations are also social/political entities. Organizations require *external legitimation* such that the firm's right to exist and mode of operation is not challenged. Organizations

Table 13.1. Political Economy, Activity Domains, and Organizing Decisions.

	External Structures and Processes	Internal Structures and Processes
Polity	GOAL: External legitimation	GOAL: Internal legitimation
	• Imposition/acceptance of social, legal, competitive values	• Establishment of core values and decision premises
	• Development of role in local and larger society	• Development of commitments, beliefs, myths
	• Establishment of position with regulatory agencies	• Development of influence and power relations
Economy	GOAL: Effectiveness	GOAL: Efficiency
	• Product, market, technology, competitive timing decisions	• Choice of structure
	• Acquisition of resources	• Development of reward, control, and incentive systems
		• Recruiting, selection practices

also require *internal legitimation* from participants such that continuity of personnel and behavior cycles are sustained. Table 13.1 summarizes major categories of behaviors and activities as they correspond to this political-economy approach.

On the basis of this political-economy framework, we propose that the following five activity domains are critical, if not exhaustive, in characterizing organizations as they pursue a strategic orientation. (1) *Core values and beliefs* set constraints as to where, how, and why a firm competes. (2) Business unit *strategy* defines the nature of products produced and markets served and establishes general time and technological constraints. (3) Intraorganization *power distributions* control the allocation of scarce resources. (4) The organization's fundamental *structure* formalizes hierarchy, role relations, and competitive emphases. (5) The nature, type, and pervasiveness of *control systems* indicate a firm's emphasis on efficiency.

These activity domains fall into a hierarchy corresponding to how pervasively they affect premises of decisions. A firm's core values are the most pervasive aspect of organizations in that they set basic constraints as to where, how, and why a firm competes. Given core values, decisions on products, markets, technology, and timing define a firm's competitive domain. Core values and domain decisions set the basic premises of decisions within the firm. These premises constrain and shape the distribution of power and the allocation of scarce resources, which, in turn, constrain choices of structures and control systems. This hierarchy also suggests a degree of coupling between activity domains. Changes in core values will be associated with cascading effects in strategy, power, structure, and controls. On the other hand, changes in control systems will be only weakly coupled with changes in structure, power, or strategy.

These activity domains individually, and as they interrelate with one another, constitute the organizational "working out" of a strategic orientation. Although this strategic orientation is imposed, or intended, in the first place by organization founders, subsequent strategic orientations may develop as a consequence of unintended or emergent interactions among the activity sets themselves (Mintzberg, 1973).

Definition 1: *Strategic orientation* is defined in terms of what business the firm is in and how it competes. This strategic orientation sets the bearing of organization activities and may vary in the degree to which it is explicit.

Though a firm's strategic orientation may or may not be explicit, it can be *described* by the set of organization activities: (1) core beliefs and values regarding the organization, its employees, and its environment; (2) products, markets, technology, and competitive timing; (3) the distribution of power; (4) the organization's structure; and (5) the nature, type, and pervasiveness of control systems.

Strategic orientation is a concept critical to our notion of convergence. It answers the question, What is it that is being converged upon? It does not, in and of itself, induce convergence. Convergence is a process that derives from socially emergent inertial dynamics and from "rational" attempts, given a strategic orientation, to accomplish the multiple constraints of organizations as political-economic systems. Whereas a strategic orientation may not be explicit, it can be described by patterns in core organization activities. For example, early Bell Telephone sold nonbusiness telephonic communication to local markets through a loosely structured organization whose core values centered on flexibility, research, and innovation. This strategic orientation was reaccomplished until after the Western Union–Bell patent agreement of 1879 when, under new ownership and management, Bell Telephone became American Bell. American Bell embarked on a fundamentally different strategic orientation emphasizing universal, low-cost service as core values delivered through a vertically integrated and highly formalized structure. This latter convergence period was continuously developed through the mid-1970s.

The core activity domains (see Table 13.1) individually and as they interrelate with one another result in differing levels of performance and inertia that are, in turn, basic factors affecting organization evolution. Behaviors and decisions in each of the four activity domains must be successfully attended to in order that the organization (a) survive, and (b) outperform competitors. Inconsistent or inappropriate activities, within any of the activity domains, will be associated with lower performance and/or failure. For example, Sears' insistence on maintaining a low-cost, "good value to the masses" product orientation in the 1950s and 1960s in the face of changing demand for more fashionable goods provided by the posh suburban shopping malls resulted in a recalcitrant low sales performance (Stryker, 1961).

In addition to successfully addressing requirements of political and economic domains independently, activities must also be consistent or coupled with each other to achieve high performance. An organization that is effective, efficient, and meaningful for its participants, but that fails to achieve an autonomy of operations, may bear the brunt of sanctions imposed by the external polity such that all operations become difficult to perform (e.g., Reverend Moon's Unification Church). Conversely, an organization such as W. T. Grant was arguably meaningful for its participants, effective in its provision of desired products to a well defined market, and certainly not in violation of social or industry norms, yet failed in its ability to achieve an efficiency of operations such that all activities were ceased. AT&T, on the other hand, achieved a consistency between external polities and effectiveness and internal polities and efficiency such that it flourished through the 1970s.

Performance, then, is a consequence *both* of appropriate activities with respect to political and economic requirements *and* of achieving consistencies in and among organization activities. Consistency within and between activity domains is not synonymous with high performance. Organizations may converge with a high degree of consistency on a strategic orientation and yet be totally oblivious to environmental demands (e.g., American automobile firms in the 1970s). Conversely, appropriate strategic orientations can be ineffectively accomplished within the firm.

In addition to performance, organization-environment and intraorganizational consistencies are associated with a second important organizational outcome, the development of a structural and socially anchored inertia. As webs of interdependent relationships with buyers, suppliers, and financial backers strengthen, and as commitments to internal participants and external evaluating agents are elaborated into institutionalized patterns of culture, norms, and ideologies, the organization develops inertia, a resistance to all but incremental change. These emergent social and structural processes facilitate convergence on a strategic orientation through the enforcement of rules and norms that constrain the premises of participants' behaviors. A high degree of competence in executing a strategic orientation may thus be developed. These convergent social and structural processes also, however, begin to impede (although *not* preclude) a firm's ability to (1) reassess environmental opportunities and constraints, and thus to initiate a strategic reorientation; and (2) even given such a reassessment, substantially disrupt the networks of interdependent resource relationships and value commitments toward implementation of a new strategic orientation. For example, the very structures, values, and systems that were so successful for AT&T from the early twentieth century through to the 1970s provide for considerable resistance in the organization's attempt to reform itself toward alignment with an increasingly competitive environment.

> Definition 2: *Convergence* is defined as a process of incremental and interdependent change activities and decisions that work to achieve a greater consistency of internal activities with a strategic orientation, and that operate to impede radical or discontinuous change.

Forces for Change and Reorientation

Despite the inertial properties of convergent periods, it is a fundamental premise of our model that organizations can and do undergo radical transformations of strategic orientations and supporting values, power systems, formal structures, and controls. To the extent that incremental modifications to values, strategies, power systems, structure, and controls fail to maintain consistencies (or to establish them in the first place), the organization will fail to achieve a sustainable level of performance, and be forced to a fundamental reordering of activities. We term this reordering a reorientation and suggest two basic forces for change: (1) sustained low performance resulting from a lack of consistency among activities in the four political-economy domains, regardless of the appropriateness of overall strategic orientation; and (2) major changes in competitive, technological, social, and legal conditions of the environment that render a prior strategic orientation, regardless of its success, no longer effective.

Organizations may converge on a strategic orientation that may or may not be consistent with environmental requirements. Under conditions where an organization fails to achieve consistency, whether with respect to the overall orientation-environment fit or with respect to lack of alignment between activities supporting the strategic orientation, low performance or early failure will result. Sustained low performance leads to either failure or crisis associated with a fundamental reordering of activities and/or restatement of strategic orientation that will lead to a transformation of supporting activities.

Competitive conditions change as a product class evolves. Critical strategic contingencies shift over the course of a product class life cycle. Those strategic orientations appropriate early in a product class will not be appropriate as the product class matures. Further, exogenous shocks may also transform competitive conditions (e.g., legal events, substitute technologies). These changes may be anticipated and a transformation of activities initiated in order to ensure alignment with a new or coming environmental context; they may be ignored until recognition is forced through performance declines resulting from lack of orientation-environment fit. Performance pressures, then, whether anticipated or actual, are the most basic forces for reorientation.

Definition 3: *Reorientations* are defined by simultaneous and discontinuous shifts in strategy (defined by products, markets, and/or technology), the distribution of power, the firm's core structure, and the nature and pervasiveness of control systems. *Re-creations* are reorientations that also involve a discontinuous shift in the firm's core values and beliefs.

Definition 4: *Convergent periods* are demarked by strategic reorientations (or re-creations). Convergent periods can be characterized by (1) duration, (2) strategic orientation, (3) turbulence (rates of change in strategy, power, structure, and controls).

Reorientations involve a series of rapid and discontinuous change in the organization that fundamentally alters its character and fabric. Quite distinct from incremental change, reorientations involve simultaneous and discontinuous changes in strategies, power distributions, structures, and control systems. Reorientations that also involve discontinuous change in core values that govern decision premises, termed re-creations, represent the most radical form of reorientation. Reorientations and/or re-creations define the end of one convergent period and usher in the next. Reorientations (or re-creations) punctuate ongoing processes of convergence.

Figure 13.1 diagrams the hierarchical relationships among activity domains that define reorientation and re-creation. Examples illuminate this distinction and demonstrate the hierarchical relationship among activities. Monsanto's diversification into specialty chemicals and bioengineering represents a strategic *reorientation* involving rapid and discontinuous changes in products and markets served, distribution of power and resources within the firm, and fundamental changes in structure and controls. Through this period, Monsanto's core values, anchored in molecular manipulation and orientation towards chemistry, remained stable. Singer, on the other hand, in its diversification into high-technology products and markets has engaged in a *re-creation*. No longer does the company intend to be perceived as a producer of quality sewing machines and furniture. Traditional Singer Sewing values and images,

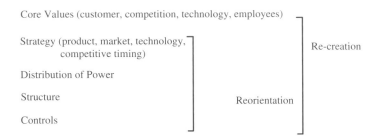

Figure 13.1. A Hierarchy of Organizing Activities.

as well as products and markets serviced, power, structure, and control systems, have been fundamentally altered in rapid order.

Organization evolution is, then, composed of sets of convergent periods punctuated by strategic reorientations (or re-creations). After the founding convergent period, each successive period is affected by prior convergent periods. Precedent and prior commitments do not simply cease when the firm attempts to reorient. Rather, history, in terms of the understandings and interpretations of previous convergent periods and reorientation crises, provides the context within which current reorientations and convergent periods operate.

Executive Leadership

Forces for convergence and reorientation are at odds. Where middle and lower-level management can sustain convergent periods under premises of the existing strategic orientation, only executive leadership can mediate between forces for convergence and forces for change and initiate a strategic reorientation. Whatever the nature of the opportunity or crisis, recognition of an actual or potential organization-environment inconsistency and direct intervention on prior convergent processes are required for a reorientation to occur. Direct intervention is required precisely because inertial factors operate to maintain status quo, often in spite of clear dysfunctional consequences. Only executive leadership can initiate and implement the set of discontinuous changes required to affect a strategic reorientation.

Executives' perceptions of opportunities and constraints guide their choice to remain in a convergent period or to initiate a reorientation. These perceptions vary systematically by the executive teams' demographic makeup, by ownership patterns, and by the length of the current convergent period. Because executives themselves, in their personal commitments and interdependences, may be constrained in their perceptions by inertial forces of a convergent period, reorientations (and re-creations) will occur most frequently after a sustained performance decline and will be most frequently initiated by outside successors.

Our model of organization evolution is, then, based on two inherently conflicting forces: internal and institutional pressures for incremental change and inertia, and pressures of low performance that emerge from disalignments (whether anticipated or realized) with environmental requirements. These opposing pressures are mediated by executive leadership, which is, in turn, also affected by convergent forces. As a result of tensions emerging between inertial processes and performance pressures, organizations evolve through relatively long convergent periods punctuated by discontinuous or metamorphic changes that lead to the next convergent period. The nature of reorientation as well as the nature of activities characterizing subsequent convergent periods is increasingly constrained by patterns established during prior periods. These ideas are summarized:

> Patterns of organizational evolution are characterized by periods of convergence
> punctuated by reorientations leading to the next convergent period. These cycles
> are driven by the emergence of tension between organizational and institutional
> forces for inertia and competitive, technological, and legal pressures on
> performance that are mediated by the perceptions and decisions of executive
> leadership.

Figure 13.2 diagrams key relationships to be considered in our analysis of organizational evolution. The following sections review relevant literature toward the development of a set of propositions that define and extend these relationships.

II. CONVERGENT PERIODS AND FORCES FOR INERTIA

Section One introduced strategic orientation as a guiding or directing principle of organizational activity that can be described in terms of decisions and behaviors relating to core values, strategy (in terms of products, markets, and/or technology), power distributions, structures, and control systems. To be successful, a firm's strategic orientation must be consistent with internal and external political and economic environments. A by-product of consistency are webs of interdependencies and commitments that are associated with increased organizational complexity and specialization and, in turn, structural and social rigidities. This section supports and elaborates these ideas. We develop a set of propositions that formalize the basic tenets of the consistency-convergence arguments. We examine convergence with respect to two principle outcomes, performance and inertia, that constitute underlying forces driving evolution.

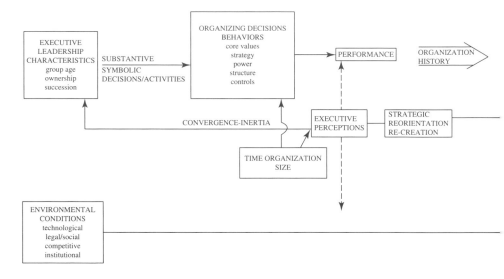

Figure 13.2. Organization Evolution: A Schematic Model.

Consistency, Convergence, and Performance

The idea that organizations pursue consistencies or alignment between patterns of activity and conditions of the external environment, and that these alignments (or lack thereof) contribute to distinct performance consequences, is not new in organization theory. Performance consequences have been examined (1) in terms of overall consistency with the external environment, which largely assumes the existence of internal consistencies; and (2) with respect to internal organizational pursuit of these consistencies. We review, as briefly as possible, the multitude of perspectives that have adopted this position. This large body of research supports the idea that consistency and convergence are basic determinants of organizational performance.

Strategic Orientation and External Consistencies

Population ecology, industrial organization economics, and strategy research each start from the premise that different contexts require different forms and/ or strategies to achieve effective performance. Although assumptions regarding units of analysis, time frames, and leverage of senior management differ, each theoretical approach emphasizes the performance consequences of achieving fit or consistency between environmental demands and organizational states.

Population ecology. Population ecologists (e.g., Carroll and Delacroix, 1982; Hannan and Freeman, 1977) focus on the dynamics of organization existence in terms of the net mortality of populations of firms over time. The unit of analysis is the population of firms that share a like form (e.g., all specialty steel

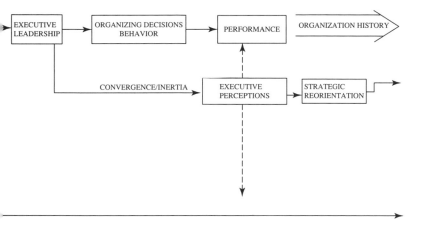

Figure 13.2. continued

firms). These populations inhabit resource niches, where several niches define a community or industry. Each niche may share scarce resources with other competing niches.

The emphasis here is very strictly on the nature of context as determinant of the type or form of organization that may thrive in the context. Organizations are assumed to adopt very early in their lives a basic strategic orientation (i.e., specialist or generalist) toward the general resource space, and, due to webs of dependencies and commitments, to be largely unable to change or reorient that stance. As a resource space is initially perceived and responded to, several orientations may characterize the activity patterns of competing populations. The environment poses a set of key survival characteristics that either fit or do not fit the activity patterns of these orientations. Survival is thus the product of natural selection. Provided the environment remains constant, or at least predictable in its pattern of change, a single form of organization will emerge as dominant in the resource space (Hawley, 1950; Stinchcombe, 1965).

Hannan and Freeman (1977) and their colleagues have thus far developed the concept of niche width as a key dimension of the organization form/environment survival relationship. Depending on whether change in environmental states is large or small and depending on whether these changes occur often or rarely, either specialist or generalist firms will possess optimal survival capability. Research in this tradition has examined the concept in terms of environmental evolution (Brittain and Freeman, 1980), net mortality rates of populations as a function of environmental conditions (Carroll and Delacroix, 1982; Freeman and Hannan, 1983), and birth rates of firms as a function of basic population dynamics (Delacroix and Carroll, 1983). Population ecology presents the most extreme version of consistency between strategic orientation and environmental conditions. Organizations do not evolve as niches change, but are replaced by new firms that are born through entrepreneurial behavior and spin-offs. The role of executive leadership is assumed to be sharply constrained after the firm is born due to severe external and internal constraints.

Industrial organization. The extensive work in industrial organization economics is complementary to the population ecology approach. Industries are the basic unit of analysis and the research paradigm has focused on *context* (e.g., entry and exit barriers, concentration ratios, size distribution of firms, elasticity of demand) and *conduct* (price, advertising levels, innovation, vertical integration), which drive economic *performance* (Baysinger, Meiners, and Zeithamel, 1981; Scherer, 1980). Firms existing in different market/competitive structures develop different configurations of economic activities and decisions to achieve competent performance. For example, Armour and Teece (1978) investigated the evolution of multidivisionalized forms in the petroleum industry and found considerable linkage between M-form structures and performance. Where population ecology focuses on inertial forces in the organization that foreclose mobility, industrial organization economics attends to deterrents to mobility (e.g., switching costs, intangible assets, capital requirements; Harrigan, 1981).

Industries can be mapped into strategic groups, groups of firms that are similar in terms of strategic approach to competitive conditions in an industry (Porter, 1980). Strategic groups face different resource constraints and exhibit different strategic and economic behavior (Hatten, Schendel, and Cooper, 1978). For example, Lenz (1978) identified strategic groups in the savings and loan industry and found that high-performing firms in each strategic group had systematically different structures, processes, and strategies, which were, in turn, consistent with environmental demands.

Porter (1980) suggests that there are three generic strategies that characterize the activity patterns of firms: cost leadership (focus on asset utilization, control, and efficiency), differentiation (focus on uniqueness, quality, and innovation), and focus (emphasis on total exploitation of a narrow market segment). Building on Spence (1979), Porter suggests that each of the strategies are optimal under different sets of competitive conditions and that these map, to some large extent, onto the life cycle patterns of an industry.

Though consistent with ecological approaches, industrial organization research more clearly specifies conduct and context over time and provides greater detail on generic types and their organizational correlates. The role of senior management is considerably expanded. Only partly constrained by historical and mobility barriers, executive leadership chooses in which strategic group to compete and the firm's strategic orientation. These choices may change as industries evolve. Management is considered able to change as industries evolve, and through strategic decisions, to be able to directly affect both strategic and structural characteristics of the firm and structural conditions of an industry (Baysinger et al., 1981). Thus organizations are viewed as capable of evolving.

Strategy. Since Chandler's (1962) seminal work on the evolution of large industrial firms, there has been substantial work on the linkages between contexts, strategy, structure, and performance at the firm level of analysis. Though similar to ecology and industrial organization approaches in its emphasis on these linkages, this research stream has focused much greater attention on managerial behavior and choice, and on the internal organizational characteristics of strategy. Chandler traced the histories of General Motors, DuPont, Sears, and Standard Oil in great detail (and seventy other firms in lesser detail) and found that increased environmental diversity was more effectively handled through divisional structures and their supporting organizational systems. The adoption of these structures, in all cases, was impeded initially due to executive commitments to the status quo, one source of inertia. The studies emphasize also, however, processes by which such inertia is overcome.

This context, strategy-structure hypothesis has stimulated a considerable amount of supporting research. Channon (1973) replicated Chandler's work on the development of the multidivisionalized firm in a European country. Rumelt (1974) has considered different kinds of diversification strategies and demonstrated performance to be associated with the degree of relatedness acquired firms bear to the acquiring organization's dominant competence. This research stream supports the linkage between environmental diversity, strategic choice, structure, and related organizational processes. It also indicates the importance of organizational inertia as an impediment to strategic change and a limit to diversification.

A second strategy research stream explicitly considers internal consistencies as critical to support of the strategic orientation/environment linkage. Miles and Snow (1978), on the basis of case studies of organizations in several distinct industries (textbooks, food processing, hospitals, and electronics), induce four generic strategic types that differ in the nature of their response to environmental conditions. Defenders pursue focused domains through emphasis on efficient operations; prospectors are flexible and innovative, constantly altering orientation according to changing conditions; analyzers operate in multiple domains, each with different approaches; and reactors simply respond as followers to the prevailing concept of industry success.

Miles and Snow (1978) argue that each strategic type is associated with its own set of values, structures, and systems, and that each type develops its own distinctive competence. Further, they argue that these strategic types (except for reactors) are stable systems with appropriate response mechanisms that can be applied even if environments change. As these generic types were hypothesized to be stable and viable under different conditions, Miles and

Snow did not discuss contextual conditions or variability. Miles (1982) and Snow and Hrebiniak (1980) found support for these strategic types and associated distinctive competences. However, Snow and Hrebiniak also found that prospectors were more prevalent and more effective in uncertain industries (e.g., electronics) while defenders were more prevalent and more effective in low-uncertainty industries (e.g., air transport).

A final research stream represents a growing overlap between industrial organization economics and strategic management domains. Strategic contingency literature argues that strategies, structures, and processes must fit industry or strategic group requirements and that these competitive requirements change over time (Hofer, 1975). Hambrick (1983) identified eight distinct subenvironments in mature industrial products industries and found that different strategic types were found to compete in the subenvironments; high-performing firms matched strategic characteristics with contextual demands. Extending this strategic contingency work, Hambrick, MacMillan, and Day (1982) found different performance levels and different strategic characteristics for firms in different cells of the BCG strategy matrix. MacMillan et al. (1982) found that within BCG cells, high-performing firms were those that matched strategic type with contextual demands. These results along with those reported by Snow and Hrebiniak (1980) indicate that it is important to distinguish between strategic groups in an industry and that different strategic groups require different strategies to achieve effective performance. Finally, these several strategy research streams also suggest that organization performance is a function of achieving internal consistency or balance between strategy, structure, processes, and values, *and* achieving an external consistency between a firm's strategy and environmental demands.

STRATEGIC ORIENTATION AND INTERNAL CONSISTENCIES

Where population ecology, industrial organization economics, and strategy research concentrate on organization-external environment relations, organization contingency literature attends to intraorganizational consistencies. This literature concentrates on the development of structures and control systems and the shaping of social and normative pressures to fit strategic/contextual demands.

In essence, the theory posits that choice of basic organizational form, specification of relevant subunits, and distribution of power and control within and between these subunits is driven by strategic organizational contingencies (Galbraith, 1977; Thompson, 1967). High-performing organizations develop specialized units to deal with critical task and environmental contingencies. For example, organizations with severe legal problems develop their own internal legal departments. Those organizations competing in heterogeneous environments develop more complex levels of structural differentiation than those firms competing in homogeneous environments. The relative influence of these different subunits hinges on the extent to which they control critical organizational contingencies (Hinings, Hickson, Pennings, and Schneck, 1974). For example, early in a product class life-cycle, market and technological issues are central, and therefore, marketing and R&D tend to be influential; manufacturing and finance are more powerful as the product class matures and the bases of competition shift to costs and efficiencies (Lawrence and Lorsch, 1967).

Given some general organizational form, different subunits also face systematically different technological and/or environmental conditions. Successful subunits facing uncertain or changing environments have more organic structures than those successful subunits facing routine environments (Duncan, 1972; Lawrence and Lorsch, 1967; Tushman, 1979). Similarly, those successful units facing nonroutine tasks have more organic structures than those units with routine tasks (Comstock and Scott, 1977; Dewar and Hage, 1978).

Finally, at the interunit level of analysis, research by Lawrence and Lorsch (1967), Comstock and Scott (1977), Van deVen, Delbecq, and Koenig (1976), and Tushman (1979) indicates that the more complex the interdependence the more complex integrating mechanisms are required for effective performance. Support for these structural contingencies is not unequivocal (e.g., Mohr, 1971; Pennings, 1975; and Schoonhoven, 1981), but there is substantial support for this multistep approach to design and to the several context-structure-performance interactions.

Closely related to organization structure is the nature of the firm's control systems. Control systems are those formal and informal mechanisms used to evaluate and monitor behavior and outputs of a social system and to allocate rewards and penalties (Dunbar, 1981; Ouchi, 1979). Child (1973) and Perrow (1979) distinguish between three basic forms of control: direct or personal control, bureaucratic control, and social or unobtrusive control. Personal control relies on direct surveillance by the relevant supervisor. This form of control is most direct; it is also inefficient and biased (due to subjective criteria and measures) and frequently an impediment to organizational growth (Filley and Aldag, 1980; Ouchi and Maguire, 1975; Penrose, 1959). Direct control tends to be supplemented with bureaucratic control and the development of norms and values that provide the core of social control in large organizations (Edstrom and Galbraith, 1977).

The literature on bureaucratic control, like the structure literature, finds that the nature of the control system should be contingent on the subunit's work requirements (Lawler and Rhode, 1980). Those tasks whose measures and transformation processes are clear are most effectively controlled through relatively close control over multiple criteria (Khandwalla, 1974; Chandler, 1977).

For tasks where the work flow is unclear or evaluation is difficult, more flexible and less bureaucratic systems are associated with greater effectiveness (Ouchi and Maguire, 1975). For example, Van deVen's (1980) study of health care organizations found that flexible, process-oriented planning and control systems were effective in formative stages of organization evolution, while more rigid procedural planning and control systems were more appropriate once there was greater clarity as to service and client demands.

For work that is difficult to evaluate and/or plan, personal and/or bureaucratic control must be supplemented with social control processes. Social, unobtrusive, or peer control hinges on the evolution of shared norms, values, and purposes that provide a common language, frame of reference, and set of premises within which complex and subtle decisions can be made even in the absence of personal and/or bureaucratic control (Normann, 1977; Ouchi, 1980; Selznick, 1957). For example, Ouchi (1981) discusses the evolution of organizational philosophies and values in Japanese organizations (and in certain types of American organizations), and argues that these philosophies help individuals and groups throughout the firm to make organizationally responsive decisions even in the context of ambiguous criteria.

Literatures from population ecology, industrial organization economics, strategic management, and organization theory are consistent to the point of near redundancy in their view of organizational competence being related to the fit between strategic orientation and internal and external environmental conditions. The research has been pairwise in nature focusing on the context-organization-performance interactions one at a time. Only Nightingale and Tolouse (1977) provide support for the joint linkages between structure, processes, and values. They provide no data, however, on contextual demands or on performance. Though widely hypothesized (e.g., Duncan and Weiss, 1979; Nadler and Tushman, 1980; Normann, 1977), the full test of organizational contingency ideas—that is, the performance consequences of achieving a fit between contextual demands and organizational states—remains for future research (Van deVen and Drazin, 1985).

Proposition One: High-performing organizations evolve consistencies both among activity domains that support a strategic orientation and between the strategic orientation and external environmental conditions.

Implicit in this consistency literature, in both internal and external emphases, is an evolutionary perspective. Whereas the research focuses on *realized* configurations of values, strategies, power distributions, structures, and controls, as these relate to performance in *given* environmental conditions, all of them, with the exception of population ecology, posit some movement toward patterned configuration. Because executives cannot know, a priori, the optimal configuration of values, strategies, power, structure, and controls, organizations do not suddenly emerge with consistencies between strategy, structure, and internal processes. Rather, organizations gradually iterate or converge to some relative equilibrium through incremental but consistent decisions of senior and midlevel management and through concomitant organization learning (Bowman, 1963; March and Simon, 1958; Quinn, 1981). Within a feasible set of strategic choices, incremental yet consistent decisions are associated with organizational competence (Child, 1977; Khandwalla, 1973). Performance is a consequence of the extent to which (a) strategic orientation is consistent with external conditions, and (b) activities engaged in to support the orientation are consonant with one another.

Convergence and Inertia

The above literature on strategic orientation, external conditions, and performance tends to concentrate on the formal structural and activity aspects of organizational phenomena. With the exception of population ecology, which assumes fundamental change to be rare if not impossible, these rational perspectives on consistency assume a general ability of organizations to restructure activities in response to changing environmental conditions. Our model also assumes such a capacity, but we explicitly recognize inertial properties that characterize convergence. It is the property of inertia in organizations that (1) coalesces activities toward a holistic convergence on strategic orientation; and (2) results in the metamorphic character of evolution. It is due to the powerful influence of inertia that fundamental change in the direction of activities occurs only via simultaneous and discontinuous interruption of ongoing activities and interrelationships. We develop several propositions that describe the origin of convergent processes and associated organizational inertia.

Internal requirements for coordinated activities and flows result in increased structural elaboration and social complexity. These patterns of structural and social decisions over time elaborate and consolidate a firm's strategic orientation. These ever more coupled and interdependent structural and social decisions increase individual and group commitments to the firm's strategic orientation and further incremental change, but reduce the probability of perceiving the need for or implementing fundamental change (Normann, 1977). For example, in tracing the evolution of Ford Motor Company, Abernathy (1978) found that after Henry Ford decided to treat his Model T as a dominant design, there were a series of incremental but consistent decisions regarding products, processes, materials, labor, vertical integration—each of which furthered Ford's strategic orientation. Abernathy argued that as organizations tailor production processes to product lines, the increased coupling and specificity of the social and technical systems permit only incremental elaboration of the existing strategic orientation. Similarly, Kimberly's (1980) study of an innovative medical school provides rich data on incremental decisions and changes that bolstered the school's strategy, systems, procedures, and values. Once developed, these complex structural and social linkages were associated with resistance to change. The linkage between social and structural complexity, resistance to fundamental change, and inertia has also been described by Grinyer and Spender (1979), Lodahl and Mitchell (1980), Smith (1982), and Miller and Friesen (1980).

The external environment is also a force for increased structural and social complexity and, in turn, resistance to anything but incremental change. As environments become more structured, institutional factors are a homogenizing and constraining force on organization-environment relations (Stinchcombe, 1965). Depending on uncertainty and dependence relations, coercive, mimetic, and professional dynamics produce homogeneity in a competitive field and are associated with incremental convergent actions and decisions within organizations (DiMaggio and Powell, 1983). For example, J. Meyer and Rowan (1977) describe the myth, ceremony, and incremental decisions in educational systems that arise from external institutional factors. Tolbert and Zucker (1983) describe the adoption of administrative structures in civil service agencies as a consequence of "rational" patterns having become institutionalized. Similarly, external forces for reliable outputs and accountability in performance generate ever more complex internal and external standard operating procedures that are also associated with incremental change and resistance to fundamental change (Hannan and Freeman, 1982).

> **Proposition Two: Internal requirements for coordinated action and flows and external requirements for accountability and predictability are associated with increased social and structural complexity.**
>
> **Proposition 2A: Increased social and structural complexity engenders patterns of interdependence among activity systems, which promotes further convergence upon an established strategic orientation and resistance to fundamental change.**

Internal coordination requirements and external requirements for accountability and predictability are, then, associated with increased structural and social complexity and interdependence, an increase in incremental change and convergence around a strategic orientation, and concomitant resistance to fundamental change. Whether labeled congealment (Boswell, 1973), dynamic conservatism (Schon, 1971), ossification (Downs, 1967), or momentum (Miller and Friesen, 1980), inherent convergent processes pull the organization towards greater stability and incremental change.

Related to this discussion of increasing structural complexity is the issue of organizational growth or size. Just as in physical systems where increases in size must be related to the system's design and shape (Sahal, 1981), so do organizations change their shapes and processes as they grow (Kimberly, 1976). Increased size is associated with increased differentiation and specialization of subunits, and with a dispersion in centers of power as different subunits mediate various organizational contingencies (Blau and Schoenherr, 1971; Thompson, 1967). Increased size is related to increased complexity in systems, hierarchy, and structures, increased formalization within and between units, and an increase in the complexity of both bureaucratic controls for routine decisions as well as political activity for nonroutine decisions (Olson, 1982; Pfeffer, 1981).

The level of technological development in a product class also affects the organization size-complexity relationship. Technology literature and work in industrial evolution finds that after a dominant design emerges in an industry, process innovation permits a greater volume of product throughput (Chandler, 1977; Sahal, 1981). Greater throughput volumes can only be accomplished through larger, more formal, more complex organizations with more influential staff units to further formalize and standardize systems and procedures. Technological evolution is, then, associated with larger, and more complex, and more bureaucratic structures, with large sunk costs and with the ascendance of a powerful technostructure.

The link between size, complexity, formalization, and resistance to change is well documented. The larger the organization the more levels in the hierarchy, the greater the use of formalized procedures, and the greater the reliance on technocrats to interpret and enforce standards. These rules and procedures take on meanings in and of themselves, and coordination through feedback is replaced by coordination through formalized and ritualized behavior (Crozier, 1964; Merton, 1968).

In these bureaucratic organizations, even though performance of routine work is efficient, the ability to handle new situations is stunted. Nonroutine decision making in large organizations is dominated by political processes within and between different interest groups. Coalitions of interests in large organizations are made up of stable, self-perpetuating groups who have a vested interest in the status quo, and who make consequential decisions slowly and with frequently biased and distorted information (Downs, 1967; Olson, 1982; Wilensky, 1967). Similarly, if size

Proposition Three: The larger the organization, the greater its structural complexity and interdependence, and the greater the emphasis on incremental as opposed to discontinuous change.

is associated with substantial capital expenditures in a complex, highly interdependent production technology, there is organizationwide resistance to anything but incremental change in procedures and processes (Abernathy, 1978).

Holding environmental conditions constant (a constraint to be relaxed in Section Three), longer convergent periods are associated with increased social and normative complexity within organizations. The passage of time permits increased elaboration of values, beliefs, and ideologies at individual, group, and organization levels of analysis. These normative outcomes are associated with patterns of interaction that are self-reinforcing, particularly if bolstered by coordinated recruiting, socialization, and training practices, and by leader behavior emphasizing a core set of values and beliefs (Argyris and Schon, 1978; Sproull, 1981). These social and normative outcomes define what Selznick (1957) has termed organizational character. The longer the convergent period, the more complex these social and normative outcomes become, and the more multilevel commitment processes are a source of resistance to change and inertia (Staw et al., 1981).

Individuals attempt to reduce uncertainty and increase the level of predictability and control in work settings. As individuals become more task proficient and as they decipher organizational mores, they build elaborate routines to gain greater predictability and control over their work settings (Crozier, 1964; Downs, 1967; Katz, 1980). Through joint decision making, individuals develop shared commitments and beliefs that justify previous actions. These shared commitments and routines are accentuated over time; thinking becomes more and more routinized. Habit becomes a substitute for thought (Weick, 1979).

Individual learning does not take place in a vacuum. Satisfying levels, frames of reference, and the generation of meaning are shaped by groups within which individuals work (Berger and Luckmann, 1967; March and Simon, 1958). Increased group age is associated with the development of shared languages, values, and norms that simplify the group's work. As with individuals, groups attempt to increase their control of their work environments through routinizing and stabilizing work flows, by minimizing their dependence on others and maximizing others' dependence on the group, and by socializing recruits to the group's norms, values, and beliefs (Dalton, 1959; Pettigrew, 1973; Van Maanen, 1976). Over time, work strategies become routinized; commitment to established practices increases as groups become more rigid in their behavior patterns and decrease both the volume and diversity of information processed (Janis, 1972; Katz, 1980; Shambaugh, 1978; Staw, 1980). For example, Katz (1982) found that older groups had significantly less intra- and extra-group communication, were less motivated, and relied on standard operating procedures more than younger groups.

These emergent social and normative processes are accentuated by organizational selection, socialization, and promotion practices. Organizations attempt to control human variability by attracting and selecting those individuals whose personal values are congruent with organizational values (Katz and Kahn, 1966; Sigelman, 1977). Once selected, recruits are inculcated with expectations, beliefs, and decision-making premises (Van Maanen, 1976). At more senior levels of the hierarchy, organizations may choose and socialize a set of executives who through training and transfers come to embody, and in turn transfer, the organization's character (Edstrom and Galbraith, 1977; Sarason, 1972). Beyond selection, socialization, and training, senior management may act directly to shape organizational norms, value, and character (Barnard, 1948; Selznick, 1957). An expanding literature on organizational character, ideology, myths, sagas, and belief systems finds that symbolic behaviors of executive leadership shape how individuals associate meaning, justification, and value to their work (Martin, 1980; Pettigrew, 1979).

Organizational values and beliefs take on a rule-like status over time. This process of institutionalization, whereby recruits are rapidly socialized and organizational values and norms are taken for granted, is driven by conformity-generating processes throughout the organization. Individual and group behavior is shaped by structures, standards, and premises of decisions; justification for these behaviors is shaped by attention to the management of symbols, settings, and meanings by senior management (Clark, 1972; Miles, 1982; Pfeffer, 1982). These social and normative processes are further bolstered by a political equilibrium that also builds on these values and also works to reaccomplish these organizational values (Pettigrew, 1973; Pfeffer and Salancik, 1978).

> Proposition Four: The longer the convergent period, the greater the social complexity and interdependence, the greater the emphasis on incremental as opposed to discontinuous change.

Several studies provide evidence of the impact of time on the existence and stability of these social and normative outcomes. Kimberly's (1980) study of a new medical center, Kaufman's (1960) study of the Forest Service, Carroll and Delacroix's (1982) work in newspaper industries, and Lodahl and Mitchell's (1980) study of new universities each document the development of organizational character, its accentuation over time, and its persistence even when environments change. Research by Morison (1966) in the navy, Miles (1982) in the tobacco industry, and by Downs (1967) in bureaucracies indicates that long convergent periods permit greater congealment of social and normative outcomes, and are associated with substantial inertia and resistance to all but incremental change.

Organizational inertia is rooted in social and structural complexity that arise and become elaborated over time during a convergent period, and as political/physical consequences of growth. Convergent periods can be characterized by their degree of turbulence; that is, rates of change in strategy, power, structure, and/or controls. Convergent periods with no turbulence have stable organizational forms with ever more incremental change elaborating a strategic orientation. Convergent periods with substantial turbulence, however, have unstable forms as the organization roots around to find a stable relation between strategy, power, structure, and controls. Turbulence within convergent periods is reflected in an increase in political and conflictual behavior, and a decrease in the complexity, coupling, and interdependence of social and structural relations. Turbulence will be associated with less social and structural rigidities, less focus on bolstering the status quo, and less organizational inertia. Convergent periods with substantial turbulence will be less constrained by inertial forces, but will have to cope with increased politics, chaos, and uncertainty.

> Proposition Five: The more turbulent the convergent period, the less the social and structural complexities, the greater the internal dissensus, and the less the multilevel resistance to fundamental change.

Convergence and Performance

Selection processes favor those organizations whose strategic orientations are consistent with internal and external environmental demands (Proposition One). Over time, and as organizations grow larger, more successful firms elaborate, extend, and bolster their strategic orientation through incremental yet consistent change (Propositions Two and Three). The longer and less turbulent the convergent periods, the greater the congealment of norms, values, as well as structures to deal with both economic and political aspects of a strategic orientation (Propositions Four and Five).

One of the outcomes of long, less turbulent convergent periods is inertial forces, which are associated with individual and organizational learning and ever more articulated and complex social and structural coordination mechanisms. Holding the environment constant (or predictable), highly inertial organizations with appropriate strategic orientations will outperform those organizations with shorter and/or more turbulent convergent periods. Inertia is, therefore, a profoundly functional organizational characteristic in stable/predictable environments. For example, during the period from 1913 to 1976, AT&T either controlled its environment or was shielded from competitive pressures. Under these stable and/or predictable conditions, a myriad of convergent, incremental decisions and actions bolstered AT&T's strategic orientation and resulted in an effective and highly inertial organization (Lawrence and Dyer, 1983). Similarly, even in more dynamic environments (e.g., computers), those more effective organizations will have longer and less turbulent convergent periods than those less effective organizations (e.g., Prime and Data General as contrasted with General Automation).

Proposition Six: Holding the external environment constant, the longer and less turbulent the convergent period, the more effective the organization.

Quite apart from the length and degree of turbulence during a convergent period, patterns of executive characteristics, recruitment, promotion, and decision-making patterns also affect performance during convergent periods. Given the importance of incremental change, focus, and consistency during convergent periods (Proposition Six), more effective organizations will have a more stable, functionally balanced, and longer tenured executive team than less effective organizations (Roberts, 1969). Further, we predict that those more effective organizations will have executive teams with relatively more homogeneous backgrounds, education, and experiences than those less effective organizations. This balance in competence, similarity in backgrounds, and stability in the executive team helps establish both required competence to compete and a consistent set of expectations and greater predictability in the organization. Similarly, even though the literature on executive succession is equivocal (Gordon and Rosen, 1981), we hypothesize that when there are entries to or exits from the executive team, these events happen sequentially (as opposed to simultaneously), and that promotion in more effective organizations is from within. These promotion patterns build in stability and predictability during the convergent period.

Because major substantive decisions are stable during nonturbulent convergent periods, we hypothesize that the dominant role of executive leadership during these periods is to manage symbols, settings, and values to further support, justify, and make more meaningful the firm's strategic orientation. As long-tenured individuals may become isolated or uncoupled from core organization values, and because recruits are a constant source of variable perspectives, the organization's character and core values must be continuously reaccomplished by executive leadership (Pfeffer, 1981; Romanelli and Tushman, 1983).

Executive leadership focuses on the management of symbols and value during convergent periods; the myriad of incremental substantive decisions in more effective firms are made by middle and lower-level managers following core premises set by senior management (Bower, 1970). Under these conditions, mid-lower level management gain commitment to the unit's strategic orientation and are able to make fine-tuned decisions on a day-by-day basis. A classical recipe for failure is when an owner/entrepreneur retains full control of strategic and mundane decisions (Buchele, 1967; Collins and Moore, 1970). These conditions promote dysfunctional dependence on the entrepreneur and trigger even greater attention by the owner/entrepreneur on incremental decisions and less time on strategic threats and opportunities. These cycles of increased dependence on the executive team leading to further executive attention to detail usually result in organizational decline (Zaleznik and Kets de Vries, 1975).

Proposition Seven: Within convergent periods, more effective organizations will have a complementary set of senior management skills, a stable executive team, a reliance on sequential internal promotion patterns, and on incremental substantive change managed by middle and lower-level management.

Taken together, Propositions Five, Six, and Seven point out the fundamental tension that results as a consequence of performance being tied dually to fit with the external environment and internal patterns of consistency and interdependence. Given a set of environmental conditions faced by a population of firms, those organizations that have evolved more convergent or less turbulent interdependencies will perform better. The very convergence, however, that enhances success becomes an impediment to change when environmental conditions shift.

III. FORCES FOR REORIENTATION AND METAMORPHIC CHANGE

Section One argued that performance pressures (whether realized or anticipated) constitute the basic force for organizational reorientations. Where Section Two argued that consistency, incremental change, and inertia are basic organizational characteristics that are accentuated in high-performing organizations, this section focuses on external and internal forces for fundamental change. This section develops the concept of reorientations as radical and discontinuous changes driven by the opposing pressures of performance and inertia. Performance pressures derive either from problems in achieving internal consistencies, from changes in the external environment that render prior patterns of consistency no longer successful, or from changes in the internal environment that redefine current, performance, and/or strategic orientation as no longer appropriate. Pressures to change or develop consistencies are forces for change; pressures to sustain developed patterns of interdependence and commitment work to reinforce the status quo. In the face of these inertial pressures, reorientations only occur through the radical disruption of convergent patterns. This section discusses changes in strategic contingencies based on external and internal processes, and develops several propositions on the existence, frequency, and characteristics of strategic reorientations.

Forces for Reorientation

Product class evolution: External forces for fundamental change. Successful organizations will not initiate fundamental change solely on the basis of intra-organizational processes. Those same social and structural factors that are associated with effective performance are also the foundations of organizational inertia. Successful organizations do evolve through fundamental changes, though, because product class conditions evolve that result in shifts in strategic contingencies over time. Product class evolution is driven by both predictable as well as unpredictable factors.

Four factors underlie the evolution of a product class: demand, technology, users, and institutional conditions (Romanelli, Tushman, and Anderson, 1983). Holding random exogenous shocks aside, each of these factors changes systematically over time from substantial uncertainty in markets, technologies, resources, and product class norms to substantial certainty in each factor. As product class conditions change, strategic contingencies faced by competing firms also change systematically.

The most basic force driving product class change is the long-run growth in demand (Hannan and Freeman, 1977; Porter, 1980). Demand growth rates directly affect technological progress, scale economies, the development of suppliers, and entry/exit barriers (Baysinger et al., 1981; Chandler, 1977; Schmookler, 1966). Although demand is difficult to predict, without increases in demand and associated volumes technology evolves slowly; there are few entries and an absence of scale economies (Scherer, 1980). Assuming demand exists, product classes evolve through introductory, growth, maturity, and decline stages based on the rate of change in demand. Holding unpredictable legal, social, and technological factors constant, a constraint relaxed below, product class demand patterns follow an S shaped pattern driven by diffusion processes and limited by demand and resource constraints (Mingley, 1981).

Technology is a basic product class resource that changes systematically over time and is a major determinant in shaping the evolution of a product class. Case studies across a range of technologies find that technological progress constitutes an evolutionary system marked by long periods of incremental change punctuated by infrequent technological breakthroughs that lead, in turn, to the next period of incremental technological change (Fusfeld, 1970; Rosenberg, 1972). If demand exists, technology evolves through its own life cycle from emergence to competing technologies to consolidation, maturity, decline, and substitution (Sahal, 1981).

There are several important characteristics of technological progress. Early technology is crude, experimental, and tentative. There is substantial technological uncertainty as multiple technologies compete with each other (e.g., gas, wood, electric, internal combustion engines). Early applications of a technology are limited and early users have a substantial role in the technology's development (Phillips, 1971; Von Hippel, 1978). After substantial technological experimentation, a dominant design emerges as a synthesis of a large number of proven concepts. A dominant design provides a stable set of design criteria with which to evaluate and extend the basic product (Abernathy, 1978). Once a dominant design is defined within a product class, technological change is then driven by bit-by-bit modifications of a relatively unchanged design (or core technology). A dominant design is like a guidepost for further technological development within a product class and seems to hold across industries (Sahal, 1981). For example, the model T, DC-3, 370 computer, and Fordson tractor all shaped the evolution of their product classes for over fifteen years.

The convergence on a dominant design is crucial in a technology's development. After a dominant design emerges, the rate of major product change decreases, while the rate of process change increases. Uncertainty shifts from the product to how the product is made (Abernathy and Utterback, 1978). Given a dominant design, firms can begin to standardize raw materials, invest in more process technology, hire and train specialized labor, and develop specialized systems to increase efficiency, increase volume, and gain the benefits of increasing scale. Increased volume, in turn, increases the rate of technological change and learning (Fusfeld, 1970). This learning drives the technology towards greater rationalization, increases the standardization of labor and equipment, and increasingly routinizes the production process (Abernathy, 1978).

As the technology and associated products become more standardized so do input requirements such that firms now buy more standardized products in greater volume from suppliers. Power relations between the firm and suppliers and buyers shift during this period towards greater organizational control and less dependence on external actors (Abernathy, 1978; Von Hippel, 1978). Declining costs and increasing standardization and quality frequently open up new markets and, in turn, increases the underlying demand base. For example, only after a dominant design emerged followed by technological standardization and decreased costs did diesel locomotives move from the passenger market, through switching locomotives, to freight locomotives (which account for 75% of industrial sales [Sahal, 1981]). Technology and technological change are, then, important determinants of product class evolution. Different technologies will have their own technological progress functions due to different physical possibilities and different demand and resource constraints (Sahal, 1981; Wheelwright and Makridakis, 1980). Technology and demand characteristics, in turn, affect the nature of users and the evolution of institutional factors.

Users also change as a product class evolves. Early in a product class it is unclear who the users might be. Once identified, innovative users need a great amount of information to build an image of the product and distinguish it from others. If demand increases, competition increases as new firms enter with their own product forms. During this growth stage, existing product criteria are supplemented with additional criteria needed to evaluate new product forms (e.g., faster, smaller). Still later as the product class matures, buyer behavior is more routinized as products are standardized and product dimensions are clear (Howard, 1977).

As a product class evolves, the characteristics of users and user decision making become more certain, routine, and amenable to measurement and influence (Urban and Hausser, 1980). The target audience shifts from the relatively few cosmopolitans/innovators early in the product class to the late majority and laggards as the product class matures (Howard and Moore, 1982; Rodgers and Shoemaker, 1971). User needs and characteristics become more predictable and certain as a product class evolves.

Institutional factors also affect the evolution of product classes. New firms in new product classes have no experience to work from and must create new roles and work relations, with a labor force with no established set of norms. These firms must custom design their organizations and build linkages with skeptical suppliers and buyers. These liabilities of newness represent social or institutional barriers to entry (Stinchcombe, 1965). Firms in mature product classes face an opposite set of institutional forces. As an industry evolves, traditions, expectations, and work associations institutionalize social and organizational characteristics of the industry (DiMaggio and Powell, 1983; Meyer and Rowan, 1977). These expectations and traditions reinforce behaviors in the product class and are a deterrent to change in the industry (Rowan, 1982; Whetten, 1980). Given these liabilities of experience, it is not surprising that major innovations come from organizations outside the industry (Cooper and Schendel, 1976).

Product class conditions evolve as a result of complex interrelations between demand, technology, users, and institutional factors. In the absence of substitute products and/or technology, product class evolution is associated with greater and greater certainty as to markets, more predictable buyer behavior, more control over supplies, and more standardized technologies. These processes are accentuated by social forces that produce industry standards and norms. Technological and user uncertainty decreases over time, but resource and demand illiberality increases as markets mature and become saturated (Romanelli, Tushman, and Anderson, 1983).

As product class conditions change, so too do crucial contingencies facing individual firms. In an emerging product class, technology and product innovativeness are critical contingencies as resources are substantial yet technological and market uncertainty is high. As the market grows and the rate of product innovation decreases, critical contingencies shift to segmenting and exploiting an evolving market. In mature and decline phases, resource constraints are substantial. Here, cost, efficiency, and stimulating latent demand become important strategic considerations (Moore and Tushman, 1982).

Proposition Eight: Product class characteristics evolve from substantial technological, user, and institutional uncertainty, and resource liberality as a product class niche opens, to technological, user, and institutional certainty and resource illiberality as the product class matures and declines.

Proposition 8A: Product class characteristics evolve through periods of incremental change punctuated by discontinuous changes sparked by (a) the emergence of a dominant design; (b) the emergence of a substitute technology or product; and (c) major legal and/or social changes.

These predictable patterns in product class evolution may be disrupted by the sudden emergence of substitute technologies and/or products, or by unexpected political/legal events. The emergence of a substitute technology drastically effects the evolution of a product class as dominant firms are frequently replaced by new entrants (Tilton, 1971). For example, jet propulsion dominated piston engines and fundamentally reordered the aircraft industry. Similarly, transistors, diesel locomotives, mechanical refrigerators, electric calculators, incandescent light bulbs, and electric typewriters each represent substitute products and/or technologies that transformed their respective product classes. Whereas technology progress functions can predict technological changes within a given technology, substitute technologies cannot be predicted (Sahal, 1981).

Unexpected legal, social, and/or political events can also transform the evolution of a product class. For example, Miles (1982) provides data on the response of the cigarette industry to legal and social threats to its existence. Similarly, Lawrence and Dyer's (1983) study of the steel, telecommunications, and hospital industries also documents the effect of legal and political events on product class evolution. In sum, product class conditions evolve through periods of incremental change punctuated by both predictable and unpredictable discontinuous changes in technology and/or legal-political factors.

Internal Forces for Fundamental Change

Performance pressures come most directly from competitive and technological pressures, but internally generated processes may also result in a redefinition of performance criteria and/or in a shift in perceptions of key strategic contingencies. Organizations are political systems, negotiated orders composed of different interest groups (Pettigrew, 1973). These negotiated orders are stable as long as performance is within some zone-of-indifference and as long as the distribution of power is stable. If organizational performance is low, inertial forces will be associated with a further decrease in performance as well as an increase in organizational turbulence. This turbulence is reflected in erratic decisions and increases in intraorganizational conflict and political behavior. Prolonged incremental change in support of an inappropriate strategic orientation leads to further crisis (and possibly failure) and to internal pressures to fundamentally change the firm's orientation. For example, Grinyer and Spender (1979) describe how extended convergence on an inappropriate strategic orientation led to declining performance, increased intraorganizational turbulence, and eventual takeover.

Proposition Nine: Sustained low performance and/or major changes in the balance of power in an organization may disrupt the negotiated order, affecting the definition of performance objectives and motivating a change in strategic orientation.

Internal pressure for fundamental change may also result from a reordering in the balance of power in an organization. If, for whatever reason, one interest group gains substantial influence over others, then this group may redefine appropriate performance targets (e.g., 20% ROI vs. 5% ROI) and/or may redefine the firm's strategic orientation. For example, in the early 1970s even while Prime was a very successful minicomputer firm, a major shift in the distribution of power and authority from engineering executives to marketing and sales executives helped transform Prime from a high-priced, focused firm to a low-cost minicomputer firm selling to multiple markets. Similarly, Pettigrew's (1973) discussion of strategic change at Michaels hinges less on performance problems or changes in competitive conditions than on shifts in power within the organization.

Reorientations: Their Existence, Characteristics, and Performance Correlates

For a given set of environmental conditions, more effective organizations achieve a consistency between environmental demands and organization states. Those organizations that do not achieve both internal and external consistencies will be outperformed (Proposition One). As organizations grow and age they develop emergent values, core beliefs, and commitments along with standard procedures that together become self-reinforcing. These emergent inertial processes operate to reaccomplish the status quo (Propositions Two, Three, Four). Given multilevel sources of inertia, organizations actively resist fundamental change; they become dynamically conservative (Downs, 1967).

Environments do change, and change quite dramatically as product classes evolve. Environmental change poses systematically different strategic contingencies over time (Proposition Eight). Similarly, major changes in the distribution of power may result in a shift in performance criteria and/or a shift in a firm's strategic orientation (Proposition Nine). These environmental and politically based forces for change run counter to inertial forces for stability.

If organizations, particularly successful organizations, resist fundamental change, how do they evolve in the face of environmental change? Population ecology models argue that inertial forces are so strong that environmental shifts will be associated with waves of exits and new entrants (Brittain and Freeman, 1980). A transformational approach to evolution argues that organizations are indeed stable and inertial systems, but that they do change relatively infrequently in quantum, discontinuous shifts from one consistency to a qualitatively different consistency (Filley and Aldag, 1980; Normann, 1977; Starbuck, 1968; Watzlawick, Weakland, and Fisch, 1974).

Building on this transformational approach to organizational evolution, we define strategic reorientations as simultaneous and discontinuous changes in strategy, power, structure, and controls. Re-creations are reorientations that also involve discontinuous shifts in core values. Because of the pervasiveness and centrality of core values, re-creations are the most severe and traumatic form of reorientation. Reorientations (or re-creations) are analogous to discontinuous shifts in organizational paradigms and are seen as illogical and paradoxical by organization members (Sproull, 1981). This approach to organizational evolution indicates that organizations proceed through relatively long periods of convergence that are punctuated by bursts of fundamental and discontinuous changes throughout the system, which lead, in turn, to the next period of incremental change and convergence.

There is substantial support for this punctuated equilibrium model of organizational evolution. Mintzberg and Waters' (1982) history of Steinberg Inc. finds convergent periods each extending for over ten years until economic and/or legal conditions presented a series of crises. Each strategic reorientation involved a series of rapid and discontinuous changes in strategy, structure, and core values. Miller and Friesen (1980a, 1980b) found internally consistent patterns or gestalts between organizational characteristics that were resistant to change. They found that when change did occur, it happened in a revolutionary fashion as one organization type was transformed to another. Biggart (1977) describes the re-creation of the Post Office Department as the old department was destroyed and replaced by the Postal Service embodying systematically different values, structures, controls, and systems. Similar metamorphic change processes that lead to a following convergent period have been reported by Grinyer and Spender (1979), Meyer and Brown (1978), Chandler (1962), Kaufman (1960), Stryker (1961), and Starbuck (1968). Although organizations may be trapped in convergent periods (e.g., Hall, 1976), this research demonstrates the nature and existence of transformational change.

> Proposition Ten: Organizations evolve through periods of incremental change (convergent periods), punctuated by reorientations, which lead, in turn, to the following convergent period.

If strategic contingencies change, if the organization's strategic orientation does not fit competitive conditions, or if political shifts result in new performance criteria, organizational inertia will drive decreased organizational performance. Prolonged attention to incremental adaptation of an inappropriate strategic orientation will lead to increased intra-organizational turbulence, further crises, and either failure or a reorientation (Normann, 1977). For example, Messinger's (1955) study of the decline of the Townsend Movement describes its executive leadership's efforts to maintain the status quo through incremental adjustments in the face of a radically changing environment. The organization did not reorient itself and declined rapidly. Kimberly (1980) and Lodahl and Mitchell (1980) also describe the impact of inertial processes and the consequences of not reorienting as environments change.

Even though external conditions may be a reason for a strategic reorientation, perception of inconsistencies and executive action are required for its occurrence. Given the pervasiveness of inertial forces, both perception and action are usually triggered only by sustained low performance, a major shift in the distribution of power, and/or organizational crises. These perceptions and the response to changing strategic requirements are shaped by the characteristics of executive leadership.

Reorientations are also sparked by fundamental changes in technological and/or legal-social conditions in a product class (Propositions Eight, 8A). The emergence of a dominant design marks a shift in emphasis from product innovation to process innovation. Strategically, a dominant design results in increased emphasis on market segmentation and a greater emphasis on cost and efficiency. The emergence of a dominant design will correspond to a shake-out in the product class as some firms make the transition from entrepreneurial firms to more rationalized operations. Successful firms will build on their core values and shift their strategies, distribution of power, structure, and controls to fit fundamentally different strategic contingencies that emerge along with a dominant design. For example, Smith (1982) traces the evolution of early AT&T in making the transition from an entrepreneurial firm to a cost- and performance-conscious firm after the emergence of a dominant design in telephonic communication. Similarly, Abernathy (1978) traces the evolution of Ford Motor Co. from an entrepreneurial firm to a cost-focused firm corresponding to the creation of the Ford Model T.

Substitute technologies and/or products represent a fundamentally different threat than a dominant design. Electronic typewriters, jet engines, and transistors were each substitute products that eventually eliminated the market for those firms wedded to the prior technology (Tilton, 1971). Because technological and/or product substitution affects a firm's core technological competence and values, and because technological substitution brings product class conditions back to substantial uncertainty, we hypothesize they will be associated with strategic re-creations and/or substantial crisis and failure rates for existing organizations (Tilton,). For example, the re-creation of Singer into a technology-based organization corresponds with computer-based processing displacing mechanical operations. Changes in strategy, power, structure, and controls were also bolstered by fundamental changes in core values at Singer.

Proposition Eleven: Reorientations will be triggered by sustained low performance, major shifts in the distribution of power within the firms, and/or by discontinuous changes in product class conditions.

Proposition 11A: The emergence of a dominant design and/or major legal/social events will be associated with reorientations, while re-creations will be most frequently triggered by substitute products and/or technologies.

Reorientations and re-creations are also triggered by discontinuous changes in legal/social conditions. For example, the Kingsbury Agreement of 1913 made AT&T into a regulated monopoly and sparked a reorientation that resulted in a convergent period lasting through the late 1970s. Fundamental changes in legal, social, and technological arenas are associated with the current re-creation of AT&T. Substantial political and social dissatisfaction with the Post Office Department led to legal changes that, in turn, resulted in the re-creation of the Post Office (Biggart, 1977). Reorientations and/or re-creations sparked by legal, social, and/or political forces are also described in Miles (1982), Mintzberg and Waters (1982), and Kaufman (1960). Legal/social changes are frequently coupled to technological discontinuities. Transformation of firms in steel, telecommunication, railroads, and power generation were each affected by the coupling of fundamental technological change (e.g., Bessemer steel process; steam engines in the railroads) and associated changes in legal/political conditions (see Chandler, 1977).

Reorientations involve metamorphic changes in internal and external relations as structures, systems, processes, and commitments are transformed and rebuilt. Reorientations involve substantial organizational uncertainty and chaos along with performance variability. During reorientation attempts, previous structures, systems, and values become part of the organization's past. These historical forces embody the organization's past procedures and values and become inertial forces that resist the implementation of new strategies and systems. An organization's history will be particularly problematic if the organization has been effective during the previous convergent period; success sows the seeds of extraordinary resistance to fundamental change. The longer and more successful the prior convergent period, the more time these inertial forces have to develop and the more pervasive the impact of organizational history (Biggart, 1977; Morison, 1966).

As old strategies, systems, procedures, and relations are replaced, as new individuals are recruited, as a new set of external and internal relations are established, reorientations expose the organization to similar liabilities of newness it incurred when the organization was born (Stinchcombe, 1965). These liabilities are, however, accentuated by organizational inertia and associated multilevel resistance to change. The longer the prior convergent period, the greater these forces for stability. Reorientations, then, involve substantial risk to the organization. To disrupt stable patterns of activities and processes, even in the face of organization-environment inconsistencies, is to disrupt the fabric of competence.

Given these inertial forces and the impact of organizational history on current behavior, we hypothesize that reorientations will be associated with an increase in organizational turbulence as the organization's economic and political subsystems react to each other. Similarly, because of the substantial difficulty in implementing reorientations, initiating reorientations increases the risk of organizational failure. Because inertial processes are accentuated over time, the degree of turbulence and the risk of failure increase the longer the duration of the prior convergent period. Because re-creations also involve shifts in core values, they are even more traumatic events than reorientations. Re-creations will engender even greater resistance to change and will become associated with even greater turbulence and risk of failure than reorientations.

Proposition Twelve: The longer and/or more successful the prior convergent period, the greater the inertial forces, the greater the degree of turbulence and risk of failure associated with a reorientation. These degrees of turbulence and risk of failure are accentuated in re-creations.

Given the force of history and the impact of inertial forces on implementing reorientations (or re-creations), it is not surprising that many firms exit the industry when a dominant design emerges or when substitute technologies and/or products appear (Utterback and Reitberger, 1982).

For high-performing organizations, reorientations are triggered by the emergence of a dominant design, substitute products and/or technologies, or by major legal/social events (see Proposition Eleven). The frequency of reorientations corresponds to the rate of change of these technological and legal/social conditions. Product classes where the rate of technical change is substantial (e.g., semiconductors) will converge on a dominant design relatively quickly and may produce substitute technologies or dominant designs more rapidly than in those product classes where the underlying technologies are changing more slowly (e.g., steel; Sahal, 1981). Within a product class, the rate of technological change varies from substantial early in the product class to incremental as the technology matures, to substantial as a new technology replaces the dominant technology (e.g., the shifts from piston-driven to jet-driven aircraft). Reorientations will be more frequent in those technologies whose rates of change are substantial and in emerging phases of a product class.

Legal-social conditions also affect product class conditions. Those product classes or phases of a product class that experience substantial legal/social uncertainty will have more frequent reorientations than those product classes with more stable legal/social conditions. It follows that those organizations uncoupled from technological and legal/social conditions (e.g., some private universities), or those organizations in stable or predictable environments, will have long uninterrupted convergent periods and will not engage in strategic reorientations (Meyer and Rowan, 1977; M. Meyer, 1978).

Although the frequency of reorientations in a product class is contingent on technological and/or legal/social uncertainty, environmental conditions do not directly cause strategic reorientations. Organizations must perceive changing strategic contingencies, choose to reorient, and effectively implement the reorientation. These perceptions, choices, and the probability of implementation are shaped by the length and effectiveness of the prior convergent period (Proposition Twelve). Environmental conditions do not cause reorientations, but high-performing organizations will engage in reorientations that correspond to technological and legal/social conditions. Effective organizations in environments with substantial technological and/or legal/social uncertainty will have more reorientations than those effective organizations in highly certain environments. Those more effective firms in stable environments will have long and nonturbulent convergent periods (Proposition Six).

> **Proposition Thirteen: The greater the rate of change in environmental conditions, the greater the frequency of reorientation.**
>
> **Proposition 13A: High-performing organizations will have reorientations corresponding to environmental conditions. Low-performing organizations will either not reorient or will reorient too frequently.**

Exhibit 13.1. Frequency of Reorientations, Product Class Uncertainty, and Organization Performance.

		Product Class Uncertainty	
		Low	High
Performance	High	Few reorientations	Many reorientations
	Low	No Reorientations or too many	

Low-performing firms will either not attempt to reorient or will reorient too frequently as they struggle to align themselves with environmental demands (see Exhibit 13.1).

Stage models dominate the literature on organizational evolution. These approaches postulate a set of distinct and historically sequenced stages (Buchele, 1967; Greiner, 1972). Reviewing nine different stage models, Quinn and Cameron (1983) induce four sequential stages in organization evolution: entrepreneurial, collectivity, formalization, and elaboration of structure.

Proposition Fourteen: Organizations do not evolve through a standard set of stages. Rather, organizations may reach their respective strategic orientations through systematically different patterns of convergence and reorientation.

Proposition 14A: High-performing organizations have longer and less turbulent convergent periods than low-performing organizations, and have reorientations corresponding to product class discontinuities.

Because environments permit several feasible strategic alternatives (Child, 1972), because of technological, social, and political uncertainty, and because of the loose coupling between one convergent period and the next, there are no generic stages through which organizations must evolve (e.g., Filley and Aldag, 1980). Rather, we hypothesize that high-performing organizations will have longer and less turbulent convergent periods than low-performing organizations, and will have reorientations that correspond to environmental discontinuities (see Propositions Six, Thirteen). Whereas different strategic orientations will dominate during different phases of a product class's evolution (Proposition One), there exists no standard, historically sequenced set of periods through which organizations must evolve to achieve effectiveness.

Highly effective organizations, those that evolve over a product class life cycle, are those that have strategic orientations corresponding to environmental demands. High-performing organizations manage both for consistency and convergence, *and* for reorientation and fundamental change. Reorientations must be continually reaccomplished as environmental conditions change; these reorientations must be initiated and implemented even in the face of inertial forces for stability. Thus those most effective organizations are those which manage periods of both stability and fundamental change.

IV. CONVERGENCE AND REORIENTATION: THE ROLE OF EXECUTIVE LEADERSHIP

Section Two focused on consistency, convergence, and inertia; Section Three turned attention to fundamental environmental change and metamorphic organizational change. This section argues that executive leadership is the primary agent capable of mediating between these contrasting forces for stability and change. Middle-level management can sustain convergent periods, but only executive leadership has the position and potential to initiate and implement a strategic reorientation. Several propositions are developed linking the role and characteristics of executive leadership to our punctuated equilibrium model of organizational evolution.

The literature on executive leadership is equivocal on the linkage between executive behavior and organizational outcomes. Arguments from population ecology (Aldrich, 1979; Hannan and Freeman, 1977), bureaucracy (Downs, 1967), and resource dependence (Pfeffer and Salancik, 1978) insist that leaders are profoundly constrained by contextual and inertial forces. Pfeffer (1981) extends these ideas and argues that the core role for executive leadership is in shaping and managing social, normative, and symbolic outcomes. Literature from organization behavior (Selznick, 1957; Thompson, 1967) and strategy (Miles, 1982) asserts, to the contrary, that executive leadership has a vital role in shaping both substantive and symbolic outcomes

Romanelli and Tushman (1983) argue that a punctuated equilibrium model of organizational evolution helps reconcile these anomalous research streams. Both substantive and symbolic decisions and actions are vital, but their relative emphases shift by organization period. During convergence periods, executive leadership concentrates on symbolic actions and behavior and leaves to middle-level managers the responsibility of implementing incremental substantive changes. Because new individuals are constantly entering the organization and because the constellation of relevant others in the external environment is constantly changing, executive leadership cannot relax vigilance regarding symbolic outcomes (Barnard, 1938; Neustadt, 1980). Legitimation, explanation, and rationalization are constant requirements of executive leadership during convergent periods (Proposition Seven). During reorientations, however, executive leadership must engage in major substantive as well as symbolic decisions as strategies, structures, systems, and commitments are reordered (Normann, 1977; Stryker, 1961).

> Proposition Fifteen: The dominant role of executive leadership switches from symbolic behavior and incremental substantive change during convergent periods to major substantive and symbolic change and activities during reorientations.

Substantive choices regarding strategy, power, structure, and controls will only be exercised during relatively infrequent and brief reorientations. Barnard's (1938) inculcation of belief and Selznick's (1957) embodiment of purpose are, however, important leadership functions during both convergence periods and during reorientations (Romanelli and Tushman, 1983). Executive strategic choice is, then, the primary mechanism through which strategic reorientations get initiated and implemented. Environments do not cause reorientations. Rather, direct responsive activity that intervenes on prior activity patterns and establishes new patterns is required for reorientations to occur. Direct executive leadership is required because internal inertial forces operate to maintain the status quo.

Executive perception and sense making are important processes affecting the decision to initiate a reorientation. Executive leadership will either continue to elaborate an existing strategic orientation or initiate a reorientation depending on their perceptions of organizational performance and/or environmental threats. Several factors affect executive perceptions of organization/environment conditions. The same institutionalization processes that operate to induce resistance to change at the organizational level operate to systematically bias executive information acquisition, distort perceptions of organization-environment relations, and adversely affect the quality of decision making under high-stress conditions (Staw et al., 1981).

Inertial processes at the individual, group, and organization levels of analysis affect executive leadership's decision making and reduce the probability of organizational responsiveness to environmental discontinuities (Kiesler and Sproull, 1982). At the individual level, prior commitments and self-justification processes affect information acquisition and interpretation to bolster the status quo. The longer and more successful the convergent period, the greater these commitment processes operate, the lower the probability that adverse information will be sent to or be heard by the executive team (O'Reilly, 1978; Wilensky, 1967). These executive leadership inertial processes are accentuated the greater the executive team is insulated from the environment either because of ownership or legal conditions. Greater organizational ownership and/or legal control work to weaken the linkage between environmental conditions and organization behavior, and are associated with increased executive tenure, increased stability of the executive team, and idiosyncratic perceptions of environmental opportunities and constraints (M. Meyer, 1978). For example, owner/managers have immense difficulty in perceiving and/or adapting to changing competitive and organizational requirements (Christensen, 1953; Collins and Moore, 1970). Zaleznik and Kets de Vries (1975) discuss the psychological and Allen and Panian (1982) discuss the structural determinants of this executive inertia and its accentuation over time.

These individual-level inertial processes are further accentuated in older and more homogeneous executive leadership teams. Increased group tenure and homogeneity increase the team's convergence on a set of norms, values, and decision-making procedures, but decrease the team's informational and resource diversity. The longer an executive team remains stable, the greater its homogeneity and the greater its prior success, the more insulated it becomes, the greater the emphasis on cohesion and conformity, and the more committed the team becomes to prior courses of action (Janis, 1972; Shambaugh, 1978).

Organizationally, the very systems, procedures, and structures that support the existing strategic orientation work to focus attention and filter information in support of the status quo (Wildavsky, 1964; Wilensky, 1967). Similarly, history, precedent, and widespread commitments to the status quo are reinforced by those executives whose career interests are best served by stability and incremental change (e.g., Morison, 1966). The longer the convergent period and/or the more successful the organization, the more pervasive these organization, group, and individual-level inertial forces.

Proposition Sixteen: The decision to initiate a strategic reorientation is shaped by the length and success of the prior convergent period and by demographic characteristics of the executive team. The longer and more successful the prior convergent period, the more homogeneous and stable the executive team, and the greater the executive team's ownership of the firm, the less likely will they initiate a strategic reorientation.

These executive inertial processes are further accentuated under high-stress conditions. Information flow is reduced and communication networks become more centralized and dependent on formal status in high-stress conditions (Tushman, 1979). What communication does exist under these conditions is frequently biased and distorted (O'Reilly, 1978). Executive groups under high-stress conditions further restrict information acquisition, increase conformity pressures, and restrict control to a few key individuals (Janis, 1972; Kiesler and Sproull, 1982). Executives under stress rely even more on routine response patterns, become more rigid, and engage in more controlling and autocratic behavior (Staw et al., 1981). These counterproductive processes are accentuated by the older and more homogeneous executive teams. Thus those situations that demand creative problem solving may, instead, trigger increased emphasis on the status quo.

In sharp contrast to convergent periods, during reorientations executive leadership must engage in a series of consequential strategic choices. Executive leadership must make a series of substantive choices and simultaneously bolster these choices with attention to symbols, values, and the establishment of a revised normative order. As important as these substantive and symbolic choices are, the decision to initiate a reorientation is an even more basic and consequential decision. Given the influence of inertial processes on managerial perceptions and the rigid response patterns under high-threat conditions (Proposition Sixteen), reorientation decisions will be most frequently made under crisis conditions and will be most frequently initiated by external executives who have systematically different characteristics than those previous executives. Internal executives will be less likely to initiate reorientations; they will be more likely to successfully implement strategic reorientations.

Executives tend not to initiate reorientations from within. Chandler (1962) suggests that the psychological hazards of adjusting to new ways are a greater impediment to major change than internal politics. Similarly, Boswell (1973), Christensen (1953), and Grinyer and Spender (1979) found that organizations initiated fundamental change only after the entrepreneur died and/or after the senior executives were replaced by outsiders. Supporting these ideas, succession literature indicates that executive succession is associated with performance crisis, and that external executive succession is associated with major change (Carlson, 1962; Helmich and Brown, 1972). Externally recruited executives can develop and hire an executive leadership group with characteristics appropriate to strategic contingencies, yet must implement substantive and symbolic changes with few ties to the old system (Gordon and Rosen, 1981). Where external executives are more likely to initiate reorientations, they face substantial resistance in its implementation.

In more effective organizations, these new executives will have backgrounds, skills, and abilities to deal with critical competitive contingencies. For example, Grinyer and Spender (1979) found that the new executive team that initiated a turnaround in a large engineering firm had those managerial and technical skills that a more cost-conscious environment demanded. Similar shifts in executive characteristics corresponding to environmental discontinuities have been described by Stryker (1961), Smith (1982), Miles (1982), and Biggart (1977). Finally, because of the trauma associated with reorientations and the necessity for coordinated action in the face of substantial uncertainty, those reorientations implemented by a team of executives with built-in working relationships will be more effective than those reorientations driven by a set of new and unacquainted managers (Roberts, 1969). Compared to convergent periods, then, reorientations will have greater executive turnover, a greater proportion of outside executives hired, and a greater number of simultaneous changes in executives.

Proposition Seventeen: Reorientations are most frequently initiated through external executive succession of multiple members of an executive team, but are more effectively implemented by internal executive leadership.

Proposition 17A: Characteristics of new executives and recruitment patterns discriminate between more and less successful convergent periods following a reorientation.

Reorientations need not be driven by external succession. Where inertial processes may forestall executive leadership's perceiving the need to reorient, executive leadership is not precluded from such perceptions and/or actions. Indeed, those reorientations which can build on prior convergent periods and use executive leadership as a visible link to the past are more likely to be successfully implemented. For example, Mintzberg and Waters (1982) describe how an executive led his retail chain through several reorientations, and personally embodied stability in core values even if strategies, systems, and procedures were fundamentally altered. Similarly, key reorientations at IBM, Xerox, AT&T, and Ford were each engineered by existing executive leadership (Mr. Watson Jr., Mr. Wilson, Mr. Vail, and Mr. Ford, respectively; Abernathy, 1978; Dessauer, 1975; Fishman, 1981; Smith, 1982). Reorientations will always be associated with the recruitment of a set of outside executives whose characteristics are appropriate to competitive conditions, but the process may itself be more effectively implemented by existing executive leadership.

CONCLUSION

This chapter has developed a model of organizational evolution based on a simultaneous consideration of forces for stability, forces for fundamental change, and the role of executive leadership in mediating between these contrasting forces. This punctuated equilibrium model of organization evolution focuses on both continuities and discontinuities in the lives of organizations, and assigns a vital role for greater understanding of organizational periods, environmental discontinuities, the impact of organizational history on current behavior, and the paradoxical roles of executive leadership.

Organizations evolve through convergent periods punctuated by strategic reorientations (or re-creations). Convergent periods are relatively long periods of incremental change that elaborate a particular strategic orientation. Convergent periods can be characterized by duration, degree of turbulence, and by strategic orientation. Convergent periods may not be associated with effective performance. Strategic reorientations involve simultaneous and discontinuous changes in strategy, power, structure, and controls. Re-creations are reorientations that also involve discontinuous shifts in core values. These metamorphic events mark the end of one convergent period and initiate the following period. Only executive leadership is able to initiate and implement strategic reorientations. These metamorphic changes are either proactive responses to changing competitive conditions or the result of crises that follow extended periods of economic decline. Because of product class uncertainty and because one period is not dependent on prior periods, organizations do not evolve through a set of sequential stages. Rather, high-performing organizations will have longer and less turbulent convergent periods and reorientations that correspond to environmental discontinuities.

Our punctuated equilibrium model of organization evolution borrows from ecological, adaptation, and transformational approaches to evolution. Environments do actively select out firms that do not align themselves with environmental constraints. Further, strategic contingencies change as environmental conditions shift over a product class life cycle. Yet, some organizations do transform themselves. Those organizations that evolve over a product class life cycle are those that initiate and successfully implement strategic reorientations. Environments select out those firms that either do not reorient, choose inappropriate reorientations, and/or can not implement strategic reorientations. Finally, for successful organizations, the period between strategic reorientations is characterized by incremental, adaptive change, as structures, systems, and processes are more finely tailored to the firm's strategic orientation.

Executive leadership takes on a vital if protean role in this punctuated equilibrium model. During convergent periods executive leadership emphasizes symbolic activities and incremental change, while during re-creations executive leadership engages in major substantive as well as symbolic activities. Beyond these substantive and symbolic behaviors, executive leadership must also choose to initiate reorientations. Given inertial forces, which are accentuated in high-performing organizations, it is the mark of inspired executive leadership to be able to encourage inertial forces during convergent periods, and at the same time to keep vigilant of technological, market, and/or legal threats and opportunities and proactively initiate and implement reorientations. The paradox of executive leadership is, then, to manage for consistency and inertia during convergent periods, and at the same time attend to competitive conditions, being prepared to make seemingly inconsistent substantive and symbolic decisions to reorient the organization as product class conditions unfold.

Organizational evolution is a complex phenomenon. Organizational processes are fundamentally different between convergent periods and reorientations. Within convergent periods, senior executives reinforce core values while middle-level management makes those necessary adaptive substantive decisions; organization change is incremental and executive succession is dominated by sequential promotions from within. During convergent periods, organization inertia increases and competitive vigilance decreases; structure frequently drives strategy. During reorientations, however, executive leadership makes consequential substantive as well as normative decisions, and organization change is traumatic. Reorientations are frequently driven by outside executives and are characterized by substantial turnover in an executive team. During reorientations, organization inertia decreases, competitive vigilance increases; strategy drives structure.

There are also important differences between convergent periods. History, precedent, and procedures from prior convergent periods, as well as interpretations of reorientations and associated crises, provide context and constraints for future convergent periods. Current convergent periods are, then, shaped by an organization's history. This punctuated equilibrium model reflects the complexity of organization evolution and helps reconcile seemingly anomalous research results. The model highlights the importance of our understanding the determinants of both organization stability and change, and our understanding the relations between environments, organizations, executive leadership, and organization history.

This period-based model provides clear direction for research on organizational evolution. Because political, technological, and economic conditions of the external environment are so important in the evolution of firms, and because these conditions vary across industries, research on organizational evolution must compare alternative fates within industries. Because an organization's prior patterns of convergence and reorientation set the stage for current behavior, research on evolution must capture these historical processes through longitudinal research designs. These historical data can be used to identify reorientations and be used to test hypotheses within and between industries.

Organizations evolve through the interaction of internal convergent forces for stability and external forces for change as mediated by executive leadership. Organizations move through convergent periods demarked by strategic reorientations. Both empirical and case research supports our thesis, but directed empirical work is needed to bolster our understanding of organizational evolution. The framework presented here provides theoretical justification for pursuing such research.

References

Abernathy, W. J. The productivity dilemma: Roadblock to innovation in the automobile industry. Baltimore: Johns Hopkins University Press, 1978.

Abernathy, W. & Utterback, J. Patterns of industrial innovation. Technology Review, 1978, 80, 41–47.

Aldrich, H. Organizations and environments. Englewood Cliffs, NJ: Prentice-Hall, 1979.

Aldrich, H. & Pfeffer, J. Environments of organizations. In A. Inkeles (Ed.), Annual Review of Sociology (Vol. 2), Palo Alto: Annual Reviews Inc., 1976.

Allen, M. P. & Panian, S. K. Power, performance, and succession in the large corporation. Administrative Science Quarterly, 1982, 27, 538–547.

Argyris, C. & Schon, D. A. Organizational learning: A theory of action perspective. Reading, MA: Addison-Wesley, 1978.

Armour, H. O. & Teece, D. J. Organizational structure and economic performance: A test of the multidivisional hypothesis. Bell Journal of Economics, 1978, 9, 106–122.

Barnard, C. The functions of the executive. Cambridge, MA: Harvard University Press, 1938.

Barnard C. Organization and management. Cambridge, MA: Harvard University Press, 1948.

Baysinger, B., Meiners, R., & Zeithamel, C. Barriers to corporate growth. Lexington, MA: Heath Co., 1981.

Berger, P. & Luckmann, T. The social construction of reality. New York: Doubleday, 1967.

Biggart, N. The creative/destructive process of organizational change. Administrative Science Quarterly, 1977, 22, 410–424.

Blau, P. The dynamics of bureaucracy. Chicago: University of Chicago Press, 1963.

Blau, P. M. & Schoenherr, R. The structure of organizations. New York: Basic Books, 1971.

Boswell, J. The rise and fall of small firms. London: Allen & Unwin, 1973.

Bower, J. L. Managing the resource allocation process. Cambridge, MA: The Harvard Business School, 1970.

Bowman, N. Consistency and optimality in managerial decision making. Management Science, 1963, 9, 310–321.

Brittain, J. & Freeman, J. Organizational proliferation and density dependent selection. In J. R. Kimberly and R. Miles (Eds.), Organizational Life Cycles. San Francisco: Jossey-Bass, 1980.

Buchele, R. Business policy in growing firms. San Francisco: Chandler Publishing, 1967.

Carlson, R. O. Executive succession and organizational change. Chicago: University of Chicago, Midwest Administration Center, 1962.

Carroll, G. R. & Delacroix, J. Organizational mortality in the newspaper industries of Argentina and Ireland: An ecological approach. Administrative Science Quarterly. 1982, 27, 169–198.

Chandler, A. D. Strategy and structure: Chapters in the history of American industrial enterprise. Cambridge, MA: MIT Press, 1962.

Chandler, A. D. The visible hand: The managerial revolution in American business. Cambridge, MA: Harvard University Press, 1977.

Channon, D. F. The strategy and structure of British enterprise. Boston: Graduate School of Business Administration, Harvard University, 1973.

Child, J. Organization structure, environment and performance: The role of strategic choice. Sociology, 1972, 6, 2–21.

Child, J. Predicting and understanding organizational structure. Administrative Science Quarterly, 1973, 18, 168–185.

Child, J. Organization. London: Harper & Row, 1977.

Child, J. & Kieser, A. Development of organizations over time. In P. C. Nystrom & W. H. Starbuck (Eds.), Handbook of Organizational Design (Vol. 1). New York: Oxford University Press, 1981.

Christensen, C. Managerial succession in small and growing enterprises. Cambridge, MA: Harvard University Press, 1953.

Clark, B. R. The organizational saga in higher education. Administrative Science Quarterly, 1972, 17, 178–184.

Collins, O. & Moore, D. The organization-makers. New York: Meredith Company, 1970.

Comstock, D. E. & Scott, W. R. Technology and the structure of subunits: Distinguishing individual and workgroup effects. Administrative Science Quarterly, 1977, 22, 177–202.

Cooper, A. C. & Schendel, D. Strategic responses to technological threats. Business Horizons, 1976.

Crozier, M. The bureaucratic phenomenon. Chicago: University of Chicago Press, 1964.

Dahrendorf, R. Class and class conflict in industrial society. Stanford, CA: Stanford University Press, 1959.

Dalton, M. Men who manage. New York: Wiley, 1959.

Delacroix, J. & Carroll, G. R. Organizational foundings: An ecological study of the newspaper industries of Argentina and Ireland. Administrative Science Quarterly, 1983, 28, 274–291.

Dessauer, J. My years with Xerox. New York: Manor Books, 1975.

Dewar, R. & Hage, J. Size, technology, complexity, and structural differentiation: Toward a theoretical synthesis. Administrative Science Quarterly, 1978, 23, 111–136.

DiMaggio, P. & Powell, W. The iron cage revisited: Institutional isomorphism and collective rationality in organizational fields. American Sociological Review, 1983, 48, 147–160.

Downs, A. Inside bureaucracy. Boston: Little, Brown, 1967.

Dunbar, R. Designs for organization control. In P. C. Nystrom & B. Starbuck (Eds.), Handbook of Organizational Design. Oxford: Oxford University Press, 1981.

Duncan, R. The characteristics of organizational environments and perceived environmental uncertainty. Administrative Science Quarterly, 1972, 17, 313–327.

Duncan, R. & Weiss, A. Organizational learning: Implications for organization design. In B. Staw (Ed.), Research in Organizational Behavior (Vol. 1). Greenwich, CT: JAI Press, 1979.

Edstrom, A. & Galbraith, J. R. Transfer of managers as a coordination and control strategy in multinational organizations. Administrative Science Quarterly, 1977, 22, 248–263.

Filley, A. C. & Aldag, R. J. Organization growth and types: Lessons from small institutions. In B. Staw and L. L. Cummings (Eds.), Research in Organizational Behavior (Vol. 2). Greenwich, CT: JAI Press, 1980.

Fishman, K. D. The computer establishment. New York: Harper & Row, 1981.

Freeman, J. Organizational life cycles and natural selection processes. In B. Staw & L. L. Cummings (Eds.), Research in Organizational Behavior (Vol. 4). Greenwich, CT: JAI Press, 1982.

Freeman, J. & Hannan, M. Niche width and the dynamics of organizational populations. American Journal of Sociology, 1983.

Fusfeld, A. The technological progress function. Technology and Forecasting and Social Change, 1970, I, 301–312.

Galbraith, I. R., Designing complex organizations. Reading, MA: Addison-Wesley, 1977.

Gordon, G. E. & Rosen, N. Critical factors in leadership succession. Organizational Behavior and Human Performance, 1981, 27, 227–254.

Greiner, L. E. Evolution and revolution as organizations grow. Harvard Business Review, July-August, 1972, 37–46.

Grinyer, P. & Spender, J. Turnaround. London: Associated Business Press, 1979.

Hall, R. H. A system pathology of an organization: The rise and fall of the old Saturday Evening Post. Administrative Science Quarterly, 1976, 21, 185–211.

Hambrick, D. C. An empirical typology of mature industrial product environments. Academy of Management Journal, 1983, 26, 213–230.

Hambrick, D. C., MacMillan, I. C., & Day, D. L. Strategic attributes and performance in the four cells of the BCG matrix—A PIMS-based empirical analysis. Academy of Management Journal, 1982, 25, 510–531.

Hannan, M. T. & Freeman, J. H. The population ecology of organizations. American Journal of Sociology, 1977, 32, 929–964.

Hannan, M. & Freeman, J. Structural inertia and organizational change. Working paper, Stanford University, 1982.

Harrigan, K. R. Barriers to entry and competitive strategies. Strategic Management Journal, 1981, 2, 395–412.

Hatten, K. T., Schendel, D. E., & Cooper, A. C. A Strategic model for the U.S. brewing industry: 1952–1971. Academy of Management Journal, 1978, 21, 592–610.

Hawley, A. H. Human ecology: A theory of community structure. New York: Ronald Press, 1950.

Helmich, D. L. & Brown, W. B. Successor type and organizational change in the corporate enterprise. Administrative Science Quarterly, 1972, 17, 371–381.

Hinings, C. R., Hickson, D. J., Pennings, J. M., & Schneck, R. E. Structural conditions of interorganizational power. Administrative Science Quarterly, 1974, 19, 22–44.

Hofer, C. F. Toward a contingency theory of business strategy. Academy of Management Journal, 1975, 18, 784–810.

Howard, J. A. Consumer behavior. New York: McGraw-Hill, 1977.

Howard, J. A. & Moore, W. J. Changes in consumer behavior over the product life cycle. In M. L. Tushman & W. L. Moore (Eds.), Readings in the Management of Innovation. Boston: Pitman, 1982.

Janis, I. L. Victims of groupthink. Boston: Houghton Mifflin, 1972.

Katz, D. & Kahn, R. The social psychology of organizations. New York: Wiley, 1966.

Katz, R. Time and work: Toward an integrative perspective. In B. Staw & L. L. Cummings (Eds.), Research in Organizational Behavior (Vol. 2). Greenwich, CT: JAI Press, 1980.

Katz, R. The effects of group longevity on project communication. Administrative Science Quarterly, 1982, 27, 81–104.

Kaufman, H. The forest ranger: A study in administrative behavior. Baltimore: The Johns Hopkins University Press, 1960.

Khandwalla, P. Effect of competition on the structure of top management control. Academy of Management Journal, 1973, 16, 285–295.

Khandwalla, P. Mass output orientation and organization structure. Administrative Science Quarterly, 1974, 19, 74–97.

Kiesler, S. & Sproull, L. Managerial response to changing environments: Perspectives on problem-sensing from social cognition. Administrative Science Quarterly, 1982, 27, 548–570.

Kimberly, J. R. Organizational size and the structuralist perspective: A review, critique and proposal. Administrative Science Quarterly, 1976, 21, 571–597.

Kimberly, J. R. Initiation, innovation, and institutionalization in the Creation Process. In J. R. Kimberly & R. H. Miles (Eds.), The Organizational Life Cycle. San Francisco: Jossey-Bass, 1980.

Kimberly, J. & Miles, R. E. The organizational life cycle. San Francisco: Jossey-Bass, 1980.

Lawler, E. & Rhode, D. Organization control. Chicago, IL: Scott Foresman, 1980.

Lawrence, P., & Dyer, D. Renewing American industry. New York: Free Press, 1983.

Lawrence, P. R. & Lorsch, J. Organization and environment. Boston: Graduate School of Business Administration, Harvard University, 1967.

Lenz, R. T. Environment, strategy, organization structure and performance: Patterns in one industry. Doctoral dissertation, Indiana University, 1978.

Lodahl, T. M. & Mitchell, S. M. Drift in the development of innovative organizations. In J. R. Kimberly & R. H. Miles (Eds.), The Organizational Life Cycle. San Francisco: Jossey-Bass, 1980.

MacMillan, I. C., Hambrick, D. C., & Day, D. I. Strategic attributes and performance in the four cells of the BCG matrix. Academy of Management Journal, 1982, 25, 733–755.

March, J. & Simon, H. Organizations. New York: Wiley, 1958.

Martin, J. Stories and scripts in organizational settings. Working paper 543, Stanford Business School, 1980.

Merton, R. K. Social theory and social structure. New York: Free Press, 1968.

Messinger, S. L. Organizational transformation: A case study of a declining social movement. American Sociological Review, 1955, 20, 3–10.

Meyer, J. W. & Rowan, B. Institutionalized organizations: Formal structure as myth and ceremony. American Journal of Sociology, 1977, 83, 340–363.

Meyer, M. Leadership and organization structure. In M. Meyer (Ed.), Environments and Organizations. San Francisco: Jossey-Bass, 1978.

Meyer, M. & Brown, C. The process of bureaucratization. In M. W. Meyer & Associates (Eds.), Environments and Organizations. San Francisco: Jossey-Bass, 1978.

Miles, R. E. & Snow, C. C. Organizational strategy, structure, and process. New York: McGraw Hill, 1978.

Miles, R. E. Coffin nails and corporate strategies. Englewood Cliffs, NJ: Prentice-Hall, 1982.

Miller, D. & Friesen, P. H. Momentum and revolution in organizational adaptation. Academy of Management Journal, 1980, 22, 591–614.

Miller, D. & Friesen, P. Archetypes of organizational transitions. Administrative Science Quarterly, 1980, 25, 268–299.

Mingley, D. Toward a theory of product life cycle. Journal of Marketing, 1981, 109–115.

Mintzberg, H. The nature of managerial work. New York: Harper & Row, 1973.

Mintzberg, H. The structure of organizations. Englewood Cliffs, NJ: Prentice-Hall, 1979.

Mintzberg, H. & Waters, J. A. Tracking strategy in an entrepreneurial firm. Academy of Management Journal, 1982, 25, 465–499.

Mohr, L. Organizational technology and organizational structure. Administrative Science Quarterly, 1971, 16, 444–459.

Moore, W. & Tushman, M. Managing innovation over the product life cycle. In Moore and Tushman (Eds.), Managing Innovation. Marshfield, Mass.: Pitman Publishing, 1982.

Morison, E. Men, machines, and modern times. Cambridge, MA: MIT Press, 1966.

Nadler, D. & Tushman, M. L. A congruence model for diagnosing organizations. Organizational Dynamics, Winter, 1980.

Neustadt, R. E. Presidential power: The politics of leadership from FDR to Carter. New York: John Wiley, 1980.

Newman, W. & Yavitz, B. Strategy in action. New York: Free Press, 1983.

Nightingale, O. & Toulouse, J. Toward a multi-level congruence theory of organizations. Administrative Science Quarterly, 1977, 22, 264–280.

Normann, R. Management for growth. New York: Wiley, 1977.

Olson, M. The rise and decline of nations. New Haven: Yale University Press, 1982.

O'Reilly, C. The intentional distortion of information in organization communication. Human Relations, 1978, 31, 173–193.

Ouchi, W. G. A conceptual framework for the design of organizational control mechanisms. Management Science, 1979, 25, 833–848.

Ouchi, W. G. Markets, bureaucracies, and clans. Administrative Science Quarterly, 1980, 25, 129–141.

Ouchi, W. G. Theory Z. Reading, MA: Addison-Wesley, 1981.

Ouchi, W. G. & Maguire, M. A. Organizational control: Two functions. Administrative Science Quarterly, 1975, 20, 559–569.

Pelz, D. & Andrews, F. Scientists in organizations. New York: John Wiley, 1966.

Pennings, J. M. The relevance of the structural-contingency model for organizational effectiveness. Administrative Science Quarterly, 1975, 20, 393–410.

Penrose, E. T. The theory of the growth of the firm. New York: Wiley, 1959.

Perrow, C. Complex organizations: A critical essay. Glenview, IL: Scott, Foresman and Co., 1979.

Peters, T. J. Symbols, patterns, and settings: An optimistic case for getting things done. Organizational Dynamics, 1978, 7, 3–23.

Pettigrew, A. M. The politics of organizational decision-making. London: Tavistock, 1973.

Pettigrew, A. M. On studying organizational culture. Administrative Science Quarterly, 1979, 24, 570–581.

Pfeffer, J. Management as symbolic action: The creation and maintenance of organizational paradigms. In L. L. Cummings & B. Staw (Eds.), Research in Organizational Behavior (Vol. 3). Greenwich, CT: JAI Press, 1981, 1–52.

Pfeffer, J. Organizations and organization theory. Boston: Pitman, 1982.

Pfeffer, J. & Salancik, G. R. The external control of organizations: A resource dependence perspective. New York: Harper & Row, 1978.

Phillips, A. Technology and market structure: A study of the aircraft industry. Lexington, MA: Heath Lexington Books, 1971.

Polli, R. & Cook, V. Validity of the product life cycle. Journal of Business, 1969.

Porter, M. E. Competitive strategy: Techniques for analyzing industries and competitors. New York: The Free Press, 1980.

Porter, M. E. Contributions of industrial organization to strategic management. Academy of Management Review, 1981, 6, 609–620.

Quinn, J. B. Strategies for change: Logical incrementalism. Homewood, IL: Irwin, 1981.

Quinn, R. E. & Cameron, K. Organizational life cycles and shifting criteria of effectiveness: Some preliminary evidences, Management Science (forthcoming).

Roberts, E. Entrepreneurship and technology. In W. Gruber & D. Marquis (Eds.), Factors in the Transfer of Technology. Cambridge, MA: MIT Press, 1969.

Rodgers, E. & Shoemaker, D. The diffusion of innovation. New York: Free Press, 1971.

Romanelli, E. & Tushman, M. L. Executive leadership and organizational outcomes: An evolutionary perspective. Working paper 508, Columbia University, 1983.

Romanelli, E., Tushman, M. L., & Anderson, P. The emergence and evolution of resource niches: A conceptual framework. New York: Columbia University, 1983.

Rosenberg, N. Technology and American economic growth. White Plains: Sharp Company, 1972.

Rowan, B. Organizational structure and the institutional environment: The case of public schools. Administrative Science Quarterly, 1982, 27, 259–279.

Rumelt, R. P. Strategy, structure and economic performance. Cambridge, MA: Harvard University Press, 1974.

Sahal, D. Patterns of technological innovation. Reading, MA: Addison-Wesley, 1981.

Sarason, S. The creation of settings and the future societies. San Francisco: Jossey-Bass, 1972.

Scherer, F. J. Industrial market structure and economic performance. Boston: Houghton Mifflin, 1980.

Schmookler, J. Invention and economic growth. Cambridge, MA: Harvard University Press, 1966.

Schon, D. Beyond the stable state. London: Temple Smith, 1971.

Schoonhoven, C. B. Problems with contingency theory: Testing assumptions hidden within the language of contingency "theory."Administrative Science Quarterly, 1981, 26, 349–377.

Schumpeter, J. A. The theory of economic development. Cambridge, MA: Harvard University Press, 1934.

Selznick, P. Leadership in administration. New York: Harper & Row, 1957.

Shambaugh, P. The development of the small group. Human Relations, 1978, 31, 283–295.

Sigelman, L. Reporting the news: An organizational analysis. American Journal of Sociology, 1977, 79, 132–151.

Smith, G. The Bell/Western Union Patent Agreement of 1879. Working paper, Winthrop Research Group, Cambridge, MA, 1982.

Snow, C. & Hrebiniak, L. Strategy, distinctive competence and organizational performance, Administrative Science Quarterly, 1980, 25, 317–326.

Spence, A. Investment strategy and growth in a new market. Bell Journal of Economics, 1979, 10, 1–9.

Sproull, L. S. Beliefs in organizations. In P. C. Nystrom & W. H. Starbuck (Eds.), Handbook of Organization Design (Vol. 1). New York: Oxford University Press, 1981.

Starbuck, W. Organizational growth and development. In J. G. March (Ed.), Handbook of Organizations. Chicago: Rand-McNally, 1965.

Starbuck, B. Organizational metamorphosis. In R. Milman & M. Holtenstein (Eds.), Promising research directions. Academy of Management, 1968, 113–122.

Staw, B. M. Rationality and justification in organizational life. In L. L. Cummings and B. Staw (Eds.), Research in Organizational Behavior, (Vol. 2). Greenwich, CT: JAI Press, 1980.

Staw, B. M., Sandelands, L. E., & Dutton, J. E. Threat-rigidity effects in organizational behavior: A multilevel analysis. Administrative Science Quarterly, 1981, 26, 501–524.

Stinchcombe, A. L. Social structure and organizations. In J. G. March (Ed.), Handbook of Organizations. Chicago: Rand McNally, 1965.

Stryker, P. The character of the executive. New York: Harper & Row, 1961.

Thompson, J. D. Organizations in action. New York: McGraw-Hill, 1967.

Tilton, J. E. International diffusion of technology: The case of semiconductors. Washington, DC: Brookings Institution, 1971.

Tolbert, P. & Zucker, L.G. Institutional sources of change in the formal structure of organizations: The diffusion of civil service reform, 1880–1935. Administrative Science Quarterly, 1983, 28, 22–39.

Tushman, M. L. Work characteristics and subunit communication structure: A contingency analysis. Administrative Science Quarterly, 1979, 24, 82–97.

Urban, G. & Hausser, J. Design in the marketing of new products. Englewood Cliffs: Prentice-Hall, 1980.

Utterback, J. & Reitberger, G. Technology and industrial innovation in Sweden, CPA, MIT, 1982.

Van deVen, A. H., Delbecq, A. L., & Koenig, R. Determinants of coordination modes within organizations. American Sociological Review, 1976, 41, 322–338.

Van deVen, A. H. Early planning, implementation, and performance of new organizations. In J. Kimberly & R. S Miles (Eds.), The Organizational Life Cycle. San Francisco: Jossey-Bass, 1980.

Van deVen, A. & Drazin, R. The concept of fit in organization theory. In L. Cummings & B. Slaw (Eds.), Research in Organization Behavior (Vol. 7). Greenwich, Conn.: JAI Press, 1985.

VanMaanen, J. Breaking in: Socialization to work. In R. Dubin (Ed.), Handbook of Work, Organization, and Society. Chicago: Rand-McNally, 1976, 67–130.

VonHippel, E. Successful industrial products from customer ideas. Journal of Marketing. January, 1978, 39–40.

Watzlawick, P., Weakland, J., & Fisch, R. Change. New York: Norton, 1974.

Weber, M. The theory of social and economic organizations. A. M. Henderson & T. Parsons (Trans. & Eds.), New York: Oxford University Press, 1947.

Weber, M. The protestant ethic and the spirit of capitalism. New York: Scribner, 1952.

Weick, K. E. The social psychology of organizing. Reading, MA: Addison-Wesley, 1979.

Wheelwright, S. & Makridakis, S. Forecasting methods for management. New York: Wiley, 1980.

Whetten, D. Sources, responses, and effects of organizational decline. In J. Kimberly & R. Miles (Eds.), The Organizational Life Cycle. San Francisco: Jossey-Bass, 1980.

Wildavsky, A. Politics of the budgetary process. Boston: Little, Brown, 1964.

Wilensky, H. Organizational intelligence. New York: Basic Books, 1967.

Zald, M. N. Political economy: A framework for analysis. In M. N. Zald (Ed.), Power in Organizations. Nashville, TN: Vanderbilt University Press, 1970.

Zaleznik, A. & Kets de Vries, M. Power and the corporate mind. Boston: Houghton Mifflin, 1975.

CHAPTER FIFTEEN

Kurt Lewin and the Planned Approach to Change

A Reappraisal

Bernard Burnes (2004)

INTRODUCTION

*Freud the clinician and Lewin the experimentalist—these
are the two men whose names will stand out before all
others in the history of our psychological era.*

The above quotation is taken from Edward C. Tolman's memorial address for
Kurt Lewin delivered at the 1947 Convention of the American Psychological
Association (quoted in Marrow, 1969, p. ix). To many people today it will seem
strange that Lewin should have been given equal status with Freud. Some fifty
years after his death, Lewin is now mainly remembered as the originator of the
Three-Step Model of change (Cummings and Huse, 1989; Schein, 1988), and
this tends often to be dismissed as outdated (Burnes, 2000; Dawson, 1994; Dent
and Goldberg, 1999; Hatch, 1997; Kanter et al., 1992; Marshak, 1993). Yet, as
this chapter will argue, his contribution to our understanding of individual and
group behavior and the role these play in organizations and society was enormous and is still relevant.

In today's turbulent and changing world, one might expect Lewin's pioneering
work on change to be seized upon with gratitude, especially given the high failure
rate of many change programs (Huczynski and Buchanan, 2001; Kearney, 1989;
Kotter, 1996; Stickland, 1998; Waclawski, 2002; Wastell et al., 1994; Watcher,
1993; Whyte and Watcher, 1992; Zairi et al., 1994). Unfortunately, his commitment to extending democratic values in society and his work on Field Theory,

Group Dynamics, and Action Research which, together with his Three-Step Model, formed an interlinked, elaborate, and robust approach to planned change, have received less and less attention (Ash, 1992; Bargal et al., 1992; Cooke, 1999). Indeed, from the 1980s, even Lewin's work on change was increasingly criticized as relevant only to small-scale changes in stable conditions, and for ignoring issues such as organizational politics and conflict. In its place, writers sought to promote a view of change as being constant, and as a political process within organizations (Dawson, 1994; Pettigrew et al., 1992; Wilson, 1992).

The purpose of this chapter is to reappraise Lewin and his work. The chapter begins by describing Lewin's background, especially the origins of his commitment to resolving social conflict. It then moves on to examine the main elements of his planned approach to change. This is followed by a description of developments in the field of organizational change since Lewin's death, and an evaluation of the criticisms leveled against his work. The chapter concludes by arguing that rather than being outdated, Lewin's planned approach is still very relevant to the needs of the modern world.

LEWIN'S BACKGROUND

Few social scientists can have received the level of praise and admiration that has been heaped upon Kurt Lewin (Ash, 1992; Bargal et al., 1992; Dent and Goldberg, 1999; Dickens and Watkins, 1999; Tobach, 1994). As Edgar Schein (1988, p. 239) enthusiastically commented: "There is little question that the intellectual father of contemporary theories of applied behavioural science, action research and planned change is Kurt Lewin. His seminal work on leadership style and the experiments on planned change which took place in World War II in an effort to change consumer behaviour launched a whole generation of research in group dynamics and the implementation of change programs."

For most of his life, Lewin's main preoccupation was the resolution of social conflict and, in particular, the problems of minority or disadvantaged groups. Underpinning this preoccupation was a strong belief that only the permeation of democratic values into all facets of society could prevent the worst extremes of social conflict. As his wife wrote in the Preface to a volume of his collected work published after his death: "Kurt Lewin was so constantly and predominantly preoccupied with the task of advancing the conceptual representation of the social-psychological world, and at the same time he was so filled with the urgent desire to use his theoretical insight for the building of a better world, that it is difficult to decide which of these two sources of motivation flowed with greater energy or vigour" (Lewin, 1948b).

To a large extent, his interests and beliefs stemmed from his background as a German Jew. Lewin was born in 1890 and, for a Jew growing up in Germany, at this time, officially approved anti-Semitism was a fact of life. Few Jews could expect to achieve a responsible post in the civil service or universities. Despite this, Lewin was awarded a doctorate at the University of Berlin in 1916 and went on to teach there. Though he was never awarded tenured status, Lewin achieved a growing international reputation in the 1920s as a leader in his field (Lewin, 1992). However, with the rise of the Nazi Party, Lewin recognized that the position of Jews in Germany was increasingly threatened. The election of Hitler as Chancellor in 1933 was the final straw for him; he resigned from the University and moved to America (Marrow, 1969).

In America, Lewin found a job first as a "refugee scholar" at Cornell University and then, from 1935 to 1945, at the University of Iowa. Here he was to embark on an ambitious program of research that covered topics such as child-parent relations, conflict in marriage, styles of leadership, worker motivation and performance, conflict in industry, group problem solving, communication and attitude change, racism, anti-Semitism, antiracism, discrimination and prejudice, integration-segregation, peace, war, and poverty (Bargal et al., 1992; Cartwright, 1952; Lewin, 1948a). As Cooke (1999) notes, given the prevalence of racism and anti-Semitism in America at the time, much of this work, especially his increasingly public advocacy in support of disadvantaged groups, put Lewin on the political left.

During the years of the Second World War, Lewin did much work for the American war effort. This included studies of the morale of front-line troops and psychological warfare, and his famous study aimed at persuading American housewives to buy cheaper cuts of meat (Lewin, 1943a; Marrow, 1969). He was also much in demand as a speaker on minority and intergroup relations (Smith, 2001). These activities chimed with one of his central preoccupations, which was how Germany's authoritarian and racist culture could be replaced with one imbued with democratic values. He saw democracy, and the spread of democratic values throughout society, as the central bastion against authoritarianism and despotism. That he viewed the establishment of democracy as a major task, and avoided simplistic and structural recipes, can be gleaned from the following extracts from his article on "The Special Case of Germany" (Lewin, 1943b):

> Nazi culture . . . is deeply rooted, particularly in the youth on whom the future depends. It is a culture which is centred around power as the supreme value and which denounces justice and equality. (p. 43)

> To be stable, a cultural change has to penetrate all aspects of a nation's life. The change must, in short, be a change in the "cultural atmosphere," not merely a change of a single item. (p. 46)

> Change in culture requires the change of leadership forms in every walk of life. At the start, particularly important is leadership in those social areas which are fundamental from the point of view of power. (p. 55)

With the end of the War, Lewin established the Research Center for Group Dynamics at the Massachusetts Institute of Technology. The aim of the Center was to investigate all aspects of group behavior, especially how it could be changed. At the same time, he was also chief architect of the Commission on Community Interrelations (CCI). Founded and funded by the American Jewish Congress, its aim was the eradication of discrimination against all minority groups. As Lewin wrote at the time, "We Jews will have to fight for ourselves and we will do so strongly and with good conscience. We also know that the fight of the Jews is part of the fight of all minorities for democratic equality of rights and opportunities" (quoted in Marrow, 1969, p. 175). In pursuing this objective, Lewin believed that his work on Group Dynamics and Action Research would provide the key tools for the CCI.

Lewin was also influential in establishing the Tavistock Institute in the UK and its journal, *Human Relations* (Jaques, 1998; Marrow, 1969). In addition, in 1946, the Connecticut State Inter-Racial Commission asked Lewin to help train leaders and conduct research on the most effective means of combating racial and religious prejudice in communities. This led to the development of sensitivity training and the creation, in 1947, of the now famous National Training Laboratories. However, his huge workload took its toll on his health, and on February 11, 1947, he died of a heart attack (Lewin, 1992).

Lewin's Work

Lewin was a humanitarian who believed that only by resolving social conflict, whether it be religious, racial, marital, or industrial, could the human condition be improved. Lewin believed that the key to resolving social conflict was to facilitate learning and so enable individuals to understand and restructure their perceptions of the world around them. In this he was much influenced by the Gestalt psychologists he had worked with in Berlin (Smith, 2001). A unifying theme of much of his work is the view that "the group to which an individual belongs is the ground for his perceptions, his feelings and his actions" (Allport, 1948, p. vii). Though Field Theory, Group Dynamics, Action Research, and the Three-Step Model of change are often treated as separate themes of his work, Lewin saw them as a unified whole with each element supporting and reinforcing the others and all of them necessary to understand and bring about planned change, whether it be at the level of the individual, group, organization, or even society (Bargal and Bar, 1992; Kippenberger, 1998a, 1998b; Smith, 2001). As Allport (p. ix) states: "All of his concepts, whatever root-metaphor they employ, comprise a single well-integrated system." This can be seen from examining these four aspects of his work in turn.

Field Theory

This is an approach to understanding group behavior by trying to map out the totality and complexity of the field in which the behavior takes place (Back, 1992). Lewin maintained that to understand any situation it was necessary that: "One should view the present situation—the *status quo*—as being maintained by certain conditions or forces" (Lewin, 1943a, p. 172). Lewin (1947b) postulated that group behavior is an intricate set of symbolic interactions and forces that not only affect group structures, but also modify individual behavior. Therefore, individual behavior is a function of the group environment or "field," as he termed it. Consequently, any changes in behavior stem from changes, be they small or large, in the forces within the field (Lewin, 1947a). Lewin defined a field as "a totality of coexisting facts which are conceived of as mutually interdependent" (Lewin, 1946, p. 240). Lewin believed that a field was in a continuous state of adaptation and that "Change and constancy are relative concepts; group life is never without change, merely differences in the amount and type of change exist" (Lewin, 1947a, p. 199). This is why Lewin used the term "quasi-stationary equilibrium" to indicate that although there might be a rhythm and pattern to the behavior and processes of a group, these tended to fluctuate constantly owing to changes in the forces or circumstances that impinge on the group.

Lewin's view was that if one could identify, plot, and establish the potency of these forces, then it would be possible not only to understand why individuals, groups, and organizations act as they do, but also what forces would need to be diminished or strengthened in order to bring about change. In the main, Lewin saw behavioral change as a slow process; however, he did recognize that under certain circumstances, such as a personal, organizational, or societal crisis, the various forces in the field can shift quickly and radically. In such situations, established routines and behaviors break down and the status quo is no longer viable; new patterns of activity can rapidly emerge and a new equilibrium (or quasi-stationary equilibrium) is formed (Kippenberger, 1998a; Lewin, 1947a).

Despite its obvious value as a vehicle for understanding and changing group behavior, with Lewin's death, the general interest in Field Theory waned (Back, 1992; Gold, 1992; Hendry, 1996). However, in recent years, with the work of Argyris (1990) and Hirschhorn (1988) on understanding and overcoming resistance to change, Lewin's work on Field Theory has once again begun to attract interest. According to Hendry (1996), even critics of Lewin's work have drawn on Field Theory to develop their own models of change (see Pettigrew et al., 1989, 1992). Indeed, parallels have even been drawn between Lewin's work and the work of complexity theorists (Kippenberger, 1998a). Back (1992), for example, argued that the formulation and behavior of complex systems as described by Chaos and Catastrophe theorists bear striking similarities to Lewin's conceptualization of Field Theory. Nevertheless, Field Theory is now probably the least understood element of Lewin's work, yet, because of its potential to map the forces impinging on an individual, group, or organization, it underpinned the other elements of his work.

Group Dynamics

The word "dynamics" . . . comes from a Greek word
meaning force . . . "group dynamics" refers to the forces
operating in groups . . . it is a study of these forces: what
gives rise to them, what conditions modify them, what
consequences they have, etc.
—(Cartwright, 1951, p. 382)

Lewin was the first psychologist to write about "group dynamics" and the importance of the group in shaping the behavior of its members (Allport, 1948; Bargal et al., 1992). Indeed, Lewin's definition (1939, p. 165) of a "group" is still generally accepted: "it is not the similarity or dissimilarity of individuals that constitutes a group, but interdependence of fate." As Kippenberger (1998a) notes, Lewin was addressing two questions: What is it about the nature and characteristics of a particular group that causes it to respond (behave) as it does to the forces that impinge on it, and how can these forces be changed in order to elicit a more desirable form of behavior? It was to address these questions that Lewin began to develop the concept of Group Dynamics.

Group Dynamics stresses that group behavior, rather than that of individuals, should be the main focus of change (Bernstein, 1968; Dent and Goldberg, 1999). Lewin (1947b) maintained that it is fruitless to concentrate on changing the behavior of individuals because the individual in isolation is constrained by group pressures to conform. Consequently, the focus of change must be at the group level and should concentrate on factors such as group norms, roles, interactions, and socialization processes to create "disequilibrium" and change (Schein, 1988).

Lewin's pioneering work on Group Dynamics not only laid the foundations for our understanding of groups (Cooke, 1999; Dent and Goldberg, 1999; French and Bell, 1984; Marrow, 1969; Schein, 1988) but has also been linked to complexity theories by researchers examining self-organizing theory and nonlinear systems (Tschacher and Brunner, 1995). However, understanding the internal dynamics of a group is not sufficient by itself to bring about change. Lewin also recognized the need to provide a process whereby the members could be engaged in and committed to changing their behavior. This led Lewin to develop Action Research and the Three-Step Model of change.

Action Research

This term was coined by Lewin (1946) in an article entitled "Action Research and Minority Problems." Lewin stated in the article: "In the last year and a half

I have had occasion to have contact with a great variety of organizations, institutions, and individuals who came for help in the field of group relations'' (p. 201).

However, though these people exhibited "a great amount of good-will, of readiness to face the problem squarely and really do something about it. . . . These eager people feel themselves to be in a fog. They feel in a fog on three counts: 1. What is the present situation? 2. What are the dangers? 3. And most importantly of all, what shall we do?'' (Lewin, 1946, p. 201).

Lewin conceived of Action Research as a two-pronged process that would allow groups to address these three questions. Firstly, it emphasizes that change requires action, and is directed at achieving this. Secondly, it recognizes that successful action is based on analyzing the situation correctly, identifying all the possible alternative solutions, and choosing the one most appropriate to the situation at hand (Bennett, 1983). To be successful, though, there has also to be a "felt need." Felt need is an individual's inner realization that change is necessary. If felt-need is low in the group or organization, introducing change becomes problematic. The theoretical foundations of Action Research lie in Gestalt psychology, which stresses that change can only successfully be achieved by helping individuals to reflect on and gain new insights into the totality of their situation. Lewin (1946, p. 206) stated that Action Research "proceeds in a spiral of steps each of which is composed of a circle of planning, action, and fact-finding about the results of the action." It is an iterative process whereby research leads to action and action leads to evaluation and further research. As Schein (1996, p. 64) comments, it was Lewin's view that "one cannot understand an organization without trying to change it." Indeed, Lewin's view was very much that the understanding and learning which process produces for the individuals and groups concerned, which then feeds into changed behavior, is more important than any resulting change as such (Lewin, 1946).

To this end, Action Research draws on Lewin's work on Field Theory to identify the forces that focus on the group to which the individual belongs. It also draws on Group Dynamics to understand why group members behave in the way they do when subjected to these forces. Lewin stressed that the routines and patterns of behavior in a group are more than just the outcome of opposing forces in a force field. They have a value in themselves and have a positive role to play in enforcing group norms (Lewin, 1947a). Action Research stresses that for change to be effective, it must take place at the group level, and must be a participative and collaborative process that involves all of those concerned (Allport, 1948; Bargal et al., 1992; French and Bell, 1984; Lewin, 1947b).

Lewin's first Action Research project was to investigate and reduce violence between Catholic and Jewish teenage gangs. This was quickly followed by a project to integrate black and white sales staff in New York department stores

(Marrow, 1969). However, Action Research was also adopted by the Tavistock Institute in Britain, and used to improve managerial competence and efficiency in the newly nationalized coal industry. Since then it has acquired strong adherents throughout the world (Dickens and Watkins, 1999; Eden and Huxham, 1996; Elden and Chisholm, 1993). However, Lewin (1947a, p. 228) was concerned that "a change towards a higher level of group performance is frequently short lived; after a 'shot in the arm,' group life soon returns to the previous level. This indicates that it does not suffice to define the objective of a planned change in group performance as the reaching of a different level. Permanency at the new level, or permanency for a desired period, should be included in the objective."

It was for this reason that he developed his Three-Step Model of change.

Three-Step Model

This is often cited as Lewin's key contribution to organizational change. However, it needs to be recognized that when he developed his Three-Step Model Lewin was not thinking only of organizational issues. Nor did he intend it to be seen separately from the other three elements that make up his planned approach to change (i.e., Field Theory, Group Dynamics, and Action Research). Rather Lewin saw the four concepts as forming an integrated approach to analyzing, understanding, and bringing about change at the group, organizational, and societal levels.

A successful change project, Lewin (1947a) argued, involved three steps.

Step One: Unfreezing. Lewin believed that the stability of human behavior was based on a quasi-stationary equilibrium supported by a complex field of driving and restraining forces. He argued that the equilibrium needs to be destabilized (unfrozen) before old behavior can be discarded (unlearnt) and new behavior successfully adopted. Given the type of issues that Lewin was addressing, as one would expect, he did not believe that change would be easy or that the same approach could be applied in all situations: "The unfreezing of the present level may involve quite different problems in different cases. Allport . . . has described the 'catharsis' which seems necessary before prejudice can be removed. To break open the shell of complacency and self-righteousness it is sometimes necessary to bring about an emotional stir up" (Lewin, 1947a, p. 229).

Enlarging on Lewin's ideas, Schein (1996, p. 27) comments that the key to unfreezing "was to recognize that change, whether at the individual or group level, was a profound psychological dynamic process." Schein (1996) identifies three processes necessary to achieve unfreezing: disconfirmation of the validity of the status quo, the induction of guilt or survival anxiety, and creating psychological safety. He argued that "unless sufficient psychological safety is created, the disconfirming information will be denied or in other way defended against, no survival anxiety will be felt, and consequently, no change will take place'' (Schein, 1996, p. 61). In other words, those concerned have to feel safe from loss and humiliation before they can accept the new information and reject old behaviors.

Step Two: Moving.   As Schein (1996, p. 62) notes, unfreezing is not an end in itself; it "creates motivation to learn but does not necessarily control or predict the direction." This echoes Lewin's view that any attempt to predict or identify a specific outcome from planned change is very difficult because of the complexity of the forces concerned. Instead, one should seek to take into account all the forces at work and identify and evaluate, on a trial and error basis, all the available options (Lewin, 1947a). This is, of course, the learning approach promoted by Action Research. It is this iterative approach of research, action, and more research that enables groups and individuals to move from a less acceptable to a more acceptable set of behaviors. However, as noted above, Lewin (1947a) recognized that, without reinforcement, change could be short-lived.

Step Three: Refreezing.   This is the final step in the Three-Step Model. Refreezing seeks to stabilize the group at a new quasi-stationary equilibrium in order to ensure that the new behaviors are relatively safe from regression. The main point about refreezing is that new behavior must be, to some degree, congruent with the rest of the behavior, personality, and environment of the learner or it will simply lead to a new round of disconfirmation (Schein, 1996). This is why Lewin saw successful change as a group activity, because unless group norms and routines are also transformed, changes to individual behavior will not be sustained. In organizational terms, refreezing often requires changes to organizational culture, norms, policies, and practices (Cummings and Huse, 1989).

   Like other aspects of Lewin's work, his Three-Step Model of change has become unfashionable in the last two decades (Dawson, 1994; Hatch, 1997; Kanter et al., 1992). Nevertheless, such is its continuing influence that, as Hendry (1996, p. 624) commented: "Scratch any account of creating and managing change and the idea that change is a three-stage process which necessarily begins with a process of unfreezing will not be far below the surface."

LEWIN AND CHANGE: A SUMMARY

Lewin was primarily interested in resolving social conflict through behavioral change, whether this be within organizations or in the wider society. He identified two requirements for success:

1. To analyze and understand how social groupings were formed, motivated, and maintained. To do this, he developed both Field Theory and
   Group Dynamics.

2. To change the behavior of social groups. The primary methods he developed for achieving this were Action Research and the Three-Step Model
   of change.

Underpinning Lewin's work was a strong moral and ethical belief in the importance of democratic institutions and democratic values in society. Lewin believed that only by strengthening democratic participation in all aspects of life
and being able to resolve social conflicts could the scourge of despotism,
authoritarianism, and racism be effectively countered. Since his death, Lewin's
wider social agenda has been mainly pursued under the umbrella of Action Research (Dickens and Watkins, 1999). This is also the area where Lewin's
planned approach has been most closely followed. For example, Bargal and
Bar (1992) described how, over a number of years, they used Lewin's approach
to address the conflict between Arab-Palestinian and Jewish youths in Israel
through the development of intergroup workshops. The workshops were developed around six principles based on Lewin's work:

> (a) a recursive process of data collection to determine goals, action to implement
> goals and assessment of the action; (b) feedback of research results to trainers; (c)
> cooperation between researchers and practitioners; (d) research based on the
> laws of the group's social life, on three stages of change—"unfreezing,"
> "moving," and "refreezing"—and on the principles of group decision making; (e)
> consideration of the values, goals and power structures of change agents and
> clients; and (f) use of research to create knowledge and/or solve problems.

> **(Bargal and Bar, 1992, p. 146)**

In terms of organizational change, Lewin and his associates had a long and
fruitful relationship with the Harwood Manufacturing Corporation, where his
approach to change was developed, applied, and refined (Marrow, 1969). Coch
and French (1948, p. 512) observed that, at Harwood: "From the point of view
of factory management, there were two purposes to the research: (1) Why do
people resist change so strongly? and (2) What can be done to overcome this
resistance?" Therefore, in both his wider social agenda and his narrower
organizational agenda, Lewin sought to address similar issues and apply similar concepts. Since his death, it is the organizational side of his work that has
been given greater prominence by his followers and successors, mainly
through the creation of the Organization Development (OD) movement (Cummings and Worley, 1997; French and Bell, 1995).

OD has become the standard-bearer for Kurt Lewin's pioneering work on
behavioral science in general, and approach to planned change in particular

(Cummings and Worley, 1997). Up to the 1970s, OD tended to focus on group issues in organizations, and sought to promote Lewin's humanistic and democratic approach to change in the values it espoused (Conner, 1977; Gellerman et al., 1990; Warwick and Thompson, 1980). However, as French and Bell (1995) noted, since the late 1970s, in order to keep pace with the perceived needs of organizations, there has been a major broadening of scope within the OD field. It has moved away from its focus on groups and towards more organizationwide issues, such as Socio-Technical Systems, organizational culture, organizational learning, and radical transformational change. Nevertheless, despite OD's attempts to modernize itself, in the last twenty years Lewin's legacy has met with increasing competition.

NEWER PERSPECTIVES ON CHANGE

By the early 1980s, with the oil shocks of the 1970s, the rise of corporate Japan, and severe economic downturn in the West, it was clear that many organizations needed to transform themselves rapidly and often brutally if they were to survive (Burnes, 2000). Given its group-based, consensual, and relatively slow nature, Lewin's planned approach began to attract criticism as to its appropriateness and efficacy, especially from the Culture-Excellence school, the postmodernists, and the processualists.

The Culture-Excellence approach to organizations, as promoted by Peters and Waterman (1982) and Kanter (1989), has had an unprecedented impact on the management of organizations by equating organizational success with the possession of a strong, appropriate organizational culture (Collins, 1998; Watson, 1997; Wilson, 1992). Peters and Waterman argued that Western organizations were losing their competitive edge because they were too bureaucratic, inflexible, and slow to change. Instead of the traditional top-down, command-and-control style of management, which tended to segment organizations into small rule-driven units, proponents of Culture-Excellence stressed the integrated nature of organizations, both internally and within their environments (Kanter, 1983; Watson, 1997). To survive, it was argued, organizations needed to reconfigure themselves to build internal and external synergies, and managers needed to encourage a spirit of innovation, experimentation, and entrepreneurship through the creation of strong, appropriate organizational cultures (Collins, 1998; Kanter, 1983; Peters and Waterman, 1982; Wilson, 1992).

For proponents of Culture-Excellence, the world is essentially an ambiguous place where detailed plans are not possible and flexibility is essential. Instead of close supervision and strict rules, organizational objectives need to be promoted by loose controls, based on shared values and culture, and pursued through empowered employees using their own initiative (Watson, 1997). They argue that change cannot be driven from the top but must emerge in an organic, bottom-up fashion from the day-to-day actions of all in the organization (Collins, 1998; Hatch, 1997). Proponents of Culture-Excellence reject as antithetical the planned approach to change, sometimes quite scathingly, as the following quotation from Kanter et al. shows: "Lewin's model was a simple one, with organizational change involving three stages: unfreezing, changing and refreezing. . . . This quaintly linear and static conception—the organization as an ice cube—is so wildly inappropriate that it is difficult to see why it has not only survived but prospered. . . . Suffice it to say here, first, that organizations are never frozen, much less refrozen, but are fluid entities with many 'personalities.' Second, to the extent that there are stages, they overlap and interpenetrate one another in important ways" (1992, p. 10).

At the same time that the Culture-Excellence school were criticizing planned change, others, notably Pfeffer (1981, 1992), were claiming that the objectives, and outcomes, of change programs were more likely to be determined by power struggles than by any process of consensus building or rational decision making. For the postmodernists, power is also a central feature of organizational change, but it arises from the socially constructed nature of organizational life:

> In a socially-constructed world, responsibility for environmental conditions lies with those who do the constructing. . . . This suggests at least two competing scenarios for organizational change. First, organization change can be a vehicle of domination for those who conspire to enact the world for others. . . . An alternative use of social constructionism is to create a democracy of enactment in which the process is made open and available to all . . . such that we create opportunities for freedom and innovation rather than simply for further domination.
>
> **(Hatch, 1997, pp. 367–8)**

The other important perspective on organizational change that emerged in the 1980s was the processual approach, which derives from the work of Andrew Pettigrew (1973, 1979, 1985, 1990a, 1990b, 1997). Processualists reject prescriptive, recipe-driven approaches to change and are suspicious of single causes or simple explanations of events. Instead, when studying change, they focus on the interrelatedness of individuals, groups, organizations, and society (Dawson, 1994; Pettigrew and Whipp, 1993; Wilson, 1992). In particular, they claim that the process of change is a complex and untidy cocktail of rational decision processes, individual perceptions, political struggles, and coalition building (Huczynski and Buchanan, 2001). Pettigrew (1990a, 1990b) maintains that the planned approach is too prescriptive and does not pay enough attention to the need to analyze and conceptualize organizational change. He argues that change needs to be studied across different levels of analysis and different time periods, and that it cuts across functions, spans hierarchical divisions, and has no neat starting or finishing point; instead it is a "complex analytical, political, and cultural process of challenging and changing the core beliefs, structure and strategy of the firm" (Pettigrew, 1987, p. 650).

Looking at planned change versus a processual approach, Dawson (1994, pp. 3–4) comments that:

> Although this [Lewin's] theory has proved useful in understanding planned change under relatively stable conditions, with the continuing and dynamic nature of change in today's business world, it no longer makes sense to implement a planned process for "freezing" changed behaviours. . . . The processual framework . . . adopts the view that change is a complex and dynamic process which should not be solidified or treated as a series of linear events. . . . Central to the development of a processual approach is the need to incorporate an analysis of the politics of managing change.

Also taking a processualist perspective, Buchanan and Storey's main criticism of those who advocate planned change is "their attempt to impose an order and a linear sequence to processes that are in reality messy and untidy, and which unfold in an iterative fashion with much backtracking and omission" (1997, p. 127).

Though there are distinct differences between these newer approaches to change, not least the prescriptive focus of the Culture-Excellence approach versus the analytical orientation of the processualists, there are also some striking similarities that they claim strongly challenge the validity of the planned approach to change. The newer approaches tend to take a holistic/contextual view of organizations and their environments; they challenge the notion of change as an ordered, rational, and linear process; and there is an emphasis on change as a continuous process that is heavily influenced by culture, power, and politics (Buchanan and Storey, 1997; Burnes, 2000; Dawson, 1994; Kanter et al., 1992; Pettigrew, 1997). Accompanying and offering support to these new approaches to change were new perspectives on the nature of change in organizations. Up to the late 1970s, the incremental model of change dominated. Advocates of this view see change as being a process whereby individual parts of an organization deal incrementally and separately with one problem and one goal at a time. By managers responding to pressures in their local internal and external environments in this way, over time, their organizations become transformed (Cyert and March, 1963; Hedberg et al., 1976; Lindblom, 1959; Quinn, 1980, 1982).

In the 1980s, two new perspectives on change emerged: the punctuated equilibrium model and the continuous transformation model. The former approach to change "depicts organizations as evolving through relatively long periods of stability (equilibrium periods) in their basic patterns of activity that are punctuated by relatively short bursts of fundamental change (revolutionary periods). Revolutionary periods substantively disrupt established activity patterns and install the basis for new equilibrium periods" (Romanelli and Tushman, 1994, p. 1141).

The inspiration for this model arises from two sources: firstly, from the challenge to Darwin's gradualist model of evolution in the natural sciences (Gould, 1989); secondly, from research showing that although organizations do appear to fit the incrementalist model of change for a period of time, there does come a point when they go through a period of rapid and fundamental change (Gersick, 1991).

Proponents of the continuous transformation model reject both the incrementalist and punctuated equilibrium models. They argue that, in order to survive, organizations must develop the ability to change themselves continuously in a fundamental manner. This is particularly the case in fast-moving sectors such as retail (Greenwald, 1996). Brown and Eisenhardt (1997, p. 29) draw on the work of complexity theorists to support their claim for continuous change:

> Like organizations, complex systems have large numbers of independent yet interacting actors. Rather than ever reaching a stable equilibrium, the most adaptive of these complex systems (e.g., intertidal zones) keep changing continuously by remaining at the poetically termed "edge of chaos" that exists between order and disorder. By staying in this intermediate zone, these systems never quite settle into a stable equilibrium but never quite fall apart. Rather, these systems, which stay constantly poised between order and disorder, exhibit the most prolific, complex and continuous change.

Complexity theories are increasingly being used by organization theorists and practitioners as a way of understanding and changing organizations (Bechtold, 1997; Black, 2000; Boje, 2000; Choi et al., 2001; Gilchrist, 2000; Lewis, 1994; Macbeth, 2002; Shelton and Darling, 2001; Stacey et al., 2002; Tetenbaum, 1998). Complexity theories come from the natural sciences, where they have shown that disequilibrium is a necessary condition for the growth of dynamic systems (Prigogine and Stengers, 1984). Under this view, organizations, like complex systems in nature, are seen as dynamic nonlinear systems. The outcome of their actions is unpredictable but, like turbulence in gases and liquids, it is governed by a set of simple order-generating rules (Brown and Eisenhardt, 1997; Lewis, 1994; Lorenz, 1993; Mintzberg et al., 1998; Stacey et al., 2002; Tetenbaum, 1998; Wheatley, 1992). For organizations, as for natural systems, the key to survival is to develop rules that are capable of keeping an organization operating "on the edge of chaos" (Stacey et al., 2002). If organizations are too stable, nothing changes and the system dies; if too chaotic, the system will be overwhelmed by change. In both situations, radical change is necessary in order to create a new set of order-generating rules that allow the organization to prosper and survive (MacIntosh and MacLean, 2001).

As can be seen, the newer approaches to change and the newer perspectives on the nature of change have much in common. One of the problems with all three perspectives on change—incrementalism, punctuated equilibrium, and continuous change—is that all three are present in organizational life and none appear dominant. Indeed, Burnes (2000) even questions whether these are separate and competing theories, or merely different ways of looking at the same phenomenon: change. He points out that sectoral, temporal, and organizational life cycle differences can account for whether organizations experience incremental, punctuated equilibrium or continuous change (Kimberley and Miles, 1980). He also draws on the natural sciences, in the form of population ecology, to argue that in any given population of organizations one would expect to see all three types of change (Hannan and Freeman, 1988). Therefore, rather like the Jungian concept of the light and dark, these various perspectives on change may be shadow images of each other, none by itself capable of portraying the whole (Matthews, 2002).

LEWIN'S WORK: CRITICISMS AND RESPONSES

From the 1980s onwards, as newer perspectives on organizational life and change have emerged, Lewin's planned approach has faced increasing levels of criticisms. This section summarizes the main criticisms and responds to them.

Criticism One

Many have argued that Lewin's planned approach is too simplistic and mechanistic for a world where organizational change is a continuous and open-ended process (Dawson, 1994; Garvin, 1993; Kanter et al., 1992; Nonaka, 1988; Pettigrew, 1990a, 1990b; Pettigrew et al., 1989; Stacey, 1993; Wilson, 1992).

Response One

These criticisms appear to stem from a misreading of how Lewin perceived stability and change. He stated:

> One should view the present situation—the *status quo*—as being maintained by certain conditions or forces. A culture—for instance, the food habits of a certain group at a given time—is not a static affair but a live process like a river which moves but still keeps to a recognizable form. . . . Food habits do not occur in empty space. They are part and parcel of the daily rhythm of being awake and asleep; of being alone and in a group; of earning a living and playing; of being a member of a town, a family, a social class, a religious group . . . in a district with

good groceries and restaurants or in an area of poor and irregular food supply. Somehow all these factors affect food habits at any given time. They determine the food habits of a group every day anew just as the amount of water supply and the nature of the river bed determine the flow of the river, its constancy or change.

(Lewin, 1943a, pp. 172–3)

Far from viewing social or organizational groups as fixed and stable, or viewing change as linear and unidimensional, it is clear that he understood the limits of stability at least as well as his critics. He argued that social settings are in a state of constant change but that, just like a river, the rate varies depending on the environment. He viewed change not as a predictable and planned move from one stable state to another, but as a complex and iterative learning process where the journey was more important than the destination, where stability was at best quasi-stationary and always fluid, and where, given the complex forces involved, outcomes cannot be predicted but emerge on a trial and error basis (Kippenberger, 1998a; Lewin, 1947a). Therefore, rather than being prescriptive, Lewin recognized the unpredictable (nonlinear) nature of change and, as Hendry (1996) notes, he adopted the same "contextualist" and learning approach favored by many of his critics. Indeed, as outlined earlier, some argue that Lewin's conception of stability and change is very similar to that of many complexity theorists (Back, 1992; Elrod and Tippett, 2002; Kippenberger, 1998a; MacIntosh and MacLean, 2001; Tschacher and Brunner, 1995).

We should also note that when Lewin wrote of "refreezing," he referred to preventing individuals and groups from regressing to their old behaviors. In this respect, Lewin's view seems to be similar to that of his critics. For example, the last stage in Kanter et al.'s model of change (1992, p. 384) is to "Reinforce and institutionalize the change." More telling, though, is that when Elrod and Tippett (2002) compared a wide range of change models, they found that most approaches to organizational change were strikingly similar to Lewin's Three-Step Model. When they extended their research to other forms of human and organizational change, they also found that "Models of the change process, as perceived by diverse and seemingly unrelated disciplines [such as bereavement theory, personal transition theory, creative processes, cultural revolutions, and scientific revolutions] . . . follow Lewin's . . . three-phase model of change" (Elrod and Tippett, p. 273).

Criticism Two

Lewin's work is only relevant to incremental and isolated change projects and is not able to incorporate radical, transformational change (Dawson, 1994; Dunphy and Stace, 1992, 1993; Harris, 1985; Miller and Friesen, 1984; Pettigrew, 1990a, 1990b).

Response Two

This criticism appears to relate to the speed rather than the magnitude of change because, as Quinn (1980, 1982) pointed out, over time, incremental change can lead to radical transformations. It is also necessary to recognize that Lewin was concerned with behavioral change at the individual, group, organizational, and societal levels (Dickens and Watkins, 1999), whereas rapid transformational change is seen as only being applicable to situations requiring major structural change (Allaire and Firsirotu, 1984; Beer and Nohria, 2000; Burnes, 2000; Cummings and Worley, 1997). Even in such situations, as Kanter et al. (1992) maintain, these "Bold Strokes" often need to be followed by a whole series of incremental changes (a "Long March") in order to align an organization's culture and behaviors with the new structure. Lewin did recognize that radical behavioral or cultural change could take place rapidly in times of crisis (Kippenberger, 1998a; Lewin, 1947a). Such crises may require directive change; again, this may be successful in terms of structural change but research by Lewin and others has shown that it rarely works in cases where behavioral change is required (Lewin, 1947b; Kanter et al., 1992; Schein, 1996; Stace and Dunphy, 2001).

Criticism Three

Lewin stands accused of ignoring the role of power and politics in organizations and the conflictual nature of much of organizational life (Dawson, 1994; Hatch, 1997; Pettigrew, 1980; Pfeffer, 1992; Wilson, 1992).

Response Three

Given the issues that Lewin was addressing, this seems a strange criticism. Anyone seriously addressing racism and religious intolerance, as Lewin was, could not ignore these issues. As Bargal et al. (1992, p. 8) note, Lewin's approach to change required "the taking into account differences in value systems and power structures of all the parties involved." This is clear from the following quotation (Lewin, 1946, p. 203):

> An attempt to improve inter-group relations has to face a wide variety of tasks. It deals with problems of attitude and stereotypes in regard to other groups and one's own group, with problems of development of attitudes and conduct during childhood and adolescence, with problems of housing, and the change of the legal structure of the community; it deals with problems of status and caste, with problems of economic discrimination, with political leadership, and with leadership in many aspects of community life. It deals with the small social body of the family, a club or a friendship group, with the larger social body of a school or school system, with neighborhoods and with social bodies of the size of a community, of the state and with international problems.

We are beginning to see that it is hopeless to attack any one of these aspects of inter-group relations without considering the others.

One also needs to be aware that French and Raven's Power/Interaction Model (French and Raven, 1959; Raven, 1965), on which much of the literature on power and politics is based, owes much to Lewin's work (Raven, 1993). French was a long-time collaborator of Lewin, and Raven studied at the Research Center for Group Dynamics in the 1950s. Both have acknowledged the importance and influence of his work on their perspective on power (House, 1993; Raven, 1993, 1999).

Criticism Four

Lewin is seen as advocating a top-down, management-driven approach to change and ignoring situations requiring bottom-up change (Dawson, 1994; Kanter et al., 1992; Wilson, 1992).

Response Four

Lewin was approached for help by a wide range of groups and organizations: "They included representatives of communities, school systems, single schools, minority organizations of a variety of backgrounds and objectives; they included labor and management representatives, departments of the national and state governments, and so on" (Lewin, 1946, p. 201).

He clearly recognized that the pressure for change comes from many quarters, not just managers and leaders, and sought to provide an approach that could accommodate this. However, regardless of who identified the need to change, Lewin argued that effective change could not take place unless there was a "felt need" by all those concerned; he did not see one group or individual as driving or dominating the change process but saw everyone as playing a full and equal part (Lewin, 1947b). He believed that only by gaining the commitment of all those concerned, through their full involvement in the change process, would change be successful (Bargal et al., 1992; Dickens and Watkins, 1999; French and Bell, 1984). Consequently, rather than arguing that Lewin saw behavioral change as a top-down process, it would be more accurate to say that Lewin recognized that it could be initiated from the top, bottom, or middle but that it could not be successful without the active, willing, and equal participation of all.

CONCLUSION

Lewin undoubtedly had an enormous impact on the field of change. In reappraising Lewin's planned approach to change, this chapter seeks to address three issues: the nature of his contribution, the validity of the criticisms leveled against him, and the relevance of his work for contemporary social and organizational change.

Looking at Lewin's contribution to change theory and practice, there are three key points to note. The first is that Lewin's work stemmed from his concern to find an effective approach to resolving social conflict through changing group behavior (whether these conflicts be at the group, organizational, or societal level). The second point is to recognize that Lewin promoted an ethical and humanist approach to change, which saw learning and involvement as being the key processes for achieving behavioral change. This was for two reasons: (1) he saw this approach as helping to develop and strengthen democratic values in society as a whole and thus acting as a buffer against the racism and totalitarianism that so dominated events in his lifetime; (2) on the basis of his background in Gestalt psychology and his own research, he saw this approach as being the most effective in bringing about sustained behavioral change. The last point concerns the nature of Lewin's work. Lewin's planned approach to change is based on four mutually reinforcing concepts, namely Field Theory, Group Dynamics, Action Research, and the Three-Step Model, which are used in combination to bring about effective change. His critics, though, tend to treat these as separate and independent elements of Lewin's work and, in the main, concentrate on his Three-Step Model of change. When seen in isolation, the Three-Step Model can be portrayed as simplistic. When seen alongside the other elements of Lewin's planned approach, it becomes a much more robust approach to change.

We can now examine the criticisms made of Lewin's planned approach to change. The main criticisms leveled at Lewin are that (1) his view of stability and change in organizations was at best no longer applicable and at worst "wildly inappropriate" (Kanter et al., 1992, p. 10); (2) his approach to change is only suitable for isolated and incremental change situations; (3) he ignored power and politics; and (4) he adopted a top-down, management-driven approach to change. These criticisms were addressed above, but to recap:

1. There is substantial evidence that Lewin (1947a, p. 199) recognized that "Change and constancy are relative concepts; group life is never without change, merely differences in the amount and type of change exist." There is also a substantial body of evidence in the social, and even physical sciences, to support Lewin's three-step perspective on change (Elrod and Tippett, 2002; Hendry, 1996).

2. As Dickens and Watkins (1999, p. 127) observed, Lewin's approach is "intended to foster change on the group, organizational and even societal levels." In the main, he saw change as a slow process of working with and through groups to achieve behavioral and cultural change. However, writers as

diverse as Quinn (1980, 1982) and Kanter et al. (1992) have recognized that an incremental approach can achieve organizational transformation. Lewin also recognized that, under certain crisis conditions, organizational transformations can be achieved rapidly (Kippenberger, 1998a; Lewin, 1947a). Nevertheless, in the main, even amongst Lewin's critics, the general view is that only structural and technical change can be achieved relatively speedily (Dawson, 1994; Kanter et al., 1992; Pettigrew et al., 1989, 1992; Wilson, 1992).

3. Given Lewin's concern with issues such as racial and religious conflict, the accusation that he ignored the role of power and politics is difficult to sustain. One of the main strengths of Field Theory and Group Dynamics is that they identify the forces within and between groups and show how individuals behave in response to these. In addition, the iterative, investigative, and learning approaches that lie at the heart of Action Research and the Three-Step Model are also designed to reveal and address such issues (Bargal and Bar, 1992).

4. The issues Lewin sought to tackle were many and varied (Cartwright, 1952; Lewin, 1948a). Lewin's sympathies were clearly with the underdog, the disadvantaged, and the discriminated against (Cooke, 1999; Marrow, 1969). His assistance was sought by a wide range of parties including national and local government, religious and racial groups, and employers and unions; his response emphasized learning and participation by all concerned (Lewin, 1946). In the face of this, the charge that he saw change as only being top-down or management-driven is difficult to sustain.

Lewin's critics have sought to show that his planned approach to change was simplistic and outmoded. By rejecting these criticisms, and by revealing the nature of his approach, this chapter has also shown the continuing relevance of Lewin's work, whether in organizations or society at large. The need to resolve social conflict has certainly not diminished since Lewin's day. Nor can one say that Lewin's approach seems dated, based as it is on building understanding, generating learning, gaining new insights, and identifying and testing (and retesting) solutions (Bargal and Bar, 1992; Darwin et al., 2002). Certainly, there seems little evidence that one can achieve peace, reconciliation, cooperation, or trust by force (Olsen, 2002). Likewise, in organizations, issues of group effectiveness, behavior, and change have not diminished in the half century since Lewin's death, though they may often now be labeled differently. However, as in Lewin's day, there are no quick or easy ways of achieving such changes, and Lewin's approach is clearly still valuable and influential in these areas (Cummings and Worley, 1997). This can be seen from the enormous emphasis that continues to be placed on the importance of group behavior, involvement, and empowerment (Argyris, 1992; Handy, 1994; Hannagan, 2002; Huczynski and Buchanan, 2001; Kanter, 1989; Mullins, 2002; Peters,

1993; Schein, 1988; Senge, 1990; Wilson, 1992). Indeed, the advent of the complexity perspective appears to be leading to a renewed interest in Lewin's work (Back, 1992; Kippenberger, 1998a; MacIntosh and MacLean, 2001; Tschacher and Brunner, 1995).

In conclusion, therefore, though Lewin's contribution to organizational change has come under increasing criticism since the 1980s, much of this appears to be unfounded and/or based on a narrow interpretation of his work. In contrast, the last decade has also seen a renewed interest in understanding and applying his approach to change (Bargal and Bar, 1992; Elrod and Tippett, 2002; Hendry, 1996; Kippenberger, 1998a; MacIntosh and MacLean, 2001; Wooten and White, 1999). In many respects, this should not come as a surprise given the tributes and acknowledgments paid to him by major figures such as Chris Argyris (Argyris et al., 1985) and Edgar Schein (1988). Above all, though, it is a recognition of the rigor of Lewin's work, based as it was on a virtuous circle of theory, experimentation, and practice, and that is best expressed by his famous dictum that "there is nothing so practical as a good theory" (Lewin, 1943–44, p. 169).

References

Allaire, Y. and Firsirotu, M. E. (1984). "Theories of organizational culture." *Organization Studies*, 5, 3, 193–226.

Allport, G. W. (1948). "Foreword." In Lewin, G. W. (Ed.), *Resolving Social Conflict*. London: Harper & Row.

Argyris, C. (1990). *Overcoming Organizational Defenses*. Boston, MA: Allen and Bacon.

Argyris, C. (1992). *On Organizational Learning*. Oxford: Blackwell.

Argyris, C., Putnam, R. and McLain-Smith, D. (1985). *Action Science: Concepts, Methods and Skills for Research and Intervention*. San Francisco, CA: Jossey-Bass.

Ash, M. G. (1992). "Cultural contexts and scientific change in psychology—Kurt Lewin in Iowa." *American Psychologist*, 47, 2, 198–207.

Back, K. W. (1992). "This business of topology." *Journal of Social Issues*, 48, 2, 51–66.

Bargal, D. and Bar, H. (1992). "A Lewinian approach to intergroup workshops for Arab-Palestinian and Jewish Youth." *Journal of Social Issues*, 48, 2, 139–54.

Bargal, D., Gold, M. and Lewin, M. (1992). "The heritage of Kurt Lewin—Introduction." *Journal of Social Issues*, 48, 2, 3–13.

Bechtold, B. L. (1997). "Chaos theory as a model for strategy development." *Empowerment in Organizations*, 5, 4, 193–202.

Beer, M. and Nohria, N. (2000). "Cracking the code of change." *Harvard Business Review*, May–June, 133–41.

Bennett, R. (1983). *Management Research*. Management Development Series, 20. Geneva: International Labour Office.

Bernstein, L. (1968). *Management Development*. London: Business Books.

Black, J. (2000). "Fermenting change: capitalizing on the inherent change found in dynamic nonlinear (or complex) systems." *Journal of Organizational Change Management*, 13, 6, 520–25.

Boje, D. M. (2000). "Phenomenal complexity theory and change at Disney: response to Letiche." *Journal of Organizational Change Management*, 13, 6, 558–66.

Brown, S. L. and Eisenhardt, K. M. (1997). "The art of continuous change: linking complexity theory and time-paced evolution in relentlessly shifting organizations." *Administrative Science Quarterly*, 42, March, 1–34.

Buchanan, D. A. and Storey, J. (1997). "Role-taking and role-switching in organizational change: the four pluralities. In McLoughlin, I. and Harris, M. (Eds.), *Innovation, Organizational Change and Technology*. London: International Thompson.

Burnes, B. (2000). *Managing Change*, 3rd edition. Harlow: FT/Pearson Educational.

Cartwright, D. (1951). "Achieving change in people: some applications of group dynamics theory." *Human Relations*, 6, 4, 381–92.

Cartwright, D. (Ed.) (1952). *Field Theory in Social Science*. London: Social Science Paperbacks.

Choi, T. Y., Dooley, K. J. and Rungtusanatham, M. (2001). "Supply networks and complex adaptive systems: control versus emergence." *Journal of Operations Management*, 19, 3, 351–66.

Coch, L. and French, J.R.P. Jr. (1948). "Overcoming resistance to change." *Human Relations*, 1, 4, 512–32.

Collins, D. (1998). *Organizational Change*. London: Routledge.

Conner, P. E. (1977). "A critical enquiry into some assumptions and values characterizing OD." *Academy of Management Review*, 2, 1, 635–44.

Cooke, B. (1999). "Writing the left out of management theory: the historiography of the management of change." *Organization*, 6, 1, 81–105.

Cummings, T. G. and Huse, E. F. (1989). *Organization Development and Change*, 4th edition. St Paul, MN: West Publishing.

Cummings, T. G. and Worley, C. G. (1997). *Organization Development and Change*, 6th edition. Cincinnati, OH: South-Western College Publishing.

Cyert, R. M. and March, J. G. (1963). *A Behavioral Theory of the Firm*. Englewood Cliffs, NJ: Prentice Hall.

Darwin, J., Johnson, P. and McAuley, J. (2002). *Developing Strategies for Change*. Harlow: FT/Prentice Hall.

Dawson, P. (1994). *Organizational Change: A Processual Approach*. London: Paul Chapman Publishing.

Dent, E. B. and Goldberg, S. G. (1999). ''Challenging resistance to change.'' *Journal of Applied Behavioral Science*, 35, 1, 25–41.

Dickens, L. and Watkins, K. (1999). ''Action research: rethinking Lewin.'' *Management Learning*, 30, 2, 127–40.

Dunphy, D. D. and Stace, D. A. (1992). *Under New Management*. Sydney: McGraw-Hill.

Dunphy, D. D. and Stace, D. A. (1993). ''The strategic management of corporate change.'' *Human Relations*, 46, 8, 905–18.

Eden, C. and Huxham, C. (1996). ''Action research for the study of organizations.'' In Clegg, S. R., Hardy, C. and Nord, W. R. (Eds.), *Handbook of Organization Studies*. London: Sage.

Elden, M. and Chisholm, R. F. (1993). ''Emerging varieties of action research: Introduction to the Special Issue.'' *Human Relations*, 46, 2, 121–42.

Elrod, P. D. II and Tippett, D. D. (2002). ''The 'Death Valley' of change.'' *Journal of Organizational Change Management*, 15, 3, 273–91.

French, W. L. and Bell, C. H. (1984). *Organization Development*, 4th edition. Englewood Cliffs, NJ: Prentice-Hall.

French, W. L. and Bell, C. H. (1995). *Organization Development*, 5th edition. Englewood Cliffs, NJ: Prentice-Hall.

French, J.R.P. Jr. and Raven, B. H. (1959). ''The bases of social power.'' In Cartwright, D. (Ed.), *Studies in Social Power*. Ann Harbor, MI: Institute for Social Research.

Garvin, D. A. (1993). ''Building a learning organization.'' *Harvard Business Review*, July–August, 78–91.

Gellerman, W., Frankel, M. S. and Ladenson, R. F. (1990). *Values and Ethics in Organizational and Human Systems Development: Responding to Dilemmas in Professional Life*. San Francisco, CA: Jossey-Bass.

Gersick, C.J.G. (1991). ''Revolutionary change theories: a multilevel exploration of the punctuated equilibrium paradigm.'' *Academy of Management Review*, 16, 1, 10–36.

Gilchrist, A. (2000). ''The well-connected community: networking to the edge of chaos.'' *Community Development Journal*, 3, 3, 264–75.

Gold, M. (1992). ''Metatheory and field theory in social psychology: relevance or elegance?'' *Journal of Social Issues*, 48, 2, 67–78.

Gould, S. J. (1989). ''Punctuated equilibrium in fact and theory.'' *Journal of Social Biological Structure*, 12, 117–36.

Greenwald, J. (1996). ''Reinventing Sears.'' *Time*, 23 December, 53–5.

Handy, C. (1994). *The Empty Raincoat*. London: Hutchinson.

Hannagan, T. (2002). *Management: Concepts and Practices*, 3rd edition. Harlow: FT/Pearson.

Hannan, M. T. and Freeman, J. (1988). *Organizational Ecology*. Cambridge, MA: Harvard University Press.

Harris, P. R. (1985). *Management in Transition*. San Francisco, CA: Jossey-Bass.

Hatch, M. J. (1997). *Organization Theory: Modern, Symbolic and Postmodern Perspectives*. Oxford: Oxford University Press.

Hedberg, B., Nystrom, P. and Starbuck, W. (1976). "Camping on seesaws: prescriptions for a self-designing organization." *Administrative Science Quarterly*, 17, 371–81.

Hendry, C. (1996). "Understanding and creating whole organizational change through learning theory." *Human Relations*, 48, 5, 621–41.

Hirschhorn, L. (1988). *The Workplace Within*. Cambridge, MA: MIT Press.

House, J. S. (1993). "John R. French, Jr.: A Lewinian's Lewinian." *Journal of Social Issues*, 49, 4, 221–6.

Huczynski, A. and Buchanan, D. (2001). *Organizational Behaviour*, 4th edition. Harlow: FT/Prentice Hall.

Jaques, E. (1998). "On leaving the Tavistock Institute." *Human Relations*, 51, 3, 251–7.

Kanter, R. M. (1983). *The Change Masters*. New York: Simon & Schuster.

Kanter, R. M. (1989). *When Giants Learn to Dance: Mastering the Challenges of Strategy, Management, and Careers in the 1990s*. London: Unwin.

Kanter, R. M., Stein, B. A. and Jick, T. D. (1992). *The Challenge of Organizational Change*. New York: Free Press.

Kearney, A. T. (1989). *Computer Integrated Manufacturing: Competitive Advantage or Technological Dead End?* London: Kearney.

Kimberley, J. and Miles, R. (Eds.) (1980). *The Organizational Life Cycle*. San Francisco, CA: Jossey-Bass.

Kippenberger, T. (1998a). "Planned change: Kurt Lewin's legacy." *The Antidote*, 14, 10–12.

Kippenberger, T. (1998b). "Managed learning: elaborating on Lewin's model." *The Antidote*, 14, 13.

Kotter, J. P. (1996). *Leading Change*. Boston, MA: Harvard Business School Press.

Lewin, K. (1939). "When facing danger." In Lewin, G. W. (Ed.), *Resolving Social Conflict*. London: Harper & Row.

Lewin, K. (1943a). "Psychological ecology." In Cartwright, D. (Ed.), *Field Theory in Social Science*. London: Social Science Paperbacks.

Lewin, K. (1943b). "The special case of Germany." In Lewin, G. W. (Ed.), *Resolving Social Conflict*. London: Harper & Row.

Lewin, K. (1943–44). "Problems of research in social psychology." In Cartwright, D. (Ed.), *Field Theory in Social Science*. London: Social Science Paperbacks.

Lewin, K. (1946). "Action research and minority problems." In Lewin, G. W. (Ed.), *Resolving Social Conflict*. London: Harper & Row.

Lewin, K. (1947a). ''Frontiers in group dynamics.'' In Cartwright, D. (Ed.), *Field Theory in Social Science*. London: Social Science Paperbacks.

Lewin, K. (1947b). ''Group decisions and social change.'' In Newcomb, T. M. and Hartley, E. L. (Eds.), *Readings in Social Psychology*. New York: Henry Holt.

Lewin, G. W. (Ed.). (1948a). *Resolving Social Conflict*. London: Harper & Row.

Lewin, G. W. (1948b). ''Preface.'' In Lewin, G. W. (Ed.), *Resolving Social Conflict*. London: Harper & Row.

Lewin, M. (1992). ''The impact of Kurt Lewin's life on the place of social issues in his work.'' *Journal of Social Issues*, 48, 2, 15–29.

Lewis, R. (1994). ''From chaos to complexity: implications for organizations.'' *Executive Development*, 7, 4, 16–17.

Lindblom, C. E. (1959). ''The science of muddling through.'' *Public Administration Review*, 19, Spring, 79–88.

Lorenz, E. (1993). *The Essence of Chaos*. London: UCL Press.

Macbeth, D. K. (2002). ''Emergent strategy in managing cooperative supply chain change.'' *International Journal of Operations and Production Management*, 22, 7, 728–40.

MacIntosh, R. and MacLean, D. (2001). ''Conditioned emergence: researching change and changing research.'' *International Journal of Operations and Production Management*, 21, 10, 1343–57.

Marrow, A. J. (1957). *Making Management Human*. New York: McGraw-Hill.

Marrow, A. J. (1969). *The Practical Theorist: The Life and Work of Kurt Lewin*. New York: Teachers College Press.

Marshak, R. J. (1993). ''Lewin meets Confucius: a re-view of the OD model of change.'' *The Journal of Applied Behavioral Science*, 29, 4, 393–415.

Matthews, R. (2002). ''Competition, archetypes and creative imagination.'' *Journal of Organizational Change Management*, 15, 5, 461–76.

Miller, D. and Friesen, P. H. (1984). *Organizations: A Quantum View*. Englewood Cliffs, NJ: Prentice Hall.

Mintzberg, H., Ahlstrand, B. and Lampel, J. (1998). *Strategy Safari*. Hemel Hempstead: Prentice Hall.

Mullins, L. (2002). *Management and Organisational Behaviour*, 6th edition. Harlow: FT/Pearson.

Nonaka, I. (1988). ''Creating organizational order out of chaos: self-renewal in Japanese firms.'' *Harvard Business Review*, November–December, 96–104.

Olsen, B. D. (2002). ''Applied social and community interventions for crisis in times of national and international conflict.'' *Analyses of Social Issues and Public Policy*, 2, 1, 119–29.

Peters, T. (1993). *Liberation Management*. London: Pan.

Peters, T. and Waterman, R. H. (1982). *In Search of Excellence: Lessons from America's Best-Run Companies*. London: Harper and Row.

Pettigrew, A. M. (1973). *The Politics of Organisational Decision Making*. Tavistock: London.

Pettigrew, A. M. (1979). "On studying organizational culture." *Administrative Science Quarterly*, 24, 4, 570–81.

Pettigrew, A. M. (1980). "The politics of organisational change." In Anderson, N. B. (Ed.), *The Human Side of Information Processing*. Amsterdam: North Holland.

Pettigrew, A. M. (1985). *The Awakening Giant: Continuity and Change in ICI*. Oxford: Blackwell.

Pettigrew, A. M. (1987). "Context and action in the transformation of the firm." *Journal of Management Sciences*, 24, 6, 649–70.

Pettigrew, A. M. (1990a). "Longitudinal field research on change: theory and practice." *Organizational Science*, 3, 1, 267–92.

Pettigrew, A. M. (1990b). "Studying strategic choice and strategic change." *Organizational Studies*, 11, 1, 6–11.

Pettigrew, A. M. (1997). "What is a processual analysis?" *Scandinavian Journal of Management*, 13, 40, 337–48.

Pettigrew, A. M., Ferlie, E. and McKee, L. (1992). *Shaping Strategic Change*. London: Sage.

Pettigrew, A. M., Hendry, C. N. and Sparrow, P. (1989). *Training in Britain: Employers' Perspectives on Human Resources*. London: HMSO.

Pettigrew, A. M. and Whipp, R. (1993). "Understanding the environment." In Mabey, C. and Mayon-White, B. (Eds.), *Managing Change*, 2nd edition. London: The Open University/Paul Chapman Publishing.

Pfeffer, J. (1981). *Power in Organizations*. Cambridge, MA: Pitman.

Pfeffer, J. (1992). *Managing with Power: Politics and Influence in Organizations*. Boston, MA: Harvard Business School Press.

Prigogine, I. and Stengers, I. (1984). *Order Out of Chaos: Man's New Dialogue with Nature*. New York: Bantam Books.

Quinn, J. B. (1980). *Strategies for Change: Logical Incrementalism*. Homewood, IL: Irwin.

Quinn, J. B. (1982). "Managing strategies incrementally." *Omega*, 10, 6, 613–27.

Raven, B. H. (1965). "Social influence and power." In Steiner, I. D. and Fishbein, M. (Eds.), *Current Studies in Social Psychology*. New York: Holt, Rinehart, Winston.

Raven, B. H. (1993). "The bases of power—origins and recent developments." *Journal of Social Issues*, 49, 4, 227–51.

Raven, B. H. (1999). "Kurt Lewin Address: Influence, power, religion, and the mechanisms of social control." *Journal of Social Issues*, 55, 1, 161–89.

Romanelli, E. and Tushman, M. L. (1994). "Organizational transformation as punctuated equilibrium: an empirical test." *Academy of Management Journal*, 37, 5, 1141–66.

Schein, E. H. (1988). *Organizational Psychology*, 3rd edition. London: Prentice Hall.

Schein, E. H. (1996). "Kurt Lewin's change theory in the field and in the classroom: notes towards a model of management learning." *Systems Practice*, 9, 1, 27–47.

Senge, P. M. (1990). *The Fifth Discipline: The Art and Practice of the Learning Organization*. London: Century Business.

Shelton, C. K. and Darling, J. R. (2001). "The quantum skills model in management: a new paradigm to enhance effective leadership." *Leadership and Organization Development Journal*, 22, 6, 264–73.

Smith, M. K. (2001). "Kurt Lewin: groups, experiential learning and action research." *The Encyclopedia of Informal Education*. http://www.infed.org/thinkers/et-lewin.htm, 1–15.

Stace, D. and Dunphy, D. (2001). *Beyond the Boundaries: Leading and Re-creating the Successful Enterprise*, 2nd edition. Sydney: McGraw-Hill.

Stacey, R. D. (1993). *Strategic Management and Organisational Dynamics*. London: Pitman.

Stacey, R. D., Griffin, D. and Shaw, P. (2002). *Complexity and Management: Fad or Radical Challenge to Systems Thinking?* London: Routledge.

Stickland, F. (1998). *The Dynamics of Change: Insights into Organisational Transition from the Natural World*. London: Routledge.

Tetenbaum, T. J. (1998). "Shifting paradigms: from Newton to chaos." *Organizational Dynamics*, 26, 4, 21–32.

Tobach, E. (1994). "Personal is political is personal is political." *Journal of Social Issues*, 50, 1, 221–44.

Tschacher, W. and Brunner, E. J. (1995). "Empirical-studies of group-dynamics from the point-of-view of self-organization theory." *Zeitschrift fur Sozialpsychologie*, 26, 2, 78–91.

Waclawski, J. (2002). "Large-scale organizational change and performance: an empirical examination." *Human Resource Development Quarterly*, 13, 3, 289–305.

Warwick, D. P. and Thompson, J. T. (1980). "Still crazy after all these years." *Training and Development Journal*, 34, 2, 16–22.

Wastell, D. G., White, P. and Kawalek, P. (1994). "A methodology for business process redesign: experience and issues." *Journal of Strategic Information Systems*, 3, 1, 23–40.

Watcher, B. (1993). *The Adoption of Total Quality Management in Scotland*. Durham: Durham University Business School.

Watson, T. J. (1997). *In Search of Management*. London: Thompson International.

Wheatley, M. J. (1992). *Leadership and the New Science: Learning About Organization from an Orderly Universe*. San Francisco, CA: Berrett-Koehler.

Whyte, J. and Watcher, B. (1992). *The Adoption of Total Quality Management in Northern England*. Durham: Durham University Business School.

Wilson, D. C. (1992). *A Strategy of Change*. London: Routledge.

Wooten, K. C. and White, L. P. (1999). "Linking OD's philosophy with justice theory: postmodern implications." *Journal of Organizational Change Management*, 12, 1, 7–20.

Zairi, M., Letza, S. and Oakland, J. (1994). "Does TQM impact on bottom line results?" *TQM Magazine*, 6, 1, 38–43.

PART THREE

DIAGNOSING THE CURRENT STATE
Editors' Interlude

P art Two gives an overview of the theoretical foundation underlying the conceptualization and understanding of organizations as social systems and the nature of organization change. The primary theory used by scholars to comprehend how change manifests in an organization is open-system theory, which is a useful framework to study the relationship between an organization and the environmental forces that impinge on it. In the context of planned organization change, "systems analysis" is a tool used to observe the interdependencies among the various components within an organization and between an organization and aspects of its external environment (customers, competitors, suppliers, and so on). This analysis is critical to determine if change in the organization is necessary, and if so, what areas and level of the organization should be the focus of the change. In other words, it is important to diagnose the current state of the organization to assess the need for change, which is the focus of Part Three.

Diagnosis consists of both data gathering and analysis. Data about the organization are acquired in several ways, among them interviews with organizational members, questionnaires, observation by a consultant or practitioner, and archival data (that is, vision and mission statements, strategic plans, and policy documents). Once data have been collected, an organizational model—a metaphorical representation of an organization—is often useful to (1) help categorize the data into manageable components, (2) enhance our understanding of problems that may exist within the current state of the organization and its interaction with the external environment, and (3) guide action for change by indicating the key levers that may influence change in other dimensions across the organization.

The first chapter in this section, by Burke (1992), is an excerpt from his book *Organization Development*. It outlines four organizational models that are based on open-system theory and are often used to diagnose for change and determine the proper intervention. The second chapter presents a more recently developed organizational model by Burke and Litwin (1992), which builds on and captures some of the best qualities of the previous models. It is a predictive model in that it deals with cause (organizational conditions) and effect (resultant behavior and performance). The Burke-Litwin Model distinguishes between transformational and transactional aspects of an organization, whereby the former carry more leverage or are more heavily weighted than the latter. In other words, change in transformational dimensions will affect change throughout the organization and is therefore essential for revolutionary change to occur. The "weighting" of dimensions allows leaders and practitioners to develop an implementation strategy based on their organization change diagnosis. They are able to determine a road map for the overall change effort by first ordering the dimensions with the most influence on the organization and then focusing on the next level of dimensions, and so on. The authors begin with background concerning the development of the model and then furnish a description of the model, its application, and support for its validity.

The third chapter, by Kraut (1996), illustrates how organizational surveys can be used to diagnose focal areas in the planning of organization change initiatives. It is the overview for his edited book on the subject and offers broad coverage of the history of organizational surveys, methodologies, and the purposes for conducting a survey. Kraut provides guidelines for creating useful and reliable surveys that are connected to organizational goals with actionable results.

The final chapter in Part Three, by Ann Howard and associates (1994) on organizational diagnosis is an integrative and concluding chapter from the authors' book *Diagnosis for Organizational Change: Methods and Models*. The authors identify several problems involved in the process of diagnosis and offer helpful illustrations for overcoming them. As the reader is led through the chapter, many of the foundational concerns about diagnosis are revealed.

In today's fast-paced world, it is more difficult than ever before to conduct a thorough organizational diagnosis. Busy executives often claim that a diagnosis takes too long, and besides, isn't it fairly evident about the change that is required? Two points need to be made here. First, without a reasonably thorough diagnosis, mistakes in implementation of the change are more likely. For example, missing the fact that many people do not have sufficient experience and expertise to make some interventions work can derail the initiative.

Second, we need to remember Kurt Lewin's dictum that the best way to understand an organization is to try to change it. The diagnosis comes from observing and perhaps collecting data about people's reactions and responses to the change. So it is possible to initiate action and diagnose at the same time. Though perhaps in a less than formal manner, one can simultaneously conduct the all-important diagnosis nevertheless.

CHAPTER SIXTEEN

Understanding Organizations

The Process of Diagnosis

W. Warner Burke (1992)

Without a framework for understanding, the data an OD practitioner collects about a client organization may remain nothing more than an array of personal comments of the who-said-what-about-whom variety. For the information to become useful, it must be treated in organizational terms. Since OD represents a systematic approach to change, and the data for diagnosis are largely in systems language, the categories for diagnosis are systems labels.

This chapter covers selected models of and theories about organizations that are useful in the diagnostic phase of OD consultation because they help to organize and systematize the potentially confusing masses of data. Among the models and theories from which the OD practitioner may choose, some are merely descriptive while others emphasize dimensions for diagnosis, thereby providing direction for change. The purpose of this chapter is to provide the practitioner with some criteria and bases for making choices.

The models and theories I have chosen to consider in this chapter are all behavior-oriented. Although some other frameworks emphasize technological, financial, or informational aspects of organizations, behavior-oriented models are more valuable for OD practice because the role of the OD practitioner is to understand what *people* do or do not do in organizations. Word processing and office technology, for example, are of interest to OD practitioners, but only in terms of the changes people will have to make, not for the electronic wizardry involved (Lodahl and Williams, 1978).

The various models we shall explore are all based on the open-system notion of input-throughput-output and all recognize that an organization exists in an environmental context and is a sociotechnical system. All recognize the same fundamentals—an open system that exists in an environment and consists of people and technology.

We shall first examine four models that are largely descriptive: a model of simplicity with structure, two models of complexity with structure, and a develop-your-own model.

ORGANIZATIONAL MODELS

Weisbord's Six-Box Model

A model is useful when it helps us visualize reality, and Weisbord's model (1976, 1978) meets this criterion very well. Weisbord depicts his model as a radar screen, with "blips" that tell us about organizational highlights and issues good and bad. Just as air traffic controllers use their radar, we too must focus primarily on the screen as a whole, not on individual blips (see Fig. 16.1).

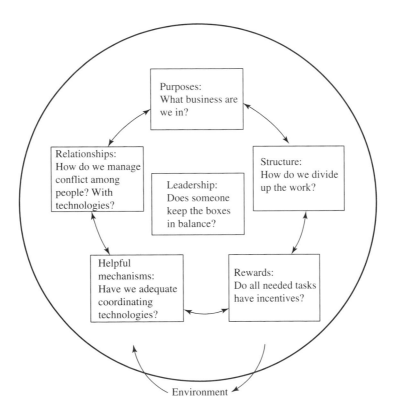

Figure 16.1. Weisbord's Six-Box Organization Model.

Source: M. R. Weisbord, "Organizational Diagnosis: Six Places to Look for Trouble with or Without a Theory," *Group and Organization Studies* 1 (1976): 430–47. Reprinted by permission.

Every organization is situated within an environment and, as the arrows in the figure indicate, is influenced by and influences various elements of that environment. In Weisbord's model, the organization is represented by six boxes: purpose, structure, rewards, helpful mechanisms, relationships, and leadership. Weisbord believes that, for each box, the client organization should be diagnosed in terms of both its formal and its informal systems. A key aspect of any organizational diagnosis is the gap between the formal dimensions of an organization, such as the organization chart (the structure box), and its informal policies, such as how authority is actually exercised. The larger this gap is, the more likely it is that the organization is functioning ineffectively.

Weisbord provides key diagnostic questions for each of the six boxes. For the *purposes* box, the two most important factors are goal clarity, the extent to which organization members are clear about the organization's mission and purpose, and goal agreements—people's support of the organization's purpose. For *structure*, the primary question is whether there is an adequate fit between the purpose and the internal structure that is supposed to serve that purpose. With respect to *relationships*, Weisbord contends that three types are most important: between individuals, between units or departments that perform different tasks, and between the people and the nature and requirements of their jobs. He also states that the OD consultant should "diagnose first for required interdependence, then for *quality of relations*, and finally for modes of conflict management" (Weisbord, 1976: 440).

In assessing blips for the *rewards* box, the consultant should diagnose the similarities and differences between the organization's formal rewards (the compensation package, incentive systems, and the like) and organization members' perceived rewards or punishments.

Weisbord makes the *leadership* box central because he believes that a primary job of the leader is to watch for blips among the other boxes and to maintain balance among them. To help the OD consultant in *diagnosing* the leadership box, Weisbord refers to an important book published some years ago by Selznick (1957), citing the four most important leadership tasks. According to Selznick, the consultant should determine the extent to which organizations' leaders are (1) defining purposes, (2) embodying purposes in programs, (3) defending the organization's integrity, and (4) maintaining order with respect to internal conflict.

For the last box, *helpful mechanisms*, Weisbord refers analogously to "the cement that binds an organization together to make it more than a collection of individuals with separate needs" (Weisbord, 1976: 443). Thus, helpful mechanisms are the processes that every organization must attend to in order to survive: planning, control, budgeting, and other information systems that help organization members accomplish their respective jobs and meet organizational objectives. The OD consultant's task is to determine which mechanisms (or which aspects of them) help members accomplish organizational purposes and which seem to hinder more than they help. When a helpful mechanism becomes red tape, it probably is no longer helpful.

Table 16.1 gives a summary of the six-box model and the diagnostic questions to be asked.

Table 16.1. Weisbord's Matrix for Survey Design or Data Analysis.

	Formal System (Work to be done)	Informal System (Process of working)
1. Purposes	Goal clarity	Goal agreement
2. Structure	Functional, program, or matrix?	How is work actually done or not done?
3. Relationships	Who should deal with whom on what?	How well do they do it?
		Quality of relations?
		Modes of conflict management?
4. Rewards (incentives)	Explicit system	Implicit, psychic rewards
	What is it?	What do people *feel* about payoffs?
5. Leadership	What do top people manage?	How?
		Normative "style" of administration?
6. Helpful mechanisms	Budget system	What are they actually used for?
	Management information (measures?)	How do they function in practice?
	Planning	How are systems subverted?
	Control	

Diagnostic questions may be asked on two levels:

1. How big a gap is there between formal and informal systems? (This speaks to the fit between individual and organization.)

2. How much discrepancy is there between "what is" and "what ought to be"? (This highlights the fit between organization and environment.)

Source: M. R. Weisbord, "Organizational Diagnosis: Six Places to Look for Trouble with or Without a Theory," *Group and Organization Studies* (1976), 1: 430–47. Reprinted by permission.

In summary, Weisbord's model is particularly useful when the consultant does not have as much time as would be desirable for diagnosis, when a relatively uncomplicated organizational map is needed for quick service, or when the client is unaccustomed to thinking in systems terms. In the latter case, the model helps the client to visualize his or her organization as a systemic whole without the use of strange terminology. I have also found Weisbord's model useful in supervising and guiding students in their initial OD consultations.

The Nadler-Tushman Congruence Model

For a more sophisticated client and when more time is available, a more complex model of organizations might be useful for OD diagnosis. In such instances, the Nadler and Tushman (1989) congruence model might serve the purpose.

Nadler and Tushman make the same assumptions as Weisbord—that an organization is an open system and therefore is influenced by its environment (inputs) and also shapes its environment to some extent by outputs. An organization thus is the transformation entity between inputs and outputs. Figure 16.2 represents the Nadler-Tushman congruence model.

Inputs. Nadler and Tushman view inputs to the system as relatively fixed; the four they cite are the *environment*, the *resources* available to the organization, the organization's *history*, and *strategies* that are developed and evolve over time. These inputs help define how people in the organization behave, and they serve as constraints on behavior as well as opportunities for action.

As we know from the works of Burnes and Stalker (1961) and Lawrence and Lorsch (1969), the extent to which an organization's environment is relatively stable or dynamic significantly affects internal operations, structure, and policy. For many organizations a very important aspect of environment is the parent system and its directives. Many organizations are subsidiaries or divisional profit centers of larger corporations, colleges within a university, or hospitals within a larger health care delivery system. These subordinate organizations may operate relatively autonomously with respect to the outside world (having their own purchasing operations, for example) but because of corporate policy may be fairly restricted in how much money they can spend. Thus, for many organizations we must think of their environments in at least two categories: the larger parent system and the rest of the outside world—government regulations, competitors, and the marketplace in general.

According to the Nadler-Tushman model, resources include capital (money, property, equipment, and so on), raw materials, technologies, people, and various intangibles, such as company name, which may have a high value in the company's market.

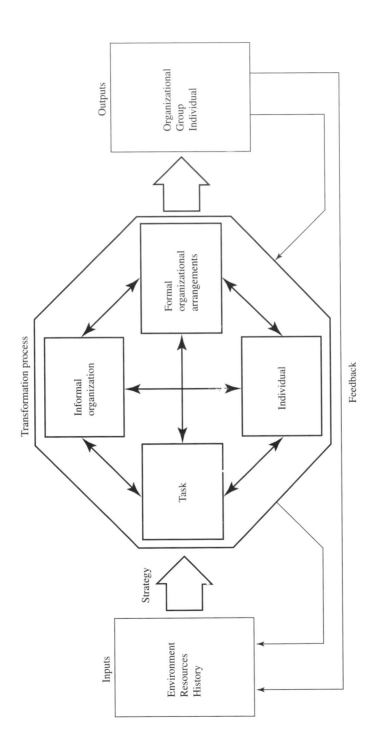

Figure 16.2. The Nadler-Tushman Congruence Model for Diagnosing Organizational Behavior.

Source: D. A. Nadler and M. L. Tushman, ''A Diagnostic Model for Organization Behavior,'' in *Perspectives on Behavior in Organizations*, edited by J. R. Hackman, E. E. Lawler, and L. W. Porter (New York: McGraw-Hill, 1977), p. 92. Reprinted by permission.

An organization's history is also input to the system. The history determines, for example, patterns of employee behavior, policy, the types of people the organization attracts and recruits, and even how decisions get made in a crisis.

Although strategy is categorized as an input in the models, Nadler and Tushman set it apart. Strategy is the process of determining how the organization's resources are best used within the environment for optimal organizational functioning. It is the act of identifying opportunities in the environment and determining whether the organization's resources are adequate for capitalizing on these opportunities. History plays a subtle but influential role in this strategic process.

Some organizations are very strategic; that is, they plan. Other organizations simply react to changes in their environments or act opportunistically rather than according to a long-range plan that determines which opportunities will be seized and which will be allowed to pass. As Nadler and Tushman point out, however, organizations have strategies whether they are deliberate and formal or unintentional and informal.

Outputs. We shall move to the right-hand side of the model to consider outputs before covering the transformation process. Thus we shall examine the organization's environment from the standpoint of both how it influences the system and how the organization operates internally.

For diagnostic purposes, Nadler and Tushman present four key categories of outputs: system functioning, group behavior, intergroup relations, and individual behavior and effect. With respect to the effectiveness of the system's functioning as a whole, the following three questions should elicit the necessary information:

1. How well is the organization attaining its desired goals of production, service, return on investment, and so on?
2. How well is the organization utilizing its resources?
3. How well is the organization coping with changes in its environment over time?

The remaining three outputs are more directly behavioral: how well groups or units within the organization are performing; how effectively these units communicate with one another, resolve differences, and collaborate when necessary; and how individuals behave. For this last output, individual behavior, we are interested in such matters as turnover, absenteeism, and, of course, individual job performance.

The Transformation Process. The components of the transformation process and their interactions are what we normally think of when we consider an organization—the people, the various tasks and jobs, the organization's managerial structure (the organization chart), and all the relationships of individuals, groups, and subsystems. As Fig. 16.2 shows, four interactive major components compose the transformation process that changes inputs into outputs:

The *task* component consists of the jobs to be done and the inherent characteristics of the work itself. The primary task dimensions are the extent and nature of the required interdependence between and among task performers, the level of skill needed, and the kinds of information required to perform the tasks adequately.

The *individual* component consists of all the differences and similarities among employees, particularly demographic data, skill and professional levels, and personality-attitudinal variables.

Organizational arrangements include the managerial and operational structure of the organization, work flow and design, the reward system, management information systems, and the like. These arrangements are the formal mechanisms used by management to direct and control behavior and to organize and accomplish the work to be done.

The fourth component, *informal organization*, is the social structure within the organization, including the grapevine, the organization's internal politics, and the informal authority-information structure (whom you see for what).

Congruence: The Concept of Fit. As Nadler and Tushman point out, a mere listing and description of these system inputs, outputs, and components is insufficient for modeling an organization. An organization is dynamic, never static, and the model must represent this reality, as the arrows in Fig. 16.2 do. Nadler and Tushman go beyond depicting relationships, however. Their term *fit* is a measure of the congruence between pairs of inputs and especially between the components of the transformation process. They contend that inconsistent fits between any pair will result in less than optimal organizational and individual performance. Nadler and Tushman's hypothesis, therefore, is that the better the fit, the more effective the organization will be.

Nadler and Tushman recommend three steps for diagnosis:

1. *Identify the system.* Is the system for diagnosis an autonomous organization, a subsidiary, a division, or a unit of some larger system? What are the boundaries of the system, its membership, its tasks, and—if it is part of a larger organization—its relationships with other units?

2. *Determine the nature of the key variables.* What are the dimensions of the inputs and components? What are the desired outputs?

3. *Diagnose the state of fits.* This is the most important step, involving two related activities: determining fits between components and diagnosing the link between the fits and the organization's outputs.

The OD consultant must concentrate on the degree to which the key components are congruent with one another. Questions such as the following should be asked:

- To what extent do the organizational arrangements fit with the requirements of the task?

- To what extent do individual skills and needs fit with task requirements, with organizational arrangements, and with the informal organization? Hackman and Oldham's job characteristics theory (1975) is a useful supplementary model for this part of the diagnosis, as is expectancy theory (Vroom, 1964; Lawler, 1973).

- To what extent do task requirements fit with both the formal and the informal organization? Information-processing models are useful supplements for this aspect of the diagnosis (Galbraith, 1977; Tushman and Nadler, 1978).

To diagnose the link between fits and outputs, the OD consultant must focus the outcome of the diagnoses of the various component fits and their behavioral consequences on the set of behaviors associated with systems outputs: goal attainment, resource utilization, and overall systems performance. Considering the component fits, or lack thereof, in light of system outputs helps identify critical problems of the organization. As these problems are addressed and changes are made, the system is then monitored through the feedback loop for purposes of evaluation.

In summary, the dimensions of the Nadler-Tushman model are quite comprehensive and have face validity. Moreover, their notion of congruence suggests certain cause-effect linkages. For example, little or no congruence between, say, strategy and structure in their model produces poor organizational performance. Also, a mismatch between what's going on in the organization's environment and strategy—for example, no plan for dealing with a recent change in government regulation—would imply a causal relationship to performance. Many other congruences or lacks thereof could be mentioned. The number of possibilities is large. Nadler and Tushman, however, do not provide ideas or, say, a formula for determining which variables in their model are central. For example, they include under a single heading organizational arrangements, quite a number of components, any one of which could easily be central. And, finally, they do not suggest any means for knowing when congruence has occurred or what levels of congruence or incongruence produce desirable or undesirable effects.

To be fair, more recently Nadler and Tushman (1989) have had some second thoughts about their congruence position: "While our model implies that congruence of organizational components is a desirable state it is, in fact, a double-edged sword. In the short term, congruence seems to be related to effectiveness and performance. A system with high congruence, however, can be resistant to change. It develops ways of insulating itself from outside influences and may be unable to respond to new situations'' (p. 195).

Tichy's TPC Framework

With his organizational framework, Tichy (1983) focuses explicitly on the management of change. He states that there are nine organizational change levers. They are the (1) external interface, or the organization's external environment; (2) mission; (3) strategy; (4) managing organizational mission/strategy processes, that is, realistically engaging the relevant interest groups; (5) task (change often requires new tasks); (6) prescribed *networks*, more or less the formal organizational structure; (7) organizational processes (communicating, problem solving, and decision making); (8) people; and (9) emergent networks, more or less the informal organization. Figure 16.3 shows how Tichy arranges these nine levers. He assumes that "organizational effectiveness (or output) is a function of the component of the model, as well as a function of how the components interrelate and align into a functioning system" (p. 72).

Even more important in Tichy's thinking about organization change is his TPC framework. The model in Fig. 16.3 is not unique. What makes Tichy's thinking unique is his overlay of the three systems—technical, political, and cultural—across the nine-lever model. He contends that there have been three dominant yet fairly distinct traditions guiding the practice of organization change. The *technical* view is rational, based on empiricism and the scientific method. The *political* view is based on the belief that organizations have dominant groups, and bargaining is the primary mode of change. The *cultural* view is the belief that shared symbols, values, and "cognitive schemes," as Tichy labels them, are what tie people together and form the organization's culture. Change occurs by altering norms and the cognitive schemes of organizational members. Taking only one or only two of these views for managing organizational change is dysfunctional. All three must be adjusted and realigned for successful change. The metaphor that Tichy uses to capture this thinking is a rope with three interrelated strands. The strands, or three views, can be understood separately but must be managed together for effective change.

For diagnostic purposes, Tichy uses a matrix like the one shown in Fig. 16.4. This format summarizes what he calls "the analysis of alignments." Tichy describes the use of the matrix this way:

> Based on the diagnostic data collected, a judgment is made for each cell of the matrix regarding the amount of change needed to create alignment. Working across the matrix, the alignment is within a system: technical, political, or cultural. Working down the matrix, the alignment is between systems. The 0

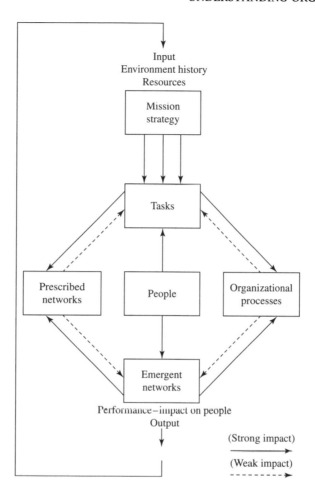

Figure 16.3. Tichy's Framework.

Source: N. M. Tichy, *Managing Strategic Change: Technical, Political, and Cultural Dynamics,* copyright ©1983 Wiley Interscience. Reprinted by permission of John Wiley & Sons.

(no change), 1 (moderate change) or 2 (great deal of change) ratings represent the amount of change needed to align that component (p. 164).

In summary, Tichy's model includes many if not most of the critical variables important to understanding organizations. His model is unique with respect to the strategic rope metaphor and is particularly relevant to OD work, since the emphasis is on change. Moreover, Tichy is clear about what he considers to be the primary organizational levers that must be pushed or pulled to make change happen effectively. Instead of congruence, alignment is the operational term. And Tichy provides a way of analyzing the key alignments

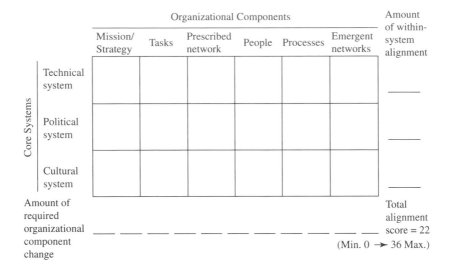

Figure 16.4. Tichy's TPC Framework.

Source: Tichy (1983). Reprinted by permission.

that are necessary according to his framework. Data are first collected and then categorized within his matrix (Fig. 16.4).

There is a human component in Tichy's model, but for the most part his framework ignores issues at the individual level. He admits this omission at the end of his book by stating that he skimmed over the psychological aspects of change. The political and cultural strands are, of course, people concerns but much broader than, say, job-person match (or alignment) and local work unit activities such as teamwork. Finally, the criticism of too much congruence potentially working against change could also apply to Tichy's insistence on alignments.

Hornstein and Tichy's Emergent Pragmatic Model

The emergent pragmatic model of organizational diagnosis (Hornstein and Tichy, 1973; Tichy, Hornstein, and Nisberg, 1977) is based on the premise that most managers and consultants "carry around in their heads" implicit theories or models about organizational behavior and about how human systems actually operate. These notions are usually intuitive, ill-formed, and difficult to articulate. Because they are largely intuitive, different observers and members of organizations have different theories, which gives rise to conflicts among consultants or between consultants and clients about what is really wrong with the organization and how to fix it.

Hornstein and Tichy have developed a procedure for helping managers articulate and conceptualize their implicit models. The procedure has managers represent the information they would seek in diagnosing an organization by selecting labels from among twenty-two samples or creating their own from twenty-eight blank labels provided. The labels include such items as informal groupings, fiscal characteristics, turnover, goals, and satisfaction of members with their jobs.

Hornstein and Tichy's approach to organizational diagnosis is shared between consultant and client and among members of the client organization. The approach is called an emergent-pragmatic theory because "the model *emerges* from an exploration of both the consultant's and client's assumptions about behavior and organizations . . . and draws on both the consultant's and client's organizational *experiences* as well as on empirical and theoretical work in the field" (Tichy, Hornstein, and Nisberg, 1977: 367; emphasis added).

Another of Hornstein and Tichy's premises is that, consciously or not, organizational consultants tend to impose their theories and models of human systems on their clients. These impositions often do not fit with the client members' perceptions and beliefs or do not jibe with the client organization's underlying values. To improve congruence, Hornstein and Tichy advocate a highly collaborative approach between consultants and clients, one that results in an emergent model representing different perspectives and experiences.

There are five phases to the emergent-pragmatic approach. The consultant guides the client group through these phases:

1. Exploring and developing a diagnostic model
2. Developing change strategies
3. Developing change techniques
4. Assessing the necessary conditions for assuring success
5. Evaluating the change strategies

To summarize, the emergent-pragmatic approach to organizational diagnosis is based on the assumption that most managers and consultants have intuitive theories about how organizations function, rather than well-formed conceptual frameworks, and the assumption that many consultants impose their models and theories on client organizations, regardless of how appropriate they may be for the particular client. Hornstein and Tichy advocate a collaborative model of diagnosis to avoid the potential negative consequences of operating on the basis of these two assumptions.

The three models described earlier—Weisbord's six-box model, the Nadler-Tushman congruence model, and Tichy's TPC framework—are generic frameworks and do not fall prey to the problems of Hornstein and Tichy's two premises. When the consultant and the client do not find the Weisbord, Nadler-Tushman, or other formal models to their liking, however, the emergent-pragmatic approach offers a clear alternative. It is a do-it-yourself model and, if both consultant and client are willing to spend the time required to do it right, a mutually satisfying and appropriate model for the client organization is likely to result.

The four models described may all be categorized as *contingency* models. They do not specify directions for change prior to diagnosis; rather, what needs to be changed emanates from the diagnosis. None of the models advocates a particular design for an organization's internal structure, a certain style of behavior, or a specific approach to management. The inventors of these models do have biases, however. Weisbord says the boxes should be in balance, Nadler and Tushman argue that the various dimensions of their model should fit with one another, as does Tichy, and Hornstein and Tichy state that the consultant and client should collaborate toward the emergence of a model that is appropriate for the given organization. These biases have more to do with the best way to diagnose than with the most important dimension to change.

References

Burnes, J.M. and G. Stalker. 1961. *The Management of Innovation*. London: Tavistock.

Galbraith, J.R. 1977. *Organization Design*. Reading, Mass.: Addison-Wesley.

Hackman, J.R. and G.R. Oldham. 1975. "Development of the Job Diagnostic Survey." *Journal of Applied Psychology* 60: 159–70.

Hornstein, H.A. and N.M. Tichy. 1973. *Organization Diagnosis and Improvement Strategies*. New York: Behavioral Science Associates.

Lawler, E.E. III. 1973. *Motivation in Work Organizations*. Monterey, Calif.: Brooks/Cole.

Lawrence, P.R. and J.W. Lorsch. 1969. *Developing Organizations: Diagnosis and Action*. Reading, Mass.: Addison-Wesley.

Lodahl, T.M. and L.K. Williams. 1978. "An Opportunity for OD: The Office Revolution." *OD Practitioner* 10(4): 9–11.

Nadler, D.A. and M.L. Tushman. 1989. "Organizational Frame Bending: Principles for Managing Reorientation." *Academy of Management Executive* 3: 194–204.

Tichy, N.M. 1983. *Managing Strategic Change: Technical, Political, and Cultural Dynamics*. New York: Wiley.

Tichy, N.M., H.A. Hornstein, and J.N. Nisberg. 1977. "Organization Diagnosis and Intervention Strategies: Developing Emergent Pragmatic Theories of Change." In W.W. Burke, ed., *Current Issues and Strategies in Organizational Development*. New York: Human Science Press, pp. 361–83.

Tushman, N.L. and D.A. Nadler. 1978. "Information Processing as an Integrative Concept in Organizational Design." *Academy of Management Review* 3: 613–24.

Vroom, V. 1964. *Work and Motivation*. New York: Wiley.

Weisbord, M.R. 1976. "Organizational Diagnosis: Six Places to Look for Trouble with or Without a Theory." *Group and Organizational Studies* 1: 430–47.

Weisbord, M.R. 1978. *Organizational Diagnosis: A Workbook of Theory and Practice*. Reading, Mass.: Addison-Wesley.

CHAPTER SEVENTEEN

A Causal Model of Organizational Performance and Change

W. Warner Burke
George H. Litwin (1992)

O rganization change is a kind of chaos (Gleick, 1987). The number of variables changing at the same time, the magnitude of environmental
change, and the frequent resistance of human systems create a whole
confluence of processes that are extremely difficult to predict and almost impossible to control. Nevertheless, there are consistent patterns that exist—
linkages among classes of events that have been demonstrated repeatedly in
the research literature and can be seen in actual organizations. The enormous
and pervasive impact of culture and beliefs—to the point where it causes
organizations to do fundamentally unsound things from a business point of
view—would be such an observed phenomenon.

To build a *most likely* model describing the causes of organizational performance and change, we must explore two important lines of thinking. First,
we must understand more thoroughly how organizations function (i.e., what
leads to what). Second, given our model of causation, we must understand
how organizations might be deliberately changed. The purpose of this chapter
is to explain our understanding so far. More specifically, we present our framework for understanding—a causal model of organizational performance and
change. But, first, a bit of background.

In our organizational consulting work, we try very hard to link the practice
to sound theory and research. The linkage typically is in the direction of theory
and research to practice—that is, to ground our consultation in what is known,
what is theoretically and empirically sound. Creation of the model to be presented in this chapter was not quite in that knowledge-to-practice direction,
however. With respect to theory, we strongly believe in the open system
framework, especially represented by Katz and Kahn (1978). Thus, any

organizational model that we might develop would stem from an input-throughput-output, with a feedback loop, format. The model presented here is definitely of that genre. In other words, the fundamental framework for the model evolved from theory. The components of the model and what causes what and in what order, on the other hand, have evolved from practice, not extensive theory or research. What we are attempting with this chapter, therefore, is a theoretical and empirical justification of what we clearly believe works. To be candid, we acknowledge that our attempt is not unlike attribution theory—we are explaining our beliefs and actions *ex post facto:* "This seems to have worked; I wonder if the literature supports our action."

Our consulting efforts over a period of about five years with British Airways taught us a lot—what changes seemed to have worked and what activities clearly did not. It was from these experiences that our model took form. As a case example, we refer to the work at British Airways later in this chapter. For a more recent overview of that change effort, see Goodstein and Burke (1991).

OTHER ORGANIZATIONAL MODELS

From the perspective of both research about organizations and consultation to organizational clients, we have experienced some frustration about most if not all current organizational models that do little more than describe or depict. A case in point is the 7S model developed by Pascale and Athos (1981) and further honed by Peters and Waterman (1982). Parenthetically, let us quickly add that by comparing our model with others, particularly those the reader may be familiar with, if not fond of, we wish to clarify the nature of our thinking and, ideally, its distinctive contribution, not cast our comments in a competitive manner.

The strengths of the 7S model are (1) its description of organizational variables that convey obvious importance—strategy, structure, systems, style, staff, skills, and shared values (as will be seen, we have incorporated these dimensions in one form or another in our model)—and (2) its recognition of the importance of the interrelationships among all of these seven variables, or dimensions. The 7S model, on the other hand, does not contain any external environment or performance variables. The model is a description of these seven important elements and shows that they interact to create organizational patterns, but there is no explication of how these seven dimensions are affected by the external environment. Nor do we know how each dimension affects the other or what specific performance indices may be involved.

Some organizational models that in our judgment are largely descriptive do at least stipulate certain "shoulds." Weisbord (1976), for example, states that the role of the leadership box in his six-box model is to coordinate the remaining five. The Nadler-Tushman (1977) model is one of congruence. They argue that for organizational effectiveness the various boxes composing their model should be congruent with one another (e.g., organizational arrangements, or structure, should be congruent with organizational strategy).

Even contingency models of organizations, which imply that "it all depends" and that there is no one best way to organize or to manage (e.g., Lawrence & Lorsch, 1969; and Burns & Stalker, 1961, before them) have certain causal implications. Organizational effectiveness is, in part, contingent on the degree of match between the organization's external environment (whether static or dynamic) and the organization's internal structure (either mechanistic or organic).

To some degree, then, models such as Nadler-Tushman and the positions taken by Burns and Stalker and by Lawrence and Lorsch suggest a cause-effect linkage. Nadler and Tushman at least imply that little or no congruence between, say, strategy and structure produces low organizational performance, and the contingency models posit that an improper match between the organization's external environment and its internal structure "causes" organizational ineffectiveness. The issue in both is that the number of items that might be congruent (or matched in the case of contingency) is great and the models provide neither a formula for determining which are central nor an objective means for knowing when congruence or matching has occurred or what levels of congruence/matching or incongruence/nonmatching produce desirable or undesirable effects. In short, our desire is for a model that will serve as a guide for both organizational diagnosis *and* planned, managed organization change—one that clearly shows cause-and-effect relationships and can be tested empirically.

With respect to the latter half of this desire, a model of organization change, we are attempting to provide a causal framework that encompasses both the what and the how—what organizational dimensions are key to successful change and how these dimensions should be linked causally to achieve the change goals. In other words, we are attempting to integrate two categories of change theory from the world of organization development (OD), what Porras and Robertson (1987) as well as Woodman (1989) refer to as (1) implementation theory and (2) change process theory. The former concerns activities that must be undertaken to affect planned change (e.g., survey feedback) and the latter refers to specific changes that need to occur as a consequence of these implementation activities (e.g., embracing a particular value such as emphasizing service to customers more than adhering rigidly to procedures regarding how to deal with customers, rather than vice versa). As these OD researchers have pointed out, theory in OD is typically either one or the other—implementation or change process. With the model presented in this chapter, we are striving for an integration of both theories.

An additional desire, as noted already, is to link what we understand from our practice to what is known from research and theory. It is clear that, for example, the 7S model came from consulting practice (see Peters & Waterman, 1982, 9–12), and we know firsthand that Weisbord's six-box model evolved from his practice. We believe that these models have valid components because they are in fact based on practice and do not convey irrelevant or the so-called ivory tower thinking. Yet these and other models do not go far enough. For example, such critical dimensions as the external environment, performance, and organizational culture are not accounted for sufficiently. Moreover, depicting organizational models as simply as possible can be beneficial, especially when attempting to explain systemic ideas to people who are relatively naïve about large organizations; however, reality is much more complex than most, if not all, models depict. And when attempting to account for organizational functioning and change at the same time, we must depict a considerable degree of complexity while maintaining coherence—no mean feat. We know of no organizational models that attempt this degree of complexity, coherence, and predictability (i.e., causality).

BACKGROUND: CLIMATE AND CULTURE

Climate

The early, original thinking underlying the model presented here came from George Litwin and others during the 1960s. In 1967, the Harvard Business School sponsored a conference on organizational climate. The results of this conference were subsequently published in two books (Litwin & Stringer, 1968; Tagiuri & Litwin, 1968). The concept of organizational climate that emerged from this series of studies and articles was that of a psychological state strongly affected by organizational conditions (e.g., systems, structure, manager behavior, etc.).

The importance of this early research and theory development regarding organizational climate was that it clearly linked psychological and organizational variables in a cause-effect model that was empirically testable. Using the model, Litwin and Stringer (1968) were able to predict *and* control the motivational and performance consequences of various organizational climates established in their research experiment. They were working with motivation analysis and arousal techniques developed by McClelland (1961), Atkinson (1958), and others over a period of more than twenty years.

Culture

In recent years there has been a great deal of interest in the concept of organizational culture. Drawn from anthropology, the concept of culture is meant to describe the relatively enduring set of values and norms that underlie a social system. These underlying values and norms may not be entirely available to one's consciousness. They are thought to describe a "meaning system" that allows members of that social system to attribute meanings and values to the variety of external and internal events that are experienced.

In this chapter, we attempt to be very explicit about the distinction between climate and culture. Climate is defined in terms of perceptions that individuals have of how their local work unit is managed and how effectively they and their day-to-day colleagues work together on the job. The level of analysis, therefore, is the group, the work unit. Climate is much more in the foreground of organizational members' perceptions, whereas culture is more background and defined by beliefs and values. The level of analysis for culture is the organization. Climate is, of course, affected by culture, and people's perceptions define both, but at different levels. We attempt to clarify more in depth these distinctions later in the chapter, as has Schneider (1985) before us. Further, we are attempting to create a model of organizational behavior within which both climate and culture can be described in terms of their interactions with other organizational variables. Thus, we are building on earlier research and theory with regard to predicting motivation and performance effects.

In addition, we are attempting to distinguish between the set of variables that influence and are influenced by climate and those influenced by culture. We postulate two distinct sets of organizational dynamics, one primarily associated with the transactional level of human behavior—the everyday interactions and exchanges that more directly create climate conditions. The second set of dynamics is concerned with processes of organizational transformation—that is, rather fundamental changes in behavior (e.g., value shifts). Such transformational processes are required for genuine change in the culture of an organization. In our effort to distinguish between transactional and transformational dynamics in organizations, we have been influenced by the writings of James McGregor Burns (1978) and by our own experience in modern organizations.

THE MODEL

Figure 17.1 is a diagram summarizing the model. As noted earlier, this model owes its original development to the work of Litwin and his associates (Litwin & Stringer, 1968; Tagiuri & Litwin, 1968) and has been refined through a series of studies directed by Burke and his colleagues (Bernstein & Burke, 1989; Michela et al., 1988). Recent collaboration has led to the current form of this model that (1) specifies by arrows which organizational variable (see the boxes) influences more directly which other variables and (2) distinguishes transformational and transactional dynamics in organizational behavior and change.

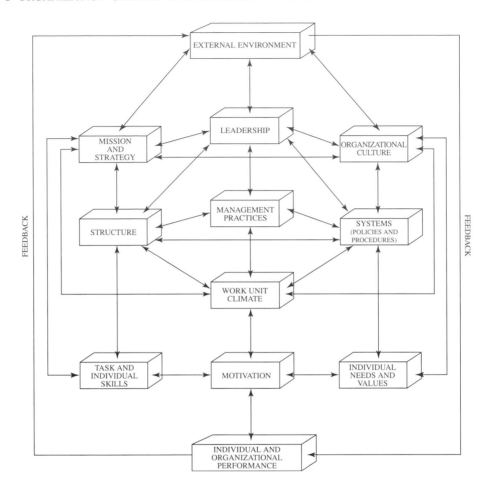

Figure 17.1. A Model of Organizational Performance and Change.

Conforming to accepted ways of thinking about organizations from general systems theory (Katz & Kahn, 1978), the external environmental box represents the input, and the individual and organizational performance box the output. The feedback loop goes in both directions: that is, organizational performance affects the system's external environment via its products and services, and the organization's performance may be directly affected by its external environment (e.g., a change in government regulations or trends on Wall Street). The remaining boxes in the model represent the throughput aspect of general systems theory.

The total of twelve boxes represent, of course, our choices of organizational variables we consider to be the most important ones. These choices were not made in isolation. We have been influenced by others' thinking. To a large degree, therefore, we have followed precedence. For example, in one form or another, and perhaps using different labels, we have incorporated the seven S's of the McKinsey model explained by Peters and Waterman (1982). The same can be said of Weisbord's model (1976) and the one by Nadler and Tushman (1977). In addition, we have attempted to account for key variables at a total system level, with such variables as mission, strategy, and culture, at a group or local work unit level (e.g., climate), and at an individual level (e.g., motivation, individual needs and values, and job-person match).

It is no doubt an understatement to say that the model is complex. At the same time, however, we recognize the need for the human mind to simplify the rich complexity of organizational phenomena. And though complex to depict and describe, our model, exhibited two-dimensionally, is still an oversimplification. A hologram would be better, but is not available.

Arrows going in both directions are meant to convey the open-systems principle. A change in one (or more) "box(es)" will eventually have an impact on the others. Moreover, if we could diagram the model such that the arrows would be more circular—the hologram idea—reality could be represented more accurately. Yet this is a *causal* model. For example, though culture and systems affect one another, we believe culture has a stronger influence on systems than vice versa. Kerr and Slocum (1987), for example, have provided data that suggest a strong linkage between corporate culture and the organization's reward system. They show how a company's reward system is a manifestation of its culture. They also point out that the organization's reward system can be used to help change the company's culture. Their data lend support to the linkage notion. We would simply take their evidence and suggest a step further by arguing that corporate culture (beliefs and values) determine the type of reward system an organization has. Yet we would strongly agree that to change culture the reward system should be used (i.e., to reward the behaviors that would reflect the new values we might wish to incorporate).

Displaying the model the way we have is meant to make a statement about organizational change. Organizational change, especially an overhaul of the company business strategy, stems more from environmental impact than from any other factor. Moreover, in large scale or total organizational change, mission, strategy, leadership, and culture have more "weight" than structure, management practices, and systems—that is, having organizational leaders communicate the new strategy is not sufficient for effective change. Culture change must be planned as well and aligned with strategy and leader behavior. These variables have more weight because when changing them (e.g., organizational mission), they affect the total system. Changing structure, on the other hand, may or may not affect the total system. It depends on where in the organization a structural change might occur.

We are not necessarily discussing at this stage where one could *start* the change, only the relative weighting of change dynamics. When we think of the model in terms of change, then, the weighted order displayed in the model is key. This point will be elaborated in the next section.

To summarize briefly so far, the model shown in Figure 17.1 attempts to portray the primary variables that need to be considered in any attempt to predict and explain the total behavior output of an organization, the most important interactions between these variables, and how they affect change. Again, in reality, all boxes would have bidirectional arrows with every other box. We are displaying with our model what we consider the most critical linkages. Later in this chapter, we define each of the variables and give some examples of typical interactions.

TRANSFORMATIONAL AND TRANSACTIONAL DYNAMICS

The concept of transformational change in organizations is suggested in the writings of such people as Bass (1985), Burke (1986), Burns (1978), McClelland (1975), and Tichy and Devanna (1986). Figure 17.2 contains a display of the transformational variables—the upper half of the model. By *transformational* we mean areas in which alteration is likely caused by interaction with environmental forces (both within and without) and will require entirely new behavior sets from organizational members.

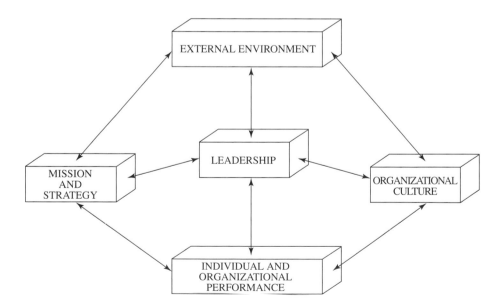

Figure 17.2. A Model of Organizational Performance and Change: The Transformational Factors.

It is true, of course, that members can influence their organization's environment so that certain changes are minimized (e.g., lobbying activities, forming or being involved in trade associations and coalitions). Our feedback loop in the model is meant to reflect this kind of influence. Our point here is that for the most part organization change is initiated by forces from the organization's external environment (e.g., changes in the competitive environment, government regulations, technological breakthroughs). Not everyone would agree with our premise. Torbert (1989), for example, argues that organizational transformation emanates from transformational leaders, not from the environment. We would agree that strong leaders make a difference, especially in the early states of their tenure. These leaders are responding, nevertheless, to forces in their organization's environment, we contend. This leader responsiveness does not mean passivity. Astute leaders are people who scan their organization's external environment, choose the forces they wish to deal with, and take action accordingly. This leadership process is neither passive nor in isolation, as Torbert's contention might imply.

Figure 17.3 contains the transactional variables—the lower half of the model. These variables are very similar to those isolated earlier by Litwin and, in part (structural effects on climate), later by Michela et al. (1988). By transactional we mean that the primary way of alteration is via relatively short-term reciprocity among people and groups. In other words, "You do this for me and I'll do that for you."

This transformational-transactional way of thinking about organizations that we are using for the model, as noted earlier, comes from theory about leadership. The distinction has been characterized as differences between a leader and a manager. Burke (1986) combined both the theorizing of Zaleznik (1977) and Burns (1978)—that is, transformational (Burns) leader (Zaleznik) and transactional (Burns) manager (Zaleznik)—to clarify further these distinctions and to hypothesize how each type, leader or manager, could empower others effectively. With respect to the model, and in keeping with the leader (transformational)–manager (transactional) distinctions, transformational change is therefore associated more with leadership, whereas transactional change is more within the purview of management.

With this broad distinction of transformational-transactional in mind, we now proceed with a more specific explanation of the model. And, at the risk of erring on the side of brevity, the next section defines each category or box in the model. With each box definition we have provided at least one reference from the literature that helps to clarify further what we mean.

External environment is any outside condition or situation that influences the performance of the organization (e.g., marketplaces, world financial conditions, political/governmental circumstances). For a broad view of the changing nature of our world economy, see Drucker (1986). For a more specific

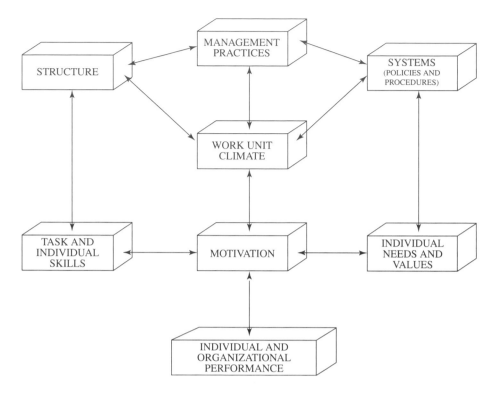

Figure 17.3. A Model of Organizational Performance and Change: The Transactional Factors.

perspective on how the external environment affects the organization, see Pfeffer and Salancik (1978).

Mission and strategy are what the organization's (1) top management believes are and has declared are the organization's mission and strategy and (2) what employees believe is the central purpose of the organization. Apparently, the mere fact of having a written mission statement is important to organizational effectiveness (Pearce & David, 1987). Strategy is how the organization intends to achieve that purpose over an extended time scale. We prefer Porter's more recent (1985) way of conceptualizing strategy (as opposed to, say, the Boston Consulting Group's way) because he links it directly to environment (industry structure), organizational structure, and corporate culture.

Leadership is executives' providing overall organizational direction and serving as behavioral role models for all employees. When assessing this category we would include followers' perceptions of executive practices and values. As our model shows, we make a distinction between leadership and management. This difference follows the thinking of Bennis and Nanus (1985), Burke (1986), Burns (1978), and Zaleznik (1977).

Culture is "the way we do things around here." This clear, simple definition comes from Deal and Kennedy (1982). To be a bit more comprehensive in our definition, we should add that culture is the collection of overt and covert rules, values, and principles that are enduring and guide organizational behavior. Understanding an organization's history, especially the values and customs of the founder(s), is key to explaining culture (Schein, 1983). Also, as stated earlier, culture provides a "meaning system" for organizational members.

Structure is the arrangement of functions and people into specific areas and levels of responsibility, decision-making authority, communication, and relationships to assure effective implementation of the organization's mission and strategy. Perhaps the classic articles on structure and no doubt some of the ones cited most often are by Duncan (1979) and Galbraith (1974). For perspectives about organizational structure and the future, see Jelinek, Litterer, and Miles (1986) and Peters (1988).

Management practices are what managers do in the normal course of events to use the human and material resources at their disposal to carry out the organization's strategy. By practices we mean a particular cluster of specific behaviors. An example of a behavioral management practice is "encouraging subordinates to initiate innovative approaches to tasks and projects." As a practice, two managers may "encourage subordinates" to the same extent, but how specifically each one does it may differ. Thus, we are following the work of such people as Boyatzis (1982), Burke and Coruzzi (1987), and Luthans (1988).

Systems are standardized policies and mechanisms that facilitate work, primarily manifested in the organization's reward systems, management information systems (MIS), and in such control systems as performance appraisal, goal and budget development, and human resource allocation. This category of the model covers a lot of ground. Some references that help to explain what we mean by the subcategories include Lawler (1981) on reward systems, Keen (1981) on MIS, Flamholtz (1979) on control systems, and Schuler and Jackson (1987) with their linkage of human resource management systems and practices to strategy.

Climate is the collective current impressions, expectations, and feelings that members of local work units have that, in turn, affect their relations with their boss, with one another, and with other units. For further clarification of what we mean by climate, see James and Jones (1974); Litwin, Humphrey, and Wilson (1978); and Michela et al. (1988).

Task requirements and individual skills/abilities are the required behavior for task effectiveness, including specific skills and knowledge required of people to accomplish the work which they have been assigned and for which they feel directly responsible. Essentially, this box concerns what is often referred to as job-person match. This domain of the model represents mainstream industrial/organizational psychology. Almost any good textbook, such as

Maier and Verser (1982), will provide thorough coverage of this category of the model. On the job side, see Campion and Thayer (1987) for an up-to-date analysis of job design, and for the person side, at the general manager level, Herbert and Deresky (1987) provide a useful perspective on matching a person's talents with business strategy.

Individual needs and values are the specific psychological factors that provide desire and worth for individual actions or thoughts. Many behavioral scientists believe that enriched jobs enhance motivation and there is evidence to support this belief, yet as Hackman and Oldham (1980) have appropriately noted, not everyone has a desire for his or her job to be enriched. For some members of the workforce, their idea of enrichment concerns activities off the job, not on the job. As the American workforce continues to become even more diverse, the ability to understand differences among people regarding their needs and values with respect to work and job satisfaction increases in importance. See, for example, Kravetz (1988) regarding changes in the workforce and Plummer (1989) on our changing values (i.e., more emphasis on self-actualization).

Motivation is aroused behavior tendencies to move toward goals, take needed action, and persist until satisfaction is attained. This is the net resultant motivation—that is, the resultant net energy generated by the sum of achievement, power, affection, discovery, and other important human motives. The article by Evans (1986) is especially relevant because his model for understanding motivation in the workplace is not only multifaceted but the facets are very similar to our model.

Individual and organizational performance is the outcome or result as well as the indicator of effort and achievement (e.g., productivity, customer satisfaction, profit, and quality). At the organizational level the work of Cameron, Whetten, and their colleagues is especially relevant to this box; see, for example, Cameron (1980) and Cameron and Whetten (1981, 1982), and at the individual level the article by Latham, Cummings, and Mitchell (1981).

CLIMATE RESULTS FROM TRANSACTIONS; CULTURE CHANGE REQUIRES TRANSFORMATION

In attempting to explain this model so far, we have encountered many questions, but perhaps most have focused on the distinction between climate and culture. An additional explanation is no doubt appropriate.

In our causal model, we argue that day-to-day climate will be a result of transactions around such issues as:

1. Sense of direction: effect of *mission* clarity or lack thereof.
2. Role and responsibility: effect of *structure*, reinforced by manager *practice*.

3. Standards and commitment: effect of manager *practice*, reinforced by *culture*.

4. Fairness of rewards: effect of *systems*, reinforced by manager *practice*.

5. Focus on customer versus internal pressures, standards of excellence: effect of *culture*, reinforced by other variables.

In contrast, the concept of organizational culture has to do with those underlying values and meaning systems that are difficult to manage, to alter, to even be aware of totally (Schein, 1985). We do not mean to use culture to describe another way of understanding the short-term dynamics of the organization. Rather, it provides us with a theoretical framework for delving into that which is continuing and more or less permanent. By more or less permanent, we mean that change can be arranged or may come about through the application of uncontrolled outside forces, but it will involve substantial upheaval in all transactional-level systems and will take time.

When we describe culture as the underlying values and meaning systems of an organization, we describe those forces that create the dimensions of climate, those underlying ideas and images around which specific attitudes and behaviors cluster. Thus, when we attempt to alter the organizational cluster, we change the climate framework (i.e., the gauge by which organizational members perceive their work climate). You might even think of such a period as involving a destabilized climate that would have quite distinctive properties of its own. The new organization culture, as it becomes accepted, would create a modified, if not entirely new set of dimensions around which climate would be perceived, described, and responded to. Take, for example, customer service. The culture change desired is one of establishing a *value* that the customer comes first, to be served as quickly and as pleasantly as possible with the highest degree of quality, and a *norm* that behavior in a given work unit should be externally oriented first (i.e., focused on customers or those whom members of the work unit serve) and internally oriented second (i.e., how members work together). The impact of this change in the culture—a significant shift of priority—on work unit climate might be to replace a former dimension of teamwork with one of interunit (or customer) relations. Or, at a minimum, this latter focus on unit relations might become an added dimension of climate.

APPLYING THE MODEL

For major organizational change to occur, the top transformational boxes represent the primary and significant levers for that change. Examples from our experience include (1) an acquisition where the acquired organization's culture, leadership, and business strategy were dramatically different from the acquiring organization, even though both organizations were in the same industry, requiring yet a new merged organization to come about; (2) a federal agency where the mission had been modified, the structure and leadership changed significantly, yet the culture remained in the 1960s (obviously a culture change effort); and (3) a high-tech firm where leadership had recently changed and was perceived negatively, the strategy was unclear, and internal politics had moved from minimal (before) to predominant (after). The hue and cry in this latter high-tech organization was something like "We have no direction from our leaders and no culture to guide our behavior in the meantime." These examples represent transformational change (i.e., the need for some fundamental shifts).

For organizations where the problems are more of a fine tuning, improving process, the second layer of the model serves as the point of concentration. Examples include some changes in the organization's structure, modification of the reward system, management development (perhaps in the form of a program that concentrates on behavioral practices), or conducting a climate survey to obtain a current measure of such variables as job satisfaction, job clarity, and degree of teamwork.

We have been involved recently with one organization where almost all of the model was used to provide a framework for executives and managers to understand the massive change they were attempting to manage. This organization, British Airways, became a private corporation in February 1987, and changing from a government agency to a market-driven, customer-focused business enterprise required quite a change indeed. *All* boxes in the model have been and still are being affected. Data were gathered based on most of the boxes and summarized in a feedback report for each executive and manager. This feedback, organized according to the model, helped executives and managers understand which of the boxes within his or her organizational domain (or "patch," as the British call it) needed attention.

It is also useful to consider the model in a vertical manner. For example, in one large manufacturing organization (Bernstein & Burke, 1989) we examined the causal chain of culture–management practices–climate. Feedback to executives in this corporation showed how and to what degree cultural variables influenced management practices and, in turn, work unit climate (our dependent variable in this case).

SOME PRELIMINARY SUPPORT FOR THE MODEL'S VALIDITY

Within the context of general system theory, all variables affect one another and the hologram notion, introduced earlier, is a useful way to visualize organizational reality. But with respect to organization change, our contention is that external environment has the greatest impact and, internally, the transformational variables (mission/strategy, leadership, culture) have the greatest impact, and next the transactional variables, etc. If we were able to conduct the statistical procedure of path analysis on all variables (boxes) of the model, the beta weights for the downwardly directed arrows would be larger than the beta weights in the opposite direction (e.g., the structure-to-climate direction would be larger than the climate-to-structure one).

What follows are citations of research studies that provide support for our organization change argument. These citations are limited to one or two per "arrow" and do not represent an exhaustive listing.

The Influence of External Environment

Because our model is based on open-systems theory, we believe in the causal nature of environments. An excellent framework for understanding this causal relationship is the one provided by Emery and Trist (1965). More specifically and recently, Prescott (1986) has empirically demonstrated how environment influences strategy and, in turn, performance. Miles and Snow (1978) have provided evidence to show that executive perceptions of their organization's environment and their consequent decision making is directly and causally linked. With respect to organizational culture, if we limit our definition of external environment to industry group, for example, then Gordon (1985), who studied utility companies and financial institutions, has shown that corporate culture is directly influenced by the industry category (external environment) of the firm.

THE TRANSFORMATIONAL VARIABLES

Chandler's classic study (1962) clearly demonstrated the differential impact of strategy or structure. More recently, Miles, Snow, Meyer, and Coleman (1978) have shown how strategy affects structure. And, as noted earlier, company mission apparently affects strategic decisions, which in turn affect performance (Pearce & David, 1987). When mission statements include corporate values and philosophy, or at least imply certain values, they also reflect the organization's culture, as Wilkins (1989) has noted. The influence of *culture* on policy and system, in this case the *reward system*, has been shown by Kerr and Slocum (1987), and Bernstein and Burke (1989) have demonstrated the impact of culture on management practices. It also seems that culture makes a difference with respect to organizational performance—that is, some cultures are more efficient than others (Wilkins & Ouchi, 1983).

It should be mentioned at this stage that we are quite aware of the fact that models may only help us to understand reality; they do not necessarily depict it. With respect to our three transformational boxes, they can be thought of more realistically as being in the minds of organizational leaders and as part of their behavior, not in organizational categories. The thinking of Tregoe and Zimmerman (1980) is helpful here. They define nine different categories of strategy, or what they call strategic driving forces: product or service offered, market needs, technology, production capability, method of sale, method of distribution, natural resources, size and growth, and profit-return on investment. They contend that any given company has only one, singular strategic driving force. This idea, incidentally, is similar to Galbraith's "center of gravity" notion (1983). The strategic driving force is a manifestation of the company leader's beliefs about how to succeed in a particular industry or line of business. Beliefs are part and parcel to corporate culture, and the leadership category is where they (strategy and culture) come together—in the minds of organization leaders and as part of their behavior. When these executives believe differently about which strategy brings success, the company is in trouble (see Burke, 1991, for a case example). Incidentally, in this organizational case, there was a clear need for transformational change—that is, in particular, change in leadership and in corporate culture. In the end, however, at best, there was only a transactional change limited largely to a modification in the organization's structure.

And, finally for this transformational category, do *leaders* make a difference organizationally? It is not difficult to find research to verify the hierarchical effect on behavior (i.e., that bosses affect subordinates). One of the early studies that showed how supervisors were directly affected by their bosses' managerial style was Fleishman's (1953). But even through mediating variables, as our model reflects, do leaders have an impact on organizational performance? Surprisingly, little research has been conducted to address this question. And the studies that have are not always consistent with one another. Salancik and Pfeffer (1977), for example, showed that turnover of mayors had little effect on the city's performance. Two more recent studies do provide support, however. Weiner and Mahoney (1981) found that leadership accounted for more variance in organizational performance than other variables, and Smith, Carson, and Alexander (1984), in a longitudinal study, showed empirically that leadership was associated with improved organizational performance.

The Transactional Variables

The variables, structure, management practices, and systems are more operational and are more incremental with respect to organization change. Although our main variable to consider as the dependent one is *climate*, structure also has a direct impact on task requirements and individual skills/abilities (job-person match). System, especially rewards, also directly affect individual needs and values.

Joyce and Slocum (1984) have shown that both management practices and structure influence climate, and an earlier study by Schneider and Snyder (1975) also demonstrated that climate is affected by the same two variables and by the reward system (i.e., pay and promotion policies). Schneider has also shown a direct linkage between management practices and climate in a series of studies in the service sector (Schneider, 1980; Schneider & Bowen, 1985).

With respect to the impact of *structure* on variables other than climate, the work of Lawrence and Lorsch (1969), of course, has shown its influence on management practices. The relationship between structure and systems has been demonstrated in numerous ways, just one example being Ouchi's study of structure and organizational control (1977). And the relationship between structure and task requirements has also been demonstrated many times, perhaps the work by Galbraith (1977, 1973) being one of the best illustrations.

Regarding the impact of *systems*, perhaps the most important subsystem of the policy and procedures (systems) box is the organization's reward system. The belief that "people do what they are rewarded for doing" is practically a cliché. Demonstrating this relationship of rewards and behavior is not as obvious and straightforward as one might presume, however. Witness the pay-for-performance controversy for a case in point. There is evidence, nevertheless.

Research on gainsharing shows linkage among management practices, climate, and motivation/performance. Gainsharing positively influences performance (Bullock & Lawler, 1984). As Hammer (1988) has noted, however, the presence of worker participation is close to being a necessary condition for success (in particular, Scanlon Plans). In other words, when management establishes a working climate of participation coupled with pay for performance, positive results occur. For more direct evidence that a participatory climate affects productivity, see Rosenberg and Rosenstein (1980).

And for evidence that reward systems affect individual needs/values, and vice versa, see Deutsch (1985). For a more specific example, see the research of Jordan (1986), a field study indicating that Deci's contention (1975) that extrinsic rewards have a negative effect on intrinsic motivation is probably correct.

Another subsystem within the policy and procedures box and one that is intertwined with the reward system is the organization's performance appraisal system. For evidence that this subsystem affects management practices and climate and, in turn, motivation and ultimately performance, see the work of Cummings (1982) and Cummings and Schwab (1973).

Yet another major subsystem within the policy and procedure box is the organization's management information system. Perhaps the latest and broadest research in this area—the impact of information technology on worker behavior—is the work of Zuboff (1988).

To summarize, these transactional dimensions are central to the model. They affect and are affected by a greater variety of variables than most other dimensions.

MOTIVATION AND PERFORMANCE

With respect to the differential impact of individual needs and values on motivation and job satisfaction, the work of Hackman and Oldham (1980) shows some of the clearest evidence. Among other findings, their research indicates that a majority of people probably have a need for growth and development on the job and therefore would respond to and be more motivated by job enrichment, but not everyone would be so motivated. Among other findings that certain psychologically based interventions affect productivity positively, Guzzo, Jette, and Katzell (1985) more recently have provided evidence that work redesign (i.e., job enrichment) does as well.

Compared with other boxes in the model, finding evidence to support our contention that congruence between persons' skills/abilities and job requirements leads to enhanced motivation and, in turn, higher performance is very easy. For a summary of this area of research, see M. J. Burke and Pearlman (1988) and for an example of impressive evidence, see Hunter and Schmidt (1982).

SUMMARY

Table 17.1 provides a summary of the studies that we have cited as preliminary support for the model's validity, particularly in terms of arrows that are in the downward direction.

A summary word of qualification: the studies we have chosen to demonstrate support for ideas about organizational performance and change are highly selective. There are no doubt numerous other studies that both support and perhaps question our arguments. The fact that evidence does not exist, however, is the point we wish to make.

The evidence that we have cited comes from disparate sources and, with respect to the model, is piecemeal. Ideally, a proper test of the model would be a study that simultaneously examines the impact of all boxes across a variety of organizations. The closest we have come so far is to examine organizational members' perceptions and beliefs: how managers' beliefs about mission and strategy, for example, relate to (if not predict) their perception and their

Table 17.1.

Dimensions of Model	Studies
External Environment ↓	Prescott (1978)
Mission and Strategy ↓	Miles & Snow (1978)
Leadership ↓	Gordon (1985)
Culture	
Mission and Strategy ↓	Chandler (1962); Miles et al. (1978)
Structure ↓	Tregoe & Zimmerman (1980)
Leadership/Culture	
Leadership ↓	Fleishman (1953)
Management Practices ↓	Weiner & Mahoney (1981); Smith et al. (1984)
Performance	
Culture ↓	Kerr & Slocum (1987)
Reward System ↓	Bernstein & Burke (1989)
Management Practices ↓	Wilkins & Ouchi (1983)
Performance	
Structure ↓	Joyce & Slocum (1984); Schneider & Snyder (1975)
Climate ↓	Lawrence & Lorsch (1967)
Management Practices ↓	Ouchi (1977)
Systems ↓	Galbraith (1977; 1973)
Task Requirements	

(continued)

Table 17.1. (continued)

Dimensions of Model	Studies
Management Practices ↓ Climate	Schneider (1980); Schneider & Bowen (1985)
Systems ↓ Climate	Bullock & Lawler (1984); Cummings (1982) Cummings & Schwab (1973); Hammer (1988); Zuboff (1988)
Management Practices ↓ Individual Needs and Values	Deutsch (1985); Jordan (1986)
Climate ↓ Motivation-Performance	Rosenberg & Rosenstein (1980)
Task-Person ↓ Motivation-Performance	M.J. Burke & Pearlman (1988); Hunter & Schmidt (1982)
Individual Needs and Values	Hackman & Oldham (1980); Guzzo et al. (1985)

subordinates' perceptions of work unit climate. To cite an actual example, at British Airways one of the performance indices used was perceived team effectiveness. Data were also collected from BA managers regarding their beliefs and perceptions about (1) team manager practices (e.g., degree of empowering behavior toward subordinates), (2) the usefulness of BA's structure toward subordinates, (3) the clarity of BA's strategy, (4) the extent to which BA's culture supports change, and (5) the team's climate (e.g., goal and role clarity). These data categorized according to just these five boxes from the model accounted for 54 percent of the variance in ratings of team effectiveness for this organization (Bernstein, 1987). We are not implying that the model always explains this degree of variance. We are illustrating how the model can be used methodologically for particular client organizations.

Figure 17.4 shows these relationships diagrammatically from the model as they were applied to the client organization, in this case BA.

In another more recent, direct attempt to test the validity of the model in assessing primarily (but not exclusively) the culture of a hospital, Fox (1990)

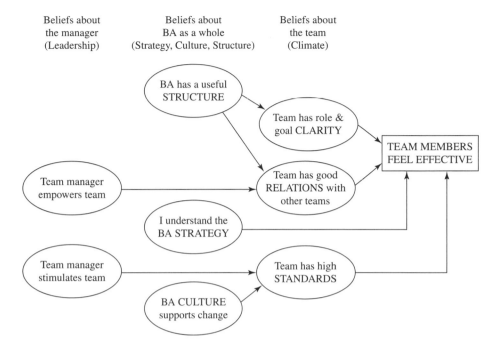

Figure 17.4. Beliefs Associated with Team Members' Perceptions of Effectiveness.

showed significant support for the causal relationships of certain dimensions (boxes). Using the model as a causal predictor, her path analysis outcomes demonstrated that leadership, culture, and management practices predicted significant variance in employees' perceptions of work unit climate and organizational performance. The two transformational dimensions, leadership and culture, were clearly the two strongest predictors.

CONCLUSIONS

By covering the choice of variables (boxes) that we have selected, we have made an attempt with this chapter to describe and define an organizational model that, at least at face value, makes good, common sense. Yet others have done this kind of modeling work as well. It is our contention, however, that we have taken an additional step by hypothesizing causality (arrows), particularly in the weighted direction—that is, top-down, the transformational then transactional factors. We have searched and have found, from the literature and from our own work, at least in part, empirical support for this hypothesized causality. We are as a consequence encouraged, and we intend to search further and conduct more research. For a recent and further application of the model in a corporate setting, see Burke and Jackson (1991).

We do not always obtain evidence that supports precisely the causal chain depicted in the model, however. We have found from our experience, for example, that on occasion perceptions regarding strategy or structure explain more variance in ratings of climate or some index of performance than do management practices, usually a heavy indicator. These occasions are when the organization is in the midst of a change in strategy, a change in structure, or both. It may also be that national differences would affect the causal chain in ways that are not quite the same as the model predicts. In the UK, for example, beliefs about "the team" and what constitutes satisfaction may not be the same as American beliefs. When given the opportunity to complain or criticize, the British seem to attribute their feelings of dissatisfaction more toward distant factors—the culture, the structure—than to factors close to home—one's teammates. Americans, on the other hand, are just as likely to criticize their team mates as they are to complain about the inadequate organizational structure.

Finding exceptions to the causal implications of the model does not detract necessarily from its usefulness. As a guide for what to look for and a predictor for what and how to manage large-scale organizational change, we have found the model invaluable. Like any other model, however, we must not allow it to determine exclusively what we diagnose or how we handle organization change. We cannot afford to allow our model to become ideology, as Morgan (1986) has warned, and that our "way of seeing is not a way of seeing".

A final note: It is interesting to point out that executives and managers more typically concern themselves with the left side of the model—more mission and strategy, structure, task requirements and individual skills/abilities, and performance (i.e., when one wants to change an organization, these are the critical dimensions). Behavioral scientists, on the other hand, are more likely to be concerned with the right side and middle—leadership, culture, systems (especially rewards), management practices, climate, individual need and values, motivation, and performance. We are criticized by the former group as only dealing with the "soft" stuff. We of course, should be concerned with *both*, and with a more effective integration of purpose and practice.

References

Atkinson, J. W. (Ed.) 1958. *Motives in fantasy, action, and society*. Princeton, NJ: Van Nostrand.

Bass, B. M. 1985. *Leadership and performance beyond expectations*. New York: The Free Press.

Bennis, W. G., & Nanus, B. 1985. *Leaders: Strategies for taking charge*. New York: Harper & Row.

Bernstein, W. M. 1987. Unpublished manuscript.

Bernstein, W. M., & Burke, W. W. 1989. Modeling organizational meaning systems. In R. W. Woodman & W. A. Pasmore (Eds.), *Research in organizational change and development*, 3: 117–159. Greenwich, CT: JAI Press.

Boyatzis, R. 1982. *The competent manager*. New York: Wiley & Sons.

Bullock, R. J., & Lawler, E. E. III. 1984. Gainsharing: A few questions and fewer answers. *Human Resource Management*, 23: 23–40.

Burke, M. J., & Pearlman, K. 1988. Recruiting, selecting, and matching people with jobs. In J. R. Campbell, R. J. Campbell & Associates (Eds.), *Productivity in organizations*, 97–142. San Francisco: Jossey-Bass.

Burke, W. W. 1986. Leadership as empowering others. In S. Srivastva & Associates (Eds.), *Executive power: How executives influence people and organizations*, 51–77. San Francisco: Jossey-Bass.

Burke, W. W. 1991. Engineered materials. In A. M. Glassman & T. G. Cummings (Eds.), *Cases in organization development*, 68–77. Plano, TX: Business Publications.

Burke, W. W., & Coruzzi, C. A. 1987. Competence in managing lateral relations. In J. W. Pfeiffer (Ed.), *The 1987 annual: Developing human resources*, 151–156. San Diego: University Associates.

Burke, W. W., & Jackson, P. 1991. Making the SmithKline Beecham merger work. *Human Resource Management*, 30: 69–87.

Burns, J. M. 1978. *Leadership*. New York: Harper & Row.

Burns, T., & Stalker, G. 1961. *The management of innovation*. London: Tavistock.

Cameron, K. S. 1980. Critical questions in assessing organizational effectiveness. *Organizational Dynamics*, 9(1): 66–80.

Cameron, K. S., & Whetten, D. A. 1981. Perceptions of organizational effectiveness over organizational life cycles. *Administrative Science Quarterly*, 26: 525–544.

Cameron, K. S., & Whetten, D. A. (Eds.) 1982. *Organizational effectiveness: A comparison of multiple models*. New York: Academic Press.

Campion, M. A., & Thayer, P. W. 1987. Job design: Approaches, outcomes, and trade-offs. *Organizational Dynamics*, 15(3): 66–79.

Chandler, A. A. 1962. *Strategy and structure: Chapters in the history of the American industrial enterprise*. Cambridge, MA: MIT Press.

Cummings, L. L. 1982. *Improving human resource effectiveness*. Berea, OH: ASPA Foundation.

Cummings, L. L., & Schwab, D. P. 1973. *Performance in organizations: Determinates and appraisal*. Glenview, IL: Scott, Foresman.

Deal, T. E., & Kennedy, A. A. 1982. *Corporate cultures: The rites and rituals of corporate life*. Reading, MA: Addison-Wesley.

Deci, E. L. 1975. *Intrinsic motivation*. New York: Plenum Press.

Deutsch, M. 1985. *Distributive justice: A social psychological perspective*. New Haven, CT: Yale University Press.

Drucker, P. F. 1986. *The frontiers of management*. New York: E. P. Dutton/Truman Talley Books.

Duncan, R. 1979. What is the right organization structure? *Organizational Dynamics* 7(3): 59–80.

Emery, F. E., & Trist, E. L. 1965. The causal texture of organizational environments. *Human Relations*, 18: 21–32.

Evans, M. G. 1986. Organizational behavior: The central role of motivation. *Journal of Management*, 12: 203–222.

Flamholtz, E. 1979. Organizational control systems as a managerial tool. *California Management Review*, 22(2): 50–59.

Fleishman, E. A. 1953. Leadership climate, human relations training, and supervisory behavior. *Personnel Psychology*, 6: 205–222.

Fox, M. M. 1990. *The role of individual perceptions of organization culture in predicting perceptions of work unit climate and organizational performance*. Unpublished doctoral dissertation, Columbia University, New York City.

Galbraith, J. R. 1973. *Designing complex organizations*. Reading, MA: Addison-Wesley.

Galbraith, J. R. 1974. Organization design: An information processing view. *Interfaces*, 4(3): 28–36.

Galbraith, J. R. 1977. *Organization design*. Reading, MA: Addison-Wesley.

Galbraith, J. R. 1983. Strategy and organization planning. *Human Resource Management*, 22: 63–77.

Gleick, J. 1987. *Chaos: Making a new science*. New York: Viking.

Goodstein, L. D., & Burke, W. W. 1991. Creating successful organizational change. *Organizational Dynamics*, 19(4): 5–17.

Gordon, G. G. 1985. The relationship of corporate culture to industry sector and corporate performance. In R. H. Kilmann, M. J. Saxton, R. Serpa & Associates (Eds.), *Gaining control of the corporate culture*, 103–125, San Francisco: Jossey-Bass.

Gordon, G. G. 1991. Industry determinants of organizational culture. *Academy of Management Review*, 16: 396–415.

Guzzo, R. A., Jette, R. D., & Katzell, R. A. 1985. The effects of psychologically based intervention programs on worker productivity. *Personnel Psychology*, 38: 275–291.

Hackman, J. R., & Oldham, G. R. 1980. *Work redesign*. Reading, MA: Addison-Wesley.

Hammer, T. H. 1988. New developments in profit sharing, gainsharing, and employee ownership. In J. P. Campbell, R. J. Campbell & Associates (Eds.), *Productivity in organizations*, 328–366. San Francisco: Jossey-Bass.

Herbert, T. T., & Deresky, H. 1987. Should general managers match their business strategies? *Organizational Dynamics*, 15(3): 40–51.

Hunter, J. E., & Schmidt, F. L. 1982. Fitting people to jobs: Implications of personnel selection on national productivity. In E. A. Fleishman & M. D. Dunnette (Eds.), *Human performance and productivity: Human capability assessment*, 1: 233–284. Hillsdale, NJ: Erlbaum.

James, L. R., & Jones, A. P. 1974. Organizational climate: A review of theory and research. *Psychological Bulletin*, 81: 1096–1112.

Jelinek, M., Litterer, J. A., & Miles, R. E. 1986. The future of organization design. In M. Jelinek, J. A. Litterer, & R. E. Miles (Eds.), *Organization by design: Theory and practice* (2nd ed.): 527–543. Plano, TX: Business Publications.

Jordan, P. C. 1986. Effects of an extrinsic reward on intrinsic motivation: A field experiment. *Academy of Management Journal*, 29: 405–412.

Joyce, W. F., & Slocum, J. W. 1984. Collective climate: Agreement as a basis for defining aggregate climates in organizations. *Academy of Management Journal*, 27: 721–742.

Katz, D., & Kahn, R. L. 1978. *The social psychology of organizations* (2nd ed.). New York: Wiley.

Keen, P.G.W. 1981. Information systems and organizational change. *Communications of the ACM,* 24(1): 24–33.

Kerr, J., & Slocum, J. W. 1987. Managing corporate culture through reward systems. *Academy of Management Executive*, 1: 99–108.

Kravetz, D. J. 1988. *The human resource revolution*. San Francisco: Jossey-Bass.

Latham, G. P., Cummings, L. L., & Mitchell, T. R. 1981. Behavioral strategies to improve productivity. *Organizational Dynamics*, 9(3): 4–23.

Lawler, E. E. 1981. *Pay and organization development*. Reading, MA: Addison-Wesley.

Lawrence, P. R., & Lorsch, J. W. 1969. *Organization and environment: Managing differentiation and integration*. Boston, MA: Division of Research, Harvard Business School.

Litwin, G. H., Humphrey, J. W., & Wilson, T. B. 1978. Organizational climate: A proven tool for improving performance. In W. W. Burke (Ed.) *The cutting edge: Current theory and practice in organization development*, 187–205. La Jolla, CA: University Associates.

Litwin, G. H., & Stringer, R. A. 1968. *Motivation and organizational climate*. Boston, MA: Harvard Business School Press.

Luthans, F. 1988. Successful vs. effective real managers. *Academy of Management Executive*, 2: 127–132.

Maier, N.R.F., & Verser, G. C. 1982. *Psychology in industrial organizations* (5th ed.). Boston, MA: Houghton Mifflin.

McClelland, D. C. 1961. *The achieving society*. Princeton, NJ: Van Nostrand.

McClelland, D. C. 1975. *Power: The inner experience*. New York: Irvington.

Michela, J. L., Boni, S. M., Schechter, C. B., Manderlink, G., Bernstein, W. M., O'Malley, M., & Burke, W. W. 1988. *A hierarchically nested model for estimation of influences on organizational climate: Rationale, methods, and demonstration*. Working Paper, Teachers College, Columbia University.

Miles, R. E., & Snow, C. C. 1978. *Organizational strategy, structure, and process*. New York: McGraw-Hill.

Miles, R. E., Snow, C. C., Meyer, A. D., & Coleman, H. J. 1978. Organizational strategy, structure, and process. *Academy of Management Review*, 3: 546–562.

Morgan, G. 1986. *Images of organizations*. Beverly Hills, CA: Sage Publications.

Nadler, D. A., & Tushman, M. L. 1977. A diagnostic model for organization behavior. In J. R. Hackman, E. E. Lawler, & L. W. Porter (Eds.), *Perspectives on behavior in organizations*: 85–100. New York: McGraw-Hill.

Ouchi, W. G. 1977. The relationship between organizational structure and organizational control. *Administrative Science Quarterly*, 22: 95–113.

Pascale, R., & Athos, A. 1981. *The art of Japanese management*. New York: Warner Books.

Pearce, J. A., & David, F. 1987. Corporate mission statements: The bottom line. *Academy of Management Executive*, 1: 109–116.

Peters, T. 1988. Restoring American competitiveness: Looking for new models of organizations. *Academy of Management Executive*, 2: 103–109.

Peters, T. J., & Waterman, R. H., Jr. 1982. *In search of excellence: Lessons from America's best-run corporations*. New York: Harper & Row.

Pfeffer, J., & Salancik, G. R. 1978. *The external control of organizations: A resource dependent perspective*. New York: Harper & Row.

Plummer, J. R. 1989. Changing values: The new emphasis on self-actualization. *The Futurist*, 23(1): 8–13.

Porras, J., & Robertson, P. J. 1987. Organization development theory. A typology and evaluation. In R. W. Woodman & W. A. Pasmore (Eds.), *Research in organizational change and development*, 1: 1–57. Greenwich, CT: JAI.

Porter, M. E. 1985. *Competitive strategy: Techniques for analyzing industries and competitors*. New York: Free Press.

Prescott, J. E. 1986. Environments as moderators of the relationship between strategy and performance. *Academy of Management Journal*, 29: 329–346.

Rosenberg, R. D., & Rosenstein, E. 1980. Participation and productivity: An empirical study. *Industrial and Labor Relations Review*, 33: 355–367.

Salancik, G. R., & Pfeffer, J. 1977. An examination of needs satisfaction models of job attitudes. *Administrative Science Quarterly*, 22: 427–456.

Schein, E. H. 1983. The role of the founder in creating organizational cultures. *Organizational Dynamics*, 12(1): 13–28.

Schein, E. H. 1985. *Organizational culture and leadership*. San Francisco: Jossey-Bass.

Schneider, B. 1980. The service organization: Climate is crucial. *Organizational Dynamics*, 9(2): 52–65.

Schneider, B. 1985. Organizational behavior. *Annual Review of Psychology*, 36: 573–611.

Schneider, B., & Bowen, D. E. 1985. Employee and customer perceptions of service in banks: Replication and extension. *Journal of Applied Psychology*, 70: 423–433.

Schneider, B., & Snyder, R. A. 1975. Some relationships between job satisfaction and organizational climate. *Journal of Applied Psychology*, 60: 318–328.

Schuler, R. S., & Jackson, S. E. 1987. Linking competitive strategies with human resource management practices. *Academy of Management Executive*, 1: 207–219.

Smith, J. E., Carson, K. P., & Alexander, R. A. 1984. Leadership: It can make a difference. *Academy of Management Journal*, 27: 765–776.

Tagiuri, R., & Litwin, G. H. (Eds.) 1968. *Organizational climate: Explorations of a concept*. Cambridge, MA: Harvard University Press.

Tichy, N. M., & Devanna, M. A. 1986. *The transformational leader*. New York: Wiley.

Torbert, W. R. 1989. Leading organizational transformation. In R. W. Woodman & W. A. Pasmore (Eds.), *Research in organizational change and development*, 3: 83–116. Greenwich, CT: JAI Press.

Tregoe, B. B., & Zimmerman, J. W. 1980. *Top management strategy: What it is and how to make it work*. New York: Simon & Schuster.

Weiner, N., & Mahoney, T. A. 1981. A model of corporate performance as a function of environmental, organizational, and leadership influences. *Academy of Management Journal*, 24: 453–470.

Weisbord, M. R. 1976. Organizational diagnosis: Six places to look for trouble with or without a theory. *Group and Organization Studies*, 1: 430–447.

Wilkins, A. L. 1989. *Developing corporate character: How to successfully change an organization without destroying it*. San Francisco: Jossey-Bass.

Wilkins, A. L., & Ouchi, W. G. 1983. Efficient cultures: Exploring the relationship between culture and organizational performance. *Administrative Science Quarterly*, 28: 468–481.

Woodman, R. W. 1989. Organizational change and development: New areas for inquiry and action. *Journal of Management*, 15: 205–228.

Zaleznik, A. 1977. Managers and leaders: Are they different? *Harvard Business Review*, 55(3): 67–78.

Zuboff, S. 1988. *In the age of the smart machine: The future of work and power*. New York: Basic Books.

CHAPTER EIGHTEEN

An Overview of Organizational Surveys

Allen I. Kraut (1996)

S urveys of employee opinions and perceptions seem quite popular nowa-days, but it was not always so. In 1953, noted industrial psychologist Morris Viteles wrote *Motivation and Morale in Industry*, and this "compre-hensive account of the latest studies and attitude surveys bearing upon the wants and needs of workers" (in the words of the dust jacket) reported that Conference Board studies of thousands of U.S. companies found barely fifty doing attitude surveys in 1944, rising to 245 in 1947. A later Conference Board study, in 1951, found 223 companies that had done surveys, of which only three had done them before 1940.

In Viteles's view (p. 246), the fourfold central purpose of the "employee-attitude survey" is to (1) learn the importance employees attach to different aspects of the work situation, (2) assess the level of employee satisfaction and morale to enable management to respond in units that require attention, (3) identify the factors determining employee satisfaction and morale, and (4) extend motivational theory. Reflecting interests of the post war era, Viteles's comments show a great concern about ways to increase productivity and to maintain "industrial harmony" (between management and workers and their unions). Yet, even now, his writing seems remarkably sophisticated in describ-ing the scientific use of surveys and their practical side. He notes that surveys raise employee expectations and quotes one executive as saying: "An attitude survey is like a hand grenade—once you pull the pin you have to do something with it. Otherwise it may hurt you rather than help you" (p. 394).

Obviously, we have come a long way in favor of surveys since then. Recent data suggest that in the 1990s, more than half of U.S. companies are using surveys of employees. A study by Delaney, Lewin, and Ichniowski (1988) surveyed seven thousand executives and received data representing 495 business units. The executives used surveys in from 38 percent to 51 percent of their units, depending on the type of employees in each unit. Another large poll, by Gallup (1988), found seven out of ten companies reporting they had done a survey of employees within the last ten years. Kraut and Freeman (1992) found survey usage reported by 78 percent of the human resource directors from seventy-five large well-managed firms.

These studies do not indicate how well or successfully the surveys are done. On anecdotal evidence, they seem to vary widely in size, frequency, types of questions, sampling strategy, form of administration, and use of the collected data. Still, by virtue of their visibility, surveys get a lot of attention and have the potential for broad impact in a company.

The term *organizational survey* describes a number of methods of systematically gathering data from the members of an organization. These methods include questionnaires, interviews, and even (unobtrusive) observation. Most questionnaires are self-administered and often paper and pencil, although this medium is rapidly being supplanted by such other media as telephones and computers. Interviews may be carried out individually (face-to-face or not) or even in focus groups.

A survey will usually have a theme, evidenced in standardized, usually close-ended questions, perhaps with some open-ended items also included. Later, the data will be formally processed, analyzed, and reported to the survey sponsors. Although there are many variations, the unifying component of organizational surveys is that they are a methodical way of gathering data from people in an organization for specific purposes.

ORIGINS

A short history of sample surveys in general (Rossi, Wright, & Anderson, 1983) shows they came into wide use in the 1920s and 1930s, primarily to determine public opinion (and political views) and to perform market research. During World War II, the U.S. government used surveys extensively to seek opinions from civilians and military personnel. The work by Samuel Stouffer and associates, *The American Soldier* (1947–1950) was an awesome example of using survey research for policy purposes.

After the war, many of the people involved in such government survey activities moved to university centers and set up survey research centers, such as the University of Michigan's Institute for Social Research, whose staff included Rensis Likert, Angus Campbell, and Leslie Kish. Although much of the effort of such groups was devoted to social science research, part of their work led to research in private-sector organizations, and gradually some of their staff and graduates left to conduct internal survey research within and for different companies.

METHODOLOGIES

With these origins, it should be no surprise that the published craft and science of survey research has been dominated by fields outside of industrial and organizational psychology. Much of what has been written comes from sociologists, public opinion pollsters, market researchers, and social psychologists, mainly for application to their own fields. Largely from academic bases, the authors cover topics like the logic of the science, research designs, sampling and multivariate statistics, question-writing, index construction, data analysis, and reporting.

One of the first comprehensive texts, *Survey Research*, authored by Charles Backstrom and Gerald Hursh-Cesar, was published in 1963 and intended for political scientists and political sociologists. A second edition came out almost two decades later, in 1981, but seems to be out of print. The popular *Survey Research Methods*, by Earl Babbie, came out in 1973 and is now in its second edition (1990). Focusing on the "logic and skills" of survey research, it has also spawned a larger text, *The Practice of Social Research*, now in its sixth edition (1992).

Along the way, we have seen some paperback texts produced primarily for public opinion pollsters, like *The Sample Survey: Theory and Practice*, written by Donald Warwick and Charles Lininger (1975), and Floyd J. Fowler's slim *Survey Research Methods* (rev. ed., 1988).

Some books, such as sociologist Donald Dillman's *Mail and Telephone Surveys: The Total Design Method* (1978), aim to present the "step-by-step details" of doing a survey. A more recent text, *Designing and Conducting Survey Research* (1992), authored by public administration faculty Louis Rea and Richard Parker, also provides step-by-step instruction for survey research.

Still other books have focused on subparts of survey research, such as market researcher Stanley Payne's classic *The Art of Asking Questions* (1951) or the more recent *Asking Questions: A Practical Guide to Questionnaire Design*, by public opinion researchers Seymour Sudman and Norman Bradburn (1982). In this vein are two other classics, Robert Kahn and Charles Cannell's *The Dynamics of Interviewing* (1957) and Leslie Kish's *Survey Sampling* (1965). A more comprehensive work, using many contributors and directed at social science research, can be found in the *Handbook of Survey Research*, edited by Peter Rossi, James Wright, and Andy Anderson (1983).

All the works just cited, along with the standard research methodology texts, have been the foundation for training industrial and organizational psychologists in survey research. Practical experience has been afforded through university-based survey research centers and graduate internships in industry. However, very few books have been written by or for those doing organizational surveys, although there have been some articles in various journals. A notable exception is Randall Dunham and Frank Smith's slender 1979 paperback, *Organizational Surveys*. Based largely on surveys done at Sears, Roebuck, it was written for managers, with the stated goal of presenting "the practical application of survey techniques" in order to provide managers "with the expertise necessary to conduct surveys properly and to use the results effectively" (p. iv). At a pragmatic level, it also served researchers well as a primer for understanding the operational and nonscientific aspects of surveys as they might be used within organizations.

CHANGING PURPOSES

In a general sense, the purposes of organizational surveys center around the themes distinguished by David Nadler: assessment and change. As Viteles's remarks showed, the early years of organizational surveys were dominated by an interest in the *assessment* of employee opinions, an interest also signaled by the subtitle of Dunham and Smith's 1979 book on organizational surveys: *An Internal Assessment of Organizational Health*. A similar theme is echoed by the title of another volume issued at about the same time, *Organizational Assessment: Perspectives on the Measurement of Organizational Behavior and the Quality of Work Life*, which was authored by three influential academically based industrial and organizational psychologists, Edward Lawler, David Nadler, and Cortlandt Cammann (1980). Signaling an emerging new emphasis, their book was part of a series on "organizational assessment and change." This shift toward an interest in change was aided by another work from the same era, titled *Feedback and Organization Development: Using Data-Based Methods*, by Nadler (1977). Although surveys were not mentioned in the title, they were obviously the source of the data being used to fuel change. Several examples and models for using survey data were detailed.

In my experience over three decades, I have seen organizational surveys performed for several different reasons, although most fit neatly under the umbrella terms of assessment or change. It is also worth noting that any particular survey may try to achieve several different purposes, which can overlap or even conflict with one another.

The major purposes of organizational surveys are described below. The order of listing begins with the purposes that are primarily assessment-related and ends with the purposes that are primarily change-related. The reader will note that some reasons for performing these surveys are a mix of both assessment and change.

To Pinpoint Areas of Concern

It is common for companies to have a generalized interest in knowing what aspects of the work setting are satisfying or dissatisfying to employees. They have a wish to "see how things are going," that is, to do an assessment in the organization. This type of evaluation may be aimed at particular issues to see what people feel good or bad about. There may be particular concerns on the minds of management, such as pay or benefits or supervision. In other cases, the interest may be in a particular group of people rather than a topic. Here the reason is to learn what groups may be "problem" units. This kind of survey can come about if poor labor relations are manifested, for example. In nonunion companies, a group petition may represent a threat of collective action, which can be very upsetting and spark management to learn what pleases or displeases different groups. Efforts may be taken to identify the attitudes associated with pro-union behaviors (the study by Hamner and Smith, 1978, is an example).

The units of interest may also be demographic groups. Unexpected increases in turnover among recent college recruits or in critical skill groups (like programmers, scientists, or engineers) can create an interest in how group staff feel about various issues. In recent years, many companies have been driven by diversity concerns to seek out the opinions of employees grouped by gender and ethnicity.

To Observe Long-Term Trends

Keeping tabs on relevant issues and significant groups over time requires multiple surveys done in comparable ways. The desire for long-term trend data may come out of interest in the impact of management attempts to make meaningful change in response to earlier survey inputs. Or it may arise from an interest in assessing changes caused by shifts in the firm's environment. Such changes can come about from sources as varied as the impact of inflation on people's evaluations of their pay, the effects of competition on feelings of job security, or people's perception of management's competence to deal with technological changes.

To some executives, such surveys are analogous to an annual physical examination. Even if one feels well, it may be worthwhile to check the status of one's vital elements of function against prior data. Here, the orientation is to prevent problems or nip them in the bud. Articles in the popular press suggesting, for example, that "employee morale" is deteriorating generally can also provoke a company's interest in surveys of trends.

To Monitor Program Impact

In a similar fashion, measuring reactions to earlier changes is a legitimate purpose of employee surveys. Such changes include reorganizations, reductions in force, relocations, and the introduction of new personnel practices (like different performance appraisals, career paths, or pay systems).

Other changes that some firms measure include the effects of shifts in ongoing programs. These shifts might include changed methods of parts distribution, different phasing of technical training, increases in pay levels, or alterations in staffing ratios. The impact of such changes may show up more starkly in some employee groups than in others or influence the ratings of some issues more than others, occasionally in unexpected ways. For example, in one company, a change in the "holidays" plan that designated three existing minor holidays as "personal choice" days, allowing them to be taken at any time an employee chose, resulted in more favorable ratings of both the holiday and vacation plans.

These after-the-fact measurements can reveal if organizational changes have had the desired or expected effects, as opposed to negative or unanticipated impacts, and can thus form a basis for making data-based corrections where needed.

To Provide Input for Future Decisions

In some organizations, surveys gather useful data to influence future management decisions. For example, one might want to know which benefit plans the employees would most like to see improved. And even if one does not want to ask this or a similar question of the staff directly, the survey can at least assess which of several plans employees are least satisfied with.

Surveys can uncover employee preferences, such as for a particular geographical location or work hours. They can also analyze needs in areas like training, tools or administrative support, support systems for balancing work and family life, and so on. Again, organizational decisions driven by systematically gathered data are more likely to be on target than someone's pet program unguided by meaningful input.

To Add a Communication Channel

As organizations grow larger or more widespread, management often expresses the need for communication systems that supplement already existing ones. The opinion survey can play that communication system role, getting around the filtering out of negative reports often seen in large organizations.

Surveys are also a means to assess if a plaintive voice is merely a squeaky wheel or really the tip of an iceberg. In addition, the practice of reporting back survey results to participants can encourage a pattern of two-way communication and can be the basis for ongoing dialogues on key issues.

To Perform Organizational Behavior Research

As the training of most organizational survey researchers is in the social sciences, it should be no surprise that many of them use surveys, at least in part, for research on topics of importance in the field of organizational behavior. The landmark leadership studies associated with Ohio State University (Stodgill & Coons, 1957) and the University of Michigan (Likert, 1961) were based on surveys done in various organizations, and other researchers have followed their example. Professional journals are full of studies on the relationship of attitudes and perceptions to outcomes like absenteeism, turnover, pro-union behaviors, and work accidents. Most of these studies are based on data from organizational surveys. The relevant questions are often only a small part of a firm's survey and may be tied to outside criteria. The research topic may be defined by the firm's interest in that topic or by the interests of the researcher. In any case, even a casual reading of the professional literature shows that organizational surveys are often used for organizational behavior research.

Progressive firms are often aware of other groups' research and will use their own regular surveys, or even specially designed surveys, to address similar issues. Although each firm's aim is to serve its own interests, such research sometimes adds substantially to general knowledge.

To Assist Organizational Change and Improvement

In progressive organizations, surveys can evolve into a way of life that encourages change through continuous organizational improvement. By using surveys for self-assessment and then to stimulate and guide desirable changes, organizations make surveys a basis for deliberate efforts at better organizational functioning.

When surveys report data for individual units, the findings focus attention on those units and their problems, sometimes known euphemistically as "opportunities for improvement." Comparisons among units, invidious or not, encourage diagnosis of and action on apparent problems. Such comparisons often focus attention on smaller units as well as larger ones and increase the possibility of unit accountability and responsiveness.

Surveys, if properly done, can thus be seen as a *discipline* in the sense that they can become a system for regularly attending to important issues, unit by unit. The discipline can extend to regular and formal systems for taking actions and reporting them. We may think of this as a discipline in the same sense that an individual's health-promoting habits—such as regularly brushing his or her teeth, getting exercise, and taking care of social and emotional needs that are at risk of being crowded out by the pressure to do more urgent tasks—are a discipline.

An investment of energy and resources is needed to produce organizational improvement built on surveys, and this investment can also pay dividends later. Obviously, time and attention must be given to the total survey process. One aspect of desirable preparation and infrastructure development is the training of managers to deal with the survey data when they receive them. Some of this training, such as how to hold an effective feedback meeting and how to diagnose and solve problems, can have an enormous spillover effect and result in managers who are more effective in many other aspects of their supervisory roles. (For example, see reports by Dodd and Pesci, 1977; and also Smith, 1976.)

The striving for organizational improvement also focuses management attention on particular aspects of organizational functioning. Many firms now use surveys as a way to measure aspects of their functioning that make them more competitive, including quality, customer satisfaction, and internal efficiencies.

Over the last decade or so, there has been a sea change in the types of issues covered in most organizational surveys. My impression, based on scores of surveys, is that "people" issues such as morale, satisfaction with various aspects of work, and industrial relations were the most popular (and sometimes exclusive) topics in the past. Work and family issues and diversity issues are more recent additions. However, it is in the business issues labeled cultural change, quality, and customer satisfaction that we see the biggest increase. The items covered under such rubrics deal with issues vital to organizational success. Their use in surveys is intended to drive and measure *changes* in the ways firms operate and succeed or fail. (A corroboration of these trends may be seen in discussions of the new items added to the Mayflower Group's core set of survey questions over the last two decades.)

To Provide Symbolic Communication

Perhaps the most important, and least understood, strategic purpose of the organizational survey is that of symbolic communication. This function is especially important in attempts at organizational change. Although symbolic communication is sometimes obvious, it is often what sociologists call a latent (or underlying and not always obvious) function. Like it or not, every aspect of the survey process sends a message to the people involved in it. Both the content and the conduct of a survey carry enormous meaning.

When a firm's staff are asked questions about their satisfaction with pay, benefits, and careers, they presume that those areas of satisfaction are important to management. If a survey asks questions about how managers are behaving, both the managers and their staffs are put on notice that those behaviors are important aspects of the manager's role.

We must recognize that the contents of a survey signal and highlight what the firm's leaders want to know about (whether it is customer satisfaction, quality, empowerment, innovation, or a similar topic). In fact, when new signals need to be called because the organization is trying to stimulate different ways of functioning, survey topics and items are powerful educational tools. They communicate to all: "This is what management is interested in. These are the issues management is paying to learn more about."

Unfortunately, when surveys are poorly done, the messages strongly communicated may be unintended ones. This often happens through the conduct (as opposed to the content) of the survey. If no feedback is given to employees, the (perhaps unintended) message that they perceive may be that management does not want to get into a meaningful dialogue, is trying to cover up the results, or has no desire to include employees in dealing with the findings. A lack of visible action may send the message, "We don't really care what you say."

Ignoring the data, taking no action, or not communicating any actions taken might seem to send no message. But a lack of a visible response to survey results actually communicates a negative message. This message may be interpreted in various ways: that employees lack importance, that the survey was a charade or ruse, or that management does not care about employees' perceptions and opinions. In any case, lack of response is a powerful, if negative, symbolic communication to employees.

However, it seems that more and more executives are using survey measures to see how their change efforts are going. They report out the results and use them to push their change agendas further. Some even use the measures as part of a scorecard for evaluating and rewarding management at different levels.

CONCLUSION

In the last half century, organizational surveys have grown from rarities to popular and potentially powerful tools for management to use. They can serve a variety of purposes, from being tools for numerous types of assessment to being levers for far-reaching organizational change.

In a fundamental shift, more organizations than ever are using surveys as strategic tools to drive and measure organizational change. Going beyond the traditional measures of morale and employee satisfaction, many firms have fashioned their surveys to carry new messages and gather new data. These innovations try to gauge how well the organization comprehends new circumstances and acts in appropriately different ways. Such measurements, providing useful knowledge on which to base and judge action, have become part of many firms' efforts to succeed in an increasingly competitive and demanding environment.

The technology for administering surveys, processing and analyzing data, and communicating the results has become enormously sophisticated. Still, we must recognize that technical and methodological skills and tools are necessary but not sufficient for organizational surveys to be successful.

A recent poll (Management Decision Systems, 1993) of one hundred firms using surveys shows several obstacles to effective practice. The leading obstacle is reported to be "failure to provide feedback and lack of action planning and follow-through." This is followed closely by "lack of middle and senior management commitment." The third obstacle, "low perceived value of the surveys," may be caused by the other two (p. 6).

The critical ingredient for fruitful organizational surveys is a wise and committed leadership. Using surveys well requires a deep understanding by top management of its reasons for doing a survey in the first place. Top management must have the will and energy to make use of the survey process. Organizations take their cues from their leaders and act accordingly.

The full magnitude of an organizational survey reveals itself over time; a survey is a process and not an event. Top management can play an important part at several points. True leaders can speak out early and shape the social reality and meaning of surveys for others in the organization. They can force attention to the results, against competing priorities. They can monitor and follow up on actions in response to survey findings. They can reward and recognize successful users of the data and act as role models.

Survey researchers working in organizations must have the professional and practical skills to conduct surveys well. But they cannot simply wait for a wise and committed executive leadership to emerge. Successful survey professionals also tutor and coach top managers on their roles in the survey process. Acting as ghostwriters, survey professionals will sometimes even draft speeches and letters from the management to support the process. Often, as part of a human resource management group, survey professionals will set up the procedures for line managers at various levels to review survey results, the action plans taken in response, and the follow-through on such plans. Although these are line management responsibilities, the survey researchers must often do behind-the-scenes work to energize and maintain the process.

It is important to recognize that survey professionals must have the understanding, interpersonal skills, and personal drive to educate and forge a partnership with top management if organizational surveys are to be well used. If the professional community is successful in creating such bonds with top management, the coming years will be very exciting indeed.

References

Babbie, E. (1990). *Survey research methods* (2nd ed.). Belmont, CA: Wadsworth.

Babbie, E. (1992). *The practice of social research* (6th ed.). Belmont, CA: Wadsworth.

Backstrom, C. H., & Hursh-Cesar, G. (1981). *Survey research* (2nd ed.). New York: Wiley.

Delaney, J. T., Lewin, D., & Ichniowski, C. (1988). *Human resource management policies and practices in American firms.* New York: Industrial Relations Research Center, Graduate School of Business, Columbia University.

Dillman, D. A. (1978). *Mail and telephone surveys: The total design method.* New York: Wiley.

Dodd, W. E., & Pesci, M. L. (1977, June). Managing morale through survey feedback. *Business Horizons*, 36–45.

Dunham, R. B., & Smith, F. J. (1979). *Organizational surveys: An internal assessment of organizational health.* Glenview, IL: Scott, Foresman.

Fowler, F. J., Jr. (1988). *Survey research methods* (Rev. ed.). Newbury Park, CA: Sage.

Gallup, G. (1988). Employee research: From nice to know to need to know. *Personnel Journal, 67*, 42–43.

Hamner, W. C., & Smith, F. J. (1978). Work attitudes as predictors of unionization activity. *Journal of Applied Psychology, 63*, 143–421.

Kahn, R. L., & Cannell, C. F. (1957). *The dynamics of interviewing: Theory, technique, and cases.* New York: Wiley.

Kish, L. (1965). *Survey sampling.* New York: Wiley.

Kraut, A. I., & Freeman, F. (1992). *Upward communications: Programs in American industry* (Tech. Rep. No. 152). Greensboro, NC: Center for Creative Leadership.

Lawler, E. E., III, Nadler, D. A., & Cammann, C. (1980). *Organizational assessment: Perspectives on the measurement of organizational behavior and the quality of work life.* New York: Wiley.

Likert, R. (1961). *New patterns of management.* New York: McGraw-Hill.

Management Decisions Systems. (1993). *Employee surveys: Current and future practices.* Darien, CT: Author.

Nadler, D. A. (1977). *Feedback and organization development: Using data-based methods.* Reading, MA: Addison-Wesley.

Payne, S. (1951). *The art of asking questions.* Princeton, NJ: Princeton University Press.

Rea, L. M., & Parker, R. A. (1992). *Designing and conducting survey research: A comprehensive guide.* San Francisco: Jossey-Bass.

Rossi, P. H., Wright, J. D., & Anderson, A. B. (1983). *Handbook of survey research.* San Diego, CA: Academic Press.

Smith, P. E. (1976). Management modeling training to improve morale and customer satisfaction. *Personnel Psychology*, *29*, 351–359.

Stodgill, R. M., & Coons, A. E. (1957). *Leader behavior: Its description and measurement*. Columbus: Ohio State University, Bureau of Business Research.

Stouffer, S. A., & Associates. (1947–1950). *The American soldier: Studies in social psychology in World War II* (Vols. 1–4). Princeton, NJ: Princeton University Press.

Sudman, S., & Bradburn, N. M. (1982). *Asking questions: A practical guide to questionnaire design*. San Francisco: Jossey-Bass.

Viteles, M. S. (1953). *Motivation and morale in industry*. New York: Norton.

Warwick, D. P., & Lininger, C. A. (1975). *The sample survey: Theory and practice*. New York: McGraw-Hill.

CHAPTER NINETEEN

Toward Integrated Organizational Diagnosis

Ann Howard and Associates (1994)

Many organizations today, facing fast-paced global competition, are re-engineering business processes and redesigning their organizations from top to bottom. No system functions independently, and no system remains unexamined. The time has come for organizational consultants to recognize that diagnosis and change efforts on one system do not function independently of other systems or the efforts of other practitioners. As Burke (1992) has stated, organizational consultation needs to evolve from implementing a set of standard tools that address small- to medium-sized organizational problems to enacting an emerging paradigm for the management of large-scale organization change.

The preceding chapters of the volume in which this chapter originally appeared gave testimony to broadening concerns and more systems thinking. For example, Ronald Zemke described how training needs analysis has expanded into the wider domain of human performance technology. Elise Walton and David Nadler wrote of enlarging organization design into organization architecture. James Walker and Thomas Bechet identified the evolution of manpower planning into strategic human resource planning. And Douglas Bray's personnel centered organizational diagnosis used individual assessments to deduce organizational problems. In other words, the authors of Howard et al.'s volume emanated from diverse focal points, but they echoed across organizational systems. Howard and her coauthors include many quotes from these authors in this final integrating chapter. This chapter considers how to unite visions of organizational change into a coherent whole. That is, how can behavioral science practitioners advance toward integrated organizational diagnosis? To answer this question, we must pose others. For example: What do client organizations expect of practitioners, and what is their view of diagnosis? What are the barriers to integrated organizational diagnosis, and how might they be overcome?

INITIATING DIAGNOSIS

Smooth implementation of the diagnostic process is inevitably affected by the client's expectations about professional help.

What Do Clients Have in Mind When They Request Professional Services?

Clients typically seek out human resources practitioners to address a specific issue, often one they equate with "trouble." According to Harry Levinson, most clients request services "when they have some form of pain. Most often, people expect some form of relief."

Similarly, Edward Lawler says, "Clients normally have in mind a fix for their problem." Elise Walton and David Nadler add that the problem identified by the client is frequently not at the heart of the issue:

> Clients often have a clear presenting problem: strategy that hasn't been implemented, confusing and expensive business processes, a vague sense that the culture is "wrong." At issue is often the level of the problem; that is, there are problems underlying problems underlying problems. We often attempt to uncover root problems, or causes, which may differ from the presenting problem and the client-developed diagnosis and may generate a different set of solutions.

Warner Burke is often summoned to help with organization change or its aftermath:

> Clients have in mind either a specific project (e.g., facilitation of an off-site meeting; a workshop for managers on, say, performance management; a consulting skills program for human resources people) or a general assignment that involves organizational change of one form or another, such as culture change (helping to revamp the vision/mission and, perhaps, strategy) and/or structural change (modifying the organization chart, which these days usually means flattening the hierarchy). Organization development [OD] people are not always called on for organization redesign purposes, but they are usually asked for help in dealing with the *consequences* of a structural change.

Although both problems and a need for change precipitate clarion calls for professional help, William Byham and Robert Rogers note that "very few clients call a consultant for diagnosis. They are attracted to a consultant by his or her reputation for conducting a training program, implementing organizational change, and so forth.''

Do Clients Resist Diagnosis?

Clients seek help for problems and change, not for diagnosis. This answer to the previous question suggests that clients believe they already have their situations diagnosed when they request help. Does this mean that they resist the suggestion that further diagnosis is needed?

Not necessarily, say the authors, at least at first. Most clients do not find diagnosis unreasonable. ''It makes logical sense to them,'' say William Byham and Robert Rogers. Adds Warner Burke, ''They recognize the need for the consultant to get a 'feel for things,' to establish rapport with key people in the client organization, and to learn their particular business and ways of doing things.'' Kimball Fisher goes even further: ''Experienced clients seldom balk at reasonable diagnostics. Some, in fact, demand it as a prerequisite to intervention.''

Another reason diagnosis may be palatable is that, in Warner Burke's words, ''All clients believe that their particular organization is unique, regardless of type and industry category. Thus, the consultant must learn—and appreciate—this uniqueness.'' Similarly, William Byham and Robert Rogers relate that ''a good diagnosis before prescription makes clients feel, and rightly so, that the prescription is tailored to their particular needs.''

This rosy view of client acceptance of diagnosis is tempered by certain restraints. Client sophistication can influence whether diagnosis will be accepted. Says Kimball Fisher, ''For those who are less committed to a long-term change or less knowledgeable about the change process, resistance to the diagnostic process is common.'' There are also practical impediments. Edward Lawler reports that ''clients generally are not enthusiastic about a diagnostic phase, particularly if it is going to be long and expensive.'' Similarly, Warner Burke remarks, ''They do not want this phase to last forever, that's for sure.''

Time pressures can be brutal in today's organizations. Says Kimball Fisher, ''There is always pressure, of course, to get results as quickly as possible, and when clients view diagnosis as a way to delay results they become anxious.'' Ronald Zemke observes that managers get paid for solving problems and want help now, and that a trainer who tells a manager to slow down and analyze the problem first is exhibiting ''behavior that can lead to involuntary retirement from the field of play. So it's easy to understand why many training people will simply hope against hope that management is right and the problem *can* be solved through training, all the while worrying over unseen sinkholes and snares, to mix a few metaphors.''

Resistance to diagnosis grows with the size of the problem being attacked, according to William Byham and Robert Rogers:

> The difficult thing is getting customers to accept a more comprehensive diagnosis (the whole problem) rather than a specific diagnosis for a particular symptom. For example, none of our clients has ever resisted doing a job analysis ahead of the development of a selection system. However, they might resist the suggestion that the job analysis should not proceed until the effectiveness of the organization structure has been investigated, because this investigation will determine how empowered employees will be and will thus shape the employees' jobs. We still have found that many will go along with the higher-level diagnosis if it is thoroughly explained.

Perhaps a fair summary statement is that clients are willing to accept diagnosis as long as its value is thoroughly explained and it can survive a cost-benefit analysis. This may still sound discouraging, but it could be worse. "More difficult to sell, however, is an evaluation of the change effort," says Edward Lawler. Ronald Zemke adds, "The too often heard retort to the suggestion of an evaluation is, 'But *you're* the expert. Just do it right the first time.'"

DIAGNOSIS AND INTERVENTION

One of the risks of diagnosis is that the problems it uncovers may not be ones clients are prepared to tackle. This poses a new line of questioning to our authors: Does diagnosis always lead to intervention? If not, why not?

Why Diagnosis May Not Lead to Intervention

The diagnosis itself may sink prospects for intervention. Says Warner Burke, "Sometimes the diagnosis is done so poorly that the action to take as a consequence is anything but clear." Adds Edward Lawler, "Sometimes diagnosis does not lead to intervention because it fails to identify and produce consensus about what kinds of changes are needed or even what the problems are."

Producing consensus can be particularly vexing to a practitioner. William Byham and Robert Rogers offer an example:

> One of the more complex problems we face is the agreement with management that is not a true agreement. Over the last few years we have encountered this especially in relation to the diagnosis of desired levels of empowerment. . . . We believe that figuring out the level of empowerment desired by the organization is critical to the diagnosis of many other systems within the organization (selection, appraisal, training, and compensation, to name a few). In casual interviews with people within the organization, there often appears to be very great agreement on empowerment goals. But later, when asking executives to deal with specific issues, we find out that there is little agreement on general direction.

This is just one example of a diagnosis going beyond superficial vision to specifics. A consultant helps executives get down to reality and see how things are going to play out in terms of people affected, other parts of the organization, and impact on the bottom line. The consultant does this through asking questions, pointing out relationships, and so forth.

Clients may disallow interventions because the diagnosis reveals problems they have difficulty facing. According to Warner Burke, occasionally the "diagnosis generates such negative feelings that the client becomes immobilized or simply unwilling to deal with the data." Harry Levinson reports similar experiences:

> Sometimes the client doesn't want to proceed further out of fear or anxiety or reluctance to get at the root of the organization's problems. Sometimes there is internal resistance, as happened once when the top management of a police department was willing to undertake consultation but the middle management certainly wasn't. Their internal conflicts got in the way.

Ronald Zemke has found similar sensitivities: "Especially paralyzing to the progress of an intervention is the diagnosis that suggests that the sponsor is an integral part of the problem. 'I hired you to fix them, not [to] blame me!' is often heard in one form or another."

Difficulty garnering political support for change is cited by Elise Wallon and David Nadler as well as by Kimball Fisher. Similarly, Douglas Bray notes that issues such as "getting management on board" and concern about "upsetting employees" may affect whether intervention will take place. Bray and Fisher also mention practical hurdles, such as time and expense.

Linking Diagnosis and Intervention

William Byham and Robert Rogers admit that although the theoretical answer to the question, "Does diagnosis always lead to intervention?" is "No," in practice they have "never known an instance where diagnosis didn't lead to intervention. Why would management bring the consultant in if they didn't feel that something needed to be done?"

Kimball Fisher likewise reports, "The large majority of clients take at least some minimum steps after the diagnosis." He, in fact, tries to ensure that this will happen: "I believe it is the practitioner's responsibility to get the client to agree to some minimum level of intervention prior to the diagnosis as part of the initial contracting discussion." Fisher also reminds us that "diagnosis is an intervention. In my experience the act of diagnosis itself changes the client system being observed. Expectations are heightened, uncomfortable concerns are raised, and unresolved issues are surfaced publicly. If some additional intervention is not taken, there is a predictable increase in skepticism and a reduction in trust." Adds Ronald Zemke, "Diagnosis creates awareness and sets up expectations among people in the organization. To ignore or discount that is to dehumanize the process." Elise Walton and David Nadler make a similar point: "The question implies a clear line between diagnosis and intervention, not often found in practice. In fact, diagnosis is intervention, and the relationship between action and discovery is often iterative and interdependent."

SEQUENCING DIAGNOSIS AND CHANGE EFFORTS

Given that practitioners embark upon diagnosis from various corners of the organizational architecture, an integrated diagnosis must consider logical priorities. Is there a preferred sequence to diagnosis/change efforts? Does it matter what aspects of organizational functioning are addressed first?

Beginning Diagnosis at the System Level

Katz and Kahn (1980), strong proponents of the open systems model, recommend that diagnosis begin at the system rather than the individual level because this will account for the greatest amount of variance. In a like vein, Rummler (1988) has said, "Put a good performer in a bad system and the system will win every time—almost" (p. 8).

Regarding reasons for beginning at the system level, Warner Burke puts it this way:

> Unless one is consulting to a particular function (e.g., human resources) for particular purposes, it is best to begin at some general management level—a business sector head, for example—and to work at the outset with understanding goals, objectives, and business purposes and how these fit with the external environment and with internal resources, capabilities, and needed changes. In other words, it is best to begin at a level where various organizational functions come together and require integration.

William Byham and Robert Rogers also emphasize initial goal setting:

> The sequence should be to figure out where you're going before you figure out how you're going to get there. Compensation, training, and so forth, are systems within the organization that help it achieve certain goals. They should not be attacked before the organization has defined the goals they are trying to achieve.

Elise Walton and David Nadler believe that failure to work from strategy and goals is common:

> We tend to follow the old "structure follows strategy" principle or, more generically, the precept that direction/vision must precede all change, must *direct* all change. Otherwise, you get "ad hocracy" and lots of little changes that add up to very little result. The tendency to start up lots of little solutions to lots of little problems and never look at the systemic needs seems to be a common mistake in U.S. industry.

Beginning Diagnosis and Change Efforts Elsewhere

Although there are strong arguments for beginning diagnosis at the system level, this is not always feasible nor necessarily desirable. ''Start with the pain the client expresses,'' says Harry Levinson. ''Even though we know that the presenting problem is often not the real one or the basic one, that's where the client hurts and what the client wants you to at least start working on. In the beginning clients may not yet understand that forces other than those they are aware of may be operating.''

Edward Lawler points out several ways in which the pay system can take the lead in organizational change efforts:

> Perhaps most frequently discussed is the Scanlon plan or some other form of gain-sharing to improve plant productivity. In these situations the initial change effort is focused on the development and installation of a gain-sharing plan that pays bonuses based on improvements in productivity. The Scanlon Plan also emphasizes building participative problem-solving groups into the organization, but the clear emphasis is on the gain-sharing formula and the financial benefits of improved productivity. The participative management structure is put in to facilitate productivity improvement, which in turn will result in gains to be shared. Not surprisingly, once gain-sharing starts and inhibitors to productivity are identified, other changes result. Typical of these are improvements in the organization's structure, the design of jobs and work, and training programs. Often these are dealt with rather swiftly and effectively because the gain-sharing plan itself provides a strong motivation to do so.

There are other reward system changes that also can trigger broader organizational change efforts. For example, the introduction of skill-based pay can stimulate a broad movement to participation because, among other things, it provides people with the skills and knowledge they need to participate. In a somewhat different vein, a dramatic change in the pay-for-performance system can be very effective in altering the strategic directions that an organization takes. For example, installing bonus systems that pay off on previously unmeasured or overlooked performance indicators can dramatically shift the direction of an organization. Similarly, installing a long-term bonus plan for executives can cause them to change their time horizons and their decision-making practices in important ways.

Sequencing Subsystem Diagnosis and Change

Where diagnosis begins only partly answers the sequencing question. After the first step, what is the best order in which to approach the remaining organizational systems? Sometimes there is an urge to do everything at once. Elise Walton and David Nadler put it this way:

We are looking at the interdependence of interventions and what that implies for our generic approaches to change. For example, a change in strategy may call for a new structure, which calls for new people with new skills. It turns out that you can't change the structure until you can change the people, and so on. The question is, How can you concurrently make all these changes?

Edward Lawler provides one example of simultaneous changes: "New participative plants represent an interesting example of participative reward systems changes being put in at the same time as other participative practices. Indeed, one reason for such plants' success is their ability to start with all their systems operating in a participative manner." Nevertheless, this type of organizational change is atypical, according to Lawler. "In a major organizational change it is difficult to alter all the systems in the organization simultaneously. Typically, one set of changes leads to another set of changes." Although reward systems change can be either a lead or a lag in the overall change process, he reports that it is most often a lag factor:

> This certainly is true in most efforts to change toward participative management. The initial thrust often is on team building, job redesign, quality circles, or some other area. It is only after these other practices have been in place for a while that the organization tends to deal with the reward system changes needed to support these new practices. Often, there is surprise that these other important changes lead to a need for revision in the reward system. The connected nature of organizations makes it almost inevitable that when major changes are made in an organization's strategic direction or management style and practices, change will also have to be made in the reward system.

Kimball Fisher looks at the linkages between systems to determine an appropriate sequence:

> Each phase of the diagnosis/change process should create a desire to complete the next phase of change. Reward system redesign, for example, is better done after (not before) organization redesign. This way it supports job structure changes and is seen as a natural extension of the previous redesign process. Similarly, communication infrastructure building should normally be changed prior to organization restructuring. If this type of sequencing is followed in creating team-based operations, for example, good information meetings normally generate interest and a desire to create teams. After team structures are in place, people are interested in creating pay and performance appraisal systems that support the new team structure. Done out of sequence, the various parts of the change effort are confusing and sometimes counterproductive.

William Byham and Robert Rogers keep their eyes on the ultimate outcome: "Regardless of where you start or the path you take, the resulting output should be as much alignment of systems with the vision and cultural goals as possible."

In summary, there are logical considerations, but no hard-and-fast rules about sequencing diagnosis and change efforts. Beginning at the system level offers some advantages, but different situations may favor other starting places and sequences. Says Edward Lawler, "It is hard to generalize about where you start a change process. I am asked this question frequently and usually resist answering it. I might add that organizations often see this resistance as a mark of a typical academic, if not an incompetent, because they think that there ought to be one way to proceed with the diagnosis/change effort."

BARRIERS TO INTEGRATED ORGANIZATIONAL DIAGNOSIS

Some of the barriers to integrated organizational diagnosis recapitulate and exacerbate the obstacles to doing any diagnosis at all. Many practical problems fall into this category. But there are also barriers unique to an integrated organizational diagnosis, which derive from the segmentation of both organizations and professional practice.

Practical Barriers

A complete diagnosis could involve collecting a staggering amount of information. Douglas Bray offers this view:

> The variety and amount of information needed to gauge the human resources health of an organization is imposing. We must measure not only the knowledge, skills, and motivation of employees but also the effectiveness of organizational efforts to enhance these and employee performance, as guided by organizational values. The many things that must be known about employees and from them cannot be learned without the use of behavioral simulations, tests, focus groups, targeted interviews, and questionnaires. Because an organization's employees are in many jobs, at several levels, and in different divisions and departments, the total diagnostic job in even a moderate-sized company would be immense even if only management-level employees were included.

Bray's personnel-centered method uses sampling to bring the scope of the diagnostic effort under control.

The time required for an integrated diagnosis can be considerable, particularly management time. William Byham and Robert Rogers characterize this issue:

> Any time you try to deal with integrated organizational diagnosis, you're dealing with the top people in the organization, and they're hard to get hold of. You have to sell the value of the diagnosis to those people so they'll take the time off to participate. Most managers understand the value of diagnosis once it is explained, but there is also a constant push to do it quicker than it can really be accomplished.

Douglas Bray raises the issue of how much diagnosis the client will stand for or pay for. "This can be very elaborate or minimal. It is important for the practitioner to differentiate real needs from what would be 'good for you.'"

James Walker and Thomas Bechet describe other practical problems that are associated with data gathering:

> The work that people do may be examined from a variety of perspectives and purposes. In many organizations jobs are analyzed and described for compensation purposes, for organization planning, for process and quality improvement, for identification of training and development needs, and for guiding future staffing and selection decisions. It makes eminent sense for a common analysis of work to serve all of these purposes.

However, these analyses are typically conducted at different times, by different people, and with somewhat different data being required. As a result, the incumbent employees and their managers are asked to provide information for different purposes at different times. And the responses change over time as work content changes.

Attempts have been made over the years to develop an integrated job analysis process, resulting in a data base that could serve multiple applications. However, it is difficult to anticipate information requirements for specific applications and to obtain credible information when there is no clear and pressing need for the information.

Because need for the information rests with those persons requesting it, the ownership of the information rests with them, not with the incumbent employees and their managers. It is preferable that employees and managers perceive the merit of a broad understanding of changing work activities and requirements, that they recognize that this information can enable them to continuously improve their performance, utilization, and development.

Organizational Silos

Organization structures can create barriers to integrated organizational diagnosis. For example, Joseph Harless, a human performance analyst, notes that there is no organizational entity identified as providing help with human performance. "Every door that we have is marked with a particular solution, like 'Training sold here,' 'Personnel selection sold here,' 'Work-process redesign sold here'" (Froiland, 1993). Warner Burke calls such structural barriers "the chimney or smokestack phenomenon, overly sectorizing business units. In other words, the lack of adequate horizontal processes."

Elise Walton and David Nadler describe how differences among organizational units can pose obstacles:

> Perspective probably encompasses the broadest range of differences, but clearly there are functional differences, one of the more notable ones being

line/staff. In this case, the question of perspective is supplemented by the actor/observer differences; that is, line managers, as actors, and staff managers, who are often the observers, tend to have very different interpretations of an event.

Another difference is in objectives, that is, in how organizational members answer the question, "How is the change likely to benefit or harm me?" To the extent that a certain diagnosis implicates their weaknesses or suggests action that may be unfavorable, individual members may have a hard time integrating with the rest of the team. As always, the issue is how to build broad ownership of the diagnosis.

Professional Silos

One encouraging note about organizational silos is that current change efforts are successfully removing many of them. The same cannot be said for professional silos. As Warner Burke (1992) has put it, "As organizational and psychological consultants, we are becoming specialists instead of generalists, yet organizational conceptualization is moving more toward systemic and holistic thinking" (p. 6).

One problem created by professional specialization is a deviation in point of view. Elise Walton and David Nadler emphasize how differences in perspective can get in the way:

> Some consultants think the customers' interests must come first whereas others think the stockholders' interests come first, and, more important, those holding one perspective may know about the other and may discount ideas that emerge from that viewpoint as "biased." These would apply to diagnosis as well as interventions prescribed. To put it in industrial/ organizational [I/O] psychologists' terms, some think rewards are important levers for change and others do not, some think change must follow a business imperative only and others do not, and so forth. We have created our own functional silos.

Harry Levinson views differences in perspective in terms of fundamental assumptions and beliefs:

> The greatest barrier to more integrated organizational diagnosis is the fact that different consultants make different assumptions about fundamentals of human motivation and behavior. If, for example, a consultant on salary structure doesn't understand the concept of ego ideal, Elliott Jaques's conceptions of cognitive capacity and mental processing, and the importance of unconscious motivation, that consultant and I will have a difficult time working together. A more common barrier is the lack of sufficient understanding of another consultant's area of expertise.

Warner Burke also considers silos of both perspective and knowledge as consequences of consultant specialization:

> Specialization means that consultants know a few things very well (e.g., compensation or training and development), but are not broadly based or sufficiently unbiased. Some push their own specific methods and forget everything else.

William Byham and Robert Rogers have similar concerns about the narrow focus of practitioners:

> The biggest barrier to integrated organizational diagnosis is in the mind of the practitioner. The consultant who is brought in to provide a service or product often tends to conduct a diagnosis only around that service or product rather than encouraging the client to "helicopter up" to consider the bigger picture before coming back down to the specific issues that need to be discussed.

Kimball Fisher adds that lack of common language and technique can make integrated diagnosis extremely difficult.

In summary, integrated organizational diagnosis faces practical obstacles such as time and expense, but these appear less intractable than the philosophical barriers. Kimball Fisher points to the mechanisms that act to keep these barriers in place: "Reward and recognition systems in both business and academia make cooperative processes unattractive. Few consultants, internal or external, are willing to make the technical, administrative, marketing, and ego compromises to coordinate with a large group of diagnosticians and change agents."

PROFESSIONAL EXPERTISE

Given the problems it creates for integrated organizational diagnosis, professional specialization warrants further scrutiny. How much specialized expertise is required to diagnose and change various aspects of organizational functioning? Can one practitioner do it all?

Practitioners as Generalists

An argument can be made for generalist practitioners, but we must first define the term. Warner Burke makes the first cut:

> The operative term is *organizational*. We cannot claim expertise in diagnosing function problems, that is, in determining, for example, what is wrong with the company's marketing strategy, why the debt-to-equity ratio is out of whack, or what is wrong with a particular manufacturing process. The exception would, of course, be human resources.

What, then, does generalized organizational expertise include? Harry Levinson expects acquaintance with the psychology of economics, psychodynamics, professional ethics, decision making and cognitive complexity, succession planning and career management, and stages in organization development. Warner Burke offers the following sampler of the kinds of principles an organizational practitioner should understand:

- How an organization is a sociotechnical system and how strategy precedes structure.
- The folly of rewarding A when the organization wants B.
- The consequences of organizational change.
- What effective teamwork is and when teams are appropriate and when they are not.
- The importance of integration as well as differentiation.
- The importance of boss-subordinate relationships in the delivery of highly satisfactory customer service.
- When an issue implicates selection and placement rather than a lack of adequate training and development.
- That training and development are needed when people are being held accountable for responsibilities they are ill-equipped to perform.

Obviously, both kinds of lists could be quite extensive, which indicates the difficulty of becoming a generalist in organizational practice. William Byham and Robert Rogers support this view:

> It takes a great deal of expertise to diagnose—much more than to prescribe or deliver. Diagnosis requires more understanding of the big picture, the various options available, and the interactions of different organizational systems, procedures, people, and so forth. One practitioner can do everything that is needed for a high-level diagnosis. But it might be quite appropriate to bring in additional specialists when the diagnosis gets down to specific areas, such as selection or training, or to subareas within those broader areas, such as assessment center methodology within selection methodology.

In contrast to intervention, diagnosis may require breadth more than depth of expertise. Says Warner Burke, "I believe strongly that the OD consultant and any I/O psychologist who works as an organizational consultant should first and foremost be a generalist when it comes to diagnosis." Douglas Bray also underlines that broad understanding is often important for diagnosis:

> The personnel-centered approach would be demanding in terms of practitioner background and skills because it seeks to cover the waterfront. When it comes to interventions that might be stimulated by diagnosis, the story is different. Here

specialization is required, whether that of personnel selection, training and development, or organization development.

Practitioners as Specialists

Although breadth aids diagnosis, it is still, in Warner Burke's words, "rare for one practitioner to be able to do it all." Edward Lawler agrees: "It is difficult for one practitioner to do a complicated organizational change process well. Not only is there an issue of required expertise, but there is an issue of finding a sounding board for ideas and issues and social support." Harry Levinson concurs:

> No practitioner can diagnose and change all aspects of an organization. A consultant needs to know what he or she doesn't know and therefore when to refer to others or to suggest to the client that other specialists should be consulted. For example, only yesterday I had to recommend to a client three consultants who could develop a compensation plan for executives.

He also raises ethical issues of trying to reach beyond one's area of expertise.

> One cannot be ethical without knowing the boundaries of one's knowledge, skill, and competence. Even if the practitioner has competence in more than one area, say, in both human resources and marketing, it is highly unlikely that he or she will have equal competence in the wide range of managerial issues that all organizations must deal with.

Ethical practice that also offers the broad coverage needed for a sound diagnosis implies supplementing one's skills with those of other practitioners. Elise Walton and David Nadler acknowledge increasing use of this approach:

> A fair amount of specialized expertise is required for our work, and we frequently find ourselves partnering with other firms that can provide specific expertise (e.g., market studies, financial assessments, in-depth survey capability). Particularly as change efforts get broader and more strategic, many different specialized skills are required.

In summary, the need for both generalized and specialized expertise makes divergent but complementary demands on different types of practitioners. In the world of I/O psychology, the "I" psychologists need to "helicopter up" (to borrow the phrase from Byham and Rogers) to the system level for a view of the forest while the "O" psychologists need to parachute down to examine the trees. Each group would benefit from reaching across the sky to the other.

Positioning Expertise in the Organization

Skills required for diagnosis and intervention may also vary depending on the level within the organization at which the consultation occurs. William Byham and Robert Rogers observe that "the skills required of diagnosticians at high levels of management are quite different from those required at lower levels. There is far less expert opinion required at higher levels and more facilitation—appropriately mixed with challenging people to really think through what they have decided." James Walker and Thomas Bechet believe this is because higher-level executives have an idea of what should be happening: "They have probably been through management training or had other exposure to organizational practitioners. Those at lower levels may never have worked with consultants before and need more content." Yet they admit that there may be a less flattering interpretation. "Senior executives look at three bullets, not the whole report. They put their trust in the consultant because they don't have time for the details."

Professional expertise may be positioned inside or outside organizational boundaries. There is accumulating evidence that the role of the internal consultant or human resources department is shifting. As one example, among members of the American Psychological Association's Division of Industrial and Organizational Psychology (the majority of SIOP members), the proportion who work in industry continues to decline, 24 percent in 1985 versus 19 percent in 1992, while those in the "other" category, primarily external consultants, shows a corresponding rise, 28 percent in 1985 versus 34 percent in 1993 (American Psychological Association, 1993; Howard, 1986).

James Walker and Thomas Bechet identify three emerging models of human resources practice: (1) internal practitioners perform routine administrative activities and consultants handle diagnosis and change efforts; (2) administrative activities are contracted out to service centers (e.g., compensation and benefits to financial departments) and internal practitioners handle many diagnosis and change efforts; and (3) both types of activities are contracted out—the hollow shell model. It is too early to determine if these waves of change will swell in one dominant course, and the model may vary by organizational size. But human resources activities do seem to be drifting away from corporate staffs and into business units, docking closer to internal customers.

Kimball Fisher warns that clients must not become detached from organizational diagnosis and change activities:

> Specialized diagnostic and change expertise is certainly more helpful as organizations become increasingly complex. To the extent that practitioners use their expertise (intentionally or unintentionally) to make the client system dependent on the diagnostician, however, they do a great disservice to their customers. The only real expert in organizational diagnosis is the client. Even if one practitioner can't do it all (which is increasingly likely), a prime ethical directive for the practitioner team is to complete its work with the client system in such a way that the latter is better able to evaluate and maintain its own well-being.

Ronald Zemke adds this humbling thought about clients:

We're learning from reengineering, quality action teams, benchmarking task forces, self-directed teams, and the like, that our "expertise" isn't such a rare commodity. Good managers, focused on gaps—differences in desired and actual states of accomplishment—can do not only adequate but excellent diagnoses *and* intervention. It suggests to me that the advisor/support role we contemporarily hound managers to adopt may be a prescription we should consider for ourselves!

WORKING TOGETHER

We have concluded that diagnosis benefits from the breadth of a generalist but that few practitioners are able to execute grand change efforts alone. They typically need the assistance of specialists—for specialized diagnoses and for interventions. Achieving the goal of integrated diagnosis, then, entails collaboration, the subject of our last question. How can practitioners work together for more integrated organizational diagnosis?

Sharing and Learning

Given the extent of professional specialization, a first priority is to enhance knowledge and communication channels among practitioners. Elise Walton and David Nadler suggest that "practitioners themselves need to build a shared language system and a better way of dialoguing about diagnosis and intervention and that personal relationships (knowing your colleague well) seem to help integration." Similarly, Warner Burke advocates "being willing to listen to and learn from one another."

Harry Levinson suggests joint panels at professional meetings "to understand the range of each other's work and the areas in which we could complement each other." He recommends inviting specialists from outside of psychology to such conferences to further extend such learning. Kimball Fisher also notes the usefulness of sharing papers and presentations.

Students of industrial/organizational psychology, organizational behavior, human resources management, and related fields should also have the opportunity to learn integrated approaches. One model of a learning tool is the computerized simulation developed for teaching occupational psychology at Glasgow Caledonian University. Students adopt the role of an external consultant invited into a company for diagnosis and development of intervention plans. Using a hypercard navigation system, they can move through the organization and consult with personnel records, memos, transcripts of interviews, and the like, to help diagnose the organization's difficulties and dysfunctions (McQueen, Wrennall, & Tuohy, 1993).

Co-Consulting

A natural next step after sharing information is sharing consulting opportunities, or co-consulting. William Byham and Robert Rogers suggest a medical analogy:

> An appropriate model might be the internist-specialist, although the job requirements would be exactly the opposite in terms of difficulty. First, the organization gets a general examination dealing with critical success factors, vision, values, and so forth, which is then followed by more specific examinations by specialists.

Kimball Fisher suggests more direct sharing of responsibility.

> A major step toward integrated diagnosis is the sharing of practice and experience among diverse practitioners. This is best facilitated when people work together on real projects. Finding a way to demonstrate how the benefits of this integration are greater than the perceived personal and organizational costs would be useful.

There are various ways that integration can offer such benefits. Simply avoiding errors that derive from myopic views of organizational problems is one potential advantage. Keeping systems in reasonable alignment, so that the effects of one change don't negate another, is another advantage. In addition, consultants who work together, or at least have the benefit of studying each other's work, may be able to augment their own diagnoses. For example, Douglas Bray shows how two facets of his personnel-centered diagnosis— evaluation of incumbents and the job inventory—directly tie to organization culture and reward systems:

> One would want to know, for example, what values the organization espouses, what efforts have been made to inculcate these values in the incumbents, and what incumbent behaviors are desired as expressions of these values before conducting the assessment process. In the individual assessment one would then seek to determine knowledge of these values, attitudes toward them, and their effect on incumbent behavior.

> With respect to rewards, the job inventory would set forth all the facts about the financial rewards available to job incumbents, the salary plan, how increments are determined, the nature of commissions or bonuses and how team or division results are factored in, and so forth. Then in the assessment of incumbents, one would evaluate such things as their knowledge of these facts and their attitudes toward the plan and its administration, as well as how financial incentives affect their motivation and job behavior.

Edward Lawler offers another model for working together: "The kind of cross-functional teams that are often put together by large consulting firms are an example of how to work together to do a more integrated organizational diagnosis. I personally favor also involving individuals from within the organization in this kind of cross-functional diagnosis."

Just as change should be managed in an integrated way, so should the change agents. According to Beckhard and Pritchard (1992), many organizational leaders are, in fact, creating a process for managing organizational and management consultants. A liaison within the company may arrange consultants' meetings periodically to exchange ideas and interact with top management. For example, a change team at TRW Systems, composed of external consultants and internal human resource managers, was credited with generating considerable synergy, coordinating changes, and successfully coping with surprises.

An Assessment Center for Organizational Diagnosis

Integrated organizational diagnosis might be likened to an assessment center with the organization, not individuals, as the assessee. Various practitioners would serve as assessors and administer the exercises (their own techniques) to address the elements of the organization. The assessors (practitioners) would meet at an integration session to pool the results of their exercises (diagnoses) and rate the organization on preestablished dimensions of individual and organizational performance. The organization's overall performance in the assessment center would be judged by how well it was achieving its critical success factors. Following the integration session, a feedback report and an integrated intervention plan could be based on the organization's diagnosed strengths and developmental needs.

Suppose, for example, that Translines, the transportation company introduced in [Chapter One of the volume in which this chapter originally appeared], called upon all of the authors of [the volume] to deliver an integrated organizational diagnosis. We would meet first with the top executives to discuss the project and work together to pin down organizational strategy and critical success factors. Harry Levinson would launch his detective's investigation of various corners of the organization, paying particular attention to why the president was having so much difficulty setting a direction for the company and why the three vice presidents were unable to operate as a team. Warner Burke would collect data for the organizational variables (the various boxes) in the Burke-Litwin model and would develop a big-picture view of how the organization could be developed. Robert Rogers and William Byham would push the top executive group toward identifying a vision and values and deciding the extent to which they really were going to promote high involvement across the major divisions. The incongruencies and misalignments among the various organization systems would be identified. Elise Walton and David Nadler would discover the negative ramifications of the organization's centralized design and investigate new grouping and linking mechanisms.

Meanwhile, Edward Lawler would investigate the behaviors reinforced by Translines' reward system and consider better designs, and Kimball Fisher would identify barriers to the functioning of quality and safety teams. Ronald

Zemke and Douglas Bray would take a look at problems in the performance not just of the area managers but of those who work with them and discern which problems could be best addressed by training or which by selection. Bray would also gather data from individual assessments on the impact of other organization systems, such as culture and rewards. James Walker and Thomas Bechet would incorporate the performance information into an investigation of systems to recruit, select, train, and decruit employees to meet the needs created by the staffing drivers that they would identify.

The assessors would meet in an integration session to evaluate the current situation in Translines and prepare an integrated diagnostic report. These integration sessions would continue at various stages of intervention. The company's progress would be measured periodically by rating its assessment dimensions, redefined to incorporate its new vision and values.

Is this scenario an unrealistic fantasy? Or does it herald the future? We hope we have convinced you that some kind of integrated organizational diagnosis is feasible and well worth pursuing. For now, just call it our vision of diagnosis for optimal organizational change.

References

American Psychological Association (1993). *Profile of division 14 members: 1993.* Prepared by the Office of Demographic, Employment, and Education Research, APA Education Directorate. Washington, DC: Author.

Beckhard, R., & Pritchard, W. (1992). *Changing the essence: The art of creating and leading fundamental change in organizations.* San Francisco: Jossey-Bass.

Burke, W. W. (1992, August). *The changing world of organization change.* Paper presented at the meeting of the American Psychological Association, Washington, DC.

Froiland, P. (1993, September). Reproducing star performers. *Training: The Human Side of Business*, pp. 33–37.

Howard, A. (1986, May). Characteristics of society members. *The Industrial-Organizational Psychologist*, pp. 41–47.

Katz, D., & Kahn, R. L. (1980). Organizations as social systems. In E. E. Lawler III, D. A. Nadler, & C. Cammann (Eds.), *Organizational assessment: Perspectives on the measurement of organizational behavior and the quality of work life* (pp. 162–184). New York: Wiley.

McQueen, R. A., Wrennall, M. J., & Tuohy, A. P. (1993). *Occupational psychology and computer simulation.* Unpublished manuscript, Glasgow Caledonian University, Department of Psychology, Glasgow, Scotland.

Rummler, G. (1988). The 10 most important lessons I've learned about human performance systems. In G. Dixon (Ed.), *What works at work: Lessons from the masters* (pp. 5–9). Minneapolis, MN: Lakewood Books.

PART FOUR

UNDERSTANDING RESISTANCE
Editors' Interlude

E veryone knows that change is *always* accompanied by *resistance*. Right? Well, maybe winning the Lotto or becoming an heir or heiress might not be resisted. So, maybe there are exceptions. *Nevertheless, anyone who has ever tried to bring about change in an individual, group, or an organization has always experienced resistance.* Try, for the moment, writing your name with the opposite hand from that which you would normally use. You will find it uncomfortable, slow, and probably somewhat irritating. You will probably still be able to read it, but it will not look much like your normal signature. If I told you that you now had to sign your name like this the rest of your life, you would probably try to find a thousand reasons why this is absurd (most of which would be legitimate), and you would challenge my authority to tell you to do it, and probably break off any further interaction. You would have successfully *resisted* my attempt to change the way you write your signature.

This simple illustration contains many of the key ingredients in resistance. A demand or request to change is placed on an individual, group, or organization; the change, if implemented, will be perceived as reducing some of the control the recipient believes she, he, or it (group or organization) has and perhaps reduce the quality of the behavior targeted for change. The handwriting illustration also raises a core question about resistance, namely, Is resistance an empirical construct or simply a metaphor used to explain why an action did not occur? This led us to explore the nature of resistance more thoroughly.

THE NATURE OF RESISTANCE

In every televised football game there comes a time when the team that has been leading fumbles or gives up the ball on downs and the other team starts making first downs and marches toward the end zone. The play-by-play commentators are quick to say "momentum has shifted," or as one colorful announcer used to say, "Big Mo" has shifted. One often wonders what commenting on momentum means in this context. Anyone with the slightest understanding of football can see that what has happened is that the team that has had difficulty advancing the ball now can do so. What does momentum add to our understanding? Is there a great spirit called momentum that favors first one team and then the other? Is there something more than the actual play of each team happening on the field? It's doubtful. Except for the "color" added by the announcer, no additional understanding is added. Momentum as a concept and as used by announcers covers any behavior that signals a change from one team's successful advancement of the ball to the other team. (We do recognize that momentum as a concept in physics has operational implications that can be measured.) Such a change could come from an interception, fumble, series of plays, and so on. It is much more informative to know that the ball changed teams because of a fumble than it is to hear Big Mo has shifted.

When we first began to look at the term *resistance* in this book, we wondered if we weren't dealing with another Big Mo. Just as with the football illustration, resistance is invoked any time a planned change goes astray. What does it add to our understanding to hear "the shop *resisted* the introduction of quality circles?" Or to hear "the employees *resisted* switching over to computer-aided die machines?" Resistance as used in these two illustrations covers phenomena that range from group and organizational norms to lack of skill exposure, to potential job loss. So, how has our knowledge increased to say a change is being resisted? Not much, unless we can identify what the form and nature of such resistance is and why it occurred.

Fortunately, the chapters in Part Four constitute a basis for research, for establishing operational parameters for the concept of resistance. The chapters transform resistance from a heuristic, such as momentum, to operational definitions that enhance understanding, and in particular planning, change.

The earliest research on resistance to organizational change comes from Kurt Lewin, whose theory of quasi-stationary equilibrium is included in the first chapter of Part Two. In that chapter Lewin discusses "social habits" in the framework of force-field analysis. He specifically proposes that, in spite of forces to change a person's behavior in a group, a social habit is likely to persist because of an "inner resistance" to change. Lewin (1951) argues that all human behavior is a result of an interaction between a person's individual needs and personality and his or her perception of the field of forces that exist in the external environment. On the basis of his observations of group dynamics, Lewin realized that sources of resistance often exist in the external work environment, that is, group and organizational structures or forces (social roles, norms, shared values, reward systems, authority structures). These forces can discourage, rather than encourage, change if they are viewed by individuals to be imposed on them. Only when these forces are perceived as directly affecting a person's needs will they be embraced or "owned." According to Lewin, resistance to change cannot be understood without an awareness of the forces that are affecting the target. In other words, Lewin emphasized that resistance to change must be examined using a systems perspective.

Building on Lewin's groundbreaking work, Coch and French published the first chapter in this section, "Overcoming Resistance to Change," in 1948. It is the first known study that specifically investigated why people resist change and how resistance can be addressed. In field studies with workers at a pajama factory in the Harwood Manufacturing Corporation, the authors examined the resistance that workers manifested when necessary changes in work methods and jobs were introduced. The resistance took the form of grievances about piece rates that went with the new methods, high turnover, very low efficiency, restriction of output, and marked aggression against management. Ultimately, the researchers found that workgroups that were allowed to participate in organizational change efforts had much lower resistance than those that did not. They therefore concluded that employee participation reduces resistance to change.

The work of Coch and French established the empirical legitimacy of the concept of resistance and suggested how it might work in planned organization change efforts. After the Coch and French studies, two papers were developed that expanded the construct of resistance; they are presented in this volume. In the first paper, by Watson (1966), considerable attention is given to the role of resistance in individual personality. He examines *homeostasis*, the tendency of human beings to maintain fairly constant physiological states; *habit*, the propensity of humans to respond to stimuli with established patterns of behavior; and *primacy*, the tendency to repeat early patterns of behavior. Watson also incorporates concepts from psychoanalytic psychology (e.g., selective perception and retention, dependence, superego, insecurity and regression, and so on). He also moves beyond the phenomenon itself and develops reasonable arguments as to why resistance occurs in social systems (today, "organization" is used more widely). In short, he sets the stage for many of the other chapters to be found in this section.

The chapter by Brehm comes from his 1966 book *A Theory of Psychological Reactance*. He proffers a theory that resistance is a response to a loss of freedom of choice. He explains that individuals resist change when they experience a lack of choice or the imposition of being forced to change (that is, move to a new state of being, adopt new behaviors, and so forth). When a person's feeling of freedom is jeopardized by a change initiative, his or her immediate response is to attempt to regain that freedom. The magnitude of this reaction is quite strong. In fact, in situations where issues of advantage and change are in conflict, people may prefer to continue on a path that is not in their best interest rather than forfeit the feeling of free choice. For example, a smoker who is *told* to cease his habit is likely to continue as usual or increase the rate of smoking, even if he knows that the habit is detrimental to his health. From Brehm's theory, we know that organization change initiatives should be introduced such that organizational members feel they have a degree of choice in determining and implementing the change. Otherwise, the initiatives are likely to be met with increased resistance.

Almost three decades after the cited research of Watson and Brehm was published, James O'Toole (1995)* wrote a book titled *Leading Change*, in which he explores why people resist change and concludes, like Brehm, that resistance stems from an objection to having the will of others imposed on oneself. Further, in the chapter included in this section, he asserts that "a sine qua non of effective leadership is the ability to overcome the resistance to change among followers." However, just as organizational members are likely to resist change imposed by their leaders, the leaders themselves are susceptible to resistance to change that is advocated by outsiders. In other words, everyone is conditioned to resisting change. O'Toole's chapter lists thirty-three popular hypotheses as to why people resist change. He then explains that a true understanding of this phenomenon in organizations must be studied at the group and organizational levels in the form of *collective resistance*. We have included four chapters in this Part Four that discuss group and organizational responses to change. Before we introduce these chapters, however, it is important to first discuss individual responses to change.

INDIVIDUAL RESPONSE TO CHANGE

The next set of chapters in this Part Four establish the thesis that resistance is as much a part of the human psyche as are needs, fear, and anger. These four chapters help the reader understand why and to what degree resistance is a basic part of the psychology of humans. They also help the reader understand the relationship between motivation and resistance.

In 1976 Harry Levinson began a discourse indicating that change is an experience of loss and that the level of resistance a person demonstrates in response to

---

*Chapter is included in the collection of readings on the *Organization Change: A Comprehensive Reader* website. www.josseybass.com/go/burke.

change is proportional to the degree of psychological importance he or she places on what is left behind or lost in the change. Levinson asserts that organizational change efforts that fail do so because the experience of individual loss is not considered by the leaders and consultants involved in the planning of change. Bridges (1986) similarly viewed change as an experience of loss, at least initially. In the chapter included in Part Four, he outlines a three-phase framework to demonstrate how people move through organizational transitions. First, people experience an "ending phase," which requires employees to let go of their current reality and any identity that is tied to it. It is characterized by loss, and as Bridges notes people are "in mourning" during this time and are likely to demonstrate behaviors indicative of grief, denial, and despair. Bridges refers to the second phase as "the neutral zone" because it lies somewhere between the past and the desired future state. It is often accompanied by an experience of intense emotions, such as confusion, loss, and uncertainty. The final phase is called "the vision" or "new beginning," as it represents the future of the organization once the change has been successfully completed. During this phase, people begin to adopt new behaviors, skills, and competencies. They form new relationships and begin to build a new identity as the vision becomes the new reality.

Todd Jick prepared Chapter Twenty-Five on "The Recipients of Change" as discussion material for a class that he was teaching at the Harvard Business School in 1990. In it, he underscores that resistance is "a part of the natural process of adapting to change" and iterates Levinson and Bridges's position that resistance is a response to a feeling of loss and a desire to protect our self-integrity. He briefly reviews frameworks that outline the phases of individual reactions to change, including Bridges's three-phase model. Although Jick agrees that such frameworks accurately depict the psychological response to change, he warns that they can be simplistic and neglect to account for individual differences with respect to the way people cope with change. He ends the chapter with suggestions for leaders and practitioners who are managing the change process that is based on this deeper understanding of the change recipients' experience.

The final chapter in this subsection of Part Four is by Sandy Piderit and was published in the *Academy of Management Review* in 2000. Piderit gives a comprehensive overview of the literature on resistance to change and proposes that individual responses to change should be viewed as multidimensional attitudes with cognitive, emotional, and behavioral components. This tripartite conceptualization reveals that resistance is more complex than previous definitions would suggest. Moreover, it emphasizes that any assessment of dispositional attitudes about resistance to organizational change must consider cognitive, emotional, and behavioral factors. In 2003 a scale was developed by Oreg to measure individuals' dispositional inclination to resist change according to Piderit's multidimensional definition of the construct. Hence, a combination of

Jick and Piderit's suggestions is answered with new research. That is, individual differences with respect to cognitive, emotional, and behavioral responses to change can now be taken into account in considering implementing organization change initiatives.

GROUP RESPONSE TO CHANGE

Over time, groups develop implicit and explicit agreements about how individuals are expected to behave in one another's presence. When they are implicit they are referred to as norms, and when explicit they are often known as rules of conduct. As with individuals, norms and rules permit a sense of control so that when violated they tend to elicit resistance. Also, as individuals interact over time in groups, the group itself can be understood in the same *general systems* terms used in Part Two of this volume. Thus, all parts of a system that are relevant to organizations (input, throughput, output, and feedback) apply and are potentially informative as to how resistance pervades groups.

The next two chapters on Bion's theory related to group dynamics by Rioch (1970) and on group development by Bennis and Shepard (1956), although different, actually go together. The theoretical work by Bion and by Bennis and Shepard helped to set the stage for what we have paid attention to and how we have understood group development in particular, and group dynamics in general, ever since.

As indicated in Rioch's chapter, Wilfred Bion is one of the early writers to extrapolate from psychological characteristics of individuals and apply them to group-level phenomena. He is credited primarily for two such characteristics: the task group and the assumption group, of which the latter has three parts: dependency, fight-flight, and pairing groups. His work with mental hospitals soon after the Second World War helped to elevate the discussion of resistance from being an exclusively individual characteristic to a group-level construct. Hence, once again the implication for the change agent targeting individuals for change is the requirement to understand such phenomena as the perceived central task of groups, the emotional dynamics of the group in terms of its values and norms.

Bennis and Shepard's theoretical piece references Bion. The authors examine "internal uncertainty" in times of change and how this uncertainty manifests itself, so to speak, in stages of dependence (authority relations) and interdependence (personal relations). They relate individual personality to group development—different people have different levels of needs—and then move on to their "phase movement" theory of how groups develop first with respect to *dependence*, from dependence-flight, to counterdependence-flight, to resolution-catharsis. Phase two concerns interdependence, with its subphase from enchantment-flight to, finally, consensual validation.

ORGANIZATION RESPONSE TO CHANGE

The theories and models of planned organization change reviewed in Part Two of this volume anticipate resistance in organization. For instance, the proposition that changing any part of a system will cause reactive responses to other parts of the system helps define the nature of resistance in organizations. Some authors following the notion of organization as a metaphor from biology compare the nature of organization to that of coral by saying that early functional requirements of organizations often become dysfunctional as the organism changes and form rigid superstructures that must be broken down in order for growth to occur.

Brown and Starkey (2000) continue to elevate individual psychodynamics to the organizational level. They invoke the metaphor that individuals and organizations are not primarily motivated to learn *or change*, to the extent that learning entails anxiety-provoking identity change. Further, they leverage the metaphors by arguing that organizations, like individuals, are prone to ego defenses, such as denial, rationalization, idealization, fantasy, and symbolization. To overcome resistance in organizations, the implication for the change agent is to understand such barriers to organizational learning and change and, through reflection and dialogue, promote the development of a more adaptive organizational self-concept.

In the *Quest of Resilience*, Hamel and Valikangas (2003) employ a construct that has again been used to characterize individuals, that of resilience. However, when used as an organizational property, it helps to differentiate organizations with a capacity for continuous change and therefore a lowered level of organizational resistance. Resilience is the ability of an organization to regularly reinvent itself, to morph into new business models, quickly. Such organizations, in the authors' view, continuously learn to identify and conquer the cognitive, strategic, political, and ideological challenges of the day. Moreover, resilient organizations are able to respond to change before the need for it becomes dire. The authors outline challenges faced by organizations that are on a "quest" to become more resilient and offer guidelines to overcome them.

CONCLUDING COMMENTS

The chapters included in Part Four are designed to increase understanding such that any undertaking to implement organization change will make planning for resistance an essential element of such plans. In planning organization change, acknowledging that resistance will occur should allow leaders and change agents to determine whether such resistance will come from contrary motivation of those being changed, poor logic, norms and values of the group to be changed, new skill requirements, organizational inertia, or perceived loss of power and influence. As a signal to planners to increase the depth and scope of their plans, resistance is an essential concept. It is not an excuse for failure.

Taken together, the papers in Part Four serve the reader as a comprehensive smorgasbord of ideas about why, how, what, and when people are likely to resist change. It would be hard to imagine being able to find an individual, group, organization, or even another culture where the change agent, armed with the knowledge in these chapters, would not be able to quickly diagnose resistance (active or passive) and act to mitigate or remove it.

Reference

Lewin, K. (1951) Field Theory in Social Science. New York: Harper.

PART FOUR A

THE NATURE OF RESISTANCE

CHAPTER TWENTY

Overcoming Resistance to Change

Lester Coch
John R. P. French, Jr. (1965)

INTRODUCTION

It has been characteristic of American industry to change products and methods of doing jobs as often as competitive conditions or engineering progress dictate. One of the most serious production problems faced at the Harwood Manufacturing Corporation has been the resistance of production workers to the necessary changes in methods and jobs. This resistance expressed itself in several ways, such as grievances about the piece rates that went with the new methods, high turnover, very low efficiency, restriction of output, and marked aggression against management.

Efforts were made to solve this serious problem by the use of a special monetary allowance for transfers, by trying to enlist the cooperation and aid of the union, by making necessary layoffs on the basis of efficiency, etc. In all cases, these actions did little or nothing to overcome the resistance to change. On the basis of these data, it was felt that the pressing problem of resistance to change demanded further research for its solution. From the point of view of factory management, there were two purposes to the research: (1) Why do people resist change so strongly? and (2) What can be done to overcome this resistance?

Starting with a series of observations about the behavior of changed groups, the first step in the overall program was to devise a preliminary theory to account for the resistance to change. Then on the basis of the theory, a field experiment was devised and conducted within the context of the factory situation. Finally, the results of the experiment were interpreted in the light of the preliminary theory and the new data.

BACKGROUND

The main plant of the Harwood Manufacturing Corporation, where the present research was done, is located in the small town of Marion, Virginia. The plant produces pajamas and, like most sewing plants, employs mostly women. The plant's population is about five hundred women and one hundred men. The workers are recruited from the rural, mountainous areas surrounding the town and are usually employed without previous industrial experience. The average age of the workers is twenty-three; the average education is eight years of grammar school.

The policies of the company in regard to labor relations are liberal and progressive. A high value has been placed on fair and open dealing with the employees, and they are encouraged to take up any problems or grievances with the management at any time. Every effort is made to help foremen find effective solutions to their problems in human relations, using conferences and role-playing methods. Carefully planned orientation, designed to help overcome the discouragement and frustrations attending entrance upon the new and unfamiliar situation, is used. Plantwide votes are conducted where possible to resolve problems affecting the whole working population. The company has invested both time and money in employee services, such as industrial music, health services, lunchroom, and recreation program. As a result of these policies, the company has enjoyed good labor relations since the day it commenced operations.

Harwood employees work on an individual incentive system. Piece rates are set by time study and are expressed in terms of units. One unit is equal to one minute of standard work: sixty units per hour equal the standard efficiency rating. Thus, if on a particular operation the piece rate for one dozen is ten units, the operator would have to produce six dozen per hour to achieve the standard efficiency rating of sixty units per hour. The skill required to reach sixty units per hour is great. On some jobs, an average trainee may take thirty-four weeks to reach the skill level necessary to perform at sixty units per hour. Her first few weeks of work may be on an efficiency level of five to twenty units per hour.

The amount of pay received is directly proportional to the weekly average efficiency rating achieved. Thus, an operator with an average efficiency rating of seventy-five units per hour (25 percent more than standard) would receive 25 percent more than base pay. However, there are two minimum wages below which no operator may fall. The first is the plantwide minimum, the hiring-in wage; the second is a minimum wage based on six months' employment and is 22 percent higher than the plantwide minimum wage. Both minima are smaller than the base pay for sixty units per hour efficiency rating.

The rating of every piece worker is computed every day, and the results are published in a daily record of production, which is shown to every operator. This daily record of production for each production line carries the names of all the operators on that line arranged in rank order of efficiency rating, with the highest rating worker at the top of the list. The supervisors speak to each operator each day about her unit ratings.

When it is necessary to change an operator from one type of work to another, a transfer bonus is given. This bonus is so designed that the changed operator who relearns at an average rate will suffer no loss in earnings after change. Despite this allowance, the general attitudes toward job changes in the factory are markedly negative. Such expressions as "When you make your units (standard production), they change your job" are all too frequent. Many operators refuse to change, preferring to quit.

THE TRANSFER LEARNING CURVE

An analysis of the after-change relearning curves of several hundred experienced operators rating standard or better prior to change showed that 38 percent of the changed operators recovered to the standard efficiency rating of sixty units per hour. The other 62 percent either became chronically substandard operators or quit during the relearning period.

The average relearning curve for those who recover to standard production on the simplest type job in the plant reaches sixty units per hour after eight weeks and, when smoothed, provides the basis for the transfer bonus. The bonus is the percent difference between this expected efficiency rating and the standard of sixty units per hour. It is interesting to note that this relearning period of an experienced operator is longer than the learning period for a new operator. This is true despite the fact that the majority of transfers—the failures who never recover to standard—are omitted from the curve. However, changed operators rarely complain of "wanting to do it the old way," etc., after the first week or two; and time and motion studies show few false moves after the first week of change. From this evidence it is deduced that proactive inhibition or the interference of previous habits in learning the new skill is either nonexistent or very slight after the first two weeks of change.

An analysis of the relearning curves for forty-one experienced operators who were changed to very difficult jobs compared the recovery rates for operators making standard or better prior to change with those below standard prior to change. Both classes of operators dropped to a little below thirty units per hour and recovered at a very slow but similar rate. These curves show a general (though by no means universal) phenomenon: that the efficiency rating prior to change does not indicate a faster or slower recovery rate after change.

A PRELIMINARY THEORY OF RESISTANCE TO CHANGE

The fact that relearning after transfer to a new job is so often slower than initial learning on first entering the factory would indicate, on the face of it, that the resistance to change and the slow relearning is primarily a motivational problem. The similar recovery rates of the skilled and unskilled operators tend to confirm the hypothesis that skill is a minor factor and motivation is the major determinant of the rate of recovery. Earlier experiments at Harwood by Alex Bavelas demonstrated this point conclusively. He found that the use of group-decision techniques on operators who had just been transferred resulted in very marked increases in the rate of relearning, even though no skill training was given and there were no other changes in working conditions (Lewin, 1947).

Interviews with operators who have been transferred to a new job reveal a common pattern of feelings and attitudes, which are distinctly different from those of successful nontransfers. In addition to resentment against the management for transferring them, the employees typically show feelings of frustration, loss of hope of ever regaining their former level of production and status in the factory, feelings of failure, and a very low level of aspiration. In this respect these transferred operators are similar to the chronically slow workers studied previously.

Earlier unpublished research at Harwood has shown that the nontransferred employees generally have an explicit goal of reaching and maintaining an efficiency rating of sixty units per hour. A questionnaire administered to several groups of operators indicated that a large majority of them accept as their goal the management's quota of sixty units per hour. This standard of production is the level of aspiration according to which the operators measure their own success or failure; and those who fall below standard lose status in the eyes of their fellow employees. Relatively few operators set a goal appreciably above sixty units per hour.

The actual production records confirm the effectiveness of this goal of standard production. The distribution of the total population of operators in accordance with their production levels is by no means a normal curve. Instead there is a very large number of operators who rate sixty to sixty-three units per hour and relatively few operators who rate just above or just below this range. Thus we may conclude that (*box 1 on next page*):

1. There is a force acting on the operator in the direction of achieving a production level of sixty units per hour or more. It is assumed that the strength of this driving force (acting on an operator below standard) increases as she gets nearer the goal—a typical goal gradient.

2. The strength of the restraining force hindering higher production increases with increasing level of production.

3. The strength of frustration is a function of the weaker of these two opposing forces, provided that the weaker force is stronger than a certain minimum necessary to produce frustration (French, 1944).

On the other hand restraining forces operate to hinder or prevent her from reaching this goal. These restraining forces consist among other things of the difficulty of the job in relation to the operator's level of skill. Other things being equal, the faster an operator is sewing the more difficult it is to increase her speed by a given amount. Thus we may conclude that (*box 2*):

In line with previous studies, it is assumed that the conflict of these two opposing forces—the driving force corresponding to the goal of reaching sixty and the restraining force of the difficulty of the job—produces frustration. In such a conflict situation, the strength of frustration will depend on the strength of these forces. If the restraining force against increasing production is weak, then the frustration will be weak. But if the driving force toward higher production (i.e., the motivation) is weak, then the frustration will also be weak. Probably both of the conflicting forces must be above a certain minimum strength before any frustration is produced; for all goal-directed activity involves some degree of conflict of this type, yet a person is not usually frustrated so long as he is making satisfactory progress toward his goal. Consequently we assume that (*box 3*):

From propositions one, two, and three we may derive that the strength of frustration (1) should be greater for operators who are below standard in production than for operators who have already achieved the goal of standard production, (2) should be greater for operators on difficult jobs than for operators on easy jobs, and (3) should increase with increasing efficiency rating below standard production. Previous research would suggest the hypothesis that (*box 4 on next page*):

An analysis of the effects of such frustration in the factory showed that it resulted, among other things, in such forms of escape from the field as high

4. One consequence of frustration is escape from the field (French, 1944).

turnover and absenteeism. The rate of turnover for successful operators with efficiency ratings above standard was much lower than for unsuccessful operators. Likewise, operators on the more difficult jobs quit more frequently than those on the easier jobs. Presumably the effect of being transferred is a severe frustration, which should result in similar attempts to escape from the field.

In line with this theory of frustration, and the finding that job turnover is one resultant of frustration, an analysis was made of the turnover rate of transferred operators as compared with the rate among operators who had not been transferred recently. For the year September 1946 to September 1947, there were 198 operators who had not been transferred recently—that is, within the thirty-four-week period allowed for relearning after transfer. There was a second group of 85 operators who had been transferred recently—that is, within the time allowed for relearning the new job. Each of these two groups was divided into seven classifications according to their unit rating at the time of quitting. For each classification the percent turnover per month, based on the total number of employees in that classification, was computed.

The results are given in Figure 20.1. Both the levels of turnover and the form of the curves are strikingly different for the two groups. Among operators who

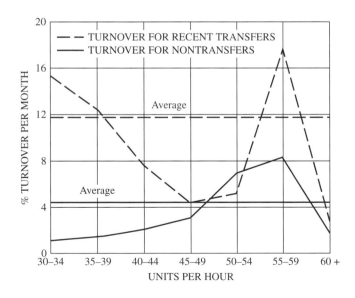

Figure 20.1. The Rate of Turnover at Various Levels of Production for Transfers as Compared with Nontransfers.

have not been transferred recently the average turnover per month is about 4.5 percent; among recent transfers the monthly turnover is nearly 12 percent. Consistent with the previous studies, both groups show the predicted very marked drop in the turnover curve after an operator becomes a success by reaching sixty units per hour or standard production. However, the form of the curves at lower unit ratings is markedly different for the two groups. As predicted, the nontransferred operators show a gradually increasing rate of turnover up to a rating of fifty to fifty-nine units per hour. The transferred operators, on the other hand, show a high peak at the lowest unit rating of thirty to thirty-four units per hour, decreasing sharply to a low point at forty-five to forty-nine units per hour. Since most changed operators drop to a unit rating of around thirty units per hour when changed and then drop no further, it is obvious that the rate of turnover was highest for these operators just after they were changed and again much later just before they reached standard. Why?

It is assumed that the strength of frustration for an operator who has not been transferred gradually increases because both the driving force toward the goal of reaching sixty and the restraining force of the difficulty of the job increase with increasing unit rating. This is in line with hypotheses one, two, and three above. For the transferred operator, on the other hand, the frustration is greatest immediately after transfer when the contrast of her present status with her former status is most evident. At this point the strength of the restraining forces is at a maximum because the difficulty is unusually great due to proactive inhibition. Then as she overcomes the interference effects between the two jobs and learns the new job, the difficulty and the frustration gradually decrease and the rate of turnover declines until the operator reaches forty-five to forty-nine units per hour. Then at higher levels of production the difficulty starts to increase again, and the transferred operator shows the same peak in frustration and turnover at fifty-five to fifty-nine units per hour.

Though our theory of frustration explains the forms of the two turnover curves in Figure 20.1, it hardly seems adequate to account for the markedly higher level of turnover for transfers as compared to nontransfers. On the basis of the difficulty of the job, it is especially difficult to explain the higher rate of turnover at fifty-five to fifty-nine units per hour for transfers. Evidently additional forces are operating.

Another factor that seems to affect recovery rates of changed operators is the cohesiveness of the work group. Observations seem to indicate that a strong psychological subgroup with negative attitudes toward management will display the strongest resistance to change. On the other hand, changed groups with high cohesiveness and positive cooperative attitudes are the best relearners. Collections of individuals with little or no cohesiveness display some resistance to change but not so much as the groups with high cohesiveness and negative attitudes toward management.

An analysis of turnover records for changed operators with high cohesiveness showed a 4 percent turnover rate per month at thirty to thirty-four units per hour, not significantly higher than in unchanged operators but significantly lower than in changed operators with little or no cohesiveness. However, the acts of aggression are far more numerous among operators with high, than among operators with low, cohesiveness. Since both types of operators experience the same frustration as individuals but react to it so differently, it is assumed that the effect of the in-group feeling is to set up a restraining force against leaving the group and driving forces toward staying in the group. In these circumstances, one would expect some alternative reaction to frustration rather than escape from the field. This alternative is aggression. Strong cohesiveness provides strength so that members dare to express aggression, which would otherwise be suppressed.

One common result in a cohesive subgroup is the setting of a group standard concerning production. Where the attitudes toward management are antagonistic, this group standard may take the form of a definite restriction of production to a given level. This phenomenon of restriction is particularly likely to happen in a group that has been transferred to a job where a new piece rate has been set; for they have some hope that if production never approaches the standard, the management may change the piece rate in their favor.

A group standard can exert extremely strong forces on an individual member of a small subgroup. That these forces can have a powerful effect on production is indicated in the production record of one presser during a period of forty days.

In the Group	
Days	Efficiency Rating
1–3	46
4–6	52
7–9	53
10–12	55
Scapegoating Begins	
13–16	55
17–20	48
Becomes a Single Worker	
21–24	83
25–28	92
29–32	92
33–36	91
37–40	92

For the first twenty days she was working in a group of other pressers who were producing at the rate of about fifty units per hour.

Starting on the thirteenth day, when she reached standard production and exceeded the production of the other members, she became a scapegoat of the group. During this time her production decreased toward the level of the remaining members of the group. After twenty days the group had to be broken up, and all the other members were transferred to other jobs, leaving only the scapegoat operator. With the removal of the group, the group standard was no longer operative; and the production of the one remaining operator shot up from the level of about forty-five to ninety-six units per hour in a period of four days. Her production stabilized at a level of about ninety-two and stayed there for the remainder of the twenty days. Thus it is clear that the motivational forces induced in the individual by a strong subgroup may be more powerful than those induced by management.

THE EXPERIMENT

On the basis of the preliminary theory that resistance to change is a combination of an individual reaction to frustration with strong group-induced forces, it seemed that the most appropriate methods for overcoming the resistance to change would be group methods. Consequently an experiment was designed employing three degrees of participation in handling groups to be transferred. The first variation involved no *participation* by employees in planning the changes, though an explanation was given to them. The second variation involved *participation through representation* of the workers in designing the changes to be made in the jobs. The third variation consisted of *total participation* by all members of the group in designing the changes. Two experimental groups received the total participation treatment. The four experimental groups were roughly matched with respect to (1) the efficiency ratings of the groups before transfer, (2) the degree of change involved in the transfer, and (3) the amount of cohesiveness observed in the groups.

In no case was more than a minor change in the work routines and time allowances made. The no-participation group, the eighteen hand pressers, had formerly stacked their work in half-dozen lots on a flat piece of cardboard the size of the finished product. The new job called for stacking their work in half-dozen lots in a box the size of the finished product. The box was located in the same place the cardboard had been. An additional two minutes per dozen was allowed (by the time study) for this new part of the job. This represented a total job change of 8.8 percent.

The group treated with participation through representation, the thirteen pajama folders, had formerly folded coats with prefolded pants. The new job called for the folding of coats with unfolded pants. An additional 1.8 minutes per dozen was allowed (by time study) for this new part of the job. This represented a total job change of 9.4 percent.

The two total participation groups, consisting of eight and seven pajama examiners respectively, had formerly clipped threads from the entire garment and examined every seam. The new job called for pulling only certain threads off and examining every seam. An average of 1.2 minutes per dozen was subtracted (by time study) from the total time on these two jobs. This represented a total job change of 8 percent.

The no-participation group of hand pressers went through the usual factory routine when they were changed. The production department modified the job, and a new piece rate was set. A group meeting was then held in which the control group was told that the change was necessary because of competitive conditions, and that a new piece rate had been set. The new piece rate was thoroughly explained by the time-study person, questions were answered, and the meeting was dismissed.

The group that participated through representatives was changed in a different manner. Before any changes took place, a group meeting was held with all the operators to be changed. The need for the change was presented as dramatically as possible, showing two identical garments produced in the factory; one was produced in 1946 and had sold for 100 percent more than its fellow in 1947. The group was asked to identify the cheaper one and could not do it. This demonstration effectively shared with the group the entire problem of the necessity of cost reduction. A general agreement was reached that a savings could be effected by removing the "frills" and "fancy" work from the garment without affecting the folders' opportunity to achieve a high efficiency rating. Management then presented a plan to set the new job and piece rate:

1. Make a check study of the job as it was being done.
2. Eliminate all unnecessary work.
3. Train several representative operators in the correct methods.
4. Set the piece rate by time studies on these specially trained operators.
5. Explain the new job and rate to all the operators.
6. Train all operators in the new method so they can reach a high rate of production within a short time

The group approved this plan (though no formal group decision was reached), and chose the operators to be specially trained. A submeeting with the "special" operators was held immediately following the meeting with the entire group. They displayed a cooperative and interested attitude and immediately presented many good suggestions. This attitude carried over into the working out of the details of the new job; and when the new job and piece rates were set, the "special" operators referred to the resultants as "our job," "our rate," etc. The new job and piece rates were presented at a second group meeting to all the operators involved. The "special" operators served to train the other operators on the new job.

The total participation groups went through much the same kind of meetings. The groups were smaller, and a more intimate atmosphere was established. The need for a change was once again made dramatically clear; the same general plan was presented by management. However, since the groups were small, all operators were chosen as "special" operators—that is, all operators were to participate directly in the designing of the new jobs, and all operators would be studied by the time-study person. It is interesting to note that in the meetings with these two groups suggestions were immediately made in such quantity that the stenographer had great difficulty in recording them. The group approved of the plans, but again no formal group decision was reached.

RESULTS

The results of the experiment are summarized in graphic form in Figure 20.2. The gaps in the production curves occur because these groups were paid on a time-work basis for a day or two. The no-participation group improved little

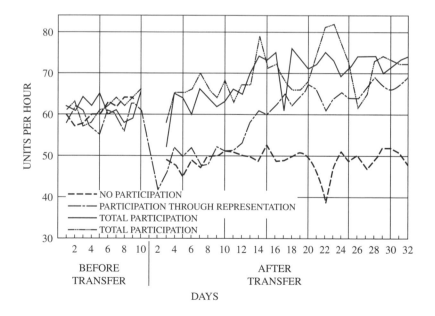

Figure 20.2. The Effects of Participation Through Representation (Group One) and of Total Participation (Groups Two and Three) on Recovery After an Easy Transfer.

beyond their early efficiency ratings. Resistance developed almost immediately after the change occurred. Marked expressions of aggression against management occurred, such as conflict with the methods engineer, expression of hostility against the supervisor, deliberate restriction of production, and lack of cooperation with the supervisor. There were 17 percent quits in the first forty days. Grievances were filed about the piece rate, but when the rate was checked it was found to be a little "loose."

The group treated with participation through representation showed an unusually good relearning curve. At the end of fourteen days, the group averaged sixty-one units per hour. During the fourteen days, the attitude was cooperative and permissive. They worked well with the methods engineer, the training staff, and the supervisor. (The supervisor was the same person in the cases of the first two groups.) There were no quits in this group in the first forty days. This group might have presented a better learning record if materials had not been scarce during the first seven days. There was one act of aggression against the supervisor recorded in the first forty days. It is interesting to note that the three special representative operators recovered at about the same rate as the rest of their group.

OVERCOMING RESISTANCE TO CHANGE

The total participation groups recovered faster than the other experimental groups. After a slight drop on the first day of change, the efficiency ratings returned to a prechange level and showed sustained progress thereafter to a level about 14 percent higher than the prechange level. No additional training was provided them after the second day. They worked well with their supervisors, and no indications of aggression were observed from these groups. There were no quits in either of these groups in the first forty days.

A fifth experimental group, composed of only two sewing operators, was transferred by the total-participation technique. Their new job was one of the most difficult jobs in the factory, in contrast to the easy jobs for the four other experimental groups. As expected, the total participation technique again resulted in an unusually fast recovery rate and a final level of production well above the level before transfer.

In the first experiment, the no-participation group made no progress after transfer for a period of thirty-two days. At the end of this period the group was broken up, and the individuals were reassigned to new jobs scattered throughout the factory. Two and a half months after their dispersal, the thirteen remaining members of the original group, having regained standard production, were again brought together as a group for a second experiment.

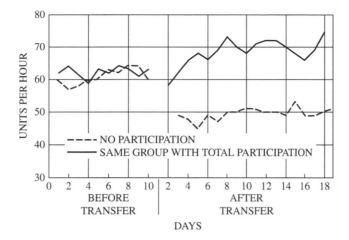

Figure 20.3. A Comparison of the Effect of No Participation with the Different Participation Procedures on the Same Group.

This second experiment consisted of transferring the group to a new job, using the total participation technique. The new job was a pressing job of comparable difficulty to the new job in the first experiment. On the average it involved about the same degree of change. In the meetings no reference was made to the previous behavior of the group on being transferred.

The results of the second experiment were in sharp contrast to the first (see Figure 20.3). With the total-participation technique, the same group now recovered rapidly to their previous efficiency rating, and, like the other groups under this treatment, continued on beyond it to a new high level of production. There was no aggression or turnover in the group for nineteen days after change, a marked modification of their previous behavior after transfer. Some anxiety concerning their seniority status was expressed, but this was resolved in a meeting of their elected delegate, the union business agent, and a management representative.

Interpretation

The purpose of this section is to explain the drop in production resulting from transfer, the differential recovery rates of the three experimental treatments, the increases beyond their former levels of production by the participating groups, and the differential rates of turnover and aggression.

The first experiment showed that the rate of recovery is directly proportional to the amount of participation, and that the rates of turnover and aggression are inversely proportional to the amount of participation. The second experiment demonstrated more conclusively that the results obtained depended on the experimental treatment rather than on personality factors like skill or aggressiveness, for identical individuals yielded markedly different results in the no-participation treatment as contrasted with the total-participation treatment.

Apparently total participation has the same type of effect as participation through representation, but the former has a stronger influence. In regard to recovery rates, this difference is not unequivocal because the experiment was unfortunately confounded. Right after transfer, the latter group had insufficient material to work on for a period of seven days. Hence their slower recovery during this period is at least in part due to insufficient work. In succeeding days, however, there was an adequate supply of work, and the differential recovery rate still persisted. Therefore, we are inclined to believe that participation through representation results in slower recovery than does total participation.

Before discussing the details of why participation produces high morale, we will consider the nature of production levels. In examining the production records of hundreds of individuals and groups in this factory, one is struck by the constancy of the level of production. Though differences among individuals in efficiency rating are very large, nearly every experienced operator maintains a fairly steady level of production, given constant physical conditions. Frequently the given level will be maintained despite rather large changes in technical working conditions.

As Lewin has pointed out, this type of production can be viewed as a quasi-stationary process—in the ongoing work the operator is forever sewing new garments, yet the level of the process remains relatively stationary (1947). Thus there are constant characteristics of the production process permitting the establishment of general laws.

In studying production as a quasi-stationary equilibrium, we are concerned with two types of forces: (1) forces on production in a downward direction, and (2) forces on production in an upward direction. In this situation we are dealing with a variety of both upward forces tending to increase the level of production and downward forces tending to decrease the level of production. However, in the present experiment we have no method of measuring independently all of the component forces either downward or upward. These various component forces upward are combined into one resultant force upward. Likewise the several downward component forces combine into one resultant force downward. We can infer a good deal about the relative strengths of these resultant forces.

Where we are dealing with a quasi-stationary equilibrium, the resultant forces upward and the forces downward are opposite in direction and equal in strength at the equilibrium level. Of course, either resultant force may fluctuate over a short period of time, so that the forces may not be equally balanced at a given moment. However, over a longer period of time and on the average the forces balance out. Fluctuations from the average occur, but there is a tendency to return to the average level.

Just before being transferred, all the groups in both experiments had reached a stable equilibrium level at just above the standard production of six-ty units per hour. This level was equal to the average efficiency rating for the entire factory during the period of the experiments. Since this production level remained constant, neither increasing nor decreasing, we may be sure that the strength of the resultant force upward was equal to the strength of the resultant force downward. This equilibrium of forces was maintained over the period of time when production was stationary at this level.[1] But the forces changed markedly after transfer, and these new constellations of forces were distinctly different for the various experimental groups.

For the no-participation group the period after transfer is a quasi-stationary equilibrium at a lower level, and the forces do not change during the period of thirty days. The resultant force upward remains equal to the resultant force downward and the level of production remains constant. The force field for this group is represented schematically in Figure 20.4. Only the resultant forces are shown. The length of the vector represents the strength of the force, and the point of the arrow represents the point of application of the force—that is, the production level and the time at which the force applies. Thus the forces are equal and opposite only at the level of fifty units per hour. At higher levels of production the forces downward are greater than the forces upward; and at lower levels of production the forces upward are stronger than the forces downward. Thus there is a tendency for the equilibrium to be maintained at an efficiency rating of fifty.

The situation for the other experimental groups after transfer can be viewed as a quasi-stationary equilibrium of a different type. Figure 20.5 gives a sche-matic diagram of the resultant forces for all the participation groups. At any

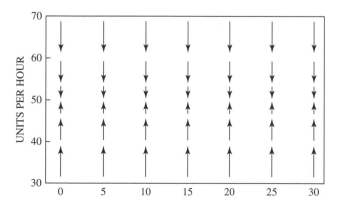

Figure 20.4. A Schematic Diagram of the Quasi-Stationary Equilibrium for the Control Group After Transfer.

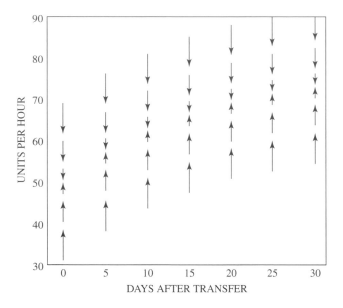

Figure 20.5. A Schematic Diagram of the Quasi-Stationary Equilibrium for the Experimental Groups After Transfer.

given level of production, such as fifty units per hour or sixty units per hour, both the resultant forces upward and the resultant forces downward change over the period of thirty days. During this time the point of equilibrium, which starts at fifty units per hour, gradually rises until it reaches a level of over seventy units per hour after thirty days. Yet here again the equilibrium level has the character of a "central force field" where at any point in the total field the resultant of the upward and the downward forces is in the direction of the equilibrium level.

To understand how the differences among the experimental treatments produced the differences in force fields represented in Figures 20.4 and 20.5, it is not sufficient to consider only the resultant forces. We must also look at the component forces for each resultant force.

There are three main component forces influencing production in a downward direction: (1) the difficulty of the job, (2) a force corresponding to avoidance of strain, and (3) a force corresponding to a group standard to restrict production to a given level. The resultant force upward in the direction of greater production is composed of three additional component forces: (1) the force corresponding to the goal of standard production, (2) a force corresponding to pressures induced by the management through supervision, (3) a force corresponding to a group standard of competition. Let us examine each of these six component forces.

1. Job Difficulty. For all operators the difficulty of the job is one of the forces downward on production. The difficulty of the job, of course, is relative to the skill of the operator. The given job may be very difficult for an unskilled operator but relatively easy for a highly skilled one. In the case of a transfer a new element of difficulty enters. For some time the new job is much more difficult, for the operator is unskilled at that particular job. In addition to the difficulty experienced by any learner, the transfer often encounters the added difficulty of proactive inhibition. Where the new job is similar to the old job there will be a period of interference between the two similar but different skills required. For this reason a very efficient operator whose skills have become almost unconscious may suffer just as great a drop as a much less efficient operator. Except for group five, the difficulty of these easy jobs does not explain the differential recovery rates because both the initial difficulty and the amount of change were equated for these groups. The two operators in group five probably dropped further and recovered more slowly than any of the other three groups under total participation because of the greater difficulty of the job.

2. Strain Avoidance. The force toward lower production corresponding to the difficulty of the job (or the lack of skill of the person) has the character of a restraining force—that is, it acts to prevent locomotion rather than as a driving force causing locomotion. However, in all production there is a closely related driving force toward lower production, namely "strain avoidance." We assume that working too hard and working too fast is an unpleasant strain, and corresponding to this negative valence there is a driving force in the opposite direction, namely towards taking it easy or working slower. The higher the level of production the greater will be the strain and, other things being equal, the stronger will be the downward force of strain avoidance. Likewise, the greater the difficulty of the job the stronger will be the force corresponding to strain avoidance. But the greater the operator's skill the smaller will be the strain and the strength of the force of strain avoidance. Therefore (*box 5*):

5. The strength of the force of strain avoidance
$$= \frac{\text{Job difficulty} \times \text{production level}}{\text{Skill of operator}}$$

The differential recovery rates of the three experimental groups in experiment one cannot be explained by strain avoidance because job difficulty, production level, and operator skill were matched at the time immediately following transfer. Later, however, when the participation treatments had produced a much higher level of production, these groups were subjected to an increased downward force of strain avoidance that was stronger than in the no-participation group in experiment one. Evidently other forces were strong enough to overcome this force of strain avoidance.

3. The Goal of Standard Production. In considering the negative attitudes toward transfer and the resistance to being transferred, there are several important aspects of the complex goal of reaching and maintaining a level of sixty units per hour. For an operator producing below standard, this goal is attractive because it means success, high status in the eyes of fellow employees, better pay, and job security. On the other hand, there is a strong force against remaining below standard because this lower level means failure, low status, low pay, and the danger of being fired. Thus it is clear that the upward force corresponding to the goal of standard production will indeed be strong for the transfer who has dropped below standard.

It is equally clear why any operator shows such strong resistance to being changed. She sees herself as becoming a failure and losing status, pay, and perhaps the job itself. The result is a lowered level of aspiration and a weakened force toward the goal of standard production.

Just such a weakening of the force toward sixty units per hour seems to have occurred in the no-participation group in experiment one. The participation treatments, on the other hand, seem to have involved the operators in designing the new job and setting the new piece rates in such a way that they did not lose hope of regaining the goal of standard production. Thus the participation resulted in a stronger force toward higher production. However, this force alone can hardly account for the large differences in recovery rate between the no-participation group and the other experimental groups; certainly it does not explain why the latter increased to a level so high above standard.

4. Management Pressure. On all operators below standard the management exerts a pressure for higher production. This pressure is no harsh and autocratic treatment involving threats. Rather it takes the form of persuasion and encouragement by the supervisors. They attempt to induce the low-rating operator to improve her performance and to attain standard production.

Such an attempt to induce a psychological force on another person may have several results. In the first place the person may ignore the attempt of the inducing agent, in which case there is no induced force acting on the person. On the other hand, the attempt may succeed so that an induced force on the person exists. Other things being equal, whenever there is an induced force acting on a person, the person will locomote in the direction of the force. An induced force, which depends on the power field of an inducing agent—some other individual or group—will cease to exist when the inducing power field is withdrawn. In this respect it is different from an ''own'' force, which stems from a person's own needs and goals.

The reaction of a person to an effective induced force will vary depending, among other things, on the person's relation to the inducing agent. A force induced by a friend may be accepted in such a way that it acts more like an own force. An effective force induced by an enemy may be resisted and rejected so that the person complies unwillingly and shows signs of conflict and tension. Thus in addition to what might be called a "neutral" induced force, we also distinguish an *accepted* induced force and a *rejected* induced force. Naturally the acceptance and the rejection of an induced force can vary in degree from zero (i.e., a neutral induced force) to very strong acceptance or rejection. To account for the difference in character between the acceptance and rejection of an induced force, we make the following assumptions (*boxes 6 and 7*):

6. The acceptance of an induced force sets up additional own forces in the same direction.

7. The rejection of an induced force sets up additional own forces in the opposite direction.

The grievances, aggression, and tension in the no-participation group in experiment one indicate that they rejected the force toward higher production induced by the management. The group accepted the stereotype that transfer is a calamity, but the no-participation procedure did not convince them that the change was necessary, and they viewed the new job and the new piece rates set by management as arbitrary and unreasonable. The other experimental groups, on the contrary, participated in designing the changes and setting the piece rates so that they spoke of the new job as "our job" and the new piece rates as "our rates." Thus they accepted the new situation and accepted the management-induced force toward higher production.

From the acceptance by the participation groups and the rejection by the no-participation group of the management-induced forces, we may derive (by six and seven above) that the former had additional own forces toward higher production whereas the latter had additional own forces toward lower production. This difference helps to explain the better recovery rate of the participation groups and the fact that they exceeded their original level of production.

5. Group Standards. Probably the most important force affecting the recovery under the no-participation procedure was a group standard, set by the group, restricting the level of production to fifty units per hour. Evidently this explicit agreement to restrict production is related to the group's rejection of the change and of the new job as arbitrary and unreasonable. Perhaps they had faint hopes of demonstrating that standard production could not be attained and thereby obtain a more favorable piece rate. In any case there was a definite group phenomenon that affected all the members of the group.

We have already noted the striking example of the presser whose production was restricted in the group situation to about half the level she attained as an individual. In the no-participation group, too, we would expect the group to induce strong forces on the members. The more a member deviates above the standard, the stronger would be the group-induced force to conform to the standard, for such deviations both negate any possibility of management's increasing the piece rate and at the same time expose the other members to increased pressure from management. Thus individual differences in levels of production should be sharply curtailed in this group after transfer.

An analysis was made for all groups of the individual differences within the group in levels of production. In experiment one the forty days before change were compared with the thirty days after change; in experiment two the ten days before change were compared to the seventeen days after change. As a measure of variability, the standard deviation was calculated each day for each group. The average daily standard deviations *before* and *after* change were as follows:

Group	Variability Before Change	Variability After Change
Experiment one		
No participation	9.8	1.9
Participation through representation	9.7	3.8
Total participation	10.3	2.7
Total participation	9.9	2.4
Experiment two		
Total participation	12.7	2.9

There is indeed a marked decrease in individual differences within the no-participation group after their first transfer. In fact the restriction of production resulted in a lower variability than in any other group. Thus we may conclude that the group standard at fifty units per hour set up strong group-induced forces, which were important components in the central-force field shown in Figure 20.4. It is now evident that for this group the quasi-stationary equilibrium after transfer has a steep gradient around the equilibrium level of fifty units per hour—the strength of the forces increases rapidly above and below this level. It is also clear that the group standard to restrict production is a major reason for the lack of recovery in the no-participation group.

The table of variability also shows that the experimental treatments markedly reduced variability in the other four groups after transfer. In participation by representation this smallest reduction of variability was produced by a group standard of individual competition for improvement in efficiency rating. Competition among members of the group was reported by the supervisor soon after transfer. This competition was a force toward higher production, which resulted in good recovery to standard and continued progress beyond standard.

The total participation groups showed a greater reduction in variability following transfer. These two groups in experiment one under total participation were transferred on the same day. Each group tried to set a better record for improvement than the other group. This group competition, which evidently resulted in stronger forces on the members than did the individual competition, was an effective group standard. The standard gradually moved to higher and higher levels of production with the result that the groups not only reached but far exceeded their previous levels of production.

Probably a major determinant of the strength of these group standards is the cohesiveness of the group (Festinger, Back, Schachter, Kelley, and Thibaut, 1950). Whether this power of the group over the members was used to increase or to decrease productivity seemed to depend on the use of participation (Schachter, Ellertson, McBride, and Gregory, 1951).

TURNOVER AND AGGRESSION

Returning now to our preliminary theory of frustration, we can see several revisions. The difficulty of the job and its relation to skill and strain avoidance has been clarified in proposition five. It is now clear that the driving force toward sixty is a complex affair; it is partly a negative driving force corresponding to the negative valence of low pay, low status, failure, and job insecurity. Turnover results not only from the frustration produced by the conflict of these two forces but also as a direct attempt to escape from the region of these negative valences. For the members of the no-participation group, the group standard to restrict production prevented escape by increasing production, so that quitting their jobs was the only remaining escape. In the participation groups, on the contrary, both the group standards and the additional own forces resulting from the acceptance of management-induced forces combined to make increasing production the distinguished path of escape from this region of negative valence.

In considering turnover as a form of escape from the field, it is not enough to look only at the psychological present; one must also consider the psychological future. The employee's decision to quit the job is rarely made exclusively on the basis of a momentary frustration or an undesirable present situation; she usually quits when she also sees the future as equally hopeless. The operator transferred by the usual factory procedure (including the no-participation group) has in fact a realistic view of the probability of continued failure because, as we have already noted, 62 percent of transfers do in fact fail to recover to standard production. Thus the higher rate of quitting for transfers as compared to nontransfers results from a more pessimistic view of the future.

The no-participation procedure had the effect for the members of setting up management as a hostile power field. They rejected the forces induced by this hostile power field, and group standards to restrict production developed within the group in opposition to management. In this conflict between the power field of management and the power field of the group, the group attempted to reduce the strength of the hostile power field relative to the strength of their own power field. This change was accomplished in three ways: (1) the group increased its own power by developing a more cohesive and well-disciplined group, (2) they secured "allies" by getting the backing of the union in filing a formal grievance about the new piece rate, and (3) they attacked the hostile power field directly in the form of aggression against the supervisor, the time-study engineer, and the higher management. Thus the aggression was derived not only from individual frustration but also from the conflict between two groups. Furthermore, this situation of group conflict both helped to define management as the frustrating agent and gave the members strength to express any aggressive impulses produced by frustration.

CONCLUSIONS

It is possible for management to modify greatly or to remove completely group resistance to changes in methods of work and the ensuing piece rates. This change can be accomplished by the use of group meetings in which management effectively communicates the need for change and stimulates group participation in planning the changes.

Such participation results in higher production, higher morale, and better labor-management relations.

Harwood's management has long felt that such field experiments are the key to better labor-management relations. It is only by discovering the basic principles and applying them to the true causes of conflict that an intelligent, effective effort can be made to correct the undesirable effects of the conflict. In addition to these practical values, therefore, this experiment also contributes to our theories of group productivity, group processes, and intergroup relations.

A CROSS-CULTURAL REPLICATION

This experiment was replicated in a similar Norwegian factory in 1956, although necessarily using somewhat different operational definitions (French, Israel, and As, 1960). Nine four-person groups were changed to producing new products with a new piece rate. The four control groups had low participation in planning the changes, but the five experimental groups were given more participation through a series of meetings that were similar to the "total participation" procedures in the previous experiment. However, this treatment probably produced somewhat weaker psychological participation (defined as the amount of influence the person perceives that he or she exerts on a jointly made decision affecting all participants).

The effects of participation on several dimensions of labor-management relations and on job satisfaction were measured by a questionnaire. It was predicted that these effects would increase with increasing legitimacy of participation and with decreasing resistance to the methods of introducing the change.

Compared to the control groups, the experimental groups showed trends in the direction of greater job satisfaction and more favorable attitudes toward management. As predicted these effects became significant when we controlled for the legitimacy of participation and for the amount of resistance to change as measured by the questionnaire. Thus participation produces improved morale only to the extent that it is legitimate (i.e., the workers feel they have as much influence as they should have). Likewise participation produces improved morale only to the extent that there is no strong resistance to the methods of introducing change.

There was no difference between the experimental and the control groups in the level of production, probably because the participation was less relevant and because there were stronger group standards restricting production.

The revised theory, specifying the conditioning variables, accounts for the results of both experiments and also for individual differences in reactions to participation.

Note

1. See Lewin (1947), p. 29.

References

Festinger, L., Back, K., Schachter, S., Kelley, H., and Thibaut, J. *Theory and experiment in social communication*. Ann Arbor, Mich.: Edwards Bros., 1950.

French, J.R.P., Jr. The behavior of organized and unorganized groups under conditions of frustration and fear, studies in topological and vector psychology, III. *University of Iowa Studies in Child Welfare*, 1944, *20*, 229–308.

French, J.R.P., Jr., Israel, J., and As, D. An experiment on participation in a Norwegian factory: Interpersonal dimensions of decision-making. *Human Relations*, 1960, *13*, 3–19.

Lewin, K. Frontiers in group dynamics. *Human Relations*, 1947, *1*, 5–41.

Schachter, S., Ellertson, N., McBride, D., and Gregory, D. An experimental study of cohesiveness and productivity. *Human Relations*, 1951, *4*, 229–238.

CHAPTER TWENTY-ONE

Resistance to Change

Goodwin Watson (1967)

All of the forces that contribute to stability in personality or in social systems can be perceived as resisting change. From the standpoint of an ambitious and energetic change agent, these energies are seen as obstructions. From a broader and more inclusive perspective, the tendencies to achieve, to preserve, and to return to equilibrium are most salutary. They permit the duration of character, intelligent action, institutions, civilization, and culture.

Lewin's concept (1951) of apparently static systems as in "quasi-stationary equilibrium" has directed attention to the importance of reducing resistance if change is to be accomplished with minimal stress. The more usual strategies of increasing pressures by persuasion and dissuasion raise tensions within the system. If the opposite strategy—that of neutralizing or transforming resistance—is adopted, the forces for change already present in the system-in-situation will suffice to produce movement. For example, administrators may try by exhortation to get teachers to pay more attention to individual differences among pupils. Or they may analyze the factors that now prevent such attention (e.g., large classes, single textbooks, standard tests) and by removing these pressures release a very natural tendency for teachers to adapt to the different individual pupils.

During the life of a typical innovation or change enterprise, perceived resistance moves through a cycle. In the early stage, when only a few pioneer thinkers take the reform seriously, resistance appears massive and undifferentiated. "Everyone" knows better; "No one in his right mind" could advocate the change. Proponents are labeled crackpots and visionaries. In the second stage, when the movement for change has begun to grow, the forces pro and con become identifiable. The position can be defined by its position in the social system and its power appraised. Direct conflict and a showdown mark the third stage, as resistance becomes mobilized to crush the upstart proposal. Enthusiastic supporters of a new idea have frequently underestimated the strength of their opponents. Those who see a favored change as good and needed find it hard to believe the lengths to which opposition will go to squelch that innovation. This third stage is likely to mean life or death to the proposed reform. Survival is seen as depending on building up power to overcome the enemy. Actually, as Lewin's force-field analysis indicates, an easier and more stable victory can be won by lowering the potency of the opposing forces. The fourth stage, after the decisive battles, finds supporters of the change in power. The persisting resistance is, at this stage, seen as a stubborn, hidebound, cantankerous nuisance. For a time, the danger of a counterswing of the pendulum remains real. Any conspicuous failure of the reform may mobilize latent opposition, which, jointed with the manifest reactionaries, could prove sufficient to shift the balance of power. Strategy in this fourth stage demands wisdom in dealing not only with the overt opponents but with the still-dissonant elements within the majority that appears, on the whole, to have accepted the innovation. Many teachers of new math today may be less than wholehearted about its value. In a fifth stage, the old adversaries are as few, and as alienated, as were the advocates in the first stage. The strategic situation is now that new change-enterprises are appearing and the one-time fighters for the old innovation (e.g., junior high schools) are being seen as resisters of the emerging change (Edwards, 1927).

At each stage of the innovation, from its inception to its defense as status quo, wise strategy requires perceptive analysis of the nature of the resistance. For purposes of this study, we shall focus first on the forces of resistance as they operate within the individual personality. Then we shall inventory the forces most easily identified in the social system. This is, of course, an arbitrary separation, used to facilitate the recognition of factors. In reality, the forces of the social system operate within the individuals and those attributed to separate personalities combine to constitute systemic forces. The two work as one.

A. RESISTANCE IN PERSONALITY

1. Homeostasis

Some of the stabilizing forces within organisms have been described by Cannon (1932) as "homeostasis." The human body has built-in regulatory mechanisms for keeping fairly constant such physiological states as temperature or blood sugar. Exercise increases pulse rate, but "resistance" to this change presently brings the heartbeat back to normal. Appetites rise, are satisfied, and the organism returns to its steady state. Raup (1925) generalized the reversion to *complacency* as the most basic characteristic of the psychological as well as the physiological behavior of humans.

The conception of organisms as naturally complacent unless disturbed by intrusive stimuli has had to be modified in recent years because of contradictory evidence showing a hunger for stimulation. Years ago, W. I. Thomas proposed the "desire for new experience" as one of the four most basic wishes underlying human behavior (Thomas and Znaniecki, 1918–1920). Observers of rats, dogs, and chimpanzees have noted an "exploratory motive" strong enough to counterbalance fear of the unknown (Hebb, 1958, p. 171). Experiments with perceptual isolation of human subjects showed that lying quietly awake in a comfortable bed, free from disturbing stimuli, soon became intolerable. People need to interact with a changing environment (Lilly, 1956).

Frequently, educational changes prove temporary. For a time, after sensitivity training, a school principal may be more open and receptive to suggestions from teachers. But with time, the forces that made the principal behave as he or she did before training return the person to his or her own more brusque and arbitrary manner.

2. Habit

Most learning theory has included the assumption that unless the situation changes noticeably, organisms will continue to respond in their accustomed way. At least one psychologist (Stephens, 1965) has argued that the *repetition* of a response—often used as a criterion for having "learned" it—offers no conceptual problem. The model resembles a machine that, unless something significant is altered, will continue to operate in a fixed fashion. There should be no need for repeated exercise or for a satisfying effect to "stamp in" the learned response; once the circuit is connected it should operate until rearranged. Once a habit is established, its operation often becomes satisfying to the organism. Gordon Allport (1937) has introduced the term "functional autonomy" to refer to the fact that activities first undertaken as a means to some culminating satisfaction often become intrinsically gratifying. The man accustomed after dinner to his chair, pipe, and newspaper may resist any change in the details of his routine. The term "bus man's holiday" reflects the fact that people sometimes enjoy continuing in free time an activity that has been part of their required work. The concept of functional autonomy is probably too inclusive. Not all activities that are often repeated take on the character of drives. We have no wholly correct basis for predicting which habits will show most intrinsic resistance to change.

Sometimes a new educational practice—e.g., a changed form of teacher's class record book or report card—arouses much resistance. After it has been established, perhaps with some persuasion and coercion, it becomes as resistant to change as was its predecessor. The familiar is preferred.

3. Primacy

The way in which the organism first successfully copes with a situation sets a pattern, which is unusually persistent. Early habits of speech may be recognized despite much effort in later life to change. A child who has several times heard a story told in certain words is likely to be annoyed if the key phrases are not repeated exactly when the story is retold. Part of the joy in familiar music is the accord between established expectations and the flow of melody and harmony. Dreams of adults are often located in the settings of childhood. Even in senility, the recent experiences fade first, and the earliest associations persist longest. All later concepts perforce build on some of the earliest generalizations.

It is often observed that teachers, despite in-service courses and supervisory efforts, continue to teach as they themselves were taught. Their image of a teacher was formed in childhood, and whenever they hear or read anything about better teaching, this is assimilated to that early and persisting concept.

4. Selective Perception and Retention

Once an attitude has been set up, a person responds to other suggestions within the framework of an established outlook. Situations may be perceived as reinforcing the original attitude when they actually are dissonant. Thus, in one famous experiment, a common stereotype associating Negroes with carrying razors led observers of a cartoon to think they had seen the razor in the hands of the African American rather than the white (Allport and Postman, 1945). Experiments with materials designed to bring about changes in attitude revealed that subjects did not hear clearly, nor remember well, communications with which they disagreed (Watson and Hartman, 1939; Levine and Murphy, 1943). It is a common observation that people usually prefer news sources, whether in print or broadcast, with which they are already in agreement (Klapper, 1960). By reading or listening to what accords with their present views; by misunderstanding communications that, if correctly received, would not be consonant with preestablished attitudes; and by conveniently forgetting any learning that would lead to uncongenial conclusions subjects successfully resist the possible impact of new evidence upon their earlier views. There are relatively few instances in which old prejudices have been changed by better information or persuasive arguments.

The thousands of teachers who are exposed in graduate courses to different philosophies of education from those the teachers are accustomed to employ may do very well at answering test questions about the new approach, but they carefully segregate in their mind the new as "theory, which, of course, would not work in the practical situation."

5. Dependence

All human beings begin life dependent upon adults who incorporate ways of behaving that were established before the newcomer arrived on the scene. Parents sustain life in the helpless infant and provide major satisfactions. The inevitable outcome is conservative. Children tend to incorporate (imitate, introject) the values, attitudes, and beliefs of those who care for them.

All teachers were once beginners in the lower grades. At that time, their teachers loomed large and influential, whether friendly or hostile. The little pupil had to conform. Later adoption of the kind of teaching the child then experienced is as natural as acceptance of a particular alphabet and number system.

There may later, in adolescence, be outbursts of rebellion and moves toward independent thought. But the typical adult still agrees far more than he or she disagrees with parents on such basic items as language, religion, politics, child-rearing, and what a school should do.

6. Superego

Freud (1922) conceived one of the basic personality functions as engaged in the enforcement of the moral standards acquired in childhood from authoritative adults. From the first ''No! No!'' said to the baby on through all the socializing efforts of parents, a code of controls is internalized. When the Oedipus complex is resolved, the child sets standards for himself corresponding to his image of the perfect and omnipotent parent. Any violation of these demanding rules is punished with a severity the energy of which is derived from the attachment to parents as this operated in the Oedipal period—age three to five.

Here, then, in the Superego, is a powerful agent serving tradition. The repressive constraints that operate—partly unconsciously—do not derive from the realities of life in the present or the preceding generation. The Superego of the child corresponds to the Superego of the parent, not to her rational conclusions based on experience. Each mother and father passes on a heritage of taboos that she or he, in childhood, acquired from ages past. An individual needs considerable ego strength to become able to cope realistically with changing life situations in disregard of the unrealistic, perfectionist demands of the Superego.

There is reason to believe that people who choose occupations in which they try to inculcate higher standards in others (clergymen, teachers, law enforcement) are persons with extra strong Superego components. They take pride in making severe demands on themselves and on others. They bitterly resist any change, which they conceive to be a relaxation of the firmest discipline and the highest expectations of perfection in performance. The influx of less able students into secondary schools and colleges has created almost intolerable conflict in teachers who still require achievement at levels few can attain.

7. Self-Distrust

As a consequence of the dependence of childhood and the stern authority of the tradition-oriented voice of the Superego, children quickly learn to distrust their own impulses. Each says, in effect, "What I would really want is bad! I should not want it!"

John Dewey, in *Human Nature and Conduct* (1922), saw the possibility of human betterment in the liberation of the creative impulses of youth. "The young are not as yet subject to the full impact of established customs. Their life of impulsive activity is vivid, flexible, experimenting, curious." What Dewey did not say is that within each young person there are powerful forces condemning and repressing any impulses that do not correspond to the established routines, standards, and institutions of society as it is and has been. The Puritan view that the enjoyable is evil gets a firm hold on children. Every clash between their desires and what adults expect of them adds an increment to each child's self-rejection: "They must be right; I must be naughty to have such terrible feelings." Thus guilt is mobilized to prevent action for change. People conclude that they are not worthy of any better life. To be "good" is to accept the *status quo ante*. Agitators and rebels speak with the voice of the evil serpent and should not be heeded.

The author, during the depth of the economic depression, found that most of a sample of unemployed men did not lay the blame for their predicament on faulty social mechanisms. Rather, they internalized the responsibility. They said, "I ought to have stayed on in school" or "It was my fault that I lost the job; I shouldn't have said what I did!" or "I should have waited to get married and have a family." Only about one in five wanted to change the economic system; the majority blamed themselves only (Watson, 1941).

Innumerable pupils, parents, teachers, and administrators have felt impulses to alter school procedures. Most of these have been stifled by a feeling suggested by the expression, "Who am I to suggest changes in what the wisdom of the past has established?"

8. Insecurity and Regression

A further obstacle to effective participation in social change is the tendency to seek security in the past. The golden age of childhood is a Paradise Lost. When life grows difficult and frustrating, individuals think with nostalgia about the happy days of the past.

The irony is that this frustration-regression sequence enters life at just the time when change would be most constructive. When old ways no longer produce the desired outcome, the sensible recourse would be to experiment with new approaches. But individuals are apt at such a time to cling even more desperately to the old and unproductive behavior patterns. They are dissatisfied with the situation, but the prospect of change arouses even more anxiety, so they seek somehow to find a road back to the old and (as they now see it) more peaceful way of life.

Demands for change in school organization and practice become acute as a result of such social changes as automation, rapid travel to other lands, or racial desegregation. The reaction of insecure teachers, administrators, and parents is, too often, to try to hold fast to the familiar or even to return to some tried-and-true fundamentals that typify the schools of the past. A candidate for state superintendent of schools in California based his successful campaign in the mid-1960s on return to the old-fashioned. The fact that California had been changing more rapidly in population, occupations, etc. than had any other state was one factor in the appeal of this program of reaction.

B. RESISTANCE TO CHANGE IN SOCIAL SYSTEMS

1. Conformity to Norms

Norms in social systems correspond to habits in individuals. They are customary and expected ways of behaving. Members of the organization demand of themselves and of other members conformity to the institutional norms. This is the behavior described by Whyte in *The Organization Man* (1956). It includes time schedules; modes of dress; forms of address to colleagues, superiors, and subordinates; indications of company loyalty; personal ambition to rise; appropriate consumption; and forms of approved participation in recreation and community life. Teachers, even more than businesspeople, have been expected to exemplify certain proper behaviors.

Norms make it possible for members of a system to work together. Each knows what to expect in the other. The abnormal or anomic is disruptive.

Because norms are shared by many participants, they cannot easily change. Above all, the usual individual cannot change them. She can get herself rejected, for deviate behavior, but the norm will persist. A laboratory experiment (Merei, 1949) showed that even a child with strong leadership qualities was required, nevertheless, to conform to the established play norms of a small group of kindergarten children. An excellent teacher who declined to submit the prescribed advance lesson plans for each week did not alter the norm; he was fired.

When one person deviates noticeably from the group norm, a sequence of events may be expected. The group will direct an increasing amount of communication toward the person, trying to alter attitude. If this fails, one after another will abandon the person as hopeless. Communication will decrease.

The person may be ignored or excluded and no longer belongs (Festinger and Thibaut, 1951).

The famous experiments, led by Lewin during the war, on altering norms of eating indicated that changes are better introduced by group decision than by expecting individuals to pioneer a practice not being used by their associates (Lewin, 1952).

The evidence indicates that if norms are to be altered, this will have to occur throughout the entire operating system. The sad fate of experimental schools and colleges (Miles, 1964) indicates the power of the larger system to impose its norms even on units that have been set apart, for a time, to operate by different standards and expectations.

2. Systemic and Cultural Coherence

The Gestalt principle that parts take on characteristics because of their relationship within the whole implies that it is difficult to change one part without affecting others. Innovations that are helpful in one area may have side effects destructive in related regions. For example, a technical change that increased the efficiency of piece-workers in a factory enabled them to earn more than supervisors were being paid, so the new technique had to be abandoned. Electronic data processing in another company altered the size and relative responsibilities of related departments, generating considerable resentment (Mann and Neff, 1961). Studying change in a city YMCA, Dimock and Sorenson (1955) concluded: "No part of institutional change is an 'island unto itself': changes in program call for changes in every other part of the institution . . . and advance in one sector cannot proceed far ahead of change in other sectors. For example, program groups cannot be changed without officer training . . . which in turn is contingent upon advisor training . . . which in turn depends upon staff reeducation. Similarly, changes in staff goals and ways of working are dependent upon administrative procedures, policies and budgets which in turn require changes in Boards and Committees." A parallel statement for school systems might indicate that a change in teacher-pupil relationships is likely to have repercussions on teacher-principal interaction, on parent-principal contacts, on pressure groups operating on the superintendent, on board member chances for reelection, and perhaps on the relationship of the local system to state or federal agencies. Any estimate of resistance that takes account only of the persons primarily and centrally concerned will be inadequate; the repercussions elsewhere may be even more influential in the survival of the innovation.

3. Vested Interests

The most obvious source of resistance is some threat to the economic or prestige interests of individuals. A school consolidation that eliminates some board members and a principal is unlikely to receive their warm support, although such cases have occurred. The most common resistance to educational improvements, which would cost money, comes from organized or unorganized taxpayers. Mort and Cornell (1941) found that desirable school innovations were most likely to be adopted by communities with high financial resources. Poverty has been—at least until the recent antipoverty program—a block to educational experimenting. This author (Watson, 1946) found likewise that YMCAs located in communities with high volume of retail sales per capita were more likely to adopt recommended new practices.

A "vested interest" may be in freedom to operate as one pleases, quite as truly as in money income or title on the door. Centralizing control of school decisions is usually unwelcome to the persons who would otherwise be making decisions in local school neighborhoods or classrooms.

Concern for school taxes and for positions on school boards is likely to center in the upper classes of the community. They are the people who have most power and influence. Newspapers and broadcasting are more accessible to them than to the underprivileged. A few powerful political or financial interests can block programs desired by a large majority of ordinary citizens. The influence of upper-class families on school policies is vividly portrayed in Hollingshead's *Elmtown's Youth* (1949).

4. The Sacrosanct

Anthropologists have observed that, within any culture, some activities are easily changed; others are highly resistant to innovation. Generally, the technology is receptive to new ideas and procedures. The greatest resistance concerns matters connected with what is held to be sacred. Some women can become managers of businesses or presidents of colleges in our male-dominated society, but they find it almost impossible to become a priest, rabbi, bishop, or pope in a conservative denomination. Translations of Scriptures into the vernacular have met strong disapproval. The ritual reading of some verses from the Bible or the recitation of a prayer is held onto with far more fervor than is spent on retention of school texts or equipment. Traditional ceremonies are apt to persist despite doubts as to their educational impact. The closer any reform comes to touching some of the taboos or rituals in the community, the more likely it is to be resisted. Introduction of improved technology in underdeveloped countries runs into formidable obstacles if it seems to impinge on religious superstitions, beliefs, or practices (Spicer, 1952).

Cultures resist almost as stubbornly alterations that enter the realm of morals and ethics. Even when few live by the traditional code, it must still be defended as "ideal" (Linton, 1945). A well-recognized illustration is the expectation of sexual continence between puberty and marriage. Kinsey may find very few youths who practice it, but schools, churches, and courts must operate as if the prescription were unquestionable.

There is a clear connection between the operation of the Superego in individuals and the taboos persisting in the culture. Both uphold impossibly high standards and react punitively to recognized infractions of the excessive demands.

5. Rejection of "Outsiders"

Most change comes into institutions from "outside." Griffiths, studying change in school systems, concluded, "The major impetus for change in organizations is from outside" (in Miles, 1964, p. 431).

Few psychological traits of human beings are so universal as that of suspicion and hostility toward strange outsiders. Kohler (1922) observed this kind of behavior among his chimpanzees on the island of Tenerife many years ago. Wood (1934) has explored, across different cultures, the mixture of curiosity and antagonism toward foreigners. A typical attack on any new proposal is that "it doesn't fit our local conditions." Struggles to improve labor and race relations have commonly been discounted as inspired by "outside agitators" or "atheistic Communists." Research, development, and engineering units are familiar with the way in which a new project is hampered if it is seen as NIH (not invented here).

The history of experimental demonstration schools is that they were often observed but seldom replicated ("This is fine, but it wouldn't work in our system"). Differences in class of children, financial support, equipment, and tradition helped to rationalize the resistance. The genius of agricultural agents a century ago led them away from model farms run by state colleges and toward demonstration projects within the local neighborhood. Farmers accepted what was being done within their county when they could not import new practices from far away.

A major problem in introducing social change is to secure enough local initiative and participation so the enterprise will not be vulnerable as a foreign importation.

SUMMARY OF RECOMMENDATIONS

Our observations on sources of resistance within persons and within institutions can be summarized in some concise principles. These are not absolute laws but are based on generalizations that are usually true and likely to be pertinent. The recommendations are here reorganized to fit three headings: (1) Who brings the change? (2) What kind of change succeeds? and (3) How is it best done?

A. Who brings the change?

Resistance will be less if administrators, teachers, board members, and community leaders feel that the project is their own—not one devised and operated by outsiders.

Resistance will be less if the project clearly has wholehearted support from top officials of the system.

B. What kind of change?

Resistance will be less if participants see the change as reducing rather than increasing their present burdens.

Resistance will be less if the project accords with values and ideals that have long been acknowledged by participants.

Resistance will be less if the program offers the kind of *new* experience that interests participants.

Resistance will be less if participants feel that their autonomy and their security are not threatened.

C. Procedures in instituting change

Resistance will be less if participants have joined in diagnostic efforts leading them to agree on what the basic problem is and to feel its importance.

Resistance will be less if the project is adopted by consensual group decision.

Resistance will be reduced if proponents are able to empathize with opponents, to recognize valid objections, and to take steps to relieve unnecessary fears.

Resistance will be reduced if it is recognized that innovations are likely to be misunderstood and misinterpreted, and if provision is made for feedback of perceptions of the project and for further clarification as needed.

Resistance will be reduced if participants experience acceptance, support, trust, and confidence in their relations with one another.

Resistance will be reduced if the project is kept open to revision and reconsideration if experience indicates that changes would be desirable.

References

Allport, G. W. *Personality: A Psychological Interpretation*. New York: Holt, Rinehart and Winston, Inc., 1937.

Allport, G. W., and L. J. Postman. The basic psychology of rumor. *Transactions of N. Y. Academy of Sciences*, Series II, 1945, 8: 61–81.

Cannon, W. B. *Wisdom of the Body*. New York: W. W. Norton & Company, Inc., 1932.

Dewey, J. *Human Nature and Conduct*. New York: Holt, Rinehart and Winston, Inc., 1922.

Dimock, H. S., and R. Sorenson. *Designing Education in Values: A Case Study in Institutional Change*. New York: Association Press, 1955.

Edwards, L. P. *The Natural History of Revolution*. Chicago: University of Chicago Press, 1927.

Festinger, L., and J. Thibaut. Interpersonal communication in small groups. *J. Abn. Soc. Psychol.*, 1951, 46: 92–99.

Freud, S. *Beyond the Pleasure Principle*. London: Hogarth Press, Ltd., 1922.

Hebb, D. O. *A Textbook of Psychology*. Philadelphia: W. B. Saunders Company, 1958.

Hollingshead, A. B. *Elmtown's Youth*. New York: John Wiley & Sons, Inc., 1949.

Klapper, J. T. *Effects of Mass Communication*. New York: The Free Press, 1960.

Kohler, W. Zur psychologie des shimpanzen. *Psychol, Forsehung*, 1922, 1: 1–45.

Levine, M. M., and G. Murphy. The learning and forgetting of controversial material. *J. Abn. Soc. Psychol.*, 1943, 38: 507–517.

Lewin, K. *Field Theory in Social Science*. New York: Harper & Row, 1951.

Lewin, K. Group decision and social change. In G. E. Swanson, T. M. Newcomb, and E. L. Hartley. *Readings in Social Psychology*. New York: Holt, Rinehart and Winston, Inc., 1952, pp. 463–473.

Lilly, J. C. Mental effects of reduction of ordinary levels of physical stimuli on intact, healthy persons. Symposium on Research Techniques in Schizophrenia. Psychiatric Research Reports 5 (June): 1–9, 1956.

Linton, R. *The Cultural Background of Personality*. New York: Appleton-Century-Crofts, 1945.

Mann, F. C., and F. W. Neff. *Managing Major Change in Organizations*. Ann Arbor, Mich: Foundation for Research on Human Behavior, 1961.

Merei, F. Group leadership and institutionalization. *Human Rela.*, 1949, 2: 23–39.

Miles, M. B. (Ed), *Innovation in Education*. New York: Bureau of Publications, Teachers College, Columbia University, 1964.

Mort, P. R., and F. G. Cornell. *American Schools in Transition*. New York: Bureau of Publications, Teachers College, Columbia University, 1941.

Raup, R. B. *Complacency: The Foundation of Human Behavior*. Crowell-Collier and Macmillan, Inc., 1925.

Spicer, E. H. *Human Problems in Technological Change*. New York: Russell Sage Foundation, 1952.

Stephens, J. A. *The Psychology of Classroom Learning*. New York: Holt, Rinehart and Winston, Inc., 1965.

Thomas, W. I., and F. Znaniecki. *The Polish Peasant in Europe and America: Monograph of an Immigrant Group*. Chicago: Univ. of Chicago Press, 1918–20.

Watson, G. *A Comparison of "Adaptable" Versus "Laggard."* New York: YMCA Association Press, 1946.

Watson, G. What makes radicals? *Common Sense*, 1941, 10: 7–9.

Watson, W. S., Jr., and G. W. Hartman. The rigidity of a basic attitudinal frame. *J. Abn. Socl. Psychol.*, 1939, 34: 314–335.

Whyte, W. H., Jr. *The Organization Man*. New York: Simon and Schuster, Inc., 1956.

Wood, M. M. *The Stranger*. New York: Columbia University Press, 1934.

CHAPTER TWENTY-TWO

A Theory of Psychological Reactance

Jack W. Brehm (1966)

Freedom of behavior is a pervasive and important aspect of human life. People are continually surveying their internal and external states of affairs and making decisions about what they will do, how they will do it, and when they will do it. They consider their wants and needs, the dangers and benefits available in their surroundings, and the ways in which they can accomplish various ends. This is not to say that behavior is always freely selected. It will frequently be true that individuals perform given acts without quite knowing why, and it will also be true that they perform acts because they knew they were not free to do otherwise. Nevertheless, most of the time people will feel that they are relatively free to engage in a variety of different behaviors and that they can select among these as they please.

There is good reason for the belief that one has freedom of action. Objectively there frequently are multiple possibilities, and subjectively there are frequently multiple needs, none of which demands immediate gratification. Thus, subjectively at least, it seems that one scans the possibilities and their effects, and then decides which of the several possibilities to take. Whether or not a person "really" has freedom, he can and almost certainly will believe that he has.

The freedom to choose when and how to behave is potentially beneficial. To the extent a person is aware of her needs and the behaviors necessary to satisfy those needs, and providing she has the appropriate freedom, she can choose behaviors so as to maximize need satisfaction. An individual, for example, who felt more thirsty than hungry and who, at the moment, was free to go either to a soda fountain or a restaurant could satisfy the dominant need by choosing to go to the soda fountain. Without the freedom to select behaviors appropriate to various needs, the satisfaction of needs would be a more haphazard affair, which would not only fail to maximize need satisfaction but could frequently result in extreme deprivation, pain, and even death. Given some minimal level of valid knowledge about oneself and the environment, freedom to choose among different behavioral possibilities will generally help one to survive and thrive.

It is reasonable to assume, then, that if a person's behavioral freedom is reduced or threatened with reduction, the person will become motivationally aroused. This arousal would presumably be directed against any further loss of freedom, and it would also be directed toward the reestablishment of whatever freedom had already been lost or threatened. Since this hypothetical motivational state is in response to the reduction (or threatened reduction) of one's potential for acting, and conceptually may be considered a counterforce, it will be called ''psychological reactance.'' The purpose of this chapter, then, is to delineate a theory of psychological reactance and to report and examine relevant evidence.

Before presenting a formal theoretical statement, it may be well to consider two hypothetical examples of the arousal and reduction of reactance. Picture first Mr. John Smith, who normally plays golf on Sunday afternoons, although occasionally he spends Sunday afternoon watching television or puttering around his workshop. The important point is that Smith always spends Sunday afternoon doing whichever of these three things he prefers; he is free to choose which he will do. Now consider a specific Sunday morning on which Smith's wife announces that Smith will have to play golf that afternoon since she has invited several of her friends to the house for a party. Mr. Smith's freedom is threatened with reduction in several ways: (1) he cannot watch television, (2) he cannot putter in his workshop, and (3) he must (Mrs. Smith says) play golf. According to the present view, Smith would be motivationally aroused to reestablish these threatened freedoms. We might therefore expect to hear him protest that there was an important television program he wanted to watch and that he had planned to do some special work in his shop. We might also expect to hear him say that he is tired of golf, that the course is not in good condition, and so forth. If the amount of reactance aroused were great, we might indeed expect Smith to spend the afternoon watching television, perhaps with the volume turned unusually high.

For a second hypothetical example, let us consider a person who is looking for a pack of cigarettes, and let us suppose that this person normally smokes Camels but also occasionally smokes Kools. Let us further suppose that on this occasion she would prefer to have Camels, and that she locates a vending machine that contains both Camels and Kools. After depositing the necessary amount of money in the machine, she is just about to reach out to pull the lever for Camels when the machine dispenses a pack of Camels. Since the machine could not have divined this preference, the individual's freedom to select her own brand has been preempted and she should experience reactance. We might expect this person to find suddenly that she is not so eager to have Camels, that if she now had her choice she might well select Kools or some other kind, and that she is displeased with vending machines. She might even put more money in the machine in order to select a pack of Kools.

It is important to note that neither of these hypothetical examples involves simple frustration, that is, blocking of the person from a preferred goal. Mr. Smith was likely to play golf anyway, and we may even make it a condition of the example that he intended to play golf prior to his wife's announcing that he had to. Similarly, the woman seeking Camels received just what she was looking for. But in both cases, according to the present proposal, these people should be motivationally aroused to resist doing or taking what they originally intended. We shall return to this point again. For the present, since a better picture has been gained through these examples of somewhat trivial events of what is meant by reactance, let us turn to a formal statement of the determinants and consequences of psychological reactance.

THE THEORY

It is assumed that for a given person at a given time there is a set of behaviors any one of which the person could engage in either at the moment or at some time in the future. This set may be called the individual's "free behaviors." Free behaviors include only acts that are realistically possible: smoking a cigarette could be a free behavior, while walking to the moon could not. Behaviors may become free in a variety of ways. One may become free to spend company money for lunches by formal agreement between oneself and the company; a person may acquire the freedom to read a book by learning how to read; one may feel free to spit on the walk because one always has done so; and one may feel free to vote because the right is guaranteed by law. In general, we may say that for specified behaviors to be free, the individual must have the relevant physical and psychological abilities to engage in them and must know, by experience, by general custom, or by formal agreement, that he or she may engage in them.

It should be noted that the concept of "behavior" is intended to include any conceivable act. A behavior might consist of selecting a choice alternative, thinking that Roosevelt was a good president, or not watching television. More generally, behaviors may be characterized as "what one does (or doesn't)," "how one does something," or "when one does something."

It will not always be clear either to an objective observer or to the individual whether or not he or she has the freedom to engage in a given behavior. This can happen because the individual has inadequate relevant information, as when he or she lacks experience in attempting to engage in the behavior in question and does not know any formal relevant rules. Lack of clarity about freedom can also occur because there is conflicting information. A jaywalker, for example, may feel free to jaywalk because he frequently does so but he may not feel free to jaywalk because to do so is illegal. While these unclarities about when a behavior is or is not free may constitute serious difficulty for the analysis of practical problems, they do not preclude clear and adequate experimental tests of the theory, for it is possible to construct situations in which specified behavioral freedoms are relatively unequivocal.

Given that a person has a set of free behaviors, she will experience reactance whenever any of those behaviors is eliminated or threatened with elimination. That is, if a person felt free to engage in behaviors A, B, and C, and then learned that she could not engage in, for example, A, she would experience reactance.

The magnitude of reactance is a direct function of (1) the importance of the free behaviors that are eliminated or threatened, (2) the proportion of free behaviors eliminated or threatened, and (3) where there is only a threat of elimination of free behaviors, the magnitude of that threat. Let us consider each of these determinants in somewhat greater detail.

1. Given that a certain free behavior has been threatened or eliminated, *the more important that free behavior is to the individual, the greater will be the magnitude of reactance.* The importance of a given behavior is a direct function of the unique instrumental value that the behavior has for the satisfaction of needs, multiplied by the actual or potential maximum magnitude of those needs. By unique is meant that no other behavior in the individual's repertoire of behaviors would satisfy the same need or set of needs. In other words, the importance of a free behavior derives from its necessity for the reduction of potentially important needs. However, it is *not* necessary for the relevant needs to be of great magnitude at all times for the free behavior to have high importance at all times. It is only necessary that the individual believe he or she *might* have the needs in question. This may become more clear if we recall the example of Mr. Smith, who was told by his wife to go play golf, and who according to the present view should therefore experience increased motivation to watch television or putter in his workshop. It was noted then, and may be reiterated here, that Smith may actually have preferred to play golf prior to his wife's pronouncement and, further, he may not, on that particular Sunday, have had an active interest in watching television or puttering. But to the extent that he believes he *might* have wanted to do either of these things, the freedom to engage in them is important and the loss of that freedom should arouse reactance.

1a. The magnitude of reactance is also a direct function of the relative importance of the eliminated or threatened behavioral freedom compared to the importance of other freedoms of the moment. Considering all of a person's free behaviors at a given time, and holding constant the absolute importance of the one that is eliminated or threatened, its relative importance increases as the absolute importance of the other freedoms decreases.

In illustration, let us suppose that a person has rated several items on an equal interval scale where 0 equals no attraction and 100 equals very high attraction, and that the items A, B, etc., have received the following ratings: A = 10, B = 20, C = 30, X = 70, and Z = 90. Here the absolute attractiveness of X, Y, and Z is greater than that of A, B, and C, and if a person had the choice alternatives X, Y, and Z, and then lost Z, he would experience more reactance than if he had the alternatives A, B, and C and then lost C. But if the absolute attractiveness of the eliminated alternative is held constant, then its relative attractiveness will determine the magnitude of reactance. If the individual had the choice alternatives A, B, and C and then lost B, he would experience more reactance than if he had the alternatives A, B, and X and then lost B. When one's choice alternatives are an orange, an apple, and a pear, he should experience a noticeable degree of reactance when someone swipes the apple; but when the choice alternatives are an orange, and apple, and an automobile, one will not care much about the loss of the apple.

2. Given the individual's set of free behaviors, *the greater the proportion eliminated or threatened with elimination, the greater will be the magnitude of reactance.* If a person believed herself free to engage in behaviors A, B, C, and D, all of which have some importance, then the elimination of both A and B would create more reactance than the elimination of either A or B alone. Or, given that behavior A is eliminated, if the original set of free behaviors consisted of A and B there will be more reactance than if the original set consisted of A, B, C, and D.

3. Given that an important free behavior has been threatened with elimination, *the greater the threat, the greater will be the magnitude of reactance.* A threat becomes greater as the likelihood increases that it could be carried out. A threat of elimination of a free behavior will frequently be located in a social source, i.e., another person. When the threat is social, the question of how great the threat is will center on the formal and informal relationships between the threatener and the person threatened. Those who have equal or greater amounts of social power than oneself can issue threats of relatively great magnitude to one's own free behaviors, while those with less power would be relatively unable to muster serious threats.

3a. When a person's free behavior, A, is eliminated or threatened with elimination, there may also be the implication that other free behaviors, say B and C, or the same behavior on future occasions, A_2 and A_3, will also be eliminated. That is, by the loss of a single free behavior there may be by implication a threat of elimination of other free behaviors either in the present or in the future. This proposition assumes, of course, that the free behaviors in question are ordered such that the loss of one implies the loss of others. The ordering may be as simple as membership in a class. For example, if a person were informed not to chew gum while at work, the person might easily imagine that other similar behaviors, such as smoking or sucking on candies, would also be eliminated. Or the dimension of implication might be such that elimination of a given behavior would imply the loss of some but not all related behaviors. Imagine, for example, a set of perquisites that correlate with job status at a hypothetical college. Assistant professors have unlimited library privileges, associate professors have the same plus an office all to themselves, and full professors have these two advantages plus a graduate assistant to help them in their work. Under these conditions, if a full professor were informed that she would no longer have an office to herself, she should also feel that her having a graduate assistant was in jeopardy though she would presumably feel there was relatively little threat of losing library privileges.

3b. Just as a free behavior may be threatened by virtue of elimination of or threat to another free behavior, so a free behavior may be threatened by the elimination of or a threat to another person's free behavior. The implication in this case relates the observed person to oneself; if the loss of a free behavior to an observed person could just as well happen to oneself, then one's own free behavior is threatened. When an observed person loses a free behavior similar to a free behavior for oneself, the greater is the implication that the loss could as easily have happened to oneself, and the greater will be the magnitude of the reactance. If, for example, co-equal secretaries worked together in an office and normally felt free to go to the water cooler for a drink whenever they felt like it, the elimination of this freedom for one should threaten the same freedom for others, leading to their experiencing reactance.

Justification and Legitimacy

If Mr. Smith says to Mrs. Brown "You cannot have Betty for babysitting this evening" when Mrs. Brown might have wanted Betty, then Brown should experience reactance. It will be obvious, however, that Brown's reaction will be affected by the justification and/or legitimacy of Smith's interference. If Smith adds that Betty's mother has gone to the hospital for an emergency operation, thus justifying the restriction, Brown will not show a strong negative reaction. If Betty is a young teenager and Smith happens to be her father, then Smith can legitimately control Betty's activities and again Brown is not likely to show a strong negative reaction.

Justification and legitimacy, however, are complicated variables from the point of view of reactance theory. They tend, on the one hand, to affect the magnitude or reactance aroused by the loss of a freedom, and they tend on the other hand to affect restraints against the effects of reactance. Let us consider these in turn.

When person A tells person B what to do, and thereby threatens a specific freedom of the latter, there may or may not be further freedoms threatened by implication, as we have already seen. One possible effect of justification is to limit the threat to a specific behavior or set of behaviors. So if Smith says that he is interfering with Brown's expectations because of a personal emergency, this keeps Brown from imagining that Smith will likely interfere on future occasions as well. Fewer of Brown's behavioral freedoms have been threatened. In a similar way, legitimacy may indicate the set of behaviors threatened since there will be a general presumption that illegitimate interference with one's freedoms is less likely to occur. There is an additional implication in the notion of legitimacy of behavioral restriction that one's freedom was equivocal anyway. In the above example, if Betty is a young teenager, then Brown could never have been sure of her freedom to have Betty babysit since she is normally subject to restrictions from her parents. Conversely, an illegitimate attempt to restrict one's freedom may be capable of arousing a great deal of reactance since it may imply a threat to a large number of free behaviors. If Smith is *not* the father of Betty and has no more legitimate control over her than does Brown, then Smith's attempted interference (without justification) also carries the implication that Smith may well attempt similar interferences on future occasions. From Brown's point of view, if Smith gets away with this, what can't he get away with?

Although justification and legitimacy may be seen as affecting the magnitude of reactance aroused by a given elimination or threat, lack of justification and legitimacy are not necessary conditions for the occurrence of reactance. A loss of freedom, no matter how well justified, should still create reactance. And if we bear in mind that legitimacy (formal rules, agreement, etc.) is only one of several sources of freedom, we can also say that a loss of freedom, no matter how legitimate, can also result in reactance.

How a person responds to reactance will doubtless be affected by both justification and legitimacy. In general, these conditions will create restraints against direct attempts at restoration of freedom. For this reason, these conditions will tend to give rise to attempts at indirect restoration of freedom, such as through behavioral or social implication, when that kind of restoration is possible.

In the above discussion we have attempted to show that although justification and legitimacy are powerful determinants of the magnitude of reactance, their total effects are complicated. They are therefore not particularly useful tools for the demonstration of reactance effects in research and they have not been employed in the research reported in the volume in which this chapter originally appeared. Rather, our attempts have been to test reactance hypotheses with justification and legitimacy held constant.

THE EFFECTS OF REACTANCE

Psychological reactance is conceived as a motivational state directed toward the reestablishment of the free behaviors that have been eliminated or threatened with elimination. Generally, then, a person who experiences reactance will be motivated to attempt to regain the lost or threatened freedoms by whatever methods are available and appropriate. It should be helpful, of course, to be somewhat more specific about the effects of reactance, and in the following paragraphs we shall indicate several distinguishable possibilities.

The Phenomenology of Reactance

Although there is no assumption that a person will necessarily be aware of reactance, it should be true that when he is, he will feel an increased amount of self-direction in regard to his own behavior. That is, he will feel that he can do what he wants, that he does not have to do what he doesn't want, and that at least in regard to the freedom in question, he is the sole director of his own behavior. If the magnitude of reactance is relatively great, the individual may be aware of hostile and aggressive feelings as well. In this connection it may be noted that reactance can be an "uncivilized" motivational state since it frequently is directed against the social acts of others. For this reason it would not be surprising to find that a person in whom reactance has been aroused would tend to deny that he was either motivated to restore freedom or upset, and he might even convince himself of this. This tendency to defend against reactance can be expected to extend to nonverbal behavior as well. As will be seen, the studies in support of reactance theory have tended to use measures that do not require people to be uncivilized, or they have measured relatively subtle uncivilized responses.

When reactance does not lead to "uncivilized" or antisocial behavior, it should tend to result in some awareness of one's increased motivation to have what was lost or threatened. That is, a person's desire for a given behavior, A, should increase as a consequence of its being eliminated, or threatened with elimination, from the set of free behaviors. Correspondingly, behavior A should appear to increase in attractiveness.

Direct Reestablishment of Freedom

The greater the magnitude of reactance, the more will the individual attempt to reestablish the freedom that has been lost or threatened. However, attempts at reestablishment can be expected to occur only to the extent that there is a realistic possibility of succeeding. In general, reactance will result in attempts at restoration of freedom when there is some equivocality about the elimination of the free behavior in question, or, in other words, where there has only been a threat of elimination. When the loss of a free behavior is irreversible, as when one's left arm has been amputated or one has been told to do something by a person with immense power over oneself, there will not normally be attempts at direct restoration.

Direct reestablishment of freedom means engaging in that behavior which one has learned one cannot or should not engage in. If behavior A has been free and one is then told not to engage in A, the resultant reactance will lead the individual to engage in A. If one's set of free behaviors consisted of A and B and one were then told to do A, the direct restoration of freedom would consist of doing B.

Where freedom is threatened by social pressure, reactance will lead one to resist that pressure. If an habitual smoker, for example, were told by a friend that he should stop smoking, the resultant reactance would operate against the otherwise persuasive effects of the friend's advice. Continuing to smoke at the same rate or at a greater rate would reestablish the freedom to smoke. Quite obviously, however, the direct social influence might be greater than the magnitude of reactance, in which case a compromise response of reduced smoking would occur.

Reestablishment of Freedom by Implication

When there are restraints against the direct reestablishment of freedom, attempts at reestablishment by implication will occur where possible. Consider again, for example, the person who has learned she can no longer chew gum on the job. She can reestablish her freedom by engaging in other behaviors of the same class, e.g., sucking on candy or smoking, or better yet, she can engage in what she would assume to be even less acceptable behaviors such as putting on lipstick, combing her hair, or eating candy bars.

Freedom can also be reestablished by social implication. If a person has lost a free behavior through social threat, then the engagement in a similar free behavior by another person like himself and "in the same boat" will tend to reestablish his own freedom. In terms of our earlier example of the co-equals who felt free to go for a drink of water whenever they wanted, if A has been told she can no longer do this and B's freedom has thereby been threatened by implication, the freedom of A will be reestablished by implication if B proceeds to have a drink as he pleases. We might plausibly expect that when possible, one of the effects of reactance will be for a person to try to get someone else to engage in a threatened or eliminated behavior.

The Role of Importance

As has been stated, the magnitude of reactance aroused by the loss of a given freedom is directly proportional to the importance of that freedom to the individual. But though importance therefore helps to determine the amount of reactance aroused, it does not serve in the reduction of reactance. This is because reactance is defined *not* simply as an unpleasant tension that the individual will reduce in any way he can, such as reducing the importance of any freedom he happens to lose, but rather as a motivational state with a specific direction, namely, the recovery of freedom. Indeed, the only reasonable expectation about the effect of reactance on the importance of a lost free behavior is that importance may increase.

Voluntary Versus Involuntary Elimination

Although the hypothetical examples used to illustrate the theory and the research to be reported all concern eliminations of freedom or threats that are involuntary, this is not meant to imply that threats and eliminations must be involuntary in order to arouse reactance. The reason that voluntary eliminations or threats have not been used in examples and research is that they involve a decision process, that is, a giving up of one or more alternatives in order to select something, which in turn would involve various conflict type and postdecisional psychological processes. Reactance theory may eventually have something of interest to say about conflict and postdecisional processes, but it would seem premature to attempt such articulation here in view of the current theories that deal with these processes (e.g., Festinger, 1957; Janis, 1959), and in view of the absence of relevant data.

RELATED CONCEPTS

The notion that people will be motivated to reestablish freedom that is threatened or eliminated is probably not new, but it has not been utilized in current experimental research in psychology. For this reason we have tried to show in our examples that this theoretical formulation deals with a special set of problems and is not to be identified with various theories dealing with somewhat similar problems such as frustration, social power, etc. Nevertheless, there are theoretical concepts related to reactance and it may help the reader to locate the present theory if these related concepts are indicated.

Although theories concerning frustration and aggression (e.g., Dollard, Doob, Miller, Mowrer, and Sears, 1939) are peripherally relevant since they deal with the blocking of goal attainment, which will sometimes also involve elimination of freedom, the most relevant concepts are those that have to do with social power. French and Raven (1959), for example, distinguish between ''resisting forces'' and ''opposing forces'' as factors that operate against positive social influence. Their definition of resisting forces as motivation instigated by the inducing force but opposite in direction is conceptually similar to the reactance formulation. However, the bases they suggest for the instigation of resisting forces are coercive measures to obtain compliance, and especially illegitimate coercion. It is only with regard to coercive inducing forces, then, that there is a close parallel between the approach of French and Raven and that of reactance theory.

Other views of social power, of course, would also tend to be relevant. For example, the analysis of power and counterpower by Thibault and Kelley (1959) could in part be translated into terms of freedom, freedom reduction, and ways of reestablishing freedom. At the same time, one fundamental difference between their approach and reactance theory is that they do not posit a motivation to gain or recover power but rather concern themselves with the reward-cost outcomes of various kinds of power relationships.

The concepts of "personal weight" and "weight reduction" (Horwitz, 1958) seem particularly relevant and close to reactance theory. Personal weight is defined as the expected power a person has in a given social relationship. When two people disagree, the legitimate outcome of the disagreement is a function of their weighted desires. When the actual outcome deviates from the legitimate outcome there is the implication that the disfavored member's weight has been reduced. Horwitz explicitly assumes that if the disfavored person does not redefine what is legitimate, the person will generate a tension system for restoring power to its expected level. As may be seen, this formulation is quite similar to reactance theory, where personal eliminations of or threats to freedom are concerned. It is obvious, of course, that the concept of personal weight was not formulated to handle interpersonal events. A second point worth noting is that although enhancement of personal weight is assumed by Horwitz to be satisfying, there is no assumption in reactance theory about reactions to increases in freedom where there has been no prior reduction.

The intention of this brief discussion of related concepts is to indicate the kinds of theoretical conceptions to which it is related, not to explore these conceptions and relationships exhaustively. There is other relevant literature, such as Heider's discussion of "retribution" (1958), but this review should suffice to locate reactance theory among previous theoretical ideas.

TESTING THE THEORY

It should be clear from the above presentation that reactance will frequently occur in response to restrictions or threats thereof imposed by social entities, and that the general effect of reactance is to produce tendencies to oppose the actual or threatened restrictions. That is, some kind of force is exerted upon a person and this gives rise to reactance, which may be seen as a second force opposing the first. This opposition of forces complicates the testing of the theory since it makes necessary that one somehow partial out the effects of the instigating force in order to detect the effects of the reactance.

To illustrate this problem more concretely, let us imagine a person who has put a coin in a vending machine and is now trying to decide whether to take candy bar A or candy bar B. Let us further imagine that a stranger then walks up and says, "Take A." This example will be recognized as a typical social influence situation in which a "persuasive communication" has been transmitted from a communicator to a communicatee. But according to reactance theory the chooser's freedom may be threatened by the attempted social influence; the more pressure is put on the person to comply, the more the freedom not to select A and to select B is threatened. Since freedom may be reestablished by selecting B (doing the opposite of what was suggested) it may be predicted that the greater the magnitude of reactance aroused, the greater will be the chooser's tendency to select B. But with the importance of the freedom to select B held constant and the magnitude of reactance aroused, the greater will be the chooser's tendency to select B. But with the importance of the freedom to select B held constant, the magnitude of reactance should be a direct function of the pressure to comply with the influence attempt. That is, as the pressure to comply increases, the pressure not to comply also increases and the resultant effect on the individual's final response is difficult to predict. In addition, where the magnitude of reactance is less than the pressure to comply, the individual will do what is suggested but less enthusiastically than if no reactance were experienced. Unfortunately, any decreases in the resultant strength or enthusiasm of compliance could be due to *resistance* against compliance just as well as to a *motive* against compliance, and resistance might easily occur independently of reactance. To demonstrate only resistance to compliance, then, will generally be more equivocal evidence for reactance than to demonstrate noncompliance, e.g., doing the opposite of what is suggested or "boomerang" attitude change. Thus, one general difficulty in testing for reactance effects from social pressure is that the magnitude of reactance must somehow be made greater than the pressures that give rise to the reactance.

In addition, as the reader has probably noticed the above social influence situation is nowhere nearly as simple as we have assumed. For the chooser may imagine that the attempted influence is because the communicator wants B for herself (and therefore B is better than A), or, accepting the communication as an indication that the communicator prefers A, the chooser may decide he does not want to be like someone who gives unsolicited advice and he would therefore tend to choose B. So even if it could be shown in this relatively simple situation that people would do the opposite of what was suggested to them, that in itself would not yield completely unequivocal evidence in support of reactance theory.

The problems are not altogether eliminated by testing the theory in impersonal situations. This may be seen if we recall the earlier example of the individual who wanted a pack of Camel cigarettes. In that case, after the money had been placed in the vending machine, a pack of Camels was dispensed without the individual's having a chance to make her selection. Although there should be no imputation of motives or preferences to the machine, psychological processes other than reactance can still occur and obscure the effects of reactance, or make interpretation difficult. Specifically, the individual has invested money in the machine and has been stuck with the pack of Camels regardless of any reactance she may experience. Because of her investment and the subsequent commitment to the pack of Camels, she may be resistant to derogating Camel cigarettes, as reactance would lead her to do. Similarly, if a person were about to choose one from several attractive choice alternatives and suddenly discovered that for quite impersonal reasons one was no longer available, one would be impelled by reactance to want that even more, but at the same time might find it painful to want something one clearly could not have.

In summary, the testing of reactance hypotheses is relatively complicated and difficult. Nevertheless, we hope to show that not only are there interesting implications of reactance theory, but also that relatively unequivocal tests can be made.

SUMMARY

The theory stated in the preceding pages holds that a person who feels free to engage in a given behavior will experience psychological reactance if that freedom is eliminated or threatened with elimination. Psychological reactance is defined as a motivational state directed toward the reestablishment of the threatened or eliminated freedom, and it should manifest itself in increased desire to engage in the relevant behavior and actual attempts to engage in it. Basically, the magnitude of reactance is a direct function of (1) the importance of the freedom that is eliminated or threatened, and (2) the proportion of free behaviors eliminated or threatened.

References

Dollard, J., Doob, L. W., Miller, N. E., Mowrer, O. H., and Sears, R. R. *Frustration and Aggression*. New Haven: Yale University Press, 1939.

Festinger, L. *A Theory of Cognitive Dissonance*. Stanford: Stanford University Press, 1957.

French, J.R.P., Jr., and Raven, B. The Bases of Power. In D. Cartwright (Ed.), *Studies in Social Power*. Ann Arbor: University of Michigan Press, 1959.

Heider, F. *The Psychology of Interpersonal Relations*. New York: Wiley, 1958.

Horwitz, M. The Veridicality of Liking and Disliking. In R. Tagiuri and L. Petrullo (Eds.), *Person Perception and Interpersonal Behavior*. Stanford: Stanford University Press, 1958.

Janis, I. L. Motivational Factors in the Resolution of Decisional Conflicts. In M. R. Jones (Ed.), *Nebraska Symposium of Motivation*. Lincoln: University of Nebraska Press, 1959.

Thibault, J. W., and Kelley, H. H. *The Social Psychology of Groups*. New York: Wiley, 1959.

INDIVIDUAL RESPONSE TO CHANGE

CHAPTER TWENTY-FOUR

Managing Organizational Transitions

William Bridges (1986)

During a presentation on organizational transition to the management team of a large aerospace corporation, a *New Yorker* cartoon was used as a handout. The cartoon showed a heavy man slouching in an overstuffed chair; his despairing wife was saying, "If Coca-Cola can change after all these years, why can't you?"

It was a nice summary of a complex and often forgotten idea: that things can and do change quickly, but that people do not—even though they are under strong pressure to do so. But events sabotaged the presentation: the day it was made, morning papers carried the story of the decision to bring back the old Coke. Such is the fate of anyone who tries to work with change!

Social and technological change is an old story in America; in some ways it is *the* American story. A hundred fifty years ago the French author Alexis de Tocqueville noted in his diary:

> Born often under another sky, placed in the middle of an always moving scene, himself driven by the irresistible torrent which draws all about him, the American has no time to tie himself to anything, he grows accustomed only to change, and ends by regarding it as the natural state of man. He feels the need of it, more he loves it; for the instability, instead of meaning disaster to him, seems to give birth only to miracles all about him.

The ability and willingness to change have always been prerequisites for taking part in the American Dream. In the Old World respect came from a valuable heritage, and any change from that norm had to be justified. In America, however, the status quo was no more than the temporary product of past changes, and it was the *resistance to change* that demanded an explanation. A failure to change with the times was more than just a private misfortune; it was a socially and organizationally subversive condition. This attitude still persists in America, particularly in the corporate world.

Change in the current corporate landscape is the rule rather than the exception. The general economy expands and contracts and everyone adjusts accordingly, with some individuals benefiting and others suffering. Foreign competition undermines the domestic auto industry, setting in motion a domino chain of effects that reaches far down into the industrial economy as a whole. Office computers and assembly line robotics make new procedures advantageous, and traditional offices and production lines are changed to take advantage of them. The government regulates some industries and deregulates others, and the affected companies respond by struggling to change their tactics, policies, and pricing. Government agencies themselves are buffeted by change as appropriations are cut and citizen concerns become more insistent; like all other parts of the organizational world, they change in order to cope with change.

It is clear that our corporations, nonprofit institutions, and public agencies need to change; what is less clear are the stages that individuals go through in the process of change. "The most critical problem executives have is that they don't understand the powerful impact of change on people," says Harry Levinson, the industrial psychologist. Like the rest of us, executives have been wise about the mechanics of change and stupid about the dynamics of transition. That stupidity is dooming many of their change efforts to failure.

THE DIFFERENCE BETWEEN CHANGE AND TRANSITION

Since *change* and *transition* are often used interchangeably, let me clarify the difference between them. *Change* happens when something starts or stops, or when something that used to happen in one way starts happening in another. It happens at a particular time, or in several stages at different times. *Organizational change* is structural, economic, technological, or demographic, and it can be planned and managed in a more or less rational model: move Activity A to Section B and close Section C, start up automated production in Department D, issue bonds to raise money to open Branch E, and so forth.

Transition, on the other hand, is a three-part psychological process that extends over a long period of time and cannot be planned or managed by the same rational formulae that work with *change*. There are three phases that people in transition go through:

1. *They have to let go of the old situation and* (what is more difficult) *of the old identity that went with it*. No one can begin a new role or have a new purpose if that person has not let go of the old role or purpose first. Whether

people are moved or promoted, outplaced or reassigned, they have to let go of who they were and where they have been if they are to make a successful transition. A great deal of what we call resistance to change is really difficulty with the first phase of transition.

2. *They have to go through the "neutral zone" between their old reality and a new reality that may still be very unclear.* In this no-man's-land in time, everything feels unreal. It is a time of loss and confusion, a time when hope alternates with despair and new ideas alternate with a sense of meaninglessness, a time when the best one can do sometimes is to go through the motions. But it is also the time when the real reorientation that is at the heart of transition is taking place. Thoreau wrote that "corn grows in the night," and the neutral zone is the nighttime of transition.

3. *They have to make a new beginning, a beginning that is much more than the relatively simple "new start" required in a change.* The new beginning may involve developing new competencies, establishing new relationships, becoming comfortable with new policies and procedures, constructing new plans for the future, and learning to think in accordance with new purposes and priorities. Traditional societies called this phase "being reborn," and such societies had rites of passage to help the individual with that "rebirth." Our society talks instead of "adjustment," but that concept does not do justice to the struggle many people go through when they begin again after a wrenching ending and a disorienting period in the neutral zone.

It is this three-phase reorientation from an old to a new way of being that organizational leaders usually overlook when they plan changes. The planners work hard to show why the changes are good; they build coalitions to support them; they work out PERT charts to schedule them; they see that the necessary funds are appropriated to pay for them; they assign managerial responsibility for implementing them. And they mumble darkly about selfishness, stupidity, and treachery when people affected by the changes slow those changes down, making the planners spend more money than they had forecast. In the end, these same people may even abort the very changes on which the organization's future depends.

An example of this resistance can be found in the Army's lengthy (and ultimately successful) attempt to replace the Colt .45 handgun with the 9 mm pistol. The Pentagon had been trying to replace the .45 for years; the first recommendations date from the 1930s. The arguments were impressive: the .45 was heavy and hard to shoot accurately; it was liable to strange malfunctions; it did not correspond to any weapon our allies used and therefore its parts were not interchangeable with any of those weapons; finally, it was designed to be used as an early-twentieth-century cavalry weapon, not a modern handgun.

With so many arguments against the .45, one may wonder why there was so much resistance to replacing it. There were in fact several reasons. A 9 mm replacement pistol would probably have been of European design; in fact an Italian design was finally selected. In addition, critics of the 9 mm scornfully called it "the women's cartridge," suggesting that the weapon debate was burdened by the deeper issue of women in the "man's army." Finally, the Army could not agree with the Air Force or the Navy on the specifications of the new weapon. It became clear that something more than technical issues was involved when the Army accused the Air Force of using "nonstandard military mud" in a test to simulate difficult firing conditions. Clearly the .45 was not just a weapon; it was a symbol of an identity. To let go of that weapon was in essence to end that identity.

It is easy to criticize this difficulty in letting go of what to most of us is outmoded "reality," but that is because we are not directly involved in the situation. One need only catch oneself holding on to an irrelevant reality to understand that problem, and anyone who works effectively with transition-related issues probably feels considerable sympathy for people who find transition difficult. My decision to work with organizations in transition probably comes in part from my own difficulties in this area, and the sympathy that these difficulties engender.

THE PHASES OF ORGANIZATIONAL TRANSITION

The "Ending Phase"

In my work over the past twelve years with more than five thousand individuals in transition, I have found that most people were very relieved to be able to identify and discuss the transitions they were going through. Such discussion surfaces without prompting, as one can see from the results of a survey of AT&T employees in the wake of divestiture. Here is a typical response: "I felt like I had gone through a divorce that neither my wife nor my children wanted. It was forced upon us by some very powerful outside forces, and I could not control the outcome. It was like waking up in familiar surroundings (such as your home), but your family and all that you held dear were missing."

Other common metaphors are death, bereavement, the loss of a limb, the destruction of a home, and the end of the world.

I have found it useful in discussing such feelings of loss to describe them as having three aspects:

1. *Disengagement*. Whatever the particulars of the situation, there is a break, an "unplugging," a separation of the person from the subjective world he or she took for granted. Some people are relatively self-contained to begin

with, and they may not be so dismayed by this break. But people whose personal security is tied to relationships and feelings of belonging, to status and role, are quite undone by disengagement. Transition management must begin with the ability to foresee the impact of disengagement and to find ways of countering its debilitating effects. It often helps to identify continuities that balance the losses, to reemphasize connections to the whole as connections to the parts are broken, to encourage people to talk about their feelings of loss, and to give temporary people temporary superiors who are sensitive to their situation. People are in mourning during this time, and so managers and supervisors need to expect the behaviors that are commonly associated with mourning: denial, anger, bargaining, grief, and the despair that comes before final acceptance.

2. *Disidentification*. One of the first losses in any transition is the sense of one's identity in the former situation. As I noted earlier, the old identity must go if there is to be space for the new one, but that fact does not keep the disidentification process from being very painful and even terrifying. One can see the impact of disidentification in companies that shift from traditional, functional organizational lines to strategic business units and thereby undermine the traditional identities of engineers, accountants, and other professionals who no longer have a clear sense of who they are. It is also painfully evident when people approach retirement and begin to wonder who they will be without their particular jobs and organizations. The problem can be converted into an opportunity, however, if people are given assistance in redefining themselves and their future directions. New training opportunities and a chance for life and career planning can often turn disidentification into the beginning of a new identity.

3. *Disenchantment*. Every reality gives meaning both to people's experience and to their way of responding to that experience. But when big changes occur, that meaning-making capacity breaks down. Things don't make sense any more—or they make only some terrible and inadmissible kind of sense, as in the suspicion that a person's job has been a sham and that that person's supervisor has been deceiving him or her all along. Such thoughts occur to almost everyone at some time or other during a painful ending, but if there really has been deception, disenchantment can become an overwhelming experience—as it was for some E. F. Hutton workers during the check-kiting investigation, or for some NASA employees in the aftermath of the shuttle explosion. The only way to deal with *disenchantment* is to allow the hurt to be expressed internally, no matter how this expression may affect the organization's leaders, and to have those leaders make an honest statement to the employees. Quick, frank, full communication is essential, as is rapid action to correct whatever situation led to the disenchantment in the first place.

The "Neutral Zone Phase"

There is no clear division between the first or "ending" phase of transition and the second, or "neutral zone," phase. The mourning for what has been lost, the confusion over identity, and the bitterness of disenchantment will flare up periodically like an underground fire that can only burn itself out. But with time there is a shift from the old task of letting go to the new task of crossing the "neutral zone," that wilderness that lies between the past reality and the one that leadership claims is just around the corner.

Neutral zone management must begin with an acknowledgment that this zone exists and that it has a constructive function in the transition process. It is difficult for most of us to make such an acknowledgment for two reasons. First, the Western mind sees the psychological emptiness of the neutral zone as something to be filled with the right content. We have no word or concept that is similar to the Japanese word *ma*, which refers to a necessary pause that one must make in waiting for the right moment for action. Where we would talk of "emptiness," the Japanese would say "full of nothing." Needless to say, the Japanese understand the neutral zone far better than we do.

Furthermore, people do not want to accept the reality of the neutral zone because they are afraid they will succumb to it. Productivity and effectiveness are likely to break down in the neutral zone, but this happens whether its existence is acknowledged or not. Talking about it simply makes people realize that they are neither isolated nor insane. Such discussion removes extraneous issues and may even speed up the process of reorientation. Thus, we can help people make sense of the neutral zone experience by describing it in terms of the following three conditions:

1. *Disorientation.* The neutral zone is an interim period between one orientation that is no longer appropriate and another that does not yet exist. This period has a function that is reminiscent of the situation in Robert Frost's poem "Directive." The poem is about a confusing journey into the backcountry of New Hampshire and the mind, a journey that leaves behind the known and leads to the discovery of something new. At one turning point in the journey, Frost says to the reader, "You're lost enough to find yourself now."

2. *Disintegration.* The neutral zone is a stage in which "everything has fallen apart." (Some variant of that phrase will be heard again and again during this phase of organizational transition.) This is potentially a creative disintegration, but it is still a very frightening experience. The breakdown of the old structure and the reality it held in place creates a sort of vacuum, a "low-pressure area" in the person and the organization that will attract bad intra- and interpersonal weather from all sides. Old issues that individuals and groups have apparently resolved suddenly return to haunt them. Long-dormant anxieties and antagonisms are stirred up, and unless people can

understand why this is happening, they are likely to conclude that "the end is at hand." At such a time there is a strong temptation to leave the organization, and many resignations can be traced to this turmoil. But if people can recognize this as a transition-generated condition that will pass, most will be able to ride it out.

3. *Discovery.* In the ancient rites of passage that used to carry a person through periods of transition, the neutral zone was spent in a literal "nowhere." There, in the desert or forest or tundra, the person could break away from the social forces that held his or her old reality in place, and a new reality could emerge. The neutral zone wilderness was believed to be a point of closer access to the spirits or the deeper levels of reality, and so the Plains Indians called the journey into the wilderness a "vision quest."

One does not have to accept the ancient beliefs to recognize that the neutral zone is still a place of discovery. Studies of creativity always emphasize that the creative solution comes from the psychological equivalent of the neutral zone. In his list of the main obstacles to creativity, the psychologist Richard Crutchfield shows that unless one can get into the neutral-zone frame of mind, one's responses are likely to be conventional rather than creative. The first two obstacles he lists have to do with problem clarity and understanding, but the remaining three are (1) rigidity and the inability to put aside popular assumptions; (2) lack of a period of incubation, so that problems can sit in the mind for a while; and (3) fear of reaction to unconventional ideas (cited in Harry Levinson, *Executive*, Harvard University Press, 1981). There is little wonder that we need to lose ourselves in the wilderness to find a new identity; in the wilderness, one can turn inward to incubate an embryonic idea, and popular assumptions and reactions to unconventional ideas no longer exist.

"The Vision" or New Beginning

Just as an organizational transition must begin with an ending, it must also end with a beginning. With our cultural bias toward the new, we Americans are always marching off on new ventures without bothering to end old ones. Perhaps that comes from our frontier days, when Americans could usually walk away from a situation and start over again elsewhere without acknowledging the ending. Whatever the reason, Americans often fail to understand that their main difficulties with making new beginnings come not from a difficulty with beginnings *per se*, but from a difficulty with endings and neutral zones. Transition managers must avoid that trap by implementing certain activities that will compensate for the losses people suffered in the ending.

1. If the loss of turf is an issue, interest-based, not position-based negotiation is essential if responsibilities and benefits are to be reallocated in ways that people feel are equitable.

2. If loss of attachments is an issue, rituals to mark those endings and team building to reattach the person in a new place are effective. In addition, the natural mourning process must not be shortened so that people may fully recover from their losses.

3. If loss of meaning is an issue, a meaning-based rather than an information-based communications campaign is important. This campaign must begin by confronting the problem that the organization is facing, rather than simply explaining the solution that the leadership has discovered.

4. If loss of a future is an issue, career- and life-planning opportunities can help people recover a sense of where they are going and discover their place in the new order.

5. If loss of a competence-based identity is an issue, training in new competencies—social as well as technical—is essential if people are to retain their confidence. The need for such training might seem obvious; however, people are often informed that they must acquire new skills without being told how to develop them.

6. If loss of control is an issue, any possible involvement in creating the future will help to compensate for the loss. This must be a real involvement, however, not a last minute, "let's-hope-they-don't-mess-up-our-plans" invitation to contribute ideas.

7. If loss itself is an issue, all such losses must be recognized and acknowledged. Nothing turns people off faster than a pep talk about how everything is happening for the best, unless it is the advice that they should "think positively" in a painful and intimidating situation.

The new beginning, when its time is ripe, must be built upon the new orientation and identity that emerge in the neutral zone. The catchword today for that new reality is "the vision," and an organization's vision of itself—as articulated by its leadership—is the foundation upon which its future must be formed. In trying to create and communicate such a vision, however, an organization's leaders must remember several things:

1. A new vision can take root only after the old vision has died and been buried. To forget that is to court the kind of backlash that Archie McGill experienced in trying prematurely to instill his vision of an innovation- and marketing-oriented culture at American Bell in the early 1980s.

2. In spite of the diagrams depicting organizations as fields full of arrows that all point the same way, a vision and the culture that develops from it do not remove all factions and forms of opposition. In fact, a culture is not a pattern of total agreement but a dialogue between opposing forces that agree on the nature of their opposition. Culture change is really a shift in the

definition of the opposition and in the terms of the dialogue, not a conversion process in which a group of Sauls see a burning bush and become single-minded Pauls.

3. Vision is a concept that appeals primarily to what Carl Jung called the "intuitive function." This way of perceiving deals not with the details of the present but with the general shape of the future. Research has shown, however, that although a high percentage of organizational leaders are "intuitive types," about three quarters of the employees in most large organizations are "sensation types." These are present- rather than future-oriented individuals who do not use intuition as often as intuitive types and who are not as impressed by its results. The vision must therefore be supplemented by a clear plan, and the big picture by many small examples, if the majority of employees are going to accept them.

4. To complicate matters further, both the vision and the plan have to be spelled out in two different forms, for another of Carl Jung's discoveries, substantiated by thousands of tests, is that people make and carry out decisions in two different ways. Some consider situations impersonally according to principles and categories. These "thinking types" will want to know how the future will work and what the logical reasons for the changes are. "Feeling types," on the other hand, decide and act on the basis of personal values and the interpersonal aspects of a situation. They will be more concerned with what the future is going to "feel like" and how everyone will fit into it. These different types "see" visions quite differently.

5. Finally, both types of people are going to feel overwhelmed if the vision and the new reality it portrays are very different from current conditions. As University of Texas psychologist Karl Weick has shown in his article "Small Wins: Redefining the Scale of Social Problems" (*The American Psychologist*, January 1984), organizations often move faster in a new direction if they follow what he calls the "Small Wins" Principle. In addition to the overall goal, the organizational leadership needs to identify a few "concrete, complete, implemented outcome[s] of moderate importance . . . [that will] produce visible results" if people are not to lose their momentum when their early efforts at making the new beginning fall short of the vision.

QUESTIONS FOR TRANSITION MANAGERS

In closing, let us look at the management of organizational transition from a somewhat more general perspective. People who are responsible for leading or managing an organizational transition need to ask themselves these questions:

1. *Have I included transition planning in my planning for the changes that lie ahead of us?* That means systematically foreseeing who will have to let go of what if the planned changes are actually going to work. It means predicting the resources that people will need for the wilderness experience of the neutral zone. Finally, it means going beyond the vision and plan for the change to a design for the process, a design in which the vision and plan are actually converted into new behavior and attitudes.

2. *Have I created a transition-monitoring system to keep track of what transition is actually doing to the organization as it unfolds through its three phases?* Only in that way can one be sure that people aren't getting lost in the shuffle, that communications are really understood, and that plans are really being put into action.

3. *Have I made sure that managers and supervisors are being trained to facil-itate transition rather than merely to "make change happen"?* Organizational leaders and outside consultants alike can too easily become enamored of "change-agentry," forgetting how much easier it is to prescribe a change in someone else than it is to effect a change in oneself.

4. *Have I really looked at how I will need to change if I am to function effectively in the new system?* Organizational leaders who do not do this are undermining their preaching with their example. Furthermore, they tend to project their own problems onto others, and fail to legitimize transition management as a critical aspect of organizational change.

5. *Have I taken pains to communicate effectively the changes and the transi-tions they will require?* There are some secondary questions here: (1) Am I giving as clear a picture as I can of the *what, when, how*, and *why* of the changes? (2) Am I recognizing that different types of people are concerned about different aspects of the change—or am I just saying what *I* would want to hear? (3) Am I remembering that no communication is complete until the send-er knows that the receiver has the correct message and has had a chance to reply? (4) Am I relying on the old communication channels to give and receive messages, or do I need to create new channels?

6. *Am I using this present transition as an opportunity to redesign the policies, procedures, systems, and structures to make the organization more transitionworthy in the future?* If not, I will have missed a great opportunity, for organizations that will lead their fields tomorrow are the ones that are now creating ways of going through transitions successfully.

In these turbulent times, the ability to change frequently and rapidly is a re-quirement for survival. However, successful change requires many individual transitions. Since unmanaged transitions lead to unmanageable change, transition management must rank as one of the key executive skills that will be needed in the years ahead.

Selected Bibliography

Bowlby, John. *Loss: Sadness and Depression* (Basic Books, 1980).

Bridges, William. *Transitions: Making Sense of Life's Changes* (Addison-Wesley, 1980).

Keirsey, David and Bates, Marilyn. *Please Understand Me: Character and Temperament Types* (Prometheus Nemesis, 1978).

Kübler-Ross, Elizabeth. *On Death and Dying* (Macmillan, 1968).

Levinson, Harry. *Executive* (Harvard University Press, 1981).

Myers, Isabel Briggs. *Gifts Differing* (Consulting Psychologists Press, 1980).

Pascale, Richard T. and Athos, Anthony G. *The Art of Japanese Management* (Simon & Schuster, 1981).

Pierson, G. W. *Tocqueville and Beaumont in America* (Oxford University Press, 1938).

Tunstall, W. Brooke. "Breakup of the Bell System: A Case Study in Cultural Transformation." In Kilmann, Ralph H. et al., eds., *Gaining Control of the Corporate Culture* (Jossey-Bass, 1985).

Van Gennep, Arnold. *Rites of Passage*. Trans. Monika B. Vizedon and Gabrielle Caffee (University of Chicago Press, 1960).

Weick, Karl E. "Small Wins: Redefining the Scale of Social Problems" (*The American Psychologist*, January 1984).

CHAPTER TWENTY-FIVE

The Recipients of Change

Todd D. Jick (1990)

"It's tough for people who have done real well to feel pushed out the door. Tough for the ego, like cutting out a big piece of yourself. Especially when you've been there for a while, you're rooted. It's who you were, part of who you are."

The comment above was made by someone in a company that was "downsized." But as the statement indicates, the person himself was downsized in a way—losing "a big piece" of himself. This image is by no means unusual; people in the throes of change often speak in terms of being diminished. They also use words like anger, betrayal, shock—in short, they describe dramatic emotions that rarely encompass the positive. They experience being unappreciated, anxious, at a minimum confused.

In contrast, much has been written about the need to embrace change with enthusiasm. We are to "foster hardiness" and be flexible; change is a challenge to confront, an adventure; we must "thrive on chaos." What accounts for this difference between actual reactions to change and what we are supposed to feel? Can this gap be bridged? Not easily.

No organization can institute change if its employees will not, at the very least, accept the change. No change will "work" if employees don't help in the effort. And change is not possible without people changing themselves. Any organization that believes change can take hold without considering how people will react to it is in deep delusion. Change can be "managed" externally by those who decide when it is needed and how it "should" be implemented. But it will be implemented only when employees accept change—and the specific change—internally.

This chapter explores how people, in general, react to change, why they do so, and how they may be able to understand their reactions better. The perspective is that of the "change," or recipient, but the ideas are helpful to change agents as well. By grasping more firmly the experience of being changed, those managing the process can gain a broader understanding of the effects—intended and unintended—of the changes they are instituting.

One point must be stressed at the outset. For some people, any interference with routine provokes strong reaction. These folks we call "set in their ways"—or worse! At the other extreme are those for whom the next mountain is always to be attacked with ferocity. These are the daredevils among us. Most people fall between these two poles, and it is with them that we are concerned. Further, the "change" we address is more than minor distribution in ways of operation; we are dealing with the kinds of change that are experienced as transformational.

REACTIONS TO CHANGE

The typical employee spends at least eight hours a day at the work place, doing, in general, fairly regular, predictable tasks. Indeed, most companies have orientation programs that emphasize the company "culture," which implies some stability. Employees usually have some sort of job description, performance appraisals that are linked to that description, and job planning reviews, all of which tacitly indicate that there is a quid pro quo. The employee does X, and if that is done well, on time, etc., the employee receives Y in compensation.

In addition to this external contract is a psychological one belonging to the organization, fitting into the work and social patterns that exist in the company. There is a political dimension here as well. For those seeking advancement in the organization there are written and unwritten "rules" of the game. "The way we do things around here" is something that career-minded employees attend to.

But what happens when the rules are changed in the middle of the game, as in the following: "So this morning we get a memo addressed to 'all staff.' It says the policy of year-end cash performance bonuses is discontinued. Just like that—30 percent of my salary! And after all the long hours I've put in during the last months."

What would we suppose this accountant might feel? In fact, one could argue that almost any reaction she has is normal and "justifiable." She has experienced a trauma.

But the "loss" a change implies need not be as definitive as the bonus situation above. A loss can be imaginary as, for example, what a change in a job description may entail. This may be a perceived loss in turf, a perceived diminution in status, in identity, or self-meaning in general. Everything that someone has built up is considered threatened; even if the change is a promotion, people can react with anxiety. In fact, people often try to perform the new job and the old one simultaneously so as not to experience the (imaginary) loss.

For most people, the negative reaction to change is related to control—over their influence, their surroundings, their source of pride, how they have grown accustomed to living and working. When these factors appear threatened, security is in jeopardy. And considerable energy is needed to understand, to absorb, and process one's reaction. Not only do I have to deal with the change per se, I have to deal with my reactions to it! Even if the change is embraced intellectually ("I finally got the promotion"), immediate acceptance is not usually forthcoming. Instead, most feel fatigued; we need *time* to adapt.

THE EVOLUTION OF CHANGE REACTIONS

Most people, of course, do adapt to change, but not before passing through some other psychological gates. Two "maps" (below) describe the complex psychological process of passing through difficult, often conflicting, emotions. Each of these approaches emphasizes a progression through stages or phases, which occurs over time and, essentially, cannot be accelerated (Table 25.1). To speed up the process is to risk carrying unfinished psychological "baggage" from one phase to the next.

Table 25.1. Frameworks to Explain Reactions to Change.

Transition Stages	*Change Stages (Risk Taking)*
Ending phase: Letting go of the previous situation (disengagement, disidentification, disenchantment)	Shock: Perceived threat, immobilization, no risk taking
Neutral zone: Completing endings and building energy for beginnings (disorientation, disintegration, discovery)	Defensive retreat: Anger, holding on, risk taking still unsafe
New beginnings: New possibilities or alignment with a vision	Acknowledgment: Mourning, letting go, growing potential for risk taking
	Adaptation and change: Comfort with change, energy for risk taking

One way to think about the reaction pattern relates to a theory based on risk taking.[1] Change, they assert, requires people to perform or perceive in unfamiliar ways, which implies taking risks, particularly those associated with self esteem—loss of face, appearing incompetent, seemingly unable or unwilling to learn, etc. People move from discomfort with risks to acceptance in four stages: shock, defensive retreat, acknowledgment, adaptation, and change. This can be likened to bereavement reactions.

In the *shock* phase, one is threatened by anticipated change, even denying its existence: "This isn't happening." The psychological shock resembles the physical—people become immobilized and "shut down" to protect themselves; yet at the same time, they deny the situation is occurring. As a result of this conflict, productivity is understandably low, people feel unsafe, timid, and unable to take action, much less risks.

We move from shock to *defensive retreat*—i.e., we get angry. We simultaneously lash out at what has been done to us and we hold on to accustomed ways of doing things. Thus, we are both keeping a grip on the past while decrying the fact that it's changed. This conflict also precludes taking risks, for we are uncomfortable and feel unsafe.

Eventually, we cease denying the fact of change, we acknowledge that we have lost something, and we mourn. The psychological dynamics include both grief and liberation. Thus, one can feel like a pawn in a game while being able to take some distance from the game, view it with some objectivity. At this point experimenting with taking risks becomes possible; we begin exploring the pros and cons of the new situation. Each "risk" that succeeds builds confidence, and we are ready for the final "gate."

Ideally, most people *adapt and change* themselves. The change becomes internalized, we move on and help others to do so; we see ourselves "before and after" the change and, even if it's a grudging acknowledgment, we consider the change "all for the best." In some cases, people actively advocate what they recently denied.

Another approach to how people come to terms with change also is based on phases, in this case three: letting go, existing in a neutral zone, making new beginnings.[2]

Ending and letting go means relinquishing the old, prechange situation, a process that involves dramatic emotions—pain, confusion, and terror. That is, we first experience a sharp break with what has been taken for granted; included in this pain is a loss of the identity we had invested in the old situation. This situational "unplugging" and loss of identity leads to a sense of disenchantment; things fail to make sense. People feel deceived, betrayed.

Such feelings lead into a second psychological phase called a *neutral zone:* a "wilderness that lies between the past reality and the one that . . . is just around the corner." People feel adrift and confused; the previous orientation no longer exists, yet the new one seems unclear. In this period of "full of nothing," we grow increasingly unproductive and ineffective. But psychologically, the neutral period is essentially for mustering the energy to go on. It is the time between ending something and beginning something else. When someone is "lost enough to find oneself" and when the past becomes put into perspective, the emotions have been experienced and dealt with and put aside—then there is "mental room" to reorient and discover the new. The third phase is the seeking out of new possibilities: *beginning* to align our actions with change.

Organizations are often tempted to push people into the "beginning" phase, not recognizing—or accepting—the need to complete the psychological work (and it *is* work) of the two previous phases. But jumping into a flurry of "beginning-type" activity—planning, pep rallies, firing up the troops—only increases people's discomfort of change. Only if sufficient attention has been paid to letting go and dwelling in the neutral zone, only if the old has been properly buried, can the new appear. People can then draw from the past and not be mired in it; they can be eager to embrace new possibilities.

These basically optimistic theories about how people eventually embrace change—although psychologically accurate—are somewhat simplistic. Most people will work through the emotional phases they delineate; some will do so more quickly than others. But others will get stuck, often in the first stages, which encompass the most keen and jagged emotions. The catchall word "resistance" is used to describe these people: they are destructive (internally or externally), and they won't move forward.

People get stuck for two basic—and obvious—reasons: "change" is not the same monolithic event that has neat and tidy beginnings and ends; and people's subjective experiences of change vary considerably as a result of individual circumstances.

Thus, frameworks that presume periods of psychological sorting out while the change is being digested are somewhat flimsy in helping us deal with multiple changes. How are we to be in "defensive retreat" with one change, in the "neutral zone" with another, while adapting to a third? If these changes are also rapid-fire—a fairly common situation in these unheaving days in the political and economic arenas—it becomes clearer why some people "resist."

For example, changes involving significant personal redirection, like job restructuring, are often accompanied by changes in a firm's ownership, leadership, and policies. All coming at once (or in rapid sequence), they can severely stress or even undo chief anchor points of meaning. These affect the previously agreed-upon ways of doing one's work, one's affiliations, skills, and self-concept. When these anchor points come under siege, most of us are likely to be immobilized and even obdurate. In a worst-case scenario, the individual going through this siege at the office is simultaneously experiencing a major change at home—a divorce, for example.

People do not always easily pass through the phases described above because, notwithstanding the psychological validity of the progression of emotions, not everyone interprets "change" in the same way; thus, experiences of "change" vary. Other personality issues must be considered as well. People who are fragile emotionally will have much greater difficulty swimming through feelings of loss; they may continually see themselves as victims. Such obscuring emotions will hinder their ability to move on. Instead, they may cycle back to shock-like or defensive behavior, never breaking out of the early phases.

ORGANIZATIONAL RESPONSES

As indicated, many firms attempt to accelerate employees' adaptation to change, for understandable reasons. Employees who are preoccupied with their internal processes are less likely to be fully productive; indeed, as the description of patterns of change reveals, people in the early phases of reacting to change often are unable to do much at all. It thus makes good "business sense" to help people cope, with a minimum of dysfunctional consequences.

Unfortunately, from the recipient's perspective, such good intentions are often considered as controlling, even autocratic. If the change is hyped too much—too many pep rallies, too many "it's really good for you and all for the best"—those of us who feel no such thing can grow increasingly isolated and resentful. How can they say everything is rosy when I feel so miserable?

Consider the following list of typical advice presented, in one form or another, for dealing with change:

- Keep your cool in dealing with others.
- Handle pressure smoothly and effectively.
- Respond nondefensively when others disagree with you.
- Develop creative and innovative solutions to problems.
- Be willing to take risks and try out new ideas.
- Be willing to adjust priorities to changing conditions.
- Demonstrate enthusiasm for and commitment to long-term goals.
- Be open and candid when dealing with others.
- Participate actively in the change process.
- Make clear-cut decisions as needed.

Seemingly straightforward and commonsensical, this advice is eminently rational and usually presented in good faith. But as we now understand, such directives—for that is what they are—fail to take into account that psychological needs must be addressed. Most people are aware of the wisdom of taking responsibility for dealing with change themselves; they recognize the importance of the "right attitude." Americans in particular pride themselves on pioneer spirit, challenges, and adventure—the can-do philosophy.

It appears, however, that most people do not want this shoved down their throats, especially when they are first grappling with the magnitude, or their perception of it, of a change's effect on them. Rather, most of us prefer some empathy, some understanding of what we are experiencing—not just advice for getting on with it.

The next two sections of this chapter explore ways in which people facing change can help themselves experience the changes less painfully and some guidelines their managers can use to help their employees (and themselves) cope with difficult parts of the change process. Although these ideas are simple, even commonplace, they look at the experience of change in its totality; they acknowledge that "change" is not merely doing A on Monday and B on Tuesday. There is a transaction between the two, and if that is ignored by either the recipient or those instituting the change then full adaptation to, and embracing of, the change itself is jeopardized.

INDIVIDUAL COPING WITH CHANGE

Given the strong emotional responses that most of us feel at the onset of a change—anger, depression, shock—and that often these are "unacceptable" emotions either to ourselves or at the workplace, we need to console ourselves that these are indeed natural reactions. People need to give themselves permission to feel what they are feeling; change always implies a loss of some kind, and that must be mourned: a job, colleagues, a role, even one's identity as it has been wrapped up in the prechange situation. Accepting and focusing on our negative reactions is not the same as wallowing in them, of course.

It has already been pointed out that dealing with change takes energy. Even more energy is required in fighting negative reactions. Thus, to accept, at the outset, that strong emotions are part and parcel of the change process is at least to avoid wasting some energy; we are better able to reduce the added strain of constantly keeping feelings at bay. In fact, one's strength is increased by letting what is natural take its course.

A corollary to accepting strong reactions to change is patience—recognizing that time is needed to come to grips with a situation and that moving through various constellations of emotions is not done in an instant. Whereas most people experience the range of emotions described earlier, there is no time clock that works for everyone. The adaptation process involves an unsettled, ambiguous period for most of us,[3] and if we accept that, at least we can function superficially—if not at our peak—until we strengthen and begin to act more meaningfully.

A major reaction to change is a feeling of losing control; what was assumed to be the norm now isn't, and we are in an in unknown land. A valuable antidote to feeling powerless is to establish a sense of personal control in other areas of our lives and to avoid as much as possible taking on other efforts that sap energy. Thus, if one accepts that adapting to change will be arduous, one husbands one's resources. This means maintaining our physical well-being and nourishing our psyches.

It is no coincidence that a new field called "managing stress" has arisen during a period of major and pervasive organizational restructuring. And the recommendations the practitioners in this area make, while simple, are useful: get enough sleep, pay attention to diet and exercise; take occasional breaks at the office; relax with friends; engage in hobbies. Making such efforts is not escapism or distracting oneself from "reality." Rather, it is a way of exerting control over one's life during a period of uncertainty.

Accepting strong emotions and acknowledging the importance of patience in dealing with change are vital; but so is developing a sense of objectivity about what is happening. We do have choices in how we perceive change, and we are able to develop the capacity to see benefits, not just losses, in new situations. Coming to accept and adapt to change is in fact a process of balancing: What have I lost, what am I gaining? Different from the "look on the bright side" exhortations frequently espoused by those who ignore the powerful emotions a change can evoke, inventorying personal losses and gains is a real step toward gathering the strength to move on.

Related to such inventorying is "diversified emotional investing." The individual balances the emotional investment in essential work-related anchor points of meaning—how work is done, affiliations, skills, self-concept in relation to the work—with emotional investments in other areas—family, friends, civic and religious activities. Thus, when one or more anchor points at the workplace are threatened, the person can remain steadier through the transition adaptation.

Admittedly, such inventorying and "diversified emotional investigating" are difficult when in the throes of strong emotions. Perhaps the best mechanism for coping with change, then, is anticipating it. No one escapes the effects of change, in the workplace or elsewhere, and those who recognize that its impact will be powerful, that the process of adaptation and change takes time, and that we all have other sources of strength are in much better shape than those who delude themselves into thinking "it can never happen to me."

MANAGING THE RECIPIENTS OF CHANGE

Obviously, the manager who has experienced change personally is potentially more effective in helping others work through their adaptation processes. But

Table 25.2. Strategies for Coping with Change.

Individuals	Managers
Rethinking resistance	Accepting feelings as natural
Permission to feel and mourn	As natural as self-protection
Taking time to work through feelings	As a positive step toward change
Tolerating ambiguity	As energy to work with
	As information critical to the change process
	As other than a roadblock
Managing stress	Giving first aid
Maintaining physical well-being	Accepting emotions
Seeking information about the change	Listening
Limiting extraneous stressors	Providing safety
Taking regular breaks	Marking endings
Seeking support	Providing resources and support
Exercising responsibility	Creating capability for change
Identifying options and gains	Making organizational support if risks clear
Learning from losses	Continuing safety net
Participating in the change	Emphasizing countless gains of change
Inventorying strengths	Helping employees explore risks, options
Learning new skills	Suspending judgment
Diversifying emotional investing	Involving people in decision making
	Teamwork
	Providing opportunities for individual growth

beyond recalling their own experiences, managers should consider three areas that are essential for easing their employees' difficulties: rethinking resistance, giving "first aid," and creating capability for change (see Table 25.2).

RETHINKING RESISTANCE

Resistance to change, as mentioned earlier, is a catch-all phrase; it describes anyone who doesn't change as fast as we do, as well as people who seemingly refuse to budge. As such, resistance per se is considered an obstacle, something to overcome at all costs. Those labeled resistant are deemed people with poor attitudes, lacking in team spirit. Not surprisingly, treating "resistance" this way serves only to intensify real resistance, thereby thwarting or at least side-tracking possibilities of change.

As the discussion of patterns of change revealed, however, resistance is a part of the natural process of adapting to change; it is a normal response of those who have a strong vested interest in maintaining their perception of the current state and guarding themselves against loss. Why should I give up what has successfully made meaning for me? What do I get in its place? Resistance, at the outset of the change process, is far more complicated than "I won't." It is much more of a painful "Why should I?"

When resistance is considered a natural reaction—part of a process—it can thus be seen as a first step toward adaptation. At the very minimum, resistance denotes energy—energy that can be worked with and redirected. The strength of resistance, moreover, indicates the degree to which change has touched on something valuable to individuals and the organization. Discovering what that valuable something is can be of important use in fashioning the change effort organizationally. One theorist puts it this way:

> First, they ["resistors"] are the ones most apt to perceive and point out real threats, if such exist, to the well-being of the system which may be the unanticipated consequences of projected changes;
>
> Second, they are especially apt to react against any change that might reduce the integrity of the system;
>
> Third, they are sensitive to any indication that those seeking to produce change fail to understand or identify with the core values of the system they seek to influence.

Because "resistance to change" is such an amorphous phrase, many attitudes labeled resistant are not that at all. Depending on the change involved, people may be learning new and difficult skills, for example. Their frustration in doing so may cause them to nay-say the effort. Calling the nay-saying resistance is a genuine error; if the effort to change is in fact being made, it should be encouraged. Further, listening to the criticism may provide clues that the training is ineffective.

There are also entirely rational reasons for resistance. By no means are all change agendas perfect, as the quote above indicates. The organization that assumes it can superimpose "change" on its employees and then labels any negative reaction "resistance" is guaranteeing that change, if it occurs at all, will hardly accomplish that purpose for which it was intended:

> One of the common mistakes made by managers when they encounter resistance is to become angry, frustrated, impatient, or exasperated. . . . The problem with

an emotional reaction is that it increases the probability that the resistance will intensify. . . . Remember that anger directed towards others is likely to make them afraid in return.[4]

In sum, rethinking resistance to change means seeing it as a normal part of adaptation, something most of us do to protect our self-integrity. It is a potential source of energy, as well as information about the change effort and direction. Instead of assuming that all "resistance" is an obstacle, managers should look carefully to see if real resistance is present, over time (i.e., there are always people who won't change and who will complain all the while). In general, however, going with the "resistance"—not condemning it but trying to understand its sources, motives, and possibly affirmative core—can open up possibilities for realizing change. Writes one expert on the subject: "Without it [resistance] we are skeptical of real change occurring. Without real questioning, skepticism, and even outright resistance, it is unlikely that the organization will successfully move on to the productive stage of learning how to make the new structure effective and useful."[5]

GIVING "FIRST AID"

Many managers find that addressing straightforward, technical issues in the change effort—such as the new department layout, who gets what training—is comparatively easy. But consciously or not, they ignore the more complex, often unpredictable concerns of the people being changed. The rationale can be a business one: "We don't have time for that, we're here to make money." Or it can be emotional: "I don't want to get involved in messy feelings; that's not my job."

For whatever reason, not allowing employees opportunities to vent feelings is overlooking a powerfully effective sopping strategy. Administering emotional first aid, particularly in the early and most difficult stages of change, validates recipients in their terms and doesn't leave them in an emotional pressure cooker. We have already seen that a major coping mechanism for the individual is acknowledging that his or her reactions are natural; when this is combined with external validation the result is profoundly effective. Indeed, when management provides opportunity for grievances and frustrations to be aired constructively, employees' bitterness and frustration may be diminished.

As the above implies, first aid, in its most powerful form, is simply listening. Nonjudgmental listening. The dominant attitude of the nonjudgmental listener is respect for what the individual is experiencing; this in turn is predicated in accepting that everyone needs time to absorb change and that complicated and even contradictory emotions belong to the early stage of the process.

First aid also means providing safety by delineating expectations and establishing informal and formal rewards for those experiencing change. It also involves identifying and clarifying what is not changing, and probing to uncover why. Where do people feel they will be taking the biggest risks? It is in these areas, as we have seen, that the most powerful concerns—and resistance—lie.

Finally, first aid means providing resources to help people through their greatest difficulties—ongoing information about the change, support and counseling where needed, particularly forums in which employees can help each other. These resources are especially critical when someone has bid farewell to the old but has yet to become attached to the new.

Listening, accepting, and supporting may seem like simple, almost basic, advice for the manager of changes. Unfortunately, all too often they are missing from the manager's toolkit for change. Such essential human interaction tends to get lost in the maze of plans, committees, and reports typically accompanying major change efforts. For the recipients to adapt fully to their new circumstances requires more than the passive response of managers, however; managers need to help changees become more capable of change.

CREATING THE CAPABILITY FOR CHANGE

Creating the capability for change is undertaken after the "bleeding" has stopped and the need for first aid lessens. The manager's dual task is to help people move into the current change and encourage them to feel confident about accepting subsequent changes.

Providing safety and rewards—a part of first aid—is also essential to creating a climate in which people will take risks. This is what good parenting is all about! In the workplace, managers who expect their employees to change, and particularly if the change is in fact multiple changes, need to make clear how the organization is willing to support their efforts. What differentiates this effort from first aid is its continuance. First aid is *first*; it is the effort that eases the pain, but it does not cure the disease, much less help prevent its occurrence.

Safety in creating the capability for change goes deeper into risk taking. Perhaps a nonevaluative period can be declared, one in which income, rank, or other aspects of job security are put on hold as employees test the waters. Having employees evaluate themselves vis-à-vis the change is another approach; in all cases, the more involvement people have in the changes that surround them, the better. It is a fundamental tenet of participative management that employees are more likely to support what they help create. Cooperation, negotiation, and compromise are critical to the implementation of any change; it is difficult to *get* cooperation, negotiation, and compromise from people who are effectively ordered to change, never listened to or supported, and then faulted if they fail to change as expected.

Rewards, in creating capabilities for change, are often implicit. Consider the popularity of programs like Outward Bound. The "rewards" in these arenas are the pride of accomplishment and the cheers from one's co-participants. Encouraging employees to take similarly difficult, albeit in many cases psychological, risks means creating environments in which they can shine—not necessarily the standard rewards of money and promotion. Creative managers who truly wish their employees to grow, who recognize the difficulties inherent in the challenge of change, and who support efforts to make change are patient along the way; their reward, in turn, is the trust of their employees— and a potentially more flexible organization.

IS CONTINUOUS CHANGE "GOOD" FOR US?

I hear change is coming, and it no longer sends shivers up my spine. I have to trust it won't clobber me. There's not really anything I can do but learn to survive and help others through it.

This note has treated "change" and its effects on employees as a first-time event: the company, having done its thing for about fifty years, suddenly throws the cards in the air, and everyone picks up from there. It is, of course, increasingly rare to find such situations. Most people are more or less continually facing major changes in their work environments, from the rapid fire of new technology and process, to new owners, perhaps foreign, to an increasing emphasis on change itself as essential. The ability to change rapidly and frequently seems to be a critical mechanism for survival, many argue.

Obviously, an organization that encourages constant change hardly has the time to do first aid, and all the rest; everyone is moving around, and no one— neither the changee nor the manager—has time to examine the psychological ramifications, much less get support. Two questions need answering in the face of such constant change: Does experience with change help people cope with it better? What are the longer-term implications of constant change for individuals and organizations?

Some evidence exists that an "inoculation effect" takes hold after confronting continuous change; people do react to the same situation, when it recurs, differently. Hurricane victims, for example, exhibit a "confidence curve" as a result of repeated experience with the phenomenon. Those who have been through a hurricane once are most stressed; they become hyperwatchful and overprepare upon even the faintest signal of a hurricane warning. They become gun-shy to the prospect of another similar event. In contrast, those who have had repeated exposure to hurricanes approach an impending storm with more equanimity.

If this analogy is transferable, then recipients—in the face of continuous change—may exhibit a learning curve. At first they will be hypersensitive but later will become more "matter of fact" and psychologically more ready for change. However, we haven't enough evidence yet to be certain of this. And some fear that the opposite effects could occur instead, whereby recipients will become more vulnerable, more resistant, and less equipped as more and more change unfolds. Moreover, if someone experiences constant change, has she or he ever completely dealt with the first one?

Perhaps the answer revolves around expectations. In some companies today, people are routinely moved in and out of projects and positions; it is the nature of the work requirements in that organization. But this is understood by all from the beginning. As such, employees harbor the expectation that there will be constant change. Indeed, some are attracted to the company because of that. If people know at the outset that frequent change, in positions, responsibilities, and the like, is in fact their job, we can suppose that a kind of self-selection takes place; those who wish that kind of experience will seek out jobs in the company, and in turn, the company will hire those who can accept that kind of mobility. With more and more companies now exhibiting continuous change, people may come to expect it and be more inured to it.

The notion of continuous change as the ideal organizational state is fairly recent, so many of its effects in the long term on individuals within such environments are not known precisely. But we all—change agents and change recipients—must develop the strength and the capability to cope with the emotions and the demands that come with this new territory. The individual and the organization share the responsibility and obligation. When both make "good faith efforts," the results can be buoying.

Notes

1. Harry Woodward and Steve Bucholz, *Aftershock* (New York: John Wiley, 1987).

2. William Bridges, "Managing Organizational Transitions," *Organizational Dynamics*, Summer 1986: 24–33.

3. Leonard Greenhalgh and Todd Jick, "Survivor Sense Making and Reaction to Organizational Decline," *Management Communications Quarterly*, 2, 3 February 1989: 305–327.

4. Ken Hultman, *The Path of Least Resistance* (Austin, Texas: Learning Concepts, 1979).

5. Ibid.

CHAPTER TWENTY-SIX

Rethinking Resistance and Recognizing Ambivalence

A Multidimensional View of Attitudes Toward an Organizational Change

Sandy Kristin Piderit (2000)

Adapting to changing goals and demands has been a timeless challenge for organizations, but the task seems to have become even more crucial in the past decade. In the for-profit sector, global population growth and political shifts have opened new markets for products and services at a dizzying pace. To respond to the pace of change, organizations are adopting flatter, more agile structures and more empowering, team-oriented cultures. As status differences erode, some employees are coming to expect involvement in decisions about organizational change. Successful organizational adaptation is increasingly reliant on generating employee support and enthusiasm for proposed changes, rather than merely overcoming resistance.

The concept of resistance to change has been widely studied, but it has limitations. Both Merron (1993) and Dent and Goldberg (1999) have argued for retiring the phrase ''resistance to change.'' The limitations of the concept can be framed in philosophical terms; for instance, critical theorists and labor policy scholars argue that the interests of managers should not be privileged over the interests of workers when studying organizational change (Jermier, Knights, & Nord, 1994). Alternatively, the limitations of the concept can be framed in practical terms; for instance, practical scholars and scholarly practitioners argue that the concept might have outlived its usefulness (Dent & Goldberg, 1999; Krantz, 1999). My purpose here is to summarize a critique of existing views of resistance to change and to advocate a view that captures more of the complexity of individuals' responses to proposed organizational changes.

In the first part of the chapter, I suggest that in studies of resistance to change, researchers have largely overlooked the potentially positive intentions that may motivate negative responses to change. I also show how studies of resistance have dichotomized responses to change and, thus, somewhat over-simplified them. Furthermore, I argue that varied emphases in the conceptualization of resistance have slipped into the literature, blurring our sense of the complexities of the phenomenon.

In the second part of the chapter, I propose a multidimensional view of responses to proposed organizational changes, capturing employee responses along at least three dimensions (emotional, cognitive, and intentional). Within this view, "resistance to a change" is represented by the set of responses to change that are negative along all three dimensions, and "support for a change" is represented by the set of responses that are positive along all three dimensions. Responses to a change initiative that are neither consistently negative nor consistently positive, which were previously ignored but are potentially the most prevalent type of initial response, can be analyzed as cross-dimension ambivalence in employees' responses to change.

In the third part of the chapter, I identify the implications of this new view for both research and practice. By highlighting the many other sets of responses that can occur, this new view shows the importance of ambivalent responses to change for research on exit, voice, loyalty, and neglect and for research on generating change within organizations.[1]

A SYNTHESIS OF PAST CONCEPTUALIZATIONS OF RESISTANCE TO CHANGE

Unfavorable Responses to Change Might Be Motivated by the Best of Intentions

In the majority of work on resistance to change, researchers have borrowed a view from physics to metaphorically define resistance as a restraining force moving in the direction of maintaining the status quo (cf. Lewin, 1952). Furthermore, most scholars have focused on the various "forces" that lead employees away from supporting changes proposed by managers. As Watson (1982) points out, managers often perceive resistance negatively, since they see employees who resist as disobedient. And as Jermier et al. put it, "The most prevalent way of analysing resistance is to see it as a reactive process where agents embedded in power relations actively oppose initiatives by other agents" (1994: 9). Even if they only see employees who oppose change as shortsighted, managers are tempted by the language of resistance to treat their subordinates as obstacles.

Thus, the label of resistance can be used to dismiss potentially valid employee concerns about proposed changes. Of course, for a long time in the practical literature about managing change processes, researchers have been advising practitioners to guard against this. For example, Mary Parker Follett pointed out in the 1920s that

> we shouldn't put to . . . workers finished plans in order merely to get their consent . . . one of two things is likely to happen, both bad: either we shall get a rubber-stamped consent and thus lose what they might contribute to the problem in question, or else we shall find ourselves with a fight on our hands—an open fight or discontent seething underneath [reprinted in Graham, 1995: 220].

Likewise, Lawrence (1954) warns managers to avoid creating resistance in subordinates by assuming that they will always be opposed to change. In the 1990s others have reissued similar warnings (Dent & Goldberg, 1999; Merron, 1993). A prominent consultant noted that the concept of resistance to change "has been transformed over the years into a not-so-disguised way of blaming the less powerful for unsatisfactory results of change efforts" (Krantz, 1999: 42).

This tendency to dismiss employees' objections to change simply may be another manifestation of the fundamental attribution error (Jones & Harris, 1967); that is, managers in charge of rolling out a change initiative blame others for the failure of the initiative, rather than accepting their role in its failure. Employees are likely to do the same thing—assigning blame for failed change attempts to their managers, rather than themselves. However, as Klein (1976) and Thomas (1989) argue, in most research on resistance to change, researchers have taken the perspective of those in charge of implementing change, and so scholars have written less about the perspectives of those with less power. Perhaps scholars, as well as practitioners, need to be cautioned against playing the blame game unwittingly.

Fortunately, in other types of literature—not yet well integrated into research on resistance to change—scholars also remind us of a wider range of reasons why employees may oppose a proposed organizational change. For instance, research on obedience to authority indicates that resistance might be motivated by individuals' desires to act in accordance with their ethical principles (Milgram, 1965; Modigliani & Rochat, 1995). Similarly, the organizational dissent literature shows that some employee resistance to organizational actions is motivated by more than mere selfishness (Graham, 1984, 1986). Also, recent studies of issue selling (Ashford, Rothbard, Piderit, & Dutton, 1998; Dutton, Ashford, Wierba, O'Neill, & Hayes, 1997) indicate that employees might try to get top management to pay attention to issues that employees believe must be addressed in order for the organization to maintain high performance.

Rarely do individuals form resistant attitudes, or express such attitudes in acts of dissent or protest, without considering the potential negative consequences for themselves. This point is documented in several studies. In the field of ethics, for instance, Clinard (1983) documents the "pressures on middle management," such as threats to their opportunities for advancement or to their job security, that can discourage managers from speaking up about ethical concerns. Meyerson and Scully (1995) dramatize the dilemmas faced by change agents when judging how far they can stretch those they wish to lead. Rodrigues and Collinson (1995) analyze the different ways in which Brazilian employees use humor to "camouflage and express their dissent" (1995: 740), as well as the times when camouflage was powerful (and the conditions under which more acerbic satire was used). Thus, frivolous expression of resistance seems unlikely, since individuals who engage in it could face severe penalties and are aware that they should tread lightly.

Hence, what some may perceive as disrespectful or unfounded opposition might also be motivated by individuals' ethical principles or by their desire to protect the organization's best interests. It is worth entertaining efforts to take those good intentions more seriously by downplaying the invalidating aspect of labeling responses to change "resistant."

Varying Emphases in the Conceptualization of Resistance

Studies of resistance would also benefit from careful attention to the concept's meaning. As Davidson argues, resistance has come to include

> anything and everything that workers do which managers do not want them to do, and that workers do not do that managers wish them to do . . . resort to such an essentially residual category of analysis can easily obscure a multiplicity of different actions and meanings that merit more precise analysis in their own right [1994: 94].

A review of past empirical research reveals three different emphases in conceptualizations of resistance: as a cognitive state, as an emotional state, and as a behavior. Although these conceptualizations overlap somewhat, they diverge in important ways. Finding a way to bring together these varying emphases should deepen our understanding of how employees respond to proposed organizational changes.

Portraying resistance in terms of behavior has been common since the earliest work on the topic. In his early theorizing, Lewin (1952) defined resistance by using a metaphor from the physical sciences. In their classic study Coch and French (1948) focused on the undesirable behaviors of workers in response to management-imposed changes in jobs and work methods. With their quasi-experiment they examined whether encouraging employee participation in planning a change would reduce resistance. Although their conceptual discussion indicated that resistance could involve undesirable behaviors and/or aggression, their measures focused on neither. Instead, the criterion they used to compare the treatment and control groups was desirable behavior, in the form of compliance with the production rate standards set by management. (Although strict compliance with the rate standards may or may not have been accompanied by undesirable behaviors or aggression, this possibility could not have been captured in the measures reported.) This study generated a large body of work on the effects of participative decision making (see McCaffrey, Faerman, & Hart, 1995, for a recent review).

More recent studies of resistance also have focused on behavior. For instance, Brower and Abolafia (1995) define resistance as a particular kind of action or inaction, and Ashforth and Mael (1998) define resistance as intentional acts of commission (defiance) or omission. Similarly, Shapiro, Lewicki, and Devine (1995) suggest that willingness to deceive authorities constitutes resistance to change, and Sagie, Elizur, and Greenbaum (1985) use compliant behavior as evidence of reduced resistance.

In contrast, other scholars have described resistance in emotional terms. For example, Coch and French (1948) acknowledged a more emotional component of resistance (aggression), and in their preliminary theory of resistance described the forces that they believed produced frustration in employees and caused the undesirable behaviors. Similarly, Vince and Broussine (1996) surveyed the responses of managers in public service organizations to a period of change in structure and financial constraints. They found that managers' responses were often paradoxically emotional. And, finally, the ideas of frustration and anxiety underpin Argyris and Schön's (1974, 1978) perspective that resistance arises from defensive routines. The approach that they advocate emphasizes the role of an external consultant in surfacing the defensiveness inherent in those routines, finding ways to minimize or dissipate the anxiety that reinforces those routines, and making time for calmer consideration of how to repair them (Argyris, 1993). As Diamond (1986) points out, although the remedy for resistance that they recommend involves a cognitive realignment of resistors' espoused theories and their theories-in-use, the underlying nature of resistance is portrayed as highly emotional.

The idea that resistance can be overcome cognitively suggests that it may include a component of negative thoughts about the change. Watson (1982) suggests that what is often labeled as resistance is, in fact, only reluctance. Armenakis, Harris, and Mossholder (1993) define resistance in behavioral terms but suggest that another state precedes it: a cognitive state they call ''(un)readiness.'' A reinterpretation of the Coch and French quasi-experiment (Bartlem & Locke, 1981) suggests that participation might have motivational and cognitive effects on resistance to change, also implying that cognition is part of the phenomenon of resistance.

Each of these three emphases in conceptualizations of resistance—as a behavior, an emotion, or a belief—has merit and represents an important part of our experience of responses to change. Thus, any definition focusing on one view at the expense of the others seems incomplete. Therefore, rather than privilege one conceptualization over the others, I seek to integrate the three alternative views of resistance to change.

A NEW VIEW OF RESPONSES TO CHANGE: AMBIVALENT ATTITUDES

These three emphases in the conceptualization of resistance to change can be reframed in a more integrative way by borrowing the concept of attitude from social psychology. Mindful adaptation of the concept might be required, because the research on attitudes does not always provide clear guidance about which dimensions of attitudes are most salient.

Multiple Dimensions of Attitudes

Early attitude theorists (Katz, 1960; Rosenberg & Hovland, 1960) argued that attitudes are structured along three dimensions, which roughly correspond with the three definitions that have dominated research on resistance to change. I label these three dimensions of attitudes the cognitive, emotional, and intentional. This conception is known as the tripartite view of attitudes (Ajzen, 1984).

In this view the cognitive dimension of an attitude refers to an individual's beliefs about the attitude object. In their review of the literature on the tripartite view, Eagly and Chaiken define this dimension as follows: "beliefs express positive or negative evaluation of greater or lesser extremity, and occasionally are exactly neutral in their evaluative content" (1998: 271). The emotional dimension of an attitude refers to an individual's feelings in response to the attitude object. Eagly and Chaiken define this dimension as the "feelings, moods, emotions, and sympathetic nervous-system activity that people have experienced in relation to an attitude object and subsequently associate with it" (1998: 272).

The third dimension of attitudes is the most complex and controversial, both because in some studies researchers find evidence of only two dimensions and because others who find a third dimension label it inconsistently. The findings of past empirical studies of the tripartite attitude structure are mixed (e.g., Bagozzi, 1978; Breckler, 1984; Kothandapani, 1971), and as Eagly and Chaiken conclude, "Evidence supports the empirical separability of three classes of evaluative responses under some but certainly not all circumstances'' (1993: 13). In the traditional tripartite view, the conative dimension of an attitude reflects an individual's evaluations of an attitude object that are based in past behaviors and future intentions to act. Some researchers place more emphasis on past behaviors, whereas others focus on future intentions. In some cases a separate attitude dimension concerning intentions or behavior has been identified, but in other cases intentions are so loosely connected with other dimensions of attitudes that they have been treated as entirely separate constructs.

In the context considered here, because an employee facing a newly proposed organizational change is responding to a novel event, the conative dimension is more likely to reflect intentions than past behaviors. (The employee might not find the change process particularly novel, but the specific proposal is likely to have some novel aspects.) Also, it seems more desirable in this applied context to treat behavior as a separate construct so that the mutual influences of attitudes and behavior on one another are not buried in an already complex set of issues. In other words, it is useful to distinguish between an intention to resist at the attitudinal level and dissent or protest at the level of actual behavior, which might or might not be planned. By ''an intention'' I mean a plan or resolution to take some action, rather than a plan to try to achieve some goal (Bagozzi, 1992).

Much of the work on resistance in labor process theory (e.g., Jermier et al., 1994), as well as some recent work on extrarole behaviors, such as taking charge (e.g., Morrison & Phelps, 1999), focuses on dissent or protest, whether intentional, habitual, or spontaneous. Distinguishing between intention and behavior will allow more careful study of the connections between the two concepts. Whether the intentional dimension is sufficiently associated with individuals' cognitive and emotional responses to be treated as a dimension of an employee's attitude remains an empirical question in the context of an attitude about a proposed organizational change.

One remaining contentious question in attitude research concerns the causal relationships among the dimensions. Fiske and Pavelchak (1986) label the two dominant positions in the debate the ''piecemeal'' and ''category-based'' views. In the piecemeal view, advanced by scholars such as Zanna and Rempel (1988), it is posited that variations in evaluation along the particular dimensions of an attitudinal response will cause variations in global attitude. In the category-based view (Ajzen, 1984; Davis & Ostrom, 1984), the global attitude is viewed as primary; changes in the global evaluation are modeled as causes of variation in the cognitive, emotional, and intentional dimensions, rather than as results of variation in those dimensions. Unfortunately, these views are still the subject of continuing debate in social psychology, and competing interpretations and new data are still being advanced.

In summary, questions of how the multiple dimensions of employee responses to change should be defined—and how they are related to one another—remain open to further clarification through empirical research. Social psychological research, however, clearly supports a multidimensional view of attitudes that can be used to integrate the inconsistent definitions of resistance that have been found in organizational studies. Thus, an employee's response to an organizational change along the cognitive dimension might range from strong positive beliefs (i.e., "this change is essential for the organization to succeed") to strong negative beliefs (i.e., "this change could ruin the company"). An employee's response along the emotional dimension might range from strong positive emotions (such as excitement or happiness) to strong negative emotions (such as anger or fear). An employee's response along the intentional dimension might range from positive intentions to support the change to negative intentions to oppose it.

The Possibility of Ambivalence in Response to a Particular Change Proposal

One key benefit of using this multidimensional definition to describe employees' attitudes toward proposed changes is that conceptualizing each dimension as a separate continuum allows for the possibility of different reactions along the different dimensions. In some cases this might only mean that beliefs about a proposed change are more positive than emotional responses to the change. However, with this definition we also recognize the possibility, in other cases, of ambivalent attitudes, where two alternative perspectives are both strongly experienced (Foy, 1985; Merton, 1976; Thompson, Zanna, & Griffin, 1995).

The simplest case of ambivalence to imagine is the case in which an individual's cognitive response to a proposed change is in conflict with his or her emotional response to the proposal. Furthermore, ambivalence within a dimension is also possible, and, in fact, ambivalence within the emotional dimension already has been reported in research. In particular, Russell (1980) and Watson, Clark, and Tellegen (1988) have presented data suggesting that positive and negative affect can co-occur. Similarly, Vince and Broussine's (1996) study of public service managers' responses to change shows that incongruent emotions, such as excitement and fear, are often experienced simultaneously.

In principle, ambivalence could occur within the cognitive or intentional dimensions as well. For instance, an employee exhibiting cognitive ambivalence might simultaneously believe that the change proposed in his or her organization is necessary for its future survival but is not yet sufficiently well researched. An employee exhibiting intentional ambivalence might plan to oppose a proposed change through anonymous comments in the suggestion box but might support the change in public because of uncertainty about how top management will respond to criticism of the change initiative. Although research does not shed any light on the likelihood of intentional ambivalence, anecdotal evidence of its occurrence can be found; Drummond's (1998) case study of a site manager's indirect opposition to the proposed closure of his facility has similar elements.

The Prevalence of Ambivalent Attitudes

The following examples of employees' responses to organizational change, drawn from interviews,[2] also illustrate the merits of assessing their attitudes toward change along three dimensions. In the first example an employee had learned that his budget for offering incentives to his distributors was disappearing. His emotional response to the announcement was quite negative. Because the budget cut was announced late in his planning cycle, the announcement shocked and frustrated him. However, he also reported a positive cognitive response to the change: he believed the change would have positive effects, since the budget for product improvements was being increased to allow his distributors to offer their customers a more attractive product. Thus, this employee's response represents an example of an ambivalent attitude toward the proposed budget change, because of the incongruity between his cognitive and emotional responses to the proposal.

A second example comes from an interview with a middle manager in a large, diversified company, who described his response to the restructuring and centralization of his organization around a new enterprisewide software system. His initial reaction to the restructuring included positive beliefs, because he felt the change was sorely needed, as well as positive emotions, reflected in expressions of enthusiasm. However, he reported increasingly negative intentions over time, and he planned to challenge his leadership to cancel the project if they would not provide the support that was needed. He later spoke out against the dangers of the "behemoth project." Although he still believed the change was needed, he was discouraged by his coworkers' lack of commitment. Thus, this manager's initial attitude can be represented as initially supportive, but it evolved to a more ambivalent state as his negative intentions solidified and his negative emotions toward his coworkers' laxity emerged.

The third example is drawn from an interview with a consultant who learned that his firm was merging with another consulting company. He initially responded with a combination of excitement and fear, demonstrating ambivalence within the emotional dimension of his response to the change. In his case that ambivalence motivated his efforts to gather information about the rationale for the merger and to assess the likelihood of job cuts in conjunction with it. Although he was not comfortable discussing the change with his superiors, because he did not want to reveal his fears and appear insecure, he and his peers were able to reassure each other through their surreptitious information gathering that the rationale for the merger was to acquire consulting skills in markets that his original firm had not already entered. As a result, he became an active supporter of the merger later on.[3]

In addition to this anecdotal evidence, there is also a theoretical reason to expect that most employees' responses to a proposed change will involve some ambivalence. We know from attitude research that the process of attitude formation often begins with ambivalence (e.g., Thompson et al., 1995). Furthermore, within the typology of alpha, beta, and gamma change, an initial response that is uniformly negative seems possible only in response to alpha changes, which involve a "variation in the level of [a] state, given a constantly calibrated measuring instrument" (Golembiewski, Billingsley, & Yeager, 1976: 134). Because some employees will already have formed an attitude toward the current point, they may be able to infer their attitude toward the proposed shift immediately.

However, as Beer and Walton (1987) point out, beta change involves developing a new understanding of what constitutes a shift on the reference dimension (or a "variation in the level of [a] state, complicated by the fact that some intervals of the measurement continuum . . . have been recalibrated," according to Golembiewski et al., 1976: 134). For example, a team trained in dialectic decision making might come to redefine what is meant by "too much conflict" in its meetings. Given the more complex process involved in making sense of a change proposal that involves such a recalibration, it seems unlikely that employees' inferences about their attitude toward a change proposal, such as the proposal to engage in a structured decision-making process, could be immediate.

Similarly, the gamma change process, which involves "a complete conceptual redefinition" (Beer & Walton, 1987: 342) and which may involve either the addition of new dimensions or the complete replacement of old reference dimensions with new ones (Porras & Silvers, 1991: 57), is even more complex. Thus, when facing beta or gamma change, employees seem more likely to engage in the formation of a new attitude, rather than simply shift their old attitude along a stable dimension. It seems reasonable to assume that most employees' initial responses to a beta or gamma change will be ambivalent.

For these reasons I conclude that conceptualizing employees' responses to proposed organizational changes as multidimensional attitudes permits a richer view of the ways in which employees may respond to change. Because of the potential for a multidimensional view of responses to change to inspire future research in such directions, I join Dent and Goldberg (1999) and Merron (1993) in arguing that we should retire the phrase "resistance to change," and I advocate a new wave of research on employee responses to change, conceptualized as multidimensional attitudes.

IMPLICATIONS FOR RESEARCH AND PRACTICE

There are five key implications of this alternative view for research and practice. First, a multidimensional view of responses to proposed change may enhance our accuracy in predicting employee behaviors that have been difficult to predict in past research.

For example, understanding exit, voice, loyalty, and neglect has continued to challenge theorists and empirical researchers (Hirschman, 1970; Janssen, de Vries, & Cozijnsen, 1998; Rusbult, Farrell, Rogers, & Mainous, 1988; Saunders, Sheppard, Knight, & Warshaw, 1992; Withey & Cooper, 1989). One premise that could aid in developing such a predictive framework is the idea that employees find it more difficult to express negative emotions than negative beliefs. (This premise is certainly implicit in Argyris and Schön's work, 1974 and 1978, although some employees may exhibit more facility than others in expressing their emotions.) From that premise it would follow that employees would be more likely to engage in voice than in loyalty or neglect when they experience ambivalence within their cognitive response to a proposed change. Because they can easily articulate their beliefs about the change, they would be more likely to share their reflections with the managers introducing the organizational change. Conversely, employees would be more likely to exhibit neglect when ambivalence occurs within the emotional dimension of their response to change or when an incongruity arises between their cognitive and their emotional reactions. Because it is difficult for them to articulate their negative emotional responses to change, they would be more likely to wrestle with their ambivalence alone or to avoid the subject entirely.

Similarly, understanding the nature of ambivalence in employee responses to change also might be useful in predicting the mode in which employees will communicate their responses to change agents and in identifying the most appropriate process for addressing their responses. For instance, when employees are experiencing emotional ambivalence rather than uniformly negative responses to a proposed change, they may be more likely to express their responses through humor (e.g., Rodrigues & Collinson, 1995) or other indirect modes of communication (e.g., Drummond, 1998). In such a case, more data about the change initiative might not be very useful, even if it can be provided efficiently in large-scale rollout meetings. Instead, more impromptu and casual conversations might be more effective in creating an atmosphere in which employees feel safe expressing their negative emotional responses openly.

Conversely, when employees are experiencing cognitive ambivalence about a proposed change but no negative emotional responses, they may be quite direct in expressing their concerns. In such a case, change agents might find that their listening ability is more important than their ability to communicate their own perspectives on the change to employees. Overselling the benefits of the change may not be effective in securing employee support, if employees already accept that the change will have some positive outcomes but feel a different perspective is required.

Of course, the merits of these premises are empirical questions, to be examined in future research on predicting employee voice, loyalty, and neglect and in research on the modes in which employee responses to change are expressed and managed.

A second key implication of the new multidimensional view of employee responses to proposed organizational changes is that the degree of ambivalence in an employee's attitude may have both desirable and undesirable consequences. Paying attention to balancing those consequences will help us understand how to manage change processes successfully. A variety of research indicates that divergent opinions about direction are necessary in order for groups to make wise decisions and for organizations to change effectively. For instance, recent research on institutionalized dissent (Cohen & Staw, 1998) shows that sometimes organizations encourage and plan for dissent and ritualize disagreement. Although the fact that organizations encourage dissent does not necessarily imply that dissent is functional, it is one reasonable explanation for the prevalence of such an organizational practice.

Furthermore, research on organizational learning indicates that disagreement and disconfirmation of expectations can be important triggers for developing knowledge. In fact, Barnett argues that "'an emphasis on failure, negative feedback, stress, or crisis' as a learning stimulus has eclipsed the potential importance of other meaningful stimuli (e.g., opportunities, people, and success)" (1994: 8) as conditions that foster learning. Similarly, research on strategic change processes indicates that disagreement can play a key role in supporting organizational renewal. Studies by Barr, Stimpert, and Huff (1992), Burgelman (1991), and Floyd and Wooldridge (1996) show that if the organization's managers do not experiment, it seems unlikely that they will be able to carry out a renewal process. The implication of all this research is that moving too quickly toward congruent positive attitudes toward a proposed change might cut off the discussion and improvisation that may be necessary for revising the initial change proposal in an adaptive manner.

It is not clear, however, whether the expression of resistance (i.e., uniformly negative responses to change) is likely to encourage continued discussion, debate, and improvisation. Indeed, the honest expression of ambivalence seems more likely to generate dialogue than the expression of either determined opposition or firm support.

Several research pieces also indicate that ambivalence and its acknowledgment might have positive effects. Pratt and Barnett (1997) argue that ambivalence is needed to stimulate unlearning (the discarding of obsolete and misleading knowledge), which is a necessary precursor to change. Similarly, Weigert and Franks argue that the expression of ambivalence in public "is likely to lead to public collective responses" (1989: 223), suggesting that acknowledging ambivalence can provide a basis for motivating new action, rather than the continuation of old routines. Furthermore, recent research on creativity indicates that "insight is primarily dependent on analogical retrieval . . . moreover, this retrieval usually is cued by some external event" (Sternberg, 1988: 3). Work by Langley and Jones (1988) and by Weisberg (1988) shows that the ability to perceive a situation from a different angle or to apply a novel analogy is often the key to finding a previously unconsidered alternative that may lead to novel behavior. All this work suggests that by fostering ambivalence and reframing our understanding of the status quo, we are better able to generate new possibilities for understanding and action.

For change agents and for theorists, the strategy of fostering ambivalence rather than support in the early stages of a change initiative invites a different view of how the first stage of a change process should play out. The first stage in creating change should be generating widespread conversation, rather than beginning the change process by engaging a small group of managers in identifying the desired change and later aiming to gain broader employee support for that proposal. This strategy is less consistent with a view of change as a planned process (Porras & Silvers, 1991) and more consistent with a microlevel perspective on change as a continuous process in which "ongoing adaptation and adjustment" occur (Weick & Quinn, 1999: 362). Some models of this type of change process are emerging, such as the trialectic view of change advocated by Ford and Ford (1994) and the five-stage process model of breakaway organizations developed by Dyck and Starke (1999). How change agents begin to generate conversation around ambivalence about new possibilities is an important question for future research on the first phase of the change process.

Ambivalence, however, must be fostered with care; we also know from other streams of research that acknowledging ambivalence might not always be optimal. On the one hand, Weigert and Franks warn that "if ambivalence is not ritually enacted and meaningfully interpreted, its power to fuel extreme responses grows" (1989: 223). On the other hand, Schwartz (1986) examined the effect of inner dialogue on personal and relational well-being and found that an inner dialogue characterized by a high ratio of positive to negative statements was associated with greater well-being.

This finding suggests that acknowledging both polarities of an ambivalent attitude toward a change proposal with equal time might be unhealthy. Thus, the question that emerges for research and practice concerns the tensions generated by fostering ambivalence: How can we balance the need for ambivalence with the need to limit its debilitating effects?

A third key implication of the new multidimensional view concerns the need to expand our research beyond our past focus on top-down organizational change. Increasingly, change processes are managed in emergent and democratic ways. However, our theorizing may not be keeping pace, except in some emerging research. For example, in the appreciative inquiry process (Cooperrider, 1998; Cooperrider & Srivastva, 1987), the proposal emerges from and is tempered and repeatedly revised by an inclusive dialogue among a large number of employees across many levels of hierarchy. In this approach the important question of what it means to respond to a "proposed change" is framed, when the nature of the change that is proposed remains ambiguous for much of the process. Here, finding answers to the questions of how multiple dimensions of an employee's responses to a change evolve over time and how such shifts are related to the effectiveness with which change is implemented seems even more important.

A fourth implication of these ideas is that employee responses to change may evolve over time, and paying attention to this evolution might yield insights about how to manage change initiatives successfully. For example, a formal change announcement from the CEO may shift employees' cognitive responses to a change quite quickly from negative to positive, but their emotional responses may require more time to shift from negative to positive, through many informal conversations after the formal rollout speech. Observing patterns of attitudes and ambivalence over time might be more useful in predicting the success of a change initiative than examining the favorability of employees' attitudes toward the change at any one point in time. The implication is that both scholars and managers need to pay more attention to the dynamic processes that help to acknowledge and sustain ambivalence without letting it impede the momentum of change.

A final implication of these ideas is that scholars who wish to understand the full range of individual responses to proposed organizational changes should assess those responses along multiple dimensions. Applied research is needed to continue the process of mindfully adapting the concept of tripartite attitudes from social psychology. Relevant methods for operationalizing the dimensions could include interviews (Piderit, 1998), surveys (Piderit, 1999), and even more novel approaches, such as drawing (Vince & Broussine, 1996).

CONCLUSION

There is power in metaphor, but the physical metaphor of "resistance to change" may have taken us as far as we can go. In this chapter I critiqued research on resistance to change for failure to take the good intentions of resistors seriously and for the varying emphases in conceptualizations of resistance. I proposed a new conception of responses to proposed organizational changes as multidimensional attitudes. This new conception is intended to encourage an appreciation for the prevalence of ambivalence in individuals' responses to change. Investigations of what motivates those responses to change also will be needed, as well as studies of both the positive and the negative consequences of ambivalence of different types.

These ideas are not all new to the field, but earlier admonitions about the benefits of employee input and the drawbacks of dismissing subordinates' responses to change were not consistently brought to center stage in organization studies. If we can do better, we will be able to offer guidance to all employees involved in change processes and not just to change agents with official authority. Our research will begin to give equal attention to top-down, planned change and to bottom-up or egalitarian change processes. Finally, we will take on the challenge of helping organization members reap the benefits of ambivalence toward change for organizations while minimizing its potentially stressful effects for individuals.

Notes

1. I gratefully acknowledge the comments of Richard Bagozzi, David Deeds, Jane Dutton, Loren Dyck, Phoebe Ellsworth, Eric Neilsen, Mary Grace Neville, Janet Weiss, and the reviewers and special issue editor on earlier versions of this work.

2. To illustrate how the tripartite definition of attitudes could be used to describe employees' responses to organizational changes, I collected stories about employees' reactions to recently proposed changes in their organization. I conducted seven interviews with professionals and five with managers. The interviewees had varied functional backgrounds, and they described their reactions to three types of organizational changes (updating work processes, developing new initiatives, and restructuring). The interview protocol appears in Piderit (1999).

3. These three employees' descriptions of their reactions to change were typical of the reactions reported in interviews, since most of the interviewees described their reactions to the organizational changes that they faced in terms of a mix of positive and negative thoughts, emotions, and behavioral intentions. Four of the twelve interviewees reported enduring ambivalence in response to the change they faced, and another five interviewees reported initial ambivalence.

References

Ajzen, I. 1984. Attitudes. In R. J. Corsini (Ed.), *Wiley encyclopedia of psychology*, vol. 1: 99–100. New York: Wiley.

Ajzen, I. 1987. Attitudes, traits, and actions: Dispositional prediction of behavior in personality and social psychology. In L. Berkowitz (Ed.), *Advances in experimental social psychology*, vol. 20: 1–63. New York: Academic Press.

Argyris, C. 1993. *Knowledge for action: A guide to overcoming barriers to organizational change*. San Francisco: Jossey-Bass.

Argyris, C., & Schön, D. 1974. *Theory in practice*. San Francisco: Jossey-Bass.

Argyris, C., & Schön, D. 1978. *Organizational learning*. Reading, MA: Addison-Wesley.

Armenakis, A. A., Harris, S. G., & Mossholder, K. W. 1993. Creating readiness for organizational change. *Human Relations*, 46: 681–703.

Ashford, S. J., Rothbard, N. P., Piderit, S. K., & Dutton, J. E. 1998. Out on a limb: The role of context and impression management in selling gender-equity issues. *Administrative Science Quarterly*, 43: 23–57.

Ashforth, B. E., & Mael, F. A. 1998. The power of resistance: Sustaining valued identities. In R. M. Kramer & M. A. Neale (Eds.), *Power and influence in organizations*: 89–120. Thousand Oaks, CA: Sage.

Bagozzi, R. P. 1978. The construct validity of the affective, behavioral, and cognitive components of attitude by analysis of covariance structures. *Multivariate Behavior Research*, 13: 9–31.

Bagozzi, R. P. 1992. The self-regulation of attitudes, intentions, and behavior. *Social Psychology Quarterly*, 55: 178–204.

Barnett, C. K. 1994. *Organizational learning theories: A review and synthesis of the literature*. Working paper, University of Michigan, Ann Arbor.

Barr, P. S., Stimpert, J. L., & Huff, A. S. 1992. Cognitive change, strategic action, and organizational renewal. *Strategic Management Journal*, 13: 15–36.

Bartlem, C. S., & Locke, E. A. 1981. The Coch and French study: A critique and re-interpretation. *Human Relations*, 34: 555–566.

Beer, M., & Walton, A. E. 1987. Organization change and development. *Annual Review of Psychology*, 38: 339–367.

Breckler, S. J. 1984. Empirical validation of affect, behavior, and cognition as distinct components of attitude. *Journal of Personality and Social Psychology*, 47: 1191–1205.

Brower, R. S., & Abolafia, M. Y. 1995. The structural embeddedness of resistance among public managers. *Group and Organization Management*, 20: 149–166.

Burgelman, R. A. 1991. Intraorganizational ecology of strategy making and organizational adaptation: Theory and field research. *Organization Science*, 2: 239–262.

Clinard, M. B. 1983. *Corporate ethics and crime: The role of middle management*. Beverly Hills, CA: Sage.

Coch, L., & French, J.R.P., Jr. 1948. Overcoming resistance to change. *Human Relations*, 1: 512–532.

Cohen, L. E., & Staw, B. M. 1998. Fun's over, fact checkers are here: A case study of institutionalized dissent in the magazine publishing industry. *Advances in Qualitative Organization Research*, 1: 105–136.

Cooperrider, D. L. 1998. *Capturing what matters most in the practice of appreciative inquiry: A positive revolution in change.* Paper presented at the annual meeting of the Academy of Management, San Diego.

Cooperrider, D. L., & Srivastva, S. 1987. Appreciative inquiry in organizational life. *Research in Organizational Change and Development*, 1: 129–169.

Davidson, J. O'C. 1994. The sources and limits of resistance in a privatized utility. In J. M. Jermier, D. Knights, & W. R. Nord (Eds.), *Resistance and power in organizations:* 69–101. New York: Routledge.

Davis, D., & Ostrom, T. M. 1984. Attitude measurement. In R. J. Corsini (Ed.), *Wiley encyclopedia of psychology:* 97–99. New York: Wiley.

Dent, E. B., & Goldberg, S. G. 1999. Challenging "resistance to change." *Journal of Applied Behavioral Sciences*, 35(1): 25–41.

Diamond, M. A. 1986. Resistance to change: A psychoanalytic critique of Argyris and Schön's contributions to organization theory and intervention. *Journal of Management Studies*, 23: 543–562.

Drummond, H. 1998. Go and say, "we're shutting": Ju Jitsu as a metaphor for analyzing resistance. *Human Relations*, 51: 741–759.

Dutton, J. E., Ashford, S. J., Wierba, E. E., O'Neill, R., & Hayes, E. 1997. Reading the wind: How middle managers assess the context for issue selling to top managers. *Strategic Management Journal*, 15: 407–425.

Dyck, B., & Starke, F. A. 1999. The formation of breakaway organizations: Observations and a process model. *Administrative Science Quarterly*, 44: 792–822.

Eagly, A. H., & Chaiken, S. 1993. *The psychology of attitudes*. Fort Worth, TX: Harcourt Brace Jovanovich.

Eagly, A. H., & Chaiken, S. 1998. Attitude structure and function. In D. T. Gilbert, S. T. Fiske, & G. Lindsey (Eds.), *Handbook of social psychology*, vol. 2: 269–322. Boston: McGraw-Hill.

Fiske, S. T., & Pavelchak, M. A. 1986. Category-based versus piecemeal-based affective responses: Developments in schema-triggered affect. In R. M. Sorrentino & E. T. Higgins (Eds.), *Handbook of motivation and cognition: Foundations of social behavior*, vol. 1: 167–203. New York: Guilford.

Floyd, S. W., & Wooldridge, B. 1996. *The strategic middle manager*. San Francisco: Jossey-Bass.

Ford, J. D., & Ford, L. W. 1994. Logics of identity, contradiction, and attraction in change. *Academy of Management Review*, 19: 756–785.

Foy, N. 1985. Ambivalence, hypocrisy, and cynicism: Aids to organization change. *New Management*, 2(4): 49–53.

Golembiewski, R. T., Billingsley, K., & Yeager, S. 1976. Measuring change and persistence in human affairs: Types of change generated by OD designs. *Journal of Applied Behavioral Sciences*, 12(2): 133–157.

Graham, J. 1984. *Abstract of a dissertation on principled organizational dissent.* Paper presented at the annual meeting of the Society for Industrial and Organizational Psychology, Toronto.

Graham, J. 1986. Principled organizational dissent: A theoretical essay. *Research in Organizational Behavior,* 8: 1–52.

Graham, P. (Ed.). 1995. *Mary Parker Follett—prophet of management: A celebration of writings from the 1920s.* Boston: Harvard Business School Press.

Hirschman, A. O. 1970. *Exit, voice, and loyalty: Responses to decline in firms, organizations, and states.* Cambridge, MA: Harvard University Press.

Janssen, O., de Vries, T., & Cozijnsen, A. J. 1998. Voicing by adapting and innovating employees: An empirical study on how personality and environment interact to affect voice behavior. *Human Relations*, 51: 945–966.

Jermier, J. M., Knights, D., & Nord, W. R. (Eds.). 1994. *Resistance and power in organizations.* London: Routledge.

Jones, E. E., & Harris, V. A. 1967. The attribution of attitudes. *Journal of Experimental Social Psychology*, 3: 1–24.

Katz, D. 1960. The functional approach to the study of attitudes. *Public Opinion Quarterly*, 24: 163–204.

Klein, D. 1976. Some notes on the dynamics of resistance to change: The defender role. In W. G. Bennis, K. D. Benne, R. Chin, & K. E. Corey (Eds.), *The planning of change* (3rd ed.); 117–124. New York: Holt, Rinehart & Winston.

Kothandapani, V. 1971. Validation of feeling, belief, and intention to act as three components of attitude and their contribution to prediction of contraceptive behavior. *Journal of Personality and Social Psychology*, 19: 321–333.

Krantz, J. 1999. Comment on "challenging 'resistance to change.'" *Journal of Applied Behavioral Sciences*, 35(1): 42–44.

Langley, P., & Jones, R. 1988. A computational model of scientific insight. In R. J. Sternberg (Ed.), *The nature of creativity: Contemporary psychological perspectives:* 177–201. New York: Cambridge University Press.

Lawrence, P. R. 1954. How to deal with resistance to change. *Harvard Business Review*, 32(3): 49–57.

Lewin, K. 1952. Group decision and social change. In G. E. Swanson, T. M. Newcombe, & E. L. Hartley (Eds.), *Readings in social psychology* (2nd ed.): 459–473. New York: Holt.

McCaffrey, D. P., Faerman, S. R., & Hart, D. W. 1995. The appeal and difficulties of participative systems. *Organization Science*, 6: 603–627.

Merron, K. 1993. Let's bury the term "resistance." *Organizational Development Journal*, 11(4): 77–86.

Merton, R. K. 1976. *Sociological ambivalence and other essays*. New York: Free Press.

Meyerson, D. E., & Scully, M. A. 1995. Tempered radicalism and the politics of ambivalence and change. *Organization Science*, 6: 585–600.

Milgram, S. 1965. Some conditions of obedience and disobedience to authority. *Human Relations*, 18: 57–76.

Modigliani, A., & Rochat, F. 1995. The role of interaction sequences and the timing of resistance in shaping obedience and defiance to authority. *Journal of Social Issues*, 51(3): 107–123.

Morrison, E. W., & Phelps, C. C. 1999. Taking charge at work: Extrarole efforts to initiate workplace change. *Academy of Management Journal*, 42: 403–419.

Piderit, S. K. 1998. *United we stand: Embedding attitudes toward change in social relationships*. Paper presented at the annual meeting of the Academy of Management, San Diego.

Piderit, S. K. 1999. *Navigating relationships with coworkers: Understanding employees' attitudes toward an organizational change*. Unpublished doctoral dissertation, University of Michigan, Ann Arbor.

Porras, J. I., & Silvers, R. C. 1991. Organization development and transformation. *Annual Review of Psychology*, 42: 51–78.

Pratt, M. G., & Barnett, C. K. 1997. Emotions and unlearning in Amway recruiting techniques: Promoting change through "safe" ambivalence. *Management Learning*, 28(1): 65–88.

Rodrigues, S. B., & Collinson, D. L. 1995. "Having fun"?: Humor as resistance in Brazil. *Organization Studies*, 16: 739–768.

Rosenberg, M. J., & Hovland, C. I. 1960. Cognitive, affective, and behavioral components of attitudes. In M. J. Rosenberg (Ed.), *Attitude organization and change*: 1–14. New Haven, CT: Yale University Press.

Rusbult, C. E., Farrell, D., Rogers, G., & Mainous, A. G. 1988. Impact of exchange variables on exit, voice, loyalty, and neglect: An integrative model of responses to declining job satisfaction. *Academy of Management Journal*, 31: 599–627.

Russell, J. A. 1980. A circumplex model of affect. *Journal of Personality and Social Psychology*, 39: 1161–1178.

Sagie, A., Elizur, D., & Greenbaum, C. W. 1985. Job experience, persuasion strategy, and resistance to change. *Journal of Occupational Behavior*, 6: 157–162.

Saunders, D. M., Sheppard, B. H., Knight, V., & Warshaw, P. R. 1992. Employee voice to supervisors. *Employee Responsibility and Rights Journal*, 3: 241–259.

Schwartz, R. M. 1986. The inner dialogue: On the asymmetry between positive and negative coping thoughts. *Cognitive Therapy and Research*, 10: 591–605.

Shapiro, D. L., Lewicki, R. J., & Devine, P. 1995. When do employees choose deceptive tactics to stop unwanted organizational change? *Research on Negotiation in Organizations*, 5: 155–184.

Sternberg, R. J. (Ed.). 1988. *The nature of creativity: Contemporary psychological perspectives*. New York: Cambridge University Press.

Thomas, R. J. 1989. Participation and control: A shopfloor perspective on employee participation. *Research in the Sociology of Organizations*, 7: 117–144.

Thompson, M. M., Zanna, M. P., & Griffin, D. W. 1995. Let's not be indifferent about (attitudinal) ambivalence. In R. E. Petty & J. A. Krosnick (Eds.), *Attitude strength: Antecedents and consequences*: 361–386. Mahwah, NJ: Lawrence Erlbaum Associates.

Vince, R., & Broussine, M. 1996. Paradox, defense, and attachment: Accessing and working with emotions and relations underlying organizational change. *Organization Studies*, 17: 1–21.

Watson, D., Clark, L. A., & Tellegen, A. 1988. Development and validation of brief measures of positive and negative affect: The PANAS scales. *Journal of Personality and Social Psychology*, 54: 1063–1070.

Watson, T. J. 1982. Group ideologies and organizational change. *Journal of Management Studies*, 19: 259–275.

Weick, K. E., & Quinn, R. E. 1999. Organizational change and development. *Annual Review of Psychology*, 50: 361–386.

Weigert, A., & Franks, D. D. 1989. Ambivalence: Touchstone of the modern temper. In D. D. Franks & E. D. McCarthy (Eds.), *The sociology of emotions*: 205–227. Greenwich, CT: JAI Press.

Weisberg, R. W. 1988. Problem solving and creativity. In R. J. Sternberg (Ed.), *The nature of creativity: Contemporary psychological perspectives*: 148–176. New York: Cambridge University Press.

Withey, M. J., & Cooper, W. H. 1989. Predicting exit, voice, loyalty and neglect. *Administrative Science Quarterly*, 34: 521–539.

Zanna, M. P., & Rempel, J. K. 1988. Attitudes: A new look at an old concept. In D. Bar-Tal & A. W. Kruglanski (Eds.), *The social psychology of knowledge*: 315–334. New York: Cambridge University Press.

GROUP RESPONSE TO CHANGE

CHAPTER TWENTY-SEVEN

A Theory of Group Development

Warren G. Bennis
Herbert A. Shepard (1956)

I f attention is focused on the organic properties of groups, criteria can be established by which phenomena of development, learning, or movement toward maturity can be identified. From this point of view, maturity for the group means something analogous to maturity for the person; a mature group knows very well what it is doing. The group can resolve its internal conflicts, mobilize its resources, and take intelligent action only if it has means for consensually validating its experience. The person can resolve internal conflicts, mobilize resources, and take intelligent action only if anxiety does not interfere with the ability to profit from is experience, to analyze, discriminate, and foresee. Anxiety prevents the person's internal communication system from functioning appropriately, and improvements in the ability to profit from experience hinge upon overcoming anxiety as a source of distortion. Similarly, group development involves the overcoming of obstacles to valid communication among the members, or the development of methods for achieving and testing consensus. Extrapolating from Sullivan's definition of personal maturity, we can say a group has reached a state of valid communication when its members are armed with

> referential tools for analyzing interpersonal experience, so that its significant differences from, as well as its resemblances to, past experience, are discriminable, and the foresight of relatively near future events will be adequate and appropriate to maintaining one's security and securing one's satisfactions without useless or ultimately troublesome disturbance of self-esteem [1950, p. 11].

Relatively few investigations of the phenomena of group development have been undertaken. This chapter outlines a theory of development in groups that have as their explicit goal improvement of their internal communications systems.[1]

A group of strangers, meeting for the first time, has within it many obstacles to valid communication. The more heterogeneous the membership, the more accurately does the group become, for each member, a microcosm of the rest of his or her interpersonal experience. The problems of understanding, the relationships, that develop in any given group are from one aspect a unique product of the particular constellation of personalities assembled. But to construct a broadly useful theory of group development, it is necessary to identify major areas of internal uncertainty, or obstacles to valid communication, that are common to and important in all groups meeting under a given set of environmental conditions. These areas must be strategic in the sense that until the group has developed methods for reducing uncertainty in them, it cannot reduce uncertainty in other areas, and thus in its external relations.

TWO MAJOR AREAS OF INTERNAL UNCERTAINTY: DEPENDENCE AND INTERDEPENDENCE

Two major areas of uncertainty can be identified by induction from common experience, at least within our own culture. The first of these is the area of *group members' orientations toward authority,* or more generally toward the handling and distribution of power in the group. The second is the area of *members' orientations toward one another*. These areas are not independent of each other; a particular set of intermember orientations will be associated with a particular authority structure. But the two sets of orientations are as distinct from each other as are the concepts of power and love. A number of authorities have used them as a starting point for the analysis of group behavior.

In his *Group Psychology and the Analysis of the Ego*, Freud noted that "each member is bound by libidinal ties on one hand to the leader . . . and on the other hand to the other members of the group" (1922/1949, p. 45). Although he described both ties as libidinal, he was uncertain "how these two ties are related to each other, whether they are of the same kind and the same value, and how they are to be described psychologically." Without resolving this question, he noted that (for the Church and the Army) "one of these, the tie with the leader, seems . . . to be more of a ruling factor than the other, which holds between members of the group" (p. 52).

More recently, Schutz (1955) has made these two dimensions central to his theory of group compatibility. For him, the strategic determinant of compatibility is the particular blend of orientations toward authority and orientations toward personal intimacy. Bion (1948a, 1948b) conceptualizes the major dimensions of the group somewhat differently. His "dependency" and "pairing" modalities correspond to our "dependence" and "interdependence" areas; to them he adds a "fight-flight" modality. For him these modalities are simply alternative modes of behavior; for us, the fight-flight categorization has been useful for characterizing the means used by the group for maintaining a stereotyped orientation during a given subphase.

The core of the theory of group development is that the principal obstacles to the development of valid communication are to be found in the orientation toward authority and intimacy that members bring to the group. Rebelliousness, submissiveness, or withdrawal as the characteristic response to authority figures; destructive competitiveness, emotional exploitiveness, or withdrawal as the characteristic response to peers prevent consensual validation of experience. The behaviors determined by these orientations are directed toward enslavement of the other in the service of the self, enslavement of the self in the service of the other, or disintegration of the situation. Hence, they prevent the setting of, clarification of, and movement toward group-shared goals.

In accord with Freud's observation, the orientations toward authority are regarded as being prior to, or partially determining of, orientations toward other members. In its development, the group moves from preoccupation with authority relations to preoccupation with personal relations. This movement defines the two major phases of group development. Within each phase are three subphases, determined by the ambivalence of orientations in each area. That is, during the authority ("dependence") phase, the group moves from preoccupation with submission to preoccupation with rebellion, to resolution of the dependence problem. Within the personal (or "interdependence") phase the group moves from a preoccupation with intermember identification to a preoccupation with individual identity to a resolution of the interdependence problem.

THE RELEVANT ASPECTS OF PERSONALITY IN GROUP DEVELOPMENT

The aspects of member personality most heavily involved in group development are called, following Schutz, the dependence and personal aspects.

The dependence aspect comprises the member's characteristic patterns related to a leader or to a structure of rules. Members who find comfort in rules of procedure, an agenda, an expert, etc., are called "dependent."

Members who are discomfited by authoritative structures are called "counterdependent."

The personal aspect comprises the member's characteristic patterns with respect to interpersonal intimacy. Members who cannot rest until they have stabilized a relatively high degree of intimacy with all the others are called "overpersonal." Members who tend to avoid intimacy with any of the others are called "counterpersonal."

Psychodynamically, members who evidence some compulsiveness in the adoption of highly dependent, highly counterdependent, highly personal, or highly counterpersonal roles are regarded as "conflicted." Thus, the person who persists in being dependent upon any and all authorities thereby provides ample evidence that authorities should not be so trustingly relied upon; yet he or she cannot profit from this experience in governing future action. Hence, a deep, but unrecognized, distrust is likely to accompany the manifestly submissive behavior, and the highly dependent or highly counterdependent person is thus a person in conflict. The existence of the conflict accounts for the sometimes dramatic movement from extreme dependence to extreme rebelliousness. In this way counterdependence and dependence, though logically the extremes of a scale, are psychologically very close together.

The "unconflicted" person or "independent," who is better able to profit from experience and assess the present situation more adequately, may of course act at times in rebellious or submissive ways. Psychodynamically, the difference between this person and the conflicted is easy to understand. In terms of observable behavior, the independent lacks the compulsiveness and, significantly, does not create the communicative confusion so characteristic of, say, the conflicted dependent, who manifests submission in that part of communication of which he or she is aware, and distrust or rebellion in that part of communication of which he or she is unaware.

Persons who are unconflicted with respect to the dependence or personal aspect are considered to be responsible for the major movements of the group toward valid communication. That is, the actions of members unconflicted with respect to the problems of a given phase of group development move the group to the next phase. Such actions are called barometric events, and the initiators are called catalysts. This part of the theory of group development is base on Redl's thesis concerning the "infectiousness of the unconflicted on the conflicted personality constellation." The catalysts (Redl calls them "central persons") are the persons capable of reducing the uncertainty characterizing a given phase. "Leadership" from the standpoint of group development can be defined in terms of catalysts responsible for group movement from one phase to the next. This consideration provides a basis for determining what membership roles are needed for group development. For example, it is expected that a group will have great difficulty in resolving problems of power and authority if it lacks members who are unconflicted with respect to dependence.

PHASE MOVEMENTS

The foregoing summary has introduced the major propositions in the theory of group development. Although it is not possible to reproduce the concrete group experience from which the theory is drawn, we can take a step in this direction by discussing in more detail what seem to us to be the dominant features of each phase. The description given below is highly interpretive, and we emphasize what seem to us to be the major themes of each phase, even though many minor themes are present. In the process of abstracting, stereotyping, and interpreting, certain obvious facts about group process are lost. For example, each group meeting is to some extent a recapitulation of its past and a forecast of its future. This means that behavior that is "regressive" or "advanced" often appears.

Phase One: Dependence

Subphase One: Dependence (Flight). The first days of group life are filled with behavior whose remote, as well as immediate, aim is to ward off anxiety. Much of the discussion content consists of fruitless searching for a common goal. Some of the security-seeking behavior is group-shared—for example, members may reassure one another by providing interesting and harmless facts about themselves. Some is idiosyncratic—for example, doodling, yawning, intellectualizing.

The search for a common goal is aimed at reducing the cause of anxiety, thus going beyond the satisfaction of immediate security needs. But just as evidencing boredom in this situation is a method of warding off anxiety by denying its proximity, so group goal seeking is not quite what it is claimed to be. It can best be understood as a dependence plea. The trainer, not the lack of a goal, is the cause of insecurity. This interpretation is likely to be vigorously contested by the group, but it is probably valid. The characteristic expectations of group members are that the trainer will establish rules of the game and distribute rewards. She is presumed to know what the goals are or ought to be. Hence her behavior is regarded as a "technique": she is merely playing hard to get. The pretense of a fruitless search for goals is a plea for her to tell the group what to do, by simultaneously demonstrating its helplessness without her, and its willingness to work under her direction for her approval and protection.

We are here talking about the dominant theme in group life. Many minor themes are present, and even in connection with the major theme there are differences among members. For some, testing the power of the trainer to affect their futures is the major concern. In others, anxiety may be aroused through a sense of helplessness in a situation made threatening by the protector's desertion. These alternatives can be seen as the beginnings of the counterdependent and dependent adaptations. Those with a dependent orientation look vainly for cues from the trainer for procedure and direction; sometimes paradoxically they infer that the leader must want it that way. Those with a counterdependent orientation strive to detect in the trainer's action elements that would offer grounds for rebellion, and may even paradoxically demand rules and leadership from her because she is failing to provide them.

The ambiguity of the situation at this stage quickly becomes intolerable for some, and a variety of ultimately unserviceable resolutions may be invented, many of them idiosyncratic. Alarm at the prospect of future meetings is likely to be group-shared, and at least a gesture may be made in the direction of formulating an agenda for subsequent meetings.

This phase is characterized by behavior that has gained approval from authorities in the past. Since the meetings are to be concerned with groups or with human relations, members offer information on these topics, to satisfy the presumed expectations of the trainer and to indicate expertise, interest, or achievement in these topics (ex-officers from the armed services, from fraternities, etc., have the floor). Topics such as business or political leadership, discrimination and desegregation are likely to be discussed. During this phase the contributions made by members are designed to gain approval from the trainer, whose reaction to each comment is surreptitiously watched. If the trainer comments that this seems to be the case, or if she notes that the subject under discussion (say, discrimination) may be related to some concerns about membership in this group, she fails again to satisfy the needs of members. Not that the validity of this interpretation is held in much doubt. No one is misled by the "flight" behavior involved in discussing problems external to the group, least of all the group members. Discussion of these matters is filled with perilous uncertainties, however, and so the trainer's observation is politely ignored, as one would ignore a *faux pas* at a tea party. The attempts to gain approval based on implicit hypotheses about the potential power of the trainer for good and evil are continued until the active members have run through the repertoire of behaviors that have gained them favor in the past.

Subphase Two: Counterdependence (Flight). As the trainer continues to fail miserably in satisfying the needs of the group, discussion takes on a different tone, and counterdependent expressions begin to replace overt dependency phase. In many ways this subphase is the most stressful and unpleasant in the life of the group. It is marked by a paradoxical development of the trainer's role into one of omnipotence and powerlessness, and by division of the group into two warring subgroups. In subphase one, feelings of hostility were strongly defended; if a slip were made that suggested hostility, particularly toward the trainer, the group members were embarrassed. Now expressions of hostility are more frequent, and are more likely to be supported by other members, or to be met with equally hostile responses. Power is much more overtly the concern of group members in this subphase. A topic such as leadership may again be discussed, but the undertones of the discussion are no longer dependence pleas. Discussion of leadership in subphase two is in part a vehicle for making explicit the trainer's failure as a leader. In part it is perceived by other members as a bid for leadership on the part of any member who participates in it.

The major themes of this subphase are as follows:

1. Two opposed subgroups emerge, together incorporating most of the group members. Characteristically, the subgroups are in disagreement about the group's need for leadership or "structure." One subgroup attempts to elect a chairman, nominate working committees, establish agenda, or otherwise "structure" the meetings; the other subgroup opposes all such efforts. At first this appears to be merely an intellectual disagreement concerning the future organization of group activity. But soon it becomes the basis for destroying any semblance of group unity. Fragmentation is expressed and brought about in many ways: voting is a favorite way of dramatizing the schism; suggestions that the group is too large and should be divided into subgroups for the meetings are frequent; a chair may be elected and then ignored as a demonstration of the group's ineffectualness. Although control mechanisms are sorely needed and desired, no one is willing to relinquish the rights of leadership and control to anyone else. The trainer's abdication has created a power gap, but no one is allowed to fill it.

2. Disenthrallment with the trainer proceeds rapidly. Group members see her as at best ineffectual, at worst damaging, to group progress. She is ignored and bullied almost simultaneously. Her interventions are perceived by the counterdependents as an attempt to interrupt group progress; by the dependents, as weak and incorrect statements. Her silences are regarded by the dependents as desertion; by the counterdependents as manipulation. Much of the group activity is to be understood as punishment of the trainer, for her failure to meet needs and expectations, for getting the group into an unpleasant situation, for being the worst kind of authority figure—a weak and incompetent one, or a manipulative, insincere one. Misunderstanding or ignoring her comments, implying that her observations are paranoid fantasies, demonstrations that the group is cracking up, references to her in the past tense as though she were no longer present—these are the punishments for her failure.

As, in the first subphase, the trainer's wisdom, power, and competence were overtly unquestioned, but secretly suspected; so, in the second subphase, the conviction that she is incompetent and helpless is clearly dramatized, but secretly doubted. Out of this secret doubt arises the belief in the trainer's omnipotence. None of the punishments meted out to the trainer are recognized as such by the group members; in fact, if the trainer suggests that the members feel a need to punish, they are most likely to respond in injured tones or in tones of contempt that what is going on has nothing to do with her and that she had best stay out of it. The trainer is still too imposing and threatening to challenge directly. There is a secret hope that the chaos in the group is in fact part of the master plan, that she is really leading them in the direction they should be going. That she may really be helpless as they imply, or that the failure may be theirs rather than hers, are frightening possibilities. For this reason subphase two differs very little in its fundamental dynamics from subphase one. There is still the secret wish that the trainer will stop all the bedlam that has replaced polite uncertainty, by taking her proper role (so that dependent members can cooperate with her and counterdependent can rebel in the usual ways).

Subphase two thus brings the group to the brink of catastrophe. The trainer has consistently failed to meet the group's needs. Not daring to turn directly on her, the group members engage in mutually destructive behavior; in fact, the group threatens suicide as the most extreme expression of dependence. The need to punish the trainer is so strong, however, that her act of salvation would have to be magical indeed.

Subphase Three: Resolution (Catharsis). No such magic is available to the trainer. Resolution of the group's difficulties at this point depends upon the presence in the group of other forces, which have until this time been inoperative, or ineffective. Only the degenerative aspects of the chain of events in subphases one and two have been presented up to this point and they are in fact the salient ones. But there has been a simultaneous, though less obvious, mobilization of constructive forces. First, within each of the warring subgroups bonds of mutual support have grown. The group member no longer feels helpless and isolated. Second, the trainer's role, seen as weak or manipulative in the dependence orientation, can also be perceived as permissive. Third, her interpretations, though openly ignored, have been secretly attended to. And as the second and third points imply, some members of the group are less the prisoners of the dependence-counterdependence dilemma than others. These members, called the independents, have been relatively ineffective in the group for two reasons. First, they have not developed firm bonds with other members in either of the warring subgroups, because they have not identified with either cause. Typically, they have devoted their energies to an unsuccessful search for a compromise settlement of the disagreements in the group. Since their attitudes toward authority are less ambivalent than those of other members, they have accepted the alleged reason for disagreement in the group—for example, whether a chair should be elected—at face value, and tried to mediate. Similarly, they have tended to accept the trainer's role and interpretations more nearly at face value. However, her interpretations have seemed inaccurate to them, since in fact the interpretations applied much less to them than to the rest of the group.

Subphase three is the most crucial and fragile in group life up to this point. What occurs is a sudden shift in the whole basis of group action. It is truly a bridging phase; if it occurs at all, it is so rapid and mercurial that the end of subphase two appears to give way to the first subphase of phase two. If it does not occur this rapidly and dramatically, a halting and arduous process of vacillation between phases one and two is likely to persist for a long period, the total group movement being very gradual.

To summarize the state of affairs at the beginning of subphase three: (1) the group is polarized into two competing groups, each unable to gain or relinquish power; (2) those group members who are uncommitted to either subgroup are ineffective in their attempts to resolve the conflict; and (3) the trainer's contributions only serve to deepen the cleavage in the group.

As the group enters subphase three, it is moving rapidly toward extinction, that is, splintering into two or three subgroups. The independents, who have until now been passive or ineffectual, become the only hope for survival, since they have thus far avoided polarization and stereotypic behavior. The imminence of dissolution forces them to recognize the fruitlessness of their attempts at mediation.

For this reason, the trainer's hypothesis that fighting one another is off-target behavior is likely to be acted upon at this point. A group member may openly express the opinion that the trainer's presence and comments are holding the group back, and suggest that "as an experiment" the trainer leave the group "to see how things go without her." When the trainer is thus directly challenged, the whole atmosphere of the meeting changes. There is a sudden increase in alertness and tension. Previously, there had been much acting out of the wish that the trainer were absent, but at the same time a conviction that she was the *raison d'être* of the group's existence—that it would fall apart without her. Previously, absence of the trainer would have constituted desertion, or defeat, fulfillment of the members' worst fears as to their own inadequacy or the trainer's. But now leaving the group can have a different meaning. General agreement that the trainer should leave is rarely achieved. However, after a little further discussion it becomes clear that she is at liberty to leave, with the understanding that she wishes to be a member of the group and will return if and when the group is willing to accept her.

The principal function of the symbolic removal of the trainer is in its effect of freeing the group to bring into awareness the hitherto carefully ignored feelings toward her as an authority figure, and toward the group activity as an off-target dramatization of the ambivalence toward authority. The leadership provided by the independents (whom the group sees as having no vested interest in power) leads to a new orientation toward membership in the group. In the discussion that follows the exit of the trainer, the dependents' assertion that the trainer deserted and the counterdependents' assertion that she was kicked out are soon replaced by consideration of whether her behavior was "responsible" or "irresponsible." The power problem is resolved by being defined in terms of member responsibilities, and the terms of the trainer's return to the group are settled by the requirement that she behave as "just another member of the group." This phrase is then explained as meaning that she should take neither more nor less responsibility for what happens in the group than any other member.

An interesting parallel, which throws light on the order of events in group development, is given in Freud's discussion of the myth of the primal horde. In his version: "These many individuals eventually banded themselves together, killed [the father], and cut him in pieces. . . . They then formed the totemistic community of brothers all with equal rights and united by the totem prohibitions which were to preserve and to expiate the memory of the murder" (1922/1949, p. 112).

The horde's act, according to Freud, was soon distorted into an heroic myth: instead of murder by the group, the myth held that the father had been overthrown single-handedly by one person, usually the youngest son. In this attribution of the group act to one individual (the hero), Freud saw the "emergence of the individual from group psychology." His definition of a hero is "a man who stands up manfully against his father and in the end victoriously overthrows him" (1939/1955, p. 9). (The heroic myth of Freud thus shares much in common with Sullivan's "delusion of unique individuality.")

In the training group, the member who initiates the events leading to the trainer's exit is sometimes referred to as a "hero" by the other members. Responsibility for the act is felt to be shared by the group, however, and out of their experience comes the first strong sense of group solidarity and involvement—a reversal of the original version, where the individual emerges from the group. This turn of events clarifies Freud's remark concerning the libidinal ties to the leader and to the other group members. Libidinal ties toward the other group members cannot be adequately developed until there is a resolution of the ties with the leader. In our terms, those components of group life having to do with intimacy and interdependence cannot be dealt with until those components having to do with authority and dependence have been resolved.

Other aspects of subphase three may be understood by investigating the dramatic significance of the revolt. The event is always marked in group history as "a turning point," "the time we became a group," "when I first got involved," etc. The mounting tension, followed by sometimes uproarious euphoria, cannot be entirely explained by the surface events. It may be that the revolt represents a realization of important fantasies individuals hold in all organizations, that the emotions involved are undercurrents wherever rebellious and submissive tendencies toward existing authorities must be controlled. These are the themes of some of our great dramas—*Antigone, Billy Budd, Hamlet,* and our most recent folk tale, *The Caine Mutiny.* But the event is more than the presentation of a drama, or an acting out of fantasies. For it can be argued that the moments of stress and catharsis, when emotions are labile and intense, are the times in the group life when there is a readiness for change. Leighton's analysis of a minor revolution at a Japanese relocation camp is worth quoting in full on this point:

> While this [cathartic] situation is fraught with danger because of trends which may make the stress become worse before it gets better, there is also an opportunity for administrative action that is not likely to be found in more secure times. It is fairly well recognized in psychology that at periods of great emotional stir the individual human being can undergo far-reaching and permanent changes in his personality. It is as if the bone structure of his systems of belief and of his habitual patterns of behavior becomes soft, is fused into new shapes and hardens there when the period of tension is over. . . . Possibly the same can be true of whole groups of people, and there are historical examples of social changes and movements occurring when there was widespread emotional tension, usually some form of anxiety. The Crusades, parts of the Reformation, the French Revolution, the change of Zulu life in the reign of Chaca, the Meiji Restoration, the Mormon movement, the Russian Revolution, the rise of Fascism, and alterations in the social sentiments of the United States going on at present are all to some extent examples" [1946, p.360].

Observers of industrial relations have made similar observations. When strikes result from hostile labor-management relations (as contrasted to straight wage demands), there is a fluidity of relationships and a wide repertoire of structural changes during this period not available before the strike act.[2]

So it is, we believe, with the training group. But what are the new values and behavior patterns that emerge out of the emotional experience of phase one? Principally, they are acceptance by each member of a full share of responsibility for what happens in the group. The outcome is autonomy for the group. After the events of subphase three, there is no more attribution of magical powers to the trainer—either dependent fantasy that she sees farther, knows better, is mysteriously guiding the group and protecting it from evil, or the very similar counterdependent fantasy that she is manipulating the group, exploiting it in her own interests, that the experience is one of "brain-washing." The criterion for evaluating a contribution is no longer who said it, but what is said. Thereafter, such power fantasies as the trainer herself may have present no different problem from the power fantasies of any other group member. At the same time, the illusion that there is a struggle for power in the group is suddenly dissipated, and the contributions of other members are evaluated in terms of their relevance to shared group goals.

Summary of Phase One

The very word *development* implies not only movement through time, but also a definite order of progression. The group must traverse subphase one to reach subphase two, and subphase three before it can move into phase two. At the same time, lower levels of development coexist with more advanced levels. Blocking and regression occur frequently, and the group may be "stuck" at a certain phase of development. It would, of course, be difficult to imagine a group remaining too long in subphase three—the situation is too tense to be permanent. But the group may founder for some time in subphase two with little movement. In short, groups do not inevitably develop through the resolution of the dependence phase to phase two. This movement may be retarded indefinitely. Obviously much depends on the trainer's role. In fact, the whole dependence modality may be submerged by certain styles of trainer behavior. The trainer has a certain range of choice as to whether dependency as a source of communication distortion is to be highlighted and made the subject of special experiential and conceptual consideration. The personality and training philosophy of the trainer determine her interest in introducing or avoiding explicit consideration of dependency.

There are other important forces in the group besides the trainer, and these may serve to facilitate or block the development that has been described as typical of phase one. Occasionally there may be no strong independents capable of bringing about the barometric events that precipitate movement. Or the leaders of opposing subgroups may be the most assertive members of the group. In such cases the group may founder permanently in subphase two. If a group has the misfortune to experience a "traumatic" event early in its existence—exceedingly schizoid behavior by some member during the first few meetings, for example—anxieties of other members may be aroused to an extent that all culturally suspect behavior, particularly open expressions of feelings, is strongly inhibited in subsequent meetings.

Table 27.1 summarizes the major events of phase one, as it typically proceeds. This phase has dealt primarily with the resolution of dependence needs. It ends with acceptance of mutual responsibility for the fate of the group and a sense of solidarity, but the implications of shared responsibility have yet to be explored. This exploration is reserved for phase two, which we have chosen to call the Interdependence Phase.

Table 27.1. Phase One Dependence—Power Relations. *

	Subphase 1: Dependence-Submission	Subphase 2: Counterdependence	Subphase 3: Resolution
1. Emotional modality	Dependence (flight)	Counterdependence (fight). Off-target fighting among members. Distrust of staff member. Ambivalence	Pairing. Intense involvement in group task
2. Content themes	Discussion of interpersonal problems external to training groups	Discussion of group organization; i.e., what degree of structuring devices is needed for "effective" group behavior?	Discussion and definition of trainer role
3. Dominant roles (central persons)	Assertive, aggressive members with rich previous organizational or social science experience	Most assertive counterdependent and dependent members. Withdrawal of *less* assertive independents and dependents	Assertive independents
4. Group structure	Organized mainly into multisubgroups based on members' past experiences	Two tight subcliques consisting of leaders, of counterdependents and dependents	Group unifies in pursuit of goal and develops internal authority system
5. Group activity	Self-oriented behavior reminiscent of most new social gatherings	Search for consensus mechanism: voting, setting up chairpersons, search for "valid" content subjects	Group members take over leadership roles formerly perceived as held by trainer

(continued)

Table 27.1. (continued)

	Subphase 1: Dependence-Submission	Subphase 2: Counterdependence	Subphase 3: Resolution
6. Group movement facilitated by:	Staff member abnegation of traditional role of structuring situation, setting up rules of fair play, regulation of participation	Disenthrallment with staff member coupled with absorption of uncertainty by most assertive counterdependent and dependent individuals. Subgroups form to ward off anxiety	Revolt by assertive independents (catalysts) who fuse subgroups into unity by initiating and engineering trainer exit (barometric event)
7. Main defenses	Projection. Denigration of authority		Group moves into phase two

*Course terminates at the end of seventeen weeks. It is not uncommon for groups to remain throughout the course in this phase.

Phase Two: Interdependence

The resolution of dependence problems marks the transfer of group attention (and inattention) to the problem of shared responsibility.

Sullivan's description of the change from childhood to the juvenile era seems pertinent here:

> The juvenile era is marked off from childhood by the appearance of an urgent need for compeers with whom to have one's existence. By 'compeers' I mean people who are on our level, and have generically similar attitudes toward authoritative figures, activities, and the like. This marks the beginning of the juvenile era, the great developments in which are the talents for cooperation, competition, and compromise [1940, pp. 17–18; emphasis ours].

The remaining barriers to valid communication are those associated with orientations toward interdependence, i.e., intimacy, friendship, identification. Although the distribution of power was the cardinal issue during phase one, the distribution of affection occupies the group during phase two.

Subphase Four: Enchantment (Flight). At the outset of subphase four, the group is happy, cohesive, relaxed. The atmosphere is one of "sweetness and light." Any slight increase in tension is instantly dissipated by joking and laughter. The fighting of phase one is still fresh in the memory of the group, and the group's efforts are devoted to patching up differences, healing wounds, and maintaining a harmonious atmosphere. Typically, this is a time of merrymaking and group minstrelsy. Coffee and cake may be served at the meetings. Hours may be passed in organizing a group party. Poetry or songs commemorating the important events and persons in the group's history may be composed by individuals or, more commonly, as a group project. All decisions must be unanimous during this period, since everyone must be happy, but the issues on which decisions are made are mostly ones about which group members have no strong feelings. At first the cathartic, healing function of these activities is clear; there is much spontaneity, playfulness, and pleasure. Soon the pleasures begin to wear thin.

The myth of mutual acceptance and universal harmony must eventually be recognized for what it is. From the beginning of this phase there are frequent evidences of underlying hostilities, unresolved issues in the group. But they are quickly, nervously smoothed over by laughter or misinterpretation. Subphase four begins with catharsis, but that is followed by the development of a rigid norm to which all members are forced to conform: "Nothing must be allowed to disturb our harmony in the future; we must avoid the mistakes of the painful past." Not that members have forgotten that the painful past was a necessary preliminary to the autonomous and (it is said) delightful present, though that fact is carefully overlooked. Rather, there is a dim realization that all members must have an experience somewhat analogous to the trainer's in subphase three, before a mutually understood, accepted, and realistic definition of their own roles in the group can be arrived at.

Resistance of members to the requirement that harmony be maintained at all costs appears in subtle ways. In open group discussion the requirement is imperative: either the member does not dare to endanger harmony with the group or to disturb the *status quo* by denying that all problems have been solved. Much as members may dislike the tedious work of maintaining the appearance of harmony, the alternative is worse. The house of cards would come tumbling down, and the painful and exacting work of building something more substantial would have to begin. The flight from these problems takes a number of forms. Group members may say, "We've had our fighting and are now a group. Thus, further self-study is unnecessary." Very commonly, the possibility of any change may be prevented by not coming together as a total group at all. Thus the members may subgroup through an entire meeting. Those who would disturb the friendly subgroups are accused of "rocking the boat."

The solidarity and harmony become more and more illusory, but the group still clings to the illusion. This perseveration is in a way the consequence of the deprivation that members have experienced in maintaining the atmosphere of harmony. Maintaining it forces members to behave in ways alien to their own feelings; to go still further in group involvement would mean a complete loss of self. The group is therefore torn by a new ambivalence, which might be verbalized as follows: (1) "We all love one another and therefore we must maintain the solidarity of the group and give up whatever is necessary of our selfish desires"; (2) "The group demands that I sacrifice my identity as a person; but the group is an evil mechanism which satisfies no dominant needs." As this subphase comes to a close, the happiness that marked its beginning is maintained only as a mask. The "innocent" splitting of the group into subgroups has gone so far that members will even walk around the meeting table to join in the conversation of a subgroup rather than speak across the table at the risk of bringing the whole group together. There is a certain uneasiness about the group; there is a feeling that "we should work together but cannot." There may be a tendency to regress to the orientation of subphase one: group members would like the trainer to take over.

To recapitulate: subphase four begins with a happy sense of group belongingness. Individual identity is eclipsed by a "the group is bigger than all of us" sentiment. But this integration is short-lived; it soon becomes perceived as a fake attempt to resolve interpersonal problems by denying their reality. In the later stages of this subphase, enchantment with the total group is replaced by enchantment with one's subgroup, and out of this breakdown of the group emerges a new organization based on the anxieties aroused out of this first, suffocating environment.

Subphase Five: Disenchantment (Fight). This subphase is marked by a division into two subgroups—paralleling the experience of subphase two—but this time based upon orientations toward the degree of intimacy required by group membership. Membership in the two subgroups is not necessarily the same as in subphase two; for now the fragmentation occurs as a result of opposite and extreme attitudes toward the degree of intimacy desired in interpersonal relations. The counterpersonal members band together to resist further involvement. The overpersonal members band together in a demand for unconditional love. Even though these subgroups appear as divergent as possible, a common theme underlies them. For the one group, the only means seen for maintaining self-esteem is to avoid any real commitment to others; for the other group, the only way to maintain self-esteem is to obtain a commitment from others to forgive everything. The subgroups share in common the fear that intimacy breeds contempt.

This anxiety is reflected in many ways during subphase six. For the first time openly disparaging remarks are made about the group. Invidious comparisons are made between it and other groups. Similarly, psychology and social science may be attacked. The inadequacy of the group as a basis for self-esteem is dramatized in many ways—from stating "I don't care what you think," to boredom, to absenteeism. The overpersonals insist that they are happy and comfortable, while the counterpersonals complain about the lack of group morale. Intellectualization by the overpersonals frequently takes on religious overtones concerning Christian love, consideration for others, etc. In explanations of member behavior, the counterpersonal members account for all in terms of motives having nothing to do with the present group; the overpersonals explain all in terms of acceptance and rejection in the present group.

Subphase five belongs to the counterpersonals as subphase four belonged to the overpersonals. Subphase four might be caricatured as hiding in the womb of the group; subphase five as hiding out of sight of the group. It seems probable that both of these modalities serve to ward off anxieties associated with intimate interpersonal relations. A theme that links them together can be verbalized as follows: "If others really knew me, they would reject me." The overpersonal's formula for avoiding this rejection seems to be accepting all others so as to be protected by the others' guilt; the counterpersonal's way is by rejecting all others before they have a chance to reject him. Another way of characterizing the counterpersonal orientation is in the phrase, "I would lose my identity as a member of the group." The corresponding overpersonal orientation reads, "I have nothing to lose by identifying with the group." We can now look back on the past two subphases as countermeasures against loss of self-esteem; what Sullivan once referred to as the greatest inhibition to the understanding of what is distinctly human, "the overwhelming conviction of self-hood—this amounts to a delusion of unique individuality." The sharp swings and fluctuations that occurred between the enchantment and euphoria of subphase four and the disenchantment of subphase five can be seen as a struggle between the "institutionalization of complacency" on the one hand and anxiety associated with fantasy speculations about intimacy and involvement on the other. This dissociative behavior serves a purpose of its own: a generalized denial of the group and its meaning for individuals. For if the group is important and valid then it has to be taken seriously. If it can wallow in the enchantment of subphase four, it is safe; if it can continually vilify the goals and objectives of the group, it is also safe. The disenchantment theme in subphase five is perhaps a less skillful and more desperate security provision with its elaborate wall of defenses than the "group mind" theme of subphase four. What should be stressed is that both subphase defenses were created almost entirely on fantastic expectations about the consequences of group involvement. These defenses are homologous to anxiety as it is experienced by the individual; i.e., the state of "anxiety arises as a response to a situation of danger and which will be reproduced thenceforward whenever such a situation recurs" (Freud, 1936, p. 72). In sum, the past two subphases were marked by a conviction that further group involvement would be injurious to members' self-esteem.

Subphase Six: Consensual Validation. In groups of which we write, two forces combine to press the group toward a resolution of the interdependency problem. These are the approaching end of the training course, and the need to establish a method of evaluation (including course grades).

There are, of course, ways of denying or avoiding these realities. The group can agree to meet after the course ends. It can extricate itself from evaluation activities by asking the trainer to perform the task, or by awarding a blanket grade. But turning this job over to the trainer is a regression to dependence; and refusal to discriminate and reward is a failure to resolve the problems of interdependence. If the group has developed in general as we have described, the reality of termination and evaluation cannot be denied, and these regressive modes of adaptation cannot be tolerated.

The characteristic defenses of the two subgroups at first fuse to prevent any movement toward the accomplishment of the evaluation and grading task. The counterpersonals resist evaluation as an invasion of privacy; they foresee catastrophe if members begin to say what they think of one another. The overpersonals resist grading since it involves discriminating among the group members. At the same time, all members have a stake in the outcome of evaluation and grading. In avoiding the task, members of each subgroup are perceived by members of the other as "rationalizing," and the group becomes involved in a vicious circle of mutual disparagement. In this process, the fear of loss of self-esteem through group involvement is near to being realized. As in subphase three, it is the independents—in this case those whose self-esteem is not threatened by the prospect of intimacy—who restore members' confidence in the group. Sometimes all that is required to reverse the vicious circle quite dramatically is a request by an independent for assessment of his own role. Or it may be an expression of confidence in the group's ability to accomplish the task.

The activity that follows group commitment to the evaluation task does not conform to the expectations of the overpersonal or counterpersonal members. Its chief characteristic is the willingness and ability of group members to validate their self-concepts with other members. The fear of rejection fades when tested against reality. The tensions that developed as a result of these fears diminish in the light of actual discussion of member roles. At the same time, there is revulsion against "capsule evaluations" and "curbstone psycho-analysis." Instead, what ensues is a serious attempt by each group member to verbalize his private conceptual scheme for understanding human behavior—his own and that of others. Bringing these assumptions into explicit communication is the main work of subphase six. This activity demands a high level of work and of communicative skill. Some of the values that appear to underlie the group's work during this subphase are as follows: (1) members can accept one another's difference without associating "good" and "bad" with the differences; (2) conflict exists but is over substantive issues rather than emotional issues; (3) consensus is reached as a result of rational discussion rather than through a compulsive attempt at unanimity; (4) members are aware of their own involvement, and of other aspects of group process, without being overwhelmed or alarmed; (5) through the evaluation process, members take on greater personal meaning to each other. This facilitates communication and creates a deeper understanding of how the other person thinks, feels, behaves; it creates a series of personal expectations, as distinguished from the previous, more stereotyped, role expectations.

The above values, and some concomitant values, are of course very close to the authors' conception of a "good group." In actuality they are not always achieved by the end of the group life. The prospect of the death of the group, after much procrastination in the secret hope that it will be over before anything can be done, is likely to force the group into strenuous last-minute efforts to overcome the obstacles that have blocked its progress. As a result, the sixth subphase is too often hurried and incomplete. If the hurdles are not overcome in time, grading is likely to be an exercise that confirms members' worst suspicions about the group. And if role evaluation is attempted, either the initial evaluations contain so much hostile material as to block further efforts or evaluations are so flowery and vacuous that no one, least of all the recipient, believes them.

In the resolution of interdependence problems, member-personalities count for even more than they do in the resolution of dependence problems. The trainer's behavior is crucial in determining the group's ability to resolve the dependence issue, but in the interdependence issue the group is, so to speak, only as strong as its weakest link. The exceedingly dependent group member can ride through phase one with a fixed belief in the existence of a private relationship between himself and the trainer; but the person whose anxieties are intense under the threats associated with intimacy can immobilize the group. (Table 27.2 summarizes the major events of phase two.)

CONCLUSIONS

Dependence and interdependence—power and love, authority and intimacy—are regarded as the central problems of group life. In most organizations and societies, the rules governing the distribution of authority and the degree of intimacy among members are prescribed. In the human relations training group, they are major areas of uncertainty. Although the choice of these matters as the focus of group attention and experience rests to some extent with the trainer, her choice is predicated on the belief that they are the core of interpersonal experience. As such, the principal obstacles to valid interpersonal communication lie in rigidities of interpretation and response carried over from the anxious experiences with particular love or power figures into new situations in which they are inappropriate. The existence of such autisms complicates all discussion unduly and in some instances makes an exchange of meanings impossible.

Stating the training goal as the establishment of valid communication means that the relevance of the autistic response to authority and intimacy on the part of any member can be explicitly examined, and at least a provisional alternative formulated by him. Whether this makes a lasting change in the member's flexibility, or whether he will return to his more restricted formula when confronted with a new situation, we do not know, but we expect that it varies with the success of his group experience—particularly his success in understanding it.

We have attempted to portray what we believe to be the typical pattern of group development, and to show the relationship of member orientations and changes in member orientations to the major movements of the group. In this connection, we have emphasized the catalytic role of persons unconflicted with respect to one or the other of the dependence and interdependence areas. This power to move the group lies mainly in his freedom from anxiety-based reactions to problems of authority (or intimacy): he has the freedom to be creative in searching for a way to reduce tension.

We have also emphasized the "barometric event" or event capable of moving the group from one phase to the next. The major events of this kind are the removal of the trainer as part of the resolution of the dependence problem, and the evaluation-grading requirements at the termination of the course. Both

Table 27.2. Phase Two: Interdependence—Personal Relations.

	Subphase 4: Enchantment	Subphase 5: Disenchantment	Subphase 6: Consensual Validation
Emotional modality	Pairing (flight). Group becomes a respected icon beyond further analysis	Fight-Flight. Anxiety reactions. Distrust and suspicion of various group members	Pairing, understanding, acceptance
Content themes	Discussion of "group history," and generally salutary aspects of course, group, and membership	Revival of content themes used in subphase 1: What is a group? What are we doing here? What are the goals of the group? What do I have to give up—personally—to belong to this group? (How much intimacy and affection is required?) Invasion of privacy vs. "group giving." Setting up proper codes of social behavior	Course grading system. Discussion and assessment of member roles
Dominant roles (central persons)	General distribution of participation for first time. Overpersonals have salience	Most assertive counterpersonal and overpersonal individuals, with counterpersonals especially salient	Assertive independents

(continued)

Table 27.2. (continued)

	Subphase 4: Enchantment	Subphase 5: Disenchantment	Subphase 6: Consensual Validation
Group structure	Solidarity, fusion. High degree of camaraderie and suggestibility. Le Bon's description of "group mind" would apply here	Restructuring of membership into two competing predominant subgroups made up of individuals who share similar attitudes concerning degree of intimacy required in social interaction, i.e., The counterpersonal and overpersonal groups. The personal individuals remain uncommitted but act according to the needs of the situation	Diminishing of ties based on personal orientation. Group structure now presumably appropriate to needs of situation based on predominantly substantive rather than emotional orientations. Consensus significantly easier on important issues
Group activity	Laughter, joking, humor. Planning out-of-class activities such as parties. The institutionalization of happiness to be accomplished by "fun" activities. High rate of interaction and participation	Disparagement of group in a variety of ways: high rate of absenteeism, tardiness, balkiness in initiating total group interaction, frequent statements concerning worthlessness of group, denial of importance of group. Occasional member asking for individual help finally rejected by the group	Communication to others of self-system of interpersonal relations; i.e., making conscious to self, and others aware of, conceptual system one uses to predict consequences of personal behavior. Acceptance of group on reality terms

Group movement facilitated by:	Independence and achievement attained by trainer rejection and its concomitant deriving consensually some effective means for authority and control. (Subphase 3 rebellion bridges gap between subphases 2 and 4)	Disenchantment of group as a result of *fantasied expectations of group life*. The perceived threat to self-esteem that further group involvement signifies creates schism of group according to amount of affection and intimacy desired. The counterpersonal and overpersonal assertive individuals alleviate source of anxiety by disparaging or abnegating further group involvement. Subgroups form to ward off anxiety	The external realities, group termination, and the prescribed need for a course grading system constitute the barometric event. Led by the personal individuals, the group tests reality and reduces autistic convictions concerning group involvement
Main defenses	Denial, isolation, intellectualization, and alienation		

these barometric events require a catalytic agent in the group to bring them about. That is to say, the trainer exit can take place only at the moment when it is capable of symbolizing the attainment of group autonomy, and it requires a catalytic agent in the group to give it this meaning. And the grading assignment can move the group forward only if the catalytic agent can reverse the vicious circle of disparagement that precedes it.

Whether the incorporation of these barometric events into the training design merely makes our picture of group development a self-fulfilling prophecy, or whether, as we wish to believe, these elements make dramatically clear the major forward movements of the group and open the gate for a flood of new understanding and communication, can only be decided on the basis of more, and more varied, experience.

The evolution from phase one to phase two represents not only a change in emphasis from power to affection, but also from role to personality. Phase one activity generally centers on broad role distinctions such as class, ethnic background, professional interests, etc.; phase two activity involves a deeper concern with personality modalities, such as reaction to failure, warmth, retaliation, anxiety, etc. This development presents an interesting paradox, for the group in phase one emerged out of a heterogeneous collectivity of individuals; the individual in phase two emerged out of the group. This suggests that group therapy, where attention is focused on individual movement, begins at the least enabling time. It is possible that, before group members are able to help each other, the barriers to communication must be partially understood.

Notes

1. This theory is based for the most part on observations made over a five-year period of teaching graduate students "group dynamics." The main function of the seminar as it was set forth by the instructors was to improve the internal communication system of the group, hence, a self-study group.

2. See Gouldner (1954), Whyte (1951). Robert E. Park, writing in 1928, had considerable insight on some functions of revolution and change (see Park, 1955).

References

Bion, W. R. "Experiences in Groups: I." *Hum. Relat.*, Vol I, No. 3, pp. 314–320, 1948a.

Bion, W.R. "Experiences in Groups: II." *Hum. Relat.* Vol. I, No. 4, pp. 487–496, 1948b.

Frenkel-Brunswik, E. "Intolerance of Ambiguity as an Emotional and Perceptual Personality Variable." In Bruner, J. S., and Krech, D. (eds.), *Perception and Personality*. Durham, N.C.: Duke Univ. Press, 1949 and 1950, p. 115.

Freud, S. *Group Psychology and the Analysis of the Ego*. Translated by J. Strachey. London: International Psycho-Analytical Press, 1922; New York: Liveright, 1949.

Freud, S. *The Problem of Anxiety*. Translated by H. A. Bunker. New York: Psychoanalytic Quarterly Press and W. W. Norton, 1936.

Freud, S. *Moses and Monotheism*. London: Hogarth Press, 1939; New York: Vintage Books, 1955.

Gouldner, A. *Wildcat Strike*. Yellow Springs, Ohio: Antioch Press, 1954; London: Routledge & Kegan Paul, 1955.

Leighton, A. H. *The Governing of Men*. Princeton: Princeton Univ. Press, 1946.

Park, R. E. "The Strike." *Society*. New York: Free Press of Glencoe, 1955.

Schutz, W. C. "Group Behavior Studies, I—III." Cambridge, Mass.: Harvard Univ., 1954. (mimeo).

Schutz, W. C. "What Makes Groups Productive?" *Hum. Relat.*, Vol VIII, No. 4, p. 429, 1955.

Sullivan, H. S. "Tensions, Interpersonal and International." In Cantril, H. (ed.), *Tensions That Cause Wars*. Urbana, Ill.: Univ. of Illinois Press, 1950.

Sullivan, H. S. *Conceptions of Modern Psychiatry*. Washington, D.C.: William Alanson White Psychiatric Foundation, 1940, 1945; London: Tavistock Publications, 1955.

Whyte, W. F., Jr. *Patterns for Industrial Peace*. New York: Harper, 1951.

CHAPTER TWENTY-EIGHT

The Work of Wilfred Bion on Groups

Margaret J. Rioch (1970)

The shift in perspective from the individual to the group is difficult to make in actual practice although it is often given lip service. It is like a shift to a higher order of magnitude, which is not easy when the lower order is in itself very complex and by no means thoroughly understood. But the shift is necessary in order to grasp social phenomena. From this perspective it is often possible to see the problems of the individual or the pair in a new light. This is well known to family therapists, who find an individual child or a marital relationship more comprehensible when seen in the framework of the entire family.

The Washington School of Psychiatry-Tavistock Conferences provide opportunities for members to study behavior in large groups of fifty to sixty, in small groups of ten to twelve, and in intergroup situations. No particular theoretical framework is prescribed, and staff members come with various theoretical points of view and from various professional orientations, including sociology, psychology, psychoanalysis, and business administration. But Bion's concepts have been especially useful to the staff since they formulate group psychological processes in integrative terms. A. K. Rice, who has directed most of the British and American conferences since 1962, was strongly influenced by his membership in a training group conducted by Bion in 1947–48, as well as by Bion's theories.

Much of the material on which Bion based his theories and many of the examples he gives come from the small groups that he conducted at the Tavistock Clinic. He does not deal exclusively with these, however, but also discusses large social institutions such as the army and the church. His interest in group processes was stimulated when, as an officer in the British Army during

World War II, he was engaged in the selection of men for leadership roles and in charge of a rehabilitation unit of psychiatric patients. He began at that time to think of treatment of the whole society of the hospital not as a makeshift to save psychiatric manpower, but as the best way to get at the malady as he perceived it, namely the inability on the part of the patients to function adequately as members of society or, in other words, as group members. He saw this inability with reference both to the hospital community and to society at large.

Because Bion's name is so much associated with groups and because he emphasized the phenomena of total fields rather than of individuals, he is sometimes thought of as having reified the idea of the group or as having talked about the group as a mythical entity instead of talking about human behavior. This is not the case. He defines a group as a function or set of functions or an aggregate of individuals. It is not a function of any one part separately, nor is it an aggregate without a function.

For example, if a dozen strangers are lying by chance in the sun on the same beach they do not constitute a group according to this definition. But if someone in the water cries for help and the twelve individuals respond by trying to save the swimmer from drowning in some kind of concerted action, however rudimentary the concertedness may be, they have become a group in that they now have a function. This may last for only a few minutes or it may turn into an organization of life savers that goes on for years.

Although Bion thinks and speaks of instincts, he does not postulate a herd instinct or a group mind. He thinks that ideas of this kind are often developed by people in groups, but that when they occur they are symptomatic of regression. In his opinion groups bring into prominence phenomena that can best be understood if one has some experience of psychotic phenomena as well as of normal and neurotic behavior. The belief that a group or group mind exists, as something other than a function of a number of individuals, appears to Bion to be a distorted figment of the imagination that emerges when people are threatened with a loss of their individual distinctiveness.

He emphasizes that people do not have to come together in the same room to form a group. In his view a hermit in a desert is inevitably a member of a group and cannot be understood unless one knows what the group is from which the person has separated geographically. People have to come together in a room in order that group phenomena may be demonstrated and elucidated, but not in order that they should exist. This is similar to the situation in psychoanalysis in which the patient has to enter into a therapeutic relationship with the analyst in order that the analyst may demonstrate and analyze the transference, but not in order that transference phenomena should exist.

Bion's central thought is that in every group two groups are present: the "work group" and the "basic assumption group." This may all sound less mysterious if one says that in every group there are two aspects, or that there are two different ways of behaving. Bion's terminology is a shortcut that may lead to the belief that he thinks of each group of ten people as consisting of twenty invisible people sitting in two separate circles and talking, now in normal rational voices and now in another voice as in O'Neill's *Strange Interlude*. And in fact he does think in this kind of metaphor. At the same time he is quite clearly aware that it is a metaphor, which some of his less poetic readers tend to forget. It does not mean that there are two groups of people in the room, but that the two groups behave as if that were the case, and he considers that this is the unconscious fantasy of the people in the group.

His concept of the work group will be described first and then that of the basic assumption group. The work group is that aspect of group functioning which has to do with the real task of the group. This exists in a committee that has come together to plan a program, or a staff of an organization that proposes to review the activities of the past year, or a small group met to study its own behavior. The work group takes cognizance of its purpose and can define its task. The structure of the group is there to further the attainment of the task. For example, if a group needed to collect dues it would appoint a treasurer. But it would not appoint a finance committee unless there were real matters of policy to be taken care of by such a committee. The number of vice presidents would be limited by the functions that vice presidents had to perform. The number of meetings would be dictated by the amount of business that had to be conducted. The leader of the work group is not the only one who has skills, and she leads only so long as her leadership serves the task of the group. The members of the work group cooperate as separate and discrete individuals. Each member of the group belongs to it because it is his will and his choice to see that the purpose of the group is fulfilled. He is therefore at one with the task of the group and his own interest is identified with its interest. The work group constantly tests its conclusions in a scientific spirit. It seeks for knowledge, learns from experience, and constantly questions how it may best achieve its goal. It is clearly conscious of the passage of time and of the processes of learning and development. It has a parallel in the individual with the ego, in Freud's sense, in the rational and mature person.

Groups that act consistently like the one just described are very rare and perhaps even nonexistent in pure culture. A large part of Bion's theory has to do with why groups do not behave in the sensible way just described as characteristic of the work group. Humans seem to be herd animals who are often in trouble with the herd. Ineffective and self-contradictory behavior seems at times to be very common in groups—even though highly effective functioning is common at other times. The work group is only one aspect of the functioning of the group. The other aspect is the one Bion calls the basic assumption group.

Bion is probably best known popularly for the names he coined for the three kinds of basic assumption groups—the dependency, the fight-flight, and the pairing groups. It should be emphasized that he himself used the word "adumbrated"—that is, vaguely outlined—to characterize his classification of these groups, and it may well be that the classification should be made differently or that other categories should be added. This is not the main point.

It is important to understand what the term *basic assumption* means, for otherwise one may get lost in the description of the three kinds that Bion adumbrated and forget the more important point, which is the commonality of all three. Basic assumption means exactly what it says—namely, the assumption that is basic to the behavior. It is an "as if" term. One behaves as if such and such were the case. In pre-Columbian days seafaring men operated on the basic assumption that the world was flat and that they might fall off its edge. Therefore they did not venture very far from the coast. So on many different levels, by observing the behavior of individuals and of groups, one can tease out the basic assumptions on which they operate. Bion uses the term to refer to the *tacit* assumptions that are prevalent in groups, not to those that are overtly expressed. The basic assumptions of the basic assumption groups are usually outside of awareness. Nevertheless, they are the basis for behavior. They are deducible from the emotional state of the group. The statement of the basic assumption gives meaning to and elucidates the behavior of the group to the extent that it is not operating as a work group.

According to Bion there are three distinct emotional states of groups from which one can deduce three basic assumptions. The first of these is the dependency basic assumption.

The essential aim of the basic assumption dependency group is to attain security through and have its members protected by one individual. It assumes that this is why the group has met. The members act as if they know nothing, as if they are inadequate and immature creatures. Their behavior implies that the leader, by contrast, is omnipotent and omniscient. A group of sick, miserable psychiatric patients, for example, and a powerful, wise, loving, giving therapist easily fit this picture. The power, wisdom, and lovingness of the therapist are, of course, not tested. The patients are often united in the belief that if they sit long enough, the wise leader will come forth with the magic cure. They do not even need to give him adequate information about their difficulties for he knows everything and plans everything for the good of the members. In this emotional state the group insists that all explanations be extremely simple; no one can understand any complexity; no one can do anything that is difficult; but the leader can solve all difficulties, if he only will. He is idealized and made into a kind of god who will take care of his children. The leader is often tempted to fall into this role and to go along with the basic assumption of the group.

But since no one really can fill this role and since anyone who is doing his job will refuse to fill it, he can never succeed in meeting the group's expectations. In failing to be the omniscient and omnipotent leader of these people who are presenting themselves as inadequate weaklings, he inevitably arouses their disappointment and hostility. The members will try for a long time to blind themselves to this and will try not to hear what he says in interpreting their dependency to them. They often try quite desperate maneuvers to wring his heart and to force him to take proper care of them. One of the most frequent maneuvers is to put forth one member as especially sick and requiring the special care of the leader. Such a member may actually be pushed by the others into a degree of distress which she had not really felt at all, but the group needs someone who will wring the leader's heart or else show him up to be an unfeeling demon. The interesting thing is that whereas the group seems to be concerned about this poor person and her trouble, it is actually more concerned about the group aim to get the leader to take care of it and to relieve its feelings of inadequacy and insecurity. A person who falls into this role can very easily be carried away by it until he oversteps the bounds, and then he may find himself abandoned by the group.

When the leader of such a group fails to meet expectations, as he is bound to do, the group searches for alternative leaders. These are often eager to accept the role, and to prove that they can do what the original leader could not do. This is a temptation the group offers to its more ambitious members. When they fall for it, they are usually in for the same fate as the original leader.

One of the frequent concerns in the dependency group has to do with greed. This is understandable enough since in manifesting the kind of childlike dependency characteristic of this basic assumption, the group members are perpetuating a state appropriate to an earlier stage of development and each one is demanding more than her share of parental care. There is often conflict in this group between the dependent tendencies and the needs of the individuals as adults. Resentment at being in a dependent state is present as well as a desire to persist in it. Although anger and jealousy are expressed, they do not usually arouse a tremendous amount of fear because of the basic assumption that a superbeing exists in the form of the leader, who will see to it that the irresponsibilities of the members will not go too far and will not have dire consequences. There is often conflict between the desire to express feelings irresponsibly and the desire to be mature and consider consequences.

The basic assumption dependency group in pure culture does not exist any more than the work group in pure culture. But the more it tends to be dominant over the work group, the more the relationship of the members to the leader takes on the characteristics of a religious cult. The work function will often then be felt as a challenge to a religion. Some of the same phenomena will occur that have occurred in the world in the conflict between science and religion, as if the claims of science were challenging the claims of religion. The words or writings of the leader become a kind of Bible and the group engages in exegesis of his works. This tends to happen particularly if the leader has already demonstrated his human inability to satisfy the demands of the group for a deity. His written words or remembered words may then be taken in place of his person.

The outside world often looks cold and unfriendly to the basic assumption dependency group. Sometimes when the members feel deserted by their leader, they forget their internal squabbles, close ranks, and snuggle up to each other like little birds in a nest. A warm groupiness develops that gives a temporary sense of comfort and security. To challenge this is heresy and is persecuted as such.

The second basic assumption group is that of fight-flight. Bion joins these together as two sides of the same coin. The assumption is that the group has met to preserve itself and that this can be done only by fighting someone or something or by running away from someone or something. Action is essential, whether for fight or for flight. The individual is of secondary importance to the preservation of the group. Both in battle and in flight the individual may be abandoned for the sake of the survival of the group. Whereas in the basic assumption dependency group the sick person may be valued for her ability to engage the leader as a person who will take care of others, in the fight-flight group there is no tolerance for sickness. Casualties are to be expected.

A leader is even more important than in other basic assumption groups because the call for action requires a leader. The leader who is felt to be appropriate to this kind of group is one who can mobilize the group for attack or lead it in flight. She is expected to recognize danger and enemies. She should represent and spur on to courage and self-sacrifice. She should have a bit of a paranoid element in her makeup if she wishes to be successful, for this will ensure that if no enemy is obvious, the leader will surely find one. She is expected to feel hate toward the enemy and to be concerned not for the individual in the group but for the preservation of the group itself. An accepted leader of a fight-flight group who goes along with the basic assumption is one who affords opportunity in the group for flight or aggression. If she does not do this, she is ignored.

This basic assumption group is anti-intellectual and inimical to the idea of self-study; self-knowledge may be called introspective nonsense. In a group whose avowed purpose or work task is self-study, the leader will find when the group is operating in basic assumption fight-flight that attempts will be obstructed either by expressions of hatred against all things psychological and introspective, or by various other methods of avoidance. The group may chit-chat, tell stories, come late, be absent, or engage in innumerable activities to circumvent the task.

In groups engaged in more overt action, it is possible to observe the close connection of panic and the fight-flight group. Bion contends that panic, flight, and uncontrolled attack are really all the same. He says that panic does not arise in any situation unless it is one that might as easily have given rise to rage. When the rage or fear are offered no readily available outlet, frustration arises that in a basic assumption group cannot be tolerated. Flight offers an immediately available opportunity for expression of the emotion in the fight-flight group and meets the demands that all basic assumption groups have for instantaneous satisfaction. Attack offers a similarly immediate outlet. Bion thinks that if the leader of such a group conforms to the requirements of the fight-flight leader she will have no difficulty in turning a group from headlong flight to attack or from headlong attack to panic.

The third basic assumption group is that of pairing. Here the assumption is that the group has met for purposes of reproduction, to bring forth the Messiah, the Savior. Two people get together on behalf of the group to carry out the task of pairing and creation. The sex of the two people is immaterial. They are by no means necessarily a man and a woman. But whoever they are, the basic assumption is that when two people get together it is for sexual purposes. When this basic assumption is operative, the other group members are not bored. They listen eagerly and attentively to what is begin said. An atmosphere of hopefulness pervades the group. No actual leader is or needs to be present, but the group, through the pair, is living in the hope of the creation of a new leader, or a new thought, or something that will bring about a new life, will solve the old problems and bring Utopia or heaven, or something of the sort. As in the history of the world, if a new leader or Messiah is actually produced, he or she will of course shortly be rejected. In order to maintain hope, the person must be unborn. Bion emphasizes the air of hopeful expectation that pervades the group. He says it is often expressed in clichés—such as, "Things will be better when spring comes"—or in simple-minded statements that some cure-all like marriage or group therapy would solve all neurotic problems. Although the group thus focuses on the future, Bion calls attention to the present, namely the feeling of hope itself, which he thinks is evidence that the pairing group is in existence even when other evidence is not clear. The group enjoys its optimism, justifying it by an appeal to an outcome that is morally unexceptionable. The feelings associated with this group are soft and agreeable. The unborn leader of this group, according to the basic assumption, will save it from feelings of hatred, destructiveness, and despair—both its own feelings and those of others. If a person or an idea should be produced by such a group hope will again be weakened, for there will be nothing to hope for. The destructiveness and hatred have not really been reduced and will again be felt.

These, then, are the three basic assumption groups Bion describes. It is clear enough how different they all are from the work group. Although each one has its own characteristics, the basic assumption groups also have some characteristics in common. Basic assumption life is not oriented outward toward reality but inward toward fantasy, which is then impulsively and uncritically acted out. There is little pausing to consider to test consequences, little patience with an inquiring attitude, and great insistence upon feeling. Basic assumption members often are confused, have poor memories, are disoriented about time. They do not really learn and adapt through experience but actually resist change, although they may shift very readily from one basic assumption to another. Often there are reminiscences about the good old days. The language of such groups is full of clichés, or repetitive phrases, and of vague and loose generalizations. Another important aspect of the basic assumptions is that they are anonymous. They are not formulated by any one member in the group and cannot be attributed to any one member. No one wants to own them. There is a kind of conspiracy of anonymity, which is facilitated by the fact that identities and names get mixed up; statements are attributed falsely or vaguely. The basic assumptions seem to be the disowned part of the individuals, and individuals seem to fear the basic assumptions as if they might take over and leave nothing of the mature, rational persons in the group. Since the basic assumptions are anonymous, they can function quite ruthlessly, which is another reason why they are feared. There is much vicarious living in a basic assumption group, particularly through roles, so that often a person becomes fixed in a role that the group needs for its own purposes and then cannot get out of. Basic assumption groups also constantly attempt to seduce their leaders away from their work function.

Neither the work group nor the basic assumption group exists in pure culture for very long. What one sees in reality is a work group that is suffused by, intruded into, and supported by the basic assumption groups. One can make an analogy to the functions of the conscious ego, which are suffused by, invaded by, and supported by the irrational and unconscious aspects of the personality. So it seems that the basic assumptions represent an interference with the work task, just as naughty, primitive impulses may interfere with the sensible work of a mature person. And this is one important side of the picture. There is another, more positive side to the basic assumptions, however, which Bion emphasizes just as much as the negative aspects, and that is the sophisticated use of the proper basic assumption by the work group. For example, a work group such as a hospital can and should mobilize the basic assumption dependency in the service of its task of taking care of sick patients. Bion identifies the church as that major institution in society which mobilizes and uses in a sophisticated way the basic assumption dependency; the army as that one which mobilizes basic assumption fight-flight; and the aristocracy as that one which is most interested in breeding and therefore mobilizes pairing. Whether or not the aristocracy can still be considered to exist, even in England, as an important institution is an open question, along with what takes its place if it does not. Bion himself does not think that the aristocracy can be considered to be a real work group that uses its basic assumption in a sophisticated way, for if the work group characteristics were dominant in the aristocracy then the interest in breeding would be manifest in some such way as a subsidy of scientific genetics research. But this is obviously not the case. If we consider the army, for example, it is clear that the relevant basic assumptions badly interfere with its function if they get out of hand. Fight-flight when engaged in simply as irrational basic assumptions leads to panic or ill-conceived attack. However, when mobilized in a sophisticated way, fight-flight represents the motive force for battle and for organized withdrawal. As indicated earlier, both the work group and the basic assumption group are abstractions; they are concepts that are useful in thinking about ways of functioning that occur in groups. Bion's idea is that both are occurring simultaneously, but to varying degrees, in all groups.

It is necessary now to introduce another one of Bion's concepts, namely that of valency. This is a term used to refer to the individual's readiness to enter into combination with the group in making and acting on the basic assumptions. A person may have a high or low valency depending on the capacity for this kind of combination, but in Bion's view it is impossible to be a human being without having some degree of valency. The thing that Bion is trying to do with all his concepts and constructions is to produce useful ways of thinking about humans in their function as social animals. In his concept of valency he is saying that everyone has the tendency to enter into group life, in particular into the irrational and unconscious aspects of group life, and that people vary in the amount of tendency they have in this direction. Bion thinks of this tendency as something manifested on a psychological plane to be sure, but something that is so basic to the human organism that it should not be thought of as purely psychological. He thinks of it as biological and speaks of it as analogous to tropism in plants rather than as analogous to more purposive behavior. By borrowing a word from physics rather than from psychology or sociology, he emphasizes the instantaneous and involuntary aspects of the kind of behavior he is talking about, which he calls instinctive. Valency in the basic assumption group corresponds to cooperation in the work group. But whereas cooperation requires thought, training, maturity, and some degree of organization in a group, valency requires none of these. It simply occurs spontaneously as a function of the gregarious quality in humankind.

Individuals vary not only in the degree of valency they manifest but in the kind to which they have the strongest tendency. With some it is toward basic assumption dependency; some toward fight-flight; some toward pairing. Every human being has the capacity for all three, but usually one or another valency predominates. This has nothing to do with whether a person has been psychoanalyzed or not. It is not possible to analyze valency out of a human being as one is supposed to be able to analyze neurosis. For effective functioning in groups, however, and especially for leadership functioning, it is desirable to know oneself well enough to know to which valency one tends. An effective society uses the valencies of its members to serve its various purposes. For example, the educator can find a good outlet for valency toward basic assumption dependency. The combat commander can use appropriately valency toward basic assumption fight-flight. The valency toward basic assumption pairing finds a useful expression in individual interviewing and, of course, in family life. There are various types of chairpersons and directors of organizations. One type will be solicitous for the welfare of its members and will take a special interest in the weaker ones or in anyone who is sick or disabled. Another will see her main function as fighting for the interests of her organization against any outside or inside attack. Another will find that she does her job best by going around after hours to each one of her members separately, convincing each one of what she wants done. When the meeting takes place everyone is already in agreement and the decisions have all been made. Any and all of these ways can be effective, though each one may be more appropriate at one time than at another.

In the naïve or unconscious fantasy, the leader of the dependency group has to be omnipotent; the fight leader has to be unbeatable and the flight leader uncatchable; the leader of the pairing group must be marvelous but still unborn. But in the mature work group, which is making a sophisticated use of the appropriate basic assumptions, the leader of the dependency group is dependable, the leader of the fight-flight group is courageous, and the leader of the pairing group is creative.[1]

For effective functioning the basic assumptions must be subservient to and used in the service of the work task. They make good servants and poor masters. The various tales about fantastic machines, demons, genii, and so forth who perform miraculous tasks for their masters until one fine day they take over and go on a binge of destruction are mythical representations of the capacity of human beings for harnessing tremendous energy effectively and at the same time of the danger of such energy when it is not harnessed. *The Lord of the Flies* provides another illustration of what happens when the work group is weak and the irresponsible basic assumption group takes over.

The work task is like a serious parent who has an eye on intelligent planning. The basic assumptions are like the fun-loving or frightened children who want immediate satisfaction of their desires. What Bion emphasizes is that both exist and that both are necessary. The basic assumption group, however, exists without effort. The work group requires all the concentration, skill, and organization of creative forces that can be mustered to bring it into full flower. The writers who derogate groups as tending to reduce the intellectual abilities of the individuals in the group are, according to Bion, talking about the basic assumption functions, not work group functions. Bion holds to a very consistent middle way between the glorification and the derogation of the group. The latter is to be found in Jung's statement, "When a hundred clever heads join in a group, one big nincompoop is the result, because every individual is trammelled by the otherness of the others." Bion holds that a group, like an individual, may be stupid and cruel or intelligent and concerned. He does not hold that great achievements are always those of the individual working in solitude. He says that in the study groups he has been in he has made interpretations of behavior just because he believes that the group can hear them and use them, and experience has borne him out. In his own words, he attributes "great force and influence to the work group, which through its concern with reality is compelled to employ the methods of science in no matter how rudimentary a form" (p. 135).[2]

Individuals seem to fear being overwhelmed by their valency for group life; or one might put it that they fear being overwhelmed by the basic assumptions. It is not uncommon in self-study or therapy groups to hear phrases like "the fear of being sucked in by quicksands," or "the fear of being homogenized," which express the fear of being immersed in the group and thus losing one's individuality. Bion thinks that there is not actually so much danger as people think there is of being overwhelmed by the basic assumptions. He has a healthy respect for people's capacities to function on a work level. He thinks that in groups met to study their own behavior, consistent interpretation of the basic assumption tendencies will gradually bring them into consciousness and cause them to lose their threatening quality. The parallel here to the psychoanalysis of unconscious impulses is clear. Presumably, the more the basic assumption life of the group becomes conscious, the more the work task can emerge into affective functioning.

But the individual in a group is not always convinced of this. Bion thinks that the task of the adult in establishing adequate contact with the life of the group or groups in which she lives is truly a formidable one. Her first, second, and often third attempts are likely to be failures and to result in regression. When individuals in a group feel that they have lost or are about to lose their individual distinctiveness, they are threatened by panic. This does not mean at all that the group disintegrates, for it may continue as a fight-flight group; but it does mean that the individual feels threatened and very likely has regressed.

Bion says clearly that he thinks of the value of a group experience as the conscious experiencing of the possibilities of the work group. This must be differentiated from the coziness and so-called closeness of feeling in the basic assumption group. The work group Bion is talking about does not depend upon great amounts of love or warm feelings or an oceanic oneness of the group members. It does depend upon the increasing and developing ability of each individual to use skills responsibly in the service of the common task. It is not anything like the "togetherness" which is a function of the fear of being alone or on one's own. In the work group, each individual is very much on his own and may have to accomplish his own part of the task in a very lonely way, as for example someone who is sent upon a secret mission or someone who has to make the ultimate policy decision where the buck stops. The reluctance to take the final responsibility for decisions and actions can be seen as a basic assumption dependency phenomenon and is not a characteristic of the work group member, especially not of the work group leader.

The anxiety one tends to feel in groups and the difficulties with which group membership faces one stem from the double danger of either being isolated like a sore thumb of the total body that may be amputated, or being swallowed up by the total body and losing oneself. When the basic assumption group is strong, the individual tends to feel either in danger of being victimized and extruded, or swallowed up in the anonymous unanimity of group feeling. The usual case, even when work elements are present, is that the individual is wavering somewhere in between the two dangers, with an uneasy sense of being in a dilemma out of which no right way can be found.

When anxiety becomes severe the group may, as Bion says, resemble the mysterious, frightening, and destructive Sphinx. The Sphinx was made up of disparate members. She had the seductive face of a woman and a body composed of parts of powerful and dangerous animals—the lion, the eagle, and the serpent. To those who wished to pass by her she posed the riddle: "What walks on four legs in the morning, two at noon, and three in the evening?" Those who could not answer she flung to their deaths over the cliff, and that included everyone until Oedipus came by and told her that it was man.

Oedipus had been to Delphi to try to find out who really were his parents; and later too, to his sorrow, he searched for the murderer of the king. He sought after knowledge even when it meant his own undoing. Not by chance was it this man who, as the legend has it, grasped immediately the concepts of time, change, and development implicit in the riddle of the Sphinx. So long as we think in static terms that there is an entity that walks on four legs or is the personality or is the group, we can never grasp the complex and apparently disparate phenomena of the world, in time, in which we live. When Oedipus grasped the complexity in an intuitive vision of the whole, the fearful Sphinx threw herself off the rock. But unfortunately she constantly climbs back up again and waits with a new riddle for a new Oedipus to come by.

When the Sphinx lies in wait with her dreadful question, representing the frightening complexity and uncertain behavior of the world, especially the world of groups, one feels terrified at what John Fowles calls "the eternal source of all fear, all horror, all real evil, man himself" (p. 448).

But the same man or the same group that has filled the world with horror at its capacity for evil can also amaze by its capacity for good. If the Sphinx were to ask, "What is it that on Monday is wrangling, cruel, and greedy; on Tuesday is indifferent and lazy; on Wednesday is effectively and intelligently collaborative?'' one could easily answer, "That is man, and it is also ten men in a group." If she asked, "What made the difference?" a few partial answers could be given. One of them is that on Wednesday the group had a clear goal to which all of its members wanted to devote themselves. Another is that the roles of the members were clearly defined and accepted. Still another has to do with the boundaries between this and other groups. But if the Sphinx were to go on and press about what to do in order that the Wednesday behavior should become more constant and the Monday and Tuesday behavior less frequent, we *might* find ourselves with no satisfactory answer, hurtling over the cliff.

Notes

1. For these formulations the author is indebted to a personal communication from A. K. Rice, who wrote approximately these words in *Learning for Leadership,* p. 72.

2. Quoted from a letter from C. G. Jung (Illing, p. 80).

References

Bion, W. R. *Experiences in Groups;* Basic Books, 1959.

Fowles, John. *The Magus;* Dell, 1967.

Illing, Hans A. "C. G. Jung on the Present Trends in Group Psychotherapy," *Human Relations* (1957) 10: 77–83.

Rice, A. K. *Learning for Leadership;* London, Tavistock Publications, 1965.

ORGANIZATION RESPONSE TO CHANGE

CHAPTER TWENTY-NINE

Organizational Identity and Learning

A Psychodynamic Perspective

Andrew D. Brown
Ken Starkey (2000)

In this chapter we seek to develop a psychodynamic perspective on the link between organizational identity and organizational learning. That an explicit link between organizational identity and organizational learning has not been made previously is probably due to the perception that organizational identity is a relatively stable and enduring feature of organizations. Gioia and Thomas suggest that we "soften the stricture on the conception of identity as more or less fixed to include a dimension of fluidity" (1996: 394). This is in line with the views of others who have depicted organizational identity as incrementally adaptive (Dutton & Dukerich, 1991) or changeable over the long term (Albert & Whetten, 1985). Arguments for the malleability of identity should not, however, be allowed to obscure the fact that learning is frequently restricted by organizations' efforts to preserve their identities (Gagliardi, 1986). If organizations appear to be in continuous states of flux, the types of change being observed are not necessarily those associated with (or constitutive of) organizational learning. That is, they are not necessarily changes that have implications for how participants conceive of their organization's identity (their organizational self-images), but can be superficial and quite possibly transitory.

The psychodynamic perspective we develop here suggests that individuals and organizations are not primarily motivated to learn to the extent that learning entails anxiety-provoking identity change. Rather, they maintain individual and collective self-esteem by not questioning existing self-concepts. In practice, this means that individuals and organizations engage in learning activities and employ information and knowledge conservatively to preserve their existing concepts of self (Baumeister, Tice, & Hutton, 1989; Baumgardner, Kaufman, & Cranford, 1990; Brockner, 1988; Brown, Collins, & Schmidt, 1988; Campbell, 1990; Rhodewalt, Morf, Hazlett, & Fairfield, 1991; Schlenker, Weigold, & Hallam, 1990). The self, we argue, is protected by ego defenses that, in contexts where change is desirable, exert a dysfunctional influence.

There are, of course, complicated issues of levels of analysis here: individual, group, and organizational (Klein, Dansereau, & Hall, 1994; Rousseau, 1985). Individual identity depends upon both one's personal identity and the identity that is shaped from one's relationships with others, although the effect of each of these two factors will differ between individuals and over time (Albert, 1977). Our argument is this: an individual is motivated to preserve/defend his or her personal identity through an individual-level need for self-esteem. Like individuals, the psychological group and organization seek to maintain self-esteem, and this generally means acting conservatively to preserve an existing identity. Organizational learning can require that individuals be prepared to challenge the group's or organization's identity. Indeed, learning may become more problematic to the extent that individuals and groups subsume their individual identity in that of the group or organization and see themselves as representative of that social category (Banaji & Prentice, 1994; Brown, 1997). Analysis of the organizational means through which individual and collective self-esteem is regulated in the service of organizational identity thus becomes an important area of inquiry, for an understanding of these dynamics will cast light on the blocks to organizational learning.

In the literature on organizational learning, researchers strive to integrate perspectives drawn from individual and organizational learning, organization and management development, strategic management, and organizational culture (Starkey, 1996). Learning is conceptualized as a virtuous circle in which new information is used to challenge existing ideas and to develop new perspectives on the future and new action routines through "organizational dialogue"—"talk that reveals our meaning structures to each other" (Dixon, 1994: 83). Current accounts of the reasons why organizations fail to learn are incomplete because, although they recognize cognitive limitations (Bettman & Weitz, 1983; Dearborn & Simon, 1958; Einhorn & Hogarth, 1986; Feldman, 1989; Hedberg, 1981; Kahneman, Slovic, & Tversky, 1982; Levitt & March, 1988; Nystrom & Starbuck, 1984; Slovic, Fischhoff, & Lichtenstein, 1977; Starbuck & Milliken, 1988), prior learning (Argyris & Schön, 1978; Miller, 1993; Weick, 1995), political games (Pfeffer, 1981), and certain cultural and structural features of organizations (Dodgson, 1993; Hedberg, 1981; Huber, 1991; Levinthal & March, 1993; Salaman & Butler, 1994) as barriers to learning, they ignore the role of psychodynamic factors in individual and organizational identity maintenance and the negative effects such factors can have on learning.

The reasons most usually given by scholars to account for organizational nonlearning are not wrong, but they would benefit from an interpretation of them as individual and collective defenses of self-esteem. Our position is that information that threatens an organization's collective self-concept is ignored, rejected, reinterpreted, hidden, or lost, and the processes by which organizations preserve their identities are, in many ways, analogous to the methods that individuals employ in defense of their own self-concepts. This argument derives from Jacques' suggestion that "institutions are used by individual members to reinforce individual mechanisms of defense against anxiety" (1955: 247), Bion and Rickman's (1943) observation that individual psychology is fundamentally group psychology, and Sofer's contention that administrative problems are the manifestation of individual psychology—that is, the "neurotic problems of persons writ large in organizational terms" (1972: 703). In this article we explore the effects on organizational identity of those processes by which organizations seek to insulate themselves from aspects of their internal and external environments and of those mechanisms through which organizational learning is made possible.

Learning to promote critical reflection upon organizational identity is a crucial but undertheorized management task. From a psychodynamic perspective, such learning involves the understanding and the mitigation of those ego defenses that tend toward a regressive retreat from a changing reality. Management's role is to promote mature and adaptive thought and action in pursuit of the collective organizational good—recognizing, of course, that what counts as the collective organizational good is both contestable and identity dependent. This involves critical reflection upon the nature of self-concepts that form the basis of organization as part of an ongoing learning process.

If skillfully managed, the outcome of critical reflection upon the nature of identity is a self-reflexive and wise organization, secure in its ability to negotiate identity change as part of its ability to negotiate identity change as part of its future strategic development. We conceptualize self-reflexivity from the perspective of the attainment of wisdom—a view that is prefigured in the psychoanalytic literature by Erikson (1965) and, importantly, by Kohut, who defines wisdom as "a stable attitude of the personality toward life and the world, an attitude that is formed through the integration of cognitive function with humor, acceptance of transience, and a firmly cathected system of values" (1978: 458–459). For Kohut, wisdom represents "the ego's ultimate mastery over the narcissistic self, the final control of the rider over the horse" (1978: 459).

In terms of the conceptual framework outlined here, the sort of organizational learning we are primarily interested in is that which constitutes a form of identity change. Our argument is that for an organization to learn, there must be an alteration in its participants' organizationally derived self-images. Organizational learning evolves through modifications, additions, and deletions of existing routines (Albert, 1992). These routines are, at least in part, constitutive of members' collective definitions of the organization's identity (organizational self-images) so that variation in one necessarily implies variation in the other (Dutton & Dukerich, 1991; Gioia & Thomas, 1996; Sproull, 1981).

Two clarifications of this general argument merit close attention before we proceed with its further elaboration. First, it is possible for organizations to engage in routine-based learning in ways that support their existing self-concepts. What we have in mind here are minor alterations to an organization's routines that essentially leave them intact. Here again, we do not wish to argue that organizational self-concept change has occurred. In short, our focus is on what Argyris (1992) has referred to as type two rather than type one learning.

Second, it should be noted that even type two change to an organization's routines does not always constitute a clear-cut change in that organization's self-concept. For example, there may be organizations in which the ability to radically alter, add, or delete core routines is an important part of their concept of self. This opens up the intriguing possibility that, in some instances, although a third party might be inclined to describe an organization as having altered its identity, the participants in that organization might prefer to describe what has occurred as identity preservation.

In this chapter we pursue these arguments in two major sections. First, we elaborate our contention that organizations fail to learn because of the operation of ego defenses that maintain collective self-esteem, focusing specifically on denial, rationalization, idealization, fantasy, and symbolization. Second, we suggest that to mitigate these ego defenses, organizations must embrace an identity as a learning organization. This involves an organization's challenging its assumptions regarding its existing identity and promoting a dialogue focused on desirable future identities—processes promoting attitudes of wisdom. Finally, we sketch five implications for further research and draw brief conclusions.

THE DYNAMICS OF IDENTITY MAINTENANCE

Agreement on the meaning of an organization for participants is closely associated with the sharing of assumptions that make routine coordinated action possible (Schein, 1985). Expressed another way, "organizational identity concerns those features of the organization that members perceive as ostensibly central, enduring, and distinctive in character that contribute to how they define the organization and their identification with it" (Gioia & Thomas, 1996: 372). Thus, there is a "continuous reciprocal functional interdependence between the psychological processes of individuals" and organizations, for individuals and the social categories they participate in are both "mutual preconditions" and "simultaneously emergent properties" of each other (Turner, 1987: 205–206).

The conservatism of the urge to maintain self-esteem means that the existing self-concept is insulated/defended from self-analysis and challenge. Organizational self-esteem derives from participants' need for self-esteem based on their organizational self-images. Like individuals, the psychological organization seeks to maximize self-esteem and, in so doing, acts conservatively to preserve its identity.

Individual and organizational concepts of self are maintained by a variety of defenses that are engaged in order to avoid psychic pain and discomfort, allay or prevent anxiety, resolve conflicts, and generally support and increase self-esteem. Automatically and unconsciously deployed, the defenses are an attempted means of coping with an otherwise consciously intolerable situation (A. Freud, 1966; S. Freud, 1949; Laughlin, 1970). Such "defensive action may be defined as any invalid addition or subtraction from concrete reality that inhibits detection and correction of error as well as detection of the unawareness that the actions are defensive" (Argyris, 1982: 230).

Up to forty-eight ego defenses have been identified (Laughlin, 1970), but here we focus initially on five: denial, rationalization, idealization, fantasy, and symbolization.[1] It is important to note that a degree of defense is characteristic of psychologically healthy individuals and organizations, who need to regulate their self-esteem in order to function adequately (Cooper, 1986; Frosh, 1991; Kohut, 1971; Shengold, 1995). Taken to one of two extremes, however, ego defenses can make a net negative contribution to psychological health and, thus, be symptoms of pathological disorder (Brown, 1997).

A continuum of organizations, therefore, may be envisaged—one extreme of which is characterized by excessively high self-esteem (overdefended organizations) and the other by extremely low self-esteem (underdefended organizations). In the former, overprotection of self-esteem from powerful ego defenses reduces an organization's ability *and* desire to search for, interpret, evaluate, and deploy information in ways that influence its dominant routines. In the latter, inadequate protection of collective self-esteem will expose the organization to fears and anxieties that militate against self-confident action and, hence, organizational learning. In healthy organizations, in contrast, the ego defenses operate to reduce doubt and uncertainty and to increase self-confidence in ways that permit complex and ambiguous phenomena to be interpreted and explained.

The role of the ego defenses in individual-level learning (Argyris, 1982; Miller, 1993), the idea that groups act to maintain and enhance their shared self-esteem (Brockner, 1988; Swogger, 1993), and the notion that organizations act to preserve their collective identities all have found support (Dutton & Dukerich, 1991; Dutton, Dukerich, & Harquail, 1994). There is also evidence for the view of organizations, their cultures, structures, and work routines as defense mechanisms against anxiety (Bion, 1968; Bion & Rickman, 1943; Jacques, 1955). For example, Menzies has described how participants in hospital organizations collectively operate psychic defense mechanisms, such as splitting, projection, and regression, in order to avoid "feelings of anxiety, guilt, and uncertainty" (1970: 124). Similarly, Miller and Gwynne have illustrated how the social structures of residential care institutions "equip members with defenses against anxiety" (1972: 124).

The link between group defenses and self-esteem also has been made (Cartwright & Zander, 1968; Janis, 1972). Thus, Cartwright and Zander (1968) have argued that highly cohesive groups provide the sort of security that heightens participants' self-esteem, whereas Janis has suggested that groupthink is, in part, a response to threats to "the self-esteem of the members of a cohesive decision-making body" (1972: 206). Here, we seek to link and extend these suggestions, arguing that the motivation to conserve and protect organizational identity is self-esteem and that the means for accomplishing this are processes analogous to the ego defenses. These defenses can prove dysfunctional for organizational learning.

Scholars have well attested the idea that organizational identity acts as a perceptual screen that affects individual members' information processing and interpretation of issues (Dutton et al., 1994; Gioia & Thomas, 1996; Whetten, Lewis, & Mischel, 1992). In a sense, we discuss the dynamics of the screening process, which supports organizational identity and how it affects fundamentally organizations' capacity to learn. At an organizational level, defenses inhibit learning through their influence on (1) the external search for information, (2) the interpretation of information, (3) the use of information, (4) the storage of information, and (5) the internal recall of information. To illustrate the process of learning inhibition, we focus on five defenses, which, for reasons of clarity, convenience, and simplicity, we analyze separately, although empirical exploration of the theory outlined here is likely to confirm that they tend to act in concert (synergistically), to reinforce each other. The definitions of the defenses provided here have been derived from a single source (Laughlin's 1970 exemplary account), in order to minimize the possibility of confusion.

Denial

To deny something is to negate or disown it. Through denial, individuals and organizations seek to disclaim knowledge and responsibility, to reject claims made on them, and to disavow acts and their consequences. Denial is a "primitive" and "magical" process that can lead to increased confidence and that can boost feelings of invulnerability, with profound implications for learning (Laughlin, 1970: 57).

The idea that belief structures can blind decision makers and compromise organizational effectiveness by leading these decision makers to deny the existence of problems has long been recognized (Walsh & Fahey, 1986; Walsh & Ungson, 1991). Employees committed to their organization's strategies and culture may find it so painful to admit that they are obsolete that they collectively "deny that there is a problem" (Miller, 1993: 121). In other organizations participants can seek to protect themselves by denying the validity of feedback data on their activities and then refusing "to test the validity of their denials" (Argyris, 1982: 165), making impossible adequate interpretation and use of available information.

Kets de Vries cites the example of a founder-entrepreneur who "refused to accept reports that sales were dropping rapidly" and "denied responsibility" for mismanagement, until "the banks eventually intervened and declared bankruptcy" (1996: 32). Miller and Gwynne have described how denial worked as an organizing principle in a residential care institution, allowing the nursing staff to deny that individual patients had different needs, that emotional bonds between patients and nursing staff were important, and that the primary task of the institution was to assist patients from "social death to physical death" (1972: 126, 179). Other authors have illustrated the tendency of individuals and organizations faced with charges of ethical misconduct to engage in various forms of denial, such as "I am not guilty," and "The event did not occur" (Bradford & Garrett, 1995; Schonbach, 1980; Semin & Manstead, 1983; Szwajkowski, 1992). Nystrom and Starbuck have discussed how "encased learning produces blindness and rigidity that may breed full-blown crises" (1984: 53). Most strikingly, Schwartz has described how "the denial of reality" became "the motivational base of organizational life for committed participants" at NASA (1987: 61), which impeded its ability to effectively recall, interpret, and use information—with disastrous consequences for the Space Shuttle *Challenger*.

Rationalization

A rationalization is an attempt to justify impulses, needs, feelings, behaviors, and motives that one finds unacceptable so that they become both plausible and consciously tolerable. This process of making what is consciously repugnant seem more acceptable involves a degree of self-deception (Laughlin, 1970), which limits self-knowledge. At an individual level, scholars have often observed that actors offer rationalized statements for their actions (Argyris & Schön, 1978; Morgan, 1986); that executives tend to deal with problems by rationalizing them "away as aberrations, as temporary, or as beyond management's control'' (Miller, 1993: 120); and that actors blind to their mental programming often react to failure with rationalized attempts to reduce dissonance, by blaming others or claiming that a certain quota of failed initiatives is inevitable (Argyris, 1982).

Collective rationalizations in the form of "selective principles," which provide categories for thought (Douglas, 1987: 69); "retrospective sense-making," which ameliorates organizational disappointments (Weick, 1995); and "organizational defensive routines," which negate threats and embarrassments (Argyris, 1992: 286), figure prominently in the organization theory literature (see also Elsbach & Kramer, 1996, and Starbuck, 1983). Janis (1972) has described how those suffering from groupthink develop a set of shared beliefs based on stereotypes and ideology that rationalize their complacency about the soundness of their policy decisions. He suggests that leading up to the Japanese bombing of Pearl Harbor, one rationalization accepted by the U.S. Navy "was that the Japanese would never dare attempt a full-scale surprise assault against Hawaii because they would realize that it would precipitate an all-out war, which the United States would surely win" (Janis, 1972: 87). Some interesting organizational examples include the New York Port Authority's defensive rationalization of its decision not to respond to the issue of homelessness (Dutton & Dukerich, 1991), the Long Island Lighting Company's attempts to rationalize its illicit activities (Ross & Staw, 1993), and General Motors' defense of the unsafe Corvair (Nader & Taylor, 1986; Wright, 1979).

Idealization

Idealization is the process by which some object comes to be "overvalued and emotionally aggrandized" (Laughlin, 1970: 123) and stripped of any negative features. It implies the exercise of an unrealistic judgment, and it results in the creation (in imagination) of a "fantastic" and "impossible" person, standard, or other entity. A classic example of this is Freud's (1949) discussion of how groups idealize their leaders. Bion (1968) builds on Freud's pioneering work to analyze the ways in which groups can idealize a leader, tradition, object, or idea to the extent that learning and work are seriously inhibited. This situation has been described as "a sort of corporate madness in which every member colludes and which stifles any independent thought or co-operative work" (De Board, 1978: 39). Sproull (1981) has commented on how criteria for the evaluation of action can be idealized as providing objective guides regarding the best or most appropriate action. Idealization is directly implicated in Gagliardi's model of organizational culture change, where he argues that idealization leads to the emotional identification of values and that it is only this "*idealization* of past successes [that] can fully explain why organizations are often unable to unlearn obsolete knowledge in spite of strong disconfirmations" (1986: 123).

In short, idealization processes help explain why organizations can exhibit habitual responses to now-defunct cues (Starbuck & Hedberg, 1977), persevere with failing strategies (Wilensky, 1967), and retain underperforming leaders (Bion, 1968). Idealization-inspired monomaniac fixation has been amply illustrated by Miller (1990) and by Starbuck, Greve, and Hedberg (1978), who have commented on numerous examples of formerly thriving companies that came to focus on just one goal, aspect of strategy, department, or even skill that they credited for their success (see also Colvin, 1982, on ITT; Halberstam, 1986, on Ford; Lyon, 1984, on Dome Petroleum; Starbuck & Hedberg, 1977, on the Facit Company; Wright, 1979, on GM).

Fantasy

A fantasy is a kind of vivid daydream that affords unreal, substitutive satisfactions. Fantasies represent an unconscious endeavor to fulfill or gratify difficult or impossible goals and aspirations (Laughlin, 1970). In organizations, shared fantasies are expressed through linguistic and visual artifacts, such as stories, myths, jokes, gossip, nicknames, graffiti, and cartoons. "Attachment to a fantasy" is a form of collective retreat into imagination, which "converts the ambiguities of history into confirmations of belief and a willingness to persist in a course of action" in ways that are "destructive for the individual organization" (March, 1995; 437).

An illustration of this has been provided by Wastell, who shows how structured methods for improving the quality of software systems can be employed ritualistically to defend against anxiety in a way that encourages withdrawal into a "fantasy world," where "the learning processes that are critical to the success of systems development are jeopardized" (1996: 25). Miller and Gwynne (1972) have argued that in many residential care institutions, fantasies concerned with processes of cure and rehabilitation are common. Bion (1968) has described various group pathologies in which collectivities focus their energies on group fantasies in order to obscure what is actually happening.

Although fantasies are substitutes for effective learning and action, this does not imply that their influence has always been diagnosed negatively. Thus, in the work of Gabriel (1991, 1995), organizations are impersonal and emotionally impoverished locales in which fantasies give vent to such powerful feelings as heroic defiance and the expiation of guilt, humanizing and offering consolation to employees for the harshness and arbitrariness of organizational life.

Symbolization

Symbolization is the process "through which an external object becomes the disguised outward representation for another internal and hidden object, idea, person, or complex" (Laughlin, 1970: 414).[2] The idea that organizations are socially constructed and, thus, essentially symbolic phenomena into which participants read meaning is one prevalent theme in the organization theory literature (Berger & Luckmann, 1966). However, most accounts of symbols in organizations represent them instrumentally, either as mechanisms for comprehension (Daft, 1983; Dandridge, Mitroff, & Joyce, 1980) or as a means by which leaders manipulate and control their organizations (Peters, 1978; Pfeffer, 1981).

What is suggested here is a view of symbols as the unconscious means of allaying anxiety and maintaining self-esteem through the distortion and concealment of unconscious thoughts, impulses, and desires. Symbols, then, place restrictions on our capacity to perceive and process information in ways that facilitate development and learning. Gabriel's (1991, 1995) analyses of myths as shields against reality; Schwartz's suggestion that ''the main activity of organization is the generation of symbols and myths which will serve as vehicles for significance and symbolic immortality'' (1985: 38); and the many suggestions that symbols allow individuals to cope with change by concealing, camouflaging, and reconciling differences (Johnson, 1990; Moch & Huff, 1983) are all suggestive of symbolization processes designed to reduce anxiety and raise self-esteem in organizations.

The pervasive importance of symbolization in organizations is suggested by Wilensky's (1967) analysis of leaders' (especially military leaders') tendency to interpret such symbols as uniforms and titles as indicators of both loyalty and ability. This form of symbolization raises these leaders' own self-esteem (because they have the most desirable titles and uniforms) and reduces their anxiety about being deceived or betrayed by others (because by wearing these badges of conformity and commitment, subordinates deserve to be listened to and trusted). In all hierarchical organizations the hierarchy itself may be regarded as evidence of symbolization, which reduces uncertainty regarding reporting relationships and decision-making powers, allocates responsibilities, and provides a sense of coherence and meaning for participants. Symbolization is reassuring but potentially self-deceptive and self-defeating: on the one hand it allows ''self-confident action and coherent life,'' but, on the other, it militates against learning processes that would reveal ''the truth about our powerlessness and finitude'' (Schwartz, 1985: 35).

To summarize, organizations often engage in defensive information processing in order to maintain individual and collective self-esteem, and, in defending collective self-esteem, organizations are preserving their existing self-concepts. In short, an organization's self-concept is the outcome of the struggle to generate and maintain self-esteem. However, it is clear that there are occasions when organizations do learn and challenge existing self-concepts. Such learning is required when an organization seeks to improve its existing capabilities, either to perform better in a static environment or to adapt to a changing environment. In psychodynamic terms, the task of management in these circumstances is to prevent a regressive retreat from reality (owing to the activation of the defense mechanisms analyzed in this section) and to develop more "mature and reality-adapted sectors and segments of the psyche [by cultivating] a variety of mature and realistic thought and action patterns" (Kohut, 1971: 197). How ego defenses, identity, and learning interact we consider in the next section.

THE DYNAMICS OF IDENTITY CHANGE AND ORGANIZATIONAL LEARNING

How identities evolve as organizations learn—that is, how organizations mitigate their ego defenses—is an important conceptual and management issue. Organizations, like individuals, frequently find instituting a fundamental identity change difficult. Crucial to this process is the development of a capacity to deal with the fundamental anxieties that the ego defenses defend against. The idea of the learning organization suggests one way of conceptualizing the identity change process. Once one embraces the identity of a learning organization, the organization accepts that identity formation is never closed and that it will develop a series of identities through time that reflect the organization's and its members' evolving self-concepts. Here, we examine the characteristics of the learning organization, with emphasis upon three features that have particular importance for promoting changes in organizational identity through time: (1) critical self-reflexivity, (2) the promotion of dialogue about future identity as an integral feature of strategic management, and (3) the attainment of an attitude of wisdom.

One feature of the organizational learning literature is that it tends to be overoptimistic regarding the weakness of barriers to learning, so it underemphasizes the difficulties involved in mitigating them. A psychodynamic perspective suggests that to promote the deeper learning necessary to engender significant identity change, we need to directly engage with the issue of how organizations can deal with the fundamental anxiety that the ego defenses defend against. A psychodynamic perspective also suggests that this is no easy task and one that, with notable exceptions (such as Argyris, 1992), theorists of organizational learning tend to underplay. As Hirschhorn has said, "In a manner that echoes Freud's pessimism in *Civilization and its Discontents*, we can only be pessimistic about our capacity to live and work in a postindustrial world. The demands on our imagination, our empathic capacities, our ability to learn seem too great" (1988: 204).

A psychodynamic perspective, therefore, does not generate an easy optimism about the magnitude of the task involved in changing identity in a way that mitigates strong, unconscious defense mechanisms. It also recognizes that, in a sense, the self-concepts of individuals and organizations derive from their ego defenses, and that it is an alteration in the relative dominance and combinations of these defenses that is implied by the very idea of identity change.

Organizations, like individuals, defend their existing identities and, in the process, reduce their opportunity to learn. Indeed, group psychodynamic theory would suggest that the process of identity change is more difficult for an organization than for an individual. In his classic study of group psychology, Freud argues that groups promote regressive behaviors that lead to a "collective inhibition of intellectual functioning and the heightening of affectivity in groups" (1949: 23). According to Freud, groups are led almost exclusively by the unconscious, with a consequent tendency for the "disappearance of conscience or of a sense of responsibility" (Freud, 1949: 14, 9–10). Bion (1968) has examined the various mechanisms through which group members defend against the anxiety of group membership, thus disrupting ego functioning and challenging the individual's self-esteem. A core task of the ego is to maintain an individual's self-image. As Eisold has made clear, "Because the ego's ability to integrate and synthesize is its source of strength and self-confidence, the core element in the identity, group membership thus necessarily disrupts and undermines the member's very sense of a stable and functioning identity. This . . . is the greatest source of anxiety [in groups]: a kind of panic arising out of a faltering, disintegrating self that is losing its very capacity to right itself" (1985: 45).

In his or her struggle to hold on to the self, the individual clings ever more strongly to his or her particular constellation of individual defense mechanisms. To allay the anxiety of group membership, individuals tend to embrace "extremely narrow identities" (Eisold, 1985: 45). In therapeutic groups the work is to ensure that members confront the regressive pressures of group membership to combat the fragmentation of self and a regressive retreat to more primitive "narrow" identities and so develop the ego's capacity for flexible and integrative behavior. Crucial here is development of a climate of trust in the group so that "members risk change because they come to trust the group as a matrix of corrective emotional experience" (Eisold, 1985: 47).

From a psychodynamic perspective, the underlying task in the management of groups and organizations is the same: to create an emotional climate in which individuals can balance the need to feel they belong to a group without losing their individual identity so that they can work toward organizational goals that enhance their self-esteem. Self-esteem is developed and maintained by finding opportunities to express one's self in organizational work valued by salient others. This is not an easy task, because the achievement of organizational goals depends upon our ability to operate effectively in workgroups, while such groups present regressive experiences that impair the capacity to function.

How are the learning defenses to be mitigated, and how is the learning that can lead to identity change to be promoted? Our understanding of the dynamics of identity change derives from the work of Berzonsky (1988) and Blasi (1988), for whom self-concept development involves the management of three interdependent components: (1) *process*, the means by which identity is encoded, elaborated, and integrated; (2) *structure*, the way identity is organized; and (3) *content*, the information from which identity is constructed (Berzonsky, 1988). If the self-concept is an answer to the question "Who and what am I?" then, in general, the answer consists of achieving a new unity among elements of one's past and expectations about the future, and this creates a deep and fundamental sense of purposeful continuity: "This is a process of integration and questioning. The answer to these questions leads to integration, a sense of basic loyalty and fidelity as well as deep, preconscious, feelings of rootedness and well-being, self-esteem, and purposefulness" (Blasi, 1988: 226–227).

Learning that promotes identity change thus involves a resynthesis or reintegration of the processual, structural, and content aspects of self in a way that defends against anxiety and satisfies the need for self-esteem.

In work "we are confronted with the regressive pull of anxiety and splitting and the developmental pull of risk taking and reparation" (Hirschhorn, 1988: 10). It is the regressive pull of anxiety that tends to dominate and makes identity change problematic. To promote identity change, therefore, organizations need to confront the psychological boundaries individuals and groups set up to contain anxiety. Hirschhorn (1988) argues that we need a new work culture that helps people contain and transmute their anxieties and in which it is acceptable for people to air their vulnerabilities. This means challenging the modern "masculine" conception of organization, which values the suppression of doubt and ambivalence and which is single-minded in the pursuit of its goals and in its unshakable understanding of its unchanging and fully formed identity. The alternative, "post-modern" organization is more "feminine," characterized by "a culture of being open to others," and "uses doubt as a springboard for learning"; its identity "is not fixed but instead unfolds over the adult life course" (Hirschhorn, 1997: 17–18). Hirschhorn describes the transition to this postmodern form of organization as a process of reparation, arguing that work offers the possibility of individual and group reparation to address and heal damaged selves: "The production of valued goods and services for others provides us with a framework for repairing our relationships" (1988: 204).

The heart of the reparation process is to develop an understanding of the individual's own purpose and to align this with the institution's purpose and with the intentions of coworkers. We have to create conditions in which we relate "in depth" to others and recover our own personal authority. In this way we create the conditions necessary for self-fulfillment at work and protect ourselves from isolation and self-estrangement (Hirschhorn, 1997).

Critical Self-Reflexivity and the Evolution of Identity Through Time

Although accepting the definition of organizational identity as "central" and "distinctive," those with an organizational learning perspective contest the view that organizational identity should be "enduring" (Albert & Whetten, 1985). Identifying the self's qualities is an integral aspect of self-regulation (Schlenker, 1985). A coherent identity is important in creating a sense of meaning, but as organizational membership and environmental context alter, so the self needs to adapt to these changes. Identity can serve to counter the existential anxiety of a "precariousness of meaning" (Alvesson, 1990: 385), but the absence of a coherent identity can cause insecurity and even a sense of helplessness (Diamond, 1992).

However, although identity provides meaning, premature closure of identity exploration processes, or too tight a closure around an overdefined identity, is inimical to the multiple and alternative meanings that make organization development possible (Lundberg, 1989). Senior management's role in the learning organization is to surface and contest existing mental models and to build shared visions of the future (Bennis, 1993; Senge, 1990). The challenge to existing mental models and the development of new visions need to include organizational identity—a questioning of the mental models that support current views of organizational identity and the development of visions concerning the nature of the new identity the organization is working toward.

We should think about identity from a temporal as well as from a structural perspective, particularly when we confront the issue of change. Organizational learning involves the reflexive consideration of what constitutes self. Learning can be construed as an ongoing search for a time- and context-sensitive identity; it alternates through phases of exploration and commitment (Marcia, 1988). Sometimes exploration of possible identities is to the fore, whereas at other times commitment to one dominant identity for a period of time prevails; even during the commitment phase, however, the limits of identity are being explored. The exploration phase concerns the consideration of alternative future directions and involves a critical, reflexive attitude to the existing identity structure, based upon current commitments. Identity development involves a lifelong process of change, composed of sequences of exploration-commitment-identity. The identity represents the "inner organization of . . . needs, abilities, values, personal history, and plans" (Marcia, 1988: 217).

Critical self-reflexivity fosters alternative perspectives of self and institution-alizes the self-questioning of the ongoing viability of existing identity. Pascale (1990) argues that "vectors of contention" are potent forces for change within organizations. Indeed, without contention there is no internal stimulus for change. Unitary cultures with too narrow a definition of their core identities that exclude the possibility of internal dissent run the risk of maladaptation to changing environments. The problems that some of Peters and Waterman's (1982) excellent companies experienced in maintaining excellence can be attributed to this failing (Carroll, 1983; Lundberg, 1989; Pascale, 1990; Ray, 1986; Soeters, 1986). Strong culture organizations with very tightly defined and adhered to configurations of core beliefs and values are destined to become dysfunctional eventually, as their rigidities and closed boundaries reduce learning capacities (Miller, 1993).

Organizational learning that is transformative modifies the cultural core of the organization and its identity (Lundberg, 1989). Organizational trans-formation requires individuals and groups who have developed alternative scenarios of the future relative to those that characterize the status quo. These alternative perspectives, outcomes of critical self-reflexivity, call into question the viability of existing identity as the environment changes. The process of learning thus depends upon an organization's ability to under-stand and manage discord.

Identity change requires genuine exploration. When the defensive routines outlined earlier are too strong, "an identity is said to be foreclosed rather than achieved, and that identity is assumed to be less flexible, more brittlely fragile, and in greater need of content-consistent social support" (Marcia, 1988: 219). The goal is not to develop one lasting "core" self. To harmonize a range of con-tradictory internal desires and external demands, one needs to encourage a more provisional identity—less foreclosed and more enabling of alternative futures— through cultivating empathy among the various manifestations of self (Mitchell, 1993). Satisfaction and the relative richness of life have a great deal to do with the dialectic between multiplicity and integrity in the experience of self—the balance between discontinuity and continuity (Dimen, 1991; Harris, 1991). Where there is too much discontinuity, there is a dread of fragmentation, split-ting, dislocation, or dissolution—dread of the "not-me"—and where there is too much continuity, there is dread of paralysis and stagnation (Mitchell, 1993).

Paralysis and stagnation can take a variety of forms. According to Sullivan (1938), the narcissistic illusion, which is a clinging to a narcissistic ideal of a perfect self, is "the very mother of illusions" (Mitchell, 1993: 106). At the roots of the narcissistic position is a fear of confronting the inevitable gap between the desire for a perfect self and the profound disappointment of never being able to realize this desire. "Is not Narcissus trying to screen out such fears through his fixation on his own image?" (Epstein, 1995: 50–52).

Another explanation of the demise of excellent companies referred to previously is that they clung to a narcissistic fantasy of an ideal self and, therefore, stagnated because they were unable to realize that there were other possible ways of being—other forms of identity that could serve them more effectively. Theirs was a fantasy of omnipotence founded upon *past* learning. However, the lessons of the past are not enough to sustain future prosperity. Individuals and organizations need to strike a balance among past, present, and future in the same way that managers need to skillfully manage the tension between continuity and discontinuity (Pettigrew, 1985).

In some companies the dread of discontinuity can reinforce a company's tendency to regress to a past identity with which it is more familiar and comfortable. For example, Xerox developed all the technologies necessary to become a leading player in the personal computer market but was unable to liberate itself from its traditional identity as a copier company, thus failing to capitalize on its technological leadership in computing (Smith & Alexander, 1988). In contrast, Intel was able to re-create itself as a microprocessor company and relinquish, with pain and difficulty, its identity as a memory chip company, even though memory chips had been so central to the company's identity that "Intel stood for memories [and] memories meant . . . Intel" (Grove, 1997: 85).

Promotion of Dialogue About Future Identity as an Integral Feature of Strategic Management

Strategic management is the facet of management most concerned with the future. Pascale defines the goal of strategic management as maintaining the requisite, most constructive level of debate in organizations—"holding the organization in question" and "posing question[s in a] search for a different frame of reference" (1990: 51, 54–55). This enables an organization to adapt, change, or transform itself according to how the future unfolds and the external environment changes (Lundberg, 1989). Creative strategic management involves critical, reflexive analysis of the organization's fundamental premises, which are encapsulated in its identity (Hurst, Rush, & White, 1989). In preparing for an essentially unknowable future, the role of top management is to "generate and institutionalize the constant self-questioning which can facilitate smooth rather than punctuated change" and "create a system-wide learning environment" (Spender & Grinyer, 1995: 913). Identity is most problematic in conditions of high uncertainty. Pascale's (1990) notion of "managing on the edge" and Hamel and Prahalad's (1994) view of strategy as "strategic intent" contest conventional notions of strategy as the search for fit with an environment that is assumed to be stable.

Perhaps the most fully elaborated view of strategic management as an ongoing learning process that embraces the need to rethink organizational identity, in a context where environmental discontinuity is assumed, is scenario planning (Schoemaker, 1993; van der Heijden, 1996). In this approach, managers are urged to relax their conventional modes of thinking and to learn by setting aside their existing frames of reference—both epistemological and ontological. The premise is that our present ways of knowing, and what we already know, form an inadequate basis for learning about an uncertain future. Scenarios essentially are new strategic narratives (Barry & Elmes, 1997)—explorations of, and the media for, exploring new identity possibilities (van der Heijden, 1996). Strategy is conceived of as a reflective, unending search for meaning, the medium for which is akin to the construction of a narrative that makes sense of both past and future and the individual's and the organization's roles in creating this (Schafer, 1992; Spence, 1982). As Weigert has said, "We have only those socially constructed identities that we can construct in our conversations with others. Identities . . . are realized in stories" (1988: 268).

What is involved in a successful process of identity development is movement from a stable position into an exploratory phase, experimenting with elements that are, initially, alien to the central core of existing identity. "Challenge" scenarios, for example, call into question the deepest assumptions about an organization and its business, challenging managers to think the unthinkable, such as the overnight obsolescence of their core business. The exploration phase is followed by a phase of resolution and integration, "characterized by an interiorization of elements that were once external" (Marcia, 1988: 222).

Scenario planning involves the assumption that the future is likely to be discontinuous and, therefore, that organizations need to be constantly rethinking their identities. Rutenberg (1985) draws on the work of Winnicott (1974) to develop a psychodynamic perspective on scenario planning, which he describes as "playful planning," the goal of which is to enable managers to develop alternative models of the future. The scenario process is characterized as a complex "game," to distinguish it from strategic planning as a form of scientific forecasting. In the scenario process executives experiment, playfully and "intently" to "envision" different possible scenarios, forcing themselves to challenge existing cognitive assumptions, "while struggling for a language by which they can talk with fellow executives about the uncertainty of a discontinuity" (Rutenberg, 1985: 3).

Play serves to challenge existing belief systems and to restructure cognitions. It facilitates experiments with identity: What kind of person am I, can I be, and do I want to be? What kind of organization? This can best be explained psychodynamically. Play creates what Winnicott (1974) terms a *transitional object*. As exemplified in the play of children, playing with such objects helps us to resolve the anxiety of coming to terms with a changing reality and an evolving personhood. In playing we experiment and role play for different futures, and we learn to cope with the anxieties these futures provoke. Psychologically, this playing takes place in an intermediate area—a "transitional space" between the inner psyche and external reality—which is a crucial area in "the perpetual human task of keeping inner and external reality separate yet interrelated" (Winnicott, 1974: 3).

Objects of play serve as important loci for reality testing in an area that lies between primary creativity and objective perception. Play serves an important learning function. Equally important, it provides relief from the strain of relating inner and outer reality.

> Play is inherently exciting and precarious. This characteristic derives *not* from the instinctual arousal but from the precariousness that belongs to the interplay in the child's mind of what is subjective (near-hallucination) and that which is objectively perceived (actual or shared reality) [Winnicott, 1974: 61].

In play, the child establishes his or her identity by satisfactorily reconciling the tension between inner desires and the reality principle.

The Wise Organization

Critical self-reflexivity and dialogues about future identity, if they are to be successful, need to re-create a more adaptive self-concept by dealing with the psychodynamic layers of experience and the barriers to learning and identity change that we discussed earlier. According to our perspective, ego defenses, exacerbated by the regressive forces of group dynamics, serve to defend a self-concept that hinders change. In this case the strength of the ego defenses constitutes a barrier to learning. Organizational learning leads to positive identity change, if it can promote a new self-concept that mitigates some of the inhibiting effects of the defenses. This process can be viewed as the attainment of an attitude of wisdom. The wise individual or organization is one who accepts that a willingness to explore ego-threatening matters is a prerequisite for developing a more mature individuality and identity. Negotiating such identity change requires a process of profound self-questioning.

Wise individuals and organizations shape and reshape identity through the ongoing construction/reconstruction of self. This is particularly important in times of discontinuity, when it is important to explore the identity "gap" (Reger, Gustafson, DeMarie, & Mullane, 1994)—the gap between the actual self (what is) and the ideal self (what can be; Ashforth and Mael, 1996)—if the individual and the organization are to learn other ways of being in the world. Some sense of continuity is important. When major change is required, a wise way to proceed in motivating people to accept the necessity of change is to demonstrate how at least some elements of the past are valued and will be preserved (Albert, 1984). As a result, one will develop a sense of one's experience over time. One can measure a new experience in terms of continuity or discontinuity with the past and present; a new experience can represent and express one's history and current state, or "reshape one's history and current state in an enriching way" (Mitchell, 1993: 131). If we "impose" coherence too early (Phillips, 1988), our self-sufficiency is likely to be short-lived, precisely because we close ourselves to alternative sources of nurturance and understanding of ourselves and of our environment.

Too limited a concept of self can lead to unwise behavior that is not consonant with the nature of the environment. Lack of a shared identity creates dissonance and makes collective action and collective sensemaking impossible—groups disintegrate, organizations become less than the sum of their parts. Wisdom, at the individual and organizational levels, is a composite of curiosity, a willingness to learn, and an openness to learn new things about one's environment that challenges the assumption that we know all that we need to know and all that could possibly be relevant to our present situation.

The overconfident attitude assumes environmental stability. The attitude of wisdom assumes complexity and engenders what Weick (1993, 1995) terms *complex sensemaking*. Collective identity is crucial in making sense of one's environment, particularly in contexts of rapid and unpredictable change. Lacking a shared identity, organizational members have, at best, a limited sense of meaning and connection with the organization and cannot consciously assess the significance of their and others' actions for the organization (Baum, 1987, 1990; Diamond, 1992; Freud, 1949; Hirschhorn, 1988; Kets de Vries & Miller, 1984; Lynch, 1988; Schwartz, 1990).

Wisdom is associated with an ability to perceive the broader picture and "the connectedness of things" (Bigelow, 1992: 147). This involves a shift in self-perception from "self as independent" to "self as part" of a larger whole (Bigelow, 1992: 147), akin to the shift in Kohlberg's (1964) stages of moral development from a perspective of self-interest to one of social cooperation. If we are wise, we learn how to compensate for our weaknesses through facilitating and benefiting from interdependencies (Bigelow, 1992). Wisdom enables people to "transcend personalistic perspectives and embrace collective and universal concerns" (Orwoll & Perlmutter, 1990: 160). From a psychodynamic perspective, wisdom is associated with "a gradual increase of realistic self-esteem, of realistic enjoyment of success; a moderate use of fantasies of achievement (merging into plans for realistic action); and the establishment of such complex development within the realistic sector of the personality as humor, empathy, wisdom, and creativeness" (Kohut, 1971: 199).

Individuals transcend ego defenses to develop empathy—"the ability to . . . accommodate to the unique feelings and thoughts expressed by one another" (Kramer, 1990: 296). Empathy permits a more objective view of external reality, a greater receptivity to the views of others, and a more mature view of the self that accommodates previously dissociated parts.

Wisdom also demands the recognition of inevitable limitations, the abandonment of "the narcissistic insistence on the omnipotence of the wish: it expresses the acceptance of realistic values" (Kohut, 1978: 454). For Kohut, wisdom is a characteristic of the mature personality, "created by the ego's capacity to tame narcissistic cathexes and to employ them for its highest aims" (1978: 460). This recalls Erikson's identification of wisdom as a "basic virtue" that is attained in the final, eighth "step" of his psychosocial stages of development: "ego integrity" (1965: 266). The "highest aims" of both Erikson and Kohut are associated with "renunciation" (Erikson) and an acceptance of "transience" (Kohut), which lead to "a shift of the narcissistic cathexes from the self to a concept of participation in a supraindividual existence" (Kohut, 1978: 456).

In summary, in managing learning in order to promote critical reflection upon individual and organizational identity, an organization's key task is to understand and mitigate the ego defenses. These defenses tend toward a regressive retreat from a changing reality. Self-knowledge involves the active contestation of the negative aspects of ego defenses, such as denial, rationalization, idealization, fantasy, and symbolization. Management's role is to promote mature and adaptive wise thought and action in pursuit of the collective organizational good. This involves critical reflection upon the nature of the various self-concepts that form the basis of organization identity as part of an ongoing learning process. Learning depends upon the surfacing of difference and subsequent reintegration of conflicting views of the nature of self in the healing of the divisions that may thus arise. If skillfully managed, the outcome is a self-reflexive and wise organization, secure in its ability to understand and accept its limits and to negotiate identity change as part of its ongoing strategic development.

IMPLICATIONS FOR RESEARCH

Here we have suggested that psychological, and especially psychodynamic, approaches to organization studies can yield insights into collective behavior. Our contention that organizations can be understood usefully in terms of the psychology of the participants they are composed of has at least six important implications for research.

First, we should note that in this chapter we have focused on a very limited number of psychodynamically derived concepts—that is, the ego defenses and how these may be overcome through processes of learning. Only a small subset of the ego defenses and learning mechanisms has been examined. The wealth of analytic concepts and frameworks in the psychology and psychodynamics literature represents a latent reservoir of ideas that can assist us in our efforts to theorize about organizations. This chapter illustrates that there is a prima facie case for investigating how we can make use of this material, by direct importation, to add to our stock of metaphors and images of organization (Morgan, 1980, 1983; Tsoukas, 1991, 1993).

Second, although we have argued that the identity of the psychological organization consists of its participants' organizationally relevant self-images, we believe that *how* participants come to possess and identify with these self-images is an important area for further research. Individuals enter organizations with an existing self-concept that they have learnt to defend. From an organizational perspective, the individual might need to learn a new self-concept to align himself or herself with organizational identity.

One influential view of organizations suggests that they are fractured and hierarchical locales in which individuals and groups are implicated in reciprocal but often asymmetric power relationships (Clegg, 1981; Pettigrew, 1992; Pfeffer & Salancik, 1974). This means that some are more able to extend their hegemony (in our terms, able to affect individuals' self-images based on the organization) more than others. In short, how self-images develop is an exercise in power. From a learning organization perspective, learning is less coercive and identity change is based upon the mutual alignment of individual and organization. Our suggestion is that in order for these processes to be surfaced, we need to focus attention on the influence and interplay of the identity narratives that characterize both individuals and organizations (Boje, 1995; Brown, 1998; Bruner, 1990). An important factor for investigation here would be the degree of resistance to change at both the individual and organizational levels. Investigations of this nature would be consonant with the next two implications for research.

Third, we have restrictedly framed this chapter as a contribution to the debate on the relationships between the concepts of organizational identity and learning. However, we believe that our conception of the psychodynamics of organizational identity has far broader implications meriting further scholarly attention. Perhaps the most obvious inquiries to which our arguments are relevant are those concerning organizational change, especially at the strategic level. It seems reasonable to suggest that an organization's strategic discourse is an integral aspect of its identity and that strategic change implies identity change (Gioia & Thomas, 1996). The difficulties inherent in altering an organization's strategic narrative (Barry & Elmes, 1997) illustrate that an understanding of the inertial power of the collective ego defenses might valuably inform research in this area. Similarly, familiarity with processes of identity change may cast some further light on how organizations are, in fact, sometimes able to reshape and reorder the themes that characterize their strategic discourse.

Fourth, our approach has relevance for research into organizational narratives. Identity manifests itself in narrative. Much of effective management depends upon language; indeed, major strategic change depends upon the "art of strategic conversation" (van der Heijden, 1996), yet research into top management conversation is rare (Pettigrew, 1992). Hambrick and Mason's (1984) "upper echelon perspective" was crucial in stressing the strategic importance of top management teams, but the tendency in this line of research has been to focus on demographic data and multivariate analysis. Demographic data can deal with structural but not dynamic phenomena. Hambrick and Mason (1984) argued for greater use of clinical studies in this area, but cross-sectional studies with inconsistent findings still predominate (Priem, 1990). The field requires a concerted effort to penetrate this overdefended space.

Fifth, the perspective we have developed in this chapter also has relevance for research into managerial wisdom. This is an underresearched topic in academic management journals (Bigelow, 1992; Waters, 1980; Weick, 1993), although it has received some attention in practitioner-oriented literature (Hurst, 1984; Lorsch & Mathias, 1987; Mintzberg, 1987). Reliable measures of wisdom have not yet been developed, but there is some agreement about the key phases that characterize its development (Sternberg, 1990). These include the generation of an ability to learn from experience (Bigelow, 1992); a movement to longer-term thinking, which deliberately extends future time horizons (Waters, 1980); and a concern with metaknowledge (Bigelow, 1992) and "epistemic cognition" (Kitchener, 1983), which includes reflection upon the "limits of knowing" created by existing ways of viewing the world. To these we would add "ontological cognition"—a critical reflection upon the status of the categories that we use to describe our current ways of being in the world (Wimsatt, 1970). From a psychodynamic perspective, Kohut suggests that the analysis of wisdom is "our ultimate challenge" (1978: 458).

Sixth and finally, the logic of our argument suggests that we need to think deeply about how we conceptualize meaning in the study of identity and in research into organizations in general. Lundberg (1989) argues that organizations have three levels of meaning: (1) a cognitive, manifest/surface level; (2) strategic beliefs; and (3) basic values and assumptions. We have argued here that there is a fourth level—a psychodynamic level—that fundamentally affects the processes and the outcomes of organizational learning and is manifested, but in an indirect fashion, as organizational identity. Analysis of the biographies and autobiographies of organizational leaders and company histories using this perspective offers a rich research potential. Such an analysis will have practical implications for more effective management practice, to the extent that it will demonstrate how increased self-awareness can promote critical reflection upon the limits of self and of an existing identity.

CONCLUSION

In this chapter we have sought to make a contribution to our field's understanding of individual and collective identities. Although this is primarily a conceptual piece focused on definitional and psychodynamic issues of identity and learning, we believe that the ideas presented herein have important practical implications for how scholars may comprehend and measure these phenomena. Specifically, we suggest that use of our conceptualizations will enable others to more adequately trace identity dynamics, such as how collective identities emerge and change over time. We recognize, of course, that the analytic perspective on identity issues that we offer is partial, and indeed merely one of many possible approaches in this field, but we remain sanguine that it offers opportunities for us to see more clearly and, thus, to explore more deeply the nature of organization and management (Weick, 1987).

Notes

1. Our decision to focus on five ego defenses was made solely because of word-length restrictions.

2. Although *symbolization* may also refer to the creation of language, with all that follows from that, here we are using the term in the restricted sense of an ego-defensive process.

References

Albert, S. 1977. Temporal comparison theory. *Psychological Review*, 84: 485–503.

Albert, S. 1984. A delete design model for successful transitions. In J. R. Kimberly & R. E. Quinn (Eds.), *Managing organizational transitions*: 169–191. Homewood, IL: Irwin.

Albert, S. 1992. The algebra of change. *Research in Organizational Behavior*, 14: 179–229.

Albert, S., & Whetten, D. A. 1985. Organizational identity. In L. L. Cummings & B. M. Staw (Eds.), *Research in organizational behavior*, vol. 7: 263–295. Greenwich, CT: JAI Press.

Alvesson, M. 1990. Organization: From substance to image? *Organization Studies*, 11: 373–394.

Argyris, C. A. 1982. *Reasoning, learning, and action*. San Francisco: Jossey-Bass.

Argyris, C. A. 1992. *On organizational learning*. Cambridge, MA: Blackwell.

Argyris, C. A., & Schön, D. A. 1978. *Organizational learning*. Reading, MA: Addison-Wesley.

Ashforth, B. E., & Mael, F. A. 1996. Organizational identity and strategy as a context for the individual. *Advances in Strategic Management*, 13: 19–64.

Banaji, M. R., & Prentice, D. A. 1994. The self in social contexts. *Annual Review of Psychology*, 45: 297–332.

Barry, D., & Elmes, M. 1997. Strategy retold: Toward a narrative view of strategic discourse. *Academy of Management Review*, 22: 429–452.

Baum, H. S. 1987. *The invisible bureaucracy*. New York: Oxford University Press.

Baum, H. S. 1990. *Organizational membership*. Albany: State University of New York Press.

Baumeister, R. F., Tice, D. M., & Hutton, D. G. 1989. Self-presentational motivations and personality differences in self-esteem. *Journal of Personality and Social Psychology*, 57: 547–579.

Baumgardner, A. H., Kaufman, C. M., & Cranford, J. A. 1990. To be noticed favorably: Links between private self and public self. *Personality and Social Psychology Bulletin*, 16: 705–716.

Bennis, W. 1993. *The invented life: Reflections on leadership and change*. Reading, MA: Addison-Wesley.

Berger, P. L., & Luckmann, T. 1966. *The social construction of reality*. Garden City, NJ: Doubleday.

Berzonsky, M. D. 1988. Self-theorists, identity status, and social cognition. In D. K. Lapsley & F. Clark Power (Eds.), *Self, ego, and identity: Integrative approaches*: 243–262. New York: Springer-Verlag.

Bettman, J. R., & Weitz, B. A. 1983. Attributions in the board room: Causal reasoning in corporate annual reports. *Administrative Science Quarterly*, 28: 165–183.

Bigelow, J. 1992. Developing managerial wisdom. *Journal of Management Inquiry*, 1: 143–153.

Bion, W. R. 1968. *Experiences in groups*. London: Tavistock.

Bion, W. R., & Rickman, J. 1943. Intergroup tensions in therapy. *Lancet*, 27: 478–481.

Blasi, A. 1988. To be or not to be: Self and authenticity, identity, and ambivalence. In D. K. Lapsley & F. Clark Power (Eds.), *Self, ego, and identity: Integrative approaches*: 226–242. New York: Springer-Verlag.

Boje, D. M. 1995. Stories of the storytelling organization: A postmodern analysis of Disney as "*Tamara*-Land." *Academy of Management Journal*, 38: 997–1035.

Bradford, J. L., & Garrett, D. E. 1995. The effectiveness of corporate communicative responses to accusations of unethical behavior. *Journal of Business Ethics*, 14: 875–892.

Brockner, J. 1988. *Self-esteem at work*. Boston: Lexington Books.

Brown, A. D. 1997. Narcissism, identity, and legitimacy. *Academy of Management Review*, 22: 643–686.

Brown, A. D. 1998. Narrative, politics and legitimacy in an IT implementation. *Journal of Management Studies*, 35: 35–58.

Brown, J. D., Collins, R. L., & Schmidt, G. W. 1988. Self-esteem and direct versus indirect forms of self-enhancement. *Journal of Personality and Social Psychology*, 55: 445–453.

Bruner, J. 1990. *Acts of meaning*. Cambridge, MA: Harvard University Press.

Campbell, J. D. 1990. Self-esteem and clarity of the self-concept. *Journal of Personality and Social Psychology*, 59: 538–549.

Carroll, D. T. 1983. A disappointing search for excellence. *Harvard Business Review*, 61(6): 78–88.

Cartwright, D., & Zander, A. 1968. *Group dynamics: Research and theory*. London: Tavistock.

Clegg, S. 1981. Organizations and control. *Administrative Science Quarterly*, 26: 545–562.

Colvin, G. 1982. The de-Geneening of ITT. *Fortune*, 105(1): 34–39.

Cooper, A. M. 1986. Narcissism. In A. Morrison (Ed.), *Essential papers on narcissism*: 112–143. New York: New York University Press.

Daft, R. L. 1983. Symbols in organizations: A dual-content framework for analysis. In P. J. Frost, L. F. Moore, M. R. Louis, C. C. Lundberg, & J. Martin (Eds.), *Reframing organizational culture*: 199–206. London: Sage.

Dandridge, T. C., Mitroff, I., & Joyce, W. 1980. Organizational symbolism: A topic to expand organizational analysis. *Academy of Management Review*, 5: 77–82.

Dearborn, D. C., & Simon, H. A. 1958. Selective perception: A note on the departmental identification of executives. *Sociometry*, 21: 140–144.

De Board, R. 1978. *The psychodynamics of organizations*. London: Tavistock.

Diamond, M. A. 1992. Hobbesian and Rousseauian identities: The psychodynamics of organizational leadership and change. *Administration & Society*, 24: 267–289.

Dimen, M. 1991. Deconstructing differences: Gender, splitting and transitional space. *Psychoanalytic Dialogues*, 1: 335–352.

Dixon, N. 1994. *The organizational learning cycle*. Maidenhead, UK: McGraw-Hill.

Dodgson, M. 1993. Organizational learning: A review of some literatures. *Organization Studies*, 14: 375–394.

Douglas, M. 1987. *How institutions think*. London: Routledge & Kegan Paul.

Dutton, J. E., & Dukerich, J. M. 1991. Keeping an eye on the mirror: Image and identity in organizational adaptation. *Academy of Management Journal*, 34: 517–554.

Dutton, J. E., Dukerich, J. M., & Harquail, C. V. 1994. Organizational images and member identification. *Administrative Science Quarterly*, 39: 239–263.

Einhorn, E. J., & Hogarth, R. M. 1986. Judging probable cause. *Psychological Bulletin*, 99: 3–19.

Eisold, K. 1985. Recovering Bion's contributions to group analysis. In A. D. Colman & M. H. Geller (Eds.), *Group relations reader*, vol. 2: 37–48. Washington, DC: Rice Institute.

Elsbach, K. D., & Kramer, R. M. 1996. Members' responses to organizational identity threats: Encountering and countering the *Business Week* rankings. *Administrative Science Quarterly*, 41: 442–476.

Epstein, M. 1995. *Thoughts without a thinker*. New York: Basic Books.

Erikson, E. H. 1965. *Childhood and society*. Harmondsworth, UK: Penguin.

Feldman, M. S. 1989. *Order without design*. Stanford, CA: Stanford University Press.

Freud, A. 1966. *The writings of Anna Freud volume II. The ego and the mechanisms of defense* (revised ed.). Madison, CT: International Universities Press.

Freud, S. 1949. *Group psychology and the analysis of the ego*. London: Hogarth Press. (First published in 1922.)

Frosh, S. 1991. *Identity crisis, modernity, psychoanalysis and the self*. Basingstoke, UK: Macmillan.

Gabriel, Y. 1991. Turning facts into stories and stories into facts: A hermeneutic exploration of organizational folklore. *Human Relations*, 44: 857–875.

Gabriel, Y. 1995. The unmanaged organization—stories, fantasies and subjectivity. *Organization Studies*, 16: 477–501.

Gagliardi, P. 1986. The creation and change of organizational cultures: A conceptual framework. *Organization Studies*, 7: 117–134.

Gioia, D. A., & Thomas, J. B. 1996. Identity, image, and issue interpretation: Sensemaking during strategic change in academia. *Administrative Science Quarterly*, 41: 370–403.

Grove, A. 1997. *Only the paranoid survive: How to exploit the crisis points that challenge every company and career*. London: HarperCollins.

Halberstam, D. 1986. *The reckoning*. New York: Avon.

Hambrick, D. C., & Mason, P. 1984. Upper echelons: The organization as a reflection of its top managers. *Academy of Management Review*, 9: 193–206.

Hamel, G., & Prahalad, C. K. 1994. *Competing for the future*. Boston: Harvard Business School Press.

Harris, A. 1991. Gender as contradiction. *Psychoanalytic Dialogues*, 1: 197–224.

Hedberg, B. 1981. How organizations learn and unlearn. *Handbook of organizational design*, vol. 1: 3–27. Oxford: Oxford University Press.

Hirschhorn, L. 1988. *The workplace within*. Cambridge, MA: MIT Press.

Hirschhorn, L. 1997. *Reworking authority*. Cambridge, MA: MIT Press.

Huber, G. P. 1991. Organizational learning: The contributing processes and the literatures. *Organization Science*, 2: 88–115.

Hurst, D. K. 1984. Of boxes, bubbles, and effective management. *Harvard Business Review*, 62(3): 78–88.

Hurst, D. K., Rush, J. C., & White, R. E. 1989. Top management teams and organizational renewal. *Strategic Management Journal*, 10: 87–105.

Jacques, E. 1955. Social systems as a defence against persecutory and depressive anxiety. In M. Klein, P. Heimann, & R. Money-Kyrle (Eds.), *New directions in psychoanalysis*: 478–498. London: Tavistock.

Janis, I. L. 1972. *Victims of groupthink*. Boston: Houghton Mifflin.

Johnson, G. 1990. Managing strategic change: The role of symbolic action. *British Journal of Management*, 1: 183–200.

Kahneman, D., Slovic, P., & Tversky, A. 1982. *Judgment under uncertainty: Heuristics and biases*. Cambridge: Cambridge University Press.

Kets de Vries, M.F.R. 1996. *Family business: Human dilemmas in the family firm*. London: Thompson.

Kets de Vries, M.F.R., & Miller, D. 1984. *The neurotic organization*. San Francisco: Jossey-Bass.

Kitchener, K. S. 1983. Cognition, metacognition, and epistemic cognition: A three-level model of cognitive processing. *Human Development*, 26: 222–232.

Klein, K. J., Dansereau, F., & Hall, R. J. 1994. Level issues in theory development, data collection and analysis. *Academy of Management Review*, 19: 195–229.

Kohlberg, L. 1964. Development of moral character and moral ideology. In M. L. Hoffman & L. W. Hoffman (Eds.), *Review of child development research*, vol. 1: 383–427. New York: Russell Sage Foundation.

Kohut, H. 1971. *The analysis of the self*. New York: International Universities Press.

Kohut, H. 1978. Forms and transformations of narcissism. In P. H. Ornstein (Ed.), *The search for self. Selected writings of Heinz Kohut: 1950–1978*, vol. 1: 427–460. New York: International Universities Press.

Kramer, D. A. 1990. Conceptualizing wisdom: The primacy of affect-cognition relations. In R. J. Sternberg (Ed.), *Wisdom: Its nature, origins and development*: 279–313. Cambridge: Cambridge University Press.

Laughlin, H. P. 1970. *The ego and its defenses*. New York: Appleton-Century-Crofts.

Levinthal, D. A., & March, J. G. 1993. The myopia of learning. *Strategic Management Journal*, 14: 95–112.

Levitt, B., & March, J. G. 1988. Organizational learning. *Annual Review of Sociology*, 14: 319–340.

Lorsch, J. W., & Mathias, P. F. 1987. When professionals have to manage. *Harvard Business Review*, 65(4): 78–83.

Lundberg, C. 1989. On organizational learning: Implications and opportunities for expanding organizational development. In R. W. Woodman & W. A. Pasmore (Eds.),

Research in organizational change and development, vol. 3: 61–82. Greenwich, CT: JAI Press.

Lynch, I. M. 1988. *Containing anxiety in institutions: Selected essays*, vol. 1. London: Free Association Books.

Lyon, J. 1984. *Dome*. New York: Avon.

March, J. G. 1995. The future, disposable organizations and the rigidities of imagination. *Organization*, 2: 427–440.

Marcia, J. E. 1988. Common processes underlying ego identity, cognitive/moral development, and individuation. In D. L. Lapsley & F. Clark Power (Eds.), *Self, ego, and identity: Integrative approaches*: 211–225. New York: Springer-Verlag.

Menzies, I.E.P. 1970. *The functioning of social systems as a defence against anxiety*. London: Tavistock.

Miller, D. 1990. *The Icarus paradox*. New York: Harper Business.

Miller, D. 1993. The architecture of simplicity. *Academy of Management Review*, 18: 116–138.

Miller, E. J., & Gwynne, G. V. 1972. *A life apart*. London: Tavistock.

Mintzberg, H. 1987. Crafting strategy. *Harvard Business Review*, 65(4): 66–75.

Mitchell, S. 1993. *Hope and dread in psychoanalysis*. New York: Basic Books.

Moch, M., & Huff, A. S. 1983. Power enactment through language and symbol. *Journal of Business Research*, 11: 293–316.

Morgan, G. 1980. Paradigms, metaphors, and puzzle solving in organization theory. *Administrative Science Quarterly*, 25: 605–622.

Morgan, G. 1983. More on metaphor: Why we cannot control tropes in administrative science. *Administrative Science Quarterly*, 28: 601–607.

Morgan, G. 1986. *Images of organization*. Beverly Hills, CA: Sage.

Nader, R., & Taylor, W. 1986. *The big boys: Power and position in American business*. New York: Pantheon.

Nystrom, P. C., & Starbuck, W. H. 1984. To avoid organizational crisis, unlearn. *Organizational Dynamics*, 12(1): 53–65.

Orwoll, L., & Perlmutter, M. 1990. The study of wise persons: Integrating a personality perspective. In R. J. Sternberg (Ed.), *Wisdom: Its nature, origins and development*: 160–177. Cambridge: Cambridge University Press.

Pascale, R. 1990. *Managing on the edge*. New York: Viking.

Peters, T. J. 1978. Symbols, patterns, and settings: An optimistic case for getting things done. *Organizational Dynamics*, 7: 2–23.

Peters, T. J., & Waterman, R. H., Jr. 1982. *In search of excellence*. New York: Harper & Row.

Pettigrew, A. 1985. *The awakening giant: Continuity and change in ICI*. Oxford: Blackwell.

Pettigrew, A. 1992. On studying managerial elites. *Strategic Management Journal*, 13(Special Issue): 163–182.

Pfeffer, J. 1981. Management as a symbolic action: The creation and maintenance of organizational paradigms. In L. L. Cummings & B. M. Staw (Eds.), *Research in organizational behavior*, vol. 3: 1–52. Greenwich, CT: JAI Press.

Pfeffer, J., & Salancik, G. R. 1974. Organizational decision making as a political process: The case of a university budget. *Administrative Science Quarterly*, 19: 135–151.

Phillips, A. 1988. *Winnicott*. Cambridge, MA: Harvard University Press.

Priem, R. L. 1990. Top management team group factors, consensus and firm performance. *Strategic Management Journal*, 11: 469–478.

Ray, C. A. 1986. Corporate culture: The last frontier of control. *Journal of Management Studies*, 23: 287–297.

Reger, R. K., Gustafson, L. T., DeMarie, S. M., & Mullane, J. V. 1994. Reframing the organization: Why implementing total quality is easier said than done. *Academy of Management Review*, 19: 565–584.

Rhodewalt, F., Morf, C., Hazlett, S., & Fairfield, M. 1991. Self-handicapping: The role of discounting and augmentation in the preservation of self-esteem. *Journal of Personal and Social Psychology*, 61: 122–131.

Ross, J., & Staw, B. M. 1993. Organizational escalation and exit: Lessons from the Shoreham nuclear power plant. *Academy of Management Journal*, 36: 701–732.

Rousseau, D. 1985. Issues of level in organizational research: Multi-level and cross-level perspectives. In L. L. Cummings & B. M. Staw (Eds.), *Research in organizational behavior*, vol. 7: 1–37. Greenwich, CT: JAI Press.

Rutenberg, D. 1985. *Playful plans*. Working paper #85–26. Queens University, Kingston, Ontario, Canada.

Salaman, G., & Butler, J. 1994. Why managers won't learn. In C. Mabey & P. Iles (Eds.), *Managing learning*: 34–42. London: Routledge.

Schafer, R. 1992. *Retelling a life*. New York: Basic Books.

Schein, E. H. 1985. *Organizational culture and leadership*. San Francisco: Jossey-Bass.

Schlenker, B. R. 1985. Self-identification: Toward an integration of the private and public self. In R. Baumeister (Ed.), *Public self and private self*: 21–62. New York: Springer-Verlag.

Schlenker, B. R., Weigold, M. F., & Hallam, J. R. 1990. Self-serving attributions in social context: Effects of self-esteem and social pressure. *Journal of Personality and Social Psychology*, 58: 855–863.

Schoemaker, P.J.H. 1993. Multiple scenario development: Its conceptual and behavioral foundation. *Strategic Management Journal*, 14: 193–214.

Schonbach, P. 1980. A category system for account phases. *European Journal of Social Psychology*, 10: 195–200.

Schwartz, H. S. 1985. The usefulness of myth and the myth of usefulness: A dilemma for the applied organizational scientist. *Journal of Management*, 11: 31–42.

Schwartz, H. S. 1987. On the psychodynamics of organizational disaster: The case of the Space Shuttle Challenger. *Columbia Journal of World Business*, 22: 59–67.

Schwartz, H. S. 1990. *Narcissistic process and corporate decay: The theory of the organizational ideal*. New York: New York University Press.

Semin, G. R., & Manstead, A.S.R. 1983. *The accountability of conduct: A social psychological analysis*. London: Academic Press.

Senge, P. 1990. *The fifth discipline: The art & practice of the learning organization*. New York: Doubleday.

Shengold, L. 1995. *Delusions of everyday life*. New Haven, CT: Yale University Press.

Slovic, P., Fischhoff, B., & Lichtenstein, S. 1977. Behavioral decision theory. *Annual Review of Psychology*, 28: 1–39.

Smith, D. K., & Alexander, R. C. 1988. *Fumbling the future: How Xerox invented, then ignored, the first personal computer*. New York: William Morrow.

Soeters, J. L. 1986. Excellent companies as social movements. *Journal of Management Studies*, 23: 299–312.

Sofer, C. 1972. *Organizations in theory and practice*. London: Heinemann.

Spence, D. 1982. *Narrative truth, historical truth*. New York: Norton.

Spender, J.-C., & Grinyer, P. 1995. Organizational renewal: Top management's role in a loosely coupled system. *Human Relations*, 48: 909–926.

Sproull, L. S. 1981. Beliefs in organizations. In P. C. Nystrom & W. H. Starbuck (Eds.), *Handbook of organizational design*, vol. 2: 167–202. New York: Oxford University Press.

Starbuck, W. H. 1983. Organizations as action generators. *American Sociological Review*, 48: 91–102.

Starbuck, W. H., Greve, A., & Hedberg, B.L.T. 1978. Responding to crisis. *Journal of Business Administration*, 9: 111–137.

Starbuck, W. H., & Hedberg, B.L.T. 1977. Saving an organization from a stagnating environment. In H. B. Thorelli (Ed.), *Strategy + structure = performance*: 249–258. Bloomington: Indiana University Press.

Starbuck, W. H., & Milliken, F. J. 1988. Executives' perceptual filters: What they notice and how they make sense. In D. Hambrick (Ed.), *Executive effect: Concepts and methods for studying top managers*: 35–65. Greenwich, CT: JAI Press.

Starkey, K. (Ed.). 1996. *How organizations learn*. London: International Thomson Business Press.

Sternberg, R. J. (Ed.). 1990. *Wisdom: Its nature, origins and development*. Cambridge: Cambridge University Press.

Sullivan, H. S. 1938. *The fusion of psychiatry and the social sciences*. New York: Norton.

Swogger, G. 1993. Group self-esteem and group performance. In L. Hirschhorn & C. K. Barnett (Eds.), *The psychodynamics of organizations*: 99–117. Philadelphia: Temple University Press.

Szwajkowski, E. 1992. Accounting for organizational misconduct. *Journal of Business Ethics*, 11: 401–411.

Tsoukas, H. 1991. The missing link: A transformational view of metaphors in organizational science. *Academy of Management Review*, 16: 566–585.

Tsoukas, H. 1993. Analogical reasoning and knowledge generation in organization theory. *Organization Studies*, 14: 323–346.

Turner, J. C. 1987. *Rediscovering the social group: A self-categorization theory*. Oxford: Blackwell.

van der Heijden, K. 1996. *Scenarios: The art of strategic conversation*. Chichester, UK: Wiley.

Walsh, J. P., & Fahey, L. 1986. The role of negotiated belief structures in strategy making. *Journal of Management*, 12: 325–338.

Walsh, J. P., & Ungson, G. R. 1991. Organizational memory. *Academy of Management Review*, 16: 57–91.

Wastell, D. G. 1996. The fetish of technique—methodology as a social defense. *Information Systems Journal*, 6: 25–40.

Waters, J. 1980. Managerial skill development. *Academy of Management Review*, 5: 449–453.

Weick, K. E. 1987. Organizational culture as a source of high reliability. *California Management Review*, 29(2): 112–127.

Weick, K. 1993. The collapse of sense-making in organizations: The Mann-Gulch disaster. *Administrative Science Quarterly*, 38: 628–652.

Weick, K. E. 1995. *Sensemaking in organizations*. Thousand Oaks, CA: Sage.

Weigert, A. J. 1988. To be or not: Self and authenticity, identity and ambivalence. In D. K. Lapsley & F. Clark Power (Eds.), *Self, ego, and identity: Integrative approaches*: 263–281. New York: Springer-Verlag.

Whetten, D. A., Lewis, D., & Mischel, L. 1992. *Towards an integrated model of organizational identity and member commitment*. Paper presented at the annual meeting of Academy of Management, Las Vegas.

Wilensky, H. L. 1967. *Organizational intelligence, knowledge and policy in government and industry*. New York: Basic Books.

Wimsatt, W. K. 1970. Battering the object: The ontological approach. In M. Bradbury & D. Palmer (Eds.), *Contemporary criticism*: 61–82. London: Edward Arnold.

Winnicott, D. W. 1974. *Playing and reality*. Harmondsworth, UK: Penguin.

Wright, J. P. 1979. *On a clear day you can see General Motors*. Grosse Pointe, MI: Wright Enterprise.

CHAPTER THIRTY

The Quest for Resilience

Gary Hamel
Liisa Välikangas (2003)

C all it the resilience gap. The world is becoming turbulent faster than
organizations are becoming resilient. The evidence is all around us. Big
companies are failing more frequently. Of the twenty largest U.S. bankruptcies in the past two decades, ten occurred in the last two years. Corporate
earnings are more erratic. Over the past four decades, year-to-year volatility
in the earnings growth rate of S&P 500 companies has increased by nearly
50 percent—despite vigorous efforts to "manage" earnings. Performance
slumps are proliferating. In each of the years from 1973 to 1977, an average of
thirty-seven *Fortune* 500 companies were entering or in the midst of a 50 percent, five-year decline in net income; from 1993 to 1997, smack in the middle
of the longest economic boom in modern times, the average number of companies suffering through such an earnings contraction more than doubled, to
eighty-four each year.

Even perennially successful companies are finding it more difficult to deliver
consistently superior returns. In their 1994 best-seller *Built to Last*, Jim Collins
and Jerry Porras singled out eighteen "visionary" companies that had consistently outperformed their peers between 1950 and 1990. But over the last ten
years, just six of these companies managed to outperform the Dow Jones Industrial Average. The other twelve—a group that includes such companies as
Disney, Motorola, Ford, Nordstrom, Sony, and Hewlett-Packard—have apparently gone from great to merely OK. Any way you cut it, success has never been
so fragile.

In less turbulent times, established companies could rely on the flywheel of
momentum to sustain their success. Some, like AT&T and American Airlines,

were insulated from competition by regulatory protection and oligopolistic practices. Others, like General Motors and Coca-Cola, enjoyed a relatively stable product paradigm—for more than a century, cars have had four wheels and a combustion engine, and consumers have sipped caffeine-laced soft drinks. Still others, like McDonald's and Intel, built formidable first-mover advantages. And in capital-intensive industries like petroleum and aerospace, high entry barriers protected incumbents.

The fact that success has become less persistent strongly suggests that momentum is not the force it once was. To be sure, there is still enormous value in having a coterie of loyal customers, a well-known brand, deep industry know-how, preferential access to distribution channels, proprietary physical assets, and a robust patent portfolio. But that value has steadily dissipated as the enemies of momentum have multiplied. Technological discontinuities, regulatory upheavals, geopolitical shocks, industry deverticalization and disintermediation, abrupt shifts in consumer tastes, and hordes of nontraditional competitors—these are just a few of the forces undermining the advantages of incumbency.

In the past, executives had the luxury of assuming that business models were more or less immortal. Companies always had to work to get better, of course, but they seldom had to get different—not at their core, not in their essence. Today, getting different is the imperative. It's the challenge facing Coca-Cola as it struggles to raise its "share of throat" in noncarbonated beverages. It's the task that bedevils McDonald's as it tries to rekindle growth in a world of burger-weary customers. It's the hurdle for Sun Microsystems as it searches for ways to protect its high-margin server business from the Linux onslaught. And it's an imperative for the big pharmaceutical companies as they confront declining R&D yields, escalating price pressure, and the growing threat from generic drugs. For all these companies, and for yours, continued success no longer hinges on momentum. Rather, it rides on resilience—on the ability to dynamically reinvent business models and strategies as circumstances change.

Strategic resilience is not about responding to a onetime crisis. It's not about rebounding from a setback. It's about continuously anticipating and adjusting to deep, secular trends that can permanently impair the earning power of a core business. It's about having the capacity to change before the case for change becomes desperately obvious.

ZERO TRAUMA

Successful companies, particularly those that have enjoyed a relatively benign environment, find it extraordinarily difficult to reinvent their business models. When confronted by paradigm-busting turbulence, they often experience a deep and prolonged reversal of fortune. Consider IBM. Between 1990 and 1993, the company went from making $6 billion to losing nearly $8 billion. It wasn't until 1997 that its earnings reached their previous high. Such a protracted earnings slump typically provokes a leadership change, and in many cases the new CEO—be it Gerstner at IBM or Ghosn at Nissan or Bravo at Burberry—produces a successful, if wrenching, turnaround. However celebrated, a turnaround is a testament to a company's lack of resilience. A turnaround is transformation tragically delayed.

Imagine a ratio where the numerator measures the magnitude and frequency of strategic transformation and the denominator reflects the time, expense, and emotional energy required to effect that transformation. Any company that hopes to stay relevant in a topsy-turvy world has no choice but to grow the numerator. The real trick is to steadily reduce the denominator at the same time. To thrive in turbulent times, companies must become as efficient at renewal as they are at producing today's products and services. Renewal must be the natural consequence of an organization's innate resilience.

The quest for resilience can't start with an inventory of best practices. Today's best practices are manifestly inadequate. Instead, it must begin with an aspiration: zero trauma. The goal is a strategy that is forever morphing, forever conforming itself to emerging opportunities and incipient trends. The goal is an organization that is constantly making its future rather than defending its past. The goal is a company where revolutionary change happens in lightning-quick, evolutionary steps—with no calamitous surprises, no convulsive reorganizations, no colossal write-offs, and no indiscriminate, across-the-board layoffs. In a truly resilient organization, there is plenty of excitement, but there is no trauma.

Sound impossible? A few decades ago, many would have laughed at the notion of "zero defects." If you were driving a Ford Pinto or a Chevy Vega, or making those sorry automobiles, the very term would have sounded absurd. But today we live in a world where Six Sigma, 3.4 defects per million, is widely viewed as an achievable goal. So why shouldn't we commit ourselves to zero trauma? Defects cost money, but so do outdated strategies, missed opportunities, and belated restructuring programs. Today, many of society's most important institutions, including its largest *commercial* organizations, are not resilient. But no law says they must remain so. It is precisely because resilience is such a valuable goal that we must commit ourselves to making it an attainable one. (See the sidebar "Why Resilience Matters.")

Any organization that hopes to become resilient must address four challenges:

1. *The cognitive challenge:* The company must become entirely free of denial, nostalgia, and arrogance. It must be deeply conscious of what's changing and perpetually willing to consider how those changes are likely to affect its current success.

2. *The strategic challenge:* Resilience requires alternatives as well as awareness—the ability to create a plethora of new options as compelling alternatives to dying strategies.

3. *The political challenge:* An organization must be able to divert resources from yesterday's products and programs to tomorrow's. This doesn't mean funding flights of fancy; it means building an ability to support a broad portfolio of breakout experiments with the necessary capital and talent.

4. *The ideological challenge:* Few organizations question the doctrine of optimization. But optimizing a business model that is slowly becoming irrelevant can't secure a company's future. If renewal is to become continuous and opportunity-driven, rather than episodic and crisis-driven, companies will need to embrace a creed that extends beyond operational excellence and flawless execution.

Few organizations, if any, can claim to have mastered these four challenges. Although there is no simple recipe for building a resilient organization, a decade of research on innovation and renewal allows us to suggest a few starting points.

CONQUERING DENIAL

Every business is successful until it's not. What's amazing is how often top management is surprised when "not" happens. This astonishment, this belated recognition of dramatically changed circumstances, virtually guarantees that the work of renewal will be significantly, perhaps dangerously, postponed.

Why the surprise? Is it that the world is not only changing but changing in ways that simply cannot be anticipated—that it is *shockingly* turbulent? Perhaps, but even "unexpected" shocks can often be anticipated if one is paying close attention. Consider the recent tech sector meltdown—an event that sent many networking and computer suppliers into a tailspin and led to billions of dollars in write-downs.

Three body blows knocked the stuffing out of IT spending: the telecom sector, traditionally a big buyer of networking gear, imploded under the pressure of a massive debt load; a horde of dot-com customers ran out of cash and stopped buying computer equipment; and large corporate customers slashed IT budgets as the economy went into recession. Is it fair to expect IT vendors to have anticipated this perfect storm? Yes.

They knew, for example, that the vast majority of their dot-com customers were burning through cash at a ferocious rate but had no visible earnings. The same was true for many of the fledgling telecom outfits that were buying equipment by using vendor financing. These companies were building fiber-optic networks far faster than they could be utilized. With bandwidth increasing more rapidly than demand, it was only a matter of time before plummeting prices would drive many of these debt-heavy companies to the wall. There were other warning signs. In 1990, U.S. companies spent 19 percent of their capital budgets on information technology. By 2000, they were devoting 59 percent of their capital spending to IT. In other words, IT had tripled its share of capital budgets—this during the longest capital-spending boom in U.S. history. Anyone looking at the data in 2000 should have been asking, Will capital spending keep growing at a double-digit pace? And is it likely that IT spending will continue to grow so fast? Logically, the answer to both questions had to be no. Things that can't go on forever usually don't. IT vendors should have anticipated a major pullback in their revenue growth and started "war gaming" postboom options well before demand collapsed.

It is unfair, of course, to single out one industry. What happened to a few flat-footed IT companies can happen to any company—and often does. More than likely, Motorola was startled by Nokia's quick sprint to global leadership in the mobile phone business; executives at the Gap probably received a jolt when, in early 2001, their company's growth engine suddenly went into reverse; and CNN's management team was undoubtedly surprised by the Fox News Channel's rapid climb up the ratings ladder.

But they, like those in the IT sector, should have been able to see the future's broad outline—to anticipate the point at which a growth curve suddenly flattens out or a business model runs out of steam. The fact that serious performance shortfalls so often come as a surprise suggests that executives frequently take refuge in denial. Greg Blonder, former chief technical adviser at AT&T, admitted as much in a November 2002 *Barron's* article: "In the early 1990s, AT&T management argued internally that the steady upward curve of Internet usage would somehow collapse. The idea that it might actually overshadow traditional telephone service was simply unthinkable. But the trend could not be stopped—or even slowed—by wishful thinking and clever marketing. One by one, the props that held up the long-distance business collapsed." For AT&T, as for many other companies, the future was less unknowable than it was unthinkable, less inscrutable than unpalatable.

Denial puts the work of renewal on hold, and with each passing month, the cost goes up. To be resilient, an organization must dramatically reduce the time it takes to go from "that can't be true" to "we must face the world as it is." So what does it take to break through the hard carapace of denial? Three things.

First, senior managers must make a habit of visiting the places where change happens first. Ask yourself how often in the last year you have put yourself in a position where you had the chance to see change close-up—where you weren't reading about change in a business magazine, hearing about it from a consultant, or getting a warmed-over report from an employee, but were experiencing it firsthand. Have you visited a nanotechnology lab? Have you spent a few nights hanging out in London's trendiest clubs? Have you spent an afternoon talking to fervent environmentalists or antiglobalization activists? Have you had an honest, what-do-you-care-about conversation with anyone under eighteen? It's easy to discount secondhand data; it's hard to ignore what you've experienced for yourself. And if you have managed to rub up against what's changing, how much time have you spent thinking through the second- and third-order consequences of what you've witnessed? As the rate of change increases, so must the personal energy you devote to understanding change.

Second, you have to filter out the filterers. Most likely, there are people in your organization who are plugged tightly into the future and understand well the not-so-sanguine implications for your company's business model. You have to find these people. You have to make sure their views are not censored by the custodians of convention and their access is not blocked by those who believe they are paid to protect you from unpleasant truths. You should be wary of anyone who has a vested interest in your continued ignorance, who fears that a full understanding of what's changing would expose his or her own failure to anticipate it or the inadequacy of his or her response.

There are many ways to circumvent the courtiers and the self-protecting bureaucrats. Talk to potential customers who aren't buying from you. Go out for drinks and dinner with your most freethinking employees. Establish a shadow executive committee whose members are, on average, twenty years younger than the "real" executive committee. Give this group of thirtysomethings the chance to review capital budgets, ad campaigns, acquisition plans, and divisional strategies—and to present their views directly to the board. Another strategy is to periodically review the proposals that never made it to the top— those that got spiked by divisional VPs and unit managers. Often it's what doesn't get sponsored that turns out to be most in tune with what's changing, even though the proposals may be out of tune with prevailing orthodoxies.

Finally, you have to face up to the inevitability of strategy decay. On occasion, Bill Gates has been heard to remark that Microsoft is always two or three years away from failure. Hyperbole, perhaps, but the message to his organization is clear: change will render irrelevant at least some of what Microsoft is doing today—and it will do so sooner rather than later. It's easy to admit that nothing lasts forever, but it is rather more difficult to admit that a dearly beloved strategy is rapidly going from ripe to rotten.

Strategies decay for four reasons. Over time they get *replicated*; they lose their distinctiveness and, therefore, their power to produce above-average returns. Ford's introduction of the Explorer may have established the SUV category, but today nearly every carmaker—from Cadillac to Nissan to Porsche— has a high-standing, gas-guzzling monster in its product line. No wonder

Ford's profitability has recently taken a hit. With a veritable army of consultants hawking best practices and a bevy of business journalists working to uncover the secrets of high-performing companies, great ideas get replicated faster than ever. And when strategies converge, margins collapse.

Good strategies also get *supplanted* by better strategies. Whether it's made-to-order PCs à la Dell, flat-pack furniture from IKEA, or downloadable music via KaZaA, innovation often undermines the earning power of traditional business models. One company's creativity is another's destruction. And in an increasingly connected economy, where ideas and capital travel at light speed, there's every reason to believe that new strategies will become old strategies ever more quickly.

Strategies get *exhausted* as markets become saturated, customers get bored, or optimization programs reach the point of diminishing returns. One example: in 1995, there were approximately ninety-one million active mobile phones in the world. Today, there are more than one billion. Nokia rode this growth curve more adeptly than any of its rivals. At one point its market value was three-and-a-half times that of its closest competitor. But the number of mobile phones in the world is not going to increase by 1,000 percent again, and Nokia's growth curve has already started to flatten out. Today, new markets can take off like a rocket. But the faster they grow, the sooner they reach the point where growth begins to decelerate. Ultimately, every strategy exhausts its fuel supply.

Finally, strategies get *eviscerated*. The Internet may not have changed everything, but it has dramatically accelerated the migration of power from producers to consumers. Customers are using their newfound power like a knife, carving big chunks out of once-fat margins. Nowhere has this been more evident than in the travel business, where travelers are using the Net to wrangle the lowest possible prices out of airlines and hotel companies. You know all those e-business efficiencies your company has been reaping? It's going to end up giving most of those productivity gains back to customers in the form of lower prices or better products and services at the same price. Increasingly it's your customers, not your competitors, who have you—and your margins—by the throat.

An accurate and honest appraisal of strategy decay is a powerful antidote to denial. (See the sidebar "Anticipating Strategy Decay" for a list of diagnostic questions.) It is also the only way to know whether renewal is proceeding fast enough to fully offset the declining economic effectiveness of today's strategies.

VALUING VARIETY

Life is the most resilient thing on the planet. It has survived meteor showers, seismic upheavals, and radical climate shifts. And yet it does not plan, it does not forecast, and, except when manifested in human beings, it possesses no foresight. So what is the essential thing that life teaches us about resilience? Just this: variety matters. Genetic variety, within and across species, is nature's insurance policy against the unexpected. A high degree of biological diversity ensures that no matter what particular future unfolds, there will be at least some organisms that are well-suited to the new circumstances.

Evolutionary biologists aren't the only ones who understand the value of variety. As any systems theorist will tell you, the larger the variety of actions available to a system, the larger the variety of perturbations it is able to accommodate. Put simply, if the range of strategic alternatives your company is exploring is significantly narrower than the breadth of change in the environment, your business is going to be a victim of turbulence. Resilience depends on variety.

Big companies are used to making big bets—Disney's theme park outside Paris, Motorola's satellite-phone venture Iridium, HP's acquisition of Compaq, and GM's gamble on hydrogen-powered cars are but a few examples. Sometimes these bets pay off; often they don't. When audacious strategies fail, companies often react by imposing draconian cost-cutting measures. But neither profligacy nor privation leads to resilience. Most companies would be better off if they made fewer billion-dollar bets and a whole lot more $10,000 or $20,000 bets—some of which will, in time, justify more substantial commitments. They should steer clear of grand, imperial strategies and devote themselves instead to launching a swarm of low-risk experiments, or, as our colleague Amy Muller calls them, stratlets.

The arithmetic is clear: it takes thousands of ideas to produce dozens of promising stratlets to yield a few outsize successes. Yet only a handful of companies have committed themselves to broad-based, small-scale strategic experimentation. Whirlpool is one. The world's leading manufacturer of domestic appliances, Whirlpool competes in an industry that is both cyclical and mature. Growth is a function of housing starts and product replacement cycles. Customers tend to repair rather than replace their old appliances, particularly in tough times. Megaretailers like Best Buy squeeze margins mercilessly. Customers exhibit little brand loyalty. The result is zero-sum competition, steadily declining real prices, and low growth. Not content with this sorry state of affairs, Dave Whitwam, Whirlpool's chairman, set out in 1999 to make innovation a core competence at the company. He knew the only way to counter the forces that threatened Whirlpool's growth and profitability was to generate a wide assortment of genuinely novel strategic options.

Over the subsequent three years, the company involved roughly ten thousand of its sixty-five thousand employees in the search for breakthroughs. In training sessions and workshops, these employees generated some seven thousand ideas, which spawned three hundred small-scale experiments. From this cornucopia came a stream of new products and businesses—from Gladiator

Garage Works, a line of modular storage units designed to reduce garage clutter; to Briva, a sink that features a small, high-speed dishwasher; to Gator Pak, an all-in-one food and entertainment center designed for tailgate parties. (For more on Whirlpool's strategy for commercializing the Gladiator line, see "Innovating for Cash" in the September 2003 issue of the *Harvard Business Review*.)

Having institutionalized its experimentation process, Whirlpool now actively manages a broad pipeline of ideas, experiments, and major projects from across the company. Senior executives pay close attention to a set of measures—an innovation dashboard—that tracks the number of ideas moving through the pipeline, the percentage of those ideas that are truly new, and the potential financial impact of each one. Whirlpool's leadership team is learning just how much variety it must engender at the front end of the pipeline, in terms of nascent ideas and first-stage experiments, to produce the earnings impact it's looking for at the back end.

Experiments should go beyond just products. Even though virtually every company has some type of new-product pipeline, few have a process for continually generating, launching, and tracking novel strategy experiments in the areas of pricing, distribution, advertising, and customer service. Instead, many companies have created innovation ghettos—incubators, venture, funds, business development functions, and skunk works—to pursue ideas outside the core. Cut off from the resources, competencies, and customers of the main business, most of these units produce little in the way of shareholder wealth, and many simply wither away.

The isolation—and distrust—of strategic experimentation is a leftover from the industrial age, when variety was often seen as the enemy. A variance, whether from a quality standard, a production schedule, or a budget, was viewed as a bad thing—which it often was. But in many companies, the aversion to unplanned variability has metastasized into a general antipathy toward the nonconforming and the deviant. This infatuation with conformance severely hinders the quest for resilience.

Our experience suggests that a reasonably large company or business unit—having $5 billion to $10 billion in revenues, say—should generate at least one hundred groundbreaking experiments every year, with each one absorbing between $10,000 and $20,000 in first-stage investment funds. Such variety need not come at the expense of focus. Starting in the mid-1990s, Nokia pursued a strategy defined by three clear goals: to "humanize" technology (via the user interface, product design, and aesthetics); to enable "virtual presence" (where the phone becomes an all-purpose messaging and data access device); and to deliver "seamless solutions" (by bundling infrastructure, software, and handsets in a total package for telecom operators). Each of these "strategy themes" spawned dozens of breakthrough projects. It is a broadly shared sense of direction, rather than a tightly circumscribed definition of served market or an allegiance to one particular business model, that reins in superfluous variety.

Of course, most billion-dollar opportunities don't start out as sure things—they start out as highly debatable propositions. For example, who would have predicted, in December 1995, when eBay was only three months old, that the online auctioneer would have a market value of $27 billion in the spring of 2003—two years *after* the dot-com crash? Sure, eBay is an exception. Success is always an exception. To find those exceptions, you must gather and sort through hundreds of new strategic options and then test the promising ones through low-cost, well-designed experiments—building prototypes, running computer simulations, interviewing progressive customers, and the like. There is simply no other way to reconnoiter the future. Most experiments *will* fail. The issue is not how many times you fail, but the value of your successes when compared with your failures. What counts is how the portfolio performs, rather than whether any particular experiment pans out.

LIBERATING RESOURCES

Facing up to denial and fostering new ideas are great first steps. But they'll get you nowhere if you can't free up the resources to support a broad array of strategy experiments within the core business. As every manager knows, reallocating resources is an intensely political process. Resilience requires, however, that it become less so.

Institutions falter when they invest too much in "what is" and too little in "what could be." There are many ways companies overinvest in the status quo: they devote too much marketing energy to existing customer segments while ignoring new ones; they pour too many development dollars into incremental product enhancements while underfunding breakthrough projects; they lavish resources on existing distribution channels while starving new go-to-market strategies. But whatever the manifestation, the root cause is always the same: legacy strategies have powerful constituencies; embryonic strategies do not.

In most organizations, a manager's power correlates directly with the resources he or she controls—to lose resources is to lose stature and influence. Moreover, personal success often turns solely on the performance of one's own unit or program. It is hardly surprising, then, that unit executives and program managers typically resist any attempt to reallocate "their" capital and talent to new initiatives, no matter how attractive those new initiatives may be. Of course, it's unseemly to appear too parochial, so managers often hide their motives behind the facade of an ostensibly prudent business argument. New projects are deemed "untested," "risky," or a "diversion." If such ruses are successful, and they often are, those seeking resources for new strategic options are forced to meet a higher burden of proof than are those who want to allocate additional investment dollars to existing programs. Ironically, unit managers seldom have to defend the risk they are taking when they pour good money into a slowly decaying strategy or overfund an activity that is already producing diminishing returns.

The fact is novelty implies nothing about risk. Risk is a function of uncertainty, multiplied by the size of one's financial exposure. Newness is a function of the extent to which an idea defies precedent and convention. The Starbucks debit card, which allows regular customers to purchase their daily fix of caffeine without fumbling through their pockets for cash, was undoubtedly an innovation for the quick-serve restaurant industry. Yet it's not at all clear that it was risky. The card offers customers a solid benefit, and it relies on proven technology. Indeed, it was an immediate hit. Within sixty days of its launch, convenience-minded customers had snapped up 2.3 million cards and provided Starbucks with a $32 million cash float.

A persistent failure to distinguish between new ideas and risky ideas reinforces companies' tendency to overinvest in the past. So too does the general reluctance of corporate executives to shift resources from one business unit to another. A detailed study of diversified companies by business professors Hyun-Han Shin and René Stulz found that the allocation of investment funds across business units was mostly uncorrelated with the relative attractiveness of investment opportunities within those units. Instead, a business unit's investment budget was largely a function of its own cash flow and, secondarily, the cash flow of the firm as a whole. It seems that top-level executives, removed as they are from day-to-day operations, find it difficult to form a well-grounded view of unit-level, or subunit-level, opportunities and are therefore wary of reallocating resources from one unit to another.

Now, we're not suggesting that a highly profitable and growing business should be looted to fund some dim-witted diversification scheme. Yet if a company systematically favors existing programs over new initiatives, if the forces of preservation regularly trounce the forces of experimentation, it will soon find itself overinvesting in moribund strategies and outdated programs. Allocational rigidities are the enemy of resilience.

Just as biology can teach us something about variety, markets can teach us something about what it takes to liberate resources from the prison of precedent. The evidence of the past century leaves little room for doubt: Market-based economies outperform those that are centrally planned. It's not that markets are infallible. Like human beings, they are vulnerable to mania and despair. But, on average, markets are better than hierarchies at getting the right resources behind the right opportunities at the right time. Unlike hierarchies, markets are apolitical and unsentimental; they don't care whose ox gets gored. The average company, though, operates more like a socialist state than an unfettered market. A hierarchy may be an effective mechanism for applying resources, but it is an imperfect device for allocating resources. Specifically, the market for capital and talent that exists within companies is a whole lot less efficient than the market for talent and capital that exists between companies.

In fact, a company can be operationally efficient and strategically inefficient. It can maximize the efficiency of its existing programs and processes and yet fail to find and fund the unconventional ideas and initiatives that might yield an even higher return. Although companies have many ways of assessing operational efficiency, most firms are clueless when it comes to strategic efficiency. How can corporate leaders be sure that the current set of initiatives represents the highest value use of talent and capital if the company hasn't generated and examined a large population of alternatives? And how can executives be certain that the right resources are lined up behind the right opportunities if capital and talent aren't free to move to high-return projects or businesses? The simple answer is, they can't.

When there is a dearth of novel strategic options, or when allocational rigidities lock up talent and cash in existing programs and businesses, managers are allowed to "buy" resources at a discount, meaning that they don't have to compete for resources against a wide array of alternatives. Requiring that every project and business earn its cost of capital doesn't correct this anomaly. It is perfectly possible for a company to earn its cost of capital and still fail to put its capital and talent to the most valuable uses.

To be resilient, businesses must minimize their propensity to overfund legacy strategies. At one large company, top management took an important step in this direction by earmarking 10 percent of its $1 billion-a-year capital budget for projects that were truly innovative. To qualify, a project had to have the potential to substantially change customer expectations or industry economics. Moreover, the CEO announced his intention to increase this percentage over time. He reasoned that if divisional executives were not funding breakout projects, the company was never going to achieve breakout results. The risk of this approach was mitigated by a requirement that each division develop a broad portfolio of experiments, rather than bet on one big idea.

Freeing up cash is one thing. Getting it into the right hands is another. Consider, for a moment, the options facing a politically disenfranchised employee who hopes to win funding for a small-scale strategy experiment. One option is to push the idea up the chain of command to the point where it can be considered as part of the formal planning process. This requires four things: a boss who doesn't peremptorily reject the idea as eccentric or out of scope; an idea that is, at first blush, "big" enough to warrant senior management's attention; executives who are willing to divert funds from existing programs in favor of the unconventional idea; and an innovator who has the business acumen, charisma, and political cunning to make all this happen. That makes for long odds.

What the prospective innovator needs is a second option: access to many, many potential investors—analogous to the multitude of investors to which a company can appeal when it is seeking to raise funds. How might this be accomplished? In large organizations there are hundreds, perhaps thousands, of individuals who control a budget of some sort—from facilities managers to sales managers to customer service managers to office managers and beyond. Imagine if each of these individuals were a potential source of funding for internal innovators. Imagine that each could occasionally play the role of angel investor by providing seed funding for ideas aimed at transforming the core business in ways large and small. What if everyone who managed a budget were allowed to invest 1 percent or 3 percent or 5 percent of that budget in strategy experiments? Investors within a particular department or region could form syndicates to take on slightly bigger risks or diversify their investment portfolios. To the extent that a portfolio produced a positive return, in terms of new revenues or big cost savings, a small bonus would go back to those who had provided the funds and served as sponsors and mentors. Perhaps investors with the best track records would be given the chance to invest more of their budgets in breakout projects. Thus liberated, capital would flow to the most intriguing possibilities, unfettered by executives' protectionist tendencies.

When it comes to renewal, human skills are even more critical than cash. So if a market for capital is important, a market for talent is essential. Whatever their location, individuals throughout a company need to be aware of all the new projects that are looking for talent. Distance, across business unit boundaries or national borders, should not diminish this visibility. Employees need a simple way to nominate themselves for project teams. And if a project team is eager to hire a particular person, no barriers should stand in the way of a transfer. Indeed, the project team should have a substantial amount of freedom in negotiating the terms of any transfer. As long as the overall project risk is kept within bounds, it should be up to the team to decide how much to pay for talent.

Executives shouldn't be too worried about protecting employees from the downside of a failed project. Over time, the most highly sought-after employees will have the chance to work on multiple projects, spreading their personal risk. However, it is important to ensure that successful projects generate meaningful returns, both financial and professional, for those involved, and that dedication to the cause of experimentation is always positively recognized. But irrespective of the financial rewards, ambitious employees will soon discover that transformational projects typically offer transformational opportunities for personal growth.

EMBRACING PARADOX

The final barrier to resilience is ideological. The modern corporation is a shrine to a single, one hundred-year-old ideal: optimization. From "scientific management" to "operations research" to "reengineering" to "enterprise resource planning" to "Six Sigma," the goal has never changed: do more, better, faster, and cheaper. Make no mistake, the ideology of optimization, and its elaboration into values, metrics, and processes, has created enormous material wealth. The ability to produce millions of gadgets, handle millions of transactions, or deliver a service to millions of customers is one of the most impressive achievements of humankind. But it is no longer enough.

The creed of optimization is perfectly summed up by McDonald's in its famous slogan, "Billions Served." The problem comes when some of those billions want to be served something else, something different, something new. As an ideal, optimization is sufficient only as long as there's no fundamental change in what has to be optimized. But if you work for a record company that needs to find a profitable online business model, or for an airline struggling to outmaneuver Southwest, or for a hospital trying to deliver quality care despite drastic budget cuts, or for a department store chain getting pummeled by discount retailers, or for an impoverished school district intent on curbing its dropout rate, or for any other organization where more of the same is no longer enough, then optimization is a wholly inadequate ideal.

An accelerating pace of change demands an accelerating pace of strategic evolution, which can be achieved only if a company cares as much about resilience as it does about optimization. This is currently not the case. Oh sure, companies have been working to improve their operational resilience—their ability to respond to the ups and downs of the business cycle or to quickly rebalance their product mix—but few have committed themselves to systematically tackling the challenge of strategic resilience. Quite the opposite, in fact. In recent years, most companies have been in retrenchment mode, working to resize their cost bases to accommodate a deflationary economy and unprecedented competitive pressure. But retrenchment can't revitalize a moribund business model, and great execution can't reverse the process of strategy decay.

It's not that optimization is wrong; it's that it so seldom has to defend itself against an equally muscular rival. Diligence, focus, and exactitude are reinforced every day, in a hundred ways—through training programs, benchmarking, improvement routines, and measurement systems. But where is the reinforcement for strategic variety, wide-scale experimentation, and rapid resource redeployment? How have these ideals been instantiated in employee training, performance metrics, and management processes? Mostly, they haven't been. That's why the forces of optimization are so seldom interrupted in their slow march to irrelevance.

When you run to catch a cab, your heart rate accelerates—*automatically*. When you stand up in front of an audience to speak, your adrenal glands start pumping—*spontaneously*. When you catch sight of someone alluring, your pupils dilate—*reflexively*. Automatic, spontaneous, reflexive. These words describe the way your body's autonomic systems respond to changes in your circumstances. They do not describe the way large organizations respond to changes in their circumstances. Resilience will become something like an autonomic process only when companies dedicate as much energy to laying the groundwork for perpetual renewal as they have to building the foundations for operational efficiency.

In struggling to embrace the inherent paradox between the relentless pursuit of efficiency and the restless exploration of new strategic options, managers can learn something from constitutional democracies, particularly the United States. Over more than two centuries, America has proven itself to be far more resilient than the companies it has spawned. At the heart of the American experiment is a paradox: unity and diversity—a single nation peopled by all nations. To be sure, it's not easy to steer a course between divisive sectarianism and totalitarian conformity. But the fact that America has managed to do this, despite some sad lapses, should give courage to managers trying to square the demands of penny-pinching efficiency and break-the-rules innovation. Maybe, just maybe, all those accountants and engineers, never great fans of paradox, can learn to love the heretics and the dreamers.

THE ULTIMATE ADVANTAGE

Perhaps there are still some who believe that large organizations can never be truly resilient, that the goal of "zero trauma" is nothing more than a chimera. We believe they are wrong. Yes, size often shelters a company from the need to confront harsh truths. But why can't size also provide a shelter for new ideas? Size often confers an inappropriate sense of invincibility that leads to foolhardy risk-taking. But why can't size also confer a sense of possibility that encourages widespread experimentation? Size often implies inertia, but why can't it also imply persistence? The problem isn't size, but success. Companies get big because they do well. Size is a barrier to resilience only if those who inhabit large organizations fall prey to the delusion that success is self-perpetuating.

Battlefield commanders talk about "getting inside the enemy's decision cycle." If you can retrieve, interpret, and act upon battlefield intelligence faster than your adversary, they contend, you will be perpetually on the offensive, acting rather than reacting. In an analogous way, one can think about getting inside a competitor's "renewal cycle." Any company that can make sense of its environment, generate strategic options, and realign its resources faster than its rivals will enjoy a decisive advantage. This is the essence of resilience. And it will prove to be the ultimate competitive advantage in the age of turbulence— when companies are being challenged to change more profoundly, and more rapidly, than ever before.

Revolution, Renewal, and Resilience
A GLOSSARY FOR TURBULENT TIMES

What's the probability that your company will significantly outperform the world economy over the next few years? What's the chance that your company will deliver substantially better returns than the industry average? What are the odds that change, in all its guises, will bring your company considerably more upside than downside? Confidence in the future of your business—or of any business—depends on the extent to which it has mastered three essential forms of innovation.

Revolution

In most industries it's the revolutionaries—like JetBlue, Amgen, Costco, University of Phoenix, eBay, and Dell—that have created most of the new wealth over the last decade. Whether newcomer or old timer, a company needs an unconventional strategy to produce unconventional financial returns. Industry revolution is creative destruction. It is innovation with respect to industry rules.

Renewal

Newcomers have one important advantage over incumbents: a clean slate. To reinvent its industry, an incumbent must first reinvent itself. Strategic renewal is creative reconstruction. It requires innovation with respect to one's traditional business model.

Resilience

It usually takes a performance crisis to prompt the work of renewal. Rather than go from success to success, most companies go from success to failure and then, after a long, hard climb, back to success. Resilience refers to a capacity for continuous reconstruction. It requires innovation with respect to those organizational values, processes, and behaviors that systematically favor perpetuation over innovation.

Why Resilience Matters

Some might argue that there is no reason to be concerned with the resilience of any particular company as long as there is unfettered competition, a well-functioning market for corporate ownership, a public policy regime that doesn't protect failing companies from their own stupidity, and a population of start-ups eager to exploit the sloth of incumbents. In this view, competition acts as a spur to perpetual revitalization. A company that fails to adjust to its changing environment soon loses its relevance, its customers, and, ultimately, the support of its stakeholders. Whether it slowly goes out of business or gets acquired, the company's human and financial capital gets reallocated in a way that raises the marginal return on those assets.

This view of the resilience problem has the virtue of being conceptually simple. It is also simpleminded. Although competition, new entrants, takeovers, and bankruptcies are effective as purgatives for managerial incompetence, these forces cannot be relied on to address the resilience problem efficiently and completely. There are several reasons why.

First, and most obvious, thousands of important institutions lie outside the market for corporate control, from privately owned companies like Cargill to public-sector agencies like Britain's National Health Service to nonprofits like the Red Cross. Some of these institutions have competitors; many don't. None of them can be easily "taken over." A lack of resilience may go uncorrected for a considerable period of time, while constituents remain underserved and society's resources are squandered.

Second, competition, acquisitions, and bankruptcies are relatively crude mechanisms for reallocating resources from poorly managed companies to well-managed ones. Let's start with the most draconian of these alternatives, bankruptcy. When a firm fails, much of its accumulated intellectual capital disintegrates as teams disperse. It often takes months or years for labor markets to redeploy displaced human assets. Takeovers are a more efficient reallocation mechanism, yet they, too, are a poor substitute for organizational resilience. Executives in underperforming companies, eager to protect their privileges and prerogatives, will typically resist the idea of a takeover until all other survival options have been exhausted. Even then, they are likely to significantly underestimate the extent of institutional decay—a misjudgment that is often shared by the acquiring company. Whether it is Compaq's acquisition of a stumbling Digital Equipment Corporation or Ford's takeover of the deeply troubled Jaguar, acquisitions often prove to be belated, and therefore expensive, responses to institutional decline.

And what about competition, the endless warfare between large and small, old and young? Some believe that as long as a society is capable of creating new organizations, it can afford to be unconcerned about the resilience of old institutions. In this ecological view of resilience, the population of start-ups constitutes a portfolio of experiments, most of which will fail but a few of which will turn into successful businesses.

In this view, institutions are essentially disposable. The young eat the old. Leaving aside for the moment the question of whether institutional longevity has a value in and of itself, there is a reason to question this "who needs dumb, old incumbents when you have all these cool start-ups" line of reasoning. Young companies are generally less efficient than older companies; they are at an earlier point on the road from disorderly innovation to disciplined optimization. An economy composed entirely of start-ups would be grossly inefficient. Moreover, start-ups typically depend on established companies for funding, managerial talent, and market access. Classically, Microsoft's early success was critically dependent on its ability to harness IBM's brand and distribution power. Start-ups are thus not so much an alternative to established incumbents, as an insurance policy against the costs imposed on society by those incumbents that prove themselves to be unimaginative and slow to change. As is true in so many other situations, avoiding disaster is better than making a claim against an insurance policy once disaster has struck. Silicon Valley and other entrepreneurial hot spots are a boon, but they are no more than a partial solution to the problem of nonadaptive incumbents.

To the question, Can a company die an untimely death? an economist would answer no. Barring government intervention or some act of God, an organization fails when it deserves to fail, that is, when it has proven itself to be consistently unsuccessful in meeting the expectations of its stakeholders. There are, of course, cases in which one can reasonably say that an organization "deserves" to die. Two come immediately to mind: when an organization has fulfilled its original purpose or when changing circumstances have rendered the organization's core purpose invalid or no longer useful. (For example, with the collapse of Soviet-sponsored communism in Eastern Europe, some have questioned the continued usefulness of NATO.)

But there are cases in which organizational death should be regarded as premature in that it robs society of a future benefit. Longevity is important because time enables complexity. It took millions of years for biological evolution to produce the complex structures of the mammalian eye and millions more for it to develop the human brain and higher consciousness. Likewise, it takes years, sometimes decades, for an organization to elaborate a simple idea into a robust operational model. Imagine for a moment that Dell, currently the world's most successful computer maker, had died in infancy. It is at least possible that the world would not now possess the exemplary "build-to-order" business model Dell so successfully constructed over the past decade, a model that has spurred supply chain innovation in a host of other industries. This is not an argument for insulating a company from its environment; it is, however, a reason to imbue organizations with the capacity to dynamically adjust their strategies as they work to fulfill their long-term missions.

There is a final, noneconomic, reason to care about institutional longevity, and therefore resilience. Institutions are vessels into which we as human beings pour our energies, our passions, and our wisdom. Given this, it is not surprising that we often hope to be survived by the organizations we serve. For if our genes constitute the legacy of our individual, biological selves, our institutions constitute the legacy of our collective, purposeful selves. Like our children, they are our progeny. It is no wonder that we hope they will do well and be well treated by our successors. This hope for the future implies a reciprocal responsibility—that we be good stewards of the institutions we have inherited from our forebears. The best way of honoring an institutional legacy is to extend it, and the best way to extend it is to improve the organization's capacity for continual renewal.

Once more, though, we must be careful. A noble past doesn't entitle an institution to an illustrious future. Institutions deserve to endure only if they are capable of withstanding the onslaught of new institutions. A society's freedom to create new institutions is thus a critical insurance policy against its inability to recreate old ones. Where this freedom has been abridged as in, say, Japan, managers in incumbent institutions are able to dodge their responsibility for organizational renewal.

Anticipating Strategy Decay

Business strategies decay in four ways: by being replicated, supplanted, exhausted, or eviscerated. And across the board, the pace of strategy decay is accelerating. The following questions, and the metrics they imply, make up a panel of warning lights that can alert executives to incipient decline.

The fact that renewal so often lags, decay suggests that corporate leaders regularly miss, or deny, the signs of strategy decay. A diligent, honest, and frequent review of these questions can help to remedy this situation.

Replication

Is our strategy losing its distinctiveness?

Does our strategy defy industry norms in any important ways?

Do we possess any competitive advantages that are truly unique?

Is our financial performance becoming less exceptional and more average?

Supplantation

Is our strategy in danger of being superseded?

Are there discontinuities (social, technical, or political) that could significantly reduce the economic power of our current business model?

Are there nascent business models that might render ours irrelevant?

Do we have strategies in place to co-opt or neutralize these forces of change?

Exhaustion

Is our strategy reaching the point of exhaustion?

Is the pace of improvement in key performance metrics (cost per unit or marketing expense per new customer, for example) slowing down?

Are our markets getting saturated? Are our customers becoming more fickle?

Is our company's growth rate decelerating, or about to start doing so?

Evisceration

Is increasing customer power eviscerating our margins?

To what extent do our margins depend on customer ignorance or inertia?

How quickly, and in what ways, are customers gaining additional bargaining power?

Do our productivity improvements fall to the bottom line, or are we forced to give them back to customers in the form of lower prices or better products and services at the same price?

ORGANIZATION CHANGE INTERVENTIONS

Editors' Interlude

The initial chapter in this Part Five on change interventions is by Blake and Mouton (1972). Their chapter is the first one because of how it is organized and written. The organizing principle of the chapter is to consider change interventions in useful categories, twenty-five as a matter of fact. Interventions can be understood according to level, in this case, and not unexpectedly the levels are individual, group, or team to include interpersonal, intergroup, organization as a whole, and society or the larger communal context. These five levels are then "crossed," forming a matrix with five types of interventions: acceptant (concerned largely with feelings), catalytic (concerned with changing a situation), confrontation (concerned with challenging the status quo), prescriptive (concerned with providing expertise), and principles, theories, and models (concerned with ideas and education). The resulting matrix of twenty-five cells is the basis for at least that many distinct interventions. As Blake and Mouton appropriately point out, however, most interventions involve two or more of these twenty-five. The authors offer examples for each of the twenty-five interventions.

INDIVIDUAL LEVEL

Having established the broad and comprehensive model of change interventions by Blake and Mouton, we follow with a subsection of four chapters that emphasize the individual level of analysis and understanding about change. Subsequent sections address the group level and the organization level.

The individual-level subsection begins with Chapter Thirty-Two, by Armenakis, Harris, and Mossholder (1993), on creating readiness for organization change. These authors describe readiness in terms of beliefs, attitudes, and intentions that organizational members express toward a specific change effort. To prepare organizational members for upcoming changes, Armenakis and his colleagues emphasize the importance of change agents' messages for change that can effect these beliefs, attitudes, and intentions of change. The authors explain that the message should include two key components: *discrepancy,* highlighting the difference between the current situation and the desired future state; and *efficacy,* making the case that the organization is capable of successfully implementing the change. The authors also cover influence strategies (management of external information, and active participation) and suggest that an organizational survey to assess readiness can be useful. They describe a typology of readiness programs in a 2x2 arrangement combining continua of (1) low to high readiness and (2) low to high sense of urgency. The result is four programs: low readiness and low urgency, low readiness and high urgency, high readiness and low urgency, and high readiness and high urgency. The chapter concludes with a case that illustrates these ideas in practice.

The next chapter, by King (1972),* illustrates the power of effective assessment for placement of individuals in an organization. In other words, selection and placement can be an intervention for change. In the case that King describes, we learn how to build a culture by selection. The case concerns a new plant within a large food company where the decision was to create its culture according to Likert's System 4, that is, a highly participative, team approach to management. People, especially first-line supervisors and team leaders, were therefore selected on the basis of their capability with and ability to work effectively within such a culture. King describes in detail a two-day process for selecting the team leaders. The process includes a plant visit, a detailed description of the new organization, role-play exercises, group decision-making tasks, simulation exercises of plant work, and a battery of psychological tests. His report at the time was written approximately nine months after the start-up of the plant. During that time only two people had left the organization, absenteeism was less than 1 percent, and productivity had exceeded original expectations. This early success was sustained, as later reported by Richard Walton in 1975, but interestingly and perhaps unfortunately the managerial and change process associated with it did not spread into the overall parent company.

---

*Chapter is included in the collection of readings on the *Organization Change: A Comprehensive Reader* website. www.josseybass.com/go/burke.

The following chapter (Thirty-Four) by Burke is an excerpt on training and development from his 1982 book on organization development (OD). The purpose of this book excerpt was to explain individual-level OD interventions that emphasize change in individuals. Burke gives some history about the emergence of individual change interventions, including sensitivity training, Gestalt therapy and training, the Managerial Grid seminar, and the Tavistock approach. The chapter concludes with an overview of more recent approaches in the form of tailor-made programs that provide individual training and development.

The last chapter of this subsection on individual-level interventions, by Witherspoon and Cannon (2004), is about executive coaching. The art of coaching has been around for a very long time. Machiavelli, after all, was a coach. Labeling this art "executive coaching" is recent, however, and many practitioners in the organization change and management development worlds call themselves coaches. Also, there has been considerable growth in writing about coaching, describing and defining the process. To include a chapter in this volume, therefore, is prudent but also means that there is much to sort through. The choice made by Witherspoon and Cannon is quite relevant for our purpose (organization change), because their chapter concerns coaching leaders in transition. They address coaching leaders' grappling with new situations, not necessarily coaching people who are new to the role of leadership itself. Their clients, then, are quite experienced but not with the situations they are facing. Witherspoon and Cannon define the objective of transition coaching as one of action learning, helping clients discern what is vital to learn (their designation is "critical issues") and what can wait, which is key to taking charge of a new position quickly and effectively. Witherspoon and Cannon also cover leadership failure. Though grounded in the relevant literature, this chapter is largely about practice, especially coaching executives in the midst of organization change.

GROUP LEVEL

There are four chapters in the subsection on group-level change interventions. The first is an overview of team building by Burke (1982). Team building has been the cornerstone of organization development since the origins of the field. This chapter explains the four primary purposes of team building (goals, roles, procedures, and relationships) with examples and outlines criteria for an effective team, such as understanding mutual agreement and identification with respect to the primary task.

Fundamental to team building in particular, and group work in general, is process consultation. Ed Schein (1999), considered the definer of and expert on process consultation, covers this helping process. As he points out, the emphasis is on "process" because *how* things occur between and among people is just as important as *what* occurs or is done, if not more so. In this introductory chapter to his book *Process Consultation Revisited: Building the Helping Relationship*, Schein initially explains two central principles of process consultation: attempting to be helpful and staying in touch with reality. He then compares process consultation with other approaches or models of helping, including three additional principles: access your ignorance, everything the consultant does is an intervention, and the client owns the problem as the solution. Schein also presents useful examples.

Following the guidelines for effective team building and using the skills of a competent process consultant, one can help to hone a high-performing team in an organization. But there may be consequences—or dilemmas, as Kanter (1983)* refers to them—of managing this kind of participative activity. In her Chapter Thirty-Eight, Kanter underscores that high-performing teams may be "well-oiled machines" but at the same time they may have closed boundaries and end up not being very cooperative with other groups and individuals who are "not members." Kanter addresses participation in general and does not focus exclusively on teams; therefore her dilemmas concern initiating a participative process, structuring and managing such a process, and decision choices. She concludes with the need for balance, that is, how participation can work best and under what conditions. Kanter then ends the chapter with ten highly useful lessons for organizations that may want more participation. For instance, she instructs such organizations to start small and expect participative teams to wax and wane; they supplement, rather than replace, the hierarchy.

For the last chapter in this subsection on group-level interventions, we move from small to large group interventions. The chapter is by Bunker and Alban (2002), two experts on the subject. It is a comprehensive overview of large group methods and includes a brief description of twelve models of large group interventions. In short, large group means getting everyone in the system or some significant proportion in the same room at the same time. These methods, though, include both internal and external parties—employees, management, suppliers, and customers. A large group intervention, as Bunker and Alban explain, is an attempt to begin a significant organization change effort with a critical mass of people to:

- Understand the need for change
- Analyze the current reality and decide what needs to change
- Generate ideas about how to change existing processes
- Implement and support change and make it work

*Chapter is included in the collection of readings on the *Organization Change: A Comprehensive Reader* website. www.josseybass.com/go/burke.

These methods have been used with a variety of organizations and for a variety of change issues, among them changes in strategy, redesign projects, changes in relationships with customers or suppliers, and so on.

Why use large group interventions? After all, the planning, logistics, and follow-up can be demanding. A primary reason is that these methods serve as an antidote for the problems of hierarchy resistance and the time required. Moreover, with their high degree of involvement, people can become committed to the change effort more deeply and quickly. Two additional reasons concern information and diversity. With these methods, people have opportunities to furnish fast and rich information to one another. Lastly, the diversity in the room can create energy and synergy that may lead to more innovative solutions to the change problem.

ORGANIZATION LEVEL

For the organization-level subsection, we include five chapters beginning with an excerpt from the Beckhard and Harris book on organizational transitions (1987). We begin with this chapter because of its clarity and popularity regarding organization change. Practically every organization change practitioner is familiar with the Beckhard and Harris three-phase model of present state, transition, and future state. Their short book, 117 pages, is an explanation of this simple, straightforward model. It may be easy to understand but difficult nevertheless to accomplish. Their book explains the model and presents several examples. They begin with challenges and a discussion of the external environment, followed by coverage of organizational dynamics, such as the organization as a social and political system. The authors then give an overview of their model, which is the chapter included in this book, where they emphasize the importance of defining the need for change and choice about whether to change. The remainder of the book explains each of the three change phases (present, transition, future) and ends with a case study and discussion of managing commitment to change and managing complexity.

In Chapter Forty-One, by Schneider, Brief, and Guzzo (1996),* total organization change is addressed primarily through the lenses of culture and climate. It may be recalled that the chapter in Part Two by Burke and Litwin covered a comprehensive model of organization change and performance. Two primary dimensions of their model are culture and climate. This chapter by Schneider and his colleagues contributes further to our understanding of the similarities yet important distinctions between the two dimensions. These authors make the case that culture can be changed through a focus on climate. They consider

---

*Chapter is included in the collection of readings on the *Organization Change: A Comprehensive Reader* website. www.josseybass.com/go/burke.

three philosophies regarding total organizational change: organization development, sociotechnical systems, and total quality management. They argue that a more thorough and lasting change will occur when the primary emphasis is on changing climate, which in turn affects the culture. The practices that top management implements and the values they communicate determine the climate and culture.

The final chapter in Part Five takes a leap beyond the organization *per se* and enters the complex world of interorganizational relations—mergers and acquisitions, joint ventures, strategic alliances, partnerships, consortia, and so forth. The chapter by Burke and Biggart comes from the 1997 book *Enhancing Organizational Performances,* edited by Druckman, Singer, and Van Cott, which constitutes a report from the Committee on Techniques for the Enhancement of Human Performance of the National Research Council, the action arm of the National Academy of Sciences. The committee spent about two years studying factors considered to be significant in affecting organizational performance, such as organization structure, culture, leadership, conflict management, and interorganizational relations. In their part of the overall committee's work, Burke and Biggart's coverage of interorganizational relations examined environmental aspects affecting cross-organizational activities, laid out a partial taxonomy for understanding the governance of interorganizational structures from least managed (for example, a consortium) to most managed (merger or acquisition) and explained life-cycle stages in these kinds of collaborations. Burke and Biggart consider the more practical aspects of these relationships by covering conditions for failure and for success. They conclude with unanswered questions, which in turn suggest future research possibilities.

To summarize briefly this Part Five, we begin with the overall framework for organization change interventions by Blake and Mouton and then proceed with chapters that address the three primary levels of interventions: individual, group, and organization. Not explicitly considered is the intergroup domain—cooperation and conflict between groups. Blake and Mouton touch on this area; intergroup dynamics are, of course, addressed broadly in the last chapter on interorganizational relations. The main point to bear in mind is the importance of understanding organization change according to levels in the organization, because resistance to change differs at the individual level from the organizational level, thus requiring other change strategies to be successful.

CHAPTER THIRTY-ONE

Strategies of Consultation

Robert R. Blake
Jane Srygley Mouton (1972)

In the process of our studies we have come to recognize that five kinds of interventions characterize what applied behavioral scientists do as they work with people in organizations. They intervene, in any of these five ways, in five settings or units of change. So a matrix of twenty-five cells is necessary to describe the significant change efforts that are going on. We would like to explain what these cells are, offer a brief bibliography to pinpoint work going on in each, and provide a few examples that describe the respective intervention/development assumptions that each contains.

You will notice that Table 31.1 is called the D/D (Diagnosis/Development) Matrix. This is because diagnosis and development are two aspects that are more or less interdependent in planned change efforts, although occasionally they need to be separated for purposes of analysis.

The *rows* of the matrix represent types of interventions. One is acceptant. The next is catalytic. A third is confrontation. The fourth is prescriptive. The fifth and last includes use of principles, theories, and models as the determinants of change. Selection of any particular intervention, of course, is a judgmental decision taken on the basis of prior diagnosis.

The *columns* of the matrix refer to settings within which change occurs. The first column identifies the individual *per se* as a unit of change. The second, or team, column refers mainly to small groups, projects, departments, and managerial "family" groups, but it also includes interpersonal relations on a one-to-one basis. The third column is for intergroup relationships. Examples of

Table 31.1. D/D Matrix.

Units of Change

Types of intervention	Individual	Team (group, project, department), Intergroup (interdivisional, headquarters-field, union-management, etc.)	Organization	Society	
Acceptant	A	B	C	D	E
Catalytic	F	G	H	I	J
Confrontation	K	L	M	N	O
Prescriptive	P	Q	R	S	T
Principles, Models, Theories	U	V	W	X	Y

This way of organizing intervention strategies led us to introduce a third dimension called focal issues. There are four: power/authority, morale/cohesion, norms/standards, and goals/objectives. See R R. Blake, and Jane Srygley Moutori, *Consultation* (Reading, Mass.: Addison-Wesley, 1976).

intergroup diagnosis/development units are interdivisional, headquarters-field, union-management, and other relationships between any organized groupings within or semiexternal to the organization. The fourth column refers to the organization considered as a whole or as a system. The fifth we have labeled "society" because of the broader implications of training and development for planned change of society at large.

ACCEPTANT INTERVENTION

Now let's go along the top. What an "acceptant" intervention does is enter into contact with the feelings, tensions, and subjective attitudes that often block a person and make it difficult for her to function as effectively as she otherwise might. The developmental objective is to enable her to express, work through and resolve these feelings so that she can then return to a more objective, and work-related orientation. This is not the whole area of counseling as it relates to therapy. It is that aspect of counseling which takes place within the framework of organizations and which is intended to help a person perform better. Certainly it is a very important application of counseling.

Here is an example of counseling with individuals from cell A in the matrix. During the 1930s, at the Hawthorne plant of the Western Electric Company, it was discovered that many employees were blocked, taut, seething with tensions of one kind or another. Generally these tensions were either work-focused or home-focused, or an intricate combination of both. For some years Hawthorne management provided a counseling service that enabled people to be aided through counseling to discharge the emotion-laden tensions. We say "to discharge" tensions, as distinct from resolving them more or less permanently. The procedure was, in effect, "Any time you feel overcome by tension, get a slip from your supervisor and go see a counselor." This is comparable—if we adopt an oil-industry analogy—to "flaring off" subterranean natural gas rather than piping it to wherever it can be productively used.

In the peak year of the program, 1948, Hawthorne's department of counseling was manned by fifty-five people. That's a large complement of counselors. This very interesting experiment has been documented by its originators, who were able to return to the scene of their effort and to study the consequences thirty years after the program began.

An example I would like to paraphrase for you is from their book (Dickson & Roethlisberger, 1966, 225–226). The situation takes place in the counselor's office. Charlie enters. He is a semiskilled worker who has been with the company for some time but has recently been transferred to a new inspection job from another one he had formerly mastered and enjoyed. He is unhappy with his new job.

COUNSELOR: Hi ya Charlie, how are you?

CHARLIE: Glad to see you. We all set to go?

COUNSELOR: Sure, any time you're ready.

CHARLIE: Well, I'm ready any time to get out of this g.d. place. *You know, you get shoved around from one place to another.*

COUNSELOR: You mean you don't have one steady job?

CHARLIE: Steady, hell. When I came from the first floor I was supposed to do this particular bank job. I stayed on that for two or three weeks, not even long enough to learn it, then I got transferred up here. . . . Of course you know what I got. It got me nothing, just this job here which was a cut [in his hourly rate of pay].

COUNSELOR: Then all that work didn't pay off?

CHARLIE: Pay off? There's no payoff at all.

As you can see in this brief example, Charlie is ventilating his feelings and frustrations and the counselor is "reflecting"; trying to aid Charlie to clarify them by feeding him back a summary of those tensions so that Charlie might get an understanding of what they are, rather than just feeling the hurt and distress of them. You will notice that the counselor is not attempting to help Charlie solve his "transfer with pay cut" problem. That's one point of application that involves counseling with an individual to promote catharsis.

In recent years—and way out from Hawthorne—the continuum of learning through experience has been extended and enriched through experimentation with action-oriented, nonverbal approaches. An advantage here is that the modalities through which an individual is able to experience self in situations are increased. Results and experiences can be more directly *felt,* in the sense that words are unnecessary to convey whatever emotions are involved. The way in which any particular approach is used, of course, determines its location in the matrix. One of the most common uses of "encountering" is in the effort to promote personal growth through individual cathartic experiences (Watson, 1972, 155–172).

Now let's look to cell B. This involves acceptant interventions at the team or group level. Here the idea is that before a team can do an effective job of dealing with its work problems, it may have to deal with emotional tensions and feelings that exist within and between its members.

Gibb has for a considerable time been aiding teams to discharge tension in a cathartic way. This example is from his account of his methods (Gibb, 1972).

He describes how, in the process of team building, he may begin with what he calls a "preparation meeting." He brings together the people who are going to be leaders of different teams in order to prepare them for their experience. Why does he start this way? "The primary constraint," he says "is, of course, fear. Participants are given . . . perhaps the first half-day to share and fully explore as many of their fears as they are able to verbalize." What help is this? "Fears dissipate as they are brought into awareness, shared with others, lived with, listed on the board, made public, and made acceptable. The public expression of the fear may take many forms" (Gibb, 1972, 38). So the effort begins with group exploration, which aims to remove these constraints so that constructive sessions can take place.

Cell C identifies approaches to planned change utilizing catharsis at the intergroup level. For example, I am sure that many readers have experienced the tensions and emotions that underlie many union-management relationships. Bickering at the bargaining table is a constant feature and, many times, the topics discussed are not the relevant ones that need to be resolved. Sometimes the relevant ones can't even be expressed! Rather, the issues that people concentrate on seemingly are brought to the table in order to provoke a fight. Often such intergroup dynamics emerge from emotions and frustrations that never get uncovered but stay beneath the surface. Catharsis at the intergroup level has as its purpose to uncover feelings that are barriers to problem-solving interaction; to provide the opportunity for them to be made public; and, in this way, to escape from their hidden effects.

Here is an example from a union-management situation we happen to be familiar with. Contract bargaining was under way. It was hopeless. It was going nowhere. We heard management voicing its frustrations and bitching about the union, and we suggested that perhaps the needed activity was to get *away* from the union-management bargaining table and to sit down together in a special conference for the sole purpose of exploring the feelings these groups held toward one another. This was done. The tensions discharged in those three days were destructive, deep-rooted, intense. The grudges and fantasies from the past that were blocking present effectiveness finally got unloaded, and this freeing-up permitted bargainers to get back to their deliberations.

Here is just one example of the many fantasies unveiled during these days. At one time, actual events that were the source of the fantasy had occurred, but now the "truth" of these events was a matter of history. At the present time the varied feelings about these events were in the realm of fantasy.

"In 1933" (this cathartic session took place in *1963*), the union told the management, "you s.o.b.'s had us down and out because of the depression. And what did you do? You cut everybody's pay in half and, having done so, then you turned us out into the yard to dig up all the pipe and repack it. How do you expect us to bargain with a bunch of cutthroats that would do that to human beings who are down?''

The managers, hearing this, did a retake and said, ''Oh, but golly, that was not *us*; that was five dynasties of management ago!'' But this disclaimer didn't mollify the union. Eventually, 1963 management walked the 1963 union back through the time tunnel in an attempt to reconstitute the thinking that 1933 management had undertaken. This was ''We shouldn't let people go home with no job. We should keep them 'whole.' We can't employ them full time because we don't have that much production scheduled— market demand is way down. Rather than laying off people *en masse*, the humane thing to do is to keep everyone on the payroll, but to make the cost burden bearable by reducing wages. Also, we have to keep them occupied somehow. With operational activities currently at such low levels, the only thing we can do that has long-term utility to it is to dig up the yard pipe and repack it.''

So the 1933 management's intentions were probably well-meant, but the union's legend regarding those intentions portrayed them as very malicious. Yet eventually the 1963 union, after reconsidering that management's dilemma, agreed that it had taken the most humane alternative open to it. So the old legend dissolved away. Only by getting this kind of emotional muck out in the open and discharged was it possible for these union and management representatives to get back to a businesslike basis of working toward a contract. That's an example of acceptant at the intergroup level.

There are many examples of acceptant interventions at the organization level, cell D.

In another company the entire management engaged in an ''acceptant'' experience prior to bargaining. The reason was that even though management, at an intellectual level, desired to interact on a problem-solving basis with the plant's independent-union representatives, there were many deeply rooted antagonistic attitudes that continually surfaced and stifled the effort. Why? The ostensibly humane attitudes of people who have received formal education sometimes only serve as a mask for deeper feelings of resentment and antipathy. Often there is a lot of hate among managerial people toward the work force. Such feelings are particularly prevalent among engineers, supervisors and foremen who have, in their own careers, only recently risen above the level of the ''blue-collar stiff.''

The consultant determined that to work solely with the bargaining committee would be insufficient as they could only move in a problem-solving direction if they had the support of the rest of management. Thus a series of conferences were held. Participants were the top one hundred members of management, who represented all levels of supervision except first and second line foremen. The stated purpose of these meetings was to develop shared convictions in regard to answering the key question, "How can we create better relations between union and management?"

Participants were put into three "cross-section" groups during each conference. Quinn, the plant manager, sat in one group. Van, the operations superintendent, sat in another group, and Wes, the personnel chief, in a third. The groups struggled with the problem of how to improve union-management relations. It was fascinating to watch because a fairly substantial cross-section of the managerial group considered the key question a hopeless one to answer: "There is no way to bring about any improvement vis-à-vis the thugs, thieves, and crooks who presently are running the union. How can you cooperate and collaborate with such a rat pack?"

Then as the question got debated, their deep-lying attitudes and feelings were expressed in detail and were looked at from many points of view. A new concept began to appear. Consciousness dawned that one can never look forward to an improvement in union-management relations unless this governing attitude—namely that the union is composed of thugs, thieves, and crooks—is erased or at least given an experimental adjournment in the minds of management. After the discharge of emotions was completed, it was concluded in group after group: "Regardless of what the union officers are personality-wise and what their history has been, the only conceivable way of bringing about a resolution of conflict is through treating the union officers as officers and according them the dignity and respect due to people who are duly elected. It is not our place to judge the people who have been chosen by their membership as lawful representatives. This is not our role. Our role is to meet with these people and to search for whatever conditions of cooperation and collaboration are possible."

As a result of this cathartic experience, it was possible thereafter for management's bargaining team to take a more collaborative stance (Blake & Mouton, 1973).

At the level of society shown in cell E, there also are mechanisms that provide for catharsis. Religious institutions are one example. More so in American history than now, but still persisting, is the role of the clergyman as one of the persons to whom people turn when in deep emotional trouble, with the expectation of his providing the disturbed person an opportunity to talk through his feelings. In addition, the doctor, teacher, and school or private counselor are often turned to for help during periods of emotional turmoil, as indeed may be true for parents as well. Beyond these, whenever there is a trauma in society it frequently happens that *ad hoc* mechanisms are created that help people work through their distressed emotional feelings. Well-remembered American examples include the two Kennedy funeral processions, which were carried by television to many parts of the world. These occasions aided people to mourn. Mourning, in this sense, means working through and discharging tensions of a painful emotional character that currently are preventing people from going on living in their customary ways. As is true in the individual case, societal catharsis mechanisms may not have any direct and systematic connection to potential problem-solving steps, although they sometimes stimulate remedial action of one kind or another.

CATALYTIC INTERVENTIONS

Let's move to the next row down: catalytic interventions. "Catalytic" intervention means entering a situation and adding something that has the effect of transforming the situation in some degree from what it was at an earlier time. That's quite different from catharsis. When a training manager or consultant is acting to induce catharsis, she is reflecting or restating the problem—or perhaps simply listening in a fashion that gives empathic support. But when a person makes a catalytic intervention, she might provide a suggestion that causes the problem to be seen in a different and more relevant perspective. Or she might suggest a procedure that will lead to a different line of action being adopted.

Here is a catalytic intervention at the individual level, cell F in the D/D Matrix. In one particular company they have a career-planning project. A young man who had been employed for some time came in to talk about his career hopes. The interviewer said, "What are your aspirations? Where would you like to end up in the company?"

The young man replied, "Well, I think I would like to be president or chairman."

Now then, the interviewer might have said something in a cathartic or reflective way. But he didn't. He said, "Well, that's an interesting aspiration. I would like to think it through with you. How many years of education do you have?"

"Six."

"How many promotions have you had in the last two years?"

"One small wage increase."

"Have you taken any courses on your own initiative?"

"No."

And as the discussion continued, the young man began to see the unrealism in his aspiration to be president. Currently there was *no* realistic possibility either in terms of some evidence of upward progression, or of autonomously achieved preparation, or in terms of anything else he was doing. The consultant thereby brought him to the choice point of whether he was prepared to make the additional sacrifices necessary for him to generate upward movement, or whether he was simply content to go on projecting an unrealistic career fantasy (Gould, 1970, 227–228). That's a catalytic intervention at the *individual* level.

Another example, which uses a laboratory setting for life/career planning, is premised on catalytic intervention at the individual level (Fordyce & Weil, 1971, 131–132).

Catalytic intervening at the *team* level, cell G, is one of the most popular applied behavioral science developments of the past twenty-five years, and has become a central intervention in industrial life. There are a whole host of names that come to mind at this point. There are people who engage in team-building sessions where the purpose of their interventions is not to direct the team or merely to reflect back members' feelings, but to facilitate the interaction process so that the team comes to have a better understanding of the problems and pitfalls it's gotten into, and so on.

The following is an example of Schein, a consultant, facilitating group action by focusing attention on how the agenda for meetings was determined.

> In the Apex company I sat in for several months on the weekly executive-committee meeting, which included the president and his key subordinates. I quickly became aware that the group was very loose in its manner of operation: people spoke when they felt like it, issues were explored fully, conflict was fairly openly confronted, and members felt free to contribute.
>
> *What did this mean to Schein?*
>
> This kind of climate seemed constructive, but it created a major difficulty for the group. No matter how few items were put on the agenda, the group was never able to finish its work. The list of backlog items grew longer and the frustration of group members intensified in proportion to this backlog.
>
> *How did members themselves diagnose the situation?*
>
> The group responded by trying to work harder. They scheduled more meetings and attempted to get more done at each meeting, but with little success. Remarks about the ineffectiveness of groups, too many meetings, and so on, became more and more frequent.
>
> *But what did it look like to Schein?*
>
> My diagnosis was that the group was overloaded. Their agenda was too large, they tried to process too many items at any given meeting, and the agenda was a mixture of operational and policy issues without recognition by the group that such items required different allocations of time.
>
> *So what did Schein propose?*
>
> I suggested to the group that they seemed overloaded and should discuss how to develop their agenda for their meetings. The suggestion was adopted after a half-hour or so of sharing feelings.
>
> *Was Schein passive and reflecting or active in a facilitative way?*
>
> It was then decided, with my help, to sort the agenda items into several categories, and to devote some meetings entirely to operational issues while

others would be exclusively policy meetings. The operations meetings would be run more tightly in order to process these items efficiently. The policy questions would be dealt with in depth.

Schein, 1969, 106

Another example of facilitative or catalytic interaction occurs between boss and subordinate as they engage in "management by objectives." Quite frequently, however, in the introduction of MbO in an organization, people other than just the boss and subordinate are used to develop and facilitate the program. Here is a description of what such facilitators do. It is taken from Humble's work with management by objectives (Humble, 1967, 60). He calls these internal people "company advisers."

> Company Advisers must be selected and trained to a highly professional standard in the various techniques. . . . An Adviser is a source of professional advice on the whole programme. He develops suitable techniques and methods with managers; counsels each individual manager in the Key Results Analysis preparation; is present at first Reviews; helps to analyse training plans. He is an "educator" and "catalyst," *not* a man who states what the standards should be, nor what the priorities are and how the problems should be solved. That is management's task.

In this description we see a clear distinction between what we later on call prescriptive interventions—where the intervention is for the purpose of telling people what to do—and the facilitative or catalytic type of intervention where the goal is to aid a process of change or development to occur.

Data-gathering procedures frequently are used in a catalytic way. This is where data are intended to add something to the situation in order to change it (Likert, 1961). When these data are returned to their users, the expert's own personal participation is best described as catalytic. Usually she doesn't tell people what the data mean, but she does ask them questions that aid them to probe meanings more directly.

Next to cell H, intergroup. Catalysis here denotes adding something *between* two groups, in order to enable existing difficulties to rise to the surface or be placed squarely on the examining table so that they can be dealt with.

An intergroup intervention example is described by Beckhard. What he describes is a situation where people from a higher level meet with people from a lower level. The goal is to aid the lower-level people to communicate with the higher-level managers, or discuss specific problems with them, or to bring forth their feelings, attitudes, opinions and ideas regarding what actually is happening in some existing situation. Usually they have been unable, on any prior occasion, to communicate their ideas directly through organizational channels.

The person who organizes and leads the meeting is acting in a catalytic way, inserting a procedure into the situation that is facilitating in the sense that it helps the situation to develop toward resolution. In the following description, the meeting leader gives an assignment to each of the groups—say, to a top-level group and a middle management group. The leader does not give directions as to what specifically should be discussed but indicates a way to get started on a facilitative discussion.

> Think of yourself as an individual with needs and goals. Also think as a person concerned about the total organization. What are the obstacles, "demotivators," poor procedures or policies, unclear goals, or poor attitudes that exist today? What different conditions, if any, would make the organization more effective and make life in the organization better? [Beckhard, 1967, 154]

Then each unit goes off and discusses this separately. Beckhard's instructions are sufficiently general to permit people to put into their discussion whatever it is that is specifically troubling them in their particular jobs and situations. Then the meeting leader, from there on, continues in a procedurally facilitative role by helping the two units collect their data, analyze their feelings and facts, evaluate and compare them, and generally make progress. A similar example of catalytic intervention with multiple membership groups is provided by Bennis (Bennis, 1972, 158–160). Sometimes this approach is called a confrontation meeting, but this is a misnomer, because it entails no confrontation of the sort correctly described by Argyris (1971), which will be discussed later. Rather, the proceedings have a "group suggestion box" quality.

At the organization level (cell I), intervention by an "ombudsman," who is empowered to bypass ordinary channels when problem solving on behalf of people who are burdened with difficulties because of some mistake or lack of response on the part of the particular company or government department, is catalytic in character, particularly in its facilitative aspects (*Commerce Today*, 1972, 29; Foegen, 1972, 289–294).

At the level of society there are many endeavors that are essentially catalytic, as specified in cell J. We wish it were possible to say they were being systematically implemented within comprehensive and coherent frameworks of development. But there are some that, considered individually, have become quite systematic by now. Taking a census every five or ten years, one that describes the state of the nation "as of" a given point in time and permits comparisons to be made across several decades, is one way of aiding citizens to review their situation, of aiding national leadership to formulate policy, and of aiding industries to see the contemporary shape of markets, population trends, and many other things. The census is a powerful force in society. So are opinion polls. These are becoming ever more significant in the eyes of the public. Unfortunately their uses are somewhat limited to political affairs, but there are many other points of application that are possible for polling mechanisms, ones that can have a catalytic effect in terms of how society sees itself conducting its affairs.

CONFRONTATION

Let us now look along the next row, which deals with *confrontation* strategies. These represent quite different intervention styles from catalysis and very different from cathartic interventions. Confrontation has much more challenge in it. It's a much more active intrusion into the life experience of other people than could possibly be implied by a catalytic approach, and certainly much more than would be implied by a cathartic one.

There's another distinction here. As you move from catharsis and catalytic approaches into the next three, what you find is that, under the first two, there is no challenge of the *status quo* by the intervener. In other words, the intervener accepts the definition of the problem, and the associated values and attitudes usually as these are given by the client, and then helps the client to adjust better to the *status quo*. Under a confrontation mode you frequently find a shifting across some kind of "gap"—the existence of this gap having been identified in the locus of the challenge that the intervener implies.

In different ways, each of the next three approaches is much more likely to cause people to challenge the *status quo* and to reject the existing situation as being less preferable than a stronger situation that could be designed to replace it. That's a very important shift in thinking—from simply aiding people to conform or adjust, to assisting people to redesign the situations in which they live and work.

First, we'll describe a confrontation type of intervention at the individual level (cell K). This occurred in a multinational company where the New York president visited the subsidiary president and said to him, in effect—though it was a whole day in the doing—"Look, Henry, I want you to know that we're very unhappy with how your company is operating. As we look at it, in comparison with other companies in our worldwide group, your profit performance is far below the best, and we just don't see you taking the vigorous action necessary to solve your problems."

Henry *said*—that is, he didn't reply to the specifics of that statement: he couldn't hear them—"If you'll look at our 1949 figures and then look at our latest performance records relative to 1949 when I took over, you'll see that over the years we have made a dramatic shift for the better."

And so they went at it, this way and that, all day, and neither heard the other. From the New York headquarters president's point of view, this was a company they would willingly sell, because they couldn't exert influence upon it. From the subsidiary president's point of view, a valiant effort over many years that had produced betterment was being disregarded. Now the confrontation was this.

The next day, one of us said to Henry, "My hearing is that two quite different *perspectives* are being employed to evaluate this company's performance. The perspective of the New York president is a here-and-now perspective. He doesn't care what you did for him yesterday, he is asking, 'What are you doing for me today?' By comparison, your perspective is historical. You're saying, 'How much better we're doing now than yesterday and last year and five years ago.' So unless you two can get onto a common perspective and reason from there, I see very little possibility of any collaborative effort occurring." Well, they did eventually get onto that common perspective basis. Once both of them understood what the central issue was, and that they weren't just totally unresponsive to each other, then some very significant changes took place in the subsidiary company, ones that are continuing to have enlivening effects. That's a confrontation that has caused development to get under way. And the *status quo* has been radically changed from what it previously had been.

Gestalt approaches, several of which are engineered to dramatize an encounter between the participant and an absent person, between two or more imaginary people, or even to dramatize ambivalent feelings within the person's own personality, are confrontational in character, even though cathartic elements are present. Conflicts, contradictions, incongruencies, and so on are focused by the situation as the intervener structures it—or directly through the intervener's own words—in such a way as to permit more insightful resolutions through the elimination of contradictions, rationalizations, etc. (Herman, 1972).

Now let's examine confrontation at the team level (cell L). An example of this comes during a team-building session conducted by Argyris. During this team-building session, and for the last several hours, members had been insisting that the company has a soft, manipulative, ineffective philosophy. Yet they had not really pinned down examples but were just talking in terms of generalities. So he said, "It is difficult to deal with such an answer, namely that the whole company is at fault. Could you give a specific example?" Nobody could. He continued very directly, saying, "OK fellows, are you going to be soft on these issues? You speak of integrity and courage. Where is it? I cannot be of help, nor you for that matter, if all you do is accuse the company of being ineffective. You said you were ready to talk—OK, I'm taking you at your word" (Argyris, 1971, 84). He is confronting them with the discrepancies between what they can be specific about and the abstractions.

Confrontation at the intergroup level (cell M) usually involves each in coming to terms with the other. This interaction is not in terms of discharge of emotional tensions—as in the example of union and management given earlier—but in terms of gaining a shared and realistic sense of what their relationship is.

Here is an example. This one involves the headquarters' Division of Manufacturing in a large company and its major plant, which is located thirty miles away. The division is headed by a vice president. A general manager runs the plant. These two had gotten more and more out of phase with each other over the years until they had nearly reached total impasse. It was very difficult for anyone to see how their misunderstandings had originated and grown into crisis proportions.

Eventually it was arranged for the vice president of manufacturing, and eight or ten people who reported to him, and the plant's general manager and the twelve people who reported to him to get together to study their relationship. The task was for each group to describe what the relationship between headquarters and the plant would be like if it were really a good one. Thereafter, they were to describe what the relationship actually was, here and now. The vice president of manufacturing's group worked in one room and put on newsprint a description of what, from their viewpoint, an ideal relationship would be like. The plant manager's group did the same thing, but in another room. Then they came back together and put their newsprints on the wall so that it could be seen by all what both sides thought a sound relationship would be like. The descriptions were similar and this similarity gave a lot of encouragement. Differences were discussed and resolved.

The next step, working separately, was for each group to describe the relationship as it actually existed here and now. They did this, and brought back their newsprints. Now it seemed like the relationship being described, as viewed from the headquarters' point of view, was "totally" different from the relationship being pictured from the plant point of view. These dramatic divergences stimulated confrontation between the two groups on the issue of what, in fact, did characterize their mutual relationship. For several days, with close management of this situation and the interaction maintained by the interventionist to avoid an uncontrolled explosion, they thrashed through many aspects until a more accurate picture of the present relationship emerged. Now it became possible for both groups to see the many deep problems that in fact existed. They then designed some strategies for improvement steps that could lead toward resolution.

There is a comprehensive description of confrontation at the organization (cell N) level (Jaques, 1951). The project was one of the innovative applied behavioral science interventions of the early postwar period and took place within the Glacier Metal Company in England. Jaques describes how he and others on his research team continually confronted the organization with the character of its internal relationships and objective performance.

At the societal level are found a good many institutionalized as well as informal mechanisms through which problems are confronted. What these are is a function of the kind of society you are looking at. The two-party system provides ways of confronting issues by challenging what's going on. When one party publicizes its point of view, the other side is confronted with the necessity of either accepting the point of view as expressed, or identifying flaws in it. This is not to imply that in *any* political system this is done particularly well. We are only suggesting that two-party mechanisms, as these link into and work through a nation's executive branch, legislatures, and public media, constitute one important way of confronting the problems of society and getting them into definition so that actions can be taken on behalf of solving them. Furthermore, the spread of the union-management confrontation mechanism into government, school, university, and professional settings has resulted in this mechanism of intervention taking on social dimensions. Beyond that the entire legal system provides mechanisms by which confrontation with redress of injustice is permitted.

PRESCRIPTIVE

Now let's consider the *prescriptive* row. These are the most forceful types of intervention, ones I rather doubt are widely practiced by training and development people. But they are widely applied by outside consultants in conjunction with managers in industry, commerce, and government. Higdon describes the prescriptive approach as used in various consulting firms such as McKinsey and Company; Arthur D. Little; Booz, Allen, and Hamilton; and many others (Higdon, 1969). The basic procedure is that management asks an expert in, and he and his associates study the situation and provide a recommended solution. The "mainstream" consultant is not working with emotions in a cathartic sense. He is not working catalytically. He is not confronting. He is telling. His recommendations would be directions, if he had the authority of rank. But he is certainly prescribing, and these prescriptions sometimes are very complete and fundamental. Often they involve changing an organization's structure, or getting out of one product line and into another, or applying a more efficient theory of business. Many times they involve firing or laying off people, and so they can have impactful consequences on the development of an organization. Sometimes the prescription is rejected out of hand. Sometimes, when taken, it results in a healthful bracing up of part or all of the organization. There have been numerous instances, however, of consultant prescriptions becoming very frustrating to the organization in terms of the difficulties and side effects left in their wake. These include lowered morale, people leaving because they no longer can give their commitment, and so on.

Here's a description of prescriptive strategy at the individual level (cell P). It is where a consultant is trying to hold up a mirror in front of a manager to help him see what he is like, and then to prescribe, in concrete and operational terms, what he'd better do. The client is a plant manager who has trouble with his chief accountant, who is a rather "cold and formal" individual. To obtain better results than he was presently getting from this man, the plant manager— a genial fatherly person who likes to develop warm personal relations with his subordinates—was advised to take a forceful, direct, impersonal approach with him. This, the consultant predicted, would resonate much better with the accountant's psyche than the manager's more typical approach had been doing. On the matter of delayed reports the manager was to say the following: "I want your report on my desk at nine o'clock Friday morning, complete in every detail, and no ifs, ands, or buts about it." Having delivered that ultimatum, he was to turn around and leave. The plant manager did just that, although, being the kind of person he was, it was hard for him to do. The new approach brought striking results. The report came in on schedule and it was one of the finest the plant manager had ever received (Flory, 1965, 158–159). The client had been told specifically how he should act and he followed it through in strict accordance with the consultant's plan. In this case it produced effective results. Incidentally, the developing area of "behavior modification" (Krumboltz, 1965) is a training strategy that has prescriptive qualities.

An example of a prescriptive intervention at the group level (cell Q) is offered by Cohen and Smith. They think this kind of intervention is most suitable toward the end of a group experience. At that time the total group is divided into subgroups of four or five members who are given the following instructions.

> In each subgroup one person will leave the room for ten minutes. During that time the remaining members will first diagnose this person's typical style of interacting with others, and secondly try to pinpoint definite, specific, helpful suggestions as to how he might be helped to engage in atypical but productive behavior both for himself and the group. I must stress the terms "definite" and "specific." Don't make abstract generalizations like "you're too much of an introvert, so try being an extrovert for a while." Instead, give him definite and specific prescriptions to carry out that are generally atypical but productive. Thus, one person might be told to express anger toward the group more directly and verbally instead of remaining quiet. The process continues until everyone has been given a "behavioral prescription." We will all meet back here in "X" minutes to see what sort of changes have occurred [Cohen & Smith, 1972, 103].

Robert's Rules of Order are prescriptive rules for conduct at the group or team level (Robert, [1876], 1970). They tell the leader how to operate meeting procedures. This rather mechanical set of criteria, if followed, prescribes the process parameters of the meeting, provides for expressions of differences, and offers a voting mechanism for resolution.

The third party arbiter is used at the intergroup level to provide for the resolution of differences, and to speed thinking toward further progress (cell R). Typically, it operates in the following way. Two groups—say, management and a union—reach an impasse. Both agree to submit the disagreement to binding arbitration. The arbitrator, characteristically a disinterested outsider, hears evidence or otherwise studies the case and renders a decision. This usually takes the form of a prescription that both sides in the dispute are obligated to take (Linke, 1968, 158–560; Lazarus *et al.*, 1965).

Prescriptive approaches at the organization level are shown in cell S. One is vividly described in a case study from *Fortune*. Top management of Philco had engaged an outside firm to study the organization and to propose needed changes. Here's how a crucial meeting was described.

> James M. Skinner, Jr., president of Philco Corp., (arrived) . . . for a momentous meeting that had been six months in the making. Waiting for Skinner in suite 1808 were nine somewhat apprehensive men from Arthur D. Little, Inc., the technical consulting firm of Cambridge, Massachusetts. . . .

> Donham spoke first, outlining in general terms what A.D.L. hoped to accomplish with its reorganization plan. What he was proposing, in brief, was a massive reorganization of Philco's marketing setup, which would make the job of marketing all of Philco's consumer products the responsibility of one division; fix profit responsibilities at precise points in the company; get day-to-day pressures off the backs of men who should be doing long-range planning; and provide much closer support for Philco's independent distributors and dealers [Thompson, 1959, 113–114].

Levinson, operating out of a psychoanalytic tradition, has described his model of organization diagnosis in step-by-step terms. The approach he depicts is prescriptive in character, as demonstrated in the following excerpt, which gives a few of the diagnostician's recommendations regarding the improvement of personnel practices at "Claypool Furniture and Appliances."

> The recommendations to be made, following the logic expressed in the last discussion, are as follows:

> *Personnel Practices* The company should establish descriptions and standards and objectives for all positions. It should develop orientation and training programs to properly prepare people for their jobs and provide appraisal devices by which personnel and their superiors can assess progress and training needs. Positions and training in supervision and management are to be included in this process. A procedure for identifying prospective managerial talent should be evolved. The representative council should be abolished, and it should be replaced by employee task forces appointed to solve specific intraorganizational

problems. Such groups, to include stock personnel, would end the isolation of the stock people and contribute to organizational identification and group cohesion.

A continuous and open evaluation of the wage and salary structure below the managerial levels should be undertaken, with the intention of creating and maintaining an equitable and competitive salary structure . . . . [Levinson, 1972, 491]

The Hoover Commission was an effort to use prescriptive techniques of diagnosis and development at the societal level. Ex-President Herbert Hoover and other members of the commission constituted a prestigious group. The presumption was that the voice of their authority behind recommendations would be sufficient, along with a responsive incumbent president, to bring about the recommended reformations in terms of restructuring the design and operations of the executive branch of the government.

The usual procedure, applied on all levels of government in the United States, is to set up a formal inquiry into existing conditions, in the hope of bringing forth concrete recommendations with a fair chance of adoption. Inquiries of this type on the federal level include the President's Committee on Administrative Management with Louis Brownlow as chairman (reporting in 1937) and the (first) Commission on Organization of the Executive Branch, headed by former president Herbert Hoover (reporting in 1949) [Willson, 1968, 632].

PRINCIPLES, THEORIES, AND MODELS

The first row of the matrix identifies diagnostic and developmental efforts that focus upon aiding people to acquire insights derived from principles, theories, or models. The assumption is that deficiencies of behavior or performance can be resolved best when people responsible for results use relevant principles, theories, or models in terms of which they themselves can test alternatives, decide upon and take action, and predict consequences. It is an approach that emphasizes intervention by concepts and ideas rather than by people.

With regard to cell U, the particular significance to an individual of theory, principles, and models is that they are capable of providing a map of valid performance against which actual behavior and actual performance can be contrasted. When gaps exist between theory specifications for sound conduct and actual behavior, then change can be introduced that reduces the gap by increasing the congruence between the two. In this sense—and also, importantly, in the sense of removing self-deception—systematic concepts involving theories, principles, or models constitute a ''theory mirror,'' which has the unique power of enabling people to see themselves, their present situations, or future potential more clearly than if reliance is on subjective notions that something feels "right," "natural," or "OK," or simply that others "approve" it. Here are some examples:

Transactional Analysis is a conceptual formulation that provides a mirror into which people can look as a way of seeing themselves. Training designs have been created that enable participants to identify "Parent," "Child," and "Adult" oriented behavior both directly and with the benefit of colleague feedback and to study and practice ways of shifting toward more adult-like behavior (Blansfield, 1972, 149–154).

Also at the individual level, there is the Kepner-Tregoe system, which provides managers with a model through which to design an analysis of any given problem and evaluate the quality of decisions they make. The objective is to reduce impulse, spontaneity, and reliance on past practice and to shift to a rationality basis for problem analysis and decision making (Kepner & Tregoe, 1965).

There are a variety of theories, principles, or models regarding individual behavior, some of which are accompanied by intervention strategies calculated to make the models functionally useful in concrete situations. Some of the more widely known include Theories X and Y (McGregor, 1960), Grid® formulations (Blake & Mouton, 1964, 1968, 1970; Mouton & Blake, 1971), and Systems 1 through 4 (Likert, 1967). However, the approach described by Likert does not involve person-to-person feedback on actual performance. Thus provisions are unavailable for penetrating and correcting self-deception.

Examples of theory orientation at the individual level include four grids (managerial, sales, customer, and marriage), each of which describes several alternative models (9–9, 9–1, 1–9, 5–5, and 1–1) as well as mixed, dominant, and backup theories. Once a person has learned the various theories, they can be used to diagnose her own behavior. In addition, she can select any theory as a model to change toward, but the most likely endorsed one is 9–9. She can then study and practice ways of increasing the congruence between actual behavior and the model (Blake & Mouton, 1968, 34–66).

Some approaches to team building (cell V) use principles, theories, and models as the basis for diagnosing and feedback and for implementing development activities. Central issues that, for the top team of a large chemical plant, demonstrated the gap between a diagnosis of their present ways of functioning and a model of what they considered ideal are shown in Table 31.2. This actual-ideal comparative diagnosis was used for designing strategies of change to be implemented within the next four months (Blake & Mouton, 1968, 120–157).

Theory, principle, and models also have proved useful in strengthening intergroup relations (cell W). Phase three of Grid Organization Development, for example, begins with two groups convening for the purpose of describing what would be an ideal model for their particular relationship. This ideal

Table 31.2. Actual vs. Ideal Top Culture in a Chemical Plant.

Actual	Ideal
Persons only do what is expected of them. Each man runs his own shop. The boss calls the shots.	Synergism is exploited, issues are talked through, and solutions and decisions based on facts are fully thrashed through to understanding and agreement.
Plans come down from the boss without opportunity to review, evaluate, or recommend changes by those who implement them.	Plans based on analysis of facts permit real issues to be treated soundly; plans are produced jointly by those who should be involved; individual responsibilities are clear.
Traditional ways of doing things are rarely questioned; they represent the tried and true operating standards.	Elements of culture are continually evaluated in the light of requirements for peak performance, and if necessary they are modified or replaced through thoughtful discussions and agreement among team members.
Results are what count, no matter how achieved.	Team members are fully committed to excellence; results are achieved because members are motivated to exceed.

model is itself based on theories of intergroup conflict and cooperation (Blake & Mouton, 1964; Blake, Shepard, & Mouton, 1964). It culminates with an *in situ* design that spells out the properties of a sound and effective relationship in a particular, concrete setting. The modeling stage is followed by implementation strategies for converting "what is" to "what should be." An example of the properties of an ideal management-union relationship as described by one company is shown in Exhibits 31.1 and 31.2.

The development of an Ideal Strategic Corporate Model in phase four of Grid Organization Development is an example of the use of models at the organization level (cell X). Phase four enables a top group, particularly, to isolate itself from the *status quo* long enough to design what would be an "ideal" company, given its realistic access to financial resources. Issues considered include, "What should be the key financial objectives that the company should strive after?" "What should be the nature of the company's business, and the nature of its markets?" "What should its structure be?" "What policies should it operate under?" Finally, "What are development requirements for getting from where it is to where it would go if it were to approach the ideal model?"

Exhibit 31.1. What a Sound Union-Management Relationship Would Be as Described by Management.

The Management Would:

Maintain open communications with the union in the following areas:

Economics of industry and company

Goals and objectives of company

Long-range company plans

How company profits are handled and distributed

Problems facing company

Growth opportunities—company and individual

Security and development of employees

Employee induction and orientation—where person fits in total scheme of things

Participate in prebargaining discussions to:

Identify and clarify current economic climate

Identify and understand company's competitive position

Assess and evaluate indexes for productivity

Identify and agree upon appropriate and objective cost of living standards

Identify and understand employee attitudes and concerns

Assess strengths and weaknesses of present contract

Identify possible obstacles and barriers that could arise during negotiations

Adopt bargaining strategy to:

Develop frame of reference for agenda

Explore problem areas jointly

Explore opportunity areas

Have more joint problem solving—e.g., on:

Evaluating impact on employees from operational changes

Work simplification

Benefits and pension programs

Techniques of training

Job safety

Handle complaints and grievances as follows:

First line supervisors would discharge responsibility for resolving complaints and grievances and act with dispatch

Participate in continuing joint efforts leading to clear interpretation and uniform application of contract clauses at working level

(continued)

Exhibit 31.1. (continued)

Maintain open door policy—union executives have free access to management executives and vice versa

Establish and maintain open, upper-level labor-management dialogue—ongoing critique

Endeavor to understand problem confronting union officers within their frame of reference in their relationship with membership

The Union Would:

Develop comprehensive understanding of specific nature of the business and concern for it

Understand and consider nature of competition as it relates to company performance and needs for change

Develop understanding of relationships of productivity to wages and benefits

Because of peculiar nature of industry, understand long-range impact on both company and employees from work stoppages

Recognize implications of taking fixed positions in approaching problems—win-lose trap

Recognize harm in intragroup (within-union) conflict resulting in company and employee backlash

Subdue personal interests in favor of overall company and union objectives

Accept responsibility to communicate facts to employees without prejudice

Source: Blake, R. R., & Mouton, J. S. *Corporate excellence through grid organization development: A systems approach.* Houston: Gulf Publishing, 1968, 181–182. Not to be reproduced without permission.

Exhibit 31.2. What a Sound Union-Management Relationship Would Be as Described by the Union.

The Management Would:

Exercise authority on complaints, grievances, questions, decisions needed, etc., without needless delay, particularly first-level managers

Adopt uniform education program for all supervisors, vertical and horizontal, on understanding, interpreting, and applying the contract

Interpret the contract in an honest and aboveboard way

Consult employees on changes in working schedules, shifts, transfers, location, etc.

Apply a system of seniority and rotation without favoritism, e.g., assigned overtime, easy jobs, time off, vacations, best working schedules, etc.

Rate employees' performance on a uniform, systematic, and fair basis and with employees told where they stand

Coordinate and communicate effectively between department supervisors to prevent needless work by employees and cut down costs and wasted effort

The Union Would:

Represent all employees fairly

Communicate problems, complaints, contract infractions to management

Have access to top management without runaround at lower levels

Be concerned with costs and amount of production

Insure employee has correct rating for skills he has and that he is paid for job he does, not the classification he has

(Union had insufficient time remaining to complete this activity.)

Source: Blake, R. R., & Mouton, J. S. *Corporate excellence through grid organization development: A systems approach.* Houston: Gulf Publishing, 1968, 183. Not to be reproduced without permission.

An example of the change in thinking about financial objectives at the corporate level during phase four is shown in Table 31.3.

The use of principles, models, and theories also can be seen at the level of society (cell Y). The Magna Charta is a well-known historical example. The U.S. Constitution describes the kind of behavior, freedom, and control that American society was expected to be modeled after. Over nearly two centuries,

Table 31.3. Genuine Concern with the Organization's Earning Capacity Results from Designing an Ideal Strategic Model.

From	*To*
Maintain or increase market share while living within a budget.	Optimal 30, minimum 20 percent pretax return on assets employed with an unlimited time horizon.
Dollar profit should improve and not fall behind last year. Return on investment computed and discussed on an after-the-fact calculation which exerted little or no influence on operational decision making.	Each business should have a specified profit improvement factor to be calculated on a business-by-business basis. The objective should be an earnings per share level which would within five years justify a price-earnings ratio of twenty to one or better.
	Share of market objectives should be established within the framework of return on assets and cash generation objectives.

Source: Blake, R. R., & Mouton, J. S. *Corporate excellence through grid organization development: A systems approach.* Houston: Gulf Publishing, 1968, 233. Not to be reproduced without permission.

several constitutional amendments have updated the model in the light of contemporary perspectives. Legislative and executive actions are always being tested against the Constitution.

Lilienthal's work in Iran can be viewed as intervention at the societal level to bring about change through assisting the eventual users to design models of "what should be" as the basis of specific implementation plans. Lilienthal is a notable industrial statesman who led first the Tennessee Valley Authority and then the U.S. Atomic Energy Commission in their beginning years. He has described his later consulting work (Lilienthal, 1969) when, with his own and his colleagues' vast knowledge of hydroelectric engineering, community rehabilitation, and agribusiness, they helped the Iranian government design a model for water and electric-power resources for the future of its then undeveloped Khuzestan province. That model is being systematically implemented through the building of dams, power irrigation systems, and so on, as well as infrastructure developments such as agricultural advisory programs, health and educational facilities, etc. This is an example of how a consultant can work, not in a prescriptive mode, but as a skillful teacher in aiding people to learn to design and implement complex models. Lilienthal thus has enabled a vast development to occur, one that otherwise would have been piecemeal, suboptimizing, and possibly impractical.

Skinner's recent writings about society are derived from theory and principles and also rest on a model concept (Skinner, 1971).

SUMMARY AND CONCLUSIONS

The D/D Matrix provides a way of encompassing a wide range of activities now under way for strengthening human performance through diagnosis and development. Illustrations of each approach have been given without trying to be inclusive.

Using this matrix, anyone who wishes to do so can identify the assumptions underlying his own work, and evaluate their probable consequences for increasing the effectiveness of individuals, groups, groups in relationships with one another, organizations, and society. The acceptant approach of emotional barrier-reduction and the catalytic approach of helping people to make progress in dealing with given situations are most likely to aid individuals and groups to do a better job within the existing *status quo*.

Confrontation and prescription are useful in a "fixed" or "frozen" situation. They provide alternatives to those currently present in the *status quo*. Both rely heavily on outside expertise.

The history of society and its capacity to identify and grapple with complex and interrelated problems of the physical environment, new technologies, and community development is significantly linked with the production and use of principles, theories, and models for understanding, predicting—and, therefore, managing—natural and human environments. Approaches to diagnosis and development that rely on the use of principles, theories, and models for understanding emotional, intellectual, and operational events provide the most powerful and impactful approach to the implementation of planned change.

It is highly unlikely that any single approach will be based solely on one intervention mode. Rather, the likelihood is that several intervention modes will be included with one of them being central or dominant. For example, the Dickson-Roethlisberger counseling program appears to have been a very "pure" individual-cathartic approach, with minor reliance on counseling as catalytic intervention. Process consultation, as depicted by Schein, relies heavily upon catalytic intervention, with some use of acceptant interventions and very infrequent use of the confrontation mode. Schein makes practically no use of the prescriptive mode, and makes theory interventions only after the fact.

The intervening in T Groups is mainly catalytic, with secondary reliance on the cathartic mode. "Encounter" relies very heavily on catharsis. Grid OD concentrates on theory, principles, and models; but it also provides at key points for confrontation, catalytic intervention, and cathartic release. Other approaches can be analyzed in a similar manner.

No one can say, in an abstract sense and without regard to a particular situation, that there is "one best way." Although principles, theories, and models constitute the strongest approach, they may lack feasibility until emotional blockages have been reduced through cathartic intervention. Or, perhaps, opening up the possibilities of systematic OD may take little more than a timely catalytic intervention that enables managers to see possibilities not previously envisaged. Statements of a similar character can be made with regard to confrontation and prescription.

In the final analysis, however, acceptant, catalysis, confrontation, or prescription constitute means to an end, rather than ends in themselves. The ultimate goal is that people become capable of effective living through utilizing principles, theories, and models as the basis of human enrichment.

References

Cell in D/D Matrix:

Argyris, C. *Organization and innovation.* Homewood, Ill.: R. D. Irwin, 1965.

Argyris, C. *Intervention theory and method.* Reading, Mass.: Addison-Wesley, 1970.

Argyris, C. *Management and organization development.* New York: McGraw-Hill, 1971.

Beckhard, R. The confrontation meeting. *Harvard Business Review*, March–April, 1967, 149–155.

Bennis, W. G. Organization development: What it is and what it isn't. In D. R. Hampton (Comp.) *Behavioral concepts in management* (second edition). Encino, Calif.: Dickinson, 1972, pp. 154–163.

Blake, R. R., & Mouton, J. S. *The managerial grid: Key orientations for achieving production through people.* Houston: Gulf Publishing, 1964.

Blake, R. R., & Mouton, J. S. *Corporate excellence through grid organization development: A systems approach.* Houston: Gulf Publishing, 1968.

Blake, R. R., & Mouton, J. S. *The grid for sales excellence: Benchmarks for effective salesmanship.* New York: McGraw-Hill, 1970.

Blake, R. R., & Mouton, J. S. *How to assess the strengths and weaknesses of a business enterprise.* Austin, Tex.: Scientific Methods, Inc. 1972, 6 vols.

Blake, R. R., & Mouton, J. S. *Diary of an OD man.* Houston: Gulf Publishing, 1976.

Blake, R. R., Shepard, H. A., & Mouton, J. S. *Managing intergroup conflict in industry.* Houston: Gulf Publishing, 1964.

Blake, R. R., Sloma, R. L., & Mouton, J. S. The union-management intergroup laboratory: Strategy for resolving intergroup conflict. *Journal of Applied Behavioral Science*, 1965, *1*, 1, 25–57.

Blansfield, M. G. Transactional analysis as a training intervention. In W. G. Dyer (Ed.) *Modern theory and method in group training.* New York: Van Nostrand Reinhold, 1972, pp. 149–154.

Cohen, A. M., & Smith, R. D. The critical-incident approach to leadership in training groups. In W. G. Dyer,(Ed.) *Modern theory and method in group training.* New York: Van Nostrand Reinhold, 1972, pp. 84–196.

Commerce Today, 2, April 3, 1972, 29.

Dickson, W. J., & Roethlisberger, F. J. *Counseling in an organization: A sequel to the Hawthorne researches.* Boston: Division of Research, Graduate School of Business Administration, Harvard University, 1966.

Flory, C. D. (Ed.) *Managers for tomorrow.* New York: The New American Library of World Literature, 1965.

Foegen, J. H. Ombudsman as complement to the grievance procedure. *Labor Law Journal*, May 1972, 23, 289–294.

Fordyce, J. J. & Weil, R. *Managing with people: A manager's handbook of organization development methods.* Reading, Mass.: Addison-Wesley, 1971.

Gibb, J. R. TORI theory: Consultantless team building. *Journal of Contemporary Business*, 1972, 1, 3, 33–41.

Gould, M. I. Counseling for self-development. *Personnel Journal*, 1970, *49*, 3, 226–234.

Herman, S.M.A. Gestalt orientation to organization development. In W. Burke (Ed.) *Contemporary organization development: Approaches and interventions.* Washington, D.C.: NTL Institute for Applied Behavioral Science, 1972.

Higdon, H. *The business healers.* New York: Random House, 1969.

Humble, J. W. *Improving business results.* Maidenhead, Berks.: McGraw-Hill, 1967.

Jaques, E. *The changing culture of a factory.* London: Tavistock, 1951.

Kepner, C. H. & Tregoe, B. B. *The rational manager.* New York: McGraw-Hill, 1965.

Krumboltz, J. D. (Ed.) *Revolution in counseling: Implications of behavioral science.* Boston: Houghton Mifflin, 1965.

Lazarus, S. *et al. Resolving business disputes: The potential of commercial arbitration.* New York: American Management Association, 1965.

PART FIVE A

INDIVIDUAL-LEVEL CHANGE INTERVENTIONS

CHAPTER THIRTY-TWO

Creating Readiness for Organizational Change

Achilles A. Armenakis
Stanley G. Harris
Kevin W. Mossholder (1993)

INTRODUCTION

Because of increasingly dynamic environments, organizations are continually confronted with the need to implement changes in strategy, structure, process, and culture. Many factors contribute to the effectiveness with which such organizational changes are implemented. One such factor is readiness for change. Readiness, which is similar to Lewin's (1951) concept of unfreezing, is reflected in organizational members' beliefs, attitudes, and intentions regarding the extent to which changes are needed and the organization's capacity to successfully make those changes. Readiness is the cognitive precursor to the behaviors of either resistance to, or support for, a change effort. Schein (1979) has argued "the reason so many change efforts run into resistance or outright failure is usually directly traceable to their not providing for an effective unfreezing process before attempting a change induction" (p. 144). Although some researchers have discussed the importance of readiness (cf. Beckhard & Harris, 1987; Beer & Walton, 1987; Turner, 1982), it has seldom been recognized as being distinct from resistance (cf. Coch & French, 1948; Kotter & Schlesinger, 1979; Lawrence, 1954). Specifically, creating readiness has been most often explained in conjunction with prescriptions for reducing resistance. For example, Kotter and Schlesinger (1979) discuss several strategies in dealing with resistance (e.g., education and communication, participation and involvement, facilitation and support, negotiation and agreement). Such prescriptions are effective in reducing resistance to the extent that they first create readiness. In essence, readiness for change may act to preempt the likelihood of resistance to change, increasing the potential for change efforts to be more effective.

Making an explicit distinction between readiness and resistance helps refine discussions of the implementation of change efforts and captures the spirit of the proactive change agent (cf. Armenakis, Mossholder, & Harris, 1990; Kanter, 1983; Kisler, 1991). Framing a change project in terms of readiness seems more congruent with the image of proactive managers who play the roles of coaches and champions of change, rather than those whose role is to reactively monitor the workplace for signs of resistance.

The purpose of this chapter is to clarify the readiness concept and examine how change agents can influence organizational members' readiness for change. Because the energy, inspiration, and support necessary to create readiness must come from within the organization, this article focuses primarily on the activities of internal change agents (i.e., organizational leaders, managers, etc.). Clearly, external change agents can also benefit from a heightened sensitivity to the creation of readiness. In addition to playing a role in providing information important to readiness creation, external change agents are often in a position to educate internal change agents regarding the importance of readiness.

As a means of fulfilling the article's purpose, the theoretical underpinnings of the readiness concept and the strategies used in creating readiness will be described and an integrative model offered. To enrich this discussion, the actual efforts of one organization to create readiness for a large-scale change are highlighted.

A READINESS MODEL

Theoretical Basis

A classic study by Coch and French (1948), traditionally described as an experiment in reducing resistance to change, demonstrated the value of allowing organization members to participate in change efforts. Four research groups were formed to represent varying degrees of participation including no participation (the comparison group), participation via representation, and total participation. The researchers found that the productivity of the experimental groups exceeded that of the comparison group and concluded that participation reduced resistance to organizational change. Interestingly, Bartlem and Locke (1981) and Gardner (1977) have subsequently identified differing readiness-creating procedures used by Coch and French with the four groups as an overlooked factor in the original research design. The comparison group was told that competitive conditions required a higher productivity standard. The new standard was explained and questions were answered. In contrast, for each of the experimental groups, a meeting was called during which the need for the change was presented in stark fashion. For example, as part of this presentation, the presence of fierce price competition was dramatized by showing two identical garments produced in the factory. One was produced in 1946 and had sold for 100% more than its match, produced in 1947. When asked to do so, the group could not identify the cheaper garment. This dramatization effectively communicated that cost reduction was a very real necessity (Coch & French, 1948).

As exemplified in the Coch and French experiment, creating readiness involves proactive attempts by a change agent to influence the beliefs, attitudes, intentions, and ultimately the behavior of a change target. At its core, the creation of readiness for change involves changing individual cognitions across a set of employees. The dynamics concerned with bringing about such changes in individuals has been explored at length in the cognitive change literature (see, e.g., Bandura, 1982; Fishbein & Azjen, 1975). It is important to note, however, that the creation of readiness for organizational change must extend beyond individual cognitions since it involves social phenomena as well. As social-information processing models suggest (cf. Griffin, 1987), any individual's readiness may also be shaped by the readiness of others. Drawing on the individual-level cognitive change, collective behavior, social-information processing, mass communications, and organizational change literatures, each aspect of this model is addressed in more detail below.

The Message

The primary mechanism for creating readiness for change among members of an organization is the message for change. In general, the readiness message should incorporate two issues: (1) the need for change, that is, the discrepancy between the desired end-state (which must be appropriate for the organization) and the present state; and (2) the individual and collective efficacy (i.e., the perceived ability to change) of parties affected by the change effort.

Discrepancy. The discrepancy aspect of the message communicates information about the need for change and should be consistent with relevant contextual factors (e.g., increased competition, changes in governmental regulations, depressed economic conditions). Creating the belief that change is needed requires showing how the current performance of the organization differs from some desired end-state (Katz & Kahn, 1978). Pettigrew (1987) emphasizes the importance of changes in external contextual factors (namely, social, economic, political, and competitive environments) in justifying the need for organizational change. He argues that the legitimacy for organizational change can be established by interpreting the effect of external contextual factors on an organization's performance. In the Coch and French experiment, the pricing discrepancy between the garments implied that the productivity standard was too low (relative to the competition) and that the challenge was to increase productivity to facilitate competitive pricing.

Others have discussed the importance of creating the awareness of a discrepancy concept, using different phraseology. For example, Nadler and Tushman (1989) refer to creating intellectual pain, the realization that something is awry. Spector (1989) advocates diffusing dissatisfaction throughout the organization to make appropriate discrepancies self-evident. Bandura (1982) frames this in terms of unfavorable personal consequences, the organizational analog of which would be the threat of a complete failure of the organization. In essence, intellectual pain, diffused dissatisfaction, and organizational failure may be used to suggest aspects of a discrepancy between the present state and some apparent or implied desired end-state.

Although the appropriateness of certain end-states, such as survival, is rarely questioned, the appropriateness of others may be. For example, successfully convincing members of an organization that changes are necessary to become number one in the industry on some measure rests on their acceptance of being number one as an appropriate end-state. Much of the recent literature on leadership vision emphasizes the importance of clarifying and gaining commitment to the end-state against which the organization is judging its present condition and justifying the need for change (cf. Bennis & Nanus, 1985). Therefore, the discrepancy message involves communicating where the organization is currently, where it wants to be, and why that end-state is appropriate.

Efficacy. Although the realization that a discrepancy exists can be a powerful motivator for change, other reactions are also possible. For example, Nadler and Tushman (1989) discuss the possibility that awareness of discrepancy can result in counterproductive energy. They warn that negative information can result in defensive reactions, like denial, flight, or withdrawal.

To minimize the possibility of a counterproductive reaction, a change agent should build the target's confidence that it has the capability to correct the discrepancy. This confidence has been referred to as efficacy (Bandura, 1982, 1986) and may be viewed as the perceived capability to overcome the discrepancy. Efficacy has been consistently found to influence thought patterns, actions, and emotional arousal. Bandura (1982) reports that individuals will avoid activities believed to exceed their coping capabilities, but will undertake and perform those which they judge themselves to be capable of. Thus, in creating readiness, one must not only communicate a salient discrepancy, but must also bolster the efficacy of organizational members regarding the proposed changes to reduce the discrepancy.

INTERPERSONAL AND SOCIAL DYNAMICS

Because a readiness effort involves convincing a collection of socially interacting individuals to change their beliefs, attitudes, and intentions in accordance with the discrepancy and efficacy aspects of the message, a change agent must understand the distinction between individual and collective readiness, as well as what influences the collective interpretation of the readiness message. This understanding can be facilitated by an integration of the literature on collective behavior (cf. Smelser, 1963), social information processing (cf. Griffin, 1987), and mass communications (cf. DeFleur & Ball-Rokeach, 1989).

Interventions to create readiness for change are attempts to mobilize collective support by building and shaping awareness across organizational members regarding the existence of, the sources of, and solutions to the organization's problems (cf. Smelser, 1963). Through the dynamics of social information processing, an organization's collective readiness is constantly being influenced by the readiness of the individuals composing it. System members look to one another for clues regarding the meaning of events and circumstances facing the organization. Any readiness-building activities must take this social exchange into account. It is important to consider that the change agent is not the sole source of discrepancy and efficacy information. The impact of any message generated by the change agent will be shaped by the social interpretation of that message.

From the mass communications literature, three theories offer insight into various social dynamics that could operate in readiness interventions: the individual differences, social differentiation, and social relationships theories (DeFleur & Ball-Rokeach, 1989).

Individual differences theory argues that the response of one individual may diverge from that of another because of differing cognitive structures. One example of this can be found in research by Kirton (1980) on the different reactions of individuals characterized as innovators or adaptors. Kirton's findings suggest that innovators are likely to respond favorably to readiness programs designed to prepare the target for fundamental change (i.e., change that requires job incumbents to use different mental processes and to develop new skills) while adaptors are more likely to respond favorably to readiness programs designed to prepare the target for incremental change (i.e., change that requires incumbents to make minor modifications in thought patterns and to fine tune existing skills). In sum, individual difference theory serves as a reminder that specific individuals may react differently to the same message.

Social differentiation theory argues that the response to influence attempts will be determined by the target's cultural or subcultural membership. Such cultural memberships may polarize the beliefs, attitudes, and intentions of members. Hierarchical differentiation (i.e., executives, managers, supervisors, and workers) or other differentiates (e.g., union/nonunion, engineers/nonengineers) shape group membership and result in psychological boundaries that may affect the beliefs, attitudes, intentions, and behaviors of members (cf. VanMaanen & Barley, 1985; Bushe, 1988). These psychological boundaries affect the ease with which readiness is evenly created across the subcultures within the organization.

Finally, social relationships theory suggests that responses to an influence attempt will hinge on the network of relationships individuals have. In particular, the influence of opinion leaders on others' sentiments can be powerful in affecting those others' readiness for change. Identifying and recognizing the influence of opinion leaders in the organization may enable the change agent to more effectively design them into the readiness intervention. Building readiness in these opinion leaders first could allow them to provide social cues for others in the organization and, in effect, act as informal change agents in disseminating the logic of the readiness program. As a result, a social information processing-based snowball effect might be generated.

Influence Strategies

Given the above conceptualization of readiness dynamics, how might a change agent intervene in the natural flow of social information processing occurring among organizational members to increase their readiness for change? Two strategies offered by Bandura (1977) and Fishbein and Azjen (1975) for influencing individual cognitions are appropriate for creating readiness for organizational change: persuasive communication (both oral and written) and active participation. A third strategy consists of the management of external sources of information. These three strategies have certain advantages and disadvantages (e.g., timeliness and manageability). The skillful change agent will capitalize on opportunities and the strengths of each strategy and utilize them in concert to influence readiness. Each of these strategies offers a lever for conveying discrepancy and efficacy information.

Persuasive Communication. Persuasive communication is primarily a source of explicit information regarding discrepancy and efficacy. However, the form of persuasive communication employed also sends symbolic information regarding the commitment to, prioritization of, and urgency for the change effort. For example, a CEO who travels to all corporate locations to discuss the need for change sends the message explicitly communicated in his or her comments and the symbolic message that the issues are important enough to take the time and resources necessary to communicate them directly. Oral persuasive communication consists of in-person speeches, either live (e.g., speaking in person or through teleconferencing technology) or recorded (e.g., audio/

videotape). Written persuasive communication consists of documents prepared by the organization (e.g., newsletters, annual reports, memos).

Lengel and Daft (1988) have assessed communication media in terms of richness, a composite dimension comprising the extent of simultaneous multiple information cues, personal focus, and timeliness of feedback. In-person is the richest medium because it establishes a personal focus and permits multiple information cues and immediate feedback. Written media (e.g., annual reports, newsletters) are considered lean, being impersonal and providing for few information cues, and no direct feedback opportunities. Between these two extremes are other media like audio/videotape and electronic mail. For nonroutine communications (i.e., ones that are emotional and difficult to express) more richness is required. Messages that are simple, straightforward, rational, and logical can be communicated via lean media.

Oral persuasive communication involves direct, explicit message transmission through meetings, speeches, and other forms of personal presentation. Live in-person presentations would be rated high in richness, according to Lengel and Daft's criteria. If this form of presentation is not feasible, a videotape of the presentation may be appropriate. For example, Eden and Kinnar (1991) recently employed both verbal persuasion and videotape presentation to boost self-efficacy and increase volunteering for a special-forces service. Elsewhere, Barrett and Cammann (1984) describe a case in which the CEO of National Steel Company conducted a series of personal meetings and prepared a videotape that would be available to all employees. The main objective was to communicate that the ongoing downturn in the steel industry (a contextual factor) was not simply a cyclical one. Thus, this CEO was creating readiness using live and video-recorded presentations.

Management of External Information. Sources outside the organization can be used to bolster messages sent by the change agent. For example, a diagnostic report prepared by a consulting firm may be used to add credibility to a message sent by the change agent. Generally, a message generated by more than one source, particularly if external to the organization, is given a greater air of believability and confirmation (Gist, 1987).

The news media is one form of external source that can play an important role in creating readiness for change. Employee knowledge about issues influencing their readiness can be affected through mass media channels like radio and television broadcasts, magazines, and newspapers. Information provided by such sources tends to have an air of objectivity and is therefore often persuasive with regard to creating readiness for change. However, though such information is persuasive, it is not easily managed by the change agent.

There are two ways in which a change agent may attempt to manage such information. First, information can be provided to the external press.

Organizations often use press releases in this manner. Warren (1984) described a case involving the president of Antioch College, who supplied the press (e.g., the *New York Times, Newsweek,* and the local newspaper) with information regarding the college's fiscal difficulties (i.e., discrepancy) and a plan (i.e., efficacy) to restore Antioch to fiscal stability. A second way a change agent can manage such media information is by making change-relevant information available by disseminating copies of selected articles, books, or film clips to organizational members. For example, many organizations distribute copies of business books that highlight particular desired messages.

Active Participation. Persuasive communication and the management of external information both emphasize the direct communication of readiness messages. Change agents can also manage opportunities for organizational members to learn through their own activities, and thereby send readiness messages indirectly. The message generated by active participation is essentially self-discovered (Fishbein & Azjen, 1975). This source of information is advantageous since individuals tend to place greater trust in information discovered by themselves. It is important to note that even though a change agent may manage opportunities for organizational members to be exposed to information that influences readiness, the message is generated through the activity and is therefore outside of the explicit control of the change agent.

One form of active participation is directly involving individuals in activities rich in information pertaining to potential discrepancy and efficacy messages. For example, participating in formalized strategic planning activities can lead to self-discovery of discrepancies facing the organization. Answering customer complaints can lead to a similar self-discovery. Furthermore, experiential learning exercises have been recognized as effective in providing change-relevant insights in training programs. For example, Kirton's (1980) work suggests that experiential learning exercises may be used to teach adaptive style individuals the appropriateness of a more innovative style.

Another form of active participation is vicarious learning. For example, a vicarious learning experience can be designed to bolster confidence that new production techniques not only offer competitive advantages but can be implemented in their own work environment. Gist, Schwoerer, and Rosen (1989) successfully applied vicarious learning in getting workers to begin using computer software. The act of observing others applying new productive techniques enhances one's confidence in adopting the innovation.

A third form active participation can take is enactive mastery. Enactive mastery can be used to prepare a target for change by taking small incremental steps. Success from the small-scale efforts can generate efficacy with regard to the challenge of implementing changes necessary for large-scale change. This logic has been discussed by Schaffer (1981) and Thompson (1981) in terms of getting clients to buy into, initiate, and sustain needed changes.

CHANGE AGENT ATTRIBUTES

The effectiveness of the influence strategies is dependent upon the change agent wielding them. Attributes such as credibility, trustworthiness, sincerity, and expertise of the change agent are gleaned from what people know about the agent and/or the agent's general reputation. Clearly, readiness-creating messages will have more influence if the change agent generating those messages has a good reputation in these domains (Gist, 1987). Conversely, when these attributes are unfavorable, the change agent's ability to create readiness for change will be hampered.

Readiness Assessment

To guide readiness building efforts, it is beneficial to assess the system's readiness. Assessments of the perceived discrepancy and efficacy of the target would be performed in gauging the state of readiness. Pond, Armenakis, and Green (1984) and Fox, Ellison, and Keith (1988) provide evidence that readiness can be assessed through survey research methodology. As described in the evaluation literature (cf. Armenakis, Field, & Holley, 1976) assessment methodologies can include the use of questionnaire, interview, and observation methods.

Whatever methods are used in sensing readiness, the change agent must respect the importance of reliability and validity issues (cf. Sackett & Larson, 1990). However, this respect should be tempered by the realization that readiness assessments may be for the purpose of discovery as much as for the purpose of confirmation. Thus, as McCall and Bobko (1990) note, a broader perspective on what is acceptable in the way of methodology may be required by the context in which the assessment is conducted. Qualitative techniques become more necessary in fluid, dynamic contexts. For example, polling opinion leaders or identifying and tracking rumors may help clarify trends that appear in survey data. Domain or taxonomic analyses, which are directed at understanding semantics, symbolic structures, and underlying perceptions of employees (McCall & Bobko, 1990), are other examples of procedures that may be useful in an attempt to determine the collective readiness of the organization. Naturally, the typical constraints of availability of time, funds, and expertise, and the importance placed on the assessment, will influence the design. If properly conducted, such assessments can reveal the need to intensify efforts,

use additional strategies to create readiness, and offer insights into how readiness messages might be modified.

A Typology of Readiness Programs

The purpose of the preceding discussion was to describe the major components
of a program for creating employee readiness for change. However, decisions
about leveraging each of the components into a readiness program should be
guided by two considerations: the extent to which employees are ready (as determined through an assessment) and the urgency of the change (the amount
of time available before changes must be implemented).

As described, employee readiness is influenced by the message transmitted
via the strategies, the change agent attributes, and the interpersonal and social
dynamics of organizational members. In addition to these planned efforts,
however, employee readiness may be influenced by at least three other factors:
unplanned media information, existing organizational conditions, and significance of the change effort. Information disseminated through the media (e.g.,
industry layoffs, increasing foreign competition, economic conditions) may affect employee readiness for change, heightening awareness of changing external contextual factors. Furthermore, existing organizational conditions affect
employee loyalty, commitment, or other feelings toward an organization and
its leaders, consequently influencing readiness. Indeed, Fox et al. (1988) found
that effective management practices (e.g., planning, delegating, communicating) influenced employee cooperation and perceived equity and were associated with higher employee readiness for implementing improvements in
procedures and problem solving. In contrast, ineffective practices were associated with lower readiness.

In addition, some changes are more intense and potentially more threatening. Fundamental change, such as changing from a functional form to a strategic business unit organization or from an assembly line to an autonomous
workgroup arrangement, requires different mental processes and the development of new skills. In contrast, incremental change, such as rearranging work
stations to capitalize on a more efficient plant layout (without reengineering
jobs), requires lesser modifications of thought processes and a simple fine tuning of job skills. Thus, employees may be less ready for fundamental than for
incremental change.

Sometimes organizational changes are urgently needed and require rapid
implementation. In such cases, a readiness program will have to be implemented that utilizes the most effective and efficient strategies. Thus, a change
agent may use only a persuasive communication strategy. In other situations,
needed changes may not be so urgent, permitting the implementation of a readiness effort broader in scope and more thorough in detail. Such a program may
involve persuasive communication as well as active participation (e.g.,

vicarious learning) and the management of external information (e.g., press releases).

By combining readiness and urgency, various combinations of change conditions can be hypothesized. Although readiness and urgency are both continuous dimensions, for the sake of clarity, programs consistent with the combinations of the extreme conditions of readiness and urgency will be described.

Low Readiness, Low Urgency. An aggressive program is appropriate when employees are not ready for organizational change yet there is ample time for creating that readiness. A comprehensive readiness program leveraging all components is appropriate for this set of conditions. A variety of rich and lean persuasive communication methods (i.e., in-person presentations, video/ audiotapes, newsletters) is suitable. Active participation experiences (e.g., visits to model manufacturing facilities) can be employed. If the organizational changes include introducing new technology (e.g., computerized systems as part of a change to autonomous workgroups), some form of enactive mastery could be appropriate. Furthermore, external information sources (e.g., press releases, speeches by recognized experts) can be incorporated into the program. Some attempt to build the credibility of the change agent may also be fruitful. For example, a CEO or other internal key figure in the change effort may participate in magazine and newspaper interviews describing previous experiences or recent awards so that credibility can be enhanced. When external change agents are involved, organizational leaders will want to select those with established reputations so their involvement will lend credibility to the anticipated changes. These actions will be expected to favorably influence opinion leaders, thus marshalling their support among other members of the change target.

Low Readiness, High Urgency. A crisis program may be appropriate when employees are not ready and there is great urgency in implementing needed organizational changes. The organization is in a crisis situation and must react immediately or face severe consequences. Obviously, this is an undesirable situation and requires drastic measures. The system needs to be jolted, which may include replacing the current change agent or augmenting this position with key personnel. Any personnel changes may be necessary in order to add credibility, trustworthiness, sincerity, and expertise. In addition, persuasive communication (e.g., in-person presentations) is required. Given time constraints, managing external information and active participation are likely to be infeasible.

High Readiness, Low Urgency. A maintenance program may be appropriate when employees are ready for change but there is little urgency in implementing needed organizational changes. The threat in this situation is that readiness may wane before changes are implemented. Therefore, the emphasis should be on maintaining readiness. Efforts should focus on keeping the discrepancy and efficacy messages current and visible. Lean persuasive communication methods (e.g., newsletters) and managed external information (e.g., magazine and newspaper press releases) may suffice as information sources. Active participation is not as critical to this program as in the aggressive program, but may still be appropriate.

High Readiness, High Urgency. A quick response program may be appropriate when employees are ready and the time available for implementing needed change is short. Thus, organizational changes can be implemented almost immediately. The challenge here is to maintain readiness energy as the change begins to unfold. Once again, persuasive communication, particularly rich persuasive communication, is appropriate. Because of the urgency of the needed changes and the high readiness state, active participation and management of external information may not be suited for this program.

The brief descriptions of these four generic readiness programs provide the salient characteristics for the extremes of the readiness and urgency conditions. For whatever reason, a change agent may elect to vary from the programs described. Attempts to leverage any combination of the components contained in the readiness model would be a matter of whether the conditions are conducive to their use. To provide a detailed comprehensive example of the readiness model, the readiness creating efforts of the Whirlpool Corporation, the world's largest manufacturer of major home appliances, are described. Whirlpool's program can be classified as an aggressive readiness program.

AN INTEGRATIVE EXAMPLE OF READINESS INTERVENTIONS

Whirlpool's leaders, Jack Sparks in 1983, succeeded by David Whitwam in 1987, began a long-term program designed to improve the company's competitiveness by fundamentally altering the organization to become more aggressive, responsive, innovative, and market-oriented. In the following discussion, a summary of the external contextual factors and the readiness-building activities of Sparks and Whitwam are reviewed.

Contextual Factors

During the 1960s and 1970s, the fierce competition within the appliance industry resulted in the consolidation of numerous companies into relatively few players, namely, Whirlpool, General Electric, Electrolux, and Maytag. The strategy adopted by Whirlpool Corporation leaders was to emphasize cost control and operational efficiency rather than market aggressiveness, growth, and globalization. Even though the supply of appliances in the United States had been largely domestically based, foreign competitors began entering the already competitive market in the 1980s. These increasingly competitive pressures were compounded when the U.S. demand for appliances leveled off. The opportunities for expansion abroad, however, were growing (Stewart, 1990).

The Message

The content of the message Sparks and Whitwam communicated to build readiness for change included discrepancy and efficacy aspects. The discrepancy part of the message was that competitive pressures were mounting and that, to remain competitive, Whirlpool would have to become more aggressive, more sensitive to the marketplace, more lean and mean, and a global player. To enhance efficacy, Whirlpool employees were sent to observe model manufacturing operations (in Japan and Korea), were reminded of other companies that had successfully implemented changes resulting in classic turnaround examples, and were assured that Whirlpool could make the fundamental changes needed to prosper in the emerging environment.

Active Participation

Three active participation interventions that were implemented to create readiness are particularly noteworthy: formalized strategic planning efforts, the Global Awareness Program, and the 75th Anniversary Celebration and Show.

Formalized Strategic Planning. One of the first actions Sparks initiated in 1983 was a formalized strategic planning process to augment the organization's traditional profit planning activities. This strategic planning activity required managers in all major operational units and functions to identify their strengths and weaknesses and for corporate managers to analyze competitors' strengths and weaknesses, industry trends, and merge the operational plans. Involvement in such activities had the effect of participants discovering the discrepancy (need for change) as well as enhancing efficacy through developing the plans necessary to capitalize on the opportunities available in the marketplace.

The Global Awareness Program. To further emphasize the increased competitiveness facing the company, the Global Awareness Program was conceived. This program, initiated in 1986, involved sending groups of employees drawn from various levels and functions to visit companies operating in Japan and Korea. The program was designed to allow employees to observe firsthand the nature of the competition they faced as well as build confidence that Whirlpool could implement the same processes. It was hoped that the experience would lead them to conclude that the changes being advocated by Whirlpool leaders were indeed appropriate. Furthermore, the fact that their competitors were operating in this manner was intended to transmit the message "if they can do it, so can we."

In addition to offering an opportunity for active participation by a subgroup of employees, the Global Awareness Program was implemented on the assumption that the participants would return and share their discoveries with their peers. Though an appreciation for the potential of social synergy was evident in several of Whirlpool's readiness interventions, this is perhaps best illustrated with the Global Awareness Program. First, specially selected subgroups (from the lowest to the highest levels in the hierarchy) were formed to participate. Then, these participants were expected to exercise their personal influence and create readiness for change. For example, discussion groups involving participants and nonparticipating co-workers were established. Furthermore, videotape technology was used to expose as many employees as possible to the program. The thirteen-minute videotape describing the program and capturing the thoughts of participants (Global Awareness Program, 1986) could be viewed not only by those who were absent at the live presentations but could be viewed in peer groups without supervisors being present.

The 75th Anniversary Celebration and Show. To celebrate the company's seventy-fifth anniversary in 1986, an elaborate Broadway-style stage production was developed. The show traveled to company locations throughout the United States and played to packed houses of employees. In addition to celebrating the company's history, the show had an implicit efficacy message for all employees. Throughout the production, several points bearing on readiness for change were emphasized: (1) Whirlpool has succeeded, and can succeed in the future, against the odds; (2) change and aggressiveness were the bedrock of the company's early history; and (3) Whirlpool cares about its people and will take care of them. These messages were not explicitly stated, but they were under the surface awaiting self-discovery and self-insight by the members of the audience.

Management of External Information Sources

External sources of information used by Whirlpool to help mold readiness consisted of increased coverage of the company's operations in business periodicals and a diagnostic analysis by a well-known consulting firm.

Business Periodical Publicity. In contrast to the traditional low-key approach taken at Whirlpool, Sparks and Whitwam made an effort to increase company coverage in the business media. This visibility effort coupled with the degree of change and increase in competitive activities by Whirlpool resulted in increased coverage and exposure. For example, during the period 1983–1990, the number of magazine articles (not including the *Wall Street Journal*) mentioning Whirlpool increased almost threefold from the average of the previous ten years. *Business Week* and *Fortune* published articles about the company's change efforts. In addition to this coverage, Whirlpool employees were constantly exposed to media bearing on issues of readiness. For example, articles regarding the company's activities and broader industry trends were routinely copied and distributed among managers.

The McKinsey and Company Structure Study. In 1987, after Whitwam's move to CEO, the consulting firm of McKinsey and Company analyzed Whirlpool's structure. Several observations were offered about the inadequacies of the current structure, and resulted in a recommended major reorganization. The details of this study remained unannounced until presented by Whitwam in the New Structure Speech described below. When released, the report served to provide an important message regarding the need for change.

Persuasive Communication

In addition to the sharing of knowledge about their overseas experiences by Global Awareness Program participants described above, several other internally generated persuasive communication efforts are notable. The majority of these efforts involved instrumental, high-profile speeches and spoken and written statements of vision.

The New Vision Speech. Probably the most visible example of persuasive communication was the New Vision Speech, personally delivered in 1986, twenty-nine times in thirteen different locations to approximately fifty-five hundred employees. A fifty-two-minute videotape (New Vision Speech, 1986) of the speech was also made so that all employees could view it as desired. The New Vision Speech was compelling for two reasons: it was the most comprehensive statement of the need for change, plan for change, and encouragement for change yet offered, and the organization's leaders had expended a great deal of time and effort to share it as widely and personally as possible.

Simply stated, the focus of the new vision message was the need for change at Whirlpool with references to other successful large-scale change efforts. Two significant external contextual factors were cited to support the need for change. First, the increase in foreign competition was described. It was noted that imports in the appliance industry had increased 400% from 1982 to 1986. Second, it was noted that the consolidation among domestic appliance manufacturers had resulted in four fierce competitors, namely, Whirlpool, Maytag, GE, and Electrolux.

Part of the message devoted to efficacy was a brief history of how Whirlpool had successfully experienced change in the past by evolving from one product (a washing machine in 1911) to the multiple product company of 1986. Furthermore, the much celebrated Chrysler Corporation turnaround was used as an example to build efficacy.

The New Structure Speech. At the February 1988 Corporate Quarterly Review (which was attended by most officers, directors, and managers), Whitwam (New Structure Speech, 1988) stressed that the old structure was not permitting Whirlpool to be competitive. Although he did not explicitly report the company's performance, his audience was aware that 1987 company performance was below projections (Zellner, 1988). Whitwam referred to the diagnostic analysis conducted by McKinsey, thus providing additional support for the impending reorganization.

Whitwam explained the company was to reorganize around the strategic business unit concept. The intended result of this reorganization was to increase accountability and stimulate a sense of ownership throughout the company, push decision making closer to the marketplace, and improve operating effectiveness and efficiency. After describing the benefits of the new structure, he challenged Whirlpool employees, telling them the company needed their patience, support, and cooperation. His determination to succeed was reflected in his exclamation that Whirlpool would not fail in the bitterly contested marketplace.

READINESS ASSESSMENT

An important part of Whirlpool's change efforts has been an attempt to track the progress of change and assess the degree of readiness and resistance to change. Specifically, Sparks and Whitwam commissioned assessments of the attitudes of the company's leadership regarding these issues. These assessments were conducted by a team of university-based researchers who surveyed the opinions of the top four levels of management throughout the organization. These assessments were used to guide the interventions designed to create readiness for large-scale change. For example, the 1986 assessment suggested that not very many employees, even in the leadership cadre, fully understood the company's vision. This finding helped in the refinement of the influence strategies used to create readiness, including the New Vision Speech.

EPILOGUE

In March 1988, Whirlpool began the implementation of the SBU reorganization. In addition, in August 1988, Whirlpool completed the negotiations for a new joint venture with N. V. Philips Gloeilampenfabricken of the Netherlands to produce and market appliances in Europe, thus becoming the world's largest global competitor in the home appliance industry. Although the home appliance industry has been sluggish, due to the nationwide downturn in housing construction, Whirlpool has been described several times in the business media as a company aggressively positioning itself to meet the challenges of a slowed domestic economy and to take advantage of the economic unification of Europe (e.g., Woodruff & Kapner, 1991).

CONCLUSION

This chapter has emphasized the importance of creating readiness as a precursor to organizational change and examined the influence strategies available to help generate readiness. Some further implications for, and contributions to, the management of organizational change are summarized below.

First, the readiness concept complements previous contributions made by Lawrence (1954), Kotter and Schlesinger (1979), and others regarding resistance to change. The potential causes of resistance should be appreciated in designing the discrepancy and efficacy content of the readiness message and in selecting the strategies for creating readiness. The findings from mass communications research are useful in understanding that individual and cultural differences are influential in the response of the target group to readiness efforts. This information can be coupled with the traditional causes of resistance (e.g., lack of trust) in designing readiness programs to address the pertinent issues in eliciting the necessary support to accomplish successful change.

Second, the readiness model suggests the importance of building readiness within the context facing the organization. For example, Whirlpool's readiness efforts, begun in 1983, were not a response to an immediate crisis but rather to anticipated challenges. Beer and Walton (1987) and Pettigrew (1987) emphasize the role of contextual factors in bringing about change. It is apparent from the Whirlpool experience that company leaders were very deliberate in incorporating the appropriate contextual factors in the message to communicate discrepancy and efficacy information.

Third, decisions about implementing readiness programs should be guided by the urgency of the change and the extent to which employees are ready for the needed change. By conceptualizing high and low urgency to implement needed organizational change in combination with high and low readiness for change, four generic readiness programs (i.e., aggressive, crisis, maintenance, and quick response) were described. This typology of readiness programs is useful because it describes various scenarios faced by change agents. Within the constraints imposed by time limitations and the readiness challenge, a change agent can understand the practicalities of readiness creation.

Fourth, the detailed description of Whirlpool's aggressive readiness program demonstrated the full complement of strategies available to change agents. A change agent can use this program as a basis from which to extract ideas and tailor a readiness program for another organization.

Fifth, this chapter argues for the active creation of readiness. Recognizing the importance of readiness, some authors have argued that change agents may direct their initial efforts to areas where organization members are ready (cf. Beer & Walton, 1987; Pond et al., 1984). The framework presented in this chapter makes a case for identifying where change is needed, and then designing a readiness program to influence the appropriate beliefs, attitudes, and intentions so that changes can be successfully implemented. Instruments designed to assess readiness can then be administered to determine the effectiveness of readiness activities. New strategies can be implemented, and messages transmitted through existing strategies can be modified to achieve the readiness intended. The creation of readiness is not necessarily a prechange concern only. Readiness must be maintained throughout the process of large-scale change, particularly since such change is composed of smaller changes that are ongoing. A single initial creation-of-readiness effort may not be adequate to maintain the required levels of readiness throughout the duration of the change process. Thus, employees need to be made ready and readiness efforts should be conducted as needed throughout the change effort.

Finally, the concepts presented in this chapter can be extended to include other change applications. For example, readiness can be aimed at the individual level, taking on more of the appearances of coaching and counseling. That is, a primary change agent, such as a CEO or some key officer, may need to ready other top officers so that they can become effective change agents for the organization as a whole.

The topic of readiness represents a rudimentary issue in the management of change, and as presented here illustrates the need for further refinement in the planned change process. The implications of overlooking the importance of readiness may very well be that an appropriate intervention may not produce the intended organization changes because organization members are simply not ready (cf. Pasmore & Fagans, 1992). It is hoped that this chapter will stimulate change agents to consciously think about and plan readiness interventions. Furthermore, urgency and readiness are concepts whose values were discussed in relative terms. Currently, the relativity of these concepts must be determined by the change agent. However, more research under conditions permitting experimental control may provide useful findings and needed guidance for the design and implementation of readiness programs.

References

Armenakis, A., Field, H., & Holley, W. Guidelines for overcoming empirically identified evaluation problems of organizational development change agents. *Human Relations*, 1976, *129*, 1147–1161.

Armenakis, A., Mossholder, K., & Harris, S. Diagnostic bias in organizational consultation. *Omega: The International Journal of Management Science*, 1990, *18*(6), 161–179.

Bandura, A. Self-efficacy: Toward a unifying theory of behavioral change. *Psychological Review*, 1977, *84*, 194–215.

Bandura, A. Self-efficacy mechanism in human agency. *American Psychologist*, 1982, *37*(2), 122–147.

Bandura, A. *Social foundations of thought and action: A social-cognitive view*. Englewood Cliffs, NJ: Prentice Hall, 1986.

Barrett, A., & Cammann, C.Transitioning to change: Lessons from NSC. In J. R. Kimberly and R. E. Quinn (Eds.), *Managing organizational transitions*. Homewood, IL: Richard D. Irwin, 1984, pp. 218–239.

Bartlem, C., & Locke, E. The Coch and French study: A critique and reinterpretation. *Human Relations*, 1981, *34*(7), 555–566.

Beckhard, R., & Harris, R. *Organizational transitions: Managing complex change*. Reading, MA: Addison-Wesley Publishing Company, 1987.

Beer, M., & Walton, A. Organization change and development. *Annual Review of Psychology*, 1987, *38*, 339–367.

Bennis, W., & Nanus, B. *Leaders: The strategies for taking charge*. New York: Harper & Row, 1985.

Bushe, G. Developing cooperative labor-management relations in unionized factories: A multiple case study of quality circles and parallel organizations within joint quality of work life projects. *Journal of Applied Behavioral Science*, 1988, *24*(2), 129–150.

Coch, L., & French, J. Overcoming resistance to change. *Human Relations*, 1948, *1*(4), 512–532.

DeFleur, M., & Ball-Rokeach, S. *Theories of mass communication*. New York: Longman, 1989.

Eden, D., & Kinnar, J. Modeling Galatea: Boosting self-efficacy to increase volunteering. *Journal of Applied Psychology*, 1991, *76*, 770–780.

Fishbein, M., & Azjen, I. *Belief, attitude, intention, and behavior: An introduction to theory and research*. Reading, MA: Addison-Wesley Publishing Company, 1975.

Fox, D., Ellison, R., & Keith, K., Human resource management: An index and its relationship to readiness for change. *Public Personnel Management*, 1988, *17*(3), 297–302.

Gardner, G. Workers' participation: A critical evaluation of Coch and French. *Human Relations*, 1977, *30*(12), 1071–1078.

Gist, M. Self-efficacy: Implications for organizational behaviour and human resource management. *Academy of Management Review*, 1987, *12*(3), 472–485.

Gist, M., Schwoerer, C., & Rosen, B. Effects of alternative training methods on self-efficacy and performance in computer software training. *Journal of Applied Psychology*, 1989, *74*(6), 884–891.

Global Awareness Program (Videotape). Benton Harbor, MI: Whirlpool Corporation, 1986.

Griffin, R. Toward an integrated theory of task design. In L. L. Cummings and B. M. Staw (Eds.), *Research in organizational behavior* (Vol. 9). Greenwich, CT: JAI Press, 1987, pp. 79–120.

Kanter, R. *The change masters*. New York: Simon and Schuster, 1983.

Katz, D., & Kahn, R. *The social psychology of organization*. New York: John Wiley, 1978.

Kirton, M. Adaptors and innovators in organizations. *Human Relations*, 1980, *3*, 213–224.

Kisler, G. *The change riders*. Reading, MA: Addison-Wesley Publishing Company, 1991.

Kotter, J., & Schlesinger, L. Choosing strategies for change. *Harvard Business Review*, 1979, *57*(2), 106–114.

Lawrence, P. How to deal with resistance to change. *Harvard Business Review*, 1954, *32*(3), 49–57.

Lengel, R., & Daft, R. The selection of communication media as an executive skill. *Academy of Management Executive*, 1988, *2*(3), 225–232.

Lewin, K. *Field theory in social science*. New York: Harper and Row, 1951.

McCall, M., & Bobko, P. Research methods in the service of discovery. In M. Dunnette and L. Hough (Eds.), *Handbook of industrial and organizational psychology* (Vol. 1). Palo Alto, CA: Consulting Psychologists Press, 1990, pp. 381–418.

Nadler, D., & Tushman, M. Organizational frame bending: Principles for managing reorientation. *Academy of Management Executive*, 1989, *3*(3), 194–204.

New Structure Speech (Videotape). Benton Harbor, MI: Whirlpool Corporation, 1986.

New Vision Speech (Videotape). Benton Harbor, MI: Whirlpool Corporation, 1988.

Pasmore, W., & Fagans, M. Participation, individual development, and organizational change: A review and synthesis. *Journal of Management*, 1992, *18*, 375–397.

Pettigrew, A. Context and action in transforming the firm. *Journal of Management Studies*, 1987, *24*(6), 649–670.

Pond, S., Armenakis, A., & Green, S. The importance of employee expectations in organizational diagnosis. *Journal of Applied Behavioral Science*, 1984, *20*, 167–180.

Sackett, P., & Larson, J. Research strategies and tactics in industrial and organizational psychology. In M. Dunnette & L. Hough (Eds.), *Handbook of industrial and organizational psychology* (Vol. 1). Palo Alto, CA: Consulting Psychologists Press, 1990, pp. 419–490.

Schaffer, R. Productivity improvement strategy: Make success the building block. *Management Review*, 1981, *70*, 46–52.

Schein, E. Personal change through interpersonal relationships. In W. Bennis, J. Van Maanen, E. Schein, & F. Steele (Eds.), *Essays in interpersonal dynamics*. Homewood, IL: The Dorsey Press, 1979, pp. 129–162.

Smelser, N. *Theory of collective behavior*. New York: Free Press, 1963.

Spector, B. From bogged down to fired up: Inspiring organizational change. *Sloan Management Review*, Summer 1989, 29–34.

Stewart, T. A heartland industry takes on the world. *Fortune*, 1990, *121*(6), 110–112.

Thompson, H. Consulting for results. *Business Horizons*, 1981, *24*(6), 62–65.

Turner, A. Consulting is more than giving advice. *Harvard Business Review*, 1982, *60*(5), 120–129.

VanMaanen, J., & Barley, S. Cultural organization: Fragments of a theory. In P. J. Frost, L. F. Moore, M. R. Louis, C. C. Lundberg, & J. Martin (Eds.), *Organizational culture*. Beverly Hills, CA: Sage, 1985, pp. 31–54.

Warren, D. Managing in crisis: Nine principles for successful transition. In J. R. Kimberly and R. E. Quinn (Eds.), *Managing organizational transitions*. Homewood, IL: Richard D. Irwin, 1984, pp. 85–106.

Woodruff, D., & Kapner, F. Whirlpool goes on a world tour. *Business Week*, June 3, 1991, 99–100.

Zellner, W. A tough market has Whirlpool in a spin. *Business Week*, May 2, 1988, 121–122.

CHAPTER THIRTY-FOUR

Training and Development

W. Warner Burke (1982)

T he primary target of interventions in training and development for OD objectives is management. Training programs and job rotation are typical. Much of OD begins with management training, usually with development of professional skills but sometimes with a personal focus as well. This latter focus has been significant in the growth of OD. Many of OD's roots are associated with individually focused interventions, T-group or sensitivity training, Maslow's hierarchy of needs theory, and individual assessment. In the early days of OD (late 1950s and early 1960s), it was difficult to distinguish what was beginning to be called organization development from sensitivity training, because the people who are considered the pioneers of OD—such as Chris Argyris, Richard Beckhard, Warren Bennis, Robert R. Blake, Lee Bradford, Paul Buchanan, Sheldon Davis, Charles Ferguson, Murray Horwitz, Douglas McGregor, Herbert Shepard, and Robert Tannenbaum—were all heavily involved in sensitivity training at the time. For early OD, the T-group was the primary intervention. This type of training evolved into what we now know as team building. I hasten to add, however, that team building is *not* a team T-group.

SENSITIVITY TRAINING

Sensitivity training may still be considered an OD intervention, but it is rarely used as such today. The change in emphasis over the decades has been considerable. When sensitivity training was brought into organizations as a developmental technique and conducted with family units—a boss and the subordinates who reported directly to the boss—the developmental objective became background and internal politics became foremost. It is difficult to tell people exactly what you may think and feel, especially about them, when you know (1) that you will have to continue working with them after the training and (2) that people, particularly bosses, tend to remember the feedback they receive, especially when it is considered negative. It is only natural to fear retribution. Organization development is still a taboo term in some organizations today because of bad experiences with sensitivity training fifteen or more years ago.

The place of sensitivity training in organization development now is marginal. Most OD practitioners who recommend sensitivity training to their clients suggest that the people involved go to a public program away from the organization, with program members who are strangers at the outset. The risks are thus lessened, of course, and the individual can feel freer to experiment with his or her behavior and to learn therefrom. The T-group learning experience should be treated as self-development without a requirement that it *prove* to be useful for the organization. Such an outcome cannot be proved anyway (J. P. Campbell and Dunnette, 1968). Whether sensitivity training will make better managers of people is yet to be determined. There is evidence, however, that it does make an individual difference (Beer, 1976; Bunker, 1965; Bunker and Knowles, 1967; J. P. Campbell and Dunnette, 1968; Lieberman, Yalom, and Miles, 1973). People learn, for example, (1) to listen to others more actively and with empathy, (2) to express their feelings more clearly, (3) to be more sensitive to others' feelings and needs, and (4) to understand more about their impact on other people.

For OD purposes, then, sensitivity training can be used to increase people's general level of interpersonal competence. This *may* have value organizationally where people must work together more collaboratively; where potential for conflict is high, such as in a matrix organization, and creative use of conflict is needed; where team building will become a major intervention for a number of people, in that prior experience with sensitivity training can expedite the objectives of team building (Crockett, 1977, 1970); and where employees must deal sensitively with customers, the general public, or fellow employees—for example, airline ticket agents, health care delivery specialists, recruiters, and counselors.

In addition to sensitivity training, some other training or educational modes and techniques may accomplish many of these same objectives for self-development. These other techniques include Gestalt therapy and training, the Managerial Grid Seminar, and Tavistock training. A brief explanation of these other alternatives follows. (There are others, of course, such as the Managerial Effectiveness Program of the American Management Association, the Levinson Institute's program, and leadership training at the Menninger Foundation and at the Center for Creative Leadership, to name a few. These programs provide some variation on one or more of the themes that populate sensitivity training or the three alternatives listed here.)

GESTALT THERAPY AND TRAINING

I have designated this approach to self-development both therapy and training because the distinction is not clear. Sensitivity training also encompasses both aspects, as there is not much difference between "getting better" and learning something new about oneself. The roots of sensitivity training are in education, however, whereas the basis of Gestalt training is both in Gestalt psychology and in a particular approach to therapy. *Gestalt* is a German word that translates roughly as "wholeness" or "totality." Since there is no precise translation, the word has been retained in English usage. Gestalt also implies the notion that a whole is something more than the sum of its parts. In Gestalt therapy, therefore, the patient is treated as a total person, a total entity, rather than by a singular analysis of his or her parts—personal history, current physical condition, attitudes about sex, or relationship with father or mother. These parts are important only as they relate to the whole—for example, how the personal history affects the person's functioning less than optimally today.

The Gestalt approach to self-development emphasizes, among other things, (1) integration of mind and body; (2) increased clarity about one's personal wants, values, and goals; (3) greater awareness of self, especially one's feelings and impact on others; and (4) resolution or completion of unfinished business. One is not whole until past experiences—an interpersonal conflict that continues to nag, the death of a friend or relative that continues to hurt, a past failure that one fears might be repeated—are resolved in some way. For more detailed discussion of Gestalt therapy, see Polster and Polster (1973) and some of the writings by the founder of this approach, Fritz Perls (Perls, Hefferline, and Goodman, 1951; Perls, 1969).

Stan Herman has advocated that OD practitioners help their clients resolve core personal and organizational problems by encouraging them (1) to accept and experience the full range of behavior—good and bad, positive and negative, love and hate, dominant and submissive—so that behavior will be based more on reality than on symptoms of problems and unauthenticity; (2) to become more aware of how they stop themselves from getting what they want (curbing their power); and (3) to stick with difficult personal or interpersonal problems until they have been resolved in some fashion (Herman, 1972). Herman argues that the more OD practitioners help their clients with these kinds of issues, the more effective they will be as employees and managers and the more effective the organization will be (Herman, 1977; Herman and Korenich, 1977).

The value of the Gestalt approach to self-development is that it emphasizes the total person. Whether this self-development pays off for the organization, as Herman argues, is yet to be determined. Many practitioners in OD are nevertheless attracted to the Gestalt approach because it treats the person as a total system in much the same manner as OD considers the organization a total system (Burke, 1980), and because it emphasizes personal growth and development—a strong value underlying OD.

THE MANAGERIAL GRID SEMINAR

Based on Blake and Mouton's (1978) model of managerial styles, the managerial grid, the seminar is a five-day training program, usually residential, that (1) teaches the model as a way of conceptualizing various managerial styles, with the emphasis on five primary ones; (2) provides opportunities for participants to receive feedback from questionnaires and from fellow participants about their relative use of the five primary styles; and (3) advocates one style, the 9,9 participative approach, as best.

The grid seminar is similar to sensitivity training and Gestalt therapy in that participants give and receive feedback from one another in the training group. The seminar differs from other training programs in that it is a more structured approach, relying heavily on the model, a tight design schedule, and questionnaires and other learning instruments, such as film.

The grid seminar is individually oriented (the training group is more of a vehicle for learning than a learning objective itself) and provides an opportunity for self-development in that a participant may learn how far he or she is from being a 9,9 manager and can plan personal change objectives accordingly.

For OD purposes, a grid seminar may be used as phase one of an overall grid organization development effort as a preliminary step in general team building that is not grid-focused, as a training intervention for management development in general, or as an intervention to facilitate an organization's movement toward participative management.

THE TAVISTOCK APPROACH

The Tavistock approach to training, like sensitivity training, emphasizes the small group. The Tavi method, as it is sometimes called, is different from sensitivity training in some significant ways, however. In a Tavistock group there is more emphasis on authority and leadership as the primary focus of learning, and the role of the trainer differs considerably from that of T-group trainers.

The Tavistock approach gets its name from the institute in London where its creators—Eric Trist, A. K. Rice, C. Sofer, and their colleagues—were located at the time it was developed in the late 1950s. The first training conference of its kind was held in England by the Tavistock Institute and the University of Leicester in September 1957 (Trist and Sofer, 1959). Influenced by the theories of Kurt Lewin and Wilfred Bion, as well as by the training methodology of the National Training Laboratories (NTL) Institute in the United States, the primary emphasis at that time was on group behavior. Over the next decade, Rice (1965) gradually shifted the learning focus to issues of authority and leadership and to organizations, not just small groups. Bion's (1961) theory about the task group and the basic assumption group also became more influential.

Whereas in sensitivity training the trainer sits in with the group and interacts personally with group members (some more than others, of course), the Tavi "educator," as he or she is called, does not become a part of the group. The educator often sits outside the group as an observer and outside commentator. This role outside the boundary of the group, whether the boundary is physical or psychological, causes a vacuum of authority and leadership within the group. How group members react to this vacuum becomes the prime focus of activity and learning. "The leader or leadership in a group can be thought of as representing or embodying the function of the group, especially its major function or primary task . . . [that is] that task which an organization or institution must perform in order to survive" (Rioch, 1965, p. 7).

The A. K. Rice Institute in the United States is the major organization providing this type of training on this side of the Atlantic. The Rice Institute educators have patterned their approach after A. K. Rice's work at the Tavistock Institute. Each year educators from both institutes work together to insure consistency and cross-fertilization.

This type of training obviously can be used to help people learn more about leadership, especially in the context of authority issues. The training is also useful for helping group members differentiate behavior that facilitates task accomplishment from behavior that impedes. For more information on this form of education, see *Group Relations Reader,* edited by Colman and Bexton (1975).

SUMMARY OF SELF-DEVELOPMENT PROGRAMS

The types of training I have covered so far in this training and development section are by no means all that is available. They represent, in my opinion, the primary programs for self-development. Other programs that might be considered in the same domain are more specific to organizational tasks or functions, such as training in management by objectives (MBO), which may aid in self-development but only as a by-product, not as the primary objective.

The programs covered so far typically exist outside the organization; managers usually must go away for these types of training. I shall now turn to programs that are internal to the organization and that are tailor-made or specifically designed for the people of a given organization—usually the managers.

TAILOR-MADE TRAINING AND DEVELOPMENT

Many large organizations, particularly those in business and industry, design and conduct their own training and development programs. These programs may consist of supervisory or sales training, for example, and rely exclusively on the training staff of the organization, or they may be for middle management, conducted by both the organization's staff trainers and outside, contracted trainers. The more the training concerns managers and executives, the more likely it is that outside instructors will be used. These in-house training and development programs take a variety of forms, ranging in length from a day to two or three weeks and covering a wide array of topics. Some companies' training departments publish annual catalogs of their program offerings. The variety of training in organizations is thus considerable, and the resources devoted to training are immense, particularly in some large corporations.

The kind of training and development most relevant for organization development is that conducted for managers and executives, especially the programs that concentrate on topics concerned with the management of people. These programs have usually been designed as a result of a needs analysis. The training staff conducts interviews with a sample of managers in the organization, asking them about their needs and preferences regarding their further development as managers or executives. After summarizing and analyzing these interview data, the training staff designs a program based on the needs and preferences mentioned most frequently. The resultant program typically consists of such topics as communication skills, performance appraisal, group dynamics or team development, managing meetings, business strategy and policy, delegation, time management, management by objectives, motivation, leadership, finance for the nonfinancial manager, and stress management. These topics are loosely coupled for the program design, and learning methods usually include combinations of lecture, case study and discussion, role-play, group problem solving, films, and perhaps a management simulation game.

A few organizations recently have taken a different approach to the design and conduct of management training and development. One such organization, Citicorp—the largest banking institution in the United States, with worldwide operations—launched a unique training program, "Managing People," early in 1977. Although a formal needs analysis was not conducted, the corporation's top management was concerned that, along with their rapid growth in the late

1960s and early 1970s, the increasing strain on managers to continue to produce profits and adapt to rapid change had caused mounting people problems in the organization. More and more people were feeling like cogs in a (money) machine. Since it was accepted by top management that people were the organization's most important resource, particular attention had to be paid to managing this resource more effectively. William Spencer, president of the corporation at that time, publicly stated in a filmed introduction to Citicorp's program: "The management of people is probably a greater skill mandated than individual brilliance. Even the most brilliant person, if there is little or no ability to manage people, is a lost cause in our operation."

Using the Forum Corporation of Boston as outside consultants, particularly George Litwin, the education and research division of Citicorp, headed by Henry Brenner, conducted a study (1) to identify the best management talent within the organization, (2) to determine the specific set of management practices that seemed to distinguish them from average managers, and (3) to design a training program based on these superior practices. A criterion group of managers was thus established by asking senior executives to identify subordinate managers within their respective groups who were outstanding and would most likely be taking their places as senior executives within the next decade. Thirty-nine such managers were identified. The researchers then asked these same senior executives to identify thirty-nine additional managers within their groups who were satisfactory managers but not as effective as the first group. The researchers next arranged for 353 subordinates of these seventy-eight managers (thirty-nine in the A group—outstanding—and thirty-nine in the B group—satisfactory) to rate their bosses on fifty-nine management practices culled from a list of hundreds. The ratings were done with five-point Likert scales. Some of the practices rated were

- Your manager communicates high personal standards informally—in conversation, personal appearance, and so forth.
- Your manager tries to make the best use of staff members' skills and abilities when making assignments.
- Your manager works with staff members (subordinates) to reach mutual agreement on their performance appraisals.
- Your manager uses recognition and praise—aside from pay—to reward excellent performance.
- The work-group meetings your manager conducts serve to increase trust and mutual respect among the work-group members.

The A group was rated significantly higher than the B group on twenty-two of the fifty-nine practices—regardless of their management situation in the corporation. Another eight practices differentiated between the two groups, but only under structured conditions of management, such as in a back-office operation of check processing. The A group practices were then used as the basis for design of the training program. Since this A group had been identified as outstanding managers, and since subordinate ratings had further identified some of the specific practices that these managers did exceptionally well, it followed (at least to Citicorp's top management) that the larger population of managers should be trained to adopt this special set of people-management practices. Prior to participation in the program, managers are rated by their subordinates on the selected practices. The five-day program then consists of training on clusters of these practices, with each training day devoted to one cluster. The five clusters are (1) getting commitment to goals and standards, (2) coaching, (3) appraising performance, (4) compensating and rewarding, and (5) building a team for continuity of performance. Training techniques include case method, role practice, group problem-solving and decision-making exercises, and occasional short lectures. For each day of the program, the managers receive a computer printout of their ratings by their subordinates on that day's cluster of practices. This feedback for the manager is the most powerful part of the training program, as managers focus their learning and improvement objectives on the practices that received the lowest ratings. In its first three years, some two thousand Citicorp managers went through the program. It continued to be popular and highly valued among Citicorp managers for many years.

Other companies, such as Firemen's Fund Insurance, have designed management training programs along the same lines as Citicorp's. Yet other organizations, such as the National Aeronautics and Space Administration, have designed and conducted successful management development programs and then later launched studies to determine profiles of their most competent administrators and managers. In such cases, the results of the competency studies are used (1) to refine the already existing training program, (2) to modify the performance appraisal system, and (3) to improve existing human resource planning systems, especially those for managers.

In this section on training and development we have explored development activities that consist of training and education, but we should not lose perspective. By far the most popular and widely used management development activity is job rotation (Digman, 1978). Providing a variety of managerial experiences across the primary functions of an organization is still considered the most important activity for developing general managers and executives.

References

Beer, M. 1976. "The Technology of Organization Development." In *Handbook of Industrial and Organizational Psychology*, ed. M. D. Dunnette, pp. 937–93. Chicago: Rand McNally.

Bion, W. R. 1961. *Experience in Groups*. New York: Basic Books.

Blake, R. R., and Mouton, J. S. 1978. *The New Managerial Grid*. Houston: Gulf.

Bunker, D. R. 1965. "Individual Applications of Laboratory Training." *Journal of Applied Behavioral Sciences* 1: 131–48.

Bunker, D. R., and Knowles, E. S. 1967. "Comparison of Behavioral Changes Resulting from Human Relations Training Laboratories of Different Lengths." *Journal of Applied Behavioral Sciences* 3: 505–24.

Burke, W. W. 1980. "System Theory, Gestalt Therapy, and Organization Development." In *Systems Theory for Organization Development*, ed. T. G. Cummings. Sussex, England: Wiley.

Campbell, J. P., and Dunnette, M. D. 1968. "Effectiveness of T Group Experiences in Managerial Training and Development." *Psychological Bulletin* 70: 73–104.

Colman, A. D., and Bexton, W. H. eds. 1975. *Group Relations Reader*. Washington, D.C.: A. K. Rice Institute.

Crockett, W. J. 1970. "Team Building-One Approach to Organizational Development." *Journal of Applied Behavioral Sciences* 6: 291–306.

Crockett, W. J. 1977. "Introducing Change to a Government Agency." In *Failures in Organization Development and Change*, eds. P. H. Mirvis and D. N. Berg, pp. 111–47. New York: Wiley.

Digman, L. A. 1978. "How Well-Managed Organizations Develop Their Executives." *Organizational Dynamics* 7(2): 63–80.

Herman, S. M. 1972. "A Gestalt Orientation to Organization Development." In *New Technologies in Organizational Development*, vol. 1, ed. W. W. Burke, pp. 69–89. San Diego: University Associates.

Herman, S. M. 1977. "The Shadow of Organization Development." In *Current Issues and Strategies in Organization Development*, ed. W. W. Burke, pp. 133–154. New York: Human Sciences Press.

Herman, S. M., and Korenich, M. 1977. *Authentic Management: A Gestalt Orientation to Organizations and Their Development*. Reading, Mass.: Addison-Wesley.

Lieberman, M. A., Yalom, I. D., and Miles, M. B. 1973. *Encounter Groups: First Facts*. New York: Basic Books.

Perls, F. S. 1969. *Gestalt Therapy Verbatim*. Lafayette, Calif.: Real People Press.

Perls, F. S., Hefferline, R. F., and Goodman, P. 1951. *Gestalt Therapy*. New York: Dell.

Polster, E., and Polster, M. 1973. *Gestalt Therapy Integrated: Contours of Theory and Practice*. New York: Brunner/Mazel.

Rice, A. K. 1965. *Learning for Leadership*. London: Tavistock.

Rioch, M. J. 1965. "Group Relations: Rational and Technique." In *Group Relations Reader*, ed. A. D. Colman and W. H. Bexton. Washington, D.C.: A. K. Rice Institute.

Trist, E. L., and Sofer, C. 1959. *Explorations in Group Relations*. Leicester University Press.

CHAPTER THIRTY-FIVE

Coaching Leaders in Transition

Lessons from the Field[1]

Robert Witherspoon
Mark D. Cannon (2004)

F ew organizational changes offer more upside potential—and downside risk—than senior-level leadership transitions. Whether leaders are newly appointed CEOs or group leaders just promoted from within, they are expected to learn fast, transition smoothly, and produce results. The actions these individuals take during their first few months in their new positions can have a major impact on their success or failure. Powerful impressions are formed in the first ninety days. Yet new leaders often lack clear, specific, actionable advice on how to take charge in a new leadership role[2] (Argyris, 2000).

Stepping into a new leadership role can be one of the most challenging times in an executive's[3] career (Ciampa & Watkins, 1999). Transitions are pivotal, in part because everyone is expecting change to occur. They are also periods of uncertainty and great vulnerability for new leaders (Betof & Harwood, 1992; Garnsey & Roberts, 1996). Typically, when an existing business appoints a new leader, both the new leader and the staff are unfamiliar with each other, and, as a result, they often waste time in trial-by-error learning that impedes organizational effectiveness. New leaders often face a number of formidable challenges in the first few months, including the need to:

- Clarify the expectations of key stakeholders—particularly if goals are confusing, conflicting, or unclear
- Learn a new environment—especially if the leader has just been brought in from the outside

- Address resistance and anxiety—especially if the leader is charged with leading a major change initiative
- Build new working relationships between peers and subordinates—particularly if others feel passed over for the position the leader now holds
- Develop detailed knowledge about the new role—especially for a leader new to the function and/or the business

The topic of how to handle these transitions is important, because transition itself is a recurring feature of most executive careers. According to Watkins (2000, p. 1), ''By the time he or she reaches the top, the typical CEO of a Fortune 100 company has made seven major transitions—moves between functions, business units, or companies. But for every successful CEO, there are many talented managers who stumble along the way, damaging their careers and the organizations they were charged to lead.''

For organizations these issues are multiplied, as hundreds or even thousands of managers transition into new jobs each year, creating a growing need for executive coaching.

An underlying problem, however, is that although the practice of executive coaching has been popular for some time and continues to grow rapidly, the theory and empirical research on the subject are still in their infancy (see, e.g., Kampa-Kokesch & Anderson, 2001). There is significant need for further clarification regarding definition (Kilburg, 1996) and standards (Brotman, 1998; Diedrich & Killburg, 2001), purpose, techniques and methodologies (Hall, Otazo, & Hollenbeck, 1999), comparison with counseling and therapy (Hart, Blattner, & Leipsic, 2001), and possibly appropriate credentials for coaches. Moreover, Goldsmith (reported in Morse, 2002, p. 22) has argued that more attention should be given to the development of coaching specializations. He argues that many authors and consultants mistakenly treat executive coaching as if it were a single generic service, ignoring the differences across situations. Similarly, in our experience we have observed that executive coaching situations can vary significantly, and each may require a somewhat different response.

As executive coaches, for example, we are often called in to help new leaders transition effectively. We know that their challenges can be extraordinary. Further, today's organizations have very high expectations for results, and these results need to be delivered in less time than ever before (Harrison & Dunnells, 1998). So, organizations are learning that they need to call in executive coaches to help new leaders succeed. In addition, everyone is learning that leaders in transition face a special set of issues compared to other, more typical coaching situations—for instance, when coaching high potentials in succession programs or senior executives at risk of derailing. The focus of this chapter, therefore, is on a specific application of executive coaching: a way to facilitate these leadership transitions through a process we refer to as *transition coaching* for newly appointed leaders. This approach is based on our own coaching experience and field research[4] on why executives stumble in transitions and how they can be helped to succeed.

COACHING NEWLY APPOINTED LEADERS

We see transition coaching as a special application of executive coaching. Our role as coaches is to help leaders learn. To this end, our working definition of executive coaching is an *action learning process to enhance effective action and learning agility* (Witherspoon 2000, p. 167). More specifically, transition coaching is designed to help the newly appointed leader to:

- Identify critical issues that they need to address during the transition period
- Define the expectations and concerns of key stakeholders (including clients, superiors, and direct reports)
- Obtain an experienced, confidential sounding board for ideas and actions before they are implemented
- Gain an outside perspective on the organizational dynamics associated with leadership transition
- Develop an "Appointment Charter" and implement transition action plans
- Communicate more effectively up and down the organization

The basic purpose of transition coaching is to assist new leaders by helping them to quickly and effectively take charge of a new position. Although the benefits to the individual executive are clear, transition coaching can also reduce the high rate and cost of failed leadership transitions at the organizational level as well.

When individuals assume a new or different leadership role, their risk of failure may be as high as 40 percent or more, according to some research (see, e.g., Betof & Harrison, 1996). Failure is often defined as demonstrating disappointing performance, voluntarily leaving the position, or being terminated within a twelve-to-eighteen-month time period. Further, considering the low success rates associated with planned organizational change, these risks are probably even higher for new leaders charged with creating major change. These failures are costly to both new leaders and their organizations. Given the increasingly pervasive influence that leaders have on their organization at higher organizational levels, the more senior the leadership transition, the higher the cost.

Leadership Failure

Drawing on studies of leadership succession, we have some insight into the key reasons why new leaders succeed and fail. In an analysis of new leaders who underperform, for example, Ciampa and Watkins (1999, pp. 15–20) identified five key challenges that most leaders must address in order to be successful:

- Establishing new working relationships
- Managing expectations
- Acquiring needed knowledge quickly
- Juggling organizational and personal transitions
- Maintaining personal equilibrium

Similarly, in their exploration of the main reasons for failure among newly appointed leaders, Manchester Consulting (1997, cited in Johnson, 2000) found three core factors: (1) failure to build partnership with peers and subordinates (reported by 82 percent of the responding organizations); (2) being "unclear or confused" about role expectations (58 percent); and (3) a basic lack of requisite political savvy (50 percent). The top two factors listed by Manchester Consulting represent a failure to successfully meet the "establishing new working relationships" and the "managing expectations" challenges listed by Ciampa and Watkins (1999) above.

Similarly, from our own experience in coaching executives, we believe the two main reasons that new leaders often derail is because they fail to (1) successfully manage key relationships and (2) clarify expectations regarding their performance—key factors that are reflected in other research as well. Gabarro (1987), for example, reports that a poor relationship with the boss and two or more subordinates is the single most prevalent cause of failed leadership successions. Similarly, Hill (1992, p. 87) reports that building effective relationships with subordinates was "unequivocally the most difficult task" that new managers faced. These findings point to the need for new leaders to better manage key relationships, especially in terms of engaging key players early in the transition process.

The second key reason for failure has to do with confused and/or unclear expectations regarding what is expected of the leader. One of the leaders in Gabarro's (1987) study, the new president of a corporate subsidiary, was unclear about whether the main priority for his organization was to build market share or to increase profitability. From our work, it appears that one way new leaders can improve their chances of success is to confirm with their new bosses and other key stakeholders the results they expect, the specific timetable for achieving these results, and how their performance will be measured— particularly over the first year.

On the basis of our fieldwork and experience as executive coaches, we choose to focus this chapter on problems associated with confused and/or unrealistic expectations for the new leader for three reasons. First, failure to set clear expectations with key stakeholders is among the most frequent ways new leaders get into trouble. Second, working with key stakeholders to clarify expectations addresses an important aspect of the relationship-building process. Thus, clarifying expectations also helps leaders to manage key relationships and thus avoid another potential transition pitfall. Finally, if these expectations are not addressed early on, avoiding the other challenges or traps may not matter that much—the new leader would be perceived as doing "too little, too late."

Transition Coaching

To help new leaders in transition, we need a common understanding about coaching goals and roles. Otherwise there can be confusion about expectations, as well as the time and effort required in the coaching relationship. To this end, we have found the Coaching Continuum Model (Witherspoon & White, 1997) to be very helpful in clarifying the primary focus for coaching, particularly at the outset of a new coaching engagement. The basic types of coaching in this model are listed below:

- *Coaching for skills*—to focus on a client's current project or tasks
- *Coaching for performance*—to focus on a client's effectiveness in a present job
- *Coaching for development*—to focus on a client's future job responsibilities and/or career
- *Coaching for an executive's agenda*—to focus on a client's broader issues, including better business results

In skills coaching, the primary focus is typically on a specific need—say, to improve a client's interpersonal skills for the purpose of developing better peer relations—and the coaching sessions tend to focus on one issue or skill at a time. In performance coaching, the primary focus is on a broader need—to improve a client's current effectiveness—and coaching sessions often address several issues and skills simultaneously. In development coaching, the primary focus is on a future need—to prepare the client for a potential position, a leadership role, or a career move—and coaching sessions often address several issues and skills. In agenda coaching, the primary focus is often on broader business and organization needs—say, leading a major change effort, managing the enterprise, or resolving significant conflict—and coaching sessions are ongoing and highly variable, depending on the issues.

Transition coaching is a special application of agenda coaching, to help the executive realize better business results. Typical clients include CEOs and heads of a business or major business function, notably leaders in transition. In his seminal research on senior-level transitions, Gabarro (1987) identified five distinct phases that emerge when a new leader takes charge: taking hold, immersion, reshaping, consolidation, and refinement. The first two—taking hold and immersion—are focused on a new leader's orientation and learning. During the taking hold phase, which may last three to six months, the new leader must learn the new role and in many cases the new organization at a very rapid pace. Often, this phase is also characterized by making significant changes in personnel and in structure and by securing some early wins. During the immersion phase, the pace of change slows and the new leader typically focuses on gaining a deeper understanding of the organization. In the reshaping phase, the new leaders use their leaning from the previous two phases to make deeper changes in the organization and to implement new concepts and strategies. Finally, the consolidation and refinement phases involve less change and focus more on securing and fine-tuning the changes that were made in the reshaping phase.

Transition coaching is typically designed to accelerate the executive's learning associated with taking hold and immersion, thus facilitating the executive's ability to arrive more quickly at the third phase, reshaping, in which the leader begins to implement his or her own business strategy.

Transition coaching begins with recognizing the major changes that have taken place in the new leader's situation, starting with the leader's new appointment. Typically, the new leader must simultaneously learn the new situation at a rapid pace as well as make wise decisions regarding what changes to make within the first few months. The change may involve a new title, role, function, business unit, and/or company; the situation is often complicated since new leaders are typically in the midst of multiple changes. Indeed, their own career transition is often a major change for new leaders, and one that typically extends over a longer period of time as the leaders adjust gradually to their new situations.

Once major changes are recognized, transition coaching requires the executive and consultant to decide where to intervene first and then to design appropriate transition activities (e.g., charter meetings, assimilation events, feedback and coaching sessions). As such, transition coaching may center on a one-time retreat or (more likely) be an intervention that lasts from three months to more than one year, as the coach and executive navigate the taking hold and immersion phases and prepare for the reshaping phase. Transition coaching helps new leaders arrive more quickly and successfully at the reshaping phase and provides a foundation on which the reshaping, consolidation, and refinement phases can evolve more smoothly and effectively.

From our fieldwork and coaching experience, we see new leaders often needing help in four key areas:

- *Managing up:* to clarify their new charter, by understanding what their boss really wants from them—including expectations of the board if the leader is the CEO
- *Managing across:* to clarify peer expectations for the new position, particularly when the new leader depends on peers to get things done
- *Managing down:* to understand staff needs and help the leader to get to know the new people and meeting with them to answer questions they might not normally ask
- *Managing the transition:* to quickly assess their new situation and plan the strategy for taking charge in their new position

The need for this assistance stems from a variety of situational factors at play in most major transitions. For instance, as Glacel (2000)[5] explains:

- *Whenever a new individual joins a team, dynamics change.* This happens even when the new individual is highly competent, well selected, and the arrival is anticipated with position reactions. Without a focused transition effort, the ''dance'' among members takes longer and decreases productivity.
- *Individuals act from unspoken assumptions.* In the absence of well-articulated assumptions from all parties, both new and old members of the organization act in ways that are often based on differing assumptions. This may cause confusion and conflict.
- *Power relationships change.* Everyone must renegotiate and reestablish individual power according to the new member's position. Both business and interpersonal relationships dictate who is in, who is out, who is close, and who is far from the power base. This shift trickles down throughout the organization to cause confusion and decreased productivity.
- *Even the most positive of changes will cause stress for individuals and the system.* New norms and changed expectations create tension within the system. Functional expectations may remain the same, but the new individual will have different ways of expressing norms and expectations that create individual and organization stress.

In senior *leadership* transitions, these situational factors are even more important. Typically, top leaders enjoy a honeymoon period of goodwill, perhaps even relief, as they are accorded unusual latitude in their early actions. But the honeymoon is also conditional, and critical missteps can end the romance. As Bacon and Spear (2003, p. 294) explain of senior-level transitions:

> Forming alliances with the wrong people, acting on bad advice, alienating key supporters, moving so quickly as to seem precipitous or reckless or so slowly as to

seem hesitant and fearful, behaving in ways that appear inconsistent with the person the organization thought it was bringing in, managing with a style that simply doesn't fit the organization's expectations or culture—all these are among the land mines that can explode a promising start.

Absent focused assistance, the adjustments by new leaders and their group members take longer and risk frustration or even failure. However, each leadership transition is unique, depending on specific situational factors—such as the key challenges facing each executive. Therefore, the exact timeline and structure of transition coaching needs to be tailored to each client situation, as illustrated later in this chapter.[6]

At the same time, situations are not so varied that we cannot identify key themes that stand out as important to address despite these differences in situations. In our experience, clarifying expectations has been essential for success across a wide variety of settings, and that is why we have made clarifying expectations the focus of this chapter.

In summary, leadership transitions follow a set of somewhat predictable phases, as Gabarro (1987) has shown. However, at the same time, each transition is in some ways unique with its own set of challenges, hazards, and opportunities. Thus, transition coaching involves assisting new leaders to understand their special strengths and weaknesses, the distinctive threats and opportunities in the transition, and what actions would be most helpful in accelerating and increasing the effectiveness of the transition. Since the first few months of their tenure can have a major impact on success or failure, this period must be managed with particular care. Powerful impressions are formed during a leader's first ninety days, and miscues can be costly and lasting. Thus, taking proactive steps early on to understand these factors and manage them appropriately is very important.

TRANSITION COACHING PRACTICE

We tailor transition coaching to the specific needs of each new leader and the organization, as noted above. As a way of framing this process, we typically begin by exploring the context and situational factors at play in each transition, with such questions as:

- What are your new position and the business reason(s) for your appointment?
- Do you come from the outside or were you promoted from within?
- Are you a designated successor—for example, the president expected to replace a retiring CEO after a trial period?
- Are you starting with an initial mandate or beginning with a blank slate?

These questions are important as a way of exploring the executive's agenda in his or her new situation. The answers to these questions can illuminate important aspects of the context that may shape the transition coaching process.

A knowledge of these situational factors helps in clarifying the purpose and priorities for transition coaching. This knowledge also provides a foundation for determining how best to work with the leader and other key players in the organization to clarify expectations and concerns and to establish a foundation for working together productively and for communicating about important issues. Since each coaching situation is different, the underlying goal should be to foster informed choice by all relevant parties.

To illustrate, consider the design for transition coaching to support two different leaders. For one client—a newly appointed CFO of a global venture firm recruited from outside the organization and charged with upgrading the operations he would inherit—the purpose of transition coaching was fourfold:

1. To provide the new leader with a structured process to confirm the expectations surrounding the CFO's appointment

2. To assist the CFO as he started to forge effective working relationships with his new boss and other key stakeholders, thus creating a basis for continued work planning and problem solving

3. To help the CFO to get to know his new staff, and to clarify their perceptions and questions about the firm's most pressing business and organizational issues

4. To engage his staff about their questions (e.g., about him and his views as an outsider) as well as the key business challenges they would face together over the coming months

Of these objectives, the first and most critical—as well as our focus here—was to confirm the CFO's charter and to build a working relationship quickly with the new boss. This was a priority not just because the failure to clarify expectations is a key reason why new leaders derail, but also due to the several particular situational factors in this case. Specifically, the new leader was coming from outside the organization and did not have prior experience with this boss. Furthermore, although he was coming in with a mandate to upgrade the function, the specific details of what exactly that would mean had not been worked out. The new leader reasoned that, without clear expectations and an effective working relationship with the new boss, even the best-laid transition plans might go awry. Thus, developing an appropriate Appointment Charter that would clarify expectations and serve as a foundation for working effectively with the new boss was a top priority. We will describe the Appointment Charter in more detail in the next section after we introduce the second client case. Other initial transition coaching steps included a "jump start" process to streamline the assimilation of the newly appointed leader. In this case, the jump start process was a one-day program designed to provide the CFO with a forum in which he and his immediate and extended teams could develop an early understanding of their respective operating styles, communication patterns, and business priorities so that they could quickly learn to work together effectively in addressing critical business issues.

For another client—the newly appointed chief security officer (CSO) of a Fortune 500 industrial firm—the purpose of transition coaching was different. As context, this new leader was named to a new position within his company, to create an enterprisewide function across the entire business. Unlike the CFO described above, this client's function was new, with little clear precedent about goals, roles, and reporting relationships.

Particularly after September 11, 2001, the company was seeing a need for upgrading security, and the board of directors had charged senior executives with creating a new management function to identify internal and external threats before they could wreak havoc. As the company's first CSO, this newly appointed leader needed both to build an enterprisewide function and to develop and maintain a flawless operational execution. Importantly, the first task meant forging effective working relationships with people in formerly disparate security areas. Importantly as well, the second task required fostering teamwork so that these people could all function at a higher level than before.

Significantly, this new leader came from within the company (also unlike the CFO above, who was brought in from the outside) and had reported to his new boss, the CIO, in a prior position (unlike the CFO, who was new to his boss). As well, an Enterprise Security Charter was already agreed to by the board and senior management, including the CIO. As such, this client's transition to his new CSO post was already governed by a specific agreement when he accepted the promotion. Even so, we jointly examined the charter to ensure its adequacy and identify any open issues or gaps that needed to be addressed. Finally, this new leader brought with him a small intact team and did not inherit a large staff (again, unlike the CFO case above).

Given this context, the purpose of transition coaching for the newly appointed CSO was:

- To provide the new leader with confidential 360 degree feedback from his superiors (including his boss and others in senior management), his peers (particularly important, for reasons below), and his team (direct reports)
- To help the new leader leverage his key strengths and work on important weaknesses, in light of his 360 degree feedback
- To help the new leader improve his working relationships, particularly up (with senior management) and across (with peers)

For this new leader, solid peer relationships turned out to be the critical success factor in his new position (see below, ''Productive Conversations'').

The Appointment Charter

The *Appointment Charter* is a specific agreement between new leaders and their boss (and other key parties, as needed), governing the leader's transition into the job. Clarifying the Appointment Charter helps the new leader meet the ''managing expectations'' and ''establishing new working relationships'' challenges (Ciampa & Watkins, 1999) that we discussed earlier. This process includes both clarifying expectations regarding priorities, objectives, and timelines and clarifying expectations as to how the boss and new leader will work together, keep each other informed, and so forth.

In the CFO's case described above, he accepted his new position subject to a mandate negotiated before he entered the organization. This mandate involved making significant changes to upgrade the finance function. In coaching sessions after his arrival, we urged him not to presume that his initial mandate would or should remain unchanged. We suggested that an Appointment Charter be drafted—even if not a written, signed document—to clarify the mandate, set expectations, and support an evolving transition process. To this end, one of us engaged the new leader in a series of questions about his appointment, and then interviewed the new leader's direct boss separately, focusing on the same questions. The questions probed expectations, surfaced assumptions that each party may or may not have communicated to the other, and explored prospects for how the parties might work together most effectively.

The premeeting questions also prompted the boss to think through the new leader's appointment in more depth and detail. Both executives also commented that this step forced them to find ways to communicate their mutual expectations more clearly.

After the session and the interview, we drafted an Appointment Charter for review in advance of the initial charter meeting. The initial charter meeting involved clarifying top strategic priorities, drafting an Appointment Charter, and planning actions for the first few months, as noted and explained in more detail below in the transition coaching plan section.

An early benefit of this charter process occurred in our coaching session with the CFO, who was challenged to make some significant changes in the organization. Although he was aware of his mandate for change prior to accepting the position, it was essential for him to further clarify expectations and negotiate new expectations as he gained a more in-depth knowledge of what it would take to upgrade the function.

A variation of this chartering process involves several confidential meetings between the executive coach and key players (stakeholders) in the organization who are considered critical to the new leader's success. One approach is to interview stakeholders individually. Another is to conduct a small group interview (for example, with the new leader's direct reports) without the new leader present, at which time the coach guarantees anonymity for those employees who voice concerns. As stated below, we probe a series of issues, starting with the leader's significant priorities over the next several months to a year. When we debrief executives from these meetings, they tell us they gain more (and better-quality) insights from these interviews than they could in six to eight months, and in some cases they gain information that might not otherwise surface at all. In some cases, they also agree to debrief others in the organization about the data, so everyone is working with the same information. In our experience, conducting these individual interviews has always been a helpful source of data and would be indicated under almost any circumstances. However, the higher up the new leader is in the organization, the more crucial these interviews are in the transition coaching process.

In comparison to the CFO, the newly appointed chief security officer focused on communicating his Appointment Charter and forging new working relationships, particularly with some disaffected peers. Our work together is described below (see section on "Productive Conversations").

Questions to Consider

For new leaders in transition, the following questions are helpful as starting points to clarify the Appointment Charter with their direct (and indirect) bosses and other key stakeholders.

- What are the critical business goals and issues facing the leader over the next six months? Over one year?

- What are the top three or four priorities in meeting those goals, short-term, midterm, and long-term?

- What are the major barriers to achieving those goals?

- What is the scope of the leader's authority? Are there any limitations?

- What gaps or concerns are the new leader's team(s) experiencing?

- Who are the key stakeholders with whom the new leader should establish working relationships? What is the current status? Are there any "hot buttons"?

- What are the specific questions the new leader should be asking or issues that should be addressed immediately?

- How can the new leader keep his or her boss informed? Scope (e.g., standing agenda, urgent matters), frequency (biweekly), format (face-to-face, by telephone), other matters (email updates)?

- How can the new leader best give and receive feedback?

- Are there any developmental needs the new leader should focus on in the first year?

- What advice would you give the new leader for working successfully here? Are there any unwritten rules? How do things *really* work around here?

- In sum, what are the three or four critical accomplishments within the new leader's first year? How will success be measured?

These questions reflect what we have experienced as some of the most relevant issues that are of concern to the parties involved in transitions. The responses to these questions, in turn, can be used to shape the new leader's Appointment Charter.

Although some clients can conduct these interviews themselves, they usually have difficulty finding time to do so given that they tend to be stretched thin already. Thus, we usually conduct these key person interviews. Another advantage to having a skilled coach conduct the interviews is that the issues raised can be sensitive, even threatening. A skilled third party who has established rapport and assurances that agreed upon confidences will be maintained, creates an environment in which less filtering takes place and more valid data are produced. Once in office, new leaders rarely obtain reliable answers to these questions, compared to an objective outside coach. For even if the new executives ask the questions, they tend to receive a polite and carefully measured response.

Too often, subordinates may wonder, "Does the boss really want to hear the painful truth, or is he or she just wanting to make me feel involved and that my voice counts by giving the impression of openness?" Few want to take the risk of offending or irritating the boss by being too forthcoming and frank about negative perceptions or bad news.

Productive Conversations

To obtain feedback for the newly appointed chief security officer, we conducted over a dozen key person interviews about his top priorities as CSO and possible pitfalls, as well as his key strengths and weaknesses for the new position. The results were an eye opener to this new leader. Although he was doing well in managing up (to his boss and the board) and managing down (to his team), the new leader was struggling with his peers, as seen by all his respondents. His superiors, for example, said the new leader risked derailment if he did not act quickly to mend these peer relationships. His peers complained that the new leader was disrupting meetings, acting like a big shot now that he had been promoted, and insensitive to others. In a marathon, full-day feedback session the new leader acknowledged his blind spot about peer relationships, and pledged to act quickly to improve. As a result, our work with the newly appointed CSO focused on forging better working relationships, particularly with some disaffected peers. In particular, our coaching helped the executive handle these challenging conversations with more confidence and skill.

We started by introducing him to the theory and practice of productive conversations. This coaching covered core concepts from Action Science and other disciplines such as the Left-Hand Column and the Ladder of Inference, and key skills, such as advocacy, inquiry, and public testing, that were developed by Argyris (1996) and others.

As context, the term "productive conversation" has acquired a specialized meaning in recent years to refer to discourse that is designed to foster inquiry, choice, and action about challenging issues. Action Science—or the theory of action approach, as it is sometimes called—emphasizes the importance of three core values in productive conversations:

1. Valid information, because effective problem solving requires valid data
2. Free and informed choice, because effective decisions require the participation of all key players
3. Internal commitment, because effective implementation requires personal responsibility and sustained commitment

Productive conversations, then, are conversations that lead to learning, based on valid information, free and informed choice, and internal commitment.[7] Often, these coaching sessions feature role-plays and casework, including the Argyris case method, as it is sometimes called, to analyze actual conversational data. For instance, we asked the CSO to write a dialogue case of an important and challenging conversation that he wanted to handle more effectively. We also assigned reading (e.g., Stone, Patton, & Heen, 1999) to illustrate key points. Later coaching sessions then helped this new leader conduct productive conversations and manage interpersonal conflict, particularly with alienated peers. Specifically, we helped this executive to prepare for his difficult meetings that involved strained relationships, to start the dialogue with less defensiveness, and to keep conversation focused on constructive problem solving, as well as improving working relationships. In particular, the CSO found the concepts of framing and reframing held great potential for his situation. With our help, he came to see framing as the spontaneous way he was seeing his challenging situations, key parties in those situations, and his role, and to realize that reframing offered him powerful new options for effective action. By focusing on his framing of these challenges he began to think about his thinking, particularly in conflict situations with his peers.

For example, we helped him to recognize how his frames about himself, his role as the leader, and his peers were driving his behavior and inadvertently contributing to the problems he was facing. Specifically, he had framed the role for himself as *task-oriented,* and needing to be efficient, action-oriented, tough-minded, and decisive. This frame led him to make quick decisions in meetings without much exploration and then to push hard on the others to accept his decisions, often without regard to the *relationship.*

Therefore, his peers did not feel their ideas had been given a fair hearing, and they were not convinced that the new leader had necessarily made the right decisions. Consequently, they did not feel committed to these decisions. By contrast, the CSO had framed his own behavior as reasonable and his conclusions as obviously correct; hence, he framed his peers as being political or as refusing to be constructive.

Once he was able to recognize these frames and how they were contributing to the problems, we were able to help him reframe (develop new frames that were more constructive). Rather than focusing primarily on the task and his own efficiency and decisiveness, he was able to balance his task orientation with the objective of developing better working relationships with his key peers so that he and they could delve deeply enough into critical issues to make intelligent decisions to which all were committed. Rather than framing himself as obviously right, the CSO was able to recognize that, although he had an informed point of view, he could still have something to learn from others. Instead of framing the others as political or refusing to be constructive, he could see that they may not have been given enough information to make an informed decision or that they may have had legitimate concerns. These reframes, along with coaching to develop his skills for handling difficult conversations, enabled him to operate much more naturally and genuinely in a manner that was more agreeable to all stakeholders.

System Issues

As we further debriefed the feedback data with this CSO, it became clear that parts of his problematic peer relationships were situational. For one thing, the new leader's promotion had leapfrogged him to a senior level in the company, passing over several former peers who were logical contenders for the position (he came to call these latter peers the "PoPos," for "passed over and pissed off"). For another, his new position required him to depend on, and oversee, others elsewhere in the organization, in formerly disparate security functions. In addition, the feedback revealed that many such peers did not understand or fully agree with the new leader's charter, and saw the board's creation of a new CSO position as an implied criticism of their prior performance. Furthermore, from this feedback and the new leader, we learned that his transition to CSO—and the resulting implications across the organization—had not been well communicated in the company. Last but not least, as we debriefed the data still further, it became clear that many of the misunderstandings with peers were probably joint and interactive. In other words, both the new leader and his peers (and sometimes others in the organization) were causing the current situation. So also, all parties would need to contribute to a solution.

Using a systems approach, we saw the new leader and his key stakeholders as a social system—a collection of parts that interacted with each other to function as a whole.[8] Consequently, we helped the new leader to identify and address such system issues with others in the organization. For instance, we met with the CSO and his boss to further clarify the Appointment Charter—by addressing issues raised by the CSO's peers—and to communicate the charter to other key stakeholders. To this end, the skills of productive conversations were instrumental in helping this new leader to deescalate difficult issues and engage in more effective two-way communications.

General Transition Coaching Plan

Our initial design for these two transition coaching engagements included (but was not limited to) a set of interrelated steps described below, essentially as discussed with each client at the start of the engagement. To this end, we distributed the items listed below as a handout to each client in their initial contracting meeting. Their situations differed, however, so we tailored these steps to each case. Following our description of the steps, typical activities, and approximate times (noted in brackets), we will provide some illustrations as to how the steps were applied differently across the CFO and CSO cases.

Step One: Contracting. The first step is to meet with you[9] as the new leader and relevant others, such as your direct boss and/or sponsor. Emphasis is placed on clarifying the business reason(s) for coaching, success criteria, confidentiality and related matters, particularly your roles and responsibilities. As part of the process, it is important to begin obtaining relevant data about you as well as background business information about your chief challenges in the new position. Over the coaching engagement, these data can be collected through a variety of means, including standardized assessments such as the MBTI,[10] FIRO-B,[11] 360 degree surveys, key person interviews, and direct observation of you at work. During the initial contracting session (typically two to four hours), it is important to clarify expectations and ensure consensus on the approach and commitment to next steps. [Initial contracting meeting(s) with you and possibly other organization members, about two to four hours.]

Step Two: Orientation. Second, we meet with you to further clarify your felt needs and the benefits of coaching to you and your organization, as well as to review how new leaders fail, and ways they succeed. In this step we define key factors for success (e.g., clear business goals, new leader Appointment Charter, strong key stakeholder relationships). We arrange for next steps (e.g., initial charter meeting), confirm relevant charter issues (e.g., your critical business priorities and pitfalls of the first six to twelve months) and advance preparation, if any (e.g., interview of your direct boss and other key parties as needed before the charter meeting). [Coaching session with you, about two to four hours.]

Step Three: Initial Charter Meeting. Next we meet with you and your boss(es) to review a draft Appointment Charter, confirm top strategic priorities, and summarize key issues. Or, if there is an existing charter, we jointly review it and identify any gaps between the written document and what is required. We also identify other stakeholders and/or clients to involve in the transition process and plan actions (e.g., early wins within their first three months), milestones and progress reviews (e.g., charter alignment meetings every quarter). [Facilitated meeting(s) with you and key stakeholders, about two hours.]

Step Four: Assessment. Assessment involves planning further data collection if needed (e.g., survey method and process), obtaining relevant data (e.g., by key person interviews), analyzing data, and preparing report(s). We also arrange for feedback to you as the new leader. [Time: variable, depending on survey method and your role in data collection and analysis.]

Step Five: Feedback and Discussion. The feedback meeting includes confirming feedback norms, previewing, reviewing, and internalizing data, interpreting results, analyzing patterns, consolidating insights (e.g., your priorities and pitfalls in your new position, your relevant strengths and weaknesses, and the resulting transition issues), and setting goals for change. [Feedback session with you, about two to four hours, or more if needed.]

Step Six: Planning. Further planning involves meeting with you to confirm goals, revise the Appointment Charter as needed, and plan actions, milestones, and progress reviews. [Planning session with you, about two to four hours.]

Step Seven: Action. The action step includes meeting with you in regular coaching sessions to work on plans, actions, and learning. We also review work from prior sessions and results to date, coach the new leader on priority needs, and revise plans as appropriate. We identify and obtain added data and input as needed and may involve others in the organization as well (e.g., key relationships, stakeholders). [Coaching sessions with you, as needed (e.g., every two to four weeks, two to four hours each) over two to three months.]

Step Eight: Progress reviews. Finally, we review progress, refine plans, celebrate success, and contract for additional work if needed and appropriate. We typically stand by for periodic follow-ups and a possible reassessment (e.g., another 360 degree survey, roughly twelve months later). [Review session with the client and relevant others, about two to four hours.]

Comparing the CFO and CSO Cases

Given the initial transition coaching plan, this section summarizes some key similarities and differences across both cases, and illustrates how we tailored the transition coaching steps to each situation.

Both coaching engagements began by jointly assessing the situation and each client's felt needs and presenting issues. How we collaborated with the CFO and the CSO—and with their key stakeholders and respective organizations—however, differed because of several key situational factors that came into focus over our initial coaching sessions. These situational factors for each executive included:

- Their key job demands
- Their familiarity with their key stakeholders, notably their managers, peers, and direct reports
- Their self-awareness and baseline managerial skills

Given important distinctions between the CFO and the CSO situations, we intervened differently in each case. The CFO faced a turnaround situation in which the new leader was expected to make significant changes in a short period of time. His key challenges were to:

- Reenergize the demoralized employees in his function
- Handle time pressures, particularly with regard to financial reporting deadlines, so as to have a quick and decisive impact
- Make certain tough calls and personnel choices early, a process he completed within the first six months

So also, the opportunity for this new leader was that everyone recognized the changes necessary (from the CEO on down).

As a seasoned executive, the CFO brought high baseline skills to his new assignment. As part of his ongoing development over the years, he had previous coaching (with one of us), a series of assessments (MBTI, FIRO-B, annual 360 degree feedback in his former function) and significant previous leadership opportunities in prior positions. Over the years, he had become a seasoned manager of both people and his finance function. As a result, the CFO was highly self-aware, competent, and confident. Hence, we concluded that a baseline assessment was not essential for his transition. His particular needs had more to do with learning a novel context—notably the new organization and new boss, and structuring a specific Appointment Charter, because although he was brought in with a mandate to bring about change, many of the details of this change had yet to be worked out. As stated in our initial meeting, he wanted a trusted executive coach who could serve as a sounding board and help him sort out his new situation; consequently, we designed coaching activities accordingly. For instance, the key person interviews for this client focused more on exploring context (e.g., his key priorities and pitfalls in the CFO position) and less on examining his relative strengths and weaknesses, which were less known to the CFO's respondents in any case because of his recent arrival to the organization. So also, we designed the CFO's Appointment Charter process to clarify expectations of the boss and establish an effective working relationship. The CFO also inherited a large staff, many of whom were experiencing low morale and were impatient to see constructive change. Since the needs of his staff also had to be addressed right away, a jump start process was used to accelerate the transition, so the CFO and his staff could quickly work together to effectively address critical business needs and issues.

To recap, the CFO faced a turnaround situation, arrived with high baseline skills that were relevant to his new assignment, and came from the outside. Hence, he had all of the requisite skills but little of the requisite context and no charter to guide his entry and transition. He needed agenda coaching to sort out his new situation and certain transition activities (such as chartering, jump start) to take charge in his new leadership role. Thus, although we continue to stay in touch with the CFO, his transition coaching activities were largely completed within his first year. By contrast, the CSO faced a start-up[12] situation. His key challenges were to build structures and systems from scratch for the new enterprise security function, and build a new high-performing team starting with the small intact team he brought with him from his prior job. So, the CSO's opportunity was that he could do things right from the start, because there was little or no prior policy or procedure.

As further contrast to the CFO's situation, the CSO knew his organization, had reported to his new boss in a previous job, and brought his own staff with him. In addition, a specific agreement regarding the responsibilities and expectations for the role had been worked out prior to his promotion into the job. To recap, he lacked some managerial skills but had the requisite context as well as a specific charter to guide his transition. Thus, there were less urgent needs to structure an Appointment Charter or build a working relationship with his boss or subordinates. Instead, his vulnerability lay in the fact that he was not well prepared to manage new peer relationships and to coordinate a wide array of individuals over whom he had no direct control. Furthermore, the CSO had previously received little leadership development training or coaching. Thus, he was unaware of the gaps between his current skills and those required of the new role. Therefore, we designed his key person interviews to focus on his relevant strengths and weaknesses in the new CSO position (as seen by his respondents). We also developed data from two assessments (the MBTI,

FIRO-B) to round out his feedback. So also, in the marathon feedback session, we triangulated this data by cross-referencing several perspectives (from the client, his respondents, and the assessments) to discover key themes from multiple perspectives. The resulting insights were extremely useful in increasing his self-understanding and motivation to develop new skills. After the feedback session, we assisted him in rebuilding relationships with alienated peers and in learning appropriate skills, particularly for more productive conversations. In another follow-up activity, we assisted this client with several system issues, as described above.

Given his need to develop significant new skills, the transition coaching lasted longer than it did for the CFO. Recognizing his longer-term needs, the CSO committed to meet regularly in coaching sessions for more than twelve months, both to address business issues (agenda coaching) and to reflect on his behavior in order to improve his effectiveness (performance coaching). As such, the CSO case was a *blended* coaching engagement that entailed more than one coaching role. At the outset of our coaching relationship, the CSO had just received his promotion and significant added responsibilities. Therefore, we started meeting frequently over the first several months to address his urgent new agenda. During the first part of each session we worked on topics of his choosing, typically transition issues. (In this phase, the primary focus was agenda coaching. The CSO devoted time and energy about evenly in the coaching sessions to learning—mainly about his new situation—and doing—mainly to consider urgent decisions, changes to initiate, and staffing and structuring issues.) Months later, after his marathon feedback session, we focused increasingly on developing new skills deemed critical for success in the CSO position. We continued to meet regularly and to review transition issues, but the focus shifted to learning significant new skills. (In this phase, the primary focus was performance coaching. During these coaching sessions the CSO devoted more time to learning, by deepening his understanding about his own behavior and acquiring significant new skills.) All this required continuing contracting, so that the CSO and his coach could shift smoothly, by moving back and forth among various coaching roles as needed. As such, the CSO case also required considerably more time and skill than did the CFO, and was more likely to create fundamental change for the new leader.

Even so, this extended coaching engagement served mainly to introduce the CSO to some core concepts and key skills for improving his interpersonal effectiveness. True, we helped him to prepare for some challenging conversations with peers, and to reflect on his framing and acting experiments in subsequent coaching sessions. However, both coach and client recognized that learning to use these new skills consistently, so as to interact more effectively with others, would require ongoing attention and sustained practice. For example, the competency of productive conversation requires several skills: raising difficult issues directly with others, responding to their reactions in more productive (and less defensive) ways, and learning to think differently in the first place. So, the challenges of developing significant new skills and sustaining change over time would require continuing time, energy, and practice, well beyond a single coaching engagement. As Chris Argyris has often said, it takes about as much practice as learning to play tennis.

REFLECTIONS ON TRANSITION COACHING: THE NEED FOR A LEARNING ORIENTATION

Most executive coaching occurs behind closed doors, and some clients are reluctant to disclose their coaching to others in their organizations. For most new leaders, however, it is particularly important to be open with relevant others in the organization about their transition coaching. Based on our experience, this type of openness and exchange can facilitate a learning orientation with several benefits:

- From the start, the new leader can demonstrate an openness to learning about the new situation before making major changes. This adds stability to the transition.

- During the transition, the leader can contract openly for new power relationships with key members in the organization. This reduces the risk of confusion and conflict and tends to accelerate a smooth transition.

- To complete the transition, the new leader can also negotiate mutual expectations with old and new key players, with the help of a third party if necessary. This gives all players an equal chance to put issues on the table and define positive relationships.

By maintaining a learning orientation, the leader conveys openness and respect and the potential for flexibility and creative collaboration. When others sense this openness, they are more likely to get involved and get on board rather than resist or take a "wait and see" approach.

As noted above, one added value of transition coaching is to foster a longer-term perspective for new leaders and their key stakeholders. According to Gabarro (1987), when executives discover that mastering a new leadership role is likely to take two to three years, they usually find this timeframe intolerably long and are desperate to figure out how to speed up the process. New managers often grossly underestimate the complexities of managerial work and the gap between their current skills and those needed to succeed as a manager (Hill, 1992). However, even seasoned executives who have been highly successful in previous engagements can easily fall into the traps mentioned previously (Watkins, 2000). In new managerial situations, experienced executives can fail to see how subtle differences between current circumstances and previous assignments will require that they behave differently in order to succeed in the new circumstances. Consequently, we find that knowing more about (1) what is required to succeed in various types of transitions and (2) how transition coaching can assist them in the process can readily facilitate the success of the newly appointed leaders.

Implications for Coaches

Consultants interested in coaching have a growing array of resources from which to draw (see Bacon & Spear 2003; Benton, 1999; Dotlich & Cairo, 1999; Fitzgerald & Berger, 2002; Goldsmith, Lyons, & Freas, 2000; Hargrove 1995; Hunt & Weintraub, 2002; Kilburg, 2000; Whitmore, 1996; Witherspoon & White, 1997). Despite this breadth of resources, the topic of executive coaching for leaders in transition has received relatively little attention in the literature. We believe transition coaching has great potential as an executive coaching specialization—particularly for consultants who bring both executive coaching and organization development (OD) skills. For as Burke (2002) has explained, the integration of two capabilities is increasingly important for helping leaders and their organizations in planning and implementing major change.[13] From our experience, we also know that timely transition coaching can add significant value to the individual clients and their organizations.

CONCLUSION

In conclusion, the quality of leadership transitions is of great and growing strategic importance today; however, the success of leadership transitions is anything but assured. Instead, transitions are vulnerable to a variety of problems and are frequently handled badly. As a result, many new leaders fall short and fail fast. These failures are at great cost to the organization and to individual careers. Transition coaching is a remarkably valuable intervention—both for speeding up key leadership transitions and, more important, for increasing the odds that new leaders take charge, learn quickly, and perform effectively in their new roles.

Notes

1. An earlier version of this chapter was presented as part of the Management Consulting Division's program at the Academy of Management meeting, Seattle, Washington, August 2003.

2. We think some of the literature about leadership transitions is a glaring example of "flawed advice," a widespread problem studied by Chris Argyris (2000, p. vii), who

concludes that most managerial advice "is simply too full of abstract claims, inconsistencies, and logical gaps to be useful as a concrete basis for concrete actions in concrete settings."

3. We use the terms *executive, new leader,* and *client* interchangeably to refer to the person being coached. Likewise we use the terms *coach* and *consultant* in this chapter to refer to our role as an outside professional coach to these individuals. Typically, we are called in by the client's organization (or "client system") for formal executive coaching, with the expectation of regular sessions (e.g., monthly or more often) over an extended term (e.g., six to twelve months or more); documented goals and completion dates (e.g., behavior change by a specified time); and tangible results (e.g., improvement as measured by a follow-up survey). In most cases, the coaching occurs in one-on-one meetings with the executive in feedback and coaching sessions of two hours or more.

4. Our coaching experience includes a wide array of sectors, industries, organizations, business units, functions, and levels within organizations. We conduct research on our practice theory of coaching, in the Argyris and Schön (1974) tradition, by examining and reflecting on the data generated in our coaching practice and sharing and comparing our data with colleagues. This approach to coaching practice theory draws on a theory of action perspective, with an emphasis on three core values— valid information, free and informed choice, and internal commitment—to understand and explain human action. Short-term, we believe that a useful practice theory for executive coaching should answer at least two questions for professional coaches: "What do I say and do in this situation?" and "What are the underlying principles that explain why I do and say this?" Long-term, we believe a coaching practice theory should seek to integrate a comprehensive theory and sound practice for executive coaching, much as Schwarz (2002) proposes for group facilitation.

5. Further information about transitions is available at <http://glacel.com/transition.html>. This material is taken from their website.

6. In addition to addressing these transition issues, of course, some new leaders may need to master new skills, even as they take charge of their new leadership role. Again, these needs depend on the situation and may be quite varied—ranging from personal skills (e.g., leading by example) to process skills (e.g., negotiation and conflict management) to people skills (e.g., managing direct reports) to purpose skills (e.g., strategic agility)—a subject beyond the scope of this chapter (see Lombardo and Eichinger, 2000, 2001, for further discussion of some of these managerial and leadership skills). See also Personnel Decision International's *Successful Manager's Handbook* (2000).

7. These core values, and many of the concepts for productive conversation, come from decades of research by Chris Argyris and others, designed to help people improve their effectiveness (cf. Argyris, Putnam, & Smith, 1985; Argyris & Schön, 1974, 1996). Argyris and the partners of Action Design—Philip McArthur, Robert Putnam, and Diana McLain Smith—have proven invaluable to our understanding of productive conversations in our work together at the Action Design Institute (accessible at http://actiondesign.com).

8. In recent years the field of systems thinking has become popular in part through the work of Peter Senge and his colleagues (Senge, 1990; Senge, Kleiner, Roberts, Ross, & Smith, 1994).

9. The steps in our general transition coaching plan are presented to "you," as the executive client.

10. The MBTI refers to the Myers-Briggs Type Indicator, which assesses personality type by assessing preferences along the following four dichotomies: introversion-extroversion, sensing-intuition, thinking-feeling, and judging-perceiving. For more information on the MBTI see Myers, McCaulley, Quenk, and Hammer (1998).

11. The FIRO-B refers to the Fundamental Interpersonal Orientations-Behavior, which assesses how personal needs influence behavior toward other individuals. For more information, see Hammer and Schnell (1999).

12. This contrast between a *start-up* transition and a *turnaround* transition corresponds to the distinctions made by Watkins (2003, pp. 61–78) in his STAR model of business evaluation. Each has its own distinct challenges and opportunities and requires a response tailored to address these distinctions.

13. Burke's recent work (2002) is the first to explicitly address coaching's role in OD interventions, to our knowledge. His concept of helping change leaders to (1) plan the change initiative and (2) help them deal with the unexpected consequences is close to our concept of agenda coaching for executives leading major change. In our view, Burke captures the essence of organization change when he talks about its nonlinear nature and "fallback loops" that symbolize the unanticipated consequences of planned change, side effects that must be addressed and corrected if the overall change initiative is to move forward. The same is true of helping executives to plan and implement individual change, in our experience.

References

Argyris, C. (1985). *Strategy, change, and defensive routines*. New York: Harper Business.

Argyris, C. (1993). *Knowledge for action: A guide to overcoming barriers to organizational change*. San Francisco: Jossey-Bass.

Argyris, C. (2000). *Flawed advice and the management trap: How managers can know when they're getting good advice and when they're not*. Oxford: Oxford University Press.

Argyris, C., & Schön, D.A. (1974). *Theory in practice; Increasing professional effectiveness*. San Francisco: Jossey-Bass.

Argyris, C., & Schön, D.A. (1996). *Organizational learning II*. Reading, MA: Addison-Wesley.

Bacon, T.R., & Spear, K.I. (2003). *Adaptive coaching: The art and practice of a client-centered approach to performance improvement*. Palo Alto, CA: Davies-Black Publishing.

Benton, D.A. (1999). *Secrets of a CEO coach*. New York: McGraw-Hill.

Betof, E., & Harrison, R.P. (1996, Spring). The newly appointed leader dilemma: A significant change in today's organizational culture. *The Manchester Review*, pp. 1–12.

Betof, E., & Harwood, F. (1992). *Just promoted: How to survive and thrive in your first 12 months as a manager*. New York: McGraw-Hill.

Brotman, I. (1998). Executive coaching: The needs for standards of competence. *Consulting Psychology Journal: Practice and Research*, *50*(1), 40–46.

Burke, W.W. (2002). *Organization change: Theory and practice*. Thousand Oaks, CA: Sage Publications.

Ciampa, D., & Watkins, M. (1999). *Right from the start: Taking charge in a new leadership role*. Boston: Harvard Business School Press.

Diedrich, R.C., & Kilburg, R.R. (2001). Foreword: Further consideration of executive coaching as an emerging competency. *Consulting Psychology Journal: Practice & Research*, *53*(4), 203–204.

Dotlich, D.L., & Cairo, P.C. (1999). *Action coaching: How to leverage individual performance for company success*. San Francisco: Jossey-Bass.

Fitzgerald, C., & Berger, J.G. (Eds.). (2002). *Executive coaching: Practices and perspectives*. Palo Alto, CA: Davies-Black Publishing.

Fitzgerald, C., & Kirby, L.K. (Eds.). (1997). *Developing leaders: Research and applications in psychological type and leadership development*. Palo Alto, CA: Davies-Black Publishing.

Gabarro, J.J. (1987). *The dynamics of taking charge*. Boston: Harvard Business School Press.

Garnsey, E., & Roberts, J. (1996). *Taking charge: What makes CEO succession work?* Practitioner research report for Saxton Bampfylde International plc.

Glacel, B.P. (2000). *Transition exercises*. <http://glacel.com/transition html> (accessed February 2004).

Goldsmith, M., Lyons, L., & Freas, A. (Eds.). (2000). *Coaching for leadership: How the world's greatest coaches help leaders learn*. San Francisco: Jossey-Bass/Pfeiffer.

Hall, D.T., Otazo, K.L., & Hollenbeck, G.P. (1999). Behind closed doors: what really happens in executive coaching. *Organizational Dynamics*, *27*(3), 39–53.

Hammer, A.L., & Schnell, E.R. (1999). *FIRO-B technical guide (A)*. Palo Alto, CA: Consulting Psychologist Press.

Hargrove, R.A. (1995). *Masterful coaching: Extraordinary results by impacting people and the way they think and work together*. San Francisco: Jossey-Bass/Pfeiffer.

Harrison, R.P., & Dunnells, N.P. (1998). The newly appointed leader dilemma. In *Proceedings of the 1998 Leadership Conference: The art & practice of coaching leaders* (pp. 249–257). Adelphi, MD: University of Maryland University College.

Hart, V., Blattner, J., & Leipsic, S. (2001). Coaching versus therapy: A perspective. *Consulting Psychology Journal: Practice & Research*, *53*(4), 229–237.

Hill, L.A. (1992). *Becoming a manager: Mastery of a new identity*. Boston: Harvard Business School Press.

Hunt, J.M., & Weintraub, J.R. (2002). *The coaching manager: Developing top talent in business*. Thousand Oaks, CA: Sage.

Johnson, J.M. (2000). Learning strategies for newly appointed leaders. In M. Goldsmith, L. Lyons, & A. Freas (Eds.), *Coaching for leadership: How the world's greatest coaches help leaders learn* (pp. 209–217). San Francisco: Jossey-Bass/Pfeiffer.

Kampa-Kokesch, S., & Anderson, M. (2001). Executive coaching: A comprehensive review of the literature. *Consulting Psychology Journal: Practice & Research*, *53*(4), 205–228.

Kilburg, R.R. (1996a). Foreword: Executive coaching as an emerging competency in the practice. *Consulting Psychology Journal: Practice & Research*, *48*(2), 59–60.

Kilburg, R.R. (1996b). Toward a conceptual understanding and definition of executive coaching. *Consulting Psychology Journal: Practice & Research*, *48*(2), 134–144.

Kilburg, R. (2000). *Executive coaching: Developing managerial wisdom in a world of chaos*. Washington, DC: American Psychological Association.

Kilburg, R.R. (2001). Facilitating intervention adherence in executive coaching: A model and methods. *Consulting Psychology Journal: Practice & Research*, *53*(4), 251–267.

Lombardo, M.M., & Eichinger, R.W. (2000). High potentials as high learners. *Human Resource Management*, *39*(4), 321–330.

Lombardo, M.M., & Eichinger, R.W. (2001). *The leadership machine*. Minneapolis, MN: Lominger Ltd.

Morse, G. (2002). Behave yourself. *Harvard Business Review*, *80*(10), 22–24.

Myers, I.B., McCaulley, M.H., Quenk, N.L., & Hammer, A.L. (1998). *MBTI manual: A guide to the development and use of the Myers-Briggs Type Indicator* (3rd ed.). Palo Alto, CA: Consulting Psychologist Press.

Schwarz, R.W. (2002). *The skilled facilitator: A comprehensive resource for consultants, facilitators, managers, trainers, and coaches*. San Francisco: Jossey-Bass.

Senge, P.M. (1990). *The fifth discipline: The art and practice of the learning organization*. New York: Doubleday/Currency.

Senge, P.M., Kleiner, A., Roberts, C., Ross, R.B., & Smith, B.J. (1994). *The fifth discipline fieldbook: Strategies and tools for building a learning organization*. New York: Doubleday/Currency.

Stone, D., Patton, B., & Heen, S. (1999). *Difficult conversations: How to discuss what matters most*. New York: Penguin.

Watkins, M. (2000). *Seven rules for new leaders*. Harvard Business School Note 9–800–288.

Watkins, M. (2003). *The first ninety days: Critical success strategies for leaders at all levels*. Boston: Harvard Business School Press.

Whitmore, J. (1996). *Coaching for performance*. London: Nicholas Brealey Publishing.

Witherspoon, R. (2000). Starting smart: clarifying coaching goals and roles. In M. Goldsmith, L. Lyons, & A. Freas (Eds.), *Coaching for leadership: How the world's greatest coaches help leaders learn* (pp. 165–185). San Francisco: Jossey-Bass/ Pfeiffer.

Witherspoon, R., & White, R.P. (1996). Executive coaching: A continuum of roles. *Consulting Psychology Journal: Practice & Research*, *48*(2), 124–133.

Witherspoon, R., & White, R.P. (1997). *Four essential ways that coaching can help executives*. Greensboro, NC: Center for Creative Leadership. Accession Number: 00012225–200110000–00002.

GROUP-LEVEL CHANGE INTERVENTIONS

CHAPTER THIRTY-SIX

Team Building

W. Warner Burke (1982)

When a work group has at least one goal that is common to all members and when accomplishment of that goal requires cooperative interdependent behavior on the part of all group members, team building may be an appropriate intervention. Dyer's (1977) three checklists are useful criteria for determining more specifically the appropriateness of team building for a work group. Studying his lists will help clarify the purposes and the nature of team building.

Using Beckhard's (1972) succinct statement of the four primary purposes of team building and Plovnick, Fry, and Rubin's (1975) elaboration as a guide, I shall now provide a more thorough explanation of team building. According to Beckhard (1972), there are four purposes of team building:

1. To set goals or priorities
2. To analyze or allocate the way work is performed according to team members' roles and responsibilities
3. To examine the way the team is working—that is, its processes, such as norms, decision making, communications, and so forth
4. To examine relationships among the team members

Beckhard points out that all these purposes are likely to be operating in a team building effort, "but unless one purpose is defined as the primary purpose, there tends to be considerable misuse of energy. People then operate from their own hierarchy of purposes and, predictably, these are not always the same for all members'' (Beckhard, 1972, p. 42). From a combination of responses to Dyer's checklists and individual interviews with group members, a diagnosis can be made that should indicate the primary purpose for an initial team building session. If the team building effort is the first for the group, the OD practitioner should determine if the focus of the first session should be setting goals or establishing priorities among team goals. If the goals and their priorities are clear, the OD practitioner should determine if the roles and responsibilities among team members are clear. If so, then the practitioner determines if working procedures and processes are clear. It is important and beneficial for the OD practitioner to use Beckhard's four purposes in the order that they are listed. The reason for this ordering of the purposes is as follows: *interpersonal* problems could be a consequence of group members' lack of clarity regarding team goals, roles, and responsibilities, or procedures and processes; problems with *procedures and processes* could be a consequence of group members' lack of clarity regarding team goals or roles and responsibilities; and problems with *roles and responsibilities* may be a result of group members' lack of clarity about team goals. To begin a team building effort with work on interpersonal relationships may be a misuse of time and energy, as it is possible that problems in this area are a result of misunderstandings in one of the other three domains. Clarifying goals, roles, and responsibilities, or team procedures and processes, may eliminate certain interpersonal problems among team members; clarifying roles and responsibilities may in itself eliminate some of the problems with the team's working procedures and processes; and clarifying team goals and their priorities may in itself eliminate certain problems team members may have with their roles and responsibilities.

We shall now consider case examples of team building interventions for each of these four purposes.

SETTING GOALS AND PRIORITIES

In the course of an OD effort with a medical school, the school's internal consultant and I, an outside consultant, were asked by one of the clinical department chairs to help with some departmental team building. In our interviews with the department members, my colleague and I diagnosed that there was a pervasive sense of no direction for the department as a whole. In a subsequent meeting with the chairman, the three of us designed an off-site session for one evening and the following day for the fifteen members of the department. Briefly, the design of this off-site meeting was as follows. The fifteen members, including the chairman, were initially divided into three groups of five people each, heterogeneously grouped. Their common tasks were (1) to determine

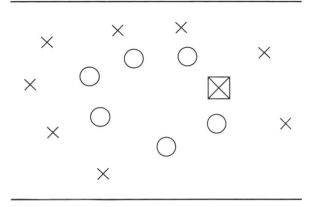

Figure 36.1. Configuration of the Second Phase of an Off-Site Meeting to Set Departmental Goals.

what they believed the departmental goals should be and (2) to select two of their members to represent them in a later plenary session. Having developed their goal statements, the three groups then assembled in the large room and the two representatives from each group met together in the center while the remaining nine department members were positioned around them as observers. Figure 36.1 depicts this arrangement of a small group of six persons working together in the center, with their colleagues gathered around them and observing.

The task for this six-person temporary executive committee was to communicate what each group had developed and to consolidate their three lists of statements into one, which would then become the statement of objectives for the department. An empty chair was provided within this inner circle of six so that, if any of the observers believed that what her or his group had developed was not being represented or thought that this temporary executive committee was going astray, the person could occupy the empty chair, state her or his position or raise an issue, wait for and possibly deal with the reaction of the executive group, and then return to observer status.

Once the executive group had consolidated the three lists into one, the total group individually ranked the statements (fourteen in this case) according to priority of importance for the department. Next, the total group individually selected its first and second choices of objectives it wished to develop into action steps for implementation. The fifteen people were then regrouped into three groups of five, according to their choices of an objective. These three groups met periodically after the off-site meeting to plan action steps for implementing the three most important objectives.

At the conclusion of the off-site meeting, each person was asked to respond to two questions, with responses arranged according to a five-point Likert scale: (1) How pessimistic or optimistic are you at the moment about the state of the department? (The one to five response ranged from "highly pessimistic" to "highly optimistic.") (2) To what extent do you believe positive change will occur as a result of this meeting? (The one to five response ranged from "not at all" to "to a great extent.") I like to ask these two questions toward the end of an off-site meeting because they provide a relatively simple way to consider the process of the meeting—people's feelings—and an opportunity to examine the degree of an individual's motivation to follow through on the steps planned for future implementation. In this case the departmental members' ratings were uniformly optimistic and positive.

The rationale for such a team building design has several elements. For such a short period of time (in this case only slightly more than one day), it is important to have as much member participation as feasible and to use the allotted time as efficiently as possible. The smaller group of six obviously could work more efficiently than the total group of fifteen, but some degree of total participation was maintained by employing the empty chair. Selecting representatives and then being able to see what they do, and also having a chance to influence their decision making, helps ensure the involvement of all department members and therefore their commitment to implementing the goals they identified. The follow-up groups did indeed meet periodically to plan action steps. A year later, in a brief interview, my colleague and I were pleased to learn that the department chairman continued to be satisfied with the progress of his department. He attributed much of this progress to the success of the off-site meeting.

ALLOCATING WORK ACCORDING TO ROLES AND RESPONSIBILITIES

Ambiguity regarding one's role and conflict between what is expected of an individual in a particular role and what that individual believes is appropriate can cause considerable confusion within a work group and anxiety for its members (Katz & Kahn, 1978). There are various techniques for gaining greater clarification of roles and responsibilities within a team. These techniques typically involve team members' (1) presenting their perceptions and understandings of their roles to one another, (2) discussing these perceptions and understandings, and (3) modifying roles as a function of increased agreement about mutual expectations. One such technique is the role analysis technique developed by Dayal and Thomas (1968). Another similar one is the job expectation technique, which is particularly useful when there is a need to integrate a new member into a team (Huse, 1980).

A technique that is particularly suitable for situations of role conflict is Harrison's (1972) role negotiation technique. Although it is most suitable for this second purpose of team building, the approach also may be used with either of the remaining two purposes, since role is not limited to formal position. According to Harrison (1972), this role negotiation technique "intervenes directly into the relationships of power, authority, and influence within the group" (p. 92). Each group member lists for each other member the things these other members (1) should do more or better, (2) should do less or stop, and (3) should continue as now. Agreements about changes are negotiated among the members and then finalized in the form of a written contract.

A technique that emphasizes the responsibilities aspects of this second purpose of team building is what Beckhard and Harris (1977) refer to as *responsibility charting*. Using a grid format, the types of decisions and actions that need to be taken are listed along the left side and those who should have some part in the decision-making process are listed across the top of the grid. Figure 36.2 shows this type of grid. The process consists of assigning an action to each of the team members whose names appear opposite an issue or decision. As the exhibit shows, there are the following

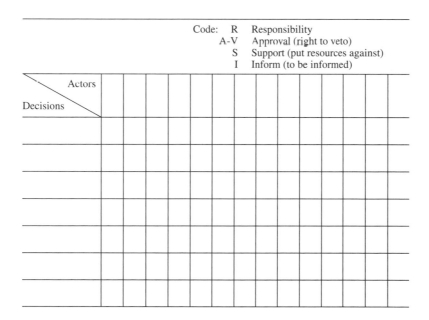

Figure 36.2. Responsibility Chart.

four types of actions: R, the *responsibility* to ensure action, to ensure that the decision is implemented; A-V, *approval* required or the right to *veto;* S, provide logistical *support* and resources; and I, must be *informed* about the decision or action. As Beckhard and Harris point out, there can be only one R on any single horizontal line. Either a consensus is reached by the team, or the boss determines who takes the responsibility.

Responsibility charting is particularly useful for new teams and for start-up situations. The process can also be used for problem solving in an ongoing team. Beckhard and Harris describe a case in which the top management team of a regional headquarters of an oil company had been having difficulty for several years in working out a new franchise relationship with some of the company's gas station owners:

> The problem was complex, and there had been all sorts of misunderstandings, conflicts, slowdowns, and differences of emphasis between staff areas. The top management—the managing director, director of marketing, director of operations, and director of finance—were concerned about this issue because it was a matter of significant investment and cost, but they had been unable to resolve it. . . . It was suggested that they do a responsibility charting exercise on the problem, which they did. As a result, they discovered that they did not have a consensus about the location of the different types of responsibilities and behaviors. This problem was relatively easy to work through [Beckhard and Harris, 1977, p. 82].

EXAMINING TEAM PROCEDURES AND PROCESSES

The third purpose of team building is to establish working procedures and processes for a newly formed team or to examine and look for ways of improving these procedures and processes if the team has already been operating as a group for some time. By *processes,* Beckhard (1972) means such things as group norms and leadership style. *Procedures* are the processes that are more directly related to goal (task) accomplishment, such as type of decision making, problem-solving technique, communication, and team structure for dealing with different agenda. The team building activity therefore involves (1) identifying the norms that are hindering effective team work and (2) changing them to different norms that will facilitate teamwork. The activity may be examining a particular team procedure that doesn't seem to be working very well. The sidebar presents a brief report of a case in which the communication procedure within a team was vastly improved by first examining the nature of the problem and then planning and implementing a new procedure for internal communications.

The Case of the Misunderstood Memo

Recently, a vice president in a large U.S. corporation was having trouble with his division managers occasionally responding inappropriately to his memos. The vice president had the choice of (1) sending his subordinates to a communications course, (2) attending a communications course himself, (3) both (1) and (2), (4) trying to live with the problem, or (5) working on the problem directly. He chose the last alternative. An external OD consultant and an internal consultant from the Employee Relations Division worked on the problem with the vice president in a team development session. They designed a work session to be held from 9:00 a.m. to lunch on a regular workday in the staff meeting room. Before the meeting, several memos from the vice president to the division managers were selected and prepared on a glass slide, which could then be shown on a screen via a projector. With the vice president and consultants present, all division managers considered several of the memos according to a certain procedure. After reading the memo on the screen, they were asked three questions: (1) What do you think the message says? (2) What priority would you give to the message: (a) HIGH, take care of the matter immediately, (b) MEDIUM, take care of the matter relatively soon, or (c) LOW, take care of it when I can get to it? (3) What action would you take?

After everyone responded to the three questions by writing their answers, each manager was asked to read his response to the total group. Considerable differences occurred among the managers. Later, the vice president explained what he meant the memo to say, what priority he desired, and what action he wanted. As might be expected, a number of misunderstandings were corrected and learning resulted, both learning on the vice president's part as well as the division managers'.

An interesting side effect resulted later in time: the vice president's memos decreased in number by 40 percent. Also, after a year of collecting relevant data, a considerable monetary savings amounting to approximately $20,000 was realized as a result of changes in communications procedures.

Source: Harvey & Boettger (1971).

EXAMINING RELATIONSHIPS AMONG TEAM MEMBERS

This fourth purpose of team building concerns identifying interpersonal problems that exist among team members and working toward some resolution of these problems. A case example of this form of team building concerned the top management group of a high-technology business organization. The climate within the group was open and spontaneous, particularly in group members' discussions of ideas and technical problems. They expressed a desire to be open with one another about their feelings and interpersonal relationships, but their individual styles and the patterns of interaction among them blocked this desire. They conformed to a nonconfronting norm when it came to interpersonal issues. This norm was reinforced by the president, who was highly analytical, rational, and sensible and was greatly admired by the subordinate team members. Eventually, a subgroup within the team emerged and began to push for facing up to the team relationship issues. They suggested that an extended meeting be held so that the group members could examine their interpersonal relationships. The suggestion was agreed to by all group members and the meeting took place.

> At this meeting each individual received some feedback from all of his colleagues about his strengths and weaknesses as they perceived them . . . [and] what bothered or pleased them about his behavior. Each individual could use this feedback any way he wished—there was no requirement for change. The feedback surfaced some historic issues that had been affecting the work of the group; for example, two people who had been competing throughout their careers maintained this competition in the group. They were perceived by all the others as sometimes robbing the group of their technical resource capability on the tasks because of their interpersonal relationship. It was agreed that the group would try to draw this to their attention whenever it arose in the future. The feedback to the president by the team was accepted and generally understood by him . . . however, the main benefit . . . was that it freed the group to produce this kind of information in the future as needed. This became a norm of the group and was perhaps the single most significant result [Beckhard, 1972, p. 31].

As illustrated in this case, when the purpose of team building is to work on relationships, a critical dimension of the process is interpersonal feedback. Regardless of the purpose we may be emphasizing in a team building effort, our ultimate goal is to improve the overall effectiveness of the team as a group. It is appropriate, therefore, for us to consider at this point some of the criteria for and characteristics of an effective group.

CRITERIA FOR AN EFFECTIVE TEAM

Douglas McGregor observed and worked with many groups, especially in a managerial context. On the basis of his research, his observations, and his consultation with these different groups, he listed what he considered the unique features of an effective managerial team (McGregor, 1967).

1. Understanding, Mutual Agreement, and Identification with Respect to the Primary Task. Team members have clarity about their ultimate purpose or mission and are committed to its accomplishment.

2. Open Communications. Team members express their ideas, opinions, and feelings openly and authentically. For further discussion of authenticity, see Herman and Korenich (1977). McGregor also points out that being absolutely open, regardless of the situation, is not the criterion for effectiveness. Openness is related to the task at hand.

3. Mutual Trust. Trust and openness go hand in hand, and openness is practically impossible to achieve without trust among team members. McGregor's (1967) definition of trust is worthy of quotation: "Trust means: 'I know that you will not—deliberately or accidentally, consciously or unconsciously—take unfair advantage of me.' It means: 'I can put my situation at the moment, my status and self-esteem in this group, our relationship, my job, my career, even my life, in your hands with complete confidence'" (p. 163).

   McGregor notes further that trust is a delicate aspect of relations, influenced more by actions than by words. Trust can be destroyed quickly and easily—one act can do it. Trust is a feeling influenced by needs, expectations, guilt, anxieties, and the like, and it is based on people's perceptions of others and their behavior, not on objective reality.

4. Mutual Support. This feature of an effective team is characterized by the absence of hostility or indifference among members and by the presence of care, concern, and active help toward one another.

5. Management of Human Differences. Group creativity typically comes from an open exchange of different ideas, opinions, and intuitions, and from an active process of integrating these differences into an outcome that represents the best of the individual contributions. Research has clearly documented that the more groups uncover and deal with their differences, the higher the quality of their decisions will be (Hall, 1971; Hall & Watson, 1970; Hall & Williams, 1966). Managing differences successfully within a group is easier said than done, of course. The key is to maintain a balance between fostering conflict of ideas and opinions and controlling these differences.

6. Selective Use of the Team. Being discriminatory about when and when not to use the team in a group endeavor for consensual decision making will help ensure time efficiency and wise use of member energy. Effective teams know when they should meet, and they know how to use their time.

I have found the following guidelines useful in deciding when to use the team for consensual decision making:

- When you do not know who has the most expertise regarding the decision to be made
- When implementation of the decision will require several people—most, if not all, members of the team
- When the facts are few—when judgment and opinion are required

These guidelines are very similar to Vroom and Yetton's (1973) more elaborate and detailed decision tree for managers' use in determining how participative to be in decision making.

7. Appropriate Member Skills. The effective team has among its membership—not just with the leader—the variety of skills that are needed for performance of the task and for maintenance of the team as a viable group. It is absolutely necessary that there be an adequate level of technical knowledge among the team's membership for task accomplishment. Just as necessary are the skills required to elicit that knowledge and integrate the various elements of it into a decision. These skills are of two types—task and maintenance. From the earlier work of Benne and Sheats (1948) and Bales (1950), Bennis and Shepard (1961) assembled a composite, representative list of these important skills and functions (see Table 36.1). The more all members of the team can develop these two sets of skills, the more effective the team is likely to be.

8. Leadership. The leadership function of an effective team is managing and integrating the other seven characteristics. It is unreasonable to assume that the leader alone can set direction, be open, trust and support team members, manage individual differences, always know when to use the team as a group, and provide all the necessary task and maintenance functions. In the effective team these characteristics become the responsibility and concern of all members. The team leader's job is to see that these characteristics are first identified and then become group norms. In addition, the team leader is the prime coordinator, seeing that the various responsibilities for effective team work are

Table 36.1. Bennis and Shepard's List.

Task Functions	Maintenance Functions
Initiating activity	Encouraging
Seeking information	Gatekeeping
Seeking opinion	Standard setting
Giving information	Following
Giving opinion	Expressing group feeling
Elaborating	Testing for consensus and commitment
Summarizing	Mediating
Testing feasibility	Relieving tension
Evaluating	

shared among members and differentiated according to subtask requirements and member talent.

Prior to McGregor's list of eight features, Likert (1961) had proposed twenty-four "performance characteristics of the ideal highly effective group." There is considerable overlap between the two lists, but four from Likert's list are different enough to be worth mentioning:

1. The values and goals of the group are integrated with and express the relevant values and needs of the members. Since the group members help to shape these values and goals (analogous to McGregor's first feature), they will be committed to and satisfied with them.

2. Group members, including the leader, believe that they as a group can accomplish the impossible. This kind of expectation stretches and challenges group members and establishes the potential for growth and development. This characteristic of an effective group is reminiscent of Vaill's (1978) "high performing systems."

3. The group understands the nature and value of constructive conformity and knows when to use it and for what purposes. Likert (1961) clarifies this characteristic: "Although it [the group] does not permit conformity to affect adversely the creative efforts of its members, it does expect conformity on mechanical and administrative matters to save the time of members and to facilitate the group's activities. The group agrees, for example, on administrative forms and procedures, and once they have been established, it expects its members to abide by them until there is good reason to change them" (p. 166).

Actually, this characteristic of Likert's helps amplify McGregor's management-of-differences feature—the process of maintaining a balance between fostering conflict and controlling it.

4. There is mutual influence among group members and especially between the members and the leader.

Likert used the word *ideal* in the preface to his list of twenty-four characteristics of an effective group. McGregor's list also can be labeled ideal. Striving for these characteristics may be idealistic for a team, but it is not necessarily unrealistic. Even approximating these ideals can improve teamwork. For team building purposes, having a standard for evaluating efforts toward a more effective team is critical, not only for direction but also for motivation as well.

By way of summary, we can define team building as an activity whereby members of a work group (1) begin to understand more thoroughly the nature of group dynamics and effective teamwork, particularly the interrelationship of *process* and *content,* and (2) learn to apply certain principles and skills of group process toward greater team effectiveness.

References

Bales, R. F. (1950). Interaction process analysis. Reading, MA: Addison-Wesley.

Beckhard, R. (1972). Optimizing team-building efforts. *Journal of Contemporary Business, 1*(3), 23–32.

Beckhard, R., & Harris, R. T. (1977). *Organizational transitions: Managing complex change.* Reading, MA: Addison-Wesley.

Benne, K. D., & Sheats, P. (1948). Functional roles of group members. *Journal of Social Issues, 4*(2), 41–49.

Bennis, W. G., & Shepard, H. A. (1961). Group observation. In W. G. Bennis, K. D. Benne, & R. Chin (Eds.), *The planning of change* (pp. 743–756). New York: Holt, Rinehart & Winston.

Burke, W. W. (1982). *Organization development: Principles and practices.* Boston: Little, Brown.

Dayal, I., & Thomas, J. M. (1968). Operation KPE: Developing a new organization. *Journal of Applied Behavioral Science, 4*(4), 473–506.

Dyer, W. E. (1977). *Team building: Issues and alternatives.* Reading, MA: Addison-Wesley.

Hall, J. (1971). Decisions, decisions, decisions. *Psychology Today, 5*(6), 51–54, 86–88.

Hall, J., & Watson, W. H. (1970). The effects of a normative intervention on group decision making performance. *Human Relations, 23,* 299–317.

Hall, J., & Williams, M. S. (1966). A comparison of decision-making performances in established and ad hoc groups. *Journal of Personality and Social Psychology, 3*, 214–222.

Harrison, R. (1972). Role negotiation: A tough-minded approach to team development. In W. W. Burke & H. A. Hornstein (Ed.), *The social technology or organization development* (pp. 84–96). San Diego, CA: University Associates.

Harvey, J. B., & Boettger, C. R. (1971). Improving communication within a managerial workshop. *Journal of Applied Behavioral Science, 7*(2), 164–179.

Herman, S. W., & Korenich, M. (1977). Authentic management: A Gestalt orientation to organizations and their development. Reading, MA: Addison-Wesley.

Huse, E. F. (1980). *Organization development and change* (Rev. ed.). St. Paul, MN: West.

Katz, D., & Kahn, R. L. (1978). *The social psychology of organizations* (2nd ed.). New York: Wiley.

Likert, R. (1961). New patterns of management. New York: McGraw-Hill.

McGregor, D. (1967). The professional manager. New York: McGraw-Hill.

Plovnick, M. S., Fry, R. E., & Rubin, I. M. (1975). New developments in OD technology: Programmed team development. *Training and Development Journal, 29*(4), 19–27.

Vaill, P. B. (1978). Toward a behavioral description of high performance systems. In M. W. McCall, Jr. & M. M. Lombardo (Eds.), *Leadership: Where else can we go?* (pp. 103–125). Durham, NC: Duke University Press.

Vroom, V. H., & Yetton, P. W. (1973). *Leadership and decision making.* Pittsburgh, PA: University of Pittsburgh Press.

CHAPTER THIRTY-SEVEN

What Is Process Consultation?

Edgar Schein (1999)

T his chapter is about the psychological and social processes that are involved when one person tries to help another person. Whether a therapist is helping a patient or working with a group, a parent is helping a child, a friend is helping another friend, or an organizational consultant is working with managers to improve some aspects of the organization, the same fundamental dynamics are involved. What goes on between a helper and the person or group being helped is what I have called *process consultation*, or PC for short.

The emphasis is on "process" because I believe that *how* things are done between people and in groups is as important as—or more important than— *what* is done. The how, or the "process," usually communicates more clearly what we really mean than does the content of what we say. Process, however, is often less familiar to us. We are less skilled in thinking about processes, in observing them in action, and in designing processes that will accomplish what we intend. In fact, we often design or participate in processes that actually undermine what we want to accomplish. To become aware of interpersonal, group, organizational, and community processes is, therefore, essential to any effort to improve how human relationships, groups, and organizations function.

In this chapter I begin to describe what PC is and the role it plays in daily life and in organization development, change, and learning. Any form of consultation implies that one person is helping another person; hence the central focus of this analysis will be on deciphering what is helpful and what is not helpful in any given human situation. I also look at PC as one of the key activities that takes place at the beginning of and throughout any organization development (OD) and learning effort. Organization development is typically defined as a planned organizationwide program, but its component parts are usually activities that the consultant carries out with individuals or groups. The mode in which these activities are carried out reflects the assumptions that underlie PC. Recent emphases on organizational learning and organizational change also make it necessary to show how PC relates to those particular activities and to build a model and a theory of helping that relates to all of those organizational processes. The central focus remains on OD, however, because I view organization development to be a general process that incorporates learning and change.

Central to any organization improvement program is the creation of a situation in which learning and change can take place by individuals and/or groups. How, then, does the consultant build readiness for learning and change? How does the consultant function as trainer, teacher, mentor, or coach in facilitating learning and change? How does the consultant work with the key individuals of an organization as part of planning an organizationwide program and/or work as a counselor when anxieties and concerns in key individuals may influence the success of the entire effort?

In dealing with these and other questions throughout the volume from which this chapter stems, I attempt to show that the mode in which the consultant chooses to operate moment-to-moment makes a major difference in how helpful the consultation will actually be. The consultant must become able to distinguish among (1) the consultant's position as an expert, telling the client what to do; (2) selling solutions that the consultant may favor or selling the use of tools that the consultant knows how to use; or (3) engaging the client in a process that will in the end be perceived as helpful to the client by both consultant and client. As we will see, these three modes rest on fundamentally different basic models of what is involved in "helping," and these in turn rest on quite different tacit assumptions about the nature of reality and the nature of help.

The field of consultation has grown remarkably in recent years, yet conceptual confusion still exists about consultants—what they actually do for organizations, how they go about doing it, and what tacit assumption they hold about giving help. For example, people who label themselves organizational consultants provide information, analyze information using special diagnostic tools, identify and diagnose complex problems, recommend solutions for the problems, help managers to implement difficult or unpopular decisions, and give managers support and comfort, or a combination of these activities.

Many analysts of the consultation process argue that the process only works when the client knows exactly what he[1] is looking for and when the consultant can deliver specific recommendations pertaining to the problem. In such a model, when clients are disappointed in the results, *they* are blamed for not having been clear in what they wanted or for being unwilling to do what the consultant recommended. In my experience, however, the person seeking help often does not know what she is looking for and indeed should not really be expected to know. All she knows is that something is not working right or some ideal is not being met, and that some kind of help is therefore needed. Any consultant process, then, must include the important tasks of helping the client figure out what the problem or issue is and—only after that—deciding what further kind of help is needed. Managers in an organization often sense that all is not well or that things could be better, but they do not have the tools with which they can translate vague feelings into the clear insights that lead to concrete actions.

The mode of consultation I describe in detail deals especially with situations of the kind just described. The consultant operating in the PC mode does not assume that the manager knows what is wrong, or what is needed, or what the consultant should do. For the process to begin constructively the only requirement is that someone wants to improve the way things are and is willing to seek help. The consultation process itself then helps the client to define the diagnostic steps that will lead ultimately to action programs and to concrete changes that will improve the situation.

MODELS OF CONSULTATION AND THE TACIT ASSUMPTIONS ON WHICH THEY REST

Consultation and helping processes can be distinguished best by analyzing the tacit assumptions they make about the client, the nature of help, the role of the consultant, and the nature of the ultimate reality in which the client and the consultant operate. The three basic models that will be discussed below can be thought of as different modes of operating and are defined by the three different roles consultants can operate in when they help a client. These models also apply to the different ways in which we provide help in our daily life when a child, spouse, or friend seeks our help. The main reason for clearly distinguishing among the three models is that *the helper must choose from one moment to the next which role to be in or which model of helping to use, but all three models imply that help is the primary function of consultation.* The focus on the concept of *helping* is so central throughout this approach to consultation that it must be stated as the first overarching principle of how to deal with others.

Principle One: Always Try to Be Helpful
Consultation is providing help. Obviously, therefore, if I have no intention of being helpful and working at it, I am unlikely to be successful in creating a helping relationship. If possible, every contact should be perceived as helpful.

The three models rest on very different assumptions about the nature of help in any given situation, however, and they have potentially very different consequences. In any situation where help is sought or offered, we must be clear about what is really going on and what helping role to adopt. We cannot be in all three roles at once, so our only choice is to be conscious of which role we want to be in from one moment to the next. This consciousness rests on our ability to decipher and experience the reality that is operating and on our ability to act on that reality. By reality I mean some sense of what is going on inside me, what is going on inside the other person or persons in the situation, and what the nature of that situation is. Wishful thinking, stereotypes, projections, expectations, prior plans, and all other forces that are based on past conceptions or psychological needs rather than here-and-now data tend to get in the way of making a wise choice of how best to help.

This concept of reality also rests on the epistemological assumption that culture and thought create the external reality in which we operate and that we are, therefore, in a perpetual process of jointly deciphering what is going on. Neither the consultant nor the person seeking help can define an objective external reality that exists outside their relationship and cultural context. But together they can approximate how their current assumptions and perceptions create that reality and how they can best deal with that reality in terms of the client's intentions to improve the situation. The second overarching principle that should guide the action of the helper/consultant, therefore, is to always deal with the here-and-now reality.

Principle Two: Always Stay in Touch with the Current Reality

I cannot be helpful if I do not know the realities of what is going on within me and within the client system; therefore, every contact with anyone in the client system should provide diagnostic information to both the client and to me about the here-and-now state of the client system and the relationship between the client and me.

Model One: The Purchase-of-Information or Expertise Model—Selling and Telling

The telling-and-selling model of consultation assumes that the client purchases from the consultant some information or an expert service that she is unable to provide herself. The buyer, usually an individual manager or representative of some group in the organization, defines a need and concludes that the organization has neither the resources nor the time to fulfill that need. She will then look to a consultant to provide the information or the service. For example, a manager may wish to know how a particular group of consumers feels, or how a group of employees will react to a new personnel policy, or what the state of morale is in a given department. She will then hire the consultant to conduct a survey by means of interviews or questionnaires and to analyze the data.

The manager may also wish to know how to organize a particular group and may need the consultant to find out how other companies organize such groups—for example, how to organize the information technology. Or the manager may wish to know particular things about competitor companies, such as their marketing strategy, how much of the price of their product is determined by production costs, how they organize their research and development function, how many employees they have in a typical plant, and so on. He will then hire the consultant to study other companies and bring back data about them. Each of these cases assumes that the manager knows what kind of information or service she or he is looking for and that the consultant is able to provide the information or service.

The likelihood that this mode of helping will work then depends on:

- Whether or not the manager has correctly diagnosed his own needs
- Whether or not he has correctly communicated those needs to the consultant
- Whether or not he has accurately assessed the capabilities of the consultant to provide the information or the service
- Whether or not he has thought through the consequences of having the consultant gather such information, or the consequences of implementing the changes that the information implies or that may be recommended by the consultant
- Whether or not there is an external reality that can be objectively studied and reduced to knowledge that will be of use to the client

The frequent dissatisfaction with consultants and the low rate of implementation of their recommendations can easily be explained when one considers how many of the above assumptions have to be met for the purchase model to work effectively. It should also be noted that in this model the client gives away power. The consultant is commissioned or empowered to seek out and provide relevant information or expertise on behalf of the client; but once the assignment has been given, the client becomes dependent on what the consultant comes up with. Much of the resistance to the consultant at the later stages may result from this initial dependency and the discomfort it may arouse consciously or unconsciously in the client.

In this model the consultant is also likely to be tempted to sell whatever she knows and is good at—when you have a hammer the whole world looks like a bunch of nails. Hence the client becomes vulnerable to being misled about what information or service would actually be helpful. And, of course, there is the subtle assumption that there is knowledge "out there" to be brought into the client system and that this information, or knowledge, will be understandable and usable by the client. For example, organizations frequently purchase surveys to determine how their employees feel about certain issues or even to "diagnose" their culture. When the "expert" information comes back in quantitative form, I have observed managers poring over the bar graph data, trying to figure out what they now *know* when they note that 62 percent of the employees think the organization has a poor career development system. What kind of information value does such a statement actually have, given the problems of sampling, the problems of questionnaire construction, the semantics of words like *career* and *development*, the ambiguity of whether 62 percent is really good or bad outside some broader context, the difficulty of determining what the employees were thinking when they answered the question, and so on? Reality in this situation is an elusive concept.

Model One: The PC Alternative

The PC philosophy, in contrast, is to immediately involve both the client and the consultant in a period of *joint diagnosis*, reflecting the reality that neither the client nor the consultant knows enough at this point of initial contact to define the kind of expertise that might be relevant to the situation. The consultant is willing to deal with an individual client or come into an organization without having a clear mission, goal, or defined problem because of the underlying assumption that any person, group, or organization can always improve its processes and become more effective if it can accurately locate the processes that make a difference to its overall performance. No organizational structure or process is perfect. Every organization has strengths and weaknesses. Therefore, the manager who senses that something is wrong because performance or morale is not what it should be should not leap into action or seek specific help until he has a clear idea of the strengths and weaknesses of the organization's present structures and processes.

The main goal of PC is to help the manager make such a diagnosis and develop a valid action plan based on it. Implicit in this goal is the assumption that the client and consultant must both remain in power. Both must share the responsibility for the insights obtained and actions planned. From the PC point of view, the consultant must not take the monkey off the client's back but recognize that *the problem is ultimately the client's* and only the client's. All the consultant can do is to provide whatever help the client needs to solve the problem himself.

The importance of *joint* diagnosis and action planning derives from the fact that the consultant can seldom learn enough about any given organization to really know what a better course of action would be or even what

information would really help because the members of the organization perceive, think about, and react to information in terms of their traditions, values, and shared tacit assumptions—that is, their organizational culture and
the particular styles and personalities of their key leaders and members.[2]
However, the consultant can help the client to become a sufficiently good
diagnostician herself and to learn how to manage organizational processes
better so that she can solve problems for herself. It is a crucial assumption
of the PC philosophy that *problems will stay solved longer and be solved
more effectively if the organization learns to solve those problems itself.* The
consultant has a role in teaching diagnostic and problem-solving skills, but
he should not attempt actually to solve the problems himself unless he is
certain that he has the requisite information and expertise. The consultant
must always deal with the reality revealed by joint diagnostic activities and
never trust his own a priori assumptions.

When we examine various other contexts in which help is sought, the
same choice must be made between operating in the expert mode or the PC
mode. When my child comes to me asking for help with a math problem,
when a student comes to me for specific information pertaining to a management problem, when a stranger on a street corner asks me for directions, when a friend asks me what movie I would recommend, when my
wife asks me what she should wear to the party, I have to process instantaneously what is really being asked and what kind of response will, in fact,
be helpful. What is the reality that is operating in the situation at that
moment?

The easiest course is to take each request at face value and apply the
purchase-of-information model—that is, answer the immediate question
using one's own expertise. But often the immediate question masks a
deeper or hidden issue. Maybe the child wants to spend some time with
me and the math problem is the only thing she could think of to get my
attention. Maybe the student has a deeper question but is afraid to ask it.
Maybe the stranger is really looking for the wrong thing but does not know it.
Maybe the friend is really testing whether or not I want to go to a movie
with him. Maybe my wife is really trying to point out something about her
wardrobe or maybe she is uncomfortable about the party to which we are
going.

The danger in answering the immediate question is that it may terminate the
conversation and the hidden issue never has a chance to surface. If I am to be
helpful, I must inquire enough to determine where the help is really needed,
and that implies starting in the PC mode. Only after I have jointly diagnosed
the situation with the other party am I in a position to determine whether my
expertise or information will, in fact, be relevant and helpful. One preliminary
generalization, then, is that *the PC mode is necessary at the beginning of any*

helping process because it is the only mode that will reveal what is really going on and what kind of help is needed.

The immediate reality is that, at the beginning of any relationship, the consultant does not know what is really being asked or is needed. It is this state of *ignorance* that is, in fact, the consultant's most important guideline for deciding what questions to ask, what advice to give, or in general what to do next. The consultant must be able to perceive what he or she does not really know, and that process has to be an *active searching out of one's area of ignorance* because we are so filled with preconceptions, defenses, tacit assumptions, hypotheses, stereotypes, and expectations. To discover our areas of ignorance can be a difficult process of weaving our way through all our preconceptions and overcoming some of our own perceptual defenses. The active word *accessing* therefore articulates the third overarching principle of helping. As we successfully access our areas of ignorance, we can engage in genuine mutual exploration; and as areas of ignorance are removed, more layers of reality are revealed, thus making it possible to define help more accurately.

Principle Three: Access Your Ignorance

The only way I can discover my own inner reality is to learn to distinguish what I know from what I assume I know, from what I truly do not know. I cannot determine what is the current reality if I do not get in touch with what I do not know about the situation and do not have the wisdom to ask about it.

Model Two: The Doctor-Patient Model

Another common generic consultation model is that of doctor-patient. One or more managers in the organization decide to bring in a consultant to "check them over," to discover if there are any organizational areas that are not functioning properly and might need attention. A manager may detect symptoms of ill health, such as dropping sales, high numbers of customer complaints, or quality problems, but may not know how to make a diagnosis of what is causing the problems. The consultant is brought into the organization to find out what is wrong with which part of the organization and then, like the physician, is expected to recommend a program of therapy or prescribe a remedial measure. Perhaps leaders in the organization discover that there is a new cure being used by other organizations such as Total Quality Programs, Reengineering, or Autonomous Work Groups, and they mandate that their organization should try this form of therapy as well to improve the organization's health. The consultant is then brought in to administer the program. In this model the client assumes that the consultant operates from professional standards; that the selling is done responsibly, based on good data that the program will provide help for the problem; that the consultant has the diagnostic expertise to apply the program only where it will help; and that the cure will take.

Notice that this model puts even more power into the hands of the consultant in that she diagnoses, prescribes, and administers that cure. The client not only abdicates responsibility for making his own diagnosis—and thereby makes himself even more dependent on the consultant—but assumes, in addition, that an outsider can come into the situation, identify problems, and remedy them. This model is of obvious appeal to consultants because it empowers them and endows them with X-ray vision. Providing expert diagnoses and prescribing remedial courses of action justify the high fees that consultants can command and make very visible and concrete the nature of the help that they claim to provide. In this model the report, the presentation of findings, and the recommendations take on special importance in identifying what the consultant does. For many consultants this is the essence of what they do, and they feel that they have not done their job until they have made a thorough analysis and diagnosis leading to a specific written recommendation.

For example, in one version of this model that is advocated for managers, the consultant uses in-depth interviews and psychological tests as part of a diagnostic phase leading to a formal, written diagnosis and a prescription for the next steps to take. Another common version has the consultant designing and administering opinion and attitude surveys to parts of the organization as a basis for diagnosing problems. The consultant is expected to know what questions to ask, what percentages of positive or negative answers constitute a problem, and what patterns of answers identify areas of potential difficulty in an organization. Sophisticated statistical techniques are often brought into play to bolster the diagnosis and to reassure the client that the consultant is indeed a diagnostic expert.

Perhaps the most common version of this model is for consultants to contract with senior executives to do extensive interviews in the client organization to find out what is going on, base their diagnosis on these data, and then recommend remedial projects to the client who initially hired them. One currently popular version of this process is to assess the competencies that are needed for success in a given job category; to compare the profile of existing competencies to databases drawn from many organizations; and, based on the observed gaps, to prescribe selection, training, and career-development programs to increase the specific competencies that have been identified as lacking.

As most readers will recognize from their own experience, this model is fraught with difficulties in spite of its popularity. All of us, as clients, have experienced how irrelevant a helper's advice or recommendations can be or how offensive it can be to be told what to do, even when we asked for the advice. All of us, as consultants, have had the experience more often than we would care to admit of having our report and recommendation accepted with a polite nod only to have it shelved or, worse, have it rejected altogether with the implication that we did not really understand the client situation at all. Clients often become defensive and belittle our recommendations by pointing out key facts we missed or by informing us that the recommended course of action has already been tried and has failed. Consultants, when operating in this doctor-patient mode, often feel that the clients are to blame—that the clients don't know what they want, that they don't recognize the truth when it is put before them, or that they resist change and don't really want to be helped. To begin to understand these difficulties and to put the PC model into perspective we must analyze some of the implicit assumptions of the doctor-patient model.

One of the most obvious difficulties with this model is the assumption that the consultant can get accurate diagnostic information on her own. In fact the organizational unit that is defined as sick may be reluctant to reveal the kind of information the consultant needs in order to make an accurate diagnosis. Quite predictably, systematic distortions will occur on questionnaires and in interviews. The direction of these distortions will depend on the climate of the organization. If the climate is one of distrust and insecurity, respondents will most likely hide any damaging information from the consultant because of fear of retaliation, something that we have seen repeatedly in the misadventures of whistle blowers. Or respondents may view the interview, survey, or test as an invasion of their privacy and provide either minimal answers or distortions based on what they consider to be the expected or safe responses. If the climate is one of high trust, respondents are likely to view contact with the consultant as an opportunity to get all their gripes off their chests, leading to an exaggeration of whatever problems may exist. In either case, unless the consultant spends a lot of time personally observing the department, she is not likely to get an accurate picture of what may be going on.

An equally great difficulty with this model is that the client is likely to be unwilling to believe that diagnosis or to accept the prescription offered by the consultant. Most organizations probably have drawers full of reports by consultants that are either not understood or not accepted by the client. What is wrong, of course, is that the doctor has not built up a common diagnostic frame of reference with his patient. They are not dealing with a common reality. If the consultant does all the diagnosing while the client waits passively for a prescription, a communication gulf will predictably arise that will make the diagnosis and prescription seem either irrelevant or unpalatable.

Even in medicine, doctors have increasingly realized that patients do not automatically accept diagnoses nor automatically do what the doctor recommends. We see this most clearly in the cross-cultural context, in which assumptions about illness or what should be done about it may differ from culture to culture. We also see this increasingly in the treatment of breast cancer, with the oncologist involving the patient in the crucial choice as to whether to have a mastectomy, a lumpectomy, a program of chemotherapy, or a program of radiation. Similarly, in plastic surgery or in the decision of whether or not to have back surgery, the patient's goals and self-image become crucial variables in determining the ultimate success of the surgery. If we take a medical version of the doctor model of consultation, we had better examine the psychiatric model in which the analysis of resistance and defenses becomes one of the major therapeutic tools.

A third difficulty with this model is that in human systems, indeed in all systems, the process of diagnosis is itself an intervention of unknown consequence. Giving psychological tests to the executive team, conducting attitude surveys in parts of the organization, and interviewing people about their perceptions of the organization influence employees by raising questions in their mind of what might be going on in the organization that warrants the introduction of consultants in the first place. Although the consultant may be acting completely innocently, the employee may conclude that management is getting ready to reorganize and lay off people. The consultant may just be doing her scientific best when she gives the tests or surveys, but the employee may feel that his privacy has been invaded or may begin to form defensive coalitions with other employees that alter the relationships within the organization. It is ironic that the elaborate precautions to make survey responses truly anonymous by having those responses mailed to neutral parties presume a level of distrust within the organization that may be a far more significant reality than whatever data the survey itself may reveal.

A fourth difficulty with the doctor-patient model is that even if the diagnosis and prescription are valid, the patient *may not be able* to make the changes recommended. In the organizational context this may in fact be the most common problem. It is often obvious to the outside consultant what should be done, but the culture of the organization, its structure, or its politics prevent the recommendations from being implemented. In many cases the consultant does not even find out about cultural and political forces until recommendations are rejected or subverted, but by then it may be too late to be really helpful.

In other words, the degree to which the doctor-patient model will work will depend on:

1. Whether or not the client has accurately identified which person, group, or department is, in fact, sick or in need of some kind of therapy

2. Whether or not the patient is motivated to reveal accurate information

3. Whether or not the patient accepts and believes the diagnosis that the doctor arrives at and accepts the prescription that the doctor recommends

4. Whether or not the consequences of doing the diagnostic processes are accurately understood and accepted

5. Whether or not the client is able to make the changes that are recommended

Model Two: The PC Alternative

The process consultation mode, in contrast, focuses not only on *joint* diagnosis but also on *passing on to the client the consultant's diagnostic and problem-solving skills*. The consultant may perceive early in her work what some of the problems in the organization may be and how they might be solved. But she typically will not share her insights prematurely for two reasons: (1) She may be wrong. If she prematurely makes a diagnosis that is incorrect, she may damage her credibility with the client and undermine the relationship. (2) She recognizes that even if she is right, the client may well be defensive, may not listen, may wish to deny what he hears, or may misunderstand what the consultant is saying and thus subvert remedial efforts.

It is a key assumption underlying PC that *the client must learn to see the problem for herself or himself by sharing in the diagnostic process and be actively involved in generating a remedy*. The reason the client must be involved is that the diagnostic process is itself an intervention and any intervention has ultimately to be the responsibility of the client and be owned by him. If tests or surveys are to be administered or if interviews are to be conducted, the client must understand and take responsibility for the decision to conduct these activities. The client must be able to explain to the possibly suspicious subordinate why this is being done and why the consultant is being brought in, or all the difficulties just described may arise.

The consultant may play a key role in helping to sharpen the diagnosis and may provide suggestions for alternate remedies that may not have occurred to the client, but she encourages the client to make the ultimate decision on what diagnostic and remedial actions to take. Again, the consultant does this on the assumption that if she teaches the client to diagnose and remedy situations himself, problems will be solved more permanently and the client will have learned the skills necessary to solve new problems as they arise.

It should also be noted that the consultant may or may not be an expert at solving the particular problems that may be uncovered. The important point in adopting the PC mode initially is that such content expertise is less relevant than are the skills of involving the client in self-diagnosis and helping him to find a remedy that fits his particular situation and his unique set of needs. The consultant must display expertise at giving help and at establishing a relationship with clients that makes it possible to be helpful and that builds a jointly shared reality in which communication is possible. The organizational consultant operating in this mode does not need to be an expert in marketing, finance, or strategy. If problems are uncovered in such areas, the consultant can help the client to find an expert resource and, more importantly, help the client to think through how best to ensure that he will get the help he needs from those experts.

The doctor-patient model, like the purchase-of-expertise model, is constantly applied by us in our daily life. When my child asks me to solve the math problem, I am strongly tempted to make an instant diagnosis of what is wrong and act on it. When my friend asks me about a movie, I make instant assumptions about his entertainment needs and give advice on what movie to see. When my student asks me to recommend some readings pertaining to her research project, I immediately think I know what kind of information she needs and suggest several books and papers. When my wife asks me what she should wear to the party, I instantly think I know what problem she is trying to solve and dispense reactions and advice accordingly. The temptation to accept the power that the other person grants you when he asks for advice is overwhelming. It takes extraordinary discipline in those situations to reflect for a moment on what is actually going on (deal with reality) and to ask a question that might reveal more or encourage the other to tell you more before you accept the doctor role (access your ignorance).

If the consultant is to be helpful, it is essential to ensure that both the other and the consultant understand what problem they are trying to solve and that they have created a communication channel in which they will understand each other so that they can solve the problem effectively and jointly. It is the ultimate purpose of PC to create such communication channels to permit joint diagnosis and joint problem solving.

The fact that *how* we go about diagnosing has consequences for the client system reveals a fourth overarching principle to be added. We must recognize that *everything the consultant does is an intervention*. There is no such thing as pure diagnosis. The common description in many consulting models of a diagnostic stage followed by recommended prescriptions totally ignores the reality that if the diagnosis involves any contact with the client system, the intervention process has already begun. How we go about diagnosing must, therefore, be considered from the point of view of what consequences our diagnostic interventions will have and whether we are willing to live with those consequences.

Principle Four: Everything You Do Is an Intervention
Just as every interaction reveals diagnostic information, so does every interaction
have consequences both for the client and for me. I therefore have to own
everything I do and assess the consequences to be sure that they fit my goals of
creating a helping relationship.

Model Three: The Process Consultation Model

Let me now summarize the main assumptions of what I am calling the process
consultation philosophy, or model. The following assumptions may not always
hold. When they do hold, when we perceive or sense that the reality is best
described by those assumptions, however, then it is essential to approach the
helping situation in the PC mode.

1. Clients, whether managers, friends, colleagues, students, spouses,
children, often do not know what is really wrong and need help in diagnosing
what their problems actually are. But only they "own" the problem.

2. Clients often do not know what kinds of help consultants can give to
them; they need to be helped to know what kinds of help to seek. Clients are
not experts on helping theory and practice.

3. Most clients have a constructive intent to improve things, but they need
help in identifying what to improve and how to improve it.

4. Most organizations can be more effective than they are if their managers
and employees learn to diagnose and manage their own strengths and weaknesses. No organizational form is perfect; hence every form of organization
will have some weaknesses for which compensatory mechanisms must be
found.

5. Only clients know what will ultimately work in their organizations.
Consultants cannot, without exhaustive and time-consuming study or
actual participation in the client organization, learn enough about the culture of an organization to suggest reliable new courses of action. Therefore,
unless remedies are worked out jointly with members of the organization
who do know what will and will not work in their culture, such remedies
are likely either to be wrong or to be resisted because they come from an
outsider.

6. Unless clients learn to see problems for themselves and think through
their own remedies, they will be less likely to implement the solution and less
likely to learn how to fix such problems should they recur. The process consultation mode can provide alternatives, but decision making about such alternatives must remain in the hands of the client because it is the client, not the
consultant, who owns the problem.

7. The ultimate function of PC is to pass on the skills of how to diagnose and constructively intervene so that clients are more able to continue on their own to improve the organization. In a sense both the expert and doctor models are remedial models whereas the PC model is both a remedial and a preventive model. The saying "instead of giving people fish, teach them how to fish" fits this model very well.

This last point differentiates the models clearly in that the expert and doctor model can be compared to single-loop, or adaptive, learning, whereas PC engages the client in double-loop, or generative, learning. One of the goals of PC is to enable the client to learn how to learn. The expert and doctor models fix the problem; the goal of PC is to increase the client system's *capacity for learning* so that it can in the future fix its own problems.[3]

The helping process should *always begin in the PC mode* because until we have inquired and removed our ignorance we do not, in fact, know whether the above assumptions hold or whether it would be safe or desirable to shift into the expert or doctor mode. Once we have begun this inquiry, we will find that one useful way to decide whether to remain in the PC role or move to one of the other modes is to determine some of the properties of the type of problem being faced by the person seeking help.[4] If both the problem definition and the nature of the solution are clear, then the expert model is the appropriate one. If the problem definition is clear but the solution is not, then the doctor has to work with the patient to develop the right kind of adaptive response using his or her technical knowledge. If neither the problem nor the solution is clear, the helper has to rely initially on process consultation until it becomes clear what is going on, what help is needed, and how it is best obtained. The decision whether a technical fix or an adaptive response will be needed will then depend on the degree to which the client or learner will have to change attitudes, values, and habits.

PROCESS CONSULTATION DEFINED

Process consultation is the creation of a relationship with the client that permits the client to perceive, understand, and act on the process events that occur in the client's internal and external environment in order to improve the situation as defined by the client.

With these assumptions in mind, we can define PC.

Process consultation focuses first on building a relationship that permits both the consultant and client to deal with reality, that removes the consultant's areas of ignorance, that acknowledges the consultant's behavior as being always an intervention, all in the service of giving clients insight into what is going on around them, within them, and between them and other people. Based on such insight, PC then helps clients to figure out what they should do about the situation. But at the core of this model is the philosophy that clients must be helped to remain proactive, in the sense of retaining both the diagnostic and remedial initiative because only they own the problems identified, only they know the true complexity of their situation, and only they know what will work for them in the culture in which they live. This can be stated as a fifth overarching principle.

Principle Five: It is the Client Who Owns the Problem and the Solution

My job is to create a relationship in which the client can get help. It is not my job to take the client's problems onto my own shoulders; nor is it my job to offer advice and solutions for situations in which I do not live myself. The reality is that only the client has to live with the consequences of the problem and the solution, so I must not take the monkey off the client's back.

The events to be observed, inquired about, and learned from are the actions that occur in the normal flow of work, in the conduct of meetings, in the formal or informal encounters between members of the organization, and in the more formal organizational structures. Of particular relevance are the client's own actions and their impact on other people in the organization, including their impact on the consultant. As counselors and therapists have found in other domains, one of the most powerful sources of insight is the interaction between the client and the consultant and the feelings this interaction triggers in both of them.[5]

Implicit in this model is the further assumption that all organizational problems are fundamentally problems involving *human* interactions and processes. No matter what technical, financial, or other matters may be involved, there will always be humans involved in the design and implementation of such technical processes, and there will always be humans involved in the initial discovery that technical fixes may be needed. A thorough understanding of human processes and the ability to improve such processes are therefore fundamental to any organizational improvement. As long as organizations are networks of people engaged in achieving some common goals, there will be various kinds of processes occurring between them. Therefore, the more we understand about how to diagnose and improve such processes, the greater will be our chances of finding solutions to the more technical problems and of ensuring that such solutions will be accepted and used by members of the organization.

SUMMARY, IMPLICATIONS, AND CONCLUSIONS

Process consultation is a difficult concept to describe simply and clearly. It is more of a philosophy or a set of underlying assumptions about the helping process that lead the consultant to take a certain kind of attitude toward his or her relationship with the client. Process consultation is best thought of as one mode of operating that the consultant can choose in any given situation. It is most necessary early in the encounter because it is the mode most likely to reveal what the client really wants and what kind of helper behavior will, in fact, be helpful. If it turns out that the client wants simple information or advice and the consultant is satisfied that she has relevant information and advice, she can safely go into the expert or doctor role. However, when she switches into that mode, she must be aware of the assumptions she is making and recognize the consequences of encouraging the client to become more dependent on her. She must also be careful not to take the problem onto her own back.

What the consultant must be really expert at, then, is sensing from one moment to the next what is going on and choosing a helping mode that is most appropriate to that immediate situation and that will build a helping relationship. *No one of these models will be used all the time. But at any given moment, the consultant can operate from only one of them.* The experienced consultant will find herself switching roles frequently as she perceives the dynamics of the situation to be changing. We should, therefore, avoid concepts like "the process consultant" and think more in terms of *process consultation* as a dynamic process of helping that all consultants, indeed all humans, find to be appropriate at certain times.

Though PC is increasingly relevant in today's organizational world, it is important to see how the model applies as well to our daily relationships with friends, spouses, children, and others who from time to time may seek our help. Ultimately what is being described here is a philosophy and methodology of the helping process and an attempt to show its relevance to organization development and learning. Central to this philosophy is a set of operating principles:

- Always try to be helpful.
- Always stay in touch with the current reality.
- Access your ignorance.
- Everything you do is an intervention.
- It is the client who owns the problem and the solution.

If the consultant/helper can operate consistently from these principles, the specific roles of when to give information, when to be a doctor, and when to remain in the process consultant role sort themselves out naturally. However, accessing ignorance and dealing with reality are not easy. These are learned skills that require conceptual models, training, and insight based on experience.

Case One: Designing and Participating in the Annual Meeting at International Oil. This case is intended to illustrate a number of the tactical complexities of staying in the process consultant mode and, at the same time, to make clear the contrast between the different modes. The reader will also note that the content of the case illustrates what is really meant by process, in that the interventions dealt almost exclusively with how things were done, not the actual content of what the group was working on.

The company is a large multinational oil and chemicals concern with headquarters in Europe. I knew a number of the people in the corporate management development group and had met one of their senior executives, Steve Sprague, years ago in an MIT executive program. My involvement resulted from the fact that some senior executives developed the desire to look at their own corporate culture and how it might or might not fit the strategic realities of the next decade. Several members of the corporate management development staff knew that I had just published some papers and a book on organizational culture.

I received a phone call from a man in the corporate staff group who was helping to design the annual three-day off-site meeting for the top forty executives of the company. The proposition was to come in for two days, listen to their internal discussions, and then lecture about culture, weaving in examples from their own discussions to provide feedback on their own culture. I was not to be actively involved at the very beginning and end of the meeting, so this was defined initially as primarily an educational intervention during the second day of the meeting. Although the overt purpose of this educational intervention was to present some formal material to the executives, a covert purpose was to involve them in thinking more realistically about their own culture and its consequences.

I was interested in this company and wanted to learn more about various company cultures, so this seemed like an ideal match. I agreed to the terms as originally stated and was then told that further briefing on the meeting would be provided by Sprague, who had become an executive vice president reporting directly to the chairman of the company. We arranged a meeting in New York during his next trip to the United States. Sprague agreed that my time and expenses were from this point on billable at my usual rates.

At the meeting Sprague talked at length about the strategic situation of the company, saying that it was critical at the annual meeting to take a real look at whether the direction on which the company had embarked still made sense, whether it should be slowed down or speeded up, and how to get the commitment of the top group to whatever was decided. I also learned at this point that Sprague was in charge of the overall design of the three-day meeting and that he not only wanted to brief me but wanted to review the entire design with me.

The initial call had focused on my lecturing on culture, but Sprague was now asking me to be an expert resource to help design the annual meeting and was now making himself the primary client. I found myself switching roles from process consultant to design expert because we were discussing the design of a meeting, a topic about which I obviously knew more than he, and we both understood this switch in role and made it explicit.

We reviewed the design of each component of the meeting in terms of Sprague's goals, and the idea emerged that for me to function as a process consultant throughout the meeting might be helpful. Since my schedule permitted attending the whole meeting, it was decided by Sprague, with my agreement, to have me play several roles throughout. I would give a short input on culture and strategy early in the meeting and define my role as one of trying to see how these topics would relate to each other as the meeting unfolded. I would do my session on culture on day two, and, most, importantly, I would run the session on day three, during which the whole group would draw out what areas of consensus they had reached about future strategic options.

These areas of consensus would deal with the business strategy, but it would be easier for me to test for such consensus than it would be for any of the insiders to do so; it would also free the chairman to play an advocacy role. It therefore made sense to both of us to have me play the consensus-tester role, and I judged that Sprague knew the personality of the chairman well enough that an outsider's assuming such a role would also be acceptable to him. Sprague's insight throughout the discussion reassured me that he had a good grasp of the issues and knew the climate of the organization well. In any case there was not time to meet the chairman, so I had to accept this role on faith.

My participation during the three days worked out as planned. The chairman was comfortable with having me present as an outside resource on process because he felt that this would permit him to focus more on the content, the strategic issues the group was wrestling with. It permitted him a degree of freedom that he ordinarily did not feel because he had played the role of consultant as well as chairman in prior meetings. He explained my role to the other executives and took ownership of the decisions to have me present in my multiple roles.

The active interventions I made focused heavily on task process. For example, I occasionally attempted to clarify an issue by restating what I had heard, asking clarifying questions, restating goals, testing consensus when conclusions seemed to be reached, and keeping a summary of areas of consensus for purposes of my formal input sessions. When it was time to present my feedback on culture, I gave some formal definitions and descriptions of culture as a set of basic assumptions but then asked the group to provide the content. Several members of the group asked more pointedly how I perceived and evaluated their culture, but I had found from past experience that it was best to remain speculative about this because even if I provided an answer that was technically correct, it might arouse defensiveness or denial. I kept emphasizing that only insiders really could understand the key cultural assumptions and invited members of the group to provide the answers.

On the final day I formally tested consensus by structuring the areas of discussion that had been covered and inviting the group to state conclusions, which I then wrote down on flip charts to make them explicit to everyone. My playing this up-front role made it possible for the chairman to be much more active in providing his own conclusions without using his formal power to override the conclusions of others. I sharpened many of the issues based on my listening during the three days and challenged the group in areas where the participants seemed to want to avoid being clear. In this role I was partly process consultant and partly management expert in giving occasional editorial comments on the conclusions being reached.

For example, the group talked of decentralizing into business units, but doing so would take power away from the units currently based in different regions. The business unit headquarters were all in the home city, so they were really centralizing as much as decentralizing. I pointed out the implications of this for various other kinds of policies, such as the movement of people across divisional or geographic lines.

The event terminated on a high note and the decision was made to revisit the results several months later. I met with Sprague to review results and learned that both he and the chairman felt that things went as expected. They felt that bringing me in as an outside resource had helped very much, both at the level of process and content.

Lessons: The consultant must be prepared to operate in whatever mode is most appropriate, given the realities of the moment. At the outset in any client relationship, the consultant must start in the process mode to discover what the client's realities are and what the consultant's relevant skills are for dealing with those realities. New roles evolve as the relationship evolves and as the client system changes. Diagnosis and intervention are completely interwoven.

Case Two: Suspended Team Building in Ellison Manufacturing. This case is intended to illustrate several elements in process consultation. I won't dwell here on how I got into the following situation, but I want to highlight the issue of joint ownership of the process, of the client's owning the problem, of the fact that everything we do—even the most innocent inquiries—are interventions with unknown consequences, and of the importance of accessing our ignorance and dealing with reality.

I had been working with the plant manager of a local plant for some months in a one-on-one counseling relationship. He wanted to think out a strategy for developing more trust among his managers and between labor and management in the plant. After several once-a-month sessions, he concluded that taking his senior management team (his immediate subordinates) to a two-day off-site meeting to build them into a team was a logical next step to take. He scheduled a working lunch with me and his organization development advisor to design the two-day meeting and to plan what my own participation in that meeting would be.

At the beginning of the lunch, I decided I needed some general information about the setting and the people, so I asked, "Who will actually attend the meeting, as you see it, and what are their roles?" (This question exemplifies what I mean by accessing my ignorance. I could not help with planning if I did not know who would be attending the meeting and in what roles.) The plant manager started down his list of subordinates, but when he got to the third name he hedged and said, "Joe is my financial person, but I am not sure he will make it; I have some reservations about his ability and have not yet decided whether or not to keep him or to transfer him." I then asked if there were any others in the group about whom he had reservations, and he said that there was one other person who had not yet proved himself and might not end up on the team.

At this point, all three of us at the lunch meeting had the same instinct, but the plant manager himself articulated it. He said, "I wonder if I ought to be having this team-building session if I'm not sure about the membership of two of the people." I asked what he thought would happen if we went ahead but then he later fired one or both of them. He concluded that this would undermine the team building and that it was not really fair to the two people about whom he was unsure.

After discussing the pros and cons of having the team-building session at all until he had made up his mind about the marginal people, we decided to postpone the meeting until he had decided, and we all breathed a huge sigh of relief that his issue had surfaced at this time rather than later.

Lessons: The crucial information came out in response to an innocent question and the inquiry process allowed the plant manager himself to reach the conclusion to cancel on the basis of his own thinking through of the issues. He regarded the lunch as a most helpful intervention even though we ended up canceling the team-building effort for the time being.

Case Three: The Unnecessary Management Meeting at Global Electric. Dealing with current and emerging realities means that the consultant must be prepared to do less as well as more. This case illustrates how useless it is to think in terms of selling services, given what may be going on in the client system.

I was asked to attend a large Swiss multinational organization's annual management conference to help the president develop a senior management committee. The divisions were operating in too isolated a fashion and, if we could use my educational input as an excuse to bring a small group together regularly, that group could gradually begin to tackle business problems.

The contact client was the director of management development and training, who briefed me during several meetings on the company's situation. They badly needed to find a vehicle to start the autonomous division managers' meeting but felt that such meetings would not work without an outsider to serve as both the excuse for the meeting—that is, the planned seminar—and as the facilitator. So an educational intervention made sense, even though the real goal was to build a more collaborative management team.

After our planning had proceeded and a date had been set some months hence, we scheduled a meeting with the president at the headquarters in Europe to discuss the details of the project. The meeting with the president revealed a somewhat different issue. He was worried that two of his key division managers were fighting all the time and undercutting each other. One of these was too dominant and the other too subservient. What he hoped to do was to bring them together in a group situation in which some feedback to both of them would "correct" their weaknesses. I was a bit skeptical about the potential of the group to do this, but he was prepared to go slowly. We decided that a seminar discussing career anchors and different management styles, a seminar similar to one that had worked well in another Swiss-German company, would serve their needs (Schein, 1985).

Two months before the seminar, I received a call from the contact client saying that they were terribly sorry but the seminar had been canceled and he would explain later. I was to bill them for any time lost; they did not know whether or not they would do the seminar later. I learned what had actually happened when I visited another client who knew the Swiss company's people well, the adventures of the Swiss company having become a topic of discussion among others in the industry.

I heard that the president had become so upset at the "weaker" manager that he had replaced him, and with that replacement most of the difficulties that had motivated the seminar seemed to have disappeared. I also learned from my contact client that my long interview with the president had partially precipitated this decision. Our meeting had made him rethink carefully what he was doing and why. He had noted my skepticism about what the group could do and so chose a different remedial course.

Lessons: Though the consultation process was brief and seemingly terminated before it began, it appears that the interventions made with the president during the planning of the educational intervention produced a level of insight that led the president to fix the problem in a way that he thought more appropriate. The consultant cannot know from one moment to the next which interventions will be crucial in producing the help that the client needs, but in this case my expertise on groups and my raising the question about whether or not the group could fix an interpersonal problem between key players apparently was decisive.

CONCLUSION: COMPLEXITIES IN DEFINING THE CONSULTANT ROLE

What these examples have illustrated is the difficulty of defining the emerging realities in a dynamic client situation, and the need to switch roles as new data emerge. Not only does the client shift in unpredictable ways but with each intervention new data are revealed that alter what it means to be helpful. Frequently the consultant has to switch to the expert mode, but then he must be able to switch back smoothly to the process consultant mode.

Many descriptions of the consulting process emphasize the need for a clearly articulated contract from the outset. The reality for me has been that the nature of the contract and who the client is with whom I should be doing the contracting shift constantly, so that contracting is virtually a perpetual process rather than something one does up front prior to beginning the consultation.

The consultant should also be clear, many models say, about precisely who the client is. I am always very clear about who the contact client is when I am first called or visited, but once I have begun to work with the contact client and we have defined a next step, the client base starts to expand in unpredictable ways.

Exercise: Reflecting on How to Help

The purpose of this exercise is to make you aware of the possibility of playing different roles when you are cast in the helper role. You can do steps one, two, and six by yourself (twenty minutes), or, if you are in a workshop setting, you can work with a partner to do all six steps (one hour).

1. Think back over the last several days and identify two or three instances of someone's asking for your help or advice.

2. Reconstruct the conversation in your own mind and identify what role you took in response to the request for help. What did the other person want? How did you respond? Could you have responded differently from the way you did respond? Does your response fall clearly into one of the models of consultation described—expert, doctor, process consultant?

3. Pair up with another person if you are in a workshop setting and recount your cases to get a reaction from the other on what they observe in your behavior.

4. Analyze their response to your story from the point of view of what role they took in response to your story and how you reacted to it.

5. Reverse roles and respond to your partner's story, and then analyze how you responded and what reactions that elicited in your partner.

6. Reflect on the roles that you seem to take naturally and spontaneously when someone seeks your help, and ask yourself whether those roles are appropriate as you look back on the situation. Are there other roles that you should learn to take?

Notes

1. "He" or "she" will be used alternately and randomly throughout the text.

2. Most of the points on organizational culture and leadership are drawn from my book on this subject and related literature that will be referred to in various chapters (Schein, 1985, 1992).

3. This terminology for learning derives originally from Bateson's concept of deutero-learning and Argyris & Schön's description of single- and double-loop learning. Perhaps the most thorough treatment is Michael's "Learning to Plan and Planning to Learn." The distinction between adaptive and generative learning has been explored by Senge in the context of how to think about organizational learning as capacity building (Argyris & Schön, 1996; Bateson, 1972; Michael, 1973, 1997; Senge, 1990).

4. Heifetz in his book *Leadership Without Easy Answers* (1994) defines adaptive work as something the leader and the follower have to do together if the problem and the solution are not clear. Comparing process consultation to a form of leadership seems entirely appropriate as situations become more complex. "What can authority do when the authority does not know the answer? In those situations, the authority can induce learning by asking hard questions and by recasting people's

expectations to develop their response ability . . . her actions are nothing if not expert, but they are expert in the management of processes by which the people with the problem achieve the resolution'' (pp. 84–85).

5. I was influenced here by the Gestalt movement. My first trainer was the late Richard Wallen, who taught me a great deal about observing what is inside me. Subsequently I was greatly influenced by Ed Nevis, who applied Gestalt principles to organizational consulting (Nevis, 1987). In my graduate training and early career, I was heavily influenced by the work of Kurt Lewin and the work of Gestalt psychologists like Koehler and Koffka.

CHAPTER THIRTY-NINE

Understanding and Using Large System Interventions

Barbara Benedict Bunker
Billie T. Alban (2002)

Several years ago, a manager from a major oil company attended a workshop in which we presented a framework for understanding twelve methods of working with organizational systems as a whole. The next day, he told us that he was so excited about the concept of "getting the whole system into the room" to address important strategic issues that he could not sleep that night. He thought that these methods could help his company solve a crisis: it was the highest-cost, lowest producer on the Gulf Coast. A consulting firm specializing in long-term strategy had told his company that if they could not turn the picture around, they should close down the Gulf Coast operation. This manager was so excited by the potential of these methods that he convinced the company to send a fourteen-person delegation to the next national conference on large group interventions. There, they heard executives describe why they had opted to use these methods for dealing with change in their companies and what results were achieved.

The delegation selected real time strategic change as a method that could work for them. For the first time in this oil company's history, everyone in this entire system—not only managers and executives, but the roustabouts from the drilling rigs, the contractors, and the suppliers—met in a room large enough to hold them; there were over twelve hundred people. First, they analyzed what was working and what was not working, and what the future would hold if things could not be turned around. Together, they created a vision of the future they desired. Together, they built a common database of information on things that needed to change. As a result, multiple task forces were set up to address the issues. The task forces were always made up of people who were part of the system they were working to change, regardless of level or function. A mechanism was established to keep task forces in touch with what was going on in other task forces and deal with overlap. There was communication to the drilling rigs in the gulf so that people who had historically been marginalized could have some voice and influence. The work, which took over two years, resulted in millions of dollars in cost savings and big increases in oil production. It created a new future for this part of the oil company.

WHAT ARE LARGE GROUP INTERVENTIONS?

In 1987, Marvin Weisbord's book *Productive Workplaces* described "getting the whole system into the room" as the best way to ensure that change in organizations would be effective and obtain commitment. This idea was already in practice in Merrelyn Emery's work on the Search Conference in Australia and in the work of Dannemiller Tyson Associates at Ford with large groups of managers.

The idea of gathering an entire organization (or a diagonal slice representative of it) to talk about, influence, or invent needed changes was new and important because organization development (OD) arose from small group research and practice in the 1950s and 1960s and tended to focus on change at the individual or group level. When the whole organization was involved, a waterfall process from top to bottom using groups at various levels was the usual practice. This proved to be both slow and time-consuming.

As the world changed and organizations were hit with more and more global competition, the demand to change faster was urgent. Change involves decisions about what must change and how, as well as a process of implementation. Practitioners knew that old methods were not bringing about change that happened quickly and was implemented quickly. As practitioners ourselves, we began to be aware of interesting developments using much larger groups that included the whole system in the early 1990s. Were these just isolated experiments, or was this a developing social innovation?

We tested our idea that something new in practice was occurring by editing a special issue of the *Journal of Applied Behavioral Science* on large group interventions in 1992. When we issued a call for papers, we were not sure we would be able to fill a whole issue. In fact, more people sent articles for review than we could publish. Reader interest in that issue was enormous and required several printings. We had clearly tapped an important emerging area of practice. As more and more people began to use large groups in their practices, more methods developed. We wrote a book (Bunker & Alban, 1997) that provided a conceptual framework for understanding what had grown to twelve methods.

Although there are numerous differences among methods, we choose to organize them by the outcome or work they do. Four methods help organizations (and communities) to plan for the future (see Figure 39.1). Four methods specialize in the redesign of work, making it more effective with attention to the social environment at the same time (see Figure 39.2). And four methods are helpful when an organization needs to solve problems, discuss difficult issues, or make decisions as a whole (see Figure 39.3).

THE SEARCH CONFERENCE
Purpose to create a future vision
Merrelyn and Fred Emery

- Set Format: Environmental Scan, History, Present, Future
- Criteria for Participants: Within System Boundary
- Theory: Participative Democracy
- Search for Common Ground
- Rationalize Conflict
- No Experts
- Total Community Discussion
- 2.5-Day Minimum
- 35 to 40+ Participants
- Larger Groups = Multisearch Conference
- 1/3 Total Time Is Action Planning

FUTURE SEARCH
Purpose to create a future vision
Weisbord and Janoff

- Set Format: Past, Present, Future, Action Planning
- Stakeholder Participation, No Experts
- Minimizes Differences
- Search for Common Ground
- Self-Managed Small Groups
- 18 Hours over 3 Days
- 40 to 80+ Participants
- Larger Groups = Multisearch Conference

REAL TIME STRATEGIC CHANGE
Purpose to create a preferred future with system-wide action planning
Dannemiller and Jacobs

- Format Custom-Designed to Issue
- Highly Structured and Organized
- Theory: Beckhard Change Model
- Common Data Base
- 2 to 3 Days + Follow-Up Events
- Use of Outside Experts as Appropriate
- Use of Small Groups and Total Community
- Self-Managed Small Groups
- 100 to 2,400 Participants
- Logistics Competence Critical
- Daily Participant Feedback
- Planning Committee and Consultants Design Events

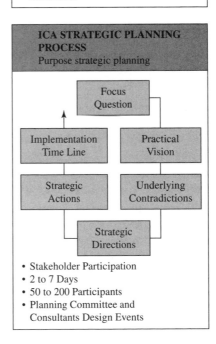

ICA STRATEGIC PLANNING PROCESS
Purpose strategic planning

- Stakeholder Participation
- 2 to 7 Days
- 50 to 200 Participants
- Planning Committee and Consultants Design Events

Figure 39.1. Large Group Methods for Creating the Future.

THE CONFERENCE MODEL® *Dick and Emily Axelrod*	FAST CYCLE FULL PARTICIPATION WORK DESIGN *Pasmore, Fitz, and Frank*

• System-Wide Preconference Education
• Design Process in Five Conferences
  – Vision
  – Customer
  – Technical
  – Design
  – Implementation
• 3+ Weeks Between Conferences
• 2+ Days for Each Conference
• Data Assist Teams Work Between Meetings to Involve Larger Organization
• 80+ Participants, Parallel Conferences for Larger Groups
	• Orientation Events Educate and Include Everyone
	• Five Meetings
	  – Future Search (2 Days)
	  – Meeting External Expectations (1 Day)
	  – Work Systems Analysis (2 to 3 Days)
	  – Work Life Analysis (1 Day)
	  – New Design and Implementation (4+ Days)
	• Up to 120 Attend Meetings
	• Parallel Design of Support Process Changes
	• 1/3 of System Participation Goal
	• Design Ratification Events Include Everyone

REAL TIME WORK DESIGN *Dannemiller and Tolchinsky*	PARTICIPATIVE DESIGN *Fred and Merrelyn Emery*
• Whole System Present at Launch and Implementation • 50 to 2,400 Participants • Process, Design, Deep Dive Conferences Representative • 1-Day Conferences on Key Administrative Support Issues • Design Team Manages Process and Does Micro-Work • Implementation Team Oversees Mini-Conferences	• Bottom-up Process • Company-Wide Education Is First Step • Management Sets Minimum Critical Specifications • Basic Principle: Each Level Coordinates and Controls Its Own Work • Each Unit Designs Its Own Work • Six Design Principles Used to Redesign Work • Multiskilling Is the Norm

Figure 39.2. Large Group Methods for Work Design.

THE IMPORTANCE OF LARGE SYSTEM INTERVENTIONS

OD is a process of using applied behavioral science knowledge and systems theory to plan and implement change in organizations. The goal is more effective organizations and a work environment supportive of human needs and development. Participation by stakeholders during organizational change was demonstrated early to be crucial in effective change processes. One way that people participate is by giving data, usually in survey or interview format, about their life in and their perceptions of the organization and its functioning.

SIMU-REAL	WORK OUT (GENERAL ELECTRIC)
Purpose real time work on current issues test future designs, learn about system *Donald and Alan Klein*	Purpose problem identification and process improvement
	• Improvement Target Selected
• Organization Selects Issue for Work	• Employee Cross-Functional Meeting
• Room Arrangement Reflects Organization's Structure	• Process: Discuss and Recommend
• People Act Their Organizational Role	• Senior Management Responds Immediately
• Periods of Stop Action and Reflection	• Champions and Sponsors Follow Through to Implementation
• Decision Process Agreed to in Advance	• Follow-Up as Needed
• 1 Day	• 1 to 2 Days
• 50 to 150 People	
• Facilitator Needs Expertise in Process Consultation	

LARGE SCALE INTERACTIVE EVENTS	OPEN SPACE TECHNOLOGY
Purpose problem solving *Dannemiller and Jacobs*	Purpose discussion and exploration of system issues *Harrison Owen*
Uses Same Methodology as Real Time Strategic Change, see description, Part One • Many Different Uses	• Least Structured of Large Group Technologies
	• Divergent Process
	• Large Group Creates Agenda Topics
	• Interest Groups Form Around Topics
	• Periodic Town Meetings for Sharing Information Across Interest Groups
	• One Facilitator Lays Out Format, Ground Rules, "Holds the Space"
	• Requires an Understanding of Large Group Dynamics
	• 1 to 3 Days

Figure 39.3. Whole System Participative Work.

Organizations need data from the full range of employees to understand how the system views itself. Unfortunately, many organizations appear not to know how to talk within themselves. These methods often allow what is known to many to become public so that it can be addressed.

Large system interventions complete the array of methods needed to intervene at all levels of organizational life. We see this new development as a natural progression in the history of trying to change organizations. Change processes usually target one or possibly two levels of intervention. Change can be planned to target individuals, interpersonal processes, groups, intergroup processes, or the organization.

Some practitioners of OD and industrial/organizational (I/O) psychology have focused at the individual level with interventions about managerial and future competencies, career development, and assessment centers. The theory is that changing the people will also change the organization.

Improving the effectiveness of groups also has been thematic over the history of OD. Early OD capitalized on early T-group research to improve group functioning using interventions such as process consultation, how to run better meetings, and team building. More recently, self-managed teams and global teams have been the focus of attention.

Working on interdepartmental issues (intergroup interventions) developed in the late 1960s, but the methods were few and typically dealt with two or at most three groups. Typical examples are Beckhard's confrontation meeting, union-management structured meetings, and work on interdepartmental tensions within organizations such as marketing and sales or manufacturing and engineering. Because they work with the whole system, large system interventions have developed new methods of working across organizational boundaries.

Until large system interventions were developed, consultants lacked methods for bringing together and working with the whole system at one time. Data-based methods such as survey feedback and generic climate surveys do collect data from and target the whole system for change. However, the intervention process is typically a waterfall from the top that takes months and addresses issues serially from the top of the organization down. Gestalt practitioners have long practiced whole systems thinking and intervention, but even they have been enabled to do much more interactive whole systems work using these new methods.

These methods also make it possible to work with the organization's environment by including stakeholders in events. Furthermore, they can be used for work across groups and organizations in communities and in complex global organizations.

We believe that these methods complete the development of methods in the field of OD practice. They are important because practitioners and clients now have choice among all possible levels of work.

KEY CONCEPTS

Data about the system have always been important in organizational change processes. In the early T-group, people shared perceptions of individual and group behavior and used these data to learn about group behavior and development. In team-building interventions, consultants interview team members and feed back summaries of the data they collect for analysis and action. At the organizational level, survey feedback, one of the central OD methods, collects data from the whole system and then feeds them back for discussion and action. In a somewhat different way, data and the processes for gathering them, analyzing them, and acting on them are central to large system interventions. In the language of these interventions, creating a common database is essential.

Creating and Analyzing the Data

Data are the information, perceptions, beliefs, and values of the people who participate in the large system intervention. This includes all the people or their representatives from the organizational system, a broad selection crossing levels and functions. It often also includes the environment outside the organization: customers, suppliers, industry experts, regulators, and other relevant stakeholders.

Small groups of seven to ten people sit at round tables, which facilitate interaction, each group composed as a microcosm of the system present at the event. Identifying the key stakeholders for the target issue and making sure that they are present at the event is critical for successful intervention.

In a series of guided activities, these groups take the data that the people present have created and analyze them. Over a series of discussions, they share their perceptions until everyone understands the issues similarly (although they may not all agree, for example, about what should be done). In the language of practitioners, everyone is reading off the same page.

Divergent Views, Conflict, and the Search for Common Ground

People from various parts of the organization come with numerous perspectives, values, and beliefs. These differences are acknowledged; however, the strategy for many of these interventions is to search for common ground, or areas where people do agree. The common psychological process in which differences emerge and then everyone focuses on trying to resolve them is circumvented. The conscious focus is areas of agreement, which often turn out to be bigger than anticipated. This common ground of agreement is the next step in everyone reading off the same page. (For an elaboration of this idea see Bunker, 1999.)

Use of Data, and Survey Feedback Use of Data

In general, there are three key differences in the use of data for large system interventions and the more familiar OD survey feedback approach.

Speed and Ownership. In large system interventions, the people who generate the data analyze and interpret them. This is a highly interpersonal process in which people are actively engaged and get immediate reactions to their data, a process that increases ownership and a sense of shared responsibility. Everything happens at one time. In survey feedback, the people who generate the data give them to others to collate and feed back a preliminary analysis. This takes time and is a more distant process because the respondents fill out questionnaires for others to analyze. It is slower because a top-to-bottom waterfall process is typically used for the feedback-discussion-action process.

Consulting Role. In the large system intervention, consultants create and facilitate the process in partnership with an active steering committee from the organization. In survey feedback, consultants contract as experts in data collection and analysis. They design questionnaires or do interviews, and they create the initial picture of the data that is fed back to the organization.

Degree of Focus. Typically, the large system intervention has a more focused agenda; people come together around a central theme or issue. Survey feedback has the ability to survey an organization about a wide array of issues at one time. It can be used for a focused issue, but more often it has a broad sweep.

Theory and Methods

By the mid-1990s, the twelve large system intervention methods described in Figures 39.1, 39.2, and 39.3 were very much in practice, and there was a great deal of interest from practitioners in understanding them and being trained to use them. Among the methods that create the future, Future Search, which was originated by Weisbord from some ideas from the Emery's Search Conference and methods from the National Training Laboratory, became very popular as a way of creating a vision for the future of organizations and communities. The Search Conference, Future Search, and the Inter-Cultural Affairs methods offer a stable format that can be learned and used by practitioners. Real Time Strategic Change, in contrast, is like a custom-tailored suit. It is designed for each client situation, often using activity modules, some of which were created by Ron Lippitt in his work in the 1970s. Real Time Strategic Change has an advantage in that it is a method that can involve much larger groups, from two hundred to two thousand, than the other future methods. It also routinely creates the option that management can bring in a draft vision of the future that participants react to and influence. In many settings, this allows management to fulfill what they see as their responsibility to lead but also allows for voice from those in the organization. In our view, all of these methods are useful and effective. Choosing the right one for a particular situation is the art form.

Among methods that are used to design work, three that were very similar in 1995 (the Conference Model, Fast Cycle Full Participation Work Design, and Real Time Work Design) have since become difficult to distinguish as separate methods. This is partly because the inventors of these methods engage in active discussions with each other about the work they are doing from their common theory base in sociotechnical systems theory of work design. It is also true that client needs modify ideal designs. Basically, these methods identify processes in the work flow that need improvement. They create a desired future state, analyze the work, and redesign how it is done and the structure that supports it so that they can create the desired state. This is done in a series of events for large groups supported by smaller task group work. Redesign projects typically take about six months to accomplish, and full implementation is often longer. Because so many people are involved, a wide sense of participation and knowing what is going on is achieved, thus reducing the sense of alienation and secrecy often associated with changes in work process (for example, downsizing).

Participative Design is a radical departure from the methods just discussed. It begins at the bottom of the organization when people design their own work and take responsibility for it. The redesign process then moves up the organization, building on the first units. After they have designed their work, the next level asks, "What is our work?" (now that their subordinates have redesigned their work). They identify what their work is and design it, and so on up to the top of the organization. This totally democratic process must be adopted by management before going forward. In addition, there is a significant period of education before any action, so that everyone in the system understands what is going to happen.

The third set of methods, those for discussion and decision making, emerged at different times and have remained relatively discrete. Simu-Real, invented by Klein in the 1970s, is a process of creating in one place the physical presence for a day of the whole system and exploring in action and stop-action episodes an issue or organizational problem.

Open-Space was invented by Owen in the 1980s as a method to create good conversations about controversial or unexplored issues in organizations and communities. In this least structured of the twelve methods, people create their own agenda in the first hour together and then proceed to explore it using rules and norms that free them from the usual hierarchical constraints.

WorkOut was invented at General Electric in the late 1980s, initially to remove requirements that took up time without adding value. Since then, it has become articulated into a method of addressing serious system problems and making decisions about them within a few months. After the problem is identified, there is intense preparation for a several-day meeting with all the stakeholders off-site. At the end of that meeting, management, including the project champion, comes to hear reports and make decisions about proposed actions. These actions are accomplished within thirty, sixty, or ninety days, by which time the problem should be under control.

Finally, Large Scale Interactive Events are a third form of the real time method (Jacobs, 1994) devoted to problem solving. This method, because of its flexibility, can be used for many objectives. For example, when tuberculosis was on the rise in New York City, especially among the poor and homeless, these practitioners designed a three-day meeting that brought together four hundred concerned stakeholders (including police, hospitals, doctors, social agencies, and homeless shelters) to plan for action. In another example, Marriott hotels used this method to deal with problems in specific hotels and to teach the staff Total Quality methods of problem analysis (Jacobs, 1994).

EMERGING TRENDS

We believe that the category system we created is useful and robust as a way of creating a conceptual framework for these methods. In our more detailed examination of the methods (Bunker & Alban, 1997), we also discuss differences among them in structure, decision-making process, number of people who can be involved in any one event, stakeholder involvement, action planning, and type of design. These differences are useful to consider when selecting a method for use (see also Holman & Devane, 1999).

Although we have no hard data on practitioner use of these methods, our central role as people who are interested in all the methods and without favorites among them keeps us in touch with many practitioners. As we move into the decade after the excitement about the discovery of these new methods, it is interesting to consider how they are being used.

Over the past five years, there has been a transition among experienced practitioners from a view that these events can be freestanding and counted on to produce enough energy to guarantee change, to a view that these events are part of a change process that needs other support. For example, in the early days of Future Search, Weisbord and Janoff taught that the energy generated in a good Future Search would carry into change processes. With experience, it is clear that although this sometimes happens, implementation should be planned carefully as the event is planned. Although these events are critical to rapid and systemwide understanding and commitment to change, the stand-alone event emphasis has moved to an understanding of how to work with these events as part of a more sustained process. Systems are difficult to change. These methods add heavy cannon to our array of weapons.

Although there have not been any radical new breakthrough methods emerging, there are practitioners who have taken these ideas and shaped them in line with their particular work and created new names for what they are doing. Most practitioners start out by learning and using one method. Gradually, many of us are using more than one method and using them in combination. For example, a system of five hospitals held Open Space meetings in their five communities before going into a Future Search and then a redesign process within each hospital. These methods are also influencing the design of conferences and meetings. The "talking heads" event typical in many organizations is being transformed into more interactional occasions using small groups at round tables.

Another current trend is experimentation with shorter events for specific client needs. This requires the good judgment of experienced practitioners because methods created and tested over several days have an internal logic and flow that can cause difficulties if they are disrupted. However, when the organizational system is coherent and shares values, there is evidence that some shorter (half- or whole-day) events can be very effective.

People also ask why appreciative inquiry (Ai), a method that developed in the 1980s, is not included in our framework. The answer is straightforward. Ai is a useful change method that is employed in both systems and units of organizations. The methods in our framework all require large group events as the core around which work is done. Ai processes can and do use large groups, but Ai did not emerge as a method based on bringing the whole system together in one room to do its work. In fact, much of Ai work is done in one-on-one interviews. Since the emergence of large system interventions, Ai practitioners, like many others, have incorporated these methods. The basic principle of gathering the whole system to do work has become influential and has stimulated modifications in a number of change methods. For the methods we are discussing, the large group event is core, not optional.

RESULTS OF USING THESE METHODS

Although there is distressingly little research about these methods, we propose from anecdotal accounts and our own experience and reflection as practitioners that change occurs in three areas that are measurable.

Measurable Outcomes

Interventions that target increased effectiveness in organizational processes or improved outcomes are most easily quantified by collecting data on the cost of the intervention and the magnitude in hard numbers of the expected changes. Unfortunately for research knowledge, organizations may do this for their own purposes but not make these data widely available. There is a tendency to hear about the success stories in dollars and cents and not to hear the same data about those that did not meet expectations.

Shifts in Perception

People arrive at large system interventions seeing the world from their own perspective and experience. In the event, they engage in focused conversations with a microcosm of the organization in small, self-managing groups. They may hear new views and information from the platform, which they are asked to discuss in these microcosm groups. These conversations build on each other, and the group becomes a unit as it works on its assigned tasks. Perceptions are often widened or changed. Rather than just seeing the organization's situation from a single department's perspective, individuals now can see it as a whole and understand much better how the whole work process, including how their own function fits with what others do. They now understand at a new level who the stakeholders are and what their interests are. In short, everyone comes away with a bigger picture of the organization. They may also understand the environment in which the organization is functioning better and why change is critical. Depending on the main issue or theme of the event, people learn from others and enlarge their perspectives.

We recall a manager from Mobil who commented about the impact that working like this had on his own way of thinking: "Whenever we have a meeting, I ask myself, 'Who should be here?'" The idea that every issue has a system of stakeholders that need to be involved is experienced so consistently that people who work this way internalize it.

Building Social Capital

A serendipitous result of this way of working is the network of relationships across the organization or community that is created. When people return to their jobs, they have widened their set of contacts across organization boundaries. In *Bowling Alone* (2000), Putnam calls these essential networks that supply information and assistance social capital. Knowing how to cross organizational boundaries is an essential skill sorely lacking in many places. A good network helps shift perceptions from *they* to *we*.

A Dearth of Research

Why is there so little research on these important new methods? One reason is clearly the complexity of measurement issues, as well as disentangling them from the many other factors affecting organizational life. Another is the privatization of research.

Most interesting to us is the possibility that this type of intervention, which involves the whole system, cannot be measured by traditional linear methods. Search-Net, an alliance of Future Search practitioners, is engaged in what they call the "ripple project," an effort to document changes that happen as a result of the energy for change generated in a large system intervention event flowing in ever-widening circles and causing change. Other practitioners report that in "reunions" several months after an event, discussion of what has happened as a result of the event was considerably advanced when people put their individual knowledge together and realized what system effects were occurring. These kinds of data could not have been discovered by sampling individuals. It took the system to understand what had happened in the system.

EMERGING FRONTIERS

In the past few years, several trends have emerged regarding the practice of large system interventions.

Before and After

Early focus was on the event itself, that is, on making gatherings of large groups of people work. A great deal was learned about designing events that engaged everyone and about the logistic requirements to support each design. As practitioners developed enough experience and felt that they had these elements under control, attention has turned to what must happen to ensure that the event and change process are successful.

Before the event, a steering committee is formed that represents a microcosm of those who will be present for the whole system meeting. They serve as a check on whether all the stakeholders have been invited and work with the practitioners who develop the design for the meeting. Their role is to give input to the design—to stand in the shoes of the people who will attend and anticipate issues and problems. Some of the issues can be addressed and resolved during the planning process; others affect how the event is organized. Sometimes the steering committee will go through a practice run of the event in order to get it right. During the event itself, they monitor how well things are going. Each day, the steering committee meets to review the day and the feedback from participants and to make adjustments in the next day's design. The steering committee, in partnership with the large system practitioners, is the control mechanism for the whole process.

Hierarchy and Democratic Participation: A Paradox

There is a history in social science research of repeated demonstrations of the importance of employee participation for commitment to change and implementation effectiveness, but much less success in getting organizations' leadership to use these methods. Why? It is not cost, because companies spend millions on consulting contracts to change organizations.

Someone has said that in America our values are very democratic but our organizations are very hierarchical. We have found that other cultures, in Scandinavia, Holland, New Zealand, and Canada, seem more comfortable with the use of these methods. Are these cultures more communitarian in nature? Do U.S. executives have a higher need for control and a greater fear of chaos? In many organizations, we experience a tension about issues of authority, a need for management control, and a desire to involve people, to give them voice. Axelrod's Terms of Engagement (2000) proposes principles for a new change management paradigm that deals with this tension.

Emery and Purser (1996) have written wisely about the contradictions of trying to run an organization in a mixed mode, that is, both hierarchically and participatively. It creates confusion in people. By contrast, Vroom and Yetton (1973) propose that decision making can work effectively in three different styles. *Authoritarian decision making* keeps the control with the person in power because he or she alone makes the decision. *Group decision making* allows group members full participation and equal power in deciding. It is democratic. And *consultative decision making,* the middle way, involves others in influencing and giving advice to the decision maker while that person still retains the power to decide. Using all three modes makes managers very effective.

The intriguing question is whether both authority and participation can be used in organizations at appropriate times or whether they are orthogonal. Anecdotally, there are stories of the effective use of both styles. For example, Carlson's raiders—a group of U.S. Marines fighting in China in the early 1940s—did the planning for their dramatic air raids around a table where each man, regardless of rank, had an equal voice. Then they went into action and implemented the raids in full military fashion. If both modes are to be used, that level of clarity about authority is essential. Organization leaders have to decide how much participation in decision making they want and at what point in the planning process. We believe many leaders and managers are not clear themselves about this issue, which can create hesitation about employing large system interventions.

Implementation Issues

It is very rare that a single event will change a system. These events are most effective as part of a process of change within an organization. The implementation issue is how decisions get fully carried out, how changes in behaviors, values, and structures become embedded in the organization.

There is a high probability that unless appropriate actions are taken, the propensity of the system will be to fall back into the bureaucratic linear mode and make decisions and do business in the old way, not the new way. For this reason, it is imperative that planning and resourcing of the implementation phase begin in the steering committee at the same time that the event is planned. After most large system intervention events, people are energized and committed to change, but they are also tired. As they go back to their demanding work settings, it is easy for plans to move slowly or erode. Linear planning and responsibility charting are ubiquitous and necessary, but they alone are not sufficient to ensure implementation. Many change efforts fail because the implementation phase is inadequately resourced. We believe that creating dedicated implementation resources is a first step. At the same time, we believe that innovative methods that are less linear and create and support the energy released by the event need more experimentation. People engaged in implementation need "reunions" and occasions to renew commitment and share information. They need to know about implementation activities and have opportunities to participate. Leadership needs to be engaged and visible in support, sending a symbolic message about the importance of this final phase. These processes must be planned in advance and also allow for the creative emergence of new ideas that can be tried to deepen the institutionalization of the change.

CONCLUSION

Numerous large system interventions are being integrated into more traditional OD practice when the change issue needs to be addressed at the system level. Because these methods are relatively recent, they are being used in change practice in many different ways. We see these experiments as useful and necessary. At the same time, research on outcomes needs development, and the role of leadership needs more attention. Finally, the important issue of implementation is a dilemma of contemporary organizational change practice, not a specific problem of these new methods.

Bibliography for Specific Methods

Appreciative Inquiry

Hammond, S. A. (1998). *The thin book of appreciative inquiry*. Plano, TX: Practical Press.

The Conference Model

Axelrod, R. H. (1993). Using the Conference Model for work design. *Journal for Quality and Participation, 16*, 58–61.

Fast Cycle Full Participation

Fitz, A. S., & Frank, G. (1999). Fast-cycle full participation organization redesign. In P. Holman & T. Devane (Eds.), *The change handbook: Group methods for shaping the future* (pp. 123–137). San Francisco: Berrett-Koehler.

Future Search

Weisbord, M. R., & Janoff, S. (2000). *Future search* (2nd ed.). San Francisco: Berrett-Koehler.

ICA Strategic Planning

Spencer, L. (1989). *Winning though participation: Meeting the challenge of corporate change with the technology of participation*. Dubuque, IA: Kendall/Hunt.

Large Scale Interactive Events

Dannemiller Tyson Associates. (2000a). *Whole-scale change: Unleashing the magic in organizations*. San Francisco: Berrett-Koehler.

Dannemiller Tyson Associates. (2000b). *Whole-scale change toolkit*. San Francisco: Berrett-Koehler.

Open Space Technology

Owen, H. (1997). *Open space technology: A user's guide* (2nd ed.). San Francisco: Berrett-Koehler.

Participative Design

Emery, F. (1995). Participative design: Effective, flexible, and successful—now! *Journal for Quality and Participation, 18*(1).

Rehm, R. (1999). *People in charge: Creating self managing workplaces*. Stroud, England: Hawthorn.

Real Time Strategic Change

Jacobs, R. W. (1994). *Real time strategic change: How to involve the entire organization in fast and far-reaching change*. San Francisco: Berrett-Koehler.

Real Time Work Design

Tolchinsky, P. D. (1999, Mar.–Apr.). A redesign of the Central Intelligence Agency. *Journal for Quality and Participation, 22*(2), 31–35.

Search Conference

Emery, M., & Purser, R. E. (1996). *The search conference: A comprehensive guide to theory and practice*. San Francisco: Jossey-Bass.

Simu-Real

Klein, D. C. (1992). Simu-Real: A simulation approach to organizational change. *Journal of Applied Behavioral Science, 28*, 566–578.

WorkOut

Leaders' Guide to WorkOut: Town Meetings. (1999). In R. Ashkenas, T. Jick, D. Ulrich, & C. Paul-Chandhury (Eds.), *The boundaryless organization field book: Practical tools for building the new organization* (Vol. 2, pp. 49–71). San Francisco: Jossey-Bass.

References

Axelrod, R. H. (2000). *Terms of engagement: Changing the way we change organizations*. San Francisco: Berrett-Koehler.

Bunker, B. B., & Alban, B. T. (1997). *Large group interventions: Engaging the whole system for rapid change*. San Francisco: Jossey-Bass.

Holman, P., & Devane, T. (Eds.). (1999). *The change handbook: Group methods for shaping the future*. San Francisco: Jossey-Bass.

Putnam, R. (2000). *Bowling alone: The collapse and revival of American community*. New York: Simon & Schuster.

Vroom, V. H., & Yetton, P. W. (1973). *Leadership and decision making*. Pittsburgh: University of Pittsburgh Press.

Weisbord, M. R. (1987). *Productive workplaces: Organizing and managing for dignity, meaning, and community*. San Francisco: Jossey-Bass.

PART FIVE C

ORGANIZATION-LEVEL INTERVENTIONS

CHAPTER FORTY

The Change Process

Why Change?

Richard Beckhard
R. T. Harris (1987)

It may be stating the obvious to say that any major organizational change involves three distinct conditions: the *future state*, where the leadership wants the organization to get to; the *present state*, where the organization currently is; and the *transition state*, the set of conditions and activities that the organization must go through to move from the present to the future (Figure 40.1).

Thinking about the change process as involving these three states helps clarify the work to be done in managing major change: *defining* the future state, *assessing* the present, and *managing* the transition.

The change process in a large complex system has several aspects:

- Setting goals and defining the *future state*, or organizational conditions desired after the change
- Diagnosing the *present condition* in relation to those goals
- Defining the *transition state*: activities and commitments required to reach the future state
- Developing strategies and action plans for managing this transition

Change management is not a neat, sequential process. The initial tasks of defining the future state and assessing present conditions demand simultaneous attention. Figure 40.1 illustrates the reciprocity of these early steps. Understandably, the question is, Where does one start?

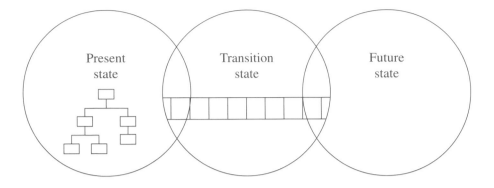

Figure 40.1. Map of the Change Management Process.

Organizational change must start by defining the need for change, for it is the question that provides the initial impetus. This chapter will focus on the issues involved in diagnosing the need for change, determining the degree of choice that exists about whether to change, and identifying what needs changing.

DEFINING THE NEED FOR CHANGE

The forces requiring change in large systems today tend to originate *outside* the organization. Changes in legislation, market demand resulting from worldwide competition, availability of resources, development of new technology, and social priorities frequently necessitate that organization managers redesign the organizational structures and procedures, redefine their procedures, redefine their priorities, and redeploy their resources. Two sample areas are discussed below.

Changes in Socioeconomics

One source of pressure for change derives from shifts in the socioeconomic makeup of the population. In both developed and developing nations, increased affluence within the population has resulted in greater demand for higher value-added products and services. In the United States the trend, some would argue, has reached the point where quality and service have replaced price as the prime criteria in the decision to buy. For businesses that have long held that the way to enhance revenue is to sell more at a lower price to gain market share and thus gain scale economies, the result tends to be loss of share to higher-priced, higher-value-added competitors. The underlying market requirements are becoming very different from those assumed by a sell solely on price strategy. The choices facing the manager in such a situation all have major implications for the organization. Any choice made will require major changes in products, quality, pricing, organizational priorities, and customer relations.

New Technology Drives

In many technology-driven industries, the pressure for change comes from within. Traditionally, technical workers—even professionally trained engineers—have accepted relatively structured roles, responsibilities, and procedures as given. Now those "knowledge workers" are demanding increased autonomy and responsibility in defining their work; more flexibility in work hours, rules, and procedures; and greater opportunities for achievement recognition. In determining an action response, the institutional manager must assess the potency of this force in light of the economic requirements of the institution, and the customers' needs.

In both examples above, the pressure for change comes from outside the management structure; nevertheless, any action taken, or lack of response, has significant consequences.

Stating the Change Problem

The need for change is frequently described in terms of "symptoms." One important dividend of a good organizational diagnosis is an accurate statement of the problem that necessitates a change. Consider a situation in which the problem is defined as "poor morale" in a department or throughout the organization, or "poor coordination" between the sales and manufacturing divisions. It would seem to follow that the change strategy should try to improve morale through some satisfaction-improvement program. Such direct strategies can work if the symptom statement describes the *fundamental* condition needing change.

A more likely-to-succeed strategy, however, would follow the diagnosis of those symptoms with the question *why*: What might be causing the problems of morale or lack of coordination? For example, a school superintendent in a large school system stated that there was a morale problem among the teachers in the district and that something must be done to improve morale. Implicit in this declaration of needs was a goal statement that if morale improves, something would be significantly better in the system. The appropriate diagnostic questions in this instance are "What would be different or better?" and "How much does it matter?"

If the answer to the first question were that higher teacher morale would improve students' reading levels, the superintendent would face one set of choices. If the answer were that teachers would not call in sick so often if morale were improved, that would be another issue. If an improvement in students' reading levels were the schools' main objective, the diagnosis would probably focus on poor teacher morale as a "cause" of the low reading levels.

If a lower absentee rate for teachers were the goal rationale, the focus would be on understanding why teachers are using their sick leave. In each instance, what needs changing is not simply the teachers' morale, but some other more primary organizational condition.

THE DEGREE OF CHOICE ABOUT WHETHER TO CHANGE

An apparently obvious, but very often overlooked, question is whether the organizational leadership can decide *whether* to make a change, or only *how* to make it. Before deciding on a change strategy, the executive must determine how much control or influence he or she has over the conditions providing the stimulus for change in the first place.

Sometimes external demands or forces provide the necessity for a change. In that case, the members of the leadership have no choice but to cope with the demand for change. Examples are legislation concerning environmental pollution, minority hiring, or allocation of public funds to health care services; new laws providing for educational parity for handicapped children; import regulations limiting product sales in a particular area; and successful union demands for increased benefits or power.

In other situations, the need for change is stimulated by forces either within or outside the organization, but nonetheless under management's general control. These include such conditions as the need for reorganization because of a reorientation from a technology-driven organization to a market-driven one, the need to add new functions and departments to a medical school due to breakthroughs in medical knowledge, the demand for increasing worker control over production, the need for increased product quality for customer satisfaction, and the need to increase control or efficiency through the introduction of new technology or office automation. In these types of situations, the manager can choose not only *how* to manage the change, but also *whether* to initiate it at all.

It might be useful to arrange the elements on a grid (see Fig. 40.2). On one axis we can list the *sources* of the factors concerned with change, such as owners/directors, legislators, employees, trade unions, special-interest and pressure groups, customers, and social values. On the other axis we can identify the *potency* of the force—high, medium, or low. Management can then array the forces operating in the situation according to both constituency and urgency. Additionally, the position of the various forces for or against the change can be designated with plus or minus signs. Such a display provides some perspective about what has to be taken into account before forming any specific action strategy.

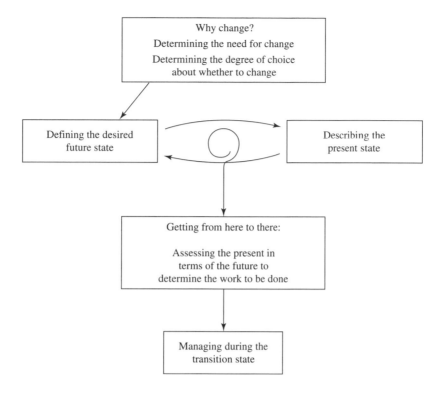

Figure 40.2. Sample Grid for Analyzing the Sources and Potency of Forces for Change.

A couple of issues are critical in conducting such an analysis. First, the management must make sure that its information about the situation is accurate and complete. The nature of the change in question should be clearly understood, and the position of each "source" regarding that change should be accurately assessed. Second, the manager's own bias and blind spots must be recognized and overcome in order for the analysis to be useful. There is often a tendency to "misperceive" or generalize about the potency of particular sources, following the assumption that these sources have always been "strong" or "weak" and that their potency in the current situation will be comparable to that in previous issues. To combat this tendency, it is often helpful to consider the future potency of each force *presuming that the management response to the demanding changes remains largely the same as at present.*

Case Illustration One: External Forces for Change—No Choice About Making the Change

The national manager of a multinational organization was faced with a dilemma. Concerned over environmental pollution, the mayors of two major cities in his host country had issued proclamations prohibiting the purchase of the type of product sold by his company and his competitors. If these proclamations became effective, the organization's business would cease completely.

In analyzing the dilemma, the manager studied several long-standing conditions. For one, his firm had a strong policy of not colluding with competitors. In addition, current company policies restricted the manager's methods of interacting with the communities in which he did business. If he obeyed the policies to the letter, he would have no alternative but to shut down his business.

To break the deadlock between company policy and local conditions, the manager had to help the firm's owners recognize the differences between the culture in which he was operating and that of the present company. Finally, he was allowed to do some "experimenting" with relationships with competitors in the host country. Under the new strategy, he met with counterparts in competing organizations. Together they were able to find a constitutional lawyer, who discovered some laws on the books of the host country limiting the power of mayors to make proclamations in restraint of trade. On the basis of this information, the managers were able to get a restraining order, which gave them time to attend to the substantive question of whether their products were in fact harmful to the environment. The manager saw that of the two competing forces acting on him—internal company policy and external local demands—he had to respond primarily to the host country forces in order to deal with the basic issue of product marketability.

In addition to a complex managerial choice of which way to move and with what consequences, the manager needed to recognize that he had no choice about whether to respond to the pressure from the host country. In most of his previous managerial actions, his orientation had been to the company—the owners. From that perspective, he had made choices about how to cope with the host country in a wide variety of situations. By analyzing the types of forces now operating and becoming aware of his lack of choice about whether to change, the manager was able to put his energy into creative strategies for how to effect the necessary change.

Case Illustration Two: Conflicting Perceptions of the Necessity for Change

The management committee and chief executive of a large manufacturing company were confronted with an increasingly serious morale problem among middle management, including the threat of unionization of the professional and technical staff. The company was a large, decentralized organization with a number of profit centers, or business divisions, and a strong headquarters organization. In the past few years, the increasing influence of the trade unions, as well as the progressive practices by the management, had resulted in changes such as new, creative work designs, improving quality of work life on the shop floor, and better compensation plans. A great deal of energy had been put into improving relationships and redistributing earnings between owners and workers, particularly those represented by trade unions. Relatively little attention had been paid to salaried nonunion staff. Those employees had been most hurt by inflation and other economic problems; their morale was at an all-time low. Many professionals and technical people, as well as junior management staff, felt that their only option was to organize and join trade unions.

Attempts to communicate this state of affairs to the organization's leadership had been stifled, either at the division management level or through central management's not "hearing" the messages. Personnel staff and others in the organization had sent several messages to the management group and to the chief executive, reporting the problem and outlining its potential implication. For a variety of reasons, the chief executive and several members of the management committee chose to treat the entire condition as a minor upset that could be smoothed over.

The chief executive had personally visited several field operations, and what he saw was, naturally, quite inconsistent with the written reports from his staff. For him, the "objective" evidence of loyal and happy people who produced, and thereby increased profitability and productivity, was clear and overriding; he was unable to see that there was real trouble afoot. Because he was approaching retirement, he did not want to initiate any major program that would upset the good performance results that had been achieved, even if a morale problem did exist, which he doubted.

The retirement of the chief executive preceded by six months the assumption of office by his successor. At the time of the announcement of the new appointment, the new chief executive, who had been on the management committee, shared the retiring chief executive's attitudes toward the morale condition; neither one saw it as a major priority for top-management effort. However, the new designate wanted to get a personal look at the general state of affairs and attitudes in the organization before he officially took office.

Aided by staff and consultants, the new chief executive arranged a series of "listening meetings," in which he would visit each field operation and listen to the concerns of groups of staff members. The membership of the groups was developed by a formula involving lateral representation in several areas as well as personnel from different hierarchical levels, meeting in a "diagonal slice" group. In addition to division managers, the status levels included middle managers, professional and technical staff, administrative and support people, shop stewards, shop workers, and new employees, so that the "diagonal slice" group was fully representative of the total field organization. During these visits, the new chief executive became acutely aware of, and deeply concerned about, the true state of affairs.

After completing his visits, he convened his top-management group and announced to his colleagues that he planned to spend up to 20 percent of his working time on the issue of employee morale. He personally took on the role of project manager, instituting a series of monthly meetings with operating managers at various levels so as to monitor continually the state of affairs. He urged heads of functions and businesses to conduct such activities as well. A senior field manager was assigned to study and recommend changes in both compensation and reward allocation to lower- and middle-management groups. He built in a feedback system through the line organization, which required his immediate subordinates to have up-to-date information on the attitudes of middle and junior management. The results included a significant improvement in morale, some changes in decision-making authority, a number of improvements in getting products to the market faster, and some significant cost savings.

In this illustration, we can compare strategies of managing the situation by two chief executives who made opposing diagnoses of the same set of forces. With the incumbent executive, the impulses for change within the organization were relayed indirectly, through memos and reports from the staff to the organization management. This information from the staff was not validated by his own experience in his routine visits to the field; therefore, his diagnosis of the strength and importance of the forces for change from the field was almost totally erroneous. By contrast, the desire of the second chief executive to find out the real situation for himself enabled him to assess more accurately the strength of the forces. His actions, his personal commitment of time and energy, and his follow-up in maintaining a flow of information throughout the system resulted from a different diagnosis of the same set of conditions. His strategy for maintaining the situation was very different from that of his predecessor.

Case Illustration Three: Management Control over Whether to Change—Misperception of Potency of Internal Forces

Case two above involved forces both internal and external to the organization. The first chief executive responded primarily (albeit inaccurately) to the internal forces; he did not recognize the potency of the environment—economic conditions—for the people in the organization. In the following case the reverse is true; the external force is very well understood. The chief executive recognizes its clear potency and chooses to respond to it actively but is unaware of the potency of the internal forces resistant to carrying out those actions.

Background and Initial Strategy. The company had long been recognized as the leading maker, in innovation and quality, of a sophisticated electronics product. The firm was organized into several decentralized divisions, each serving a different industry. The company's image of product quality and reliability had long enabled each division to maintain higher prices and profit margins than competitors. Recently, however, due to increased price and quality competition, the firm's share of market began to drop. The chief executive decided that in order to protect its profit margins and market share, his organization should take a strongly customer-centered posture and focus attention on developing a strong value-added product and customer service component. He wanted the organization managers at all levels to be actively concerned with increasing service component. He made his position very clear to his top-management group (division general managers and corporate staff vice-presidents) and personally visited the field to talk with plant managers, sales managers, and engineering design managers. He wrote and distributed several memos and papers that defined his philosophy about this new image for the company, and he offered corporate staff resources to assist the divisions in carrying out an active program.

Diagnosis. After a year of operating under this change strategy, it became very clear to the chief executive that it was not working. Diagnosis revealed that although the chief executive officer had the *official* authority and power as the leader of the organization, the *actual* power to change behavior was more widely distributed. The CEO did not "own" anyone who invented, manufactured, sold, or serviced a product; nor did he "own" any customers. *His* attitudes and values were seen by middle managers as much less relevant than those of the division senior managers; the middle managers were responding according to their perception of what behavior was rewarded or punished in the organization; the CEO's exhortations and personal biases did not affect them, particularly since many of his immediate subordinates did not echo his position. On the contrary, the general managers were all from engineering or manufacturing backgrounds and believed that quality and technological innovation should be their sole considerations. In their view, engineering should design the product right, manufacturing should efficiently provide high-quality products, and sales should sell the quality and sophistication of the product. Value-added features such as increased service and attention to customer convenience were viewed as nice but expendable amenities; given declining revenues, the general managers felt they could not afford to increase the service organization or pay much attention to customer convenience. On reflection, the CEO realized that he had contributed to this perception. During top-management meetings, the bulk of the time was always spent focusing on cost control and on pushing sales volume; little time was ever left to discuss the customer-service agenda. The result was that the division general managers and their subordinate managers felt safe in following a "minimum compliance" strategy of doing the minimum to appease the chief executive.

Revised Strategy and Action Steps. On recognizing the situation, the CEO set about directly to change the organization's behavior. At that time, one of the division general manager positions fell vacant, and the CEO decided to assume his duties himself while he sought replacement. This gave him the opportunity to role-model what he expected from his other general managers and to learn firsthand what worked and what didn't. Within the division he was running, he met with all managers and again outlined his agenda. They identified goals, actions, and timetables for getting started on this new trust. In his CEO role, he made it a norm to start every meeting with a report from each executive on what his or her division had achieved in the area of customer service enhancement—and he always reported first on his own division. He placed responsibility on all staff vice-presidents to treat the operating divisions as "customers" and to report on what they were doing to provide value-added service to the divisions.

He used the company's annual senior management conference, attended by the top sixty people in the firm, as a companywide sharing of experiences, lessons learned, and plans on the topic of "customer caring." He announced at this three-day event that customer caring would be the theme for senior management conferences not just this year but for the foreseeable future.

In preparation for the conference, each division conducted a telephone survey of its customers on their perceptions of the company's products, service, and degree of caring about the customer's needs. The results were tabulated, and at the end of the first season of the conference each general manager was assigned to report the *companywide* findings on certain aspects of the survey. Division groups defined visions and goals consistent with becoming a "customer driven" organization. Next, functional groupings (across divisions) discussed how they could support those visions. Each division then devised strategies and actions for the next six months for achieving the stated goals. Finally, each of the sixty division managers present stated, one by one in front of the entire group, what personal actions he or she promised to take in the following thirty days in support of the division's plan.

The CEO required each manager to submit his or her action commitments in writing within three days and asked for a one-page report in six weeks describing what had been done and what was planned for the next two-month period. He announced that the entire group would reconvene in five or six weeks describing what had been done and what was planned for the next two-month period. He also announced that the entire group would reconvene in five or six months to share their experiences and plan the next steps. Three days later, one hour before the close of business, the chief executive called the four managers whose written action premises he had not received, and told them to have their reports on his desk within twelve hours. News of this action traveled throughout the organization, including overseas locations, within twenty-four hours.

The message was received loud and clear. Over the next several months, behaviors changed dramatically: engineers were out visiting customers, manufacturing people were meeting with customer service staff, sales representatives were visiting plants, and executives were regularly calling customers.

Here the executive manager did not initially recognize that his control over whether or not to make the change he desired was constrained by the behavior and attitudes of people in the organization.

SUMMARY

We have argued that the first order of concern in developing a change strategy must be determination of the *need for change*. This means locating and assessing the sources of pressure to change the present situation, differentiating forces that are external to the organization from internal ones and from those that are personal agendas of the top management.

It is especially important to recognize the pressures that derive from the personal "gut" feelings of top leaders. Often there are no salient external pressures (recent and projected short-term market performance is satisfactory) and no significant internal pressures (staff morale is high and systems are operating smoothly); yet the top leader senses the need for a major change in corporate orientation, values, or culture. Pressures for change from the chief executive are no less legitimate than from anywhere else, although they probably have different consequences in terms of initial support for change. Whatever the source of pressure, we have found that conducting an analysis to determine both the need for change and sources and levels of support or resistance to change is a critical initial agenda for top leadership.

It is also helpful to sort out the degree of choice that exists about *whether to change*. The point is simple: situations arise in which an organization has little or no choice about whether to change, such as new legislation, market shifts, or the introduction of new technology within the industry. The degree of managerial choice is largely around *how to change*, not whether to change. In other instances, such as new market opportunities, acquisition possibilities, participation in voluntary social programs, and even changing corporate culture, there may exist a managerial choice

Nature of changes demanded: _____

	Owners	Legislature	Employees	Trade Unions	Social Values
High					
Medium					
Low					

(vertical axis label: Potency of Forces)

Figure 40.3. Change Management: Determining the Need for Change.

about both whether *and* how to change. Being clear about the degree of choice that exists is helpful in that it directs attention to the areas where management can have an impact.

We can now add these two initial analysis tasks to the map of the change process shown in Figure 40.1 (see Figure 40.3).

CHAPTER FORTY-TWO

Interorganizational Relations

W. Warner Burke
Nicole W. Biggart (1997)

T wo medium-size banks in a large U.S. metropolitan area recently came to the same conclusion: each was too small to withstand the market power of its larger competitors. Neither had the resources to compete or to grow and, moreover, both were prime takeover targets for large banks wanting a presence in their metropolitan market. Faced with a future of stagnation at best, and dismemberment at worst, the two banks decided to merge. Today, the combined institution is twice the size of the former banks and is one of the largest savings banks in the United States. The new bank has the size to be a major player in its market and is now pursuing efficiencies of scale and scope never before possible.

This type of interorganizational relationship, and other forms of organizational collaboration and linking together, represent an increasingly common strategy for the survival and growth of corporations as they seek to defend against competitive attack, enter into new markets, and gain access to developing technologies. Interorganizational cooperation, although largely reported as a Wall Street phenomenon, has by no means been confined to the business community, however. New roles for the military in the post-cold war era, such as peacekeeping missions and disaster relief, have increased the importance of multinational operations and posed a significant challenge to the military's cooperation with local relief agencies such as the Red Cross and local government agencies. Even nations, traditionally concerned with issues of sovereignty, have entered into collaborations with each other in the belief that cooperation in both political and economic ventures is often better than independent action. The North American Free Trade Agreement (NAFTA) and the European Union (EU) represent a new level of international interdependence among neighboring states.

Although corporations, local agencies, military forces, and nations have long attempted to cooperate with or co-opt each other, it is only in the last two decades that relations between organizations have become recognized as a critical tactic for organizational survival, growth, and success in a hostile or challenging environment (Harrigan, 1985, 1986; Gomes-Casseres, 1988; Paré, 1994; Fligstein, 1990; Bleeke and Ernst, 1995).

At least three factors are contributing to this increase in partnerships, networks, consortia, and federations, in addition to mergers and acquisitions. First, businesses compete in a global context today, and the trend is not expected to abate. With this kind of competition—more challenging and rapidly changing—organizational leaders are seeing wisdom in joining forces. Second, there is greater competition for scarce resources today, so more and more are competing for less and less; sharing costs, risks, and scarce resources is making sense to many organizational leaders. Third, there is growing recognition that collaborative behavior, in contrast to competition and individualism, may often (but not always) be a better way to operate.

Today, firms, government agencies, and states are apt to be seen by both researchers and practitioners as involved in a complex web of organizational relations, formal and informal, intended and unintended, that can help or hinder their ambitions. With this awareness has come an explosion of research and conceptualization, if not theory, by social scientists and management scholars that has attempted to understand the forces that prompt organizations to connect with each other and the conditions under which interorganizational relations are likely to succeed or fail. Although at this point there is more theory than evidence, the data suggest that differences of situation, orientation, purpose, culture, and power can affect the outcome of an ostensibly good match.

In this chapter, we characterize the voluminous writings on interorganizational relations of all types. This body of work is large and growing but can be divided into two distinct literatures: (1) macro environmental studies of the political and competitive aspects of relations between and among organizations, and (2) micro studies of the processes by which organized groups relate to each other and the factors that are likely to lead to a successful collaboration. We should point out that this chapter is based primarily on literature generated in the United States. There is an equally large and growing body of literature on interorganizational relations that is more international; see, for example, such recent sources as Gerybadze (1994), Kuman and Rosovsky (1992), and Yoshino and Rangan (1995).

The chapter begins with a characterization of the environmental research, including the history of the analysis of interorganizational relations, the ways in which researchers have conceptualized organizational environments, and the forces that increasingly push organizations to collaborate with each other. It then goes on to discuss the research concerning the processes of interorganizational relations, including the wide range of reasons that organizations collaborate, a taxonomy of types of interorganizational structures that are possible, life-cycle stages in cooperative relations, and a number of other relevant factors, including culture, leadership, evaluation, intergroup relations, and boundary stresses. Finally, we consider the conditions under which various forms of organizational connections are likely to succeed or fail. We end with questions for further research and the committee's conclusions in this area.

ENVIRONMENTAL ASPECTS OF INTERORGANIZATIONAL RELATIONS

Early theories of management were intent on perfecting the modern production organization by developing principles of efficient management and applying scientific analysis to organizational problems (Perrow, 1992). Although several schools of thought developed over the first half of the twentieth century, they all had in common a focus on the organization as an independent entity to be managed. Successive theories shifted the focus from the production system to the social system, but for the most part they proceeded from a belief that management science, properly applied, could control the forces necessary to maximize productivity.

This focus on the organization as the unit of analysis, with manipulable variables, began to shift after World War II, when systems theory, taken from biology, was applied to organizations. Systems theory encouraged researchers to look first at organizations as cybernetic systems capable of self-regulation and eventually as systems that interact with their environment (Boulding, 1956). This "open systems" perspective on organizations encouraged a new focus for research about organizations and their environments. As Scott put it, "The environment is perceived to be the ultimate source of materials, energy, and information, all of which are vital to the continuation of the system. Indeed the environment is even seen to be the source of order itself" (1987: 91). It became clear to researchers and practitioners that much of what an organization needs to succeed is outside the organization itself.

An awareness of the world outside a particular organization has led researchers to realize that much of an organization's environment consists of other organizations. A focus on organizations and their environments stimulated research on how organizations sharing an environment as either competitors or potential allies are affected by their neighbors in organizational space. Although some of the research is abstract, much of it has prescriptive implications for organizations attempting to manage their relations with other organizations in order to ensure survival, gain market power, and otherwise improve their performance.

Conceptualizing Organizational Environments

Organization Sets, Fields, and Networks. In the 1960s and 1970s, organizational scholars began conceptualizing relations between organizations in order to study them. Several levels of analysis have become standard ways of discussing interorganizational relations. The first, the *organizational set*, is an application of a social psychological model, the role set, to an organization. Just as an individual has a set of different roles he or she plays with other people— spouse, parent, worker, friend—an organization is conceived as having a set of relations with other organizations (Blau and Scott, 1962).

Organizational set analysis concentrates on the relationships of a single organization to see how those relationships affect its activities and performance. In many situations, however, organizational outcomes are the consequences of groups of organizations acting in ways that affect each other. Variously called, with somewhat different meanings, the action set (Aldrich and Whetten, 1981), the interorganizational field (Warren, 1967), and the industry system (Hirsch, 1975), this unit of analysis looks at relationships among groups of organizations that interact over time in ways that affect each other.

Hirsch's comparative analysis of the recording and pharmaceutical industries demonstrates the impact of the structure of an *interorganizational field* on the overall performance of an industry (1972; see also 1975). Although both pharmaceutical and recording companies have important similarities—for example, gatekeepers (physicians and disc jockeys) who mediate between themselves and their customers—the drug industry has been far more successful than recording companies in protecting their interests in patent protection, distribution, and pricing. Hirsch's study points to the superior collective efforts of drug companies in pursuing common interests, compared with the disorganized and misdirected efforts of recording companies that attempted to bribe disc jockeys in what became known as the payola scandals. He attributed at least some of the drug industry's higher profitability to the character of the relationships among organizations in the industry. Similarly, Miles and Cameron's study of the cooperative strategies employed among the Big Six firms within the tobacco industry (1982) demonstrates the effects on profitability of organized efforts among ostensible competitors.

Although organizational sets and interorganizational fields are still important conceptual categories, much recent research utilizes the concept of an *organizational network*. Network analysis differs from organizational set and industry analysis in seeking not only to identify the relationships among organizations but also to examine the character and structure of those relationships, usually by modeling them mathematically (Nohria and Eccles, 1992). The premise is that the networks within which an organization is embedded both constrain and provide opportunities for action. Organizational actions, and hence performance possibilities, are to a large degree explained by an organization's position within a network of organizations.

One body of research looks primarily at nonprofit community service organizations (Laumann and Papi, 1976; Galaskiewicz, 1979; Knoke and Rogers, 1979) and has the advantage of looking closely at the multiple and overlapping ties between organizations in a community, usually a geographically bounded setting. These studies tend to show how interdependencies among organizations that exchange money, people, political support, and other resources come to shape possibilities for action. Focusing on a geographic region, however, limits researchers' ability to assess the impact on performance of forces and organizations outside the region.

Much of the recent interest in strategic alliances, joint ventures, and other forms of interorganizational relationships came about as an attempt to facilitate or manage network relations, increasingly possible since the Reagan administration's weaker enforcement of antitrust laws and the passage of legislation permitting some forms of research consortia. Another important factor shaping network research is the observation that new high-technology industries, notably biotechnology and electronics, are characterized by intense patterns of formal and informal network relations. Barley and colleagues (1992: 317) note that, in these industries, scientific advances come so quickly that "even well-heeled corporations cannot hope to track, much less fully exploit, relevant scientific advances by relying solely on the published literature and their own research operations. Instead, relevant technical knowledge is more efficiently obtained by direct access to research conducted elsewhere" and made available through interorganizational relations.

The authors note, too, that whereas some high-technology industries such as electronics build on scientific communities such as chemistry and physics that have been integrated into industrial manufacturing since the nineteenth century, biotechnology is founded on a wholly new community of participants. Recent advances in recombinant DNA and hybridoma cell formations suddenly brought cutting-edge molecular biology into the center of the pharmaceutical and agricultural industries. In biotechnology, far more than electronics, however, strategic alliances between small research firms and well-funded larger corporations are common because of the expense of clinical trials necessary for government approval of bio-technology products. They conclude that "the way in which a firm partici-pates in the network is integral to its strategy for survival and growth" (p. 343).

Another and perhaps the most important factor in prompting research on organizational networks is the observation that business networks have been widely successful in the global economy. Whereas the U.S. economy is based on a belief that competitive individualism is the appropriate principle for exchange relations among economic actors—a principle that is institutional-ized in laws and practices such as arms-length bidding relations between sup-pliers and buyers, antitrust regulation, and insider-trading laws (Williamson, 1992; Biggart and Hamilton, 1992)—this principal does not exist in many other successful economies.

Regime Analysis. Another approach to analyzing interorganizational coopera-tion—international regimes—was developed from the need to understand co-operation in the less structured global system. An international regime is a set of explicit or implicit principles, norms, rules, and decision-making procedures around which actor expectations converge and that help coordinate actor be-havior (Krasner, 1982; see also Mayer et al., 1993). Some examples are the re-gimes surrounding nuclear nonproliferation, the law of the sea, and the nascent international environmental regime (Young, 1989). Regime analysis represents a movement away from purely institutional analysis (Kratochwil and Ruggie, 1989) to one that looks at a broader and sometimes less formal pattern of cooperation (Kahn and Zald, 1990).

Organizations play several roles in the regime. Certainly, cooperation among organizations can be the driving force behind the development of an international regime, or define its structure; an example is the coordination among national health agencies, nongovernmental organizations, and the World Health Organization. Yet organizations, and cooperation among them, can also be the *consequence* of or institutionalized manifestation of coordina-tion between different groups or states in the world. International cooperation can also occur outside or independent of organizations, providing the analyst with a broader conception of behavior than is present by a pure concentration on institutional behavior. A focus on organizations and cooperation is also enhanced by understanding the broader milieu in which organizations operate and cooperation emerges (Haas, 1980). The limitations of the regime frame-work, however, include its difficulty with accommodating change, its being too issue-specific to permit generalizations, and its limited applicability to more structured, less anarchic environments than global politics (for a more detailed critique of this approach, see Strange, 1989).

Collaboration as an Organizing Principle

Although competition, not collaboration, has historically been the organizing principal for organizations and markets, particularly in the United States, there is growing evidence of collaboration and other forms of managed interdependence among firms and not-for-profit organizations in the United States. Firms in a market are more likely to compete, and not collaborate, when the market is stagnant or declining and resources are increasingly scarce (Porter, 1980). Competition is also more likely in situations in which institutional factors—such as a legal system that supports antitrust regulation—or deeply rooted distrust among members of an industry militates against collaboration.

A number of forces, many of which are on the increase around the world, prompt organizations to collaborate with each other. Resource dependency theory (Pfeffer and Salancik, 1978) argues that, because a focal organization must depend on other organizations for the inputs it needs to survive, it may be in its interest to attempt to manage the organizations on which it is dependent. They argue that mergers and acquisitions, which represent total control of another organization, are only the most extreme of an array of strategies that organizations can employ to coordinate with or impose their interests on other organizations. They may use a series of "bridging strategies" (Scott, 1987: 209) to lock in the supplies or support of another firm, including contracting, strategic alliances, and co-optation, the incorporation of important external agents into the firm, for example by forming interlocking boards of directors (Palmer, 1983; Mizruchi and Schwartz, 1986).

Transaction cost economics (Williamson, 1992) agues that, under conditions of high uncertainty and small numbers of alternative suppliers, collaboration can improve cost-effectiveness and therefore improve the profitability and competitive performance of an organization. Other economists argue that collaboration weakens an organizational field by reducing competition (Scherer, 1980; Caves, 1982), thus leading to higher prices and less innovation. Ouchi and Bolton (1988), however, found in a study of microelectronics and other industries that participation in collaborative research and development (R&D) ventures strengthened the firms' global competitiveness.

Although much of the recent impulse for mergers and acquisitions was fueled by the development of the junk bond market in the 1980s and the use of purely financial criteria to mate corporate partners, a decade of failed alliances has made organizational executives less sanguine about entering into this type of long-term, permanent acquisition. In fact, research suggests that as many as half of all domestic mergers and acquisitions are financial failures (Paré, 1994). It is now clear that successful collaborations among organizations, even those with ostensibly good financial or strategic reasons to collaborate, are difficult to achieve. Financial synergy may be a necessary component of a successful relationship for a market-based firm, but compatible leadership style, strategic orientation, and culture are necessary as well, as discussed below (Sankar et al., 1995; Fedor and Werther, 1995). This is no less true of not-for-profit organizations, especially those with a strong missionary culture such as religious organizations and the military, in which value clashes can doom an alliance (Wallis, 1994).

FRAMEWORKS FOR UNDERSTANDING INTERORGANIZATIONAL PROCESSES

Reasons for Collaborating

Both research and practice show that organizations enter into relations with each other for a wide range of reasons: (1) long-range survival (Burke and Jackson, 1991); (2) gain in market power (Porter, 1990); (3) synergy (Kanter, 1989); (4) risk sharing (Bleeke and Ernst, 1993; Harrigan, 1986); (5) cost sharing; (6) subcontracting and outsourcing (Porter, 1990); (7) technology sharing (Harrigan, 1986); and (8) knowledge of a market.

As steps toward linking up with another organization begin, the parties involved are faced with at least two clear yet perplexing paradoxes, of vulnerability and control (Haspeslagh and Jemison, 1991). Organizations have to decide how much they will cede control to their partner.

The paradox of vulnerability—trust versus self-preservation—is concerned with whether or not the recent proliferation of interorganizational collaborations represents a new spirit of cooperation or a new level of cost cutting and market exploitation. From one perspective, collaboration is valuable in and of itself, opening gateways to such activities as organizational learning and transformation. To facilitate this transformation, however, partners must openly share information about strategic objectives, organizational resources, and internal challenges, which paradoxically increases vulnerability to acquisition, loss of market share, proprietary control of valued resources, and other sources of strategic advantage. Thus, collaboration can be seen as both promoting and threatening an organization's long-term stability and viability. Nevertheless, an avoidance of collaboration may also represent a costly choice, with inefficiencies and insufficient learning possibilities. The challenge is to find the right partner (one with complementary resources, compatible business and cultural characteristics, and similar philosophies regarding business goals and the collaboration's role in achieving them) yet not to be so protective of organizational resources that the collaboration becomes impossible.

The paradox of control—stability versus synergy—concerns the tension faced by managers of interorganizational relations between the impulse to control the outcome of the collaboration and the potential synergy that can result from the absence of tight controls and management. Although a clear division of authority and decision making in interorganizational relations may reduce potential conflicts arising from partners' differing strategies, cultures, and work systems, a clear division may also reduce the likelihood that genuinely new perspectives and possibilities will emerge from the relationship. An organization therefore risks undermining the synergistic objectives that led it to enter a collaboration in the first place when it institutes tight controls that may be intended to guarantee success. This is especially true when a collaborating organization uses less measurable objectives for indicating success, such as organizational learning and management and work styles.

A PARTIAL TAXONOMY OF INTERORGANIZATIONAL GOVERNANCE STRUCTURES

As a guide to understanding interorganizational relations, we present a taxonomy of interorganizational governance structures, based on work by Kahn (1990) and Harrigan (1986). Although not all-encompassing, it is comprehensive enough to provide a road map for how to understand interorganizational relations. The following taxonomy moves from relatively less interdependent relations to relations in which interdependence and its management are key.

Mutual service consortia: research and development (R&D) partnerships. Organizations pool their resources to procure access to information, technology, or some other service too costly to acquire alone (Kanter, 1994). Tasks (including financial support) are distributed among the participants, and the proceeds are returned to participants according to the terms of the agreement. No separate entity is created for the management of this relationship.

Cross-licensing and distribution arrangements. Organizations enter into agreements formalizing the limited sharing of technology or other product attributes such as brand names or markets. These arrangements are strictly contracted and bounded in scope and duration.

Joint ventures. Two or more organizations ("owners") combine varying resources to form a new, distinct organization (the "venture") in order to pursue complementary strategic objectives. This new organization is jointly owned and managed, and proceeds are distributed between the venture and owners according to a formula agreed on by the owners.

Strategic alliances. Similar to ventures, two or more organizations combine resources in pursuit of mutual gain. However, in a strategic alliance, a new firm is not created. Although interdependence is, of course, required for a joint venture to work effectively, the characteristic of interdependence is essentially the same as that required for any organization, whereas for a strategic alliance to work effectively, two distinct organizations must learn to cooperate and depend on each other.

Value network partnerships. Organizations join forces to capitalize on potential efficiencies in the production and/or distribution process (Porter, 1990). Whereas each participating organization is responsible for one area of the production system, the participating organizations are highly dependent on one another for the ultimate delivery of their product. This form of collaboration concerns the alliance of certain organizational functions such as production, and typically not multiple functions that encompass more of a particular business or business units as in a strategic alliance.

Internal ventures. An organization acts independently to create a distinct entity, from within its own ranks, for the purposes of expansion, innovation, or diversification. These are often established with the goal of capitalizing quickly on entrepreneurial initiatives coming from members of the organization's work force. When action is then taken to establish a joint venture with another organization, the description above of a joint venture would then apply.

Mergers and acquisitions. A special case of interorganizational relations; when they are established, problems of interdependence between organizations become issues of within-group functioning and are directly related to organizational performance. Acquisitions are preferred to ventures and alliances when shared ownership of initiatives is not desired.

Table 42.1 presents the types of interorganizational relations, along with some of the situational determinants of their formation and their likely outcomes (Harrigan, 1986; Porter and Fuller, 1986).

Situational Determinants

In the design of an interorganizational relation's governance structure, three questions are key: (1) What are the reasons for collaborating? (2) How will both risks and benefits be distributed? (3) What will be the indicators for successful achievement of participants' mutual goals? The response to these three questions suggests the degree of managed interdependence appropriate to the relationship between partners and, indirectly, the ideal governance structure for the relationship.

Table 42.1. Taxonomy of Cooperative Interorganizational Relationships.

Degree of Managed Interdependence	Inter-organizational Relationship	Strategic Purpose	Ownership/ Division of Proceeds	Issues/ Obstacles	Boundary Characteristics	Key Psychological Phenomena Affecting Visibility	Milestones for Success
Least managed	Market (competitive)		(Limited or unmanaged interfirm cooperation in marketplace)				
	Mutual Service Consortium, Research & Development Partnerships	Contracted pooling of resources for shared access to valued commodity: market technology, process	No shared ownership/ negotiated division of proceeds	Possible development of competitive conflict (shared product/market)	Stable, contained interface, high constituent power, committee, slow-moving	Perceptions of equity, competitor benefits	Negotiated distribution of consortium outputs, quantifiable, static
	Cross-licensing and Distribution Arrangements	Limited sharing of technology and markets	No shared ownership/ negotiated distribution of proceeds	Loss of control of knowledge, re: technology and markets	Stable, contained interface, high constituent power, committee, slow-moving	Perceptions of equity, competitor benefits	Performance of both organizations

(continued)

Table 42.1. (continued)

Strategic Alliance	Reciprocal exploitation of resources for less specified mutual gain	Varying shared ownership and managerial control/negotiated distribution of proceeds between owners	Firms risk ownership and organizational identity, because relationship leveraged by equality/inequality of shared investment/commitment and distribution/evolution of bargaining power	Boundary-spanning project team(s), multiple interfaces, varying constituent power, high-stress on boundary-role persons	Perceptions of equity (need measurement systems), perceptions of power, compatibility of cultures, intergroup trust and competition, resistance to cooperation at operational level	Venture performance, value added to owners is negotiated, benchmarked, monitored, revised (monitoring and control systems needed)
Joint Venture	Reciprocal exploitation of resources for specific mutual gain in presence of compatible strategic objectives	Varying shared ownership and managerial control/negotiated distribution of proceeds between venture and owners	Conflict between owners, between owners and venture likely to develop as each organization's performance, priorities, and environment change. Firms risk valued assets because relationship leveraged by equality/inequality	Hybrid organization/culture buffers cooperating partners, venture identity distinct from parent organizations, varying constituent power as a function of dependence and bargaining agreement constraints	Perceptions of equity (need measurement systems), perceptions of power, compatibility of cultures (including management style, work norms, and values), owner-venture competition, resistance to cooperation at an operational level	Venture performance, value added to owners is negotiated, benchmarked, monitored, revised (monitoring and control systems needed in owner organizations and in venture)

Value Network Partnership	Reduce environmental variability, streamline production and delivery systems (raise competitor entry costs)	No shared ownership/ contracted provisions of products, services	of shared investments/ commitment and distribution/ evolution of relative bargaining power; Dilemmas of control and synergy; Possible lock-in with standardization/ competitive pressures for innovation; Conflict, re: cost-effectiveness of provided product services, allocation of profit	Perceptions of equity (need measurement systems); Perceptions of power; Intergroup trust and competition, resistance to cooperation at operational level	Multiple interfaces: sharing of systems, information, processes, and resources; Varying constituent power, high stress on boundary role persons	Market share, profit margins, other markers of organizational performance and efficiency; Partner relations persons, and perceptions
Internal Venture	Capitalize on internal entrepreneurial initiatives, exploit opportunities	Negotiated internally	Dilemmas of control and maximized return; Conflicts, re: management	Intergroup competition and envy, resistance to cooperation at operational level	Multiple interfaces: sharing of systems, information processes, and resources	Venture performance; Value added to owners is negotiated,

(continued)

Table 42.1. (continued)

		requiring faster response without sharing resources	control, resource provision and output distribution	Varying constituent power, high stress on boundary role		benchmarked, monitored, revised (monitoring and control systems needed)
Most managed	Merger/Acquisition	Merger with/ acquisition of competitor or affinity organization in support of strategic objectives	No shared ownership/division of proceeds	Interorganizational dynamics become intraorganizational challenges	Boundary expansion/ subsumption	Perceptions of power, perceptions of implications for performance and related impacts on cooperation, compatibility of cultures	Organization performance

Note: Adapted from R. L. Kahn (1990) for concept of managed interdependence dimension and Harrigan (1986) for strategic functions of most relationship types.

Strategic Purpose. Some collaborative initiatives are extremely limited in objective and scope. They involve a relatively passive pooling of resources for the participants' mutual benefit. For instance, participants might share information regarding a particular technology or economic developments in a specific market or region. In the private sector, relationships of this kind usually take the form of mutual service consortia or R&D partnerships. Relationships involve relatively little risk on the part of the participants. They are bounded in scope and often in time as well. Mutual service consortia and R&D partnerships can provide extremely valuable resources to their participants but demand very limited cooperation.

Similarly, when an organization shares a specific asset with another organization, as in cross-licensing or distribution arrangements, the interface between participating organizations is relatively specific and contained. Cross-licensing and distribution arrangements usually involve the licensed use of another organization's technology, production or distribution methods, or brand name, with the purpose of bolstering organizational performance.

A more complex and interdependent relationship is necessary when a collaboration involves reciprocal exploitation of resources in pursuit of mutual gains. There are two related models for such a relationship: the joint venture and the strategic alliance. Joint ventures involve the creation of a distinct organizational entity for managing the overlapping goals of the sponsoring organizations. Strategic alliances attempt to avoid potential conflicts by limiting the power of the (new) organization responsible for the founders' mutual gain, but relations of this type often have the effect of exacerbating tensions between the founders (Harrigan, 1986).

Attempts to capitalize on linkages in the value network by strengthening relationships among suppliers, producers, distributors, etc. take the form of value network partnerships. Relationships of this type are undertaken to increase organizational efficiencies. For business organizations, they have the added indirect benefit of increasing industry competitiveness by raising the costs of competitor entry (Porter, 1990).

When an organization wishes to capitalize on internal initiatives or to sponsor pursuit of a goal that is not supported by existing systems, internal ventures can serve as valuable models. In an internal venture, a new endeavor can be sponsored without the sharing of resources with outside organizations. The paradox of control is especially important to internal ventures, as organizations struggle to sponsor initiatives that are by definition beyond their typical realm of expertise.

Moves to gain control over competitors or affiliates by expanding organizational boundaries clearly fall under the acquisition model. Similarly, the conditions under which mergers are to be emulated is straightforward—mergers involve the creation of a new organizational entity through the dissolution and recombination of previously existing boundaries.

Ownership of Responsibility. The more a relationship is managed, the more ownership of responsibility and the division of proceeds are shared. The exception to this statement is the case of a merger or acquisition in which the former separate ownership becomes one. In the middle of the continuum are joint ventures and strategic alliances. According to Yoshino and Rangan (1995), there are basically three types of ownership structures in strategic alliances: (1) nonequity, in which neither partner owns a part; (2) equity stake in the other partner; and (3) a separate alliance company, a joint venture that both partners fund (usually fifty-fifty). They suggest that the best ownership structure for an alliance is one that fits the overall strategy of the collaboration; if goals are limited, then the ties can be comparatively loose. If the alliance is critical to long-term success, then a tighter structure is warranted. The point is that the degree of ownership and the division of proceeds should be linked directly to the mission and strategy of the respective partners.

Obstacles to Cooperation. Issues and obstacles to cooperation between and among interorganizational relationships can be far-ranging. This is true both in practice as well as in the literature. Oliver (1990) has identified five critical contingencies that affect different types of relationships, such as trade associations, joint ventures, and corporate-finance interlocks. The five are asymmetry, reciprocity, efficiency, stability, and legitimacy. We can use her schema to consider briefly issues and obstacles to cooperation:

1. *Asymmetry.* A potential obstacle is an imbalance of power and control between or among the partnering organizations. This is the case when one of the partners wants to dominate the other so that desired resources can be controlled by the dominant partner.

2. *Reciprocity.* More or less the opposite of asymmetry, the assumption being that cooperation and collaboration are emphasized as opposed to domination; obstacles will arise if there is perceived inequality in, for example, sharing of resources; trust is the key to this relationship aspect. Reciprocity more often occurs when the partners are pursuing a new venture rather than merely sharing resources (see, for example, Pfeffer and Nowak, 1976).

3. *Efficiency.* Often relationships are formed to improve internal efficiencies for one or both of the organizations; a strategic alliance between two hospitals, for example, might result in the purchase of one high-technology diagnostic tool instead of two and thereby reduced costs.

Again, both hospitals must experience better efficiencies for this dimension of the relationship to be perceived as equitable; otherwise there is a major obstacle.

4. *Stability.* When one of the partners, for example, copes with its external environmental uncertainties far better than the other, then there is the potential for imbalance in the relationship. If one of these partners spends more time, energy, and money on market research in order to reduce uncertainty in the external environment, then the possibility of an obstacle to the relationship arises.

5. *Legitimacy.* The partners are attempting to enhance their reputations, images, and prestige in their environments by joining together; with the passage of time, one of the partners may benefit more than the other, which sets up an obstacle to further cooperation.

These categories of Oliver's are informed by and summarize many studies and so contribute to a better understanding of interorganizational relationships. In practice, there are other ways of categorizing potential obstacles to effective relationships (e.g., cross-cultural barriers). Furthermore, over time in a relationship things change, often as a consequence of the rapidly changing environment.

Likely Outcomes

The choice of organizational governance structure—joint venture, consortia, merger, etc.—has profound effects on many aspects of the collaborating organizations. We explore briefly the consequences of these choices according to (1) boundary characteristics, (2) psychological dynamics, and (3) milestones for success.

Boundary Characteristics. As the structure chosen for an interorganizational relationship shifts from least managed to most managed, boundaries of interdependence between and among the partners become less distinct. Boundary roles can be seen in terms of two forms of negotiation: the bargainer and the representative (Druckman, 1977; Walton and McKersie, 1965). At the least managed end of the continuum, the individuals who are relating across organizational boundaries have two duties: to represent and to bargain. Moving toward more managed interdependence, bargaining becomes even more salient. At the merger stage, the bargainers do their jobs and then "blend or integrate themselves out of role existence."

Psychological Dynamics. Findings from cognitive psychology contribute to our understanding of interorganizational relationships. For example, Schwenk (1994) points out that the biases of decision makers can heavily influence the degree of success in interorganizational relations, for example through over-confidence (see also Nisbett and Ross, 1980).

Perceived equity may be an issue. In a recent merger of two financial firms, the early slogan was that it was a "merger of equals." Members of each firm would be treated fairly and end up in the merged organization with parity. A few months following the merger, it was clear that the assumption of equity was violated. Of the top nineteen executive positions, sixteen were filled by members of one of the previous firms and only three came from the other organization. This outcome, as might be expected, caused a significant setback in the progress of the merger. Had the original position been one of acquisition instead of merger, different expectations and perceptions regarding equity would have been established. Being acquired does not, as a rule create expect-ations of parity. In a joint venture, issues of equity are typically specified clear-ly. As we move toward the least managed end of the continuum, matters of equity are easier to manage because the partners do not interact with one an-other as intensively.

Milestones for Success. For commercial enterprises, the milestones are expressed in financial terms, such as increased market share, new products de-veloped as a result of the collaboration, an expansion of the distribution sys-tems, etc. For consortia or R&D partnerships, milestones are much more varied. Increasing the talent pool, accumulating more knowledge faster, having access to information formerly unavailable, and saving on costs of conducting certain lines of research are but a few of the possible indicators for success in collaborations outside the commercial sector.

LIFE-CYCLE STAGES IN COLLABORATIONS

Regardless of the eventual structure of a particular cooperative agreement between organizations, clear patterns characterize the process by which two organizations negotiate an interorganizational arrangement. The movement through these processes can be thought of in terms of a life cycle of interorgani-zational relations. Figure 42.1 presents a schema for such a life cycle, based on observation of a number of organizations; the shaded boxes indicate processes that occur continuously during the life of an agreement between organizations.

Preengagement Stage

The preengagement stage refers to the state of the organizations prior to the initiation of a particular collaborative endeavor. In business relations, this stage usually involves the voluntary selection of another organization with

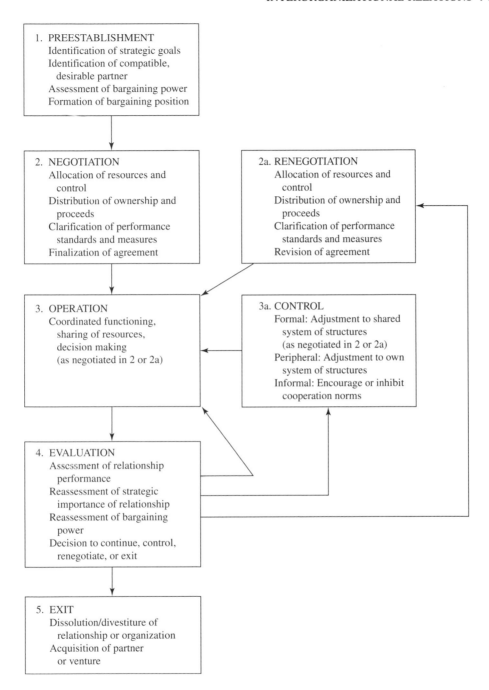

1. PREESTABLISHMENT
   Identification of strategic goals
   Identification of compatible,
     desirable partner
   Assessment of bargaining power
   Formation of bargaining position

2. NEGOTIATION
   Allocation of resources and
     control
   Distribution of ownership and
     proceeds
   Clarification of performance
     standards and measures
   Finalization of agreement

2a. RENEGOTIATION
   Allocation of resources and
     control
   Distribution of ownership and
     proceeds
   Clarification of performance
     standards and measures
   Revision of agreement

3. OPERATION
   Coordinated functioning,
     sharing of resources,
     decision making
     (as negotiated in 2 or 2a)

3a. CONTROL
   Formal: Adjustment to shared
     system of structures
     (as negotiated in 2 or 2a)
   Peripheral: Adjustment to own
     system of structures
   Informal: Encourage or inhibit
     cooperation norms

4. EVALUATION
   Assessment of relationship
     performance
   Reassessment of strategic
     importance of relationship
   Reassessment of bargaining
     power
   Decision to continue, control,
     renegotiate, or exit

5. EXIT
   Dissolution/divestiture of
     relationship or organization
   Acquisition of partner
     or venture

Figure 42.1. Life Cycle of Cooperative Interorganizational Relationships.

which to collaborate. In the public sector, it is far more likely that collaboration is mandated, as in the case of peacekeeping efforts between allies or the coordination of disaster relief efforts by state and local agencies. Private-sector firms sometimes find themselves forced to collaborate, however; for example, corporate headquarters in pursuit of a particular goal might mandate that a subsidiary collaborate with another subsidiary or with an outside organization.

When collaboration is a voluntary option, an organization's leaders have the luxury of assessing collaboration as a means for achieving long-term goals. An organization may also be on the receiving end of an offer to collaborate, prompting reassessment of their organizational strategy in order to respond to a proposal. The approached organization also enters the pre-engagement stage.

Potential or mandated partners should then be evaluated for compatibility. The first approach to evaluation assesses similarities of management and business philosophies, abilities to communicate, and interpersonal trust; the second approach is an assessment of the organizations' relative bargaining power in the relationship. Intangible factors, including each partner's perceptions of the other's reliability, trustworthiness, and culture, will exert an influence on initial bargaining positions. When the choice to ally with another organization is voluntary, intangible factors weigh more importantly in deciding whether or not to proceed with a relationship. Even when the relationship is not mandated, however, evaluation during the preengagement stage can identify areas of concern that might be addressed in the formal governance agreement created by the partners.

These assessments will affect each organization's perception of the distribution of power, dependence, and control in the relationship and thus the choice of bargaining position as the agreement concerning governance of the relationship is being negotiated. Because in this initial stage partners may not be entirely forthcoming with one another about their formulas for determining the strategic value of the relationship, many partners may not even come to realize that their respective assessments of the relationship's value and potential arise from widely differing evaluation systems. As a result, partners who may be quite compatible may never proceed to negotiation or may fail to capitalize on these potentials as they enter their relationship. Similarly, partners who initially appear compatible may proceed to negotiate a relationship that, upon closer examination, would be deemed inappropriate.

Negotiation Stage

If partners advance to the point at which they discuss formally the allocation of responsibilities, resources, and authority that would exist in the relationship, they have begun, at least informally, to manage their interdependence. In the negotiation stage, the provision of inputs to and the division of proceeds from the relationship being created is negotiated. If either inputs or proceeds are relatively intangible (for instance if one organization is offering to teach a participative management style as one of many inputs, and the counterpart organization offers insight into marketing to a new segment), then specific measures by which to assess the relationship's performance have to be created. These measures will need to be true to the interests of the participating parties, but also relevant to the performance of the collaboration and not so difficult to measure that they overburden the new system with excessively bureaucratic monitoring and measurement systems. The negotiation stage thus demands the management of the paradox of control: systems that support the achievement of collaborative objectives must be created, yet these systems must be flexible enough to allow both expected and unforeseen benefits of the collaboration to emerge.

Negotiators on behalf of the partnering organizations are in the difficult position of protecting the interests of their host organizations as well as the viability of the partnership (Adams, 1976). Cultural differences, and other differences in perspective, will have considerable impact on the effectiveness of negotiations in satisfying these dual objectives (Bontempo, 1991). Difference in cultural expectations regarding negotiation behavior, measurement, record keeping, and control systems and in approaches to strategic planning can all be expected to clash at the negotiation table. Furthermore, characteristics of negotiators' host organizations will have an influence on the course of negotiations; cultural characteristics such as need for control, trust of outsiders, and perceptions of relative power will influence the expectations placed both on negotiators and on the range of negotiating behaviors available to them (Druckman and Hopmann, 1989).

Operation Stage

After the agreement has been finalized, the collaboration proceeds to the third stage, operation, in which the agreement is implemented. The relationship now consists of an exchange of resources across organizational boundaries; if the relationship is a joint venture, the owners work with the venture as an independent system rather than a theoretical entity. Even if a new formal organization has not been created, the reality of working across organizational boundaries at many functional levels is likely to be quite different from the experience of courtship and negotiation. In order to facilitate cooperation at managerial and operational levels of the organization, employees need to be informed of the strategic value of the collaboration (Kanter, 1994), criteria for evaluating the relationship's success, and the relationship of their jobs to these criteria. New behavior by managers and other employees also needs to be structurally supported and systematically rewarded. Managers and operational employees are in a situation similar to that in which negotiators found themselves, with their loyalties at least partially divided between fulfillment of their responsibilities to their home organization and support of the collaboration. This tension can result in a serious threat to the collaboration's viability, especially if employees are receiving mixed signals about their roles in the collaboration or about senior management's commitment to its success.

Several other cultural and psychological phenomena can be expected to influence cooperation between collaborating organizations. Compatibility of work norms has a powerful effect on cooperation between the groups. The degree to which work-related behaviors such as timing, quality, and sharing of information and other resources are met influences employees' willingness to cooperate in the future.

The perceptions that members of the participating groups have of each other also affect their likelihood of cooperation. When group relations are characterized by a climate of trust, group members are more likely to help one another; if there are perceptions of competitiveness or ill will, discrimination against outgroup members is far more likely (Flippen et al., 1995). Smith and Berg (1987) indicate that a focus on the mutual stake that interdependent groups share helps to reduce intergroup resentments.

Evidence of the importance of perceived future achievement in mitigating resistance to intergroup cooperation (Haunschild et al., 1994), supported by social identity theory (Tajfel, 1981, 1982), suggests that members' perceptions of interorganizational endeavors coincide with their own goals. This can be achieved through the use of communication systems that reinforce the strategic importance of the interorganizational effort. Social identity theory research also points to factors that increase people's positive feelings about dissimilar groups. The works of Singer et al. (1963), Fishbein (1963), Druckman (1968), and Brewer (1968) can be taken together to indicate that more favorable attitudes are expressed toward dissimilar others from groups that are perceived to be (1) allies, (2) similar to one's own group, (3) comparably skilled or advanced, and (4) interested in membership in one's own group (Druckman, 1994). Intraorganizational communications can support the likelihood of intergroup cooperation by highlighting or encouraging any of these factors.

Evaluation

Regardless of specific criteria, though, evaluation of a multiorganizational relationship's performance occurs continuously on an informal basis, and it should be undertaken formally by all participant organizations on a periodic schedule. However measured, mutually satisfactory performance lays the groundwork for ongoing cooperation. Whenever possible, evaluation measures should be shared between collaborating organizations in order to reduce erroneous attributions regarding causes of successes and deficits in performance.

Renegotiation, Control, or Exit

If managers from each of the collaborating organizations are satisfied with the evaluation and decide that no response is necessary, the collaboration will probably continue as before, with managerial attention once more focused on the operation phase of the relationship life cycle. Given the dynamism of today's economic and political environment, and the fact that learning occurs almost inevitably as a result of collaboration experience, evaluation will probably indicate either major or minor opportunities for adjustment. If the need for adjustment is large, and the bargaining agreement permits, managers can approach their partners for renegotiation of the relationship. Objectives of the renegotiation are identical to those of the negotiation stage. Psychological aspects of this phase are similar also, except that all parties to the negotiation have a better idea of the likely behavior of their counterparts in the relationship; these experiences supplement their organizations' culturally determined approaches to cooperation and collaborating, which influenced behavior during negotiation.

When renegotiation is not an option, or in situations in which more minor adjustments to the collaboration are indicated, participant organizations can use control mechanisms to influence the functioning of the collaboration. Control mechanisms can be invoked either to promote or to inhibit the collaboration's effectiveness.

Many relationships, especially between public organizations, are bounded by specific time duration or the purposes of accomplishing a joint project and dissolve when these criteria have been satisfied. If the relationship was not specifically bounded in this way, and partnership performance is unsatisfactory to a partner with sufficient bargaining power to terminate it, or if the environment has changed so radically that the collaboration is no longer relevant to the participants' strategic goals, the cooperative interorganizational relationship will end.

In relationships between public organizations, success or failure in the accomplishment of mutual goals can have effects on the sponsoring organizations and *their* relationships (see Figure 42.1). When organizations have even a remote possibility of future collaboration, the importance of an amicable exit should be clear, given the role of group relations in laying the groundwork for cooperation. Of obvious importance in the dissolution of interorganizational relations is the avoidance of unduly scapegoating a particular partner for its shortcomings. The role of responsible and factual systemic analysis of problems and widespread communication of both findings and corrective action taken cannot be overemphasized.

OTHER FACTORS

Culture Clash and Change

Difference in values, expectations, and behavioral norms of communication and negotiation affect the possibility of cooperation during any contact between two organizations. Because corporate culture can be expected to exert a stronger effect on work behavior than either national or ethnic culture (Kotter and Heskett, 1992), cultural differences may be a factor in both domestic and international relationships between organizations. Thus, international relationships between organizations are more (but not exclusively) subject to the issues of difference that are present in any negotiated relationship between two or more organizations. Similarly, those who wish to improve the viability of domestic collaborations can apply much of the work regarding national and ethnic cultural differences.

   In designing collaborations, then, managers should be well informed about a number of cultural variables that will have an impact on relationship viability. Especially when more interdependent relationships are being considered, they should possess as much information as possible regarding their own organization's corporate and national/ethnic culture: which characteristics are relatively stable and which more ephemeral, how these characteristics might augment or impede achievement of strategic goals, and how members of other cultures view their own.

Leadership

Organization leaders play a critical role in the success of any collaborative relationship between two organizations in a number of ways. First, leaders' assessments of their strategic goals and the best ways to pursue these goals will constrain the type of partner sought, as well as at what point in an organization's and industry's life cycle such collaborations are pursued. Second, the personal styles and business philosophies of organizational leaders can play a critical role in initial negotiations of collaboration as well as the partner ultimately chosen. In this sense, leaders can be seen (at least partly) as manifestations of, and actors on behalf of, their own organizational culture. Whereas interpersonal compatibility among leaders may be a good indicator of success, this is probably so because it bodes well for the effectiveness of the contact among the organizations they represent rather than because of their own working relationships. The leader is an important symbolic element of the organizational community, and the success of a relationship between organizations will depend on his or her clear communication of goals and expectations for the collaboration, as well as the strategic value of the collaboration. Such communication throughout all participant organizations will be critical to operational success (Kanter, 1994). Appreciation of the relationship among leadership, culture, management behavior, and ultimate performance can vastly improve an organization's chances of embarking on and maintaining a successful relationship with other organizations (see, for example, Burke and Litwin, 1992; Burke and Jackson, 1991).

Evaluation

Successful management of interorganizational relations must therefore often include the possibility of review and renegotiation of agreements regarding strategic objectives, investments, provision of other resources, distribution of ownership, and division of proceeds. However, in order to avoid conflict, the organizations must agree on measures of the outcome variables on which these decisions will be based before the collaboration begins to operate. New measures can be added to the relationship systems during subsequent negotiations, and ineffective ones removed. This clarification of measurement systems supports circumspect and well-founded decision making regarding collaboration management. Once again, the paradox of control emerges as a challenge during the creation of performance measures that reflect the interests of all involved parties—measures should support the system, not choke it. Nevertheless, appropriately chosen measures can help to reduce the likelihood of inaccurate appraisals of poor or solid performance, as well as the perceptions of inequitable distributions of inputs and proceeds between the participating groups.

Intergroup Relations

Intergroup relations are typically examined and understood in the context of conflict and competition for scarce resources (e.g., Levine and Campbell, 1972; Alderfer, 1977; Rice, 1969). However, in the creation of collaborative alliances, organizations are attempting simultaneously to manage this competition and their shared or overlapping interests. The work of group relations theorists can contribute to the identification of phenomena that may help to overcome this challenge. For instance, organization members' perceptions of other organizations and *their* members can be expected to exert a strong influence on their abilities to exploit opportunities and resources offered by those organizations. Although perceptions of members of other organizations as outsiders may be inevitable, at least in initial stages of contact, the experience of "outsider-ness" can be either potentially threatening and undermining or potentially enhancing and thus valuable. Perceptions of outsiders can thus influence the viability of any collaborative endeavor undertaken by two organizations.

These perceptions can be modified or controlled in a number of ways. First, information about the potential benefits accruing to the organization as a result of the collaboration must be widely available. Second, dissemination of the performance indicators discussed above can help reduce what may be unfounded perceptions of discrepancy in cost-benefit yields, thus facilitating cooperation between group members.

Finally, Haunschild and colleagues (1994) have demonstrated that members' expectations about how contact with another group will have an impact on their own performance exert a strong influence on the group's openness to reframing its identification to include another group. Wilder (1986) has indicated that biases against another group can be weakened by individuating outgroup members, encouraging cross-categorization (these objectives can be achieved by forming work groups that cut across previously existing boundaries between groups), introducing a common enemy or overarching goal (i.e., highlighting the strategic importance of cooperation between groups), and removing situational cues associated with group membership. Managers can thus shape the meaning of the collaboration by focusing on expected performance benefits, making structural and systemic adjustments to support the achievement of these goals, and removing cues that detract from cooperation.

Stresses on Boundary Role Persons

The paradox of vulnerability and maintaining a climate of trust, open communication, and information sharing while at the same time protecting the host organization's autonomy and security presents a challenge for executives charged with managing interorganizational relationships.

Those performing in boundary positions are also responsible to both constituents in their host organizations and to their counterpart boundary managers in other organizations. Negotiation and the transfer of information and other resources across organizational boundaries occur within a boundary transaction system (Adams, 1976), wherein actions taken by constituents within organizations, as well as those taken by boundary managers, can have effects on the outcomes experienced by both organizations. Synergies resulting from the relationship depend largely on an organization's openness to influence from its own employees operating in clearly defined boundary roles. If there is resistance to the exercise of this influence, the relationship will be effectively contained, and potentially valuable information will not be distributed throughout the organization.

Conditions for Failure and Success

Obstacles to the success of relationships between organizations are real indeed, but they are not insurmountable. Organizational leaders who hope to capitalize on the opportunities available through collaboration and also to develop their organization's reputation as a desirable partner should consider both conditions that lead to failure and those that contribute to success.

Conditions for Failure. First and foremost, if there is insufficient clarity about goals and how to measure progress toward these goals, the relationship is doomed.

Should power and control between the partners be imbalanced, the relationship is not likely to last; that situation would indicate that an acquisition or a dissolution of the arrangement is in order. It may be that, in certain matters, one partner has more power and control than the other. Such imbalance in certain areas may be acceptable as long as the imbalance is favorable to the other partner in other areas.

If one partner has more expertise, status, and/or prestige than the other, the relationship is likely to be short-lived.

If one or more of the partners is overly confident and unrealistic about the future success of the relationship, believing that he or she has sufficient control over variables external to and within the partnership, then conditions are ripe for failure.

If things change without contingency plans, especially for renegotiating the relationship, the partnership is likely to deteriorate. Flexibility is key.

A lack of perceived equity in the relationship of any kind—a fair distribution of important jobs to both partnering organizations, for example—will lead to serious problems.

These six conditions are neither discrete nor complete. Nevertheless, they represent some of the most significant conditions for failure in interorganizational relations.

Conditions for Success. The most important condition for success in an interorganizational relationship is having a goal or a set of goals that are clear and achievable only through the cooperative efforts of both partners. Social psychologists who have studied intergroup competition, conflict, and collaboration point to the critical function of what has come to be called a superordinate goal—a goal that neither partner could achieve separately but by joining together they can.

It is also imperative that this goal or set of goals be measurable. The question that must be answered is, "How will we know that we are making progress toward goal achievement, for example, a year from now?" Other important conditions include:

- *A balance of power and control in the relationship.* If one of the partners is too dominant, then the consequences are more like an acquisition, with one absorbing the other and the other as an entity essentially going out of existence.

- *Mutual gain.* Each partner benefits from the relationship; the gain for each may be quite different (e.g., one obtains needed technology, the other realizes significant cost savings) as long as both clearly benefit.

- *Committed leaders.* When leaders of the partnering organizations demonstrate a strong belief in the efficacy of the relationship and show cooperative, collaborative behavior, others in the respective organizations are likely to follow suit.

- *Alignment of rewards.* Making certain that organizational members are rewarded for cooperating, for partnering-type behavior.

- *Respect for differences.* Like individuals, no two organizations are the same; organizational members must therefore work hard to overcome biases and stereotypes and be rewarded when they do.

- *Good luck.* Things change, and partnering organizations sometimes have some control over the changes and sometimes not; a natural disaster can, for example, destroy a budding joint venture in agriculture. Thus, the importance of contingency plans and maintaining a degree of flexibility and a willingness to renegotiate is clear.

UNANSWERED QUESTIONS

If recent newspapers and magazine articles are indicative, the trend toward some form of interorganizational relationship will continue and probably even increase. More and more industries, especially the mature ones (e.g., chemicals, pharmaceutical, banks, etc.), are consolidating and therefore many additional mergers and acquisitions can be expected. There also appears to be a growing reliance on other, less permanent forms of relationships such as networks and alliances. If this shift from a more permanent relationship (e.g., merger and acquisition) to less permanence (e.g., network, consortium, or alliance) is indeed true, why such a shift? Understanding more about this trend would be an excellent research agenda.

Assuming a shift to less permanence in relationships, two reasons to examine them via research present themselves. First, experience with and observation of a number of organizations suggests that most mergers and acquisitions prove to be unsuccessful, and economies of scale and promised synergies are not realized. The two (or more) cultures remain untouched, and eventually what looked like a promising synergy becomes a disappointment. Why enter a relationship that is likely to be unsatisfactory? With consolidation occurring in many industries, ultimate survival is a primary reason. Also, mergers and especially acquisitions mean that more control by senior executives can be exercised. These are strong attractions for permanent relationships. Understanding these different dynamics—that is, why mergers and acquisitions continue unabated when a successful outcome is questionable—would be a useful addition to our knowledge of interorganizational relations.

Second, to compete effectively in a turbulent, global marketplace, to keep the peace in a volatile society that may be falling apart, or to consolidate resources in a city that is losing industries and key professional and technical people, organizations today have to be highly flexible. Decisions must be made quickly and then perhaps changed in a matter of months if not days. This growing need for rapid decision making and adaptability flies in the face of permanence.

Research is needed, particularly research that is based on methods of rapid data gathering and analysis, to gain a better understanding of these trends and how ongoing they are likely to be.

In her review of key articles in the literature, Auster (1994) proposed five more specific needs for future theory and research: (1) conceptual clarity, (2) broadening units of analysis, (3) expanding the time frame of analysis, (4) investigating the complementarity of structure and process, and (5) expanding levels of analysis. These five areas for further study suggest rather clearly where the gaps are in the research literature so far, and consequently where more research is needed. Practice has outrun theory and research in this field, and there is a growing mountain of popular books and articles on strategic alliances, joint ventures, and the like. These publications can suggest executives' concerns and important areas for research. This literature is built largely on anecdotes and consultants' experiences. Scholarly research can subject many of these ideas and beliefs to systematic evaluation.

CONCLUSIONS

The discussion in this chapter suggests the following conclusions:

- The success of firms may be tied to how well they are linked with other firms in their environment. Industries like tobacco, pharmaceuticals, and electronics are profitable in part because competitors collaborate, within legal limits, in pursuing issues of common interest.

- The performance of an organization may be linked to its position in a network of relations—whether, for example, it is able to tap into networks for information or whether it is relatively isolated.

- The best unit of analysis for research on business performance—especially in Asia, some parts of Europe, and in highly networked industries like biotechnology—may be the network and not the individual firm.

- Organizations typically enter into alliances either to accomplish a goal that cannot be achieved alone or to distribute costs.

- Successful collaborations are the result of a well-managed process that is negotiated through predicable stages, from a preengagement state to an evaluation stage, and possible renegotiations or exit from the relationship. The chances of success are increased to the extent that the process passes through all these stages.

- Collaborations are more likely to fail when goals for the alliance are not clear or measurable, when there is a power or expertise imbalance between the organizations, and when organizations are inflexible in the face of changing circumstances.

- Political and military organizations are often forced to collaborate with partners for reasons other than the choice of organizational leaders. Research is necessary to understand how best to prepare these organizations and their personnel for alliances and alien forces, states, and organizations that may be very different culturally and operationally and with whom they do not have a predisposition to ally.

- Research is needed to understand the conditions for successful collaboration between nonmarket organizations in which financial measures of success are not available and issues of ideology and mission are especially salient in the overall political environment or context.

References

Adams, J. S., 1976. The structure and dynamics of behavior in organizational boundary roles. In *Handbook of Industrial and Organizational Psychology,* M. D. Dunnette, ed. Chicago: Rand McNally.

Alderfer, C. P., 1977. Group and intergroup relations. In *Improving Life at Work*, J. R. Hackman and L. L. Suttle, eds. Santa Monica, CA: Goodyear.

Aldrich, H., and D. Whetten, 1981. Organization sets, action sets, and networks: Making the most of simplicity. In *Handbook of Organizational Design*, P. C. Nystrom and W. Starbuck, eds. New York: Oxford University Press.

Auster, E. R., 1994. Macro and strategic perspectives on interorganizational linkages: A comparative analysis and review with suggestions for reorientation. *Advances in Strategic Management* 10B: 3–40.

Barley, S. R., J. Freeman, and R. C. Hybel, 1992. Strategic alliances in commercial biotechnology. In *Networks and Organizations: Structure, Form and Action*, N. Nohria and R. Eccles, eds. Boston: Harvard Business School Press.

Biggart, N. W., and G. Hamilton, 1992. On the limits of a firm-based theory to explain business networks: The western bias of neoclassical economics. In *Networks and Organizations: Structure, Form and Action*, N. Nohria and R. Eccles, eds., pp. 471–490. Boston: Harvard Business School Press.

Blau, P., and R. W. Scott, 1962. *Formal Organizations,* San Francisco: Chandler.

Bleeke, J., and D. Ernst, eds., 1993. *Collaborating to Compete: Using Strategic Alliances and Acquisitions in the Global Marketplace,* New York: Wiley.

Bleeke, J., and D. Ernst, 1995. Is your strategic alliance really a sale? *Harvard Business Review* 73(1): 97–105.

Bontempo, R., 1991. *Behavioral Decision Theory and the Negotiation Process: Effects of Agenda and Frame.* Doctoral dissertation, University of Illinois.

Boulding, K. E., 1956. General systems theory: The skeleton of science. *Management Science* 1: 197–208.

Brewer, M. B., 1968. Determinants of social distance among East African tribal groups. *Journal of Personality and Social Psychology* 10: 279–289.

Burke, W. W., and P. Jackson, 1991. Making the SmithKline Beecham merger work. *Human Resource Management* 30: 69–87.

Burke, W. W., and G. Litwin, 1992. A causal model of organization performance and change. *Journal of Management* 18(3): 532–545.

Caves, R., 1982. *American Industry: The Social Structure of Capitalism,* Cambridge, MA: Harvard University Press.

Druckman, D., 1968. Ethnocentrism in the inter-nation simulation. *Journal of Conflict Resolution* 12: 45–68.

—— 1977. Boundary role conflict: Negotiation as dual responsiveness. *Journal of Conflict Resolution* 21: 639–662.

—— 1994. Nationalism, patriotism, and group loyalty: A social psychological perspective. *Mershon International Studies Review* 38: 43–68.

—— and P. T. Hopmann, 1989. Behavioral aspects of mutual security negotiations. In *Behavior, Society and Nuclear War,* Volume I, P. Tetloch et al., eds. New York: Oxford University Press.

Fedor, K. J., and W. B. Werther, 1995. Making sense of cultural factors in international alliances. *Organizational Dynamics* 23(4): 33–48.

Fishbein, M., 1963. The perception of non-members: A test of Merton's reference group theory. *Sociometry* 26: 271–286.

Fligstein, N., 1990. *The Transformation of Corporate Culture,* Cambridge, MA: Harvard University Press.

Flippen, A. R., H. A. Hornstein, W. E. Siegal, and F.E.A. Weitzman, 1995. *A Comparison of Similarity and Interdependence as Triggers for Ingroup Formation.* Unpublished paper, Teacher's College, Columbia University.

Galaskiewicz, J., 1979. *Exchange Networks and Community Politics,* Beverly Hills, CA: Sage.

Gerybadze, A., 1994. *Strategic Alliances and Process Redesign: Effective Management and Restructuring of Cooperative Projects and Networks,* Berlin: Walter de Gruyter.

Gomes-Casseres, B., 1988. Joint venture cycles: The evolution of ownership strategies of USMNEs 1945–1975. In F. J. Contractor and P. Lorange, eds., *Strategies in International Business,* Lexington, MA: D. C. Heath.

Haas, E., 1980. Why collaborate?: Issue linkage and international regimes. *World Politics* 32: 357–405.

Harrigan, K. R., 1985. *Strategies for Joint Ventures,* Lexington, MA: Heath.

——— 1986. *Managing for Joint Venture Success,* Lexington, MA: Lexington Books.

Haspeslagh, P. C., and D. B. Jemison, 1991. *Managing Acquisitions,* New York: Free Press.

Haunschild, P. R., R. L. Moreland, and A. J. Murrell, 1994. Sources of resistance to mergers between groups. *Journal of Applied Social Psychology* 24(13): 1150–1178.

Hirsch, P., 1972. Processing fashions and fads: An organization-set analysis of cultural industry systems. *American Journal of Sociology* 77: 639–659.

——— 1975. Organizational effectiveness and the institutional environment. *Administrative Science Quarterly* 20: 327–344.

Kahn, R. L., 1990. Organizational theory and international relations: Mutually informing paradigms. In *Organizations and Nation-States: New Perspectives on Cooperation,* R. L. Kahn, and M. N. Zald, eds. San Francisco: Jossey-Bass.

Kahn, R. L., and M. N. Zald, 1990. *Organizations and Nation-States: New Perspectives on Cooperation,* San Francisco: Jossey-Bass.

Kanter, R. M., 1989. Becoming PALS: Pooling, allying and linking across companies. *The Academy of Management Executive* 3: 183–193.

——— 1994. Collaborative advantage: The art of alliances. *Harvard Business Review* 72(4): 96–108.

Knoke, D., and D. L. Rogers, 1979. A block-model analysis of interorganizational networks. *Sociology and Social Research* 64: 28–52.

Kotter, J. P., and J. L. Heskett, 1992. *Corporate Culture and Performance,* New York: Free Press.

Krasner, S., ed. 1982. *International Regimes,* Ithaca, NY: Cornell University Press.

Kratochwil, F., and J. Ruggie, 1989. International organization: The state of the art. In *The Politics of International Organizations: Patterns and Insights,* Paul F. Diehl, ed., pp. 17–27. Pacific Grove, CA: Brooks/Cole.

Kuman, S., and H. Rosovsky, eds., 1992. *Cultural and Social Dynamics,* Vol. 3. Stanford, CA: Stanford University Press.

Laumann, E. O., and F. U. Papi, 1976. *Networks of Collective Action,* New York: Academic Press.

Levine, R. A., and D. T. Campbell, 1972. *Ethnocentrism,* New York: Wiley.

Mayer, P., V. Rittberger, and M. Zurn, 1993. Regime theory: State of the art and perspectives. In *Regime Theory and International Relations,* V. Rittberger, ed., pp. 391–430. Oxford: Clarendon Press.

Miles, R., and K. S. Cameron, 1982. *Coffin Nails and Corporate Strategies,* Englewood Cliffs, NJ: Prentice-Hall.

Mizruchi, M., and M. Schwartz, eds., 1986. *The Structural Analysis of Business,* Cambridge, England: Cambridge University Press.

Nisbett, R., and L. Ross, 1980. *Human Inference: Strategies and Shortcomings of Social Adjustment,* Englewood Cliffs, NJ: Prentice-Hall.

Nohria, N., and R. Eccles, eds., 1992. *Networks and Organizations: Structure, Form and Action,* Boston: Harvard Business School Press.

Oliver, C., 1990. Determinants of interorganizational relationships: Integration and future directions. *Academy of Management Review* 15(2): 241–265.

Ouchi, W. G., and M. K. Bolton, 1988. The logic of joint research and development. *California Management Review* 30: 9–33.

Palmer, D. R., 1983. Broken ties: Interlocking directorates and intercorporate coordination. *Administrative Science Quarterly* 28: 40–55.

Paré, T. P., 1994. The new merger boom. *Fortune* 130(110): 95–106.

Perrow, C., 1992. *Complex Organization: A Critical Essay,* Glenview, IL: Scott Foresman.

Pfeffer, J., and P. Nowak, 1976. Joint ventures and interorganizational interdependence. *Administrative Science Quarterly* 11: 398–418.

Pfeffer, J., and G. R. Salancik, 1978. *The External Control of Organizations,* New York: Harper and Row.

Porter, M. E., 1980. *Competitive Strategy,* New York: Free Press.

——— 1990. *The Competitive Advantage of Nations,* New York: Free Press.

——— and M. Fuller, 1986. Coalitions and global strategy. In M. E. Porter, ed., *Competition in Global Industries,* Boston: Harvard Business School Press.

Rice, A. K., 1969. Individual, group, and intergroup processes. *Human Relations* 22: 565–584.

Sankar, C. S., W. R. Boulton, N. W. Davidson, and C. A. Snyder, with R. W. Usery, 1995. Building a world-class alliance: The universal card—TSYS case. *Academy of Management Executive* 9: 20–29.

Scherer, F. M., 1980. *Industrial Market Structure and Economic Performance,* Chicago: Rand McNally.

Schwenk, C. R., 1994. Commentary: Macro and strategic perspectives on interorganizational linkages. *Advances in Strategic Management* 10B: 41–46.

Scott, W. R., 1987. *Organizations: Rational, Natural, and Open Systems,* Englewood Cliffs, NJ: Prentice-Hall.

Singer, J. E., L. S. Radloff, and D. M. Wark, 1963: Renegades, heretics, and changes in sentiment. *Sociometry* 26: 178–189.

Smith, K. K., and D. N. Berg, 1987. *Paradoxes of Group Life,* San Francisco: Jossey-Bass.

Strange, S., 1989. Cave hic dragones: A critique of regime analysis. In *The Politics of International Organizations: Patterns and Insights,* P. F. Diehl, ed., pp. 51–65. Pacific Grove, CA: Brooks/Cole.

Tajfel, H., 1981. *Human Groups and Social Categories: Studies in Social Psychology,* Cambridge, England: Cambridge University Press.

——— 1982. Social psychology of intergroup relations. *Annual Review of Psychology* 33: 1–39.

Wallis, A. D., 1994. Value barriers to coordination of human services networks, In *Proceedings of the Annual Meeting of the Association of Researchers in Non-Profit Organizations and Voluntary Action* (ARNOVA).

Walton, R. E., and R. B. McKersie, 1965. *A Behavioral Theory of Labor Negotiations,* New York: McGraw-Hill.

Warren, R. L., 1967. The interorganizational field as a focus for investigation. *Administrative Science Quarterly* 12: 396–419.

Wilder, D. A., 1986. Social categorization: Implications for creation and reduction of intergroup bias. In L. Berkowitz, ed., *Advances in Experimental Social Psychology* 19: 291–355.

Williamson, O., 1992. Markets, hierarchies, and the modern corporation: An unfolding perspective. *Journal of Economic Behavior and Organization* 17: 335–352.

Yoshino, M. Y., and U. S. Rangan, 1995. *Strategic Alliances: An Entrepreneurial Approach to Globalization,* Boston: Harvard Business School Press.

Young, O., 1989. The politics of international regime formation: Managing natural resources and the environment. *International Organization* 43: 349–375.

PART SIX

KEY ROLES IN PLANNED ORGANIZATION CHANGE

Editors' Interlude

P lanned organization change is complex—a rather obvious understatement. To help sort through some of the complexity, it is useful to think about and plan organization change according to necessary roles that are key and primary to the process of implementation. Two of the most important roles, if not *the most* important, are leadership and teamwork. We begin with leadership and then proceed to cover group behavior, considering both the interdependence of the individual with the group and the group as a whole, emphasizing teamwork. It is appropriate to begin with leadership, because without this process planned change is not likely to occur. Further to the point, the mark of effective leadership is the extent to which the individual in a leadership position can pull together a group of people to accomplish tasks and reach goals as a team. Leadership effectiveness is a function of leader-follower accomplishments—together.

Bearing in mind that leadership is by definition reciprocal—no follower, no leader—we begin with Chapter Forty-Three, Rioch's (1971)* examination of followers and leaders, and the nature of that reciprocity. Steeped in the classics, the Bible (see the title of her article), Bion's theory of group dynamics,

---

*Chapter is included in the collection of readings on the *Organization Change: A Comprehensive Reader* website. www.josseybass.com/go/burke

and an analysis of charisma, Rioch helps us to understand our natural tendency as followers, particularly in times of change—moving toward some unknown, to become dependent on an all-powerful leader. She concludes with the admonition that authority, which must be exercised for change to occur, is best realized through a concerted effort of leader and followers toward task accomplishment.

With Burke's (2008) "Leading Organization Change," we consider the role of the leader more directly and specifically. He conceives of the role as having four phases: (1) a prelaunch phase examining highly important psychological factors for any change leader before proceeding, such factors as self-awareness, motives, and values; (2) a launch phase, with focus on communication, initiating key activities, and dealing with resistance (see also Part Four in this volume); (3) a postlaunch phase that emphasizes the implementation details of organization change, such as deploying multiple interventions, the leaders being willing to (a) take the heat (resistance and criticism from followers), (b) provide consistency in word and deed, (c) persevere, and (d) constantly repeat the message of why we are changing the ways that we do things; and (4) a final phase that is about sustaining the change—the most difficult stage of all, concerning momentum and such activities as dealing with unanticipated consequences of interventions, choosing successors, and launching yet again new initiatives.

The next chapter (Forty-Five) addresses self-managed groups. Not always, of course, but often aspects of organization change are about structure and organization redesign. Also often, these changes include flattening the hierarchy and decentralization. This means less dependence on individual leaders and managers and more reliance on groups, hopefully becoming teams, that take more responsibility for management and leadership themselves. In this chapter, "The Psychology of Self-Management in Organizations," Hackman (1986) addresses in some depth the implications organizationally and individually of self-management. He describes the key features of self-management, focusing of course on the group aspects and how authority is distributed. He further describes primary behaviors that differentiate self-managed units from work-unit behavior in more traditional organizations, and he explores conditions that support effective self-management by citing relevant research and theory. Hackman concludes with implications for organizational leadership.

The fourth and final piece in this grouping about leadership, self-management, and teamwork is by Katzenbach and Smith (1993),* on "The Discipline of Teams." Again a practice-oriented chapter, the authors first define what a team is: a group of individuals who share and are committed to a common purpose with associated performance goals, who have complementary skills, and who hold one another accountable for the work to be done. Then Katzenbach and Smith move on to the team functions. They cover what they consider to be the four primary elements that make teams function: (1) common commitment and purpose, (2) performance goals, (3) complementary skills, and (4) mutual accountability. Finally, they classify teams in three ways: teams that recommend things, teams that make or do things, and teams that run things.

To summarize, this Part Six consists of four chapters and covers two critical roles in planning and implementing organization change: leadership and teamwork. The two chapters that directly address leadership approach the topic from a deep psychological perspective (Rioch) and from a practical, phased approach (Burke). The two other chapters concern group behavior in the form of self-managed groups (Hackman) and teamwork (Katzenbach and Smith).

CHAPTER FORTY-FOUR

Leading Organization Change

W. Warner Burke (2008)

Leadership matters. Evidence shows that leaders can either hurt badly or destroy completely an organization. The Enron case is clearly a significant example. Evidence also shows that leaders can measurably help their organizations and can add value. Examples of change leaders who made positive differences for their organizations are described in this chapter. Also described, and what serves as the structure for this chapter, is a simple phase model for planning and leading organization change. The purposes of this chapter, therefore, are to (1) provide a framework, a phase model, for planning and leading change; (2) describe actual case examples of organization change emphasizing the leader's role; and (3) suggest with the model and case examples that large-scale transformations of organizations, although fraught with potential peril, can indeed be accomplished.

PHASES OF ORGANIZATION CHANGE
AND THE LEADER'S ROLE

The following descriptions of *how* to bring about organization change are derived from theoretical ideas and from experience in consulting with CEOs who were serving as change agents. What follows is written in a prescriptive fashion for the sake of clarity. Caveats are therefore not presented.

An interesting paradox about organization change is that we plan as if the process is linear when, in reality, it is anything but linear. It is useful, nevertheless, to think about the planning process in terms of phases. After all, phases are not totally discrete; they overlap. But we must bear in mind that as planned organization change is implemented, (1) more than one phase occurs at the same time, that is, they are not temporally mutually exclusive; and (2) contingency plans need to be in place, because rarely does anything turn out as planned. Unanticipated consequences occur. It's not possible to think of everything!

THE PRELAUNCH PHASE

Leader Self-Examination

Leadership is personal. The process concerns the use of self, how to be persuasive, how to deal with resistance, and how to be political, in the best sense of the phrase: how to embody the vision of where one wants the organization to go. It is important, therefore, for the leader who is about to begin a significant change effort to take some time at the outset to reflect. This reflection can be considered in three categories: self-awareness, motives, and values.

Self-Awareness. There is growing evidence that self-awareness is related to performance; that is, high performers tend to have a greater overlap between how they see themselves and how others see them than do moderate and low performers (Atwater & Yammarino, 1992; Church, 1997). It behooves leaders who want to bring about a successful change effort to be as cognizant as possible of themselves in personal domains such as the following:

• *Tolerance for ambiguity.* The courses that organization change will take are not exactly predictable; being able to live with this kind of ambiguity is important.

• *Need for control.* It is difficult to be a "control freak" and lead change effectively; organization change is messy, sometimes chaotic, and seemingly out of control; thus, being clear about what one can control and needs to control and what one is not likely to be able to control is critical.

• *Understanding how feelings affect behavior.* What is one's typical reaction when others disagree or challenge or when others resist the change that the leader feels strongly about? Knowing oneself in these ways helps the leader manage himself or herself more effectively, especially in trying circumstances.

• *Personal dispositions.* Most people know whether their preference is extraversion or introversion, but what about other dimensions, such as need for closure and intuition compared with sensing? (These are components of the Myers-Briggs Type Indicator [MBTI] measure, based on Jung's personality theory.) There is some evidence, for example, that intuition (trusting one's hunches, future orientation, and conceptual tendency) is more related to leader behavior than is sensing (being fact-based, concrete, and practical); see, for example, Van Eron and Burke (1992). When the MBTI was used with the top team of a large global corporation a few years ago, nine of the eleven scored intuitive, including the CEO. For a brief account of this team-building activity, see Burke and Noumair (2002).

• *Decision making.* It is highly valuable to understand the differences between times when one as a leader needs to take the reins and decide and times when one needs to loosen control and involve others as a part of self-knowledge.

Additional examples could be catalogued here, but the point is to give a flavor of some of the more important aspects of self-awareness for leadership purposes, not to provide an exhaustive list.

Motives. Knowing one's motives is, of course, a part of self-awareness, but for this section, the emphasis is on which motives are the more important ones for leading change.

O'Toole (1999), one of our paramount thinkers and writers in the arena of organization change, makes the interesting point that ambition is the "only inherent character trait [that] is essential for effective leadership" (p. 1). This word, for some, maybe most people, conjures up negative feelings. An ambitious person, especially one with high ambition, is to be avoided. But O'Toole argued that a certain amount of ambition is good. O'Toole used the words "appropriately ambitious." As he stated, "Even the saintly Mohandas K. Gandhi had ambition" (p. 2). Gandhi even admitted it himself. So let us agree with O'Toole that having the appropriate amount of ambition is not only a good quality but may also indeed be a necessary motive for effective organization change leadership. Of course, the important issue here is, what is appropriate? O'Toole did not define *appropriate*, but he stated that the change leader needs to have a "healthy dissatisfaction with the status quo" (p. 2) and then change it. He also points to the importance of having this ambition in the service of an organization change goal. In a sense, then, he was agreeing with Zaleznik's (1977) idea that a leader is one who experiences no difference between personal goals and those of the organization.

Using McClelland's (1965, 1975) three major motives—need for achievement, power, and affiliation—as discussion points, we can probably agree, first, that having at least a moderate (if not high) need to achieve is critical to success as a leader of change. Second, McClelland's need-for-power concept is not unlike O'Toole's notion of ambition. In this case, a certain amount of need for power would seem to be necessary for change leadership. If one does not want to influence others, one is not likely to be very effective at it. The McClelland and Burnham (1976) study puts the need for power into context. Using subordinates' ratings of their organization's degree of clarity and amount of team spirit as indices of successful management, McClelland and Burnham found that if a manager was high in power motivation, low in need for affiliation, and high in inhibition (that is, the power need was socialized, mature, and not expressed for self-aggrandizement), the organization's degree of clarity was greater (subordinates knew the goals and what was expected of them) and the team spirit was higher.

There are good reasons for this. Managers who have a high need for affiliation usually want to be liked and to be popular. As a result, their decision making tends to be impulsive, being done to please someone at the moment rather than in rational support of the overall good of the organization. Managers with a high need for power that is personally oriented are not builders of the institution, according to McClelland and Burnham (1976). They tend to demand personal loyalty from their subordinates—loyalty to them as individuals rather than to the organization. The institutional managers are the most successful because they encourage loyalty to the institution rather than to themselves. As a result, the successful manager creates a climate with clarity, team spirit, and opportunities for accomplishment.

The profile of the desirable institutional manager thus has three major elements: high need for power, low need for affiliation, and high inhibition. In addition, successful institutional managers like organizations and are oriented toward them. They typically join more organizations and feel greater responsibility for developing them than others. They enjoy work, they like the discipline of work, and they have a preference for getting things done in an orderly fashion. They place the good of the organization above self-interest. They are judicious; that is, they have a strong sense of fairness. They are generally more mature, less ego-centered, and less defensive. They are also more willing to seek advice from experts, and they have longer and broader vision of the future.

Finally, McClelland and Burnham (1976) pointed out that successful managers tend to have a style of management characterized by participative and coaching behavior; that is, they are concerned with the needs and development of their subordinates. In summary, according to McClelland and Burnham:

> The general conclusion of these studies is that the top manager of a company must possess a high need for power, that is, a concern for influencing people. However, this need must be disciplined and controlled so that it is directed toward

the benefit of the institution as a whole and not toward the manager's personal aggrandizement. Moreover, the top manager's need for power ought to be greater than his need for being liked by people.

Finally, effective change leaders need to have an above-average level of energy and be capable of (1) working long hours when needed, (2) interacting with lots of people, and (3) energizing others. Of the thousands of citations in Stodgill's (1974) and later Bass's (1990) handbook on leadership, one of the few consistent findings was that effective leaders are typically high-energy people.

Values. Alignment of individual needs and values with the organization's culture (norms and values) is likely to enhance motivation and in turn performance. This alignment is all the more important for the CEO and other change leaders in the organization. But what if we are attempting to change the culture? Then, it is a matter of modifying current values or establishing an entirely new set of values. Establishing these values to undergird and provide direction for the change effort is the responsibility of the CEO/change leader. Not that the values need to come directly from the CEO; the establishing process can involve many people. But in the end, the values must be compatible with the CEO's personal values because he or she must embody them and live them daily in the organization. In the case of Dime Bancorp it was a matter of establishing new values (drawn from the mission statement). An internal Dime task force did the work of drafting the new mission statement, but the CEO, Larry Toal, was highly involved. He attended many of the meetings and in the end was committed to the mission statement; and because the new values were elicited from the mission statement, Toal's commitment to the values was easily achieved.

In another merger, that of SmithKline Beecham, values were created to help establish the new culture, as with Dime. In this case, the top team of the global company initiated the work of establishing the values. Bob Bauman, CEO of the newly merged company (SmithKline from the United States and Beecham from the United Kingdom) at the time, 1989, described in his own words the value-generation process (Burke & Trahant, 2000):

> So the executive committee and I went away again, this time to define the values that would make up that culture. Obviously, there were certain values that were critical to our company. Innovation, for example, was critical. We didn't have much trouble getting people to agree on that. . . . There was no disagreement that customers were critical and that our customer base was changing. . . . HMOs were coming in, which brought up the question, "Who's the buyer now, the HMO or the doctor?" and "How do we bridge this gap?" So we knew we had to start thinking more about customers and had to do a better job—not just in providing good drugs but also in how we managed and serviced our customers.

We extended our discussion of customers incidentally to include not just the outside world but also our own organization. Because we thought it important to say that everyone in the company has a customer. I had a customer on the Board. I had customers in dealing with members of the executive committee. We agreed that people on the manufacturing line, in R&D—people everywhere inside the company—had customers. . . . Another value we believed in was winning. We wanted to create a winning attitude inside the company, so we thought performance was important. And there was some feeling in our early discussions that we weren't driving as hard in the area of performance as we needed to. . . . We agreed we wanted to be winners and perform better than our competitors. . . . Another value that was clearly agreed to but harder to articulate was people. We knew we had to have the best people we could find and that they were key to our competitive advantage. So as part of articulating this value, we emphasized that people needed to contribute to the goals of the organization; we wanted to give everyone a chance to influence and participate in how work was done and how it got measured. And we wanted people to feel ownership for continuously improving the ways they worked on the job.

Finally, we agreed to the value of integrity. It's something we felt we possessed and that was important to the nature of our industry. We felt five values was the right number. We believed that if we got too many it would be very hard to drive them all through the organization [pp. 64–66].

The Dime example was a bottom-up process of determining mission and values, whereas the SmithKline Beecham case was more top-down. Both worked because each organization operationalized its set of values by putting them into behavioral language and then building a multirater feedback program so that all key managers received feedback on behaviors that reflected the values. For more detail on the SmithKline Beecham example, see Bauman, Jackson, and Lawrence (1997); Burke (2000b); Burke and Jackson (1991); and Wendt (1993).

The External Environment

Another critical element of the prelaunch phase is for the CEO and other top leaders in the organization to monitor and gather as much information about their organization's external environment as possible. This would include information such as changing customer needs, changing technology in one's industry, changing government regulations, what competitors are up to, and what is occurring in the general economy both domestically and worldwide. And according to strategy guru Michael Porter (1985), it would also include understanding the bargaining power of customers, suppliers and unions, and threats of (1) new entrants into the marketplace and (2) substitute products or services. The CEO and his or her team must then determine how to respond to what the environment is telling them and how to establish a more effective alignment for their organization.

This prelaunch activity conforms, of course, to (1) the reality that for their survival organizations are dependent on their external environment and (2) the theoretical principles of open-system theory. Moreover, organization change occurs primarily as a reaction to some change in the environment. Rarely, if ever, do board members, CEOs, and their executive colleagues sit around a boardroom table together and decide to change the organization without regard to the organization's position in or degree of alignment within its external environment. Reading that environment accurately and reacting accordingly is indispensable.

Several decades ago, in their classic paper on the causal texture of organizational environments, Emery and Trist (1965) discussed four kinds of environments for organizations:

1. Placid, randomized
2. Placid, clustered
3. Disturbed, reactive
4. Turbulent fields

They stated that the world seemed to be moving more toward the turbulent type. They were quite correct, of course; today, most organizational environments are turbulent. Their point further stressed the importance of reading the environment as accurately as possible so that timely and appropriate organizational responses could be made to ensure survival.

The CEO/change leader's responsibility here is to prepare for the organization change as thoroughly as possible, by taking the time and expending the effort to gather environmental information carefully and accurately and then to analyze this information before jumping into the change process too quickly. Impulsive behavior by the CEO at this stage of the change process is to be avoided, if not at all other stages as well.

Establishing the Need for Change

If people in the organization see or feel no need for change, they are not likely to embrace the idea. CEOs and other senior executives are often in a better position to monitor the external environment and therefore are likely to see the need for change sooner and more clearly than the majority of organizational members. They are often in a better position, but not always. Technical people down in the organization may see a technological change coming before senior management does. Often, the sales force and others in the organization who have direct contact with customers see a need to serve them differently before senior management does. Regardless of where the awareness of a need for change originates, it remains the CEO's responsibility to communicate that need to organization members. And the communication must be convincing. An example helps to clarify these points.

British Aerospace (BAe), a multibillion-dollar aircraft and defense industry enterprise, was formed in 1977 by putting together six defense and aerospace organizations under one corporate roof. The firm at that time was a government-owned company, but two years later Prime Minister Margaret Thatcher declared that BAe would become a private, stock-owned corporation, as she later did with British Airways and other nationalized industries during the 1980s. BAe was Thatcher's first nationalized company to become privatized. In a sense, BAe was a holding company with six previously autonomous organizations, which had rich histories dating back to World War II and before and possessed quite different corporate cultures. Richard Evans (now Sir Richard), having grown up in one of the six firms of the British aircraft corporation, became CEO on New Year's Day, 1990. He inherited six baronies, each of which viewed itself with considerable pride. After all, "that beautiful bird," as Evans called the Concorde, came from the earlier parts of BAe, as did other highly regarded aircraft (e.g., the Comet, the world's first commercial jet) and sophisticated defense weaponry. Also, by 1990, BAe had a number of joint ventures with French and German companies in the manufacture of the Airbus commercial aircraft. So, Evans took over a healthy organization from the standpoint of sales, profit, and future customer orders.

One year later, however, things were considerably worse. The stock price had plummeted, orders were down (after all, the cold war was over), and capital, especially cash, was badly needed. Evans began to cut costs—he laid off thousands of employees, for example—to divest some of the businesses and to take severe write-offs. But productivity and innovation remained strong, at least in most of the former six companies, and there were many talented people in the ranks. But for some reason, these strengths could not be fully realized.

Monitoring BAe's external environment, Evans saw three large "blips on the radar," as he called them. One came from Boeing, a major competitor. They produced a new version of their 737 that was superior to the Airbus, at least at that time. A second blip was the fact that the capacity of European aerospace and defense firms far exceeded demand. And finally, there was the abysmal performance of BAe's shares on the stock market. These "blips" caused Evans to act yet again; he believed this time that a significant change needed to occur within the company to respond effectively. There were other needs for change as well—for example, correcting the silo effect of the six baronies that made up BAe. Evans believed that a major culture change was the right action to take. To use Gersick's (1991) language, change in the "deep structure" of BAe was in order. To use Evans's words (Evans & Price, 1999):

Why did I think that a culture change was the answer? There were of course many operating and strategic fixes that we could do (and did) to improve our competitive standing and our share price. But when you added all these up, and when you looked at the competitive abilities of rivals, there was a shortfall. I couldn't quantify it. I simply had a gut feeling, a conviction that the underlying reason for our deficiencies lay in the culture of the company [p. 10].

The new culture desired was one that would integrate the various businesses so that, for example, consistent, common approaches could be taken across the corporation. Another change objective was to lessen the rivalries that existed among the former six companies.

So, relying on the wisdom and experience of his new nonexecutive chairman of the board, Bob Bauman, who knew a thing or two about large-scale organization change (recall that he had led the merger of SmithKline Beecham a few years earlier) and the expertise of external consultants, Evans launched the change effort. Working with his top one hundred or so executives, Evans's initial work was on crafting a new mission statement with an appropriate list of corporate values. This early work went fairly well, but some of the executives were simply not convinced that all this effort and the occasional angst were worth it. Many of them had been through "culture change" before. Again, to quote Evans (Evans & Price, 1999):

In the eyes of many of BAe's top managers, the lack of a "burning platform" weakened my argument that change was urgently needed. How could I make them see that the present good times were not symptomatic of the way things would be five years hence? The easier way was to present them with scenarios of likely futures. For this job, I turned to one of our top line executives, John Weston, then managing director of Military Aircraft, now my successor as Chief Executive. I seconded him from his regular duties and gave him carte blanche to analyze the company from end to end and then report his findings.

With characteristic thoroughness, John documented "The Case for Change." His report probed every single part of the business, its macroeconomic environment, its competitive structure, the state of technology, and so forth. Time and again he documented a stark conclusion: our business units' rate of progress and future prospects of performance gains were inadequate, given the emergent threats in the external environment. What's more, even if we took a whip to them to urge them to improve sales and profits and squeeze the cash flow, any conceivable improvement would not change the analysis substantially. At the end of the day, BAe would be trailing and not setting the industry tempo.

Because John Weston was the divisional head of our largest and most profitable business unit, his call to action could not easily be dismissed. If he saw the writing on the wall, so might everyone else. "We wanted to give them the macroeconomic and geopolitical picture right between the eyes. The paradigm for defense and aerospace markets was changing dramatically, and we had to learn superior skills and ways of reacting," says Weston [p. 17].

The case was indeed made and the culture change at BAe went forth. The rest is history. Later, BAe became quite successful, its stock price more than triple what it had been in 1993. One of its major products, the Airbus, became a formidable competitor with Boeing. Moreover, Evans was knighted in 1996 for his role as CEO in the turnaround of BAe. For the full story of how a CEO may make the case for change and other aspects of successful organization change, see Evans and Price (1999) and Chapter Nine in Burke and Trahant (2000).

Providing Clarity of Vision and Direction

The final point of the prelaunch phase is to craft a vision statement and, in so doing, provide clear direction for the organization change effort. One of the best statements about vision has been articulated by James O'Toole (1999):

> A robust vision mobilizes appropriate behavior. It uses memorable, simple concepts that make clear what needs to be different about tomorrow. It describes the distinctive competencies needed to deliver on the desired end state (for example, "Here's what we have to do differently in order to succeed"). Often, a vision will make choices clear by making the case for change as either an opportunity or a burning platform (for example, "If we don't change in this way, the company won't survive."). That's not asking much, is it?
>
> Leaders don't even have to create visions themselves (although many do). But, at a minimum, they must initiate a process for developing a vision and then engage themselves fully in generating buy-in. Shared commitment to a vision can be built either through wide-scale participation in the act of its creation or through involvement immediately thereafter in its dissemination. . . . We're not talking quantum mechanics here. This is simple stuff—so simple that many leaders gloss over the basics. For example, by definition, vision has to do with "seeing, sight, and sensing with the eyes." Recognizing that simple fact, effective leaders make their visions, well, visual. Remember Ronald Reagan's budget message when he explained that a trillion bucks amounts to a stack of dough as high as the Empire State building? By using that visual reference, he got Americans to see that federal spending amounts to real money! In doing so, he changed the terms of the national debate and, for the first time, created a majority in support of lower taxes. It was his most effective moment as a leader [pp. 302–303].

Perhaps the paramount vision statement was delivered by Martin Luther King Jr. in his "I have a dream" speech on the steps of the Lincoln Memorial. He used striking imagery, for example, of children holding hands, that his listeners could "see." The following are short examples of vision and direction provided by change leaders who have been referenced already:

- At the time of the SmithKline Beecham merger, chairman of the board Henry Wendt's (1993) conceptualization of what a truly global corporation looks like and his and CEO Bob Bauman's crafting of "the Promise" (the merged company's vision statement) provided both the vision and the mission for the future. Their clarity of direction was critical to the success of the change that was, at the time, the largest cross-border merger ever. For the full story, see Bauman, Jackson, and Lawrence (1997), Burke (2000b), and Chapter Four in Burke and Trahant (2000).

- At British Airways, it was Colin Marshall's clear emphasis on what the new culture should be—one that was customer-focused and market-driven—that provided the necessary vision for what needed to be reached.

- At the BBC, it was John Birt's description of "Extending Choice" that showed the way to the future and the new corporation.

- At British Aerospace, it was Dick Evans's resolve to see that a mission and vision statement was crafted by the top one hundred executives that set the stage for organization change. As O'Toole (1999) noted above, the CEO may not write the vision and mission statement himself or herself, but the responsibility for seeing that the job is done is clearly the CEO's. The way Evans did it took time, to be sure, but "at the end of the day," as the British are fond of saying, he had commitment.

By way of a quick summary, recall that in the Burke-Litwin model (see Chapter Seventeen of this volume) a distinction is made between mission and vision, with vision being associated more with the leadership box or model category. But it is the change leader's or CEO's responsibility to see that both mission and vision are crafted, because both set the tone and the clarity of direction. Without direction, both in terms of who we are and who we want to be in the future, desired organization change will not occur.

THE LAUNCH PHASE

Communicating the Need

Usually, the CEO is the one who delivers the message about the need for change—but not always. In the BAe example, Dick Evans called on his number two person, John Weston, to deliver the case for change. He made this decision for at least two reasons. First, he had already launched the organization change by involving the top one hundred executives in the crafting of a new corporate mission statement and in making the choice of values for the corporation as a whole. Although these executives did the work he asked them to, Evans was not convinced that their hearts were in it. And besides, some of them seriously questioned the whole process. In other words, Evans wasn't certain that his credibility as the change leader was as solid as it needed to be. Moreover, some of his executives had been through culture change in their respective businesses and were not exactly sanguine about going through the whole process again unless there was a compelling reason to do so.

Second, in making the case for change and communicating the message, Evans believed that Weston would have more credibility because, unlike Evans, who came from marketing and sales, he was an engineer and a "numbers guy," as were many of the BAe executives. It would be abundantly clear that Weston had done his homework and knew what he was talking about. This decision by Evans did indeed work, and the buy-in for the organization change began to emerge. The point is that although the CEO does not necessarily have to be the message deliverer, seeing that the delivery occurs, especially by another change leader colleague, is nevertheless his or her responsibility.

In the British Airways case, it was Colin Marshall, the CEO, who delivered the message. In fact, he delivered it again and again, making certain that he came across as consistent with the message each time he gave it and that he was absolutely serious and committed.

Initial Activities

A significant activity to conduct at the outset of organization change is an event that will capture attention, provide focus, and create the reality that the change effort now launched is not merely an exercise. A quote from Marshall, of British Airways, gives first his rationale and then an example of an initial activity (Burke & Trahant, 2000):

> But to get people to work in new ways, we needed a major change in the company's culture. That meant refocusing everyone on the customer, on the marketplace, and away from the exclusively engineering and operations focus we'd had. That had to be done, of course, without sacrificing safety, technical, or maintenance standards. And that proved tricky. People had difficulty understanding why I kept hammering away at the need to focus on customers while also saying, "We've got to fly these aircraft at a very high technical standard, too." The focus before had always been on the technical side alone, but I made the point repeatedly that we had to do both. It was at this point that we saw the explicit need for a culture-change program. . . . The first thing we did was to launch a program called "Putting People First" . . . a two-day seminar. We took roughly 150 employees at a time and drew people from various departments within BA and from various geographical areas. The program focused on how one creates better relationships with people, with one's fellow employees, with customers, even with members of one's own family [p. 95].

Another example comes from a venerable British organization, the BBC. John Birt, the CEO ("director general" is the proper title), authorized a one-day workshop on "Extending Choice," the new mission and vision for the corporation. The day was devoted to, first, an overview and explanation of extending choice, and second, small-group meetings so that questions could be raised and discussions could be held about how this new "extended" mission affected each of them in their respective roles.

At BAe, the initial activity, as noted above, was the off-site meetings of the top one hundred executives to craft the corporate mission statement and to choose the values.

At SmithKline Beecham, the initial activity to help shape the newly merged culture for the CEO, Bob Bauman, and the ten executives directly reporting to him was working on the mission and value decisions and team building. The team building at the top had two purposes: to get this top group to work together more effectively and, what was perhaps more important, to serve as role models for the rest of the global corporation. Part of the team-building process was (1) use of the MBTI to help the executives learn about their own and their colleagues' communicating, information processing, and decision-making preferences and (2) participation in a multirater feedback process on leadership practices to obtain a clearer understanding of how their self-perceptions of their leadership compared with the perceptions of others, particularly peers and those directly reporting to them. Subsequently, both the MBTI and the multirater feedback process permeated the entire managerial population of the company.

Finally, at Dime Bancorp, the initial activities that launched the organization change (a result of a merger) consisted of (1) establishing a task force of fifteen people who represented all business units and all levels in the hierarchy to draft a new corporate mission statement, (2) determining a new business strategy led by the CEO, and (3) team building for the newly formed top team.

It should be obvious from these examples that the early activity of organization change can take a variety of forms. The point is that a focused symbolic and energizing event (or multiple events occurring at about the same time) is a highly useful way of launching large-scale and planned organization change.

Dealing with Resistance

Recall that in Part Four of this volume, resistance to organization change is considered at three levels: individual, group, and the larger system. The prudent change leader will be well aware of the nature of resistance to change and the forms that resistance behavior can take at each organizational level. Recall further that at the individual level it is important that the change leader be wary of imposing change on people and to find ways for organizational members to have choice and be as involved in the process as possible.

At the group level, recall that protecting one's turf, closing ranks, and demanding a new structure or leadership can be common forms of resistance. Seeing to it that activities in a group setting to achieve closure with the past (for example, having a symbolic funeral) can help in dealing with resistance. Also, recomposing a group with new membership can help, and of course so can any activity that involves people in key decision making. For example, a highly influential group early in the merger process of SmithKline Beecham was the "merger management committee." Selected by the CEO, this group had the responsibility of selecting who the executives would be for the key positions in the corporation, and unique was the rule instituted by Bauman, the CEO, that no member of the committee could be named for any of these executive jobs. Objectivity was therefore more assured in the decisions of who was selected. Even though none of these committee members could have any of the plum positions they were working with, they were highly motivated and strongly committed to the task. After all, they were involved in an activity that would have far-reaching effects on the corporation. A delayed reward for these members was Bauman's making certain that they were eventually placed in important roles and positions for the corporation. The purpose of this brief case was to provide an example of how to involve people in the change process.

At the larger-system level, recall that resistance can take the form of "This too shall pass"—that is, "We've seen this kind of initiative, or fad, before and it won't last this time, either." Also there are diversionary tactics; for example, "Other mainstream business needs are far more important than this change thing." It was suggested earlier that coping with these forms of resistance might involve making a strong, compelling case for the change (as in the BAe example) and exerting strong leadership—not in a dictatorial way, but leading with persistence and with clarity of direction, passion, and vision, a point to be emphasized in the next section.

POSTLAUNCH: FURTHER IMPLEMENTATION

Once the organization change has been launched, it becomes quickly apparent to the change leader that so-called change management is an oxymoron. This particular phase of organization change—postlaunch—is difficult for many CEOs. After all, they typically have control needs that are considerably above average, and now matters seem out of control. CEOs can easily experience feelings of (1) anxiety ("What have we unleashed here?") and (2) ambivalence in decision making; some organizational members feel the excitement of change unleashed and want to run free, whereas others are asking for the CEO to step in and exercise control, usually taking the form of a cry for structure ("What's my new job Who will be my boss?"). When control needs are aroused by such pleas for structure, many CEOs will want to step in and establish the new order. Because followers are asking for an antidote for all this uncertainty, the advice of Ronald Heifetz (1994) is most appropriate. In essence, he suggested three actions. First, hold the collective feet to the fire, that is, to be persistent about what it is going to take to make the change successful (e.g., living with ambiguity about exactly how everything is going to work out). Second, draw the system out of its comfort zone, but attempt to contain the associated stress so that it does not become dysfunctional (recall the work of Bridges, 1986). Third, deal with avoidance mechanisms that usually emerge during this time, such as blaming, scapegoating, and appealing to authority figures for answers.

During the postlaunch phase, it may also seem to the change leader that the process has taken on a life of its own. In fact, theory associated with living systems holds that when disturbance occurs (the launch phase), "the components of living systems self-organize and new forms and repertoires emerge from the turmoil" (Pascale, Milleman, & Gioja, 2000, p. 6). The CEO/change agent must persevere but be patient at the same time so that creativity and innovation "can do their work," or "magic," as some might call it, and allow for new forms to emerge. New forms may mean any number of things, including new ways of doing work, different values, new structures, new products, services, or business lines, getting into, if not establishing, new markets, acquiring a business never considered before, and so on.

Some more specific actions need to be considered for this postlaunch, change implementation phase as the change leader begins to deal with (1) his or her feelings of both excitement and anxiety, (2) follower behaviors of all varieties, and (3) seeming disorder. Though not exhaustive, the following five points are some key actions change leaders need to bear in mind.

Multiple Leverage

In large organizations particularly, change is too complicated for one action (intervention) to do the job. Many managers believe, for example, that changing the organizational structure will suffice. In a study of organization change some years ago, failure was most often associated with change of structure when that was essentially all that occurred (Burke, Clark, & Koopman, 1984). Moreover, in recent coverage of seven case studies of successful organization change, two of the summary points that are relevant here were as follows (Burke, 2000a):

1. Time and again, these cases illustrate the absolute necessity of strong leadership for change to occur. We see change leaders in living color here. There is no substitute for visionary leadership in times of change. By definition, if there is leadership, there are followers.

2. In addition to determining how the phases of organization change work, all these cases show the deployment of multiple interventions. True organization change is too complicated for one intervention. Multiple sources of influence are required.

Examples of levers for change from these case studies included process reengineering, crafting mission statements, developing a new process of supply chain management, training and development, crafting corporate values and leadership behaviors that were manifestations of the values, new pay-for-performance systems, developing a "safety" culture, changing a plant in a chemical company, team building, and establishing self-directed work groups.

Taking the Heat

When organization change is launched, it is safe to say that not everyone will be happy with the idea. In fact, some may be quite upset and angry, looking for a target, a person or a group to blame "for this mess we're about to get ourselves into." The change leader is the most obvious target. Recently, a college president who had launched an organizational change five years earlier sat through two meetings with full professors, listening to—and absorbing—their wrath about how poorly the change had been led and why it was such a stupid idea in the first place.

Dick Evans, of BAe, described one of his heat-receiving episodes this way (Burke & Trahant, 2000):

> But I got a lot of pushback from people. People asked, "Why do we need to do this? We're operating perfectly well. We all have big change programs to deal with in our own businesses. Why do we need to do all this other stuff?" Many seriously thought and believed that I had some sort of hidden agenda and [they] simply wanted to be told what to do so they could go away and do it [p. 146].

Pushback, as Evans described it, is to be expected—not from everyone, perhaps only a minority, but heat is generated nevertheless, especially if those who are pushing back are opinion leaders in the organization. These are the times when the change leader must use as much self-control as she or he can muster, working hard (1) to listen, (2) not to be defensive, and (3) to display the patience of Job.

Consistency

During the early days of change, the change leader's behavior is scrutinized by followers. Does the change leader really mean it? Is this for real? Or is this initiative like all the rest, just another fad that will soon pass? In a recent change at a large nonprofit organization, the most frequently asked question by followers in the hallways or at lunch has been "Does he (the change leader) really mean it?" This is, of course, a question about consistency in an organization change effort—despite Ralph Waldo Emerson's derogatory comment about consistency, to wit, "A foolish consistency is the hobgoblin of little minds adored by little statesmen and philosophers and divines." The key to this quote, however, is Emerson's adjective *foolish,* and consistency of word and deed by the change leader in the organization's change process is anything but foolish.

Perseverance

"Staying the course" is essentially what is meant by this term. Many potential change leaders falter when the going gets tough. A whimsical but illustrative comparison is that organization change is like losing weight. The first five or ten pounds are easy, but the next five or ten are much, much tougher. The early days of organization change, compared with later, are easy. People are excited and say things like "Finally, things are going to get better around here." But a year later, the change effort may have bogged down, the excitement is gone, and fatigue has set in. This is time for considerable perseverance on the part of the change leader. Perhaps the master of perseverance was Colin Marshall, at British Airways. Here's a perfect example, in his own words (Burke & Trahant, 2000):

> I made a particular point of attending every one of these "Managing People First" sessions. I spent two to three hours with each group. I talked with people about our goals, or thoughts for the future. I got people's input about what we needed to do to improve our services and operations. The whole thing proved to be a very useful and productive dialogue. We found it so valuable, in fact, that in cases when I was away, we offered people the opportunity to come back and have a follow-up session with me. So I really did talk to all 110 groups in that five-year period [p. 99].

A part of leadership in an organization change effort, then, is to stay the course, to continue to encourage people, to exude energy and enthusiasm for continuing down the change path, and to find ways to continue communicating the message.

Repeating the Message

First, what is it that you repeat? The message is the vision and the mission, but to be most effective a story needs to be told that incorporates the vision and mission and values. The work of Howard Gardner (1995) is decidedly helpful in this regard. He deliberately uses the term *story* or *narrative* instead of *message* or *theme* because, as he states, he wants to accomplish the following:

> To call attention to the fact that leaders present a dynamic perspective to their followers: not just a headline or snapshot, but a drama that unfolds over time, in which they—leaders and followers—are the principal characters or heroes.

Together they embarked on a journey in pursuit of certain goals, and along the way and into the future, they can expect to encounter certain obstacles or resistances that must be overcome. . . . The most basic story has to do with issues of identity. And so it is the leader who succeeds in conveying a new version of a given group's story who is likely to be effective. Effectiveness here involves fit—the story needs to make sense to audience members at this particular historical moment, in terms of where they have been and where they would like to go [p. 14].

The change leader tells the story time and again, because people need to be reminded of what it is that they are doing—and why. In addition to this reminding, it is critical that the change leader tell the story to followers in person, face-to-face, not over the Web, in a video, on a written document, or on CD-ROM. Why? Dialogue with followers is essential. Questions need to be answered, or at least responded to, and nuances may need elaboration. In the SmithKline Beecham merger, Henry Wendt, the chairman, and Bob Bauman, the CEO, traveled all over the world meeting with employees face-to-face to tell their story, which was the SmithKline Beecham "Promise": the company's promise to customers, employees, and stockholders.

Another example of a change leader telling the story personally, face-to-face, to five thousand people is the case of Roger Goldman, who turned around a retail banking situation that was not only in the red but overall moribund in its performance. In his words (Burke & Trahant, 2000):

I went on the road for a year to explain my vision of the bank to over 5,000 people in 800 profit centers and support offices. I did this to get people's support and to explain what we needed them to do if we were to be successful. In our case, it was about serving customers, communities, and our fellow employees. "Everyone has to give 110 percent," I told employees. "We're going to reinvent people's jobs and hold everybody more accountable for results" [p. 193].

By way of summary, consider the wonderful children's television show "Blue's Clues." The same episode is repeated four times after the initial presentation on Monday of each week. The creators of this program have discovered that for the four- or five-year-old, repetition is critical for the child's learning. By Friday, the child "gets it." To learn something, adults in organizations may not need four iterations. Actually, they may need more! The point is this: organization change with all its complexities and nuances needs to have focus, proper emphases on priorities, and explanation, particularly of "why we are doing these highly disruptive activities." Repeating this story time and again (message, vision, mission) is one of the most important functions of the change leaders.

Finally, we shall conclude this section on further implementation, the post-launch phase, with a cautionary note from Dick Evans, CEO of BAe (Evans & Price, 1999):

One danger that besets change programs is the curse of superficiality, or too much faith in the power of positive thinking. One day top management says, "Let's have a change program." And after cranking out mission and vision statements, backed with a heavy communications program, hey presto, they've done it. What are omitted from these narratives are the tensions, ambiguities, conflicts, and frustrations that inevitably arise in the implementation phase. These difficulties get swept under the rug, only to return later—most likely in a more virulent form [p. 16].

To mitigate the danger that Evans emphasizes, change leaders need to use multiple levers for the transformation, take the heat from followers from time to time, provide consistency in terms of words and deeds, persevere even to the point of risking being called stubborn, and repeat the message again and again.

SUSTAINING THE CHANGE

Before considering thoughts about sustaining organization change once things are fully launched and under way (such as unanticipated consequences, momentum, and further new initiatives), let us examine some recent thinking that is highly relevant and applicable. Earlier, in the section "Postlaunch: Further Implementation," a short quote was cited from Chapter Four by Pascale, Milleman, and Gioja (2000). The overall premise of the book is that recent knowledge, particularly in the life sciences, can inform our understanding of organizations in general, and management, leadership, and organization change in particular. Their premise is quite similar to the reasoning underlying the present volume. Pascale et al. made the point that so-called chaos theory is not applicable to organizations, for they are not chaotic. But organizations are complex—that is, complex adaptive systems—and what they label as "the new science of complexity" is the applicable theory. These ideas are congruent with nonlinear complex system theory discussed in Svyantek and Brown's (2000) chapter in Part Seven and and Gersick's (1991) concept of deep structure in Part Two. Pascale and his colleagues have distilled from complexity theory and the life sciences (biology, medicine, and ecology) "four bedrock principles" (2000) that they consider to be applicable to organizations, especially business enterprises. These principles are as follows:

1. *Equilibrium* is a precursor to death. When a living system is in a state of equilibrium, it is less responsive to changes occurring around it. This places it at maximum risk.

2. In the face of threat, or when galvanized by a compelling opportunity, living things move toward the *edge of chaos*. This condition evokes higher

levels of mutation and experimentation, and fresh new solutions are more likely to be found.

3. When this excitation takes place, the components of living systems *self-organize*, and new forms and repertoires emerge from the turmoil (referred to earlier).

4. Living systems cannot be *directed* along a linear path. Unforeseen consequences are inevitable. The challenge is to *disturb* them in a manner that approximates the desired outcome.

These principles are useful for our thinking about the importance of sustaining an organization change effort. This thinking is organized according to four considerations: unanticipated consequences, momentum, choosing successors, and launching yet again new initiatives.

Unanticipated Consequences

Referred to earlier in this chapter was the paradox of planning organization change in a linear, phased way of thinking, yet realizing that the change process itself is not linear. This means that when the change is launched, equilibrium is disturbed, and seeming chaos occurs; that is, many and different reactions to the disturbance happen simultaneously, and the system moves to the edge of chaos, as Pascale et al. (2000) put it. Some examples of this kind of reaction include the following: (1) different organizational units interpret the change vision and direction to fit their needs, and therefore, the implementing of their part of the change becomes different from that of all other units (this is not necessarily bad but is often unanticipated); (2) some people who were expected to resist actually embrace and become champions of the change— and vice versa; and (3) desired and expected outcomes for a part of the overall change effort simply do not occur. The scary part is going to the edge, but the main point to remember here is that living systems are quite capable of evoking new forms and solutions and of self-organizing with gradual movement (however, not linear) to a new state of equilibrium. Reaching a new state of equilibrium is essentially what Lewin (1947) meant with his third stage of organization change, refreeze (see Chapter Five). Also recall Weick and Quinn's (1999) reconceptualizing of Lewin's three-stage model in Chapter Fourteen calling for unfreezing after a rebalancing to ensure innovation and find new ways of ensuring continuous change, which is applicable to our thinking here. The point is that after a disturbance, living systems again seek equilibrium, and Pascale et al. warned that equilibrium "is a precursor to death." The important word in their phrase is *precursor*, which means that death is not necessarily immediate. There is some allowable, if not necessary, time for things to resettle after the disturbance. But for the organization change to maintain momentum, resettlement must not be allowed to last.

Momentum

Writing in 1991 about the successful change effort at British Airways, Goodstein and Burke stated:

> It may be that BA's biggest problem now is not so much to manage further change as it is to manage the change that has already occurred. In other words, the people of BA have achieved significant change and success; now they must maintain what has been achieved while concentrating on continuing to be adaptable to changes in their external environment—the further deregulation of Europe, for example. Managing momentum may be more difficult than managing change [p. 16].

A few year later, BA's performance began to deteriorate, in part from the lack of maintaining sufficient momentum and in part because of Colin Marshall's successor—choosing successors being the subject of the following section.

Maintaining the change momentum is critical because the natural movement toward equilibrium has to be countered. Finding new ways to recognize and reward change champions in the organization and celebrating achievements clearly helps to maintain momentum. The broader principles, however, are as follows: to counter equilibrium, Pascale et al. (2000) state rather provocatively that two forces—the threat of death and the promise of sex—can prevail. The desire to survive is powerful. If you question this, think how difficult it is to end a committee in your organization that was supposed to be ad hoc. Darwinian principles suggest that living systems do not evolve on their own but change as they respond to forces in the external environment. Living systems that survive do so because they mutate; that is, they adapt to the changing forces in their respective environments.

To maintain momentum, then, the change leader must constantly monitor the organization's external environment, being alert to changing forces that require adaptation to ensure survival.

The "promise of sex" leads us to the third ingredient for sustaining the change effort.

Choosing Successors

Another form for countering equilibrium is to prevent homogeneity, according to Pascale et al. (2000):

> Sexual reproduction maximized diversity. Chromosome combinations are randomly matched in variant pairings, thereby generating more permutations and variety in offspring. [This] benefits a living system [because] harmful [bacteria] find it harder to breach the diverse defenses of a population generated by sexual reproduction than the relatively uniform defenses affected [by a process such as mitosis or cloning] [p. 29].

This principle from the science of living systems suggests that change leaders would do well to counter equilibrium and sustain the change effort by infusing "new blood" into their organizations, that is, not cloning themselves. The point is that although a complete overhaul of the people involved in the change would be absurd, having some proportion (20 percent? 30 percent?) who are new to the effort (hired from the outside or shifted over from other parts of the organization) counteracts the support equilibrium such as tired thinking, solidified norms, and "group-think."

One of the reasons that Colin Marshall's successor at British Airways, Robert Ayling, did not succeed as CEO was that he had been with the organization for a long time and was peripheral to the change effort that had proceeded under Marshall's leadership. In other words, Ayling was not one of the change leaders and had remained tied to the old system. Examples of effective succession include the one at BAe from Evans to Weston and the more recent change at GE from Welch to Immelt.

Much has been written about problems of succession and infusing new thinking into an organization. For an overview of some of the central issues, see Levinson (1994).

Launching Yet Again New Initiatives

Finally, it is critical to identify and implement new initiatives that will renew organizational members' energy, spark new ways of thinking, and continue to propel the organization farther down its path of change after some unspecified time into the change effort. These new initiatives, of course, need to be in line with the original change objectives, provided the external environment is not signaling to the organization that something more drastic needs to happen to ensure survival.

Examples of new initiatives in the service of sustaining the overall change effort might be the following:

Acquisition of another organization or business

Creating a new business line or new product, or both

Establishing a strategic alliance or joint venture with another organization (which might even be a competitor or former competitor)

Starting a new program that will help to improve quality and reduce costs

Deploying current products and services into markets not yet penetrated; for example, a chemical, metal, or ceramic product that has been sold and marketed only to other businesses can now be considered as a product sold directly to an individual customer

The important point is for the change leader to be clear and deliberate about disturbing the system with new initiatives so that equilibrium does not take over. Incidentally, it is imperative for the change leader to cause these disturbances even if the organizational members plead for the change to come to some end point or conclusion. Conclusion needs to occur only for specific initiatives, not for the overall change effort.

SUMMARY

To specify what leaders actually do and what they need to do as change leaders, contrasts and comparisons were made between leadership and management and power and authority. Leadership was considered in terms of transformational (more related to organization change that is discontinuous) and transactional (more associated with continuous change).

An additional refinement of what is considered as leadership addresses the distinction of organizational levels, the point being that the executive is our primary focus. For this emphasis, the work of Zaccaro (2001) was particularly helpful. In his survey of the literature, he delineated four different yet overlapping conceptual perspectives about executive leadership: (1) conceptual complexity, having to deal with ever more complex and changing environments; (2) behavioral complexity, the leader's multiple roles in dealing with multiple constituencies; (3) strategic decision making, stressing the importance of congruence between the organization and its environment; and (4) visionary-inspirational, emphasizing the charismatic, transformational, and visionary aspects of leadership. The point was made that what is required to be an effective change leader is highly complex and demanding; therefore, all four of these perspectives are relevant.

Following is a summary of the way in which the leader's role and function in organization change was specified in this chapter according to four primary phases:

1. The prelaunch phase
   - Leader self-examination
   - Gathering information from the external environment
   - Establishing a need for change
   - Providing clarity of vision and direction
2. The launch phase
   - Communication of the need for change
   - Initiating key activities
   - Dealing with resistance

3. Postlaunch phase or further implementation
   - Multiple leverage
   - Taking the heat
   - Consistency
   - Perseverance
   - Repeating the message
4. Sustaining the change
   - Dealing with unanticipated consequences
   - Momentum
   - Choosing successors
   - Launching yet again new initiatives

References

Atwater, L., & Yammarino, F. (1992). Does self-other agreement on leadership perceptions moderate the validity of leadership predictions? *Personnel Psychology, 45,* 141–164.

Bass, B. M. (1990). *Bass and Stodgill's handbook of leadership* (3rd ed.). New York: Free Press.

Bauman, R. P., Jackson, P., & Lawrence, J. T. (1997). *From promise to performance: A journey of transformation at SmithKline Beecham.* Boston: Harvard Business School Press.

Bridges, W. (1986). Managing organizational transitions. *Organizational Dynamics, 15*(1), 24–33.

Burke, W. W. (2000a). SmithKline Beecham. In D. Giver, L. Carter, & M. Goldsmith (Eds.), *Best practices in organization and human resources development handbook* (pp. 103–118). Lexington, MA: Linkage.

Burke, W. W. (2000b). The broad band of organization development and change: An introduction. In D. Giver, L. Carter, & M. Goldsmith (Eds.), *Best practices in organization and human resources development handbook* (pp. 5–10). Lexington, MA: Linkage.

Burke, W. W., Clark, L. P., & Koopman, C. (1984). Improve your OD project's chances for success. *Training and Development Journal, 38*(8), 62–68.

Burke, W. W., & Jackson, P. (1991). Making the SmithKline Beecham merger work. *Human Resource Management, 30,* 69–87.

Burke, W. W., & Noumair, D. A. (2002). The role and function of personality assessment in organization development. In J. Waclawski & A. H. Church (Eds.), *Organization development: Data-driven methods for change* (pp. 55–77). San Francisco: Jossey-Bass.

Burke, W. W., & Trahant, B. (2000). *Business climate shifts: Profiles of change makers.* Boston: Butterworth Heinemann.

Capra, F. (1996). *The web of life.* New York: Anchor.

Church, A. H. (1997). Managerial self-awareness in high-performing individuals in organizations. *Journal of Applied Psychology, 82,* 281–292.

Emery, F. E., & Trist, E. L. (1965). The causal texture of organizational environments. *Human Relations, 18,* 21–32.

Evans, R., & Price, C. (1999). *Vertical take-off: The inside story of British Aerospace's comeback from crisis to world class.* London: Nicholas Brealey.

Gardner, H. (1995). *Leading minds: An anatomy of leadership.* New York: Basic Books.

Gersick, C.J.G. (1991). Revolutionary change theories: A multilevel exploration of the punctuated equilibrium paradigm. *Academy of Management Review, 16,* 10–36.

Heifetz, R. A. (1994). *Leadership without easy answers.* Cambridge, MA: Belknap Press of Harvard University Press.

McClelland, D. C. (1965). Achievement and entrepreneurship: A longitudinal study. *Journal of Personality and Social Psychology, 1,* 389–392.

McClelland, D. C. (1975). *Power: The inner experience.* New York: Irvington.

McClelland, D. C., & Burnham, D. H. (1976). Power is the great motivator. *Harvard Business Review, 54*(2), 100–110.

O'Toole, J. (1999). *Leadership A to Z: A guide for the appropriately ambitious.* San Francisco: Jossey-Bass.

Pascale, R. T., Milleman, M., & Gioja, L. (2000). *Surfing the edge of chaos: The laws of nature and the new laws of business.* New York: Crown Business.

Porter, M. (1985). *Competitive advantage: Creating and sustaining superior performance.* New York: Free Press.

Stodgill, R. M. (1974). *Handbook of leadership: A survey of theory and research.* New York: Free Press.

Svyantek, D. J., & Brown, L. L. (2000). A complex-systems approach to organizations. *Current Directions in Psychological Science, 9,* 69–74.

Van Eron, A. M., & Burke, W. W. (1992). The transformational/transactional leadership model: A study of critical components. In K. E. Clark, M. B. Clark, & D. P. Campbell (Eds.), *Impact of leadership* (pp. 149–167). Greensboro, NC: Center for Creative Leadership.

Wendt, H. (1993). *Global embrace: Corporate challenges in a transnational world.* New York: Harper Business.

Zaccaro, S. J. (2001). *The nature of executive leadership: A conceptual and empirical analysis of success.* Washington, DC: American Psychological Association.

Zaleznik, A. (1977). Managers and leaders: Are they different? *Harvard Business Review, 55*(3), 67–78.

CHAPTER FORTY-FIVE

The Psychology of Self-Management in Organizations

J. Richard Hackman (1986)

A couple of years ago a senior manager at Cummins Engine Corporation visited my class on organizational design to talk with students about the company's innovative plant in Jamestown, New York. One of the students asked, quite reasonably, for the visitor's views about the circumstances under which a self-managing organizational design, such as the one at Jamestown, would be preferred over a traditional organizational structure. "I'm not going to answer," he responded, "because that's last year's question. The question for today's managers is not *whether* to design organizations for high involvement and self-management, but *how* to do it, and how to do it well."

In 1984, the Harvard Business School celebrated its seventy-fifth anniversary by hosting a series of symposia on management. At the symposium on productivity and technology, Richard E. Walton, a senior professor at Harvard, took the occasion of the celebration to suggest that we may be in the midst of some revolutionary changes in how people are managed in work organizations. He pointed out that the major premise underlying work force management traditionally has been that efficiency can be achieved best by imposing management control over workers' behavior. Today, in response to massive evidence that control-oriented management models can produce outcomes that subvert the interests of both organizations and the people who work in them, a new work force management model is appearing. The premise of the emerging model is that organizations must elicit the commitment of their employees if they are to achieve a sustainable competitive advantage in contemporary markets. The change from a control to a commitment organizational model, Walton argued, portends a fundamental change in how organizations are designed and managed. Rather than relying on top-down management controls to elicit and enforce desired behavior, organizations in the future will rely heavily on member self-management in pursuing collective objectives.

What we have here is a senior corporate manager and a distinguished organizational scholar agreeing that something significant is afoot in the design and management of work organizations. And although the changes they foresee may not turn out to be as powerful or widespread as they suggest, it behooves organizational psychologists to understand as much as they can about the manifestations, precursors, and implications of organizational self-management. That is what this chapter is about.

I begin by exploring the key features of self-managing performing units, with special attention to how authority is distributed between those who execute work and those whose responsibilities are mainly managerial. I then identify the key behaviors that distinguish self-managing from traditional organizations, and review evidence on the relative effectiveness of self-managing organizational units. Next I turn to the major conceptual question of this chapter: What conditions foster and support a kind of self-management that will contribute both to personal well-being and to the achievement of collective objectives? Existing research and theory suggest five such conditions, each of which is described and discussed. I conclude with an exploration of the implications of the material for organizational leadership and for research and theory on the psychology of work behavior.

VARIETIES OF ORGANIZATIONAL SELF-MANAGEMENT

The Allocation of Organizational Authority

Four different functions must be fulfilled when work is done in an organization. First, of course, someone must actually *execute* the work—applying personal energy (physical or mental) to accomplish tasks. Second, someone must *monitor* and *manage* the work process—collecting and interpreting data about how the work is proceeding and initiating corrective action as needed. Third, someone must *design* the performing unit and arrange for needed organizational supports for the work—structuring tasks, deciding who will perform them, establishing core norms of conduct in the work setting, and making sure people have the resources and supports they need to carry out the work. And finally, someone must *set direction* for the organizational unit—determining the collective objectives and aspirations that spawn the myriad smaller tasks that pervade any organization.[1]

Self-managing organizations (or organizational units) can be defined in terms of how authority for these four functions is distributed. To do this, three terms must be clarified. The term *manager* refers to individuals whose responsibilities have primarily to do with directing and structuring the work of others; the term *member* refers to individuals whose primary responsibilities are to perform that work.[2] And the term *performing unit* refers to the people who have been assigned responsibility for accomplishing some specified task or set of tasks. Generally, I will speak of performing units as if they consisted of several individuals working interdependently on a common task—an organizational form that is common in organizations that aspire to self-management (Walton & Hackman, 1986). It should be kept in mind, however, that a performing unit can be as small as a single individual, or it can consist of a large number of people who share responsibility for a major piece of organizational work.

Four types of performing units are identified in Figure 45.1. In a *manager-led* unit, members have authority only for actually executing the task; managers

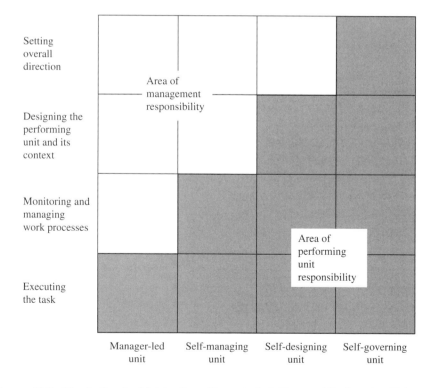

Figure 45.1. The Authority Matrix: Four Characteristic Types of Performing Units.

monitor and manage performance processes, structure the unit and its context, and set overall directions. This type of unit has been common in U.S. industry since the "scientific management" ideas of Taylor (1911) took hold early in the century. Managers manage, workers work, and the two functions should never be confused.

In a *self-managing* unit, members have responsibility not only for executing the task but also for monitoring and managing their own performance. This type of unit is often seen in new plants designed in accord with what Walton calls the commitment model (see, for example, Lawler, 1978) and is commonplace in managerial and professional work (e.g., a team of research assistants who share responsibility for collecting a set of interviews and observations).

Members of *self-designing* units have the authority to modify the design of the unit itself or aspects of the organizational context in which the unit functions. Managers set the direction for such units but assign to members full authority to do what needs to be done to get the work accomplished. Examples of self-designing units include some top management task forces (e.g., a team created to develop a new program and given free reign in determining how the design work will be structured, supported, and carried out) or an individual who is given autonomous responsibility for some task (e.g., "find 10,000 square feet of additional office space within two miles of headquarters, and get it ready for occupancy by June") with the right to corral helpers and call on organizational resources as needed to accomplish that task.

Finally, members of *self-governing* units have responsibility for all four of the major functions listed in Figure 45.1: they decide what is to be done, structure the unit and its context, manage their own performance, and actually carry out the work. Examples of self-governing units include certain legislative bodies, corporate boards of directors, advisory councils of community service agencies, worker cooperatives, and sole proprietorships.

The figure is presented as if the columns represent distinct types of performing units, but that is merely a convenience. In fact, the horizontal axis of the figure is a continuum reflecting increasing amounts of authority held by unit members relative to managers. In practice, units often fall on the column boundaries or have responsibility for only parts of certain functions. This chapter is concerned mainly with units in the "self-managing" column; however, I will speculate occasionally about the implications of the material for self-designing and self-governing units.

Behavioral Signs of Self-Management

How would one know if members of a performing unit were behaving as self-managers? What behaviors would one expect to see there that might be absent, or less frequent, in a manager-led unit? I list five behavioral signs, which are arranged from the most basic self-managing behaviors to those that one would find only in relatively mature self-managing units. I also provide some examples of positive and negative instances of each behavior, taken from a relatively new airline whose top management has a thoroughgoing commitment to self-management. These examples were generated by airline managers in seminars on the topic. The diversity of behavior seen in the company illustrates the varieties and vagaries of the concept and suggests that it can be difficult to elicit and sustain self-management, even when starting an organization from scratch.

1. People take *personal responsibility* for the outcomes of their work and show in their behavior that they feel personally accountable for the results of what they do.

One instance of individuals accepting personal responsibility for outcomes occurred during peak travel season, when a developing weather system raised the possibility that a jumbo jet on an overnight transcontinental trip might be seriously delayed or diverted to an alternate airport. If that occurred, hundreds of customers would be inconvenienced. Two individuals decided to remain in the airline's offices overnight (even though they had already completed a regular work day) to track the aircraft as it flew through the night and to call others to work if problems developed that would require special arrangements to get customers to their destinations. It turned out that the flight arrived nearly on time, and the passengers never knew that two people had spent the night standing by in case their assistance was needed.

A negative instance involved a flight that did experience weather and air traffic control delays. The cockpit and cabin crews on this aircraft had completed six hours of flying (which is what the schedule originally had called for), but there was still one round trip to be made. Although all crew members were still permitted by Federal Aviation Administration regulations to continue flying, they departed the aircraft, leaving others to figure out how to find a crew to fly the last trip.

If personal responsibility for outcomes has been accepted by an organization member, one often observes expressions of pride and overt celebration when the work turns out well—and overt dismay and self-criticism when it goes poorly. Self-management probably cannot be sustained unless reasonably intense feelings of personal responsibility for outcomes are present; without them, the temptation to "self-manage myself home" on a bad day may be nearly impossible to resist.

2. People *monitor* their own performance continuously, actively seeking data and feedback to learn how well they are accomplishing their tasks.

Cockpit crews enjoy a feedback-rich environment. Aircraft instrumentation, air traffic control, and company operations together keep crew members very well informed about how they are doing with the technical aspects of their flying task. Less feedback is available to pilots about their contributions to other organizational objectives, and one crew I observed decided to do something about that. After the aircraft had reached cruising altitude, all systems had been checked, and the crew was in a relatively relaxed attitude with the autopilot engaged, the co-pilot turned to the captain and said, "OK, let's figure our how we're doing on this one." The crew members then calculated an estimate of the total cost of the flight, multiplied the number of customers on board by the fare for the trip, subtracted the first number from the second, and found that they were losing about $4,500 on the trip. At that point, the captain got on the public address system and told the customers that, although the company really liked flying people to the destination city, there were not quite enough of them on this flight to break even. He asked the customers to tell him or the cabin crew about anything that was unsatisfactory in the service they were providing, so they could improve their performance and attract more people from that city to the airline. This crew was obviously paying attention to available data about performance; beyond that, members took an initiative to obtain additional information that could be used to improve it.

A negative instance involves a situation where performance-relevant data were already collected, summarized, and available—but people systematically ignored them. One group in the airline is charged with selecting the correct number of reservations to accept for each flight, using a set of standard formulas to establish the number of people who will "no show" for flights. Early in the airline's history, flights originating in one city on a certain day of the week were sometimes being oversold, resulting in people with confirmed reservations being denied boarding. Although company reports documented this problem, the planning group did not examine those data. Only after staff in that city (who had to deal with the angry customers who were left on the ground) complained to a member of senior management did the problem come to the attention of planning group members.

3. People *manage* their own performance, taking corrective action at their own initiative to improve their performance.

When a flight is delayed, customers typically crowd around the check-in counter listening for news, seeking help or advice, or complaining about what is happening. Under these conditions, it is difficult for staff members to deal with whatever is causing the problem. One organization member decided that the crowding problem had to be solved in order to serve the customers well and convened an informal group of colleagues to consider ways of dealing with it. The group decided that the best solution was to get inconvenienced customers away from the counter and give them special attention. Members found some unused space nearby, got some chairs and a telephone put in the space, and revised the counter operating plan so that one or more team members could give full attention to customers' questions and complaints in the holding area during irregular operations—thereby allowing the rest of the counter team to work on the cause of the difficulty. No senior managers were involved in either the diagnosis of the problem or in the action planning.

A negative instance also involves on-ground service, this time at a city distant from the airline's hub of operations. Flights often departed from this city without all customers' bags on board. That happens occasionally in the airline business, but it was happening at this city more frequently than at others in the system. It was clear that responsibility for the problem lay with the staff in the city, and they were aware that they were not doing well with bags (customers are quick to complain when their bags do not arrive at their destination, and those complaints find their way back to the city staff). Yet no action to correct the problem was taken by staff members, and when queried about the problem, one response was "I don't know what the trouble is. We're following standard bag handling procedures." That individual showed no inclination to investigate and attempt to find a solution to the problem.

4. When people do not have what they need to perform well, they actively *seek from the organization* the guidance, help, or resources they need for excellent performance—and they do so assertively and constructively.

Sometimes people feel responsible for work outcomes, have data showing that performance is substandard, and are eager to take corrective action; but they find that they do not have the authority to fix whatever is at the root of the performance problem. How do self-managers behave in such circumstances?

In one instance, a manager who was responsible for certain operational matters found, as the airline grew, that he was unable to handle personally the significant increase in his day-to-day workload. He concluded (after trying various alternative strategies for managing the work) that he needed some additional people to help coordinate his part of the operation, but he did not have the authority to make staff assignments. Moreover, the president of the company was deeply and publicly committed to a flat, lean organization with as few people as possible assigned to staff support activities.

The manager first sought the advice of his colleagues and an outside consultant. Some new ideas developed in these discussions, which he tried but which did not solve the problem. He then developed a plan for creating a small staff support group, tested it against the overall values and aspirations of the company, and finally proposed it to the president. The president had serious concerns about the idea and refused to approve it. The manager then sought further counsel from his colleagues, redesigned the plan to take account of the president's objections, and brought it once again to the president. Eventually he succeeded in obtaining the staff support he needed to accomplish the work for which he was responsible.

By contrast, a group in the financial area of the airline found, as the company grew, that its office was increasingly inadequate for the volume of work that flowed in. Paper was everywhere, there were no file cabinets in which to organize and store it, and people were sitting in every available space (including the floor) trying to process the work. Perhaps because of the president's stated opposition to large support groups and plush offices, or perhaps because of the "can do" attitude that permeated the airline, no one took an initiative to secure the physical space and equipment that was needed to get the work done accurately and on time. Only when complaints from senior managers about the performance of the unit became numerous and painful did the group raise the issue of its inadequate work environment.

Whereas the financial group tolerated less-than-acceptable performance rather than initiating action to secure needed resources, others in the organization have responded by letting their feelings of frustration build to an explosive level. One person who had struggled for months with inadequate equipment finally charged into the president's office unannounced, laying out all his frustrations and complaints angrily and in vivid detail. The president initially was speechless (he was hearing about the problems for the first time), but when he recovered he responded in kind—resulting in an interaction that was constructive neither for the two parties nor for the organization as a whole. Because of the ambivalence many people have about dealing with organizational authorities, it is often difficult for organization members, even those in units that are committed to self-management, to seek absent and needed resources from senior managers in a way that is both assertive and constructive.

5. People take initiatives to *help people in other areas* improve their performance, thereby strengthening the policies and performance of the organization as a whole. And they make sure that their own responsibilities are being met before reaching out to help others.

Each employee of the airline I have been discussing is expected to work in more than one functional area; people who fly also work in accounting or marketing, and so on. When a pilot came into the reservations office to help out, he discovered that it took much of the time he had available merely to get through the reservations manual (the document that explains reservations policies and procedures). Because he assumed that the same would be true for other pilots taking a turn in the reservations office, he undertook (on his own time) to write a brief summary of the manual, covering only the essentials of reservation practice and using language he referred to as "pilot talk." This minimanual increased the amount of productive time relative to preparation time for others who assisted with reservations.

The ideal of helping out in other areas also can be a trap. One individual whose primary staff work was in training determined that he could lend a valuable hand in corporate recruiting. So he volunteered to go on a number of road trips to solicit employment applications and screen candidates. The problem was not that recruiting did not need or appreciate his help; in fact, he provided valuable assistance to that area. The problem was that his own major area, training, was not in good shape when he left it temporarily to help out the recruiters. Whether knowingly or not, this individual used a relatively high-order self-management value (helping other areas) to escape the imperatives of more basic values (taking responsibility for the outcomes of one's own work, and monitoring and managing one's performance to ensure that the work is accomplished well).

Self-Management and Unit Effectiveness

The previous section identifies and illustrates the behaviors that operationalize self-management. Do organizations perform better or worse when these behaviors are commonplace within them? Do people fare better or worse in self-managing organizational units? To address these questions, I must first define what is meant by "better" and "worse."

Unit Effectiveness Defined. There are, of course, many dimensions on which one could assess the effectiveness of a self-managing performing unit, and one's choice of dimensions is, implicitly but necessarily, a statement of what one values. My view is that the effectiveness of a performing unit depends on its standing on three dimensions (adapted from Hackman, 1986; Hackman & Walton, 1986).

1. The degree to which the unit's productive output (that is, its product or service) meets the standards of quantity, quality, and timeliness of the people who receive, review, or use that output. If, for example, a self-managing unit generated a product that was wholly unacceptable to its legitimate client, it would be hard to argue that the unit was effective—no matter how unit members evaluated their product, or how it scored on some objective performance index. Although it is uncommon for researchers to rely on system-defined (rather than objective) performance assessments, reliable objective performance measures are actually quire rare in work organizations—and even when they do exist, what happens to a unit usually depends far more on others' assessments of its output than on those measures.

2. The degree to which the process of carrying out the work enhances the capability of organization members to work together interdependently in the future. Consider, for example, a self-managing team that functions in a way that makes it impossible for members to work together again—perhaps because mutual antagonism becomes so high that members would choose to accept collective failure rather than share knowledge and information with one another. Alternatively, members of a team can become extraordinarily skilled at working together, even increasing the unit's performance capability (for example, a string quartet or athletic team whose members learn to anticipate one another's next moves and initiate appropriate responses to those moves

even as they occur). Even when a unit is temporary (such as a one-shot task force), one could examine changes in its performance capability over time in judging its overall effectiveness.

3. The degree to which work experiences contribute to the growth and personal well being of unit members. Some jobs, and some teams, block individuals' development and frustrate satisfaction of their personal needs; others provide many opportunities for learning and need satisfaction. Even when the official purpose of an organizational unit has nothing to do with personal development, the impact of the work experience on individual members would be included in an assessment of its effectiveness.

In summary, measuring the performance of a self-managing unit always involves much more than simply counting outputs. Not only must social and personal criteria be considered but even assessments of task outcomes are complex because they depend on system-specified (rather than research-specified) standards. Although these three dimensions could be used in judging effectiveness in any organization, they are particularly salient for organizations that aspire to self-management. If a unit is poor on the second and third dimensions, for example, both the ability and the willingness of unit members to engage in self-managing behaviors surely would diminish over time. On the other hand, a unit that stands high on all three criteria has at least a chance of entering a self-reinforcing cycle of improved task performance, unit capability, and member learning and satisfaction.

The relative weight given each of the three dimensions will vary across circumstances. If, for example, a temporary self-managing team were formed to perform a single task of extraordinary importance, then the second and third dimensions would be of little relevance in judging the team's effectiveness. On the other hand, tasks sometimes are created mainly to help members gain experience, learn some things, and become competent as a performing unit (see, for example, Eisenstat's 1984 analysis of a "core skills" production unit that was created during the start-up of an individual plant specifically to build employees' skill and experience as members of self-managing metalworking teams). The task of such units may be more an excuse for the unit than the reason for it, and assessments of effectiveness in such cases would depend far more on the second and third dimensions than on the first.

The Relative Effectiveness of Self-Managing Units. Does self-managing enhance or depress unit performance on the three criterion dimensions? For a sampling of research evaluating the efficacy of self-management in work organizations, see Gunn (1984); Poza and Marcus (1980); Wall, Kemp, Jackson, and Clegg (n.d.); Walton (1980); and collections of cases edited by Lindenfeld and Rothschild-Whitt (1982) and by Zwerdling (1980). There is also a growing body of evidence on self-management in nonwork settings. Kanfer

(1984), in assessing self-management as a clinical tool, has shown how social system variables affect the success of such applications. Even in medicine, where physicians traditionally have controlled all aspects of patient treatment, there is increasing interest in patient self-management. For example, Check (1982) reported that when patients directly control the amount of morphine they receive after an operation, pain relief is improved, and far less of the drug is used than when it is administered by medical staff. Despite the fact that numerous research reports describe and analyze self-management successes and failures, evidence bearing directly on the question is scant. In fact, the question is probably unanswerable. Comparative studies of existing self-managing and traditional organizations inevitably invite numerous alternative interpretations of whatever is found (because of inescapable confounds involving labor markets, technologies, senior managers, organizational histories, and so on). And there will never be trustworthy findings from true experiments comparing self-managing and manager-led units in real work organizations. For one thing, the level of experimenter control required in such studies (e.g., to randomly assign people to units and units to conditions) will not be tolerated by most managers who have work to get out. Moreover, if an organization were found in which managers would relinquish such control to experimenters, there would be serious questions about the external validity of any findings obtained there (Hackman, 1985).

My observations of self-managing units suggest that they frequently are found at both ends of the effectiveness continuum. That is, poorly designed self-management units are easily outperformed by smoothly functioning traditional units—in part because there are no organizational controllers around to provide early warning that problems are developing or to mandate corrective action. One the other hand, self-managing units that function well can achieve a level of synergy and agility that never could be preprogrammed by organization planners or enforced by external managers. Members of such units respond to their clients and to each other quickly and creatively, resulting in both superb task performance and ever-increasing personal and collective capability. Self-managing units, then, are somewhat akin to audio amplifiers: whatever passes through the device—be it signal or noise—comes out louder.

Thus, a question of potentially greater practical and conceptual interest presents itself: What factors account for the difference between those self-managing units that perform superbly and those whose performance is abysmal? As I explore this more tractable question, it quickly will become apparent that creating, maintaining, and working in self-managing units generally requires more expertise and commitment than are needed in traditional units. The skills required to get along in a traditional organization, whether as a manager or a rank-and-file member, are relatively well learned by most people in the U.S. work force. Moreover, commonly held expectations about how one should behave at work generally are more congruent with life in manager-led units than with what is required of self-managers.

As the founding members of many cooperative organizations have learned through painful experience, effective self-managing units cannot be created simply by exhorting democratic ideals, by tearing down organizational hierarchies, or by instituting one-person-one-vote decision-making processes. Instead, it appears that certain conditions must be in place for a self-managing unit to have a real chance of achieving a high standing on the three criterion dimensions discussed previously.

I examine those conditions next. In doing so, I will give more attention to the first criterion dimension (i.e., acceptable task outcomes) than to the latter two (improved unit capability, and individual growth and well-being). This is because one of the best ways to help a unit achieve a high standing on the social and personal criteria is to foster its task-performance effectiveness. Indeed, it may be next to impossible for a unit to succeed on the social and personal criteria while it is failing on its task.

CONDITIONS THAT FOSTER AND SUPPORT EFFECTIVE SELF-MANAGEMENT

Existing research, theory, and organizational practice identify five general conditions that appear to foster and support unit effectiveness through self-management: (1) clear, engaging direction; (2) an enabling performing unit structure; (3) a supportive organizational context; (4) available, expert coaching; and (5) adequate material resources. As will be seen, the conditions are not direct, proximal causes of performance outcomes, but rather they serve to increase the likelihood that self-managing units will perform effectively. One must be careful not to think of them in traditional cause-effect terms.

Each of the conditions consists of a number of successively more detailed conditions, which represent the means by which it is operationalized (in research) or enacted (in practice). Although I discuss some of these subconditions here (particularly to illustrate differences in how the conditions apply to individual self-managers versus self-managing teams, and larger organizational units), I focus on the general processes by which the conditions shape self-management and performance effectiveness.

Clear, Engaging Direction

Effective self-management is not possible unless someone exercises authority to set direction for the performing unit. This assertion may sound a bit strange, in that self-management and the exercise of authority often are seen as being competing and inconsistent control strategies. I hope to show that the opposite is true, that the appropriate use of authority is essential in creating conditions for self-management.

Except in self-governing performing units (see Figure 45.1), the overall directions for performance are established by representatives of the larger organization in which a performing unit operates. Those who own an enterprise for example, or who act on their behalf, have the right to determine organizational objectives—to say, in effect, "This is the mountain we will climb. Not that one, this one. And while many aspects of our collective endeavor are open for discussion, choice of mountain is not among them."

Will such an assertion de-power and alienate organization members? On the contrary, having a clear statement of direction tends to be empowering, for three related reasons. First it *orients* organization members toward common objectives, thereby facilitating coordinated action in pursuing them. Ambiguity about what the collectivity exists to achieve is lessened, which reduces the amount of time and energy people spend arguing about questions of purpose or wallowing around trying to figure out what is supposed to be accomplished. When direction is made clear, some people may discover that it is not to their liking—a stressful state of affairs, but one that ultimately is constructive. As some people decide not to join the unit and others decide to leave, the unit should be populated increasingly by individuals who are interested in aligning themselves with collective directions. A far more difficult situation exists when organizational directions are distasteful or alienating to the majority of members and potential members. There is no real possibility for effective self-management in such a situation, and organizational control of member behavior is likely to be a continuing problem that may never be satisfactorily resolved (Walton & Hackman, 1986).

Second, clear direction *energizes* people, even when the goals that are articulated may not rank highest on members' personal lists of aspirations. People seek purpose in their lives and are energized when an attractive purpose is articulated for them. Consider, for example, the impact of President John F. Kennedy's statement "We will go to the moon," or that of Reverend Martin Luther King's "I have a dream" speech. On a less grand scale, but for similar reasons, a clear statement of organizational direction can energize people by adding to the meaning and purpose they find in their work. Some purposes are, of course, more engaging than others. Research suggests that engagement is enhanced when aspirations have three attributes: (1) they are consequential, that is, what is to be accomplished has a visible and substantial impact on others, be they customers, co-workers, or other unit members (Hackman & Oldham, 1980; Manz, in press); (2) they stretch members' energy and talent, that is, achieving them is neither routine nor impossible (Atkinson, 1958; Lacke, Soari, Shaw, & Latham, 1981; Walton, 1985; Zander, 1980); and (3) they are simultaneously rich in imagery and incomplete in detail, thereby providing room for members to add their own meanings to the aspirations (Bennis & Nanus, 1985; Berlew, 1979; Cohen, 1985; House, 1977).

Finally, a clear statement of direction *provides a criterion* for unit members to use in testing and comparing alternative possibilities for their behavior at work. Because self-managers are not given detailed, step-by-step behavioral prescriptions, it is imperative that they have some clear set of values or aspirations to use in evaluating ways they might proceed. Without clear direction, there will be high variation in work behavior as people rely mainly on trial and error to identify appropriate work strategies. The result, in many cases, will be heightened frustration, loss of efficiency, and poor coordination among individuals and units.

Setting a clear and engaging direction for self-managers is a more difficult and risky business than one might expect. Because it necessarily involves the exercise of authority, ambivalence and anxiety typically are aroused for both those who give direction and those who receive it. A common strategy for managing ambivalence and anxiety is to wholly embrace one or the other side of the difficult issue. So, in traditional organizations, managers sometimes are observed making decisions and giving orders in ways that make it completely clear to everyone who is in charge, even when that turns out to close off the ideas and involvement of others.

In organizations that aspire to self-management, on the other hand, managers sometimes decline to take a position on anything, even if that turns out to blur the direction of the enterprise and withhold from its members the guidance they need to manage their own behavior. It is clear that the order-giving syndrome is inappropriate for the management of self-managers. Perhaps less obvious is the fact that a managerial style in which consensus is relentlessly pursued is just as inappropriate. To chart a course between the Scylla of authoritarian behavior and the Charybdis of abdication is a significant intellectual and emotional challenge for many managers of self-managers.

A second pitfall in setting direction has to do with the focus of managerial authority. Although it is fully appropriate for people in positions of legitimate authority to be insistent about ends, they must take care not to exercise their authority regarding the specific means by which those ends are to be sought. To do so will compromise members' feelings of personal control over their life at work, with predictable and negative motivational consequences (Langer, 1983; Seligman, 1975). So, to return to the mountain-climbing metaphor, an effective direction setter will be clear and unapologetic about the choice of mountain to be climbed and about the broad limits on the behavioral latitude of individual climbers on the team. On the other hand, he or she will suppress any inclination to dictate how each stream should be crossed on the way up the mountain, or to ask individuals to await instructions at each fork in the trail.

Making this distinction, and behaving in accord with it, also turns out to be a considerable challenge for many managers of self-managers.

The voluminous literature on leadership and management includes little research that specifically examines the direction-setting function of leaders. Although authoritative (not authoritarian) direction setting is a potent device for orienting and energizing self-managers toward the achievement of collective objectives, not much is known about how those activities actually take place in work organizations.

As important as clear, engaging direction is in creating conditions for effective self-management, it is far from the whole story. I turn now to ways that the structure of a self-managing unit can either undermine good direction or exploit its positive potential.

An Enabling Performing-Unit Structure

Individuals or teams that know where they are supposed to be going have three hurdles to surmount in order to get there. They must (1) exert sufficient *effort* to get the task accomplished at acceptable levels of performance, (2) bring adequate levels of *knowledge and skill* to bear on the task work, and (3) employ *task performance strategies* that are appropriate to the work and to the setting in which it is being performed (Hackman, 1986).

To illustrate the idea of a performance strategy, consider an individual self-manager who decides to free-associate about task solutions in his or her first encounter with the task, reflect for a week about the ideas that came up, and then do a rough draft of the product. Or he or she might decide to spend considerable time checking and rechecking for errors after learning that the client cares a great deal about product quality. If the performing unit were a team, it might decide to divide into two subgroups, each of which would do part of the overall task, with the final product to be assembled later. All of these choices involve task performance strategy.

I refer to the three hurdles as the "process criteria of effectiveness." They are not the ultimate test of how well a group has done (I addressed that earlier), but they turn out to be of great use both in assessing how a performing unit is doing as it proceeds with its work and in diagnosing the nature of the problem if things are not going well. One can readily ask, for example, whether observed difficulties are rooted in an effort problem, a talent problem, or a strategy problem. And, as I will show later, the answers that emerge can be useful in determining what might remedy the problem and thereby improve unit effectiveness.

Although valuable as indicators, the process criteria do not provide useful points of intervention for improving unit effectiveness. For one thing, direct managerial interventions aimed at increasing effort, improving the utilization of talent, or making performance strategies more task-appropriate may undermine the self-managing character of the performing unit. Moreover, existing evidence suggests that direct process interventions have little or no reliable impact on unit performance (Kaplan, 1979; Woodman & Sherwood, 1980). There are, however, certain structural features of performing units that can increase the chances that the unit will achieve a high standing on the process criteria. Three such features (task design, unit composition, and sent expectations about member behavior), have special relevance to the process criteria.

Task Design. Existing research and theory on self-management (e.g., Cummings, 1978; Hackman, 1986; Hackman & Oldham, 1980) suggests that the effort an individual self-manager (or members of a self-managing team) will apply to the work depends significantly on the design of the task that is being performed. Specifically, people try hard to perform well when the following three task-induced states are present:

1. Performers experience the task as *meaningful,* a state that is fostered when (a) the task requires use of a variety of relatively high-level skills; (b) the task is a whole piece of work with a beginning, end, and readily discerned outcomes; and/or (c) the task has outcomes that are consequential for other people (be they other organization members or external clients).

2. Performers experience *personal responsibility* for the outcomes of the work, a state that is fostered when the task provides substantial autonomy for performers to decide how the work will be carried out (in effect, allowing them to personally or collectively own the work, rather than merely execute work on behalf of someone else).

3. Performers experience *knowledge of the results* of their work, a state that is fostered when executing the task generates trustworthy and informative feedback about work progress and outcomes.

When a task has these properties, performers are more likely to engage in self-rewarding behaviors when they find that they have done well (and in self-punishing behaviors when they do poorly), a state of affairs that has been referred to as "internal work motivation" (Hackman & Oldham, 1980, Ch. 4). Internal motivation is a means for sustaining task-focused effort in the absence of external controls and direct supervision, and contributes to one's overall perceptions of self-efficacy (Bandura, 1977). It is, therefore, a key ingredient in a self-managing performing unit.

This emphasis on task design runs counter to traditional wisdom about motivated work behavior. One often hears managers report that some person is "lazy" or "hard-working" or that members of some team "have a norm of not working very hard" or of "always giving their best." It is true that people have different chronic energy levels, but there is not much one can do about that. And although norms do emerge in groups that encourage especially high or low effort, such norms usually develop as a reaction to how things are set up, as a means of coping with the group task and work situation. Thus, if the work is routine and unchallenging, of dubious importance, and wholly pre-programmed with no opportunity for feedback, it is likely that individuals will slack off and that groups will develop antiproductivity norms. Improving the design of the work is usually a better way to deal with such a state of affairs than attempting directly to modify individual motivation or group norms.

The task dimensions discussed are applicable both to work designed for individual self-managers and for self-managing teams. The different referent of those dimensions in the two cases is critical. In the first instance, one is dealing with the properties of a task intended to be performed by one person, whereas in the second the focus is on a (usually larger) piece of work that is assigned to an intact team—or, possibly, to an even larger unit such as a department or division. Care must be taken to make sure the dimensions that are used to char-acterize the work are applied at a level of analysis consistent with the unit that is performing the work.

In promoting effort by creating conditions for self-motivation, task design reinforces the benefits of clear, engaging direction; indeed, the two conditions serve partially redundant functions and have effects that in many instances cannot be clearly distinguished from one another. Although this may seem to be a problem (at least for those who seek unitary, independent causes of phe-nomena), it will become increasingly evident that social systems do not follow the rules of experimental design; many of the more interesting and important things that happen in social systems are the result of multiple, redundant, non-independent forces.

Unit Composition. The first of the process criteria (effort) depends signifi-cantly on how the work itself is designed; the second (knowledge and skill) depends primarily on the people who are assigned to that work. The basic assertion is obvious: the best way to increase the knowledge and skill brought to bear on a piece of work is to have one or more highly talented people per-form that work. Some complications arise, however, when that general propo-sition is applied to work done by individual self-managers and by self-managing teams.

First, knowledge and skill are more consequential in self-managing units than in traditional units. Self-managers have responsibility for decision making about the work, not just executing it, which means that what people know (and know how to do) has high leverage on unit outcomes. In addition, consequen-ces are higher for the performers themselves if organizational conditions foster-ing self-management are in place. Assume, for the moment, that a performer understands and is engaged by the direction for the enterprise and that the task he or she is performing is well designed. The person should have high internal work motivation, feeling pleased when the work goes well and unhappy when it does not. Now, if the performer does not have the talent required to perform the task well, he or she will be unhappy most of the time, more unhappy than if self-managing conditions were not present. Because feeling bad about oneself is not a state of affairs that most people choose to maintain, the eventual result is likely to be psychological or behavioral withdrawal from the work or the organization.

Second, some people are more responsive to opportunities for self-management at work than others. It has proven difficult to isolate specific individual characteristics that empirically distinguish those who respond eagerly to motivationally engaging tasks from those who balk at them (O'Connor, Rudolf, & Peters, 1980; White, 1978), and little is known about the dynamics by which individual differences in readiness for self-managing work emerge developmentally and change over time as a function of work experiences. Nonetheless, organizations that aspire to self-management generally do take the selection and placement of members extremely seriously, attending to their apparent interest in and psychological readiness for such work as well as to more traditional measures of task-relevant knowledge and skill. Although such organizations have been criticized (e.g., by Fein, 1974) on the grounds that their success may be due more to their favorable selection ratio than to any organizational innovations, evidence to date suggests that careful assessment of the readiness of people for work in self-managing units is a well-warranted organizational practice (Walton, 1980).

Additional complexities arise when individuals are being selected for membership on self-managing teams. When work is assigned to a team, one must attend not merely to the qualities and qualifications of individual members but also to the composition of the team *qua* team. Although there has been relatively little research in recent years on issues in team composition (for reviews of early work on the topic, see Haythorn, 1968; and Schutz, 1961), existing evidence suggests that the following factors are significant in considering the composition of a self-managing team:

- Team size (many teams in organizations are far larger than they need to be and, for effectiveness, should be)
- The balance between homogeneity and heterogeneity of members' skills (when people are either too similar to one another or too different from one another, performance problems often develop)
- Members' competence in working cooperatively with other people (some minimum level of social skill is required to accomplish tasks that require coordination among members and to manage the interplay between individual desires and group goals)

Sent Expectations About Behavior. A performing unit's standing on the third process criterion (appropriateness of task performance strategies) is perhaps most powerfully shaped by the expectations that senior managers communicate to unit members. Two expectations are critical. First, unit members must understand that they are responsible for regulating their own behavior. This is, of course, the core expectation for any self-managing unit. Unless members accept it, they will be unlikely to adjust their performance strategies as circumstances change—perhaps persisting too long with whatever strategy they began with or waiting too long for instructions from someone else about what behaviors are appropriate. The second critical expectation is that the unit members are obligated to continuously assess the performance situation (with particular attention to changes in the task or environment) and to actively plan how they will proceed with the work based on those assessments.

These expectations, even when accepted and acted upon by unit members, do not directly cause performance strategies to become more appropriate. As with the other conditions I have discussed, they merely increase the chances that unit members will discover and implement ways of proceeding with the work that fit well with the requirements and opportunities in the task and situation—a better fit, perhaps, than otherwise would be the case.

Expectations that encourage active scanning and planning usually must be communicated vigorously to the performing unit, because it is far from a sure thing that they will occur naturally. Many individuals and teams operate under the assumption that they are the mere executors of work that others are responsible for decision making about how and when their behaviors should be adjusted. This assumption may make sense given members' previous organizational experiences, but the result is that situation scanning and strategy planning rarely occur spontaneously (Hackman & Morris, 1975).

For individual self-managers, these sent expectations are part of his or her work role and therefore are viewed as a structural feature of the organizational system (Kahn, Wolfe, Quinn, Snoek, & Rosenthal, 1964). Researchers are increasingly interested in the processes by which individuals regulate behavior within their work roles (e.g., Luthans & Davis, 1979; Manz, Mossholder, & Luthans, in press; Manz & Sims, 1980). Although research on self-regulation has provided many ideas about *how* a person can control his or her behavior, it has less to say about the conditions under which people actually do engage in behavioral self-management—an issue informed by a record study by Brief and Hollenbeck (1985). These researchers assessed the extent of self-regulation by a group of insurance agents in order to determine its effect on job performance. They found a low incidence of the activities posited by social learning theorists as critical to self-regulation. This finding further supports the view that self-regulatory behaviors are likely to occur only when they are specifically encouraged. In organizations, one of the most powerful and efficient ways to accomplish this is to structure an explicit expectation of self-management into individuals' formal work roles.[3]

For self-managing teams, the issue is once again more complex. Here there must be collective self-regulation, not just the creation of a set of individual role expectations. Groups regulate collective and member behavior through norms about behavior, that is, shared expectations about what will and will not be done in the group that are enforced by behaviorally contingent approval and disapproval (Jackson, 1965). Key norms tend to form very early in the life of a group and are sustained until something fairly drastic occurs that forces team members to reconsider what are and are not appropriate behaviors. Thus, expectations sent to a group early in its life (for example, when members first meet) can create a relatively enduring group structure. In the present instance, of course, those expectations would have to do with the team's responsibility for self-regulation and for ongoing situational scanning and strategy planning.

As an example of how such norms can contribute to performance effectiveness, consider a team of cabin attendants from the airline I discussed earlier. This team had been sent and had accepted expectations that members were to manage themselves within broad constraints (primarily having to do with safety procedures) and that they were to tailor the way they provided cabin service as necessary to achieve a set of clear corporate objectives. I observed this crew on two very different flights. The first was a flight to Florida on a sunny day. The plane was only half full of people, most of whom appeared to be on holiday. As people were boarding the plane, the crew got a sense of its clientele, had a brief conversation, and decided to have some fun. The cooperation of the cockpit crew was secured, and all the way to Florida various games were played (such as guessing the city over which the plane was flying) and service was provided in a light-hearted way with lots of informal conversation between crew and customers.

The second flight was a much shorter trip to an industrial city on a stormy day. The plane departed late because of the weather, and every seat was taken. Instead of vacation garb, there were newspapers, attaché cases, and people who looked preoccupied and distinctly impatient. On this flight, the crew was fast, efficient, and altogether businesslike. The crew, in each case, took a look at the performance situation and adapted its strategy for carrying out its work to be as appropriate as possible to that situation, given overall corporate objectives. It provides a sharp contrast with cabin attendants in some other airlines, where crews are required to behave strictly in accord with standard, management-specified service routines.

Summary. A summary of three structural features that foster achievement of the process criteria of effectiveness is provided in Figure 45.2. When these

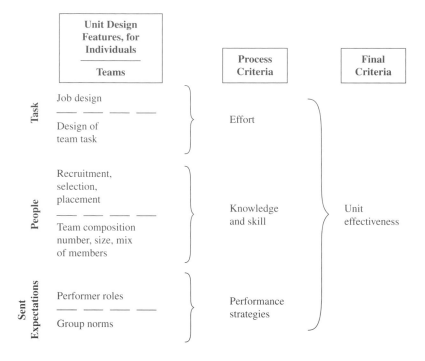

Figure 45.2. Design Features That Foster Achievement of the Process Criteria.

features are present—a motivating task, a well-composed unit, and sent expectations that support proactive self-regulation—then the chances increase that self-managers will exert sufficient effort on the task, bring sufficient knowledge and skill to bear on it, and choose or develop a performance strategy that is appropriate to the task and the situation.

Achieving a high standing on the process criteria, in turn, increases the chances that a unit ultimately will be effective—that is, clients will judge its work satisfactory, the performance capability of the unit will improve over time, and individual members will learn from their work experiences and find them personally satisfying.

When the two ingredients I have discussed so far are present (the performing unit has clear, engaging direction and an enabling structure), a solid basis for effective self-management is established. This is not, however, the whole story, because performing units do not operate in an organizational vacuum. There are two kinds of support that can help a unit exploit the potential provided by good direction and structure: those provided by formal organizational systems and those provided through hands-on coaching and consultation. I will discuss them in turn.

A Supportive Organizational Context

Although organizational supports may seem mundane, their presence (or absence) can dramatically foster (or limit) the effectiveness of a self-managing performance unit. Three specific features of the organizational context are particularly significant in supporting self-managing units. It will be no surprise that the first of the three has mainly to do with the effort self-managers apply to the work, the second with the knowledge and skill they bring to bear on it, and the third with the appropriateness of the task performance strategies they use in executing it.

The Reward System. A reward system that recognizes and reinforces excellent unit performance can complement and amplify the motivational incentives of a well-designed task. Which specific rewards will work best, of course, depends on what the unit members value. Sometimes simple recognition of excellence will suffice; in other cases, more tangible rewards will be required. But whatever the rewards, their impact on effort will be greater if they are contingent on performance, that is, if they are provided only when they are earned.

Two other features of supportive reward systems in self-managing organizations merit special mention. First, the rewards must preserve performers' "line of sight" (Lawler, 1981). It is not sufficient for performance-reward contingencies simply to exist; performers must perceive that their behavior makes a difference in the outcomes they receive. Devices such as stock ownership and profit sharing, common in organizations that aspire to self-management and organizational democracy, may have limited impact in larger organizations, where the link between what an individual does on a day-to-day basis and his or her eventual financial benefits is so remote as to be difficult to discern. Just as a citizen may ask "What difference does my one vote make?" so may a self-manager in a large enterprise wonder how much of a difference coming to work today or persevering with a difficult customer will make in his or her share of the profits. It usually is necessary, therefore, either to break large self-managing units down into smaller groups that serve as the basis for member rewards or to install multiple-level reward systems that provide immediate as well as long-term rewards and recognition.

Second, the system must be appropriate to the self-managing unit. When the work is designed for individual self-managers, an individually focused reward system may be fully appropriate. But when the performing unit is a self-managing team, consequences should focus on the performance of the team as a whole. When this principle is violated (for example, by providing rewards to individual team members based on managers' judgments of their relative contributions to the group product), dissension and conflict often develop within the group. This is the dilemma of the athletic coach, who must try to motivate the team as a whole while simultaneously cultivating and reinforcing individual performance. And it is a problem routinely faced by managers of work teams in organizations where the reward system traditionally has focused on identifying and recognizing excellent individual performers.

When the performing unit is a team, the destructive effects of rewarding individual contributions rather than unit performance can be substantial. Therefore, if it is not feasible to provide performance-contingent rewards to the group as a whole, it may be better to base rewards on the performance of the next-larger unit (such as a department or division) or not to use contingent rewards at all than to invite the divisiveness that can develop when members of a team are put into competition with one another for scarce and valued rewards (Lawler, 1981).

The Education System. Sometimes members of a performing unit collectively have all the knowledge and skill they need for optimum task performance. More commonly, there are aspects of the work for which outside expertise would be helpful. The education system of the organization can help fill in gaps in member talent and contribute to the development of members' own knowledge and skill.

For this potential to be realized, two conditions must be met. First, relevant educational resources, which can include technical consultation as well as training, must exist somewhere in the organization. Second, a delivery system must be in place to make those resources accessible to the unit. This may sound like a straightforward organizational design problem, but it often turns out to be a thorny political issue, particularly when unit members are rank-and-file members who never have had the right to call on staff resources. In effect, staff experts become the providers of service to clients whom they previously may have viewed as subordinate to them. Such reversals of traditional roles are never easy to negotiate.

The particular kind of assistance required depends on both task requirements and specific unit needs, and the appropriate form of the assistance varies as well. Sometimes a one-shot technical consultation will suffice; sometimes a continuing consulting relationship will be needed; and sometimes a formal training program will be more appropriate. Whatever the content of the assistance provided and the vehicle used to deliver it, the objective of the education system is the same: to help units that do not have the full complement of knowledge and skill required for excellent task performance obtain it.

The Information System. The information system of an organization is critical to a performing unit's ability to plan and execute a task-appropriate performance strategy. If a unit cannot obtain clear information about its performance situation, or if it does not have access to data about the likely results of alternative approaches to the task, it may develop a way of proceeding that seems reasonable to group members but that turns out to be grossly inappropriate when executed.

To develop a good performance strategy, unit members need a clear map of the performance situation. It is essentially important for members to have information about (1) task requirements, constraints, and opportunities that may limit or channel strategic options; (2) the resources that are available for use; and (3) the people who will receive, review, or use the group product, including the standards they are likely to employ in assessing its adequacy. Consider, for example, a self-managing manufacturing team that is deciding how to approach a complex assembly task. One possibility might be a cyclic strategy, in which all members build components for a period of time and then assemble final products (producing a relative flood of output), followed by another component-building period, and so on. How would this strategy compare to one in which some members build components continuously while others are dedicated to final assembly? To choose between these strategies, the group needs information about the timing of demand for their product, the availability of space for storing components and completed products, and the cost of obtaining and holding parts for use in batch production. It would be quite risky to choose a strategy without this information.

As was the case for educational resources, the delivery of information often turns out to be a major roadblock in supporting self-managers. In many organizations, information is shared only on a "need to know" basis. If rank-and-file members traditionally have been merely executors of the work with no responsibility for monitoring and managing their own performance, then historically they had no legitimate need for strategy-relevant information. Even when member roles are redefined to include self-managing responsibilities, senior managers may persist in a view that is unnecessary (or too risky) to share confidential strategy-relevant information with them—a stance that can compromise unit effectiveness, particularly in a fluid and competitive environment, but one that also can be difficult to change.

Expert Coaching and Consultation

The organizational supports I have discussed so far typically are provided relatively impersonally, through the normal operation of organizational systems. Additional support can be provided to self-managers directly, through hands-on coaching and consultation by their leaders (Fournies, 1978; Thomas, 1979). Coaching is an especially critical support for self-managers, who must learn how to regulate their behavior in often uncertain work situations (Mills, 1983).

Consistent with the general framework I have been using, I will focus on ways that coaching and consultation can affect the standing of a performing unit on the three process criteria. How, for example, can a leader or consultant help members avoid unnecessary losses of effort, misapplications of talent, or implementation of flawed performance strategy? And, on the positive side, how can members be helped to strengthen their commitment to hard, effective work on the task, increase their task-relevant knowledge and skill, and invent uniquely appropriate strategies for proceeding with the work? Although the objectives of coaching are the same whether the work is done by an individual self-manager or by a self-managing team, the nature of the consultation will vary substantially in the two cases.

Consider first individual self-managers. Earlier I discussed individual differences in psychological readiness for self-managing work, and in capability to do the work well, as two factors to be considered in recruiting, selecting, and placing self-managers. No matter how good those practices are, there always will be a less-than-perfect match between the person and the work. Direct coaching can help an initially skeptical or confused self-manager become aware of opportunities for personal satisfaction and growth present in the work and provide support and assistance as the individual learns how to exploit those opportunities. Moreover, a coach can help a self-manager hone and develop his or her task-relevant knowledge and skill, thereby shrinking any gap between a person's talents and the requirements of the task. Helping people accept their roles as self-managers has particularly high leverage for individuals who have worked mainly in traditional enterprises. These people may not know how to monitor and adjust their behavior in response to a changing task or situation or how to go about inventing and testing alternative work strategies. These skills are key to effective self-management, and a good coach can significantly assist people in acquiring them.

Teams, like individuals, often need coaching in self-management skills, particularly when team members have relatively little (or predominantly negative) experience with collaborative work. Too often a task is tossed to group members with the assumption that "they'll work it out among themselves." And too often members do not know how to do that. A leader or consultant can do much to promote team effectiveness by helping members learn how to work together as self-managers.

The role of the help provider is not to dictate to group members the "one right way" to go about their collaborative work, but rather to help members learn (1) how to minimize the "process losses" that invariably occur in groups (Steiner, 1972) and (2) how they might work together in ways that generate synergistic process gains (for a detailed discussion of process losses and gains, see Hackman & Morris, 1975, or Hackman, 1986). Specific kinds of help that might be provided include the following:

- *Effort:* helping members minimize coordination and motivation decrements (process losses that can waste effort) and helping them build commitment to the group and its task (a process gain that can build effort)

- *Knowledge and skill:* helping members avoid inappropriate weighting of members' ideas and contributions (a process loss) and helping them share expertise and learn from one another (a process gain)

- *Performance strategies:* helping members avoid flawed implementation of performance plans (a process loss) and helping them invent creative ways of proceeding with the work (a process gain)

This focus on process losses and gains that are specifically relevant to task accomplishment contrasts with group process consultations that seek to minimize intermember disagreement and promote harmonious group relations. There is no consistent evidence that group performance is facilitated by smooth, conflict-free relations among members; indeed, research suggests that working through conflicts over ideas promotes both group creativity and member satisfaction (Hoffman, 1978). So, despite the fact that turbulent intermember relations may appear to impede performance, it often is wiser to let such turbulence run its course. Rather than help members resolve their disagreements as quickly as possible, then, a consultant might encourage them to stay engaged with their ideational conflicts and to attempt to remedy only those process issues that are compromising the team's level of effort, its utilization of member talent, or its management of performance strategy.

In summary, coaching can help both individual self-managers and self-managing teams become more effective, but it is neither a cure-all nor an always-appropriate activity. If, for example, the direction provided to performers is poorly articulated or alienating, if the performing unit has serious structural flaws, or if the organizational context undermines rather than reinforces excellence, then it is highly unlikely that direct, hands-on coaching will be of much help. The leader's attention, in such cases, might more appropriately focus on getting the overall performance situation squared away, therefore creating a setting in which coaching can have a real chance of improving unit effectiveness.

Even when performance conditions are positive, self-managing units are not always receptive to coaching interventions. For example, in charting the life cycles of a number of self-managing task forces, Gersick (1984) found that there were certain times in teams' lives when they were receptive to consultation and coaching from outsiders (for example, around the midpoint of the work) and other times when they were not (for example, in the period between the first meeting and the midpoint, when members were almost wholly preoccupied with internal matters and seemingly uninterested in outside help). It appears that the timing of coaching interventions can sometimes be as important as their content in determining their impact.

The kind of coaching contemplated here has little in common with traditional performance appraisal programs in organizations. Such programs are structured organizational devices for assessing on a regular basis the acceptability of the work people do. Although assessment results may prompt training and development activities, they usually have direct consequences for individuals' compensation and advancement as well. By contrast, I have been discussing a coaching role in which performers are helped, on line, to learn how to behave so as to accomplish their work at high levels of excellence—and to improve their own skills and capabilities in the process. The term *coach* was selected deliberately, to suggest behaviors intended to help others perform as well as they can, in an enterprise to which both the coach and the performer are committed. In this view, coaching involves persistence, repetition, and constant vigilance for opportunities to help self-managers improve themselves and their performance. It is a cooperative venture between performers and leaders that is always unfinished, and it is an activity of great potential benefit to all parties—albeit one that may be impossible to do well if the performing unit and its organizational context are not properly set up in the first place.

Adequate Material Resources

I have now discussed four conditions that are critical to the effectiveness of self-managing performing units: direction, structure, context, and coaching. The fifth and final condition is also the simplest: having the wherewithal required to get the work done, such as money, space, staff time, tools, and so on. This condition is not particularly interesting conceptually, and until relatively recently it has been almost wholly overlooked by organizational researchers. Yet insufficient material resources often are a major roadblock to performance effectiveness in self-managing units (see, for example, Peters & O'Connor, 1980). Even units that have a clear and engaging direction, and whose performance situation promotes the process criteria, eventually will fail if they do not have (and cannot get) the resources they need to do their work. Among the saddest kinds of failures are those experienced by well-designed and well-supported self-managing units whose members understand their objectives and are committed to achieving them, but who cannot obtain the resources they need to fulfill their promise.

Conclusion: Five Conditions That Support
Effective Self-Management

To summarize, here are the five conditions that together promote the effectiveness of self-managing units:

Points of Leverage

Process Criteria of Effectiveness	Unit structure	Organizational context	Coaching and consultation
Ample effort	Motivational properties of the unit task	Organizational reward system	Help with motivation, commitment, and coordination issues
Sufficient knowledge and skill	Composition of the unit	Organizational education system	Help with the use and development of members' talents
Task-appropriate performance strategies	Sent expectations about scanning/planning	Organizational information system	Help with the invention and implementation of strategic plans

Figure 45.3. Points of Leverage for Creating a Favorable Performance Situation.

1. The overall direction for the work is clear and engaging.
2. The structure of the performing unit fosters competent performance, through the design of the task, the composition of the unit, and sent expectations regarding the management of performance processes.
3. The organizational context supports competent work, through the reward, education, and information systems.
4. Expert coaching and consultation are available and are provided at appropriate times.
5. Material resources are adequate and available.

The first condition provides the overall frame within which the unit operates and, when present, amplifies the constructive impact of the remaining conditions. The final condition provides the means for getting the work done. If it is present, execution can proceed smoothly and according to plan; if it is not, performance will be undermined even when all the other conditions are in place.

The middle three conditions—structure, context, and coaching—together increase the chances that a self-managing unit will achieve the three process criteria of effectiveness. The relationship between these conditions and the process criteria is illustrated in Figure 45.3. For each of the process criteria, some aspect of unit structure, some feature of the organizational context, and some type of process assistance is identified as having particular relevance.

For *effort*-related issues, one would consider (1) the motivational structure of the task, (2) the reward system of the organization, and (3) individual and group dynamics having to do with motivation, commitment, and co-ordination.

For *talent*-related issues, one would consider (1) unit composition, (2) the education system of the organization, and (3) individual and group dynamics having to do with the development and use of members' talents.

For *strategy*-related issues, one would consider (1) roles and norms relevant to the management of performance processes, (2) the information system of the organization (i.e., whether the unit gets the data it needs to design and implement an appropriate strategy), and (3) individual and group dynamics having to do with the invention and implementation of new ways of proceeding with the work.

The view of self-management I have sketched here is broad and encompassing. Rather than focus on the immediate causes of specific self-managing behaviors, I have attempted to identify a set of general conditions that, taken together, foster effective self-management. When these conditions are present, one should find good alignment between individual and collective objectives, autonomous monitoring and managing of work activities by unit members in pursuit of those objectives, and a high level of satisfaction (by both unit members and their clients) with what transpires and what is achieved. By contrast, most existing research and theory on self-management in organizations is based on principles of social learning theory (Bandura, 1971) as applied to shaping up one's own behavior (Mahoney, 1974; Watson & Tharp, 1977). The emphasis in that work is on strategies people can use to increase the frequency of constructive behaviors that they rarely exhibit or to decrease the frequency of dysfunctional behaviors that they often exhibit (see, for example, Brief & Hollenbeck, 1985; Luthans & Davis, 1979; Manz and Sims, 1980).

The two approaches, heretofore distinct in the literature, complement one another (see for example, Manz, in press). Recognition of the importance of social system conditions can enrich the design and interpretation of research on the psychology of self-regulation, for example, by identifying circumstances when self-regulation is likely to be observed and when it is likely to be associated with effective work performance. The social learning theorists' research on the dynamics of self-regulation, on the other hand, can illuminate in detail the psychological and behavioral processes that occur within the broad orienting and enabling conditions I have set forth here. I hope that future research and theory on self-management will exploit the complementarities of the two approaches in ways that both deepen conceptual understanding of the phenomena and advance practical knowledge about how to create and maintain effective self-managing units.

LEADERSHIP IN SELF-MANAGING UNITS

According to Manz and Sims (1984, p. 410), there is an inherent contradiction in thinking about the leadership of self-managers. "How," they ask "does one lead employees who are supposed to lead themselves?" In working through the dilemma they set for themselves, Manz and Sims have proposed the concept of the "unleader": someone who "leads others to lead themselves" (p. 411). Although the idea of the unleader is novel, it is common for those who write about self-management to take the view that there is relatively little need for leadership in such units, that leaders should help unit members get the work under way and then fade into the background as quickly as possible. I take a contrary view and argue that leadership is both more important and a more demanding undertaking in self-managing units than it is in traditional organizations.

The approach to self-management that I have been discussing lends itself rather naturally to a functional analysis of leader roles and behavior. As articulated by McGrath (1962), the key assertion in the functional approach to leadership is this: "[The leader's] main job is to do, or get done, whatever is not being adequately handled for group needs" (p. 5). If a leader manages, by whatever means, to ensure that all functions critical to both task accomplishment and group maintenance are adequately taken care of, then the leader has done his or her job well. By leaving room for an indefinite number of specific ways to get a critical function accomplished, the functional approach avoids the need to delineate the specific behaviors that a leader should exhibit in given circumstances—a trap into which it is all too easy for leadership theorists to fall.

Yet the functional approach is generic almost to a fault: it could apply to virtually anybody leading virtually anything. To apply the approach, one needs a theory that specifies what is critical to the effectiveness of the group or organization being led. I have attempted to provide such a specification for self-managing units (that is, in terms of the five enabling conditions I have been discussing) and will now draw on that material to explore what is required of those who lead self-managers.

Critical Leadership Function

The critical leadership functions for a self-managing unit are *those activities that contribute to the establishment and maintenance of favorable performance conditions.* Following the framework proposed by McGrath (1962, p. 17), this involves two types of behavior: (1) monitoring, or obtaining and interpreting data about performance conditions and events that might affect them; and (2) taking action to create or maintain favorable performance conditions.

For the monitoring function, a leader would ask the following: Does the unit have clear and engaging direction? Is it well structured? Does it have a supportive organizational context? Are ample coaching and process assistance available? Does it have adequate material resources? Although I have framed these questions in the present tense, the monitoring function includes not only assessments of the present state of affairs (diagnosis) but also projections about how things are changing and what deleterious or fortunate events may be about to occur (forecasting).

Action taking follows these assessments of the group and situation and involves behaviors intended to create favorable performance conditions or to remedy problems (or exploit opportunities) in existing conditions. Sometimes the focus of such actions will be within the unit (as when the leader works with members to help them understand the significance of their task or learn better ways of coordinating their activities). Other times external action will be required (as when the leader negotiates a change in the organization's compensation system to provide rewards for excellent performance or when he or she helps establish a relationship between the unit and a consultant from elsewhere in the organization).

These leadership functions can be arranged in a matrix, as in Figure 45.4. There are two types of functions (monitoring and action taking) for each of the five enabling conditions (direction, structure, context, coaching, and resources). For the monitoring function, both diagnosis and forecasting are specified; for the action-taking function, both internal and external targets are specified.

Although the leader's responsibility is to ensure that these functions are fulfilled, this does not mean that he or she must handle them personally. Leadership is appropriately shared in self-managing units, and as such units mature unit members typically assume responsibility for an increasing number of leadership functions (Walton & Schlesinger, 1979). Thus, there is no single set of leader behaviors that are always desirable and appropriate; nor will any single style of leadership be generally effective.

Does this view of leadership invite the development of a complex tale of contingencies that explicate the specific leader behaviors that should be exhibited in various circumstances? On the contrary, the five enabling conditions provide a relatively straightforward and theory-specified set of tests that a leader can use in managing his or her own behavior. Figure 45.5, by highlighting the substantive focus of a leader's monitoring activities, shows how the approach would work in practice.

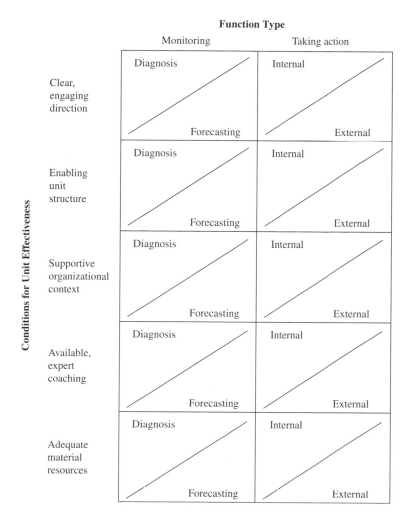

Figure 45.4. Summary of Critical Leadership Functions for Self-Managing Units.

First a leader would assess the outcome states at the right of the figure, and then work backwards to identify (and ultimately do something about) performance conditions that may be contributing to performance problems or missed opportunities. "How is the unit doing?" the leader would ask. "Are there signs of problems in the task work, in members' ability to work together interdependently, or in the quality of individuals' experiences in the unit?" When problems, unexploited opportunities, or negative trends are noted, he or she would examine the process indicators in the center of the figure to learn more about what may be going on.

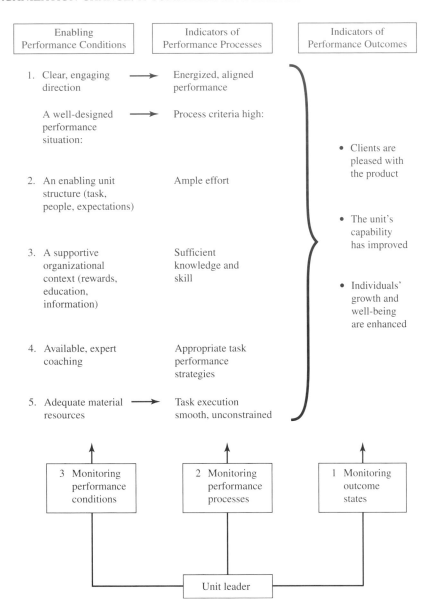

Figure 45.5. The Unit Leader's Monitoring Function: A Summary.

Then, guided by the answers to the diagnostic questions, the leader's attention would turn to the conditions at the left of the figure. "Which performance conditions most need strengthening? How are we doing in direction, in structure, in context supports, in hands-on assistance, in resources?" If it turns out that performance conditions are suboptimal, the leader's challenge is to invent (the word is chosen deliberately) ways of behaving that may remedy a deficiency or exploit an unrealized opportunity. The five enabling conditions I have been discussing would serve as criteria for a leader to use in comparing and evaluating alternative behaviors. This invent-and-test strategy is far easier to use than one that requires a leader to learn a table of contingencies specifying exactly what behaviors should be exhibited in what particular circumstances and then to regulate his or her behavior in accord with that table. The present strategy also should encourage innovation and creativity in leader behavior.

Leaders always act in accord with some model (even if implicit, and even if wrong) that specifies what behaviors are associated with what outcomes. Typically, the models used by leaders (and studied by researchers) focus on interactions that take place between leaders and unit members. In the model I have proposed here, only two of the five key conditions (setting direction, and coaching/consultation) involve leader-unit relations centrally; the other three (structuring the unit, tuning the organizational context, and providing material resources) are oriented toward the situation in which the unit functions. If this model has validity, then effective leaders would be observed to spend at least as much of their time and energy working with peers and senior managers as they do with unit members, monitoring and taking action vis-à-vis all five of the performance conditions. A leader who attempts to foster unit effectiveness primarily through hands-on work with unit members when the surrounding performance situation is flawed and unsupportive would be predicted to fail.

Designing Leader Roles

Should the leader roles be designed to foster competent leadership in self-managing units? The logic for addressing this question is the same as that used in considering the design of performing units. The major difference is that this time the focus is on the role of the leader, not the unit itself. Specifically, one would first generate a number of alternative ways to structure leader roles for the unit being considered. Then, with several possibilities on the table, each would be assessed to determine which show the greatest promise of getting the critical leadership functions fulfilled for that particular unit. Considerations include the following:

- From what perch would a leader be best able to provide direction to the unit? Will he or she be setting direction, or merely translating and communicating it? How much authority needs to be built into the role to legitimize and support the direction-setting function?

- How can leadership roles be designed so as to foster rather than undermine the autonomy a unit has in managing its own affairs? Would designating a formal leader within the unit make it harder or easier to maintain an appropriate balance between collective direction and unit autonomy?

- How much external influence will the leader require to create supportive structural and contextual conditions and to marshal needed resources? How can the role be designed to strengthen the leader's influence outward and upward?

- What information will the leader require, and with whom will he or she need to coordinate on a regular basis? Can access to critical information and contact with key co-workers be built into the role?

Once questions such as these are reviewed, it is likely that one or another of the alternative designs under consideration will emerge as dominant (or, perhaps, a new and better alternative will come up in the testing process). It often turns out in practice that leadership functions can best be fulfilled when a unit has both a defined internal leader (who is also a working unit member) and an external manager who may have responsibility for several units. There is, however, no generally best design for leadership roles in self-managing units. As was the case for the design of performing units, the right answer is to have a design process that will generate an answer that is right for particular organizational circumstances.

Training Leaders of Self-Managers

How can leaders of self-managing units develop the knowledge and skill they need to perform their roles well? Once again, McGrath's (1962) paper on leadership functions is helpful. He suggests that one can develop a matrix, with the critical functions as rows and the knowledge and skills required to fulfill those functions as columns. For leaders of self-managers, the matrix is as follows:

Critical Leadership Functions	Required Knowledge	Required Skills
Monitoring and taking action regarding:	+ – – – – – – – – + – – – – – – – +	
1. Setting direction	+ – – – – – – – – + – – – – – – – +	
2. Designing the unit	+ – – – – – – – – + – – – – – – – +	
3. Tuning the context	+ – – – – – – – – + – – – – – – – +	
4. Coaching and consulting	+ – – – – – – – – + – – – – – – – +	
5. Providing resources	+ – – – – – – – – + – – – – – – – +	

In designing a leadership training program, then, one first would determine which functions have the greatest leverage for the work to be done, and then proceed to fill in the cells with the actual knowledge and skills that are required to fulfill those functions. The specific context of the cells will necessarily depend on the properties of the work to be done and the organization in which it will be done. In some organizations, for example, political skills will be needed to obtain organizational supports and resources; in others, those supports may be abundantly available or obtainable simply by asking. As another example, consider the support leaders provide unit members through online coaching and process assistance. In some organizations, there will be great need for such help and no one available to provide it but the leader; in others, members may be experienced and expert in self-management (and therefore less in need of assistance), and moreover there may be a staff of organization development professionals on call to lend a hand if asked. Obviously, the need for leader training in process skills will vary as a function of such circumstances.

There are, nonetheless, some knowledge and skills that may be of general value in leading self-managers. Here are some ideas about what these might be, presented separately for the leader's monitoring and action-taking functions.

Monitoring

To effectively diagnose the state of a performing unit and forecast likely future problems and opportunities, a leader needs knowledge about the key conditions for effective performance. In addition, he or she must understand how these conditions are linked to the process criteria and to unit effectiveness. I have attempted to provide some guidance about such matters in this chapter, and I suspect that it would be a reasonably straightforward task to develop a training course for unit leaders based on this material.

Leadership *skills* that may help leaders of self-managers perform well include:

- Data gathering skill: the ability to collect data about social systems that are reliable and valid

- Diagnostic and forecasting skill: the ability to apprehend complexity and make sense of it, drawing on both data and existing knowledge in shaping one's conclusions

- Hypothesis testing skill: the ability to use data to conduct assessments of the relative validity of alternative hypotheses about the state of a social system (or, for forecasting, about its likely future state)

Action Taking. In taking action to help a self-managing unit perform well, a leader needs knowledge about both (1) the key levers that are available (or can be made so) to improve performance conditions, and (2) timing considerations that condition when various interventions are likely to "take" (versus when they may fall on barren ground and have little effect).

Among the skills required for competent action taking by leaders of self-managers may be:

• *Envisioning skill:* the ability to envision desired end states and to articulate and communicate them to others.

• *Inventive skill:* the ability to think of numerous nonobvious ways of getting something done.

• *Negotiation skill:* the ability to work persistently and constructively with peers and superiors to secure resources or assistance needed to support one's subordinates.

• *Decision-making skill:* the ability to choose among various courses of action under uncertainty, using all perspectives and data that can be efficiently obtained to inform the decision.

• *Teaching skill:* the ability to help others learn both experientially and didactically.

• *Interpersonal skill:* the ability to communicate, listen, confront, persuade, and generally to work constructively with other people, particularly when people's anxieties are high.

• *Implementation skill:* the ability to get things done. At the simplest level, knowing how to make lists, attend to mundane details, check and recheck for omitted items or people, and follow plans through to completion. At a more sophisticated level, the ability to constructively and assertively manage power, political relationships, and symbols to get things accomplished in social systems.

It is, I suspect, entirely feasible to develop training that will help leaders develop the knowledge and skill they need to fulfill the critical leadership functions. Yet there are some individuals for whom such training would be a waste of time—individuals who, perhaps, should not be invited to serve as leaders or self-managers. With that possibility in mind, let me turn finally to the problem of selecting people for leadership roles in self-managing units.

Selecting Leaders of Self-Managers

Are there general qualities or traits that can be used to differentiate people who are likely to develop into first-rate leaders of self-managers from those who will never be effective in such roles? Although I am mindful of the pessimistic conclusions that have emerged from decades of research on leadership effectiveness traits, I believe that relatively stable individual differences in potential for leading self-managers do exist, and that these differences can be assessed.

There are three qualities that might be measured when people are being considered for leadership roles, qualities that probably are not trainable in the short term. These qualities have little in common with those that have been studied in trait-oriented leadership research, and I offer them in a speculative spirit.

1. *Courage:* a willingness to buck the tide (and social norms) when necessary to create conditions required for effectiveness. To help a unit address and modify dysfunctional dynamics, a leader may need to challenge group norms and disrupt established routines—and may risk incurring some anger in doing so. To improve a unit's contextual supports or to increase the resources available to it, a leader may need to rock the organizational boat, and may risk a loss of esteem with his or her peers and superiors in doing so. Such behaviors require courage.

2. *Emotional maturity:* the ability to move toward anxiety-arousing states of affairs in the interest of learning about them and doing something about them (rather than moving away to get the anxiety reduced as quickly as possible).

3. *Clear and appropriate personal values:* an internalized commitment to both organizational effectiveness and human well-being. Leaders who are confused about what they personally value find it difficult to choose among competing options for action. Although almost any clear set of values can be used as the basis for managing one's own behavior, one cannot be agnostic about the content of those values in considering how to select leaders of self-managers. Only individuals who genuinely value both collective outcomes and the growth and satisfaction of unit members are likely to invent and implement conditions that promote the two values simultaneously—something that surely is necessary if a self-managing unit is to be effective over the long term.

This list may seem a bit strange to organizational scientists who typically do not deal with things such as courage, emotions, and values. But stranger still, perhaps, is the fact that excellent leaders in self-managing units tend to have many, if not all, of these very qualities. It would appear to be well worthwhile to give new thought to old questions about how candidates for leadership positions might be assessed on such difficult-to-measure but potentially significant attributes.

CONCLUSION

The model of self-management that I have presented in this chapter emphasizes the creation of conditions that direct, enable, and support effective performance, but that also leave a great deal of behavioral latitude for unit members and their leaders. It deals with multiple, nonindependent factors that have redundant influences on a set of outcomes that also are not independent.

This kind of approach can jar scientific sensibilities. Scientists are trained to look for the true causes of phenomena in which they have interest. When a performing unit performs particularly well or poorly, for example, a scientist would attempt to rule out as many explanations as possible and eventually pin down the real causal agent. Standard scientific methods are appropriate for many purposes, but there are at least three reasons why they can mislead researchers who are interested in social system effectiveness.

First, influences on performance effectiveness do not come in separate, easily distinguishable packages. They come, instead, in complex tangles that often are as difficult to straighten out as a backlash on a fishing reel. Trying to partial out the effects of each possible determinant of unit effectiveness, then, can lead one to the conclusion that no single factor has a very powerful effect— a conclusion reached by more than one reviewer of the literature on work performance. Each possible cause loses its potency when studied in isolation from other conditions also in place for the units under study.

Second, there are many different ways unit members can behave and still perform work well, and even more ways to be nonproductive. Systems theorists call this aspect of organized endeavor "equifinality" (Katz & Kahn, 1978, p. 30). According to this principle, a performing unit can achieve the same outcome from various initial conditions and by a variety of means. Equifinality supports the view that leading self-managers centrally involves creating conditions that amply support effective performance, but in a way that leaves plenty of room for unit members to develop and implement their own idiosyncratic strategies for accomplishing the work. There is no single strategy that will work equally well for different units, even units that have nearly identical official tasks.

Third, social systems develop and enact their own versions of reality and then act in accord with the environment they have helped create. A unit's redefinition of reality, which cannot be prevented, can either blunt or enhance the impact of specific actions taken by a researcher or manager to influence it. This issue is especially salient for self-managing units because of the latitude self-managers have in making sense of their performance situation and in deciding how they will behave within it.

Together, these difficulties suggest that traditional scientific models in which specific external causes are tightly linked to specific, well-defined effects may have to give way to an alternative kind of theorizing, one that is more congruent with the facts of life in social systems. I have attempted in this chapter to describe one such an approach. I conclude by discussing the implications of that approach for practice, for theory, and for research methodology.

Implications for Practice

Working in a self-managing unit is somewhat akin to driving from New York to Chicago rather than taking a train. When driving, you have many alternative routes; if one of them is blocked, there are still many ways to get to Chicago. A train, however, has only one set of tracks; and if there is an obstruction on them, you cannot proceed until it is removed. As long as organizational structures and policies provide self-managers with enough room to maneuver around whatever obstacles they encounter, unit performance can be fully acceptable even in the face of management errors and suboptimal organizational conditions.

Those who design self-managing units also enjoy maneuvering room. The conditions I have been discussing can take multiple forms, and there are multiple ways to create and install them. For example, one can think of many ways a piece of work could be designed and still foster internal work motivation; so are there many ways a reward system could be structured and still provide positive consequences contingent on unit performance. The same is true for the other conditions we have considered. This feature of self-managing work systems both invites managerial creativity in organizational design, and allows specific design features to be adapted to idiosyncratic realities of the work place.

Because the five enabling conditions are in many ways redundant, they can to some presently unknown extent substitute for one another. Rather than attempting to optimize a design, then, those who are setting up a self-managing unit would be well advised to deliberately foster redundancy and interdependence among positive performance conditions, thereby creating an overdetermined performance system that can continue to function satisfactorily even if some of its components fail.

It is, of course, far easier to create a self-managing unit from scratch than to change over an existing system. Moreover, there is reason for skepticism about the viability of converting a performing unit from manager-led to self-managing using the planned change strategy traditionally favored by organization development professionals. Such programs typically involve sequential chains of activity, with each successive step depending on successful completion of the prior one—and the truth about the strength of chains is well known.

An alternative strategy for moving an existing organization toward self-management involves waiting for, and then vigorously exploiting, naturally occurring opportunities for change. This approach (which is described in more detail by Hackman & Oldham, 1980, in their Chapter Ten) requires three things of change advocates. First, they must know where they want to go; that is, they must be clear about their organizational and human resource values and aspirations. Second, they must understand the conditions that are required to promote effective self-management, a matter about which I hope this chapter has been helpful, and one that is critical in focusing one's change activities on the highest-leverage targets. And finally, they must be sensitive to realities of timing and politics—factors that, perhaps more than any other, determine when one should take action and when it is wiser to lie in wait for a more favorable opportunity.

Implications for Theory

Throughout this chapter, I have argued that behavior and performance in self-managing units are overdetermined. That is, they are shaped by multiple, non-independent factors whose influence depends in part on the fact that they are redundant. Standard cause-effect models obviously are inappropriate for construing such phenomena, as are contingency models of the "X is a cause of Y, but their relationship is moderated by Z" variety. Multivariate models, designed specifically for analyzing causally complex phenomena, would seem a reasonable alternative. Yet if self-managing systems do operate as suggested here, so many key assumptions of these models would be violated so severely that they would be of little use (cf. James, Mulaik, & Brett, 1982). One could, of course, select variables and structure research situations to make sure that these assumptions are not violated, but then one would be in the unfortunate situation of altering the phenomena to make them more suitable for study with the tools that happen to be available. Somehow, the substantive horse must be put back in front of the methodological cart. First, better ways of theorizing about influences on work performance must be found, and then appropriate ways of gathering and analyzing data to test those ideas can be located or invented.

What kinds of conceptual models would be most useful in furthering an understanding of performance in self-managing organizational units? One intriguing lead is provided in the theory of multiple possibilities set forth by Tyler (1983). Whereas contingency theory assumes that if one knew the right moderating variables it would be possible to predict and control behavior in virtually any situation, multiple possibility theory holds that such an aspiration is ill-conceived. Instead, the theory maintains, there are many possible outcomes that can emerge in any situation, and the particular outcome that is actualized is not completely determined by the causal factors that precede it. Thus, multiple possibility theory envisions a world with some "play" in the system, and it encourages attention to human choice as a factor that transforms multiple possibilities into single courses of action.

Multiple possibility theory fits nicely with the phenomenon of self-management and also complements the systems theorists' notion of equifinality discussed earlier. Where equifinality asserts that the same outcome can occur in response to many different causes, multiple possibility theory posits that the same cause can generate a variety of different outcomes. Taken together, the two notions provide an alternative to stimulus-response models in which situational causes are tightly linked to behavioral effects, whether directly ("Introduce this management practice and performance will improve") or contingently ("Performance will improve, but only for certain kinds of people under certain circumstances").

If the notions of equifinality and multiple possibilities were taken seriously, would that signal an abandonment of "scientific" approaches to understanding work behavior? Not at all. But it would require that scholars of organizations generate qualitatively different kinds of models to deal with performance in social systems and that they also invent some new methods for assessing the validity and usefulness of those models.

Implications for Method

The methodological challenges posed by the approach to understanding work behavior and performance I have been discussing are considerable. How, for example, can one study nonindependent influences on performance in ways that will yield more than mere descriptions of what has transpired—that will, instead, offer insight into the dynamics of organizational conditions that foster and support effective self-management? What methods can be used to learn about factors that have powerful cumulative influences on work behavior, but whose effects are almost impossible to discern at any given moment in time? How can one tap into self-reinforcing cycles of increasingly good or poor performance in ways that reveal how those cycles feed themselves?

One strategy for approaching such questions would be to bring the case study out of the management school classroom and put it to work in scholarly pursuits. It is true that case studies, as traditionally prepared, often give too much credence to the interpretations favored by their authors. Selective emphasis of material, and decision making about what data to include and exclude are real problems (although these problems are shared by writers of quantitative empirical studies to a far greater extent than is usually admitted). Are there ways to present case studies that invite disconformation and tests of alternative interpretations? Would it be possible, for example, to carry out competing analyses for each interpretation of a given case, one that seeks to support the interpretation as convincingly as possible and one that attempts to cast the greatest possible doubt on it? Would such an approach to case analysis and presentation foster learning by other scholars and contribute to the accumulation of knowledge across cases?

Another possibility, heretofore used more by coroners, detectives, and aircraft accident investigators than by scholars of organizations, is the "modus operandi" method (Scriven, 1974). If one can generate a list of the *possible* causes of some outcome or event and has some knowledge about the special "signature" of each one, then it often is possible to use logical, historical, and microexperimental techniques to identify the *probable* causes of that outcome, even when it is complexly determined or overdetermined. The modus operandi approach, which as far as I know has not been used in the study of work performance, provides an interesting alternative to standard quasi-experimental and correlational designs for organizational studies.

Whatever new devices are developed for use in studying self-managing social systems, I suspect that they will require careful, systematic descriptions of the phenomena under study, interpretations that cross traditional levels of analysis (that link individual, group, organizational, and environmental variables), and renegotiation of the turf boundaries that presently keep psychologists from having to worry about contextual and structural influences on behavior (and that free scholars in other disciplines from worries about psychological dynamics that affect the phenomena in which they have special interest). Eventually, there may even be greater recognition of the value of multiple perspectives on the same data from people in different groups with different stakes in how those data are interpreted. What will be seen less and less, I hope, are analyses of the causes of performance outcomes that isolate causal agents from the social systems in which they operate and research strategies that require the phenomena to accommodate to the methodology rather than vice versa.

The practical, conceptual, and methodological challenges that have emerged from this exploration of the psychology of self-management are substantial— and obviously are not ones for which I have ready answers. I am optimistic, nonetheless, that in these challenges lies the potential for developing scholarly models of work performance that are considerably more congruent with the realities of social systems than are the deterministic contingency models presently in favor in organizational psychology. Moreover, as the challenges are confronted, I have hope that some guidelines for managerial action will emerge, guidelines that will be both powerful in affecting work performance and usable by people who design and manage purposive social systems of many varieties—including, but certainly not limited' to, organizations that aspire to self-management.

Notes

1. These functions deal specifically with the management of work performance, and they define the domain of coverage for this chapter. Matters having mainly to do with organizational governance (e.g., the mechanisms used to determine major organizational policies) are not specifically addressed here. The performance and

governance systems of an organization are, nonetheless, interdependent in many respects, and the direction-setting function is a key point of linkage between them.

2. Managers often are viewed as "bosses" or "executives" who spend much of their time in offices planning, deciding, and issuing orders. Organization members (commonly called "rank-and-file employees" or "workers") are thought to spend most of their time actually generating the products or delivering the services that the organization exists to provide. These views are too restrictive. A plant manager in industry, or an agency director in government, may simultaneously function as a manager (vis-à-vis more senior executives). This chapter presents a way of understanding self-management that is applicable to all organization members, not just those who perform front-line tasks.

3. Organizations where this is done would seem to be especially good sites for research on the psychological dynamics of self-regulation because the phenomena of interest should be more abundant there than in traditional, manager-led units.

References

Atkinson, J. W. (1958). Towards experimental analysis of human motivation in terms of motives, expectancies, and incentives. In J. W. Atkinson (Ed.), *Motives in fantasy, action, and society.* Princeton, NJ: Van Nostrand.

Bandura, A. (1971). *Social learning theory.* Morristown, NJ: General Learning Press.

Bandura, A. (1977). Self-efficacy. Towards a unifying theory of behavioral change. *Psychological Review, 84,* 191–215.

Bennis, W., & Nanus, B. (1985). *Leaders: The strategies for taking charge.* New York: Harper & Row.

Berlew, D. E. (1979). Leadership and organizational excitement. In D. A. Kolb, I. M. Rubin, & J. M. McIntyre (Eds.), *Organizational psychology* (3rd ed.). Englewood Cliffs, NJ: Prentice-Hall.

Brief, A. P., & Hollenbeck, J. R. (1985). An exploratory study of self-regulating activities and their effects on job performance. *Journal of Occupational Behavior, 6,* 197–208.

Check, W. A. (1982). Results are better when patients control their own analgesia. *Journal of the American Medical Association, 247*(7), 945–947.

Cohen, S. G. (1985). *The beginning of a model of group empowerment.* Unpublished manuscript, Yale University, School of Organization and Management, New Haven, CT.

Cummings, T. G. (1978). Self-regulating work groups: A socio-technical synthesis. *Academy of Management Review, 3,* 625–634.

Eisenstat, R. A. (1984). *Organizational learning in the creation of an industrial setting.* Unpublished doctoral dissertation, Yale University, New Haven, CT.

Fein, M. (1974). Job enrichment: A reevaluation. *Sloan Management Review, 15,* 69–88.

Fournies, F. F. (1978). *Coaching for improved work performance*. New York: Van Nostrand Reinhold.

Gersick, C.J.G. (1984). *The life cycles of ad hoc task groups: Time, transitions, and learning in teams*. Unpublished doctoral dissertation, Yale University, New Haven, CT.

Gunn, C. E. (1984). *Workers' self-management in the United States*. Ithaca, NY: Cornell University Press.

Hackman, J. R. (1985). Doing research that makes a difference. In E. E. Lawler, A. M. Mohrman, S. A. Mohrman, G. E. Ledford, & T. G. Cummings (Eds.), *Doing research that is useful for theory and practice*. San Francisco: Jossey-Bass.

Hackman, J. R. (1986). The design of work teams. In J. W. Lorsch (Ed.), *Handbook of organizational behavior*. Englewood Cliffs, NJ: Prentice-Hall.

Hackman, J. R., & Morris, C. G. (1975). Group tasks, group interaction process, and group performance effectiveness: A review and proposed integration. In L. Bernowitz (Ed.), *Advances in experimental social psychology* (Vol. 8). New York: Academic Press.

Hackman, J. R., & Oldham, G. R. (1980). *Work redesign*. Reading, MA: Addison-Wesley.

Hackman, J. R., & Walton, R. E. (1986). Leading groups in organizations. In P. S. Goodman (Ed.), *Designing effective work groups*. San Francisco: Jossey-Bass.

Haythorn, W. W. (1968). The composition of groups: A review of the literature. *Acta Psychologica, 28*, 97–128.

Hoffman, L. R. (1978). Group problem solving. In L. Berkowitz (Ed.), *Group processes*. New York: Academic Press.

House, R. J. (1977). A 1976 theory of charismatic leadership. In J. G. Hunt & L. L. Larson (Eds.), *Leadership: The cutting edge*. Carbondale: Southern Illinois University Press.

Jackson, J. (1965). Structural characteristics of norms. In I. D. Steiner & M. Fishbein (Eds.), *Current studies in social psychology*. New York: Holt.

James, L. R, Mulaik, S. A., & Brett, J. M. (1982). *Causal analysis: Assumptions, models, and data*. Beverly Hills, CA: Sage.

Kahn, R. L., Wolfe, D. M., Quinn, R. P., Snoek, J. D., & Rosenthal, R. A. (1964). *Organizational stress: Studies in role conflict and ambiguity*. New York: Wiley.

Kanfer, F. H. (1984). Self-management in clinical and social interventions. In R. P. McGlynn, J. E. Maddux, C. D. Stoltenberg, & J. H. Harvey (Eds.), *Interfaces in psychology: Social perception in clinical and counseling psychology*. Lubbock, TX: Texas Tech Press.

Kaplan, R. E. (1979). The conspicuous absence of evidence that process consultation enhances task performance. *Journal of Applied Behavioral Science, 15*, 346–360.

Katz, D., & Kahn, R. L. (1978). *The social psychology of organizations* (2nd ed.). New York: Wiley.

Langer, E. J. (1983). *The psychology of control*. Beverly Hills, CA: Sage.

Lawler, E. E. (1978, Winter). The new plant revolution. *Organizational Dynamics*, 31–39.

Lawler, E. E. (1981). *Pay and organization development*. Reading, MA: Addison-Wesley.

Lindenfeld, F., & Rothschild-Whitt, J. (Eds.). (1982). *Workplace democracy and social change*. Boston: Porter Sargent.

Locke, E. A., Soari, L. M., Shaw, K. N., & Latham, G. D. (1981). Goal setting and task performance: 1969–1980. *Psychological Bulletin, 90,* 125–152.

Luthans, F., & Davis, T.R.V. (1979, Summer). Behavioral self-management: The missing link in managerial effectiveness. *Organizational Dynamics*, 42–60.

Mahoney, M. J. (1974). *Cognition and behavior modification*. Cambridge, MA: Ballinger Publishing.

Manz, C. C. (in press). Self-leadership: Toward an expanded theory of self-influence processes in organizations. *Academy of Management Review*.

Manz, C. C., Mossholder, K. W., & Luthans, F. (in press). An integrated perspective of self-control in organizations. *Administration and Society*.

Manz, C. C., & Sims, H. P. (1980). Self-management as a substitute for leadership: A social learning theory perspective. *Academy of Management Review, 5,* 361–367.

Manz, C. C., & Sims, H. P. (1984). Searching for the "unleader": Organizational member views on leading self-managed groups. *Human Relations, 37,* 409–424.

McGrath, J. E. (1962). *Leadership behavior: Some requirements for leadership training*. Washington, DC: U.S. Civil Service Commission.

Mills, P. K. (1983). Self-management: Its control and relationship to other organizational properties. *Academy of Management Review, 8,* 445–453.

O'Connor, E. J., Rudolf, C. J., & Peters, L. H. (1980). Individual differences and job design reconsidered: Where do we go from here? *Academy of Management Review, 5,* 249–254.

Peters, L. H., & O'Connor, E. J. (1980). Situational constraints and work outcomes: The influences of a frequently overlooked construct. *Academy of Management Review, 5,* 391–397.

Poza, E. J., & Marcus, M. L. (1980, Winter). Success story: The team approach to work restructuring. *Organizational Dynamics*, 3–25.

Schutz, W. C. (1961). On group composition. *Journal of Abnormal and Social Psychology, 62,* 275–281.

Scriven, M. (1974). Maximizing the power of causal investigations: The modus operandi method. In W. J. Popham (Ed.), *Evaluation in education: Current applications*. Washington, DC: American Educational Research Association.

Seligman, M. (1975). *Helplessness: On depression, development, and death*. San Francisco: W. H. Freeman.

Steiner, I. D. (1972). *Group process and productivity*. New York: Academic Press.

Taylor, F. W. (1911). *The principles of scientific management*. New York: Harper.

Thomas, G. (1979). *The advisor: Emissary from Teachers' Center to classroom*. (Teachers' Centers Exchange Occasional Paper No. 6). San Francisco: Far West Laboratory for Educational Research and Development.

Tyler, L. E. (1983). *Thinking creatively*. San Francisco: Jossey-Bass.

Wall, T. D., Kemp, N. J., Jackson, P. R., & Clegg, C. W. (n.d.) *An outcome evaluation of autonomous work groups: A long-term field experiment* (Memo No. 649). Sheffield, UK: University of Sheffield, MRC/ESRC Social and Applied Psychology Unit.

Walton, R. E. (1980). Establishing and maintaining high commitment work systems. In J. R. Kimberly & R. H. Miles (Eds.), *The organizational life cycle*. San Francisco: Jossey-Bass.

Walton, R. E. (1985). From control to commitment: Transformation of workforce management strategies in the United States. In K. B. Clark, R. H. Hayes, & C. Lorenz (Eds.), *The uneasy alliance: Managing the productivity-technology dilemma*. Boston: Harvard Business School Press.

Walton, R. E., & Hackman, J. R. (1986). Groups under contrasting management strategies. In P. S. Goodman (Ed.), *Designing effective work groups*. San Francisco: Jossey-Bass.

Walton, R. E., & Schlesinger, L. S. (1979, Winter). Do supervisors thrive in participative work systems? *Organizational Dynamics*, 24–38.

Watson, D. L., & Tharp, R. G. (1977). *Self-directed behavior*. Belmont, CA: Brooks/Cole.

White, J. K. (1978). Individual differences and the job quality-worker response relationship: Review, integration, and comments. *Academy of Management Review, 3*, 267–280.

Woodman, R. W., & Sherwood, J. J. (1980). The role of team development in organizational effectiveness: A critical review. *Psychological Bulletin, 88*, 166–186.

Zander, A. (1980). The origins and consequences of group goals. In L. Festinger (Ed.), *Retrospections on social psychology*. New York: Oxford University Press.

Zwerdling, D. (1980). *Workplace democracy*. New York: Harper Colophon.

PART SEVEN

BUILDING KNOWLEDGE OF CHANGE THROUGH ASSESSMENT

Editors' Interlude

Once planned organization change is under way and interventions are being implemented, how can we tell if we are making any progress toward the change goal(s)? If the kinds of problems that we are now working on are new and different from those a year ago, that may be a sign of progress. If organizational members complain about the lack of sufficient progress in the change effort, that paradoxically may be a sign of progress. After all, people are complaining about appropriate concerns instead of whining about, say, their workload. Although these "signs" may be encouraging and make us feel good, to be more certain about progress we need to have in place more rigorous methods of evaluation. Part Seven illustrates these more rigorous methods and also addresses issues about these methods.

We begin with Chapter Forty-Seven, by Beckhard and Lake (1971), which is based on a study conducted back in the 1960s. This report of team intervention, "Short- and Long-Range Effects of a Team Development Effort," is included in the present volume because it shows how to conduct a rigorous study of organization change and because of its uniqueness: a longitudinal study that covered a span of about four years. Such studies covering this amount of time are rare indeed. Beckhard and Lake's report describes a team management development intervention as a strategy for dealing with (1) an overly centralized decision-making structure and operation as well as (2) changes in the organization's external environment that were having a significant impact on the internal environment of the organization . Productivity improved, turnover and absenteeism decreased, and a new electronic data processing system was successfully introduced. The research showed that techniques considered to be organization development can indeed work.

The next chapter, by Golembiewski, Billingsley, and Yeager, was an award-winning article when published in 1976 and it is clearly just as relevant today as it was then. The authors distinguish among three types of change, which they label alpha, beta, and gamma, denoting levels of change from simple to complex. An alpha change is a difference, assessed before and after, that occurs along some constant dimension of perceived reality. If, for example, a comparative measure of, say, degree of tolerance for conflict among team members shows an increase in tolerance, we might conclude that whatever change was introduced worked. As we know, this type of before-and-after self-report is quite common.

But what if a decrease in tolerance for conflict occurred, or no change at all? Change may have happened nevertheless—what Golembiewski and his colleagues call a beta change. It may be that as a consequence of the change intervention team members recalibrated the dimension of perceived reality, that is, their *standard* for how to consider conflict change, thinking now that dealing with conflict is not as simple as they might have originally thought.

A gamma change involves a redefinition or reconceptualization of some organizational domain. This involves movement from one state of behaving and operating based on certain deeply held beliefs and values to another state. Culture change would be illustrative. Thus it is highly important that we be as clear as possible about exactly what we are measuring. It is not as simple or direct and straightforward as it may seem.

Although it is important to be as clear as possible about what we are measuring, or what the dependent variable needs to be, this decision is not easy. Theory may help with this kind of decision. The next chapter, "Explaining Development and Change in Organizations," by Van de Ven and Poole (1995), is included here for this possibility of helping with choice about what to measure. Can we understand the change effort best, for example, through a *life-cycle* lens, one of the four theories about organization change that Van de Ven and Poole explain? If life-cycle theory seems to explain a lot about our change effort, then considering the organization's history, age, and where it stands in its industry are key variables. An example of life-cycle theory is Greiner's "Evolution and Revolution as Organizations Grow" (1998); see www.jossey bass.com/go/burke. On the basis of this theory or model, what we may want to measure, for example, is the crisis of autonomy and whether delegation, perhaps a dependent variable, is working.

The other three theories that Van de Ven and Poole explain are (1) *teleological,* with the focus being purpose, goals, or some end state (having a mission statement would be integral to such a perspective); (2) *dialectical*, with a focus on conflicting values, outside forces having a serious impact on the organization, and competition being about domination and control; and (3) *evolutionary* theory, with the focus being on competition for scarce resources and change as an ongoing, evolving process. As might be expected, these theories are not discrete; there is overlap and interdependence. In fact, Van de Ven and Poole summarize sixteen such combinations.

In Chapter Fifty, Beer and Walton (1987) point to central issues about research on organization change. Their chapter is a comprehensive review of organization change and development and covers many topics other than issues of research. For our purposes here we will focus on their section regarding "problems in research on intervention methods," but the reader is encouraged to read the entire chapter; it covers the field of organization change and development quite thoroughly.

With respect to Beer and Walton's concerns about research on organization change (intervention methods), they highlight four major problems. First is the problem of causation. Most researchers rely on scientific methods and attempt to identify the effects of certain interventions, such as structure change or survey feedback. But these interventions affect only parts of an organization. They are nested within the larger system and are consequently affected by many other variables. Determining cause and effect is therefore very difficult if not impossible. Second, most research is a snapshot rather than a longitudinal perspective. In other words, the problem is one of determining how permanent a change might actually be. Third, most research about organization change attempts to be as precise as possible, yet obtaining meaning from and interpreting data are not precise. Moreover, quantitative methods are not helpful for understanding results that typically have multiple causes. Fourth, the research may not fit the needs of the users. Researchers are cautious and reluctant to generalize. Users want practical advice, not statements that begin with, "Well, it depends." Beer and Walton recommend "action science" in place of traditional science, that is, involving the users in the research, practicing self-corrective learning, and focusing on studies that occur over time rather than in a one-time snapshot fashion.

Yet traditional science need not be discarded; perhaps these methods can be expanded in new and creative ways. The next chapter in Part Seven, "A Complex-Systems Approach to Organizations," by Svyantek and Brown (2000), helps us deal with larger system issues when conducting organizational research. They rely on nonlinear ways of thinking about research and point out that organizational behavior can rarely be explained by traditional methods of analysis, that is, considering a system only in terms of its component parts. Explaining behavior in system terms requires understanding patterns of interconnections and that these patterns will vary. Measuring variables over time and three-dimensionally is more the way of the future if we can combine scientific methods with nonlinear system theory.

Comparatively new to the world of organization change is the field of organizational learning. If organizations have the capacity to learn, then they can change. By "comparatively new," we mean within the last thirty years, but the surge in this field occurred in the 1980s and 1990s. Pioneers in this field are Argyris and Schön. The chapter by them included in Part Seven is from their book about the field, *The Evolving Field of Organizational Learning II,* which was published in 1996. In the first chapter of their book, they address the question of whether organizations can and do learn, and they distinguish between a learning product (essentially the *content* of learning) and a learning process (essentially acquiring, processing, and storing information). After considerable elaboration of the original question and this product-process distinction, Argyris and Schön conclude that organizations do indeed learn through a process of organizational members' collectively acquiring information, interacting with one another while exchanging thoughts and ideas regarding the acquired information, and then acting together on some formulation if not reformulation of the information such that new behavior and ways of doing things emerge. Then, in the book chapter included in this volume, they expound on what they refer to as two branches of the field, namely "the learning organization" and "organizational learning." The former branch is more about practice and the latter is more academic. With respect to the practice branch, the learning organization, Argyris and Schön show association between this branch of the field and sociotechnical systems, organizational strategy, production, economic development, systems dynamics, human resources, and organizational culture. The second half of their chapter covers the scholarly literature of organizational learning and addresses questions of contradiction (e.g., is organizational learning a real phenomenon?), whether organizational learning is a meaningful notion and if it is always beneficial, and whether real-world organizations learn productively. They conclude that "The problems raised by the two branches of the literature are largely complementary: what one branch treats as centrally important, the other tends to ignore."

In summary, Part Seven stresses the importance of testing our long-held assumptions (Argyris and Schön), determining as rigorously as possible whether we are making any progress with our change interventions (Beckhard and Lake), and whether we are making these determinations correctly (the remainder of the chapters by Golembiewski and colleagues; Van de Ven and Poole; Beer and Walton; and Svyantek and Brown).

CHAPTER FORTY-SEVEN

Short- and Long-Range Effects of a Team Development Effort

Richard Beckhard
Dale G. Lake (1971)

O f the many planned, behavior-science-based improvement efforts in organizations, very few include any measurement of change. The measures that are available usually entail collecting data during or immediately after the "intervention" or program.

This chapter describes an attempt to create a team approach to management during a period of change from mechanized bookkeeping to electronic data processing in a large commercial bank.[1] During the course of this effort, a period of one year, "hard" and "soft" measures of changes were collected. Four years later, a similar set of measures were again collected, in a follow-up study. In essence, the follow-up study indicated that a large number of changes and improvements reported at the end of the first year continued over the succeeding three years.

An examination of the environment within which the change effort took place will precede a brief description of the effort. Next, an examination will be made of the findings of changes in the group undergoing the change effort, and the group's performance will be compared with two "control" groups or divisions engaged in similar work in the organization. Finally, there will be a summary of the follow-up study four years later and, again, a presentation of performance comparisons with the control groups.

BACKGROUND

Historically, the bank was managed in a benevolent, autocratic mode—low pay, good benefits, supervision of varied quality (with very direct supervision at the lower levels) and a class society with very limited communications.

The upper-level management of the organization felt that upgrading the quality of supervision at middle management levels would increase productivity, and introducing more modern systems would meet the changing demands. These efforts to introduce new methods were not working well due to a high degree of resistance among "old line" managers at all levels, but particularly in middle management.

The training management, on the other hand, believed that there was a need for a major change in the whole atmosphere of the organization—particularly in middle levels of supervision—if any significant improvement was to occur. The turnover rate was extremely high, and in the preceding few years the recruitment effort had slipped. The bank was able to recruit good men and women from the better colleges but recently had been losing them, at an alarming rate, after only the first few years. High-potential young people did not see the bank as an exciting place to work. There had also been an increasing number of resignations of effective middle managers.

The training people felt that if real improvement was to occur, an essential first condition was for the upper-level management to look at its own attitudes, style, and managerial behavior. They felt there would have to be a change in the attitudes and values at the "top" if anything significant were to occur in the "middle."

Over a period of two years, a number of strategies, directed toward changing the attitudes of the upper-level management, had been considered or tried by the change agents in the training department. First, there were discussions about initiating the planned changes with the upper-level managers. The response had been, "As we've told you, the problem is not with us; we know we've got difficulties in the organization or we wouldn't be after you to fix them. The problem is with the middle management—go and work with them."

The second strategy considered was to initiate an attitude survey, on the assumption that the data would make clear to the upper-level management that what was needed was change on their part. After discussing this strategy with outside consultants, the training people recognized that such a report might simply increase resistance and defensiveness.

A third strategy was to hold a meeting of the upper-level management with their counterparts in other organizations that had engaged in some successful planned-organizational improvement programs. Descriptions and favorable results of these efforts impressed the management of the bank and led the change agents to try a fourth strategy.

The fourth strategy was to expose the upper-level management, in a nonthreatening way, to some current thinking about organizational values, motivation, and effectiveness. Luncheons were arranged with leading thinkers in the field. The management's response to this effort was that these were interesting meetings and very informative, but the inputs were somewhat theoretical and not particularly applicable to the bank's situation.

Eighteen months after these attempts, a fifth strategy was suggested: a pilot project to see if significant difference could be made in the climate, operating effectiveness, and productivity of a small segment of the organization through a planned "intervention." This was to be a basis for considering larger efforts. Top management agreed to support this experiment and the total change effort began.

INTERVENTION STRATEGY

In the securities division of the organization there were two groups whose work was heavily independent: Mortgage Production and Methods. Relationships and work effectiveness were not satisfactory in these groups. The task of the methods specialists was to try to help Mortgage Production upgrade its work methods. As a part of a bankwide plan, much of the work currently handled through mechanized bookkeeping was going to be computerized. The Methods group had the specific task of getting the computer installed and operating in the Mortgage Production.

It was decided to engage in a one-year project with a team composed of the management of these two groups. The stated purposes were improving their operational effectiveness as a problem-solving unit and facilitating the introduction of the computer into Mortgage Production.

The team engaged in the pilot project was composed of nine managers from the Mortgage and three from the Methods group. We will call this group the "experimental team." The steps taken with the experimental team included preparatory work for everyone on the team before the first of three off-site meetings with the group.

As part of this preparation, each of the members of the team went to a sensitivity training laboratory. After this, the team met with the consultant for half a day. The consultant described the goals and the possible outcomes of the project and asked each member of the experimental group to submit an anonymous letter to him listing the obstacles to more effective operation of this team, of the environment around this team, and of the total bank. Then the consultant organized the information from the letters as a basis for initial analysis with the team. During the first weekend conference, the consultant began the meeting by reporting back a summary of the information from the letters. The group then discussed the list of problems, set priorities, and began to work on them. These problems included such items as:

- Style of the group's supervisor
- Relationships between a supervisor and his section heads

- Relationships between operations groups and methods specialists
- The status (perceived as being low) of this group compared to other groups in the bank
- Relationships between this group and bank management

As a result of individual exposure to the sensitivity training, a large number of real problems, and the *fact* of the meeting, there was a high commitment among members to confront the problems and to try to improve the state of affairs. Discussions were frank, open, and sometimes painful.

By the end of the weekend the group had decided:

- To continue meeting monthly at the bank (without a consultant)
- To create three task forces to work on some internal problems
- To have the supervisor of mortgage operations call a meeting of his two counterparts to establish an ongoing interdepartmental communications mechanism
- To contact the central personnel department for some help in rectifying poor personnel practices and procedures

Six months later, a second weekend conference was held with the consultant attending; in the interim, the team had met monthly and carried out most of their action plans. This conference with the consultant was planned by the team and included an agenda of priority problems that they believed required more time than was available in their monthly meetings. They worked on these problems and set action plans to be carried out during the following six months. In order to reduce the number of monthly meetings, a steering committee of three people was authorized to appoint task forces of "resources" from the group to work on specific problems.

The total group met again six months later with the consultant to review the year's work and to assess future needs. They decided that there was no further need for meetings for a year because work was being handled through the appropriate task forces. They also decided that there was a need for the group to meet as a whole with the administrative group "uptown," to develop ways of increasing collaboration and communication between the two organizations.

EVALUATING THE CHANGE EFFORT

The original evaluation design, created by Matthew B. Miles of Teachers College, Columbia University, had a number of unique features. First, after an initial meeting in which Miles agreed to do the evaluation, there was no further communication between the change agent, Beckhard, and Miles.

This arrangement was designed in order to negate any bias or inadvertent confirmation of expectancies that might result if the change agent and evaluator were in close communication. Second, Miles consistently employed multiple measurement techniques in order to increase confidence in the results. A number of components were used.

First, the members of the management team were interviewed, before and after the training, to collect data on operations and problems of the team as perceived by its members. Prior to the first off-site meeting, team members indicated that they preferred *not* to be interviewed as part of the study; hence, no "pre-intervention" interviews were held. A year later, however, they were very open to participating in the research (this itself may be regarded as an outcome of the project), and each team member was interviewed. These "post-intervention" interviews focused upon the nature of the changes that had taken place.

A second feature of the design involved interviews with managers from other parts of the bank who had occasion to give or receive work from the experimental group. These interviews provided an indication of how the other groups who formed the immediate environment of the management team reacted to its effectiveness. In addition, the head of the securities division, the intermediate manager above the team, was interviewed (before and after the intervention) about his perceptions of the team and its work.

In a third component of the study, team members' subordinates, primarily clerical-level personnel, were surveyed using a questionnaire that asked for their attitudes toward work, their morale, the perceived effectiveness of their sections, how much they interacted with others on the job, and their perceptions of the leadership behavior of their own section head. This instrument was administered before and after the activity to subordinates of the experimental team and in two control divisions.

A fourth part of the study involved the scrutiny of data already being collected by the firm as a regular part of operations. These data consisted of turnover, absenteeism, and productivity.

Many questions were left unanswered by the original design: How durable are the results of team training? What happens to the team when the outside consultant has withdrawn? Are the original experimental team members able to disseminate team management practices to their subordinates? Can a successful team development effort in one part of the organization be disseminated to higher levels of management throughout the bank?

Because such questions were left unanswered, the consultant, the personnel manager, and another researcher decided to repeat some of the measurement procedures of the original design. Four years after the team training activity, data were recollected through interviews with the team managers, questionnaires to their subordinates, and productivity measures.

Leavitt, in a 1965 study, noted that four major variables may interact to effect organizational change processes. The variables are called Task, People, Technology, and Structure. For Leavitt, the People, Technology, and Structural variables can also become change strategies, and each one developing its own cadre of specialists who utilize them to improve organizational Task performance. The data in this study show, quite conclusively, how interdependent each of the three change strategies is for an organizational development effort. These data demonstrate a team development effort (the People approach), altered work-flow procedures (the Structural approach), to make the transition from mechanized bookkeeping to electronic data processing (the Technological approach) smoother and more efficient.

DATA RESULTS

In the individual interviews with team members, there was almost unanimous agreement that prior to team development there had been cumbersome decision making, divisional protectiveness, lack of promotional opportunity, and poor communication. One team member describes these conditions: ''There used to be a need to protect your own division; whenever a new job came up the first impulse was to reply with some stock answer such as 'We don't have the equipment or men to handle that type of job.' 'It would increase our overall load too much,' etc.''

When asked to indicate what changes occurred during the year of team training, managers were quick to say that they could recall no instances of events, activities, or procedures that had changed for the worse. Positive changes included:

- Improved communication, for example, staff being more directly aware of new information needed by the line.
- More flexible structural arrangements were created by adding another division to head the management team.
- A personnel man was added.
- New promotion policies came into effect.
- There was enhanced self-direction and ability of the team to accept responsibility for coping with turnover, training, absenteeism, and orientation.
- There was increased motivation to produce, which was related to reduction of perceived unreasonable pressures from the uptown division of the bank.
- There was more capacity to accept and deal with the technological changes in the organization such as the switch to Electronic Data Processing.

Table 47.1. Amount and Sources of Change.

Respondent	No. of Changes	Approximate Distribution Attributed to		
		Source I Sr. Officers	Source II Team	Source III Self & Subs.
1	24	25%	70%	5
2	22	33	65	
3	22	15	85	
4	20	10	90	
5	19		80	10*
6	17	25	75	
7	17	20	80	
8	17	20	70	10
9	17		75	*
10	14		80	15*
11	13		90	5*
12	12		95	*
13	11	5	95	
14	11	15	80	5
15	10		90	5*
	246			
	16.4			

*In arriving at this distribution a change was tabulated only when it was described and an example was given. In scoring the interview schdule this is tabulated as one change.

The number and source of the changes described by the fifteen team managers are displayed in Table 47.1.

PRODUCTION

After the intervention, the managers reported that they felt personally more productive because they were able to control their own workflow. For instance, four of those interviewed reported that prior to the team training, whenever an important new job came along, they were advised by their supervisor, "You had better do this job yourself rather than trust it to one of your clerks." Thus, much of their time was spent doing work that their subordinates were competent to do. Following team development, three of the four respondents reported positively. A sample: "I have more time for planning now; procedural write-ups used to lag behind schedule, now they are ahead of time. I have more time because my assistants do much more. I do more administrative work now and am less involved in immediate problems of operations."

Data from subordinates of the team members demonstrate impact on perceptions that have been shown to be related to changes in productivity. In the questionnaire, subordinates were asked to indicate how closely their superior (one of the team members) watched their work. In comparing subordinates of team members to subordinates from the control division, we find that team members' subordinates indicated they were watched less closely. Also, positive differences were found on two items between subordinates of team members and control: "He has reasonable expectations about amount of work" and "He explains reasoning behind changes in methods."

However, it must be concluded that results from subordinates are not as clear as the manager's own attitude shifts, or other data on productivity to be discussed subsequently.

Four managers immediately above the management positions of the persons involved in team training also were interviewed. They also perceived differences in productivity of the team managers. One felt that the improved ability to cope with pressure resulted from better cooperation between Mortgage Production and Mechanized Books (two divisions that were represented in the team). Another mentioned that he had not had to intervene at all during the team development year on behalf of his subordinates in order to obtain needed services. Previously, this was a common occurrence. All four noticed an increased tendency for Mortgage Production to take a more universal view of problems than they had before. One manager reported, "They no longer try to pin blame on someone. They try to do what is best for all."

Finally, before turning to the actual data on productivity, it should be noted that all of the above *perceptions* were reported to researchers prior to the existence of actual data on productivity.

Independently of the other research activities, the work measurement division of the bank was routinely collecting productivity data on the experimental division (Mortgage Production and two comparable divisions, Sequential Security and Housing Investment). The results are described in Figure 47.1.

The work measurement staff noted that in comparing the three divisions the following should be pointed out:

1. The Sequential Security work load is fairly consistent and its effectiveness depends on the number of people in the section over which management has no control. Overall the productivity is constant for the year.

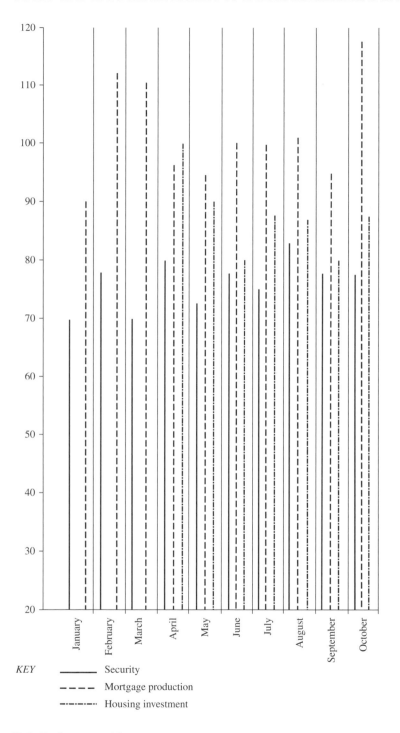

Figure 47.1. Performance Measurement.

2. Housing Investment work load varied during this period, yet the hours applied to measure work remained constant, indicating no effort to increase the effectiveness. On a yearly basis the effectiveness of this division is decreasing.

3. Mortgage Production demonstrated an increase in effectiveness, which probably can be traced to the organization improvement program. The officers became more aware of the needs for establishment of control over the work flow, which resulted in greater productivity.

TURNOVER AND ABSENTEEISM

There are additional data on absenteeism and turnover that support and influence the data just reported on productivity. Although the ultimate success of the management team training program could quite justifiably be judged by whether routine measurements of variables such as productivity, turnover, or absenteeism showed improvement, certain assumptions are involved in such a decision: (1) that the variables involved are meaningful ones as shown on *a priori* or empirical bases; (2) that the measure made are valid ones; (3) that the variables are subject to control by management during the one year period of the study; and (4) that other concomitant variables, such as morale, attitudes toward work, and perceptions of leadership, do not show a net decrease "at the expense" of changes found in these areas (the "short-run," "long-run" problems).

In Table 47.2, comparisons show that although Mortgage Production turnover was considerably higher than that in the two control departments and the bank as a whole in 1963, the rate was reduced sharply by the end of 1964, bringing it nearly into line with the bankwide rate. Meanwhile, turnover (both measures) was increasing in Sequential Security and in Housing Investment and Advisory Operation (total measure) and indeed in the bank as a whole. The relative percentage increase or decrease over the 1963 base shows this quite clearly. In general, then, Mortgage Production was bucking a bankwide trend toward increased turnover. It may be argued, of course, that turnover reduction is easier when higher rates of turnover are present. This should probably be considered in assessing these differences.

As of the end of the third quarter of 1963 (beginning of the effort), Mortgage Production had more days lost per individual and a higher percentage of absenteeism than the control divisions. However, by the end of 1964 (end of planned intervention), this picture showed a striking difference: Mortgage Production was lowest in days lost, and in percentage of absenteeism. The relative change (1963–1964 differences expressed as a percentage increase or decrease over the 1963 base) show this quite sharply: Mortgage Production showed clear

Table 47.2. Turnover Statistics.

	12/31/63 Controllable Rate	12/31/63 Total t/o Rate	9/30/64	9/30/64 Controllable Rate	9/30/64 Total t/o Rate Controllable (Percent)	1963–1964 Improvement Total (Percent)
Mortgage Production	33.83	39.80	29.05	31.96	14.1	19.6
Housing Investment and Advisory Operation	19.11	22.59	15.55	23.84	18.6	−5.5
Sequential Security	16.13	20.34	26.72	33.18	−65.8	62.5
Total Bank	21.35	26.30	25.36	29.70	−18.8	−13.2

(Data supplied December 22, 1964)

improvement, while Sequential Security stayed fairly steady and Housing Investment and Advisory Operation dropped (Table 47.3).

Having examined the "hard" data of productivity, turnover, and absenteeism, it is now important to look at those changes that preceded and help to cause these results.

COMMUNICATION

Interview of the team managers revealed that hostility, fear, distrust, and a lack of openness distorted the flow of communication prior to the team development effort. For instance, one division manager reported, "Whenever I used to receive a request for work, I first really had to decide whether my division should really be doing this job or whether we were just being a scapegoat for the division requesting the work. It hurts your business when you question whether a request is valid or not."

Team training led to an appreciation of how difficult communication is and what can be done to improve it. This is revealed in a comment from a team member: "Our personal relations with the methods division have really improved. The actual amount of information being passed back and forth is fantastic. So our study of communications problems in the team has helped immensely."

Table 47.3. Illness Absenteeism.

	9/30/63 Total					9/30/64 Total					1963–64 Improvement (Percent)	
	N	Days Available	Days Absent	Average Days Absent*	Percent Absent	N	Days Available	Days Absent	Average Days Absent**	Percent Absent**	In Average Days Absent	In Percent Absent
Merger Production	101	6.363	146	1.45	2.29	99	6.534	107	1.08	1.64	25.5	28.3
Housing Investment and Advisory Operation	114	7.182	138	1.21	1.92	130	8.580	203	1.56	2.36	28.9	−22.9
Sequential Security	139	8.757	182	1.31	2.08	145	9.570	188	1.30	1.96	0.8	5.8

*This ratio represents the average days lost per individual, and is arrived at by dividing the total days absent by the number of individuals in the department.

**This percentage of absenteeism is arrived at by dividing the number of days absent by the number of available work days in the quarter.

The top manager in the experimental team commented:

> I actually see fewer people now than before the team was begun, but I know they are more free to come to see me now. I now go out of my way to explain the background of my decision; before I took it for granted that they would know.

> At the same time there is more likelihood of their accepting a directive at face value now, which I guess indicates that they trust me more.

Others expressed feelings of being able to influence others and be influenced themselves.

> Now we go to the other division staff directly and get their views, which speeds up our work-flow. There was a time when I felt no one else knew my work well enough to help.

> It used to be that the only time you heard from above around here was when you were getting hell. Now he seeks me out on work and personnel decisions and when I make a request for a salary increase it takes, or I know why.

Feedback on work performance, especially deficient work performance, was an important area for improving communications.

> When I first started with my unit heads I had difficulty being critical of them. I had to work myself up into a state of anger before I could really tell them that they had done a poor job. The result was that they usually thought that I was mad at them and not their work. In the team I learned that when someone else criticized me they didn't do it to punish—they did it to be helpful. Now I have learned to criticize my subordinates without getting angry which helps them to correct their mistakes and improve their own work. In the long run this has helped me because their own performances are interdependent with my own.

Furthermore, the team mangers indicated that there was much more sharing of each other's special resources across the division involved and there was, generally, wider participation in decision making.

> Decisions used to be made in the central office; I gave all supervisors back their responsibility to make decisions. Now, all they do is appraise [sic] me of the decision unless it's a policy decision.

> Now, when I make a decision the first thing I do is consider who will be involved in carrying out the decision and I call them in for a discussion of the decision.

> Now I can go to any division within the department for help in making a work decision. Previously, there might have been a working problem you couldn't discuss with another supervisor.

> It used to be that meetings were taboo; now they are considered advantageous.

Those immediately above the managers involved were also encouraged by the team to work on improving communication. As one vice-president stated,

"Mortgage Production feels that communication could be better. I must go along with them. We don't forewarn them fast enough. We see that now."

In comparing the subordinates of the experimental team with those in a comparison or control division, it was found that experimental group employees had more contact with peers in their own sections in both years than control group employees; control group people had more contact than experimental with people outside their sections. Although there was not much change in these items in either group, the general tendency was toward more increase in contact with those outside the sections in the experimental group than in the control group. This observation supports data from the independently conducted higher management interviews. They reported improvement in the Mortgage Production team communication with them.

Turning now to amount of interaction with one's own section head, we find (Table 47.4) that in both 1963 and 1964 employees in the control group conferred more frequently with their section heads than did employees in the experimental group. But between 1963 and 1964, the percentage of control group employees who spoke to their section heads a few times a week or more moved from 76 percent to 66 percent, a net drop of 10 percentage points. At the same time, in the experimental group, the percentage in this category increased from 67 percent to 74 percent, 7 percentage points. The frequency of "once a week or less" shows it decreases for experimental group section heads for the control group. Thus, it seems clear that experimental group section heads were perceived as increasing their contact with employees, while perceived contact with control group section heads decreased. The reader is reminded that not

Table 47.4. Frequency with Which Employees Confer with Section Head, by Year and by Experimental and Control Groups.

	Experimental Group			Control Group		
	1963 %	1964 %	Differences (Points)	1963 %	1964 %	Differences (Points)
Frequency of content						
More than once a day	23	24	1	40	34	−6
About once a day	14	15	1	18	10	−8
A few times a week	30	35	5	18	22	4
Once a week or less	32	26	−6	24	33	9
N equals	(90)	(105)		(147)	(164)	
No answer				(3)	(1)	

Table 47.5. Employees' Preferred Change in Frequency of Conferring with Section Head, by Experimental and Control Group, 1963 and 1964.

	Experimental Group			Control Group		
	1963 %	1964 %	Differences (Points)	1963 %	1964 %	Differences (Points)
Employees' preferences						
Should confer more	20	16	−4	16	23	7
Should confer same as now	77	83	−2	83	75	−8
Should confer less	3	1	−2	1	2	1
N equals	(90)	(105)		(148)	(164)	
No answer				(4)	(3)	

only did experimental group contact improve, but employees also felt their work was less pressured and less closely supervised; this suggests that the contact was more egalitarian.

Supporting evidence for increased upward contact in the experimental group and decreased contact for control group is shown in Table 47.5. The percentage of control group employees who feel that they should confer with their section heads more frequently increased between 1963 and 1964 from 16 percent to 23 percent, while during this period the percentage of experimental group employees who felt the same way decreased from 20 percent to 16 percent. Thus not only has contact increased, but actual and ideal contact were getting closer together in the experimental group and farther apart among controls.

Even a cautious interpretation of the data from subordinates of the team managers shows a perception of increased upward influence because these subordinates' ratings improved markedly on such items as "His evaluation carries weight in getting promotions," "He would go to bat for me," and "He wants me to come to him with work complaints" (compared with their prescores and with the control division postscores on these same items).

STRUCTURAL AND TECHNOLOGICAL

The following work-flow arrangements were described by the team, subsequent to their participation in the development effort:

Electronic Data Processing was installed and used to replace certain mechanical bookkeeping procedures.

Parts of two divisions were combined so that any given account could be handled from beginning to end by a single working unit.

Promotion policies were enlarged and several team members were promoted during the year. For instance, one manager reports, ''We created three subgroups within my unit; each unit has a supervisor; this permits more advancement within the unit and pushes responsibility for training down the line.''

''Linking-pin'' positions were created of people who knew what the demands in two different divisions were. These new positions help to facilitate the progress of accounts through complex operations involving their divisions.

The team also assumed the additional function of long-range planning and goal setting. During its first year after the planned improvement effort was initiated, it focused effort on reorganization, personnel orientation and training, developing operational effectiveness, and expanding the team concept.

Plans were made to change the image that was implicit in their title (''production''). That title seemed to connote the assembly line of an industrial plant. They desired an image that was congruent with their own, which suggested that the work requires creativity and intellectual skill.

In the area of personnel and training, the team planned to develop closer ties with the staff service personnel division in order to facilitate the flow of information, including opportunities to test their understanding of feedback and to share their responses to feedback. The team planned to create additional opportunities for promotion within the division, as well as providing more extensive orientation to the goals of the bank for new employees, and reviewing turnover, salary administration, absenteeism, hiring, and firing.

Operationally, the team hoped to develop better communication with its sister divisions, the Administration and Investment branches, and also planned to make changeover to electronic data processing as smooth and as effective as possible. It planned to develop ways of confronting operating problems as a team whenever two or more divisions were involved. They expected this to increase the efficient use of funds. Also, they hoped to provide for their efficient functioning by making provisions for agenda development, subcommittee work, and the development of procedures for formalizing its own policies.

Finally, the team wanted to initiate the team concept of management development throughout the bank (keeping in mind the value of mixing levels of supervision in any particular team), to increase its self-development and push this downward to subordinates, and to develop the norm whereby each senior person has trained someone who could replace him or her upon very short notice.

STABILITY OF THE CHANGE EFFORT

The change efforts since 1964 are as far-reaching as those reported above. Two other related groups in the trust division have begun similar programs of team development, and from all three groups (these two and the original team) a permanent management team for coordination purposes was formed. A similar team was developed at the section manager level (the next lower managerial level).

New communications mechanisms link the organization, including closed circuit television for weekly joint conferences (the divisions "live" at different locations in the same city). The original group and one of the others held a joint meeting to resolve a number of relationship problems that had emerged from the two individual team development programs. These two groups then met with representatives of the third group to resolve additional relationships and procedural problems. New relationships were established between this entire division and the corporate staff of the bank, particularly with the personnel department.

One year after the end of the experiment, the top thirty managers in the organization went to a four-day workshop. They examined their own functioning and its effects on the total bank effort. Outputs of that top management meeting included a change in the recruitment structure, the development of a management trainee position, some changes in the reward system for young men, and the appointment of task forces to examine the entire reward system. Bankwide management training and development efforts were started. Today there is a consulting group of several applied behavioral scientists working with various units in the bank, and offsite team development meetings of operating units are a regular part of the operating method.

A description of the stability of this project in team management is not complete without collecting data after any "halo" effects have had a chance to wear off. For this reason, in 1968, four years after the original intervention, one of the authors, Lake, and the project manager of the first research effort, with the assistance of the director of personnel, conducted follow-up interviews with the team managers, collected data from subordinates, and data on turnover absenteeism, and productivity, experimental, and control divisions.

Before reviewing these additional data, some *caveats* are in order. First, although it would have been possible to compute exact statistical tests of difference between subordinates' sources on a questionnaire in 1963, 1964, and 1968, and to present the data according to "significant" differences, a closer examination suggested this to be an inappropriate practice. The items requesting subordinates' perceptions of the team manager are most clearly interpreted if they are separated by managers and taken from only those subordinates who filled out the questionnaire on all three occasions. Such a procedure seemed inappropriate since we were interested in impact on the overall department, not in differences between managers. Presenting aggregate data should actually work against "hoped for" directions because differences will tend to balance out.

Second, comparison with the original control group is certainly inappropriate as it has undergone personnel changes since 1964 as well. Finally, in a strictly technical sense, the 1968 results cannot be described as *caused* by the original team training. Instead, we relied upon the managers to describe the state of the department in 1968 and make any associations they thought appropriate to the original team training.

LONG-TERM RESULTS

An early goal of the team was to improve the promotion policies within the department. Managers reported that the very first promotions occurred during the team-training year, in 1964. Since then, thirteen of the original sixteen team members have been promoted, some more than once. Two members of the team hold top positions in the department and although they could not be promoted they were advanced in rank. The sixteenth member of the team left the bank.

Team management today means something quite different from its original conception in 1963. The original team, a heterogeneous group representing a cross-section of local divisions, seldom meets more than once or twice a year. Now, teams are *not* composed of members from different divisions but are homogeneous. For instance, each manager interviewed reported being a member of at least three different working teams within a division, but frequently served as a liaison for his team with teams in other divisions.

Another development of the team concept has been to create interdepartmental teams (at all levels of management) to work on specific interface problems. When the problems are resolved, the teams are dissolved. These interdepartmental teams usually use an outside consultant initially, but subsequent work is supported by specially trained personnel staff from within the bank.

In general, the managers report that teams are much more problem-oriented. They are also more short-lived. One manager described what appears to be the norm of the department: "People believe in getting together when they have problems around here now, and that *is* different."

All managers report that they have tried to push the team concept downwards. If this were so, one would expect that their subordinates would see them as egalitarian, open to influence, and able to influence others. The

Table 47.6. Subordinates' Perception of Team Managers in 1968 (N = 130).

	Extremely Well	Very Well	Moderately Well	Not Very Well	Not Well at All
25. He has reasonable expectations about the amount of work I should do	40%	32%	19%	5%	4%
26. He isn't interested in helping me get ahead in the company	11	8	12	21	48
28. He wants me to come to him if I have a complaint about my work	49	27	11	6	7
30. He doesn't want to give a new employee as much help as he needs to learn	10	7	17	25	41
32. He treats me as a person rather than just someone to get the job done	40	32	12	9	7
34. When I have a new job to do, he explains it carefully in detail	39	21	20	10	10
36. His evaluation of how his employees do their jobs carries a lot of weight in getting them promotions	36	36	19	3	6
39. If I had an idea of how to change things for the better, he would not want to hear about it	9	9	9	20	53

data in Table 47.6 from subordinates support these predictions. It shows quite clearly that subordinates perceive they are able to influence their supervisors, and that their supervisors are also able to influence upward (Item 36).

Table 47.7. Turnover Statistics.

	Controllable Rate			Total Rate		
	12/63	12/64	12/68	12/63	9/64	12/68
Mortgage Production (experimental)	33.83	19.05	38.79	39.80	31.96	40.61
Housing Investment and Advisory Operations	19.11	15.55	36.08	22.59	23.84	38.66
Sequential Securities (operations)	16.13	26.72	54.86	20.34	33.18	54.86
Total Bank	21.35	25.36	45.90	26.30	29.79	51.04

Most of the managers interviewed expressed concern regarding the current state of turnover. As one manager stated, "It is remarkable that we are able to maintain any people within the department because of our being invaded by the brokers on 'The Street'; they buy off our systems analysts as fast as we can train them." Their concern is appropriate because turnover has increased since 1964 (see Table 47.7). However, it should be noted that Mortgage Production is *well below* the total bank turnover rate (even though the Mortgage Production rate is somewhat inflated because of the increased demand for systems analysts throughout the industry).

Productivity has remained high. Work measurement statistics shown in Table 47.8 continue to show outstanding performance by Mortgage Production.

A number of the managers interviewed thought that absenteeism would increase during the last year because the entire area of the country had been hit with debilitating viruses. Again their perceptions were accurate as seen in Table 47.9 (see also Table 47.3).

Finally, in the 1968 interviews, all managers reported that it was no longer necessary to send persons to sensitivity training prior do doing effective work in teams. The reasons were not entirely clear, although it seems evident that

Table 47.8. Productivity Index 12/31/68.

	Standard Productivity Index*
Mortgage Production	94.5%**
Housing Investment and Adv. Oper.	71.8%
Sequential Security	85.2%
Install. Loan Collections	87.3%

* As of first quarter 3/31/69

** Note that the index has been revised so that it is not possible to go over 100% as it was in 1964.

Table 47.9. Illness Absenteeism Compared for Three Measurement Periods.

	9/30/63 Average Days Absent	N	9/30/64 Average Days Absent	N	12/31/68 Average Days Absent	N
Mortgage Production	1.45	101	1.08	99	2.57	183
Housing Investments and Advisory Operations	1.21	114	1.56	130	2.47	124
Sequential Security	1.31	139	1.30	145	3.09	102

the entire department was characterized as being more open, more willing to take the risks, more authentic and more able to engage in interpersonal confrontations. It would seem that the values learned in sensitivity training have become the department norms.

CONCLUSION

This report describes team management development as a strategy for coping with overly centralized decision making and changes in the external environment that require changing the internal environment. It illustrates how a specific pilot intervention, such as team development, can be a way of spreading an organizational development effort to all of management within the organization. This effort is eased by good documentation that is made public.

This team effort development became a vehicle for facilitating (1) changes in work-flow arrangements such as combining persons from more than one division in order to provide continuity for the processing of major accounts, (2) the efforts to improve productivity and at the same time reduce turnover and absenteeism, and (3) the introduction of electronic data processing.

In addition the team development activities resulted directly in more flexible decision making, increases in influence below and above the team, an enhanced sense of self-direction for the managers involved, and concern for the entire bank's problems.

Note

1. The research was conducted by Matthew B. Miles, Teachers College, Columbia.

CHAPTER FORTY-EIGHT

Measuring Change and Persistence in Human Affairs

Types of Change Generated by OD Designs

Robert T. Golembiewski
Keith Billingsley
Samuel Yeager (1976)

There is a truism about applied research that an inadequate concept of change leads to diminished or misguided applied research. Hence this chapter urges distinguishing kinds of change, distinctions that are suggested by experience and also are supported with evidence generated by exotic statistical and computational techniques in which we have been engaged. An immediate payoff of making such distinctions is more definite reliance on existing research findings, whose interpretation is necessarily related to their underlying concept of change. More central still, the goal is to facilitate the design and evaluation of efforts to improve the human condition and the quality of life, especially in organizations.

Initially, conceptual clarification of "change" will show that at least three kinds seem distinguishable. Later, data from a study of a "successful" flexitime intervention will be used to test these conceptual clarifications. Detailed statistical analysis will support the broad position that a unitary concept of change is inappropriate and may be seriously misleading.

By extending the boundaries of the known, applied research can contribute to the further development of scientific knowledge, as well as fulfilling its stated goal of bettering the human condition. But applied research contributes in both senses only to the degree that one can ascertain whether a particular intervention has "succeeded" or "failed." That knowledge not only requires measuring the "quantity" of change but especially demands confidence in the concept of change that underlies the measurement.

Our focus here is on what is measured in experimental designs, such as those in organization development (OD), and especially in those designs placing heavy reliance on self-reports. More specifically, this paper deals with the paradox underlying a dilemma emphasized by Bereiter, who asks:

> When scores on a test are observed to change, how can one tell whether it is the persons who have changed or the tests? If the correlation between pretest and posttest is reasonably high, we are inclined to ascribe change scores to changes in the individuals. But if the correlation is low, or if the pattern of correlations with other variables is different on two occasions, we may suspect that the test does not measure the same thing on the two occasions. Once it is allowed that the pretest and posttest measure different things, it becomes embarrassing to talk about change. There seems no longer any answer to the question, change *on what*? [1963, p. 11].

By discussing change in experimental (OD) contexts—via the application of modern technologies for data processing and analysis—this chapter accepts the challenge of Bereiter's central question and seeks to provide perspective on the broad issues of persistence and change in human affairs.

Change on what? Change for what? Our focus has serious implications for the OD practitioner, who cannot avoid these questions. Sometimes such value-laden questions get short shrift in technically oriented treatments or as a result of self-interest, as Ross (1971) reminds us forcefully. Yet the practitioner today recognizes that OD interventions are value-loaded (Tannenbaum & Davis, 1970; Golembiewski, 1972, esp. pp. 59–110). As such, OD interventions are far less involved with raising the level of indicators of some relatively stable system than with seeking to change basic concepts of the quality of organizational life that should and can exist.

SOME DISTINCTIONS BETWEEN TYPES OF CHANGE

Our point of entry to confronting the central, indeed crucial, complexities of change will be conceptual. After defining the three types of change in summary fashion, we shall further distinguish them by examples.

> ALPHA CHANGE involves a variation in the level of some existential state, given a constantly calibrated measuring instrument related to a constant conceptual domain.

> BETA CHANGE involves a variation in the level of some existential state, complicated by the fact that some intervals of the measurement continuum associated with a constant conceptual domain have been recalibrated.

> GAMMA CHANGE involves a redefinition or reconceptualization of some domain, a major change in the perspective or frame of reference within which

phenomena are perceived and classified, in what is taken to be relevant in some slice of reality.

Alpha Change

Most OD designs seem to recognize only alpha changes, measured by self-reports, using pretest/posttest designs, with or without comparison groups. Symbolically, such designs may be described as

$$O1 \ X \ O2$$

where O = observation and X = experimentation intervention. That is, the usual design selects some frame of reference or criterion, with ''change'' being estimated by fluctuations in the levels of self-reports triggered by the intervention. Alpha changes, then, are conceived as occurring along *relatively stable dimensions of reality* that are defined in terms of discrete and constant intervals. Note that alpha changes can be nonrandom, as established by some test of statistical significance, or they can be random only. And alpha changes may be very large or very small, or anywhere in between. The only requirement is that alpha change occur *within a relatively fixed system or state*, defined in terms of stable dimensions of reality as estimated by a measurement continuum whose intervals are relatively constant.

A parent taking a baby to the shoe store is interested in alpha change. The frame of reference is growth in baby's feet between this visit and the preceding one. The crucial measurement of change occurs within a relatively fixed system of stable dimensions of reality (our conventional concepts of ''length'' and ''width'') as defined by indicators whose intervals are more or less constant (the calibrated marks on the measuring rod against which the baby's foot is compared).

Beta Change

Beta changes involve the recalibration of the intervals used to measure some stable dimension of psychological space, as in preintervention versus postintervention responses. This contrasts with alpha changes, which are measured along more or less invariant intervals tapping a stable dimension of reality.

If beta change had occurred, a parent could not know how much a child's feet had grown between visits to the shoe store. It would not be meaningful to compare the two measurements because the intervals on the measuring rod had somehow changed.

A beta change on a rod for measuring feet is not very likely, of course, although such rods do expand and contract some. Social measuring rods can ''expand'' and ''contract'' significantly, however, even as their conceptual definition remains the same. That is, beta changes imply potentially variable responses to shifting indicators of a stable dimension of reality. Note that the reference here is to a phenomenon beyond test-retest reliability, for change in the measuring intervals is often *an intended effect of an OD intervention*, as contrasted with some defect of the measuring instrument. That is to say, OD efforts indeed can change the very measuring instrument being used to measure the change.

Oversimplifying, perhaps, instruments soliciting self-reports are more rubber yardsticks than they are equivalents of the "standard foot" in the Bureau of Standards. That is, self-reports are rooted in socioemotional or cultural definitions, or in an individual's knowledge-experiences, which provide anchoring points to rate "the degree of participation in decision making," for example. OD efforts typically can both have an impact on such cultural definitions and significantly modify or enlarge an individual's knowledge or experiences. In this sense, applying the same instrument before and after a successful OD intervention—while assuming that the intervals along which self-reports are made are the same or very similar—may be rather like applying a given survey research instrument to several different cultures, as conventionally understood. Any resulting data must be compared and analyzed very carefully, if at all (Ward, 1974, esp. p. 199).

It may seem like splitting hairs to some to distinguish beta change from alpha, because both deal only with changes in condition within a relatively stable state. But beta change does point up a significant and generic problem in interpreting behavioral research, as an extended illustration will establish. Consider the two sets of descriptions of an organization unit in Figure 48.1, before (designated Now I) and after (Now II) an OD intervention.[1] In a first

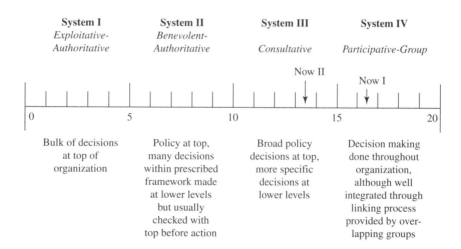

Figure 48.1. Pre- and Posttest Means on a Representative Item from Likert's Profile of Organizational Characteristics.

hypothetical case, assume that only alpha change has occurred. Even here, the figure does not support a single or simple conclusion. The Now II score is consistent with an OD "failure" in one sense, as well as with a "success" in another. The OD intervention may be said to be a failure because Now II is lower than Now I, and OD interventions should induce changes toward System IV. Or the OD intervention can be taken to be *successful* because the respondents at Now II have a more realistic view of how things really are, a firmer descriptive base for subsequent ameliorative action.

Matters get more complicated if the possibility of beta change is acknowledged. Consider employees whose pattern of responses following an OD intervention was like that in Figure 48.1 (Golembiewski & Carrigan, 1973). Things in their organization units were not worse than before the intervention, respondents reported in interviews supplementing their questionnaire responses; in fact, things had substantially improved. In effect, the OD experience may have encouraged respondents to recalibrate Likert's intervals after the intervention in at least two ways: (1) respondents made different estimates of reality, given a clearer perception of what exists; and (2) respondents changed their intervals for measuring value-loaded terms in the instrument, such as "throughout the organization," "well-integrated," and "overlapping."

We hypothesize that the OD experience had "lengthened" the psychological space between some intervals of the Likert instrument, while preserving the essential conceptual content of Likert's "managerial systems." The OD program had, in effect, shown respondents how much "integration" there was and could be, and they recalibrated the System III and IV portions of Likert's scale. One respondent added: "I don't need to be educated about what a '3' score is! I've seen that often enough." Likert's intervals were in part "rubber yardsticks," subject to expansion and contraction as personal and group standards were affected by the OD intervention. Consequently, even though respondents verbally report "more participation" at Now II, their postintervention scores are lower than for Now I. The content of the "participative group" interval had stretched "faster" or "further" than actual participation had increased, as it were. For the technical development of a similar notion, see McGee's (1966) emphasis on "elastic distances" in multidimensional scaling.

Presumably, if the OD intervention had involved a month in an equivalent of Auschwitz, respondents would have recalibrated the System I portion of the Likert Profile.

There are numerous other issues associated with the "interval problem" highlighted by beta change. For example, the "response instability" that has sometimes been taken to signal a "nonattitude" in political research (Converse, 1970; Iyengar, 1973) could in fact reflect a beta change. The difference is critical: "nonattitudes" can be treated cavalierly as opinionative ephemera, but a beta change, in contrast, may signal an important change in the intervals a rater uses to differentiate a given psychological domain. Other significant issues (Pepper & Prytulak, 1974) also seem relatable to beta effects.

Gamma Change

Gamma change is conceived as a quantum shift in ways of conceptualizing salient dimensions of reality. This totally differentiates it from beta change, which refers only to variation in the intervals measuring a relatively stable dimension of reality.

This third kind of change involves the basic *redefinition of the relevant psychological space* as a consequence of an OD intervention. In sum, gamma change is "big bang" change. It refers to a change from one state to another, as contrasted with a change of degree or condition within a given state. Thus "freedom" for blacks in 1960 may have been defined, in part, as not having to ride in the back of the bus. By 1970, such "freedom" seems to have expanded to include success at lowering bus fares, increasing the number of black drivers, and having an impact on the design of urban mass-transit systems. Measuring gamma change is extraordinarily difficult since the preintervention instrument is no longer appropriate; the postintervention response is "off the scale."

Thus, if gamma changes occur as the result of an OD program, clearly interpretations of results are chancy in the extreme, and research takes on an Alice-in-Wonderland quality. For example, issues of instrument validity become enormously complicated when phrased in these terms: valid for measuring which kind of change?

Bowers's (1973) study of fourteen thousand respondents in twenty-three organizations helps illustrate the importance of distinguishing gamma from beta and alpha change. Among other tendencies, Bowers reports that survey feedback interventions were associated with "statistically significant improvement on a majority of measures" based on The Survey of Organizations Questionnaire (TSOQ), while laboratory training interventions were "associated with declines" on similar measures (p. 21). In the absence of knowledge about the distribution of types of change, however, it is not possible to conclude whether Bowers's results demonstrate the greater potency of survey feedback. Alternatively, survey feedback may have triggered alpha changes, which TSOQ picked up, while laboratory training could have induced beta changes or gamma changes, which TSOQ did not pick up. This interpretation is consistent with the different "depths of intervention" associated with survey feedback and laboratory training, respectively. Moreover, Bowers's instrument does seem more sensitive to alpha changes, as all such instruments must be. Relatedly—although this need not be the case—TSOQ apparently was based on factorial studies of organizational samples (Taylor & Bowers, 1967) other than those in the 1973 study. It is not known to what degree the factorial solutions that might be obtained from this 1973 sample would be congruent with the 1967 baseline solutions. Nor is it known what degree of congruence exists between factorial solutions of pretest versus posttest responses to TSOQ in the 1973 sample, which could provide a clue about the incidence of beta changes or gamma changes.

Along with other points of concern (Torbert, 1973), then, interpretation of Bowers's results is made problematic by the lack of knowledge as to the kinds of change involved. In the case of both survey research and laboratory training interventions, that knowledge is profoundly significant in interpreting Bowers's results. Other research instruments reflect the same problem.

Typical descriptions of OD that seek to induce a new "social order" or "culture" into an organization convince us that gamma changes are the prime intended consequences of OD interventions. They imply not only recalibration of intervals but also new content for concepts describing the quality of organization life. Yet gamma changes are also likely to be masked by common measuring instruments whose conceptualization and operationalization are typically rooted in concepts of alpha change.

Since gamma changes may be thought of as reflecting fundamental changes in conceptualizations/expectations, as a basic redefinition of the content of the referents tapped by most available measures of organization and individual processes they severely complicate the interpretation of the results of OD efforts.

A COUSINLY CONCEPT FROM COUNSELING

An added perspective on the usefulness of distinguishing kinds of change is provided by a recent distillation of the literature on counseling. When Watzlawick, Weakland, and Fisch (1974, esp. pp. 10–11) distinguish "first-order" change from "second-order" change, they explain that the former "occurs within a given system which itself remains unchanged," while the latter "changes the system itself." A nightmare illustrates their distinction: "A person having a nightmare can do many things in his dream—run, hide, fight, scream, jump off a cliff, etc.—but no change from any one of these behaviors to another would ever terminate the nightmare."

These many changes within the system are *first-order changes*—comparable to our alpha changes described above. The authors continue: "The one way *out of* a dream involves a change from dreaming to waking . . . a change to an altogether different state."

This illustrates second-order change, which seems to us much like gamma change. The authors could easily have defined a third type, an analog of beta change: via dream analysis, a person might learn that recurring dreams are more revealing than scary. Having thus expanded the nonscary or less-scary intervals of a personal rating scale, an individual might stay in the dream state yet change her reaction to it. This is the sense of beta change.

We agree that Watzlawick et al.'s (1974) distinction between two orders of change is significant, perhaps even momentous. They note (pp. 27–28) that failure to distinguish between the two types of change can cause the "most perplexing, paradoxical consequences," as in "some of the tragicomic controversies between experimental psychologists and psychiatrists." Many of these controversies could be avoided by active recognition that when experimental psychologists "talk about change, they usually mean first-order change . . . while psychiatrists, though not often aware of this, are predominantly concerned with second-order change." The difference is great. The former deals with a change in condition; the latter deals with a change in state or, perhaps, with a "change of change."

ANALOGIES FROM THE SEVERAL SCIENCES

Other considerations also encourage the search for beta and especially gamma effects. First, and very briefly, a substantial feature of recent advances in the physical sciences has involved a basic conceptual distinction between changes in condition and changes in state, between what is here called alpha change as contrasted with gamma change. Consider complex homeostatic systems, for example. They may experience a bewildering variety of changes in their conditions, in highly variable order, and yet preserve their essential steady state (Ashby, 1954, 1956). On the other hand, common wisdom acknowledges that systems can sometimes be at such a developmental point that even minor changes in condition induce a profound change in state. Hence the expressions, "the straw that broke the camel's back," "the critical incident that induced a psychotic reaction," or "the push we need to get over the hump." Failure to distinguish the two kinds of change implies inadequate description and, possibly, dangerous prescriptions for action.

A variety of convenient analogies imply the ubiquitous character of the distinction between change in condition within a state and change in state. Consider the three states of H_2O, which are a function of temperature. As is well known, considering the condition of temperature only, H_2O has two major properties:

1. H_2O will remain in one of the three states of solid, liquid, or gas over a considerable temperature range induced by a substantial gain (or loss)

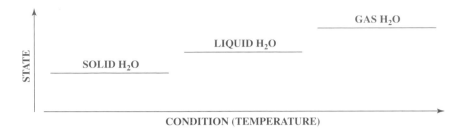

Figure 48.2. An Illustration of Changes in Condition and State.

> of calories; as it were, H_2O in each of its three forms can experience *major changes in condition without a change in state*.

2. At three critical temperatures, the addition or subtraction of a specific number of calories will induce a *change in the state* of H_2O with little or no effect on its condition as measured by temperature.

The crude sense of this analogy from physical science is given in the stepwise model sketched in Figure 48.2. The condition (temperature) is linear.

Each of the states of H_2O persists over a substantial range of conditions, in contrast, but discontinuously jumps to different states at certain critical points.

The three types of change introduced above can be related to a stepwise model of change in Figure 48.3. The illustrative case is clearest for alpha change and gamma change. That is, the larger vector A→B below is associated with a major change in condition but no change in state. This vector may reflect either alpha or beta change; it is clearly not gamma change. In contrast, the smaller vector C→D represents a minor change in condition but

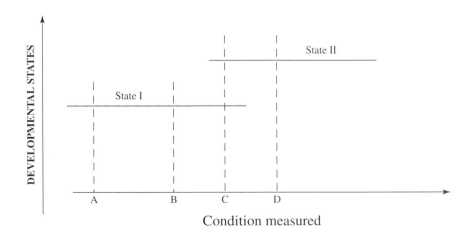

Figure 48.3. An Illustration of Alpha Change in Condition and Gamma Change in State.

induces a major change in state. In the latter case, that is, a small change induces a gamma change. A very large change also might be necessary to induce a gamma effect, depending upon the initial condition of the system.

Much common wisdom in OD and experiential education also suggests the value of distinguishing changes in condition-within-a-state from changes in state. Thus considerable time and effort may be expended in team development before "anything happens," and then quickly a team will "take off" and "go into orbit." Similar notions inhere in common concepts of developmental phases in laboratory education, as in Hampden-Turner's (1966) cyclical model of individual change, in all phase models such as that of Bennis and Shepard (1956), or in Lewin's venerable notion of unfreezing→choice or change→ refreezing (Zand and Sorensen, 1975). To illustrate, Lewin's model clearly implies several different states, and it is important to distinguish which one exists at any point. Specific behaviors or interventions appropriate in the unfrozen state of consciousness or development might be impactless or even seriously counterproductive in the frozen state.

The graphics in Figure 48.3 assume too much, of course. Analysis would be simple if we really could define and distinguish State I from State II. But all we have are vectors with known magnitudes. However, such vectors might reflect any of the three kinds of change.

EVIDENCE OF GAMMA EFFECTS IN OD EFFORTS

Today, we simply do not know how to distinguish the three types of change in any reasonably rigorous and consistent way. Too much is left to the imagination. Our purpose here is to take a small step toward what we need to know. It was noted above that OD interventions are centrally involved with seeking change in the concepts of the quality of organizational life that should and can exist, and far less concerned with raising the level of relatively stable parameters or dimensions. Thus gamma changes—not alpha—are the prime intended effects of such interventions.

We draw attention to the need to distinguish gamma change, in effect, by establishing the inadequacy of alpha or beta changes in accounting for the variation in one specific set of data. The data come from an OD structural intervention, the installation of a flexi-time system of work hours (Golembiewski, Hilles, & Kagno, 1974). The design may be schematized as:

	N	Day 1	Day 15	Short-post Test Day 195	Long-post Test Day 375
Experimentals	32	O_1	X	O_2	O_3
Comparisons	18	O_1		O_2	O_3

where O = observations via self-reports on a standard questionnaire, and X = flexi-time installation. The self-reports on each of eighteen attitudinal items are responses on Likert-like continua of seven equal-appearing intervals, with the extreme positions being anchored by brief verbal descriptions.

Factor Analysis: Search for Congruence and Incongruence

Overall, the search for gamma effects will employ factor-analytical techniques, whose resulting matrices will be tested for congruence. The reliance on factor analysis can be explained nontechnically. Factor analysis essentially seeks to isolate the major dimensions of reality necessary to economically account for the variance in scores on some large set of variables. For example, assume a factor analyst is given one thousand measurements (in inches) of objects she does not know are shoe boxes. Given a little skill and insight, the analyst should conclude that three major factors or dimensions of reality are statistically necessary to account for the variance in those one thousand measurements; and she probably would be able to recognize that those dimensions have properties like our concepts of "length," "width," and "height." For a similar demonstration, see Muhsam (1951). Using factor analysis to study changes in attitudes is similar to the example above, save in two regards: the required factorial structures are likely to be more complex, and no one knows what the underlying "object" really looks like.

These properties of factor analysis encourage our reliance on it. Any major incongruence between the factorial structures representing each set of questionnaire data gathered at several points in time, that is, is interpreted as a change in the dimensions of reality necessary to account for the variance in the sets of responses. And, of course, gamma change is defined as basic change in those dimensions of psychological space.

Specifically, six matrices are involved: one for each of the three administrations of the standard questionnaire for Experimentals only, and one for each of three administrations including all Experimentals and Comparisons taken together.[2] Responses from Comparisons only are not factor-analyzed, since $N = 18$, which is not sufficiently greater than the number of questionnaire items to encourage confidence in any resulting factorial solutions. The six factorial structures will be compared both "within" and "between": within each of the three observations for Experimentals as well as for Experimentals plus Comparisons, and between the three individual observations for Experimentals. Specifically:

- The essential congruence of factorial structures for the Experimentals over the three administrations will imply that gamma effects did not occur.

- The essential congruence of factorial structures for Experimentals plus Comparisons for each of the three questionnaire administrations will imply that gamma effects did not occur.

As noted, it was not possible to compare directly the factorial structures of Experimentals versus Comparisons.

Five major points require emphasis before introducing data. First, factor analysis will be used to help isolate gamma change, *defined as the substantial incongruence of pairs of between-wave factorial structures* as determined by Ahmavaara's technique. Put otherwise, no major changes in factorial structures are expected when only alpha changes occur. Even changes as large as one or two standard deviations from the preintervention mean may reflect only changes in the condition of a stable state rather than changes in state. Only changes in state, or gamma changes, are expected to generate major incongruence between pairs of factorial structures. Beta changes are essentially like alpha changes in this regard.

Second, this chapter reports on only one factor-analytical variant, PFA-2.[3] Any evidence of gamma effects is almost certainly not an artifact of a specific factorial procedure, however. A separate paper establishes that three other factorial variants generate essentially the same structures as PFA-2 (Golembiewski, Billingsley, & Yeager, 1975).

Third, the OD intervention studied was clearly impactful. That is, substantial patterns of intended change were observed in comparisons of pretest, short-post, and long-post scores, when the base of comparison was:

- An item-by-item analysis of a standard questionnaire soliciting eighteen separate responses at three points in time.

- An analysis of changes along seven dimensions apparently tapped by eighteen items, as determined by factor analysis[4] of responses to Wave 1 of the standard questionnaire, which structure was then used to score responses at three points in time.

- An analysis of changes along six dimensions apparently tapped by the eighteen items as determined by factor analysis[4] of responses to Wave 2 of the standard questionnaire, which structure was then used to score responses at three points in time.

- An analysis of changes along five dimensions apparently tapped by the eighteen items, as determined by factor analysis[4] of responses to Wave 3 of the standard questionnaire, which structure was then used to score responses at three points in time.

Fourth, estimating the congruence between factorial solutions involved one strategic choice, since the several factorial procedures did not generate an equal number of factors in all cases. PFA-1, for example, using Kaiser's (1960) criterion of an eigenvalue > 1.0 to govern the extraction of factors, generated seven factors for O_1, six for O_2, and five for O_3. In all three cases, the factors with eigenvalues > 1.0 accounted for some 70 percent of the variance. The convention was adopted to use seven factors, even where this means disregarding Kaiser's rule.[5]

Fifth, the procedure for comparing factorial structures is straightforward, if complex. For details, see the Appendix.

Statistical Procedures

Six tests are made of the notion that variation in the flexi-time dataset can be explained only by gamma effects. Better said, perhaps, it will be shown that alpha or beta effects are not sufficient to explain that variation.

First, the within-wave congruence of the structures isolated by the four factor-analytic procedures is compared. A substantial congruence will make it difficult to argue that any relationships below are artifacts of any specific factorial procedure.

Second, between-wave congruence is determined, using the total batch of Experimentals plus Comparisons. Estimates of the variance in common between pairs of factorial structures will be used to estimate their congruence. Major reductions of common variance are consistent with the interpretation that gamma changes occurred in Waves 2 and 3 as a result of the experimental intervention.

Third, a similar analysis is conducted for Experimentals only. Crudely, lower between-wave congruence of factorial structures for $N = 32$ Experimentals is expected. Such an effect is consistent with the interpretation that gamma changes occurred. That is, the exclusion of Comparison subjects—who experience only random changes over the observational period Wave 1 to Wave 3—will remove a portion of the common variance that probably served to somewhat inflate the estimates of congruence of factorial structures for Experimentals plus Comparisons, or $N = 50$.

Fourth, the congruence of factorial structures is tested for a randomly diminished N. This permits an estimate of the stability of factorial structures as well as of their dependence on the size of N. The substantial congruence of within-wave structures will imply that any patterns isolated in the first three analytical approaches are not simple artifacts of N.

Fifth, a test will be conducted concerning the impact on between-wave comparisons of the present convention of setting at seven the number of factors to be extracted. The congruence of structures with five, six, and seven factors is tested. If allowing the number of factors to vary does not much affect the congruence of between-wave factorial structures, the implied conclusion is that gamma effects account for any substantial incongruence isolated by research emphases two and three above (it was found that within-wave comparisons are affected only slightly by the convention of considering seven factors, but no data on the point are reported in this chapter.)

Sixth, an estimate is made of the effects of limiting to five the number of iterations of the structures derived from PFA-2. The congruence of a random sample of structures will be ascertained when iterations are set at five versus ninety-nine. High congruence of pairs of factorial structures will imply that the major convenience of limiting iterations to five did not stop data manipulation when further substantial convergence of individual structures was still possible. Hence any major incongruence isolated in emphases two and three above will be credibly assignable to systemic effects such as gamma changes.

Congruence of Within-Wave Structures (N = 50 and N = 32). To summarize briefly, it is easy to establish that the four factor-analytical procedures described above essentially isolate the same structures within each of the three questionnaire waves (Golembiewski, Billingsley, & Yeager, 1975). Conveniently, the summary below of r^2 implies a very substantial intrawave congruence of structures extracted by the four factorial procedures, given that the square of the product-moment correlation coefficient provides an estimate of the common variance between the structures of any two procedures. In sum:

Wave 1: product-moment r^2, $\overline{X} = .9524$

Wave 2: product-moment r^2, $\overline{X} = .9850$

Wave 3: product-moment r^2, $\overline{X} = .9929$

The average r^2 permits the estimate that the eighteen within-wave comparisons of pairs of structures generated by the four factorial procedures share more than 97 percent of their variance in common, on the average.

This pattern holds for an N of fifty; the pattern for N = thirty-two is similar. For details, again consult Golembiewski, Billingsley, and Yeager (1975).

This is impressive congruence, and it implies that any results below are almost certainly *not* artifacts of the single factorial strategy focused on below.

Congruence Between Waves, All Subjects. The factorial structures change enough between waves to suggest that alpha or beta changes are not adequate to account for the low congruence between the pretest factorial structure and the two postintervention structures. For PFA-2 only, the product-moment correlation coefficients in Table 48.1 imply that about 67 percent of the between-wave variance can be thought of as common. The pattern is similar for the other three factorial procedures, although they account for somewhat less of the variance (around 64 percent).

The table suggests a qualified but stout conclusion. The interwave differences might be accounted for in several ways, and not only as signs of the

Table 48.1. Congruence of Between-Wave Factorial Structures for Experimentals Plus Comparisons (N = 50, Paired Comparisons of Three Waves, PFA-2).

	Interclass Correlation	Product-Moment Correlation	Estimated Common Variance
Wave 1 vs. 2	.7903	.8055	64.9%
Wave 1 vs. 3	.8054	.8186	67.0
Wave 2 vs. 3	.8255	.8356	69.7

fundamental variation in conceptual space here designated as gamma change. To be sure, no absolute criteria establish the point at which interwave changes become great enough to signal gamma changes. Yet the "loss" of some 30 percent of variance in comparisons of the congruence of factorial structures for the three waves of questionnaires has a compelling quality to us and, if nothing else, implies the inadequacy of alpha or beta change as an explanation.

Several reasons reinforce this conclusion. First, it is difficult to credit most of the interwave variations to measurement error. Second, the reduction in variance seems large enough to imply major changes in the dimensions of the relevant psychological space, as contrasted with variations in the level of relatively stable dimensions or with variations in the measurement intervals associated with some stable dimensions of reality. The latter are beta changes, and the former are alpha changes. We presume they would not show up as the major incongruencies in factor-analytical structures reflected in Table 48.1. Third, the $N = 50$ batch of subjects represented in the table contains both Experimentals and Comparisons. Other data convincingly demonstrate that Comparisons reflected only random variation in their three waves of self-reports. In a major sense, then, the 67 percent estimate of common variance between factorial structures no doubt understates the impact of the experimental intervention in changing the relevant psychological space as measured by comparisons of factor-analytical structures at three points in time.

Congruence Between Waves, Experimentals Only. Fortunately, it is possible to test this last surmise. Table 48.2 presents some relevant data using only the Experimental subjects. As expected, the estimate of common variance falls, to an average of 51 percent from 67 percent.

The table supports two conclusions. Its pattern is consistent with the conclusion that gamma changes did occur in the data batch. Moreover, the reduced estimate of common variance in $N = 32$ is both expected and large enough to further undercut the credibility of the proposition that alpha or beta effects alone are capable of accounting for the diminished congruence of factorial

Table 48.2. Congruence of Between-Wave Factorial Structures for Experimentals Only
(N = 32, Paired Comparisons of Three Waves, PFA-2).

	Interclass Correlation	Product-Moment Correlation	Estimated Common Variance
Wave 1 vs. 2	.6121	.6533	42.7%
Wave 1 vs. 3	.7581	.7768	60.3
Wave 2 vs. 3	.6711	.7023	49.3

structures. If a 30 percent "loss" in interwave common variance is not sufficient to establish the likelihood of gamma effects, then a 50 percent "loss" provides very much more formidable support for that conclusion.

Congruence of Within-Wave Structures for Variable N. It may be the case, of course, that the lower percentage of common variance in the case of $N = 32$ vs. $N = 50$ is an artifact of the variation in N itself, rather than an effect of excluding the Comparisons. This dependence of within-wave factorial structures on the size of N was tested in a very demanding way.[6] The test reveals common and stable factorial structures that are substantially independent even of major changes in N. This finding does double duty. It prohibits gaining a cheap victory over Table 48.1 by doubting or denying the stability of the underlying factorial structures. Moreover, the summary data above clearly imply that a reduction in N by itself cannot account for the pattern in Table 48.2.

Congruence of Between-Wave Structures for Variable Number of Factors. As noted, the convention above was to compare the first seven factors in all structures, even in the case of an eigenvalue < 1.0. This convenient convention does not seem to do violence to the data, as a test case implies. To illustrate with PFA-1 only, for Experimental plus Comparisons, the congruence of factorial structures was established when the number of factors for Wave 1 = 7, for Wave 2 = 6, and Wave 3 = 5. In sum:

	Interclass Correlation	Product-Moment Correlation	Estimated Common Variance
Wave 1 vs. 2	.8218	.8326	69.3%
Wave 1 vs. 3	.7996	.8139	66.2
Wave 2 vs. 3	.8544	.8612	74.2

The estimated common variance is somewhat higher above than in Table 48.1, but the average common variance increases only from 67 to 70 percent when the number of factors is varied to include only those with eigenvalues > 1.0. The effect is small, and in the expected direction. Consequently, the convention of setting the factors to be compared at seven had the effect of lowering the variance in common between pairs of structures, but not much.

The test case suggests that very little of the incongruence between structures reflected in Table 48.1 can be attributed to its convention of setting at seven the number of factors to be compared. As in Table 48.1, moreover, the incongruence is great enough to suggest that alpha or beta changes alone cannot reasonably account for it.

A similar analysis for Experimentals only ($N = 32$) leads to a similar conclusion about Table 48.2. In this case, the number of factors with eigenvalues > 1 for Wave 1 = 7, for Wave 2 = 5, and for Wave 3 = 6. The results indicate that it is possible to account for only a small part of the incongruence between factorial structures in Table 48.2 as a consequence of setting the number of factors considered at seven. In sum:

	Interclass Correlation	Product-Moment Correlation	Estimated Common Variance
Wave 1 (7 factors) vs. 2 (5 factors)	.7741	.7895	62.3%
Wave 1 (7 factors) vs. 3 (6 factors)	.6852	.7150	51.1
Wave 2 (5 factors) vs. 3 (6 factors)	.6223	.6631	44.0

Recall that Table 48.2 indicates that only about 51 percent of the variance, on average, is shared in common among the several paired comparisons of between-wave factorial structures for Experimentals only. Allowing the number of factors to vary (as the data immediately above show) does not much affect the estimate of common variance, which increases, but only to 52.5 percent. This pattern implies that very little of the between-wave incongruence in factorial structures can reasonably be assigned to the convention of setting the number of factors at seven in most analyses in this chapter. Moreover, the pattern also supports the interpretation that the between-wave incongruence in factorial structures is large enough to suggest gamma effects.

Congruence of Within-Wave Structures When Iterations = 5 vs. 99. As a final test, it seems obvious that the SPSS convention to limit iterations to five had a small impact on this analysis. Specifically, ten sample tests were run involving all three waves, $N = 50$ and 32, and number of factors equal to five, six, or seven, as appropriate. The basic comparison involves determining the congruence of pairs of factorial structures when iterations are cut off at five and when they are allowed to run to a maximum of ninety-nine. The ten resulting estimates of common variance cover a narrow and high range, from 96.96

to 100 percent, with a grand mean of 98.80. This very high degree of congruence implies that the convenience of limiting iterations to five is not analytically troublesome.

CONCLUSIONS AND IMPLICATIONS

Although the data do lead us to conclusions that are intriguing—and challenging—we encourage moderation in interpretation. Most important, the data do seem to indicate that something like gamma changes did occur in the population examined. And there are substantial reasons for presuming that patterns in the data were probably not determined by (1) random causes, (2) a single factorial procedure only, (3) dependence upon the level of N, (4) the basic convention of considering seven factors for each wave, or (5) the convenience of limiting to five the number of iterations seeking to maximize congruence of each structure.

The results above may reflect the impact of other factors not considered here, of course. For example, there are several ways to estimate congruence other than the method used here, even though preliminary work requires no modification of the present conclusions. Here note only that specialists of good will can differ profoundly as to what is the most appropriate measure of congruence. However, despite interpretive problems, a major test of an alternative way of determining congruence provides no clear support for the hypothesis that the present results are artifacts of the specific measure of congruence used. The ratio of subjects to items in the present data batch is at best 2.6 : 1, which is in the lower half of recommended ratios. Normally, this would suggest a question about the results above. In this case, the patent stability of the factorial structures when N is allowed to vary suggests that the problem is not significant.

It seems safest to highlight only two conclusions of the preceding analysis.

First, the analysis implies the real possibility of gamma changes. Essentially, the complex analytic procedures imply that the OD intervention changed in major ways the psychological dimensions that employees used to evaluate their work site. Not only did the several factorial structures differ substantially between waves but a number of alternative explanations for those differences also were tested and discarded. Essentially, those two facts constitute our case for the need to distinguish gamma effects.

We do not describe the specifics of the gamma change. That would involve the verbal interpretations of the several factorial structures, which would burden this analysis with massive detail. Rather, we rely on the summary statistics to indicate the major incongruencies between factorial structures. Our focus was on comparing clusters of factors rather than on interpreting individual factors.

Second, reaching this point has been trying enough—and especially for the reader impatient with statistical complexity—but extensions of this line of research promise no easier pieces. Thus it will be exceedingly difficult to establish the existence of gamma changes, as well as to satisfactorily differentiate gamma from alpha and beta changes. But the present results suggest strongly that the effort is necessary, since alpha or beta changes cannot credibly account for the major incongruence in structures reported here.

To the degree that the preceding analysis is close to reality, it has profound implications for experimental research designs in the social sciences. Here we recommend other tests of this analysis, as well as an interim exercise of prudence that can ameliorate our present lack of knowledge about kinds of change.

Seven themes are especially noteworthy in these regards.

First, this analysis implies that prodigious energies in the behavioral sciences have been applied to the wrong methodological issues. Consider the sophisticated but inconclusive effort directed at the question of how change is to be measured (Cronbach & Furley, 1970; Van Meter, 1974, among many others). This analysis suggests strongly that the first question should be, What kind of change is being measured? Few students (e.g., Buss, 1974) deal with this prior question, however. Most studies seem to assume that only alpha change is relevant. That assumption seems clearly inappropriate for successful OD interventions, and the same may be true of many natural-state or contrived experiments.

Second, this analysis suggests that one useful strategy for measuring change is to test for incongruence in the dimensions of the perceived psychological domains, as by comparing the results of factor analyses before and after an OD intervention. This is relatively simple, and avoids many of the formidable problems of calculating meaningful change scores.

Going one step further will present major complexities, to be sure. It is one thing to estimate incongruence between two structures, and quite another to label and compare the individual factors in those structures. The first task is mechanical, if involved. The second task is a major art form in behavioral science. Our study took the easier route. It does not deal with the specific changes in individual factors induced by the flexi-time intervention. It was a matter of doing the simplest things first, as it were.

Third, there is a hard message for much OD research in this analysis. Specifically, interpreting any results of existing research is chancy in the absence of knowledge about types of change, which is seldom available. Even research designs that surpass the usual norms for rigor and care are suspect in this regard. For example, one better-than-average OD research design factor analyzes questionnaire responses at time one, and then uses the resulting matrix to score the initial responses as well as the responses generated by another administration of the same questionnaire at time two, following an OD intervention. "Change," then, is defined as differences in the T2 and T1 scores. This design may be variously misleading in the cases of beta and especially of gamma change, however, as the analysis above should establish.

Fourth, this focus on types of change implies the strategic value of time series designs or some such variants as time-lagged designs (Campbell, 1963). These two kinds of designs may be sketched as:

I. $O_1 \times O_2 \, O_3 \ldots$
II. $O_1 \times O_2 \, O_3 \ldots$ $O_1 \times O_2 \, O_3 \ldots$ $O_1 \times O_2 \, O_3 \times \ldots$

where O = observation and X = experimental intervention. Of course, the explanatory power of both designs is enhanced if controls or comparisons are provided. Beta effects and gamma effects seem far more difficult to isolate in simple $O_1 \times O_2$ designs.

Fifth, the analysis above implies the value of statistical procedures that seek to isolate dimensions of reality, that promise to help uncover major covariants in nature. In combination with a time-series design, for example, such procedures can be applied to help determine if basic changes in the relevant psychological space have occurred over the interval of multiple observations. Changes in such space imply gamma changes, of course.

A number of statistical procedures are useful for meeting this requirement of seeking dimensions of factors of reality, and thus of facilitating the discovery of gamma effects. Particularly useful are such technologies as factor analysis, hierarchical decomposition, and discriminant function analysis. They share one major feature: they are data-economical in that they seek the major factors or dimensions necessary to account for the variation in any dataset. In sum, such techniques conserve data. In contrast, many scaling techniques are data-wasteful. They ask, given some set of items, such as those tapping attitudes, which subset of them can be arrayed in scalelike fashion? In effect, such approaches imply substantial data loss.

The awkwardly named "catastrophe theory" also may be useful. It deals with *discontinuous change* of various sorts, the kind here called gamma change, especially in social and behavioral contexts. Catastrophe theory thus contrasts with most existing mathematics, which, as in the calculus, deals with *continuous change*. In the interests of deeper probing of discontinuous change for our day and time, the reader may recall that the abstruse catastrophe theory—the darling of many of today's mathematicians—recently received wide coverage in the mass media (*Newsweek*, 1976).

Sixth, more "clinical" attention might be devoted to subjects as they respond to measuring instruments requiring self-reports. The perception of respondents that they are using "rubber yardsticks" might be variously parlayed into a kind of early-warning system that alerts analysis to beta or gamma changes in experimental design.

Seventh, scaling techniques less sensitive to metric-level assumptions also could profitably be used to seek underlying structures in this type of analysis. Such approaches include smallest-space analysis (SSA) and nonmetric multi-dimensional scaling.

There is a long trail ahead of this line of research. Hopefully, the first few steps taken were in a useful direction.

APPENDIX

A Description of Ahmavaara's Procedure for Comparing Factorial Structures

Overall, the first seven factors generated by each factor-analytic application are taken to constitute a seven-dimensional subspace of the total space encompassed by the eighteen variables. Since the variables used to derive each factor matrix are the same and the individuals are the same, each matrix defines a separate subspace in the same overall space.

The procedures for comparing factorial solutions for a common dataset can be described briefly. Note that the approach is generally the same whether the comparison of pairs of structures is between-wave or within-wave. The former compares the congruence of the factorial structure generated by the same procedure in each of two waves of self-responses; the latter compares the two structures generated by pairs of alternative factorial procedures within a single wave of responses.

Ahmavaara's (1954) method of rotating one factor matrix into the space of another in order to compare them was utilized since it efficiently reduces the "noise" inherent in prior rotations of either matrix. Convincing evidence strongly implies the especial usefulness of Ahmavaara's procedure, compared to a substantial number of alternative procedures that might have been used (Pinneau & Newhouse, 1964). To suggest that usefulness, Hamilton (1967, p. 107) notes that Ahmavaara's method is "the simplest, neatest and most elegant [but] it has been little used and little referred to."

Ahmavaara's procedure begins with the development of a transformation matrix L of the matrices being compared, X being the "problem" and Y the "target" matrix, respectively. Ahmavaara describes L in these terms:

> The columns represent the common factors of the matrix Y, the order being the same in L as in Y. On the other hand, the rows of L represent the common factors of X, the order of factors being again the same in Ln as in X. The elements of Ln then indicate the cosines of the angles between the factors of the different studies or, more accurately, between the vectors representing these factors.

Consequently, if some element of L is exactly equal to unity, the respective factors of the two studies are identical [1954, p. 56].

Factor vectors of the same size are created by recalculating L in normalized form.

Subsequently, a check matrix C is derived by multiplying each element of L by its corresponding element in X, the problem matrix. This is the best least-squares fit of the first matrix into the second.

Finally, the interclass correlation and product-moment correlation coefficients between the check matrix C and the target Y are computed. These coefficients are critical in the analysis. The interclass correlation indicates the degree to which the two structures are similar in both pattern and magnitude. Product-moment coefficients indicate the degree of similarity in patterning only, and the square of these coefficients indicates the percentage of variance the two structures being compared have in common.

Notes

1. The terminology relates to Rensis Likert's (1967) *Profile of Organizational Characteristics*. The Profile seeks two kinds of self-reports: Now responses, which solicit data about how respondents actually see their organization unit; and ideal responses, which seek information about how respondents feel their organization should be. The focus throughout this chapter is on purported descriptions of existential states only, that is, on *Now responses*.

2. To test the possibility that any results were artifacts of a single factor-analytical technology, in addition, the analysis to be reported here was replicated for four variants: Principal Factoring without Iterations, or PFA-1; Principal Factoring with Iterations, or PFA-2; ALPHA Factor Analysis; and RAO, or Canonical Factor Analysis. For a detailed description of the differences between these techniques, see McDonald (1970). All four techniques are conveniently available in SPSS, or Statistical Package for Social Scientists. Results will be reported here basically for PFA-2. For evidence of the very substantial congruence of the structures generated by PFA-2 and the three other factorial variants listed above, see Golembiewski, Billingsley, and Yeager (1975).

3. To briefly describe PFA-2, or Principal Factoring with Iterations, the main diagonal of the correlation matrix is replaced with the communality estimates, or squared multiple correlations between the variable and the rest of the variables. The estimates of communality are iteratively improved by factoring again with the calculated communality estimates derived from the preceding solution. This process is continued until the estimates of communality converge, or until the differences between successive estimates is negligible. The SPSS program is set for five iterations or fewer, because the CDC 6400 implementation of SPSS used here capitalizes on the 60-bit accuracy of the 6400's word size. A note on the printout alerts analysts

if five iterations do not suffice for absolute convergence. As a major convenience, all analysis below deals with structures for variants two to four, which have been iterated five times or less. A later section demonstrates that ninety-nine iterations provide almost exactly the same structure as five iterations. Hence the present analytical convenience has small costs.

4. Specifically, the factorial procedure was PFA-1 followed by VARIMAX rotation.

5. This convention has several motivators. Primarily, the convention facilitates the convenient replication of the results reported here. In addition, it reduces the potential for error when comparing matrices of larger or smaller size, respecting the advice of Kaiser et al. (1971, esp. pp. 411–412 and 421). Moreover, the choice of seven factors permits the inclusion in Waves 2 and 3 of several items that load heavily on factors 6 and 7 only. Finally, had the decision been to consider only the first five factors generated by each procedure, substantial portions of variance would have been lost in analyses of Waves 2 and 3. Adding the sixth and/or seventh factor did not contribute much to the total variance in Waves 1 and 2, in contrast. Data concerning the effects of the decision to focus on seven factors will be presented below. For now, note only that the convention was not analytically troublesome.

6. Subjects were randomly eliminated so that five independent subpopulations of thirty-five were isolated for each of the three waves. PFA-1 was then applied to these fifteen subpopulations as well as to the total population ($N = 50$), and the resulting factorial structures were compared for within-wave congruence. The results of this severe test strongly imply that variation in N itself does not determine the pattern reflected by Tables 48.1 and 48.2. Specifically, in one of the fifteen comparisons considering seven factors in all cases:

	Interclass Correlation	Product-Moment Correlation	Estimated Common Variance
Wave 1, N = 35 vs. Wave 1, N = 50	.9427	.9437	89.1%
Wave 2, N = 35 vs. Wave 2, N = 50	.9415	.9427	88.9
Wave 3, N = 35 vs. Wave 3, N = 50	.9734	.9737	94.8

In sum, more than 90 percent of the estimated variance in this illustrative case can be considered common in the underlying structures. The average for all subpopulations tested was about 88 percent, which is impressive congruence, especially given the severity of the test.

References

Ahmavaara, Y. Transformation analysis of factorial data. *Annals of the Academy of Science Fennicae,* Series B, 1954, 881 (2), 54–59.

Ashby, W. R. *Design for a brain*. New York: Wiley, 1954.

Ashby, W. R. *An introduction to cybernetics*. London: Chapman & Hall, 1956.

Bennis, W. G., & Shepard, H. A theory of group development. *Human Relations*, November 1956, 9, 415–437.

Bereiter, C. Some persisting dilemmas in the measurement of change. In Chester W. Harris (Ed.), *Problems in measuring change*. Madison: University of Wisconsin Press, 1963, pp. 3–20.

Beyond calculus: "Catastrophe theory." *Newsweek*, January 19, 1976, 54–55.

Bowers, D. G. OD techniques and their results in 23 organizations: The Michigan ICL study. *Journal of Applied Behavioral Science*, 1973, 9 (1), 21–43.

Buss, A. R. Multivariate model of quantitative, structural, and quantistructural ontogenetic change. *Development Psychology*, 1974, 10, 190–203.

Campbell, D. T. From description to experimentation: Interpreting trends as quasi-experiments. In Chester W. Harris (Ed.), *Problems in measuring change*. Madison: University of Wisconsin Press, 1963, pp. 212–242.

Converse, P. E. Attitudes and non-attitudes. In Edward R. Tufte (Ed.), *The quantitative analysis of social problems*. Reading, Mass.: Addison-Wesley, 1970, pp. 168–189.

Cronbach, L. J., & Furley, L. How we should measure "change"—Or should we? *Psychological Bulletin*, 1970, 74 (1), 68–80.

Golembiewski, R. T. *Renewing organizations*. Itasca, Ill.: F. E. Peacock, 1972.

Golembiewski, R. T., Billingsley, K., & Yeager, S. *The congruence of factor-analytic structures: Comparisons of four procedures and their solutions*. Unpublished manuscript, University of Georgia, 1975.

Golembiewski, R. T., & Carrigan, S. B. Planned change through laboratory methods. *Training and Development Journal*, March 1973, 27, 18–27.

Golembiewski, R. T., Hilles, R., & Kagno, M. A longitudinal study of flexi-time effects. *Journal of Applied Behavioral Science*, 1974, 10 (4), 503–532.

Hamilton, M. Comparisons of factors by Ahmavaara's method. *British Journal of Mathematical and Statistical Psychology*, 1967, 2, 107–110.

Hampden-Turner, C. W. An existential "learning theory" and the integration of t-group research. *Journal of Applied Behavioral Science*, 1966, 2 (4), 367–386.

Iyengar, S. The problem of response stability: Some correlates and consequences. *American Journal of Political Science*, November 1973, 17, 797–808.

Kaiser, H. F. The application of electronic computers in factor analysis. *Educational and Psychological Measurement*, 1960, 20, 141–151.

Kaiser, H. F., & Caffrey, J. Alpha factor analysis. *Psychometrika*, March 1965, 30, 1–14.

Kaiser, H. F., Hunka, S., & Bianchini, J. Relating factors between studies based upon different individuals. *Multivariate Behavioral Research*, October 1971, 6, 409–421.

Likert, R. *The human organization*. New York: McGraw-Hill, 1967.

McDonald, R. P. The theoretical foundations of principal factor analysis, canonical factor analysis, and alpha factor analysis. *British Journal of Mathematical and Statistical Psychology,* May 1970, 23, 1–21.

McGee, V. E. The multidimensional analysis of "elastic" distances. *British Journal of Mathematical and Statistical Psychology,* November 1966, 19, 181–196.

Muhsam, H. V. The factor analysis of a simple object. *Journal of General Psychology,* July 1951, 45, 105–110.

Pepper, S., & Prytulak, L. S. Sometimes frequently means seldom: Context effects in the interpretation of quantitative expressions. *Journal of Research in Personality,* June 1974, 8, 95–101.

Pinneau, S. R., & Newhouse, A. Measures of invariance and compatibility in factor analysis for fixed variables. *Psychometrika,* September 1964, 29, 271–281.

Rao, C. Estimation and tests of significance in factor analysis. *Psychometrika,* June 1965, 30, 93–111.

Ross, R. OD for whom? *Journal of Applied Behavioral Science,* September 1971, 7, 580–585.

Stewart, D., & Love, W. A general canonical correlation index. *Psychological Bulletin,* 1968, 70 (3), 160–163.

Tannenbaum, R., & Davis, S. Values, man, and organization. In Warren H. Schmidt (Ed.), *Organizational frontiers and human values.* Belmont, Calif.: Wadsworth, 1970.

Taylor, J., & Bowers, D. G. *Survey of organizations.* Ann Arbor, Mich.: CRUSK, Institute for Social Research, University of Michigan, 1967.

Torbert, W. Some questions on Bowers' study of different OD techniques. *Journal of Applied Behavioral Science,* September 1973, 9, 668–671.

Van Meter, D. S. Alternative methods of measuring change: What difference does it make? *Political Methodology,* Fall 1974, 1, 125–139.

Ward, R. T. Culture and the comparative study of politics, or the constipated dialectic. *American Political Science Review,* March 1974, 68, 190–201.

Watzlawick, P., Weakland, J. H., & Fisch, R. *Change: Principles of problem formation and problem resolution.* New York: W. W. Norton, 1974.

Zand, D., & Sorensen, R. E. Problems in the measurement of organizational effectiveness. *Administrative Science Quarterly,* December 1975, 20, 532–545.

CHAPTER FORTY-NINE

Explaining Development and Change in Organizations

Andrew H. Van de Ven
Marshall Scott Poole (1995)

T his chapter introduces four basic theories that may serve as building blocks for explaining processes of change in organizations: life cycle, teleology, dialectics, and evolution. These four theories represent different sequences of change events that are driven by different conceptual motors and operate at different organizational levels. This chapter identifies the circumstances in which each theory applies and proposes how interplay among the theories produces a wide variety of more complex theories of change and development in organizational life.

Explaining how and why organizations change has been a central and enduring quest of scholars in management and many other disciplines. The processes or sequences of events that unfold in these changes—such as transitions in individuals' jobs and careers, group formation and development, and organizational innovation, growth, reorganization, and decline—have been very difficult to explain, let alone manage. To understand how organizations change, management scholars have borrowed many concepts, metaphors, and theories from other disciplines, ranging from child development to evolutionary biology. These concepts include punctuated equilibrium, stages of growth, processes of decay and death, population ecology, functional models of change and development, and chaos theory. This variation has created a theoretical pluralism that has uncovered novel ways to explain some organizational change and developmental processes. However, the diversity of theories and concepts borrowed from different disciplines often encourages compartmentalization of perspectives that do not enrich each other and produce isolated lines of research (Gioia & Pitre, 1990). As Poggie (1965: 284) said, "A way of seeing is a way of not seeing."

It is the interplay between different perspectives that helps one gain a more comprehensive understanding of organizational life, because any one theoretical perspective invariably offers only a partial account of a complex phenomenon. Moreover, the juxtaposition of different theoretical perspectives brings into focus contrasting worldviews of social change and development. Working out the relationships between such seemingly divergent views provides opportunities to develop new theory that has stronger and broader explanatory power than the initial perspectives.

Some integration is thus desirable, but it must preserve the distinctiveness of alternative theories of organizational change and development. We contend that such integration is possible if different perspectives are viewed as providing alternative pictures of the same organizational processes without nullifying each other. This can be achieved by identifying the viewpoints from which each theory applies and the circumstances when these theories are interrelated. This approach preserves the authenticity of distinct theories, and at the same time it advances theory building, because it highlights circumstances when interplays among the theories may provide stronger and broader explanatory power of organizational change and development processes (Van de Ven & Poole, 1988; Poole & Van de Ven, 1989).

We apply this approach in three parts of this chapter. On the basis of an interdisciplinary literature review, Part One introduces four basic types of process theories that explain how and why change unfolds in social or biological entities: life-cycle, teleological, dialectical, and evolutionary theories. These four types represent fundamentally different event sequences and generative mechanisms—we will call them motors—to explain how and why changes unfold. Part Two arranges these four ideal-type process theories into a typology by distinguishing the level and mode of change to which each theory applies. Part Three considers how the typology is useful for understanding a variety of specific theories of change processes in organizations. We contend that all specific theories of organizational change and development can be built from one or more of the four basic types. Although some theories can be reduced to one of the motors, most are predicated on the interplay of two or more motors. We consider a scheme of sixteen logical explanations of organizational change and development based on various combinations of the four motors and some exemplars.

We believe this framework is useful in several ways. First, it is a step toward more parsimonious explanations of organizational change and development. It uncovers similarities in seemingly different theories of change or development and highlights the "differences that make a difference" in explanations. The four motors serve as theoretical "primitives" facilitating the integration of related explanations. Second, the framework serves normative functions. The four basic theories provide useful standards to evaluate the form, completeness, and tightness of specific developmental theories. Third, this framework promotes new theories by identifying possible explanations of organizational change and development that do not yet exist in the literature. Fourth, the framework supports inductive research by identifying characteristics of the four motors and the conditions under which they are likely to operate. Rather than working from preconceived change theories, we can test the existence of the primitive motors in order to see which fits the complex phenomenon being examined. This testing helps to prevent the self-fulfilling prophecies that may occur when a researcher expects a certain number of stages of development or a certain process; it is too easy to find evidence in complex processes for whatever one expects and therefore to ignore other motors (Poole, 1981).

Throughout this chapter, we refer to process as the progression (i.e., the order and sequence) of events in an organizational entity's existence over time.[1] *Change*, one type of event, is an empirical observation of difference in form, quality, or state over time in an organizational entity. The *entity* may be an individual's job, a work group, an organizational strategy, a program, a product, or the overall organization. *Development* is a *change process* (i.e., a progression of change events that unfold during the duration of an entity's existence—from the initiation or onset of the entity to its end or termination). Finally, we refer to a *process theory* as an explanation of how and why an organizational entity changes and develops. This explanation should identify the generative mechanisms that cause observed events to happen and the particular circumstances or contingencies behind these causal mechanisms (Harre & Madden, 1975; Tsoukas, 1989).

We have chosen abstract and general definitions because we wish to open the field to a wide range of theories. Also, we wish to avoid the common assumption that all development represents progress from a lower, simpler state to a higher, more complex one. This is one possible path development may follow, but it is not the only one. Organizational development can also follow a regressive path, as in the case of organizational decline (Kimberly & Miles, 1980), or a pathological path, as in Merton's (1968) vicious cycle of bureaucracy.

I. FOUR IDEAL-TYPE DEVELOPMENTAL THEORIES

We conducted an interdisciplinary literature review to identify alternative theories used to explain processes of change in the social, biological, and physical sciences.[2] We found about twenty different process theories that vary in substance or terminology across disciplines. By inductively examining the substance and intellectual heritage of these theories, we found that most of them could be grouped into four basic schools of thought. Each of these four schools has a rich and long-standing intellectual tradition, although various disciplines use different terminologies. We will refer to them as life-cycle, teleology, dialectics, and evolution theories. Table 49.1 outlines the four types of process theories in terms of their members, pioneering scholars, event progressions, generative mechanisms, and conditions under which they are likely to operate. These theories provide fundamentally different accounts of the sequence of events that unfold to explain the process of change in an organizational entity.

This section describes the four process theories in their pure ideal-type forms. As discussed in Part Three, scholars often combine elements of these ideal types to explain observed processes of change in specific areas or contexts. However, in such cases it is very easy for the conceptual basis of specific theories to become obscure. As Kaplan (1964) warned, borrowing concepts from different theories without understanding the theoretical "roots" of these concepts can produce confounded explanations.

Life-Cycle Theory

Many management scholars have adopted the metaphor of organic growth as a heuristic device to explain development in an organizational entity from its initiation to its termination. Witness, for example, often-used references to the life cycle of organizations, products, and ventures, as well as stages in the development of individual careers, groups, and organizations: startup births, adolescent growth, maturity, and decline or death. Life-cycle theories include developmentalism (Nisbet, 1970), biogenesis (Featherman, 1986), ontogenesis (Baltes, Dittman-Kohli, & Dixon, 1986), and a number of stage theories of child development (Piaget, 1975), human development (Levinson, 1978), moral development (Kohlberg, 1969), organizational development (Kimberly & Miles, 1980), group decision-making stages (Bales & Strodtbeck, 1951), and new venture development (Burgelman & Sayles, 1986).[3] Next to teleology, life cycle is perhaps the most common explanation of development in the management literature.

According to life-cycle theory, change is immanent that is, the developing entity has within it an underlying form, logic, program, or code that regulates the process of change and moves the entity from a given point of departure toward a subsequent end that is prefigured in the present state. Thus, the form that lies latent, premature, or homogeneous in the embryo or primitive state becomes progressively more realized, mature, and differentiated. External environmental events and processes can influence how the entity expresses itself, but they are always mediated by the immanent logic, rules, or programs that govern the entity's development (Van de Ven & Poole, 1988: 37).

Table 49.1. Families of Ideal-Type Theories of Social Change.

Family	Life Cycle	Evolution	Dialectic	Teleology
Members	Developmentalism, ontogenesis, metamorphosis, stage & cyclical models	Darwinian evolution, Mendelian genetics, saltationism, punctuated equilibrium	Conflict theory, dialectical materialism, pluralism, collective action	Goal setting, planning; functionalism, social construction, symbolic interaction
Pioneers	Comte (1798–1857), Spencer (1820–1903), Piaget (1896–1980)	Lamarck (1744–1829), Darwin (1809–1882), Mendel (1822–1884), Gould & Eldridge (1977)	Hegel (1770–1831), Marx (1818–1883), Freud (1856–1939)	Mead (1863–1931), Weber (1864–1920), Simon (1916–)
Key metaphor	Organic growth	Competitive survival	Opposition, conflict	Purposeful cooperation
Logic	Imminent program, prefigured sequence, compliant adaptation	Natural selection among competitors in a population	Contradictory forces, thesis, antithesis, synthesis	Envisioned end state, social construction, equifinality
Event progression	Linear & irreversible, sequence of prescribed stages in unfolding of immanent potentials present at the beginning	Recurren-, cumulative, & probabilistic sequence of variation, selection, & retention events	Recurrent, discontinuous sequence of confrontation, conflict, and synthesis between contradictory values or events	Recurrent, discontinuous sequence of goal setting, implementation, & adaptation of means to reach desired end state
Generating force	Prefigured program/rule regulated by nature, logic, or institutions	Population scarcity, competition, commensalism	Conflict & confrontation between opposing forces, interests, or classes	Goal enactment consensus on means cooperation/ symbiosis

The typical progression of change events in a life-cycle model is a unitary sequence (it follows a single sequence of stages or phases), which is cumulative (characteristics acquired in earlier stages are retained in later stages) and conjunctive (the stages are related such that they derive from a common underlying process). There is such a progression because the trajectory to the final end state is prefigured and requires a specific historical sequence of events. Each of these events contributes a piece to the final product, and they must occur in a prescribed order, because each piece sets the stage for the next. Each stage of development is seen as a necessary precursor of succeeding stages.

Life-cycle theory parallels the approach of the gross anatomist in biology, who observes a sequence of developing fetuses, concluding that each successive stage evolved from the previous one. Hence, Nisbet (1970) claimed that organizational development is driven by some genetic code or prefigured program within the developing entity. Flavell (1982) expanded Nisbet's interpretation by discussing a number of historically driven processes of cognitive development, in which each stage logically presupposes the next, such as when the development of manipulative skills precedes writing. There is no reason to suppose organizational systems could not have such processes as well.

Life-cycle theories of organizational entities often explain development in terms of institutional rules or programs that require developmental activities to progress in a prescribed sequence. For example, the U.S. Food and Drug Administration regulates a sequence of steps that all firms must follow to develop and commercialize a new drug or biomedical product. Other life-cycle theories rely on logical or natural sequences in the development of organizational entities. For example, Rogers (1983) posited five stages of innovation: need recognition, research on problem, development of idea into useful form, commercialization, and diffusion and adoption. The order among these stages is necessitated both by logic and by the natural order of Western business practices.

Teleological Theory

Another school of thought explains development by relying on teleology, or the philosophical doctrine that purpose or goal is the final cause for guiding movement of an entity. This approach underlies many organizational theories of change, including functionalism (Merton, 1968), decision making (March & Simon, 1958), epigenesis (Etzioni, 1963), voluntarism (Parsons, 1951), social construction (Berger & Luckmann, 1966), adaptive learning (March & Olsen, 1976), and most models of strategic planning and goal setting (Chakravarthy & Lorange, 1991).

According to teleology, development of an organizational entity proceeds toward a goal or an end state. It is assumed that the entity is purposeful and adaptive; by itself or in interaction with others, the entity constructs an envisioned end state, takes action to reach it, and monitors the progress. Thus, proponents of this theory view development as a repetitive sequence of goal formulation, implementation, evaluation, and modification of goals based on what was learned or intended by the entity. The theory can operate for an individual or for a group of individuals or organizations that are sufficiently like-minded to act as a single collective entity. Teleology inherently affords creativity because the entity, consisting of an individual or group, has the freedom to enact whatever goals it likes.

Unlike life-cycle theory, teleology does not prescribe a necessary sequence of events or specify which trajectory development of the organizational entity will follow. However, this theory implies a standard for judging change: development is something that moves the entity toward its final state. Some teleological models incorporate the systems theory assumption of equifinality (i.e., there are several equally effective ways to achieve a goal). In this theory, there is no prefigured rule, logically necessary direction, or set sequence of stages in a teleological process. Instead, proponents of this theory focus on the prerequisites for attaining the goal or end state: the functions that must be fulfilled, the accomplishments that must be achieved, or the components that must be built or obtained for the end state to be realized. These prerequisites can be used to assess if an entity is developing; that is, it is growing more complex or more integrated, or it is filling a necessary set of functions. We are able to make this assessment because teleological theory posits an envisioned end state for an entity, and we are able to observe movement toward the end state vis-à-vis this standard.

Although teleology stresses the purposiveness of the actor or unit as the motor for change, it also recognizes limits on action. The organization's environment and resources constrain what it can accomplish. Some of these constraints are embodied in prerequisites defined by institutions and other actors in the entity's environment. Individuals do not override natural laws or environmental constraints, but they make use of such laws or constraints to accomplish their purposes (Commons, 1950; Gibson, 1988).

Once an entity attains its goal, this does not mean it stays in permanent equilibrium. Goals are socially reconstructed and enacted on the basis of past actions (Weick, 1979). Influences in the external environment or within the entity itself may create instabilities that push it toward a new developmental path. Theories that rely on a teleological process cannot specify what trajectory the development of an organizational entity will follow. Proponents of such theories can at best list a set of possible paths and then rely on norms of decision rationality or action rationality (Brunsson, 1982) to prescribe certain paths.

Dialectical Theory

A third school, dialectical theory, begins with the Hegelian assumption that the organizational entity exists in a pluralistic world of colliding events, forces, or contradictory values that compete with each other for domination and control. These oppositions may be internal to an organizational entity because it may have several conflicting goals or interest groups competing for priority. Also, oppositions may be external to the organizational entity as it pursues directions that collide with the direction of other organizations. In any case, a dialectical theory requires two or more distinct entities that embody these oppositions to confront and engage one another in conflict.

In a dialectical process theory, stability and change are explained by reference to the balance of power between opposing entities. Struggles and accommodations that maintain the status quo between oppositions produce stability. Change occurs when these opposing values, forces, or events gain sufficient power to confront and engage the status quo. The relative power of an antithesis may mobilize an organizational entity to a sufficient degree to challenge the current thesis or state of affairs and set the stage for producing a synthesis. So, for example, an entity subscribing to a thesis (A) may be challenged by an opposing entity with an antithesis (Not-A), and the resolution of the conflict produces a synthesis (which is Not Not-A). Over time, this synthesis can become the new thesis as the dialectical process continues. By its very nature, the synthesis is a novel construction that departs from both the thesis and antithesis.

However, there is no assurance that dialectical conflicts produce creative syntheses. Sometimes an opposition group mobilizes sufficient power to simply overthrow and replace the status quo. Thus, also, many organizations persist by maintaining sufficient power to suppress and prevent the mobilization of opposition groups. In the bargaining and conflict management literature, the desired creative synthesis is one that represents a win-win solution, whereas either the maintenance of the thesis or its replacement with an antithesis is often treated as a win-lose outcome of a conflict engagement (Neal & Northcraft, 1991). In terms of organizational change, maintenance of the status quo represents stability, but its replacement with either the antithesis or the synthesis represents a change, for the better or worse.

Evolutionary Theory

Although evolution is sometimes equated with change, we use evolution in a more restrictive sense to focus on cumulative changes in structural forms of populations of organizational entities across communities, industries, or society at large (Aldrich, 1979; Campbell, 1969; Hannan & Freeman, 1977).[4] As in biological evolution, change proceeds through a continuous cycle of variation, selection, and retention. Variations, the creations of novel forms of organizations, are often viewed to emerge by blind or random chance; they just happen (Aldrich, 1979; Campbell, 1969). Selection of organization occurs principally through the competition for scarce resources, and the environment selects entities that best fit the resource base of an environmental niche (Hannan & Freeman, 1977). Retention involves forces (including inertia and persistence) that perpetuate and maintain certain organizational forms. Retention serves to counteract the self-reinforcing loop between variations and selection. Weick (1979) and Pfeffer (1982) noted that variations stimulated the selection of new organizational forms, but retention maintained previous forms and practices. Thus, evolution explains change as a recurrent, cumulative, and probabilistic progression of variation, selection, and retention of organizational entities. This motor is prescribed in the sense that one can specify the actuarial probabilities of the changing demographic characteristics of the population of entities inhabiting a niche. Although one cannot predict which entity will survive or fail, the overall population persists and evolves through time, according to the specified population dynamics.

In organization and management applications, evolutionary theory often depicts global changes in organizational populations (e.g., Carroll & Hannan, 1989), although Burgelman (1991) and Singh and Lumsden (1990) adopted the evolutionary model to explain strategy making within organizations, and Weick (1979) and Gersick (1991) applied parts of evolutionary theory at a micro level to explain the social-psychological processes of organizing. Whatever the organizational level, an evolutionary model can be used to focus on processes of variation, selection, and retention among numerous organizational entities.

Alternative theories of organizational evolution can be distinguished in terms of how traits are inherited, the rate of change, and the unit of analysis. Organizational scholars who adopt Darwinian evolution (e.g., Hannan & Freeman, 1977, 1989; McKelvey, 1982) argue that traits are inherited through intergenerational processes, whereas those who follow Lamarck (e.g., Boyd & Richerson, 1985; Burgelman, 1991; Singh & Lumsden, 1990; Weick, 1979) argue that traits are acquired within a generation through learning and imitation. A Lamarckian view on the acquisition of traits appears more appropriate than strict Darwinism for organization and management applications. As McKelvey (1982) pointed out, strict Darwinists have developed no adequate solutions to operationally identify an organizational generation.

Darwinian theorists emphasize a continuous and gradual process of evolution. In *The Origin of Species*, Darwin (1936: 361) wrote, "as natural selection acts solely by accumulating slight, successive, favourable variations, it can produce no great or sudden modifications; it can act only by short and slow steps.'' Other evolutionists posit a saltation theory of evolution, such as punctuated equilibrium (Arnold & Fristrup, 1982; Gould & Eldridge, 1977). Whether change proceeds at gradual versus saltation rates is an empirical matter. Thus, the rate of change does not fundamentally alter the theory of evolution (as it has been adopted by organization and management scholars).

The paleontologist Gould (1989) argued that another basic distinction between Darwinian evolution and his punctuated equilibrium theory is hierarchical level. Astley (1985) and Baum and Singh (1994) made this distinction, but Tushman and Romanelli (1985) did not. Gould (1989) pointed out that classical Darwinism locates the sorting of evolutionary change at a single level of objects. This sorting is natural selection operating through the differential births and deaths of organisms, as exemplified in many studies on organizational birth and death rates by population ecologists. (See reviews in Carroll & Hannan, 1989; and Hannan & Freeman, 1989.) Gould's punctuated equilibrium model adds a hierarchical dimension to evolutionary theory by distinguishing this sorting (the growth or decline of organisms of a given species through differential birth and death rates) from speciation (the process by which new species or a subgenus is formed): ''Speciation is a property of populations [and adaptation is a property of organisms within a population], . . . while extinction [a sorting process] is often a simple concatenation of deaths among organisms'' (Gould, 1989: 122).

II. A TYPOLOGY OF CHANGE PROCESS THEORIES

Life-cycle, teleology, dialectical, and evolutionary theories provide four internally consistent accounts of change processes in organizational entities. Where and when do these theories apply to explain development in organizational entities? To address this question, it is useful to emphasize four distinguishing characteristics in the preceding discussion of the four theories. In each theory (1) process is viewed as a different cycle of change events, (2) which is governed by a different ''motor'' or generating mechanism that (3) operates on a different unit of analysis and (4) represents a different mode of change. Figure 49.1 provides a metatheoretical scheme for illustrating and distinguishing the four ideal-type theories in terms of these four characteristics. We will now discuss these distinguishing characteristics.

Cycles and Motors of Change

As the cells of Figure 49.1 illustrate, in each theory the process of development is viewed as unfolding in a fundamentally different progression of change events and is governed by a different motor.

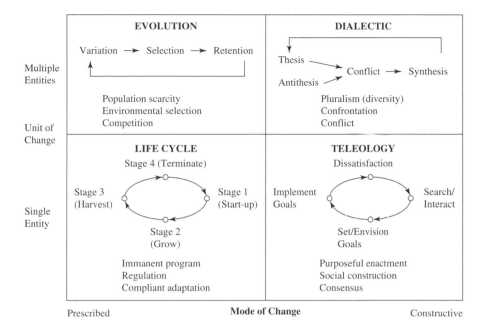

Figure 49.1. Process Theories of Organization Development and Change.

1. A life-cycle model depicts the process of change in an entity as progressing through a necessary sequence of stages. An institutional, natural, or logical program prescribes the specific contents of these stages.

2. A teleological model views development as a cycle of goal formulation, implementation, evaluation, and modification of goals based on what was learned by the entity. This sequence emerges through the purposeful social construction among individuals within the entity.

3. In dialectical models of development, conflicts emerge between entities espousing opposing thesis and antithesis that collide to produce a synthesis, which in time becomes the thesis for the next cycle of a dialectical progression. Confrontation and conflict between opposing entities generate this dialectical cycle.

4. An evolutionary model of development consists of a repetitive sequence of variation, selection, and retention events among entities in a designated population. Competition for scarce environmental resources between entities inhabiting a population generates this evolutionary cycle.

Figure 49.1 shows two analytical dimensions that are useful for classifying these developmental progressions in the four ideal-type process theories: the unit and the mode of change.

Unit of Change

Change and developmental processes go on at many organizational levels, including the individual, group, organization, population, and even larger communities of organizations. This nesting of entities into larger organizational entities creates a hierarchical system of levels. Figure 49.1 collapses this nested hierarchy of levels into whether the change in question focuses on the development of a single organizational entity or on the interactions between two or more entities. This classification highlights two different angles for studying change at any given organizational level: (1) the internal development of a single organizational entity by examining its historical processes of change, adaptation, and replication, and (2) the relationships between numerous entities to understand ecological processes of competition, cooperation, conflict, and other forms of interaction. A similar classification was used by Baum and Singh (1994) in their dual hierarchy framework. It distinguished between interactions among organizational entities in an ecological hierarchy and adaptation and replication processes within the genealogical history of an entity.

Evolutionary and dialectical theories operate on *multiple entities*. Evolutionary forces are defined in terms of the impact they have on populations and have no meaning at the level of the individual entity. Dialectical theories require at least two entities to fill the roles of thesis and antithesis. Even if researchers conceptualize the dialectic as occurring within a single person or organization, as does Riegel's (1975) dialectical theory of child development, the motor focuses on the interaction between two entities: the child and his or her environment. The explanatory model is thus dropped a level, and entities are distinguished within the child's mind and the world. Notwithstanding level, the explanation must distinguish at least two (and in Riegel's case four) entities that engage in the dialectic.

Conversely, life-cycle and teleological theories operate on a *single entity*. Life-cycle theory explains development as a function of potentials immanent within the entity. Although environment and other entities may shape how this immanence is manifested, they are strictly secondary. The real push to development comes from within the single, whole developing entity. Teleological theories, too, require only a single entity's goals to explain development. A teleological theory can operate among many members of an organization when there is sufficient consensus among the members to permit them to act as a single organizational entity. Similar to life-cycle theory, interactions between entities may influence the course of development, but this is subsidiary to the teleological motor that drives individual entities to enact an envisioned end state.

Thus, as long as the entity undergoing change has a discrete identity, one can decompose the entity within a nested organizational hierarchy to examine its members or one can aggregate the entity into its larger system without losing any of the theory's explanatory power. However, if researchers decide to examine processes of change between several distinct organizational entities, they move to either a dialectical or an evolutionary theory, because they must specify laws, rules, or processes by which the entities interact.

Mode of Change

The four motors also can be distinguished in terms of whether the sequence of change events is prescribed a priori by either deterministic or probabilistic laws, or whether the progression is constructed and emerges as the change process unfolds. A *prescribed* mode of change channels the development of entities in a prespecified direction, typically of maintaining and incrementally adapting their forms in a stable, predictable way. A *constructive* mode of change generates unprecedented, novel forms that, in retrospect, often are discontinuous and unpredictable departures from the past. A prescribed mode evokes a sequence of change events in accord with a preestablished program or action routine. A constructive mode, in contrast, produces new action routines that may (or may not) create an original (re)formulation of the entity. Life-cycle and evolutionary theories operate in a prescribed modality, while teleological and dialectical theories operate in a constructive modality.

A prescribed mode tends to create what Watzlawick, Weakland, and Fisch (1974) termed *first-order change*, or change within an existing framework that produces variations on a theme. The processes that produce these variations are prescribed and predictable because they are patterned on the previous state. Over the longer term, small changes may cumulate to produce a larger change in degree or quality of the entity. The uncertainty experienced by people undergoing such changes is relatively low, because they typically perceive sufficient continuity to anticipate and discern the direction of change. From his biological frame of reference, de Rosnay (1970) viewed prescribed motors as concerned with ontogenesis, involving the reproduction of entities similar to the original line.

Life-cycle and evolutionary theories incorporate a prescribed mode of change. During the life cycle, the immanent form is realized by steps, and although some steps may seem like a radical morphogenic change, there is an underlying continuity due to the immanent form, logic, program, or code that drives development. Due to its immanent motor, very seldom do frame-breaking changes or mutations arise in life-cycle models. Evolutionary accounts rely on the statistical cumulation of small individual events to gradually change the nature of the larger population. Although a person tends to think of mutations as sudden, dramatic changes, in actuality the evolutionary system operates according to prescribed rules that determine whether the mutation "takes" and change occurs. The apparent exception to this statement, punctuated equilibrium, actually conforms to a prescribed mode of change on closer examination. In the punctuated equilibrium model of biological evolution, posited by Gould and Eldridge (1977), species emergence at the micro level is sudden, but the diffusion of species that ultimately alters the characteristics of populations occurs through many individual events spread over quite long periods of time (on the order of millions of years; Gould, 1989). The application of punctuated equilibrium models to organizational change by Tushman and Romanelli (1985) departs from this account and, as we will discuss in Section Three, is actually a mixture of two of the theory types we have defined (see also, Poole & Van de Ven, 1989).

A constructive mode tends to generate what Watzlawick and colleagues (1974) termed *second-order change*, which is a break with the past basic assumptions or framework. The process is emergent as new goals are enacted. It can produce highly novel features; the outcome is unpredictable because it is discontinuous with the past. Those undergoing such changes may experience a high degree of uncertainty and a need to make sense of the changes. From a biological perspective, de Rosnay (1970) characterized a constructive mode of change as a phylogenetic process that leads to the generation of originals and the emergence of new species.

Teleological and dialectical motors incorporate a constructive mode of development. By their very nature, teleological processes seek to diverge from the current order; a process that has as its goal to preserve the status quo would be a theory of statics, not dynamics. Because goals can be changed at the will of the entity and because the prerequisites may be attained in many ways, teleological theories project a situation that is in principle unpredictable and may result in discontinuity (Von Wright, 1971). As a result, a teleological motor projects fundamental and novel changes in the entity.

However, there is an apparent problem. Many theories that draw on teleology also explicate gradual processes by which the goals are realized. For example, Chakravarthy and Lorange (1991) described corporate strategic planning as a stagewise, incremental process. Such gradual accounts of goal implementation actually combine two of the ideal types, teleological theory and life-cycle theory, to form a composite model. In Section Three, a number of such composites are discussed. In its pure form, however, the twin features of intentionality and the ability to change goals at will make teleological theories inherently emergent and creative.

Dialectical theory also incorporates a constructive mode of change. The sequence by which the thesis and antithesis confront and engage each other in a conflict struggle is highly uncertain; events leading to confrontation of opposites and resolutions may occur intermittently over the course of development. The result is a synthesis that breaks the current frame and represents second-order change. It produces a revolutionary change, resulting in a new entity that is an original rather than the reproduction of some prior state or entity.

Summary

The two dimensions of unit and mode of change classify the four theories in terms of their action and process. They differ from other dimensions often used to classify theories of organizational change, such as incremental versus radical change (e.g., Tushman and Romanelli, 1985), continuous versus discontinuous change (e.g., Meyer, Goes, & Brooks, 1993), first-order versus second-order change (Meyer et al., 1993), and competence-enhancing versus competence-destroying change (Abernathy & Clark, 1985). These dimensions classify organizational changes by their consequences or outcomes, rather than by their starting or process conditions. One advantage of the typology is that it is possible to identify the motor(s) of a change process before it has concluded.

Antecedent and outcome dimensions of change processes may be related in an actuarial or statistical sense, but not in a causal manner. Statistically one should expect the vast majority of incremental, continuous, and competence-enhancing changes to follow the operations of a prescribed mode, just as radical, discontinuous, and competence-destroying changes should follow from a constructive mode. These temporal relationships may not be causal. For example, the infrequent statistical occurrence of a discontinuous and radical mutation may be caused by a glitch in the operation of a prescribed life-cycle motor of change. So also, the scale-up of a teleological motor designed to create a fundamental strategic reorientation of a company may fizzle, resulting only in incremental change.

Situating the four ideal motors of change and development on the two dimensions accentuates their differences and enables researchers to describe them in their pure forms. Each of the four motors depends on a different set of conditions, which are depicted in Table 49.2. Determining whether these conditions are satisfied enables researchers to make an initial judgment concerning whether a given type of motor explains development in a particular situation.

However, as our examples illustrate, theories of organizational change and development seldom include the ideal types in their pure forms. To understand how the ideal types figure in theoretical "practice" and to appreciate their utility, we will now consider specific theories that focus on particular types of organizational changes. For the sake of clarity, we will refer to the ideal-type theories as *motors* of change and reserve the term *theory* for the complex, specific theories that have been developed by various researchers.

Table 49.2. Logically Possible Theories of Organizational Change and Development.

	Interplays Among Generating Mechanisms			
	Prescribed Motor Within Entity	Constructive Motor Within Entity	Constructive Motor Between Entities	Prescribed Motor Between Entities
	Immanent Program	Purposeful Enhancement	Conflict & Synthesis	Competitive Selection
Single-Motor Theories				
1. Life cycle (Cameron & Whetten, 1983)	**Yes**	No	No	No
2. Teleology (March & Simon, 1958)	No	**Yes**	No	No
3. Dialectics (Benson, 1977)	No	No	**Yes**	No
4. Evolution (Hannan & Freeman, 1977)	No	No	No	**Yes**
Dual-Motor Theories				
5. Design hierarchy theory (Clark, 1985)	**Yes**	**Yes**	No	No
6. Group conflict (Coser, 1956; Simmel, 1955)	No	**Yes**	**Yes**	No
7. Community ecology (Astley, 1985)	No	No	**Yes**	**Yes**
8. Adaptation-selection models (Aldrich, 1979)	**Yes**	No	No	**Yes**
9. Org. growth & crisis stages (Greiner, 1972)	**Yes**	No	**Yes**	No
10. Org. punctuated equilibrium (Tushman & Romanelli, 1985)	No	**Yes**	No	**Yes**
Tri-Motor Theories				
11. Partisan mutual adjustment (Lindblom, 1965)	**Yes**	**Yes**	**Yes**	No
12. ?	No	**Yes**	**Yes**	**Yes**
13. ?	**Yes**	No	**Yes**	**Yes**

14. Social psychology of organizing (Weick, 1979)	**Yes**	**Yes**	No	**Yes**
Quad-Motor Theories				
15. ? Human development progressions (Riegel, 1976)	**Yes**	**Yes**	**Yes**	**Yes**
16. ? Garbage can (Cohen, March, & Olsen, 1972)	No	No	No	No

Conditions for Operation of Change Theories

For a Life-Cycle Motor

A singular, discrete entity exists that undergoes change, yet maintains its identity throughout the process.

The entity passes through stages distinguishable in form or function.

A program, routine, rule, or code exists in nature, social institutions, or logic that determines the stages of development and governs progression through the stages.

For a Teleological Motor

An individual or group exists that acts as a singular, discrete entity, which engages in reflexively monitored action to socially construct and cognitively share a common end state or goal.

The entity may envision its end state of development before or after actions it may take, and the goal may be set explicitly or implicitly. However, the process of social construction or sense making, decision making, and goal setting must be identifiable.

A set of requirements and constraints exists to attain the goal, and the activities and developmental transitions undertaken by the entity contribute to meeting these requirements and constraints.

For a Dialectical Motor

At least two entities exist (each with its own discrete identity) that oppose or contradict one another.

The opposing entities must confront each other and engage in a conflict or struggle through some physical or social venue, in which the opposition plays itself out.

The outcome of the conflict must consist of either a new entity that is different from the previous two, or (in degenerate cases) the defeat of one entity by the other, or a stalemate among the entities.

For an Evolutionary Motor

A population of entities exists in a commensalistic relationship (i.e., in a physical or social venue with limited resources each entity needs for its survival).

Identifiable mechanisms exist for variation, selection, and retention of entities in the population.

Macropopulation characteristics set the parameters for microlevel variation, selection, and retention mechanisms.

III. THEORIES OF COMPLEX DEVELOPMENT AND CHANGE PROCESSES

Specific Theories as Composites of the Ideal Types

Most specific theories of organizational change and development are more complicated than the ideal types. This is so for two reasons. First, because the organizational context of development and change extends over space and time in any specific case, it is possible for more than one motor to come into play. Organizational development and change are influenced by diverse units and actors, both inside and outside the organization. The spatial dispersion of units and actors means that different influences may be acting simultaneously on different parts of the organization, each imparting its own particular momentum to the developmental process. In some cases, more than one change motor may influence development and change. Development and change also take time to occur. As time passes, there is opportunity for different motors to come into play, especially given the dispersion of influences. The resulting observed process is multilayered and complex. Attempts to explain this process with a single motor run the risk of oversimplification and selective attention to one aspect of the change process at the expense of others.

A study of the development of a new organizational entity engaged in the development of a biomedical innovation, the cochlear implant, by Van de Ven and Garud (1993) illustrated this complexity. This innovation was shaped by change processes occurring on numerous fronts. A teleological process seemed to explain the course of development of the implant in the firm's R&D lab. In a different sphere, the action of top managers in purposefully selecting and funding it was also consistent with a teleological model, but the decision premises and timing of managerial interventions moved at a different pace than efforts of the development team. At a certain point in its development, the product had to be approved by the FDA, which required a sequence of proposals, clinical trials, and regulatory reviews and approvals. This prescribed sequence, which embodied a life-cycle motor, came into play later than the teleological motors, but it was so important that the other two centers of change had to rearrange their efforts to meet its requirements. A fourth influence operated at the larger field of researchers and clinicians concerned with hearing health: the firm's pioneering implant design was initially supported by the field, but evidence mounted that led most researchers and clinicians to switch allegiance to a competing firm's design. The complex interplay of these different motors, which operated in different times and places, created a complicated developmental sequence that was difficult to understand, until these diverse influences were sorted out.

A second reason for the complexity of specific organizational change and development theories is the inherent incompleteness of any single motor. Each motor pictured in Figure 49.1 has one or more components whose values are determined exogenously to the model. For example, in the evolutionary model, it is assumed that variations arise randomly, but the process that gives rise to variation remains unspecified. In the dialectical model, the origin of the antithesis is obscure, as is the source of dissatisfaction in the teleological model, and the processes that trigger start-up and termination in the life-cycle model. Other motors can be used to account for the origin of these events. For instance, the selection process in the evolutionary model can be used to account for termination in the life cycle; the implementation step in the teleological cycle can trigger the start-up event in the life cycle and the antithesis in the dialectic. The synthesis in the dialectic could be the source of variation in the evolutionary cycle. There are many other possible interrelations. In short, events from other models are useful to remedy the incompleteness of any single model of change.

We will argue that most specific theories of organizational development and change are actually composites of two or more ideal-type motors. This decomposition of complex theories into simpler ones has several precedents. In cognitive science, Newell (1973) and Simon (1979), among others, have argued that complex behavior can be generated by the interplay of a few simple motors. In organization science, March (1981) and Masuch (1985) have shown that a few substitutions of one simple change sequence by another equally simple process can create exceedingly complicated and intractable action cycles. Poole (1983, 1985; Poole & Roth, 1989) found empirically that seemingly complex patterns of behavior in group decision making result from the interplay of life-cycle and teleological motors. Common among these approaches is the identification of simple motors whose interplay creates a complex phenomenon.

An Array of Composite Theories of Development and Change

Each ideal type theory describes a generative mechanism or motor of change. Combinations of these motors create, in effect, hybrid change theories. The simplest form of combination is to determine which of the generating mechanisms underlying the four ideal types are evident or in operation in a given applied theory of organizational change in the literature. By specifying the presence (operation) or absence (nonoperation) of the four motors in a given situation, an array of sixteen logically possible explanations of organizational change and development becomes apparent. This array, shown in Table 49.2, is analogous to examining the simple main and interaction effects of each of the four motors on alternative applied theories in the management literature.

The first four alternatives represent the main effects of the generating mechanisms underlying our four ideal-type theories: the immanent program of life-cycle theory, purposeful enactment of teleological theory, conflict and synthesis of dialectical theory, and competitive selection of evolutionary theory. These "single-motor theories" apply to cases when only one of the four change motors is in operation.

The next twelve alternatives represent interaction effects of the interdependent operation of two or more of the four generative mechanisms. Alternatives five through ten are called *dual-motor theories* because they represent cases when only two of the four change motors are in operation in a given organizational change process. Alternatives eleven through fourteen represent four logically possible *tri-motor theories*, when three of the four change motors operate interdependently. Alternative fifteen is a *quad-motor theory*, which represents the most complex situation when all four generating mechanisms operate interdependently in a given situation. Finally, alternative sixteen represents the null set, when no motor is operating.

The left column of Table 49.2 lists exemplary theories for some of the sixteen logically possible conditions in which an organizational change or developmental process may unfold. The rows with a "?" are conditions where we could not find an exemplary theory in the literature; they represent opportunities for new theory building. Admittedly, the authors of these exemplary theories or models may not agree with our classification, because they did not have our framework in mind when they developed their theories. However, we contend that the framework provides a useful new way to understand and discriminate between alternative theories of organizational change and development in the literature. Specifically, we propose that what distinguishes these alternative theories is their incorporation of different combinations of the four motors of change.

Space limitations prevent us from providing a systematic discussion of theories representing each of the sixteen logically possible combinations of the four motors of change. Instead, we present several examples of how complex theories can be constructed from the interplay of a few simple motors of change.

Row 5: Interaction of life-cycle and teleological motors. Clark (1985), building on the work of Utterback and Abernathy (1975), developed a theory of the gradual evolution of technologies. Abernathy and Utterback had proposed that the evolution of technological production proceeded from an early, "fluid" state to one that is highly "specific" and rigid. Product innovations predominate early in this evolution, but once the nature of the product is determined, process innovations increase and will dominate until rigidity extinguishes innovation. The rise and fall of product innovations is succeeded by the rise and fall of process innovations because of the logic of the production, which pushes firms to try to optimize and standardize first the nature of a successful product, and, once the product is set, the procedures for producing it. The result is increasing rigidity throughout the life of the product.

To explain how changes in technologies come about, Clark discussed the interaction between designers and customers, which establishes functional prerequisites for the product. This teleological process is in interplay with another life-cycle motor, the technical design hierarchy. Clark (1985: 241) argued that all technical design is hierarchical, because "there are choices in the development of a design that create precedents and are logically prior to other choices. These precedents create constraints that give rise to further search for alternative designs." Once an organization takes a certain technical path, this forecloses other paths and opens up a hierarchy of subproblems. Interaction between designers and customers influences progression through a hierarchy; the natural direction of movement is down the hierarchy until the technical agenda is fulfilled, but customer demands may encourage designers either to move back up the hierarchy and pursue other paths, or to jump to a different aspect of the design problem. Hence, Clark's (1985) theory provides for the interplay of teleological and life-cycle motors nested within the overall life-cycle progression from product to process emphases.

Row 9: Interaction of life-cycle and dialectical motors. In one of the earliest models of organizational development, Greiner (1972) proposed five stages to the life cycle of organizational growth through creativity, direction, delegation, coordination, and collaboration. Each of these stages culminates in a different dialectical crisis (of leadership, autonomy, control, red tape, and ?), which propels the organization into the next stage of growth. Thus, the model is grounded in temporal interactions between life-cycle and dialectical theories of change. In the main, the model is rooted in a life-cycle theory of change, in which "historical forces [organization age, size, growth rate, and stages of evolution and revolution] shape the future growth of organizations" (Greiner,

1972: 166). Greiner used dialectical theory to explain, "as a company progresses through developmental phases, each evolutionary period creates its own revolution" (1972: 166). Reflecting on his model, Greiner observed:

> My model is a reasonably explicit attempt to combine unitary life cycle with dialectical theories—but not teleological. For me, life cycle explains the "form" of the unitary stages, while the dialectics explain the underlying dynamics of movement. For example, I put the "crises" in the model because I could not find data showing the stages as naturally and automatically evolving one after the other. Thus, it is not a model where a future life or end state is assured. . . . My reason for saying it is not teleological is that there is no envisioned end state that pulls the process—for me it is the current dynamics within the organization that are driving it forward—convergence around the thesis of each stage and then running into resistance (antithesis) and requiring reorientation for the conflict to be resolved. The model in fact has no ending and concludes with a question mark. . . . I also think it is the dialectics that added the power struggle reality and made the article so successful in managerial reaction [Greiner, quoted in Van de Ven, 1992: 184].

Row 10: Interaction of teleological and evolutionary motors. Tushman and Romanelli's (1985) punctuated equilibrium model of organizational metamorphosis can be viewed as a product of alternating cycles in the operation of an evolutionary motor of change at a population level of analysis for relatively long convergent periods, punctuated by relatively short and infrequent operations of a teleological motor of change by top managers at the organizational level. During the convergence period, an evolutionary process of competitive selection works to elaborate the structures, systems, controls, and resources of organizations toward increased environmental coalignment. Reorientations represent periods of discontinuous change where an organization's strategies, power, structure, and systems are fundamentally transformed by and realigned toward the purposive actions of executive leaders (Tushman & Romanelli, 1985: 173).

In the punctuated equilibrium model, the authors use time as the avenue for incorporating both evolutionary and teleological motors in a theory of organizational change. Purposeful enactment by top managers is used to explain the creative process of occasional organizational reorientations, whereas prescribed evolutionary processes explain long periods of organizational convergence with its environment. According to Tushman and Romanelli (1985), in no instance should one expect to find both motors of change operating at the same time in a given organization because they are mutually exclusive. Thus, time provides the vehicle for incorporating opposing change motors in Tushman and Romanelli's punctuated equilibrium model of organizational change. Admittedly, the model does not specify the interplay between the two motors in much detail. It is unclear what sparks the transition from the convergence to the transformational period and vice versa.

Row 14: Interaction of life-cycle, teleological, and evolutionary motors. Weick's (1979) theory of organizing is an ambitious attempt to explain organizing in dynamic fashion. Weick's well-known model for equivocality reduction has three stages—enactment, selection, and retention—which form a life cycle for the organizing process. This cycle repeats many times during the course of an organizing episode. As behavior cycles are selected and retained, there is considerable room for the initiative and creativity of individuals to influence the process, opening the way for the influence of a teleological motor. The assumptions of the teleological motor are reflected in Weick's definition of organizing as the development of a shared grammar. In addition to the life cycle and teleological motor, there also is an evolutionary process at work. Even though individual instances of equivocality reduction follow the three stages, over many repetitions an evolutionary motor operates that selects and retains certain organizational forms over others. This evolutionary motor, strongly influenced by Campbell's (1969, 1974) theory of intellectual evolution, shapes the course of organizing over the longer term.

Again, time is a key mediator of different motors in Weick's theory. The immediate process of organizing is driven through a life-cycle motor and influenced by a teleological motor of participants' choices of adaptations and retentions. However, over the longer run, these short-term actions contribute to an evolutionary process through which different practices, structures, and ideas are selected and retained.

Row 15: Interaction of all four motors of change. The most complex and sophisticated explanation of change and development in Table 49.2 is one that incorporates interactions from all four generating mechanisms. We have found no example of this composite in the organization and management literature. To illustrate how it might work, we will briefly discuss Riegel's (1975) theory of human development. Riegel distinguished between four progressions of life events, which are analogous to our four generating mechanisms of organizational change: (1) an inner-biological progression of life-cycle events such as birth, illness, cell growth, and death; (2) an individual-personality progression in the psychological development of individuals, in terms of their wishes and duties, plans and skills, and needs for belonging and identity; (3) a cultural-sociological progression of an individual's conformity or deviance with the culture, language, institutions, and customs of the organizations in which the individual participates; and (4) an outer-physical progression of events, such as natural disasters, social demography, or economic cycles that an individual may encounter. Riegel (1975: 392) pointed out that events within and between these progressions are not always synchronized. Developmental crises occur whenever two sequences are out of step. He identified sixteen developmental progressions that can be produced by asynchronies along the four developmental progressions, which can result in either destructive outcomes or constructive leaps in development. Riegel went on to state:

> Once generated, these new developments can transform the previously contradictory interactions of conflicting events into a coordinated, synchronized pattern of interactions and change. As synchrony is reestablished, a form of individual and social progress is achieved. And yet with each successful new development, new questions and discrepancies emerge and, in this process, produce a continuous flux of contradictions and developmental change [1975: 385].

Riegel's theory of human development provides a rich example of what a theory of organizational development might look like if it focused on the crises produced by asynchronies in the operation of life-cycle, teleological, dialectical, and evolutionary motors of change.

Benefits of the Framework for Theory and Research

The approach outlined in this chapter contributes to organization theory in at least four respects. First, it offers a parsimonious explanation of a wide variety of organizational development and change theories. The four ideal-type motors serve as theoretical primitives, and the complexities of the developmental process can be analyzed as the interplay among these primitives. This interplay makes it possible to discern commonalities among a broad range of specific theories that might otherwise be overlooked. Some review articles, such as Cameron and Whetten's (1983) discussion of organizational life-cycle models, have attempted to do this for a limited range of developmental theories. The current framework extends this projection to the entire breadth of organization development and change.

Second, the framework also can serve as a heuristic for critique and reformulation. In an adequate theory, each ideal-type motor should be represented in its full-fledged form, and the relationships among motors should be fully specified. The framework encourages scholars to identify aspects of motors or relationships that are incompletely described in a given theory. In such cases, it would be necessary to spell out the remainder and fill in details. We hope the framework will promote clearer and more explicit theories of development and change.

Third, the framework points out previously unexplored explanations of organizational change and development. In particular, we could not find examples of theories in the management literature for rows twelve, thirteen, and fifteen of Table 49.2. These "missing" rows represent opportunities for theory building, perhaps through novel applications of theories or metaphors from other contexts. For example, we introduced Riegel's theory of human development to illustrate the structure of a theory of organizational development that incorporates interactions from all four change motors.

Finally, the framework provides a foundation for empirical research. As our example of cochlear implants showed, it is not always clear from the outset what forces are influencing a complex developmental process. Indeed, if it is true that the interplay of multiple forces often drives development, then conducting research with a simple a priori theory in mind actually may impede adequate explanation. The researcher may look only for indicators of that particular theory, ignoring other possible explanations. In the best case, this myopia results in an incomplete account of development and change; in the worst case, the researcher may incorrectly reject his or her model because complexities introduced by other motors covered over evidence of its adequacy. An alternative approach is to collect very rich data and canvass it for several alternative motors of change, as done by the Minnesota Innovation Research Program (Van de Ven, Angle, & Poole, 1989). To do this, the researcher must first determine which of the four motors are operating by testing whether the conditions summarized in the sidebar "Conditions for Operation of Change Theories" are present. If more than one motor is operating, the second step is to examine how they are related. This two-step approach, which we call *template matching*, avoids the narrowness imparted by adherence to a simple developmental theory, while keeping a strong theoretical basis for research. Template matching is sensitive to the context of organizational development and change. It promotes the development of explanations commensurate with the complexity of a given process. Moreover, because explanations are cast in terms of the four ideal-type motors and their interplay, this approach promotes the development of more general theories of development and change.

IV. CONCLUSION

This chapter introduced a typology of four ideal-type theories of organizational development and change: life cycle, teleological, dialectical, and evolutionary. These four theories have rich intellectual traditions and offer fundamentally different explanations of change and development processes. Each theory relies on its own motor of change, which can be mapped as a distinct action cycle. However, observed change and development processes in organizations often are more complex than any one of these theories suggests because conditions may exist to trigger interplay among several change motors and produce interdependent cycles of change. Even though each of these types has its own internal logic, complexity and the potential for theoretical confusion arise from the interplay among different motors.

On the basis of the presence or absence of the generating mechanisms underlying the four ideal-type theories, we develop a framework of sixteen logically possible explanations of organizational change and development. As the examples illustrate, this framework provides a systematic way to compare and contrast alternative theories of organizational change in the management and organization literature. It also promotes theory construction by identifying logical combinations that have previously not been developed.

An important extension of the framework is to more fully examine the types of relationships that might hold between the four change motors. Several types warrant investigation. First, there is the degree of *nesting* of motors. In some cases motors may operate on the same level of analysis (e.g., the organizational level). However, it is possible that one motor may be nested within the other, for example, when one characterizes the development of the organization as a whole, while the other pertains to the actions of individuals within the organization, or when one depicts the development of an industry and another the development of individual organizations in that industry. When motors are at the same level of analysis, relationships among them represent simple influences; however, when motors are nested, working out the relationships among them requires specifying macro-micro links. A second key relationship is the *timing* of the motors. Motors may operate simultaneously, or they may alternate at different times. If they operate simultaneously, the degrees of amplitude or influence of each motor on a change process over time should be examined. Third, we must consider the degree of *complementarity* among motors. Motors may reinforce or contradict one another. Baum and Singh (1994) provided a constructive approach to examine these relationships by specifying the vertical and horizontal relationships between ecological and genealogical hierarchies in levels of organizational systems.

As these types of relationships suggest, the *relative balance* between the constructive and prescribed motors operating at different levels of analysis are likely to play a major role in explaining patterns of stability and change in an organization. For example, when an institutionally prescribed motor dominates the development of an organization, it may suppress or dampen internally generated variety to the degree that the organization begins to act more rigidly and more predictably. When a constructive motor dominates through either teleological or dialectical processes, the organization may be unable to suppress rival subsystems that rise up from within, creating too much variety to integrate into one system. In other words, positive feedback between constructive and prescribed motors reinforces change and can produce exploding complexity, whereas negative feedback counteracts the effects of change events and is likely to produce a moving equilibrium in organizational development.

More precisely, temporal shifts in the relative balance between positive and negative feedback loops in the operation of different change motors can push an organization (1) to flow toward a fixed-point equilibrium, (2) to oscillate in a periodic sequence between opposites, (3) to bifurcate far from equilibrium and spontaneously create new structures, or (4) to behave in a random fashion. First, as just stated, organizational stability occurs when a negative feedback loop exists between the operation of prescribed and constructive motors of change. For example, the institutional routines or the established goals of the organization are sufficient to keep the creation of new programs or conflicts between alternative programs within limits so that the organization does not fly apart from too much novelty and thereby produce incremental adaptations flowing toward a stable equilibrium. Second, organizational cycles, fads, or pendulum swings occur when the relative influence of positive and negative feedback loops between change motors alternate in a periodic pattern and push the organization to oscillate somewhat farther from its stable equilibrium orbit. Such recurrent cycles are exemplified in some models of vicious circles in organizations (Masuch, 1985), group entrainment processes (McGrath & Kelly, 1986), and creative destruction (Schumpeter, 1942). Third, organizational transformations and spontaneous novel structures can be produced when strong imbalances occur between constructive and prescribed change motors, which may push the organization out of its equilibrium orbit and produce bifurcations (Prigogine & Stengers, 1984) or catastrophes (Zeeman, 1976), leading to chaotic patterns of organizational change. Finally, the behavior of change motors in a developing organization may be so complicated and indeterminate as to render deterministic modeling infeasible; the best one can do is to stochastically model the behaviors as a random process. Stochastic models based on the theory of random processes allow researchers to make better predictions than they could make without a model (Eubank & Farmer, 1990).

As this discussion suggests, a major extension of the framework is to develop and study nonlinear dynamical systems models of organizational change and development, which may be produced by feedback loops among two or more simple motors of change. Organizational researchers have tended to focus on linear or cyclical models of organizational development and have treated other seemingly random patterns as either truly stochastic processes (Tuma & Hannan, 1984) or as various forms of "error" distributions messing up their experiments (Abraham, Abraham, & Shaw, 1990). Advances in dynamic systems theory provide mathematical tools for examining chaos as an alternative explanation of organizational change and development processes. These advances have been introduced into the management and organizational literature by Cheng and Van de Ven (in press), Cottrell (1993), Koput (1992), and Polley (1993).

As Koput (1992) stated, a dynamic model is one where the variables (here the operation of the change motors) at a given time are a function (at least in part) of the same variables at an earlier time. Nonlinearity implies that there are feedback loops that vary in strength (loose or tight coupling) and direction (positive or negative) over time between opposing forces or demands. Such nonlinear dynamic models are often path-dependent or sensitive to initial conditions. This sensitivity means that small initial differences or fluctuations in trajectories of variables may grow into large differences over time, and as they move far from equilibrium they bifurcate or branch out into numerous possible pathways resembling a chaotic decision tree. In a chaotic state the pathways that are taken in the branching cannot be predicted; they represent spontaneously created new structures that emerge in a seemingly random order. What is impressive about such chaotic processes is that they have a hidden order that typically consists of a relatively simple nonlinear system of dynamic relationships among only a few variables (Eubank & Farmer, 1990). We close "out on a limb" by speculating that underlying the indeterminate and seemingly random processes of development often observed in organizational entities there exists such a relatively simple system of nonlinear dynamic relationships among a few of the motors of change examined here.

Finally, although much can be said in favor of the analytical, heuristic, and research potential of this framework, one common objection will be that it seems overly reductionistic. Can all models of development be reduced to four relatively simple motors and their interactions? The typology is based on an extensive search through hundreds of works, and the four motors emerged as the "least common denominators" of the change theories reflected in those works, reflecting essential differences among these theories. Certainly, the ultimate determinant will be researchers' experience with the typology, using it to analyze existing theories and determining what, if anything, is left out.

Notes

1. Our developmental view of process should not be confused with two other uses of *process* in the management literature. Here, *process* refers to either (1) the underlying logic that explains a causal relationship between independent and dependent variables in a variance theory or (2) a category of concepts of organizational actions (e.g., rates of communications, work flows, decision-making techniques, or methods for strategy making). These concepts or mechanisms may be at work to explain an organizational result, but they do not describe how these variables or mechanisms unfold or change over time.

2. This review was assisted by a computerized literature search across disciplines using *change* and *development* as keywords. To our surprise, more than one million articles have been published on the subject in the disciplines of psychology, sociology, education, business, and economics, as well as biology, medicine, meteorology, and geography. Of course, not all these articles addressed theories of change or development; the vast majority focused on other substantive issues and dealt

with change processes in a cursory fashion. To cope with this prolific literature, we reviewed about two hundred thousand titles and perused about two thousand abstracts, which led us to carefully read about two hundred articles that were useful in identifying about twenty process theories of development or change.

3. The classification of management and organization literature into the life-cycle and other ideal types of theories in this article is very loose and done for illustrative purposes. Because little attention has been given to underlying theories of change processes in the management and organization literature, it is difficult to know what specific theories of change the authors of cited works had in mind.

4. There are many different theories of evolution. Some scholars (e.g., March, 1994) have taken a very broad view (*evolution* equals our definition of *development*, or the dynamic sequence of changes over time). We take a more restrictive meaning and focus on adoptions of biological evolutionary theories. This restriction avoids historical confusions between early sociological evolutionism and biological evolutionism. Sztompka (1993) pointed out that early sociologists (e.g., Comte & Spencer) adopted the metaphor of organic growth (but not Darwinian or biological ideas) to examine the life span of society from its rudimentary state toward increasingly differentiated and "higher" levels. (This early sociological evolutionism is closer to a life-cycle theory than it is to biological evolutionary theory.) Some absurd extremes were drawn with this theory, and Nisbet (1970) and others attacked it; thus, most contemporary social scientists have adopted the biological evolutionary theories of Darwin, Lamarck, Gould, and Mendel. We focus only on biological evolution and distinguish its contemporary versions in the organizational and management literature.

References

Abernathy, W. J., & Clark, K. B. 1985. Innovation: Mapping the winds of creative destruction. *Research Policy*, 14: 3–22.

Abraham, F. D., Abraham, R. H., & Shaw, C. D. 1990. *A visual introduction to dynamical systems theory for psychology*. Santa Cruz, CA: Aerial Press.

Aldrich, H. 1979. *Organizations and environments*. Englewood Cliffs, NJ: Prentice Hall.

Arnold, A. J., & Fristrup, K. 1982. The theory of evolution by natural selection: A hierarchical expansion. *Paleobiology*, 8: 113–129.

Astley, W. G. 1985. The two ecologies: Population and community perspectives on organizational evolution. *Administrative Science Quarterly*, 30: 224–241.

Bales, R. F., & Strodtbeck, F. L. 1951. Phases in group problem-solving. *Journal of Abnormal and Social Psychology*, 46: 485–495.

Baltes, P. B., Dittman-Kohli, F., & Dixon, R. A. 1986. Multidisciplinary propositions on the development of intelligence during adulthood and old age. In A. B. Sorensen, F. E. Weinert, & L. R. Sherrod (Eds.), *Human development and the life course: Multidisciplinary perspectives:* 467–507. Hillsdale, NJ: Erlbaum.

Baum, J.A.C., & Singh, J. V. 1994. *Evolutionary dynamics of organizations*. New York: Oxford University Press.

Benson, J. K. 1977. Organizations: A dialectical view. *Administrative Science Quarterly*, 22: 1–21.

Berger, P. L., & Luckmann, T. 1966. *The social construction of reality*. Garden City, NY: Doubleday.

Boyd, R., & Richerson, P. J. 1985. *Culture and the evolutionary process*. Chicago: University of Chicago Press.

Brunsson, N. 1982. The irrationality of action and action rationality: Decisions, ideologies, and organizational actions. *Journal of Management Studies*, 19: 29–34.

Burgelman, R. A. 1991. Intraorganizational ecology of strategy making and organizational adaptation: Theory and field research. *Organization Science*, 2: 239–262.

Burgelman, R. A., & Sayles, L. R. 1986. *Inside corporate innovation: Strategy, structure, and managerial skills*. New York: Free Press.

Cameron, K., & Whetten, D. 1983. Models of the organizational life cycle: Applications to higher education. *Review of Higher Education*, 6(4): 269–299.

Campbell, D. 1969. Variation and selective retention in socio-cultural evolution. *General Systems*, 16: 69–85.

Campbell, D. 1974. Evolutionary epistemology. In P. A. Schilpp (Ed.), *The philosophy of Karl Popper*: 413–463. LaSalle, IL: Open Court Press.

Carroll, G., & Hannan, M. T. 1989. Density delay in the evolution of organizational populations: A model and five empirical tests. *Administrative Science Quarterly*, 34: 411–430.

Chakravarthy, B. S., & Lorange, P. 1991. *Managing the strategy process*. Englewood Cliffs, NJ: Prentice Hall.

Cheng, Y., & Van de Ven, A. In press. The innovation journey: Order out of chaos? *Organization Science*.

Clark, K. B. 1985. The interaction of design hierarchies and market concepts in technological evolution. *Research Policy*, 14: 235–251.

Cohen, M. D., March, J. G., & Olsen, J. P. 1972. A garbage can model of organizational choice. *Administrative Science Quarterly*, 17: 1–25.

Commons, J. R. 1950. *The economics of collective action*. Madison: University of Wisconsin Press.

Coser, L. A. 1956. *The functions of social conflict*. New York: Free Press.

Cottrell, T. 1993. *Nonlinear dynamics in the emergence of new industries*. Unpublished paper, University of California, Berkeley.

Darwin, C. 1936. *The origin of species*. New York: Modern Library.

de Rosnay, J. 1970. Evolution and time. *Main Currents*, 27: 35–47.

Etzioni, A. 1963. The epigenesis of political communities at the international level. *American Journal of Sociology*, 68: 407–421.

Eubank, S., & Farmer, D. 1990. An introduction to chaos and randomness. In E. Jen (Ed.), *1989 lectures in complex systems: SF1 studies in the sciences of complexity*, vol. 2: 75–190. Reading, MA: Addison-Wesley.

Featherman, D. L. 1986. Biography, society, and history: Individual development as a population process. In A. B. Sorensen, F. E. Weinert, & L. R. Sherrod (Eds.), *Human development and the life course: Multidisciplinary perspectives:* 99–149. Hillsdale, NJ: Erlbaum.

Flavell, J. H. 1982. Structures, stages, and sequences in cognitive development. In W. A. Collins (Ed.), *The concept of development: The Minnesota symposia on child psychology:* 1–28. Hillsdale, NJ: Erlbaum.

Gersick, C. J. 1991. Revolutionary change theories: A multilevel exploration of the punctuated equilibrium paradigm. *Academy of Management Review*, 16: 10–36.

Gibson, E. J. 1988. Exploratory behavior in the development of perceiving, acting, and the acquiring of knowledge. *Annual Review of Psychology*, 39: 1–41.

Gioia, D. A., & Pitre, E. 1990. Multiparadigm perspectives in theory building. *Academy of Management Review*, 15: 584–602.

Gould, S. J. 1989. Punctuated equilibrium in fact and theory. *Journal of Social and Biological Structures*, 12: 117–136.

Gould, S. J., & Eldridge, N. 1977. Punctuated equilibria: The tempo and model of evolution reconsidered. *Paleobiology*, 3: 115–151.

Greiner, L. 1972. Evolution and revolution as organizations grow. *Harvard Business Review*, 50(4): 37–46.

Hannan, M. T., & Freeman, F. 1977. The population ecology of organizations. *American Journal of Sociology*, 82: 929–964.

Hannan, M. T., & Freeman, F. 1989. *Organizational ecology*. Cambridge, MA: Harvard University Press.

Harre, R., & Madden, E. A. 1975. *Causal powers*. Totowa, NJ: Littlefield, Adams.

Kaplan, A. 1964. *The conduct of inquiry: Methodology for behavioral science*. New York: Chandler.

Kimberly, J., & Miles, R. 1980. *The organizational life cycle*. San Francisco: Jossey-Bass.

Kohlberg, L. 1969. Stage and sequence: The cognitive-developmental approach to socialization. In D. A. Goslin (Ed.), *Handbook of socialization theory and research:* 347–480. Chicago: Rand McNally.

Koput, K. 1992. *Dynamics of innovative idea generation in organizations: Randomness and chaos in the development of a new medical device*. Unpublished doctoral dissertation, University of California School of Business, Berkeley.

Levinson, D. J. 1978. *The seasons of a man's life*. New York: Knopf.

Lindblom, C. E. 1965. *The intelligence of democracy*. New York: Free Press.

March, J. G. 1981. Footnotes to organizational change. *Administrative Science Quarterly*, 26: 563–577.

March, J. G. 1994. The evolution of evolution. In J. Baum & J. Singh (Eds.), *Evolutionary dynamics of organizations:* 39–49. New York: Oxford University Press.

March, J. G., & Olsen, J. P. 1976. *Ambiguity and choice in organizations.* Bergen, Norway: Universitetsforlaget.

March, J. G., & Simon, H. A. 1958. *Organizations.* New York: Wiley.

Masuch, M. 1985. Vicious cycles in organizations. *Administrative Science Quarterly*, 30: 14–33.

McGrath, J. E., & Kelly, J. R. 1986. *Time and human interaction: Toward a social psychology of time.* New York: Guilford Press.

McKelvey, B. 1982. *Organizational systematics: Taxonomy, evolution, classification.* Berkeley: University of California Press.

Merton, R. 1968. *Social theory and social structure.* New York: Free Press.

Meyer, A. D., Goes, J. B., & Brooks, G. R. 1993. Organizations reacting to hyperturbulence. In G. P. Huber & W. H. Glick (Eds.), *Organizational change and redesign:* 66–111. New York: Oxford University Press.

Neal, M. A., & Northcraft, G. B. 1991. *Behavioral negotiation theory: A framework for conceptualizing dyadic bargaining.* In L. L. Cummings & B. M. Staw (Eds.), *Research in organizational behavior,* vol. 13: 147–190. Greenwich, CT: JAI Press.

Newell, A. 1973. Production systems: Models of control structures. In W. G. Chase (Ed.), *Visual information processing:* 463–562. New York: Academic Press.

Nisbet, R. A. 1970. Developmentalism: A critical analysis. In J. McKinney & E. Tiryakin (Eds.), *Theoretical sociology: Perspectives and developments:* 167–206. New York: Meredith.

Parsons, R. 1951. *The social system.* New York: Free Press.

Pfeffer, J. 1982. *Organizations and organization theory.* Boston: Pitman.

Piaget, J. 1975. *The child's conception of the world.* Totowa, NJ: Littlefield, Adams.

Poggie, G. 1965. A main theme of contemporary sociological analysis: Its achievements and limitations. *British Journal of Sociology*, 16: 283–294.

Polley, D. 1993. *Chaos as metaphor and science: Applications and risks.* Paper presented at the annual meeting of the Academy of Management, Atlanta, GA.

Poole, M. S. 1981. Decision development in small groups I: A test of two models. *Communication Monographs*, 48: 1–24.

Poole, M. S. 1983. Decision development in small groups III: A multiple sequence theory of decision development. *Communication Monographs*, 50: 321–341.

Poole, M. S. 1985. Tasks and interaction sequences: A theory of coherence in group decision-making. In R. Street & J. N. Cappella (Eds.), *Sequence and pattern in communicative behavior:* 206–224. London: Edward Arnold.

Poole, M. S., & Roth, J. 1989. Decision development in small groups V: Test of a contingency model. *Human Communication Research*, 15: 549–589.

Poole, M. S., & Van de Ven, A. H. 1989. Toward a general theory of innovation. In A. H. Van de Ven, H. Angle, & M. S. Poole (Eds.), *Research on the management of innovation:* 637–662. New York: HarperCollins.

Prigogine, I., & Stengers, S. 1984. *Order out of chaos.* New York: Heinemann.

Riegel, K. F. 1975. From traits and equilibrium toward developmental dialectics. In J. Cole & W. S. Arnold (Eds.), *Nebraska symposium on motivation:* 349–407. Lincoln: University of Nebraska Press.

Riegel, K. F. 1976. The dialectics of human development. *American Psychologist*, 31: 689–700.

Rogers, E. 1983. *Diffusion of innovations* (3rd ed.). New York: Free Press.

Schumpeter, J. A. 1942. *Capitalism, socialism, and democracy.* New York: Harper & Row.

Simmel, G. 1955. Der steit. [Chapter 4 in *Soziologie*]. In K. H. Wolff & R. Bendix (Trans.), *Georg Simmel: Conflict & the web of group affiliations:* 11–123. New York: Free Press. (Original work published 1908)

Simon, H. A. (Ed.). 1979. *Models of thought.* New Haven, CT: Yale University Press.

Singh, J. V., & Lumsden, C. J. 1990. Theory and research in organizational ecology. *Annual Review of Sociology*, 16: 161–195.

Sztompka, P. 1993. *The sociology of social change.* London: Basil Blackwell.

Tsoukas, H. 1989. The validity of idiographic research explanations. *Academy of Management Review*, 14: 551–561.

Tuma, N. B., & Hannan, M. T. 1984. *Social dynamics: Models and methods.* San Diego, CA: Academic Press.

Tushman, M. L., & Romanelli, E. 1985. Organizational evolution: A metamorphosis model of convergence and reorientation. In B. M. Staw & L. L. Cummings (Eds.), *Research in organizational behavior*, vol. 7: 171–222. Greenwich, CT: JAI Press.

Utterback, J. M., & Abernathy, W. J. 1975. A dynamic model of process and product innovation. *Omega*, 3: 639–656.

Van de Ven, A. H. 1992. Suggestions for studying strategy process: A research note. *Strategic Management Journal*, 13: 169–188.

Van de Ven, A. H., Angle, H. L., & Poole, M. S. 1989. *Research on the management of innovation: The Minnesota studies.* New York: Ballinger/Harper & Row.

Van de Ven, A. H., & Garud, R. 1993. Innovation and industry development: The case of cochlear implants. In R. Burgelman & R. Rosenbloom (Eds.), *Research on technological innovation, management and policy*, vol. 5: 1–46. Greenwich, CT: JAI Press.

Van de Ven, A. H., & Poole, M. S. 1988. Paradoxical requirements for a theory of organizational change. In R. Quinn & K. Cameron (Eds.), *Paradox and transformation:*

Toward a theory of change in organization and management: 19–80. New York: HarperCollins.

Von Wright, G. H. 1971. *Explanation and understanding.* Ithaca, NY: Cornell University Press.

Watzlawick, P., Weakland, J. H., & Fisch, R. 1974. *Change: Principles of problem formation and problem resolution.* New York: Norton.

Weick, K. E. 1979. *The social psychology of organizing* (2nd ed.). Reading, MA: Addison-Wesley.

Zeeman, E. C. 1976. Catastrophe theory. *Scientific American*, 234(4): 65–83.

CHAPTER FIFTY

Organization Change and Development

Michael Beer
Anna Elise Walton (1987)

Applying theory from psychology and organizational behavior, organization development (OD) comprises a set of actions undertaken to improve organizational effectiveness and employee well-being. These actions or "interventions" are typically designed and sequenced by an OD consultant following his or her diagnosis of an organization's needs and shortcomings. The toolkit these practitioners draw on ranges broadly from organizationwide changes in structure and systems to psychotherapeutic counseling sessions with groups and individuals. OD, measured as something that professional OD consultants do, appears to be growing moderately.

The application of OD by managers rather than OD consultants has grown even further. In the past five years, general management literature and practice have absorbed many of the concepts, values, and methods OD propounds. This can be seen in the widespread application, and in some cases institutionalization, of innovative plant designs, participative management approaches, collaborative approaches to union-management relations, the use of task forces and other organizational overlays to identify and solve problems, and the frequent practice of off-site team-building or mission-building sessions (Beer & Spector, 1984). We see OD concepts strongly emerging in the burgeoning general management literature, specifically via culture and leadership concepts. OD concepts can also be seen in the increasingly common view of organizations as open systems.

Major environmental changes have focused management attention on managing discontinuities in organizations' lives. Revitalization, turnaround, innovation, and the management of decline are becoming major topics in both general management and OD literature. Human resource management has also absorbed many of OD's precepts, and organizations increasingly realize human resources can be critical strategic and competitive factors.

As the knowledge base of organizational behavior and psychology filters into general management literature, we believe OD must broaden itself. Theorists and practitioners must move away from programs in which the consultant orchestrates interventions to programs in which general manager, staff groups, and consultants work together to manage change, to redirect organizational efforts and performance. The OD practitioner may have specialized behavioral-science expertise but will also need expertise in understanding and interpreting environmental changes. The OD consultant will support changes initiated by general managers.

Thus as a field organization development will have to become concerned with the theory and practice of managing the continual adaptation of internal organizational arrangements to changes in the external environment. In this capacity, intervention methods become episodes in a long-term process, and consultants become actors in a process orchestrated by general managers. This conception of the field has profound implications for research methodology, theory building, and practice. As its techniques have become staples of modern corporate management, the status of OD becomes more difficult to ascertain. This broader definition makes it impossible to state how widely OD is practiced, since the field no longer has professional boundaries.

Here we review the status of OD as consultant-centered intervention, the traditional focus of OD, OD-related trends in general management literature, recent literature on organizational adaptation and realignment, trends in human resource management and their OD implications, and finally, the implementation of change.

OD AS CONSULTANT-CENTERED INTERVENTION

There have been no new breakthroughs in intervention methodologies. Rather, variations on the basic idea of surfacing information and feeding it back for discussion by organizational members continue to be developed. Survey and questionnaire methodologies appear to be growing in popularity. New surveys have been introduced (Kilmann, 1984; Sashkin, 1985) and established ones are still being utilized (Kleiner, 1983; Levine, 1983; Gavin, 1984). Various forms of team building and the use of collateral organizations are also widely employed (Kanter, 1983; Beer & Spector, 1984). Process consultation appears in the literature less frequently than the above. We suspect it is a less bounded intervention and therefore more difficult to research with traditional methodologies.

Sashkin et al. (1984) note that some types of OD, specifically structural interventions according to contingency theory, third-party consultation, and sociotechnical systems changes, have not become as popular. They believe the popular approaches have clear goals and are highly structured. The client knows what the consultant will be doing at any given time.

We do not review new applications of traditional intervention methods because we do not regard extensions of intervention methodology as the frontier of progress in the practice or theory of OD. Moreover, as we discuss in the section on managing change, the manager and/or consultant, their assumptions about organizations, and their skills in managing an organic change process are probably more important than methodology in the final analysis. It is probably because effective change managers or consultants are in such short supply that Sashkin finds more structured methods in greater use.

Recent Research and Evaluation of OD Efforts

In the past five years, several articles (Nicholas, 1982; Roberts & Porras, 1982; Vicars & Hartke, 1984; Nicholas & Katz, 1985; Guzzo et al., 1985; Macy et al., 1986) have reviewed the OD and organization change literature to assess the relative effectiveness of typical interventions. These researchers looked at studies of team building, laboratory training, survey feedback, technostructural interventions, and process consultation.

Vicars and Hartke (1984) evaluated fifteen recent studies relative to an earlier study (Morrison, 1978) and noted an increase in validity criteria and noticeably more controls. They also noted that OD evaluations often encountered several rival hypotheses; change results from maturation, history, self-selection, and so forth.

Nicholas (1982) reviewed sixty-four studies and assessed the comparative impact of the interventions on "hard criteria," which ranged from costs and productivity to quality and absenteeism. He noted limitations in the research findings—e.g. outcomes could be the result of intervention duration or the time of posttest (immediately following the intervention or several years later). Nicholas concluded that "the single most apparent finding of this research is that no one change technique or class of techniques works well in all situations" (p. 540).

Katzell and Guzzo (1983) in a literature review of 207 psychologically based productivity experiments reported that 87 percent found some evidence of some productivity improvement. Guzzo et al. (1985) performed a meta-analysis of 98 of these experiments and found worker productivity increased by nearly one-half standard deviation.

Macy et al. (1986) meta-analyzed fifty-six empirical organization change and work innovation experiments and found an across-study positive and significant relationship with productivity. They found that reward system changes had no significant relationship with productivity and had significant negative relationships with leadership and work involvement measures. Autonomous and semiautonomous work groups, team building, and training related positively and significantly to productivity but were negatively associated with eleven dependent variables (including leadership, work involvement, general attitude, and satisfaction measures).

Both Guzzo et al. (1985) and Macy et al. (1986) note that most published reports lack the quantitative data necessary for meta-analysis. Both also qualify their findings by recognizing the bias toward publishing positive outcomes.

Measuring attitudinal change has proved tricky. A fair amount of research (Roberts & Porras, 1982; Porras, 1985; Van de Vhert et al., 1985) is going into investigating the types of change: alpha (or "real change" but no conceptual shift), beta ("scale recalibration" or shift due to changes in expectations), and gamma (a complete conceptual redefinition of the phenomena). These distinctions derive from a study (Golembiewski et al., 1976; see Chapter Forty-Eight of this volume) that observed rating declines after an intervention. The study argued that these declines occurred because participants had undergone a conceptual shift; their standards of evaluations had changed. Armenakis et al. (1983) claimed that this is now the focus of OD research, displacing earlier concerns about experimental design and statistical methods.

In sum, investigators have felt the need for, and have begun to use, quantitative data, sophisticated research designs, and statistical procedures aimed at accurate measurement of change. Nicholas & Katz (1985) and Armenakis et al. (1983) add that more frequent measurements are needed. Seashore et al. (1983) published a major text cataloging current methods and techniques. Researchers of this bent argue that in future lean times OD practitioners will need hard data to justify their projects to management by bottom-line criteria.

Despite more sophisticated research methods, OD research results are still inconclusive. One can find support for many different conclusions, among the results reported in the studies. Why should this be so?

Problems in Research on Intervention Methods

This research suffers from four problems. First, the research aims to isolate causation. By relying on normal science, this research tries to identify the results of a single intervention (though the intervention may combine technologies of team building, technostructural changes, etc.) and overlooks the systemic nature of organization. Exogenous variables and intervening events will always prevent any powerful conclusions. For example, influential figures change (Roberts & King, 1985), or management changes production methods or makes material changes (Passmore & Friedlander, 1982; Fiedler et al., 1984). Even worse, normal science methodology can damage the experiment itself. Blumberg and Pringle (1983) describe a sociotechnical intervention, including job redesign and worker participation in a unionized mine, in which the "control" group found out about the experimental group. The "control" miners so resented the experimental group's advantage that they voted to prevent further changes in the workplace.

Traditional research methods make assumptions that may be entirely inappropriate for field research. For example, the concept of control groups or uninformed subjects may diminish the value of the information (survey responses may be more "thoughtless") or halt the experiment altogether (via control-group hostility). Normal science rests on replication, something unquestionably impossible in field research. Finally, events may be multicausal, the constellation of causes being of significance. Thus, it would be impossible to identify the precise effect of a given action.

Second, much of the research overlooks time and is not sufficiently longitudinal. By assessing the events and their impact at only one nearly contemporaneous moment, the research cannot discuss how permanent the changes are. As noted above, different posttest times may support different experimental conclusions.

Third, the research is "flat." While being precise about methodology and instruments, it is often imprecise in depth and description of the intervention and situation. The nature and history of the occupational groups involved are often not explored. The environmental context is overlooked. Notably, one study compares two interventions eight years apart. The environmental context may have changed, thus affecting the intervention's effects. Quantitative description may not be the best method for understanding a multicausal phenomenon.

Fourth, the research does not fit the needs of its users. This is surprising given the action research tradition of OD. Noting that research knowledge has been slow to transfer to practice, the "crisis in utilization" is increasingly coming under scrutiny (Lindblom & Cohen, 1979; Legge, 1984; Lawler et al., 1985; Kilmann et al., 1983). Good science may be antithetical to good action. More complex statistical techniques and more complex quasi-experimental designs, in attempts to achieve more precision and tighter scientific "proof," neglect the "social construction" of knowledge in the social sciences. The complexity of the subject material and the existence of nonrational responses to data will inhibit acceptance of even the most tightly controlled experiments. As Legge (1984) notes, the best predictor of utilized knowledge is the "personal factor," the interest the users have in the evaluation study. Beer (1980) argued that managers make decisions about OD not on the basis of evaluation research but on suitability to their agenda. Rather than create increasingly esoteric designs and increasingly narrow inferences, OD might do better to aim research at needs identified by managers and utilize language managers can understand.

OD research seems to be at a turning point. As long as OD researchers emulate traditional science methodology, they will confine themselves to isolated episodes of change. By evaluating a specific intervention, they neglect the interrelatedness of elements in a system, and because the organization is a system, exogenous variables will prevent any powerful conclusions.

Rather than attempt to find the perfect quantitative methodology and "scientifically" prove its value, OD should attempt to build a different model of knowledge. Argyris et al. (1985) proposed action science. Critiquing traditional science methods, they argued for the combination of action and thinking to achieve double-loop, or self-corrective learning. Schön (1983) called for similar methodology. The call for rejection of typical positivistic assumptions is growing (Carnall, 1982; Morgan, 1983; Legge, 1984; Peters & Robinson, 1984). This would require a new format of journal reporting as well. What we are recommending is a return to the action research traditions of OD with full participation of the client in the research but with much longer time frames and the inclusion of rich descriptions of context and system dynamics.

Pettigrew provided a persuasive critique and useful counterexample of mainstream OD research and literature. Reviewing the history of and research on OD, he concluded that "theory and practice of change in organizations would continue to remain as circumscribed and ill developed as long as change is studied and thought about as episodes and projects separate from the ongoing processes of continuity and change of which those change projects are at heart" (p. 26). His book *The Awakening Giant: Continuity and Change in ICI* provides an in-depth look at the history from 1960 to 1983 of Imperial Chemical Industries and four OD groups operating in it. Pettigrew, too, concluded that more longitudinal studies must be conducted.

Our critique of OD research is, of course, also a critique of OD's preoccupation with consultant-centered intervention methods. If research designs that define change too narrowly can be misleading, defining change as a single intervention at a given point in time is too confining. We have therefore decided not to review new intervention methods in depth and instead turn now to the general manager's problem of developing organizations to improve competitiveness and employee well-being.

OD AS GENERAL MANAGEMENT

Managers are learning that they must manage change. Increasing international competition, deregulation, the decline of manufacturing, the changing values of workers, and the growth of information technology have changed the concepts and approaches managers must use. As Beckhard (1969) and Bennis (1969) argued early on, these changes require adaptive, flexible organizations and skilled managers to manage these changes.

Many OD concepts have filtered into the management literature, and OD techniques are being addressed to the manager (Dyer, 1983; Kirkpatrick, 1985). Specifically, OD's concept of explicitly intervening to manage norms and culture is emerging in management journals. OD's views on leadership and managing "soft" (style versus systems) change are emerging in the leadership literature. The systemic view of organizations has also received attention.

Culture

OD has long recognized the importance of culture and considered culture management to be within its purview, but it has never developed the concept. Almost completely separate from the OD literature, a group of writings on organizational culture has sprung up. Much of it asserts a positive correlation between type of organizational culture and organizational effectiveness (Ouchi, 1981; Deal & Kennedy, 1982; Denison, 1984). Not surprisingly, these cultures look much like Beckhard's (1969) definition of a healthy organization. Delegating, results-oriented, information-sharing, developmental, egalitarian, employee-centered cultures are believed to enhance adaptiveness, productivity, innovation, and performance (Kanter, 1983; Denison, 1984; Walton, 1985). This view was brought to the practicing public in Peters and Waterman's popular book *In Search of Excellence* (1982). Reviewing the characteristics of excellent companies, Peters and Waterman cited the elements of these companies' shared values: achieving productivity through people, the importance of people as individuals, tolerance of failure, and informality to promote communication. Performance is achieved via expectations and peer review rather than management direction and sophisticated control systems.

Surveying several companies, and relying on extensive field experience, Kanter (1983) found certain companies more adaptive and innovative. These companies engendered a culture of pride and encouraged their employees to take risks. Innovators were not separated from the mainstream organization (as some earlier literature had recommended) but integrated their ideas and proposals into the organization by involving the important stakeholders. The innovative organization promotes high levels of collaboration between functions.

In addition to type of culture, the strength of culture can be important. Wilkins and Ouchi (1983) suggested that strong cultures (clan mechanisms) may enhance organizational efficiency only under conditions of uncertainty and ambiguity (hence high "transactions" costs), stability of membership, and reasonably equitable and inescapable reward systems. If these conditions do not exist, markets or hierarchies may better meet the firm's need for internal integration.

A flood of literature on managing corporate culture resulted from the popularization of culture as a competitive advantage. Current theory suggests that managers spread culture through stories, symbolic acts, and other "soft" techniques (Peters & Waterman, 1982; Kanter, 1983; Kilmann, 1984; Sathe, 1985; Schein, 1985), much as Barnard (1938) and Selznick (1957) said long ago. The literature offers managers a "culture audit" (Wilkins, 1983), which can identify problems and actionable areas for management. The Kilmann-Saxton Culture Gap Survey (Kilmann et al., 1985) identifies differences between desired and actual culture and lays out a five-track program for redirecting the culture. Kilmann (1984) claims that any effort to manage change without such a comprehensive program is an ill-fated attempt at a quick fix.

Efforts directed at managing culture alert us to the problem of defining culture. Schein (1985) argued that popular notions of culture reflect culture rather than describe its essence (norms, observed behavioral regularities, dominant values, philosophy, climate, etc.) He argued that culture is multilayered. The essence of culture may be found in the organization's embedded, preconscious, basic assumptions and beliefs about human nature, the nature of the world, and so forth. On a second, observable level, culture manifests itself as values, which are testable only by social consensus. Values are about how things ought to be done, or what works. When a value is agreed upon by a group, the group begins the process of cognitive transformation, in which the value becomes a belief or assumption, taken for granted rather than debatable. On the surface layer are artifacts and creations, which include things like art, technology, and behavioral patterns; these have meaning but are often not decipherable.

But how manageable is culture? Can a five-track program like Kilmann's (1984) enable managers to gain control of corporate culture? Or is culture more powerful than managers, so that "culture controls the manager more than the manager controls the culture" (Schein, 1985, p. 315)? It has been argued that cultural change cannot be managed and that special events that trigger change require managers to be temporarily out of control (Deal, 1985). Changing and managing are incompatible. We suspect (as we will argue below in more depth) that the idea of planned change, long advocated by OD, requires reexamination and reformation. Preprogrammed approaches such as the five-track Culture Gap Survey are not likely to accord with how managers think and act (Kotter, 1982) any more than Grid OD did.

Research suggests that culture may be more resilient than implied by the exhortations to manage it. Researchers examining the "cultural relativity" of change programs have generally found that interventions and technology that suit the host culture are most effective. In their earlier OD review, Faucheux et al. (1982) noted that different cultures (U.S., European, Latin American) have developed different change technologies and that cross-cultural transfers of change technology have proved difficult and slow. Established change techniques used to intervene in culture directly have failed to overcome cultural resistance, suggesting that culture may be a lag rather than a lead variable.

Schein pointed out that the role of culture tends to vary with an organization's life cycle stage. For the youthful company, culture is often seen as a competitive advantage to be nurtured. For the mature company, culture may be a barrier to innovation; it may diminish integration and be a phenomenon to be managed and turned around. Change methods differ in appropriateness depending on the organization's life-cycle stage. For example, revolutionary change through outsiders may help an organization move from early growth to midlife, planned change and organization development may be most useful during organizational midlife, and coercive persuasion may suit a mature organization facing destruction or a turnaround. We believe that a theory or OD relevant to the general manager will only achieve usefulness if change problems, strategy, and tactics are tied to a life-cycle framework.

Leadership

OD has long recognized the importance of leadership in managing change. A vision, a new model for managing (Beer, 1980), a "picture of the future" (Beckhard & Harris, 1977) have been considered powerful means by which leaders might motivate behavior change.

Management literature has focused recently on the role of leadership in managing major corporate transformations. In line with OD ideas, this research has found the envisioning skills of the executives to be critical in managing change. Anderson et al. (1985) studied seventeen companies that had undergone revitalization; each company transformed itself from a substandard into a superior performer in a period of five to ten years. A key factor in these change efforts was the existence of a "championing" leader. Such leaders fight persistently for their ideas, are more ideological than their business-as-usual counterparts, manage by symbols, set an example of championing leadership for potential leaders throughout the corporation, and use rewards and interchampion competition as motivators.

Bennis and Nanus (1985) interviewed ninety renowned figures in business, government, labor, academics, and the arts. They found little commonality in behavior, dress, or speech but identified four themes in action. First, leaders got their followers' attention through a vision, agenda, or focus; second, they gave meaning to events and actions through communication, thus developing "shared meanings" among their followers. They engendered trust through positioning, being reliable, and sticking to their goals, and they used their own optimism and positive self-regard to inspire others. Followers benefited through feelings of significance, competence, community, and enjoyment.

These formulations share several themes. First, the leaders articulate and propagate a vision or agenda. Second, the leader assigns meaning and significance to events, expectations, and the vision, and in so doing structures a cognitive world. In this sense, the leader achieves results not through formal structure or formalized control systems but by creating an understanding of reality that motivates behavior. Much as OD has argued, the manager creates a set of expectations that powerfully influence behavior in the organization.

Key to these formulations is the notion that leaders empower others, a value long held by OD (Kanter, 1983; Burke, 1985). Bennis and Nanus's leaders "empower others to translate intention into reality and sustain it" (p. 80). Sashkin (1985) noted that "research is consistent in suggesting that effective leaders involve subordinates rather than dominating and . . . give away power . . . leaders achieve goals through others, and unless the others have the power to do what the leader wants done, such achievements are not likely" (p. 5).

The implication of this research is clear. Managers' leadership, not OD consultants', is central to managing major cultural transformations. Unfortunately, none of the research on leadership has specified the skills required of transformational leaders. This specification is required before managers can be helped to develop them, if indeed they are developable. A beginning has been made by Sashkin (1985) and Burke (1985) in profiling leadership style via a questionnaire. Research is also required on the role OD consultants can play in helping managers lead or in symbolically representing the leaders' desire for change.

Open Systems Analysis

OD maintains that the organization is an open system, that it interacts with its environment to maintain a state of fit between internal arrangements and the environment (Katz & Kahn, 1966; Lawrence & Lorsch, 1967; Beer, 1980; Burke, 1985). In this view, OD has asserted the organization's need for "environmental mapping" or "mapping the demand system" (Beckhard & Harris, 1977). Here the organization looks at the transactions that occur across the organization/environment interface and assesses the importance of those transactions.

Popular management books are now arguing that organization effectiveness is a state of fit or congruence between business strategy and several internal organizational arrangements such as systems, structure, management style, skills, staff, and shared values (Pascale & Athos, 1981, Peters & Waterman, 1982).

The open-systems view receives even greater attention through stakeholder and network concepts. Recent writings have recognized the importance of stakeholder relationships to management strategy. Freeman (1984) explicitly described techniques for identifying important stakeholders and managing stakeholder relationships (p. 130). Stakeholder input is achieved via the inclusion of "boundary spanners" in the strategic planning process (Freeman, 1984, p. 79). Freeman considered proactive stakeholder management capability critical to managing organizational change. Others have argued for formal inclusion of stakeholders in the corporate governance processes (Auerbach, 1984).

OD practitioners are expanding open-systems theory and applying stakeholder concepts in diagnosis and action planning (Roberts & King, 1985; Porras, 1985). Golembiewski (1985) has found it important to involve stakeholders in major public projects. Kilmann (1983) has used stakeholder analysis to formulate theories and test assumptions in research. The concept of networks has received greater attention. Mandrell (1984) found network analysis valuable in developing roles for managers in a public project.

Senge (1985) has used systems-dynamics thinking and computer technology, previously applied to the creation of a microeconomic model, to the development of a systems-dynamic model of organizations. From interviews with managers of innovative, adaptive organizations, he constructed a computer model that specifies system characteristics crucial for creating and maintaining an adaptive organization, one in which information for decision making is widely shared. This model supports much of OD's assumptions about adaptive organizations. With a computer model, he plans to train executives in systems dynamics so that they can manage organizations more effectively. This line of research promises to make some breakthroughs in how general managers learn to develop organizations.

OD AS CREATING ADAPTIVE ORGANIZATIONS

OD has long been concerned with fostering organizational adaptation to environmental changes. Management literature is increasingly interested in the organization-environment interface as well. The literature has expanded its focus to deal with issues of revitalization and decline.

Designing Innovative Organizations

Stimulated by the competitive crisis, an emerging stream of research (Tushman & Katz, 1980; Kanter, 1983; Lawrence & Dyer, 1983; Nord & Tucker, 1986) on innovation and entrepreneurship speaks to the question of adaptation and revitalization. Although this research notes the importance of cultural factors, it also considers the key dilemma of integration and differentiation in developing innovative organizations (Lawrence & Lorsch, 1967; Lawrence & Dyer, 1983).

Early ideas on innovation suggested that product-planning groups be separated and "protected" from the organization at large. Kanter (1983) suggested more recently that such segmentation may be counterproductive and create barriers to innovations. Innovators must sell ideas into the organization for them to be successful.

Rubenstein and Woodman (1984) accorded critical importance to the boundary-spanner role. Boundary-spanning roles, such as territorial sales person or public relations representative, are considered conducive to innovation since these employees bring environmental information into the firm. Even though the boundary spanner may be a useful source of information, innovation may be more successful if all members are boundary spanners (Tushman & Katz, 1980).

Research on innovation has also focused on the introduction of new technology. Graham and Rosenthal (1986) studied the implementation of flexible machining centers (FMCs) in eight companies. They found those sites that built flexibility into their human systems to be satisfied with results. Specifically, organizations need human flexibility in the composition and organization of product teams, the relations between in-house and vendor teams, and the selection, compensation, and organization of the FMC workforce. Flexibility indicators included broad skill mixes, cross-training, cross-functional cooperation, team building, and so forth. Zuboff (1985) distinguished between technologies that "informate"—bring together information so as to enhance workers' ability to think and act—and technologies that automate—technologies that minimize required skills and remove the need for thinking workers. Informating technologies are said to enhance organizational flexibility. Thus, Zuboff alerts us to the opportunities provided by new information technology for extending decisions down the hierarchy (creating a healthy and adaptive organization).

Nord and Tucker (1986) examine the implementation of an "administrative innovation," the offering of NOW accounts in large and small banks and in savings and loans. They find that successful implementations shared four characteristics: (1) flexibility with regard to roles, decision making, and communication routes; (2) power concentrated somewhere (high or low); (3) technical readiness and access to technical and social competence (talent for pulling together people to solve problems); and (4) attention to the views of those directly responsible for implementation. These characteristics of successful implementations, except perhaps for the findings about power, might easily have been OD prescriptions.

The above findings suggest that some OD technology may be on target, some not. For example, getting input from those involved in implementation sounds like OD, while a particular cultural style is not requisite for implementation. In fact, it may be that technology and technological readiness are lead variables, while style may be a lag variable. The value of this type of research is that it translates general principles from OD into situation-specific prescriptions while clarifying the role of power in managing change, an area neglected by OD. Much more of such research is needed.

In order to achieve faster, more flexible internal communication routes, some organizations are restructuring, becoming flatter. These organizations have fewer power differential (fewer titles, levels, status distinctions, reward differentials, etc.) and rely on teams to accomplish tasks. Autonomous work groups responsible for a whole task have become popular. This trend parallels OD's precepts that decision making should occur at the level closest to the information (Beckhard, 1969). There is continuing interest in organizational overlay, matrix organization, parallel organizations, and collateral organizations (Zand, 1974). The overlaps enhance the permeability at the organization's boundaries and thus allow the corporation to become more adaptive.

Rubenstein and Woodman (1984) noted the advantages of the collateral organization for individuals in the form of fulfillment, heightened perceptions, and connections to senior management. The organization benefits from enhanced disaster preparedness, decision-making ability at lower levels, the receipt of better information, and transmission of the ethos of senior management down to lower levels of the organization.

Interorganizational Relations

In their efforts to adapt to competitive forces organizations are increasingly looking to joint ventures and other interorganizational arrangements. These arrangements are subject to problems of intergroup relationships that OD has been concerned with for a long time. Gray (1985) has begun investigating conditions that enhance interorganizational collaboration. Van de Ven and Walker (1984) have looked at the dynamics of interorganizational cooperation and found that increased communications promote positive feelings and resource exchanges but also increase resource dependence. Johnson et al. (1983) have described the innovative linkage model used between university, government, and the criminal justice system.

Buono et al. (1985) looked at the pre- and postmerger attitudes in two savings banks. Owing to changes in the industry, most employees recognized the need for the merger, though there was evidence for postmerger ethnocentrism and irrational resistance. They note that management "managed" the hard factors more than the soft factors. Though the merger was between equals, one culture eventually dominated. Buono found that attitudes toward hard factors (compensation, hours of work, training policies, etc.) changed less than attitudes toward organizational commitment and top management style.

Sales and Mirvis (1984) analyzed the features of managing an acquisition. They identified phases of cultural adjustment: first, employees feel anger, grief, dread, or anxiety; second, cross-cultural contact promotes change; third, acculturation occurs when the two cultures come to terms with each other. Sales and Mirvis anticipated conflict due to power difference, a one-directional flow from the buyer, and resistance from the subdominant group.

Organizational Decline

The 1974 to 1975 and 1981 to 1982 recessions and the declining performance of major U.S. industries have focused the attention of managers and consultants on the task of managing decline. Decline, too, is organization development, possibly as natural as growth or revitalization. Research and theory on decline have grown substantially, though some argue more needs to be done (Nicoll, 1983).

Undoubtedly, decline creates high organizational stress, and management is likely to observe irrational responses (Sutton, 1983; Krantz, 1985). Hostility, denial, and anger may be part of the emotional climate, but depression, sadness, fear, and embarrassment may be more powerful factors. Sutton (1983) notes, too, that lack of acceptance may be rational if possibilities for saving the company exist. Managers face many dilemmas: how to handle blaming (place it on external environment, accept it themselves, scapegoat others), which activities to sustain and which to disband, what and how much advance information to give to customers and employees, offering hope or taking it away (Sutton, 1983). The results of different strategies are still unclear, though some generalizations seem possible. Management will need to spend more time on employees' personal concerns. It may be hard to contain information and rumors. Management may be unable to divert all blame from itself. Performance can decline but may well improve, due to increased management effort to deal with the feelings and perceptions of employees.

Cummings et al. (1983) identified transorganizational systems as one positive response to managing decline. Conditions likely to facilitate the development of transorganizational systems included environmental turbulence, interdependence, lack of exit options, altruism, or mandates. Cummings et al. reviewed transorganizational systems between similar organizations (such as the Microelectronics and Computer Technology company formed by semiconductor companies) or between dissimilar organizations (such as the Jamestown Labor-Management-Government system). They outlined strategies for setting up and running transorganizational systems. Trist (1983) suggested that interorganizational collaboration may be required to handle some of the complex problems facing organizations today. Cummings (1984) has begun exploring the opportunities for transorganizational development.

This research could bear fruit if it helps managers and consultants guide organizations through business or industry changes. It follows our general predisposition toward the development of OD theory that can help general managers manage major transitions or transformations in the life cycles of their organizations.

OD AS HUMAN RESOURCE MANAGEMENT

As organizations have struggled in an increasingly competitive economy, superior human resources are increasingly seen as a competitive advantage. This has culminated in substantial interest in developing high-commitment work systems that will attract, motivate, and retain superior employees. Indeed the term *human resources* is coming to represent an integration of personnel administration, labor relations, and organization development, with OD the senior partner. The human-resource function and the practice of human-resources management (HRM) are absorbing the values and often the practices of OD (Beer & Spector, 1984).

Human-resource managers have been struggling to define a new change-oriented function for their departments. There is an increasing tendency for human-resources personnel to be consultative, aiding with problem solving on key issues and helping management identify new trends (Finlay, 1984, Harris & Harris, 1983, Lippitt et al., 1983). Many are noting that human resource managers must model nondefensive behavior (Argyris, 1985) and implement change in the human resource function to demonstrate that they, as part of the organization, must change.

Human resource managers with an OD orientation have gained power as organizations attempt to change labor relations from adversarial to collaborative. OD technology has been applied in "relationship by objectives," or in third-party consultation directed at mediating grievance and arbitration disputes (Goldberg & Brett, 1983). Solberg (1985) described GM's Black Lake experience, in which labor and management got together to sanction, discuss, and discover quality-of-work-life objectives. He described a deeply emotional and personal experience brought about by close interaction between union leaders and managers. This event had dramatic impact on the rest of the organization. Isolated experiments with job enrichment, sociotechnical designs, and quality of work life have given way to concerted efforts by corporations to change the nature of their relationship with employees and unions. Much of this work draws on OD values and technology.

Quality-of-work-life programs continue to flourish, although the name is not as much in vogue. Walton (1985) estimates that over one thousand plants in the United States may now be involved in major system redesign. These include special efforts to recruit, select, orient, and train employees so that they fit into an organization that requires higher levels of involvement, responsibility, and interpersonal competence. That requirement comes from the design of autonomous work groups and/or the use of special problem-solving groups. Skill-based compensation systems are also being designed to support the employee growth and development so critical for the functioning of work teams in which individuals rotate jobs and perform vertical tasks. In our view a false distinction has arisen between quality-of-work-life programs, as these plant innovations are sometimes called, and OD. Both the design of a high-commitment work system in a new plant and the transformation of an older plant employ OD concepts, values, intervention methods, and practitioners. Both are organizational development.

Through an examination of six cases in which he was a consultant, Walton (1980) was able to identify the dynamics of developing innovative greenfield plants. He found that in the early stages these plants face a human resource gap. The employees lack the technical or interpersonal skills demanded by the new work system. Training and stress reduction are the key organization development tasks. In later stages there is a human resource surplus where maintaining challenge and excitement are the key organization development tasks. More research that specifies the dynamics of organization development is needed.

Compensation systems are increasingly being used by management to revitalize organizations. Lawler (1981) has argued that changes in compensation systems can be a lead variable in OD. Scanlon plans and skill-based pay systems are used as examples. Beer et al. (1984) argued that in most instances pay system redesign should not be used to lead change; better management and leadership can often accomplish the same thing without incurring some of the problems that result from rising expectations.

Employee ownership through employee stock ownership plans (ESOPs) has been tried as a means of increasing employee commitment and of helping failing companies (Simmons & Mares, 1983; Kuttner, 1985). By making employees owners, ESOPs are expected to achieve greater productivity, greater interest in the business, and heightened flexibility on both management and union sides. (Some ESOPs have been undertaken merely for the tax advantage associated with them.) Research shows that ownership without a climate of participation is unlikely to have a dramatic impact on performance (Long, 1982; Bradley, 1983). Indeed only when employee ownership or gains sharing is preceded or accompanied by extensive organization development are basic relationships between management and labor likely to change. Much more research is needed on the role of pay, gains sharing, and ownership in organization development, an area of research pioneered by Lawler (1981) and Frost et al. (1974) but not continued by others.

OD AS IMPLEMENTING CHANGE

What does the research and practice tell us about managing change? What precursors can indicate change opportunities? The introduction of new business strategies, technology, and administrative practices in response to specific changes in the environment demand that general managers become more competent in these matters. Below, we consider what we have learned about managing change.

Where Does Change Start?

Argyris (1985a) argues it starts with the individual. He offers a five-phase model for bringing about individual changes. Organizations do not develop self-corrective learning because they do not distinguish between espoused theories and theories in use. Though managers may espouse new, adaptive dictates (take risks, communicate openly), their behavior gives contraindications (failure and honesty are punished). This creates mixed messages, which are undiscussable. Because they are undiscussable, they cannot be changed. Only by confronting individuals with their inconsistencies will organizations develop the ability to critique current practice and develop double-loop, or self-corrective, learning. To do this, Argyris suggests that consultants start small and at the top. Many others have focused on individual change, particularly on trying to change the behavior of leaders and managers, claiming that this is where OD change starts.

Others disagree, and suggest that organization change comes about from change in systems and structures (Greenbaum et al., 1983, Macy et al., 1986). The argument here is that systemic change is needed to support changes in individual behavior. For example, Taimo and Santalainen (1984) compared the results of Grid OD training and found that it was less successful in Finland, where it fit poorly with organization structure and culture, than in the United States. Even in the United States individual approaches to organization change, most notably the T group movement of the 1960s, have failed.

Yet even systemwide efforts have failed. Researchers note that sociotech and other interventions are often not institutionalized and fade out after two years (Walton, 1978; Beer, 1979; Goodman & Dean, 1982). This has led some to argue that change needs to start at the industry level. For example, Sandeberg (1983) consulted to unions about technology introduction and noted the need for workers and unions alike to be better informed so as to approach industry-wide new technology implementation proactively, rather than have the circumstance defined by management. Related are the findings of Roggemma (1983), who concluded that despite intensive efforts to change practices in the shipping industry, inertia and existing industry structure and institutional forces made lasting change impossible.

Obviously change must occur at the individual, organizational, and industry level for it to be institutionalized. More research is needed, however, on the problems and opportunities created by starting at one or the other of these levels, and the most effective sequencing of change once it starts at each of these levels.

Can Change Be Planned?

This question strikes at the very heart of OD assumptions. In increasing numbers, researchers and practitioners are expressing doubt (Lippitt et al., 1985). Management literature parallels this emerging consensus. Quinn's (1980) study of strategic planning at ten large companies led him to call the process "logical incrementalism." In this conception, managers make plans that work imperfectly and attract a great deal of attention, disagreement, and support. The response of the system then affects and redirects the plan. Even managers have a hard time following grand plans (Pettigrew, 1985) and must sometimes be out of control. Change is not brought about by following a grand master plan but by continually readjusting direction and goals. Research is needed on the structures and processes organizations must develop to allow an organic planning process to take place.

What Causes Change?

If change cannot be planned, then what causes change? Though this question has no simple answer, it seems possible that OD has focused too narrowly on planned, internal efforts and neglected the role of environmental factors. Yet environmental factors may play a critical role in actual change. In a history of General Motors, Fox (1984) suggested that although DuPont placed several of GM's senior managers, had substantial equity in the firm, and continually pressed for changes, GM did not change until environmental contingencies forced change upon it. Dyer's research (1985) suggests that external events and crises precipitate changes far more than planned events. Precipitating events may often be anticipated but not controlled by managers.

Some (Anderson et al., 1985, Fry & Killing, 1985) are suggesting a taxonomy of change based on environmental factors. For example, a turnaround may occur after the organization has performed poorly over a long period. In this situation, where dissatisfaction and the perceived need to change are likely to be high and thus resistance lower, change may proceed quickly. In a revitalization situation, performance is mediocre and expected to decline. However, the perceived need to change is less acute; hence slower change must be planned around likely resistance. In the case where mediocre performance has not yet occurred but is anticipated, change is likely to be even more difficult and must proceed at an even slower pace.

What Are the Roles in Change?

The faster pace of change is highlighting the centrality of the manager in managing change. Increasingly, OD practitioners are realizing the limitations on consultants' power and recognizing that it is best to have the manager at center stage. Pettigrew (1985) noted that when consultants take greater control of process than management, or when the consultant has a highly visible role, the change process meets management resistance. Dyer (1983) argued that "organization development specialists (both internal and external) can assist in the process, but it should be managed by those who are ultimately responsible for all organizational consequences" (p xiv). Cole (1982) pointed out that change has been better institutionalized in Japan and Sweden, countries in which managers drive the change with little assistance from external consultants.

Our view is that the manager must be central to change management and that OD must become a general management skill. The leader is more an architect than a director. He or she creates the environment (systems, strategy, models, symbols, etc.) in which motivation for change will flourish. In this formulation, the leader/manager of an adaptive organization develops a vision of the future and attempts to infuse the organization with that vision, thereby motivating action and change. The manager must be flexible, willing to redraw plans and policies based on the new information and system reactions. The manager needs a sense of timing, the ability to seize opportunities for change from the inevitable crises that occur in a firm's life. The leader must be able to pick consultants who will help him or her, particularly those who can provide strengths where he or she is weak. As yet, relatively little empirical research has been done on the leadership function in managing change. We also have focused on the titular head of the organization and neglected to investigate a broad set of leaders and the roles they play in change.

Role of "Change Targets"

The individuals to be affected by organizational change have been involved with some success in planning and implementing that change. Elden (1983) used a diagonal slice of the organization to assess internal relationships and describe more complex interrelationships between them than do employees higher in the organization. Levine (1983) described a self-developed quality-of-work-life (QWL) measure whose items reflected the most common statements by organization members about their work life. Levine demonstrated that this instrument had more criterion and convergent validity compared with the Job Diagnostic Survey and saw distinct advantages to using the self-developed measure. This survey did not take job constructs as givens and was therefore less likely than the JDS to imply technological determinism.

Interventions are increasingly using teams for data gathering, analysis, and intervention. Friedlander and Schott (1981) described the use of groups as the intervention agent. In this model, the consultant's role is to help group members define tasks and roles, help with data collection, help develop team skills, and aid in understanding the larger organization in systems terms. Lundberg and Glassman (1983) used internal experts, relying on an informant panel for an organizational diagnosis. This is a promising approach to organization interventions, one that takes the consultant out of the limelight.

The Role of the Consultant

The consultant facilitates the managers' actions, providing them with data, skills, and suggestions. The consultant must be an expert in identifying opportunities for motivating change and clarifying visions. Consultants must help managers and staff learn. Naturally occurring events may be more educative and significant than the traditional interventions (laboratory, survey).

This suggests consultants must develop a better sense of what enables learning. In his study of how managers think, Isenberg (1984) found that acting and thinking may not be separable events. He argued that managers do not follow a classical rational problem-solving model but work on several problems at a time and may act on a problem before thinking about it. This again suggests that learning must be integrated with action. Certainly readiness is a key ingredient.

OD needs a new concept of the consultant's role. We believe it must become less purist, less programmed, and less value-laden. Current conceptions of consulting roles and plans are often too grandiose, developing research, knowledge, and practice that empower the consultant rather than the client.

Less Purist. OD practitioners often describe their role as neutral, as consulting to the entire "system," and as antithetical to the power politics that pervade organizations. Recent research is critiquing this concept of OD, noting vast difference between OD as written and as practiced (Lovelady, 1984). Mendenhall and Oddou (1983) noted that many programs try to teach Theory Y principles but use a Theory X style themselves.

McLean et al. (1982) noted that many reports of OD projects may be misrepresentative. Their study of OD consultants' practices identified numerous actions, ranging from overt "power plays" to unconsciously "acting like an expert," that directly contradicted consulting norms presented in the literature. They also concluded that change does not occur in the linear planned phases of typical OD, and that the best consultants are able to take advantage of events, identifying opportunities to foster change. They identified two types of consultants: the centered consultant, who is opportunistic, takes a long-range view, has high tolerance for ambiguity, realizes organizations are messy, and is gratified with small successes; and the unintegrated consultant, who controls the client's definition of situations and events, is reluctant to exploit natural opportunities, and uses theory as a blueprint for truth.

Many (Carnall, 1982; Pettigrew, 1985) criticize OD's naïveté in the field of politics. Margulies and Raia (1984) argued that OD has neglected politics, yet politics are a key to success in consulting. Arguing that the consultant cannot be neutral, they outlined how consultants can help clients with the political aspects of problems. Jones (1984) cautioned consultants to look at politics skeptically and to question their clients' perceptions of organizational politics. Brown (1982) noted the difficulty of consulting to a group embroiled in internal conflict and described how politics can undermine the consultant's efforts.

Less Programmed. Research on change clearly argues that change does not obey the linear, phased plan of the manager or consultant. Change does not occur in single episodes or interventions. Preprogrammed phase models may be unrealistic. McLean et al. (1982) noted that the planned-change model is still used but often breaks down in three typical ways. The cycle (contracting, data collection, analysis, and feedback) results in insufficient data for action and cycles back to data collection; an educational program is set up as a precursor to change activities but detracts from objectives and becomes an end rather than a means; and a steering group may get bogged down analyzing its own process and neglect the problem it was formed to solve (p. 87–89). This raises questions about the more programmed (Blake & Mouton, 1981; Kilmann, 1984) approaches.

McLean et al. (1982) pointed out that the opportunities for powerful interventions arise irregularly and unannounced. The skillful practitioner uses naturally occurring events to enhance the pressure for change. This suggests, too, that consultants need to be opportunistic and develop political skills.

Programs must consider the environment and the situation. In a fast-changing environment, managers learn primarily by doing (Boulden & Lawlor, 1982; Eisenstat 1984). A flexible consultant working with managers to solve problems on the job might thus stimulate more of what Eisenstat has called behavioral learning (through doing) as opposed to representational learning (through language) typically delivered by standardized training programs.

These findings suggest that managers and consultants must design interventions that are embedded in the work situation and tailored to it. Such interventions demand that consultants become effective in diagnosing problems and designing and managing experiences that permit inductive learning. The field will have to develop guidelines for designing and managing learning experiences. These would be the equivalent of a contingency theory of intervention.

Plans must also suit the readiness of the client system. Readiness refers to the social, technological, or systemic ability of a group or organization to change or try new things. Programs need to identify where change is possible, rather than attempt to impose change on a highly resistant, unready system. Schlesinger and Oshry (1984) and Jick and Ashkenas (1985) have argued that in order to effect long-term changes, planners must start small, exploit early successes, and seek to tie the elements of change to existing systems and structures.

In assessing a program's impact on a client system, OD consultants must also consider the magnitude of change. Organizations are constantly changing, adding new products, reorganizing, modifying strategy, in a sense fine tuning the existing organization. Tushman et al. (in press) observed two basic types of organizational change: converging change, which consists of iterative improvements toward an essentially unchanged goal; and frame-breaking change, in which the system drastically reorganizes and redirects itself. They argued that major redirections must be undertaken quickly and powerfully to avoid getting bogged down in politics. Converging change may be managed in a more consensual process.

Throughout our discussion, we have raised the question of lead versus lag variables. Change methods and organizational values appropriate for one organizational situation may be dysfunctional at another phase in the life cycle. Interventions effective in a stable environment may be inefficient in unstable environments. An organization with a powerful culture may use a technological change as a lead intervention, and follow with cultural change. This variability suggests a problem for advocates of a one-best-way approach.

Each consultant may need to specialize in what fits his or her style and experience. Schön (1983) maintained that the best professionals know more than they can put into words. To meet the challenges of their work, they rely less on graduate school theory than on their experience in responding to problems that arise in practice. This suggests that OD consultants, or for that matter managers concerned with knowing what they have learned, need to spend time in reflection to develop their own theory of change.

Less Value-Laden. Some practitioners believe that a return to the simple value of democratic management would create organizational effectiveness, yet evidence suggests that such management may be neither universally advantageous nor universally desired.

Even OD interventions designed to create more open and participative organizations may have negative outcomes for individuals. Walters (1984) points out that OD may reduce an individual's freedom, privacy, or self-esteem. For example, consultants may not inform survey respondents of possible negative outcomes (a powerful manager may retaliate after receiving negative feedback); team building or confrontation may dragoon people into revealing private or interpersonal information, imposing on their freedom and privacy for the presumed advantage of improved team performance. These interventions may benefit the organizations but harm the individual (Gavin, 1984).

The evidence that certain organizational forms or styles foster organizational effectiveness is inconclusive. Though many advocate the open, participative organization, others have found that these attributes do not always correlate with success. Some situations simply may not allow integration of employee and organizational needs. The best organizational style and form is contingent on the organization's task, what it needs to do to succeed in its environment. Moreover, advocacy of values by OD practitioners has not worked well, as evidenced by the rise and decline of many corporate OD efforts. If corporations today are adopting OD values in their efforts to revitalize, they are doing so because environmental pressures are pushing them to do so.

IN CONCLUSION

In the introduction we said our conception of the field involves a reconsideration of its research methodology, theory building, practice, and values. Here we return to a brief discussion of this conception.

Theory building in the field has always been weak. We believe this stems from the traditional focus of the field. Rather than cataloging the technology of organizational change, we need to catalog how external forces create the opportunities for change. Rather than assume that there is a single way to change organizations, a way consistent with our technology and values, we should develop a contingency theory of organization change. Such a theory would specify alternative change strategies appropriate to an organization's stage of development. It would highlight the skills required of the leader, OD consultant, and other supporting change agents as well as their relationship to each other and the task of change, with particular emphasis on what they must know about the business of the organization and its politics. The theory would deal with time frames more explicitly than current theories, and it would specify how continuity of leadership and consultation relate to effective adaptation. In short, we need a theory of organizational adaptation that incorporates *all* types of interventions, applying them to the management of the numerous crises all organizations face. Such a theory could benefit from the general-management orientation of business policy and could contribute to that field ideas about leadership, organizational culture, and change.

The primary research methodology appropriate to this orientation would not be that of normal science, which attempts to answer little questions precisely. Instead we would be more concerned with broader longitudinal designs, creating knowledge that could be used. We suggest a return to the action research traditions of the field, but with a longer time frame and a more thorough investigation of the context in which episodes occur. OD need not become lax in its search for knowledge, but we must recognize that our sphere of inquiry is fundamentally different from that of normal science. We cannot borrow the tools and techniques of another paradigm; we must develop our own.

The practice of OD must also change. We suggest the focus should move away from structured and preprogrammed consultant-centered interventions. The general manager is the central character in the drama of organization development. OD practitioners must therefore be more concerned with the selection and development of these leaders. They must also adopt the perspective of the general manager. This means knowledge of the business and task, understanding of the competitive environment and the opportunities for change and development it provides, and much more sophistication in diagnosis, politics, and intervention design suited to the situation. All of this raises serious questions about the source and development of OD consultants and their relationship to general managers and the human resource function.

Tension has always existed in the field between a concern for effectiveness and a concern for the well-being of employees. Our review suggests that in some ways this tension has been eased by the natural evolution of organizations, pushed by competitive forces, toward the values of OD. But we do not believe this evolution has come about because OD practitioners have been successful in imposing their values on organizations, nor that future evolution toward the healthy organization will come from OD practitioners who advocate humanistic values. OD practitioners—general managers and consultants alike—would be well advised to retain a normative vision for long-term guidance while adopting a situational perspective in diagnosing organizational problems and taking action to improve them. As with many human endeavors, managing this paradox is the critical skill.

References

Anderson, D.G., Phillips, J.R., Kaible, N. 1985: *Revitalizing Large Companies*. Working Paper. Cambridge, MA: Mass. Inst. Technol. 35 pp.

Argyris, C. 1985a: *Strategy, Change, and Defensive Routines*. Boston: Pitman. 368 pp.

Argyris, C. 1985b: *Reinforcing Defensive Routines: An Unintended Human Resources Activity*. Draft. 24 pp.

Argyris, C., Putnam, R., Smith, D.M. 1985: *Action Science*. San Francisco/London: Jossey-Bass. 480 pp.

Armenakis, A.A., Bedian, A.G., Pond, S.B. III. 1983: Research issues in OD evaluation past, present and future. *Acad. Manage Rev.:* 8 320–28.

Auerbach, J. 1984: *The Now and Future Business Corporation*. Working paper. Boston: President & Fellows, Harvard College.

Barnard, C.I. 1938: *The Functions of the Executive*. Cambridge MA: Harvard University Press. 334 pp.

Beckhard, R. 1969. *Organization Development Strategies and Models*. Reading, MA: Addison-Wesley. 119 pp.

Beckhard, R., Harris, R.T. 1977. *Organizational Transitions Managing Complex Change*. Reading, MA: Addison-Wesley. 110 pp.

Beer, M. 1979. The longevity of organization development. In *Organization Change Sourcebook I: Cases in Organization Development*, ed. B. Lubin, L.D. Goodstein, A.W. Lubin, pp. 62–65. La Jolla, CA: Univ. Assoc.

Beer, M. 1980. *Organization Change and Development: A Systems View*. Santa Monica: Goodyear. 367 pp.

Beer, M., Spector, B. 1984. Human resource management: the integration of industrial relations and organization development. In *Research in Personnel and Human Resources Management*, ed. K.M. Rowland, G.R. Ferris, pp. 261–97. San Francisco: JAI Press.

Beer, M., Spector, B., Laurence, P.R., Mills, D.Q., Walton, R.E. 1984. *Managing Human Assets*. New York: The Free Press. 209 pp.

Bennis, W. 1969. *Organization Development: Its Nature, Origins, and Prospects*. Reading, MA: Addison-Wesley. 87 pp.

Blake, R.R., Mouton, J.S. 1981. *The New Managerial Grid*. Houston: Gulf. 329 pp.

Blumberg, M., Pringle, C.D. 1983. How control groups can cause loss of control in action research: The case of Rushton Coal Mine. *J. App. Behav. Sci.:* 19 409–25.

Boulden, G., Lawlor, A. 1982. Surviving in a changing world: The nature of change and its application. *Leadership Organ. Dev. J.:* 38–9.

Bradley, K. 1983. *Worker Capitalism: The New Industrial Relations*. Boston: MIT Press. 192 pp.

Brown, C.M. 1982. Administrative succession and organizational performance: The succession effect. *Admin. Sci. Q.:* 27 1–16.

Buono, A., Bowditch, J.L., Lewis, J.W. III. 1985. When cultures collide: The anatomy of a merger. *Hum. Relat.:* 38 477–500.

Burke, W.W. 1985. *Leadership as Empowering Others*. New York: W. Warner Burke Assoc. 31 pp.

Carnall, C.A., 1982. *The Evaluation of Organizational Change*. Brookfield, VT: Gower. 130 pp.

Cole, R.E. Diffusion of participatory work structures in Japan, Sweden, and the United States. In *Change in Organizations*, ed. P. Goodman and Associates, pp. 166–225. San Francisco/London: Jossey-Bass.

Cummings, T.G. 1984. Trans-organization development. *Res. Organ. Behav.:* 6.

Cummings, T.G., Blumenthal, J., Greiner, L. 1983. Managing organizational decline: The case for transorganizational systems. *Hum. Resour. Manage.:* 22(4) 377–90.

Deal, T.E. 1985. Cultural change opportunity, silent killer, or metamorphosis? In *Gaining Control of the Corporate Culture*, ed. R.H. Kilmann, M.J. Saxon, R. Serpa, pp. 292–331. San Francisco/London: Jossey-Bass.

Deal, T., Kennedy, A. 1982. *Corporate Cultures*. Reading, MA: Addison-Wesley. 232 pp.

Denison, D.R. 1984. Bringing corporate culture to the bottom line. *Organ. Dvn.:* 13 4–22.

Dyer, W.G. 1983. *Contemporary Issues in Management and Organization Development*. Reading, MA: Addison-Wesley. 231 pp.

Dyer, W.G. 1985. The cycle of cultural evolution in organizations. In *Gaining Control of the Corporate Culture*, ed. R.H. Kilmann, M.J. Saxon, R. Serpa, pp. 200–29. San Francisco/London: Jossey-Bass.

Eisenstadt, R.A. 1984. *Organizational learning in the creation of an industrial setting.* PhD thesis. Yale Univ., New Haven, CT. 240 pp.

Elden, M. 1983. Democratization and participative research in developing local theory. *I. Occup. Behav.:* 4 21–33.

Faucheux, C. Amado, G., Laurent, A. 1982. Organizational development and change. *Ann. Rev. Psychol.:* 33 343–70.

Fiedler, F.E., Bell, C., Chemers, M., Patrick. D. 1984. Increasing mine productivity and safety through management training and organization development: A comparative study. *Basic Appl. Soci. Psychol.:* 5 1–18.

Finlay, J.S. 1984. Diagnose your HRD problems away. *Train. Dev. J.:* 38 50–52.

Fox, W. 1984. General Motors: DuPont's tough OD case. *Group Organ. Stud.:* 9 71–80.

Freeman, R.E. 1984. *Strategic Management: A Stakeholder Approach*. Boston: Pitman. 276 pp.

Friedlander, F., Schott, B. 1981. The use of task groups and task forces in organizational change. In *Groups At Work*, ed. R. Payne, C. Cooper, pp. 191–218. New York: Wiley.

Frost, C.F., Wakeley, J.H., Ruh, R.A. 1974. *The Scanlon Plan for Organization Development: Identity, Participation, and Equity*. East Lansing, MI: Mich. State Univ. Press. 197 pp.

Fry, J.N., Killing, J.P. 1985. *Strategic Analysis and Action*. Englewood Cliffs, NJ: Prentice-Hall.

Gavin, J.F. 1984. Survey feedback: The perspectives of science and practice. *Group Organ. Stud.:* 9(1) 29–70.

Goldberg, S.B., Brett, J.M. 1983. An experiment in the mediation of grievance. *Monthly Labor Rev.:* 106 23–29.

Golembiewski, R.T., Billingsley, K., Yeager, S. 1976. Measuring change and persistence in human affairs: Types of change generated by OD designs. *J. Appl. Behav. Sci.:* 12 133–57.

Goodman, P., Dean, J.W. 1982. Creating long term change in organizations. In *Change in Organizations*, ed. P. Goodman and Associates, pp. 166–225. San Francisco/London: Jossey-Bass.

Graham, M.B.W., Rosenthal, S.R. In press. Flexible manufacturing systems require flexible people. In *Human Systems Management*.

Gray, B. 1985. Conditions facilitating interorganizational collaboration. *Hum. Relat.:* 38(10) 911–86.

Greenbaum, H.H., Holden, E.J. Jr., Spartaro, L. 1983. Organizational structure and communications processes: A study of change. *Group Organ. Stud.:* 8(1) 61–82.

Guzzo, R.A., Jette, R.D., Katzell, R.A. 1985. The effects of psychologically based intervention programs on worker productivity: A meta-analysis. *Personnel Psychol.:* 38 275–92.

Hackman, R., Oldham, G.R. 1975. Development of the job diagnostic survey. *J. Appl. Psychol.:* 60 159–170.

Harris, P.R., Harris, D.L. 1983. Twelve trends you and your CEO should be monitoring. *Train. Dev. J.:* 37 62–69.

Isenberg, D.J. 1984. How senior managers think. *Harv. Bus. Rev.:* 62 80–90.

Jick, T.D., Ashkenas, R.N. 1985. Involving employees in productivity and WWL improvements: What OD can learn from the manager's perspective. In *Contemporary Organization Development; Current Thinking and Applications*, ed. D. D. Warrick, pp. 218–30. Glenview, IL: Scott, Foresman.

Johnson, K.W., Frazier, W.D., Ruddick, M.R. 1983. A change strategy for linking the worlds of academia and practice. *J. Appl. Behav. Sci.:* 19 439–60.

Jones, S. 1984. The politics of problems intersubjectivity in defining powerful others. *Hum. Relat.:* 37 881–94.

Kanter, R.M. 1983. *The Change Masters: Innovation and Entrepreneurship in the American Corporation.* New York: Simon & Schuster. 432 pp.

Katz, D., Kahn, R.L. 1966. *The Social Psychology of Organizing.* New York: Wiley. 838 pp.

Katzell, R.A., Guzzo, R.A. 1983. Psychological approaches to productivity improvement. *Am. Psychol.:* 38 468–72.

Kilmann, R. 1984. *Beyond the Quick Fix: Managing Five Tracks to Organizational Success.* San Francisco/London: Jossey-Bass. 300 pp.

Kilmann, R.H. 1983. A dialectic approach to formulating and testing social science theories: Assumptional analysis. *Hum. Relat.:* 36(1) 1–22.

Kilmann, R., Sacton, M.J., Serpa, R., eds. 1985. *Gaining Control of the Corporate Culture.* San Francisco/London: Jossey-Bass. 451 pp.

Kilmann, R.H., Thomas, K.W., Slevin, D.P., Nath, R., Jerrell, L., eds. 1983. *Producing Useful Knowledge for Organizations.* New York: Praeger. 731 pp.

Kirkpatrick, D. 1985. *How to Manage Change Effectively.* San Francisco/London: Jossey-Bass. 280 pp.

Kleiner, B. 1983. The interrelationship of Jungian modes of mental functioning with organizational factors: implications for management development. *Hum. Relat.:* 36(11) 997–1012.

Kotter, J.P. *The General Managers.* New York/London: Free Press. 221 pp.

Krantz, J. 1985. Group process under conditions of organization decline. *J. App. Behav. Sci.:* 21 1–18.

Kuttner, R. 1985. Sharing Power at Eastern Air Lines. *Harv. Bus. Rev.:* 6 91–101.

Lawler, E.E. 1981. *Pay and Organization Development*. Reading, MA: Addison Wesley.

Lawler, E.E., Mohrman, A.M. Jr., Mohrman, S.A., Ledford, G.E. Jr., Cummings, T.G., eds. 1985. *Doing Research That Is Useful for Theory and Practice*. San Francisco/London: Jossey-Bass. 371 pp.

Lawrence, P.R., Lorsch, J.W. 1967. *Organizations and Environment: Managing Differentiation and Integration*. Homewood, IL: Irwin. 279 pp.

Legge, K. 1984. *Evaluating Planned Organizational Change*. Orlando Academic. 243 pp.

Levine, M.F. 1983. Self-developed QWL measures. *J. Occup. Behav.:* 4 35–46.

Lindblom, C.E., Cohen, D.K. 1979. *Usable Knowledge, Social Science and Social Problem Solving*. New Haven: Yale Univ. Press. 129 pp.

Lippett, G., Lippett, R., Lafferty, C. 1983. Cutting edge trends in organizational development. *Train. Dev. J.:* 38 59–62.

Lippitt, G.L., Langseth, P., Mossop, J. 1985. *Implementing Organizational Change*. San Francisco/London: Jossey-Bass. 184 pp.

Long, R.J. 1982. Worker ownership and job attitudes: A field study. *Ind. Relat.:* 21 196–215.

Lovelady, L. 1984. Change strategies and the use of OD consultants to facilitate change II: The role of the internal consultant in OD. *Leadership Organ. Dev. J.:* 5 2–12.

Lundberg, C.C., Glassman, A.M. 1983. The informant panel: A retrospective methodology for guiding organizational change. *Group Organ. Stud.:* 3(2) 249–64.

Macy, B.A., Hurts, C.C.M., Izumi, H., Norton, L.W., Smith, R.R. 1986. Meta-analysis of empirical work improvements and organizational change experiments: Methodology and preliminary results. Presented at Natl. Acad. Manage., 46th Ann. Meet., Chicago, IL. 101 pp. 52.

Mandrell, M. 1984. Application of network analysis to the implementation of a complex project. *Hum. Relat.:* 37 659–79.

Margulies, N., Raia, A.P. 1984. The politics of OD. *Train. Dev. J.:* 38 20–23.

McLean, A.J., Sims, D.B.P., Mangan, I.L., Tuffield, D. 1982. *Organization Development in Transition: Evidence of an Evolving Profession*. New York: Wiley. 131 pp.

Mendenhall, M., Oddou, G. 1983. The integrative approach to OD: McGregor revisited. *Group Organ. Stud.:* 8 291–301.

Morgan, G., ed. 1983. *Beyond Method: Strategies for Social Research*. Beverly Hills, CA: Sage. 424 pp.

Morrison, P. 1978. Evaluation in OD: A review and assessment. *Group Organ. Stud.:* 3 42–70.

Nicholas, J. 1982. The comparative impact of organization development interventions on hard criteria measures. *Acad. Manage. Rev.:* 9 531–43.

Nicholas, J., Katz, M. 1985. Research methods and reporting practices in organization development: A review and some guidelines. *Acad. Manage. Rev.:* 10 737–49.

Nicoll, D. 1983. Organization declines as an OD issue. *Group Organ. Stud.:* 7 165–78.

Nord, W.R., Tucker, S. 1986. *Implementing Radical and Routine Innovation*. Lexington, MA: Lexington Books. 416 pp.

Ouchi, W.G. 1981. *Theory Z: How American Business Can Meet the Japanese Challenge*. Reading, MA: Addison-Wesley. 283 pp.

Pascale, R.T., Athos, A.G. 1981. *The Art of Japanese Management*. New York: Simon & Schuster. 221 pp.

Passmore, W., Friedlander, F. 1982. An action research program for increasing employee involvement in problem solving. *Admin Sci. Q.:* 27 343–62.

Peters, M., Robinson, V. 1984. The origins and status of action research. *J. Appl. Behav. Sci:* 20 113–24.

Peters, T., Waterman, R.H. 1982. *In Search of Excellence*. New York: Harper & Row. 360 pp.

Pettigrew, A. 1985. *The Awakening Giant: Community and Change in ICI*. Oxford/New York: Blackwell. 542 pp.

Porras, J.I. 1985, March. *OD Research Paper #802*.

Quinn, J.B. 1980. *Strategies for Change: Logical Incrementation*. Homewood, IL: Irwin. 222 pp.

Roberts, N., King, P. 1985. *The Stakeholder Audit: A Key Political Tool in the Change Process*. Draft.

Roggemma, J., Smith, M.H. 1983. Organizational change in the shipping industry: Issues in the transformation of the basic assumptions. *Hum. Relat.:* 8 765–90.

Rubenstein, D., Woodman, R.W. 1984. Spiderman and the Burma Raiders: Collateral organization theory in action. *J. Appl. Behav. Sci.:* 20 1–21.

Sales, A.L., Mirvis, P.H. 1984. When cultures collide: Issues in acquisition. In *Managing Organizational Transitions*, ed. J.R. Kimberly, R.E. Quinnpp, pp. 107–33. Homewood, IL: Irwin.

Sandeberg, A. 1983. Trade union-orientated research for democratization of planning in work life—Problems and pitfalls. *J. Occup. Behav:* 4 59–71.

Sashkin, M. 1985. *Visionary Leadership: A New Look at Executive Leadership*. Washington, D.C.: Off. Educ. Res. Improve. 9 pp.

Sashkin, M., Burke, R.J., Lawrence, P.R., Pasmore, W.A. 1984. Organization development approaches: Analysis and application. In *Contemporary Organization Development, Current Thinking and Applications*, ed. D. D. Warrick. Glenview, IL: Scott, Foresman. 502 pp.

Sathe, V. 1985. *Culture and Related Corporate Realities*. Homewood, IL: Irwin. 579 pp.

Schein, E. 1985. *Organizational Culture and Leadership*. San Francisco: Jossey-Bass. 357 pp.

Schlesinger, L.A., Oshry, B. 1984. Quality of work life and the manager: Muddle in the middle. *Organ. Dyn.:* 13 4–19.

Schon, D.E. 1983. *The Reflective Practitioner: How Professionals Think in Action*. New York: Basic Books. 374 pp.

Seashore, S.E., Lawler, E.E., Mirvis, P.H., Camman, C., eds. 1983. *Assessing Organizational Change: A Guide to Methods, Measures, and Practices*. New York: Wiley.

Selznick, P. 1957. *Leadership in Administration*. White Plains, NY: Row, Peterson. 162 pp.

Senge, P.M. 1985. *System dynamics, mental models, and the development of management intuition*. Presented at the 1985 Int. Syst. Dyn. Conf. Keystone, CO.

Simmons, J., Mares, W. 1983. *Working Together*. New York: Knopf. 319 pp.

Solberg, S.L. 1985. Changing culture through ceremony: An example from GM. *Hum. Resour. Manage.:* 24 329–40.

Sutton, R.I. 1983. Managing organizational death. *Hum. Resour. Manage.:* 22 391–412.

Taimo, R., Santalainen, T. 1984. Some evidence for the cultural relativity of organization development programs. *J. Appl. Behav. Sci.:* 20(2) 93–111.

Terpstra, D.E. 1982. Evaluating selected OD interventions: The state of the art. *Group Organ. Stud.:* 94 402–17.

Trist, E. 1983. Referent-organizations and the development of inter-organization domains. *Hum. Relat.:* 36(3) 269–84.

Tushman, M., Katz, R. 1980. External communication and project performance as an investigation into the role of gatekeepers. *Manage. Sci.:* 26 1071–85.

Tushman, M., Newman, W.H., Romanelli, E. In press. Convergence and upheavals managing the unsteady pace of organizational evolution. *Calif. Manage. Rev.:* 28.

Van deVen, A., Walker, G. 1984. The dynamics of interorganizational coordination. *Admin Sci. Q.:* 29 598–621.

Van deVliert, E., Huismans, S.E., Stok, J.J.L. 1985. The criterion approach to unraveling beta and alpha change. *Acad. Manage. Rev.:* 10 269–74.

Vicars, W. M., Hartke, D.D. 1984. Evaluating OD evaluations: A status report. *Group Organ. Stud.:* 9(2) 177–88.

Walters, G.A. 1984. Organizational development and individual rights. *J. Appl. Behav. Sci.:* 20 423–39 (Special issue).

Walton, R.E. 1978. The Topeka story, part II. *Wharton Mag.:* 3 36–41.

Walton, R.E. 1980. Establishing and maintaining high commitment work systems. In *The Organizational Life Cycle: Issues in the Creation, Transformation, and Decline of Organizations*, ed. J.R. Kimberly, R.H. Miles, and Associates. San Francisco/London: Jossey-Bass.

Walton, R.E. 1985. From control to commitment in the workplace. *Harv. Bus. Rev.:* 63 76–84.

Wilkins, A.L. 1983. The culture audit: a tool for understanding organizations. *Organ. Dyn.:* 12 24–38.

Wilkins, A.L., Ouchi, W.G. 1983. Efficient cultures exploring the relationship between culture and organizational performance. *Admin. Sci. Q.:* 28 468–81.

Zand, D.E. 1974. Collateral organizations: A new change strategy. *J. Appl. Behav. Sci.:* 10(1) 63–89.

Zuboff, S. 1985. Technologies that informate implications for human resource management in the computerized industrial workplace. In *HRM Trends and Challenges*, ed. R.E. Walton, P.R. Lawrence, pp. 103–40. Boston: Harv. Bus. Schl. Press.

CHAPTER FIFTY-ONE

A Complex-Systems Approach to Organizations

Daniel J. Svyantek
Linda L. Brown (2000)

Nonlinear systems theory proposes that the behavior of systems in the world is affected by many variables that interact strongly with each other, whereas more traditional systems theory assumes that a few variables, interacting weakly with each other, determine the behavior of systems (Liebovitch, 1998). The nonlinear view of systems used to describe complex systems' behavior originated in the physical sciences of physics and chemistry and is commonly known as chaos theory or complexity theory.

Researchers use nonlinear methods to describe the behavior of *complex systems* (Gallagher & Appenzeller, 1999), which are those systems whose behaviors cannot be explained by breaking down the system into its component parts. Explaining the behavior of a complex system requires understanding (1) the variables determining the system's behavior; (2) the patterns of interconnections among these variables; and (3) the fact that these patterns, and the strengths associated with each interconnection, may vary depending on the time scale relevant for the behavior being studied (e.g., if reaction time is being measured, the time scale in which changes occur might be in milliseconds, whereas for change in corporate performance the timescale might be in months or years; Koch & Laurent, 1999).

There are some basic differences between traditional and complex-systems approaches to behavior. Traditional approaches emphasize the use of linear methods (e.g., regression) in which independent variables are used to make predictions about a system behavior (i.e., the dependent variable). The data gathered tend to consist of (1) individual measures of the predictor variables gathered at time 1 and (2) individual measures of the system behavior gathered at some later time. The predictions made tend to be molecular and quantitative. The value of these predictions is based on the statistical significance of, and variance accounted for by, the predictor variables. The results of such an experiment are then used to draw inferences about behavior at a future time or in a different context. Nonlinear methods utilize a different approach to analyze data. The data gathered consist of multiple measurements of both independent and dependent variables, and these data are then graphed. The predictions made are more molar and qualitative than the predictions in traditional approaches. The value of these predictions is based on the degree to which a consistent pattern of behavior is found in the system across the repeated measurements. The results of such an experiment are to make predictions that are context-specific.

For example, consider the relationship between organizational culture and job performance and the differences between traditional and complex-systems approaches. There are several instruments for measuring organizational culture. Each instrument consists of different scales assessing such things as the reward practices within a company, the supportiveness of the company in satisfying its employees' needs, the degree to which conflict exists within the group, and the degree to which work standards are well defined. The traditional approach generally involves giving out a survey to the employees of an organization and relating the obtained scores to some measure of job performance. The results are then used to make predictions about future states for the company in question (and usually for other companies). These predictions are made on the basis of one discrete measured episode of behavior. Complex-systems approaches are founded on the idea that this single measurement does not provide enough data to understand the system's behavior or make predictions about future states of the system. Such approaches might possibly use the surveys of organizational culture, but multiple measurements would be taken and the results would be graphed.

We propose that the description of behavior in social systems (e.g., leadership) may be improved through the use of heuristic concepts derived from understanding complex systems in other sciences that emphasize the historical nature of systems and the patterns of behavior found in them. Nonlinear concepts that have explanatory value for understanding social systems are the *phase space* and *attractor*.

PHASE SPACES AND ATTRACTORS

A phase space can be used to describe a complex system after its behavior has been measured on multiple occasions. The phase space is used to map the

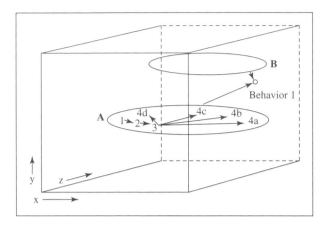

Figure 51.1. Example of a Three-Dimensional Space, Two Attractors (for Organizations A and B), Possibilities for Internal Behavior Change (Points 1, 2, 3, and 4a–d), and a Potential System Behavior, 1, Residing in the Phase Space.

coordinates of the variables defining the behavior of the system (Liebovitch, 1998). For example, Figure 51.1 shows a phase space represented by the three-dimensional box labeled X, Y, and Z. These dimensions represent three variables that define a complex system's behavior. Point 1 represents an instance of behavior at one point in time; its coordinates are X_1, Y_1, and Z_1 (i.e., the location of this point in this three-dimensional phase space). An example of such a phase space was described by Richter (1986). Richter created a simple model showing how individuals' behavioral responses in a situation are affected by their levels of aggressiveness (X), fear (Y), and guilt (Z). Knowledge of these variables allowed Richter to create a phase space describing change in individual responses across time. Variation in responses to a stressful situation across time will tend to be associated with different levels of these three variables. The goal of this analysis is to use repeated measurement of behavior to elucidate how a person's responses change in accordance with his or her personal level of aggressiveness and situational changes in fear and guilt.

One of the seeming contradictions of the study of complex systems is that macro-level prediction of a system's behavior is possible from seemingly random micro-level behaviors of the system (Liebovitch, 1998). Multiple measurements across time define a pattern of behavior exhibited by the complex system in the phase space. This pattern of behavior is the attractor, which represents stable boundaries for the system and a feasible set of alternatives for the system's behavior across time (Liebovitch, 1998). Thus, one can predict that the system's future behavior will remain within the attractor in the phase space.

Attractors have two primary characteristics; *sensitivity to initial conditions* and *stability*. Sensitivity to initial conditions has two implications for the behavior of complex systems. First, the developmental history of complex systems is critical to understanding their current states. This means that two systems with very similar starting conditions may arrive at different outcomes. Even very small, unmeasured differences can lead to divergence. Sensitivity to initial conditions makes it unlikely that two systems will follow the same historical path unless the starting conditions for both can be described as exactly the same (Abraham, Abraham, & Shaw, 1990).

The mechanism underlying sensitivity to initial conditions is positive feedback (Arthur, 1999). Positive feedback refers to the supportiveness of an environment for a particular behavior or outcome; this positive feedback increases the probability of that behavior vis-à-vis another behavior consistent with the set of behaviors contained in the phase space. The fit between environmental constraints and system characteristics important to survival may be due to very small or chance factors. Arthur (1999) proposed that an organization's early entry into a market, independent of any superiority of the organization's product, may have the effect of increasing the probability that this product will become the dominant design for the market and keep competitors from entering that market. For example, the QWERTY keyboard configuration is less than optimal for typing speed. It is the dominant design for typewriters and computer keyboards, however, because of chance factors that allowed typists using QWERTY to type faster than typists using other configurations in an early contest in the late-nineteenth century. This dominant configuration acts to keep other more well-designed key configurations from being used for modern computers because the initial superiority led people to choose the QWERTY system preferentially. This positive feedback defined the fit between QWERTY and this environmental niche and now prevents other configurations from entering this environmental niche.

This form of positive feedback is one mechanism that leads to the exaggeration of differences in complex systems having essentially the same starting conditions. Therefore, the attractors developed by two complex systems with similar starting conditions are not predictable in advance. For example, in Figure 51.1, attractors A and B may have developed from nearly identical starting conditions.

The second implication of sensitivity to initial conditions is that within one system micro-level behavior is unpredictable across time (Liebovitch, 1998). In Figure 51.1, points 1, 2, 3, and 4 (a–d) represent four measurements of the system taken at equal intervals. For points initially close to point 1 at time 1 (e.g., points 2 and 3), quantitative prediction may be possible using linear methods (e.g., regression). Such predictions work well for short increments of time and linear changes in the variable being measured. However, as time goes on, the location of behavior on the attractor rapidly becomes unpredictable because of unmeasured and unaccounted-for variables within the system. The system's behavior may jump from point 3 to point 4a, 4b, 4c, or 4d with equal probability. Therefore, although traditional regression approaches allow one to predict point 2 from point 1 and point 3 from points 1 and 2, the same regression approaches fail when one attempts to predict the movement from points 1, 2, and 3 to point 4.

This abrupt change is the *butterfly effect* (Liebovitch, 1998). It is important to remember that the butterfly effect can occur at any time between any two points on the attractor. The butterfly effect is one of the defining characteristics of nonlinear systems. It shows the value of distinguishing between qualitative and quantitative prediction in complex systems. Quantitative prediction is possible for the state of the system in the short term (e.g., prediction from point 1 to point 2 to point 3). The behavior of the system over these time intervals can be modeled using linear approaches. Qualitative prediction comes from understanding the system's attractor in the phase space. Although point 4 is not directly predictable from points 1, 2, and 3, one can still predict that it will remain in the space defined by the attractor. Therefore, although points 4a, 4b, 4c, and 4d are equally probable, they will remain on the attractor. A prediction outside the space defined by the attractor will not be made.

An attractor represents a stable pattern for a complex system. Stability is the second property of nonlinear systems (Bak, 1996). A complex system, even after drastic disturbance by its environment, tends to return to its original attractor. This stability helps determine a system's fitness, which is defined as the system's resilience, or ability to absorb change and disturbance and still maintain its basic pattern (Holling, 1976). This stability occurs because complex systems do not exist in a vacuum; they interact with each other. For example, assessing a person's level of aggressive behavior must involve taking into account the other individuals in his or her environment. Behavioral interactions define role expectations for aggression among individuals and these role expectations become stable over time. Change becomes difficult because it is not simply one individual's behavior that must be altered. Rather, the behavior of all individuals in the system must be changed. Bak (1996) has proposed that a complex system achieves its peaks of fitness during periods of stasis, that is, periods when individuals are competing for resources within a stable, integrated network. Adaptation in such a system does not change the relative performance position of the individuals making up the complex system. In effect, continual adaptation by agents is necessary for them to maintain their relative position within the network. For example, the yearly sales positions of the companies in the American automobile industry (i.e., Chrysler, Ford, and General Motors) have been shown to be consistent across time using time-series analysis. The actual sales of these companies fluctuated, but their relative position remained constant across a twenty-five-year period; General Motors remained first, Ford second, and Chrysler third (Svyantek & DeShon, 1992).

This stability makes it difficult to predict, however, the degree to which any single disturbance will affect behavior in the system. Environmental disturbances of a complex system may have minimal effect, cause a revolutionary change in the system by creating a new attractor, or cause the collapse of the system. The most likely outcome of an environmental disturbance, however, appears to be a return to the original attractor when the disturbance is removed (Bak, 1996).

ATTRACTORS AND ORGANIZATIONS

It is possible to define phase spaces for at least some social behaviors (e.g., as in Richter, 1986). An organization's culture defines a stable pattern of behavior for the organization across time and is analogous to a complex system's attractor (Svyantek & DeShon, 1993).

Organizational culture exhibits the characteristics of attractors outlined earlier. First, organizational culture is very sensitive to initial differences in starting conditions. Schein (1985), for example, stated that the organizational founders often have a critical effect on the organizational culture that will develop in new organizations. Similar organizational technologies and structures may have widely divergent cultures based on the personalities of and roles played by the founders. The mechanism through which this founder effect operates is probably positive feedback, in which initial differences in the management styles of the founders, for example, become amplified within the organizations and lead to different organizational culture patterns. Second, organizational culture, once formed, appears to be very stable. This stability persists in the face of efforts to change the culture to increase economic performance (Barney, 1986). It derives from the fact that organizational cultures have two functions: internal integration and external adaptation (Svyantek, 1997).

Internal integration defines what it means to be a member of an organization and provides a context for the interactions of individuals and groups within the organization (Svyantek, 1997). For example, consider the phase space in Figure 51.1. Patterns of behaviors related to traditional organizational culture or organizational climate variables (e.g., the reward practices, the degree to which the organization is supportive of its employees) may define the position of the organization in the phase space by providing the information relevant for plotting on the x-, y-, and z-axes. There will be differences in this position between different organizations (here, A and B). Over time, each organization's attractor is defined. Once this attractor is developed and becomes fixed, it is resistant to change. These core values will then be replicated across generations of organizational members through institutionalized selection, socialization, and reward practices (Schneider, Goldstein, & Smith, 1995.)

The adaptation function of culture allows the complex system to interact with its external environment and survive, (Svyantek, 1997). This function is more plastic than the level concerned with internal integration and is concerned with the transmission of information relevant to external adaptation by the organization. Changes in the adaptation function are fairly easily copied by organizations that have different core cultures but are in the same industry (e.g., if one automobile company comes out with a new type of vehicle, such as the minivan, other automobile companies can copy this). These changes do not change the relative performance levels of the companies, but they must occur to maintain the companies' relative positions in the industry. The behaviors associated with the external function of culture are more variable and, therefore, less diagnostic of the true nature of the organizational attractor than are the behaviors associated with the integrative function.

In addition, systems with different attractors may exhibit the same behavior because of environmental constraints (e.g., legal constraints on equal employment opportunity policies may alter the hiring practices of organizations). For example, in Figure 51.1, organizations A and B have different attractors yet exhibit the same observable behavior, behavior 1. The attractors for the two organizations reside in different portions of the phase space, yet each is constrained to adopt the behavior because of environmental pressures. The degree to which this behavior is consistent with the two organizational attractors is represented by the lengths of the arrows from the attractors to the behavior. From the standpoint of an external observer, behavior 1 provides more valid information for making future predictions about the core culture of organization B than about the culture of organization A (because behavior 1 is closer to B's attractor than to A's attractor). For example, suppose that behavior 1 is hiring a minority applicant. It is likely that the core culture defining organization A's attractor will not be as supportive of minorities after hiring as is the core culture of organization B. If the environment (in this case, the legal environment) is constraining the system's behavior, behavior 1 has different information value for a minority applicant hired by organization A and a minority applicant hired by organization B. Minority applicants hired by organization B are more likely to receive training and socialization (e.g., mentoring) that are helpful to their careers; minority applicants hired by organization A may not be provided with the same training and socialization necessary to succeed. Therefore, minority applicants making decisions about which company to accept a job in are faced with the problem that a behavior required by law (hiring) has little diagnostic value for their careers. In effect, this one behavior is inadequate to define an attractor, and only through future interactions with the two organizations would the minority applicants come to understand the core values making up the organizational attractors.

A key to understanding which function of organizational culture an observed behavior provides information about is to study behaviors across time and across contexts. If the observed behavior is indicative of the integrative level of culture (the organization's attractor), there will be little movement of the behavior in the phase space if the context changes (e.g., the external hiring practices and internal socialization practices of organization B will remain consistent with each other if the laws mandating equal opportunity are overturned). If the behavior is indicative of the adaptation function of organizational culture, when the context changes, the observed behavior changes. Therefore, if a behavior is diagnostic of the integrative cultural level defining the attractor, it will be maintained across changes in the environment, but if a behavior is diagnostic of the adaptive cultural level, it is likely to change and be replaced by a new behavior when the environment changes.

IMPLICATIONS

One problem with the study of social behavior as a complex system is that most data sets available consist, at best, of a few dozen data points across time. There is no clear agreement, however, on how large a data set is required. The estimates of repeated measures required to define an attractor range from ten to five billion (Liebovitch, 1998).

Complex systems must be studied across time to find the patterns of underlying order defining their attractors. Currently, the organizational data most appropriate for analysis with the methods used to study complex systems are outcome measures. These data are mapped using *phase space diagrams*. A phase space diagram illustrates the way in which a system transforms itself over time (Abraham et al., 1990) and requires repeated measurements to understand patterns of variability in the data being gathered. It is particularly useful for showing the temporal evolution of a nonlinear system's behavior because it creates an image of the system's behavior over time. The simplest phase space is one in which change in some variable across time is of interest to the evaluator (Liebovitch, 1998). The phase space diagram shows whether or not behavior on this variable varies across time and the amount of variation that occurs.

We (Svyantek & Brown, 1999; Svyantek & Snell, 1999) have used phase space diagrams to define the attractors for organizational outcome variables.

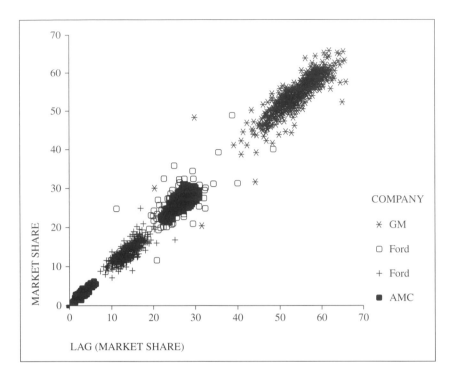

Figure 51.2. Relative Market Share for the American Automobile Industry (1965–1992) Plotted Using a Lag Diagram Pairing Market Share for the Current Time Period (y-Axis) with Lagged Market Share from the Previous Time Period (x-Axis).

Figure 51.2 shows a phase space diagram used to investigate market share performance of U.S. automobile manufacturers across the twenty-seven-year period from 1965 to 1992 (Svyantek & Brown, 1999). This phase space diagram shows that the market shares of U.S. automobile manufacturers were stable over this period. Thus, stability, one of the defining characteristics of a complex system, appears to be identifiable using phase space diagrams for organizations.

The discussion of complex systems suggests that traditional research methods used to study organizations in the field may need to be reassessed. The social-system data most amenable to study using nonlinear research methods (e.g., the phase space diagram) are outcome measures, such as market share. Other organizational constructs (e.g., organizational culture) are typically not measured in ways that would allow the use of such nonlinear methods. For example, organizational culture might be studied using a survey that describes the culture at a discrete point in time. Organizational culture, however, is typically viewed as a consistent pattern of values and norms that is passed between organizational members across time (Barney, 1986; Schneider et al., 1995), and longitudinal data are necessary to study such variables.

Understanding a complex system, therefore, requires understanding the historical processes and interactions that led to the development of consistent patterns of behavior across time. The study of organizations (and social systems in general) as complex systems requires that researchers take a much more longitudinal, historical, and in-depth, context-specific approach. Both the current state and the history of a complex system must be known if investigators are going to describe organizational attractors and improve prospects for changing these attractors.

Future research on the relevance of complex-systems concepts and complex-systems methods for understanding human social behavior should focus on developing new research methods suited to studying the internal workings of human social systems across time. These methods will require some means of gathering multiple measurements of variables such as organizational culture to define organizational attractors and will probably be expensive and time-consuming. Only through the development of such new methods, however, will the new science of complex systems realize its full potential for explaining human social behavior.

Recommended Reading

Abraham, F.D., Abraham, R.H., & Shaw, C.D. (1990). (See References)

Gallagher, R., & Appenzeller, T. (1999). (See References)

Gleik, J. (1987). *Chaos: Making a new science*. New York: Viking.

Hastings, A., Hom, C.L., Elner, S., Turchin, P., & Godfray, H.C.J. (1993). Chaos in ecology: Is Mother Nature a strange attractor? *Annual Review of Ecology and Systematics, 24*, 1–33.

Liebovitch, L.S. (1998). (See References)

References

Abraham, F.D., Abraham, R.H., & Shaw, C.D. (1990). *A visual introduction to dynamical systems theory for psychology*. Santa Cruz, CA: Aerial Press.

Arthur, W.B. (1999). Complexity and the economy. *Science, 284*, 107–109.

Bak, P. (1996). *How nature works*. New York: Springer-Verlag.

Barney, J.B. (1986). Organizational culture: Can it be a source of sustained competitive advantage? *Academy of Management Review, 11*, 657–665.

Gallagher, R., & Appenzeller, T. (1999). Beyond reductionism. *Science, 284*, 79.

Holling, C.S. (1976). Resilience and stability of ecosystems. In E. Jantsch & C.J. Waddington (Eds.), *Evolution and consciousness: Human systems in transition* (pp. 73–92). Reading, MA: Addison-Wesley.

Koch, C., & Laurent, G. (1999). Complexity and the nervous system. *Science, 284,* 96–98.

Liebovitch, L.S. (1998). *Fractals and chaos simplified for the life sciences.* New York: Oxford University Press.

Richter, F.M. (1986). Non-linear behavior. In D.W. Fiske & R.A. Shweder (Eds.), *Metatheory in social science: Pluralisms and subjectivities* (pp. 284–292). Chicago: University of Chicago Press.

Schein, E.H. (1985). *Organizational culture and leadership.* San Francisco: Jossey-Bass.

Schneider, B., Goldstein, H.W., & Smith, D.B. (1995). The ASA framework: An update. *Personnel Psychology, 48,* 747–773.

Svyantek, D.J. (1997). Order out of chaos: Non-linear systems and organizational change. *Current Topics in Management, 2,* 167–188.

Svyantek, D.J., & Brown, L.L. (1999). *Stasis and punctuations in organizational evolution: An investigation of stability in the American automobile industry.* Manuscript submitted for publication.

Svyantek, D.J., & DeShon, R.P. (1992). Leaders and organizational outcomes in established industries: An analysis of Lee Iacocca and the American automobile industry. In K. Clark, M. Clark, & D. Campbell (Eds.), *The impact of leadership* (pp. 293–303). Greensboro, NC: Center for Creative Leadership.

Svyantek, D.J., & DeShon, R.P. (1993). Organizational attractors: A chaos theory explanation of why cultural change efforts often don't. *Public Administration Quarterly, 17,* 339–355.

Svyantek, D.J., and Snell, A.S. (1999). Knowledge out of chaos: Using phase spaces for the qualitative evaluation of organizational change. In M.P. Cunha & C.A. Marques (Eds.), *Readings in organization science: Organizational change in a changing context* (pp. 523–540). Lisboa, Portugal: Instituto Superior de Psicologia Aplicada.

CHAPTER FIFTY-TWO

The Evolving Field of Organizational Learning

Chris Argyris
Donald A. Schön (1996)

We divide the literature that pays serious attention to organizational learning into two main categories: the practice-oriented, prescriptive literature of "the learning organization," promulgated mainly by consultants and practitioners, and the predominantly skeptical scholarly literature of "organizational learning," produced by academics. The two literatures have different thrusts, appeal to different audiences, and employ different forms of language. Nevertheless, they intersect at key points: their conceptions of what makes organizational learning "desirable" or "productive"; their views of the nature of the threats to productive organizational learning; and their attitudes toward whether—and if so, how—such threats may be overcome.

In the following sections, we describe the main currents of thought at work in the two branches of the organizational learning literature, and identify some of the controversial issues.

THE LITERATURE OF "THE LEARNING ORGANIZATION"

Although this literature takes many forms, its underlying conception of a central ideal is broadly shared. This ideal includes notions of organizational adaptability, flexibility, avoidance of stability traps, propensity to experiment, readiness to rethink means and ends, inquiry orientation, realization of human potential for learning in the service of organizational purposes, and creation of organizational settings as contexts for human development. Different authors articulate the ideal in different ways and single out different issues as central to its realization.

For example, David Garvin's review of literature on the learning organization (1993) pays special attention to ideas of systematic experimentation, movement from "superficial knowledge to deep understanding," "comprehensive frameworks," for the evaluation of progress, and the "opening up of boundaries [to] stimulate the exchange of ideas." In their review article, Ulrich, Jick, and Von Glinow (1993) also emphasize—in contrast to demonstration projects that too often become "sequestered showcases"—the importance of the "ability to move lessons learned from experience and experiments across boundaries," including boundaries of time and geography, levels of hierarchy, functional units, and links in the supplier-firm-customer value chain. These authors focus on continuous improvement, competence acquisition, experimentation, and boundary spanning. They stress the need for managers to make a visible commitment to the generation and generalization of organizational learning by incorporating it in strategic intent, measuring it, monitoring it, investing in it, talking about it in public, and giving it symbolic expression.

Within such a broadly shared background of assumptions and values, views of the learning organization differ according to the organizational functions to which the authors give primary attention. In each subfield, authors tend to stress different features of the ideal and to concentrate on different enabling prescriptions for its achievement.

Sociotechnical Systems

Sociotechnical systems—also known as the Quality of Work Life, or Industrial Democracy Movement—grew out of the postwar activities of the Tavistock Institute in England. It was extended in the 1960s and 1970s by the work of Einar Thorsrud, David Philip Herbst, and their colleagues in Norway, along with Fred Emery in Australia and many others. Gradually, the status of sociotechnical systems has shifted from fringe movement to established profession.

Its conception of a learning organization focuses on the idea of collective participation by teams of individuals, especially workers, in developing new patterns of work, career paths, and arrangements for combining family and work lives. According to this view, individuals (workers and their supervisors) can and must learn to redesign their work, and upper-level managers must learn to create the contexts within which they can do so.

Organizational Strategy

This field, some twenty-five years old, created by management consultants and academics in schools of business and management, takes its root metaphor from the military: organizations, like nations, engage in warlike games of competition for markets. Organizational strategy was originally conceived as a kind of planning aimed at formulating broad policies based on appreciation of a firm's position in relation to its markets, competitors, technologies, materials, and skills. As the field matured and the idea of strategy penetrated governmental and nonprofit sectors, concepts of the strategic game have become dynamic. Effective strategy tends now to be seen as requiring continual development of new understandings, models, and practices. Attention has shifted from planning to implementation of plans and then to the interaction of planning and implementing in a process explicitly described as organizational learning.

In a recent review of the literature on corporate strategy, Edward Bowman (1995) traces the intellectual development of the field, asking "how people in organizations . . . can understand and/or prescribe decision processes." Bowman makes a broad distinction between "rational" and "natural" approaches to the analysis of strategic decision making (a distinction that Overmeer also takes as central to his discussion of strategy and learning). For Bowman, the rational approach, which he associates mainly with economists and management scientists, adopts a "Cooks-tour" view of planning where all is calculated in advance. The "natural" approach uses the narrative, case-based methods of behavioral theory to describe a "Lewis-and-Clark" view of planning that follows the "habitual, unfolding, trial-and-error, learned, isomorphic patterns of decision processes." Bowman argues for an integration of the natural and the rational through a synthesis of economic and behavioral theory.

Production

In the 1970s and 1980s, as the United States slowly and painfully became aware of the competitive challenge posed by Japan, Germany, Korea, and other nations, and as attention focused on the need for continual improvement in the quality of products and production processes, authors in this field began to speak of learning.

For example, *Dynamic Manufacturing* (1988), by Hayes, Wheelwright, and Clark, carries the subtitle "Creating a Learning Organization," which the authors apply not only to the production process but to the performance of the organization as a whole. The authors claim that "companies that are quick both to learn new things and to perfect familiar things, that adapt imaginatively and effectively to change, and that are looked up to by their competitors because of their ability to lead the way into new fields, tend to have certain attributes in common. Moreover, companies with these attributes tend to be excellent throughout" (p. 25).

Economic Development

After World War II, the field of economic development, in close connection with the rise of international development agencies such as the World Bank, emerged. This field has been dominated by economists, especially macroeconomists, but a few of its influential practitioners have emphasized the development of institutions on which national economic development depends.

Albert Hirschman's *Exit, Voice, and Loyalty* (1970) is subtitled "Responses to Decline in Firms, Organizations, and States." Hirschman sees all such institutions as inherently subject to deterioration in the form of "lapses from efficient, rational, law-abiding, virtuous or otherwise functional behavior" (p. 1). He is concerned with two principal mechanisms of recuperation: the "exit" option, through which "some customers stop buying the firm's products or some members leave the organization," and the "voice" option, through which "the firm's customers or the organization's members express their dissatisfaction directly to management or to some other authority to which management is subordinate, or through general protest addressed to anyone who cares to listen."

In both cases, the basic schema is that of signal and response: customers or organization members signal their dissatisfaction by exit or voice and managers respond.

The recuperative processes with which Hirschman is concerned have many of the attributes of the organizational learning processes described above: they affect the organization as a whole, they operate continually throughout the life of the organization, and they involve the detection and correction of decline, deterioration, or dysfunction. Hirschman's view of development—of organizations, regions, or societies—contains an elusive theory of social learning, one that evinces itself most clearly in the three books that grew out of his experience as an economic development consultant (see Rodwin & Schön, eds., 1995). In Hirschman's normative, practice-oriented theory of development, his diagnoses and prescriptions hinge on what would now be called "structural enablers": institutional structures of incentives that compel or attract individuals to learn to produce behavior conductive to development.

Systems Dynamics

The systems modeling discipline first developed by Jay Forrester in the 1960s on the basis of servomechanism and control theory—and applied in grand sequence first to industry and then to cities and finally to the world—has turned in recent years to organizational learning. Peter Senge, one of Forrester's best-known followers, has published *The Fifth Discipline* (1994), subtitled "The Art and Practice of the Learning Organization." Senge's treatment of the subject unites systems thinking with organizational adaptation and with the realization of human potential in a mixture that has a distinctly Utopian flavor. On the one hand, he asserts, "the rate at which organizations learn may become the only sustainable source of competitive advantage" (p. 3). On the other hand, he envisages learning organizations where people continually expand their capacity to create the results they truly desire, where "new and expansive patterns of thinking are nurtured, where collective aspiration is set free, and where people are continually learning how to learn together" (p. 2).

Senge's prescriptive approach combines the methodology of systems dynamics with certain ideas adapted from our theory-of-action perspective, notably an awareness of the importance of the "mental models" held by organizational practitioners, including those that constrain or facilitate reliable inquiry into organizational processes.

Human Resources

In recent years, writers in the field of human resources have picked up the language of the learning organization, stressing the development of the human capability for questioning, experimenting, adapting, and innovating on the organization's behalf. Characteristically, writings in this subfield emphasize the mutually reinforcing interactions between enhanced opportunity for individual development within organizations and enhanced organizational capability for competitive performance.

For example, Jones and Hendry (1992), researchers at Warwick University in England, base their review of the literature on a pivotal distinction between "an incremental approach" to training and development and a "fundamental mind shift." They envisage a stage of "transformation" toward the latter where "learning focuses on managing personal change and self-assessment," management structures flatten, managers become more like coaches, thinkers and doers come together, everyone learns to go after the root causes of problems rather than assigning blame, and "the whole organization becomes committed via personal involvement." Beyond this stage the authors describe an as-yet-unrealized ideal of "transfiguration" in which people give priority to a concern for society's general welfare and betterment. They question why organizations exist in their present forms and treat their organizations as representing "a way of life to be cherished because of its values."

Organizational Culture

Organizational culture is a term whose currency among practitioners in present-day organizations rivals that of *organizational learning.* Managers have learned to speak of "our culture" as familiarly and with as little sense of the problematic as they speak of "our kind of people." Edgar Schein's *Organizational Culture and Leadership* (1985) offers the most careful attempt to provide a clear analysis of the meaning of organizational culture, and its second edition (1992) links organizational culture to the ideal of a learning organization. Schein argues that in a world of turbulent change, organizations have to learn ever faster, which calls for a learning culture that functions as "a perpetual learning system" (p. 372). The primary task of a leader in contemporary organizations is to create and sustain such a culture, which then, especially in mature organizations, feeds back to shape the leader's own assumptions.

Schein defines leadership as "the attitude and motivation to examine and manage culture" (p. 374). He regards the organization as the group and analyzes organizational culture as a pattern of basic assumptions shared by the group, acquired by solving problems of adaptation and integration, working "well enough to be considered valid and, therefore, to be taught to new members as the correct way to perceive, think, and feel in relation to those problems." In organizational learning, basic assumptions shift in the heads of the group members. The job of a learning leader is to promote such shifts by helping the organization's members to "achieve some degree of insight and develop motivation to change" (p. 390).

A learning leader must assess the adequacy of the organization's culture, detect its dysfunctionality, and promote its transformation, first by making his or her own basic assumptions into "learning assumptions" and then by fostering such assumptions in the culture of the organization. Among the most important learning assumptions: people want to contribute and can be trusted to do so; one should advocate one's own not-knowing, becoming a learner and trying to get others to do likewise, thereby diffusing responsibility for learning; and "the process of learning must ultimately be made part of the culture." Leaders can foster a learning culture by envisioning it and communicating the vision, by rewarding those pockets in an organization that represent the desired assumptions, and by fostering their creation through cultural diversity.

Acting in these ways is a large part of what Schein means by "managing the culture." He believes cultural change *can* be managed, although he is aware that it also depends on changed assumptions found to work in effectively adapting to the external environment and producing "comfort" in the internal one. Schein does not address the possible conflict of these managerial strategies (for example, promulgating a vision versus accepting one's own not-knowing) or what happens when changed assumptions fail to work.

Schein seems to be aware that managing a culture contains a hint of internal inconsistency (cultures are usually seen as growing up and evolving, rather than as objects of direct control), and he tries to argue simultaneously that the culture of an organization can be shaped by its leader, evolves in response to selective pressures exerted by external and internal environments, and can persist in the face of its not working. To some extent, Schein tries to reconcile these propositions by reference to different stages in an organization's life cycle. Specifically he recognizes that the culture of a mature organization may contain dysfunctional, taken-for-granted assumptions, products of past successes that "operate as silent filters on what is perceived and thought about" (p. 382). He observes, for example, "that the overt and espoused values that are stated for [organizational] solutions (e.g., TQM) often hide assumptions that are not, in fact, favorable to the kind of learning I have described."

When a culture becomes dysfunctional, learning leaders must be careful to "look inside themselves to locate their own mental models and assumptions before they leap into action" (p. 373). In order to avoid "unwittingly undermining [their] own creations," leaders must cultivate insight into their unconscious conflicts as well as into their conscious intentions. Consultants, in turn, can foster such insight by "helping the leader make his own sense of what is going on in himself and his organization," functioning as "cultural therapists" who help the leader figure out "what the culture is and what parts of it are more or less adaptive" (p. 387).

But Schein does not grasp the full burden of paradox inherent in the idea of managing a culture toward the ideal of a learning organization. He focuses on the danger that organizational cultures are inherently stability-seeking. He does not focus, directly and critically, on the issue of the *controllability* of a culture—the degree to which it may be subject to design causality—nor does he specify how learning assumptions such as not-knowing, trust in others, and "Theory Y assumptions about human nature" can actually be imparted to human beings. He addresses the limits of culture management mainly through his notion of "cultural humility," i.e. the recognition that culture is partly affected by powerful forces that may lie beyond a leader's direct control.

Some writings on the learning organization—like those of Schein, Senge, and the sociotechnical theorists—make significant contributions. They describe a range of types of organizational learning. They offer prescriptions that are useful at least as guides to the kinds of organizational structures, processes, and conditions that may function as enablers of productive organizational learning; for example:

- Flat, decentralized organizational structures
- Information systems that provide fast, public feedback on the performance of the organization as a whole and of its various components
- Mechanisms for surfacing and criticizing implicit organizational theories of action, cultivating systematic programs of experimental inquiry
- Measures of organizational performance
- Systems of incentives aimed at promoting organizational learning
- Ideologies associated with such measures, as among them total quality, continuous learning, excellence, openness, and boundary crossing

On the other hand, the literature on the learning organization is inattentive to the gaps emphasized in the arguments of the learning skeptics. It ignores the analytic difficulties posed by the very idea of organizational learning. It treats the beneficence of organizational learning as an axiom. It does not give serious consideration to processes that threaten the validity or utility of organizational learning. And it gives short shrift to the difficulties of implementation, the phenomena that undermine attempts to achieve the ideal or cause such attempts to be short-lived.

These gaps and difficulties are fundamentally dependent on the behavioral worlds of organizations that make for limited learning systems. Writers on the learning organization tend to focus on first-order errors, from mistaken or incomplete action strategies and assumptions of the sort that practitioners ordinarily detect and try to correct. They tend to be selectively inattentive to second-order errors, which are due to the organizational designs that make people systematically unaware of the behavioral phenomena that underlie the production and reproduction of first-order errors. We refer here, for example, to defensive routines, mixed messages, taboos on the discussability of key issues, games of control and deception, and organizational camouflage. As we have argued, reflection on such phenomena and the theories-in-use that underlie them is essential both to the task of explaining the limitations of organizational learning and to the design of interventions that can overcome those limitations.

THE SCHOLARLY LITERATURE OF ORGANIZATIONAL LEARNING

This literature—intentionally distant from practice, nonprescriptive, and value-neutral—focuses on just those questions the first branch ignores: What does "organizational learning" mean? How is organizational learning at all feasible? What kinds of organizational learning are desirable, and for whom and with what chance of actual occurrence? The scholars of organizational learning generally adopt a skeptical stance toward these questions. Their skepticism tends to revolve around three main challenges:

1. There are those who argue that the very idea of organizational learning is contradictory, paradoxical, or quite simply devoid of meaning.

2. A second challenge to the idea of organizational learning accepts it as a meaningful notion. What it denies is that organizational learning is always (or ever) beneficent.

3. A third kind of skepticism about organizational learning questions whether real-world organizations do learn productively, and whether, in principle and in actuality, they are capable of coming to do so.

Organizational Learning Is Contradictory

When we begin by assuming that individuals are the only proper subjects of learning and that we know what we mean when we say that individuals learn, then we are likely to be puzzled and disturbed by the notion that learning may also be attributed to organizations. Indeed, some researchers have argued, as Geoffrey Vickers did, that if the term "organizational learning" means anything, it means learning on the part of individuals who happen to function in an organizational setting. From this perspective, to say that an organization learns is to commit what the philosopher Gilbert Ryle called a "category mistake."

Yet even a cursory reading of the recent literature suggests that the disposition to regard organizational learning as a paradoxical idea was far more vigorous twenty years ago than it is now. Economists such as Marin (1993), Herrnstein (1991), and Holland and Miller (1991) have begun to introduce learning into economic discourse, making explicit the references to learning that have long been implicit in such branches of economics as the theory of the firm, which treats the firm as a decision maker optimizing to a utility function; and theories of free-market competition, which give an essential place to gains in efficiency and productivity stimulated by market forces. Contemporary researchers in the fields of organization theory and strategy concern themselves with high-level, intraorganizational entities such as management or R&D and seem relatively untroubled by sentences in which "organization" is the subject and "learning" the predicate. For example, Fiol and Lyles (1985) define learning, whether undertaken by individual or organizational agents, as "the process of improving actions through better knowledge and understanding" (p. 803). Organizations learn, in the sense proposed by Levitt and March (1988), when they "encode inferences from history into routines that guide behavior" (p. 319). Huber (1989) suggests that "an organization has learned if *any of its components* have acquired information and have this information available for use, either by other components or by itself, on behalf of the organization" (p. 3).

One increasingly influential research tradition, derived from the work of Campbell (1969) and Nelson and Winter (1982), draws on the Darwinian language of evolution, adaptation, and natural selection. Researchers in this tradition see organizational learning as a process in which whole organizations or their components adapt to changing environments by generating and selectively adopting organizational routines. For example, Robert Burgelman (1994) describes business firms as "ecologies of strategic initiatives, . . . which emerge in patterned ways and compete for limited organizational resources so as to increase their relative importance within the organization. Strategy results, in part, from selection and retention operating on internal variation associated with strategic initiatives" (p. 240).

In Burgelman's description, the agents that generate and select internal variations are collective entities labeled managers, departments, or top management.

It matters greatly, of course, in Burgelman's theory as in the theories of others mentioned above, whether entities defined at relatively high levels of social aggregation are taken to be uniquely appropriate or at least sufficient for the study of organizational adaptation and learning, or whether they are seen as needing to be complemented by a view that reveals how individuals enter into these processes. Many sociologically oriented researchers who see organizational learning as an intraorganizational phenomenon avoid the difficulties of bridging between individual and organizational phenomena by consistently treating agents and processes of learning at a relatively high level of social aggregation.

We insist, on the contrary, that a theory of organizational learning must take account of the interplay between the actions and interactions of individuals and the actions and interactions of higher-level organizational entities such as departments, divisions, or groups of managers. Unless a theory of organizational learning satisfies this criterion, it cannot contribute to knowledge useful to practitioners of organizational learning; nor can it explain the phenomena that underlie observed limitations to organizational learning. A few researchers share our view. For example, Daniel Kim (1993) has observed:

> Although the meaning of the term 'learning' remains essentially the same as in the individual case, the learning process is fundamentally different at the organizational level. A model of organizational learning has to resolve somehow the dilemma of imparting intelligence and learning capabilities to a nonhuman entity without anthropomorphizing it [p. 12].

Anyone who adopts such a position faces the rather daunting task of explaining how the "fundamentally different" processes carried out by individual and by higher-level entities can interact to yield the phenomena we are prepared to recognize as organizational learning. Clearly, although organizational learning has long since become an idea in good currency, it is no less problematic for organization theorists than when it languished at the margins of the field. Indeed, it holds a special interest for us just because it stretches the boundaries of our ordinary understandings of individual and organization.

What, then, are the possible modes of explaining the interplay between individuals and higher-level entities that constitute organizational learning? Should we imagine that individuals who play certain organizational roles (perhaps those who exercise greatest authority or control over action) can learn from their experiences and that when enough of them do so the organization as a whole can be said to learn? Should we think of organizations as groups of individuals, recognizing that groups are real entities irreducible to the individuals who make them up? Should we then attribute to such groups a capacity for thinking, inquiring, experimenting, and learning? Should we think of organizations as cultures that consist of systems of beliefs, values, technologies, languages, common patterns of behavior, shared representations of reality;

and should we then use learning to designate certain processes of cultural change? Should we think of organizations as cognitive constructs—perhaps theories in their own right—so that organizations may be said to learn when their members contribute to the cumulative accretion or modification of these constructs?

A key concept for us is that of inquiry, the intertwining of thought and action carried out by individuals in interaction with one another on behalf of the organization to which they belong in ways that change the organization's theories of action and become embedded in organizational artifacts such as maps, memories, and programs. A key question for us, then, is the meaning of the phrase "on behalf of the organization." We argue that it is possible for individuals to think and act on behalf of an organization because organizations are political entities, in a fundamental sense of that term. Collectivities become organizational when they meet three constitutional capabilities: to make collective decisions (so that groups of individuals can say "we" about themselves), to delegate authority for action to an individual in the name of the collectivity, and to say who is and who is not a member of the collectivity. Under these conditions, it makes conceptual sense to say that individuals can act on behalf of an organization. It also makes conceptual sense to say that on behalf of an organization individuals can undertake learning processes (organizational inquiry) that can, in turn, yield learning outcomes as reflected in changes in organizational theories of action and the artifacts that encode them.

But our emphasis on organizational inquiry as linking interpersonal and organizational phenomena in organizational learning and our insistence on the importance of the behavioral worlds that constrain or facilitate organizational inquiry have led some critics of the views we first expressed in our 1978 book to dismiss our approach as one that deals exclusively with the interpersonal or social-psychological dimension of organizational life. For some critics, indeed, our approach to organizational learning is about individuals and not about organizations at all.

Clearly, the issue underlying the controversy over our approach to organizational learning or over any attempt to treat organizational learning in terms of the interaction between individuals and organizations hinges, first, on what level or levels of aggregation one chooses to treat as distinctively organizational and, second, on the features one selects as critically important to learning at the level of aggregation in question. As we have noted, some researchers focus on clusters of organizations grouped together in larger systems, such as markets or ecologies within which learning is predicated of whole organizations (the firm or the state) or even the larger clusters to which they belong. For other observers, such as Nelson and Winter, and Burgelman, attention focuses on the interactions of larger entities (departments, divisions, top management) within organizations. For some organization theorists, such as

Crozier (1963), or theorists of policy implementation (Pressman & Wildavsky, 1973; Bardach, 1980), the key focus is on games of freedoms, interests, and powers that unfold among groups of individuals who occupy kinds of roles within organizations. For other theorists, such as Hirschman, the focus is on structures of incentives, created in part through the operation of the mechanisms of exit and voice that drive changes in organizational performance.

For theorists of a social-psychological bent, such as Schein (1992), attention focuses on individuals in interaction with one another within the settings organizations provide. Some researchers, following the directions set out in Marvin Minsky's *The Society of Mind* (1987), treat individuals themselves as organizations whose thought and action must be conceived in terms of the interplay of intrapsychic microagents in direct analogy with the operation of complex computer programs.

The issue of choice of level(s) of aggregation and the closely related issue of selective attention to features at any given level seem to occupy in the realm of organizational phenomena a place analogous to the one they occupy in the realm of theories of material objects. Physicists, mechanical engineers, materials scientists, and physical chemists focus on strikingly different levels of aggregation (for example, galaxies, bridges, composite materials, molecules) and give privileged status to different descriptions of phenomena discovered at these levels. In part, their different foci of attention reflect what they happen to be interested in and, in part, the purposes to which their respective inquiries are addressed. At certain key points, however, their research interests intersect, especially when the researchers are concerned with questions about the prospective guidance of technological practice. For example, civil engineers who are interested in the behavior of large-scale structures may consult materials scientists or even physical chemists, when their research leads them to think about metal fatigue or about the sources of the propagation of cracks in concrete. It remains controversial and intellectually fruitful whether descriptions of the behavior of higher-level entities, such as machines, can be reduced to descriptions of the behavior of lower-level entities, such as materials or molecules (Polanyi, 1967), or whether or in what particular ways it is both feasible and useful to develop theories of the behavior of higher-level entities without worrying much about the lower-level phenomena that might be adduced to account for that behavior.

In the broad and varied field of research on organizational learning, different interests and purposes also lead researchers to focus on different levels of aggregation and on different features of the phenomena discovered at any given level. We have argued that intersections among individual, interpersonal, and higher levels of aggregation become critically important if we wish to understand, and all the more so if we wish to redesign, the practices of organizational life, as carried out by individuals who inhabit organizations and bear responsibility for contributing to organizational performance, including especially the performance of organizational learning. But researchers on organizational learning are far from agreement on this point. There is disagreement not only about the nature of the kinds of interactions among individual, interpersonal, and higher-level entities that may be involved in organizational learning but also whether an adequate theory of organizational learning demands an account of such interactions.

Organizational Learning Is a Meaningful Notion but Not Always Beneficent

Once organizational learning is taken as a neutral term rather than as a normative ideal, it is obvious to us, and others, that it need not be for the good, given some view of the good. In the Nazi period, Eichmann's bureaucracy clearly became more efficient at carrying out its evil mission and may be said, with some plausibility, to have "learned" to do so. But the ethical critique of organizational learning varies with the kinds of evil to which the critic believes organizations are particularly disposed.

Some authors treat the ideal of the learning organization as an instance of contemporary rhetorics of "high-performance organizations," (see Kunda, 1992; who refers, in turn, to Bendix, 1956; Van Maanen, 1988; and Goffman, 1959.) They claim that organizational power elites use the ideal of the learning organization as they use other rhetorical ideals as cunning vehicles of normative control to gain the compliance—indeed, the commitment—of subordinates, and in ways that may be good for those in control but bad for those who are subordinated to them. As Kunda puts it:

> Normative control is the attempt to elicit and direct the required efforts of members by controlling the underlying experiences, thoughts, and feelings that guide their actions. Under normative control, members act in the best interests of the company . . . [because] they are driven by internal commitment, strong identification with company goals, intrinsic satisfaction from work . . . elicited by a variety of managerial appeals, exhortations, and actions. . . . In short, under normative control it is the employee's self . . . that is claimed in the name of corporate interest [p. 11].

Finally, some authors criticize organizational learning because they claim that much of it, perhaps even the greater part, is in the service of stability rather than change. On this view, organizations learn to preserve the status quo, and learning of this sort is the enemy of organizational change and reform (Fiol & Lyles, 1985; Levitt & March, 1988).

All such criticisms rest on the idea that organizational learning is not a value-neutral activity but proceeds from values, has implications for values, and is subject to critique in terms of a conception of what is good or right, and for whom. These implications, which seem obvious once they are stated, come to light only when organizational learning is stripped of its normative aura and considered as subject to evaluation in particular contexts on the basis of particular criteria of goodness or rightness. In short, we cannot escape the need to declare what kinds of organizational learning we will take to be desirable or undesirable and why.

DO REAL-WORLD ORGANIZATIONS LEARN PRODUCTIVELY?

In order to speak of an organization learning, we must see it as a more or less coherent agent. And we must also see it as capable of acting rationally, at least in the sense of being able to remember past events, analyze alternatives, conduct experiments, and evaluate the results of action. But some authors claim that these attributions have little or no validity for organizations as we find them in the world. We categorize their doubts in terms of threats to coherent action, valid inference, and efficacy.

Threats to Coherent Action

Some theorists have argued that organizations are actually pluralistic systems, little more than stage settings for performances by agents such as professions, disciplines, or social groupings that by their very nature cut across organizational boundaries. Some authors see organizations as political systems, made up of subgroups, each with its own interests, freedoms, and powers, crucially engaged in battles for control or avoidance of control and incapable of functioning holistically as agents of learning (Crozier, 1963; Bardach, 1980). In his middle period, March, along with various coauthors (Cohen & March, 1974; March & Olsen, 1976), proposed that organizations are inherently chaotic, at best organized anarchies. His "theory of the garbage can" presents decision making in terms of ideas, interests, images, and values in search of problems, rather than in terms of problem solvers actively searching for ideas, images, and values. Where the garbage can is in operation, it is hard to see how organizations can be considered capable of coherent action or inquiry.

Again, these lines of argument appear to have had more weight twenty years ago in the full flush of the reaction against unreflective theories of organizational rationality (e.g., Perrow, 1979) than they do at present. Although attributions of organizational incoherence still present themselves as sources of doubt about claims made in the name of organizational learning, they tend no longer to be taken a priori as reasons for outright rejection of the idea. Rather, it seems, there is a growing sentiment that the degree of coherence manifested in organizational action or inquiry is an empirical matter to be ascertained at particular places and times. A case in point is March's transition from viewing organizations as "organized anarchies" to the far more modulated position he has expressed in his more recent writings, where he suggests that there are periods in which institutional reform can be pursued through "integrative processes . . . that treat conflict of interest as the basis for deliberation and authoritative decision rather than bargaining" (March, 1989, p. 142).

Threats to Valid Inference

Across the wide-ranging descriptions of organizational learning processes presented in scholarly literature, there is a consistent emphasis on rational inference, inference in the form of lesson drawing from observations of past experience, inference about the causal connections between actions and outcomes, and inference from cycles of trial and error. A number of authors, including some of those noted above, base their skepticism on "threats to valid inference," which seem to them to make real-world organizational learning a dubious proposition.

March, who defines organizational learning as "encoding inferences from history into routines that guide behavior" (Levitt and March, 1988, p. 319), has been prolific in identifying threats to the validity of such inferences. For example (1988, pp. 322–323), he underlines the importance of "competence traps," wherein organizations falsely project into the future the strategies of action that have worked for them in the past. He calls attention to various sources of ambiguity that undermine organizational judgments of success or failure:

> The lessons of experience are drawn from a relatively small number of observations in a complex, changing ecology of learning organizations. What has happened is not always obvious, and the causality of events is difficult to untangle. What an organization should expect to achieve, and thus the difference between success and failure, is not always clear [p. 323].

He describes instances of "superstitious learning" that "occur when the subjective experience of learning is compelling, but the connections between actions and outcomes are misspecified" (p. 325).

March also identifies a "dilemma of learning" that constitutes a family of threats to valid inference. When learning proceeds gradually through "small, frequent changes and inferences formed from experience with them," then a likely outcome is the reinforcement or marginal change of existing routines. Such behavior "is likely to lead to random drift rather than improvement" (Lounamaa & March, 1987). On the other hand, when organizations learn from "low probability, high consequence events," then inferences about them are often "muddled with conflict over formal responsibility, accountability, and liability" (Levitt and March, 1989, p. 334). The upshot is that "learning does not always lead to intelligent behavior. The same processes that yield experiential wisdom produce superstitious learning, competence traps, and erroneous inferences" (p. 335).

In this line of argument, March treats learning in the narrow sense of drawing lessons from history as an alternative to other models of decision making, such as rational choice, bargaining, and selection of variations. He argues that under some circumstances learning may prove inferior to its alternatives, although he adds the caveat that the alternatives may also make mistakes and it is, therefore, "possible to see a role for routine-based, history-dependent, target-oriented organizational learning" (p. 336). (From our point of view, all of March's alternate strategies may enter into the processes of *inquiry* around which we build our broader approach to organizational learning. The relative vulnerabilities of lesson drawing from history would be relevant not to the general question of the cognitive capability for learning in real-world organizations but to the problem of choosing, in any given context, what strategy of inquiry to pursue.)

A very different kind of threat to the validity of inference in organizational inquiry stems from the observation that organizational learning depends on the interpretation of events, which depends, in turn, on frames, the major story lines through which organizational inquirers set problems and make sense of experience. Framing is essential to interpretive judgments, but because frames themselves are unfalsifiable, organizational inquirers may be trapped within self-referential frames. Padgett (1992) writes that "the collectively constructed frame or 'membrane' through which information and rewards are assembled and received" is an "axiomatic construction of the world" that is "reciprocally tied to the constitution of the observer." Communication across divergent, self-referential frames is bound to be problematic.

However, Schön and Rein (1994) explore the frame conflicts that underlie persistent policy disputes, for example, those that revolve around welfare, homelessness, or the costs and benefits of advanced technology. They argue that in actual policy practice inquirers may be capable of reflective inquiry into the frames that underlie their divergent positions and can sometimes hammer out, in particular situations, a pragmatic resolution of their conflicting frames.

Threats to Effective Action

Even if organizational inquirers are sometimes able to draw valid inferences from historical experience or current observation, their inferences may not be converted to effective action. A number of contemporary researchers (Fiol & Lyles, 1985; Kim, 1993) call attention to the fact that learning outcomes may be fragmented or situational and may never enter into the organizational mainstream. In earlier research, proponents of the "behavioral theory of the firm" (Cyert & March, 1963; March, 1963; Simon, 1976) described dysfunctional patterns of organizational behavior that undermine productive organizational learning. They noted that organizations depend on control systems that set up conflicts between rule setters and rule followers, which leads to cheating, and that in such an organizational world "everyone is rational and no one can be trusted."

"Fragmented" learning outcomes are closely related to "conditions for error." And the dysfunctional, defensive patterns of behavior described by Simon, Cyert, and the early March are closely related to the patterns we have ascribed to limited learning systems. The question is how we should view such phenomena. Should we consider them along the lines of the behavioral theory of the firm, as pervasive and inherent features of organizational life that it is the business of organizational researchers to "discover" rather than to change? Or should we treat them as critically important impediments to productive learning that call for, and may be malleable in response to, double-loop inquiry?

CONCLUSION

Our review of the two-pronged literature of organizational learning leaves us with challenges to the beneficence, the feasibility, and the meaningfulness of organizational learning. Proponents of the learning organization are not worried about the meaningfulness of organizational learning and take its desirability to be axiomatic. They prescribe a variety of enablers through which they claim that organizations can enhance their capability for productive learning, but they do not inquire into the gaps that separate reasonable prescription from effective implementation.

Skeptical researchers into organizational learning present, from a variety of perspectives, important reasons for doubt. Some of them have raised questions about the paradox inherent in the claim that organizations learn, which hinges on assumptions about relationships among individual, interpersonal, and higher levels of social aggregation. Other writers have challenged the desirability of organizational learning, arguing that organizations may learn in ways that foster evil ends or reinforce the status quo, or arguing that the ideal of the learning organization may be used to support a subtler and darker form of managerial control. Still other researchers observe and categorize phenomena that function as impediments to valid inference and effective action.

The problems raised by the two branches of the literature are largely complementary: what one branch treats as centrally important, the other tends to ignore. Both branches do concern themselves with the capability of real-world organizations to draw valid and useful inferences from experience and observation and to convert such inferences to effective action. But authors of a prescriptive bent tend to assume, uncritically, that such capabilities can be activated through the appropriate enablers, and learning skeptics tend to treat observed impediments as unalterable facts of organizational life.

References

Bardach, E. (1980). "On Designing Implementable Programs." In *Pitfalls of Analysis*, G. Majone and E.S. Quade, eds. Chichester, England: John Wiley and Sons.

Bendix, R. (1956). *Work and Authority in Industry*. New York: Harper and Row.

Bowman, E. (1995). "Next Steps for Corporate Strategy." In *Advances in Strategic Management*, P. Shrivastava, C. Stubbart, A. Huff, and J. Dutton, eds. Greenwich, Conn.: JAI Press, Inc.

Burgelman, R. (1994, March). "Fading Memories: A Process Theory of Strategic Business Exit in Dynamic Environments." In *Administrative Sciences Quarterly*, vol. 39: pp. 24–56.

Campbell, D. (1969). "Variation and Selective Retention in Socio-Cultural Evolution." In *General Systems*, vol. 16: pp. 69–85.

Cohen, M.D., and March, J.G. (1974). *Leadership and Ambiguity*. Princeton: Carnegie Foundation for the Advancement of Teaching.

Crozier, M. (1964; original publication, 1963). *The Bureaucratic Phenomenon*. Chicago: University of Chicago Press.

Cyert, R.M., and March, J.G. (1963). *A Behavioral Theory of the Firm*. Englewood Cliffs, N.J.: Prentice Hall.

Fiol, C.M., and Lyles, M.A. (1985). "Organizational Learning." In *Academy of Management Review*, vol. 10: pp. 803–813.

Garvin, D. (1993, July-August). "Building a Learning Organization." *Harvard Business Review*, vol. 4: pp. 78–91.

Hayes, R.H., Wheelwright, S.C., and Clark, K.B. (1988). *Dynamic Manufacturing: Creating a Learning Organization*. New York: The Free Press.

Herrnstein, R.J. (1991). "Experiments on Stable Suboptimality in Individual Behavior." In *Learning and Adaptive Economic Behavior*, vol. 81, no. 2: pp. 360–364.

Hirschman, A. (1970). *Exit, Voice, and Loyalty: Responses to Decline in Firms, Organizations, and States*. Cambridge, Mass.: Harvard University Press.

Holland, J.H., and Miller, J.H. (1991). "Artificial Adaptive Agents in Economic Theory." In *Learning and Adaptive Economic Behavior*, vol. 81, no. 2: pp. 365–370.

Huber, G.P. (1989). "Organizational Learning: An Examination of the Contributing Processes and a Review of the Literature." Prepared for the NSF-sponsored Conference on Organizational Learning, Carnegie-Mellon University, May 18–20.

Jones, A.M., and Hendry, C. (1992). *The Learning Organization: A Review of Literature and Practice*. Coventry, UK: Warwick Business School, University of Warwick.

Kim, D. (1993). "Creating Learning Organizations: Understanding the Link Between Individual and Organizational Learning." OL&IL Paper v3.5, MIT Sloan School of Management, Massachusetts Institute of Technology, Cambridge, Mass.

Kunda, G. (1992). *Engineering Culture*. Philadelphia: Temple University Press.

Levitt, B., and March, J.G. (1988). "Organizational Learning." *Annual Review of Sociology*, vol. 14: pp. 319–40.

Lounamaa, P., and March, J.G. (1987). "Adaptive Coordination of a Learning Team." *Management Science*, vol. 33: pp. 107–23.

March, J.G., and Olsen, J. (1976). *Ambiguity and Choice in Organizations*. Bergen, Norway: Universitetsforlaget.

March, J.G., and Olsen, J. (1989). *Institutions Rediscovered*. New York: The Free Press.

Marin, D. (1993). "Learning and Dynamic Comparative Advantage: Lessons from Austria's Post War Pattern of Growth for Eastern Europe." Paper prepared for the 17th Economic Policy Panel, Copenhagen, April 22–23, 1993.

Minsky, M. (1987). *The Society of Mind*. New York: Simon and Schuster.

Nelson, R., and Winter, S.G. (1982). *An Evolutionary Theory of Economic Change*. Cambridge, Mass.: The Belknap Press of Harvard University Press.

Padgett, J.F. (1992, February). "Learning from (and about) March." *Organization Science*, vol. 3: pp. 744–748.

Polanyi, M. (1967). *The Tacit Dimension*. New York: Doubleday (Anchor).

Pressman, J., and Wildavsky, A. (1793). *Implementation*. Berkeley: University of California Press.

Rodwin, L., and Schön, D.A., eds. (1994). *Rethinking the Development Experience: Essays Provoked by the Work of Albert Hirshman*. Washington, D.C.: The Brookings Institution.

Schein, E. (1985; second edition, 1992). *Organizational Culture and Leadership*. San Francisco: Jossey-Bass Publishers.

Schön, D.A., and Rein, M. (1994). *Frame Reflections: Toward the Resolution of Intractable Controversies*. New York: Basic Books.

Senge, P. (1990). *The Fifth Discipline: The Art and Practice of the Learning Organization*. New York: Doubleday.

Simon, H. (1976). *The Sciences of the Artificial*. Cambridge, Mass.: MIT Press.

Ulrich, D., Jick, T., and Von Glinow, M.A. (1993, Autumn). "High-Impact Learning: Building and Diffusing Learning Capability." *Organizational Dynamics*: pp. 52–66.

Van Maanen, J. (1988). *Tales of the Field*. Chicago: University of Chicago Press.

PART EIGHT

SOME CONCLUSIONS AND FUTURE NEEDS
Editors' Interlude

SOME CONCLUSIONS

Looking across the previous seven parts and the chapters included for each, and especially considering their content over time, we can identify certain shifts that have occurred in the past half century. These shifts signify change in emphasis, not one replacing the other. At least five shifts, in no particular order, seem clear enough for us to consider.

1. *From individual and group to the larger system, including interorganizational.* We have greater clarity that organization change is more likely to occur when we intervene at the larger (if not total system) level than when we are attempting to bring about change by focusing only on the individual or group. Do we need to pay attention to individuals and groups? Of course, but as they relate to and serve the whole. The era of mergers and acquisitions, strategic alliances, joint ventures, and related interorganizational activities has only begun. These activities are not exactly passing fads.

2. *From theory steeped in behavioral sciences to cell biology and open systems theory, chaos theory, and nonlinear complex system theory.* Again the point is that we are not abandoning the behavioral sciences; it's more a matter of increasing the level and complexity of our understanding. Moreover, this shift helps us with the first one above, that is, to understand more thoroughly systems in their totality, for example how work units interact differently in the midst of large-scale system change.

3. *From resistance to change as a nuisance to greater understanding that resistance is natural and not always bad.* There are individual differences regarding one's tendency to resist (Oreg, 2003), and different forms of resistance and it is important to remember that resistance is better than apathy. At least with resistance there is energy and people care about something. It's a matter of rechanneling that energy. Besides, how can you manage apathy?

4. *From the traditional scientific method for determining whether change has occurred to action science involving the client (or end user) in the process.* Again this shift is not necessarily one replacing the other. Refer to Chapter Fifty-One in this volume, where Svyantek and Brown show how to expand our traditional scientific methods to deal more effectively with nonlinear phenomena. Also recall that Beer and Walton, in the same Part Seven, explained why traditional methods are not likely to work.

5. *From groups and work units nested within the hierarchy to self-managed groups that are less constrained by formal hierarchy.* The trend that continues from the 1980s is to reduce hierarchy, to flatten the organization. The work of Eliot Jaques (e.g., Jaques, 1989) provides credible evidence that any organization, regardless of size, should have no more than seven layers in the hierarchy. With less hierarchy the span of control for any given manager is likely to increase, making management much more difficult and complicated. Thus, the need for reliance on self-managed groups. In other words, this shift is likely to continue.

To summarize: these shifts are the clearer ones to us; there are no doubt other, perhaps subtler, ones that we will see more clearly in the future. Also, it bears repeating that these are shifts, not replacements. It is more a matter of increasing complexity, e.g., incorporating into our thinking and planning chaos theory as well as behavioral science theory.

SOME FUTURE NEEDS

In a chapter on emerging themes from writings about leading and managing people in organizations, Peterson and Sancovich (2003) offer some thoughtful suggestions regarding needs for the future. Although they are not addressing planned organization change, what they suggest has implications for change. Their themes or emerging needs are:

1. *The need to embrace paradox.* Even in a world of rapid change, some things need to remain unchanged and stable. It seems clear that organizational members in the midst of considerable change can cope much better if at the same time they know what is not going to change, at least for the time being.

2. *Dynamic organizations are better suited to some people than to others.* Some individuals are more open to change and less resistant than others (Oreg, 2003). The chapter by King in Part Five demonstrated that with careful selection processes a better fit between individual skills and attitudes and organizational needs and goals can be achieved. The point is no doubt obvious: individual differences are very important considerations when planning and implementing change.

3. *Managers and leaders need to be able to deal with ambiguity.* Organization change produces unintended consequences (Burke, 2008), results from an intervention that were not expected—in other words, creating ambiguity. Again there are individual differences. Selecting individuals who are more tolerant about dealing with ambiguity may be better choices for leading change.

4. *Knowledge is a flow more than a fixed asset.* Organizations produce far more data and information than can be used. It is therefore critical to understand which bits of information are the most timely and have the highest priority. The need is to manage knowledge effectively.

In addition to these four emerging themes and needs from Peterson and Sancovich's synthesis (2003), we have chosen to add four more, in this case more directly related to organization change:

1. *Sustaining change.* The more difficult aspect of planned organization change than initiating the effort is to sustain it, the final phase of Burke's four that begin with prelaunch, launch, and postlaunch (see Part Six). Sustaining the change once it is under way is the most difficult aspect of planned organization change. What, for example, is momentum? How do you recognize it in the first place and then support the process? We need some answers to these questions.

2. *Ideal design and structure.* We have not found the ideal organizational design and structure. Perhaps such does not exist. But organizational executives keep searching and trying this structure versus that one. Furthermore, many managers seem to believe that if you change the structure, the organization as a consequence will be changed. We know better. Our future need is to learn more about structure, especially informal structures, such as networks, and why the number 150 seems to work so well (that is, never having an organizational unit larger than 150 people). The research behind this figure comes from the work of Dunbar (1992) and Wegner (1991) and the experience of the company Gore Associates; see Burke (2008).

3. *What we still don't know.* For all that has been written about leadership, we remain to some extent in the dark. But glimmers of light are on the horizon and need to be pursued, particularly with respect to leading change. One such glimmer is early evidence that self-awareness is related to performance; the

greater one's self-awareness the higher the leader's performance. Also recall our two key roles for change: leadership and teamwork. One definition of an effective leader is how well he or she selects and manages a team. Perhaps leadership effectiveness should be measured in terms of what followers accomplish, and not so much in terms of what the leader does. More understanding in this kind of direction would be useful and exciting.

4. *Our final need is for greater flexibility.* Coming back to the beginning, the chapter in Part One by Foster and Kaplan, they showed us that twenty-first century organizational environments are changing more rapidly than organizations can respond. They suggested that the reason for this lag was "cultural lock-in," the organization's culture being too calcified to cope rapidly enough with the external changes. They argued that organizations should not be *built to last*, taking a critical jab at the popular book by Collins and Porras with that title, but instead should be "built to change." Now we have a book by Lawler and Worley (2006) with that title. Flexibility is the key, according to these authors. Their book, though an important contribution, is only the beginning of what is needed regarding our knowledge and practice. As they note, for example, strategy should be an everyday process, not a one-time event or activity once a year.

These eight needs for the future are not a definitive list. They represent what comes across, perhaps tacitly, in many of the chapters included in this volume. Many other needs for the future could be included. It is our hope that this book of readings will stimulate readers to find these other needs for the future and not just settle for our list.

References

Burke, W. W. (2008). *Organization change: Theory and practice*. 2nd Ed. Thousand Oaks, CA: Sage.

Dunbar, R.I.M. (1992). Neocortex size as a constraint on group size in primates. *Journal of Human Evolution*, *20*, 469–493.

Jaques, E. (1989). *Requisite organization*. Arlington, VA: Cason Hall.

Lawler, E. E. III, & Worley, C. G. (2006). *Built to change: How to achieve sustained organizational effectiveness*. San Francisco: Jossey-Bass.

Oreg, S. (2003). Resistance to change: Developing an individual difference measure. *Journal of Applied Psychology, 88*, 680–693.

Peterson, R. S., & Sancovich, A. C. (2003) Emerging themes from a new paradigm. In R. S. Peterson and E.A. Mannix (Eds.), *Leading and managing people in the dynamic organization* (pp. 253–261). Mahwah, NJ: Erlbaum.

Wegner, D. (1991). Transactive memory in close relationships. *Journal of Personality and Social Psychology, 61*, 923–929.

NAMES INDEX

SUBJECT INDEX

CREDITS

Grateful acknowledgement is made to the following for permission to reprint previously published materials.

Chapter One:

"The Casual Texture of Organizational Environments" by F.E. Emery and E.L. Trist in *Human Relations, 18*, pp. 21–32. Copyright © 1965. Reproduced by permission of Sage Publications, Ltd.

Chapter Two:

"Changing Organizations" from *Changing Organizations* by Warren G. Bennis, 1966, the first Douglas Murray McGregor Memorial Lecture of the Alfred P. Sloan School of Management, Massachusetts Institute of Technology. Cambridge, Mass.

Chapter Three:

"Survival and Performance in the Era of Discontinuity" from *Creative Destruction* by Richard N. Foster and Sarah Kaplan. Copyright © 2001 by McKinsey & Company, Inc., United States. Used by permission of Doubleday, a division of Random House, Inc.

Chapter Four:

"Management and the Scientific Renaissance" from *Surfing the Edge of Chaos* by Richard T. Pascale, Mark Millenmann, and Linda Gioja. Copyright © 2000 by Richard T. Pascale, Mark Millemann, and Linda Gioja. Used by permission of Crown Business, a division of Random House, Inc.

Chapter Five:

"Quasi-Stationary Social Equilibria and the Problem of Permanent Change" by Kurt Lewin in *The Planning of Change* edited by Warren G. Bennis, Kenneth

D. Benne, and Robert Chin. Copyright © 1961 by Holt, Rinehart and Winston, Inc. Originally published as "Group Decision and Social Change" in *Readings in Social Psychology*, edited by Theodore M. Newcomb and Eugene L. Hartley. Copyright © 1947 by Holt, Rinehart and Winston, Inc.

Chapter Six:

"The Mechanisms of Change" by Edgar H. Schein in *The Planning of Change*, 2nd ed., edited by Warren G. Bennis, Kenneth D. Benne, and Robert Chin. Copyright © 1961, 1969 by Holt, Rinehart and Winston, Inc. Reprinted from *Interpersonal Dynamics*, edited by Warren G. Bennis, Edgar H. Schein, F. Steele, and D. Berlow (Homewood, IL: The Dorsey Press), 1964, pp. 362–378.

Chapter Seven:

"General Strategies for Effecting Changes in Human Systems" by Robert Chin and Kenneth D. Benne in *The Planning of Change*, 4th ed., edited by Warren G. Bennis, Kenneth D. Benne, and Robert Chin. Copyright © 1985 by CBS College Publishing. Copyright © 1976 by Holt, Rinehart and Winston. Copyright © 1961, 1969 by Holt, Rinehart and Winston, Inc.

Chapter Eight:

"Toward a Theory of Motive Acquisition" by David C. McClelland in *American Psychologist*, XX, No. 2, pp. 321–333. Copyright © 1965 by the American Psychological Association. Reproduced with permission. No further reproduction or distribution is permitted without written permission from the American Psychological Association.

Chapter Nine:

"Nature Intervenes: Organizations as Organisms" by Gareth Morgan in *Images of Organization*, 2nd ed., pp. 33–71. Copyright © 1997 by Sage Publications, Inc. Reprinted by permission of Sage Publications, Inc.

Chapter Ten:

"Sociotechnical Systems: Origin of the Concept" by Eric L. Trist in *Perspectives on Organization Design and Behavior*, edited by A.H. Vande Ven and H. Murray. Copyright © 1981. Reprinted by permission of John Wiley & Sons, Inc.

Chapter Eleven:

"Evolution and Revolution as Organizations Grow" by Larry E. Greiner, commentary and revision of *Harvard Business Review* Classic, "Evolution and Revolution as Organizations Grow." Reprinted by permission of *Harvard Business Review*, May–June, 1998. Copyright © 1998 by Harvard Business School Publishing Corporation; all rights reserved.

Chapter Twelve:

"Revolutionary Change Theories: A Multilevel Exploration of the Punctuated Equilibrium Paradigm" by Connie J.G. Gersick in *Academy of Management Review*. Copyright © 1991. Reprinted by permission of The Academy of Management.

Chapter Thirteen:

"Organizational Evolution: A Metamorphosis Model of Convergence and Reorientation" by Michael L. Tushman and Elaine Romanelli in L.L. Cummings & B. M. Staw, eds., *Research in Organizational Behavior, 7*, 171–122. Copyright © 1985. Reprinted by permission of Elsevier.

Chapter Fourteen:

"Organizational Change and Development" by Karl E. Weick and Robert E. Quinn is reprinted with permission from the *Annual Review of Psychology*, Volume 50, pp. 361–386. Copyright © 1999 by Annual Reviews. www .annualreviews.org.

Chapter Fifteen:

"Kurt Lewin and the Planned Approach to Change: A Reappraisal" by Bernard Burnes in *Journal of Management Studies*, vol. 41, issue 6, pp. 977–1002. Copyright © 2004. Reprinted by permission of Blackwell Publishing.

Chapter Sixteen:

"Understanding Organizations: The Process of Diagnosis" in *Organization Development: Normative View*, 1st ed., by W. Warner Burke. Copyright © 1987. Reprinted by permission of Pearson Education, Inc., Upper Saddle River, NJ. In Chapter Sixteen, Table 16.1, Weisbord's Matrix for Survey Design or Data Analysis: From "Organizational Diagnosis: Six Places to Look for Trouble with or Without a Theory" by M.R. Weisbord in *Group and Organization Studies*, 430–447. Copyright © 1976. Reprinted by permission of Sage Publications, Inc. Figure 16.2, The Nadler-Tushman Congruence Model for Diagnosing Organizational Behavior: From "A Diagnostic Model for Organization Behavior" by D.A. Nadler and M.L. Tushman in *Perspectives on Behavior in Organizations*, edited by J.R. Hackman, E.E. Lawler, and L.W. Porter. Copyright © 1977 The McGraw-Hill Companies, Inc. Reprinted with permission. Figure 16.3, Tichy's Framework: From *Managing Strategic Change: Technical, Political, and Cultural Dynamics* by N.M. Tichy. Copyright © 1983 Wiley Interscience. Reprinted with permission of John Wiley & Sons, Ltd. Figure 16.4, Tichy's TPC Framework: From *Managing Strategic Change: Technical, Political, and Cultural Dynamics* by N.M. Tichy. Copyright © 1983 Wiley Interscience. Reprinted with permission of John Wiley & Sons, Ltd.

Chapter Twenty-Five:

"The Recipients of Change" is reprinted by permission of Harvard Business School Press from *Note in the Recipients of Change* by Todd D. Jick. Copyright © 1990 by Harvard Business School Publishing Corporation; all rights reserved.

Chapter Twenty-Six:

"Rethinking Resistance and Recognizing Ambivalence: A Multidimensional View of Attitudes Toward an Organizational Change" by Sandy Kristin Piderit in *Academy of Management Review*. Copyright © 2000. Reprinted by permission of The Academy of Management.

Chapter Twenty-Seven:

"A Theory of Group Development" by Warren G. Bennis and Herbert A. Shepard in *Human Relations*, 9, (4), pp. 415–437. Copyright © 1956. Reproduced by permission of Sage Publications, Ltd.

Chapter Twenty-Eight:

"The Work of Wilfred Bion on Groups" by Margaret J. Rioch in *Psychiatry, 33,* 56–66. Copyright © 1970. Reprinted by permission of Elsevier.

Chapter Twenty-Nine:

"Organizational Identity and Learning: A Psychodynamic Perspective" by Andrew D. Brown and Ken Starkey in *Academy of Management Review*. Copyright © 2000. Reprinted by permission of The Academy of Management.

Chapter Thirty:

"The Quest for Resilience" by Gary Hamel and Liisa Valikangas is reprinted by permission of *Harvard Business Review*, September, 2003. Copyright © 2003 by Harvard Business School Publishing Corporation; all rights reserved.

Chapter Thirty-One:

"Strategies of Consultation" from *Strategies of Consultation* by Robert R. Blake and Jane Srygley Mouton. Copyright © 1972. Austin, TX: Scientific Methods, Inc. In Chapter Thirty-One, Exhibit 31.1, What a Sound Union-Management Relationship Would Be as Described by Management: Blake, R.R. & Mouton, J.S. *Corporate excellence through grid organization development: A systems approach.* Houston: Gulf Publishing, 1968, 181–182. Exhibit 31.2, What a Sound Union-Management Relationship Would Be as Described by the Union: Blake, R.R. & Mouton, J.S. *Corporate excellence through grid organization development: A systems approach.* Houston: Gulf Publishing, 1968, 183. Table 31.3, Genuine Concern with the Organization's Earning Capacity Results from

Chapter Forty-Seven:

''Short- and Long-Range Effects of a Team Development Effort'' by Richard Beckhard and Dale G. Lake is reprinted with the permission of The Free Press, a Division of Simon & Schuster Inc. from *Social Intervention: A Behavioral Science Approach*, Edited with introductions by Harry A. Hornstein, Barbara Benedict Bunker, W. Warner Burke, Marion Grindes, and Roy J. Lewicki. Copyright © 1971 by The Free Press. All rights reserved.

Chapter Forty-Eight:

''Measuring Change and Persistence in Human Affairs: Types of Change Generated by OD Designs'' by Robert T. Golembiewski, Keith Billingsley, and Samuel Yeager in *Journal of Applied Behavioral Science, 12*, 133–157. Copyright © 1976. Reprinted by permission of Sage Publications, Inc.

Chapter Forty-Nine:

''Explaining Development and Change in Organizations'' by Andrew H. Van de Ven and Marshall Scott Poole in *Academy of Management Review*. Copyright © 1995. Reprinted by permission of The Academy of Management.

Chapter Fifty:

''Organizational Change and Development'' by Michael Beer and Anna .Elise Walton is reprinted with permission from the *Annual Review of Psychology*, Volume 38, pp. 339–367. Copyright © 1987 by Annual Reviews. www.annualreviews.org.

Chapter Fifty-One:

''A Complex-Systems Approach to Organizations'' by Daniel J. Svyantek and Linda L. Brown in *Current Directions in Psychological Science, 9*, 69–74. Copyright © 2000. Reprinted by permission of Blackwell Publishing.

Chapter Fifty-Two:

''The Evolving Field of Organizational Learning'' by Chris Argyris and Donald A. Schon in *Organizational Learning II: Theory, Method and Practice*. Copyright © 1996. Reprinted by permission of Pearson Education, Inc., Upper Saddle River, NJ.